'This outstanding volume includes insights from every leading scholar doing thought provoking research on digital journalism. Everything you need to know about the state of contemporary journalism: the why, the how, and with what effect— it's all here, in this engaging and forward thinking *Companion to Digital Journalism Studies*.'

Zizi Papacharissi, Professor and Head, Department of Communication, University of Illinois at Chicago, USA

'Bob Franklin and Scott Eldridge have created a foundational text for the development of Digital Journalism Studies as an emerging interdisciplinary field of study. *The Routledge Companion to Digital Journalism Studies* is a masterful collection, addressing key ideas, issues and concerns shaping the field and exploring conceptual, professional, methodological and ethical considerations related to Digital Journalism Studies. Framed globally, this must-read text includes 58 original articles, which focus on the implications of economic, cultural, social, political and technological conditions facing Digital Journalism Studies while addressing key changes in the way people now engage with news and information.'

Bonnie Brennen, Nieman Professor of Journalism, Marquette University, USA

'The world of news and journalism is changing fast as the Internet has become a common means of news gathering and distribution. *The Routledge Companion to Digital Journalism Studies* offers a comprehensive collection of essays analysing "digital journalism" and "Digital Journalism Studies" and makes an irreplaceable and timely contribution to the field. Very familiar concepts like news and journalism are now up for complete overhaul, and this essential compilation of original work provides a major input to this task.'

Peter Golding, Emeritus Professor, Northumbria University, UK

THE ROUTLEDGE COMPANION TO DIGITAL JOURNALISM STUDIES

The Routledge Companion to Digital Journalism Studies offers an unprecedented collection of essays addressing the key issues and debates shaping the field of Digital Journalism Studies today.

Across the last decade, journalism has undergone many changes, which have driven scholars to reassess its most fundamental questions and, in the face of digital change, to ask again: 'Who is a journalist?' and 'What is journalism?' This *Companion* explores a developing scholarly agenda committed to understanding digital journalism and brings together the work of key scholars seeking to address key theoretical concerns and solve unique methodological riddles.

Comprised of 58 original essays by distinguished academics from across the globe, this *Companion* draws together the work of those making sense of this fundamental reconceptualization of journalism and assesses its impacts on journalism's products, its practices, resources, and its relationship with audiences. It also outlines the challenges presented by studying digital journalism and, more importantly, offers a first set of answers.

This collection is the very first of its kind to attempt to distinguish this emerging field as a unique area of academic inquiry. Through identifying its core questions and presenting its fundamental debates, this *Companion* sets the agenda for years to come in defining this new field of study as Digital Journalism Studies, making it an essential point of reference for students and scholars of journalism.

Bob Franklin is Professor of Journalism Studies at the Cardiff School of Journalism, Media and Cultural Studies. He is the founding editor of the journals *Digital Journalism*, *Journalism Practice* and *Journalism Studies*. His most recent book is *The Future of Journalism: In an Age of Digital Media and Economic Uncertainty* (2015).

Scott A. Eldridge II is an Assistant Professor of Journalism Studies and Media at the University of Groningen, Netherlands. His research and publications focus on changing concepts of journalism and the challenges to journalism's identity presented by emerging digital actors. He is Reviews Editor for the journal *Digital Journalism* and is on the editorial boards of *Digital Journalism* and the *Journal of Applied Journalism & Media Studies*.

Contributors: Laura Ahva, Tanja Aitamurto, Stuart Allan, Marco T. Bastos, Annika Bergström, Henrik Bødker, Tanja Bosch, Peter Bro, Meredith Broussard, Axel Bruns, Matt Carlson, Lilie Chouliaraki, Irene Costera Meijer, Nello Cristianini, Juliette De Maeyer, Lina Dencik, Nicholas Diakopoulos, Murray Dick, Monika Djerf-Pierre, David Dowling, Martin Eide, Scott A. Eldridge II, Ivar John Erdal, Terry Flew, Bob Franklin, Jose A. García-Avilés, Celeste González de Bustamante, Tim Groot Kormelink, Ágnes Gulyás, Folker Hanusch, Raymond A. Harder, Jonathan Hardy, Uwe Hasebrink, David Hedley, Ulrika Hedman, Lea Hellmueller, Alfred Hermida, Kristy Hess, Arne Hintz, Michiel Johnson, Andy Kaltenbrunner, Aljosha Karim Schapals, Michael Karlsson, Nete Nørgaard Kristensen, Thomas B. Ksiazek, Thomas Lansdall-Welfare, Ainara Larrondo, Justin Lewis, Seth C. Lewis, You Li, Wiebke Loosen, Asmaa Malik, Pere Masip, Brian McNair, Klaus Meier, Toby Miller, Mette Mortensen, Merja Myllylahti, Joyce Y. M. Nip, Chris Paterson, Steve Paulussen, John V. Pavlik, Limor Peer, Chris Peters, Robert G. Picard, Jeannine E. Relly, David Ryfe, Jan-Hinrik Schmidt, Ivor Shapiro, Helle Sjøvaag, Prasun Sonwalkar, Guy Starkey, Steen Steensen, Edson C. Tandoc Jr., Einar Thorsen, Neil Thurman, Hilde Van den Bulck, Tom Van Hout, Sarah Van Leuven, Travis Vogan, Karin Wahl-Jorgensen, Melissa Wall, Lisa Waller, Stephen J. A. Ward, Oscar Westlund and Jenny Wiik.

THE ROUTLEDGE COMPANION TO DIGITAL JOURNALISM STUDIES

Edited by Bob Franklin
and Scott A. Eldridge II

Routledge
Taylor & Francis Group

LONDON AND NEW YORK

First published 2017
by Routledge
2 Park Square, Milton Park, Abingdon, Oxon OX14 4RN

and by Routledge
711 Third Avenue, New York, NY 10017

Routledge is an imprint of the Taylor & Francis Group, an informa business

British Library Cataloguing-in-Publication Data
A catalogue record for this book is available from the British Library

Library of Congress Cataloging-in-Publication Data
Names: Franklin, Bob, 1949– editor. | Eldridge, Scott A., II editor.
Title: The Routledge companion to digital journalism studies /
edited by Bob Franklin and Scott A. Eldridge II.
Description: London ; New York : Routledge, 2017. | Includes
bibliographical references and index.
Identifiers: LCCN 2016006772 | ISBN 9781138887961 (hbk) |
ISBN 9781315713793 (ebk)
Subjects: LCSH: Online journalism. | Digital media. |
Journalism—Technological innovations.
Classification: LCC PN4784.O62 R68 2017 | DDC 070.4—dc23
LC record available at http://lccn.loc.gov/2016006772

ISBN: 978-1-138-88796-1 (hbk)
ISBN: 978-1-315-71379-3 (ebk)

Typeset in Goudy
by Book Now Ltd, London

CONTENTS

Contents

ILLUSTRATIONS

Figures

Tables

CONTRIBUTORS

Laura Ahva is a Research Fellow interested in journalistic practice, audience studies, and participation. She has published in various journals, including *Journalism*, *Digital Journalism*, and *Journalism Practice*. She is based in the School of Communication, Media and Theatre at the University of Tampere in Finland.

Tanja Aitamurto is the Deputy Director and a Brown Fellow at the Brown Institute for Media Innovation at the School of Engineering at Stanford. She examines how collective intelligence, whether gathered by crowdsourcing, crowdfunding, or co-creation, impacts journalism, governance, and media innovations. More about her work at www.tanjaaitamurto.com.

Stuart Allan is Professor of Journalism and Communication as well as Head of the School of Journalism, Media and Cultural Studies at Cardiff University, UK. His publications include *Citizen Witnessing: Revisioning Journalism in Times of Crisis* (2013) and *The Routledge Companion to News and Journalism* (2012).

Marco T. Bastos is a Lecturer in media and communications at City, University of London and an affiliate of the Duke Network Analysis Center and the Data Science Initiative of the University of California at Davis. His research focuses on sociological aspects of digital media with a substantive interest in the cross-effects between online and offline social networks.

Annika Bergström is an Associate Professor at the Department of Journalism, Media and Communication at the University of Gothenburg. Her research focuses on audience development within the areas of internet news and online participation regarding politics and user-generated content in the journalistic context.

Henrik Bødker is an Associate Professor at the Department of Media and Journalism Studies at Aarhus University in Denmark. He has published on various intersections between popular culture and media, e.g. music and magazines. His most recent work focuses on aspects of online journalism.

Tanja Bosch is a Senior Lecturer in the Centre for Film and Media Studies at the University of Cape Town, where she teaches communication theory, qualitative research methods, and broadcast journalism. She conducts research on youth and identity, new media, and radio studies.

Peter Bro is Professor and Director of the Centre for Journalism, University of Southern Denmark, which has around 5–600 students and a staff of 25 researchers and lecturers. He is a member of the board of one of Denmark's largest media companies and primarily writes about new journalistic norms and forms.

Meredith Broussard is an Assistant Professor at the Arthur L. Carter Journalism Institute of New York University. Her research focuses on artificial intelligence in investigative reporting, with a particular interest in using data analysis for social good.

Axel Bruns is a Professor in the Digital Media Research Centre at Queensland University of Technology. He is Vice-President of the Association of internet Researchers; author of *Blogs, Wikipedia, Second Life and Beyond* (2008) and *Gatewatching* (2005); and an editor of the *Routledge Companion to Social Media and Politics* (2016) and *Twitter and Society* (2014).

Matt Carlson is an Associate Professor of communication at Saint Louis University. He is author of *Journalistic Authority* and *On the Condition of Anonymity*, and a co-editor with Seth C. Lewis of *Boundaries of Journalism* and *Journalists, Sources, and Credibility* with Bob Franklin.

Lilie Chouliaraki is Professor of Media and Communications at the London School of Economics and Political Science. She has written extensively on human suffering as a problem of communication, on digital witnessing, and the ethics of spectatorship. Her recent books include *The Spectatorship of Suffering* (2006/2011) and *The Ironic Spectator* (2013; Outstanding Book Award 2015, International Communication Association).

Irene Costera Meijer is a Professor of Journalism Studies at the VU University Amsterdam, the Netherlands. She is the principal investigator of two research projects—"The New News Consumer: User-Based Innovation to Meet Paradigmatic Change in News Use and Media Habits" (2013–2018) and "Rethinking Quality Journalism in the Digital Age" (2010–2015).

Nello Cristianini is a Professor of Artificial Intelligence at the University of Bristol since March 2006. He has wide research interests in the areas of data science, artificial intelligence, machine learning, and applications to computational social sciences, digital humanities, and news content analysis.

Juliette De Maeyer is an Assistant Professor at the Department of Communication at Université de Montréal, where her research focuses on the intersection of journalism and technology, on the discourses about technological change in journalism, and on the materiality of newsmaking.

Lina Dencik is a Senior Lecturer at the School of Journalism, Media and Cultural Studies at Cardiff University. Her research looks at the interplay between developments in media and social and political change, with a particular focus on globalization and resistance. Her publications include *Media and Global Civil Society* (2012) and *Critical Perspectives on Social Media and Protest* (co-edited with O. Leistert, 2015).

Nicholas Diakopoulos is an Assistant Professor in the Philip Merrill College of Journalism at the University of Maryland, College Park. His research and teaching are in computational and data journalism with an emphasis on algorithmic accountability, narrative data visualization, and social computing in the news.

Murray Dick is a Lecturer in multimedia journalism at Newcastle University, UK. His research interests are primarily concerned with journalistic practice, but also include sociologies of online journalism and of visual data journalism (infographics), information management, journalism history, and journalism pedagogy.

Monika Djerf-Pierre is a Professor at the Department of Journalism, Media and Communication at the University of Gothenburg, Sweden, and Adjunct Professor of Journalism at Monash University, Australia. Her main research fields are journalism, media history, political communication, risk and crisis communication, and gender studies.

David Dowling is an Associate Professor at the University of Iowa School of Journalism and Mass Communication and specializes in publishing industries and the culture of media production. The author of six books, his articles have appeared in such journals as *Convergence*, *Genre*, *American Journalism*, *Digital Humanities Quarterly*, and *Digital Journalism*.

Martin Eide is a Professor at the Department of Information Science and Media Studies, University of Bergen, Norway. He has published several books and articles on press history and on the social impact of journalism. His latest project has been *Journalistic Reorientations: Online Challenges to Journalistic Ontology*.

Scott A. Eldridge II is an Assistant Professor of Journalism Studies and Media at the University of Groningen, Netherlands. His research and publications focus on changing concepts of journalism and the challenges to journalism's identity presented by emerging digital actors. He is Reviews Editor for the journal *Digital Journalism* and is on the editorial boards of *Digital Journalism* and the *Journal of Applied Journalism & Media Studies*.

Ivar John Erdal is an Associate Professor at Volda University College, Norway. His research focuses on digital journalism and convergence, and has appeared in journals such as *Journalism Studies*, *Convergence*, and *Journalism Practice*.

Terry Flew is a Professor of Media and Communications at Queensland University of Technology (QUT). He has authored books and articles on a variety of journalism and media-related topics, including *Media Economics* (2015). He is a chief investigator of the Digital Media Research Centre at QUT, Chair of the ICA Global Communications and Social Change Division, and a member of the ICA Executive Board.

Bob Franklin holds the Chair in Journalism Studies at the Cardiff School of Journalism, Media and Cultural Studies, Wales. He is founding editor of the international peer-reviewed journals *Digital Journalism*, *Journalism Practice*, and *Journalism Studies*.

Jose A. García-Avilés is Head of Journalism at the University Miguel Hernández (Spain). He has been researching media convergence since 2002 and has published extensively on newsroom convergence in Spain and Europe. He has lectured in the International Media Innovation Management based in Berlin and was visiting scholar at the Columbia University Journalism School.

Celeste González de Bustamante is an Associate Professor in the School of Journalism at the University of Arizona and an 1885 society distinguished scholar. She is the author of "*Muy* buenas noches," Mexico, Television and the Cold War (2012) and co-editor of *Arizona Firestorm: Global Immigration Realities, National Media, and Provincial Politics* (2012). She is the current president of *La red de periodistas de la frontera* (Border Journalism Network).

Tim Groot Kormelink is a PhD candidate in Journalism Studies at the VU University Amsterdam, the Netherlands. His research is mainly concerned with storytelling and news use in the context of everyday life.

Ágnes Gulyás is a Reader in Digital Transformations at the School of Media, Art and Design, Canterbury Christ Church University, UK. Her research focuses on changes in media production and consumption in the digital age, in particular how these affect communities. Her publications include articles in *Digital Journalism*; *Media, Culture & Society*; *Critical Survey*; as well as a co-edited book (with Hammer) *Public Service Media in the Digital Age*.

Folker Hanusch is Professor of Journalism at the University of Vienna, as well as an Adjunct Professor at Queensland University of Technology. His research interests are in the study of journalism culture and comparative communication research, topics on which he has published widely.

Raymond A. Harder is a member of the research groups Media, Policy & Culture (MPC) and Media, Movements and Politics (M²P) at the University of Antwerp, Belgium. He is working on a PhD project, funded by the University of Antwerp Research Fund, on the role of social media in reshaping the flow of news stories.

Jonathan Hardy is Professor of Media and Communications at the University of East London. He writes on media industries, marketing and communications policy, and is the author of *Critical Political Economy of the Media* (2014), *Cross-Media Promotion* (2010), and *Western Media Systems* (2008).

Uwe Hasebrink is Director of the Hans Bredow Institut for Media Research and a Professor at the University of Hamburg. He has published extensively on audience research, including individual media use and media repertoires, the convergence of media from the user's perspective, and consequences of online media for classical media, as well as other areas of media research. Since 2015 he has been the coordinator of the EU Kids Online research network.

David Hedley is Managing Editor of *UToday*, the daily newsletter at the University of Calgary in Canada. He worked in newsrooms for 30 years in writing, editing, assigning, and design roles and recently completed a master's degree at the Royal Roads University School of Communication and Culture.

Ulrika Hedman is a journalist and a PhD candidate in journalism and media studies at the University of Gothenburg. Her research interests include the profession of journalism, social media in journalism, and journalists–audience dialogue and interaction.

Lea Hellmueller is Assistant Professor and Director of the Global Media Research Center at the University of Houston. She is the author of *The Washington, DC Media Corps in the*

21st Century (2014) and the co-principal investigator of the Journalistic Role Performance around the Globe project.

Alfred Hermida is an Associate Professor and Director of the School of Journalism at the University of British Columbia, Canada. He is author of *Tell Everyone* (2014), co-author of *Participatory Journalism* (2011) and co-editor of *The Sage Handbook of Digital Journalism* (2016). His research has been published in *Journalism Studies, Journalism Practice, Journal of Computer-Mediated Communication*, and *Journal of Broadcasting and Electronic Media*.

Kristy Hess is a Senior Lecturer in journalism at Deakin University, Australia. Her research focuses on the future of local media in a digital world and its relationship to civic life and social order.

Arne Hintz is a Senior Lecturer at the Cardiff School of Journalism, Media and Cultural Studies, Cardiff University. His research connects communication policy, media activism, and technological change. He has led the collaborative research project "Digital Citizenship and Surveillance Society." His publications include the co-edited volume *Beyond WikiLeaks* (2013).

Michiel Johnson is a member of the research groups Media, Policy & Culture (MPC) and Media, Movements and Politics (M²P) at the University of Antwerp, Belgium. His PhD research is funded by the FWO (Research Foundation–Flanders) and focuses on the influence of social media on the journalist–source relationships in economic journalism.

Andy Kaltenbrunner, political scientist, is co-founder and Director of the research center Medienhaus Wien. He is a media-advisor, researcher, and Visiting Professor at universities and academies in Europe and the United States and developed Vienna's first MA program for journalists at the University of Applied Sciences (FHW, 2003) and the executive MA program "International Media Innovation Management" at Deutsche Universität für Weiterbildung Berlin (2011).

Aljosha Karim Schapals is a Research Associate at the Digital Media Research Centre of Queensland University of Technology (QUT) in Brisbane, Australia. Previously, he worked as a Research Assistant at the Information Law & Policy Centre, University of London, as well as working as a Visiting Lecturer in the Department of Journalism at City University London. His research interests lie in the changes taking place in news production and consumption as a result of the internet, with a particular focus on citizen journalism, politics and social media.

Michael Karlsson is a Professor at Karlstad University, Sweden, and is researching online journalism and methods. He has widely published in journals such as *Journal of Computer-Mediated Communication, New Media & Society*, and *Journalism Studies*.

Nete Nørgaard Kristensen is an Associate Professor at the Department of Media, Cognition and Communication, University of Copenhagen. She is the author and co-author of several books and articles on journalists and news sources, political journalism, media and war, cultural journalism, and cultural critique in journals such as *Communication, Culture and Critique, Digital Journalism, Journalism Practice, Journalism*, and *Northern Lights*.

Thomas B. Ksiazek, Northwestern University, is an Associate Professor in the Department of Communication at Villanova University. His research interests include digital media use, news audiences, journalism studies, and network analysis.

Thomas Lansdall-Welfare is a researcher in computer science at the University of Bristol focusing on applications of big data and text mining. Recent projects include monitoring trends in public mood via Twitter and large-scale analysis of online news media content.

Ainara Larrondo is a Senior Lecturer at the Faculty of Social Sciences and Communication of the University of the Basque Country (Spain, Bilbao). She is an active member of several funded research projects focusing on online journalism, with expertise in media convergence, newswriting, active audiences, and organizational web communication.

Justin Lewis is a Professor of communication at Cardiff School of Journalism, Media and Cultural Studies, and Dean of Research for the College of Arts, Humanities and Social Sciences. He has written widely about media, culture, and politics. His latest book is *Beyond Consumer Capitalism* (2013).

Seth C. Lewis is the Shirley Papé Chair in Electronic Media in the School of Journalism and Communication at the University of Oregon. He has published widely on the digital transformation of journalism, and is editor of *Journalism in an Era of Big Data: Cases, Concepts, and Critiques* (forthcoming) and co-editor of *Boundaries of Journalism: Professionalism, Practices, and Participation* (2015).

You Li is an Assistant Professor of journalism at Eastern Michigan University. Her research interests include media history, media sociology, and media management. Her recent publications were featured in *Journalism and Mass Communication Quarterly*, *Newspaper Research Journal*, and *Journalism Practice*.

Wiebke Loosen is a Senior Researcher for journalism research at the Hans Bredow Institute for Media Research (Hamburg, Germany) and a Lecturer at the University of Hamburg. Her main research interests cover journalism's transformation in the digital age as well as research methods and methodology.

Asmaa Malik is an Assistant Professor at the School of Journalism at Ryerson University in Toronto, Canada. Malik teaches digital and entrepreneurial journalism and is a former editor at *Toronto Star* and *The Montreal Gazette*, where she was the deputy managing editor in charge of the news organization's digital strategy.

Pere Masip is a Senior Lecturer at the School of Communication and International Relations Blanquerna at Ramon Llull University (Barcelona). His research interests are online journalism and impact of digital technologies in journalistic practices. He is currently leading a research project focusing on audience's motivation to participate on news media.

Brian McNair is Professor of Journalism, Media and Communication at Queensland University of Technology (QUT), Brisbane, Australia. He is a chief investigator of the Digital Media Research Centre at QUT and has authored books and articles on a variety of journalism and media-related topics, including *News & Journalism in the UK*, 5th edition (2009).

Klaus Meier holds the chair for "Journalism Studies I" at the Catholic University Eichstaett-Ingolstadt (Germany). His research explores editorial management, innovations in news-rooms, convergence, quality and ethics, digital journalism, and journalism education. He is a board member of "Forum Journalismus und Medien" Vienna and of the journal *Digital Journalism*.

Toby Miller is Emeritus Distinguished Professor, University of California, Riverside; Sir Walter Murdoch Professor of Cultural Policy Studies, Murdoch University; Profesor Invitado, Escuela de Comunicación Social, Universidad del Norte; Professor of Journalism, Media and Cultural Studies, Cardiff University/Prifysgol Caerdydd; and Director of the Institute of Media and Creative Industries, Loughborough University London.

Mette Mortensen is an Associate Professor at the Department of Media, Cognition and Communication, University of Copenhagen. She has written the monographs *Kampen om ansigtet: fotografi og identifikation* (*Facial Politics: Photography and Identification*, 2012) and *Eyewitness Images and Journalism: Digital Media, Participation, and Conflict* (2015) and co-edited several books and special issues. She has published articles in journals such as *The International Journal of Cultural Studies*, *Global Media and Communication*, *Digital Journalism*, and *Journalism Practice*.

Merja Myllylahti is a researcher and media Lecturer at Auckland University of Technology (AUT). She is also a project manager for AUT's Journalism, Media and Democracy Research Center. Her research interests lie in digital media ownership, digital media economics, digital media business models and paywalls. Her latest academic work has been published in *Digital Journalism* and *Nordicom*.

Joyce Y. M. Nip is a Senior Lecturer in the Department of Media and Communications as well as the Department of Chinese Studies, University of Sydney. She is editorial board member of *Journalism Practice* and *Digital Journalism*.

Chris Paterson researches at and leads the MA in International Communication at the University of Leeds. He co-edited, with David Domingo, two volumes of *Making Online News* (2008, 2011), authored or edited four additional books about international journalism, and has most recently co-edited *Advancing Media Production Research* (2016).

Steve Paulussen is an Assistant Professor in media and journalism studies at the Department of Communication Studies at the University of Antwerp in Belgium. He is a member of the research group Media, Policy & Culture.

John V. Pavlik is a Professor of journalism and media studies at Rutgers University. Pavlik has written widely on the impact of new technology on journalism, media, and society. Pavlik's PhD (1983) and MA (1980) in mass communication are from the University of Minnesota.

Limor Peer is Associate Director for Research at the Institution for Social and Policy Studies at Yale University. She is working on research communication, reproducibility, and data quality in the social sciences. In her prior position at Northwestern University's Media Management Center, she supervised research on media audience, content, and management strategy.

Chris Peters is an Associate Professor of media and communication at Aalborg University's Copenhagen campus. His research explores the ways people get and experience information in everyday life and the sociocultural impact of transformations in the digital era. His publications include *Rethinking Journalism*, *Rethinking Journalism Again*, and *Retelling Journalism*.

Robert G. Picard is North American Representative of the Reuters Institute at the University of Oxford, a fellow of the Royal Society of Arts, and an affiliated fellow of the Information Society Project at Yale University. He has authored and edited 30 books.

Jeannine E. Relly is an Associate Professor in the School of Journalism at the University of Arizona. Her research focuses on democratic institutions in countries in conflict and political transition. Dr. Relly currently is head of the International Communication Division of the Association for Education in Journalism and Mass Communication. Before joining the academy, Dr. Relly reported for a dozen years along the Mexico–US border and in the Caribbean.

David Ryfe is Professor and Director of the School of Journalism and Mass Communication at the University of Iowa. He publishes widely in the areas of deliberative practice, political communication, and the history and sociology of news. His most recent book, *Can Journalism Survive?* (2012), offers an ethnographic investigation of how American journalists are responding to the disruption of their industry.

Jan-Hinrik Schmidt is a Senior Researcher for Digital Interactive Media and Political Communication at the Hans Bredow Institute (Hamburg, Germany). His main research interests cover social media and their impact on the public sphere, as well as the communicative construction of software technologies.

Ivor Shapiro is a Professor at the School of Journalism, Ryerson University in Toronto, Canada. His research on professional identity and ethics in journalism has been published in *Journalism Studies*, *Newspaper Research Journal*, *Canadian Journal of Communication*, *Journalism Practice*, and as chapters in several books. A former magazine writer and editor, he teaches media ethics, law and feature reporting.

Helle Sjøvaag is a Research Professor at the University of Bergen, Norway. Research areas include journalism, digital methods, media diversity, and regulation. She has published extensively in international journals, including in *Journalism Studies*, *Convergence*, and *International Journal of Cultural Policy*.

Prasun Sonwalkar is a London-based journalist, reporting the UK and Europe for *Hindustan Times*. A Commonwealth Scholar and Press Fellow of Wolfson College, Cambridge, he holds a PhD from the University of Leicester and previously taught at the University of the West of England, Bristol. His research has appeared in various journals and edited collections. Before moving to the UK, he held several key positions on *The Times of India*, *Business Standard*, and *Zee News*.

Guy Starkey is Professor and Associate Dean, Global Engagement, at Bournemouth University. His publications include *Local Radio, Going Global*, second edition, *Radio in Context*, second edition, *Radio Journalism* (with Professor Andrew Crisell), and *Balance and Bias in Journalism: Representation, Regulation and Democracy*.

Steen Steensen Professor of Journalism and Head of the Department of Journalism and Media Studies at Oslo and Akershus University College of Applied Sciences. His research on digital journalism has been published in numerous books and journals, including *Journalism Studies*, *Journalism*, and *New Media & Society*.

Edson C. Tandoc Jr. is an Assistant Professor at the Wee Kim Wee School of Communication and Information at the Nanyang Technological University in Singapore. His research focuses on the sociology of message construction in the context of news and social media.

Einar Thorsen is Principal Lecturer in Journalism and Communication at Bournemouth University. His research focuses on online journalism, crisis news, and digital communication security. He has co-edited *Media, Margins and Civic Agency* and *Media, Margins and Popular Culture* (with Jackson, Savigny, and Alexander, 2015), and two volumes of *Citizen Journalism: Global Perspectives* (with Stuart Allan, 2009, 2014).

Neil Thurman is a Professor of communication with an emphasis on computational journalism in the Department of Communication Studies and Media Research, LMU Munich. Previously he worked at City University London where he led master's programs in journalism, media and globalization and in electronic publishing. Neil's research focuses on the changes taking place in news production and consumption as a result of the internet.

Hilde Van den Bulck is full Professor of Communication Studies and head of the research group Media, Policy & Culture at the University of Antwerp in Belgium. She combines expertise in media structures and policies, focusing on public service media, with expertise in media culture and identity. She has published widely on these topics.

Tom Van Hout is Assistant Professor and Academic Director of the Institute of Professional and Academic Communication at the University of Antwerp. He specializes in qualitative approaches to discourse in the professions and has published peer-reviewed work on news sourcing, journalistic voice, professional competence, and media linguistics.

Sarah Van Leuven is an Assistant Professor at the Department of Communication Sciences at Ghent University, Belgium. She is head of the research group Center for Journalism Studies and on the steering committee of the Journalism Division of the Netherlands-Flanders Communication Association. She specializes in quantitative approaches to journalism studies and has published on the public sphere, sourcing practices, and international news coverage.

Travis Vogan is an Assistant Professor in the School of Journalism and Mass Communication and the Department of American Studies at the University of Iowa. He is the author of *Keepers of the Flame: NFL Films and the Rise of Sports Media* (2014) and *ESPN: The Making of a Sports Media Empire* (2015).

Karin Wahl-Jorgensen is a Professor in the Cardiff School of Journalism, Media and Cultural Studies, Cardiff University. She is the author or editor of five books, most recently *Disasters and the Media* (2012, with Simon Cottle and Mervi Pantti). She is currently finalizing *Emotions, Media and Politics* (forthcoming).

Melissa Wall is Professor of Journalism at California State University—Northridge where she researches participatory media. She is the editor of *Citizen Journalism: Valuable, Useless or Dangerous?* and the creator of the Pop-Up Newsroom, a temporary, virtual newsroom that engages students in global reporting collaborations.

Lisa Waller is a Senior Lecturer in the School of Communication and Creative Arts, Deakin University, Australia. Her research is concerned with how news media shapes society, from Indigenous Affairs policy to the administration of justice and everyday life in regional and rural settings and beyond.

Stephen J. A. Ward is Distinguished Lecturer in Ethics at the University of British Columbia, a fellow of the School of Journalism and Mass Communication at the University of Wisconsin, and Courtesy Professor in the School of Journalism at the University of Oregon. He is founding director of the Center for Journalism Ethics at the University of Wisconsin and former director of the Graduate School of Journalism at the University of British Columbia.

Oscar Westlund is an Associate Professor at the University of Gothenburg and was recently research leader for the media inquiry at the Government Offices of Sweden, Swedish Ministry of Culture (2015–2016). He researches and has published extensively on the production, management, distribution, consumption, technologies, and policy relating to journalism and news. He also serves the editorial board of five international journals.

Jenny Wiik is a lecturer and researcher at the Department of Journalism, Media and Communication at the University of Gothenburg. Her research interest concerns journalism as a profession and the challenges of this profession in a time of technological, political, and economic change.

ACKNOWLEDGMENTS

As an intellectual endeavor, this companion has been an exciting process and an enjoyable editorial project. However, we would certainly not be able to present this volume to you, nor draw together the chapters in this volume, without the shared enthusiasm of the contributors whose work is found on these pages. There are 85 authors who have lent their intellectual work to this text, without whom this field would a be far less dynamic and interesting space. From its very inception, the strength of this *Companion* has been in its community of contributors and it has benefited from the feedback of authors who, in conversations both digital and in person, offered new insights into ways of thinking about Digital Journalism Studies. Their contributions have made this field a robust, critical, and reflective place and an exciting one. Without a doubt each of these contributors has also benefited from the support and contributions of their own colleagues and those working in Digital Journalism Studies beyond these pages. We would especially like to thank Natalie Foster at Routledge for supporting our ambitions and for helping us spark this academic endeavor from its earliest stages. Thanks also to Sheni Kruger, whose support has helped bring this companion to publication. In that spirit, we would also like to thank the anonymous reviewers whose feedback on our initial proposal helped launch this project. Finally, we would also like to thank colleagues in Cardiff at the School of Journalism, Media and Cultural Studies and in Sheffield at the Department of Journalism Studies who have supported this project from its proposal to its final publication. Their feedback has enriched this project in so many ways. We hope they know who they are.

Bob Franklin and Scott A. Eldridge II
Sheffield, January 2016

INTRODUCTION
Defining Digital Journalism Studies

Scott A. Eldridge II and Bob Franklin

This *Companion* brings together scholars from across the globe whose work is contributing to the emerging field of Digital Journalism Studies. In developing this book, we have set out to illustrate how Digital Journalism Studies has developed as a discrete and conceptually rich field of scholarly research with its own agenda of questions and modes of inquiry. We argue that 'digital' is no longer simply an adjectival descriptor or mere appendage to 'journalism' to be deployed when news and information move from paper to screen, nor is it merely a vague reference to the newest media technologies. As the chapters in this volume demonstrate, the theoretical richness of this field and the depth of its scholarship are evident in the ways it extends far beyond describing new technologies or highlighting their place in our mediated world. For us and for the contributors to this volume, Digital Journalism Studies is a field devoted to exploring fundamental changes in the ways that journalism is produced, engaged with, and critically understood. While Digital Journalism Studies does point to the ways in which journalism has become closely interconnected with new digital technologies, and scholars have gone to great lengths to describe that shifting relationship, to understand its place in academic studies, we have curated a collection of essays that discusses its theoretical, methodological, and professional and practical dimensions but significantly also makes the case for the emergence of Digital Journalism Studies as a new field of scholarly inquiry. This emergent area of academic scholarship supersedes rather than merely complements journalism studies and is driven not solely but largely by journalists' and journalism's accommodation to the emergence of digital technologies.

It might be thought that any book-length study of such a dynamic field risks being outdated before it leaves the press, but the contributions here tell a different story. The theoretical and conceptual challenges explored in Part I (Conceptualizing Digital Journalism Studies), for example, point to fundamental areas of inquiry that define Digital Journalism Studies as a coherent academic field reaching across disciplines, revisited through exploring the issues and debates in Part IV (Digital Journalism Studies: Issues and Debates), where pressing concerns for journalism's changing landscape are interrogated. Furthermore, the geographical case studies in the penultimate section (Global Digital Journalism) remind us that not all matters 'digital' are universally prominent, while the methods explored in the section 'Investigating Digital Journalism' poke, prod, and unravel the ways that new and immanent research methods and questions of analysis separate Digital Journalism Studies from other areas of academic inquiry. Elsewhere, chapters unpack the ways we can make sense of new forms of content in vast spaces through analysis of web traffic and content and in local and hyperlocal spaces where digital journalism has found strength, while others contend with new ways that a practicing journalist operates in a digital age.

For this opening chapter, we revisited the work of the authors within this volume and of colleagues contributing to Digital Journalism Studies beyond these pages to shine light on Digital Journalism Studies' core demands. These include definitional debates concerning where the boundaries lie not only for digital journalism as a media form but also for this academic field. It engages with the complexities that underline its ongoing development and challenges in its future. If the mission of Digital Journalism Studies is to reach across cultural, journalistic, socio-economic, and technological borders to paint a more holistic picture of the ways scholars and practitioners alike are grappling with changes emerging at a pace and scale previously unseen, this chapter endeavors to trace the priorities that are defining this scholarly work. As the contributions in this collection make clear, this demands new approaches to research and prompts new questions about the journalism world.

The formation of a field

In the early part of this century, initial attempts to make sense of the internet and journalism tended to focus acutely on the technological shifts that underscore digital journalism. Early forays into understanding journalism in online contexts looked at the internet as providing radical new means of communication and similarly radical ways of communicating. Concepts such as the 'Network Society' developed by Manuel Castells (2000) came to the foreground and underlined views of digital spaces as more 'horizontal' or 'flatter,' as 'decentralized' as plural online communities replaced more traditional, top-down, hierarchical journalistic organizations. The work of authors such as Dan Gillmor (2004) popularized the idea that digital platforms' low capital demands created greater access and opportunities for self-publishing, and journalism was declared to be a shared practice open to everyone. The first stages of journalism going online were reflected in discussions of newspapers and broadcasters moving to digital platforms. Early writing offered initial overviews of the ways journalism was taking advantage of digital opportunities. However, amid this work, including notable contributions that have enriched our understanding—such as the work of Pablo Boczkowski in his book *Digitizing the News* (2004)—in the early twenty-first century, proclamations of an internet 'revolution' were plentiful and the enthusiasm for new approaches to communicating online hard to ignore. What was missing, however, was a more critical and nuanced engagement with the complexities of these changes. The polarization between those optimistic about digital opportunities or pessimistic about the changes to 'legacy' journalism on occasion seemed to resemble the manichaeistic 'Boo-Hiss' shouts of the Victorian music hall audience—a sort of "internet good, old fashioned media (especially newspapers) bad." A mood captured neatly by Chyi, Lewis, and Zheng's (2012) analysis of what they termed 'the crisis of journalism frame'.

However fevered, the emphasis on novelty and revolution lent itself to descriptive writing, and technological shifts and radical change were discussed from this 'novelty' perspective. Arguably this was a misleading focus that was insufficient for assessing the impact on journalism and journalism studies that accompanied the digital turn (Eldridge, 2015). As James Curran writes in *Misunderstanding the Internet*, the enthusiastic view that the internet would 'change the world' (2012: 34) was hard to ignore, that is, until its egalitarian promise started to prove less-than-fulfilled (Domingo, *et al.* 2009; Fico, *et al.* 2013). While new language was being crafted to describe online opportunities such as 'Web 2.0' or commercial 'click and mortar' operations, in the early part of the twenty-first century there were few critical voices developing understanding beyond focusing on the potential of new technologies, including journalistic technologies. As Curran suggests: "The central weakness of this theorizing is that it assesses the impact of the internet not on the basis of evidence but on the basis of inference from internet technology" (2012: 8).

The attention paid to enthusiasm over analysis presented a challenging reality for scholars who were interested in journalism. For Digital Journalism Studies as an emerging academic field, this is no less a challenge. Technological novelty continues to pose a challenge for scholars, as they face the dual demands of making sense of the dynamics of digital journalism as they emerge, while also describing an excitingly expansive range and variety of digital innovations. In order to construct the boundaries of this nascent field, this *Companion* grapples with both of these demands as it logs, archives, and critically assesses the fundamental shifts in all aspects of journalism, its professional practices, and products, and the audiences for these products.

While this might sound like a fraught balance between identifying change and understanding its impact on journalism, it has become clear that scholarship has progressed beyond identifying these intellectual dilemmas and has moved toward building a rich theoretical engagement and understanding. In doing so, and through this *Companion*, we can register not only the core demands of the academic work explored by its scholars but also define the points of reference for future work understanding digital journalism and digital journalism scholarship.

Taking the work of Boczkowski noted above, for instance, his recent book with Eugenia Mitchelstein—*News Gap* (2013)—explores not only content 'gone digital' but reorients that discussion towards understanding news media operating online from the people's perspective. Oscar Westlund, in this volume and in previous work (2013), has introduced new avenues for understanding digital engagement from the 'personal' perspective as well, and does so by contending with newer and newer ways of going online and reaching audiences through mobile, smart, and tablet devices. Similarly, while in the early part of this decade Clay Shirky (2003) explored bloggers and questions of power in online communities, Tanja Aitamurto reorients our discussion of 'communities' and 'crowds' in terms of their sourcing and funding power in her chapter here. These are a few of the myriad approaches scholars are taking to move beyond Curran's warning of a skewed overemphasis on the technological. Viewed through these varied lenses, we argue that a greater understanding is beginning to develop that defines the field of Digital Journalism Studies and its scholarship.

Conceptualizing an interdisciplinary field

Introducing the journal *Digital Journalism*, itself a locus for shaping this field and this *Companion*, the Editor noted how scholars and journalists alike have "become increasingly aware, across the last few years, of fundamental changes which have been restructuring all aspects of journalism and journalism studies" (Franklin, 2013: 1). This restructuring, of course, reflects the ubiquity of digital technologies and digital journalism, but it also focuses on the ways in which their prominence has been a disruptive development that poses an array of challenging questions. This has prompted new ways of thinking not only about journalism but also about the relationships between journalists and organizations and the people and societies they communicate with. It is, in many ways, a field that can be marked in part by new points of reference and ways of describing its dynamics.

Our first priority is a conceptual one, and at its core we concern ourselves with defining what we are talking about when we refer to 'digital journalism' and Digital Journalism Studies.

In many ways, Digital Journalism Studies can be understood through the way it has embraced unclear definitional boundaries around journalism as it has experienced radical change in the past few decades. Definitions of journalism have been elusive (although certainly plentiful), and Ivor Shapiro has called our attention to scholars' tendency "to envision journalism in dramatically different ways" (2014: 555); he joins Asmaa Malik here to illustrate that definitional clarity continues to present both "a challenge and a promise". These include reoriented journalism–audience relationships, where we now speak of "the people formerly known as the audience" (Rosen, 2006), empowered by digital opportunities for both producing and using content as 'produsers' (Bruns, 2007); such technologically driven opportunities also give rise to Mark Deuze's equivalent characterization of "the people formerly known as the employers" (2009). Yochai Benkler (2011) describes this as a 'Networked Fourth Estate' and by doing so illustrates how the juxtaposition of digital ways of working have collided with normative understandings of journalism's societal role. This has shaken the primacy of traditional news media organizations, and orientations of media power have included up-from-below practices of 'citizen witnessing' (Allan, 2013) and blurred entertainment and information in new ways (Bastos, this volume). In response to a wider array of media actors, traditional media see themselves confronted by bloggers engaged in 'black market journalism' (Wall, 2004) and digitally native journalists seen as 'interlopers' (Eldridge, 2014). All of this is to say that Digital Journalism Studies is confronted with an array of changing dynamics that texture the way we engage with media, news, and information in a digital world.

The conceptualization of Digital Journalism Studies goes beyond a new lexicon. Digital journalism has changed binary relationships between producers of journalism and the people they purport to serve. Part of that challenge comes from the theoretical foundations that academics work with for exploring digital journalism and their bases in cultural, political, sociological studies, communication, and other disciplines. For this we turn to the work of Laura Ahva and Steen Steensen, who mapped journalism research and its disciplinary approaches (Steensen and Ahva, 2015) and devote their attention in this *Companion* to mapping Digital Journalism Studies as an interdisciplinary field. Embracing this argument, scholars have identified how prominent discourses that have shaped this field and debates between narratives of 'evolution' or 'revolution,' and in many ways the maturation of Digital Journalism Studies, are marked by work that has moved from debating these oppositional polarities of change. The work of Henrik Bødker (2015) on digital cultures of circulation, Thomas Ksiazek and Limor Peer (2011) on civility online, Lea Hellmueller and You Li (2015) on participation, and Meredith Broussard (2015) on computational reporting represent just some of the vast interdisciplinary approaches to understanding digital journalism that extend beyond scales of change to provide a more nuanced exploration of shifts in patterns of engagement with digital content, audience behavior, and tensions around previously distinct communicative roles.

Within Digital Journalism Studies we trace troublesome questions concerning what makes a journalist a journalist. This is the focus of Eldridge's chapter in this volume and has been explored elsewhere, including recent publications by Matt Carlson and Seth Lewis (2015), Karin Wahl-Jorgensen (2013), and Mark Coddington (2014). Scholars approach these new dynamics by assessing how digital journalists position themselves in society and how that rests on certain norms of authority, public interest, and legitimation of information for fulfilling democratic priorities. In this we see scholarship focusing on new actors and forms of communication engaging with the rich legacy of journalism research and its own threads through political theory, computer science, and sociological studies. Research within Digital Journalism Studies has made it clear that tensions over the primacy of journalistic identity itself forms an area of inquiry, apparent in Jane Singer's (2005) writing more than a decade ago of 'j-bloggers' and still relevant for discussions of digital 'interlopers' nowadays (Eldridge, 2014).

Martin Conboy in *Journalism Studies: The Basics* (2013) notes the tension that journalism organizations face as they try to balance information provision, entertainment, and commercial viability. As was true in the 'pre-digital' era, digital journalism and Digital Journalism Studies have been marked in part by the way this balance has been upended. Scholars tackling tensions between commercial imperatives are confronted with competing dynamics of openness and the accessibility of communicative avenues. While the popular notion that "we're all journalists now" (Jardin, 2004) might be under-realized, making sense of the way digital platforms offer diffuse information sources amid more traditional organizational constraints continues to present challenges. Digital Journalism Studies is at pains to understand these realities as they impact upon journalism's digital and analog sustainability. Merja Myllylahti in her chapter here unpacks the questions of profitability and paywalls—clearly not saviors of the newspaper industry—as news media wrestle with changing commercial realities in digital contexts. While addressing these questions has not produced 'saviors,' it has provided a richer understanding for journalism and journalists in digital spaces and adds to a growing wealth of research data. Robert Picard and Jonathan Hardy have also taken up this challenge, exploring digital journalism from commercial and political economy perspectives. While these arguments continue what has been a strong academic vein within journalism and media studies—in the work of Robert McChesney, James Curran, or Victor Pickard, for instance—the disruption of digital technologies has drawn the political and the economic into a new lens. As Picard notes, journalists working in digital journalism need to understand the business of journalism more than they had to before. From a critical political economy stance (CPE), Jonathan Hardy draws out critiques of trying to replicate old business models online and points to blurred editorial/commercial divides, making the case for supporting digital journalism as a public good.

Of course, the field is not only defined by the scholars in this volume and annual surveys by research centers including the Reuters Institute for the Study of Journalism at Oxford University, the Pew Center in Washington, DC, and other studies produced globally have brought the discussion to more public audiences beyond the academy. However, we argue that scholars like Myllylahti, using methodological approaches advocated within this volume by Michael Karlsson and Helle Sjøvaag, and Annika Bergstrom and Jenny Wiik, allow us to carry our understanding beyond descriptions of data and usage practice toward more reflective and critical discussions of digital change, including what we can learn of journalistic practice and digital journalism's viability.

In exploring these facets of Digital Journalism Studies, there are clear threads that link the scholarship in Digital Journalism Studies to that of Journalism Studies. While as a field we are similarly interested in understanding the practices of reportage, the content of journalism, and the theoretical bases for understanding that Journalism Studies has established, the dynamics of digital change and disruption make it impossible to see these as the same academic field. However, in the same way that a debate over digital 'evolution' or 'revolution' illserves discussions of digital journalism, the development of Digital Journalism Studies has drawn on (rather than rejected) this earlier work.

We can look at the work of Murray Dick as one example that illustrates this allegiance between Digital Journalism Studies and Journalism Studies. Dick has pointed to infographics as long-standing visual/textual features of journalism (2015), and he writes of their pervasiveness online and of the popularity they engender. Similarly, while 'data' have always been a feature of journalism with its ever-present emphasis on facticity (Conboy, 2013), the scale to which it has taken prominence in digital journalism and has come to define digital society more broadly presents a wholly unique area of inquiry for the field of Digital Journalism Studies.

Identifying Digital Journalism

If we can address conceptual challenges to define the underpinnings of Digital Journalism Studies, our second challenge seems to be, on the one hand, evidencing what makes digital journalism unique, both in terms of description—what does digital journalism look like?—and, more significantly, in terms of the fundamental demand of how we make sense of changing journalistic forms and the practices that lead to their creation. This is a wide-ranging set of demands, which we have broken down into several categories, including 'Developing Digital Journalism Practice' (Part V), and 'Digital Journalism Content' (Part VIII).

The focus on 'Big Data' evident in discussions of infographics, computational journalism, and algorithms poses new questions for digital journalism research around its social, cultural, and technological dimensions, as Seth Lewis explores in this volume. It has become an obtrusive component of journalistic practice as well, with coding and algorithms factoring into everyday routines—John Pavlik (Chapter 26) writes this has played out in the shifting practices of journalists in data-driven environments. Where digital journalism might be dismissed as an unnecessarily new categorization, the rise of computer-assisted and 'robot journalism' suggests otherwise. Making sense of data as a journalistic source, Nick Diakopolous argues data and digital possibilities are enabling journalists and organizations to develop new tools and media. Matt Carlson, on the other hand, suggests (Chapter 22) that data, and in particular the way they enable automation of some journalistic work, points to a hybrid journalism in the future. Juliette De Maeyer (Chapter 30), however, cautions us that the impact of dynamic technological innovation on journalistic routines has long featured in discussions of digital journalism practice, yet the exact roles and structure of some of these digital artifacts, including hypertext, remain unclear.

How this all plays out for users forms an interesting discussion within this field, as well as the ways we look at traditional forms from new digital perspectives, and informs our approach to understanding digital futures. David Dowling and Travis Vogan, for example, make a compelling and critical assessment of transitioning genres of journalism as long-form stories move online, identifying the opportunities and missteps made as outlets embrace new forms of multimedia digital storytelling. In a different light, Tanja Bosch explores how social media have enabled new connections between audiences and journalists working on more traditional platforms like radio. These and other contributions show that our foci within Digital Journalism Studies can explore not only what is new but also how traditional media have adapted to these digital opportunities, as Jose García-Aviles, Klaus Meier, and Andy Kaltenbrunner attest. They can also make sense of globally relevant questions within focused cases, whether looking at expansive online networks that connect audiences in interactive fora, as Neil Thurman and Aljosha Karim Schapals write in their study of journalists live-blogging, but also the way internet technologies have enabled 'hyperlocal' journalism within small communities, assessed by Kristy Hess and Lisa Waller. This has registered fundamental changes to journalism culture, as Folker Hanusch explores, as well as shifts in the previous boundaries of genres and forms, including with digital radio and podcasts, the focus of Guy Starkey's contribution.

The work of researchers looking in these new areas reminds us as well that practice and content in digital journalism pose challenges far beyond cataloguing new forms of journalism. This includes social media, how it is used by journalists (as Ágnes Gulyás and Alf Hermida explore), as well as the way its prominence has changed the status of journalism in different parts of the world, an area Joyce Nip focuses on in a case study of Weibo use in China. An emphasis on data poses challenging questions around individual agency, while compelling debates about morality and ethics are present throughout new forms of understanding and communicating as we explore our increasingly digital societies. For a field that tangles with the technological, human, political, and commercial nature of journalism, Digital Journalism Studies engages directly with these challenges in the questions about government surveillance as more and more activity permeates digital spaces (see the contribution by Arne Hintz, Karin Wahl-Jorgensen, and Lina Dencik). For practice, the risks of intrusion are more acute for sources working within digital technologies, or with journalists around digital dynamics; Einar Thorsen is instructive on this in his chapter on whistleblowing. In practice, this has had an effect not only on the way we talk about digital journalism but in the way journalists interact online in some of the more fraught if not repressive and even life-threatening environments which Celeste González de Bustamante and Jeannine Relly explore in their discussion of journalists' uses of social media while reporting along the US–Mexico border.

Just the same (but brand new)

Journalism's normative dimensions have been an aspect of journalism studies previously, and we have found their continued presence in the development of Digital Journalism Studies. Familiarity with terms such as 'the Fourth Estate' or journalism as a 'watchdog' with authority over information is evident in concepts like gatekeeping and agenda setting which have not disappeared in the digital contexts. Peter Bro unpacks the latter two dimensions in his chapter and examines how these stalwarts of journalism's normative dimensions are being challenged by the development of new digital forms that minimize their prominence (Bro, 2008). Martin Eide, looking at norms of transparency and accountability, argues that certain normative underpinnings when discussed in the digital context have—if not new—increased importance for trust in digital journalism. This presents an extant challenge when it comes to journalistic ethics, as Stephen J. A. Ward discusses here, where "a widely accepted digital journalism ethics does not exist" (35). Though new ideas continue to emerge, the way that digital journalism draws both organizational and professional ethics into discussion with personal ethics extends to the way we 'look' at the world, either as ironic spectators (Chouliaraki, 2013) or 'witnesses' (Allan, 2013). Both Lilie Chouliaraki and Stuart Allan engage with the ways new actors are contributing to digital journalism in considering dynamics of 'witnessing.' Lilie Chouliaraki discusses the way digital journalism has borne witness to death and destruction globally, an argument that centers our attention on questions of agency as both subjects and objects of 'spectatorship' but also on the powerful images produced using digital technologies. This question of visual 'witnessing' and its digital aspects is no longer the sole domain of the journalist. Moreover, as Stuart Allan explores in his chapter on citizen photojournalism here and in his 2013 book *Citizen Witnessing*, the role of new users has challenged (if not changed) the professional boundaries around photojournalism in a digital space.

Academic fields of study are at their best when they prioritize big questions (and the pursuit of big answers) while being sure to answer questions about 'how' those answers are developed. Perhaps because of its technological threads, Digital Journalism Studies has not developed with any such absence. The works of Thomas Lansdall-Welfare, Justin Lewis, and Nello Christianini, picking up on previous research they conducted with Ilias Flaounas, Omar Ali, Saatviga Sudhahar, Sen Jia, and Nick Mosdell (2013), have shown us that computer science can enrich our understanding of digital journalism in unique ways through massive, and previously inconceivable, automated analysis of digital content. The road they have paved has allowed us to consider new methods for analyzing social media content, which made waves as part of the study of Twitter with Farida Vis' research on 'Reading the Riots' (2013) and continues to strengthen our understanding of the ways digital content and social media form part of our journalistic world, as scholars have now applied these techniques to analyze as many as 1.8 billion tweets for their news function and to make sense of geopolitical conflicts (Malik, 2016). Drawing threads from Journalism Studies through to Digital Journalism Studies, Tom van Hout and Sarah van Leuven take the concepts of 'churnalism' first explored by Justin Lewis, Andy Williams, and Bob Franklin (2008) to show how software and digital affordances offer new ways to map the production of news content out of public relations material 'live.' As methods for understanding digital journalism and its social, cultural, and technological dimensions, we have expanded significantly our understanding of the way people interact with digital content and research including the work by Irene Costera Meijer and Tim Groot Kormelink in their chapter here and their previous research studies which have introduced exciting explanations of the ways people engage with digital content. When we broaden our explorations to ask what this means for our understandings of audiences, the work of Wiebke Loosen and Jan-Hinrik Schmidt reorient familiar discussions of news 'proximity' within Digital Journalism Studies.

Conclusion

For many years now we have seen the word 'digital' appended to all types of technologies, and it has not been absent in discussions surrounding journalism. Digital content has become commonplace, we talk about audiences of digital 'natives' who also populate universities and are now entering the workplace, while journalism itself has seen rapid and widespread change as digital newsrooms and digital journalists become the norm; journalists working in 'non-digital media' have become an endangered species in the Global North. One of the unique struggles of trying to make sense of digital journalism, a field very much defined by the scale and pace of change, is remaining comprehensive when change is ever-present. In shaping this companion, we have balanced the demands of remaining broad in range and deep in scholarly analysis of the relevant dynamics of Digital Journalism Studies. In foregrounding the innovative studies and themes that are defining Digital Journalism Studies as a field, the concerns of chapters and their thematic and scholastic approach favor work 'at the edge.' Within these pages, the *Routledge Companion to Digital Journalism Studies* offers a collection of essays addressing these and other key issues and debates which shape the field of Digital Journalism Studies. With the proliferation of digital media, journalism has undergone many changes, which have driven scholars to reassess its most fundamental questions. In the face of digital change, we ask again—'Who is a journalist?' and 'What is journalism?'—and, in exploring the many facets of these questions in a digital era, have continued to map new areas of inquiry and explore new aspects of journalism. This *Companion* seizes on the developing scholarly agenda committed to understanding digital journalism and brings together the work of those seeking to address key theoretical concerns and solve unique methodological riddles.

Within Digital Journalism Studies, we have embraced these new challenges and developed new ways of understanding these shifts. As scholars, the authors here have recalibrated the way we make our observations of the digital world, and through the work of the contributors here and our colleagues in the field, we can focus less on the digital patina of new forms of journalism and develop new understandings. This has also allowed us to be innovative and critical and to develop theoretically rich work in ways previously unknown. Within this volume we have embraced scholarship at the leading edge of research, but to a contributor we are all keenly away that in this nascent field there are ever more exciting dynamics on the horizon. As editors, we are equally aware that the contributors we have gathered here are pushing beyond the limits they have outlined in their chapters and will soon be asking new questions, joined by new researchers who have embraced this field with equal enthusiasm.

We are content to be offering a first set of answers, but eager to address further questions about the future of Digital Journalism Studies in the certain knowledge that there is so much more to come.

Structure

In this *Companion* you will find a collection of invited essays from academics across the globe to explore what makes Digital Journalism Studies unique. Reflections on the changes that have faced the practice, the product, and the study of digital journalism are addressed by those invested in making sense of these substantive changes.

Part I focuses on the need to explore the ways in which key themes and ideas, which have been central to journalism studies, require theoretical reconsideration in the context of digital media and change. This requirement includes detailed consideration of bedrock questions such as 'What is journalism?' and 'Who is a journalist?' as well as how the interdisciplinary tenets of Digital Journalism Studies have taken shape. This section also addresses the need to reassess fundamentally the nature and role of journalism ethics in the digital age, alongside considerations of the possible redundancy of traditional concepts such as gatekeeping, their metamorphosis in the new digital setting for journalism, along with the moral questions that confront our increasingly digital world.

Part II offers a collection of essays exploring the necessity for innovative research design and methodological approaches to enable research-based scholarly studies of the changes in digital journalism's products and practices. Chapters address the hitherto unseen challenges of analyzing digital and changeable content, observing journalistic production, managing copious amounts of data, and assessing user and audience activity. However, they also highlight the affordances of technologies for researching digital journalism, for tackling large data sets in real time, and for developing understandings that were previously inconceivable.

Part III considers the new business models and emerging financial strategies established to resource and sustain a viable and democratic as well as digital journalism. Chapters reassess journalism's business models and the changes to its traditional revenue streams, but go further to look at new forms of reaching audiences and monetizing content, as well as those tools such as aggregators which can prove a hindrance as well as local markets with their unique dynamics. Sustainability extends to capture questions of political economy, as well as the trials (and sometimes errors) of journalism organizations adapting to online change.

Part IV addresses some of the key debates which have characterized the emergence of Digital Journalism Studies, including the significance of mobile news for digital journalism, the impact of social media on breaking and sourcing news, and considers the 'networked' character of these spaces. We also explore the acceptability and role of 'actants,' data, and of robots in the processes and with these the growing significance of transparency and accountability tools in evaluating the digital news environment. These debates are not limited to concerns of production, and the audience is brought into these debates in assessing online comments and the expression of free speech, the complex nature of citizen journalism, whether it is effective, and the ways citizen journalists contribute to news agendas.

Part V explores the notable changes which have occurred across all aspects of journalism practice, especially journalists' relationships with sources, their uses of hypertext and an assessment of its emergence, as well as a more nuanced analysis of the impact of web analytics on journalists' editorial autonomy and the development of wholly new editorial formats and practices such as live-blogging.

Part VI focuses on the radical reshaping and recasting of relationships between journalists and their audiences along with the fundamental scholarly reappraisal and rethinking of that relationship in Digital Journalism Studies. Chapters explore new conceptual understandings of this relationship via discussions of seminal ideas that revisit the unidirectional relationship between news media and audiences, the emergence of concepts such as audience repertoires, as well as news 'on the move' and the changing dynamics of proximity and distance. This revisiting of the audience engages with the shifting vocabulary and changed relationships between audiences as consumers, readers, and citizens to capture the changing reading practices that characterize audiences' wide-ranging habits in the digital journalism setting.

Part VII considers the broad social, political, and journalistic implications of social media for traditional theorizing of the key concept of the public sphere. Chapters analyze the role of various social media (Twitter, YouTube, and Facebook) as sources for journalists as well as the changing understanding of citizens as reporters or breakers of news, but also consider journalists' differential uses of social media and the extent to which their uses of social media have been 'normalized' into journalists' routine professional practice.

Part VIII examines the content of digital journalism with a focus on how traditional/legacy media have adapted to the digital revolution via convergent and multiplatform working. Particular chapters deal with the metamorphosis of newspapers to online platforms and broadcast journalism's increasing production of podcasts. Other chapters examine the dynamics of change for specific content such as infographics considering their prevalence and popularity, digital photojournalism and changing amateur/professional boundaries, and the impact of new and digital ways of telling stories for long-form narrative journalism online.

In *Part IX*, scholars whose work in Digital Journalism Studies focuses on Africa, Australia, China, Europe, India, and Latin America explore developments in the journalism industry and journalism practice in their particular regional setting with its unique patterns of media organization and ownership, contending with relations between state, media, and nonstate actors. The difference in the ways Digital Journalism manifests in these areas as well as the impact on journalism practices, roles, cultures, and histories is explored. The concern is to assess the degree to which the transition to a digital journalism is occurring across diverse global communities and unpacks both the promise engendered by digital journalism in countries around the world, as well as its limitations and risks that come with hyperconnected societies.

In *Part X*, a final set of chapters points to the problematic challenges in digital journalism's contemporary and near future that remain on research agendas. With the reach of digital technologies, new risks have been introduced which have had an effect on the nature of journalism and whistleblowing, as have issues of surveillance and government intervention when access to the same infrastructure that makes digital journalism intriguing also poses uncertainty. We close with a conventionally but perhaps too gloomily titled 'Epilogue' exploring the ecological and ethical implications of digital journalism and digital approaches to making sense of the world, emphasizing what we miss when we lean on dominant understandings of digital change.

References

Allan, S. (2013) *Citizen Witnessing*. Cambridge, UK: Polity Press.

Benkler, Y. (2011) "A Free Irresponsible Press: WikiLeaks and the Battle Over the Soul of the Networked Fourth Estate." *Harvard Civil Rights-Civil Liberties Law Review* 46: 311–397.

Boczkowski, P. (2004) *Digitizing the News: Innovation in Online Newspapers*. Cambridge, MA: MIT Press.

Boczkowski, P. and Mitchelstein, E. (2013) *The News Gap*. Cambridge, MA: MIT Press.

Bødker, H. (2015) "Journalism as Cultures of Circulation." *Digital Journalism* 3(1): 101–115.

Bro, P. (2008) "Normative Navigations in the News Media." *Journalism* 9(3): 309–329.

Broussard, M. (2015) "Artificial Intelligence for Investigative Reporting: Using an Expert System to Enhance Journalists' Ability to Discover Original Public Affairs Stories." *Digital Journalism* 3(6): 814–831.

Bruns, A. (2007) "Produsage." In *Proceedings of the 6th ACM SIGCHI Conference on Creativity & Cognition*, Washington, DC, pp. 99–106.

Carlson, M. and Lewis, S. (eds) (2015) *Boundaries of Journalism: Professionalism, Practices and Participation*. Abingdon, UK: Routledge.

Castells, M. (2000) *The Rise of the Network Society*. Oxford, UK: Wiley-Blackwell.

Chouliaraki, L. (2013) *The Ironic Spectator*. Cambridge, UK: Polity Press.

Chyi, H.I., Lewis, S.C. and Zheng, N. (2012) "A Matter of Life and Death? Examining How Newspapers Covered the Newspaper 'Crisis.'" *Journalism Studies* 13(3): 305–324.

Coddington, M. (2014) "Defending Judgment and Context in 'Original Reporting': Journalists' Construction of Newswork in a Networked Age." *Journalism* 15(6): 678–695.

Conboy, M. (2013) *Journalism Studies: The Basics*. Abingdon, UK: Routledge.

Curran, J. (2012) "Reinterpreting the internet." In Curran, J., Fenton, N. and Freedman, D. (eds) *Misunderstanding the Internet*. Abingdon, UK: Routledge, pp. 3–33.

Deuze, M. (2009) "The People Formerly Known as the Employers." *Journalism* 10(3): 315–319.

Dick, M. (2015) "Just Fancy That: An Analysis of Infographic Propaganda in the Daily Express, 1956–1959." *Journalism Studies* 16(2): 152–174.

Domingo, D., Quandt, T., Heinonen, A., Paulussen, S., Singer, J. and Vujnovic, M. (2009) "Participatory Journalism Practices in the Media and Beyond: An International Comparative Study of Initiatives in Online Newspapers." In Franklin, B. (ed.) *The Future of Newspapers*. London, UK: Routledge, 203–218.

Eldridge, S. (2014) "Boundary Maintenance and Interloper Media Reaction: Differentiating between Journalism's Discursive Enforcement Processes." *Journalism Studies* 15(1): 1–16.

Eldridge, S. (2015) "Change and Continuity: Online Media through History's Lens." In Conboy, M. and Steel, J. (eds) *The Routledge Companion to British Media History*, Abingdon, UK: Routledge, pp. 528–538.

Fico, F., Lacy, S., Wildman, S., Baldwin, T., Bergan D. and Zube, P. (2013) "Citizen Journalism Sites as Information Substitutes and Complements for United States Newspaper Coverage of Local Governments." *Digital Journalism* 1(1): 152–168.

Flaounas, I., Ali, O., Lansdall-Welfare, T., De Bie, T., Mosdell, N., Lewis, J., et al. (2013) "Research Methods in the Age of Digital Journalism: Massive-Scale Automated Analysis of Newscontent – Topics, Style and Gender." *Digital Journalism* 1(1): 102–116.

Franklin, B. (2013) "Editorial." *Digital Journalism* 1(1): 1–5.

Gillmor, D. (2004) *We the Media; The Rise of Citizen Journalists*. Sebastopol, CA: O'Reilly Media.

Hellmueller, L. and Li, Y. (2015) "Contest over Content: Longitudinal Study of the CNN iReport Effect on the Journalistic Field." *Journalism Practice* 9(5): 617–633.

Jardin, X. (2004) "We're All Journalists Now." *Wired*, 8 November. Available from: http://archive.wired.com/culture/lifestyle/news/2004/08/64534.

Ksiazek, T. and Peer, L. (2011) "YouTube and the Challenge to Journalism: New Standards for News Videos Online." *Journalism Studies* 12(1): 45–63.

Lewis, J., Williams, A. and Franklin, B. (2008) "A Compromised Fourth Estate?" *Journalism Studies* 9(1): 1–20.

Malik, M. and Pfeffer, J. (2016) "A Macroscopic Analysis of News Content in Twitter." *Digital Journalism*. DOI:10.1080/21670811.2015.1133249

Rosen, J. (2006) "PressThink: The People Formerly Known as the Audience." Available from: archive.pressthink.org/2006/06/27/ppl_frmr_p.html

Shapiro, I. (2014) "Why Democracies Need a Functional Definition of Journalism Now More than Ever." *Journalism Studies* 15(5): 555–565.

Shirky, C. (2003) "Power Laws, Weblogs and Inequality." In Lebkowsky, J. and Ratcliffe, M. (eds) *Extreme Democracy*, Lulu.com, pp. 46–52.

Singer, J. (2005) "The Political J-Blogger: 'Normalizing' a New Media Form to Fit Old Norms and Practices." *Journalism* 6(2): 173–198.

Steensen, S. and Ahva, L. (2015) "Theories of Journalism in a Digital Age." *Journalism Practice* 9(1): 1–18.

Vis, F. (2013) "Twitter as a Reporting Tool for Breaking News: Journalists tweeting the 2011 UK Riots." *Digital Journalism* 1(1): 27–47.

Wahl-Jorgensen, K. (2013) "Is WikiLeaks Challenging the Paradigm of Journalism? Boundary Work and Beyond." *International Journal of Communication* 8: 2581–2592.

Wall, M. (2004) "Blogs as Black Market Journalism: A New Paradigm for News." *Interface: The Journal for Education, Community and Values* 4(2). Available from: http://bcis.pacificu.edu/journal/2004/01/edit.php

Ward, S. J. A. (2017) "Digital Journalism Ethics." In Franklin, B. and Eldridge II, S. (eds) *The Routledge Companion to Digital Journalism Studies*. Abingdon, UK: Routledge, pp. 35–43.

Westlund, O. (2013) "Mobile News: A Review and Model of Journalism in an Age of Mobile Media." *Digital Journalism* 1(1): 6–26.

PART I

Conceptualizing digital journalism studies

1

WHAT'S DIGITAL? WHAT'S JOURNALISM?

Asmaa Malik and Ivor Shapiro

This book offers several valuable perspectives on the continuing evolution of digital journalism. If you are holding it in your hands and flipping its pages, you are well aware of the limitations of ink and paper. If, however, you are reading it on a mobile device and swiping the screen to get to the next paragraph, you may wonder why this chapter is not being updated even as you read it.

Therein lie both the challenge and the promise of the field we are discussing—and a clue to its definition. The two words *digital journalism* contain at least two sets of definitional problems. First, the idea of *journalism*—as in something distinct from multiple alternative sources of information about news and public affairs—has become increasingly harder to pin down. As for the idea of *digital*, it must surely refer to more than merely the means by which information is disseminated, since printed pages and broadcast news have been available on digital platforms for several years.

Credible arguments could therefore be made that practically all journalism is digital today and that practically all nonfiction (or practically none of it) is journalism. In what follows, we will argue otherwise, on both counts. In our view, *journalism* continues to be distinguished from other nonfiction by a small collection of somewhat easily recognized characteristics. Meanwhile, *digital* refers not so much to means of production and reception but to content itself—its voice and reach, the manner and stages of its evolution, and its potential impact. Conversely, *analog* journalism, although in decline, lives on, in static productions for both print and audio-visual platforms.

Yet, we must concede right away that, just as the border between journalism and other nonfiction may be porous, so is that between digital and analog journalism. Some news begins digitally and either ends with production in a newspaper or newscast or treats that static production as a way station toward a further stage of evolution. Elsewhere, news that begins in legacy form ends up as social material to be fought over, corrected, or enhanced. Either way, as we will show, the shadow of that seemingly simple modifier, *digital*, extends over substantive transformations in the process, technique, and norms of journalism itself.

First, however, as with any modified noun phrase, we begin the task of definition with the noun. We cannot isolate what *digital journalism* is until we clearly understand what *journalism* is—and, thereby, what it is not.

Defining 'journalism'

The idea of defining journalism has become increasingly controversial in this century, as the "boundaries between journalism and other forms of public communication" become less intuitive (Deuze, 2007: 141). Much of the debate stems from a worry over according special status to a class of practitioners (Gant, 2007; Hartley, 2000: 41; Ingram, 2011; Rosen, 2011), which raises yet more problematic questions over whether or not journalists comprise a 'profession' (Allison, 1986, 1986; Banning, 1999; Deuze, 2005; Merrill, 1986). This knot is neatly sliced, however, when one restricts the project to defining a set of practices (journalism) rather than a class of practitioners (journalists) (Zelizer, 2004: 42–43). Shapiro, who described this practice-focused approach as 'functional definition,' proposed that journalism "comprises the activities involved in an independent pursuit of accurate information about current or recent events and its original presentation for public edification" (2014: 561).

The most tenuous part of Shapiro's proposal is the phrase *independent pursuit* and particularly, in a digital context, the word *pursuit*. Not one but at least two distinct types of activity may be encompassed under the heading of journalism, and they are classically referred to as *reporting* and *commentary*. Many legacy newspapers, especially in the anglophone tradition that Hallin and Mancini (2004) termed the North Atlantic or liberal national media systems, divide editorial teams, workflows, and products into 'news' and 'opinion,' with different editorial standards and workflows pertaining to each. The degree to which political ideology shapes journalists' activities varies widely across the globe, mirroring a range of culturally oriented professional identities that Hanitzsch (2011) classified under four headings: populist disseminators, detached watchdogs, critical change agents, and opportunist facilitators—with Anglo-American cultures leaning toward the second type. In addition, journalists' autonomy will naturally be constrained by the sensibilities and power of their bosses, the publishers. But, whatever the degree of alignment between practice and ideology, journalists' work will at various times be concentrated either on description (as performed by reporters, editors, and chase producers, for example) or on commentary (columnists, reviewers, op-ed editors). The latter group does not so much *pursue* information as analyze and opine on the information that colleagues, competitors, or other discoverers have brought to light.

We therefore adopt Shapiro's definition with the addition of three words, thus: "Journalism comprises the activities involved in an independent pursuit of, or commentary upon, accurate information about current or recent events and its original presentation for public edification." This definition contains five complementary tests that must *all* be satisfied to achieve its definitional purpose.

First, is the work *independent?* We distinguish this idea from one with which it is commonly confused, *objectivity*, by focusing on economic interests in the relationship between author and content. The root idea is that a direct material interest in a certain outcome should not drive what is deemed to be interesting or truthful. This is, by far, the most controversial of the five tests in an age which tends to think of independence as epistemologically impossible. Yet, many journalists continue to recognize themselves by self-imposed ethical constraints or 'ideal-typical traits' (Deuze, 2007: 163) that include the core idea that journalistic public service is something distinct from public relations, or propaganda.

Second, is a concern for *accuracy* central to the project? Whether pursuing information or commenting on it, does the work show evidence of an aspiration (at least) to factual truthfulness? The degree of rigor in verification may vary greatly depending on the work's authorial approach, medium, purpose, and subject matter (Shapiro *et al.*, 2013), but absent a clear interest in accuracy, it will be difficult to make a claim that the work is journalistic in any accepted sense.

Is the subject matter *current or recent events?* Although past events form part of the context of many works of journalism and may even inspire such works (e.g. on significant anniversaries), it is this test, above all, that draws a line between works of journalism and of historiography.

Is the presentation *original?* The measure here is not subjective or form-focused (as art reviewers might use the word) but rather quite literal: has the work involved new thinking, research, or creative effort, or is it merely a collection (aggregation) of others' work? This test is, of course, highly relevant in defining journalism in the age of the social Web: a news organization like Reported.ly—which actively curates and verifies social media posts to construct breaking news narratives—will make a better claim to creating journalism than, for example, Google Search.

Finally, is the content presented for *public edification?* The word journalism is not fitting in reference to communication among experts within their private areas of expertise. Rather, journalism seeks, by definition, "to broaden the boundaries within which information is known and understood" (Shapiro, 2014: 560).

In our view, a work that passes all five of the above tests is, by definition, journalism. But is it *digital?* That depends on a whole other set of questions.

Finding 'digital' journalism

The first appearance of journalism in online form has been attributed to Canada's *The Globe and Mail*, which in 1979 began publishing news electronically on the same day as its print edition; the next year, the *Columbus Dispatch* published the United States' first online newspaper (Zelizer and Allan, 2010: 104). Today, the digital dissemination of journalism is ubiquitous (Barthel, 2015), but, in order to get beyond a merely technological definition, we will use our exploration of the various spaces in which we intuitively recognize 'digital' journalism to note common features that appear to be defining.

Charting this rapidly shifting landscape carries the risk that many of the examples we cite might be mere memories by the time this book is printed! But for now, at least, we find ourselves able, relying largely on our own experience, to distinguish seven types of manifestation in which journalism seems a way that, at least intuitively, seems distinct from legacy or analog forms. We will list each of these digital spaces with, in each case, a few implications that begin to distinguish the nature of digital users' and creators' experience.

Web publications are both digital journalism's stalwarts and harbingers of its broader nature. Starting from the first attempts of news organizations to publish 'shovelware' on the Web in the late twentieth century, the online experience offered users new opportunities to curate their own news experience using topical headline lists and intertextual links to previously reported material (Scott, 2005: 93). Today, the multimedia site of a typical large news organization serves as a hub for the latest news and feature coverage with a view to further distribution via cross-platform channels and social networks. It includes blogs and live blogs, digital-only videos and newscasts, podcasts, and photo galleries. The *New York Times* website, for example, is not only home to breaking news text and multimedia content but also features information-rich, interactive graphics that help readers understand everything from presidential campaign tactics to real estate investment strategies.

Social networks

The internet homepage, once considered a news organization's most valuable digital asset, has lost its prominence as people turn to social media platforms such as Twitter, Facebook, and Snapchat for links to news and information (Thompson, 2014). These networks allow readers to use lists, feeds, tags, and other devices to tailor the information they receive by interest and by influencer and allow publishers to reach directly into users' feeds to provide information of predictable interest (Evans, 2015; Shaw, 2015). Digital journalism on social platforms has unprecedented potential for wide distribution of content, as users not only share curated and recommended information within their personal and global networks but also use them to comment and share their takes on the news of the day. Conversely, journalists often tap into the discussions and debates that take place on social networks to take the pulse of audiences.

Search results and the complex search engine algorithms behind them affect the ways that people find news online. Several factors, including keywords and headlines, can contribute to the algorithmic ranking of search results (Richmond, 2008). And when they turn up false reports and questionable or reputation-damaging information, search results can have lasting consequences, for example, on news subjects' attempts to restart their lives.

Mobile web and publications

Responsive design allows websites to change in layout and architecture depending on viewers' devices, without changing the content available. However, some organizations have created unique web- and application-based publications for mobile devices, allowing journalism content to morph as it moves across platforms. *The Montreal Gazette*, for example, convened a smartphone team dedicated to creating and repackaging stories, breaking news alerts, and multimedia based on the habits of mobile users. By 2015, two of Canada's largest newspapers, *La Presse* and *The Toronto Star*, had launched tablet publications to package and display news and feature stories that maximize the platform's visual impact. Still other news organizations have entered into exclusive relationships for their content. In 2015, *Vice* magazine's newscast, *Daily Vice*, first became available in its entirety to customers of a specific mobile carrier, with only an abridged version online (Dobby, 2014).

Mobile and desktop applications

Another way readers and viewers engage with digital journalism is through applications that aggregate content and push notifications on mobile and desktop devices (Weiss, 2013). Applications such as Circa offer readers a rewritten take on developing stories using several online sources and notify them of any updates to stories they indicate an interest in. Others, such as Al-Jazeera's *AJ+*, use a strong sense of graphic design to share information via 'cards,' featuring facts, data visualizations, and conversation-starting questions, which prompt users to comment on trending news topics. Most mobile and desktop applications are native, keeping users within the boundaries of one news organization and its content, relying on user loyalty and personalization to drive engagement (Newman, 2014).

Wearable technology offers emerging platforms for digital journalism. Increasing functionality allows physical data and location information to dictate the content delivered to users. In that sense, they may be able to detect a need for news and information before it has even been articulated. The now-discontinued Google Glass prototype delivered headlines of geo-located news as wearers walked through a city (Cellan-Jones, 2015). This was succeeded by wrist-worn devices including the Apple and Android watches which capture a snapshot of the user's vital statistics and use that data to deliver information tailored for that person in that moment. The Oculus Rift virtual reality headset promises to deliver immersive journalism experiences, such as *The Des Moines Register*'s 'Harvest of Change' project, which deposits the viewer into a 3D version of an endangered Iowa farm, replete with hay bales, animals, and tractors (Gayomali, 2014). Other interactive clothing-related technologies seem likely to follow.

Commenting

As with the previous examples, comments on digital news stories and multimedia are not limited to the originating news organization's website. The conversation is carried through social media networks and mobile publications and applications. When it comes to digital journalism, the potential for immediate engagement cannot be underestimated. Users not only comment on news and multimedia, but they can point out inaccuracies and bring additional expertise and context to the stories. Some news sites use Facebook plug-ins, for example, to ensure commenters use their real identities; others have turned off commenting features on controversial stories or have done away with them altogether, citing concerns about incivility and cyberbullying (Hochberg, 2014). Still other outlets, such as the *New York Times*, use active moderation to post only the most germane comments on original stories (Sullivan, 2012).

Distinguishing characteristics

Having identified where digital journalism is currently found, we are in a position to begin isolating features that distinguish this universe substantively from the journalism that existed up until the dawn of the internet. While not all of the following seven characteristics are evident or significant in all digital journalism all the time, we argue that they may all make a substantive difference to the content and impact of the work. Among other things, digital journalism across diverse platforms has the following characteristics.

Interactive

The relationship between digital publishers and consumers is two-way. Readers are able to draw attention to inaccuracies and offer their expertise. In 2010, *The Guardian* and the *Washington Post* asked their readers to help them analyze, interpret, and visualize information from the 90,000 classified documents publicly released by WikiLeaks documents (Chokshi, 2010). Crowd-funded news organizations, such as *The Tyee* in British Columbia, allow readers to donate money for specific topics they would like journalists to investigate. Conversely, analytics tools allow news organizations to glean huge amounts of information about audiences and their viewing habits.

Unfinished

Any work of journalism may go through many versions and forms before it is published, but it is the possibility of future permutations that distinguishes digital. At least since the Oklahoma City bombing on April 19, 1995, which has been described as a 'journalistic Bastille Day' for the "sudden liberation of newspapers from the time-constraints associated with print" (Zelizer and Allan, 2010: 104–105), journalists have gained experience with breaking news in bits rather than full stories. A live blog covering an ongoing event, such as a public hearing or a trial, may be continually updated for months. An article that begins as a breaking news report can be rewritten throughout the day to reflect new information discovered by its authors plus readers' corrections, clarifications, and additions. Indeed, digital journalism increasingly reaches news consumers in unmediated form: a 2012 Pew Research Center report found that 35 percent of news videos produced by news organizations and posted to YouTube were comprised of raw and unedited footage (Journalism and Media Staff, 2012). This unmediated quality is also a characteristic of unedited live blogs and live tweets, as well as of live streams from news events, such as press conferences.

Long-lasting

The potential lifespan of a digitally published work is counted in decades or centuries versus the days or weeks of analog news. In many cases, the headline and the link are automatically sent to Twitter and saved to online, research, and proprietary archives. Within minutes of its first appearance, a news story will be tweeted and retweeted and posted in Facebook newsfeeds. Sometimes readers will create screen-grabs of particularly noteworthy articles and circulate *them*. While several news outlets, such as BuzzFeed, use tracking codes to follow their content through various networks, there remains a strong potential for stories to go on and have lives of their own (Robischon, 2015).

Global

Just as digital content's reach seems practically infinite in time, so too in (earthly) space. Even if news is created to reflect local interests, sharing via social media gives it the opportunity to be distributed independently of its originating platforms and news sources. An individual's geographic proximity to a breaking news event no longer determines how long it will take for them to receive information. Social media and news alerts, for example, allow immigrants to keep up with real-time information from their homelands via on-the-ground sources, rather than relying on foreign correspondents' reports. The English language *The Montreal Gazette* counts among its digital readers sizeable numbers of anglophone ex-Montrealers, whereas French is the predominant language in the paper's home province of Quebec.

Personal

The language of the internet is a conversational one; journalism with personality is apt to be most widely read. Starting in 2006, the *Guardian*'s Comment Is Free area invited writers from around the world to post edited stories about current affairs; the *Huffington Post* allows guest bloggers to post lifestyle and relationship stories directly onto the site. News reporters, too, have been affected by the shift from a more omniscient, neutral tone to a more familiar one. Though their voices are still generally expected to be more muted in news stories, the cultivation of a digital persona allows them to selectively reveal other dimensions of their personalities. For example, a crime reporter may write a straight news story about a dramatic arrest for the website or smartphone, but in her Twitter posts, she may report from the scene in a more conversational tone, adding context as events unfold.

Unsiloed

Not for some time have news consumers needed journalists as gatekeepers of information (Bruns, 2005; Singer, 2014). In the absence of this hegemony, media organizations now readily link to competitors' work and other sources to help offer a one-stop experience. Journalism in the digital age exists alongside other media forms, including personal blogs, advocacy writing, and advertorial content. A search on a world leader's name will yield links to a smattering of news stories along with links to his official page, a Wikipedia article, his YouTube channel, and Twitter feed. Digital users therefore must learn how to filter results like these for actual news as opposed to self-disseminated propaganda or may filter in only news and information that is in accordance with their personal beliefs and political views.

An evolutionary moment

Since digital journalism often evolves from analog beginnings, a useful step toward definition may be taken by asking: what happens *at the moment* at which analog work turns digital? Several types of transformation can be gleaned from the descriptions above.

Digital journalism is born, we suggest, when the author–audience *relationship* becomes more interactive and engaged and when a work's completeness or limitation becomes a question or challenge, rather than a fact. On the other hand, at that same moment of birth, the *impact* of a work becomes permanent enough to achieve lasting impact, for good or ill.

These moments are not merely interesting transformations in the communication process; they have consequential significance. Video may be especially compelling when it is disseminated as raw footage, and readers' interactions with data in multimedia visualizations may provoke far greater emotional response—and attain greater credibility—than is possible in the analog experience (Grim and Wing, 2015). There is an intimacy involved with reading and watching a story like the *New York Times* breakthrough 'Snow Fall' project, which combined interactive graphics, videos, and a multi-part text story into an almost immersive experience about a deadly avalanche (Dowling and Vogan, 2015). Without the distractions of television breaks or newspaper advertising, audiences become able to engage with news content in the privacy of their own computers. Further, the innately human impulse to share a personal experience with a friend or a relative is easily facilitated with the help of social media sharing tools.

A further transformation occurs when the quest for accuracy is seen as a work in progress rather than a *fait accompli*: an inaccurate story may be updated with correct information and a correction may be appended. Eaves and Owen put it this way: "As good as a 21-year-old Ivy League [fact-checking] intern may be, he or she will never be as clever or knowledgeable as the combined fact-checking capacity of thousands of readers" (2010: 42–43). And the *unsiloed* availability of news may result in consumers receiving mostly information that confirms their prejudices; people tend to gravitate toward information that confirms their attitudes (Knobloch-Westerwick, 2009: 443–444) and to take control over the diversity of online information sources to increase their exposure to opinions consistent with their own views, although this does not necessarily mean losing contact with other opinions (Garrett, 2009: 691–694).

On the other hand, the *longevity* and *ubiquity* of digital news products may result in misinformation, as news reports proliferate without either context and beyond reach of corrections. This is further complicated by the fact that news websites have been found to dedicate more time and resources to propagating questionable claims than verifying or debunking them (Silverman, 2015). Once a story is posted to an online publication, Google instantly indexes it and makes it discoverable. Meanwhile, the consequences of that same longevity place additional pressure on publishers. Whereas analog archives document news content, however flawed, as originally published, content that publishers regret can now be made to disappear. In February 2015, the *Toronto Star* published a controversial story about alleged ill-effects of the HPV vaccine, Gardasil—and unpublished it almost three weeks later, effectively deleting the story from Google search results (Braganza, 2015). Meanwhile, courts in some jurisdictions have recognized 'the right to be forgotten,' according to which individuals can have specific information about them deleted from search engines (Gibbs, 2014).

Definition as work-in-progress

When we began work on this chapter, we assumed that by its end, having first identified the boundaries of the digital journalism space and then diagnosed its characteristics, we would arrive at a definition in the literal, exclusionary sense. We would, we assumed, propose a series of hurdles or tests for the existence of digital journalism, in the vein proposed above for journalism itself. After all, the act of definition is generally seen as "quite literally exclusive: any definition of 'dogness' must exclude cats" (Shapiro, 2014: 555).

But, having come this far, we find ourselves short of our goal. To pursue the canine metaphor, it is as if we have identified that the four-legged mammal in question is carnivorous, domesticated, capable of barking, and possessed of muzzle and tail—but we have not arrived at the genus-defining line between *Canis* and *Felis*. We might know digital journalism when we see it, almost as readily as we can tell a dog from a cat, but we cannot (yet) present a series of tests that a work of journalism must pass in order to be, substantively, digital.

If this is an admission of defeat, it is only partial. To present a series of characteristics that are *commonly present* in the genus is, we suggest, at least an important step toward definition. But, alternatively, a series of recognizable characteristics may be seen as simply a different type of definition itself—one that is inclusive rather than exclusive.

In this more optimistic view, the definition of our problematic adjective is structurally different from that of the noun. On the one hand, the activities that comprise *journalism* may be recognized by the presence of *all* of the following: an independent relationship between author and subject matter, a central concern for accuracy, an interest in current or recent events, a degree of originality in presentation, and an audience beyond those already 'in the know.' The definition of *digital*, on the other hand, is inclusive. It consists not of a series of hurdles but of a range of landmarks. We propose, therefore, that digital journalism may be recognized by the presence of *some combination of* interactive engagement, author–audience collaboration, contingent publication, resilient impact, and global reach.

An inclusive definition of this kind may be viewed as appropriate not only to the inclusive culture of the digital sphere but also to the contingent state of evolution in the form itself. The concept of digital journalism is so new that the word 'digital' is missing from an otherwise comprehensive set of keywords in news and journalism studies compiled just 5 years before this writing (Zelizer and Allan, 2010). In that light, how could the definition but be unfinished? The chapter you are reading is, after all, the very opposite of digital: we, the authors, wrote it in mid-2015 in Toronto, Canada, and here it sits, warts and all, for your consideration in the place that you occupy at the moment. Had our work been done digitally, we might perhaps have come this far, presented it for your consideration, and then collaborated with you and a global universe of readers to take it further, and make it better.

As it stands, the best we can do is appeal to our common digital opportunities to invite your reaction. You will find us on whatever has replaced Twitter, Facebook, etc., by the time of this reading. See you on the internet.

Further reading

Major contributions to the unfinished work of defining journalism have been made by Mark Deuze's (2005) "What is journalism? Professional identity and ideology of journalists reconsidered." A more global understanding of the various ways in which journalism is understood, practiced, and published may be found in Hallin and Mancini's (2004) *Comparing media systems: Three models of media and politics* and Thomas Hanitzsch's (2011) "Populist disseminators, detached watchdogs, critical change agents and opportunist facilitators: Professional milieus, the journalistic field and autonomy in 18 countries." Jane Singer has been exploring for many years the difference that the internet makes to journalists' traditional 'gatekeeping' function—most recently in her 2014 paper, "User-generated visibility: Secondary gatekeeping in a shared media space."

References

Allison, M. (1986) "A Literature Review of Approaches to the Professionalism of Journalists." *Journal of Mass Media Ethics* 1(2): 5–19.

Banning, S.A. (1999) "The Professionalization of Journalism: A Nineteenth-Century Beginning." *Journalism History* 24(4): 157–163.

Barthel, M. (2015) "Newspapers: Fact Sheet." State of the News Media 2015, *Pew Research Center*, 29 April. Available from: http://www.journalism.org/2015/04/29/newspapers-fact-sheet/ (accessed 29 May 2015).

Braganza, C. (2015) "The Toronto Star's Gardasil Controversy: A Timeline. *J-Source*, 12 February." Available from: http://j-source.ca/article/toronto-stars-gardasil-controversy-timeline.

Bruns, A. (2005) *Gatewatching: Collaborative Online News Production*. 1st edn. New York, NY: Peter Lang Publishing.

Cellan-Jones, R. (2015) "Google Glass Sales Halted but Firm Says Kit is Not Dead." *BBC News*, 15 January. Available from: http://www.bbc.com/news/technology-30831128 (accessed 29 May 2015).

Chokshi, N. (2010) "The WikiLeaks Crowdsourcing Begins." *The Atlantic*, 26 July. Available from: http://www.theatlantic.com/technology/archive/2010/07/the-wikileaks-crowdsourcing-begins/60402/.

Deuze, M. (2005) "What Is Journalism? Professional Identity and Ideology of Journalists Reconsidered." *Journalism* 6(4): 442–464.

Deuze, M. (2007) *Media Work*. Digital Media and Society Series, Cambridge, UK: Polity Press.

Dobby, C. (2014) "Bad Language and Leather: Rogers-Vice Partnership Targets Millennials." *The Globe and Mail*, 30 October. Available from: http://www.theglobeandmail.com/report-on-business/rogers-vice-media-to-partner-on-100-million-venture/article21380037/ (accessed 31 May 2015).

Dowling, D. and Vogan, T. (2015) "Can We 'Snowfall' This?" *Digital Journalism* 3(2): 209–224.

Eaves, D. and Owen, T. (2010) "Missing the Link: How the Internet is Saving Journalism." In Benedetti, P., Kierans, K. and Currie, T. (eds) *The New Journalist: Roles, Skills, and Critical Thinking*. Toronto, ON: Emond Montgomery Publications, pp. 39–62.

Evans, P. (2015) "Facebook's Instant Articles Service Launches with 9 Major Web Publishers." *CBC News*, 13 May. Available from: http://www.cbc.ca/1.3072156 (accessed 22 May 2015).

Gant, S. (2007) *We're All Journalists Now*. New York, NY: Free Press.

Garrett, R.K. (2009) "Politically Motivated Reinforcement Seeking: Reframing the Selective Exposure Debate." *Journal of Communication* 59(4): 676–699.

Gayomali, C. (2014) "How an Iowa Newspaper is Using Oculus Rift for Big, Ambitious Journalism." *Fast Company*, 22 September. Available from: http://www.fastcompany.com/3035851/world-changing-ideas/how-an-iowa-newspaper-is-using-oculus-rift-for-big-ambitious-journalism (accessed 22 May 2015).

Gibbs, S. (2014) "Google Hauled in by Europe Over 'Right to be Forgotten' Reaction." *The Guardian*, 24 July. Available from: http://www.theguardian.com/technology/2014/jul/24/google-hauled-in-by-europe-over-right-to-be-forgotten-reaction (accessed 22 May 2015).

Grim, R. and Wing, N. (2015) "Here's a News Report We'd Be Reading If Walter Scott's Killing Wasn't on Video." *The Huffington Post*, 8 April. Available from: http://www.huffingtonpost.com/2015/04/08/walter-scott-shooting-without-video_n_7024404.html (accessed 13 May 2015).

Hallin, D.C. and Mancini, P. (2004) *Comparing Media Systems: Three Models of Media and Politics*. New York, NY: Cambridge University Press.

Hanitzsch, T. (2011) "Populist Disseminators, Detached Watchdogs, Critical Change Agents and Opportunist Facilitators: Professional Milieus, the Journalistic Field and Autonomy in 18 Countries." *International Communication Gazette* 73(6): 477–494.

Hartley, J. (2000) "Communicative Democracy in a Redactional Society: The Future of Journalism Studies." *Journalism* 1(1): 39–48.

Hochberg, A. (2014) "Facing a Flood of Incivility, News Sites Make Reader Comments Harder to Find." *Poynter Media Innovation*, 15 December. Available from: http://www.poynter.org/news/media-innovation/308039/facing-a-flood-of-incivility-news-sites-make-reader-comments-harder-to-find/ (accessed 22 May 2015).

Ingram, M. (2011) "Defining Journalism is a Lot Easier Said than Done." *GIgaom*, 15 December. Available from: https://gigaom.com/2011/12/15/defining-journalism-is-a-lot-easier-said-than-done/.

Journalism and Media Staff (2012) "Edited Footage vs. Raw Footage." *Pew Research Center*, 16 July. Available from: http://www.journalism.org/2012/07/16/edited-footage-vs-raw-footage/ (accessed 22 May 2015).

Knobloch-Westerwick, S. (2009) "Looking the Other Way." *Communication Research* 36(3): 426–448.

Merrill, J.C. (1986) "Professionalization: Danger to Freedom and Pluralism." *Journal of Mass Media Ethics* 1(2): 56–60.

Newman, N. (2014) *Executive Summary and Key Findings of the 2014 Report*. Digital News Report 2014, Reuters Institute for the Study of Journalism. Available from: http://www.digitalnewsreport.org/survey/2014/executive-summary-and-key-findings-2014/ (accessed 13 September 2014).

Richmond, S. (2008) "How SEO is Changing Journalism." *British Journalism Review* 19(4): 51–55.

Robischon, N. (2015) "BuzzFeed Unveils Pound to Show How You Really Share Content." *Fast Company*, 27 April. Available from: http://www.fastcompany.com/3045484/buzzfeed-unveils-pound-to-show-how-you-really-share-content (accessed 29 May 2015).

Rosen, R.J. (2011) "Why We Should Stop Asking Whether Bloggers are Journalists." *The Atlantic*, 13 December. Available from: http://www.theatlantic.com/technology/archive/2011/12/why-we-should-stop-asking-whether-bloggers-are-journalists/249864/ (accessed 13 October 2014).

Scott, B. (2005) "A Contemporary History of Digital Journalism." *Television & New Media* 6(1): 89–126.

Shapiro, I. (2014) "Why Democracies Need a Functional Definition of Journalism Now More than Ever." *Journalism Studies* 15(5): 555–565.

Shapiro, I., Brin, C., Bédard-Brûlé, I. and Mychajlowycz, K. (2013) "Verification as a Strategic Ritual." *Journalism Practice* 7(6): 657–673.

Shaw, L. (2015) "Snapchat Discover Hosts Original Video from CNN, Vice and ... AT&T?" *The Globe and Mail*, 28 January. Available from: http://www.theglobeandmail.com/technology/tech-news/snapchat-discover-hosts-original-video-from-cnn-vice-and-att/article22672544/ (accessed 22 May 2015).

Silverman, C. (2015) *Lies, Damn Lies and Viral Content*. A Tow/Knight Report, Tow Center for Digital Journalism. Available from: http://towcenter.org/wp-content/uploads/2015/02/LiesDamnLies_Silverman_TowCenter.pdf.

Singer, J.B. (2014) "User-Generated Visibility: Secondary Gatekeeping in a Shared Media Space." *New Media & Society* 16(1): 55–73.

Sullivan, M. (2012) "Questions and Answers on How the Times Handles Online Comments from Readers." *The New York Times*, 15 October. Available from: http://publiceditor.blogs.nytimes.com/2012/10/15/questions-and-answers-on-how-the-times-handles-online-comments-from-readers/ (accessed 22 May 2015).

Thompson, D. (2014) "What the Death of Homepages Means for the Future of News." *The Atlantic*, 15 May. Available from: http://www.theatlantic.com/business/archive/2014/05/what-the-death-the-homepage-means-for-news/370997/.

Weiss, A.S. (2013) "Exploring News Apps and Location-Based Services on the Smartphone." *Journalism and Mass Communication Quarterly* 90(3): 435–456.

Zelizer, B. (2004) *Taking Journalism Seriously: News and the Academy*. Thousand Oaks, CA: Sage.

Zelizer, B. and Allan, S. (2010) *Keywords in News and Journalism Studies*. New York, NY: McGraw-Hill.

2
DECONSTRUCTING DIGITAL JOURNALISM STUDIES

Laura Ahva and Steen Steensen

This chapter discusses the formation and state of digital journalism studies as a field of research. Our point of departure is that journalism studies is an interdisciplinary field that draws inspiration and conceptual tools from many research traditions, most notably from those of political science, sociology, history, language studies, as well as cultural analysis (Zelizer, 2004), but increasingly also from fields like science and technology studies (STS) and economics. All these disciplinary traditions thus play a role in how journalism is being analyzed. With the increased need to understand the significance of "online, multimedia or cross-media, convergent, and otherwise distinctly digital journalism" (Deuze, 2008a: 199), the discrete field of digital journalism studies emerged at the start of the new millennium. The aim of this chapter is to offer an overview of the emergence of this field of research and discuss its interdisciplinarity as well as assess its current standing and possible blind spots.

We begin the chapter by spelling out how digital journalism studies has evolved from being dominated by a discourse of *revolution*, via *evolution*, to a discourse of *deconstruction*, which, we argue, currently dominates the field. Today, when news is something you find in your personalized social media feed and decisions about 'newsworthiness' are, at least to some extent, left to third-party algorithmic manipulation, digital journalism studies is marked by the need to address fundamental questions about what the object of its inquiry really is and how journalism can be deconstructed in order to make sense of this in a digital age. This current discourse of deconstruction is marked by increased theoretical awareness through interdisciplinarity because the domain of digital journalism can neither be understood solely through a single disciplinary tradition nor can it be left to mere empirical examination.

This chapter then presents and discusses a meta-analysis (research on research) on articles published in the recently (2013) launched journal *Digital Journalism* which will be compared with a similar meta-analysis of articles in the journals *Journalism Studies* and *Journalism: Theory, Practice & Criticism*. This analysis aims at uncovering the main paths of theorizing within digital journalism studies. We find that digital journalism studies is marked by four strong research traditions borrowing from sociology, political science, cultural studies, and STS. The dominating discourse of deconstruction currently found in digital journalism studies thus seems shaped by influences from these disciplinary traditions.

Digital journalism studies from revolution to deconstruction

In an early review of online journalism research, Kopper, Kolthoff, and Czepek (2000) concluded that empirical research at that time was difficult to find and that most of the empirical inquiries were market-driven and non-academic, interested in how one could make a profit out of journalism on the web. This research, along with the more prediction-based and non-empirical academic research at the time, was predominantly normative. The potentials and threats of digital technology in general, and of the internet in particular, were seen as major game-changers that would *revolutionize* journalism.

We find a typical articulation of this discourse of revolution in a 1997 *Columbia Journalism Review* essay written by John Pavlik:

> Since networked new media can be interactive, on-demand, customizable; since it can incorporate new combinations of texts, images, moving images and sound; since it can build new communities based on shared interests and concerns; and since it has the almost unlimited space to offer levels of reportorial depth, texture and context that are impossible in any other medium—new media can transform journalism.
>
> (1997: 30)

Such statements dominated the academic discourse about online journalism from the mid- to late 1990s, a period Domingo (2008) has identified as the 'utopian wave' of online journalism research. This discourse of revolution and utopianism was enmeshed in a 'web' of technological determinism that spilled over to the next wave of academic research, labeled by Domingo 'the descriptive/empirical wave.' The empirical investigations of this wave of research continued to be marked by a discourse of revolution, as the main aim seemed to be assessing the impact of new, digital technology on journalism. The results, however, curbed the early enthusiasm. Online journalism, as it turned out, did not utilize new, digital technology to the same extent scholars had previously predicted (for overviews, see Domingo, 2006; Steensen, 2011).

The discourse of revolution was therefore balanced with a counterdiscourse that emphasized the resilience of journalistic practices and cultures—a discourse of *evolution*. Researchers emphasized that old practices and cultures of journalism were resilient to change and that journalism was not drastically transformed by digitalization. Instead, it was slowly evolving. Deuze (2008b: 110) framed this discourse of evolution in the following manner:

> [T]echnology is not an independent factor influencing the work of journalists from the outside, but must be seen in terms of its implementation, and therefore how it extends and amplifies previous ways of doing things.

The discourse of evolution emphasized that new technology cannot change journalism overnight, as it is only one of many factors that shape how journalism evolves. Researchers started to pay more attention to the long lines of development within journalism, also in pre-internet times, and argued that newsroom cultures are conservative (e.g. Boczkowski, 2004; Deuze, 2008b; Heinonen, 1999; Scott, 2005), and this discourse was thus marked by linear thinking concerning the development of digital journalism.

However, the evolutionary discourse also implied a search for new theoretical approaches with which to understand both how journalism evolved and why technology did not create rapid changes. Central to this development was what Domingo (2008) labeled the 'constructivist wave' of research into online journalism. Researchers started to question technological determinism with more rigor and were instead interested in doing in-depth (often ethnographic) case studies with the aim of understanding 'innovation as an open process' (Domingo, 2008: 17) with various players involved. This wave of research was largely inspired by the publication of Boczkowski's seminal book *Digitizing the News* (2004), which introduced perspectives from STS to journalism studies, thus allowing for a greater theoretical understanding of the interplay among technology, materiality, and social practice related to the production of online journalism. As Boczkowski later stated in a reflection on his work with *Digitizing the News*, "I realized that technology was a vastly under-explored territory in journalism scholarship" (2015: 2).

The trend of theorizing 'the digital' was thus initiated by the constructivist wave and the discourse of evolution, and it has continued in what we here identify as the discourse of *deconstruction* that today seems to dominate the field. Digital journalism studies has by now reached a point of maturity in which theorizations about the phenomenon are increasingly called for, not only to understand the many emerging and changing practices and cultures of journalism but also to investigate the essence of journalism in the digital age. In other words, digital journalism is no longer seen only as something that is constructed within technical, social, cultural, and economic structures; it is seen as a domain that needs to be deconstructed in order for us to understand the new meanings that journalism acquires within the entire digital mediascape. Boczkowski, for instance, has argued a need to shift "the stance of theoretical work from tributary to primary" (2011: 162), suggesting that theorizing digital journalism is not only a means to reach an end, it is the very end one wishes to reach in order to rediscover what journalism is and might be.

Several books published recently address this need to deconstruct and reconceptualize journalism, and their titles alone are clear expressions of a discourse of deconstruction. In *Rebuilding the News*, Anderson (2013) argues that the classical newsroom is no longer the epicenter of newswork; bloggers, citizen journalists, and social networks are, alongside journalists, important actors in the new 'news ecosystem.' In *Rethinking Journalism* (Peters and Broersma, 2013), the authors argue that the problems journalism is faced with today are far more structural than previously voiced and that there is a need to fundamentally rethink what journalism is. In *Boundaries of Journalism* (Carlson and Lewis, 2015), journalism's demarcations toward other professions and businesses are deconstructed, as are previously established internal boundaries between different journalistic genres and groups of journalists. Carlson's (2015: 2) notion in the book's introduction serves as an apt example of the dominant discourse, as he points out the continuous need to deconstruct and then reconstruct journalism:

> Journalism is not a solid, stable *thing* to point to, but a constantly shifting denotation applied differently depending on context. Whatever is distinct about journalism must be continuously constructed.

We must, however, note that the very brief history of digital journalism research outlined above is a construction in itself. Inquiries into digital journalism are not as clear-cut, periodical, and linear as our narrative might suggest. For instance, normative perspectives on digital journalism still thrive (Kreiss and Brennen, 2015), and technological determinism is still apparent in the field, as is the discourse of revolution (Steensen, 2011). The need for greater theorization and deconstruction was also articulated quite early on, for instance by Heinonen (1999) and Singer (1998).

Furthermore, the STS perspective introduced as part of the evolutionary discourse has been further developed and refined and is now one of the paths through which digital journalism is currently deconstructed. However, technology is only one option among many, and there are other possible paths for theorization. In the following section, we will therefore identify these paths as the ways in which different disciplinary perspectives have paved the way for researchers to study digital journalism.

The disciplinary paths of digital journalism studies

To investigate these paths and the interdisciplinary nature of digital journalism as a research field, we conducted an analysis of article abstracts published in the one journal dedicated to the sub-field of digital journalism studies, namely *Digital Journalism* (Taylor & Francis). We analyzed the abstracts of all articles published in the journal from the inaugural issue published in 2013 to issue number 3 in 2015 (73 abstracts in total).

In the following discussion, we will also draw from an earlier set of keyword and abstract analysis of articles published in the two most significant journals dedicated to journalism studies—*Journalism: Theory, Practice and Criticism* (Sage) and *Journalism Studies* (Taylor & Francis). The keyword analysis covered all articles published from the inaugural issues of both journals in 2000 through 2013, and the abstract analysis covered the volumes of 2002 and 2003 (90 abstracts) and the volumes of 2012 (105 abstracts) from both journals (for more details on the sample, see Steensen and Ahva, 2015). The aim of these analyses was to map the disciplinary perspectives of journalism studies from the era of digitalization toward the more coherent field of digital journalism studies.

Our method in the abstract analysis was simple: we read the sampled abstracts closely and coded each according to what we interpreted to be their main disciplinary 'home' or inclination. We based our coding on Zelizer's (2004) description of the dominant disciplinary perspectives in journalism studies: *political science, sociology, history, language,* and *cultural analysis*. In addition, we included *economy, philosophy, law,* and *technology* (cf. Zelizer, 2004: 8) as disciplinary perspectives that influence journalism studies (see Steensen and Ahva, 2015, for details on the coding process).

This categorization is of course dubious in that the borders between disciplines are not always clear. However, we found it useful to anchor our analysis in existing frames to avoid losing our analytical focus in the interdisciplinary contours of the field. Furthermore, in the following discussion, we will take a step away from the disciplines themselves and try to elaborate the emerging paths of theorizing within digital journalism studies. While doing this we will also accompany our discussion with additional examples from digital journalism literature.

Before moving to the results, it is important to note that the inherently interdisciplinary nature of (digital) journalism studies leaves ample room for research that does *not explicitly* adhere to any particular theoretical framework or that can be easily traced back to a distinct disciplinary tradition. In the earlier set of our journal analysis, this became apparent in the large amount of publications that did not draw on any explicitly named theories in their abstracts or keywords (Steensen and Ahva, 2015: 11). This finding may be a sign of empiricism—a tendency to justify argumentation with strong empirical evidence only. Or it can, as Siapera and Veglis (2012: 10; see also Steensen and Ahva, 2015) suggest, be a sign that a substantial strand of research into digital journalism follows the path of grounded theory. This approach aims to produce typologies and models via data collection and analysis, thus contributing to middle-range theory building. While acknowledging this, we wish to next focus on the more explicit role given to theoretical approaches and their disciplinary roots in digital journalism studies.

Sociology of digital journalism

According to previous reviews (e.g. Domingo, 2008: 18–19; Siapera and Veglis, 2012: 10) as well as our own analysis, sociology seems to hold strong as the central disciplinary tradition from which digital journalism studies draws. According to our analysis of abstracts from *Journalism* and *Journalism Studies*, 30 percent of all articles in the entire sample (N = 195) fell in line with the sociological tradition. The situation was almost similar with the newer set of abstracts (2013–2015; N = 73) from *Digital Journalism*: here 31 percent drew from sociology. Sociology was thus the most popular discipline in all the journals. In fact, Deuze (2008a) has suggested the 'sociology of online news' as a framework that can offer avenues for studying how technologies, regulation and policies, industries and organizations, career paths, market structures, as well as audience conceptions emerge in the professional practices of digital journalism.

Our analysis suggests that a dominant theoretical sociological framework is professionalism. This framework has offered conceptual tools to study journalists' professional role perceptions, values and norms, as well as work practices in the digital era (see Singer, 2003). According to our mapping, this type of research within digital journalism studies focuses, for example, on emerging professional practices, the impact of new technologies and media (such as social media) on journalists' attitudes, the evolving forms of gatekeeping, and the transformation of news values in the digital age. Also, the blurring of boundaries often pointed to in contemporary digital journalism studies (see Carlson and Lewis, 2015) is often related to professionalism and analyzed through the sociological framework of 'boundary work' (Gieryn, 1999). Another trend is to analyze professionalism in a global context related to different 'cultures' of journalism, a concept Hanitzsch (2007) has deconstructed into three essential constituents: the institutional roles, epistemologies, and ethical ideologies of journalism. In addition, classical sociological theorists, such as Pierre Bourdieu, continue to play a role in how digital journalism is theorized (Siapera and Spyridou, 2012).

Political science and digital journalism

In our initial analysis of *Journalism* and *Journalism Studies*, we found that political science was the most dominant perspective of publications in the first set of abstracts from 2002 to 2003 (32 percent). However, over time we noticed a trend where political science as the typical disciplinary backbone of journalism research was giving way to sociology: the proportion of studies affiliated with political science decreased to 25 percent in 2012. Our analysis of the recent abstracts in *Digital Journalism* reinforces this trend: the political science framework was apparent in only 7 percent of the abstracts from 2013 to 2015.

However, this does not indicate that theoretical frameworks associated with the political science tradition (such as agenda setting, democracy theories, public sphere, and public opinion) have lost their relevance in digital journalism studies. For example, as Natalie Fenton (2012: 120) puts it: "neither journalism nor the internet *creates* democracy and democracy does not invent journalism or indeed the internet." Therefore, she calls for continued attention to the ways in which the processes of democratization—as well as de-democratization—are apparent in the digital context. Furthermore, questions of civic engagement and political participation are increasingly discussed in relation to digital journalism (e.g. Correia, 2012) but also 'beyond' it, in the broader context of digital and connective media environment, since the position of a 'citizen journalist' is globally opening itself to various actors, such as activists (see Allan and Thorsen, 2009).

So, even if the political communications paradigm seems weak in (an admittedly limited sample of) *Digital Journalism*, we note that these theorizations are developed in the context of other journals and publications, perhaps because the research questions are also reaching beyond journalism to the entire digital media landscape, such as theorizations related to the concept of 'mediatization' (e.g. Strömbäck and Esser, 2014). This strand of research is interested, for example, in the questions of how 'the media logic' is shaping political communication and affords possibilities to bypass the traditional gatekeeping of journalism with the help of social media, such as Twitter (e.g. Ekman and Widholm, 2015). As such, the notion of 'public sphere' is currently deconstructed in political communication studies at large, especially related to the interplay among politics, journalism, and social media (see Moe and Enli, 2013).

User-oriented cultural analysis of digital journalism

What seems clearly different for digital journalism studies when compared to journalism studies more broadly is the position given to audiences or users in research. This means that whereas reception studies or audience studies have for a long time been seen as separate from 'traditional' journalism studies, users have played a central part in how digital journalism has been theorized from the start due to the interactive and participatory possibilities afforded by the web. This has resulted in the deconstruction of the producer/consumer paradigm that is especially clear in the tradition of cultural analysis.

According to our analyses, the studies affiliated with cultural analysis have maintained their position as the third most popular disciplinary reference for journalism studies and digital journalism studies research, just after sociology and political science in *Journalism Studies* and *Journalism*, and after sociology and technology in *Digital Journalism*. We have named this approach here as user-oriented cultural analysis. Within this label, we find studies that theorize digital journalism from the perspective of user cultures—the habits, routines, and rituals of the online audiences that are adapting to and shaping the contours of the increasingly mobile and cross-media environment defined by digital technology (Picone, Courtois, and Paulussen, 2015).

This approach draws, for example, on anthropology (e.g. Bird, 2011) and cultural studies (and also partly from language studies, e.g. Hartley, 2012). For example, Graeme Turner (2010) from the cultural studies perspective wishes to avoid jumping to conclusions about the democratizing effects of digital journalism, but rather wishes to discuss the increased appearance and agency of ordinary people in the media—the demotic—including journalism-like practices such as blogging but also that of entertainment (Turner, 2010: 71–97). Hartley (2012: 59–93), in turn, advocates theorizing digital journalism through cultural studies in order to understand how popular culture as the source of popular self-representation is shaping journalism via digital, online, and self-made media, such as blogging, user-generated content, Web 2.0 applications, and e-zines.

However, it should be noted that user orientation's prevalence in digital journalism studies extends beyond its conspicuous role in cultural studies, and user-focused research is found in research that draws from all the mentioned disciplines. For instance, there are studies on user-generated content or mediated (political) engagement that are sociologically or politically oriented, too.

Socio-materiality of digital journalism

The fourth main disciplinary perspective in digital journalism studies is that of technology. According to our analysis, the trend of technologically oriented theorization seems to be on the rise. In *Journalism* and *Journalism Studies*, technology as a disciplinary background appeared as a minor (sixth place) but thriving perspective: its proportion rose from 3 percent in 2002 and 2003 to 7 percent in 2012. It is perhaps of no surprise that in *Digital Journalism* (2013–2105) technology holds the second place with 19 percent. It seems reasonable that theories related to technology, such as innovation theory, social construction of technology, anthropology of technology, and especially STS-inspired socio-material perspectives such as actor–network theory, have been in the repertoire of digital journalism studies from the start (for summaries, see Domingo, 2008: 20–25; Siapera and Veglis, 2012: 11–12). With these theories, scholars have aimed to understand how technology and journalism are shaping each other.

Altogether, the growing popularity of Bruno Latour's (2005) actor–network theory for the study of digital journalism (e.g. Anderson, 2013; Primo and Zago, 2015) seems to suggest that there has been a neglect in earlier journalism studies in taking into account the ways in which materiality (both physical materiality such as machinery, telephones, screens, desks, etc., and non-physical materiality such as applications and algorithms, etc.) plays a role in the journalistic process, or rather in the formation of the news network (Domingo, Masip, and Costera Meijer, 2015). Boczkowski (2015: 65) argues that journalism studies is currently undergoing a 'material turn' in which researchers aim to "reveal the broad spectrum of actors" implicated in the news-making process, and "the spatially distributed network of connections—that include the newsroom as one key locale, but not the only one—from which the news emerges."

In this increased emphasis on materiality and technology, the concept of the network has become popular, focusing on the ways the digital environment has provided possibilities for tracing the associations between various actors, for example, in how page visits (the act of clicking, reading, or checking) leave traces that can be tracked and measured. Furthermore, the promises of 'big data' for journalism research and practice have evoked discussion among scholars, and steps have been taken from merely technological or empirical research toward a more holistic understanding—embracing aspects of epistemology, expertise, ethics, and economics—of big data in the context of digital journalism (Lewis and Westlund, 2015).

Discussion

The analysis above shows that digital journalism studies today approaches its object of inquiry through deconstructive theoretical perspectives predominantly adopted from sociology and STS, but also from political science and cultural studies. This result suggests that digital journalism studies as a field of research is indeed multidisciplinary. This kind of spread identified here reflects a varied theoretical toolkit for digital journalism studies to draw from. However, when we compare the discourse of deconstruction that we identified as the dominant register in the beginning of the chapter and the results of our analysis, we can see that digital journalism studies has entered this current discursive environment through rather traditional research avenues. This is clear especially as sociology remains the predominant disciplinary perspective of journalism studies.

It should be mentioned, though, that the interdisciplinary nature of digital journalism studies goes beyond our categorizations. Whereas the perspectives of philosophy, economy, and history were all reasonably well represented in the analysis of *Digital Journalism* with 4 percent each, the emerging perspectives in the category of 'other' were also equally represented by, for example, visual studies (4 percent) and geography (3 percent). A slight surprise was the fact that the perspective of language was so marginal with only 1 percent of articles belonging to this tradition. This seems to suggest that studies focusing on strictly textual aspects of journalism are currently not at the heart of digital journalism studies, at least not in this particular journal.

In other words: The theoretical deconstruction of journalism in the digital age seems to leave behind some blind spots, especially related to perspectives from the humanities, like theoretically informed qualitative analysis of text. It may seem as if the availability (and to a degree, the hype) of big data has pushed quantitative, statistical analysis of media texts to the forefront, thus leaving perspectives like genre theory and sociolinguistics behind. Genre theory would, for instance, push researchers to highlight the importance of previously established conventions and expectations to a text production system like journalism, in order for it to uphold its social function (Steensen, 2013). Overlooking such perspectives might therefore make digital journalism studies prone to emphasize change and innovation over continuity and legacy.

Furthermore, even though perspectives from STS have contributed greatly to problematizing (and challenging) technological determinism, this trait still holds a firm, albeit more subtle, grip on digital journalism studies. In the growing body of socio-material research on digital journalism, materiality is often reduced to mean elements of technology, thus promoting technological matter over other things that matter.

Conclusion

This overview of digital journalism studies as an emerging research field has focused on three different discursive moves and located how digital journalism studies research has conceptualized its research object by drawing from various disciplinary traditions. Our discussion locates digital journalism studies as a cross-disciplinary field, with sociology, political science, cultural analysis, and technology providing the four strongest research pillars. These disciplinary perspectives have provided the most typical routes through which digital journalism has been theorized from the start of the 2000s, but these four are not the only research avenues. The current state of research reflects the idea that *inter*disciplinarity, in its fullest sense, makes possible, even desirable, the combination of elements from various traditions to theorize digital journalism. These combinations, we believe, are gaining ground in digital journalism studies, especially if the research field continues to take the challenge of deconstruction seriously.

Further reading

Pablo Boczkowski's seminal book *Digitizing the News* (2004) provides an early example of how perspectives from STS can be applied to digital journalism studies. The two volumes (2007 and 2011) of *Making Online News* edited by Chris Paterson and David Domingo provide rich evidence of how ethnographic methods can pave the way for theory-building in digital journalism. Readers interested in current theorizations of digital journalism may find the double special issue of *Digital Journalism* (3: 1, 2015) and *Journalism Practice* (9: 1, 2015) edited by Steen Steensen and Laura Ahva and entitled "Theories of journalism in the digital age" an interesting read. In this double special issue, over 20 scholars offer their takes on theories that might help to understand journalism in the digital era. To understand better the ways in which journalism today is deconstructed due to processes of digitalization, Matt Carlson and Seth C. Lewis's edited volume *Boundaries of Journalism* (Routledge, 2015) offers a good starting point.

References

Allan, S. and Thorsen, E. (2009) *Citizen Journalism: Global Perspectives*. New York, NY: Peter Lang.

Anderson, C.W. (2013) *Rebuilding the News: Metropolitan Journalism in the Digital Age*. Philadelphia, PA: Temple University Press.

Bird, S.E. (2011) "Seeking the Audience for News: Response, News Talk, and Everyday Practices." In Nightingale, V. (ed.) *The Handbook of Media Audiences*. Oxford: Blackwell Publishing Ltd., pp. 489–508.

Boczkowski, P. (2004) "The Processes of Adopting Multimedia and Interactivity in Three Online Newsrooms." *Journal of Communication* 54(2): 197–213.

Boczkowski, P.J. (2011) "Epilogue: Future Avenues for Research on Online New Production." In Domingo, D. and Paterson, C. (eds) *Making Online News, Volume 2: Newsroom Ethnographies in the Second Decade of Internet Journalism*. New York, NY: Peter Lang, pp. 161–168.

Boczkowski, P.J. (2015) "The Material Turn in the Study of Journalism: Some Hopeful and Cautionary Remarks from an Early Explorer." *Journalism* 16(1): 65–68.

Carlson, M. (2015) "Introduction: The Many Boundaries of Journalism." In Carlson, M. and Lewis, S. (eds) *Boundaries of Journalism: Professionalism, Practices and Participation*. Oxon, UK: Routledge, pp. 1–18.

Carlson, M. and Lewis, S. (eds) (2015) *Boundaries of Journalism: Professionalism, Practices and Participation*. Abingdon: Routledge.

Correia, J.C. (2012) "Online Journalism and Civic Life." In Siapera, E. and Veglis, A. (eds) *The Handbook of Global Online Journalism*. Chichester, UK: Wiley-Blackwell, pp. 101–118.

Deuze, M. (2008a) "Epilogue: Toward a Sociology of Online News." In Paterson, C. and Domingo, D. (eds) *Making Online News: The Ethnography of New Media Production*. New York, NY: Peter Lang, pp. 199–210.

Deuze, M. (2008b) "The Professional Identity of Journalists in the Context of Convergence Culture." *Observatorio (Obs*)* 2(4): 103–117.

Domingo, D. (2006) "Inventing Online Journalism. Development of the Internet as a News Medium in four Catalan Online Newsrooms." PhD dissertation. Universitat Autònoma de Barcelona.

Domingo, D. (2008) "Inventing Online Journalism: A Constructivist Approach to the Development of Online News." In Paterson, C. and Domingo, D. (eds) *Making Online News: The Ethnography of New Media Production*. New York, NY: Peter Lang, pp. 15–27.

Domingo, D., Masip, P. and Costera Meijer, I. (2015) "Tracing Digital News Networks." *Digital Journalism* 3(1): 53–67.

Ekman, M. and Widholm, A. (2015) "Politicians as Media Producers." *Journalism Practice* 9(1): 78–91.

Enli, G.S. and Moe, H. (2013) "Special Issue: Social Media and Election Campaigns: Key Tendencies and Ways Forward." *Information, Communication & Society* 16(5): 637–645.

Fenton, N. (2012) "De-democratizing the News? New Media and the Structural Practices of Journalism." In Siapera, E. and Veglis, A. (eds) *The Handbook of Global Online Journalism*. Chichester, UK: Wiley-Blackwell, pp. 119–134.

Gieryn, T.F. (1999) *Cultural Boundaries of Science: Credibility on the Line*. Chicago, IL: University of Chicago Press.

Hanitzsch, T. (2007) "Deconstructing Journalism Culture: Toward a Universal Theory." *Communication Theory* 17(4): 367–385.

Hartley, J. (2012) *Digital Futures for Cultural and Media Studies*. Chichester, UK: Wiley-Blackwell.

Heinonen, A. (1999) "Journalism in the Age of the Net." *Changing Society, Changing Profession*. Tampere: Acta Universitatis Tamperensis, 685.

Kopper, G.G., Kolthoff, A. and Czepek, A. (2000) "Research Review: Online Journalism – A Report on Current and Continuing Research and Major Questions in the International Discussion." *Journalism Studies* 1(3): 499–512.

Kreiss, D. and Brennen, J.S. (2015) *Normative Theories of Digital Journalism*. Paper presented at 2015 Conference of the International Communication Association, San Juan, Puerto Rico, 20–25 May.

Latour, B. (2005) *Reassembling the Social: An Introduction to Actor-Network-Theory*. New York, NY: Oxford University Press.

Lewis, S.C. and Westlund, O. (2015) "Big Data and Journalism." *Digital Journalism* 3(3): 447–466.

Paterson, C. and Domingo, D. (eds) (2007) *Making Online News: The Ethnography of New Media Production*. New York, NY: Peter Lang.

Pavlik, J.V. (1997) "The Future of Online Journalism: A Guide to Who's Doing What." *Columbia Journalism Review*, July/August, 30–36.

Peters, C. and Broersma, M. (eds) (2013) *Rethinking Journalism: Trust and Participation in a Transformed News Landscape*. Abingdon: Routledge.

Picone, I., Courtois, C. and Paulussen, S. (2015) "When News is Everywhere: Understanding Participation, Cross-Mediality and Mobility in Journalism from a Radical User Perspective." *Journalism Practice* 9(1): 35–49.

Primo, A. and Zago, G. (2015) "Who and What Do Journalism?" *Digital Journalism* 3(1): 38–52.

Scott, B. (2005) "A Contemporary History of Digital Journalism." *Television New Media* 6(1): 89–126.

Siapera, E. and Spyridou, L. (2012) "The Field of Online Journalism: A Bourdieusian Analysis." In Siapera, E. and Veglis, A. (eds) *The Handbook of Global Online Journalism*. Chichester, UK: Wiley-Blackwell, pp. 1–17.

Siapera, E. and Veglis, A. (2012) "Introduction: The Evolution of Online Journalism." In Siapera, E. and Veglis, A. (eds) *The Handbook of Global Online Journalism*. Chichester, UK: Wiley-Blackwell, pp. 1–17.

Singer, J. (1998) "Online Journalists: Foundations for Research into Their Changing Roles." *Journal of Computer-Mediated Communication* 4(1): n.p.

Singer, J. (2003) "Who Are These Guys? The Online Challenge to the Notion of Journalistic Professionalism." *Journalism* 4(2): 139–163.

Steensen, S. (2011) "Online Journalism and the Promises of New Technologies." *Journalism Studies* 12(3): 311–327.

Steensen, S. (2013) "Balancing the Bias: The Need for Counter-Discursive Perspectives in Media Innovation Research." In Storsul, T. and Krumsvik, A.H. (eds) *Media Innovations: A Multidisciplinary Study of Change*. Gothenburg, Sweden: Nordicom, pp. 45–59.

Steensen, S. and Ahva, L. (2015) "Theories of Journalism in a Digital Age." *Digital Journalism* 3(1): 1–18.

Strömbäck, J. and Esser, F. (2014) "Introduction: Making Sense of the Mediatization of Politics." *Journalism Studies* 15(3): 243–255.

Turner, G. (2010) *Ordinary People and the Media: The Demotic Turn*. London, UK: Sage.

Zelizer, B. (2004) *Taking Journalism Seriously: News and the Academy*. Thousand Oaks, CA: Sage Publications.

3

DIGITAL JOURNALISM ETHICS

Stephen J. A. Ward

To speak of digital journalism ethics is to speak in the future and normative tense. A widely accepted digital journalism ethics does not exist, but new ideas are emerging as journalists revise their norms and aims. Amid a media revolution, a framework is being constructed to replace a pre-digital professional ethics articulated a century ago. Therefore, we should not rest content with describing the state of journalism ethics. We should not presume that the traditional professional ethics can be simply extended to news media today. Journalism ethics should be future-orientated, full of proposals for what journalism ethics *ought* to be. The task is to define what responsible journalism means in a digital, global world. I follow this understanding of the task of ethics. Surveying trends, I identify seminal concepts that, brought together, constitute a new mindset—a pragmatic understanding of the function and justification of journalism ethics. As I will explain, this mindset sees future journalism ethics as discursive in method, 'imperfect' in epistemology, and integrative in developing new principles.

The creation of digital, global media, with many new players and platforms around the world, has undermined a pre-digital consensus on journalism ethics while raising new normative questions. Who is a journalist? What are the principles of digital journalism ethics? How should journalists use new media and engage communities? What sort of journalism is appropriate for a media-linked world where stories have global impact?

The old mindset

Good answers to these questions will require a new mindset. A mindset is a set of ideas for understanding (and dealing practically with) a practice or problem. For instance, I may understand journalism ethics from a free press standpoint, arguing that freedom of expression trumps other values such as not causing offence. Or, I may understand ethics from an absolutist mindset, arguing that principles must be universal and unchanging. A mindset is not one's specific ethical beliefs; it is a view of the nature of those beliefs.

The old mindset of Western pre-digital ethics continues to influence ethical thinking, long after the emergence of digital media. So, what was (and is) the dominant mindset of pre-digital journalism ethics and why does it need to be reformed? The answer is that the mindset is unsuited to the new media ecology and therefore fails to provide adequate guidance for practitioners. The mindset is unsuited for two reasons: (1) it views journalism ethics as primarily the careful observance of pre-established, static principles for a (once) stable practice, not the more dynamic process of participating in an evolving discourse about (and reinvention of) principles in an unstable journalism environment; and (2) it favors untenable, dualistic formulations of key media principles, such as objectivity, constructing a 'wall' between fact and value, reporting and interpreting, reporting and social engagement.

With regard to (1), the influential code of the Society of Professional Journalists (SPJ) in the United States is based on a view of ethics primarily as firm content (SPJ, 2014). It organizes many norms under four principles—tell the truth and report it, be independent, minimize harm, and be accountable. The code says little about ethics as method or the skills of ethical reasoning. It encourages all journalists to apply its universal principles to situations and to (somehow) balance the principles where they conflict.

With regard to (2), the pre-digital ideal of news objectivity reduced objectivity to reporting 'just the facts' in a detached, neutral manner (Ward, 2005). The formulators of this ideal presumed that a strict separation of fact and value in reporting was possible and that all other factors—interpretation, perspective, and engagement—were biasing factors that reporters should avoid entirely. Anything beyond stating facts was subjective opinion. Therefore, pre-digital ethics did not develop norms and best practices for good interpretive and engaged story-telling—key features of today's global, digital journalism. Moreover, pre-digital ethics is unsuited to a global journalism because it was constructed for non-global media. For pre-digital ethics, journalism ethics expresses what journalists owe their fellow citizens. Journalism ethics stops at the border (Ward, 2010).

Therefore, the pre-digital mindset struggles to guide a new journalism that is increasingly perspectival, socially engaged, and global in reach. It is no surprise, then, that traditional principles cannot be extended to new forms of journalism or are rejected by new practitioners.

A new mindset: pragmatic humanism

For the rest of this chapter, I propose a mindset for our ongoing media revolution, avoiding static, dualistic principles. I call it pragmatic humanism because it regards principles, pragmatically, as fallible and evolving standards for doing journalism for humanity. The new mindset guides the invention of new principles and the reinterpretation of existing values that remain valid, such as truth-telling, editorial independence, and promoting democracy.

Pragmatic humanism is a holistic set of notions of three kinds: (1) *functional notions* about the nature and aims of journalism; (2) *epistemic notions* about the nature and justification of ethical claims; (3) *structural notions* about how to organize new ethical beliefs into new codes. The ideas are drawn from many places—philosophy, ethics, sociology, communication studies. The ideas are held by a heterogeneous band of journalists, ethicists, and citizens.

Functional notions

The new mindset makes process and participation as important as firm content and the indoctrination of principle. At a time of cross-border tensions, politically and culturally, *how* journalists discuss, invent, and modify their values should be as much a part of journalism ethics as defending the established ideas of a dominant group or culture. A primary function of journalism ethics in a global era is to encourage dialogue—informed, reasonable, global discourse on journalistic values and practices.

Discourse ethics has been a defining aspect of much contemporary moral theorizing due to the influence of Rawls (1972) and Habermas (2001). Ethical discourse is a genuine 'give and take' among moral equals in communication across differences. It is a "communicative form of moral conduct" (Makau and Marty, 2013: 79). At the heart of discourse ethics is evolution, enrichment, and fair negotiation. It explores an *ethics-to-be*, able to deal with new conditions, new issues. For a mindset focused on defending pre-established principles, ethics as evolving discourse is of minor value. Why discourse at length if we already know what our principles are?

Dialogic discourse in journalism ethics is of paramount value. Modern societies are redolent with diverse conceptions of the good that come into conflict through media. Ethics as discourse is an alternative to conflict, dogmatism, or the tyranny of one group's morality. Recasting journalism ethics as open-ended discourse is a step toward an ethics for a plural world.

Journalism ethics as discourse implies that ethics is often emergent—the emergence of new moral values and attitudes. Social and technological changes bring forward new practices, priorities, and values. The new values become an emergent ethic that questions existing values. Journalism ethics today is a prime example of emergent ethics. It is a zone of contestation between new and old values. Before the digital revolution, professional practitioners came to think of their ethics as stable and settled. Disagreement or uncertainty were negative signs, indicating some weakness in the accepted ethics. The new mindset takes a contrary position: emergence, disagreement, and uncertainty is a natural part of ethics.

The new mindset also shifts the focus of journalism ethics from the 'micro' to the 'macro' level. The micro level consists of questions about what an individual journalist should do in specific situations, for example, grant anonymity to a source. The macro level consists of questions about the performance of a nation's news media system or the global news media system. The global nature of today's news media immerses journalism ethics in the macro issues of political morality, including issues of power, inequality, media ownership and diversity, digital divides, and how news media cover global issues. For the new mindset, journalism ethics is scarcely distinguishable from the communication policies and norms required by interconnected societies. Therefore, another primary function of journalism ethics is to be a catalyst for discourse on this macro, global level.

Epistemic notions

An epistemology is a conception of the nature of knowledge and the standards of good inquiry. An epistemology of ethics is a conception of the nature of ethical knowledge and the standards of good ethical inquiry. I recommend an epistemic perspective that I call imperfectionism (Ward, 2015). Imperfectionism develops themes in American pragmatic philosophy (see Albrecht, 2012) from John Dewey to Richard Rorty. My imperfectionism is defined by a commitment to (1) falliblism and (2) interpretism.

Falliblism is the view that there are no "metaphysical guarantees to be had that even our most firmly-held beliefs will never need revision" (Putnam, 1995: 21). Humans are imperfect inquirers. Their beliefs are fallible and never certain. The complexity of the world resists perfect results. Moreover, the cognitive capacity of humans is flawed by bias and other infelicities. Imperfectionism sees beliefs as hypotheses on how to understand phenomenon or proposals on how to regulate conduct. Falliblism is not extreme skepticism. It does not require us to doubt *everything*. It only requires us to be ready to doubt *anything*—if good reason to do so arises.

Falliblism rejects the pervasive metaphor of absolutism, influential in pre-digital ethics, that our beliefs and standards need infallible, foundational principles, the way a house needs an unmoving foundation. Falliblism prefers the metaphor of knowledge as the current results of ongoing inquiry, where inquiry is a ship already under sail (Quine, 1960: 124). As we sail along, some beliefs strike us as questionable. We use some of our beliefs to question other beliefs. But we cannot question all of our beliefs at the same time. Falliblism dovetails with the idea of emergent ethics and the value of experiment. If we are fallible and situated, we can expect ethics to be an area of emergent and contested belief. We improve our beliefs through new experiences and discourse with others. We explore and experiment. The imperfectionist respects many forms of thinking, even if they fail to reach certainty or eliminate disagreement. Well-grounded belief and valuable reasoning exists between the absolute and the arbitrary in ethics and other domains.

Interpretism helps to explain why we are fallible and how we evaluate ethical beliefs. Interpretism starts from the premise that humans have no direct cognitive contact with reality or the world. We always understand the world through conceptual schemes and symbols. We do not first apprehend pure facts about the world and *then* interpret them. There is no dualism of observation and interpretation. Everything we cognize, describe, explain, or know is an interpretation of experience. Knowledge is well-tested interpretation. Inquiry is construction of interpretations. Evaluative notions, like objectivity, are standards for evaluating interpretations. Therefore, all forms of journalism and all journalism stories and articles are interpretations, and journalistic norms are tools for evaluating these narratives.

Interpretation is the way that fallible inquiry and belief-formation occur in ethics and in journalism ethics. At the most general level, ethics is based on normative interpretations of types of action, professions, and practices (Ward, 2015). A normative interpretation says *how*, ethically speaking, a type of conduct ought to be carried out by stating the social point of the activity—the activity seen in its best light (Dworkin, 1986). Norms and principles are justified insofar as they promote this purpose. In Western journalism ethics, the purpose is normally expressed by what I call 'publicism': journalism in its best light advances the public good, not just the interests of individuals or groups. That public good is usually conceived of as the good of a self-governing public in a democracy. Therefore, journalistic norms are justified if they advance democratic journalism. Any value claim, practice, or principle should promote or be consistent with journalism's public responsibilities. We are not free to make up any type of interpretation about an established practice. Our interpretations of journalism, to be taken seriously, need to account for paradigmatic examples of the practice, be consistent with the history of the practice, start from shared understandings, and advance arguments that are plausible to practitioners and resolve problems. Normative interpreters work between the absolute and the arbitrary. Within the Western tradition, different interpretations of the point of journalism can be found among modern journalists, from Walter Lippmann and Edward R. Murrow to Hunter S. Thompson and current citizen journalists. The current fragmentation in journalism ethics can be understood as a clash of normative interpretations of journalism.

Why is imperfectionism, with its twin concepts of fallibism and interpretism, important for a mindset tasked with the construction of a new journalism ethics? Because the imperfectionist approach is an epistemology specifically 'designed' to make sense of inquiry and ethical belief-formation in a changing, pluralistic world. Imperfectionism avoids the false dilemma of either an unbending absolutism or an arbitrary subjectivism. It encourages us to learn from others and to enter into dialogue. Rather than look for absolute foundations amid the winds of change, imperfectionism encourages us to participate in a global, open-ended discourse.

Imperfectionism reminds us that the task of journalism ethics is not to preserve and protect but to reflectively engage the future with fresh minds and fresh ideas.

Structural notions: integration

To complete my analysis, I turn to structural issues. To the ideas of discursive method and imperfectionism, I add the idea of an integrative approach to developing multimedia codes of ethics.

The integrative approach responds to a worry not about content—what will the new norms be?—but about the scope and structure of any new ethics. In terms of scope, the question is: To what extent will any new ethics be able to gain the agreement of a substantial number of journalists? In terms of structure, the related question is: Will journalism ethics of the future consist only of separate and different codes for specific types of journalism practice, say a code for social media journalism, a code for investigative journalism, a code for newspaper journalism, and so on. Or will it be possible to construct, in addition to specific codes, a general or universal code that applies to most journalists, based on common values? Now that a pre-digital consensus has broken down, can journalism ethics, like humpty dumpty, be put together again?

Perhaps, integration will fail because too few journalists agree on too few principles.

Even the ideal of integration is contested. There is debate whether a journalism-wide ethics is possible or desirable. The debate is between what I call integrationists and fragmentists. An integrated ethics has unifying principles and aims that are widely shared by practitioners. A fragmented ethics lacks unifying notions. It is characterized by deep disagreement among practitioners about aims, principles, and best practices. In journalism, fragmentation is the proliferation of different views about the purpose of journalism and its main norms. To speak metaphorically, a fragmented journalism ethics is not a mainland where values connect to a hub of principles. Instead it is an archipelago of isolated 'islands' or value systems embraced by different types of journalists in different cultures. The current state of journalism ethics tends to resemble a normative archipelago. The islands are the fragments of a former, unified pre-digital professional ethics.

Integrationists believe journalists should share a set of aims and principles. Integrationists believe the reintegration of journalism around shared values is possible and desirable. Fragmentists believe fragmentation is not only a fact about journalism ethics but is also a positive state of affairs. Integration smacks of journalistic conformity and homogeneity.

In journalism, it may appear that only fragmentation is occurring, since the differences attract publicity. However, if we look closer, both integration and fragmentation are occurring. There is a movement toward integration in the revision of codes of ethics. Many major news organizations—from the BBC (2015) in the United Kingdom to the SPJ—have or are working on substantial updates of their editorial guidelines. These revisions are integrative insofar as they show how their principles apply to new practices. Fragmentation also carries on. The view that social media journalism has its own norms has been a mantra since online journalism emerged (Friend and Singer, 2007).

I reject fragmentism as a negative force. It divides journalists into camps, weakening their ability to join in common cause, for example, against threats to a free press. For the public, fragmentation may be understood as the view that there is no such thing as journalism ethics, only each journalist's values, and this may be a reason to support draconian press laws. Fragmentation makes a hash of the important idea of journalistic self-regulation since the latter requires regulation by a society-wide group of journalists who follow common principles. If each journalist, or each type of journalists, can construct their own ethics, without the restraint of a common code, journalistic self-regulation is not possible. Furthermore, the public will struggle to keep fragmented practitioners accountable because there are no agreed-upon principles for the evaluation of media conduct. Under the flag of fragmentation, dubious forms of journalism can be rationalized by appeal to personal values.

Fragmentism undermines the public basis of journalism ethics, noted above. Fragmentists, in rejecting integration, seem to assume mistakenly that the source of authority for journalism ethics is the good of each individual journalist or each island of journalists. Moreover, fragmentists lack a vocabulary for discussing how journalists, together, promote the public good because, by their own assumption, there are *no* general, 'cross-island' principles or duties.

Has the media revolution undermined the validity of publicism in journalism ethics? The answer is no. Journalism remains a social practice with impact on others. Things are less clear today because many citizen journalists do not belong to professional journalistic associations and therefore do not fall under the latter's codes of ethics. Yet, this difficulty is not a reason to reject the idea of public journalism ethics. Publicism applies to all forms of journalism practice. Its scope is not limited to professional mainstream journalists.

Publicism, as a regulating norm, needs to be redefined for digital, global journalism. Yet any redefinition must take seriously the responsibilities of journalism on the level of social and institutional practice. Publicism blocks the idea that bloggers, users of Twitter, or anyone who engages in journalism are free to make up their own idiosyncratic ethics—or not bother with ethics at all. Journalism ethics does not 'belong' to journalists. It belongs to citizens—what they need from their journalists. Journalists have no special authority to announce, *ex cathedra*, journalism's values and what it will accept as restraints on its publishing. Journalists must face the tribunal of the public, not just their own conscience, when their conduct comes into question. They need to provide reasons that other citizens would accept, from a public point of view.

I am an integrationist. Yet I believe any new integration must be guided by a sophisticated mindset that recognizes unity and diversity as permanent, valuable, and linked features of journalism ethics. An integrative approach should avoid polar opposites—treating ethics as only fragmented islands of value or treating ethics as only homogenized principles that ignore differences. An integrated approach seeks unity in difference. It grounds journalism ethics in common, general principles that serve the public good and are realized in multiple ways by various forms of journalism in different media cultures. Differences in best practices and norms are allowed, as long as they are consistent with the unifying principles. In short, local differences are ethically permissible variations of common principles. Responsible journalists do not share one unique set of ethical beliefs. What they share is an *overlap* of basic values such as truth-telling and acting as a watchdog on power. Local media cultures give these abstract principles a concrete (and varying) meaning for specific contexts.

For example, how investigative journalists, daily reporters, and social media journalists honor the unifying principles of truth-seeking, freedom of the press, accuracy, and independence can differ within acceptable limits. Journalists from Canada to South Africa will define differently what they mean by serving the public or the social responsibility of the press. Articulating this nexus of the global and local is an important feature of current theorizing in global ethics (Christians *et al.*, 2008). It should be part of the reconstruction of journalism ethics.

An integrative approach also must address the widely shared feeling that, in today's media world, codes of ethics that consist mainly of abstract principles no longer provide proper guidance for practice. Such codes say little about the 'personalization' of journalism ethics—the need to articulate norms for specific media platforms and specific types of journalism. For example, it is no longer sufficient to ask journalists to be accurate in a general manner, say by checking facts. How is accuracy to be realized in fast-moving online journalism, from 'live blogging' events to tracking reports on social media? Here, again, we encounter a debate within journalism ethics. And, again, the choice is often framed in terms of a dilemma: to construct either a depersonalized ethics for all journalists or a personalized ethics for types of journalism.

The depersonalized view was evident in the 2014 revision of the SPJ code of ethics. The ethics committee decided to maintain the code's de-personal approach—one that character- izes many pre-digital codes. The code is designed to be universal and intended to apply to all journalists in all situations—rich in content with many principles and norms and de-personal in being platform-neutral. The code does not name specific types of journalism. The commit- tee rejected a personalized approach that expresses norms for types of journalism and their distinct problems.

In contrast, a recent project of the Online News Association (ONA) in the United States used the personalized approach to help members create ethical guidelines. The project, which began in 2014, stressed common process, not common content. The ONA decided that, in an era of multiple forms of journalism, the best strategy was to personalize the process—to give each online journalist or outlet the 'tools' to construct their own editorial guidelines. The ONA Website encouraged its members to 'build your own ethics.' This process has been dubbed 'DYI (Do It Yourself) ethics' (ONA, 2014). The toolkit starts with a small set of common principles that the ONA thinks most journalists would consider fundamental, such as tell the truth, do not plagiarize, and correct your errors. Then journalists are asked to make a choice between (a) traditional objective journalism, where "your personal opinion is kept under wraps," and (b) transparency journalism, "meaning it's fine to write from a certain political or social point of view as long as you're upfront about it" (ONA, 2014). The toolkit then provides guidance on constructing guidelines for about 40 areas of practice where 'honest journalists' might disagree, such as removing items from online archives, use of anonymous sources, and verification of social media sources.

The DIY approach appears to be a positive, inclusive, and democratic approach, suited to a plural media world. To others it is a regressive response since journalism ethics needs strong content. It needs to stand behind principles and not retreat to a 'process' that, like a smorgas- bord, allows everyone to pick and choose what values they like.

I believe the future of journalism ethics is not a choice between de-personal and personal approaches. That is a false dilemma. Even the ONA approach is not a pure form of personal- ized ethics. It is an inventive hybrid of de-personal and personalized approaches, although the emphasis is solidly on the latter. Any adequate code in the future will have to combine both approaches in a creative and mind-stretching exercise. What would an integrated code of journalism ethics look like? It would consist of four levels:

Level 1: De-personalized, general principles expressing what every responsible journalist should affirm insofar as they serve the publics of self-governing democracies.

Level 2: More specific norms that fall under the principles, like the SPJ code, only there is no ban on mentioning forms of journalism or formulating rules for new practices.

Level 3: Case studies and examples of how the norms of levels 1 and 2 are applied in daily journalism, such as how to minimize harm, without a focus on new media issues.

Level 4: A set of guidelines and protocols for new media practices and platforms. This level would be a work in progress, evolving as we improve our ethical thinking in this area.

This code should be a 'living' document, existing online so that it can be constantly improved and updated in light of public discussion on issues and trends.

Unlike the personalization approach, the code would be rich in content, from the principles on levels 1 and 2 to the applications and leading-edge discussions on levels 3 and 4. Unlike the de-personalized approach, it would do more than state abstract principles for all. It would weave fundamental principles into a multi-level code.

Conclusion

I have argued that the construction of digital, global journalism ethics begins with the adoption of a new mindset for ethics in general and journalism ethics in particular. The mindset of pragmatic humanism proposes that digital, global journalism ethics be discursive in method, imperfectionist and non-dualistic in epistemology, and integrationist in developing new ethical content. The mindset rejects pre-digital ideas of journalism ethics as primarily fixed content, absolutist and dualistic in epistemology, and de-personal in developing new ethical content. However, an ethical mindset is only a first step. It is, by nature, a set of abstract ideas and general attitudes. A mindset is an approach to determining ethical content; it is not the content itself. In other writings, I have proposed principles grounded in a cosmopolitan ethics that promotes a global humanity (Ward, 2010).

Moreover, this chapter, focused on mindset, does not examine other emerging features of the new journalism ethics, such as the global ethics movement (Ward, 2013) and the important fact that citizens around the world are now engaged in journalism ethics through critical interchanges hosted by global online networks. Journalism ethics is no longer 'closed' to members of professional media organizations (Ward and Wasserman, 2015). It is open to all.

Moreover, as citizens create media content, they rub up against long-standing questions in journalism ethics. Journalism ethics becomes a 'media ethics for everyone,' part of a larger communication ethics. These trends will shape developments in journalism and media ethics.

Given the trends surveyed, the task is clear: We need to create a new, more complex, and conceptually deeper ethics for an expanding world of journalism that is professional and non-professional, mainstream and non-mainstream, online and offline, local and global.

Further reading

This chapter has developed ideas from work in global media ethics. For insight into how the 'local and global' combine in global ethics, read Christians *et al.*'s article "Toward a Global Media Ethics." Two other pieces, my book *Radical Media Ethics and Global Journalism Ethics*, and an article I wrote with Herman Wasserman titled "Open Ethics" explain in detail the shape of a digital, global journalism ethics. Friend and Singer's *Online Journalism Ethics* is a good source for the early development of a digital journalism ethics, and Makau and Marty's *Dialogue and Deliberation* explores the meaning and possibility of dialogic democracy.

References

Albrecht, J.M. (2012) *Reconstructing Individualism: A Pragmatic Tradition from Emerson to Ellison*. New York, NY: Fordham University Press.
BBC (2015) *Editorial Guidelines*. Available from: http://www.bbc.co.uk/editorialguidelines/.
Christians, C.G., Rao, S., Ward, S.J.A. and Wasserman, H. (2008) "Toward a Global Media Ethics: Theoretical Perspectives." *Ecquid Novi: African Journalism Studies* 29(2): 135–172.
Dworkin, R. (1986) *Law's Empire*. Cambridge, MA: Harvard University Press.

Friend, C. and Singer, J. (2007) *Online Journalism Ethics: Traditions and Transitions*. Armonk, NY: M. E. Sharpe.

Habermas, J. (2001) "Discourse Ethics: Notes on a Program of Philosophical Justification." In Lenhardt, C. and Nicholsen, S.W. (trans.) *Moral Consciousness and Communicative Action*. Cambridge, MA: MIT Press, pp. 43–115.

Makau, J.M. and D.L. Marty. (2013) *Dialogue and Deliberation*. Long Grove, IL: Waveland Press.

Online News Association (ONA) (2014) *Build Your Own Ethics Code*. Available from: http://journalists. org/resources/build-your-own-ethics-code.

Putnam, H. (1995) *Pragmatism*. Cambridge, MA: Blackwell.

Quine, W.V.O. (1960) *Word and Object*. Cambridge, MA: The MIT Press.

Rawls, J. (1972) *A Theory of Justice*. Oxford, UK: Oxford University Press.

Society of Professional Journalists (SPJ) (2014) *SPJ Code of Ethics*. Available from: http://www.spj.org/ ethicscode.asp.

Ward, S.J.A. (2005) *The Invention of Journalism Ethics: The Path to Objectivity and Beyond*. Montreal, Québec: McGill-Queen's University Press.

Ward, S.J.A. (2010) *Global Journalism Ethics*. Montreal, Québec: McGill-Queen's University Press.

Ward, S.J.A. (ed.) (2013) *Global Media Ethics: Problems and Perspectives*. Malden, MA: Wiley-Blackwell.

Ward, S.J.A. (2015) *Radical Media Ethics: A Global Approach*. Malden, MA: Wiley-Blackwell.

Ward, S.J.A. and Wasserman, H. (2015) "Open Ethics: Towards a Global Media Ethics of Listening." *Journalism Studies* 16(6): 834–849. DOI: 10.1080/1461670X.2014.950882.

4

THE DIGITAL JOURNALIST

The journalistic field, boundaries, and disquieting change

Scott A. Eldridge II

Championing some of the biggest news stories of the early twenty-first century, WikiLeaks' editor-in-chief Julian Assange describes his organization as part of a "healthy, vibrant and inquisitive journalistic media" (WikiLeaks, 2015) that embraces the values of the 'fourth estate' (Lynch, 2012). Meanwhile, journalists and media critics describe him as a hacker, an activist, and a 'provocateur' (Carr, 2010; Shafer, 2012), who is dismissed by others as a 'seething jerk' (Shafer, 2010), a "self-publicising prig with messianic tendencies" (Evans, 2011), and the leader of the 'Wikicult' (Moore, 2010). News stories repeatedly characterize WikiLeaks as "a stateless organization that operates in an online world without borders" (Carr, 2011), and although Assange sees himself as a member of the journalistic field, he is described as a technological rogue on "the hacktivist fringe of the internet" (*Guardian*, 2010).

The subject of both academic and journalistic attention, Assange has emerged as an emblematic but confrontational figure in digital journalism and as a prominent figure in a group of digital actors who have challenged the status quo of the journalistic field. By positioning their work at the leading edge of innovative journalism and taking advantage of an expanse of digital approaches to share news and information online, emerging digital actors pursuing journalistic work have irritated and blurred the traditional boundaries of the journalistic field.

Adopting unconventional approaches to achieve journalistic ends, these 'interlopers' (Eldridge, 2014) also challenge scholars to revisit existing understandings of the nature of both journalism and journalists. For digital journalism studies, these 'would-be journalists' highlight a divisive aspect of digital change by drawing attention to the parameters of the journalistic field. This chapter argues that such boundary disputes help to make sense of a field that until recently appeared relatively stable, but is currently very much in flux.

Digital interlopers

In a previous work, I categorized new digital entities that challenge the boundaries of the journalistic field as 'interloper media,' drawing attention to the way new actors who self-identify as journalists are portrayed as transgressing journalistic boundaries and misappropriating professional identities (Eldridge, 2013, 2014). For digital journalism studies, they represent a competition between an established set of journalists, presenting the journalistic field as a defined space of belonging built on familiar norms and values, and new actors who adopt journalistic identities. This binary view of the field distances new actors who offer alternative views of that space through in-group/out-group discourses (Eldridge, 2014: 13). Stoking tensions over what it means to belong to the journalistic field and prompting boundary disputes, discourses marginalizing interlopers play out through explicit discussions of belonging (Coddington, 2012; Wahl-Jorgensen, 2014), along with more subtle boundary work in everyday news texts (Eldridge, 2013, 2014).

Boundary disputes prompted by the emergence of digital journalists build on traditional understandings of journalism and rely heavily on normative understandings of what defines journalism (Steel, 2013). Boundaries also depend on a recognition of journalism based on traditional measures of the field that are shared internally, by journalists, and more broadly in society; in this construction of the journalistic field, interlopers and some digital journalists present threats to this existing journalistic order.

Whether discussing journalistic bloggers on 'J-blogs' (Singer, 2005), journalists' use of social media (Artwick, 2013), interactive live-blogs (Thurman and Schapals, this volume), or the work of more activist-oriented interloper media such as WikiLeaks (Eldridge, 2014), the work of new digital journalists is increasingly commonplace. However, despite close proximity between these new actors and the journalistic field—notably when WikiLeaks' work was communicated through the *New York Times*, the *Guardian*, and other media—the journalistic identity of interloping digital journalists remains marginalized; blogs can now be found across legacy media, yet terms like 'blogger' and 'blogosphere' are still used as derisive labels by some (Sullivan, 2013). This in part reflects the technological newness and independence of interlopers. In the past 15 years, the emergence of political bloggers has shown that others are able to cover elections without the traditional press corps (Eldridge, 2013); 'accidental journalists' and 'citizen witnesses' have emerged to offer new avenues to news and information (Allan, 2013); and those like Assange who identify as journalists are finding new ways to release information to the world.

While these dynamics signal that radical approaches to digital journalism from non-characteristic digital journalists can succeed, new actors continue to be treated as outside the journalistic field and simultaneously antagonize journalistic standard bearers. As Karin Wahl-Jorgensen argues, new digital actors demonstrate how "new technologies can be harnessed for the purpose of free expression and circulation of information—core journalistic values in which the profession remains heavily invested, and willing to fight for" (2014: 2588), yet in doing so they provoke contests over legitimacy and authority. These clashes can be understood through the symbolic constructions of the journalistic field (Bourdieu, 1994, 2005) and the discursive construction of boundaries to reinforce journalistic belonging (Bishop, 1999, among others).

Fields and boundaries: symbolic constructions of journalism

Pierre Bourdieu's work on field theory and on the journalistic field underpins a significant amount of work in journalism studies and digital journalism studies. For exploring the ways emerging approaches to journalism have challenged journalistic 'belonging,' field theory describes society through differentiated fields which when recognized internally and externally by members of society provide social boundaries around the work of social actors. For those fields where other structural and regulatory definitions may be less applicable, as with journalism, the outward articulation of boundaries to define journalism plays a prominent role in distinguishing the field from other social actors.

Bourdieu describes the journalistic field in part as a space defined by 'action and reaction' (2005: 30), by which he means a societal space defined by its constituent members offering a 'dominant vision' of journalism, and an equally dominant contrast of what journalism is not (2005: 42). This dominant vision defining its boundaries rests on shared presuppositions and agreed-upon complicities concerning what it means to be a journalist. These underscore the field's ability to define its unique space in society. Bourdieu's work has enabled scholars to advance theoretical work that accounts for new digital actors contending with journalistic concepts. This offers both a theoretical grounding for discussing journalistic identity as well as exposing where traditional definitions of journalism fail to reflect modern realities.

However, since Bourdieu's work was developed, the journalistic field has become an increasingly messy definitional space (it is worth noting that Bourdieu's development of field theory pre-dates the emergence of digital technologies and online media and his work on the journalistic field was a posthumous publication). Even so, in theorizing the journalistic field, he captures its historic struggle with maintaining boundaries against other definers of social reality, including those in the academy and politics who 'do battle' in presenting the defining narratives of the social world (Bourdieu, 2005: 31). Bourdieu sees journalism as a field in constant engagement to remain relevant; expressed differently, while journalism has long defined its societal role as necessary for the functioning of society, it has never been alone in that role and competes with other fields to present "a legitimate vision of the social world" (Bourdieu, 2005).

As Rodney Benson argues, while external dynamics are key in shaping fields, including the journalistic field, fields do enjoy a strong degree of autonomy to maintain internal order—"a microcosm within a macrocosm" (2006: 188). Fields operate with their own sets of rules, rules that are the result of historic struggles to establish and maintain distinction externally while reinforcing order internally.

These clashes have led different social actors to visibly reinforce the boundaries of their respective fields. While externally this remained critical for societal recognition, it is the internal order and the "ongoing production of difference" (Benson, 2006: 189) that has come to define the journalistic field. In this particular struggle, the 'symbolic weight' of traditional members of the field gives them an out-sized advantage in shaping the field's parameters and elements of inclusion and exclusion (2006: 190). In other words, we all recognize a newspaper as journalism, as we would a prominent broadcaster and even a legacy news media website, in part because of their dominance in *reinforcing* that 'vision' of the journalistic field. Interlopers and other digital actors, by contrast, are only able to *challenge* this dominant narrative.

From the vantage point of field theory, traditional journalists find themselves in conflict with new digital actors due in part to the way journalists have defined their societal space around a set of taken-for-granted criteria (for Bourdieu, these would be journalism's specific doxa). Built on traditional constructs and ideal-typical values associated with the 'Fourth Estate,' the journalistic field depends on its criteria being recognizable both internally and externally—journalism as something 'we know when we see' (Donsbach, 2010: 38). While journalism has, arguably, never been a truly uniform or coherent space, challenged in fact by differences between popular and elite newspapers, broadcast journalists, the periodical press, and myriad other peculiarities, across these nuances there has traditionally been at least a tacit agreement that members of the field were "participating in the same game" (Bourdieu, 2005: 36):

The most irreducible adversaries have in common that they accept a certain number of presuppositions that are constitutive of the very functioning of the field. In order to fight one another, people have to agree on the areas of disagreement. There is a kind of fundamental complicity among the members of a field.

(Bourdieu, 2005)

However, tacit unanimity and journalistic identity built on criteria that are often unspoken have left the field open to challenges from new digital actors who see their work as journalism. As Silvio Waisbord notes, until relatively recently, "no other occupation or consolidated profession pretended to be in the same business as journalism. Such absence of competition somewhat protected journalism from potential challenges" (2013: 139–140). Digital actors have challenged that protected status.

Consequently, definitions of being a journalist are enforced through hefting traditional journalists' 'social weight' to reject interloper claims. This builds distinctions through public articulations of what journalism is and is not around traditional values and through in-group/out-group distinctions of belonging. "Though seemingly vague, [these] 'fuzzy' oppositions are very fundamental in that when a whole society has them in its head, they end up defining reality" (Bourdieu, 2005: 37). Beyond underscoring "'fuzzy' oppositions," these contests over belonging to the journalistic field also reflect clashes over the legitimacy claims of traditional members of the field. For interlopers, however, the results of these clashes have wider implications:

Being deemed a "legitimate" journalist accords prestige and credibility, but also access to news sources, audiences, funding, legal rights, and other institutionalized perquisites. Also, struggles over what is appropriate journalism bear on the actual news products as some practices are held to be worthy while others are rejected.

(Carlson, 2015: 2)

In a struggle over legitimacy and resources, digital interlopers continue to challenge the boundaries of the journalistic field and assert their journalistic identity in ways that compel scholars to make sense of their digital approaches to journalism.

Journalism's boundaries

Having discussed the contested nature of the journalistic field in the face of interloping digital journalists, this chapter now turns to discuss the nature of journalistic boundaries as discursive performances and the way these have focused on digital, interloping journalists. By performances, I mean that boundaries exist primarily through the amplification of difference between journalists and digital journalists and gain meaning through contestation. Referred to as boundary disputes or boundary work, these are "symbolic contests in which different actors vie for definitional control to apply or remove the label of journalism" (Carlson, 2015: 2). Boundaries and their performances become pronounced at moments of intensity, as with the furor around WikiLeaks, but are also the product of an ongoing need to define journalism's boundaries (Bourdieu, 2005: 33), and maintained through "less intensive peer monitoring" (Benson, 2006: 198).

The field's need to promote and maintain distinction drives boundary work that materializes through "claims to authority" (Gieryn, 1983: 781) over the right to call oneself a journalist. When the primacy of the journalistic field is challenged, boundaries of inclusion move beyond tacit acknowledgment of belonging and are made prominent in news texts and public discourses. These can emerge in spot-lit and obvious discussion of journalism (Bishop, 1999; Cecil, 2002; Coddington, 2012; Wahl-Jorgensen, 2014), while at other times boundaries come through more subtle distinctions of difference.

I argue and evidence in previous work that there are two levels where the 'symbolic contest' of boundaries can be found, describing these levels as 'overt' and 'covert' constructions of journalistic identity (Eldridge, 2014: 14). The first of these, overt discourses, draw lines around the journalistic field in order to maintain internal order and reinforce internal rules (Benson, 2006). Overt discourses reinforce belonging through a familiar set of sign-posted discussions of norms and criteria of professionalism described as boundary work. These are rooted in the sociological work of Thomas Gieryn (1983, 1999) and developed in journalism studies by Ron Bishop (1999, 2004), Dan Berkowitz (2000), and others.

To tie this discussion of boundaries to Bourdieu's discussion of fields, when boundaries emerge in newspaper texts, media criticism pieces, and other critical outlets such as editorials and columns as sign-posted discussions of journalism, they (a) benefit from the social weight traditional journalistic media have in promoting a dominant vision of journalism, (b) rely on ideal-typical definitions of journalism, and (c) present a version of the field that leaves little room for interloping actors who self-identify as journalists. In this sense, the performance of journalistic boundaries is made clear through the opinionated tone of columns adopting forceful language of belonging and non-belonging, and the discussion of journalism and media is drawn immediately to the readers' attention through headlines or dedicated spaces (Eldridge, 2014: 2).

As "the outward-facing expression of journalistic identity" (Eldridge, 2014: 3), such overt boundary maintenance is understood from the work of Ron Bishop (1999), who explores boundaries maintained between 'good' and 'bad' journalism and presented in ways "meant to be seen" (1999: 91). Bishop describes discourses that cordon off the tarnished reputation of tabloid journalists, insulating elite newspapers from the popular press as it struggled to distinguish its work from paparazzi after the death of Princess Diana. This presents "an inwardly focused self-policing of the profession of journalism by associated in-group members" (Eldridge, 2014: 2). While this creates difference, it still recognizes that both good and bad journalists are "participating in the same game" (Bourdieu, 2005: 36) and shore up the boundaries of journalism by creating a hierarchy of 'good' and 'bad' journalism or ostracizing the 'bad apples' (Cecil, 2002) who have failed to live up to journalistic ideals. By and large, this maintains standing among familiar journalistic forms and actors, even if the self-policing seems overwrought and ineffective (Bishop, 2004).

At the second level of distinction, I argue that covert discourses of journalistic belonging and non-belonging perform underanalyzed but critical boundary work in the journalistic field's efforts toward "reinforcing the power and primacy of journalism's self-declared societal role" (Eldridge, 2014: 6). Interwoven in news texts that are not otherwise sign-posted as discussions of journalism, such boundaries define legitimacy by describing journalists through a "familiar lexicon of belonging" (2014: 8), reflective of the field's specific doxa (Bourdieu, 2005: 37). Conversely, these discourses project a non-journalistic identity on interlopers. Covert discourses offer more nuanced forms of marginalization, describing emerging media work as emotive, rumor-laden, and approached with an activist's edge to further separate the journalistic field from interlopers.

At both levels, distinction is developed not only through explicitly juxtaposing competing claims of belonging or evaluating interlopers' performance of journalistic work but rather through a mixture of discourses that amplify the journalistic work of traditional members of the journalistic field alongside the absence of such descriptors for digital interlopers (Eldridge, 2014: 14). Examples of this contrast through absence can be found in descriptions of digital journalists as engaged in out-group activities, such as hacking. Digital journalists are also framed as less-than-serious in their treatment of information, describing the content of blogs as "cyberwhispers" (Rutenberg, 2008), contrasting the paradigm of facticity at the core of journalistic work (Conboy, 2013: 2). Emphasizing journalism-as-labor, publications by WikiLeaks are only viewed as journalistic when exposed to journalistic routines by traditional members of the field: "The field reports chime with allegations made by the *New York Times* writer Peter Maass, who was in Samarra at the time" (Leigh and O'Kane, 2010). This poses a 'normalization problem,' where journalistic contributions of these new actors and digital forms are only considered valid when enveloped by traditional members of the field. Providing further narratives of journalism-as-labor, the time-intensive 'combing through' (Leigh, 2010) and 'sifting' (*Guardian*, 2010) of digital material distinguishes traditional routines of cultural production by 'legitimate' members of the journalistic field from interlopers like Assange, who "dumps 92,000 new primary source documents into the laps of the world's public with no context" (Exum, 2010).

Pre-dating WikiLeaks and Assange, similar dynamics could be found in the treatment of independent news bloggers, described as frenzied and reactive: "the blogosphere at full tilt" (Seelye, 2008). Operating against the guiding paradigms of the journalistic field of objectivity and veracity, the 'blogosphere' is a place where truth and facticity are less important and often rumor-focused: "whether the story is true is still unknown, but it didn't take long for the right-wing blogosphere to embrace it" (Parker, 2008). Such descriptions of what I describe as interlopers in my work are threaded through news coverage going back to the early twenty-first century, distancing new actors from traditional journalists (Eldridge, 2013; Singer, 2003). As performances of journalistic identity and as reinforcements of the field's guiding doxa, these reify the field's boundaries along traditional measures that rebuff digital challenges.

Prominent performances of boundary building also emerge when traditional journalists amplify valorized ideals of the journalistic field. Such discourses draw on normative dimensions of the 'Fourth Estate', even as these are often based more on idealization than realization (Hampton, 2010). In these cases, news texts offer a vision of journalism as a force in society imbued with values of social responsibility, public interest, and a commitment to veracity alongside context. This came to the foreground in one of the more contentious aspects of the WikiLeaks collaboration with the *Guardian* and the *New York Times*, as each claimed it was their initiative to redact personal identifiers in the published releases, and as such each sought to promote their own social responsibility and public interest ideals as responsible watchdogs (Eldridge, 2014: 13). In other narratives, the role of journalists spiriting away information on encrypted drives (Leigh and Harding, 2011), with the interloper made passive as an intermediary or conduit (Davies, Steel, and Leigh, 2010), actively describe journalists seeking truth and making information prominent while minimizing the agency of digital actors.

When news texts valorize the journalist in a laudable, almost heroic, manner, the journalistic field is also defined through an ideal-typical portrayal of the journalist. Whether foregrounding institutional expertise and reminders of journalism-as-labor (Conboy and Eldridge, 2015; Eldridge, 2013, 2014; Örnebring, 2010) or emphasizing normative 'Fourth Estate' ideals (Hampton, 2010), these discourses build boundaries by washing over interloper claims that their work is also responsible, publicly interested, and contextualized (Benkler, 2011: 322). These examples and previous work show that when distinguishing between a dominant vision of the journalistic field and interlopers, boundaries are built through one or both of two key dynamics to present a singular perspective of the journalist: the expression of a 'held' identity from the speaking journalists and a 'projected' identity as non-journalists on interlopers (Eldridge, 2014: 12). Unwilling to incorporate new approaches to fulfilling its journalistic roles, this reflects what Bourdieu describes as an inherent conservatism to a field's dominant vision, one that resists change and mutes discord in favor of 'agreed upon complicities' (2005: 36).

As a result, journalistic boundaries are presented as an immovable construct. Consequently, for digital actors to challenge these boundaries is to swim against a rather forceful tide.

Digital dissonance

New and emerging digital journalists challenge us to conceptualize the journalistic field as vast, rather than finite, and define journalism beyond familiar and once distinct genres and forms (Eldridge, 2015). This approach sees journalism as a diffuse set of media products from a wide range of social agents—including a wider range of journalists—now active in creating news products and journalistic content. Yochai Benkler (2011, 2013a) points to this as the product of a 'networked fourth estate,' with myriad actors contributing to journalistic processes. His argument develops first as a defense of WikiLeaks' work as journalistic and Julian Assange as a journalist, later in support of WikiLeaks' source Chelsea Manning (Benkler, 2013b). Benkler (2011) initially argues that a more networked fourth estate is a place where new actors can contribute to journalistic endeavors. Moreover, he denounces "more established outlets' efforts to denigrate the journalistic identity of the new kids on the block to preserve their own identity" (2011: 315).

Benkler's thesis—that the field of journalism is expanding in a digital era—challenges the normative insularity of journalism's and the field's self-defined boundaries described above. Through invoking a similarly persistent array of ideals, standards, and criteria of belonging, Benkler argues, new actors operating within this digital space make it clear that continuing to view journalism narrowly ignores certain digital realities. He also identifies a key characteristic of these new digital actors, arguing that they can simultaneously hold a journalistic identity alongside activist, movement building, or otherwise alternative identities (Benkler, 2013b).

However, while Benkler sees these within a networked fourth estate, the idea of new actors holding variable identities where only one is 'journalistic' rankles traditional journalists. Notably, when asked about such variable identities, journalists I have interviewed for previous studies describe this as 'spear-carrying' and incompatible with journalistic identities. Journalists expressly differentiate between technical and more 'everyday' definitions of journalism and, while praising the activism of interlopers, see digital work as worthy of protection but not of being ordained journalism. Others argue that if Assange (in this case) was a journalist he would not have fallen out with the rest of the field's members, describing a sense of belonging to an in-group and playing 'the same game' as other journalists (Bourdieu, 2005: 44). This reinforces Donsbach's (2010) reflection that journalism seems to be something we define as such if and when society is broadly familiar with its actors and products.

While Benkler's argument drives a progressive wedge through narrow definitions of journalism, it risks underappreciating digital journalists struggling to have their work considered journalism in its own right. The extent to which there is an acceptance of interlopers' journalistic contribution is often limited to supporting roles. WikiLeaks, for instance, is portrayed

as innovative and revolutionary when it provides a new avenue for digital 'sources,' so long as that information is then legitimated by other journalists with professional expertise (Eldridge, 2013: 292; 2014: 11). While normalization of new media forms and journalists is not uncommon (Lasorsa, Lewis, and Holten, 2012; Singer, 2003), in terms of power and authority their journalistic contribution is marginalized when emerging from outside the traditional boundaries of the field (Eldridge, 2013). Joining blogs as new journalistic possibilities, the normalization of social media has also been widespread (see Paulussen, Harder, and Johnson, this volume), as has the adoption of PGP—or 'Pretty Good Privacy'—keys and 'secure drop' software that give news organizations new ways to wrap the previously distinct whistleblowing offers of WikiLeaks into their routine practices. As one journalist told me in an interview, "the genius of Julian Assange is he's provided a template that can be imitated by others and that other people can copy, perhaps not with his flair for self publicity."

It is in this last phrase—where the critical distinction between acceptance of interlopers through normalization and valuing these actors as journalists on their own—where problems emerge. A suggestion that interlopers need first to conform to recognizable features of the field confirms that new actors and digital functions are still viewed as 'lesser-than,' as subaltern voices. Glenn Greenwald was a prominent object of this view, when his reporting on Edward Snowden in the *Guardian* was portrayed as 'lesser-than' when he was dismissed as an activist and potentially criminal by David Gregory, the host of NBC's 'Meet the Press,' and as a 'blogger' in the *New York Times* (Sullivan, 2013).

To return to Benkler (2011, 2013), while progressive in arguing that traditional members of the field are too sensitive concerning their established order, describing interlopers as journalistic rather than journalists presents a twin risk when digital journalists are valued solely in a role of support. This materializes in the difference between labeling something as 'journalism,' versus 'journalistic,' where the former is a member of the field in its own right and the latter might be a 'source' or conduit or a technological hub for whistleblowers (all descriptions ascribed to WikiLeaks). In other words, new digital journalists that challenge the ways we approach and understand journalism in a digital age should not only gain credibility when brought into the journalistic fold or placed in service to recognizable members of the journalistic field (Artwick, 2013; Lasorsa, Lewis, and Holten, 2012).

Conclusion: challenging a fragile field

Under duress as new actors claiming journalistic identity, the dimensions of the journalistic field can be challenged in part because they rely on the acceptance of journalism as familiar and distinct (Bourdieu, 2005). This distinction has become harder to maintain as barriers to publication, investigation, and reporting have been lowered online, and digital technologies continue to be embraced by even the most traditional of journalistic organizations.

When *New York Times* public editor Margaret Sullivan defends Greenwald as a 'proud, rather than apologetic' blogger, she recognizes that even while she adopts the term for her own work from time to time, the use of 'blogger' is often a pejorative. Sullivan nodded to the superior air with which the label is applied to marginalize new digital journalists, noting, "when the media establishment uses the term, it somehow seems to say, 'You're not quite one of us'" (Sullivan, 2013).

There is a great deal of analytical space in the phrase 'not quite one of us,' and as this chapter has argued, this distinction becomes a de facto definer of the dimensions of the journalistic field. This privileges an ideal-typical understanding of journalists that disadvantages digital actors for their newness, dismissing alternative actors as 'lesser-than' members of the journalistic field. Increasingly, however, the journalistic field is a difficult space to define. Even for traditional members of the field, digital change has woven into the practices and production of journalism; the field's cultural products—news—include a wider tapestry of media forms, and the field producing this work is equally varied. Bourdieu writes of the journalistic field agreeing to its boundaries in part because of agreed-upon complicities that 'smooth over' difference, and yet internally and externally difference is increasingly difficult to ignore.

As more and more digital journalists take unfamiliar approaches to journalism while aligning their work with the traditional milieus of the journalistic field (Hanitzsch, 2011), they continue to introduce diversity into the journalistic field. What remains unclear is whether we will continue to find examples where they are dismissed for being too amateur (Singer, 2005), too colloquial (Eldridge, 2013), too anti-establishment (Eldridge, 2014), or simply too disruptive to be seen as peers; whether the tensions around what defines journalism will remain; or whether interlopers will eventually be seen as journalists and no longer as parasitic 'fleas on the dog' (Carr, 2008) living off traditional media.

Further reading

For more on journalism and its boundaries, Matt Carlson and Seth Lewis' edited collection *Boundaries of Journalism* (2015) offers a wide-ranging discussion of the lines between and around journalism. For more on the journalistic field, including Pierre Bourdieu's discussion of the journalistic field, see Rodney Benson and Erik Neveu's *Bourdieu and the Journalistic Field* (2005). Benedetta Brevini, Arne Hintz, and Patrick McCurdy's edited volume *Beyond WikiLeaks* (2013) offers a comprehensive collection of academic and journalistic views on the WikiLeaks' challenge to journalism's status quo.

References

Allan, S. (2013) *Citizen Witnessing: Revisioning Journalism in Times of Crisis*. Cambridge, UK: Polity Press.

Artwick, C.G. (2013) "Reporters on Twitter: Product or Service?" *Digital Journalism* 1(2), 212–228.

Benkler, Y. (2011) "A Free Irresponsible Press: WikiLeaks and the Battle Over the Soul of the Networked Fourth Estate." *Harvard Civil Rights-Civil Liberties Law Review* 46: 311–397.

Benkler, Y. (2013a) "WikiLeaks and the Networked Fourth Estate." In Brevini, B., Hintz, A. and McCurdy, P. (eds) *Beyond WikiLeaks: Implications for the Future of Communications, Journalism and Society*. Basingstoke, UK: Palgrave MacMillan, pp. 11–34.

Benkler, Y. (2013b) "In the Matter Of: United States vs. PFC Bradley E. Manning (Unofficial Transcript)." *Freedom of the Press Foundation* 17(10): 1–166.

Benson, R. (2006) "News Media as a 'Journalistic Field': What Bourdieu Adds to New Institutionalism and Vice Versa." *Political Communication* 23(2): 182–202.

Berkowitz, D. (2000) "Doing Double Duty: Paradigm Repair and the Princess Diana What-a-Story." *Journalism* 1(2): 125–143.

Bishop, R. (1999) "From Behind the Walls: Boundary Work by News Organizations in Their Coverage of Princess Diana's Death." *Journal of Communication Inquiry* 23(1): 90–112.

Bishop, R. (2004) "The Accidental Journalist: Shifting Professional Boundaries in the Wake of Leonardo DiCaprio's Interview with Former President Clinton." *Journalism Studies* 5(1): 31–43.

Bourdieu, P. (1994) "Structures, Habitus, Power: Basis for a Theory of Symbolic Power." In Dirks, N.B., Eley, G. and Ortner, S.B. (eds) *Culture/Power/History: A Reader in Contemporary Social Theory*. Princeton, NJ: Princeton University Press, pp. 155–199.

Bourdieu, P. (2005) "The Political Field, the Social Science Field, and the Journalistic Field." In Benson, R. and Neveu, E. (eds) *Bourdieu and the Journalistic Field*. Cambridge, UK: Polity Press, pp. 29–47.

Carlson, M. (2015) "Introduction: The Many Boundaries of Journalism." In Carlson, M. and Lewis, S.C. (eds) *Boundaries of Journalism: Professionalism, Practices and Participation*. Abingdon, UK: Routledge, pp. 1–18.

Carr, D. (2008) "In Denver, a Thousand Little Pieces." *The New York*, 1 September, p. C1.

Carr, D. (2010) "Journalists, Provocateurs, Maybe Both." *The New York Times*, 25 July, p. B1.

Carr, D. (2011) "WikiLeaks' Founder, in a Gilded British Cage." *The New York Times*, 26 September, p. B1.

Cecil, M. (2002) "Bad Apples: Paradigm Overhaul and the CNN/Time 'Tailwind' Story." *Journal of Communication Inquiry* 26(1): 46–58.

Coddington, M. (2012) "Defending a Paradigm by Patrolling a Boundary: Two Global Newspapers' Approach to WikiLeaks." *Journalism & Mass Communication Quarterly* 89(3): 377–396.

Conboy, M. (2013) *Journalism Studies: The Basics*. Abingdon, UK: Routledge.

Conboy, M. and Eldridge, S. (2015) "Morbid Symptoms: Between a Dying and a Re-Birth (Apologies to Gramsci)." *Journalism Studies* 15(5): 566–575.

Davies, N., Steel, J. and Leigh, D. (2010) "See No Evil: Secret Files Show How US Ignored Iraq Torture." *The Guardian*, 23 October.

Donsbach, W. (2010) "Journalists and Their Professional Identities." In Allan, S. (ed.) *The Routledge Companion to News and Journalism*. Abingdon, UK: Routledge, pp. 38–59.

Eldridge, S. (2013) "Perceiving Professional Threats: Journalism's Discursive Reaction to the Rise of New Media Entities." *The Journal of Applied Journalism & Media Studies* 2(2): 281–299.

Eldridge, S. (2014) "Boundary Maintenance and Interloper Media Reaction: Differentiating between Journalism's Discursive Enforcement Processes." *Journalism Studies* 15(1): 1–16.

Eldridge, S. (2015) "Change and Continuity: Historicizing the Emergence of Online Media." In M. Conboy and J. Steel (eds) *The Routledge Companion to British Media History*. Abingdon, UK: Routledge, pp. 528–538.

Evans, L. (2011) "Compelling Revelations." *The Spectator*, 1 October.

Exum, A. (2010) "Getting Lost in the Fog of War." *The New York Times*, 26 July.

Gieryn, T. (1983) "Boundary-Work and the Demarcation of Science from Non-Science: Strains and Interests in Professional Ideologies of Scientists." *American Sociological Review* 48(6): 781–795.

The Guardian (2010) "The War Logs: The Leak: About the Logs." *The Guardian*, 25 July.

Hampton, M. (2010) "The Fourth Estate Ideal in Journalism History." In Allan, S. (ed.) *The Routledge Companion to News and Journalism*. Oxon, UK: Routledge, pp. 3–12.

Hanitzsch, T. (2011) "Populist Disseminators, Detached Watchdogs, Critical Change Agents and Opportunist Facilitators. Professional Milieus, the Journalistic Field and Autonomy in 18 Countries." *International Communication Gazette* 73(6): 477–494.

Lasorsa, D., Lewis, S. and Holten, A. (2012) "Normalizing Twitter: Journalism Practice in an Emerging Communication Space." *Journalism Studies* 13(1): 19–36.

Leigh, D. (2010) "The Leak: One Tiny Memory Stick, One Big Headache for the United States." *The Guardian*, 29 November.

Leigh, D. and Harding, L. (2011) *WikiLeaks: Inside Julian Assange's War on Secrecy* London, UK: Guardian Books.

Leigh, D. and O'Kane, M. (2010) "Front: US Turned Over Captives to Iraqi Torture Squads." *The Guardian*, 25 October.

Lynch, L. (2012) "That's Not Leaking, It's Pure Editorial." *The Canadian Journal of Media Studies* 2012(Fall): 20–40.

Moore, S. (2010) "Anarchy Rules, But It's about a Lot More than Just Lobbing Things at Police." *The Guardian*, 18 December.

Örnebring, H. (2010) "Technology and Journalism-as-Labour: Historical Perspectives." *Journalism* 11(1): 57–74.

Parker, K. (2008) "The Final Hours." *The Washington Post*, 31 October.

Rutenberg, J. (2008) "The Man Behind the Whispers about Obama." *The New York Times*, 13 October.

Seelye, K. (2008) "In Political Coverage, Nothing Succeeds Like Success." *The New York Times*, 23 October.

Shafer, J. (2010) "Why I Love WikiLeaks." *Slate.com*. Available from: http://www.slate.com/articles/news_and_politics/press_box/2010/11/why_i_love_wikileaks.html

Shafer, J. (2012) "WikiLeaks' 16th Minute." *Reuters*. Available from: http://blogs.reuters.com/jackshafer/2012/01/18/wikileaks-16th-minute/

Singer, J.B. (2003) "Who are These Guys? The Online Challenge to the Notion of Journalistic Professionalism." *Journalism* 4(2): 139–163.

Singer, J.B. (2005) "The Political J-Blogger: 'Normalizing' a New Media form to Fit Old Norms and Practices." *Journalism* 6(2): 173–198.

Steel, J. (2013) "Leveson: Solution or Symptom? Class, Crisis and the Degradation of Civil Life." *Ethical Space* 10(1): 8–14.

Sullivan, M. (2013) "As Media Change, Fairness Stays Same." *The New York Times*, 26 October.

Wahl-Jorgensen, K. (2014) "Is Wikileaks Challenging the Paradigm of Journalism? Boundary Work and Beyond." *International Journal of Communication* 8: 2581–2592.

Waisbord, S. (2013) *Reinventing Professionalism: Journalism and News in Global Perspective*. Cambridge, UK: Polity Press.

WikiLeaks (2015) "About." Available from: https://wikileaks.org/What-is-Wikileaks.html

5

THE TIME(S) OF NEWS WEBSITES

Henrik Bødker

Journalism constitutes a series of interrelated practices for the social construction of time. It arrests the ordinary and the unusual in various forms of texts that create feelings of simultaneity, help to define the contemporary, outline possible futures, and shape our understanding and memories of the past. News institutions are thus constituted by certain rhythms, or news cycles, that structure working practices in relation to the publication of different types of journalistic products. These rhythms and products, in turn, are both structured by and help structure the lives of news consumers as well as their conceptions of the temporal processes that undergird the social and cultural framework of their communities. The journalistic texts that are most closely related to the present, that is, news, are often considered to be the core of journalism and are defined through such terms as breaking, scoops, up-to-date, live, updated less than a minute ago, and so on. Related to this core are thus journalistic texts, genres and publications at a greater temporal distance from the present—features, portraits, documentaries, magazines, etc.

News, time, and the internet

In relation to societal processes, journalistic publications have therefore always been interwoven with the rhythms of daily life. And seen against the digital possibilities in terms of breaking news, it is hardly possible to imagine a nineteenth-century media landscape in which 'quarterlies' lost terrain because their "publication rhythm became increasingly anachronistic relative to the perceived pace of life" (Mussell, 2012: 41). A significant development in relation to news has been precisely a steadily decreasing interval of publication from annual, to quarterly, to monthly, fortnightly, weekly, several days a week, daily, hourly, and—with many online news sites—to every other minute. As news and communication more generally is intricately tied to the prevalent cultures of temporality at any given time, as Innis (1973) underlines in 'The Bias of Communication,' this alignment of news with broader rhythms of life has been central in both commentary and research on the acceleration of society. This acceleration is intimately tied to capitalism, competition, and technology. In relation to this Hassan (2014) writes: "Through the networking of computer processing power, and through the pervasion of networks throughout every register of economy, culture, and society, a new temporality affects the human relationship with time" (7).

And 'the super-commodity of information' (Sloterdijk quoted in Hassan, 2012: 4) as well as the continuous updating and the 'always-on' and 'on-demand' character of the internet, caused some commentators to argue that "[t]the internet seems to struggle with time: apart from newness, nowness, it lacks a temporal context" (Nye, quoted in Webster, 2012: 47). This lack of a temporal context may be conceived very broadly as 'time-less time' in Castells' (in)famous phrase, which refers to ways in which the global flow on the internet "dissolves time by disordering the sequence of events and making them simultaneous, thus installing society in eternal ephemerality" (2003: 497). As a technological infrastructure, the internet may indeed encourage what Scholte calls 'transplanetary' and 'supraterritorial' relations (2005: 60–64) that somehow may 'dissolve time'; Nowotny indeed argues that of the various "'social constructions' [...] which leave their mark on artefacts [...] the built-in dimension of time is surely one of the most fundamental dimensions" (1995: 93). Yet, "network time [...] is not total or monolithic" (Hassan, 2014: 9); and people engage with this infrastructure not from 'timeless' locations but from within 'social time,' that is, specifically located cultural negotiations between body time, natural time, wider cultural time regimes, and, linked to that, technological temporalities, for example, time built into clocks and media (see Adam, 2006: 71, and throughout).

This means that, if we follow Leong *et al.* (2009: 1277), "to examine a given collective experience of internet time, one first needs to trace just who and/or what comprises the collective, and therefore whose time is being examined." In a broad sense, journalists constitute such a collective, and the comment above about the internet struggling with time is made precisely by someone (from within television) who used to have much more control of time and/or scheduling and consequently argues that the internet has a problem because "it is not *entrained* [synchronized] to our human rhythm" (Nye, emphasis in the original). While newspapers used to, in the words of Innis, have 'a monopoly over time' (1973: 60), this has been gradually undermined by other media, most recently the internet. And seen from within journalism, this may be seen as a challenge to what Keightley, in a different context, calls 'ordered duration' (2012: 2) and which consequently puts a strain on established working rhythms, and, perhaps, in a wider sense, on political processes. It may, however, also be seen as an escape from what Carey (with reference to Innis) calls journalism's "telescoping [of] time into a one-day world" (1992: 163). Under the heading 'Real Time = Continuity,' Stevens (2006) actually argued in the *Nieman Reports* that for "the first time, a communications medium mirrors life." How one evaluates such shifts ultimately depends on 'whose time is being examined' and what processes one looks at. In this chapter, my focus will be on how news websites constitute time. In doing so, I take my cue from Leong *et al.*'s overall argument that "we should approach network temporality as a multiplicity of times derived from relations between different elements" (2009: 1279) where, since this is a first step, I take elements to mean only "the textual elements which in a strict sense constitute the website as textual phenomenon" (Brügger, 2010: 13). The overall impetus for this is a wish to nuance the overall tendency to subsume discussions on time and digital media under the concepts of '[s]peed, acceleration and immediacy' (Keightley, 2012: 3).

Within journalism studies, there is a long tradition of discussing speed and its consequences in terms of work practices. This is arguably linked to what Anderson (2012: 1007–1008) calls the 'internalism' of 'journalism scholarship,' namely its "tendency to consider the problems of journalism ... from the point of view of the journalism profession." Another, and related, reason is the strong tendency to see journalism as the "relay of a certain kind of information" (Zelizer, 2008: 88) and therefore focus, in the word of Keightley (2012: 4), on "the communicative time of technologies with reference to the speed of information transfer." But journalism is not only communication; it is also culture as Zelizer (2008) argues in tandem with Carey's (1992) distinction between the transmission and ritual view of communication. Time is, in the transmission view, linked to "one of the most ancient of human dreams: the desire to increase the speed and effect of messages as they travel in space" (Carey, 1992: 15). Temporality in the ritual view is, contrary to the negation of space, linked to the 'maintenance of society in time' (1992: 18). Despite an increased speed of transmission and an ever closer monitoring of the present, journalism still forms the base for the continuity and durability of communities by arresting time in various forms of texts, which then inform collective memory and which accumulate as cultural heritage and material for the writing of history. With regard to the internet, this is linked to a range of new ways of textually ordering duration and memory.

Online news sites as serials

Despite increasingly smaller intervals of updating, and the pushing of what Schudson in predigital times called the 'fetishism of the present' (Schudson, 1986: 81), online news sites may still be understood as a continuation of the printed serial, a 'genre' which Mussell (2012) argues is characterized by the aspects of 'miscellaneity and seriality': "As miscellanies, newspapers and periodicals provide something with each of their textual components; as serials, they offer something new with each issue" (2012: 30). With regard to news websites, however, the notion of an issue becomes more unstable: firstly, there is no fixed periodicity— although the date arguably has retained some of its cultural significance; and, secondly, the various textual elements (within different sections) are updated at varying intervals and, in addition to that, each journalistic product may go through various stages of updating. While in print, a new issue constituted a discrete entity within which (almost) all the textual elements were new, the online publication is rather a continuous process of overlapping and accumulating editions.

Yet, despite such differences, each news site (like print publications) still constitutes its temporality by using "the repetition of certain (predominantly formal) features to negotiate between the demands of continuity and novelty" (Mussell, 2012: 24). Serials, both print and online, are thus intimately tied to 'our temporal being' in the sense that "[e]vent-generated change [i.e. news] and patterns of cyclical recurrence [i.e. the publication] [...] compromise the grids of [our] temporal reference" (Hassan, 2012: 16). Yet, in terms of newspapers and periodicals "what stays the same is often overlooked for what is different," Mussell argues in relation to print publications (2012: 30), although this is arguably also the case for the digital. The masthead—its font, size, and color—of, for instance, the URL theguardian.com is thus just as significant a marker of temporarily as is the running line of breaking news. Or, expressed differently, the constitution of temporality and thus meaning is found in the specific negotiations between what stays the same and what changes. The significance and timeliness of breaking news on a site like theguardian.com is thus to be understood in relation to the duration and legitimacy signified by the masthead as well as other recurrent structures.

The news website thus constitutes time on two interrelated levels: within discrete and coherent pieces of news (or textual elements); and as interrelations between textual elements (written, static images, moving images and sound) within or across webpages. Here I lean on the terminology developed by Brügger (2010) in his discernment of the website as an analytical object; and the two levels just described correspond to what Brügger calls, respectively, the 'morphological' and the 'syntactical.' Although "[w]e routinely ignore the ways in which time is organized, represented and communicated in media content" (Keightley, 2012: 4), there has been some focus on (primarily) the morphological level within journalism studies. Barnhurst (2011) has drawn out important aspects of temporality from a larger longitudinal study of American print journalism. His overall argument is that textual references to time have widened over the last century rather than narrowed to become more present-focused (which is an often-heard narrative from both journalists and critics). Bell (1995: 315) analyzed temporality within printed news texts and argued that many news stories "move to and fro in time, from historical or recent background, to verbal reaction to lead events." The overall argument here was that the constitution of temporality within each discrete article was highly complex and necessitated a keen sensibility that was linked to the seriality of the publication and—not least—to the temporality of the issues covered (something to which I will return). And, a more recent study by Tenenboim-Weinblatt and Neiger (2014) looks at how print journalism compares with that of online in terms of temporal direction. The result, based on empirical data from Israel, is—perhaps surprisingly—that online news articles were mainly focused on the present and the past, while print is more directed towards the future.

Such studies focus on how important aspects of the temporality of journalism are constituted by arresting time through language. In relation to this, Adam (2006) writes:

> Written language shares with art the principal temporal relations of fixing and stabilizing what is transient and ephemeral through the externalization, disembodiment and decontextualization of knowledge.
>
> (Adam, 2006: 120)

Following this, one could say that any journalistic product, for example, a text, a broadcast, or a website, halts the passage of time by momentarily fixing events and their social relations. But in relation to the timeliness of this freezing, there is, says Schudson, 'always a need for context' (1986: 86) as also remarked upon above in connection with Bell's analysis of the 'news time.' So, while fixing in time is a 'decontextualisation of knowledge' or, in the words of Carey (by way of Innis), a "telescoping [of] time into a one-day world" (1992: 163), it is simultaneously a recontextualization in terms of being inserted into a serial and with that linked to duration and repetition. From this perspective, temporality is—in addition to the markers of time within discrete journalistic texts—a product of interrelations between the different textual elements within the serial as well as in between the discrete issues. In relation to this, it is important to point out that the textual arresting of time is also a constitution of time in the sense that "acts are events that emerge and *make* the present, simultaneously making the past and future, instead of [simply marking] a motion from past to future" (Barnhurst, 2011: 118). And this 'making' of the past and future—by 'arresting the present'—is intricately linked to the social aspects of news in the sense, as Schudson's argues, that "news stories would not be stories at all if some degree of shared historic depths could not be assumed" (1986: 84). "'Timeliness' operates not," argues Schudson, "by Greenwich mean time but by a cultural clock, a subtle and unspoken understanding of what is timely and genuinely 'new'" (1986: 82) and a "timely event [thus] participates in a larger trend of some significance" (1986: 83). Another way to say this is that most news events are what could be called 'resonant incident(s)' (Lemann, 2014: 73) in the sense that they gain meaning from, or are contextualized by, on-going, public, or semi-public conversations linked to underlying cultural currents. Duration is here (re)established in the sense that "[s]tories that matter are stories that persist and take different turns over days or weeks or longer" as Schudson points out (Schudson, 1986: 89). Thus, to sum up, while most news is focused on the present, the covered events are re-temporalized through the actual news discourse and its position within a periodical with a specific negotiation between novelty and continuity and, linked to that, to more or less explicit on-going societal conversations. It is in relation to such aspects that online news, at the syntactical level, establishes new modes of temporality.

Accumulation, searchability, and commentary

As a periodical, news websites negotiate between novelty and continuity in ways that are rather different from what takes place in print. The speed of transmission and the shorter intervals of publication are significant aspects of this; and so is interactivity, which is important in relation to commentary and searchability. But before discussing these aspects in relation to time, I wish to start by focusing on what seems the most important difference from the printed serial and that is the accumulation of content. In a digital environment, yesterday's news thus no longer (only) stockpiles as paper waste or clippings in scrapbooks but rather accumulates as dispersed digital and traceable layers—incorporated into or accompanying new texts. Many news stories thus seem to be dragging along their own genealogies. What is novel about the news website in terms of temporality is thus that it is a closer and closer monitoring of the present *and* a continuous (but uneven) accumulation and reuse of the preceding monitoring; and this combination of chronicling and archiving is a trait that the news site shares with the web, which has been described as "unique mixture of the ephemeral and the permanent" (Schneider and Foot, 2004: 115).

The most visible way of accumulation is the way most news stories are accompanied by, or contain, links to preceding and otherwise related stories. The story here appears as an installment in the unfolding of an event that has a prehistory, is covered now, and most likely will be written about again tomorrow. This is a digital manifestation of Schudson's notion of a 'continuous present' where "the 'developing' story [that] unfolds over time offers a newspaper version of 'the continuous present' tense" (1986: 89). What he means here is how important stories develop over time while "the time span enlarges backward and forward, [and] the reverberations to past and future become the new context of the story" (1986). What concerned Schudson was precisely, as touched upon above, how the most relevant news is part of or helps to constitute 'an event with duration' (1986: 88). In the printed newspaper, this duration was manifested as more or less implicit references within discrete journalistic texts and, importantly, related to that, to an accumulated knowledge or memory within the readership. The recognition of references and thus the duration of the event were consequently largely dependent on a more continuous engagement with the news in general and with its coverage in a particular publication. It was precisely within this continuous engagement that Mussell locates much of the cultural significance of printed serials. Here, both stories as duration and underlying cultural currents could be thought of as a kind of intangible substance that "in the spaces between individual issues" was part of creating the 'virtual identity' of a given serial (Mussell, 2012: 115).

Something similar may be the case for online periodicals. A major difference here, however, is that the duration of the coverage is manifest not only as textual references within discrete journalistic texts but also as hyperlinks either next to or within stories. The news event and its chronology are thus explicitly manifest as easily accessible and navigable textual elements. The 'burden' of a continuous engagement with the news in general and with a particular periodical is lessened, or externalized, through an almost instant archive through which a reconstructing of the unfolding of the event is made possible. Hyperlinks, as Adamic reminds us, "express social relationships in a public space for others to see" (2008: 227) and a list of links to preceding and/or contextualizing articles thus arguably signify, even if these possibilities are not pursued, a newspaper's ability to pursue a particular event and this duration—in a somewhat circular way—adds significance to the last piece in the unfolding of the story.

Barnhurst is concerned with something similar when he interprets arguments in the *Nieman Reports* about how stories no longer stand alone and says that "the interconnections of web information embed stories in a matrix with the past and [thus] create a different relationship with the present" (2011: 112). What this means for the understanding of news needs to be researched in more detail. It seems safe to say, however, that there is a growing cultural awareness, developed partly through social media, of news as something constantly unfolding. On March 18, 2015 news about the terrorist attack in Tunisia on NPR.org was thus marked 'Developing Story' while the welcoming page at Twitter.com states: "Get in-the-moment updates on the things that interest you. And watch events unfold, in real time, from every angle" (consulted on March 24, 2015). Already in 2003 Hassan saw the notion of 'real-time' as "a slogan to make us believe that this or that product or application must be super-efficient because it operates on the exciting-sounding plane of 'real-time'" (2003: 231). Instead, he proposes the term 'network time,' which he sees as 'digitally compressed clock-time' (2003: 233), which—as I argue—is accompanied by a growing awareness of news as unfolding through complex relations within, between, and across different media, for example, breaking on Twitter, discussed on blogs and Facebook, and followed and developed by legacy news institutions.

In addition to accompanying or incorporated links, such progressive layering of content is available through various search functions that scan the web and/or only the texts within a particular online publication. This allows a filtering of the available articles according to specific terms and/or journalist. Something similar is often available in relation to each article where the former articles by the journalist can be listed according to date. Such functions help buttress the legitimacy of the publication and/or journalist by portraying their investment in certain issues over time. In addition, of course, it allows readers to pursue the coverage of the past. The articles that have accumulated digitally are usually readily retrievable but for more and more newspapers "the digitalization of their archives represents an important revenue stream at a time when their financial future appears uncertain" (Mussell, 2012: 52). Thus, while libraries are busy digitizing newspapers and increasingly have to relate to journalism offered as a cultural heritage by private news institutions, these will—if, paradoxically, some of journalism's future may be found in its stored pasts—have to offer increasingly engaging modes of retrieving and contextualizing the past.

On some level, comments are an inherent part of the temporal contextualization discussed above in the sense that they accompany the journalistic productions that precede a particular story and in relation to each of these stories they have their own temporal unfolding. Most importantly in this context, however, is that—in contrast to the written periodical—they introduce a temporality that is linked to, but rather different from, that of the news institution. The most conspicuous aspect of this is that each comment is anchored in somebody's present in the sense that it signifies a more or less immediate reaction to the reading of an article and/or preceding comments to this article. This means that most comments are written in the present tense—much like news headlines. Schudson writes that "[n]ewspaper headlines are almost always in the present tense, but newspaper stories are invariably written in the past tense" (1986: 89). It takes time to verify, source, construct, and contextualize, which is why news is not written in real-time—apart from 'live' coverage or blogging in which stories are updated in small snippets at short intervals. Comments are not in need of verification; or, rather, the verification is part of an unfolding process through which comments are upheld, challenged, or simply left alone.

Apart from offering interpretations and competing headlines to the running news, comments are also a way to monitor and portray audience relevance and activity, as are the number of times shared and lists of 'popular right now.' Apart from having implications for the production of content, such measures and their online manifestations are a way to portray—in almost real-time—the relevance or resonance of part of the news coverage. This, then, adds another but related temporality to the 'extended present' discussed earlier.

Seen in relation to the ways in which the printed news serial constituted temporality, one can thus argue that novelty and duration are textually manifested in new ways through which there is both a much closer monitoring of the present and its unfolding and the social impact of this *and* a more sustained integration of (and possible interaction) with various pasts. Rather than simply a matter of speed and acceleration, news sites should rather be seen as digital structures that both signify and allow for the construction of complex temporalities arising from the interrelations between different textual elements on the site: masthead, sections, breaking news, contextualizing articles, most read lists, comments, and searches. While this 'multiplicity of times' (Leong *et al.*, 2009: 1280) exists as textual potentialities, the actualization through trajectories of usage makes this even more complex, and this is linked to emerging patterns of news consumption.

The temporalities of news consumption

While printed newspapers to some extent relied on a continued engagement in terms of situating stories within an event with duration, most online news users are more fickle. In terms of meaning, this is partly ameliorated by the ways in which the digital helps to place stories into a context. But the internet contains an abundance of constantly updated and easily accessible content in addition to what in a conventional way can be called news. The competition for attention has thus been tremendously intensified along with various ways to increase the 'stickiness' of websites, that is, the ability to keep users on a particular site. For journalism, this is obviously important since both the number of visitors and the time consumed are important parameters for selling advertising. This has put an increased focus on community making through which news institutions wish to develop more sustaining social relations with their audience. Thus, while the printed newspaper (ideally) could be seen as a manifestation of a community (city, region, nation state), the move to the internet has sent newspapers looking for a community. And, for society, this is also important because a continued engagement with (common) news is believed to be a constituent element of democracy. This has caused a continued engagement with the social implications of an increasingly competitive 'marketplace of attention' (Webster, 2014).

Against the background of a steadily accelerating society (touched upon briefly above), time has thus become an increasingly scarce resource, and the consumption of media is, more than other commodities, linked to the temporal unfolding inherent in reading, listening, and viewing. "Contrary to the consumption of time that also occurs with other products and services, (the price of which is independent of time in most cases)," Nieto (2003: 128) argues that, "in the information market the value of the content is intimately linked to the amount of people's time that it is capable of attracting." In relation to news, this has been linked to the alignment of different social situations with particular media (radio and newspapers over breakfast, newspapers on the train to and from work and perhaps at lunch, and then television at night). Such rhythms are still somewhat in place. Yet, the internet—along with mobile devices—allows for news consumption to be inserted into many more and smaller pockets of time throughout the day. The consumption of news is thus increasingly temporally fragmented and/or unhinged from specific social situations in the sense that "news usage seems hardly separable from other practices": "no one will find it odd anymore when people do a 'checking cycle' while getting up or during social experiences like having a drink or grabbing a bite" (Meijer and Kormelink, 2014: 12). This is linked to the internet being "a normal, everyday backdrop to almost everything we do in daily life," which is what makes Hassan (2012: 4) argue the "[i]nternet itself is nearing its perpetual vanishing point." This is, however, not "[t]he end of the news habit?" as Bird rhetorically asks (2010: 419) but rather a "certain intensification in the experience of time" (Meijer and Kormelink, 2014: 12) since updating and thus something new is an important aspect of experiences of temporality (see also Meijer and Kormelink, this volume).

Such developments have been accompanied by discussions about engagement and distraction. And this is linked to recurrent discussions, both popular and academic, about how the internet, its abundance, easy availability of content, and instantaneous transmission induce 'pathologies of speed' (Hassan, 2014: 7) and/or, as Nicholas Carr (in)famously asked in *The Atlantic* in 2008, whether "Google is Making Us Stupid?" What concerns Carr is how the "crazy quilt of internet media" may "be weakening our capacity for the kind of deep reading that emerged when an earlier technology, the printing press, made long and complex works of prose commonplace." This is, says Hassan (2014: 10), a "speed-up of the physical and cognitive functioning of individuals as a direct response to the demands of capitalist competition that have shifted decisively to the realm of information flows." And although Carr's 'deep reading' may never have been vital for the cultural significance of news, there is no doubt, as Meijer and Kormelink argue based on a synthesis of a range of studies, that many people increasingly engage through "Checking, Sharing, Clicking and Linking" (2014) in addition to (or instead of) reading, listening, and viewing as more extended temporal practices. The social impact of "such new user routines cannot," they argue, "be adequately assessed at present times" (2014: 13).

Future times

How journalism as digital texts (in a broad sense) constitutes time is a highly complex and constantly developing process along with the advent of new modes of presentation, new devices, and apps and new practices of news consumption. This article has briefly discussed some of the new ways in which the news website contains a multitude of intersecting and developing temporalities. This needs further study and this requires a nuanced employment of the various and complex methodologies available for working with the archived web. The preliminary analysis presented in this article builds on a recording of www.theguardian.com/uk for 24 hours from June 6 to 7 as well as 19 versions (within the same time span) of the site stored at the Danish Web Archive (http://netarkivet.dk). What such materials can only hint at, however, and what indeed also needs further study are the everyday practices through which various textual possibilities and technologies are translated into social time embedded in different cultural contexts.

Further reading

In relation to the broad intersections between media and time, I have found Emily Keightley's work and her edited volume *Time, Media and Modernity* very helpful. James Mussell's thoughts on the seriality of periodicals in his *The Nineteenth-Century Press in the Digital Age* have been important for thinking about news as a set of processes drawn out in time and so have Michael Shudson's thoughts on the 'extended present' in his 1986 article "Deadlines, Datelines, and History."

References

Adam, B. (2006) *Time*. Cambridge, UK: Polity Press. (Original work published 2004)

Adamic, L.A. (2008) "The Social Hyperlink." In Turow, J. and Tsui, L. (eds) *The Hyperlinked Society: Questioning Connections in the Digital Age*. Ann Arbor, MI: University of Michigan Press, pp. 227–249.

Anderson, C.W. (2012) "Towards a Sociology of Computational and Algorithmic Journalism." *New Media & Society* 15(7): 1005–1021.

Barnhurst, K. (2011) "The Problem of Modern Time in American Journalism." *Kronoscope* 11(1–2): 98–123.

Bell, A. (1995) "News Time." *Time & Society* 4(3): 305–328.

Bird, S.E. (2010) "News Practices in Everyday Life: Beyond Audience Response." In Allan, S. (ed.) *The Routledge Companion to News and Journalism*. London, UK: Routledge, pp. 417–427.

Brügger, N. (2010) *Website Analysis: Elements of a Conceptual Architecture*. Aarhus, Denmark: Papers from The Centre for Internet Research.

Carey, J.W. (1992) *Communication as Culture: Essays on Media and Society*. London, UK: Routledge. (Original work published 1989)

Castells, M. (2003) *The Rise of the Network Society*. Oxford, UK: Blackwell. (Original work published 1996)

Hassan, R. (2003) "Network Time and the New Knowledge Epoch." *Time & Society* 12(2/3): 225–241.

Hassan, R. (2012) *The Age of Distraction: Reading, Writing, and Politics in a High-Speed Networked Society*. New Brunswick, NJ: Transaction Publishers.

Hassan, R. (2014) "A Temporalized Internet." *The Political Economy of Communication* 2(1): 3–16.

Innis, H.A. (1973) *The Bias of Communication*. Toronto, ON: University of Toronto Press. (Original work published 1951)

Keightley, E. (2012) "Introduction: Time, Media, Modernity." In Keightley, E. (ed.) *Time, Media and Modernity*. Basingstoke, UK: Palgrave MacMillan, pp. 1–22.

Lemann, N. (2014) "A Call for Help: What the Kitty Genovese Story Really Means." *The New Yorker*, March 10, pp.73–77.

Leong, S., Mitew, T., Celletti, M. and Pearson, E. (2009) "The Question Concerning (Internet) Time." *New Media & Society* 11(8): 1267–1285.

Meijer, I.C. and Kormelink, T.G. (2014) "Checking, Sharing, Clicking and Linking." *Digital Journalism* 3(5): 664–679. DOI: 10.1080/21670811.2014.937149.

Mussell, J. (2012) *The Nineteenth-Century Press in the Digital Age*. London, UK: Palgrave Macmillan.

Nieto, A. (2003) "Media Markets as Time Markets: The Case of Spain." In Albarran, A. and Arrese, A. (eds) *Time and Media Markets*. London, UK: Routledge, pp. 127–144.

Nowotny, H. (1995 [1994]) *Time: The Modern and Postmodern Experience*. Cambridge, UK: Polity Press. (Original work published 1994)

Nye, J. (2012) "Tapping Out an Age-Old Rhythm." *Viewing 24/7*, 22 August. Retrieved from: http://viewing247.com/?s=age+old+rhythm (accessed 27 March 2015).

Schneider, S.M. and Foot, K.A. (2004) "The Web as An Object of Study." *New Media & Society* 6(1): 114–122.

Scholte, J.A. (2005) *Globalization*. New York, NY: Palgrave.

Schudson, M. (1986) "Deadlines, Datelines, and History." In Manoff, R.K. and Schudson, M. (eds) *Reading the News*. New York, NY: Pantheon, pp. 79–108.

Stevens, J.E. (2006) "Taking the Big Gulp." *Nieman Reports* (Winter): 66–69.

Tenenboim-Weinblatt, K. and Neiger, M. (2014) "Print Is Future, Online Is Past: Cross-Media Analysis of Temporal Orientations in the News." *Communication Research*. DOI: 10.1177/0093650214558260.

Webster, J.G. (2014) *The Marketplace of Attention: How Audiences Take Shape in a Digital Age*. Cambridge, MA: MIT Press.

Zelizer, B. (2008) "How Communication, Culture, and Critique Intersect in the Study of Journalism." *Communication, Culture & Critique* 1(1): 86–91.

6

DIGITAL FOOTAGE FROM CONFLICT ZONES

The politics of authenticity

Lilie Chouliaraki

Digital witnessing, the visual engagement with distant suffering through mobile media by means of real-time recording, uploading, and sharing, poses new epistemic challenges in the management of the visibility of conflict death in Western media (Mortensen, 2015). These are challenges about the status of death images (are they authentic?), our relationship to them (what should we feel towards them?), and the power relationships within which they are embedded (who dies and how does this matter?). Central to these new challenges is the rise of 'amateur' recordings of conflict[1] as a testimonial act—an act of representation that publicizes conflict death from the local eyewitness perspective so as to mobilize emotion and invite a response, be this revenge, outrage, contempt, fear, or empathy (Chouliaraki, 2015). While such testimonial acts were earlier the privilege of journalistic professionals, the rise of 'amateur' actors has complicated the remediation of testimonies of death on Western news platforms.

This is, at least partly, because digital witnessing is not simply about local actors' use of cameras to record death but, importantly, about the participation of these actors in the very death scenes they produce as potential victims, benefactors, or perpetrators.

Digital witnessing is, in this sense, defined by the new status of the camera not only as a tool for the professional reporting of conflict but, simultaneously, as a weapon in the very conduct of conflict, where those who record are precisely those who may be killed, as civilians, or those who kill, as militants, in the course of recording—what Mortensen calls the 'mediatization' of conflict death (2015). Drawing on Gaddafi's death video, Al-Ghazzi hints precisely at this intimate implication of the camera in the very dynamics of conflict, by speculating on a causal relationship between the dictator's death and the participation in it of those who filmed it: "one cannot help but wonder," he says, "whether and how al-Quaddafi's or Hussein's fates would have changed if the rebels did not have cell phones with them to tape their capture and execution" (2014: 441). Rather than attempt, like Al-Ghazzi, such a causal link between 'amateur' media and the act of killing, however, I approach mediatized death as primarily a symbolic practice of representation, which, by implicating the actors of death in the production of their own spectacle, blurs the very boundary between the two; so that, as Butler puts it, we can no longer "separate [...] the material reality of war (death) from those representational regimes through which it operates and which rationalize its own operation" (2009: 29).

Digital witnessing and the remediation of mediatized death

It is, I argue, precisely this blurring of boundaries, characteristic of mediatized death in the post-Arab Spring conflict zones, that brings about a sense of radical doubt in the status of the death spectacle in Western journalism. This is because, unlike embedded war journalism, which boasts unlimited access to the realities of conflict yet regulates its spectacles through strict norms of taste and decency (Campbell, 2004), 'amateur' footage offers intimate views of the battlefield yet provides no guarantee of truth. Instead, it promotes its unedited footage as the 'real thing,' rendering it a crucial news source for Western platforms—keen as these are to reclaim some of their waning institutional legitimacy through the raw authenticity of popular testimony (Kristensen and Mortensen, 2013). How exactly Western news, in the case of UK press, authenticates and remediates this uncensored imagery of conflict death, how, that is, it enacts a particular politics of authenticity, is the analytical focus of this chapter.

I explore this problematic by focusing on three instances of mediatized death in post-Arab Spring conflict reporting: Gaddafi's death portrait (2011), the Jihadist beheadings (2014), and Syrian civilian victims (2013), which, as we shall see, together constitute a comprehensive (though not exhaustive) typology of digital witnessing in the UK press. Following a theoretical overview of the implications of remediating digital witnessing in the West, I proceed with an analytical discussion of the politics of authenticity involved in the remediation of these cases; I demonstrate that this politics does not simply entail technical controls of verification but actively recontextualizes and reconstitutes 'amateur' footage as authentic, in the course of reporting it. Authenticity, I therefore claim, becomes here a matter of affective resonance—a symbolic process that regulates the emotional potential of mediatized death in ways that resonate with Western sensibilities, thereby tactically amplifying, challenging, or ignoring the testimonial potential of the source. In the process, affective resonance simultaneously positions each life lost within a continuum of lives-worth-living: from the dehumanization of the Arab leader to the suspended humanization of civilian casualties and to the hyper-humanization of the beheaded Westerner as a 'hero.' This politics of authenticity can, from this perspective, be seen as a key dimension of the exercise of power of Western journalism in that, by establishing a global hierarchy of human lives, it contributes to perpetuating the already existing geopolitical asymmetries between the West and its 'others.'

The ambivalent implications of remediation: between doubt and authenticity

At the heart of the epistemic doubt surrounding the 'amateur' footage of conflict death lies the synergy between the proliferation of digital cameras and the implication of civilians in conflict zones (Mortensen, 2015; see also Sumiala and Hakola, 2013). Digital witnessing participates here in a complex visual ecology of conflict that brings together the nonprofessional and professional actors of conflict in a radical democratization of our 'right to look' (Mirzoeff, 2011). Even though, as we shall see, this democratization is usually associated with civilian testimonies only, insofar as digital witnessing is also practiced by NGOs and military actors (as both allies and enemies of the West), the democratization of the 'right to look' should be seen as inextricably linked to a parallel democratization of 'the right to kill'—a right that is "no longer the sole monopoly of states" or "regular armies" (Mbembe, 2003: 16–17), but has today become the practice of fragmented and conflicting armed groups across battlefields.

Consequently, the concept of gatekeeping that had traditionally been used as a key journalistic mechanism for the management of doubt through state-controlled protocols of verification (Bennett, 2004) proves today to be inadequate. Remediation refers instead to a more complex process of managing doubt that takes into account not only the increasing quantity of pictures available but, importantly, the rival values that inform them; for, as Pötzsch puts it, digital or iwar is not only marked by "new technologies of [...] vision and cognition" but also by "new ways of executing violence on behalf of implicitly universalized sets of norms and values" (2015: 91). Digital witnessing, it follows, raises the question of the authenticity of mediatized death not only insofar as it communicates nonprofessionalized and unauthorized content but also insofar as, in so doing, it also communicates multiple and conflicting 'universalized norms and values' around whose life is worthy of commemoration and whose death is, what Butler calls, 'grievable' (2009). It is precisely as a response to this dual question that the management of authenticity should be seen as more than a problem of source verification. It should instead be approached as, at once, a profound skepticism towards the moral invitation of such footage for us to feel for the dead *and* as a technology of power that, in defining whose life is worthy of our emotion or whose is not, classifies conflict death along the lines of a hierarchy of grievability.

While, however, the role of digital witnessing as the West's primary mode of engagement with conflict death is well established (Allan, 2013; Chouliaraki, 2013; Mortensen, 2015; Sumiala, 2013), the question of doubt remains underexplored: it is either taken for granted as an inevitably corrosive dimension of digital witnessing or ignored in favor of an unthinking optimism towards the authenticity of the 'amateur.' Both positions ultimately leave remediation outside their remit of critical attention. On the one hand, the positive argument treats digital witnessing as the manifestation of an authentic popular perspective on conflict—what I earlier referred to as the emergence of 'the right to look,' in that people's cameras enable those who were once 'the objects of surveillance' to now "turn their eyes, ears and voice on the powerful" (Fuchs, 2011: 13). This emphasis on 'amateur' footage as an instrument of public transparency informs the democratization of conflict reporting argument, where digital witnessing is welcome because it breaks with the professional monopoly of the news and introduces, what Hoskins and O'Loughlin term, 'a new fragility' in Western reporting—a fragility "fed by the potential of images [...to] shutter attempts to develop or sustain a version of warfare around which public and political opinion can cohere" (2010: 22). Digital witnessing, however, does not only work to democratize official war narratives through the authenticity of 'amateur' stories. Its testimonies further humanize those who speak from conflict zones, by remediating their suffering and inviting Western publics to stand by them in solidarity. Doubt here is ignored in favor of the systematic appreciation not only of the new authenticity but also the new 'humanity' of conflict: 'the camera-phone,' as Andén-Papadopoulos argues, "permits entirely new performative rituals of bearing witness, ... effectively mobilizing [this] footage as graphic testimony in a bid to produce feelings of political solidarity" (2014: 753).

On the other hand, there is the negative argument, which, instead of appreciating the authenticity of 'amateur' footage, is critical of such footage on two accounts: as a technology of 'seeing,' it gives rise to concerns of citizen surveillance, whereas as a narrative of war, it leads to the sentimentalization and depoliticization of conflict. Turning the celebration of technology argument on its head, this approach is skeptical of mobile cameras for being less about the 'right to look' and more about the 'obligation to be seen.' Given that digital footage inevitably entails an element of peer-to-peer monitoring, this perspective shows suspicion towards the mediatization of death as, potentially, a new site of state surveillance, where "important security-related practices are privatized and outsourced [...] beyond the grasp of government agencies" yet operate to their advantage (Pötzsch, 2015: 87). This suspicion around the potential of digital technology to dehumanize those it reports through the scrutinizing visibility of the camera further bifurcates into doubt about the potential of 'amateur' content to personalize rather than politicize and rationally debate conflict reporting: "the focus on experiences and feelings of individual players in the tales of war and terror," claim Kampf and Liebes, "is only one aspect of a larger trend of inability to discuss social and political issues" (2013: 15).

In summary, the controversy around digital witnessing revolves around the potential of mediatized death either to overcome doubt and act as a moralizing force that democratizes Western journalism and humanizes conflict victims, or to accentuate skepticism and act as a regulative force that dehumanizes people and depoliticizes conflict news. While the optimism of the former perspective refers to 'amateur' testimonials that emphasize their potential for authentic voice-giving but ignore the remediating effects of Western journalism, the pessimism of the latter is culpable of the reverse: it overemphasizes journalism's remediating impact on Western publics at the expense of the connectivities that may potentially be enabled by the authentic testimonials of civilians. Instead of a priori privileging one over the other position, I take my starting point on the shared premise of both perspectives, namely that digital witnessing is a key symbolic terrain for the mediation of conflict death, and I treat this terrain as inherently unstable, asking questions about the politics of authenticity through which such instability is settled: How does the remediation of mediatized death in Western media validate and legitimize 'amateur' testimonials? Under which conditions may the remediation of digital witnessing act as a humanizing force on the conflict deaths it reports? and which are the political implications of the remediation of digital witnessing for the Western mediascapes?

Remediations of digital witnessing: the politics of authenticity

In addressing these questions, I draw on three cases studies of mediatized death: the beheading of a Western citizen (2014), the death of Gaddafi (2011), and the mass killing of Syrian civilians (2013). All three are maximally newsworthy (front page news) while, at the same time, they share a similar geopolitical context, the post-Arab Spring conflicts (2011–2015), helping us to establish continuities and discontinuities between them against a common historical background.

Witnessing as vindication/dehumanization

Gaddafi's death, on October 20, 2011, was partly captured on the digital cameras of Libyan militia and went viral shortly after: no lethal shooting was recorded but his weak and bloodied body, already injured by a grenade, is seen to be violently pushed around. Even though the footage became an extraordinary sensation in social media, the absence of a visual record of death gave rise to controversy. Central to it was the authenticity of the footage.[2] Unable to establish any definitive evidence of the manner of killing itself,[2] however, the newsworthiness of this footage ultimately operated less as testimony to an event and more as marker of emotional proximity. What the chaotic scenes of violence communicated with evidential certainty, in other words, was not the moment of Gaddafi's death but the affective dynamics through which Libyan soldiers acted upon him: negative emotions of intense hate and aggression (in the imagery of pushing, pummeling, and shouting soldiers), thereby giving rise to a regime of witnessing as vindication—a regime waiting to be translated into a new story in UK news and to invite Western publics to engage with its emotional intensities in ways that endorse, ignore, or denounce them.

How is this regime of witnessing remediated in UK press? The consistent presence of Gaddafi's face across front pages confirms the tactical use of, what Zelizer calls, the about-to-die trope as an authenticating device ('yes, he is dead'), which allows Western journalism to reclaim authority over politically controversial events (2010). This universal presence of Gaddafi's death or near-death across front pages, however, suggests that, for the UK press, it was more important to show Gaddafi dying than to respect the privacy of his last moments. Despite its news value, then, this public exposure deprives the dead body of its human dignity, leading to, what Campbell (2004) calls, a misrecognition of the victim's humanity and reproducing historical asymmetries between the dignified dead of the West and the indignity of its 'others.'

In light of this visual consensus, differences among the UK newspapers' remediation of Gaddafi's death can be classified along three categories—each investing the image with a different claim to authenticity. In the first (the *Daily Mail*, the *Daily Mirror*), the about-to-die imagery, framed in Gaddafi's last words, 'Don't shoot': we witness him dying but we also get to know his last reaction. Through this combination, Gaddafi is here a figure suspended between a reluctant humanization that demystifies him as a powerless individual pleading for his life and explicit humiliation that exposes him as weak and cowardly in the face of death: "don't shoot…" In the second category (the *Independent*, the *Guardian*, the *Daily Telegraph*) about-to-die imagery is signified through words such as 'end,' 'death,' and 'no mercy' together with evaluative vocabularies of 'merciless tyrant' and 'dictator': Gaddafi is here no longer just a dying man; he stands for any despotic regime. His humanity is thus fully annulled by this very subsumption under the category of 'dictator' while his death turns into a moral tale that invites us to reflect on the destiny of others like him. The final category, consisting solely of the *Sun*, accompanies an about-to-die Gaddafi with the sentence "That's for Lockerbie…" This statement draws upon the nation's collective memory of the Libya-executed 1988 PanAm plane bombing over Scotland. In so doing, it invites 'us' to recognize Gaddafi's death as a legitimate and long-awaited act of vindication, asserting a truth that is primarily ideological: 'Gaddafi becomes here a trophy of revenge in a conflict between 'us' and 'them.'

Their differences granted, these various remediations of mediatized death in UK press converge toward a relatively homogenous regime of witnessing that, instead of challenging the affective potential of aggression and revenge characteristic of the militants' own footage, confirms and legitimizes this potential. By foregrounding violence, tyranny, and criminality as the truth claims through which Western publics are encouraged to engage with this death, vindictive witnessing not only establishes an affective affinity with its source but also a similar moral orientation to the victim's humanity. Gaddafi thus emerges as an absolute 'other,' subjected to, what Butler (2009) calls, 'symbolic defacement': a fully dehumanized figure, whose brutal killing leaves us uninvolved if not relieved.

Witnessing as commemoration/hyperhumanization

If Gaddafi's death accomplishes the symbolic defacement of a tyrant, Alan Henning's beheading is about the actual defacement of a Western citizen—a British taxi driver who volunteered as a humanitarian worker in the Syrian conflict zone.[3] Filmed on October 3, 2014 by his perpetrators, ISIS jihadists, the video differs from the previous one—pointing to the semiprofessional, rather than fully 'amateur' status of its actors. Rather than chaotic and improvised, it was carefully staged following the tripartite structure of the decapitation genre: justification (the jihadist mentioning the Western alliance against ISIS), execution (denunciatory statements against the UK government by victim and perpetrator before the latter places a knife in the victim's throat), and anticipation (announcement of next execution).

The verification of the video's source and content was established through a forensic examination of the recording by intelligence services as well as technology experts, but the remediation of the footage by UK media addressed a broader skepticism towards its content as an intimidation tactic of jihadist propaganda (Conway, 2012). Its politics of authenticity focused, therefore, on the suppression of disgust and terror, which were inherent in the theatrical staging of Alan Henning's about-to-die scene. It is precisely these affective states, set in motion through imagination rather than the actual act of decapitation (which was never part of the recording), that situates the footage within a regime of, what we may call, traumatic witnessing.

How is traumatic witnessing remediated in the UK newspapers? Their online versions did use video stills of the execution but, for the first time since the beheadings began 2 months earlier, no newspaper uploaded the footage link onto their platforms—an act of defiance against the manipulative strategy of the perpetrators. Print versions followed a similar tactic.[4] Unlike the Gaddafi news, which authenticated his death by combining explicit imagery with narratives of contempt, contemplation, or revenge, the marginalization of similar imagery here recontextualized Henning's death in one single narrative of commemoration that turned the victim into an iconic figure: someone with an all-too-human identity and simultaneously emblematic of universal values. It is the combination of language use, where Henning is described in ordinary terms as, for instance, a 'Salford driver' (the *Independent*) with images of him posing by his humanitarian aid vehicle (the *Independent*), or holding a Syrian baby (the *Guardian*, the *Sun*, the *Daily Mail*), that construct him as a compassionate volunteer and an exceptional philanthropist—a 'hero' (the *Sun*). This construction of a humanitarian icon is further situated within a dominant nationalist framework, through the extensive use of national identification markers such as 'Brit nr2' (the *Sun*), 'Second Briton' (the *Daily Mail*), 'British hostage' (the *Daily Telegraph*)—all of which represented Henning's death as part of an unfolding tragedy of national loss.

Unlike Gaddafi's annihilated humanity that, in different degrees, activated a vindictive regime of witnessing relatively resonant with that of its source, Henning's heroic humanity fully refracts the affective potential of existential fear, inherent in the jihadist video, into a radically different, hybrid affect of sober national pride. This politics of authenticity activated a commemorative regime of witnessing, which hyperhumanized Henning; while he was presented as a human being like 'us,' an ordinary 'Salford' driver who 'just wanted to help,' he was also celebrated as an ideal version of 'us,' a humanitarian 'hero' worthy of national commemoration.

Witnessing as outrage/suspended humanization

The footage of the Syrian gas attack in Damascus, killing approximately 1700 people, on August 22, 2013, was recorded by the Violence Documentation Centre (VDC), a body of opposition activists committed to documenting violence against civilians. These 'amateur' witnesses followed the NGO practice of bearing witness to war crimes but were not outsiders to the death scenes; they were, at once, benefactors and fellow sufferers to those they filmed. The videos recorded the suffering of Syrian civilians, including large numbers of children in hospital areas where they sought help after the attack. Focusing not on single individuals, as the previous examples, but on groups of people, these records included, but did not exclusively consist of, about-to-die images, as some people would eventually recover yet others were already dead.

The verification process was managed by Western experts, for instance, at the EU Institute for Security Studies in Paris, who established the veracity of the footage on the grounds that the respiratory and neurological symptoms of the victims could not have been staged.[5]

Simultaneously, the 'amateur' aesthetic of unedited shots and jerky camera movements also contributed to conveying a compelling authenticity of affect—that of outrage. By inviting the world to 'be there' next to the horrific suffering of children, the footage situated its claims to truth within a regime of humanitarian witnessing as denunciation, inviting us to feel indignation towards the perpetrators.

How is this regime remediated in the UK press? All six newspapers[6] of August 22, 2013 recontextualized the video and/or included video stills or a photograph gallery of the aftermath of the attack in their online versions—with some explicitly addressing the 'taste and decency' challenge posed by such gruesome imagery.[7] Only three of them, however, moved the online story onto the front page of their print versions.[8] Of those three, the *Daily Mirror* used close-up imagery of dead faces with a headline, 'Now they are gassing children,' pointing to Assad as the killer. Even though both the *Independent* and the *Guardian* also hosted shots of lined-up dead, they did so within more complex visual compositions that also included living figures; while the *Independent* established authenticity through a narrative of evil and devastating loss that caused enormous grief to Syrian families—Syria's 'darkest day,' as the subtitle proclaims, the *Guardian* focused on an elderly figure holding a baby wrapped in white linen among rows of dead, assigning to the image the status of evidence of a 'war crime'— through its association to Saddam Hussein's 1988 gas attack in Kurdistan ('chemical attack worst since Saddam Hussein').

If the Damascus gas attack claimed authenticity by mobilizing various types of meaning at the service of emotional (they are gassing children), moralistic (darkest day), and legalistic (gas attack...worst since Hussein) narratives of denunciation, the visualization of the dead told a more complicated story. To begin with, half of the print platforms ignored the story, thereby effecting a 'radical defacement' of the dead—a denial to even recognize the loss of these lives (Butler, 2009). Meanwhile, the common feature of the remaining three front pages is the *en masse* visibility of the dead. Even though this very visibility as the object of indignant testimony undoubtedly granted some recognition to those victims, the presence of their faces (even when justified) nonetheless broke the 'taste and decency' code reserved for the protection of Western victims, signaling a differential distribution of the rights to privacy between 'their' and 'our' dead. Moreover, this collective imagery, even if it did stir emotions on the basis of its sheer numbers, did not personalize these dead: we know nothing about their lives and histories.[9] Consequently, we may be appalled by their mass killing but we were not invited to relate to their humanity. This, at once, discontinuous and intrusive remediation of Syria's mass deaths works to situate them within an unstable regime of witnessing that mobilized some sense of outrage towards the persecutor but not necessarily empathy towards the victims.

At the same time, the association of the persecutor with the figure of Assad proves to be itself problematic, as this rushed vilification of the government ultimately failed to take into account the ambivalent dynamics around the identity of the persecutor: Assad or the rebels.[10] Much of the international debate around the option of a UN intervention in Syria gravitated, consequently, on assigning blame and debating the UN's Responsibility to Protect mandate rather than on the predicament of the victims.

In summary, unlike the previous cases, the politics of authenticity in the Syrian civilians story configured an ambiguous emotionality—neither universally resonant, as in Gaddafi's vindictive witnessing, nor categorically dissonant, as in Henning's commemorative one. The affect of outrage, so compellingly registered in the source footage, was here selectively taken up, with only half of the press prioritizing it as a case of humanitarian testimony, while this very half was, simultaneously, itself reluctant to protect the dignity of the dead as human beings. It is this double reluctance, informed by a fundamental instability of the quality of humanity among the Syrian dead, that we may refer to as suspended humanization—a form of humanization that reflects a partial resonance in the remediation of affects between source footage and its Western remediation. A possible consequence of such remediation is that it proposes a less assertive and more uneven moral engagement with the Syrian victims—one that cannot take the value of their human life for granted, nor fully recognize and commemorate their humanity.

The remediation of 'amateur' footage and its politics of authenticity

Like past spectacles, digital witnessing, the act of engaging with 'amateur' actors' camera recordings of conflict death, also invites its publics to acknowledge death as a moral event that requires a response. Yet, it differs from past spectacles in that it injects into the practice of witnessing an accentuated sense of doubt: How would we know it's authentic? What should we feel towards it? This is because, given the multiple actors filming in conflict zones, digital witnessing breaks with the professional monopoly of the journalist and becomes a site of struggle where competing value-charged spectacles vie for visibility. How Western news establishes the truth of these digital spectacles and remediates them as credible newsworthy facts, how, in other words, it activates a politics of authenticity, becomes, therefore, an important research focus in the current news landscape.

Looking into the remediations of three key cases of 'amateur' footage in the UK press, I examined how doubt around the status and engagement with mediatized death is addressed online and in print. Two insights emerged. First, the remediation of mediatized death relies upon emotion as a key site for its politics of authenticity. This thematization of emotionality, in turn, points to an emerging conception of authenticity that, more than the factual accuracy of source verification, now privileges affective resonance as a key mechanism for establishing the truth of conflict death. Second, processes of affective resonance entail uneven allocations of the symbolic attributes of humanity among the dead. It is, in turn, those differential processes of humanization that render digital witnessing central to the classification of conflict deaths across a continuum of grievabilities in Western news platforms.

These two insights point to the need to retheorize digital witnessing in ways that neither overemphasize nor ignore the specificities of remediation, as existing literature does. Against the negative argument, my discussion shows that the new prominence of affective resonance partly confirms Liebes and Kampf's (2013) point on the prioritization of sentiment over expert judgment and the subsequent depoliticization of conflict reporting in Western journalism. But it also goes beyond it. Specifically, if the emphasis on the 'affective' underlines the new emotionality of the news, 'resonance' points instead to a significant continuity in past and present journalism, namely to the institutional process of 'normalization,' by which news agendas are finely tuned to harmonize with the priorities of, what Singer terms, the national or cultural status quo (2013). The clearest example of 'normalization' is the uneven remediation of the Syrian massacre, where uncertainty about the appropriate affective resonance with this historical event resulted in the suspended humanizations of its victims. Pace Liebes and Kampf, then, far from a depoliticization of conflict reporting, the rise of emotionality as the news' new politics of authenticity, constitutes instead a deeply political act albeit one that operates in more insidious ways than in the past.

Indeed, against the positive argument, my discussion shows that the appreciation of digital witnessing as a democratization of journalism fails to take into account precisely these new operations of power that take place in and through 'amateur' footage. While the democratization perspective takes its point of departure in a conception of Western journalism as a pluralistic space that potentially catalyzes acts of solidarity, digital witnessing highlights another dimension of this space as a site for the production of new geopolitical classifications of humanity. The Syrian testimony stands, again, as the clearest example of this classification: in contrast to Libya, where unanimity against the ousting of Gaddafi as a tyrant led to an almost-united front of a Western alliance against his regime, suspicion around the political topography of the Syrian conflict (whose side to take?) contributed to selective and tactical remediations of civilian deaths in the West. Perhaps some of the ensuing international controversy on the possibility of a UN intervention in Syria, and the eventual cancellation of such a project, may have partly something to do with this twilight presence of the humanity of the Syrian victims in the global mediascape. Pace the positive argument, then, the new visibility of digital witnessing does not necessarily imply new norms of recognition but may, instead, reproduce old norms of misrecognition—with tragic consequences for war victims, who ultimately bear the consequences of our differential exposure to their sufferings.

In conclusion, empirical, case-based analysis of the politics of authenticity of 'amateur' footage allows us to challenge the dilemmatic debate around digital witnessing as either a wholly negative force of depoliticization or as a positive catalyst of democratization in Western journalism. This context-sensitive analysis demonstrates instead that there is substantial variation in the ways that the testimonial voices of digital witnessing are remediated in Western media. It is, therefore, important to study this variation in order to identify the new possibilities for agency that are also enacted through it. My contribution to this line of research has, here, been to show how such variation participates in the reproduction of hierarchies of grievability, rendering digital witnessing a new symbolic terrain for the exercise of power over human life and death.

Further reading

For more on the digital mediation and 'witnessing,' my book *Ironic Spectator* (2013) explores the ways we mediate human tragedies. Stuart Allan's (2013) *Citizen Witnessing* offers an in-depth discussion of 'amateur' and 'citizen' mediation and the role of the nonprofessional in digital news. Finally, for more on the specific area of media around death, terror, and war, Barbie Zelizer's book *About to Die* (2010) explores the use of images in conveying emotionally laden news stories.

Notes

1 The use of 'amateur' refers to local actors who engage in digital recordings of conflict without having the formal training or qualification to produce professional news imagery from relevant specialized institutions (e.g. civilians, NGOs, local citizen journalists, soldiers, militants). The quotation marks point to the inevitable limitations of the term, insofar as certain local actors, such as ISIS, blur the boundaries between amateur and professional by producing media artifacts of semiprofessional (beheadings) or professional (social media use) quality (Nissen, 2014).
2 See Human Rights Watch report (2012): http://world.time.com/2012/10/18/how-did-gaddafi-die-a-year-later-unanswered-questions-and-bad-blood/
3 *Daily Mirror* updates: http://www.mirror.co.uk/news/world-news/alan-henning-beheading-recap-updates-4374968 and http://www.mirror.co.uk/news/world-news/alan-henning-beheading-isis-release-4375267

The *Daily Mail*: http://www.dailymail.co.uk/news/article-2780017/BREAKING-NEWS-British-ISIS-hostage-Alan-Henning-beheaded-new-video-released-terror-group.html and http://www.dailymail.co.uk/news/article-2780147/The-ordinary-taxi-driver-killed-ISIS-terrorists-Murdered-Alan-Henning-travelled-Syria-help-child-refugees-war-torn-country.html

The *Daily Telegraph*: http://www.telegraph.co.uk/news/worldnews/middleeast/syria/11140503/What-Alan-Henning-beheading-video-tells-us-about-Islamic-State.html

The *Guardian*: http://www.theguardian.com/uk-news/2014/oct/03/alan-henning-isis-syria-video-murder http://www.theguardian.com/world/2014/oct/05/isis-murder-alan-henning-british-muslim-community

The *Independent*: http://www.independent.ie/world-news/europe/alan-henning-beheading-isis-video-appears-to-show-murder-of-british-aid-worker-30636929.html and http://www.independent.co.uk/news/uk/home-news/alan-henning-murder-an-ordinary-man-possessed-of-an-extraordinary-kindness-9774147.html

The *Sun*: https://twitter.com/TheSunNewspaper/status/518309837189697538 and http://www.thejournal.ie/alan-henning-execution-1705892-Oct2014/

4 For instance, the *Independent*, October 5, 2014; as discussed by the *Huffington Post*: http://www.huffingtonpost.co.uk/2014/10/05/islamic-state-independent_n_5934086.html

5 http://www.hrw.org/sites/default/files/reports/syria_cw0913_web_1.pdf

6 The *Independent* 'Syria's darkest day? Opposition blames Assad forces as up to 1,300 killed in 'poison gas attacks': http://www.independent.co.uk/news/world/middle-east/syrias-darkest-day-opposition-blames-assad-forces-as-up-to-1300-killed-in-poison-gas-attacks-8777527.html

The *Guardian* 'Syria conflict: chemical weapons blamed as hundreds reported killed': http://www.theguardian.com/world/2013/aug/21/syria-conflcit-chemical-weapons-hundreds-killed

Daily Mirror 'Syria: Slaughter of the innocents as children among over 1,000 civilians gassed to death': http://www.mirror.co.uk/news/world-news/syria-chemical-weapons-attack-children-2203679

The *Daily Telegraph*: BBC license pay. Image of British young woman losing a leg in NYC crash.

The *Daily Mail*: Exposed. Health Supplement con. Image: Davidson won't face court over sex assault claims by 10 women.

The *Sun*: Boris bonking nus boss bedded broke brass (sex scandal explosed). (No online headlines available—Showing BBC Headlines Instead for August 22, 2013.)

7 The *Daily Mirror*, August 22, 2013: http://www.mirror.co.uk/news/world-news/syria-chemical-weapons-attack-children-2203679

The *Daily Telegraph* and the *Sun*'s online versions are no longer available.

8 The BBC license fee (the *Daily Telegraph*), a health supplements fraud (the *Daily Mail*) and a municipality of London sex scandal (the *Sun*).

9 In contrast, for instance, to the Peshawar killings in December 2014, which were personalized and historicized in Western news; for instance through individual portraits of each schoolchild-victim in the *Independent* website: http://www.independent.co.uk/news/world/asia/peshawar-attack-the-faces-of-the-innocent-children-killed-by-taliban-gunmen-9931606.html

10 http://www.independent.co.uk/voices/comment/did-syria-gas-its-own-people-the-evidence-is-mounting-8783590.html

References

Al-Ghazzi, O. (2014) "'Citizen Journalism' in the Syrian Uprising: Problematizing Western Narratives in a Local Context." *Communication Theory* 24(4): 435–454.

Allan, S. (2013) *Citizen Witnessing: Revisioning Journalism in Times of Crisis*. Cambridge, UK: Polity Press.

Andén-Papadopoulos, K. (2014) "Citizen Camera-Witnessing: Embodied Political Dissent in the Age of Mediated Mass Self-Communication." *New Media & Society* 16(5): 753–769.

Bennett, W. L. (2004) "Global Media and Politics: Transnational Communication Regimes and Civic Cultures." *Annual Review of Political Science* 7: 125–148

Butler, J. (2009) *Frames of War: When is Life Grievable?* London and New York: Verso.

Campbell, D. (2004) "Horrific Blindness: Images of Death in Contemporary Media." *Journal for Cultural Research* 8(1): 55–74.

Chouliaraki, L. (2013) "Re-Mediation, Inter-Mediation, Trans-Mediation: The Cosmopolitan Trajectories of Convergent Journalism." *Journalism Studies* 14(2): 267–283.

Chouliaraki, L. (2015) "Digital Witnessing in War Journalism: The Case of Post-Arab Spring Conflicts." *Popular Communication: The International Journal of Media and Culture* 13(2): 105–119.

Conway, M. (2012) "From al-Zarqawi to al-Awlaki: The Emergence and Development of an Online Radical Milieu." *CTX: Combating Terrorism Exchange* 2(4): 12–22.

Fuchs, C. (2011) "New Media, Web 2.0 and Surveillance." *Sociology Compass* 5(2): 134–147.

Hoskins, A. and O'Loughlin, B. (2010) *War and Media: The Emergence of Diffused War*. Cambridge, UK: Polity Press.

Kampf, Z. and Liebes, T. (2013) *Transforming Media Coverage of Violent Conflicts: The New Face of War*. London, UK: Palgrave McMillan.

Kristensen, N.N. and Mortensen, M. (2013) "'Amateur' Sources Breaking the News, Metasources Authorizing the News of Gaddafi's Death: New Patterns of Journalistic Information Gathering and Dissemination in the Digital Age." *Digital Journalism* 1(3): 352–367.

Mbembe, A. (2003) "Necropolitics." *Public Culture* 15(1): 11–40.

Mirzoeff, N. (2011) *The Right to Look: A Counterhistory of Visuality*. Durham, NC: Duke University Press.

Mortensen, M. (2015) *Journalism and Eyewitness Images: Digital Media, Participation and Conflict*. Abingdon: Routledge.

Nissen, T.E. (2014) "Terror.Com. IS's Social Media Warfare in Syria and Iraq." *Contemporary Conflicts* 4(4): 1–8.

Pötzsch, H. (2015) "The Emergence of iWar: Changing Practices and Perceptions of Military Engagement in a Digital Era." *New Media & Society* 17(1): 78–95.

Sumiala, J. (2013) *Media and Ritual: Death, Community and Everyday Life*. London, UK: Routledge.

Sumiala, J. and Hakola, O. (2013) "Introduction: Media and Death." *Thanatos* 2(2): 3–7.

Zelizer, B. (2010) *About to Die: How News Images Move the Public*. New York, NY: Oxford University Press.

7

GATEKEEPING AND AGENDA-SETTING

Extinct or extant in a digital era?

Peter Bro

"Nearly all studies of agenda-setting have focused on the effects of news on readers and viewers. As important, however, is a more thorough understanding of how the media products themselves are put together," wrote Maxwell E. McCombs and Donald L. Shaw (1976: 19) in the wake of a symposium about agenda-setting in the middle of the 1970s. The symposium was inspired by the authors own seminal article, "The agenda-setting function of the Mass Media" (1972) that showed a strong correlation between the issues that were in the headlines of the media and on the minds of the audience during the presidential election in 1968. The original article from 1972 sparked a widespread scholarly interest in the notion of agenda-setting in the following decades, and the result has been numerous publications in the preceding decades; among them, a special issue of *Journal of Communication* on the 25th anniversary where McCombs and Shaw took stock of what they rightly termed 'a successful theory' (1993: 58).

From the very beginning, however, McCombs and Shaw acknowledged that it was not only important to look into the effects of the news media (1976: 19). It was also important to look at the function and influencing factors of the news media; and in their article from the symposium, they referred directly to the work of David Manning White (1950). White had studied which news stories were selected—and rejected—for publication by a wire editor at a regional newspaper, and in a subsequent interview White had asked the wire editor to reflect upon the reason for his decisions. The editor was dubbed 'Mr. Gates,' since White thought of the editor as a gatekeeper, who decided what "national and international news" from the wire services should be published (1950: 384). The concept of gatekeeping has in its own right prompted numerous publications, conferences, and seminars, both before and after McCombs and Shaw reminded the readers of its existence in 1976, and over the last 50 years literally hundreds of studies of 'gatekeeping' and 'agenda-setting' have followed, and in many publications both concepts appear together.

Over time the two groundbreaking studies and the concepts they helped to introduce within journalism studies have been termed "milestones in mass communication research" (Lowery and DeFleur, 1995), 'classics,' and 'household names'; and this is not only the case for researchers. The concepts have also become familiar among those news reporters and audiences who were subjects of the original studies. However, in the past decades the reach and relevance of the concepts have been discussed as digital means, methods, and technologies for the production, publication, distribution, and consumption of news have developed, and the relations between news reporters, their sources, and audiences have been affected accordingly. This development challenges journalism researchers to revisit these two separate but, in many instances, intertwined concepts, and this chapter describes and discusses in what way the concepts—and the theoretical, methodological, and empirical foundations on which they were founded—still make sense and enjoy relevance in the twenty-first century.

Intellectual and conceptual inheritance

The concepts of gatekeeping and agenda-setting had limited news value at the time they were introduced more formally within journalism studies. David Manning White went to great lengths in his introduction to "The 'Gate Keeper': A Case Study in the Selection of News" (1950) to clarify the conceptual descend. "It was the late Kurt Lewin …" White writes in the opening line of his article and describes how the social scientist Lewin was the first to suggest that one could apply the concept of gatekeeping to the study of "a news item through the certain communication channels … dependent on the fact that certain areas within the channels functioned as 'gates'" (383). White also mentions how Wilbur Schramm made an 'observation central' to the gatekeeper study, when he wrote about the number of 'choices and discards,' which has to be made between a communicator and a later receiver (Schramm, 1949: 289)— and how Schramm helped finalize White's eventual article.

McCombs and Shaw also pay academic homage to thoughts and texts by colleagues. First and foremost, they singled out Bernard Cohen, who famously noted in *The Press and Foreign Policy* (1963) how the press "is significantly more than a purveyor of information and opinion. It may not be successful much of the time in telling people what to think, but it is stunningly successful in telling its readers what to think about" (1963: 13). Part of the statement was included in their first article, "The Agenda-Setting Function of Mass Media" (1972), where McCombs and Shaw for the first time presented the concept and their empirical material from the 100 residents from Chapel Hill they studied in 1968. Here, they found that "voters tend to share the media's *composite* definition of what is important" (1972: 184) and that there was a strong correlation ($r > 0.9$) between the agenda in the media and in the minds of their respondents. But the statement from Cohen was also included in many subsequent articles, anthologies, and other publications throughout the years alongside other research colleagues who had inspired and helped to lay the intellectual groundwork for their agenda-setting study.

In this context, however, the important point is not the intellectual—and perhaps more to the point: the conceptual—inheritance White, McCombs, and Shaw themselves drew inspiration from but rather the inheritance they left for others and how this inheritance has developed over the years. This has been a success McCombs and Shaw themselves have reflected upon a number of times. In "The Evolution of Agenda-Setting Research: Twenty-Five Years in the Marketplace of Ideas" (1993), they wrote: "(T)he hallmark of a successful theory is its fruitfulness in continually generating news questions and identifying new avenues of scholarly inquiry" (1993: 58), with a line borrowed from James Conant (1951), and in the remaining part of the anniversary article they document the apparent success by the growth of literature, the integration of subfields, and the ability to generate new research problems across a variety of communication settings (1993: 65). This is the point the authors—joined by David Weaver—also make in similar publications.

The 25th anniversary was not only celebrated in the form of an article but also in an anthology: *Communication and Democracy: Exploring the Intellectual Frontiers in Agenda-Setting*. Here, the editors note in the prologue: "Agenda setting has remained a vital and productive area of communication research over a quarter-century because it has continued to introduce new research questions into the marketplace of ideas and to integrate this work with other theoretical concepts and perspectives about journalism and mass communication" (McCombs, Shaw, and Weaver, 1997: xiii). Among these, the tradition of gatekeeping was singled out as one of the other areas where a theoretical merger had taken place. But the concept of gatekeeping has also in itself left an enduring intellectual legacy and given way to hundreds of subsequent studies. Even if White largely left it to colleagues to document, describe, and discuss the continual academic importance of gatekeeping. While McCombs and Shaw—occasionally joined by other colleagues—themselves have helped to trace their conceptual legacy throughout the decades, other researchers have in time functioned as curators and continual developers for the concept of gatekeeping.

Criticism of gatekeeping and agenda-setting

Hundreds of publications might refer to each of the two original studies, but the popularization of the two concepts has often come with critique. As Stephen Reese and Jane Ballinger have noted, "(c)lassic studies might capture the imagination" but they "may not be the most advanced in either theory or method" (2001: 642), and with a particular reference to White's study, they have noted how the original gatekeeper article ascribed to the news media a simplistic function where gatekeepers are basically left with decisions about what is 'in or out' (Reese and Ballinger, 2001: 647). This individualistic and one-way linear view of gatekeeping was one of the findings from White's study that was almost instantly criticized. On the basis of an interview, White had concluded that the wire editor was 'highly subjective' in his decisions (1950: 390), but other studies soon showed that there was often a more subtle—and at other times a more steadfast—social control going on in the news rooms (see, e.g. Breed, 1955). Other studies and researchers criticized White for glossing over the complexities of the news production and selection process, where interaction between, for example, news sources and news reporters and between editors and news reporters affect the final products.

New definitions of what gatekeeping is, who gatekeepers are and when gatekeeping takes place have surfaced over the decades, and two of the most ardent researchers and chroniclers of the development of gatekeeping, Pamela Shoemaker and Tim Vos, have somewhat modified the process of gatekeeping. They have suggested in the opening line of their *Gatekeeping Theory* that gatekeeping could be described as the "process of culling and crafting countless bits of information into the limited number of messages that reach people every day, and it is the center of the media's role in modern public life" (2009: 1). The original agenda-setting study has been met by similar criticism about its failure to grasp the complexities in terms of the function and effects of the news media. Denis McQuail, whose own work was referenced (Blumler and McQuail, 1969) in the first agenda-setting article by McCombs and Shaw, has noted that research within the field tends to leave agenda-setting with the status of a plausible but unproven idea, because correlation is no proof of causal connections between media content and effects (2000: 456).

Other—albeit often sympathetic—critics have noted how there are several types of agenda-setting that needs to be taken into account: 'public agenda setting,' 'policy agenda setting,' and the 'media agenda setting' (Rogers and Dearing, 1988). While still other critics have conducted their own studies that lead to contradictory findings in varying contexts—ranging from minimal to massive effects (see, e.g. van Aelst and Walgrave, 2011)—which prompts discussions about what the effect on various types of agendas might be contingent upon: the agenda-type, the issues, the media, the audience, etc. In both instances, the criticism of the original studies failure to grasp the complex workings of the relation between the press, politics, and the public have only grown as—what some researchers have described as 'seismic' and even 'tectonic'—changes have appeared. The criticism has perhaps been most apparent with the notion of gatekeeping, not least because White's study was based on a particular—now extinct—technological platform and an adjacent sub-profession, namely the wire-editor. For even if some writers have been correct in stating that in reality the world has been online since the introduction of that very telegraph on which the wire editor in White's study based his work, the internet of the twenty-first century is very different from 'the Victorian Internet' (Standage, 1998).

The digital development has resulted in changes inside and outside the newsroom that have lead researchers to write that the concept of gatekeeping has lost its 'wit,' is 'undermined,' has 'collapsed,' has been 'busted,' is 'dead,' and even 'gone.' One practitioner, a former industry leader, for instance, claimed that "Thanks to the internet, the role of media gatekeeper has gone" (cf. Allan, 2006: 169), whereas researchers have conducted studies that have shown how the gates in the media in certain instances—like during scandals—have collapsed, which has lead them to conclude: "if there are no gates, there can be no gatekeepers." Others have predicted that the idea of gatekeeping is not only gone or collapsed, but has 'died' altogether (cf. Shoemaker and Vos, 2009: 130) with the development of the internet that, in the words of yet another observer, has "busted open the system of gates and gatekeepers" (Rosen, 2006: 1). All of which are gloomy statements that often stem from the main point that the scarcity of space in the newspaper that forced Mr. White to reject many news stories has vanished on the internet, plus the internet makes it still easier for other people and professions to produce, publish, and distribute news.

The same criticism has met the concept of agenda-setting that was originally studied by McCombs and Shaw. For in an era with an abundance of news media, news material, and news providers, some observers have noted that it is increasingly difficult for news organizations to set the agenda outside newsrooms. In both instances, some critics have called for a retirement of these two classic concepts, while even some researchers who have been less inclined to dismiss the continued importance of the two original concepts, have begun to neologize other concepts which they feel are more descriptive of the effect, function, and influencing factors of the news media in the twenty-first century. Among these are 'gate watchers,' 'gatecrashers,' 'gate jumpers,' 'second-order gatekeeping,' 'reverse gatekeeping,' 'algorithmic gatekeeping,' and 'gate programmers,' whereas researchers within the area of agenda-setting have suggested new concepts such as 'agenda-building,' 'agenda-melding,' and the perhaps best known supplementary concept of 'second-order agenda setting' that emphasizes the news media potential effect in terms of telling readers, listeners, and viewers 'how to think about an issue' rather than 'what to think about.'

Reading through the research literature in the twenty-first century and the adjacent statements from news media owners, editors, and individual reporters, one cannot help but wonder if the concepts of gatekeeping and agenda-setting should rightly be considered extinct—or extant. But as one of the main curators of the concept of gatekeeping, Tim P. Vos has written in a book-length defense of the continued importance of the concept—on the 65th anniversary of the publication of White's study—transition is not necessarily termination (2015: 11), and he makes an important point. For reviewing the key studies that take the new technological developments into account, it becomes apparent that even if Heinderyckx is right in noting that 'gatekeeping is diversifying' (2015: 256), there seems to be some recurring features in the ways in which gatekeeping might be said to take place—including who the gatekeepers are. Rather than being irrelevant, the concept of gatekeeping seems to have been used to encompass an increased variety of different principles and practices in journalism, and when one reviews the literature about gatekeeping and agenda-setting and relates these works to contemporary journalism, three models stand out: the first is based on a process of information, the second on communication, and the third on elimination.

Models of information, communication, and elimination

The methodological approach White followed in the original gatekeeper study gave him and his readers a limited vantage point for understanding the function and influencing factors of journalism. Following the initial inspiration from Kurt Lewin, who was the first to suggest that news reporting could be approached within the framework of channels, flows, and gatekeepers, White primarily concerned himself with what was 'in' and 'out' (1950: 383). Pursuing this interest led him to look at the work of a wire editor, who more than most people and sub-profession in a news room can be viewed as having just such a function. This methodological approach bequeathed us a model where the relation between the three main actors in agenda-setting—pointed out by Rogers and Dearing as part of the criticism of the original agenda-keeping study—namely the public, the press, and policy-makers, appears as a linear one-way flow from senders via mediators to receivers. In this model of information (see Figure 7.1), editors and reporters are left with decisions about what to include and exclude, and the content included is what potentially can prompt an agenda among the public.

Researchers sometimes seem to forget that White was more aware that the process of news reporting was a 'complex process of communication' (1950: 390) than might have come across in his study. White was primarily interested in what he termed the 'final gatekeeper,' and in the introduction to "The Gate keeper: A Case Study in the Selection of News," he explained how there are several other gatekeepers involved in the chain of communication: "From reporter to rewrite man, through bureau chief to 'state' file editors, at various press associations" (1950: 384). This is an important point to remember when looking at the model of information where several gatekeepers are involved within each of the three main actor categories. There can be several gatekeepers within each of them who can hinder or help the news flow to others, and just like news stories can pass through several gates within the media, as White mentioned, there can be several gates that a news story passes through among both citizens and more authoritative decision-makers, for example, in the form of opinion leaders among the audience, who can pass news along to friends, family, and other people with whom they are familiar.

Research dating back to McCombs and Shaw even suggests that agenda-setting might not only take place from media to audience but also from media to media. Going through the published data from the original gatekeeper study, McCombs and Shaw "showed … how deeply Mr. Gates himself was influenced by what came over the wires. What the wire services ran heavily he ran heavily" (1976: 20). Their point was that the agenda-setting effect may not only have an effect between the main actors but also within the individual groups of actors. But the relations between members of the public, the press, and policy-makers are not only marked by a one-way linear flow, where news reporters function as gatekeepers and have an agenda-setting effect on a passive audience, which was something that researchers already noted shortly after the publication of White's and McCombs and Shaw's studies. Reviewing the research within the areas of gatekeeping and agenda-setting—and simply paying attention to what takes place in the news media in this century—it becomes apparent that the model based on information is not the only one in existence. There is also a second model based on communication (see Figure 7.1).

The second model comes across in a number of statements from researchers and practitioners over the past years. 'Big Media' have 'treated the news as a lecture,' while in future "news

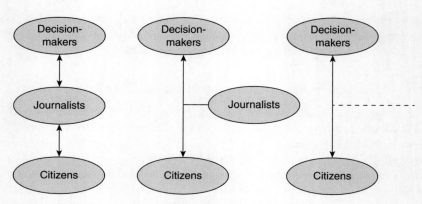

Figure 7.1 Models of information, communication, and elimination.

reporting and production will be more of a conversation, or a seminar. The lines will blur between producers and consumers," Dan Gillmor (2006: xxiv) has written, and he has not only prophesied about the effects of the emergence of the internet in the 1990s but has also experimented with the new technologies and techniques the internet brought along—and taught them at journalism schools. Researchers like Axel Bruns have also written about a 'flattened hierarchy' (2005: 15), where news sources and audiences of the past become more connected by the media in the present, and at times practitioners and professors have worked together in an attempt to document and even experiment with new ways of gatekeeping and agenda-setting. Indeed, in the 1990s a new movement within the field of journalism saw the light as academics and practitioners started working together in what Michael Schudson has described as the 'best-organized movement' in the history of American journalism (1999: 118).

The movement has been termed everything from *public journalism* to *conversational journalism* (see, e.g. Rosen, 1999), and it was originally based on a widespread sentiment that people employed in news media had "to reposition ourselves in the political process. We have to distance ourselves from the people we write about and move ourselves closer to the people we write for" (Broder, 1990). This repositioning included attempts to reconnect different actors—including the news media—in society, and from the very beginning there were discussions about how journalists should—and could—involve "citizens in shaping a news agenda" (1996: 71). In time, the name of the movement might have become less important, but technology has certainly helped to make the ideal become a very real set of principles and practices. Researchers, firmly grounded within traditions of agenda-setting and gatekeeping, write about new more 'participatory,' 'collaborative' types of journalism. Their point is that in a new media environment many news media "… have applied various informal means of involving citizens in the agenda-setting process, such as by conducting in-depth interviews, focus groups, and roundtable discussions," as one of the observers of this development has noted (Haas, 2007: 33).

Others have noted how the news media are "learning how to adapt to a more collaborative media environment in which journalists share the creation and dissemination of the news with users," as Alfred Hermida has described it (2011: 179). This scholarly work includes an interest in how people outside the newsrooms not only play a part in the production of news stories but also in the selection and rejection in terms of what should be distributed. For in the digital era, the 'final' and 'terminal' gatekeeper White was originally interested in is increasingly a friend, a family member, or someone else familiar, and as research has shown, these gatekeepers outside the newsrooms might have their own conceptions about what news to select and reject before they publish and distribute it to others. These new gatekeepers and gateways by which the news is produced, published, distributed, and consumed do not only include new persons and professions. Programs, portals and popular search engines, and other types of digital means, methods, and technologies have become the gatekeeper between many producers and consumers of news, and in the process the very definition of what news is, who selects its, and attempts to set the agenda with it has changed.

"More and more news sources such as political leaders, governmental agencies, political parties, business corporations, and so on, are … seeking to reach publics directly. The internet is giving would-be communicators new opportunities to make their voices heard without depending on the news media," one contributor to the anthology, *Communication and Democracy*, noted (Takeshita, 1997: 27), and these possibilities are not monopolized by those decision-makers that in the first and second models are reliant on the news media if they wish to promote an agenda among themselves, the media, or the general public. The new digital infrastructure has given what some observers have described as 'the former audience' (Gillmor, 2006) new possibilities for connecting with other private citizens and even authoritative decision-makers when they share news stories from their own personal or professional lives by way of the means, methods, and platforms made possible by the internet. This is a model in which the news media, as we have known them ever since the invention of journalism in the nineteenth century (see, e.g. Chalaby, 1998), is in immediate danger of disappearing as the prime gatekeeper in society, and where it is left to members of the public or authoritative decision-makers to set the agenda within each-others groups and among one-another.

Future curating of the gatekeeping and agenda-setting concepts

The three models detailed above can hardly capture all the complexities of the transition that journalism is going through—and the varied ways in which gatekeeping and agenda-setting take place in a digital era. But models can help highlight important characteristics—and at best help to track changes in time and space as both news reporting and research develops. In this regard, the three models for the ways in which gatekeeping and agenda-setting take place supplement rather than substitute for one another. From the viewpoint of the press, private citizens, and authoritative decision-makers, all three models can co-exist. Many news organizations engage in a number of different relations with their sources and audiences at the same time. These are relations that at times will be based on information and at other times communication. Similarly with private citizens and authoritative decision-makers, whose relations among themselves and between themselves can change continuously depending on the media—news media, social media, or others—they base their relations with other people and professions on. All of which can change who—and what—functions as gatekeepers and who—and what—gets to set the agenda among various people and professions.

It is also important to note that the models are not a result of a continual development that evidently will end up in a situation, where the third model is predominant. For in a broader historical perspective, the model of elimination simply marks a return to a previous era within the media rather than a new, hitherto unknown one. For in the past—and it is still so in many countries—the news media were owned, organized, and under orders to prompt particular political, commercial, or other interests. This is a model that marks a return to, what Schudson has described as a time where "governments, businesses, lobbyist, candidates, churches, and social movements deliver information directly to citizens" (1995: 1). So even if there are differences between the applicability of the three models between various regions of the world and individual nations, between news organizations, and even between persons in the same news room, each model seeks to encompass a different notion of the function, influencing factors and effect of the people and professions involved in, what David Manning White already in 1950 described as a "complex process of communication" (White, 1950: 390). This process has not become any less complex in the current digital era.

Further reading

This chapter is grounded on the two seminal articles that helped introduce the concepts of 'agenda-setting' and 'gatekeeping' within the realm of journalism studies. David Manning White published "The 'Gate Keeper': A Case Study in the Selection of News" in *Journalism Quarterly* in 1950, and Maxwell McCombs and Donald Shaw published "The agenda-setting function of the press" in *Public Opinion Quarterly* in 1972. Both articles have since been reprinted a number of times and they have in turn inspired hundreds of other studies and subsequent publications. Of particular importance in the context of new technological developments are Axel Bruns' *Gatewatching* from 2005, Pamela Shoemaker and Tim P. Vos's *Gatekeeping Theory* from 2009, and Tim P. Vos and Francois Heinderyckx's anthology *Gatekeeping in Transition* from 2015. As for the agenda-setting tradition, Donald Shaw and Maxwell McCombs have themselves closely followed the diffusion of the concept for decades and the development can be tracked in the latest edition of *Setting the Agenda* (McCombs, 2014).

References

Allan, S. (2006) *Online News*. London, UK: Open University Press.
Blumler, J.G. and McQuail, D. (1969) *Television in Politics*. Chicago, IL: University of Chicago Press.
Breed, W. (1955) "Social Control in the Newsroom." *Social Forces* 33(4): 326–335.
Broder, D. (1990) "Democracy and the Press." *The Washington Post*, 3 January.
Bruns, A. (2005) *Gatewatching: Collaborative Online News Production*. New York, NY: Peter Lang.
Chalaby, J.K. (1998) *The Invention of Journalism*. London, UK: Macmillan Press.
Cohen, B. (1963) *The Press and Foreign Policy*. Princeton: Princeton University Press.
Conant, J. (1951) *Science and Common Sense*. New Haven, CT: Yale University Press.
Gillmor, D. (2006) *We the Media*. Sebastopol, CA: O'Reilly.
Haas, T. (2007) *The Pursuit of Public Journalism: Theory, Practice, and Criticism*. New York, NY: Routledge.
Hermida, A. (2011) "Fluid Spaces, Fluid Journalism." In Singer, J.B., Hermida, A., Domingo, D., Heinonen, A., Paulussen, S., Quandt, T., et al. (eds) *Participatory Journalism: Guarding Open Gates at Online Newspapers*. Oxford, UK: Wiley-Blackwell, pp. 177–191.
Lowery, S. and DeFleur, M. (1995) *Milestones in Mass Communication Research: Media Effects*. London: Pearson.
McCombs, M.E. and Shaw, D.L. (1972) "The Agenda-Setting Function of the Press." *Public Opinion Quarterly* 36(2): 176–187.
McCombs, M. and Shaw, D. (1976) "The Agenda-Setting Function of Mass Media." *The Public Opinion Quarterly* 36(2), 176–187.
McCombs, M. and Shaw, D. (1993) "The Evolution of Agenda-Setting Research: Twenty-Five Years in the Marketplace of Ideas." *Journal of Communication* 43(2): 58–67.
McCombs, M.E., Shaw, D.L. and Weaver, D. (1997) *Communication and Democracy: Exploring the Intellectual Frontiers in Agenda-Setting Theory*. Mahway, NJ: Lawrence Erlbaum Associates.
McQuail, D. (2000) *Mass Communication Theory*. London, UK: Sage Publications.
Reese, S. and Ballinger, J. (2001) "The Roots of a Sociology of News: Remembering Mr. Gates and Social Control in the Newsroom." *Journalism & Mass Communication Quarterly* 78(4): 641–658.
Rogers, E. and Dearing, J. (1988) "Agenda-Setting Research: Where Has It Been, Where Is It Going?" In Anderson, J.A. (ed.) *Communication Yearbook 11*. Newbury Park, CA: SAGE, pp. 555–594.

Rosen, J. (1999) *What Are Journalists For?* New Haven, CT: Yale University Press.

Rosen, J. (2006) "Web Users Open the Gates." *The Washington Post*, 19 June.

Schramm, W. (1949) "The Nature of News." *Journalism Quarterly* 26(3): 259–269.

Schudson, M. (1995) *The Power of News*. Cambridge, MA: Harvard University Press.

Schudson, M. (1999) "What Public Journalism Knows about Journalism but Doesn't Know about 'Public.'" In Glasser, T. (ed.) *The Idea of Public Journalism*. New York, NY: Guildford Press, pp. 118–133.

Shoemaker, P. and Vos, T. (2009) *Gatekeeping Theory*. New York, NY: Routledge.

Standage, T. (1998) *The Victorian Internet*. New York, NY: Berkley Books.

Takeshita, T. (1997) "Exploring the Media's Roles in Defining Reality." In M. McCombs, D. Shaw, and D. Weaver (eds) *Communication and Democracy*. London: Lawrence Erlbaum, pp. 15–28.

van Aelst, P. and Walgrave, S. (2011) "Minimal or Massive? The Political Agenda-Setting Power of the Mass Media According to Different Methods." *The International Journal of Press/Politics* 16(3): 295–313.

Vos, T.P. and Heinderyckx, F. (2015) *Gatekeeping in Transition*. New York, NY: Routledge.

White, D.M. (1950) "The 'Gate Keeper': A Case Study in the Selection of News." *Journalism Quarterly* 27(3): 383–390.

PART II

Investigating digital journalism

8

RETHINKING RESEARCH METHODS FOR DIGITAL JOURNALISM STUDIES

Helle Sjøvaag and Michael Karlsson

Journalism studies, and for that matter any research field, works on the premise of certain shared ontological assumptions of the basic components and categories of the field and their relationships. In short, there is a set of things that 'exists for a discipline' and, subsequently, others that do not exist for a discipline (Turk, 2006: 187). Occasionally, however, these assumptions are altered and the old paradigm is challenged. To illustrate this, we can look at gatekeeping theory which today is established within the field although this has not always been the case.

The theory essentially entered journalism studies with White's seminal 1950 case study (White, 1997) and was later developed by scholars such as Gaye Tuchman with her classic study on 'the news net,' routines, and strategic rituals (Tuchman, 1972). These studies were not only theoretically innovative but also, more importantly in this context, methodologically innovative. Gatekeeping could not have been appropriately understood unless White had access to the news items that 'Mr. Gates' discarded. Tuchman's ethnographic study, an approach previously uncommon in the field, allowed the sociological dimensions of gatekeeping to appear. Extensive observations in the newsroom revealed patterns of professional practice that were not visible during shorter visits or could not be uncovered by means of interviews or surveys. Thus, innovative use of method revealed important dimensions of journalism practice and the development of theory. In fact, the emergence of the entire communication research field is closely intertwined with methodological development through Lazarsfeld and colleagues' invention of 'the focused interview' and pioneering use of panels and content analysis (Katz, 1987; Merton and Kendall, 1946).

On the ontology and epistemology of journalism studies

Classic journalism studies have taken categories such as producers, newsrooms, contents, channels of distribution, and audiences as more or less for granted. These are clear and discrete entities that can be studied using a number of established methods—surveys, content analysis, interviews, ethnography, and experiments. Contemporary research, however, has begun to question how journalism studies views these entities theoretically. Terms such as liquid news (Deuze, 2008; Karlsson, 2012), the exploding newsroom (Anderson, 2011), produsage (Bruns, 2008), content farms, aggregation, and curation (Bakker, 2012) have been introduced to describe concepts that challenge the established research regime. Either as new approaches to old things or implying that something completely new has been added to journalism, these have unsettled previous ontological assumptions.

With these challenges follow questions about the epistemology of digital journalism studies. To what extent are the available methods appropriate to acquire knowledge about new components of journalism and their relationships? Do we need completely new methods, can we tweak the old ones, or are the established methods robust enough to account for the changes in the current digital media environment? This chapter, for the purpose of rethinking research methods, takes the need for new methods as its point of departure.

Neff (2015: 75), commenting on communication research and its relation to 'things,' argues that, "the field has yet to develop a rich theoretical language and methodological toolkit for studying the things of social life on their own terms." Similarly, Rodgers (2015: 12) contends that journalism studies must develop ways to study software systems "as genuine objects of journalism" that are shaping journalism. And while putting objects at the center has been criticized for distracting researchers from the social context of technology (Gray, 2012, in Anderson and De Maeyer, 2015), Anderson and De Maeyer (2015: 4) argue that departing from objects can reveal the material affordances of technology uses within journalistic organizations. Similarly, we would argue that an object orientation can reveal the material affordances of methodologies. A key question, then, is how new methods can be and have been developed.

Two dimensions of research methods for digital journalism

We argue that there are at least two interconnected dimensions in digital journalism—consequences of digitization and digital objects per se—with ramifications for digital journalism research methods. The first dimension is related to consequences of digitization. To this dimension belong issues related to changes that have followed from digitization though not entirely embedded in digital media. These include the delocalization of the newsroom and the overlapping relationship between producer and user. Anderson (2011), for instance, vividly suggests that the newsroom is exploding as news work now is conducted in public in a dynamic relationship with actors conventionally situated outside the newsroom. Newsroom ethnography assumes that important dimensions of journalism are produced in a secluded area—distinct from the outside world to which one must gain access in order to unpack the black box (Hemmingway, 2004). The 'inside' is not as clear as it used to be either, as media companies increasingly outsource production to temporary workers or even offshore (Deuze, 2009). Crowdsourcing conflates the borders and makes it challenging to study where journalistic texts originate and what qualities they possess (Muthukumaraswamy, 2010). Similarly, Steensen (2013) demonstrates that sometimes journalism is really a conversation between journalists and audience, without the journalists being the major contributor. One step further from in-house production, citizen journalists create additional methodological challenges, since their publishing modes typically bear little resemblance to the traditional ways in which available methods are honed (Carpenter, 2010). Conducting ethnography and interviews becomes more difficult as the 'actors' who create news become harder to pin down, and the 'space' where news is produced has ceased to exist as an object of study. It seems that the newsroom itself—understood as a place where news production is taking place—is disintegrating while still having a core occupied by professional journalists that may reside in a specific locale. Thus, journalistic production in a newsroom still exists and can still be studied but this is not sufficient for understanding, as we will discuss later, when new actors enter and alter the field.

Another consequence of digitization relates to the fragmentation and elusiveness of the audience in general. Survey research is increasingly hampered by peoples' exclusive cell phone use, dwindling overall response rates, sampling bias, and increasing costs (Groves, 2011; Link and Lai, 2011). People are consuming news at great rates, yet the established methods do not provide adequate means of assessing new consumption patterns.

The second dimension of digital journalism research relates to the 'digital objects' themselves, such as news aggregators, search engines, content management systems, third-party intermediaries, liquid content, and hyperlinked interconnectedness. This chapter focuses mostly on this second dimension. Objects that are, in themselves, completely new or qualitatively different and need to be understood on their own terms—terms that existing methods have not been designed to measure. This is not to argue that these digital objects will, by definition, change journalism but rather to highlight aspects of journalism that fly below the radar. By finding methods that can explore 'digital objects' that not only produce news but also render news accessible to audiences through digital interfaces, researchers will be able to see how and to what extent these are conditioned by social context or alter it.

As digital journalism studies is a relatively new field, there is a dire need to begin to develop these methods. Important steps have already been taken but much remains to be done. Consequently, this chapter now moves to identify problems and argue for the necessity of developing new approaches to understanding digital journalism.

Digital objects and their methods

With the digitization of journalistic production, the tools used to create, disseminate, and access news stories not only condition the process by which news work is done but also condition the manner in which researchers can access, store, and analyze processes that are now largely automated. Essentially emerging to the unembedded as black boxes (c.f. Stavelin, 2013), computerized structures, programs, and digital rendering systems that are man-made to suit a specific purpose, also shape the approaches available for scientific enquiry.

Uncertainties for research range from how news stories are prioritized on a website to how to determine item and corpus boundaries. To the former, as algorithms familiar with your browsing preferences present individualized daily news menus (e.g. Thurman and Schifferes, 2012), it has become difficult to access what we have previously understood as editorialized news agendas. Similarly, difficulty in determining item and corpus boundaries presents a challenge for collecting increasingly temporally and spatially fluid digital journalistic data (Sjøvaag and Stavelin, 2012). Such uncertainties about sampling accuracy accentuate the usefulness of conceptualizing the elements of digital journalistic features as objects in themselves. Objects are something that a computer can capture. The question becomes how those objects are recognized and defined. A news item broken down into smaller units of digital objects can facilitate a more accurate procedure for assembling the fluid elements of texts that are seemingly both linked and autonomous. It can more accurately break up items in the process of storing news data for later processing and analyzing and can also facilitate reassemblage of items, compound separate units, and aggregate sectioned data according to the parameters in the analysis design. Once operationalized, digital objects can be coded automatically based on established parameters that can enable comparisons across corpora.

Thinking of digital news features as objects or a collection of objects enables the researcher to create new structures of data that can be analyzed using digital objects of the researcher's own making. Through designing algorithms and programs to look specifically for aspects of news relevant to the analysis including geographic tags, named entities such as organizations or political parties, topic distribution, sentiments, and clusters of words that can point to argumentation structures, deliberative standpoints, or changes in discourse over time can all be approached (e.g. Gamson and Modigliani, 1989). Because online and mobile news is digitally structured and because digital structures can be different across publishers and across time, finding and capturing the elements that make up a news story requires continuous inductivity in designing methodologies. Conceptualizing the elements of digital journalism production, dissemination, and reception as objects enables or even necessitates such an inductive methodological framework. This is important not least because the digital realm is fraught with emerging (and disappearing) features. Hence, in 'objectifying' the study of online or mobile journalism, digital research methodologies emerge as fluid aspects in and of themselves, particularly when the concept of 'objects' is applied to the study of production and reception.

Thinking about online or mobile journalism as consisting of objects accessible to digital methods both in collection and analysis creates certain challenges along the Lasswellian communication spectrum of sender/channel/message/receiver. 'Objectifying' each step in the process as digitally accessible to computational research methods essentially highlights the outdatedness of Harold Lasswell's (1948) analytical framework, not least because news production and consumption is now a much more intricate social process involving input, reciprocity, and peer-to-peer communication at every step of the process. While this both enables and to some extent accentuates possible moments of interference—both of the human and the technical kind—on the road from a previously autonomous sender to a largely isolated receiver, it also endangers a possible augmentation of the digital to a point where social aspects are overlooked. For this reason, methods for digital journalism studies—while necessarily inductive in their lookout for 'newness'—also need to be grounded in theory. Only then can methodological innovation add to the theoretical development of the field. In the following section, we outline a few emerging approaches for digital journalism research that exemplify how approaching digital news features as objects helps to advance research into the impact of digitization on editorial media.

Relationships and navigation: link analysis

Networked media are largely characterized by hyperlinks connecting nodes together. In fact, without the hyperlink and hypertext, there would be no 'web' in the World Wide Web. A link is itself an object (Manovich, 2001)—a defining property of the web that indicates content substitution or complementation, content aggregation, and traffic generation (Dellarocas, Katona, and Rand, 2013). Accordingly, hyperlinks and hyperlinking practices bring a new dimension to journalism and journalism studies. In a digital journalism context, links are understood as expanding news stories with background (Steensen, 2011) or sources (Tsui, 2008), signaling transparency of method, and ideally inspiring trust (Buebules, 2002; De Maeyer, 2013). In analyzing links in digital news texts, researchers already approach links as objects, usually combining quantitative and qualitative approaches (De Maeyer, 2013), content and network analysis, looking for the intention of the link as a citational, navigational, social, or commercial object (Ryfe, Mensing, and Kelley, 2016). Inherent in researching the linking practices of legacy news organizations online is the jurisdictional protectionism that is grounded in financial considerations—keeping browsers within the boundaries of controlled editorial contexts (Chang *et al.*, 2012).

However, conceptualizing links as intentional objects is increasingly challenged by the growing prevalence of social media. Therefore, methods also need to account for the different functions that links entail (e.g. Coddington, 2012; Ryfe et al., 2016), and whether links are created by humans or computers (De Maeyer, 2013). Link studies are also complicated by search engines such as Google, now considered part of the link ecosystem and something that digital journalism studies needs to unpack (Örmen, 2016) with personalization taken into account (Thurman and Schifferes, 2012). Whereas hyperlinks are clearly defined, accessible objects, they also infer movement or possibilities of use (Brügger, 2009), creating a need to define the depth and scope of the object of study. While treating nodes, links, and search algorithms as digital objects facilitates methodological access to clearly defined items, this object orientation also reveals the affordances of digital methods in analyzing web connectivity. Consequently, link analysis allows for investigating the relationship between sites and the strength and directions of those relationships, but also offers new challenges for the researcher (Weber and Monge, 2011; Weber, 2012). In that sense, link analysis provides a methodological tool to assess the relative importance of a news site or a news item in any macro- or micro-media ecology, whether it is the question of mapping patterns between sites or social media platforms (Sormanen *et al.*, 2016). Not least since external links seem to grow in importance over time (Karlsson, Clerwall, and Örnebring, 2015; Weber, 2012).

Automation and 'big data'

Techniques for analyzing large amounts of digital data produced primarily by editorial institutions are also in rapid development as the harvesting of web data becomes more uniform and easily accessible. Yet at the dawn of a new methodological landscape, most of the 'big data' methods used to scrape data from databases, APIs, and 'liquid' journalistic sites come from information sciences, informatics, and computational social science. Using algorithms designed for textual analysis, researchers can use topic modeling methods to render the topical contents of large corpora (Elgesem, Steskal, and Diakopoulos, 2015); named entity recognition (NER) to map the distribution and frequency of words, such as proper names, organizations, and locations (Mansouri, Affendey, and Mamat, 2008); natural language processing (NLP) to perform corpus-based discourse analysis (Touileb and Salway, 2014); sentiment analysis can establish opinions in the news; and automated content analysis (ACA) (Günther and Scharkow, 2014) can map frequency and distribution of topical content. Hugely helpful to the study of large textual corpora such as those produced by online media, these methods are also inherently weak, the tradeoff being that computational power can easily substitute scale for depth (boyd and Crawford, 2012). Furthermore, not only are these techniques still in development, interpretive textual methods also tend to produce low reliability (Mahrt and Scharkow, 2013). For this reason, use of 'big data' methods for digital journalism research needs a hybrid design, combining media approaches with computational methods (Lewis, Zamith, and Hermida, 2013; Lewis *et al.* in this volume).

The threshold for embracing 'big data' methods is therefore obvious; most humanities or social science–trained journalism scholars do not possess the skills or technical knowledge to design, run, and process the computer programs needed to perform automated analyses on large sets of media texts. While these methods facilitate 'objectifying' digital journalistic features in online media, it takes a clear understanding of the logics and processes by which these methods operate to properly analyze findings without turning the methodology into yet another black box. However, as it is unlikely that automating entire methodological procedures, without human input, would be sufficiently valid for the social scientific study of news (Mahrt and Scharkow, 2013; Zamith and Lewis, 2015), interdisciplinary cooperation is essential in this development. Researchers are also increasingly met with challenges to capture fluid, 'live' and 'moving' digital objects (Karlsson, 2012), such as dynamic scrolling, rolling news feeds, content management systems (Rodgers, 2015), intelligent agents, and 'robots' (Anderson, 2011; Clerwall, 2014; van Dalen, 2012), whose behaviors cannot be so easily frozen (Karlsson and Strömbäck, 2010). While we need to develop 'best practice' approaches for digital journalism research, the rapid technological development of the web as a space for journalistic output means we need to keep our methodological departures sufficiently inductive.

Third-party intermediaries—hubs, nodes, and peripheries in the news ecology

Another area where studies are scarce is making sense of how the distribution of content is fundamentally altered when digitized. Journalism has commonly been located in one space that people visit (web) or has been distributed to them (press, radio, and TV). The rise of various social media platforms entails that journalism is increasingly dispersed, as digital media allow users and social actors to create, like, and share (and reshare) news through their networks, a process that both decentralizes and recentralizes information (Anderson, 2010; Domingo and Le Cam, 2014; Gerlitz and Helmond, 2013). Likewise, the rise of aggregators (Bakker, 2012) means that the news that people encounter might be published in another place and context than its origin. Thus, the reach or circulation of news becomes harder to estimate. A story that makes the front page may not pick up speed in networks and vice versa. Or perhaps more aptly stated, as increased opportunities to monitor traffic patterns will prevent media outlets from missing big social media events, it will be more difficult to establish when, where, how, and why important journalistically relevant events take place within these networks. All in all, these new patterns are due to the increase of prominence of what can be referred to as third-party intermediaries. That is, actors conceived of as individuals, organizations, or technological platforms, which were previously excluded from the direct media/journalist–audience relationship now have a more potent platform and an (unequal) opportunity to disrupt, redirect, or reverse the flow of information between (for a lack of better terms) media and their audiences.

The practice of spreading news also entails how discussing and making news meaningful takes place in many different and temporal spaces (Bødker, 2015) where a broad range of institutionalized third-party intermediaries (Heise, 2013) such as Facebook might host such interactions for briefer or longer time spans. These are practices we know little about, that are even difficult to find, measure, store, or analyze in the first place (not least because of legal issues)—not to mention the concomitant difficulties in estimating their social significance and value. Yet, this is indeed how some contemporary news is produced, distributed, and consumed. Thus, there is need to develop methods that allow for, first of all, finding but also assessing the spatial, temporal, and cultural spread of different third-party intermediaries as both technical systems and social agents. Furthermore, there is need to compare the roles of different intermediaries both on their own merits and in relation to legacy media. A few studies have already emerged. Adopting a computational approach, Sormanen *et al.* (2016) study activities such as shares, posts, comments, and links in a Facebook protest group over a period of time and consider how the members of the group relate to the public debate. Other studies (Anderson, 2010; Bødker, 2015; Domingo and Le Cam, 2014) have a (single) case-centric approach to uncover how news is created and circulated through and between different platforms and actors. Utilizing a variety of methods—search engines, interviews, content analysis, link analysis, and ethnography—in order to discern the contours, these studies are united in their efforts to go beyond "news production within institutions" and established characteristics such as producer, distributor, channel, and consumer to focus instead on "the circulation of news in ecosystems" (Anderson, 2010: 291).

Challenges and the road ahead

There are more areas of research to study than can be covered in this chapter, including the role of robots, algorithms, and content management systems in the production of news to name only a few. Regardless, the principal issue is the same: how do journalism researchers create an epistemology suitable for digital journalism studies when there is an abundance of challenges and a near absence of methods or even a widespread acknowledgement of the issues at hand?

The task will not be easy and sometimes even counterproductive as some of the tweaked, novel, and innovative methods will, in all probability, fail. Yet, there are not really any alternative options to trying new paths as the existing methods have reached the end of the road. This chapter points towards the richness of using new approaches and the difficulties in predicting what will follow from using new (and unapproved) methods.

In moving ahead, we argue for a tolerance within the research community towards experimenting with methods that might entail 'messy but productive' solutions (Karpf, 2012: 642) while also try developing agreed-upon tools, protocols, and approaches (Herring, 2010). A key problem will be to determine how to develop new methodological approaches and how and when to apply them. But this would not be the first time that communication scholars have faced and solved those problems. The innovative studies that lead to the introduction and development of gatekeeping theory were enabled through novel methodological approaches. Great discoveries lie ahead.

Further reading

The object orientation that this chapter assumes has been inspired by C. W. Anderson and Juliette De Maeyer's introductory article "Objects of Journalism and the News," published in a special issue of *Journalism* in 2015. The critical dimensions concerning big data that we raise have previously been well conceptualized in danah boyd and Kate Crawford's article "Critical Questions For Big Data," published in *Information, Communication & Society* in 2012, whereas David Karpf offers a qualified discussion about the need for and problems with changing a methodological paradigm in "Social Science Research Methods in Internet Time," published in *Information, Communication & Society* in 2012. We also recommend for further reading De Maeyer's 2013 article "Towards a Hyperlinked Society: A Critical Review of Link Studies" from *New Media and Society*, which provides a useful overview of research on hyperlink.

References

Anderson, C.W. (2010) "Journalistic Networks and the Diffusion of Local News: The Brief, Happy News Life of the 'Francisville Four.'" *Political Communication* 27(3): 289–309.

Anderson, C.W. (2011) "Blowing up the Newsroom: Ethnography in the Age of Distributed Journalism." In Domingo, D. and Paterson, C. (eds) *Making Online News, Volume 2. Newsroom Ethnographies in the Second Decade of Internet Journalism.* New York, NY: Peter Lang, pp. 151–160.

Anderson, C.W. and De Maeyer, J. (2015) "Objects of Journalism and the News." *Journalism* 16(1): 3–9.

Bakker, P. (2012) "Aggregation, Content Farms and Huffinization." *Journalism Practice* 6(5–6): 627–637.

Bødker, H. (2015) "Journalism as Cultures of Circulation." *Digital Journalism* 3(1): 101–115.

boyd, d. and Crawford, K. (2012) "Critical Questions for Big Data." *Information, Communication & Society* 15(5): 662–679.

Brügger, N. (2009) "Website History and the Website as an Object of Study." *New Media & Society* 11(1–2): 115–132.

Bruns, A. (2008) *Blogs, Wikipedia, Second Life, and Beyond: From Production to Produsage*. New York, NY: Peter Lang.

Buebules, N.C. (2002) "The Web as a Rhetorical Place." In Snyder, I. (ed.) *Silicon Literacies: Communication, Innovation and Education in the Electronic Age*. London, UK: Routledge, pp. 75–84.

Carpenter, S. (2010) "A Study of Content Diversity in Online Citizen Journalism and Online Newspaper Articles." *New Media & Society* 12(7): 1064–1084.

Chang, T., Southwell, B.G., Lee, H. and Hong, Y. (2012) "Jurisdictional Protectionism in Online News: American Journalists and Their Perceptions of Hyperlinks." *New Media & Society* 14(4): 684–700.

Clerwall, C. (2014) "Enter the Robot Journalist: Users' Perceptions of Automated Content." *Journalism Practice* 8(5): 519–531.

Coddington, M. (2012) "Building Frames, Link by Link: The Linking Practices of Blogs and News Sites." *International Journal of Communication* 6: 2007–2026.

Dellarocas, C., Katona, Z. and Rand, W. (2013) "Media, Aggregators, and the Link Economy: Strategic Hyperlink Formation in Content Networks." *Management Science* 59(10): 2360–2379.

De Maeyer, J. (2013) "Towards a Hyperlinked Society: A Critical Review of Link Studies." *New Media and Society* 15(5): 737–751.

Deuze, M. (2008) "The Changing Context of News Work: Liquid Journalism and Monitorial Citizenship." *International Journal of Communication* 2: 848–865.

Deuze, M. (2009) "The People Formerly Known as the Employers." *Journalism* 10(3): 315–318.

Domingo, D. and Le Cam, F. (2014) "Journalism in Dispersion: Exploring the Blurring Boundaries of Newsmaking through a Controversy." *Digital Journalism* 2(3): 310–321.

Elgesem, D., Steskal, L. and Diakopoulos, N. (2015) "Structure and Content of the Discourse of Climate Change in the Blogosphere: The Big Picture." *Environmental Communication* 9(2): 169–188.

Gamson, W.A. and Modigliani, A. (1989) "Media Discourse and Public Opinion on Nuclear Power: A Constructionist Approach." *American Journal of Sociology* 95: 1–37.

Gerlitz, C. and Helmond, A. (2013) "The Like Economy: Social Buttons and the Data-Intensive Web." *New Media & Society* 15(8): 1348–1365.

Groves, R.M. (2011) "Three Eras of Survey Research." *Public Opinion Quarterly* 75(5): 861–871.

Günther, E. and Scharkow, M. (2014) "Recycled Media: An Automated Evaluation of News Outlets in the Twenty-First Century." *Digital Journalism* 2(4): 524–541.

Heise, N. (2013) "'Bridging Technologies': Intermediating Functions of Technical Objects within the Relationship of Journalism and Audience." *Objects of Journalism*. London, UK: ICA Pre-conference.

Hemmingway, E.L. (2004) "The Silent Heart of News." *Space and Culture* 7(4): 409–426.

Herring, S. (2010) "Web Content Analysis: Expanding the Paradigm." In Hunsinger, J. Klastrup, L. and Allen, M. (eds) *International Handbook of Internet Research*. Dordrecht, Netherlands: Springer, pp. 233–249.

Karlsson, M. (2012) "Charting the Liquidity of Online News: Moving Towards a Method for Content Analysis of Online News." *International Communication Gazette* 74(4): 385–402.

Karlsson, M., Clerwall, C. and Örnebring, H. (2015) "Hyperlinking Practices in Swedish Online News 2007–2013: The Rise, Fall, and Stagnation of Hyperlinking as a Journalistic Tool." *Information, Communication & Society* 18(7): 847–863.

Karlsson, M. and Strömbäck, J. (2010) "Freezing the Flow of Online News: Exploring Approaches to the Study of the Liquidity of Online News." *Journalism Studies* 11(1): 2–19.

Karpf, D. (2012) "Social Science Research Methods in Internet Time." *Information, Communication & Society* 15(5): 639–661.

Katz, E. (1987) "Communications Research Since Lazersfeld." *The Public Opinion Quarterly* 51(2): 25–45.

Lasswell, H.D. (1948) "The Structure and Function of Communication in Society." In Bryson, L. (ed.) *The Communication of Ideas*. New York, NY: Institute of Religious and Social Studies, pp. 37–51.

Lewis, S.C., Zamith, R. and Hermida, A. (2013) "Content Analysis in an Era of Big Data: A Hybrid Approach to Computational and Manual Methods." *Journal of Broadcasting and Electronic Media* 57(1): 34–52.

Link, M.W. and Lai, J.W. (2011) "Cell-Phone-Only Households and Problems of Differential Nonresponse Using an Address-Based Sampling Design." *Public Opinion Quarterly* 75(4): 613–635.

Mahrt, M. and Scharkow, M. (2013) "The Value of Big Data in Digital Media Research." *Journal of Broadcasting and Electronic Media* 57(1): 20–33.

Manovich, L. (2001) *The Language of New Media*. Cambridge, MA: MIT Press.

Mansouri, A., Affendey, L.S. and Mamat, A. (2008) "Named Entity Recognition Approaches." *International Journal of Computer Science and Network Security* 8(2): 339–344.

Merton, R.K. and Kendall, P.L. (1946) "The Focused Interview." *American Journal of Sociology* 51(6): 541–557.

Muthukumaraswamy, K. (2010) "When the Media Meet Crowds of Wisdom." *Journalism Practice* 4(1): 48–65.

Neff, G. (2015) "Learning from Documents: Applying New Theories of Materiality to Journalism." *Journalism* 16(1): 74–78.

Örmen, J. (2016) "Googling the News: Opportunities and Challenges Pertaining to Studying Google Search Results." *Digital Journalism* 4(1): 107–124.

Rodgers, S. (2015) "Foreign Objects? Web Content Management Systems, Journalistic Cultures and the Ontology of Software." *Journalism* 16(1): 10–26.

Ryfe, D., Mensing, D. and Kelley, R. (2016) "What Is the Meaning of a News Link?" *Digital Journalism* 4(1): 41–54.

Sjøvaag, H. and Stavelin, E. (2012) "Web Media and the Quantitative Content Analysis: Methodological Challenges in Measuring Online News Content." *Convergence* 18(2): 215–229.

Sormanen, N., Niskala, N., Rohila, J., Lauk, E., Uskali, T., Jouhki, J. and Penttinen, M. (2016) "Paradigm Shift: Towards a Computational Approach in Data Gathering and Analysis in Social Scientific Research—Case Facebook Groups." *Digital Journalism* 4(1): 55–74.

Stavelin, E. (2013) *Computational Journalism: When Journalism Meets Programming.* Doctoral thesis. University of Bergen, Bergen.

Steensen, S. (2011) "Online Journalism and the Promises of New Technology: A Critical Review and Look Ahead." *Journalism Studies* 12(3): 311–327.

Steensen, S. (2013) "Conversing the Audience: A Methodological Exploration of How Conversation Analysis Can Contribute to the Analysis of Interactive Journalism." *New Media & Society* 16(8): 1197–1213.

Thurman, N. and Schifferes S. (2012) "The Future of Personalization at News Websites." *Journalism Studies* 12(5–6): 775–790.

Touileb, S. and Salway, A. (2014) "Constructions: A New Unit of Analysis for Corpus-Based Discourse Analysis." *PACLIC* 28: 634–643.

Tsui, L. (2008) "The Hyperlink in Newspapers and Blogs." In Turow, J. and Tsui, L. (eds) *The Hyperlinked Society: Questioning Connections in the Digital Age.* Ann Arbor, MI: University of Michigan Press, pp. 70–84.

Tuchman, G. (1972) "Objectivity as a Strategic Ritual." *The American Journal of Sociology* 77(4): 660–679.

Turk, Ž. (2006) "Construction Informatics: Definition and Ontology." *Advanced Engineering Informatics* 20(2): 187–199.

van Dalen, A. (2012) "The Algorithms Behind the Headlines." *Journalism Practice* 6(5–6): 648–658.

Weber, M.S. (2012) "Newspapers and the Long-Term Implications of Hyperlinking." *Journal of Computer-Mediated Communication* 17(2): 187–201.

Weber, M.S. and Monge, P. (2011) "The Flow of Digital News in a Network of Sources, Authorities, and Hubs." *Journal of Communication* 61(6): 1062–1081.

White, D.M. (1997) "The 'Gate Keeper': A Case Study in the Selection of News." In Berkowitz, D. (ed.) *Social Meanings of News.* Thousand Oaks, CA: Sage, pp. 63–71.

Zamith, R. and Lewis, S.C. (2015) "Content Analysis and the Algorithmic Coder: What Computational Social Science Means for Traditional Modes of Media Analysis." *The Annals of the American Academy of Political and Social Science* 659(1): 307–318.

9

AUTOMATING MASSIVE-SCALE ANALYSIS OF NEWS CONTENT

Thomas Lansdall-Welfare, Justin Lewis, and Nello Cristianini

In this chapter we address one of the key questions in contemporary journalism and communication studies: how can we detect macroscopic trends in the vast troves of media data made available by digital technology? To do so, we ask: how well can computational methods apply content, framing, or discourse analysis to huge samples? This work is part of the emerging field of computational social sciences (Lazer *et al.*, 2009), and our approach combines expertise in computer science with quantitative and qualitative approaches in journalism and media studies.

Much of the focus on 'big data' in media and communications has been on newer forms of social media, such as the analysis of massive social networks (Watts, 2007); the study of friendships by using mobile phone data (Eagle, Pentland, and Lazer, 2009); the discovery of patterns in email exchange (Echmann, Moses, and Sergi, 2004); the study of player interactions in online games (Szella, Lambiotte, and Thurner, 2010); and the study of mood within social media (Lansdall-Welfare, Lampos, and Cristianini, 2012). At the same time, the growth of the digital humanities—based on digital archives of cultural forms—has allowed scholars to explore the content of millions of books, creating new forms of disciplinary fusion such as 'culturomics' (Michel *et al.*, 2011).

This chapter presents a number of large-scale investigations of millions of articles of online news content. Our aim, in part, is to demonstrate how automated approaches can access and analyze both semantic and stylistic properties of content, thereby opening up the possibility of transforming the analysis of media content to cover huge data sets.

Analysis based on human coding can draw upon complex semiotic frameworks—human coders can have sophisticated cultural and idiomatic repertoires and interpretive skills. It is, however, time consuming and costly. While traditional media content analyses can sometimes produce sample sizes of a few thousand, they generally require coding teams working over a period of several months to produce the data (e.g. Lewis and Cushion, 2009).

If we can begin to introduce sophistication into machine-based forms of analysis, it gives us access to huge samples, allowing the kinds of comprehensive, longitudinal forms of analysis often beyond the reach of conventional content analysis. We explore the application of modern Artificial Intelligence (AI) techniques, including data mining, machine learning, natural language processing, and computer vision for the large-scale automated analysis of news media content. In order to demonstrate these approaches, we chose three areas of analysis—writing style, gender representation, and narrative analysis—with some fairly predictable outcomes. Our aim, in part, was to replicate earlier findings on a larger scale. Despite these fairly modest aims, the research presented here nonetheless adds both nuance and detail to our understanding of media, opening up the possibility of analyzing vast news corpora for much less predictable questions.

Methods

We based our analyses on state-of-the-art AI techniques including data mining (Liu, 2007), statistical machine learning (Shawe-Taylor and Cristianini, 2004), and natural language processing (Manning and Schutze, 1999). The collections of news articles for each of the studies presented here were obtained from the web using our news content analysis system (Flaounas *et al.*, 2011), before being automatically coded and annotated using a variety of techniques, outlined below.

Readability

Our assessment of the readability of news articles was based on the Flesch Reading Ease Test scoring method (Flesch, 1948). Readability cannot be entirely reduced to a set of linguistic properties, but it provides a useful framework in which certain properties (such as shorter words or sentences) are likely to be associated with higher levels of readability. To validate this approach, we added a set of articles from the children's BBC current affairs program Newsround. As expected, the Newsround news items were the most readable in our sample (with a mean readability score of 62.50 and standard error of the mean equal to 0.27).

Topic classification

News articles were automatically coded and annotated according to their topic, using the well-established approach of Support Vector Machines (SVM) from the field of machine learning (Cristianini and Shawe-Taylor, 2000). This involved training a machine to perform the annotation, in much the same way a researcher would have to train human coders. We trained one SVM classifier for each topic we wanted to detect. To train classifiers we used two well-known corpora, from Reuters and the *New York Times*.

Named Entity Recognition

References to any number of different types of entity can be found in texts by making using of Named Entity Recognition (NER) techniques. This involves a combination of pattern matching within the text, while using various linguistic clues and applying rules known as 'grammars' in the open source tool Gate (Cunningham *et al.*, 2002). Information about specific types of entity, such as people, can also be extracted. For other non-standard types of entity, we make use of gazetteers to list the entities we are interested in extracting.

Sentiment detection

For each of the references to an 'entity' we extracted from news articles using the open source tool Gate (Cunningham *et al.*, 2002), we wanted to determine their sentiment in the text. The sentence containing each reference was assessed for its sentimental content using an opinion lexicon containing 6,800 polarized sentiment terms. A sentence containing a reference to an entity is then defined as positive if it contains more positive words than negative words and vice versa.

Linguistic subjectivity

While many forms of language can express subjectivity, our focus was on the most overt subjective linguistic expressions—words such as 'terrible' or 'wonderful,' for example—which are typically adjectives expressing a sentiment. We categorized an adjective as subjective if its subjectivity weight is above 0.25 in Senti-WordNet (Baccianella, Esuli, and Sebastiani, 2010), a standard database for scoring the subjectivity of words. If a word has many different weights, we used their average weighting. For each article, we measured the linguistic subjectivity of their title and their first three sentences. Adjectives were found by parsing the text based on the 'Stanford Log-linear Part-of-Speech Tagger' (Toutanova *et al.*, 2003).

Gender bias in texts

We identified the gender of people named in the text of news articles using the open source tool Gate (Cunningham *et al.*, 2002). We validated our tools for gender detection by using the Freebase database (Bollacker *et al.*, 2008), which contains information about the gender of many celebrities in a computer-readable format. We found 38,480 entities in Freebase that match exactly our systems entries. From those entities, the gender was correctly detected for 79.4 percent by our system; 18.9 percent were left unlabelled; with 1.6 percent of the entities having an incorrect gender label (errors were balanced among males and females).

Gender bias in images

Images occurring in news articles were classified by gender according to the largest face in each image. Faces were first detected by applying face recognition (Jones and Viola, 2003) to the images using standard computer vision software (Bradski, 2000). Each face was then categorized by gender using our gender classification algorithm (Jia and Cristianini, 2015), which obtains an accuracy of over 95 percent on the standard Labeled Faces in the Wild data set.

Narrative analysis

Subject-Verb-Object (SVO) triplets are extracted from news articles by resolving co-references and performing anaphora resolution on the text, before dependency parsing the text using the Malt parser (Nivre *et al.*, 2007). From each parse, triplets that match the form SVO are extracted and formed into a network where each subject or object is represented as a node, with connecting edges showing the verb relating them. Action clouds for an entity are generated from the triplet networks by aggregating together the verbs from triplets where a particular entity forms the subject or object of the triplet. This allows two action clouds to be generated for each entity, one for the actions performed by the entity and one for the actions performed on the entity.

Findings

Using combinations of these automated techniques, we conducted a number of studies concentrating on big data analysis of news content, exploring differences in writing style between topics, gender representation in news outlets, and between mediums of communication, framing of issues, and changes in narrative surrounding entities, drawing on news content from millions of news articles published by hundreds of outlets in a wide range of countries over several years.

Writing style in news content

In the first study (Flaounas *et al.*, 2013), we analyzed 2,490,429 articles gathered from 498 online English language news outlets, from 99 different countries, between January 1, 2010, and October 31, 2010. Each article in the corpus was classified automatically into 15 different generic news categories such as Crime or Sport. The articles were then assessed for readability (i.e. the ease of reading an article) and for linguistic subjectivity (based on the ratio of sentimental adjectives over the total number of adjectives).

Aggregating the readability and linguistic subjectivity scores for articles by topic category (Figure 9.1), we can see that, as we might expect, articles about Sport, Art and Fashion were the most readable. While we might have expected Science and Business reporting to use more difficult technical language, we found that articles about politics are the least readable of any genre. If this is not altogether surprising, it does raise some important questions.

Journalists tend to assume that topics like Business or Science are more esoteric and difficult for their readers. As a consequence, they either write for specialist audiences or try to make them accessible to a general audience. Politics, on the other hand, is (by definition in a democracy) addressed to general readers—and yet these results suggest this is, in linguistic terms, the most esoteric, least accessible form of journalism. This may partly explain high levels of public disengagement with politics (Lewis, Inthorn, and Wahl-Jorgensen, 2005).

Figure 9.1 also shows that articles about Fashion and Art use the most expressive adjectives (these topics obviously lend themselves to adjectival judgment). Topics such as Business,

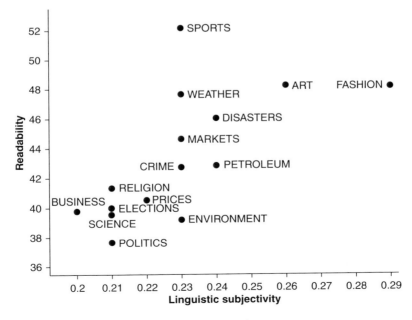

Figure 9.1 Comparison of topics based on their writing style.

Politics, and Elections appear to use the least overtly subjective language. This does not mean that coverage of business or politics is *necessarily* more impartial—extensive literatures within media and journalism studies (e.g. 'framing' or discourse analysis) show that objectivity cannot be reduced to adjectival counts, but it does suggest a set of cultural norms about the use of language within different news genres and shows how computational analysis can be *part of* the analysis of objectivity.

These findings confirm that the language of news varies according to topic, and that, as Martin Conboy writes: "Within specialist sections of the newspaper, sports, fashion and entertainment for instance, there is more latitude for the language to show traces of opinion and even judgement of taste" (Conboy, 2007). It might also confirm that certain subjects are more suited to a narrative and conversational approach (see, e.g. Connel, 1998; Jacobs, 1996) while the less obviously subjective story topics are constrained by the relative complexity of the subject matter.

We also found that there is a significant correlation between readability and linguistic subjectivity (Spearman correlation = 73.49 percent; $p = 0.0018$). In other words, the more readable a topic is, the more linguistically subjective it tends to be. While there are many possible explanations for this, it does open up the possibility that these two stylistic features have become associated with one another in journalistic conventions. This, in turn, allows us to imagine new conventions that break down these associations—so, for example, political coverage that strives for high readability *without* linguistic subjectivity (a stylistic combination achieved, our findings suggest, by sports coverage).

Other findings in the study (Flaounas *et al.*, 2013) included a comparison of 15 leading UK and US newspapers. This indicated (predictably) that tabloid newspapers were, overall, both more subjective and more readable, with the *Sun* topping the table on both counts. Interestingly, this matches UK regulator Ofcom's surveys on the perceived bias of news outlets (Ofcom, 2014), which suggested that broadsheets are trusted more than tabloids, with the *Sun* regarded as the least objective and trustworthy newspaper in the UK. While there may be other, more subtle ways in which bias is manifested, these findings suggest that the use of subjective language is a trigger (though not a guarantee) for people to assume media bias.

Gender representation in the media

The analysis of the representation of gender has a long history within media and cultural studies, often involving complex judgments of stereotyping and language as well as more straightforward measures such as the relative incidence of male and female journalists, sources and other actors (e.g. Carter, Branston, and Allan, 1998).

Using the same corpus of articles as the study on writing style, we investigated the gender imbalances among the most frequently mentioned people in the textual content of the news articles. Of the 1,000 most mentioned people in our data set, the vast majority were men, a finding very much in line with traditional content studies.

Figure 9.2 allows a more fine-grained analysis of gender bias in news. Previous work on gender bias has found sports coverage to be a bastion of patriarchal assumptions (Alexander, 1994; Bishop, 2003; Eastman and Billings, 2000), something our findings confirm. This provides a weighty endorsement to more traditional studies (e.g. Len-Rios *et al.*, 2006, based on articles from two newspapers for a period of three weeks), reporting similar findings.

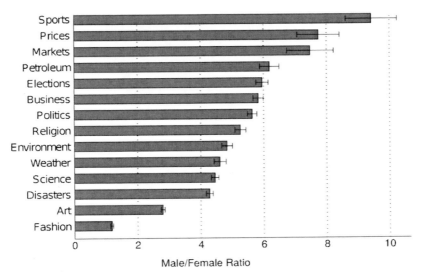

Figure 9.2   Comparison of topics based on their male/female ratio in text.

Business or business-related topics (Prices, Markets, and Petroleum) are also heavily male-dominated, while political coverage appears to become (even) more male dominated during elections. Fashion reporting is the least male-dominated form of news, although even here women are still outnumbered by men. Since this is a genre traditionally about women for women, this suggests a deep-rooted gender bias across news reporting as a whole, one that is exacerbated but not explained by the dominance of men at the top of 'real world' professions like business and politics.

While most automation of news content analysis is currently based on Natural Language Processing, the rapidly maturing field of Computer Vision will enable us to also analyze the content of images in the news. As a proof of concept, a recent study (Jia, Lansdall-Welfare, and Cristianini, 2015) investigated gender bias in images of online newspapers on a vast scale. Using images appearing in 885,573 news articles from 882 news outlets in a period of four months between 19 October 2014 and 19 January 2015, they again found gender imbalance between different topics with similar results (Figure 9.3). There are some interesting nuances here, however: the gender imbalance increases (proportionately) when images are shown in the coverage of politics, while decreasing a little in the coverage of sport. The fact that women do better in images than text in the coverage of sport tends to reinforce stereotypical representations, since sporting images tend to feature young, conventionally attractive women.

Other findings in the study (Jia, Lansdall-Welfare, and Cristianini, 2015) indicated that tabloid-style outlets have a higher gender bias in Fashion and Weather topics than their broadsheet-style counterparts, whereas broadsheet-style outlets have a comparatively higher gender bias in Markets, Petroleum, Religion, Sports, and Technology; and that while the Daily Mail has a large proportion of Politics articles by topic classification (a high gender bias topic), overall as an outlet it had the lowest gender bias. Again, given the nature of the Mail's online content, this may simply reinforce stereotypical representations.

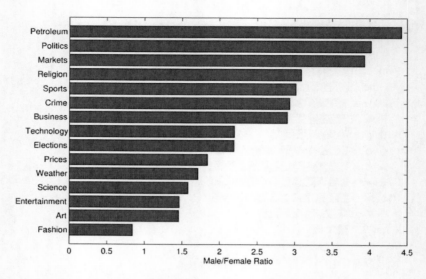

Figure 9.3   Comparison of topics based on their male/female ratio in images.

Large-scale narrative analysis

It is possible to identify key actors and issues in a corpus of articles and determine the relationships between them. This type of analysis is known as Quantitative Narrative Analysis, or QNA for short (Earl *et al.*, 2004). By forming SVO triplets from the narrative of news articles, it is possible to capture relationships in media coverage.

In a recent study (Sudhahar, Veltri, and Cristianini, 2015), such approaches uncovered the political spectrum of actors and their key issues automatically from 130,213 news articles covering the 2012 US presidential elections, as shown in Figure 9.4. In Lansdall-Welfare *et al.*, (2014), we scaled up this QNA approach to analyze the framing of issues in science-related news articles using 5,195,010 news articles gathered from the web between 1 May 2008 and 31 December 2013. We applied sentiment detection and narrative analysis, among others, to the news articles and discovered interesting patterns in the way certain issues and topics were represented in media.

We found, for example, that the sentiment surrounding the issue of nuclear power shifted from being positive to negative following the Fukushima disaster in March 2011 (Figure 9.5). Before the disaster, nuclear power was portrayed as a viable alternative to fossil-based energy sources in the debates taking place within many countries at the time. Following the disaster, our findings suggest that nuclear power was cast in a negative light, with the story focusing on the public's perception of the technology and its association with thyroid cancer.

Figure 9.6 shows the verb clouds of the actions being performed on nuclear power in the triplet network before and after the disaster took place, highlighting the shift from one of mainly 'embracing,' 'supporting,' and 'needing' nuclear power to the frequent appearance of 'abandoning,' 'scrapping,' and 'replacing' it.

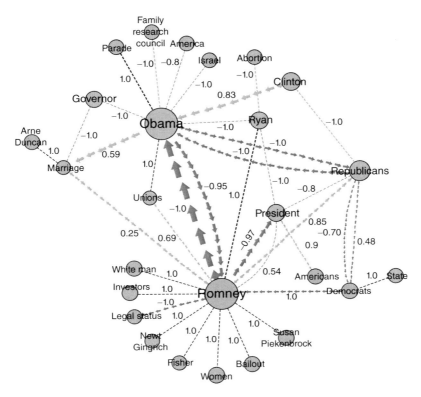

Figure 9.4 A subset of the US elections network in Sudhahar, Veltri, and Cristianini (2015) showing the political affiliation of key actors and issues.

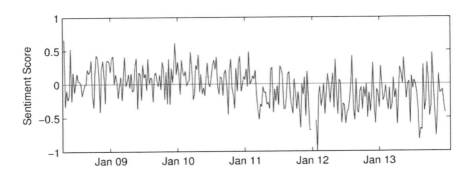

Figure 9.5 Normalized difference in the number of positive to negative sentences containing 'Nuclear Power'.

Figure 9.6   Verbs related to 'Nuclear Power' as an object before (left) and after (right) the Fukushima disaster in March 2011.

Conclusion

The studies reviewed here involved millions of news articles and close to one million images, numbers that can be scaled up even further. Further studies have demonstrated how machine translation technology has also reached a level of performance, which enables us to usefully analyze large multilingual corpora (Flaounas *et al.*, 2010).

The automation of news content analysis will not replace the human judgment needed for fine-grained, qualitative forms of analysis. It does, however, open up new possibilities:

- It enables researchers to conduct analysis on massive samples, reducing possibilities of bias—whether perceived or real—in sample selection. The data on gender bias, for example, are compelling, showing clear patterns across huge data sets.
- Automatic detection of objects and their analysis in the content of images can be leveraged for new large-scale studies into the images that accompany the traditional media text.
- Machine-based analysis (such as the cluster analysis of newspapers) can detect unforeseen linguistic patterns, while content analysis generally relies on anticipating linguistic frameworks in order to look for them.
- The portrayal of many different types of entity mentioned in news can be tracked over years, enabling us to track changes in the framing of issues or topics. So, for example, we could see how the changes in the coverage of nuclear power responded to a specific event. While this particular change is fairly predictable, this analysis is capable of detecting less predictable shifts in the ways in which issues are reported.
- By significantly increasing sample size, we can conduct far more fine-grained explorations of variables over time.
- Once analytical frameworks have been developed and baseline data have been produced, they can be repeated in future research easily and at low cost.

This level of macroanalysis is needed now more than ever, since the range of communication outlets available to people—together with trends towards concentration of ownership (Bagdikian, 2000; McChesney and Nichols, 2010)—makes it increasingly difficult to isolate one media form. So while it was possible, hitherto, to focus on a dominant communications medium like television to explore the relationship between media content and public understanding/opinion, the contemporary media environment makes this more difficult.

The work of George Gerbner and the Cultural Indicators project, for example, tried to isolate television as an information system (Morgan, 2002). Their very reasonable premise was that television's impact could be explored when heavy television viewers expressed understandings of the world that matched television's dominant representations—especially where these diverged from real-world comparisons. While television remains a dominant medium, which may have a profound impact on the stories we use to understand the world (Miller, 2009), such impacts may now be masked by cross-media ownership patterns combined with the presence of multiple media outlets. It is distinctly possible, in such a world, that light television viewers—whether they get their information from a newspaper, a website, or a podcast—are receiving much the same stories as those told by television. In this context, finding no differences between light and heavy viewers does not mean television has no influence. It may simply mean that both television and other media outlets are telling similar stories about the world and that both are equally influential.

Our approach raises the possibility of exploring the whole range of media outlets and identifying, in all their complexity, moments of similarity and divergence—a cultural indicators project writ large across a multidimensional media world. It also allows us to explore systematically the genealogy of stories and ideas, tracking their emergence and passage through different media over time. So, for example, we can explore the relationship between news outlets and the burgeoning world of blogs to see how ideas travel between them or between different kinds of media (such as social media, online, print, and broadcast) to see which media play an agenda setting role. We can, quite literally, track news as it emerges and develops across all news and communication forms.

Even at this exploratory stage, however, some of our findings throw up some intriguing patterns alongside the more predictable results that shed light on debates and raise some interesting questions. So, for example, the failure of many citizens to engage with political news (Lewis, Inthorn, and Wahl-Jorgensen, 2005) or with environmental problems like climate change may, in part, reflect the fact that these news topics tend to be written in less readable language than most others. Indeed, the failure of many citizens (notably those in countries like the United States and the United Kingdom) to understand what climate change is or the scale of the scientific consensus and alarm about it (Lewis and Boyce, 2009) may not simply be a product of efforts to make it appear controversial. The fact that the least readable topics—the environment and politics—are precisely the places where climate change is most likely to be discussed may also play a role in maintaining this confusion.

We can also begin to separate different linguistic features that allow new kinds of journalistic writing. It may be possible, for example, for political coverage to strive for greater levels of readability while retaining low levels of subjectivity—in short, to be popular rather than populist.

These are early days for this form of analysis, and our findings remain suggestive. The ability to extract automatically the key actors of the news narrative, generating a network of their interactions (Sudhahar, Franzosi, and Cristianini, 2011), or to compare the preferences of readers with those of editors on a large scale (Hensinger, Flaounas, and Cristianini, 2012), allows us to begin to develop these findings. While certain things remain beyond the scope of the analyses described here (identifying a stereotypical gender representation, for example), further research may allow us to develop more sophisticated machine-based tools that can be taught the same kinds of interpretative frameworks used by human coders.

Further reading

For more on computational analysis, see Ilias Flaounas *et al.*'s 2010 article in *PLoS One* "The Structure of EU Mediasphere" (2010) and Flaounas *et al.*'s 2013 article "Research Methods in the Age of Digital Journalism: Massive-scale Automated Analysis of News-content—Topics,

Style and Gender" in *Digital Journalism*. For more on the compatibility of quantitative and qualitative research methods, see Justin Lewis' 2008 chapter "Thinking by Numbers: Cultural Analysis and the Use of Data."

Acknowledgments

We thank Ilias Flaounas, Omar Ali, Saatviga Sudhahar, Sen Jia, and Nick Mosdell for their contribution to some of the studies covered in this chapter. Thomas Lansdall-Welfare and Nello Cristianini are supported by the EU-funded project ThinkBIG (FP7-IDEAS-ERC 339365).

References

Alexander, S. (1994) "Newspaper Coverage of Athletics as a Function of Gender." *Women's Studies International Forum* 17: 655–662.

Baccianella, S., Esuli, A. and Sebastiani, F. (2010) "SentiWordNet 3.0: An Enhanced Lexical Resource for Sentiment Analysis and Opinion Mining." *Seventh Conference on International Language Resources and Evaluation* 25: 2200–2204.

Bagdikian, B.H. (2000) *The Media Monopoly*. Boston, MA: Beacon Press.

Bishop, R. (2003) "Missing in Action: Feature Coverage of Women's Sports in Sports Illustrated." *Journal of Sport and Social Issues* 27: 184–194.

Bollacker, K., Evans, C., Paritosh, P., Sturge, T. and Taylor, J. (2008) "Freebase: A Collaboratively Created Graph Database for Structuring Human Knowledge." In *Proceedings of the 2008 ACM SIGMOD International Conference on Management of Data*, Vancouver, Canada, 9–12 June, pp. 1247–1250. New York: ACM.

Bradski, G. (2000) "The Opencv Library." *Doctor Dobbs Journal* 25(11): 120–126.

Carter, C., Branston, G. and Allan, S. (1998) *News, Gender and Power*. London, UK: Routledge.

Conboy, M. (2007) *The Language of the News*. London, UK: Routledge.

Connel, I. (1998) "Mistaken Identities: Tabloid and Broadsheet News Discourse." *Javnost—The Public* 5(3): 11–31.

Cristianini, N. and Shawe-Taylor, J. (2000) *An Introduction to Support Vector Machines and Other Kernel-Based Learning Methods*. Cambridge, UK: Cambridge University Press.

Cunningham, H., Maynard, D., Kalina, B. and Valentin, T. (2002) "GATE: A Framework and Graphical Development Environment for Robust NLP Tools and Applications." In *Proceedings of the 40th Anniversary Meeting of the Association for Computational Linguistics*, Philadelphia, PA, pp. 168–175. Stroudsburg: ACL.

Eagle, N., Pentland, A. and Lazer, D. (2009) "Inferring Friendship Network Structure by Using Mobile Phone Data." *Proceedings of the National Academy of Sciences* 106: 15274–15278.

Earl, J., Martin, A., McCarthy, J.D. and Soule, S.A. (2004) "The Use of Newspaper Data in the Study of Collective Action." *Annual Review of Sociology* 30: 65–80.

Eastman, S.T. and Billings, A.C. (2000) "Sportscasting and Sports Reporting: The Power of Gender Bias." *Journal of Sport and Social Issues* 24: 192–213.

Echmann, J.-P., Moses, E. and Sergi, D. (2004) "Entropy of Dialogues Creates Coherent Structures in E-mail Traffic." *Proceedings of the National Academy of Sciences* 101: 14333–14337.

Flaounas, I., Ali, O., Lansdall-Welfare, T., De Bie, T., Mosdell, N., Lewis, J., et al. (2013) "Research Methods in the Age of Digital Journalism: Massive-Scale Automated Analysis of News-Content—Topics, Style and Gender." *Digital Journalism* 1(1): 102–116.

Flaounas, I., Ali, O., Turchi, M., Snowsill, T., Nicart, F., De Bie, T., et al. (2011) "NOAM: News Outlets Analysis and Monitoring System." In *Proceedings of the 2011 ACM SIGMOD International Conference on Management of Data*, Athens, Greece, 12–16 June, pp. 1275–1278. New York: ACM.

Flaounas, I., Turchi, M., Ali, O., Fyson, N., De Bie, T., Mosdell, N., et al. (2010) "The Structure of EU Mediasphere." *PLoS ONE* 5: e14243.

Flesch, R. (1948) "A New Readability Yardstick." *Journal of Applied Psychology* 32: 221–233.

Hensinger, E., Flaounas, I. and Cristianini, N. (2012) "What Makes Us Click? Modelling and Predicting the Appeal of News Articles." In *Proceedings of the 1st International Conference on Pattern Recognition Applications and Methods*, Vilamoura, Algarve, 6–8 February, pp. 41–50. Portugal: SciTePress.

Jacobs, R.N. (1996) "Producing the News, Producing the Crisis: Narrativity, Television and News Work." *Media, Culture & Society* 18: 373–397.

Jia, S. and Cristianini, N. (2015) "Learning to Classify Gender from Four Million Images." *Pattern Recognition Letters* 58: 36–41.

Jia, S., Lansdall-Welfare, T. and Cristianini, N. (2015) "Measuring Gender Bias in News Images." In *NewsWWW 2015—2nd Workshop on Web and Data Science for News Publishing*, Florence, Italy, 19 May.

Jones, M. and Viola, P. (2003) *Fast Multi-View Face Detection*. Tech. Rep. TR2003-96. Cambridge, MA: Mitsubishi Electric Research Laboratories.

Lansdall-Welfare, T., Lampos, V. and Cristianini, N. (2012) "Effects of the Recession on Public Mood in the UK." In *Proceedings of the 21st International Conference Companion on World Wide Web*, Lyon, France, 16–20 April, pp. 1221–1226. New York: ACM.

Lansdall-Welfare, T., Sudhahar, S., Veltri, G. and Cristianini, N. (2014) "On the Coverage of Science in the Media: A Big Data Study on the Impact of the Fukushima Disaster." *Big Data, 2014 IEEE International Conference on Big Data*, Washington, DC, 27–30 October, pp. 60–66. IEEE.

Lazer, D., Pentland, A.S., Adamic, L., Aral, S., Barabasi, A.L., Brewer, D., et al. (2009) "Life in the Network: The Coming Age of Computational Social Science." *Science* 323(5915): 721–723.

Len-Rios, M. E., Rodgers, S., Thorson, E. and Yoon, D. (2006) "Representation of Women in News and Photos: Comparing Content to Perceptions." *Journal of Communication* 55(1): 152–168.

Lewis, J. (2008) "Thinking by Numbers: Cultural Analysis and the Use of Data." In Bennett, T. and Frow, J. (eds) *Handbook of Cultural Analysis*. London, UK: Sage.

Lewis, J. and Boyce, T. (2009) "Climate Change and the Media: The Scale of the Challenge." In Boyce, T. and Lewis, J. (eds) *Climate Change and the Media*. New York, NY: Peter Lang.

Lewis, J. and Cushion, S. (2009) "The Thirst to Be First: An Analysis of Breaking News Stories and their Impact on the Quality of 24-Hour News Coverage in the UK." *Journalism Practice* 3(3): 304–318.

Lewis, J., Inthorn, S. and Wahl-Jorgensen, K. (2005) *Citizens or Consumers: The Media and the Decline of Political Participation*. Milton Keynes, UK: Open University Press.

Liu, B. (2007) *Web Data Mining, Exploring Hyperlinks, Contents, and Usage Data*. New York, NY: Springer.

Manning, C. and Schutze, H. (1999) *Foundations of Statistical Natural Language Processing*. Cambridge, MA: MIT Press.

McChesney, R.W. and Nichols, J. (2010) *The Death and Life of American Journalism: The Media Revolution that Will Begin the World Again*. New York, NY: Nation Books.

Michel, J.-B., Shen, Y.K., Aiden, A.P., Veres, A., Gray, M.K., the Google Books Team, et al. (2011) "Quantitative Analysis of Culture Using Millions of Digitized Books." *Science* 331: 176–182.

Miller, T. (2009) *Television Studies: The Basics*. New York, NY: Routledge.

Morgan, M. (ed.) (2002) *Against the Mainstream: The Selection Works of George Gerbner*. New York, NY: Peter Lang.

Nivre, J., Hall, J., Nilsson, J., Chanev, A., Eryigit, G., Kübler, G., et al. (2007) "MaltParser: A Language-Independent System for Data-Driven Dependency Parsing." *Natural Language Engineering* 13(2): 95–135.

Ofcom (2014) *News Consumption in the UK: 2014 Report*. Available from: http://stakeholders.ofcom.org. uk/binaries/research/tv-research/news/2014/News_Report_2014.pdf (accessed June 2014).

Shawe-Taylor, J. and Cristianini, N. (2004) *Kernel Methods for Pattern Analysis*. Cambridge, UK: Cambridge University Press.

Sudhahar, S., Franzosi, R. and Cristianini, N. (2011) "Automating Quantitative Narrative Analysis of News Data." *JMLR: Workshop and Conference Proceedings* 17: 63–71.

Sudhahar, S., Veltri, G.A. and Cristianini, N. (2015) "Automated Analysis of the US Presidential Elections Using Big Data and Network Analysis." *Big Data & Society* 2(1): DOI: 10.1177/2053951715572916.

Szella, M., Lambiotte, R. and Thurner, S. (2010) "Multirelational Organization of Large-Scale Social Networks in an Online World." *Proceedings of the National Academy of Sciences* 107: 13636–13641.

Toutanova, K., Klein, D., Manning, C. and Singer, C. (2003) "Feature-Rich Part-of-Speech Tagging with a Cyclic Dependency Network." In *Proceedings of HLTNAACL*, pp. 252–259. Stroudsburg: ACL.

Watts, D. (2007) "A Twenty-First Century Science." *Nature* 445: 489.

10

THE ETHNOGRAPHY OF DIGITAL JOURNALISM

Chris Paterson

Digital journalism has developed as a genre of media production with a variety of characteristics which make it both distinct from and similar to whatever 'journalism' had previously been (a matter determined both by whom you ask and what they see as the purpose of this particular form of story-telling). Yet two decades from its advent, we are often constrained in understanding digital news manufacturing (but is it 'journalism'?) through an entrenched reliance on a remarkable era of newsroom research centered in the 1970s: the tradition of the ethnographic sociology of news production.

The US sociologists Gaye Tuchman (1978, 2014) and Herbert Gans (1979), political scientist Edward Epstein (1973), and British social scientist Philip Schlesinger (1978, 1980), in particular, used their long-term systematic observation of journalistic work—and the organizational structures surrounding it—to provide richly detailed, vividly described, and well-theorized examinations of how people within particular large media organizations followed—day in and day out—a rigid set of working practices (the 'routines' of news production) which created the world's daily diet of news. The research of Buckalew (1970), Warner (1970), Altheide (1976), Golding and Elliott (1979), and Fishman (1980) was also influential. These scholars helped us all not just to see that 'the news' is nothing more, and nothing less, than a set of stories told (and sold) to the public by a small group of people who have declared themselves uniquely qualified to do so, but also to understand, and reliably predict, why the news looked as it did.

Why immerse?

At the time this seemed a controversial, or even unnecessary, exercise. Had not Warren Breed (1955) and David Manning White (1950) adequately explained, in providing the foundations of gatekeeping theory, how stories get into newspapers—and how institutional policy made news less of a 'reflection of reality' than many assumed (Shoemaker and Reese, 2014: 35)? Did we really need sociologists to spend weeks, months, or years minutely examining and theorizing journalistic work to tell us something more? As Reese explains, by the end of the 1960s, scholars were less inclined to accept 'functionalist' explanations of communication at face value; thanks to the work of Goffman (1974), Berger and Luckman (1966), and later, Gitlin (1980) and Hall (1992), we increasingly understood that media present certain, ideologically loaded, interpretations of the world (at the expense of other interpretations) and that those collectively shape what we all regard as 'real.' If that were the case, intensive examination of the processes of news making was essential.

Tuchman would write decades later in a forward to the latest edition of Shoemaker and Reese's iconic *Mediating the Message*:

> looking back, I don't think that the authors of those newsmaking studies—Mark Fishman, Herbert Gans, Todd Gitlin, Harvey Molotch, Michael Schudson, and I—realized that we were documenting what Dan Hallin has since called the "high modernism" of American journalism, a period when newsworkers pledged obedience to codes of professionalism and claimed their news coverage was independent of the financial interests of the large corporations, then beginning to consolidate their grasp on the media landscape and eventually to hold it in thrall.
>
> *(Tuchman, 2014: xi)*

That body of research explained a great deal about why the 'news' of that period looked the way it did, why it represented certain interests in society better than others, and why it considered a fairly narrow range of happenings in the world to be 'news.' News values research (Galtung and Ruge, 1970), emerging around the same time, demonstrated that we can fairly accurately plot what news workers are going to write about each day and what they will discard as 'un-newsworthy,' but it frustratingly told us nothing about working practices which consistently shape news in a particular way. Yet from the 1980s until only the past decade, interest in long-term ethnographic research into newsrooms had faded. Vitally, for a brief moment, that early body of work permitted some limited understanding of the social construction of our world: why we carry certain shared 'pictures in our heads' of the way the world is (as put by Berger and Luckman, 1966; Fishman, 1980; Tuchman, 1978; Walter Lippman, 1922).

Reliance on those older studies to explain contemporary digital news production processes has begun to seem less adequate. Relationships between publishers of information and their sources have become all the more complex and all the more crucial, and information production is far more widely disbursed, and often informalized, than in the days when a fairly small number of large broadcasters and newspapers dominated news production. But newsrooms—while these might now be defined more broadly—still often remain the principle locations of the collective decision making and working practices which generate the information we tend to label as 'news,' and the locations where an often difficult and painful transition from analogue to digital journalism continues to take place. Has the relevance of these earlier works of news sociology faded because contemporary digital newsrooms bear an ever decreasing resemblance to newsrooms of the late 1960s and 1970s? Moller Hartley's (2011) ethnographic study of Danish online newsrooms, for example, suggests not, as it builds usefully on Tuchman's categories of news to explore how contemporary journalists routinize the handling of 'breaking news' in predictable ways, but Hartley also found that the explanatory theory offered by Tuchman required some elaboration to account for the modern speed of news production and other attributes of online news.

Importantly, this early ethnographic sociology of news uniquely explained the news process while avoiding the trap of the 'attitudinal fallacy' (Jerolmack and Khan, 2014). In the context of news, that is the resilient but naïve faith that what journalists say about their work (in interviews with researchers or in surveys) explains a significant amount about the manufacturing of the news. It is a trap in any social research to allow the phenomenon under examination to describe itself, but it is especially ironic in the examination of journalism that social researchers often simultaneously critique journalists' claims to have access to a 'truth' beyond the reach of the rest of us, while easily accepting as objective reality journalists' (necessarily) subjective interpretations of their own practice. Jerolmack and Khan survey a body of research demonstrating that what people say is more often than not a poor predictor of what they do, in support of their argument that surveys and interviews too often confuse attitudes with actual behavior (2014). Put simply, this is a good argument that, if you want to understand why journalism is manufactured in the way it is, you need to systematically observe the process: you need to engage with the ethnographic sociology of news production.

Many researchers who embrace an observational, ethnographic approach to understanding how 'the news' is created also treat interviewing and other research methods (document analysis, news content research, examination of the audience/users) as necessary, complementary approaches to gathering data which allow the researcher to both describe the processes they seek to understand in richer detail and with greater nuance, and to 'triangulate,' comparing information discovered through one approach with information gleaned by another, moving ever closer to a (never fully obtainable) accurate and rich description. Epstein (1973) was perhaps the first news researcher to effectively employ a multi-method approach, involving interviews, observation, and content analysis, as well as detailed analysis of the institutions he wrote about. His use of content analysis enabled him to contrast interview data with actual television news output and find revealing discrepancies.

The essential failing of ethnography, particularly as argued by positivists, is that it represents a phenomenon from a single perspective and offers little opportunity for confirmation by other researchers. But the ethnographer of journalism will rarely claim to reveal and explain everything, instead seeking only to describe their research setting as comprehensively as is possible. As expressed by Clifford (Clifford and Marcus, 1986), the hope is only to reveal a 'partial truth' in. Ethnography is a process of translating cultural meanings and social practices which are relevant to the subjects of the research—in this case, mostly journalists—into richly detailed interpretations which will be recognizable to broader audiences. Engaging in this translation honestly requires taking care not to overly interpret or assume meaning without cause.

The ethnography of news production has borrowed from, and been grounded in, the theory and research methodologies of anthropology, sociology, organizational studies, critical media studies, and more recently, the study of professions (Abbott, 1993). But few ethnographers of media production fail to mention the inspiration and guidance of cultural anthropologist Clifford Geertz (1973), who is widely credited for reviving interest in long-term, immersive 'fieldwork' as the means to understand unfamiliar human cultures. Exploitative, paternalistic, and ethnocentric—as well as scientifically dubious—accounts of primitive and exotic 'others', which became a prominent feature of popular magazines like *National Geographic* in the 1950s, had required reassessment of the role of the anthropologist and the processes by which one culture learns about another.

Clifford and Marcus (1986) focused on published, highly polished accounts of social life which they termed the 'poetics of ethnography,' whereas for Geertz the key to successfully enabling one culture to understand another was a set of richly detailed and elegantly crafted field notes of observations. 'Thick description' (Geertz, 1973) is the painstaking art of minutely and precisely describing the social processes witnessed by the ethnographer: noting the most mundane details of what people do and how they interact and finding an effective balance between describing them in writing that is engrossing, detailed, and neutral and writing that identifies those observations which most matter and clearly ascribing meaning to them.

In the context of newsroom research, this might be done through noting, and exploring, moments of tension where cracks appear in the efficient news production machinery: a senior journalist causally remarking to a junior colleague 'I wouldn't have done it that way,' a multi-skilled journalist making one less verification telephone call than they had hoped to in order to have enough time to produce their story for multiple media platforms, an editor swearing under her breath because an accounting department email has just demanded cuts to the cost of planned coverage (examples from this author's ethnographic experience).

Indeed, one of the greatest values of ethnographic data, differentiating it from data obtained by other means, is its ability to reveal inconsistencies and conflicts in the actions of informants. Schlesinger (1980) reflected on his own ethnographic research, writing that ethnography uniquely permits the observation of moments of crisis, those occasional intra-organizational struggles about how to frame news, requiring the revision of news production routines. A journalist might helpfully recount in an interview with a researcher how some effort to aspire to the highest ideal of good journalism had to be compromised by the realities of economics or politics (or just because her editor didn't like her approach) but revealing such moments of tension (a) isn't always in the interests of interviewees and (b) is, as noted earlier, also nothing more than a subjective interpretation of an occurrence. Interviews, and on a larger scale, surveys, can give researchers clues to points of tension in the machinery of journalism (Kohut's [2000] revealing survey of self-censorship is a case in point), but only extended, systematic observation of news production practices can reveal these in a way in which they can be reliably described and analyzed. As both the product and practice of journalism became 'digital', the tradition of long-term researcher immersion in the news production process had faded. The new genre of 'online news' evolved amid a great deal of hype about its potential to be something far greater than its predecessor, but with little ongoing collection of empirical data to explain what it actually is. For example, a decade ago, Deuze, Neuberger, and Paulussen (2004) noted a distance between the ideals shared by online journalists and their practices, but observed that little empirical evidence had been published about the reasons for this distance. Digital journalism was becoming the dominant way people learn about the world, yet research into how it is made remained sparse. But many scholars have since focused their efforts on the (predominately or exclusively) digital newsroom and the domains of news production increasingly stretching far beyond newsrooms.

The limited ethnographically informed research into news production settings which blend traditional news forms with digital production processes and digital modes of news delivery—the central characteristic of 'convergent' news production—has demonstrated that new news production suffers from many of the same constraints as old news production, only with new constrains like 24-hour production cycles, 'shovel-ware' dependence on public relations and wire services to meet content production targets (Paterson and Domingo, 2008), the constant burden of immediacy (Weiss and Domingo, 2010) and, the most recent trend to bewitch and beguile news workers, the chase of the proper web metrics (Anderson, 2011b).

In his writing on the transition to online news at a Dublin newspaper, Anthony Cawley managed in a few paragraphs to both richly convey the atmosphere of the newsroom he was examining and vividly and clearly explain the importance of what he was witnessing—the effect of print to digital transition for one journalist:

> The newsroom looks like a normal print newsroom: messy desks, coffee mugs, background noise of ringing telephones, scenery of PC screens displaying stories in various stages of completion. The journalists are a bit young and casually dressed, but little else stands out. On Anderson's desk are the normal tools of a print journalist: a notebook, a pen, a telephone, his contacts book, a telephone book, a tape recorder, and a PC. His work practices resemble those of a print journalist: he calls sources, press offices, organisations, writes down what they say and assembles the story into an inverted pyramid structure.

One difference is significant, however. Each time he finishes a run at a story—adds fresh information or reaction—he publishes the update directly himself. A reader who has been paying close attention this morning would have seen the G8 arrest story evolve from bare facts, to having reaction from a source close to the arrested man, to having official confirmation of his deportation, to having his flight and expected arrival time. Anderson controls the information gathering process, the writing, the sub-editing and the publication of his story. He controls stages where, conventionally, a sub-editor, a page setter or a printer would have assumed responsibility on the story's journey from the newsroom to the public domain. This is an online newsroom, Anderson is an online journalist, and the traditional demarcation of news production doesn't apply.

(Cawley, 2008: 47)

Process

Paterson and Domingo summarized the benefits of ethnography in the examination of online news in this way:

- Gathers a huge amount of very rich first-hand data.
- The researcher directly witnesses actions, routines, and definitions of technology and social relations.
- The researcher can gain a confident status with the actors, obtaining insiders' points of view.
- The researcher can witness conflicts and processes of evolution.
- Analysis of the gathered data allows a comprehensive description of the social use of a technology and offers insights to understand the factors involved in its social construction and shaping. (Paterson & Domingo, 2008: 5)

The first challenges in taking an ethnographic approach to news production research come before a researcher approaches any news organization for permission to observe their work. Like all good research, clear, well-crafted research questions are vital at the outset, and it is these which would determine if observational research is appropriate and where it should take place. If the question is why the content produced by a media organization is as it is, an ethnographic approach might be the only viable research tool.

If the researcher's hope is to explain all news production or the production practices across a certain type of news (net-native sports news sites in the German language, for example), there might be little reason to expect that close analysis of practices at one exemplar from this group would reliably explain anything about the practices of the whole group. But, conversely, extended ethnographic analysis across several, or many, organizations—in the hope of assessing differences and better grasping a broader truth about a whole class of media producers—is normally impossible for individual researchers.

Might one simply compress observation to a few days, and thereby improve one's chances of getting in? US news ethnographer David Ryfe has argued that ethnographic newsroom research which falls short of many months, and even years, of observation, has little hope of capturing the dynamics of newsroom change and capturing subtle details of how production processes and specific journalistic cultures shape our news. But he makes this point with the acknowledgement that contemporary realities for research students and professional academics make such long-term field research exceedingly rare (Ryfe, 2016).

But time with a news organization is also dependent on the extent to which the institution will allow itself to be observed, and that is a matter for negotiation once the doors to some observation have been opened. Schlesinger (1980) reflected on the challenging process of gaining the access to conduct long-term observational research within media organizations, observing that it is usually challenging, and that access, when granted, can be tenuous. Paterson observed in the introduction to his partially ethnographic study of television news agencies that a longstanding obstacle to genuinely ethnographic production research "is that organizations risk criticism when they permit independent analysis of what they do: what makes sense in the context of their business may look irresponsible or arrogant to people outside of that context" (2011a: xi). Suspicion and caution about the purpose of media production research from inside media organizations continues to be an obstacle for researchers, although there are few records to indicate how much of an obstacle, since researchers tend not to publish accounts of their struggles to gain access or the refusals they receive.

Paterson and Zoellner (2010) commented on the usefulness of some prior professional media or journalism experience in gaining research access based on a small survey of production researchers who generally agreed this offers an important advantage. Munnik (2016) and Garcia (2008) both helpfully reflect on the challenge; Munnik in the increasingly familiar context of seeking access to media organizations which were especially defensive and reclusive following a series of scandals involving the UK media.

With an alien culture laid out before them, ethnographers are challenged to know where to focus their observations and how to use them to draw conclusions about journalistic work. That process is simplified through the application of a clear theoretical framework to understand journalistic work. Ida Willig has explained the value of Pierre Bourdieu's reflexive sociology in providing greater insight into ethnographic newsroom research (Willig, 2013), and Bourdieu himself has suggested the utility of viewing journalistic work as a 'field' and has reflected on the process of participant observation (2003). Willig suggests that Bourdieu's field theory provides a framework to "analyse journalistic practice at the same time as macro contexts outside of the newsroom" and suggests a key advantage of doing so is a "consistent, theoretical framework incorporating the analytical concepts highly applicable in empirical research" (2013: 384). Others have found this approach unhelpful and have grounded their work in other theoretical frames such as gatekeeping (Paterson, 2011a), actor-network theory (Domingo, 2008), and others.

Well-theorized newsroom research by Paulussen *et al.* (2011), Domingo (2008), and Ryfe (2012), among others, has helpfully shifted the discourse about convergence from technological or organizational determinism to an approach focusing on human agency and the varying ways news workers are adapting to technological challenges. Geens conducted research for 4 months at a Flemish regional news website in Belgium and confirmed earlier research which found that the convergent (what Geens terms 'Post-Fordist') newsroom job descriptions have changed dramatically from traditional news production, with most people in the converged newsrooms having many tasks and goals as opposed to just one or two main tasks, with hierarchies, relationships, and criteria for reward all becoming more complex (Paulussen *et al.*, 2011).

This author sought to move beyond major news providers to seek understanding of how the principal sources of the raw components of their stories were manufactured by news agencies such as the *Associated Press*, *Reuters*, and *Agence France Press*, which for a century had produced for the world's media the easily digestible bits of information which make up all the reporting which a news organization cannot do on its own. Observation in the newsrooms of three international television news agencies provided a first-hand glimpse of the internal struggles and practices which determine which television pictures of global events every other media outlet in the world has to work with each day; effectively, what ingredients are available from hour to hour to the chefs (the editors at every television station globally) to make that dish we readily consume each day: television news (Paterson, 2011a: x). As news agencies transition into a fully digital age, they still set the agenda for global media (Lewis, Williams, and Franklin, 2008; Paterson, 2007), but research has failed to keep pace with understanding how their non-stop, multi-media, global digital news product is created (Paterson, 2011b).

We learn from the accounts of the ethnographers that cooperation between old and new media is uncommon—that in fact new media journalists continue to mostly operate independently of old media and are normally considered to have a lower status than old media journalists. The new breeds of journalists are often chained to their desks and tend to communicate exclusively through their computers. As Deuze (2008: 204) expressed it "a picture emerges of an atomized profession, isolated and connected at the same time, yet also blind to each other (and thus itself), and the wider society it operates in." There is not integration, but frequently division and distance. Extended ethnographic research into combined legacy media (print, television, radio) and new media news operations often found that online news professionals were lacking authority and legitimacy within their organizations and growing frustrated at their lack of status. But as Deuze (2008) suggests, their 'liquid,' flexible, and changing identities mirror the 'liquid,' constantly shifting nature of the news of the online news product, as media work generally becomes ever more precarious (Gill and Pratt, 2008). And Anderson (2011a, 2013) has demonstrated by innovatively (and metaphorically, it must be said) 'blowing up the newsroom' that news production is increasingly distributed across many actors and different kinds of institutions, but these networks of production—the news ecosystem—can be richly described and plotted.

Conclusion

As the recent comprehensive and long-term ethnographic research projects of Usher (2011, 2014), Ryfe (2012), Domingo (2008), Boczkowski (2004), and others have shown, it *is* possible to gain access to new (net-native) and to fast changing traditional (legacy) news organizations and comprehensively explore and theorize their news manufacturing processes using the tools of immersive ethnography. As the definitions of 'news' and of 'newswork' become ever more elastic, it will be increasingly difficult to determine the most useful target of ethnographic research, just at these changes make such research ever more important. But more is needed than the patience and will to engage in such research: media institutions must remain willing to exhibit accountability through permitting intrusive investigation (and not seeking to censor it when it has been done), and academic institutions and funding bodies must recognize that there remains no better way to understand the creation of our 'shared reality' and to provide the resources and time for it to happen.

Further reading

The two volumes of *Making Online News* (2008, 2011) edited by this author and David Domingo collected research from around the world from within fast evolving digital newsrooms. Usher's explanation of her research in *Making News at the New York Times* (2014) will be useful to prospective ethnographers of the digital newsroom. Cottle (2007) provided an overview of the role of ethnography in journalism and its future directions, and the 2016 collection, *Advancing Media Production Research*, attempts to expand the horizons of ethnographic production research through new approaches to method and theory and attempts to cross methodological, disciplinary, and genre boundaries.

References

Abbott, A. (1993) *The System of the Professions: An Essay on the Division of Expert Labor*. Chicago, IL: University of Chicago Press.

Altheide, D. (1976) *Creating Reality: How TV News Distorts Events*. Beverly Hills, CA: Sage.

Anderson, C.W. (2011a) "Blowing up the Newsroom: Ethnography in the Age of Distributed Journalism." In Domingo, D. and Paterson, C. (eds) *Making Online News, Newsroom Ethnographies in the Second Decade of Internet Journalism*. New York, NY: Peter Lang, pp. 151–60.

Anderson, C.W. (2011b) "Between Creative and Quantified Audiences: Web Metrics and Changing Patterns of Newswork in Local US Newsrooms." *Journalism* 12(5): 550–566.

Anderson, C.W. (2013) *Rebuilding the News: Metropolitan Journalism in the Digital Age*. Philadelphia, PA: Temple University Press.

Berger, P.L. and Luckman, T. (1966) *The Social Construction of Reality: A Treatise in the Sociology of Knowledge*. Garden City, NY: Anchor Books.

Boczkowski, P.J. (2004) *Digitizing the News: Innovation in Online Newspapers*. Cambridge, MA: MIT Press.

Bourdieu, P. (2003) *Distinction: A Social Critique of the Judgement of Taste*. London, UK: Routledge.

Breed, W. (1955) "Social Control in the Newsroom: A Functional Analysis." *Social Forces* 33: 326–335.

Buckalew, J. (1970) "News Elements and Selection by Television News Editors." *Journal of Broadcasting* (Winter): 47–54.

Cawley, A. (2008) "News Production in an Irish Online Newsroom: Practice, Process, and Culture." In Paterson, C. and Domingo, D. (eds) *Making Online News: The Ethnography of New Media Production*. New York, NY: Peter Lang, pp. 45–60.

Clifford, J. and Marcus, G. (1986) *Writing Culture: The Poetics and Politics of Ethnography*. Berkeley, CA: University of California Press.

Cottle, S. (2007) "Ethnography and Journalism: New(s) Departures in the Field." *Sociology Compass* 1(1): 1–16.

Deuze, M. (2008) "Epilogue: Toward a Sociology of Online News." In Paterson, C. and Domingo, D. (eds) *Making Online News: The Ethnography of New Media Production*. New York, NY: Peter Lang, pp. 199–210.

Deuze, M., Neuberger, C. and Paulussen, C. (2004) "Journalism Education and Online Journalists in Belgium, Germany, and the Netherlands." *Journalism Studies* 5(1): 19–29.

Domingo, D. (2008) "When Immediacy Rules: Online Journalism Models in Four Catalan Online Newsrooms." In Paterson, C. and Domingo, D. (eds) *Making Online News: The Ethnography of New Media Production*. New York, NY: Peter Lang, pp. 113–126.

Epstein, E.J. (1973) *News from Nowhere: Television and the News*. New York, NY: Random House.

Fishman, M. (1980) *Manufacturing the News*. Austin, TX: University of Texas Press.

Galtung, J. and Ruge, M. (1970) "The Structure of Foreign News." In Tunstall, J. (ed.) *Media Sociology*. London, UK: Constable.

Gans, H.J. (1979) *Deciding What's News: A Study of CBS Evening News, NBC Nightly News, Newsweek, and Time*. Evanston, IL: Northwestern University Press.

Garcia. E.P. (2008) "Print and Online Newsrooms in Argentinean Media: Autonomy and Professional Identity." In Paterson, C. and Domingo, D. (eds) *Making Online News: The Ethnography of New Media Production*. New York, NY: Peter Lang, pp. 61–76.

Geertz, C. (1973) *Interpretation of Cultures*. New York, NY: Basic Books.

Gill, R. and Pratt, A. (2008) "In the Social Factory? Immaterial Labour, Precariousness and Cultural Work." *Theory, Culture & Society* 25(7–8): 1–30.

Gitlin, T. (1980) *The Whole World is Watching: Mass Media in the Making and Unmaking of the New Left*. Berkeley, CA: University of California Press.

Goffman, E. (1974) *Frame Analysis: An Essay on the Organization of Experience*. Cambridge, MA: Harvard University Press.

Golding, P. and Elliott, P. (1979) *Making the News*. New York, NY: Longman.

Hall, S. (1992) "Encoding, Decoding." In During, S. (ed.) *The Cultural Studies Reader*. London, UK: Routledge, pp. 90–103.

Hartley, J.N. (2011) "Routinizing Breaking News: Categories and Hierarchies In Danish Online Newsrooms." In Domingo, D. and Paterson, C. (eds) *Making Online News, Newsroom Ethnographies in the Second Decade of Internet Journalism*. New York, NY: Peter Lang, pp. 73–86.

Jerolmack, C. and Khan, S. (2014) "Talk Is Cheap: Ethnography and the Attitudinal Fallacy." *Sociological Methods & Research* 43(2): 178–209.

Kohut, A. (2000) "Self-Censorship: Counting the Ways." *Columbia Journalism Review*, May/June, pp. 42–43.

Lewis, J., Williams, A. and Franklin, B. (2008) "A Compromised Fourth Estate? UK News Journalism, Public Relations and News Sources." *Journalism Studies* 9(1): 1–20.

Lippman, W. (1922) *Public Opinion*. New York, NY: Macmillan.

Munnik, M.B. (2016) "When You Can't Rely on Private or Public: Using the Ethnographic self as Reference." In Paterson, C., Lee, D., Saha, A. and Zoellner, A. (eds) *Advancing Media Production Research*. Basingstoke, UK: Palgrave Macmillan, pp. 147–160.

Paterson, C. (2007) "International News on the Internet: Why More is Less." *The International Journal of Communication Ethics* 4(1/2): 57–65.

Paterson, C. (2011a) *The International Television News Agencies: The World from London*. New York, NY: Peter Lang.

Paterson, C. (2011b) "Convergence in the News Wholesalers: Trends in International News Agencies." In Domingo, D. and Paterson C. (eds) *Making Online News Newsroom Ethnographies in the Second Decade of Internet Journalism*. New York, NY: Peter Lang, pp. 129–140.

Paterson, C. and Domingo, D. (2008) *Making Online News: The Ethnography of New Media Production*. New York, NY: Peter Lang.

Paterson, C., Lee, D., Saha, A. and Zoellner, A. (eds). (2016) *Advancing Media Production Research*. Basingstoke, UK: Palgrave Macmillan.

Paterson, C. and Zoellner, A. (2010) "The Efficacy of Professional Experience in the Ethnographic Investigation of Production." *Journal of Media Practice* 11(2): 97–109.

Paulussen, S., Geens, D. and Vandenbrande, K. (2011) "Fostering a Culture of Collaboration: Organizational Challenges of Newsroom Innovation." In Domingo, D. and Paterson C. (eds) *Making Online News: Newsroom Ethnography in the Second Decade of Internet Journalism*. New York, NY: Peter Lang, pp. 4–14.

Ryfe, D.M. (2012) *Can Journalism Survive? An Inside Look at American Newsrooms*. Cambridge, UK: Polity Press.

Ryfe, D.M. (2016) "The Importance of Time in Media Production Research." In Paterson, C., Lee, D., Saha, A. and Zoellner, A. (eds) *Advancing Media Production Research*. Basingstoke, UK: Palgrave Macmillan, pp. 38–50.

Schlesinger, P. (1978) *Putting "Reality" Together: BBC News*. London, UK: Constable.

Schlesinger, P. (1980) "Between Sociology and Journalism." In Christian, H. (ed.) *Sociology of the Press and Journalism*. Keele, UK: University of Keele.

Shoemaker, P. and Reese, S.D. (2014) *Mediating the Message*. New York, NY: Routledge.

Tuchman, G. (1978) *Making News: A Study in the Social Construction of Reality*. London, UK: Free Press.

Tuchman, G. (2014) "Forward." In Shoemaker, P. and Reese, S.D. (eds) *Mediating the Message*. New York, NY: Routledge, pp. ix–xii.

Usher, N. (2011) "Redefining Public Radio: Marketplace in the Digital Age." In Domingo, D. and Paterson C. (eds) *Making Online News: Newsroom Ethnography in the Second Decade of Internet Journalism*. New York, NY: Peter Lang, pp. 45–56.

Usher, N. (2014) *Making News at The New York Times*. Ann Arbor, MI: University of Michigan Press.

Warner, M. (1970) "Decision-Making in Network Television News." In Tunstall, J. (ed.) *Media Sociology*. London, UK: Constable, pp. 158–167.

Weiss, A.S. and Domingo, D. (2010) "Innovation Processes in Online Newsrooms as Actor-Networks and Communities of Practice." *New Media & Society* 12(7): 1156–1171.

White, D.M. (1950) "The Gate Keeper." *Journalism Quarterly* 27: 383–390.

Willig, I. (2013) "Newsroom Ethnography in a Field Perspective." *Journalism: Theory, Practice and Criticism* 14(3): 372–287.

11

INVESTIGATING 'CHURNALISM' IN REAL-TIME NEWS

Tom Van Hout and Sarah Van Leuven

Popularized by industry insider Nick Davies, 'churnalism' refers to the recycling of prepackaged public relations and press agency copy as news. In *Flat Earth News*, Davies (2008: 59) paints a bleak picture of "journalists who are no longer out gathering news but who are reduced instead to passive processors of whatever material comes their way, churning out stories whether real event or PR artifice, important or trivial, true or false." Davies' narrative is one of seemingly irreversible decline. Corporate interests have grown profit margins at the expense of staff numbers and news quality. Industrial concentration, uncertain labor conditions, standardization, and digital media technologies have caused fewer journalists to serve more media. Journalists themselves are no longer committed to uncovering truths. Instead, they rely on second-hand information and spread pseudo-news. Almost certainly a diagnosis of a terminal illness.

Davies' feather ruffling book, billed and received as a dog eat dog attack on journalism, is largely based on a study of UK print journalism (Lewis, Williams, and Franklin, 2008a). To verify the causality of ready-made source material in news reporting, the authors performed keyword-based content analyses of two single-week samples comprising 2,207 newspaper stories of UK domestic news and their respective public relations and news agency source materials. The study found that no less than 70 percent of all articles published in UK print journalism rely to varying degrees on prepackaged information. This source reliance was attributed to four interconnected 'rumors' which, taken together, contextualize changes in UK print journalism: (i) journalists have become news processors instead of generators; (ii) market demands force smaller workforces to produce more output; (iii) journalists have become less wary of PR copy; and (iv) editorial independence in UK newsrooms has decreased. The authors back up these claims with employment figures, profit margins and pagination patterns at UK national newspapers, and interview data. Lewis, Williams, and Franklin (2008a: 29–30) found that:

> approximately half (49 percent) of news stories published in the quality press and analysed for this study were wholly or mainly dependent on materials produced and distribute [sic] by wire services with a further fifth (21 percent) of stories containing some element of agency copy.

Furthermore, journalistic reliance on PR materials (Lewis, Williams, and Franklin, 2008a: 30):

> is similarly striking with almost a fifth (19 percent) of stories deriving wholly (10 percent) or mainly (9 percent) from PR sources. A further 22 percent were either a mix of PR with other materials (11 percent) or mainly other information (11 percent) while 13 percent of stories appeared to contain PR materials which could not be identified.

These findings provide evidence for the commercialization of news media, increased productivity demands in UK newsrooms, the instrumental role of news subsidies, and evolving editorial standards in print journalism. However, when framed in a narrative of decline that laments the erosion of first-hand reporting and succumbs to romanticizing a bygone era populated by fiercely independent news hounds, we feel that Davies' take on news media is overly pessimistic and ultimately unproductive for understanding digital journalism.

Critical issues

Studies in different national settings have consistently linked higher workloads to increased reliance on prepackaged news sources (e.g. Carsten, 2004; Machill *et al.*, 2006; Reich, 2010). The debate on this development can be seen to spread between two poles, the first one seeing churnalism as a threat to the public service ideal of journalism—the reassuring but lofty idea that journalism safeguards democracies from corruption, falsehood, and malgovernance by exposing wrongdoing, providing unbiased information, and mobilizing the public. For instance, Jackson and Moloney (2015) argue that churnalism is characteristic of the broader 'PR-isation' of the news industry in which 'editorial subsidies' or 'page-ready content'—an updated and more extreme version of 'information subsidies' (see Gandy, 1982)—threaten independent journalism and democratic processes. Such claims are difficult to verify. The dearth of longitudinal studies suggests that we do not have much with which to compare contemporary journalistic practices. A notable exception is Reich's (2014: 363) study of sourcing practices in the Israeli press (studying 2001, 2006 and 2011), which demonstrates that "the changes found are too selective, modest and not always in the expected directions to be considered as a transformation of news routines and practices."

The second pole draws attention to the transition from legacy to digital news media and understands that journalism is no longer exclusively defined by eyewitness reporting. This is not to say that reporting news is considered irrelevant or that journalists no longer self-identify as knowledge mediators. However, the balance is shifting. A recent survey among Belgian journalists shows that 80 percent regularly (41.5 percent) to always (38.4 percent) work in the newsroom, with fieldwork being the exception rather than the norm (Van Leuven, Deprez, and Raeymaeckers, 2015). From this perspective, what Davies disqualifies as churnalism is but one aspect of a changing media ecology in which "newsmaking today is as much about managing multiple fast-moving flows of information already in circulation as it is about locating and sharing 'new' news" (Boyer, 2013: 2). Technological innovations support the transition from traditional, on-the-spot reporting to a combination of filtration and curation of existing information, and, to a lesser extent, slow journalism or long form journalism. Several studies show that journalists churn short news items so they can invest time in desk and field research. In addition, analysis and contextualization of events are increasingly viewed as the main task of journalists, while the direct reporting of facts is 'outsourced' to wire services and PR services (Broersma, 2009; Knight, 2011). This shift towards monitoring, filtering, and repurposing of content already in circulation forces attention to an understudied yet central aspect of contemporary newsroom praxis: office-based screenwork. In what follows, we discuss data collection procedures and analytic frameworks that have been used to measure reliably or otherwise convincingly study digital news production and sourcing practices.

Main research methods

Two methodological approaches to churnalism can be distinguished in terms of three sets of tensions: (i) offline versus online procedures for data collection; (ii) textual versus participant driven procedures for data analysis; and (iii) empirical breadth and statistical significance versus empirical depth and qualitative insight. The first approach content analyzes news texts by freezing news flows. The focus is on large samples of semiotic material (usually textual) which are then coded, quantified, or qualified. The second approach tracks, documents, and maps news flows across time and space. This approach often uses mixed methods to qualify professional practices from the perspectives of participants or to model the complexity and contingency of news flows in real time. We take both approaches in turn, starting with content analysis.

Freezing the flow

The general aim of content analysis is to make "replicable and valid inferences from texts (or other meaningful matter) to the contexts of their use" (Krippendorff, 2004: 18). Quantitative content analysis does so by systematically reducing manifest content to numbers and deriving meaning from this. Qualitative content analysis is equally systematic but reduces textual characteristics to key ideas or topics. For instance, in their study of online news flows, Karlsson and Strömbäck (2009) use content analysis to qualify and quantify the immediacy and interactivity of online news by (i) monitoring story updates using screen shots and manual downloads of front pages; (ii) using software to measure how often new stories appear on the top of the front page; and (iii) counting the number of top stories news sites publish or update during set intervals.

To illustrate how content analysis can be used to study churnalism, we draw on recent research on source reliance in foreign news. A costly and time-consuming endeavor, foreign news is an easy target for cost-cutting and hence churnalism. Indeed, news organizations are increasingly replacing their network of correspondents with home-based journalists who thus largely depend on news agency copy and (to a lesser degree) PR content (Hafez, 2009). Van Leuven, Deprez, and Raeymaeckers (2014) examined the extent to which churnalism occurred in the foreign news output of four Belgian newspapers over a period of 15 years (1995–2010) by quantifying the use of prepackaged media sources (news agency copy and recycled news articles from other media brands) and information subsidies or PR content (press releases, press conferences, information from spokespeople, and corporate websites) in 4,515 foreign news articles. Findings show that news agency copy, recycled news articles, and information subsidies were incorporated in respectively 25, 20.5, and 11.1 percent of the analyzed articles. These numbers are significantly lower than what Lewis, Williams, and Franklin (2008b) report. Differences may be attributed to national contexts (UK versus Belgium), empirical focus (domestic versus foreign news), and methodological approaches.

Van Leuven, Deprez, and Raeymaeckers (2014) used a rather conservative measure of churnalism for reasons of replicability and validity, taking into account only those instances where media sources and information subsidies were explicitly mentioned in the news output.

In contrast, Lewis, Williams, and Franklin (2008b) counted not only those instances where PR materials or agency content were explicitly used, but also those cases where a text (fragment) resembled PR. In those cases, researchers were required to follow a number of possible leads to determine whether or not PR played an agenda-setting role. This issue points to an important limitation of quantitative content analysis for the analysis of churnalism. News stories tend to carry few traces of their production process because journalists are expected to produce news and not bother their audiences with a detailed meta-analysis of all steps in the writing process. As a result, quantitative content analysis can only provide a partial overview of sourcing routines.

Conversely, qualitative content analysis provides a means to trace source material in the final news output more comprehensively. Van Leuven, Deprez, and Raeymaeckers (2013) present the findings of an input–output analysis (Lams, 2011), a specific type of qualitative content analysis in which media sources and PR materials (the input) and news articles (the output) are compared. It fits in with the claim of a growing group of researchers that news production is increasingly an 'outsourced' practice and that, consequently, news production analysis needs to include the source materials that anticipate the news production process (Dinan and Miller, 2009; Grünberg and Pallas, 2012). This study examined the extent to which 138 press releases from the international NGO *Médecins Sans Frontières* (MSF) published between 1995 and 2010 were adopted in foreign coverage by four Belgian newspapers. The authors traced 105 news articles that bore a clear resemblance to 55 of the 138 press releases (40 percent success rate). This resemblance comprised a verbatim reproduction of (parts of) the press release, but even if no sentences were literally copied and pasted, it was still clear from the overall content or particular point of view that the journalist had used information from the press release. Yet 76 of those 105 articles contained additional news gathering and were primarily (i.e. more than half) written by newspaper or news agency journalists. Moreover, Belgian newspapers integrated fewer MSF press releases in their news output in 2010 than in 1995. This does not necessarily mean that Belgian journalists produced little, and less, churnalism in those 15 years. The study is based on one case and the article sample is too small to generalize the findings. There are several alternative explanations for these findings such as the fact that the competition for news access between NGOs has evolved to the detriment of MSF with new players entering the field. Most importantly, the findings show that churnalism should not be treated as a universal and unstoppable shift towards more prepackaged news but instead represents a more nuanced and moderate evolution in different degrees in various contexts.

Even though the comparison between input and output provides additional insight into the news production process, content analysis is not sufficient to accomplish a full understanding of the context and processes inside and outside the newsroom that influence news gathering and news production such as certain editorial guidelines, social relations and hierarchies in the newsroom, or budgetary considerations. Furthermore, content analysis can show if the journalist has copied and pasted prepackaged information, but it remains unclear how extensively the journalist checked this information against other sources first (Broersma, 2009).

Tracking the flow

A second set of approaches tracks the flow of online news in real time and virtual space. For instance, Kautsky and Widholm (2008: 88) use a screen capture software protocol "to analyse different versions of websites as they appear in sequence, arguing that the versionality of online news opens a window into the text which allows us to peek into the discourse practice of online news." They find that CNN's online news coverage comprises three modes of reporting: establishment, intensification, and closure. A second example is the computer-assisted, fieldwork-driven approach to news production combining newsroom ethnography and applied linguistics (Perrin, 2013; Van Hout, 2015). Rather than keyword searches and judgments on textual overlap between source and target text, this approach studies news production as a process: how it exploits semiotic modes and institutional practices and how it materializes and unfolds over time and space. The material dimension of writing news often goes unnoticed—not in the least because we take the technological mediation of news for granted—but it is ingrained in the design of computer programs, information networks, and software applications, precisely the technologies that shape global information flows and hence the news we consume.

One of the signal strengths of this approach is that it enables the detailed analysis of not just texts but also the social practices around texts (Lillis, 2008) as this involves:

- *news producers*: their engagements with the technologies of production; their social position, sociotechnical role, and status in the newsroom; their personal inclinations;
- *situated encounters*: story meetings; telephone conversations; human–computer interaction; source–media interaction; peer group talk; the material setting of and physical arrangements at particular newsrooms;
- *institutions*: how institutional stakeholders (companies, PR agencies, newswires, and governments) shape, sustain, and are reproduced by the news production process; how these stakeholders 'manage' news flows.

Methodologically, a combination of data collection procedures is used to investigate how journalists write from sources in real time. These include computer-assisted writing process data, interviewing, participant observation, and collecting photographs and documents. Some of these procedures are conducted simultaneously, others sequentially. For instance, in his groundbreaking work on news writing, Perrin (2006) developed a three-tiered methodology known as *progression analysis* that tracks the writing process across three sequential phases of production: the situational context of the writing process (or macro level), the movement of writing throughout the composition phase (or meso level), and the writer's consciously applied revising strategies (or micro level). The macro level contextualizes the writing task in a situational 'portrait' by way of standardized interviews and participant observation. The meso level employs S-notation (Kollberg and Severinson-Eklundh, 2001) to map revisions made during the writing process and to visualize those revisions in so-called progression diagrams. The micro level uses an interview protocol for eliciting an ongoing narrative from the authors about their writing, which forms the critical mass for comparing what journalists say about their writing practices and how they write on screen.

Taking a page from Perrin's methodology, Van Hout (2010, 2015) used a similar methodological combination during his fieldwork at the business desk of a national newspaper in Belgium. To examine how reporters write from sources in real time, he used two software applications. Inputlog (Leijten and Van Waes, 2013) is a keystroke logging tool for Microsoft Windows that records keystrokes, mouse movements, window navigation, and dictated speech. Camtasia Studio© is an online screen recorder that was used to make screen videos of the writing processes. Both applications were used with the informed consent of the journalists in question. Moreover, the software ran in the background and did not interfere with normal computer operations. The writing logs and screen videos were combined with observational, textual, and interview data in an attempt to follow the story from the moment it entered the newsroom until the moment it was filed for copy-editing. During fieldwork, a four-step data collection protocol was developed.

Story identification

This involves monitoring incoming emails, following the newswires, and attending the newsdesk story meeting to identify stories within the newsbeats of the participating reporters. During the story meeting, a list is kept of the stories that these reporters were or had been assigned.

Reporter confirmation

Immediately following the story meeting, the reporters are asked what stories they are working on and how their assigned stories are sourced. If an assigned story is based on a press release or a newsfeed, the researcher asks for permission to record the writing process and for copies of the source texts.

Data recording and storage

When signaled by the reporter, both software applications are activated from the moment the reporter starts writing until (s)he files the story for copy-editing. The software is then turned off and the logging and screen recording files are stored on the central newsroom server.

Retrospective interviewing

After the writing session was completed, the reporter is asked to comment on the Camtasia screen video during a brief stimulated retrospective interview.

From the data inventory, a core set of 18 news production processes was extracted. Each case was based on prepackaged information such as press releases and press agency copy. Every logged story comprised at least four data files: the Inputlog data file, the Camtasia screen video, an audio file of the retrospective interview, and copies of the source texts. In addition, copies of the story budget (a list of planned stories for that particular day), printouts of the press releases, email messages, and interview notes made by the reporters were included. Rough transcripts were made of the screen videos and the retrospective interviews. Inputlog logging files were also included. Data analysis proceeded inductively and contrastively through "a focused iterative process of data interrogation which aims to interweave the findings that emerge from each dataset" (Moran-Ellis *et al.*, 2006: 54). This allows for a detailed reconstruction of how reporters accomplish routine writing tasks at speed: how they locate, organize, and 'trim' selected source texts; how they source, naturalize, copy, and add information; and how they revise the text-produced-so-far to 'knock' the story into shape. These accounts naturalize churnalism as a "reproductive process in which professionals contribute to glocalized news-flows by transforming source texts into public target texts" (Perrin, 2013: 54).

The wider theoretical relevance of this sort of knowledge remains important not only to document how journalism is changing but also to understand what can be gained and lost from a move to a fully fledged digital journalism (Van Hout, 2015). The methodology of real-time tracking and virtual lurking highlights the writing process as an under-researched, but, as a result of keystroke logging software, researchable feature of journalistic practice in real time. The trade-off lies in the amount of data this approach generates, and hence the time it takes to analyze the different types of data.

Recommendations for future directions

Despite the central role of sources in the news production process, Broersma and Graham (2012: 406) underline that sourcing is an under-researched practice especially when it comes to "the conventions of how sources are included in news texts." Researchers have mainly employed content analysis and ethnographic studies to meet this criticism, but both approaches have limitations. Qualitative content analysis and ethnographic research are too labor-intensive to be executed on a large scale, and moreover, some exchanges between journalists and sources, such as phone calls, are unobservable (Reich, 2014). Quantitative content analysis of news sourcing is equally labor-intensive and delivers limited return-on-investment as it only provides insight in explicit uses of sources and churnalism (Van Leuven, Deprez, and Raeymaeckers, 2014). However, in the current digital environment, many tasks that are performed manually can be automated to save time. Like journalism, academic research is adapting to the new digital environment and experimenting with new opportunities for data collection and data analysis:

> The automation of many tasks in news content analysis will not replace the human judgement needed for fine-grained, qualitative forms of analysis, but it allows researchers to focus their attention on a scale far beyond the sample sizes of traditional forms of content analysis. Rather than spending precious labour on the coding phase of raw data, analysts could focus on designing experiments and comparisons to test their hypotheses, leaving to computers the task of finding all articles of a given topic, measuring various features of their content such as their readability, use of certain forms of language, sources, etc.
>
> (Flaounas *et al.*, 2012: 111; see also Lewis, Zamith, and Hermida, 2013)

Reconstruction interviews, developed in detail by Reich (2009, 2010, 2014) are probably the best method for analyzing news sourcing in a quantitative manner. Journalists are asked to describe in detail how a relatively large sample of their own, recent articles was produced "answering a series of questions regarding every contribution made by every type of source, textually and orally, inside the newsroom or outside, etc." (Reich, 2010: 804). The interviewer uses a registration form so that the journalists' sourcing routines and the inputs of different sources can be systematically reconstructed for each article and for each journalist. To minimize socially desirable answers, sources are detached from specific articles and assigned to categories such as 'PR practitioner' or 'senior official.' This creates an open climate in which journalists may be less reluctant to talk about churnalism practices (Reich, 2010, 2014).

In sum, it is essential to look beyond the potential of individual research methods for future studies of churnalism. Considering the dynamic and increasingly complex nature of news sourcing, we underwrite the call for more mixed-method research (Moran-Ellis *et al.*, 2006). The integration and combination of traditional and innovative, online and offline research methods will yield a more complete understanding of sourcing practices in the era of screenwork.

Further reading

This chapter was inspired by Lewis, Williams, and Franklin's political economy of UK print journalism (2008a, 2008b) and by Jackson and Moloney's (2015) interview study of UK PR professionals' views on media technology, change, and power. Boyer (2011) provides an insightful behind-the-scenes look at 'slotting,' or incoming news filtering, in a German news agency. Van Hout and Macgilchrist's (2010) follow a news story from its entry in the newsroom through the review process during a story meeting and the writing process up to the point the story is filed for copy-editing. Reich (2014) presents a longitudinal study of sourcing practices in the Israeli press using face-to-face reconstruction interviews. A complete reading of this research method is available in Reich (2009).

References

Boyer, D. (2011) "News Agency and News Mediation in the Digital Era." *Social Anthropology* 19: 6–22.

Boyer, D. (2013) *The Life Informatic: Newsmaking in the Digital Era.* Ithaca, NY: Cornell University Press.

Broersma, M. (2009) "De Waarheid in Tijden Van Crisis: Kwaliteitsjournalistiek in Een Veranderend Medialandschap." In Ummelen, B. (ed.) *Journalistiek in Diskrediet.* Diemen, Netherlands: AMB, pp. 23–39.

Broersma, M. and Graham, T. (2012) "Social Media as Beat: Tweets as News Source During the 2010 British and Dutch Elections." *Journalism Practice* 6(3): 403–419.

Carsten, R. (2004) "Everyone in Journalism Steals from Everyone Else: Routine Reliance on Other Media in Different Stages of News Production." In *Paper presented at annual conference of The International Communication Association*, New Orleans, LA, 27 May.

Davies, N. (2008) *Flat Earth News.* London, UK: Chatto & Windus.

Dinan, W. and Miller, D. (2009) "Journalism, Public Relations, and Spin." In Wahl-Jorgensen, K. and Hanitzsch, T. (eds) *The Handbook of Journalism Studies.* New York, NY: Routledge pp. 250–264.

Flaounas, I., Ali, O., Lansdall-Welfare, T., De Bie, T., Mosdell, N., Lewis, J., et al. (2012) "Research Methods in the Age of Digital Journalism." *Digital Journalism* 1: 102–116.

Gandy, O. (1982) *Beyond Agenda Setting: Information Subsidies and Public Policy.* Norwood, MA: Ablex.

Grünberg, J. and Pallas, J. (2012) "Beyond the News Desk: The Embeddedness of Business News." *Media, Culture & Society* 35(2): 216–233.

Hafez, K. (2009) "Let's Improve 'Global Journalism!'" *Journalism* 10(3): 329–331.

Jackson, D. and Moloney, K. (2015) "Inside Churnalism: PR, Journalism and Power Relationships in Flux." *Journalism Studies* 1–18. DOI: 10.1080/1461670X.2015.1017597.

Karlsson, M. and Strömbäck, J. (2009) "Freezing the Flow of Online News." *Journalism Studies* 11: 2–19.

Kautsky, R. and Widholm, A. (2008) "Online Methodology: Analysing News Flows of Online Journalism." *Westminster Papers in Communication and Culture (WPCC)* 5: 81–97.

Knight, M. (2011) "The origin of stories: How journalists find and create news in an age of social media, competition and churnalism." In *Paper presented at the Future of Journalism Conference*, Cardiff, UK, 8–9 September.

Kollberg, P. and Severinson-Eklundh, K. (2001) "Studying Writers' Revising Patterns with S-Notation Analysis." In Olive, T. and Levy, C.M. (eds) *Contemporary Tools and Techniques for Studying Writing.* Dordrecht, Netherlands: Kluwer Academic Publishers, pp. 89–104.

Krippendorff, K. (2004) *Content Analysis. An Introduction to its Methodology.* London, UK: Sage.

Lams, L. (2011) "Newspapers' Narratives Based on Wire Stories: Facsimiles of Input?" *Journal of Pragmatics* 43: 1853–1864.

Leijten, M. and Van Waes, L. (2013) "Keystroke Logging in Writing Research: Using Inputlog to Analyze and Visualize Writing Processes." *Written Communication* 30: 358–392.

Lewis, J., Williams, A. and Franklin, B. (2008a) "Four Rumours and an Explanation: A Political Economic Account of Journalists' Changing Newsgathering and Reporting Practices." *Journalism Practice* 2: 27–45.

Lewis, J., Williams, A. and Franklin, B. (2008b) "A Compromised Fourth Estate? UK News Journalism, Public Relations and News Sources." *Journalism Studies* 9: 1–20.

Lewis, S.C., Zamith, R. and Hermida, A. (2013) "Content Analysis in an Era of Big Data: A Hybrid Approach to Computational and Manual Methods." *Journal of Broadcasting & Electronic Media* 57: 34–52.

Lillis, T. (2008) "Ethnography as Method, Methodology, and 'Deep Theorizing': Closing the Gap Between Text and Context in Academic Writing Research." *Written Communication* 25: 353–388.

Machill, M., Beiler, M. and Schmutz, J. (2006) "The Influence of Video News Releases on the Topics Reported in Science Journalism: An Explorative Case Study of the Relationship Between Science Public Relations and Science Journalism." *Journalism Studies* 7: 869–888.

Moran-Ellis, J., Alexander, V.D., Cronin, A., Dickinson, M., Fielding, J., Sleney, J., et al. (2006) "Triangulation and Integration: Processes, Claims and Implications." *Qualitative Research* 6: 45–59.

Perrin, D. (2006) "Progression Analysis: An Ethnographic, Computer-Based Multi-Method Approach to Investigate Natural Writing Processes." In Van Waes, L., Leijten, M. and Neuwirth, C.M. (eds) *Writing and Digital Media*. Oxford, UK: Elsevier, pp. 175–181.

Perrin, D. (2013) *The Linguistics of Newswriting*. Amsterdam, Netherlands: John Benjamins.

Reich, Z. (2009) *Sourcing the News*. Cresskill, NJ: Hampton Press.

Reich, Z. (2010) "Measuring the Impact of PR on Published News in Increasingly Fragmented News Environments." *Journalism Studies* 11: 799–816.

Reich, Z. (2014) "'Stubbornly Unchanged': A Longitudinal Study of News Practices in the Israeli Press." *European Journal of Communication* 29: 351–370.

Van Hout, T. (2010) "Sourcing Business News: A Case Study of Public Relations Uptake." In Franklin, B. and Carlson, M. (eds) *Journalists, Sources, and Credibility: New Perspectives*. London, UK: Routledge, pp. 107–126.

Van Hout, T. (2015) "Between Text and Social Practice: Balancing Linguistics and Ethnography in Journalism Studies." In Snell, J., Shaw, S. and Copland, F. (eds) *Linguistic Ethnography: Interdisciplinary Explorations*. London, UK: Palgrave Macmillan, pp. 71–89.

Van Hout, T. and Macgilchrist, F. (2010) "Framing the News: An Ethnographic View of Financial Newswriting." *Text & Talk* 30: 147–169.

Van Leuven, S., Deprez, A. and Raeymaeckers, K. (2013) "Increased News Access for International NGOs? How MSF Press Releases Built the Agenda of Flemish Newspapers (1995–2010)." *Journalism Practice* 7: 430–445.

Van Leuven, S., Deprez, A. and Raeymaeckers, K. (2014) "Towards a More Balanced News Access? A Study on the Impact of Cost-Cutting and Web 2.0 on the Mediated Public Sphere." *Journalism* 15: 850–867.

Van Leuven, S., Deprez, A. and Raeymaeckers, K. (2015) "Journalistic Sourcing Practices in Times of Churnalism and Twitter: A Survey of Flemish Professional Journalists (2008–2013)." *Tijdschrift Voor Communicatiewetenschap* 43: 64–83.

12

DIGITAL JOURNALISM AND BIG DATA

Seth C. Lewis

Exactly how *big* is big data? And, to what extent is that 'bigness' a material, technological phenomenon or a social, mythological one—or both? What precisely is meant by the term 'big data' at all? As we take up these and other questions in this chapter, consider the contemporary situation:

> A company called Planet Labs has recently deployed a network of 100 toaster-sized satellites that will take daily high-resolution images of everywhere on earth. The goal is to launch thousands—a persistent near-real-time surveillance tool, available to anyone online. They call these satellites Doves.
>
> *(Owen, 2015: para. 11)*

Owen goes on to describe how driverless cars, such as those developed by Google, can collect nearly 1 GB of data each second, gathering data from the world around them. The popular notion of the 'the internet of things,' where smart devices are commonplace, brings data collection into our homes. The ramifications of this are also clear: "A warning came with a recent Samsung smart TV about discussing 'personal or other sensitive information' in its vicinity" (Owen, 2015), highlighting both the ever-present nature of data collection and the possible risks involved.

Big data, indeed, is big—in the sheer *volume* of digital information involved, as well as the *velocity* and *variability* of structured and unstructured data that must be analyzed, not to mention the potential *value* that may be derived through such processes (Dumbill 2012; Shah, Cappella, and Neuman, 2015; Stone, 2014). At the same time, the term big data, like other buzzwords, is both ubiquitous and incoherent—seemingly everywhere and yet never entirely clear. To rely on big data as a concept, therefore, means acknowledging at the outset that it is a problematic one worth deconstructing, as a number of scholars have shown (e.g. Crawford, 2013; Crawford *et al.*, 2014; González-Bailón, 2013).

Nevertheless, it is also fair to say that something meaningful is afoot in the development of technology and society: the staggering growth in digital trace information produced by and about human (and natural) activity, all bound up in and made possible by the broad diffusion of internet connectivity, mobile devices, 'smart' machines, tracking tools, digital audience information systems, always-on sensors, and cheap computing storage. "In a digitized world, consumers going about their day—communicating, browsing, buying, sharing, searching—create their own enormous trails of data" (Manyika *et al.*, 2011: 1). "This data layer," another observer has suggested, "is a shadow. It's part of how we live. It is always there but seldom observed" (quoted in Bell, 2012: 48). Technological advances have made it easier than ever to *observe* such data and to organize, analyze, and visualize massive collections of these digital traces (Manovich, 2012). This, in turn, is connected to broader trends that have lowered barriers to, while accelerating forms of, data-mining writ large, whether conducted by corporations, governments, Silicon Valley startups, or researchers.

The upshot has been a rapid push for 'big-data solutions' across many sectors of society, in the belief that more observations at less cost may lead to better decision-making (described in Crawford *et al.*, 2014). Simultaneously, however, there has been a chorus of concerned voices highlighting the implications of big data for matters of privacy, surveillance, ethics, bias, manipulation, and power imbalances in a world dominated by algorithms and automation, as in Owen's (2015) ominous account above (see also boyd and Crawford, 2012; Crawford *et al.*, 2014; Gillespie, 2014). Thus, big data, encompassing "a complex amalgamation of digital data abundance, emerging analytic techniques, mythology about data-driven insights, and growing critique" (Lewis and Westlund, 2015b: 447), is of major importance for how we think about the nature of digital information: how it is captured, configured, and ultimately made visible in society.

For these reasons, big data is of great relevance for journalism. This is both because journalism is a key mode of digital information work, one increasingly reliant on data, code, and machines (Lewis and Westlund, 2016), and because of journalism's traditional role as sense-maker in society, a function that remains quite relevant even in a fragmenting media landscape (Hindman, 2009). The extent to which journalism changes (or not) in relation to big data, and the extent to which journalism can adequately chronicle larger social changes that may occur on account of big data, matters a great deal indeed. And so, drawing on my previous work on this subject (Lewis, 2015; Lewis and Westlund, 2015b), this chapter sets out a basic framework for understanding the relationship between big data and journalism—that is, between this messy assemblage of data-centric practices, philosophies, and possibilities, on the one hand, and journalism as professional field, mode of practice, and media industry, on the other.

I proceed first by briefly unpacking big data as a phenomenon. Then, I explain big data's relevance to and relationship with journalism, in light of historical developments and contemporary concepts and case studies. Finally, I conclude with a slight twist of perspective: a consideration of what these developments mean for the *study* as well as the practice of news.

Defining big data[1]

Big data, as a concept, assumes different meanings in different contexts and for different purposes, from policing to city planning to predicting preferences for all manner of consumer products (Crawford *et al.*, 2014). In strict computing terms, big data refers to data sets that are too large for standard computer memory and software to process. Beyond technical specifications, however, big data can refer as much to *processes* surrounding data, and to the resulting *products* of information about a great many people, places, and things, as to the scope of data itself. As Mayer-Schönberger and Cukier (2013: 6) describe it: "Big Data refers to our new-found ability to crunch a vast quantity of information, analyze it instantly, and draw sometimes astonishing conclusions from it."

More relevant for social researchers, however, big data can be defined as a social, cultural, and technological phenomenon, one that sits at the interplay of three dynamics: technology through the maximizing of computational power and algorithmic accuracy; analysis, or the use of large data sets to identify patterns; and mythology, or "the widespread belief that large data sets offer a higher form of intelligence and knowledge that can generate insights that were previously impossible, with the aura of truth, objectivity, and accuracy" (boyd and Crawford, 2012: 663). The third of these—mythology—calls up a critical stance that is essential but often lost amid the oft-inflated expectations in many business, policy, and even some scholarly circles for big data 'solutions' (Morozov, 2013). Such a critique means worrying less about the 'bigness' of data and attending more to how data comes to be seen as 'big' in social relevance and normative valence. This also means recognizing the discursive work being performed by the term itself: 'big data' may be as much a marketing term and a techno-utopian vision as it is an actual thing (cf. Gillespie, 2014). It is important, therefore, to consider in whose interests, toward what purposes, and with what consequences the very term 'big data' is used. On the other hand, problematic though it may be, big data remains the most succinct way of referring to a larger and complicated set of factors at play in technology and society as well as in journalism.

In this chapter, I define big data in light of boyd and Crawford's conception of a social, cultural, and technological phenomenon, as one representing various philosophies, practices, and promises. For journalism, big data embodies emerging ideas about, activities for, and norms connected with data sets, algorithms, computational methods, and related processes and perspectives connected to *quantification* as a key paradigm of information work (Coddington, 2015a; Lewis, 2015). Big data, in this sense, is neither good nor bad for journalism but rather freighted with potential and pitfall, depending on how it is imagined and implemented and crucially toward what purposes and in whose interests.

The context of journalism, as occupation and media industry

While conversations about the importance, meaning, and application of big data have been a key feature for some time in domains accustomed to working with large-scale data sets, such as healthcare (Fiore-Gartland and Neff, 2015) and the sciences (Shah *et al.*, 2015), the media industries, including journalism, increasingly are taking notice of big data for its editorial as well as commercial implications. And, like in other sectors of society, there is no shortage of hope and hype surrounding big data for/in journalism, flavored with some degree of hesitation about consequences (see Lewis and Westlund, 2015b). As one industry report puts it boldly, "'Big Data' strategies are the Next Big Thing for media companies" (Stone, 2014: 1). It goes on to note the wide-ranging possibilities:

> For newspapers, television, magazines and Internet-only publishers, Big Data strategies can include audience analytics to enable a better understanding and targeting of customers; tools to understand public and private databases for journalistic storytelling; tools to manage and search the exploding amount of video, social media and other content; tools to target advertising and ad campaigns; tools to automate the production of text and video stories, tools to identify waste and enable efficiencies; and much more.

Furthermore, the report suggests, "The opportunity for employing Big Data strategies are many: to better understand cross-platform audiences, create powerful data journalism stories, streamline business processes and identify new products and services to offer customers" (Stone, 2014: 1). In this and other industry accounts, there is often a persistent promise that big data could provide the ultimate win-win: improved journalism *and* improved ways of paying for it. Let us briefly consider the historical context for these data-centric aspirations and the broader intertwining of editorial and commercial possibilities (see Lewis and Westlund, 2015a; Westlund and Lewis, 2014).

Journalism has long been familiar with data and databases as a key object of news work, as evident in decades of computer-assisted reporting (CAR) and even older forms of information visualization (Fink and Anderson, 2014; Howard, 2014). But the database—which Manovich (2000) boldly suggests is to the digital era what narrative, in novels and cinema, was to the modern era—has assumed a particularly conspicuous role in contemporary journalism (Schudson, 2010). Indeed, the larger turn toward digitization of information in recent times has been connected with a greater role in journalism for the techniques of computer and data sciences: from programming and algorithms to machine learning and probability models (Diakopoulos, 2015), as well as the ethos of open-source software development and its emphasis on making data sets transparent and interactive (Lewis and Usher, 2013; Parasie and Dagiral, 2013). Thus, data, whether 'big' in the sense of being too complex for traditional database management software or simply 'big' in its potentially transformative import, has taken on particular relevance for news (Anderson, 2013; Coddington, 2015a). "The open question in 2014," one report noted, "is not whether data, computers, and algorithms can be used by journalists in the public interest, but rather how, when, where, why, and by whom" (Howard, 2014: 4).

There is equal if not greater interest in big data from the commercial side of news organizations. During a moment of intense financial pressure, as legacy media struggle with declining revenues and fragmenting audiences, the ability to harness and appropriate big data, often in the form of digital audience analytics, has captured the hopes of marketers everywhere (Turow, 2011), most certainly in the context of media companies hoping to develop more algorithmically tailored content and services (Couldry and Turow, 2014). Many a conference program, like that sponsored by the World Publishing Expo in 2013, has promised to teach news publishers how to "turn big data into revenue"—part of a broader belief in some circles that "big data analytics can save publishing" by helping publishers not only better understand their audiences but also retool their entire approach to marketing and advertising online (Soloff, 2011). As big data assumes significance on the commercial side, technologists increasingly are needed to identify and appropriate suitable tech systems and solutions. These technologists, in turn, form an important bridging function in negotiating technical systems and solutions across the editorial and business domains of the organization (Lewis and Westlund, 2015a; Westlund, 2011), potentially complicating sharp divisions that have long existed (or been assumed to exist) between news and business/marketing departments (Coddington, 2015b). Altogether, to invoke big data in the context of journalism as professional practice and commercial enterprise is to recognize the varied ways in which news media organizations are seeking to make sense of, act upon, and derive value from the growing variety of digital data writ large.

The results of such efforts are only just coming into focus. Stone's (2014) *Big Data for Media* report, citing a number of case studies, suggests that big data strategies can serve both editorial and marketing needs. The *Huffington Post* uses big data to improve the user experience through better story recommendations, headline optimization, and comment moderation, as well as to improve advertising efficiency. *BuzzFeed* uses machine learning to predict social hits: "we know what's viral before it takes off," the site's chief data scientist said (quoted in Stone, 2014: 7). Viral success, of course, has been a key component of *BuzzFeed*'s tremendous revenue growth. Meanwhile, the *Financial Times* has focused on better collecting and analyzing registration data via its metered paywall, allowing the newspaper to deliver better customer service, targeted advertising, and new product offerings based on reader interests, in addition to adjusting its content strategies to better reflect reader preferences for desktop, mobile, and tablet platforms at different times of day (see Stone, 2014). Moreover, some startup news organizations have found market distinction in focusing on data-centric storytelling, as in the likes of *Vox* and *FiveThirtyEight* (Lewis and Westlund, 2015b). Increasingly, data-intensive automated journalism (Carlson, 2015) is becoming a key strategy for cutting costs and redeploying human resources, as evident in the *Associated Press* outsourcing its routine business reporting on financial earnings reports to algorithms that automatically generate thousands of stories each month.

Cases, concepts, critiques

Amid such excitement, however, it should be acknowledged that journalistic institutions are not working with big data in the same way that astronomers, biologists, and corporate data-miners manage vast troves of data. Those in news working with large data sets tend to be the 'usual suspects' in the U.S. or northern Europe (Fink and Anderson, 2014), perpetuating longstanding divides between (digital) resource-rich and resource-poor institutions, even as data journalism as concept and practice is expanding rapidly around the globe (Gray *et al.*, 2012). Moreover, scholarly critiques are needed to temper too much optimism, and scholarly concepts are required to develop a more theoretically grounded understanding of the big data phenomenon and its implications for journalism. It was with this in mind that Oscar Westlund and I suggested four conceptual starting points, ones developed through our review of the broader communication literature on big data and ones with particular resonance for journalism: *epistemology, expertise, economics,* and *ethics* (see Lewis and Westlund, 2015b).

These Four E's, we argued, suggest key perspectives through which to understand the present and potential applications of big data for journalism's professional logic and its industrial production. These concepts work in tandem with our previously outlined Four A's model, covering the interrelationships that exist in cross-media news organizations among diverse types of social *actors* (e.g. journalists, businesspeople, and technologists), technological *actants* (e.g. algorithms and content management systems), and *audiences* (e.g. whether conceived of as passive or active), all interpolated through the *activities* of media production and distribution (Lewis and Westlund, 2015a). Seen in this broader light, it becomes more apparent what big data could mean not only for journalists but also for business and information technology (IT) teams; for the relationships between humans and machines; and for various classifications of and interactions with audiences across multiple platforms of distribution. Altogether, big data may have important consequences for journalism's ways of *knowing* (epistemology) and *doing* (expertise), as well as its negotiation of *value* (economics) and *values* (ethics). As quantitative journalism becomes more central to journalism's professional core (Coddington, 2015a), and as computational and algorithmic techniques likewise become intertwined with the business models on which journalism is supported, critical questions will continually emerge about the socio-material relationship of big data, journalism, and media work broadly. To what extent are journalism's cultural authority and technological practices changing in the context of (though not necessarily because of) big data? And how might such changes be connected with news audiences, story forms, organizational arrangements, distribution channels, and news values and ethics, among many other things?

A starting point for exploring such questions may be found in a number of empirical studies that have emerged recently, including those published in a special issue of *Digital Journalism* on "journalism in an era of big data" (see Lewis, 2015). Several articles explore matters of algorithms, automation, and 'autonomous decision-making' (Diakopoulos, 2015; see also Westlund's [2013] model of journalism) and the journalistic consequences of such developments for organizational and professional norms and routines. In one study, Young and Hermida (2015) examine the emergence of automatically generated crime coverage at the *Los Angeles Times*. The development of such 'robo-posts,' they argue, raises questions about "how decisions of inclusion and exclusion are made, what styles of reasoning are employed, whose values are embedded into the technology, and how they affect public understanding of complex issues" (2015: 384). In a related work, Carlson (2015) explains what begins to happen as "the role of big data in journalism shifts from reporting tool to the generation of news content" in the form of what he calls 'automated journalism' (2015: 419). The term refers to "algorithmic processes that convert data into narrative news texts with limited to no human intervention beyond the initial programming" (2015: 416). Among the data-oriented practices emerging in journalism, he says, "none appear to be as potentially disruptive as automated journalism" (2015: 416), insofar as it calls up concerns about the future of journalistic labor, news compositional forms, and the very foundation of journalistic authority. Analyzing *Narrative Science* and journalists' reactions to its automated news services, Carlson shows how the case reveals fundamental tensions not only about the work practices of human journalists but also what a future of automated journalism may portend for "larger understandings of what journalism is and how it ought to operate" (2015: 429). Among other issues going forward, he says, "questions need to be asked regarding whether an increase in algorithmic judgment will lead to a decline in the authority of human judgment" (2015: 429). Meanwhile, in separate empirical studies, Dörr (2015) found that automated journalism can adequately perform key tasks of professionals on a technical level, and Clerwall (2014) discovered that news consumers could not easily discern between software-generated content and similar news stories written by journalists.

Before rushing headlong into robot journalism, however, quantitative journalism in its most basic form is still searching for institutional footing in many parts of the world. In exploring the difficulties for data journalism in French-speaking Belgium, de Maeyer *et al.* (2015) offer a reminder that the take-up of such journalism is neither consistent nor complete. Their research examines the various obstacles, many of them structural and organizational, that hinder the development of data journalism in that region. The study shows how uneven and sometimes incoherent the path of experimentation may be at the intersection of big data and journalism.

Toward future research: big data for the study of news

This chapter has addressed what big data, as a social, cultural, and technological phenomenon, means for journalism—for its editorial products as well as commercial needs, for its epistemology and expertise, its economics and ethics, and its professional authority and social standing in an era of algorithms and automation. But, in closing, we might shift our gaze to consider what these developments—the rise of data, code, and computer programming as central modes of information gathering and analysis—also mean for the *study* of news. The study of news takes many forms, of course, but there are at least two dominant lines of research: First, analyses of *who journalists are and how they work*—that is, the sociology of roles, routines, organizations, occupations, systems, and other influences that shape news production; and second, analyses of *what journalists produce and how it reflects the world*—that is, the textual/content analysis of patterns, themes, and frames evident in news, and the likely outcomes for audiences associated with such content. While not mutually exclusive, these two streams of research help reveal what big data could portend for the study of news, whether from a traditionally sociological or content-centric perspective—in addition to other, non-human, non-textual domains of communication that deserve exploration.

Such considerations about future research need to be situated in light of what is happening across the social sciences. Big data has afforded easy retrieval of large-scale 'natural' social data, or evidence of how people act in the world, such as on social media, without scientific intervention. Big data is also connected with advances in storage capacity, processing power, and analytic engines that have allowed researchers to explore such social data in a way not previously possible. All of which raises the question: "how can scientists best use computational tools to analyze such data, problematical as they may be, with the goal of understanding individuals and their interactions within social systems?" (Shah *et al.*, 2015: 6). As explored throughout the special issue edited by Shah and colleagues (2015), this question is of both practical and conceptual concern. Practically speaking, computational social science involves technical skill sets that are mostly unfamiliar to communication scholars—such as machine learning, natural language processing, and others necessary to work with data measured in terabytes or petabytes, using algorithms to generate patterns and draw inferences, etc. Conceptually speaking, scholars are working to understand what such data sets and dynamics mean for the future of hypothesis testing and scientific advancement, at a time when some claim that abundant data means the 'end of theory' (Shah *et al.*, 2015: 11; see also boyd and Crawford, 2012; Couldry and Turow, 2014; González-Bailón, 2013).

Considering the two key lines of news research, it is apparent that big data has immediate and pressing implications for *content* studies. The ability to harness news content at scale and analyze it (at least in part) using automated means of 'algorithmic coders' (Zamith and Lewis, 2015), machine learning (Burscher *et al.*, 2015), and natural language processing raises fundamental questions about the role of content analysis in an era of big data (Lewis, Zamith, and Hermida, 2013; Schwartz and Ungar, 2015). For studies of journalistic *practice*, however, it's far less clear how computationally driven methods would supplant let alone complement traditional modes of social (often qualitative) analysis. Nevertheless, insofar as journalistic practice becomes increasingly interconnected with and dependent on technology (Lewis and Westlund, 2015a; 2016), scholars too may need to become more fully conversant in data, code, and related technologies in order to investigate meaningfully the human–machine interplay in contemporary news media organizations. Moreover, as human–machine communication becomes an increasingly salient feature (Jones, 2014)—that is, as journalists talk not only with each other *through* machines but also talk *to* machines as key parts of their work—scholars will need to develop new practical and conceptual toolkits for exploring these developments and what they will mean for the journalism of the future.

Further reading

This chapter has drawn on examples published in a 2015 special issue of *Digital Journalism* (Volume 3, Issue 3) entitled, "Journalism in an Era of Big Data: Cases, Concepts, and Critiques." Beyond the introductory (Lewis, 2015) and concluding (Lewis and Westlund, 2015b) essays that synthesize the literature, the special issue includes important conceptual contributions such as Coddington's (2015a) typological comparison of computational journalism, data journalism, and computer-assisted reporting, and key empirical contributions such as Young and Hermida's (2015) exploration of algorithms entering news production at the *Los Angeles Times*. Aside from the special issue, Anderson's (2013) essay provides a fundamental baseline for interpreting big data in relation to news. More broadly, Mayer-Schönberger and Cukier (2013) provide a basic overview of big data, while the many writings of Crawford (e.g. Crawford *et al.*, 2014) pointedly critique the social implications of big data. Finally, Shah *et al.* (2015) is a useful starting point for understanding the development of computational social science in light of big data.

Note

1 Here and elsewhere, this chapter draws on some material published in Lewis (2015) and Lewis and Westlund (2015b).

References

Anderson, C.W. (2013) "Towards a Sociology of Computational and Algorithmic Journalism." *New Media & Society* 15(7): 1005–1021.

Bell, E. (2012) "Journalism by Numbers." *Columbia Journalism Review* 51(3): 48–49.

boyd, D. and Crawford, K. (2012) "Critical Questions for Big Data: Provocations for a Cultural, Technological, and Scholarly Phenomenon." *Information, Communication & Society* 15(5): 662–679.

Burscher, B., Vliegenthart, R. and De Vreese, C.H. (2015) "Using Supervised Machine Learning to Code Policy Issues: Can Classifiers Generalize Across Contexts?" *The ANNALS of the American Academy of Political and Social Science* 659(1): 122–131.

Carlson, M. (2015) "The Robotic Reporter: Automated Journalism and the Redefinition of Labor, Compositional Forms, and Journalistic Authority." *Digital Journalism* 3(3): 416–431.

Clerwall, C. (2014) "Enter the Robot Journalist: Users' Perceptions of Automated Content." *Journalism Practice* 8(5): 519–531.

Coddington, M. (2015a) "Clarifying Journalism's Quantitative Turn: A Typology for Evaluating Data Journalism, Computational Journalism, and Computer-Assisted Reporting." *Digital Journalism* 3(3): 331–348.

Coddington, M. (2015b) "The Wall Becomes a Curtain: Revisiting Journalism's News–Business Boundary." In Carlson, M. and Lewis, S.C. (eds) *Boundaries of Journalism: Professionalism, Practices, and Participation.* New York. NY: Routledge.

Couldry, N. and Turow, J. (2014) "Advertising, Big Data and the Clearance of the Public Realm: Marketers' New Approaches to the Content Subsidy." *International Journal of Communication* 8: 1710–1726.

Crawford, K. (2013) "Think Again: Big Data." *Foreign Policy*. Retrieved from http://foreignpolicy.com/2013/05/10/think-again-big-data/ (accessed 10 May 2013).

Crawford, K., Miltner, K. and Gray, M.L. (2014) "Critiquing Big Data: Politics, Ethics, Epistemology." *International Journal of Communication* 8: 1663–1672.

de Maeyer, J., Libert, M., Domingo, D., Heinderyckx, F. and Cam, F.L. (2015) "Waiting for Data Journalism: A Qualitative Assessment of the Anecdotal Take-Up of Data Journalism in French-Speaking Belgium." *Digital Journalism* 3(3): 432–446.

Diakopoulos, N. (2015) "Algorithmic Accountability: Journalistic Investigation of Computational Power Structures." *Digital Journalism* 3(3): 398–415.

Dörr, K. (2015) "Mapping the Field of Algorithmic Journalism." *Digital Journalism*. DOI: 10.1080/21670811.2015.1096748.

Dumbill, E. (ed.) (2012) *Planning for Big Data*. Sebastopol, CA: O'Reilly Media.

Fink, K. and Anderson, C.W. (2014) "Data Journalism in the United States: Beyond the 'Usual Suspects.'" *Journalism Studies* 16(4): 467–481.

Fiore-Gartland, B. and Neff, G. (2015) "Communication, Mediation, and the Expectations of Data: Data Valences Across Health and Wellness Communities." *International Journal of Communication* 9: 1466–1484.

Gillespie, T. (2014) "The Relevance of Algorithms." In Gillespie, T., Boczkowski, P.J. and Foot, K.A. (eds) *Media Technologies: Essays on Communication, Materiality, and Society*. Cambridge, MA: MIT Press, pp. 167–193.

González-Bailón, S. (2013) "Social Science in the Era of Big Data." *Policy & Internet* 5(2): 147–160.

Gray, J., Chambers, L. and Bounegru, L. (2012) *The Data Journalism Handbook*. Sebastopol, CA: O'Reilly Media.

Hindman, M.S. (2009) *The Myth of Digital Democracy*. Princeton, NJ: Princeton University Press.

Howard, A.B. (2014) *The Art and Science of Data-Driven Journalism*. New York, NY: Tow Center for Digital Journalism, Columbia University.

Jones, S. (2014) "People, Things, Memory and Human-Machine Communication." *International Journal of Media & Cultural Politics* 10(3): 245–258.

Lewis, S.C. (2015) "Journalism in an Era of Big Data: Cases, Concepts, and Critiques." *Digital Journalism* 3(3): 321–330.

Lewis, S.C. and Usher, N. (2013) "Open Source and Journalism: Toward New Frameworks for Imagining News Innovation." *Media, Culture & Society* 35(5): 602–619.

Lewis, S.C. and Westlund, O. (2015a) "Actors, Actants, Audiences, and Activities in Cross-Media News Work: A Matrix and a Research Agenda." *Digital Journalism* 3(1): 19–37.

Lewis, S.C. and Westlund, O. (2015b) "Big Data and Journalism: Epistemology, Expertise, Economics, and Ethics." *Digital Journalism* 3(3): 447–466.

Lewis, S.C. and Westlund, O. (2016) "Journalism and Technology." In Witschge, T., Anderson, C.W., Domingo, D. and Hermida, A. (eds) *The SAGE Handbook of Digital Journalism*. New York, NY: Sage.

Lewis, S.C., Zamith, R. and Hermida, A. (2013) "Content Analysis in an Era of Big Data: A Hybrid Approach to Computational and Manual Methods." *Journal of Broadcasting & Electronic Media* 57(1): 34–52.

Manovich, L. (2000) "Database as a Genre of New Media." *AI & Society* 14(2): 176–183.

Manovich, L. (2012) "Trending: The Promises and the Challenges of Big Social Data." In Gold, M.K. (ed.) *Debates in the Digital Humanities*. Minneapolis, MN: The University of Minnesota Press, pp. 460–475.

Manyika, J., Chui, M., Brown, B., Bughin, J., Dobbs, R., Roxburgh, C., et al. (2011) "Big Data: The Next Frontier for Innovation, Competition, and Productivity." *McKinsey Global Institute* 1–137.

Mayer-Schönberger, V. and Cukier, K. (2013) *Big Data: A Revolution that will Transform How We Live, Work, and Think*. Boston, MA: Houghton Mifflin Harcourt.

Morozov, E. (2013) *To Save Everything, Click Here: The Folly of Technological Solutionism*. New York, NY: PublicAffairs.

Owen, T. (2015) "The Violence of Algorithms: Why Big Data is Only as Smart as Those Who Generate it." *Foreign Affairs*. Retrieved from https://www.foreignaffairs.com/articles/2015-05-25/violence-algorithms (accessed 25 May 2015).

Parasie, S. and Dagiral, E. (2013) "Data-Driven Journalism and the Public Good: Computer-Assisted-Reporters and 'Programmer-Journalists' in Chicago." *New Media & Society* 15(6): 853–871.

Schudson, M. (2010) "Political Observatories, Databases & News in the Emerging Ecology of Public Information." *Daedalus* 139(2): 100–109.

Schwartz, H.A. and Ungar, L.H. (2015) "Data-Driven Content Analysis of Social Media: A Systematic Overview of Automated Methods." *The ANNALS of the American Academy of Political and Social Science* 659(1): 78–94.

Shah, D.V., Cappella, J.N. and Neuman, W.R. (2015) "Big Data, Digital Media, and Computational Social Science: Possibilities and Perils." *The ANNALS of the American Academy of Political and Social Science* 659(1): 6–13.

Soloff, D. (2011) "How Big Data Analytics Can Save Publishing." *Advertising Age*. Retrieved from http://adage.com/article/digitalnext/big-data-analytics-save-publishing/231363/ (accessed 5 December 2011).

Stone, M.L. (2014) *Big Data for Media*. Oxford, UK: Reuters Institute for the Study of Journalism.

Turow, J. (2011) *The Daily You: How the New Advertising Industry is Defining Your Identity and Your Worth*. New Haven, CT: Yale University Press.

Westlund, O. (2011) *Cross-Media News Work: Sensemaking of the Mobile Media (R)evolution.* Gothenburg, Sweden: University of Gothenburg.

Westlund, O. (2013) "Mobile News: A Review and Model of Journalism in an Age of Mobile Media." *Digital Journalism* 1(1): 6–26.

Westlund, O. and Lewis, S.C. (2014) Agents of Media Innovations: Actors, Actants, and Audiences. *The Journal of Media Innovations* 1(2): 10–35.

Young, M.L. and Hermida, A. (2015) "From Mr. and Mrs. Outlier to Central Tendencies: Computational Journalism and Crime Reporting at the *Los Angeles Times*." *Digital Journalism* 3(3): 381–397.

Zamith, R. and Lewis, S.C. (2015) "Content Analysis and the Algorithmic Coder: What Computational Social Science Means for Traditional Modes of Media Analysis." *The ANNALS of the American Academy of Political and Social Science* 659(1): 307–318.

13

EXPLORING DIGITAL JOURNALISM WITH WEB SURVEYS

Annika Bergström and Jenny Wiik

The past decade has witnessed a growing interest in exploring the profession of journalism at an aggregate level, which has triggered a number of national as well as comparative studies. The expanding possibilities offered by web surveys have contributed to this development. Survey design is a feasible way to gather generalizable data about both journalists and their audiences in order to track developments related to changing media structures. The statistical data facilitate comparisons between countries as well as over time. Web surveys can also be useful in distinguishing subgroupings within national contexts based, for example, on gender, age, and type of work place.

It is becoming increasingly common to study journalists, from several perspectives: their professional boundaries (Lewis, 2012), views (Mitchell, Holcomb, and Purcell, 2015; Wiik, 2014), and features (Hovden, 2008; Stigbrand and Nygren, 2013), as well as in relation to, and interaction with, audiences (Andersson, 2013). The use of web surveys in this research is constantly expanding and offers great potential for future studies. One important, large-scale study within the field is the so-called Worlds of Journalism study, currently collecting data via several modes or methods: web and telephone survey as well as personal interviews (e.g. Hanitzsch *et al.*, 2010).

Web surveys are also commonly used in audience research. The audience has been found to play a significant role in journalistic practice and constitutes an important external influence (Loosen and Schmidt, 2012, this volume; Napoli, 2011). Images of the audience are also shaping journalistic routines and are embedded in the news-making process (DeWerth-Pallmeyer, 1997; Vobic, 2014). Further, the audience pays for journalistic content and, aside from owners and advertisers, constitutes the base on which journalism relies financially (McQuail, 2005; Picard, 2002). The audience is, however, increasingly disloyal, fragmented, and diverse (McQuail, 2005), which means that quick and easy, but reliable research methods are preferred to the more traditional telephone interviews.

There are, thus, substantial benefits to be derived from using web surveys in the area of digital journalism, such as their considerable potential for economy as well as speed in delivering findings. Online surveys also allow the use of multimodal features and have been shown to attract groups beyond those which are reached by traditional surveys, which might be helpful in achieving satisfying response rates and representativeness when combined with mail or telephone surveys. The survey mode will most likely continue to evolve, both in response to societal changes and in response to technological developments. Newer modes have tended to supplement rather than replace existing methods (Couper, 2011).

However, while it is evident that web surveys could be an attractive tool in gathering data about journalists and their audiences, they are, like other survey modes, associated with certain biases concerning instance sampling and data quality. This chapter sets out to reveal under what circumstances web surveys can be an alternative in studies of journalists and audiences, and what factors must be taken into account to achieve representative, generalizable data of significance to the research field of digital journalism studies. Different ways of finding the right sample of respondents will be discussed, both in the area of journalists and among their audiences.

Conducting web surveys

The main purpose of conducting surveys is to find answers to questions with the highest data quality possible. Traditionally, larger surveys have been conducted either by mail or telephone surveys, but nowadays both journalists and their audiences are constantly connected via various platforms and consequently online communication offers an effective and cost-savvy way to reach them. In this pursuit of robust, valid, and reliable estimates of known population parameters, there are a number of aspects to consider. Survey errors, for example, can occur in populations, sampling, design of survey instrument, from response rate and representativeness, when handling and presenting data. All these aspects of maintaining high data quality may in turn be challenged by falling response rates, the increasing use of opt-in web panels, and a greater diversity of survey distribution on new technological platforms.

Driving forces for including web methods in data collection are the pressures to reduce administration costs, attempts to reduce measurement errors, and technological developments leading to new data collection procedures (Dillman, Smyth, and Christian, 2009). Sometimes, web surveys are used in combination with other mode designs. Mixed modes have the potential for extending the reach of a survey by encouraging participation across a broader mix of the population (De Leeuw, 2005; Dillman, Smyth, and Christian, 2009; Holmberg *et al.*, 2010; Shih and Fan, 2007). It is easy to conduct a study on the web and there are many easily handled tools for web surveys.

Web surveys are self-administered and can be designed with different levels of interactivity. The self-administrative modes indicate a high respondent control over when and in what way to answer and also provide a high degree of privacy (Couper, 2011). Via interactivity, web surveys provide greater flexibility in terms of channels of communication. Even though most web surveys present questions verbally, it is possible to use audio and video formats when presenting the survey content. Web surveys also allow for a wide range of advanced features such as randomization of question orders, conditional questions, etc., making it easier to customize a bespoke survey for individual respondents (Tourangeau *et al.*, 2013).

Different modes of research may, however, attract different respondents. Generally, web survey respondents are significantly younger than their mail survey equivalents. There is an inverse correlation between preference for web-based responses and the age of the respondent (Börkan, 2009; Carini *et al.*, 2003; Diaz de Rada and Dominguez-Álvarez, 2013; Kwak and Radler, 2002). Internet response, moreover, is found to be more attractive to male than female respondents, which in some cases has led to web surveys involving fewer female respondents (Carini *et al.*, 2003; Kwak and Radler, 2002).

It is evident from survey research literature that differences can occur for identically worded questions depending on research mode. Measurement effects seem to be strongest on socially desirable topics, since respondents act according to social norms and tend to give culturally acceptable answers (Couper, 2011; Dillman and Christian, 2005; Jäckle *et al.*, 2010). One example is when audiences are asked to rate their interest in various news content, which commonly leads to a tendency to over-estimate the person's own interest in political stories and opinion material. It is also well established that in international research, people tend to over report their own voting behavior, since the social norm in most countries is that you should vote (Granberg and Holmberg, 1991). Among journalists, there is the matter of professional ideals and standpoints, which to a high degree are subject to presumptions. It could be legitimate to support the watchdog ideal, for instance, while in many countries it is not legitimate for journalists to support commercial ideals as elements of the professional role (Wiik, 2010).

Self-administered forms of data collection perform better than interview modes on this matter (De Leeuw, 2005), and computer-mediated surveys may yield more honest responses on items of a sensitive nature (Carini *et al.*, 2003). Given that you control how representative the sample is, web surveys might be preferable when studying certain aspects of attitudes or behavior within the field of digital journalism. Previous research is rather inconsistent on when and how web survey mode might differ from other modes and in what respect (Bergström, 2015).

Another advantage is that completion rates for web-based questionnaires usually are higher than for paper-based questionnaires and that e-questionnaires contain fewer missing responses (Barrios *et al.*, 2011; Diaz de Rada and Dominguez-Álvarez, 2013; Dillman, Smyth, and Christian, 2009; Evans and Mathur, 2005; Kwak and Radler, 2002). Additionally, it seems that people tend to answer open-ended questions to a larger extent in web surveys and that the answers are generally longer (Barrios *et al.*, 2011).

There is, however, evidence in previous research that information technology–related questions are coming out better in web than in mail surveys (Carini *et al.*, 2003; Kwak and Radler, 2002), which might bias results on digital journalism both from the journalist's and the audience's perspective. In times characterized by downsizing editorial staff and by faith of audiences turning to digital platforms, overestimated digital habits in web surveys might not serve as a satisfying basis for strategic decisions.

Another drawback with web surveys, no matter the device chosen by the respondent when answering, is that the internet as a dynamic medium opens up for multitasking drawing the attention of the respondent from the survey (De Leeuw, 2005) and preventing respondents from carrying out the cognitive process necessary to respond to each question (Diaz de Rada and Dominguez-Álvarez, 2013). It is also likely that the never ending flow of the internet makes it easy to miss or ignore e-mail invitations to web surveys relative for instance interviewer request (Tourangeau *et al.*, 2013).

Altogether, web survey tools are becoming more popular when studying both journalists and their audience. To fully understand if and how internet differs from other modes, controlled comparisons between modes and thorough analysis of representativity are needed using a variety of topics to enhance the generalizability of findings (De Leeuw, 2005). The following sections deal with specific advantages and obstacles of conducting web surveys among journalists and audiences respectively.

Surveying journalists

The past decade has witnessed an explosive development in surveying journalists both nationally and comparatively (Wiik, 2010; Weaver and Willnat, 2012, 2014). Measurement methods vary but web surveys are becoming increasingly popular. One of the most important studies in this tradition is the 'Worlds of Journalism study' (e.g. Hanitzsch *et al.*, 2010), which has employed both web and telephone surveys. One of the biggest challenges involved in surveying online journalists is to define the population. What is a journalist today? And is there a difference between 'online journalists' and other journalists? Deuze, Neuberger, and Paulussen (2004) defined online journalists as "those media professionals who are directly responsible for the internet content of news ventures" (2004: 20). On the one hand, we could argue that all journalists these days are online journalists to some extent. On the other hand, the professional role is itself becoming increasingly blurred in many countries (Carlson and Lewis, 2015; Eldridge, this volume), whereas the theoretical considerations should be regarded even more carefully than before. Either way, researchers still face the challenge of collecting journalists' names and addresses as journalistic staff or groups fluctuate quite frequently. Traditionally limited in options from a common approach of asking editors' permission to contact their staff or possibly collecting names from newspaper web sites or similar online resources, social and online media have introduced new (if not straightforward) means of identifying respondents. There are different ways to find journalists, and while searching the web can be very time-consuming, social media often provide groups of journalists that the researcher can approach. On Facebook, for instance, journalists appear in professional discussion groups where researchers can make appeals for participants in research studies. These groups, however, often include non-journalist members and appeals are usually met with skepticism. Still, one Swedish study managed to gather thousands of names by starting in a Facebook forum (Hjort, Oskarsson, and Szabó, 2013), while others have used the union membership register (Andersson and Wiik, 2013), more or less official Twitter accounts (Hedman, 2015), or journalist groups at Linked In (Alejandro, 2010), to reach journalists online.

To draw a sample, researchers should preferably know all individuals in the population. This almost always causes problems, since such lists never match perfectly because people are missing from the list, incorrect names are included, contact information is missing, and the researcher invariably ends up with some kind of coverage error. If researchers are working with probability sampling, they need to control these various errors that can occur from such approaches. Where there is a complete list of the individuals in the population, the researcher wishes to study, they can draw a random sample. Mostly, this is not the case, however, and they need to use some other method for sampling, such as multistage sampling or clusters.

When surveying journalists with a web survey method, it is nearly impossible to select a random sample of individuals accessing the net. It is thus common to rely on self-selection by respondents or simply put a survey questionnaire on a web page. In both cases, there is a considerable risk of producing biased estimates (Bethlehem, 2015). A way to deal with coverage and sampling problems with internet samples is to maintain web panels from which samplings can be made. It can, however, be hard to determine how well the panelists represent the general population. A way to handle this would be to use different data collection modes and probability samples for the recruitment of panel members (De Leeuw and Hox, 2008).

The potential bias reported above reflecting the likelihood of different groups choosing different survey modes can be resolved by controlling for variables of importance (Carini *et al.*, 2003). Many of the technology-related problems mentioned above are invalid when studying journalists. In most Western countries and in most journalistic contexts, journalism professionals are heavy internet users and can be reached easily via the web (Hedman and Djerf-Pierre, 2013). Problems might occur, however, related to both ethics and representativeness in spite of the theoretically benign preconditions. Nevertheless, online research tools continue to develop rapidly and new technical opportunities continue to emerge. Online often means mobile and previous research points to an opportunity for reaching young people via mobile devices. Data quality equals that of desktop respondents. Device adapted questionnaires may therefore turn out to be useful in the future (Toepoel and Lugtig, 2014).

Surveying audiences

Population is a central concept when working with surveys, without regard to the mode choice. Researchers need to define the group of people they want to predict. It could be the whole population of a specific country, a certain professional group, a group of users of specific media content, etc. Total population samples are rare for both financial and administrative reasons. Instead, researchers typically draw a sample of the population. If the ambition is to find differences between binaries such as young and old, or male and female, researchers can work with smaller samples but still reach statistically significant results. But if they wish to present a total picture of the variations in news consumption practices between generations in rural and urban areas, for example, they will need a greater number of responses to achieve statistical significance.

Turning to web surveys, there are a few issues which might strengthen or harm the data quality of audience research. Responding via the web requires some degree of familiarity with computers and digital features (Shin *et al.*, 2012). When studying large populations, it is important to be aware of access to, and familiarity with computers and digital features since web access is unevenly distributed both between countries (Internet World Stats) and also between groups within a country or sometimes a population (Norris, 2001; van Deursen and van Dijk, 2014).

After controlling for internet access and computer skills, some sociodemographic factors, such as age, have turned out to affect respondents' willingness to complete a web survey (Fan and Yan, 2010). Further, respondents who are more likely to be adaptive to new technologies tend to be overrepresented in web surveys (Kwak and Radler, 2002; Smyth *et al.*, 2014). If the demographic profile for internet respondents is distinctive from that of respondents to other modes, the response rate gains may be offset by measurement errors (Bates, 2001; Dillman *et al.*, 2009; Revilla, 2014).

Another issue related to web surveys is the opportunity to put up self-selected panels or to invite people on a certain web site to complete a web survey. By letting go control of sampling and random selection, researchers cannot control representativeness and consequently loose the possibility of predicting more general behaviors or opinions. When searching for audience behavior in terms of, for instance, new media replacing or complementing legacy media (Chan and Leung, 2005; Dimmick, 2003), or attitudes to, and use of interactive features in news reporting (Bergström and Wadbring, 2015), it is hard to draw any significant conclusions if you cannot make a thorough analysis of respondents and dropouts.

In many contexts, there is the problem of achieving a randomly selected sample. In many countries, there are no public registers to provide researchers with contact information about citizens. Moreover, where the situation is more favorable in this respect, as in Sweden for instance, e-mail addresses are not systematically gathered in public registers. In that case, researchers must distribute survey invitations by mail, encouraging people to log in and complete the web survey instead of just sending a link to the survey via e-mail.

Traditionally, studying the use of journalistic content has been more or less routine since media forms have been separated from each other. With converging media techniques and converging content, it has become increasingly difficult to separate media forms and media content. It has also become a challenge for the users themselves to identify their use and to express frequency in a questionnaire. How do you, for instance, keep track of your own internet use when you are constantly online? It seems that it is no longer possible to answer according to frequency scales such as 'several times a day' or similar.

Previous research could quite easily pose questions about watching television, listening to the radio, or reading newspapers. In today's media landscape, all of these channels are made available on the internet not only by former providers but also by new actors. Media forms, channels, and content are converging, and it is hard to tell where, for instance, newspaper reading ends and television watching starts in an online context. With digital, mobile technology, media audiences are hard to capture, no matter of survey mode. New design is needed, more clearly identifying whether the research questions deals with certain kind of content or genre, platforms of use, or specific content distributors. Before, these perspectives most often were strongly correlated.

To sum up, audience research might be conducted with web surveys or a mix of web and other data collection modes. There are several advantages with choosing digital methods of collecting audience data, such as reaching internet-savvy groups who would not be likely to engage with a mail or telephone survey. Researchers need to pay attention to sampling and representativeness, however, if the aim is to keep track of audience behavior in a constantly changing media landscape or to evaluate interactive features within news journalism. The easy availability of web tools might make them tempting to use without really considering the bias that might go with the choice.

Conclusion

We have in this chapter examined both the benefits and flaws of web surveys when studying digital journalism. In general, the benefits present the strongest features of web surveys; they are cheap, easy to handle, and save time. This has led to an increase in the number. As Couper observes, "there is a growing realization that willing and able respondents are becoming an increasingly scarce commodity" (Couper, 2011: 902). Both the journalistic profession and media audiences are in many countries very extensively encouraged to participate in research studies, and this might cause tiredness and *ennui* among potential respondents.

There is furthermore a risk that the apparent easiness of the web survey format causes sloppiness when constructing questions and selecting respondents. Easily available responses might harm problematizing among journalists as well as journalism researchers. There might be inflation not only in the number of surveys but also in the number of unconsidered issues.

The overall increase of surveys has led to the circulation of a large amount of data, calling for sharper analytical skills among scholars as well as the public. This also applies to journalists themselves, who increasingly are tempted to use online survey tools in the generation of news. Almost every newspaper worth its salt has a 'question of the day' on its website, again generating a lot of data but these are rarely statistically significant. Misinterpretations of such data are more rule than exception, and the need for journalists to improve their analytical skills in this area has never been greater. But when using data gathered by others, journalists need to assess it critically before making headlines of insignificant opinion changes or voting behavior. It is also extremely important to be cautious about audience data when relying on them for strategic planning within the media business. Relying on skewed samples or data sets might lead to unnecessary anxiety or incorrect actions. It thus becomes increasingly important that journalists learn the basics of survey construction, statistical data treatment, and necessary analytical skills tied to this. Journalism schools should therefore consider strengthening these modules, something which many already have done.

Overall, this points to the conclusion that while web survey tools are providing fruitful new ways to study both journalists and their audiences, there are also a number of challenges. The challenges are both general to all survey studies and specific to the field of digital journalism. The loose boundaries of the profession, the high turnover of journalistic staff, and the fragmentation of news media users all present problems for the survey form. But these problems are not unique to the web survey method. As long as researchers keep control of populations and samples, digital survey tools might provide data on the same quality level as data from other collection modes.

Further reading

For further exploration of web tools in journalism research, C. W. Anderson's 2011 article "Between Creative and Quantified Audiences: Web Metrics and Changing Patterns of Newswork in Local U.S. Newsrooms" offers a critical understanding of how quantifying the audience relates to newsroom practices. Specific to surveys, Couper and Miller's "Web Survey Methods. Introduction" is a valuable problematization of the diversity of web surveys.

Ari Heinonen's 2011 chapter "The Journalist's Relationship with Users: New dimensions to conventional roles," puts the somewhat ambivalent relation between journalists and audiences in focus. Finally, Jaana Hujanen addresses the issue of audience-oriented journalism and the neglected area of audience research methods within journalism in the 2008 article "RISC Monitor Audience Rating and its Implications for Journalistic Practice."

References

Anderson, C.W. (2011) "Between Creative and Quantified Audiences: Web Metrics and Changing Patterns of Newswork in Local U.S. Newsrooms." *Journalism* 12(5): 550–566.

Andersson, U. (2013) "Maintaining Power by Guarding the Gates: Journalists' Perceptions of Audience Participation in Online Newspapers." *Journalism and Mass Communication* 3(1): 1–13.

Andersson, U. and Wiik, J. (2013) "Journalism Meets Management." *Journalism Practice* 7(6): 705–719. DOI: 10.1080/17512786.2013.790612.

Alejandro, J. (2010) *Journalism in the Age of Social Media*. Oxford, UK: Reuters Institute of the Study of Journalism.

Barrios, M., Villarroya, A., Borrego, Á. and Ollé, C. (2011) "Response Rates and Data Quality in Web and Mail Surveys Administered to PhD Holders." *Social Science Computer Review* 29(2): 208–220.

Bates, N. (2001) "Internet versus Mail as a Data Collection Methodology from a High Coverage Population." In *Proceedings of the Annual Meeting of the American Statistical Association*, Atlanta, Georgia, 5–9 August.

Bergström, A. (2015) "Same, Same But Different: Effects of Mixing Web and Mail Modes in Audience Research." *Digital Journalism* 4(1): 142–159.

Bergström, A. and Wadbring, I. (2015) "Beneficial Yet Crappy: Journalists and Audiences on Obstacles and Opportunities in Reader Comments." *European Journal of Communication* 15(2): 137–151.

Bethlehem, J.G. (2015) "Challenges of Web Surveys and Web Panels." Paper presented at the fourth Baltic-Nordic Conference on Survey Statistics, Helsinki, 24–28 August.

Börkan, B. (2009) "The Mode Effect in Mixed-Mode Surveys: Mail and Web Surveys." *Social Science Computer Review* 28(3): 371–380.

Carini, R.M., Hayek, J.C., Kuh, G.D., Kennedy, J.M. and Ouimet, J.A. (2003) "College Student Responses to Web and Paper Surveys: Does Mode Matter?" *Research in Higher Education* 44(1): 1–19.

Carlson, M. and Lewis, S.C. (2015) *Boundaries of Journalism: Professionalism, Practices and Participation, Shaping Inquiry in Culture, Communication and Media Studies*. London, UK: Routledge.

Chan, J.K. and Leung, L. (2005) "Lifestyles, Reliance on Traditional News Media and Online News Adoption." *New Media & Society* 7(3): 357–382.

Couper, M.P. (2011) "The Future of Modes of Data Collection." *Public Opinion Quarterly* 75(5): 889–908.

Couper, M.P. and Miller, P.V. (2008) "Web Survey Methods. Introduction." *Public Opinion Quarterly* 72(5): 831–835.

De Leeuw, E.D. (2005) "To Mix or Not to Mix Data Collection Modes in Surveys." *Journal of Official Statistics* 21(2): 233–255.

De Leeuw, E.D. and Hox, J.J. (2008) 'Self-Administered Questionnaires: Mail Surveys and Other Applications.' In De Leeuw, E.D., Hox, J.J. and Dillman, D.A. (eds) *International Handbook of Survey Methodology*. New York and London: Psychology Press, pp. 239–263.

Deuze, M., Neuberger, C. and Paulussen, S (2004) "Journalism Education and Online Journalists in Belgium, Germany, and the Netherlands." *Journalism Studies* 5(1): 19–29.

DeWerth-Pallmeyer, D. (1997) *The Audience in the News*. Mahwah, NJ: Lawrence Erlbaum Associates, Publishers.

Diaz de Rada, V. and Dominguez-Álvarez, J.A. (2013) "Response Quality of Self-Administered Questionnaires: A Comparison between Paper and Web Questionnaires." *Social Science Computer Review* 32(2): 256–269.

Dillman, D.A. and Christian, L.M. (2005) "Survey Mode as a Source of Instability in Responses across Surveys." *Field Methods* 17(1): 30–52.

Dillman, D.A., Smyth, J.D. and Christian, L.M. (2009) *Internet, Mail, and Mixed-Mode Surveys. The Tailored Design Method*. Hoboken, NJ: John Wiley & Sons, Inc.

Dimmick, J.W. (2003) *Media Competition and Coexistence: The Theory of the Niche*. Mahwah, NJ: Lawrence Erlbaum.

Evans, J.R. and Mathur, A. (2005) "The Value of Online Surveys." *Internet Research* 15(2): 195–219.

Fan, W. and Yan, Z. (2010) "Factors Affecting Response Rates of the Web Survey: A Systematic Review." *Computers in Human Behavior* 26(2): 132–139.

Granberg, D. and Holmberg, S. (1991) "Self-Reported Turnout and Voter Validation." *American Journal of Political Science* 35(2): 448–460.

Hanitzsch, T., Hanusch, F., Mellado, C., Anikina, M., Berganza, R., Cangoz, I., et al. (2010) "Mapping Journalism Cultures Across Nations." *Journalism Studies* 12(3): 273–293.

Hedman, U. (2015) "When Journalists Tweet: Disclosure, Participatory, and Personal Transparency." In *ICA 2015: Communication Across the 'Life Span'*. San Juan, Puerto Rico, 21–25 May.

Hedman, U. and Djerf-Pierre, M. (2013) "The Social Journalist: Embracing the Social Media Life or Creating a New Digital Divide?" *Digital Journalism* 1(3): 368–385.

Heinonen, A. (2011) "The Journalist's Relationship with Users: New Dimensions to Conventional Roles." In Singer, J.B., Hermida, A., Domingo, D., Heinonen, A., Paulusen, S., Quandt, T., et al. (eds) *Participatory Journalism. Guarding Open Gates at Online Newspapers*. Malden, MA: Wiley-Blackwell, pp. 34–56.

Hjort, M., Oskarsson, S. and Szabó, M. (2013) *Jättekliv eller tidsfördriv – En studie i hur svenska journalister använder sociala medier som arbetsverktyg* [Giant Step or Pastime – A Study of How Swedish Journalists Use Social Media as a Business Tool]. Gothenburg: The Department of Journalism, Media and Communication, University of Gothenburg.

Holmberg, A., Lorenc, B. and Werner, P. (2010) "Contact Strategies to Improve Participation via the Web in a Mixed-Mode Mail and Web Survey." *Journal of Official Statistics* 26(3): 465–480.

Hovden, J.F. (2008) *Profane and Sacred. A study of the Norwegian Journalistic Field*. Bergen, Norway: University of Bergen.

Hujanen, J. (2008) "RISC Monitor Audience Rating and its Implications for Journalistic Practice." *Journalism* 9(2): 182–199.

Internet World Stats, 2015-05-07. Retrieved from www.internetworldstats.com.

Jäckle, A., Roberts, C. and Lynn, P. (2010) "Assessing the Effect of Data Collection Mode on Measurement." *International Statistical Review* 78(1): 3–20.

Kwak, N. and Radler, B. (2002) "A Comparison between Mail and Web Surveys: Response Pattern, Response Profile and Data Quality." *Journal of Official Statistics* 18(2): 257–273.

Lewis, S.C. (2012) "The Tension Between Professional Control and Open Participation." *Information, Communication & Society* 15(6): 836–866.

Loosen, W. and Schmidt, J-H. (2012) "(Re-)discovering the Audience." *Information, Communication & Society* 15(6): 867–887.

McQuail, D. (2005) *McQuail's Mass Communication Theory*. 5th edn. London, UK: Sage.

Mitchell, A., Holcomb, J. and Purcell, K. (2015) "Investigative Journalists and Digital Security. Perceptions of Vulnerability and Changes in Behavior." *Pew Research Centre*. Retrieved from http://www.journalism.org/2015/02/05/investigative-journalists-and-digital-security/.

Napoli, P.M. (2011) *Audience Evolution. New Technologies and the Transformation of Media Audiences.* New York, NY: Columbia University Press.

Norris, P. (2001) *Digital Divide: Civic Engagement, Information Poverty and the Internet Worldwide.* Cambridge, UK: Cambridge University Press.

Picard, R.G. (2002) *The Economics and Financing of Media Companies.* New York, NY: Fordham University Press.

Revilla, M. (2014) "Comparison of the Quality Estimates in a Mixed-Mode and a Unimode Design: an Experiment from the European Social Survey." *Quality & Quantity* 49(3): 1219–1238.

Shih, T-H. and Fan, X. (2007) "Response Rates and Mode Preferences in Web-Mail Mixed Mode Surveys: A Meta-Analysis." *International Journal of Internet Science* 2(1): 59–82.

Shin, E., Johnson, T.P. and Rao, K. (2012) "Survey Mode Effects on Data Quality: Comparison of Web and Mail Modes in a U.S. National Panel Survey." *Social Science Computer Review* 30(2): 212–228.

Smyth, J.D., Olson, K. and Millar, M.M. (2014) "Identifying Predictors of Survey Mode Preference." *Social Science Research* 48: 135–144.

Stigbrand, K. and Nygren, G. (2013) *Professional Identity in Changing Media Landscapes: Journalism Education in Sweden, Russia, Poland, Estonia and Finland.* Huddinge: Södertörns högskola. Journalistikstudier vid Södertörns högskola.

Toepoel, V. and Lugtig, P. (2014) "What Happens If You Offer a Mobile Option to Your Web Panel? Evidence from a Probability-Based Panel of Internet Users." *Social Science Computer Review* 32(4): 544–560.

Tourangeau, R., Conrad, F.G. and Couper, M.P. (2013) *The Science of Web Surveys.* New York, NY: Oxford University Press.

van Deursen, A. and van Dijk, J. (2014) "The Digital Divide Shifts to Differences in Usage." *New Media & Society* 16(3): 507–526.

Vobic, I. (2014) "Audience Conceiving among Journalists: Integrating Social-Organizational Analysis and Cultural Analysis through Ethnography." In Patriarche, G., Bilanzic, H., Jensen, J.L. and Jurisic, J. (eds) *Audience Research Methodologies: Between Innovation and Consolidation.* New York and London: Routledge, pp. 19–36.

Weaver, D. and Willnat, L. (eds) (2012) *The Global Journalist in the 21st Century.* Abingdon, UK: Routledge.

Weaver, D. and Willnat, L. (2014) *The American Journalist in the Digital Age.* Bloomington: School of Journalism, Indiana University.

Wiik, J. (2010) *Journalism in Transition.* Gothenburg: Department of Journalism, Media and Communication, University of Gothenburg.

Wiik, J. (2014) "Towards the Liberal Model." *Journalism Practice* 8(5): 660–669. DOI: 10.1080/17512786.2014.883112.

PART III

Financial strategies for digital journalism

14

FUNDING DIGITAL JOURNALISM

The challenges of consumers and the economic value of news

Robert G. Picard

The business of journalism is an uncomfortable subject for many journalists and one they prefer to disregard whenever possible. Because the news industry enjoyed a rising tide of funding as advertising expenditures increased decade-by-decade during in the twentieth century, the question of how journalism could be funded did not arise for them, allowing most journalists to ignore the business aspects of news provision. The swelling revenue from advertising allowed journalists to disregard the fact that the news they produced was also being sold to consumers in a market transaction, but that its price was well below the cost of gathering, preparing, copying, and distributing the news product. Considered in revenue terms, the primary business of newspaper publishing in the twentieth century was advertising not news.

The movement of news to digital platforms, however, is forcing journalists to pay greater attention to the business of news and to wrestle with issues involving the economics of journalism, the commercial value of news, how news audiences behave, what prices consumers will pay, how payment will be structured, and what opportunities exist for non-market funding.

This chapter addresses issues involving the funding of digital journalism. To understand those issues, it is important for readers to distinguish between the terms *funding model* and *business model*. They are too frequently and erroneously used synonymously by many in journalism, but represent distinct concept and issues. The term *funding model* refers to how an enterprise makes money, but this is only one part of the firm's broader *business model* that specifies the firm's business logic, value proposition, value configuration, processes and relationships, and customer interactions (Picard, 2011a). Those issues are crucial for making the funding model successful. This chapter will use the term funding to refer to income/revenue received and funding model for the revenue configuration that makes it possible.

How digital operation alters the economics of journalism

The need for funding is directly linked to the costs of producing and distributing news and how the shift to digital operation affects those costs is important.

Digital journalism alters the cost structures that exist when journalism is practiced in print (Picard, 2011b). Digital operations do so by ending costs that previously existed for making newspaper copies and delivering them. In physical production (print), profitable operation is pursued by managing variable costs. This requires seeking efficiency in the unit costs of producing copies through economies of scale and reducing transaction costs. The environment provides significant advantages to newspapers with larger numbers of customers. In digital operations, however, serving additional digital copies has little cost effect and competitors tend to operate with relatively similar cost structures regardless of the number of customers. Costs are primarily affected by the scale and scope of content provided rather than the scale and scope of copying and distribution costs. In this environment, managing fixed costs becomes the challenge.

Although digital journalism reduces the costs of production and distribution, it does not equally reduce the costs for gathering and processing news, and news organizations have threshold level production and distribution costs that must be borne regardless whether they serve smaller or larger digital audiences.

In the past, legacy news providers benefited from monopolistic structures created by their production and distribution cost structures, temporal constraints, and distribution distance barriers and by mass audiences that were created to attract advertiser revenues. Digital media cost structures and features overcame those barriers, however, allowing smaller audiences to become economically efficient and many sizes of enterprises to compete effectively because disadvantages created by varying production and distribution economies of scale no longer affect them.

The digital shift, however, has had a significant effect on revenue by dramatically reducing advertising funding that provided the bulk of income for print operations. Digital operations have created a near endless supply of advertising opportunities that lower the prices advertisers pay for reaching digital audiences and do not carry the types of retail advertising that existed in print. Consequently, advertisers spend less in digital than they did for print, and news providers are unable to obtain the levels of revenue from digital that they received from print.

Journalism has never been a commercially viable product

Answering questions about how to fund digital journalism in the twenty-first century requires reflecting upon how journalism has been financed in the past. Historically, the gathering, production, and distribution of news was never a stand-alone, self-financing commercial activity. It has always relied on subsidy funding from other profitable activities that benefited from the news activities.

Four clear financing models are visible over the centuries. News was initially paid for by emperors and monarchs in an imperial finance model during ancient times and that model evolved into a commercial elite finance model during the Middle Ages, in which large international traders paid for news. The rise of merchant classes led to a social elite financing model in the eighteenth and nineteenth centuries, which then transformed into the mass media financing model base of the nineteen and twentieth centuries (Picard, 2013). The latter model was based on mass-produced news that required enterprises to keep content prices low and filling papers with content to attract large audiences—including many readers more interested in sports, entertainment, cooking, and other topics rather than news. These audiences were then sold to advertisers who provided the bulk of newspaper revenue (Picard, 2011a).

The elements of the model came about because it was recognized that a limited number of people would pay for news and the level they were willing to pay was relatively low—facts that have always made journalists uncomfortable. The challenge of most people being unwilling to pay for news was outlined by Walter Lippmann in 1922:

Nobody thinks for a moment that he ought to pay for his newspaper.[...] He will pay a nominal price when it suits him, will stop paying whenever it suits him, will turn to another paper when that suits him.[...] It is not a business pure and simple, partly because the product is regularly sold below cost..... The citizen will pay for his telephone, his railroad rides, his motor car, his entertainment. But he does not pay openly for his news[...]he will pay indirectly for the advertisements of other people, because that payment, being concealed in the price of commodities is part of an invisible environment that he does not effectively comprehend.[...] The public pays for the press, but only when the payment is concealed.

(1922: 175)

Funding digital journalism is confronting this unwillingness to pay again, especially because the overall funding of all digital media relies primarily on market funding, and digital media provide maximum advantages to branded content providers that can generate large numbers of unique users and views of their digital pages.

What do we know about digital news consumers?

The behavior of digital news consumers is critical for establishing effective funding models for digital journalism.

The fundamental principles of the market assert that sellers need to provide consumers with products and services that consumers want and hence sellers can be successful only if their offerings deliver greater value than their competitors. Aligning producers and consumers is central to commercial success, but studies have shown that journalists and news consumers differ significantly about what news is of interest (Boczkowski and Peer, 2011; Lee and Chyi, 2014), in good part because journalists perceive their efforts as servicing non-market functions. This creates a challenge in digital operations because the ability to finance news operations by other than market transactions between producer and consumer is more limited than in print and broadcasting.

Our understanding of patterns of behavior of digital news users has increased significantly in recent years and is important in developing and assessing funding models.

It is clear that news consumers are using multiple devices to access digital news (Chyi and Chadha, 2012; Reuters Digital News Report, 2015), but that mobile is rapidly becoming the central platform for news distribution. Mobile use is creating additional consumption among those who do not use legacy news sources (Dimmick, Feaster, and Hoplamazian, 2010; Reuters Digital News Report, 2015), that news publishers viewing mobile primarily as complementary content distribution risk displacement (Nel and Westlund, 2012), but that digital and mobile news can have displacing and complementary effects that are influenced by user ages (Westlund and Färdigh, 2015).

This is occurring because mobile news has relative advantage, utility, and ease of use (Chan-Olmsted, Rim, and Zerba, 2013), that accessibility and information-seeking motives influence mobile news consumption (Shim *et al.*, 2015) and that the degree of press freedom of established media influences demand for mobile news (Wei *et al.*, 2014). A study examining the interplay among demographics, online news use, format preference, and its effect on consumers' paying intent for news suggests that consumers do not always use what they prefer and that they are not always willing to pay for what they use (Chyi and Lee, 2013).

Willingness to pay for news remains a challenge in digital news. An early survey conducted in 2002 reported that 70 percent of internet users could not understand why anyone would pay for online content (Jupiter Media Metrix, 2003). A 2010 survey documented internet users' unenthusiastic response to paying for newspaper content on the web; in fact 60 percent of online users reported they were willing to pay zero dollars for their favorite newspaper online (Chyi, 2012). Willingness to pay rises somewhat when apps and tablets are involved but are highly influenced by local market conditions (Picard, 2014).

Contemporary research reveals that payment for digital news currently tops out at about 15 percent of digital users: 6 percent of digital users pay for news in the UK, 7 percent in Germany, 10 percent in the US, 11 percent in Australia, and 14 percent in Finland, for example (Reuters Institute, 2015).

This indicates that a small number of users will pay for regular access to a steady stream of well-curated news and information; most will not. Most consumers are content with the basic material available free from broadcast and cable channels, digital aggregators, and other digital sources. Increasingly many do not seek news, but are willing to rely on news reaching them through social media and serendipitous exposure.

The research indicates that if digital news providers want to rely on consumers who want regular, curated news and information to pay most of the costs of gathering, producing, and disseminating, the content will have to accept a smaller number of users paying a higher price or reduce the price by undertaking other activities that produce revenue. News providers that are targeting the largest group of consumers—those unwilling to pay, who seek news less frequently or use it when it is shared with them or discovered in another way—will need to rely on strategies that bring extremely large number of consumers into regular contact with their content on multiple platforms so they can provide advertisers with access to individual consumers and aggregated audiences.

Constructing a strategy to achieve desired income involves trade-offs between sales revenue and traffic-driven ad revenue. Paid content drives content sales revenue and free content drives traffic and increases advertising sales. Producing the highest possible revenue for a news enterprise may result from content sales, advertising sales, or a combination of the two.

What we know about payments today is that willingness to pay is affected by the digital platform used and the extent to which free competitors providing similar news are available. Paid apps for mobile and tablets gain better consumer acceptance than general online payments, and news organizations operating in larger markets have advantages in gaining acceptance from sufficiently large numbers of consumers to make pay systems a success. Market leaders—especially large legacy media news providers—have brand and content advantages in moving to payment.

What methods for content payment are in place?

Providing paid content to consumers requires news organizations to select a content payment model and create an access structure to obtain payment. The choices of payment model are unique to individual news providers dependent on the market structures, consumer demand, marketing strategies, and payment infrastructures available to them.

A widely used approach is the *freemium model* in which some content is provided free and some requires payment. This is a classic up-selling strategy, but requires high quality, attractive content for the paying. The freemium model permits use of different prices for differential access to content. News organizations using this model provide some content free to support brand maintenance and to help market their paid access plans. The free content tends to be less exclusive than paid content and sometimes is an abbreviated version of the paid content. The model generates traffic for ad revenue on both the free and paid content because both are carrying advertising. Using this model require managers to identify content that is kept for paid customers and to decide how long it may be kept from those who do not pay.

Another widely used approach employs the *metered model*, a form of the freemium model that limits free access to a number of articles and multimedia presentations to encourage making a switch to regularly paying for greater content. It requires monitoring use by individual consumers, asking for payment at certain levels of use, and then blocking access if they do not pay. This practice of course reduces traffic to the news organization's platforms that generate advertising revenue. In the past, many publishers employed metering techniques that allowed consumers to view 10–15 free articles or multimedia presentations monthly. But many have now reduced that number to five articles per month. The metered model supports brand maintenance and marketing for paid access.

Another strategy used by some news providers is to operate separate free and paid sites as different brands with the paid edition including premium content, more stories, in-depth articles, columnists, and archives. There is clear evidence that paywalls that keep non-paying customers from content reduce website traffic between 85 and 95 percent and that metered systems reduce traffic 5–15 percent.

Digital operations make a variety of purchased access options possible: single article, 1-day access, 1-week access, monthly subscription, quarterly subscription, and annual subscription. They are not equally beneficial for news organizations, however, because digital payment systems create transaction cost challenges. The costs of managing transactions, accounting and auditing, and conveying funds for digital purchases can incur expenses that are higher than the actual cost of the content purchased. In addition, the number of customers a firm attracts matters because cost inefficiencies develop when serving news organizations that have fewer transactions, making them more expensive to serve.

These issues arise when deciding how payment for content will be accepted. Cash and check payments incur high costs for handling and accounting and high fees from banks and other financial intermediaries. These may generate costs between £1.50 and £10 per item. Debit cards/credit cards are more cost effective, but involve costs assessed by credit card processers and banks that make them undesirable for payments for small transactions. Prepaid accounts lower costs because all activity is electronic and automatic and can be managed internally or externally by non-bank intermediaries. Nevertheless internal processing costs of 0.20p to 0.30p per transaction are common in such systems.

Some news organizations with larger numbers of customers and sales transactions may be able to manage the costs effectively and operate pay systems of their own, but other firms may need to take part in cooperative pay systems that overcome transaction cost challenges by collectively creating economies of scale and lowering transaction costs.

Two general payment patterns are emerging worldwide: one based on subscription and the other on single access or micro purchases. The subscription approach has its strongest use in countries such as Denmark, Germany, Japan, and the United States. Purchasing limited time access to content or making micro purchases is highest in countries such as Brazil, Italy, Spain, and the United Kingdom. These patterns align with the national traditions of how print newspapers have conventionally been purchased.

Non-market funding models are working for some news providers

Commercial news provision is not the only way news can be provided in the digital age, because digital technologies make it possible for many different types of organizations to engage in news and information provision. Not-for-profit operating models are being pursued by many digital news organizations, relying on a variety of non-market funding models and mix sources of funding (Knight Foundation, 2013; Sirkkunen and Clare Cook, 2012).

Foundations, particularly in the United States, have stepped in to help to establish and support digital not-for-profit news providers and provide funding for specific types of coverage in both not-for-profit and for-profit news providers (Westphal, 2008). Most foundations supporting journalism were established by wealthy individuals looking to improve their communities or funding activities in specialty areas such as education, health care, and energy. Although there is interest in promoting more foundation funding of local news start-ups in the United Kingdom, few foundations have moved into that role and support from public organizations is being encouraged (Carnegie UK Trust, 2014). Even where foundation funding is more widely available, it is not expected to become a long-term funding solution because donors typically do not like to provide continuing operational support and tend to change their funding emphases over the years (Levy and Picard, 2011; Picard, 2014; Shaver, 2010).

Patronage has long been a funding model for activities that are not commercially viable. Nobility, aristocracy, and wealthy individuals have funded cultural and other endeavors in areas that interested them and brought them attention. Mozart, for example, relied on funding from Austrian Count Franz von Walsegg to compose his Requiem Mass in D Minor, and the Earl of Southampton was a regular patron of Shakespeare's poetry.

Not-for-profit digital journalism enterprises are relying heavily on patronage for startup and operating funds. *ProPublica*, the leading digital investigative journalism news organization in the United States, was established with and receives annual support from the patronage of Herbert and Marion Sandler, whose wealth came from financial services. The *Voice of San Diego*, a digital news provider of in-depth local news coverage and investigative journalism, receives it largest funding as patronage from a retired venture capitalist who now engages in philanthropy. In the United Kingdom, the Bureau of Investigative Journalism operates with the patronage of David and Elaine Potter, whose wealth derived from the software industry. There are also many individuals who provide lesser patronage donations to established not-for-profit journalism enterprises.

A number of news enterprises offer memberships and seek small gifts from those who consume their services. Best known for using this model are public radio and television stations in the United States, but digital media such as *Texas Tribune* and *MinnPost* use memberships as one of the revenue streams. Although it is a form of patronage, it represents, at best, 'poor man's patronage' because the average gifts are small and come from persons without significant wealth.

Mixed funding is becoming the norm for not-for-profit news providers and they are increasingly reliant on multiple sources of funding (Knight Foundation, 2013). They obtain foundation grants, patronage donations, pursue memberships, develop revenue from events, have some advertising income, and providing commercial services within their expertise such as developing advertising campaigns and providing web hosting and web design services for small firms.

Some digital news providers that require payment are trying to bundle the payment with payments made for other services, including premium credit cards, bank accounts, and pay television subscriptions. Such firms are sometimes willing to do so because it allows them to provide something extra as an incentive to pay their prices.

Some observations

Funding commercial and not-for-profit journalism is both possible and sustainable in the digital realm, but it will have different sources and level compared to journalism of the late twentieth century. News enterprises will have to be smarter and more aggressive in seeking revenue because it will not 'walk through the door' in the hands of advertisers as it previously did.

Large commercial firms are making significant progress in obtaining digital funding. Digital revenues, for example, now account for 40 percent of the revenue of the *Guardian* and *Observer* (Jackson, 2015). Not all news organizations will be equally successful, however, because there is limited space in the national and international advertising and subscription markets for news providers. The market structures and advertising dynamics are making it difficult for more than 3 to 4 news providers to obtain significant revenues in their national market and the global market.

Other news providers are struggling to find revenue in the market. Online advertising produces only 10–15 percent of the price print advertising previously delivered and mobile advertising can barely produce 2 percent of that price. These weaknesses in advertising funding are forcing news organizations to rely heavily on a mix of funding, with different providers pursuing varying strategies that produce dissimilar reliance on various forms of funding.

Digital native news providers are struggling overall for revenue and, for the most part, remain small and typically serve niche topics or locales (Bruno and Nielsen, 2012; Sirkkunen and Cook, 2012). The choices of organizational structures and funding are influenced by the backgrounds of those starting digital news organizations and this can reduce their effectiveness as business enterprises (Naldi and Picard, 2012).

A few digital native news providers are growing rapidly and producing significant revenue. In the United States, for example, Vox Media and BuzzFeed have become so successful that employees are attempting to unionize to better share in the wealth they are producing. Although producing and distributing news and journalism, the two are targeting more general audiences rather than serious news consumers. A few other commercial successes are evident—Mediapart in France, for example, that are intent on providing high quality news in the digital environment.

Funding digital journalism requires news enterprises to reduce their reliance on advertising funding, develop better insight into consumers and their willingness to pay for digital journalism, gain a clearer understanding of the economic value of news, and to consider multiple ways of financing digital operation. Pursuing multiple methods will not be simple, however, because it requires firms to develop internal structures and obtain knowledgeable personnel to support those functions—making news organizations look very different than they have in the past.

Further reading

For more understanding of business and economic issues facing media firms and digital media, readers may consult my book *The Economics and Financing of Media Companies* and my report *Mapping Digital Media: Digitization and Media Business Models*. For an excellent overview of consumption and payments for news, see *Reuters Digital News Report 2015*. For information about how digital news startups are faring, read Esa Sirkkunen and Claire Cook's *Chasing Sustainability on the Net: International Research on 69 Journalistic Pure Players and their Business Models* and/or Nicola Bruno and Rasmus Nielsen's *Survival is Success: Journalistic Online Start-ups in Western Europe*.

References

Boczkowski, P.J. and Peer, L. (2011) "The Choice Gap: The Divergent Online News Preferences of Journalists and Consumers." *Journal of Communication* 61(5): 857–876.

Bruno, N. and Nielsen, R. (2012) *Survival is Success: Journalistic Online Start-ups in Western Europe*, RISJ Challenges Series, Reuters Institute for the Study of Journalism, University of Oxford.

Carnegie UK Trust (2014) *The Future's Bright: The Future's Local Findings from the Carnegie UK Trust's Neighbourhood News initiative*. Dumferline, Scotland: Carnegie UK Trust.

Chan-Olmsted, S., Rim, H. and Zerba, A. (2013) "Mobile News Adoption Among Young Adults: Examining the Roles of Perceptions, News Consumption, and Media Usage." *Journalism & Mass Communication Quarterly* 90(1): 126–147.

Chyi, I. (2012) "Paying for What? How Much? And Why (Not)? Predictors of Paying Intent for Multiplatform Newspapers." *International Journal on Media Management* 14(3): 227–250.

Chyi, I. and Chadha, M. (2012) "News on New Devices: Is Multi-Platform News Consumption a Reality?" *Journalism Practice* 6(4): 431–449.

Chyi, I. and Lee, A.M. (2013) "Online News Consumption: A Structural Model Linking Preference, Use, and Paying Intent." *Digital Journalism* 1(2): 194–211.

Dimmick, J., Feaster, J.C. and Hoplamazian, G.J. (2010) "News in the Interstices: The Niches of Mobile Media in Space and Time." *New Media & Society* 13(1): 23–39.

Jackson, J. (2015) "Guardian and Observer Publisher Reduces Losses as Digital Revenues Rise." *The Guardian*, 30 July. Available from: http://www.theguardian.com/media/2015/jul/30/guardian-observer-publisher-guardian-news-media

Jupiter Media Metrix (2003, January 6) "Bumpy Road from Free to Fee: Paid Online Content Revenues to Reach Only $5.8 Billion by 2006, Reports Jupiter Media Metrix." Retrieved from: http://www.prnewswire.com/news-releases/bumpy-road-from-free-to-fee-paid-online-content-revenues-will-only-reach-58-billion-dollars-by-2006-reports-jupiter-media-metrix-76496177.html

Knight Foundation (2013) *Finding a Foothold: How Nonprofit News Ventures Seek Sustainability*. Miami: Knight Foundation.

Lee, A.M. and Chyi, H.I. (2014) "When Newsworthy is Not Noteworthy: Examining the Value of News from the Audience's Perspective." *Journalism Studies* 15(6): 807–820.

Levy, D. and Picard, R.G. (2011) *Is There a Better Structure for News Providers? The Potential in Charitable and Trust Ownership*. Oxford, UK: Reuters Institute for the Study of Journalism, University of Oxford.

Lippmann, W. (1922) *Public Opinion*. New York, NY: Harcourt, Brace and Co.

Naldi, L. and Picard, R.G. (2012) "'Let's Start an Online News site': Opportunities, Resources, Strategy, and Formational Myopia in Startups." *Journal of Media Business Studies* (4): 47–59.

Nel, F. and Westlund, O. (2012) "The 4C's of Mobile News: Channels, Conversation, Content and Commerce." *Journalism Practice* 6(5–6): 744–753.

Picard, R.G. (2011a) *The Economics and Financing of Media Companies*. 2nd ed. New York, NY: Fordham University Press.

Picard, R.G. (2011b) "Mapping Digital Media: Digitization and Media Business Models, Reference Series No. 5." London, UK: Open Society Foundations Media Programme.

Picard, R.G. (2013) "State Aid for News: Why Subsidies? Why Now? What Kinds?" In Murschetz, P. (ed.) *State Aid for Newspapers: Theories, Cases, Actions*. Berlin, Germany: Springer, pp. 49–57.

Picard, R.G. (2014) "New Approaches to Paid Digital Content." In Newman, N. and Levy, D. (eds) *Reuters Institute Digital News Report 2014: Tracking the Future of News*. Oxford, UK: University of Oxford, pp. 80–92.

Reuters Institute (2015) *Reuters Digital News Report 2015*. Oxford, UK: Reuters Institute for the Study of Journalism, University of Oxford.

Shaver, D. (2010) "Online Non-Profits Provide Model for Added Local News." *Newspaper Research Journal* 31(4): 16–28.

Shim, H., Kyung, H.Y., Lee, J.K. and Go, E. (2015) "Why Do People Access News with Mobile Devices? Exploring the Role of Suitability Perception and Motives on Mobile News Use." *Telematics and Informatics* 32(1): 108–117.

Sirkkunen, E. and Cook, C. (eds) (2012) *Chasing Sustainability on the Net: International Research on 69 Journalistic Pure Players and their Business Models*. Tampere, Finland: Tampere Research Centre for Journalism, Media and Communication, University of Tampere.

Wei, R., Lo, V.H., Xu, X., Chen, Y.N. K. and Zhang, G. (2014) "Predicting Mobile News Use among College Students: The Role of Press Freedom in Four Asian Cities." *New Media & Society* 16(4): 637–654.

Westphal, D. (2008) "The State of Independent Local Online News: Start-ups Look for Foundation Support." *Online Journalism Review*, 3 November. Available from: http://www.ojr.org/ojr/people/davidwestphal/200811/1568/

Westlund, O. and Färdigh, M.A. (2015) "Accessing the News in an Age of Mobile Media: Tracing Displacing and Complementary Effects of Mobile News on Newspapers and Online News." *Mobile Media & Communication* 3(1): 53–74.

15

RESOURCING A VIABLE DIGITAL JOURNALISM

Jonathan Hardy

Much academic enquiry into financing journalism looks to the precarious prospects for sustaining commercial models. In contrast, this chapter explores arguments which suggest that a viable journalism requires alternatives to commercial funding. Mainstream debate across industry and the academy accepts, often as a premise, that journalism can only flourish as a commercially delivered product operating in highly volatile and adverse market conditions (Grueskin, Seaves, and Graves, 2011). Various radical perspectives respond that the commercial model is broken, is the agency of crisis for news media and cannot serve as the basis for sustaining a diverse public journalism. These differ in how far mainstream, market media are repudiated, but common to the critical perspectives explored in this chapter is their contribution to serious debate about the qualities of journalism that need to be sustained and fostered and about the ways in which this may be achieved.

Diagnosing problems in news journalism

Since the debate on the digital phase of the 'crisis' of news media intensified around the mid-2000s, several aspects are clearer. First, conditions vary between media systems, and consequently both diagnosis and remedy need to be situated. A survey of ten countries (Newman and Levy, 2014), for example, found weekly newspaper purchases relatively stable at 49 percent, but economic disruption was greatest in countries where the majority of sales were from newsstands or shops (UK, Spain, Italy, Brazil) compared to home delivery via subscription (Japan, Denmark, Finland, Germany). Second, even in the advanced economies where the epithet of crisis is most pertinent, the general trend has been decline rather than collapse, with important differentiation between news sectors and competing enterprises (Franklin, 2009: 1–13). Third, the debate tends to conflate print and broadcasting-based media, which makes some sense in examining trends across the convergent, commercial media of the United States but far less so when addressing the mixed systems of Europe with relatively strong public service media (PSM) alongside commercial publishers. Fourth, the Euro-American literature has tended to ignore the growth of paid newspaper markets across fast-growing economies in Asia, Africa, and Latin America (Franklin, 2009). Nevertheless, the common feature across media systems whose newspaper market was larger before digitalization has been an irreversible decline in print revenue, accompanied by cost-cutting to manage that decline. In the UK, circulation fell by 25 percent between 2005 and 2010 in the 'quality' press, and by 17 percent in the popular press (Enders Analysis, 2011). Digital revenue growth has failed to compensate for print decline while adding to costs (PEW, 2015).

Making what viable?

When considering how to resource journalism, it is important to identify what should be resourced. There is a rich literature on normative models of journalism (Christians *et al.*, 2009) and a burgeoning literature on the expansion and transformation of 'journalistic activities' from citizen journalism and professional-amateur (pro-am) hybrids to self-mass communication. Both Western liberal and radical perspectives espouse a monitorial journalism that is "committed to public enlightenment and sufficiently independent and capable of holding agencies of power in society to account—economic, political, and military" (Christians *et al.*, 2009: 240). The differences are best understood if, following Baker (2002), we identify how various models of democracy privilege different media jobs. Radical democratic perspectives extend liberal norms to argue for media to enhance the material conditions and voice of those lacking power. Media should facilitate processes of deliberation and exchange but also aid self-constitution and mobilization by social movements and interest groups (Curran, 2002: 217–247). Radical democrats have proposed that this can be achieved by having a combination of media sectors, differentially organized and financed, generating different communication spaces, forms, and styles. Curran (2002) provides the best exposition of such a normative model, proposing a core public service sector encircled by private, social market, professional, and civil media sectors. This seeks to ensure that the media system is not controlled by either the state or market but has mutually influencing parts that strengthen media independence, enhance diversity, and promote quality. Such normative models were constructed to address problems in Anglo-American media systems in the mass media era, yet they can serve as guides for considering suitably pluralistic arrangements today.

Critiques of commercial models

Critiques of commercial journalism stretch from the early growth of commercial systems in the nineteenth century (McChesney and Scott, 2004) to the rise of 'market-driven' media and hypercommercialism from the 1970s (McChesney, 2013; McManus, 1994). Waves of corporate consolidation, aided by liberalization of ownership regulations, left commercial news production in the hands of debt-laden, financialized corporations with decreasing tolerance to subsidize loss-making reporting and whose corporate logics undermine journalistic independence and investigative capacity alike (Almiron, 2010). As profitability declined, capital began to abandon news journalism, shifting to more profitable activities, including classified ad websites (McChesney, 2013). The crisis has laid bare the fundamental tensions between capitalism and democracy, between "communication groups subject to financial logics and who can, and indeed do, exercise political action, and … the need that democracy and society have for an independent, rigorous and professional journalistic practice" (Almiron, 2010: 158).

The problematic tendencies of commercial media may be expected to increase on current trajectories. Studies show reductions in the resources for paid journalism, more reliance on public relations materials, more dependence on established sources, and less resources to investigate independently, leading to dangerous levels of 'churnalism' (Davies, 2008). Joining established critiques of the ways commercialization undermines news values (Bennett, 2011) are those that concern the dynamics of monetizing digital journalism. One report (Silverman, 2015: 144) finds "The business models and analytics programs of many large news websites create an incentive for them to jump on, and point to, unverified claims and suspect viral stories. This approach is receiving some pushback and is by no means universal, but the sites pursuing this strategy are large and drive a significant number of social shares for their content."

Advertising

One of the most salient areas of critique concerns advertising. The deal, whereby advertising paid for journalism to attract readers who would see their ads, has been unravelling since the early 1990s as marketers have found more direct, information-rich, and cost-effective ways to track and target consumers online. Efforts to make good the loss of advertising by more effective retailing through paywalls, micropayments, and subscription have so far largely failed (Myllylahti, 2014: ch. 16). Successful monetization online is mostly restricted to products serving elite or specialist audiences, where there are attributes of high-value content (relatively non-reproducible and/or fast), scarcity in supply, valued user interface, and enhanced cross-platform availability. In the absence of significant growth in subscriptions, "news organisations are focusing on maximizing revenue from those who are prepared to pay" (Newman and Levy, 2015: 12). For general, public-facing journalism cultures of 'free' prevail (Chyi and Lee, 2013) and are expected to continue. "[T]here is no evidence that large numbers of consumers will ever pay for commoditized news that is freely available elsewhere" (Kaye and Quinn, 2010: 177). A survey by the Internet Advertising Bureau (Jackson, 2015) found UK adults were prepared to pay only 92p a month to access news websites, less than they were prepared to spend on email, search engines, or online video. A ten-country survey (Newman and Levy, 2015) found only 11 percent reported they had paid for digital news in the last 12 months. Pay models have tended to stall after reaching a small segment of their total consumer market willing to pay for content.

The failure to raise revenue from consumers has meant even greater dependence on advertising. Digital journalism is at the apex of two key trends in media–advertising relationships: toward the disaggregation of advertising and media and toward the greater integration of advertising within media. The characteristic relationship of media and advertising in the mid-twentieth century was integration with separation: advertising was physically integrated with the media product but separated from editorial content. That separation principle was generally upheld by news journalists, supported by managers, underpinned by self-regulatory codes across media and advertising, and subject to stronger statutory regulation in sectors like European broadcasting.

Media and advertising integration is not new, but the digital environment has brought increased pressures from marketers, met with increased accommodation (McChesney, 2013: 155; Turow, 2011). The emergent forms are *integration without separation*, which extends from branded entertainment and product placement to advergames and sponsored social media, but this coexists with trends toward *disaggregation* of media and advertising. Marketers are less dependent on the intermediary role of media, can track and target consumers directly, and demand to reduce their subsidy to media by paying only the costs of delivering an advert onto a selected platform (Hardy, 2014; Turow, 2011). Both integration and disaggregation reflect a strengthening shift toward marketer power in an era of increased media dependence on advertising finance.

For digital journalism, the fastest growing form of ad-integration is 'native advertising,' a form of branded content that is produced by or on behalf of a marketer and appears within or alongside publishers' own content offering. Ads mimic the editorial content surrounding them and follow the form and user experience associated with the context in which they are placed. In the UK, content and native advertising grew to £509 million in 2014 to account for 22 percent of all display ad spend, part of the 14 percent increase in total digital advertising spending to a record £7.2 billion (Jackson, 2015). Billed as the savior for newspapers losing traditional ad revenue, marketers were expected to spend $4.3 billion in 2015, with publishers from the *New York Times* to the *Guardian*, the *Daily Mail*, Mashable, and Refinery29 deploying editorial staff to create native ads (Sebastian, 2014). For US news brands, digital advertising and marketing services were two areas of modest growth, while revenue from traditional advertising continued to fall (NAA, 2014). The growth of native advertising reflects new pressures and opportunities, shifts in governing values across established media, and the spreading influence of formats and business models from the inaptly named 'pure players,' digital-only publishers like Buzzfeed and Huffington Post that attract a younger audience via social media and mobile (Newman and Levy, 2014).

There are long-standing critiques of the influence of advertising finance on media, source dependency, and intensifying PRisation of media (Davies, 2008; Jackson and Moloney, 2015). What is euphemistically called native advertising blends and amplifies all these concerns. The most pertinent charge is that there is a powerful imbalance in the resources to fund effective public communications. Professional journalism promised to ameliorate that imbalance by producing communications according to values that serve democratic and cultural life—accuracy, balance and editorial independence from vested interests amongst them. The expansion of native advertising is symptomatic of the erosion of that communication space. Is sponsored content an acceptable trade-off in order to finance high-cost newsgathering and reporting? What is evident is that sponsored content itself favors resource-rich, commercial sources, advertiser-friendly coverage, 'best-selling' stories, and soft news. As this model becomes more prevalent, it increases resource imbalances, undermines news values, and threatens a cure worse than the disease. Neither the safeguards of new professional 'norms and practices' (Picard, 2015: 280), more distributed, investigative capabilities confronting brands nor sponsor identification regulations redress the erosion of journalistic channels when marketers can command editorial forms and merge 'earned,' 'owned,' and 'paid' media. Market entrants like Demand Media are among the leading proponents of integrated advertising and content farming, while the absence of alternative finance drives social enterprise journalism down the same road.

Other critiques shape the debate on alternatives, the most prominent of which have addressed corporate media ownership and control, reinforced by fine-grained studies of working conditions, job losses, and eroding workplace security (see Hardy, 2014). Opinions divide over the extent to which established institutions, journalistic tasks, and paid jobs should be protected, but there are sharp criticisms of the way more celebratory accounts of network journalism (Beckett, 2008) fail to deal adequately with resource inequalities and their ongoing structuring effects. The optimistic view of a new social journalism tends to downplay the impact of resource-cuts on commercial journalism, the limited social make-up of active bloggers and citizen journalisms, problems of exposure diversity, and the dependence of new journalism on professional newsgathering. The alternative media models draw on resources that define and can in part sustain them: voluntary labor, networking, and network effects (Benkler, 2006). But these are underresourced and precarious, and Critical Political Economy (CPE) scholars make a powerful case against overestimating their reach, impact, and transforming potential, while huge disparities between these and dominant commercial communications remain (McChesney, 2013).

Together these are reasons why the radical CPE tradition seeks solutions for a viable journalism beyond the commercial model. It is important to stress, though, that context matters. Commercial enterprises may be privately owned, publicly traded, but may also take forms like the *Guardian*, a loss-making liberal publication, cross-subsidized by profitable businesses and owned by a charitable trust. Commercialism must also be investigated within a wider field of influences that include institutional, legal-regulatory and governance arrangements, the cultures and values shaping professional (and pro-am) practices, market dynamics, and user behavior.

Funding public journalism

The radical tradition contests commercial funding and seeks alternatives, but is not alone in arguing that the commercial model is not sustaining journalism. The private companies on which democracies have relied for the provision of public goods, such as public affairs journalism, are widely regarded as being in crisis. Even when the focus is on saving journalistic activity rather than industries or platforms, other ways of funding journalism will have to be found.

The following section outlines various proposals to draw on public, private, and civil society resources to fund journalism. While some focus on supporting entirely non-profit organizations that do not disburse profits to private interests, others countenance support for private media where these are subject to public oversight. The main sources of private sector funding have been consumers, marketers, investors, corporate finance, or debt. The main alternative source has been public funding, including direct and indirect subsidies for news publishers and funding for PSM (by combinations of license fees, state funding, or commercial revenues). Another source has been civil society, including funding from foundations and charitable trusts, funding from trade unions, NGOs, charities, and other 'third sector' organizations (Picard, 2015). There are also sources that extend engagements beyond identifications of consumer, citizen or member, such as crowd-funding (Carvajal, García-Avilés, and González, 2012) although much hailed initiatives like www.spot.us have been short-lived, failing to attract sustainable funding (Johnson, 2015). In all cases, there can be cross-subsidy, with funds or resources derived from one area financing activities in another.

Industry levies and taxes

If there is 'market failure' to provide a public good in sufficient qualities, there are grounds for regulatory interventions to tax the profits of communication service providers to fund journalism. The main levy proposals advanced have been aimed at (a) digital content providers (search engines, content aggregators); (b) digital service providers (mobile and broadband ISPs); and (c) commercial publishers. Most prominent has been the so-called 'Google tax' in France (Zelnick, Taubon, and Cerutti, 2010), a proposed tax of 1–2 percent on revenue generated from online display ads to fund the press, although controversially not new online ventures. This led to Google establishing a €60 million fund to finance digital innovation, following fraught negotiations in which Google threatened to stop indexing European news sites (*The Guardian*, 2013). However, there are greater challenges in collecting revenues from search engines and aggregators than for alternative proposals to tax ISPs whose revenues are derived from peoples' willingness to pay for broadband services to access content, even if not for the content itself. Leigh (2012) proposed a £2 levy on the monthly bills of UK broadband subscribers, although one of the strongest objections was to his suggestion that this be distributed to newspapers in proportion to their online readership.

Even modest levies can generate significant resources. A 1 percent levy on the total revenue of UK telecoms, according to 2010 data, would generate £405 million, argues the MRC (2011: 7). Moreover, "Far from being 'stealth taxes,' these would be open and transparent mechanisms applied to a range of operators—which could include ISPs, broadcasters, mobile phone operators and hardware companies—in order to raise much needed revenue to fill news 'gaps'" (7). The proceeds of such levies could fund non-profit online journalism or local news hubs, disbursed by accountable grant-making agencies.

Indirect public funding

Other proposals draw on traditions of indirect state support. This has particular resonance in the US where free-market orthodoxies sought to eclipse not only contemporary proposals for public subsidy but their historical presence. In a politically charged excavation, McChesney and Nichols (2010) uncover the early Republic's support for printing and postal subsidies for newspapers, that applied regardless of viewpoint and flourished up to the mid-nineteenth century, and estimate their equivalent contemporary value at around $30 billion a year, far greater than the $400 million federal subsidy for public broadcasting. Despite the promoted image of US press freedom as derived from solidly free market foundations, the level of actual indirect support has been calculated as $1.2 billion a year (Cowan and Westphal, 2010).

Indirect support is common across Western Europe, including reduced costs for postal carriage, favorable rates for public utilities such as telecommunications, and reductions in business taxes. This indirect support is worth hundreds of millions of Euros per year representing "a much more significant form of public support for the media than is commonly realised"; as a total proportion of public spending, it ranges from around 7 percent in Germany, where 90 percent of support is to PSM, up to 45 percent in Finland (Nielsen and Linnebank, 2011: 5). Such public subsidy is taken by firms that are often the fiercest critics of 'state' funded PSM. Indirect support also goes overwhelmingly to incumbent, private sector organizations. A few countries give direct aid to news brands although indirect aid remains the larger share; direct subsidies make up 0.1 percent in Finland, 1 percent in France, and 13 percent in Italy (Nielsen and Linnebank, 2011: 18). These subsidies are generally popular too. In November 2013 when a newly elected right-wing government in Norway tried to remove the country's press subsidies the proposals were roundly rejected by parliament. Norway's subsidies are mostly directed at papers with low advertising revenues and have helped to sustain far greater diversity than a fully market system would support, including meeting around a third of the revenue for the left-wing daily *Klassekampen* (Class Struggle) (McChesney, 2014). In 2014 147 newspapers received direct subsidies worth NOK 345 million, most of which was production grants, awarded in proportion to papers' circulation and market position; indirect support, notably exception from sales tax, amounts to nearly six times that figure (Mathisen, 2013).

The main forms of indirect subsidy, however, relief from VAT/sales taxes on print sales and print advertising, are declining in value as ad sales and paid circulation fall, prompting calls for digital subsidies. The European Newspaper Publishers Association (2015) calls on the EU "to provide Member States with the possibility of applying zero, super-reduced and reduced VAT rates for digital press, while maintaining the existing rates for printed press." There has been no substantial public funding dedicated to digital-only news media, except in France which provides support for ventures that employ at least one professional journalist regularly (Nielsen and Linnebank, 2011). However, innovative subsidies for entry-level journalism jobs have been introduced in the Netherlands. UK reformers have recommended direct subsidy to fund a single, entry-level reporter for local news organizations dedicated to coverage of local politics in the town hall and in the community (MRC, 2011). These various social market approaches advocate market intervention to address systemic market failure.

For advocates of public subsidy a key debate is whether any share should be directed to commercial news providers. Some favor direct over indirect subsidies as ways of targeting aid and intervening "in more precise and cost-efficient ways to support specific parts of what private sector media companies do" (Nielsen and Linnebank, 2011: 24). By contrast, McChesney argues against any form of 'corporate welfare' for US commercial media which "makes decreasing sense as capitalists abandon the field" and instead argues public subsidy should support the establishment of a "nonprofit, noncommercial, competitive, uncensored, and independent press system, embracing digital technologies" (McChesney, 2014). McChesney and Nichols (2010) build on Dean Baker's proposal to grant every American over 18 up to $200 of government money annually to direct to any non-profit medium they selected, subject to conditions: the recipient must be a recognized non-profit, take no commercial advertising and any content produced by the subsidy must enter the public domain freely, with no copyright protection. This would "amount to a $30 billion public investment with no government control over who gets the money" and would "promote all sorts of competition as well, as entities would be competing for the monies" (McChesney, 2014). A milder variant proposes to encourage tax-deductible citizen-donations (Downie and Schudson, 2009), but this source of income currently remains small and would be less dependable.

Other approaches seek to support alternatives to commercial enterprises and derive direct and indirect benefits from that status in respect of taxation, business and related costs. In the UK there are proposals to allow more newspapers to become charitable trusts, governed by charitable purposes and trading as non-profit distributing entities. Another proposal is for local newspapers to be given the status of community assets. Here the emphasis shifts from the economic benefits of status toward safeguards against the closure or sale of enterprises regarded as providing important services for the community. A third proposed structure is that of co-operative ownership. Co-operative ventures must serve to benefit members as their principal purpose rather that to generate profits *per se*, and being funded by readers and members protects against dependency on sources "that may not have the same interests (or longevity) as the outlet's reader community" (MRC, 2011: 11). In the US, the non-profit news sector ranges from the national *ProPublica* and *Consumer Reports* to the community-based *Voice of San Diego* and *MinnPost* and employed 1,300 by 2010, yet is underfunded and lacks sustainable business models (McChesney, 2013: 196–202).

Public duties for commercial providers

Another route is based on revitalized regulation to place public service obligations on commercial providers. UK reformers have proposed that commercial firms with significant market share should help to ensure media plurality by adhering to agreed standards, such as protecting journalistic independence and editorial output, in tandem with upper limits on ownership in the total media market, and national and regional news markets, so that no single voice can control more that 20 or 30 percent (CPBF, 2015):

> Any publisher with a 15 per cent share in a designated market should be subject to a Public Interest test … Ownership concentration above the 15 per cent threshold may be permitted if publishers meet certain obligations, such as investment in newsgathering or original programming, upholding codes of practice, and protecting editorial independence.

Such proposals have gained support from social democratic and socialist parties, trade unions and others. By contrast, most commercial news enterprises oppose new regulatory or financial obligations, yet their calls for subsidy and support open up space for negotiation.

Civil society resources

Can funding from foundations and charitable trusts rescue public interest journalism? Some innovative online ventures have been nurtured. However, the sums involved are miniscule set against the wider problem of post-news industry viability and even small ventures can burn through large grants rapidly, a critical issue when most grant funding is time-limited; *openDemocracy* spent £4.35 million between 2001 and 2008 from grants and donations, even though based principally on volunteer journalistic labor (Curran, 2011: 95–96). A Knight Foundation (2015: 4) report on 20 non-profits it supported found most depended on grant funding and "few appear to be rapidly approaching a sustainable business model." While predominantly beneficial, Foundation support is also relatively unaccountable and influenced to varying degrees by its source in corporate profits or the family behests of aristocrats and plutocrats. Proposals to tap civil society resources include developing community radio and media hubs for pro-am collaborations. Some of these require state resources and public subsidy but others seek to connect professional journalists, civil society organizations and citizen journalists in news hubs, for sustainable hyperlocal and local journalism (MRC, 2011).

Public service media and plurality

The use of grants and civil society resources can support innovative models of journalism and contribute to pluralism. Yet they do not provide sufficient resources to finance sustained public interest news journalism (McChesney and Nichols, 2010). With the commercial system failing, resourcing a viable journalism that includes a sizeable body of salaried journalists will require building on PSM. The internet offers tremendous possibilities to refresh PSM's mandate, from accessible, location-based news and entertainment services for all, to digital public spaces for debate (Curran, 2011; BBC, 2015). Most public service broadcasters have expanded into online news publishing, though some have been restricted. In the UK, the main BBC TV channel remains the top news source used by 53 percent of adults, with the BBC website app the third most used news source (24 percent) (Ofcom, 2014: 3). With sufficient funding, PSM can provide high-quality news and information, subject to regulation to support professionalism, impartiality and internal pluralism.

Will financing PSM undermine commercial operators and hasten their decline, eroding pluralism? According to some commercial media associations, public subsidy undermines the viability of market-based media by 'crowding out' commercial players and constraining private enterprise (European Newspaper Publishers Association, 2015). Yet, the evidence of press subsidies shows that this need not be the case. Targeted public subsidies in Finland, Italy and France have helped "the press increase its reach, helped smaller publications survive, and helped bigger ones increase both their profits and their potential to do public good" (Nielsen and Linnebank, 2011: 9). A report by KPMG likewise found that the BBC does not crowd out local newspapers, concluding that adoption of the internet had a larger effect on these businesses than any attributable to BBC online provision (BBC Trust, 2015: 12); BBC investment in online decreased between 2010 and 2015 when it remained less than 6 percent of license fee spending (£201 million of £3.62 billion). Instead of crowding out private media, PSM can create valuable incentives for them to innovate. However, the use of public money must be accountable, transparent and supported by on-going studies into what balance of incentives and obligations can best sustain news plurality across markets.

PSM resources will need to be better integrated with non-profits, social enterprises and even commercial providers (subject to public interest regulation) to support the kind of plural media system outlined earlier. In 2015 the BBC piloted Local Live streams that incorporate local press and 'hyperlocal' links and direct users to BBC and external content. Identifying local journalism as "one of the biggest market failures in news" the BBC proposed more 'open' partnerships with publishers, sharing content and links, alongside increased investment in local online news (BBC, 2015: 21). In response, the News Media Association (2015: 58) opposed BBC 'encroachment' into local news markets and called for greater access to BBC content, funding, and promotion to direct users to commercial news brands' ad-funded sites. Others want the license fee 'top sliced' to fund public journalism but this putatively progressive proposal overlaps with neoliberal agendas to shrink PSM. It also clashes with efforts to sustain PSM jobs and conditions as integral to the goals of robust journalism, better training, access and workplace diversity (Hardy, 2015).

Resourcing a viable journalism will need public subsidy, support for social enterprise, and public interest obligations on large communication providers in a system of incentives and controls that include ownership regulation and levies. There needs to be well-funded digital journalism committed to professional norms, insulated from political or commercial pressures, internally pluralist and organized around serving publics. That requires accountable public institutions but journalism also needs a dynamic, pluralistic environment. Radical democrats are right to argue for diversified media systems that capture the benefits of different arrangements and sectors. The case for PSM at the core remains strong. But there must be diversity and competition within PSM, and greater interlinking with a flourishing sector of non-profits that draw on individual creativity, community voice, and civil society resources. There is also greater scope to pool resources between PSM and commercial media, in areas such as local journalism, subject to public interest governance. A mixed system has other merits. No single source of support meets all objections to its impact on building a sustainable and stable financial model. Public subsidy will remain politically contested, opposed by powerful industry voices, susceptible to poor governance and sensitive to volatile economic and political conditions. Any proposals for reform must also be rooted in understanding the histories, institutional cultures and political economies of the media systems they are recommended for. All these proposals emanate from the argument that journalism is a public good, required by society but which the market left to itself will not provide in sufficient quality and quantity; "Like other public goods, if society wants it, it will require public policy and public spending. There is no other way" (McChesney, 2014).

Further reading

A good overview of trends is Janet Jones and Lee Salter's (2012) *Digital Journalism*. London, UK: Sage. Also recommended is Bob Franklin (ed.) (2013) *The Future of Journalism: Developments and Debates*. Abingdon, Oxon: Routledge. For responses to the crisis of American news media, see Robert McChesney and Victor Picard (eds) (2011) *Will the Last Reporter Please Turn Out the Lights: The Collapse of Journalism and What Can be Done to Fix It*. New York, NY: The New Press.

References

Almiron, N. (2010) *Journalism in Crisis: Corporate Media and Financialization*. Cresskill, NJ: Hampton Press.

Baker, C.E. (2002) *Media, Markets, and Democracy*. Cambridge, UK: Cambridge University Press.

BBC (2015) *The Future of News*. Available from: http://newsimg.bbc.co.uk/1/shared/bsp/hi/pdfs/29_01_15future_of_news.pdf (accessed 30 October 2015).

BBC Trust (2015) *Response to the DCMS Charter Review Consultation*. Available from: http://downloads.bbc.co.uk/bbctrust/assets/files/pdf/about/how_we_govern/charter_review/dcms_response.pdf (accessed 30 October 2015).

Beckett, C. (2008) *SuperMedia: Saving Journalism So It Can Save the World*. Oxford, UK: Wiley-Blackwell.

Benkler, Y. (2006) *The Wealth of Networks*. New Haven, CT: Yale University Press.

Bennett, W.L. (2011) *News: The Politics of Illusion*. 9th edn. Chicago, IL: University of Chicago Press.

Carvajal, M., García-Avilés, J. and González, J. (2012) "Crowdfunding and Non-Profit Media: The Emergence of New Models for Public Interest Journalism." *Journalism Practice* 6(5–6): 638–647.

Christians, C., Glasser, T., McQuail, D., Nordenstreng, K. and White, R. (2009) *Normative Theories of Media: Journalism in Democratic Societies*. Urbana, IL: University of Illinois Press.

Chyi, H. and Lee, A. (2013) "Online News Consumption: A Structural Model Linking Preference, Use, and Paying Intent." *Digital Journalism* 1(2): 194–211.

Cowan, G. and Westphal, D. (2010) *Public Policy and Funding the News*. Los Angeles, CA: USC Annenberg.

CPBF (2015) *A Manifesto for Media Reform*. Available from: www.cpbf.org.uk/files/media_manifesto_2015.pdf (accessed 30 October 2015).

Curran, J. (2002) *Media and Power*. London, UK: Routledge.

Curran, J. (2011) *Media and Democracy*. London, UK: Routledge.

Davies, N. (2008) *Flat-Earth News*. London, UK: Chatto and Windus.

Downie, L., Jr. and Schudson, M. (2009) "The Reconstruction of American Journalism." *Columbia Journalism Review*, 19 October. Available from: http://www.cjr.org/reconstruction/the_reconstruction_of_american.php (accessed 30 October 2015).

Enders Analysis (2011) *Competitive Pressures on the Press: Presentation to the Leveson Enquiry*. Available from: http://www.endersanalysis.com/content/publication/competitive-pressures-press-presentation-leveson-inquiry (accessed 30 October 2015).

European Newspaper Publishers Association (2015) *Issues*. Available from: http://www.enpa.be/en/issues_3.aspx (accessed 30 October 2015).

Franklin, B. (2009) *The Future of Newspapers*. London, UK: Routledge.

Grueskin, B. Seaves, S. and Graves, L. (2011) *The Story So Far: What we Know about the Business of Digital Journalism*. New York, NY: Columbia Journalism School.

Hardy, J. (2014) *Critical Political Economy of the Media*. Abingdon, Oxon: Routledge.

Hardy, J. (2015) "'Counting on Plurality' Means Adding to the BBC." *Open Democracy*, 29 April. Available from: https://www.opendemocracy.net/ourbeeb/jonathan-hardy/'counting-on-plurality'-means-adding-to-bbc (accessed 30 October 2015).

Jackson, D. and Moloney, K. (2015) "Inside Churnalism." *Journalism Studies*. DOI: 10.1080/1461670X.2015.1017597.

Jackson, J. (2015) "UK Adults Willing to Pay Only 92p a Month to Access News Websites." *The Guardian*, 9 April. Available from: http://www.theguardian.com/media/2015/apr/09/uk-news-web-sites-iab-digital-ad-spend-2014 (accessed 30 October 2015).

Johnson, K. (2015) "Why Crowdfunded Journalism Pioneer Spot.Us Died." *MediaShift*, 19 March. Available from: http://www.pbs.org/idealab/2015/03/why-crowdfunded-journalism-pioneer-spot-us-died/ (accessed 30 October 2015).

Kaye, J. and Quinn, S. (2010) *Funding Journalism in the Digital Age*. New York, NY: Peter Lang.

Knight Foundation (2015) *Gaining Ground*. Available from: http://knightfoundation.org/features/non-profitnews-2015-summary/ (accessed 30 October 2015).

Leigh, D. (2012) "A £2-a-Month Levy on Broadband Could Save Our Newspapers." *The Guardian*, 23 September. Available from: http://www.theguardian.com/media/2012/sep/23/broadband-levy-save-newspapers (accessed 30 October 2015).

Mathisen, G. (2013) "In Norway, a Slow Road Toward Subsidies for Digital Media." *European Journalism Centre*. Available from: http://ejc.net/magazine/article/in-norway-a-slow-road-toward-subsidies-for-digital-media#.VXQgMOcVgmE (accessed 30 October 2015).

McChesney, R. (2013) *Digital Disconnect*, New York: The New Press

McChesney, R. (2014) "Sharp Left Turn for the Media Reform Movement." *Monthly Review* 65(9), February. Available from: http://monthlyreview.org/2014/02/01/sharp-left-turn-media-reform-movement/ (accessed 30 October 2015).

McChesney, R. and Nichols, J. (2010) *The Death and Life of American Journalism*. Philadelphia, PA: Nation Books.

McChesney, R. and Scott, B. (eds) (2004) *Our Unfree Press: 100 Years of Radical Media Criticism*. New York, NY: New Press.

McManus, J. (1994) *Market-driven Journalism*. Thousand Oaks, CA: Sage

Media Reform Coalition [MRC] (2011) *Funding Models for News in the Public Interest*. Available from: http://www.mediareform.org.uk/wp-content/uploads/2013/04/Funding-briefing-paper.pdf (accessed 30 October 2015).

Myllylahti, M. (2014) "Newspaper Paywalls—The Hype and the Reality: A Study of How Paid News Content Impacts on Media Corporation Revenues." *Digital Journalism* 2(2): 179–194.

NAA (Newspaper Association of America) (2014) "Business Model Evolving, Circulation Revenue Rising." 18 April. Available from: http://www.naa.org/Trends-and-Numbers/Newspaper-Revenue/Newspaper-Media-Industry-Revenue-Profile-2013.aspx (accessed 30 October 2015).

Newman, N. and Levy, D. (2015) *Digital News Report*. Oxford, UK: Reuters Institute for the Study of Journalism. Available from: http://reutersinstitute.politics.ox.ac.uk/publication/digital-news-report-2015.

Newman, N. and Levy, D. (2015) *Reuters Institute Digital News Report*. Available from: http://www.digitalnewsreport.org/ (accessed 30 October 2015).

News Media Association (2015) *UK News Provision at the Crossroads*. Available from: http://www.news-mediauk.org/write/MediaUploads/PDF%20Docs/OandO_NMA_-_UK_news_provision_at_the_crossroads.pdf (accessed 30 October 2015)

Nielsen, R. and Linnebank, G. (2011) *Public Support for the Media: A Six-Country Overview of Direct and Indirect Subsidies*. Oxford, UK: Reuters Institute for the Study of Journalism.

Ofcom (2014) *News Consumption in the UK: 2014 Report*. London, UK: Ofcom.

PEW (2015) *State of the News Media*. Available from: http://www.journalism.org/files/2015/04/FINAL-STATE-OF-THE-NEWS-MEDIA1.pdf (accessed 30 October 2015).

Picard, R. (2015) "Twilight or New Dawn of Journalism." *Digital Journalism* 2(3): 273–283.

Sebastian, M (2014) "Native Ad Spending to Jump Despite Marketer Reservations." *Adage*, 21 November. Available from: http://adage.com/article/digital/native-ad-spending-jumps-marketers-reservations/295956/ (accessed 30 October 2015).

Silverman, C. (2015) *Lies, Damn Lies and Viral Content*. New York, NY: Tow Centre for Digital Journalism. Available from: http://towcenter.org/research/lies-damn-lies-and-viral-content/ (accessed 30 October 2015).

The Guardian (2013) "Google Sets Up £52m Fund to Settle French Publishing Row." 1 February. Available from: http://www.theguardian.com/technology/2013/feb/01/google-52m-fund-help-french-publishers (accessed 30 October 2015).

Turow, J. (2011) *The Daily You*. New Haven, CT: Yale University Press.

Zelnick, P., Taubon, J. and Cerutti, G. (2010) *Creation et Internet*. Rapport au Ministre de la Culture et de la Communication. Available from: http://www.ladocumentationfrancaise.fr/var/storage/rapports-publics/104000006.pdf (accessed 30 October 2015).

16

NEWSPAPER PAYWALLS AND CORPORATE REVENUES

A comparative study

Merja Myllylahti

This chapter explores how charging for digital news may support news publishers' revenues and newsroom structures. Proliferation of digital subscriptions started after traditional, print-based business models of the Western newspaper publishers began to falter. After the 2007–2008 global financial crisis, newspapers' advertising revenues declined sharply, and their newsrooms shrank as a consequence. In this context, newspapers' search for new revenue streams intensified, and they started to monetize online news content. Since 2012, news publishers in multiple countries such as the United States, Britain, Brazil, Germany, Japan, and Australia, have introduced charges for their online readers. In 2014, 73 percent of 45 largest global newspaper publishers had introduced a paywall (Marsh, 2014).

A paywall can be defined as a subscription model which limits public's access to all or to some digital news content, if no fee is paid. A hard paywall refers to a model that only allows readers to access content via subscription; a metered model allows public to read a certain number of articles without a charge before paying; and a freemium model allows free access to a selection of content, but charges for premium content. A metered model is the most common paywall employed by Western newspapers.

News revenue models have become a critical research area for the academy as the struggles of news publishers have continued and as these models impact on newsroom structures and editorial jobs. Costa has noted that "To produce quality journalism and perpetuate their role as independent, critical moderators among increasingly diffuse centres of power, they [newspapers] must come to terms with a new business model" (Costa, 2013: 92). The focus of the earlier academic studies, related to the paid online news content, has been in people's willingness to pay (Chyi, 2005, 2012). More recently researchers have started to explore paywalls in the context of revenue, content, audience, and wider society (Chiou and Tucker, 2013; Brandstetter and Schmalhofer, 2014; Myllylahti, 2014; Pickard and Williams, 2013; Sjøvaag, 2015). In 2014, Myllylahti noted that paywalls might impact on wider society by stating that "Charging for [online] news content has the potential to create a new digital divide between those who can afford to pay for news, and those who cannot" (Myllylahti, 2014: 190–191). Similarly, Pickard and Williams observed that digital subscriptions "Further inscribe commercial values into newsgathering processes; and, by extension, they may further constrict the scope of voices and viewpoints in the press" (2013: 14).

A 2014 study of eight countries found that paywalls, on their own, were not a viable business model for news publishers. The study found that digital-only subscriptions contributed approximately 10 percent towards news publishers' revenue (Myllylahti, 2014). The findings were in line with the PwC's views. In 2014, the consultancy group estimated that digital subscriptions would make 8 percent of the total global circulation revenue by 2018 (PwC, 2014). In 2015, news publishers believed that 20 percent of their future earnings would come from metered paywalls (eight from hard paywalls). Additionally, a survey conducted by the *Guardian* and SurveyMonkey revealed that news publishers expected 29 percent of their future income to come from online advertising (Berliner, 2015).

Research by Chiou and Tucker (2013) demonstrates that paywalls may impact on news readership. Their analyses of three American local newspapers discovered that the introduction of paywalls impacted negatively on readership, especially among young people. Financial newspapers, such as *The National Business Review* (NBR) in New Zealand, have argued that paywalls aid the quality of their journalism as their readers would not pay for clickbait journalism. The paper's journalist Chris Keall has noted that "People won't pay for churnalism, advertorial, or a story on Kate Middleton they can see on 10,000 other sites" (Keall, 2014). However, in their study, Brandstetter and Schmalhofer (2014) observed that the business and finance section of the German online news site *welt.de* offered very little unique content after the paper implemented a paywall. On the other hand, Sjøvaag's (2015) study of three Norwegian newspapers found that the papers had put commentary, analysis, and feature articles behind a paywall, but general news content was freely accessible. The publishers considered that as the production of features and analysis required more time to produce, this required a bigger investment. In this case, it could be argued that a paywall may protect the 'quality' of journalism—if publishers are willing to invest on it.

Growth in subscriptions, but not necessarily in advertising

In order to explore how newspapers digital subscription numbers have evolved and how paywall revenues have developed, a document analysis was conducted. The data were mainly derived from news publishers' annual reports. None of the news corporations analyzed here provided additional information when asked, demonstrating sensitivity around digital income numbers. When evaluating digital subscriptions, the data were gathered a year after each corporation implemented a paywall and then again in 2014. As the disclosure about the digital subscription revenues was poor, available data were used and compared to data provided by earlier academic research. The data concerning digital advertising revenue were examined when, and as, relevant data were retrievable. In general, it can be stated that the document analysis is an efficient research method. As Bowen (2009) observes, documents are a stable and an exact research source even when they may lack in detail and certain information. News publishers and newspapers analyzed here included:

- The New York Times Corporation (US)—the *New York Times*
- News Corp (UK)—*The Times* and the *Sunday Times*, the *Sun*
- Pearson (UK)—*Financial Times*
- Schibsted (Norway)—*Aftenposten*
- Axel Springer (Germany)—*Die Welt*
- Sanoma (Finland)—*Helsingin Sanomat*
- Fairfax Media (Australia)—*The Age* and *The Sydney Morning Herald*

These corporations were chosen for analysis as they represent some of the largest newspaper publishers in the United States, Britain, Scandinavia, Europe, and Australasia. The newspapers explored include general newspapers, tabloid, and financial journals. Most of the newspapers examined have introduced a metered paywall, and these include: the *New York Times* (2011), *Die Welt* (2013), *Helsingin Sanomat* (2012), the *Financial Times* (2007), *The Age* and *The Sydney Morning Herald* (2013), and *Aftenposten* (2013). *The Times, The Sunday Times* (2010), and the *Sun* (2013) have a hard paywall. It is worth noting here that many of these corporations also have other publications behind paywalls, and they have not been taken into account here. For example, FT Group's *The Economist* and Axel Springer's *Bild* also charge for access, and News Corp also have paywalled newspapers in the United States and Australia.

The *Financial Times* has gained substantially in paid digital subscriptions since it introduced charges for its online content. The paper's digital-only subscriptions grew from 109,609 in 2007 to 504,000 in 2014, an increase of 359 percent. Other newspapers explored introduced their paywalls much later, and therefore data concerning them only cover a 1- or 2-year period, and their growth numbers are naturally lower. As Figure 16.1 demonstrates, the *New York Times* has gained 36 percent in digital-only subscriptions since it started to charge for online access. The paying digital audience of *The Times* and *The Sunday Times* (combined) has grown 53 percent, the *Sun*—92 percent, *Helsingin Sanomat*—23 percent, *Die Welt*—6.3 percent, and *The Sydney Herald* and *The Age* (combined)—132 percent. However, it should be noted that in the case of *Helsingin Sanomat* it is not clear if its numbers include bundled or digital-only subscriptions. Schibsted has introduced paywalls for its newspapers in Sweden and Norway, but it does not break down numbers for its digital subscribers. The company has not disclosed how many people are paying for the digital *Aftenposten*, but it has been suggested that the number is in the region of 90,000 (INMA, 2014).

As seen here, in 2014 the *New York Times* was leading in terms of digital subscription with 910,000 readers, followed by the *Financial Times* with 504,000 digital-only subscriptions. The British tabloid newspaper the *Sun* had rapidly increased its paying digital reader base, which in 2014 was 225,000. These outlets have enjoyed strong growth, but how sustainable

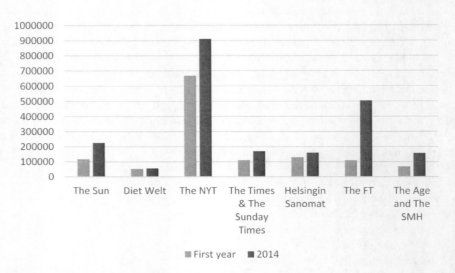

Figure 16.1   Growth in paid digital subscriptions since paywall launch.

Sources: Axel Springer, The NYT Company, News Corp, Sanoma, Pearson, Fairfax Media.

it is? In 2014, Bourgeault observed that the *New York Times* was "Starting to experience a slowdown in digital subscription growth" (Bourgeault, 2014). Similarly, the *Financial Times'* decision in early 2015 to abolish its metered model (after eight years from its implementation) is somewhat telling. The company introduced one month's paid-for-trials for its digital news content offering its readers an access for a 'nominal sum' (Jackson and Plunkett, 2015). The *Financial Times'* chief executive officer John Ridding explained the change by stating that "The theory is that within that they can build a habit, and then become a subscriber" (Jackson and Plunkett, 2015). Ridding believed that by offering trials it could "increases subscription rates by between 11 percent and 29 percent," making the system more efficient than a metered paywall (Jackson and Plunkett, 2015).

Evaluating paywall revenue proved challenging—only The New York Times Company and Fairfax Media disclosed transparent data about their digital-only subscription income. As seen in Figure 16.2, The New York Times Company's revenue from digital-only subscription packages grew from 111.7 million in 2012 to 169 million in 2014, an increase of 51.6 percent. In 2014, paywall made 10.6 percent of the company's total revenue, compared to 7.2 percent in 2011 (Myllylahti, 2014).

Fairfax Media launched digital subscriptions for its general newspapers *The Age* and *The Sydney Morning Herald* in 2013 after putting its financial newspaper the *AFR* behind a paywall in 2011. In 2014, Fairfax made AUD$24 million revenue out of these three paywalls, and this represented 2 percent of the company's total revenue (Fairfax Media, 2014). Pearson does not disclose how much revenue the *Financial Times* makes out of its digital subscriptions, and neither do Schibsted, News Corporation, or Sanoma give details about their stables. In 2015, the standard digital sub-scription package for FT.com was US$310 a year. Based on this pricing and the number of 207,000 digital-only subscribers, the paywall income of FT.com in 2010 can be estimated as US$64 million, representing 9.2 percent of the FT Group's total sales of US$698 million. Using the same pric-ing mechanism and the digital-only subscription number of 504,000, FT.com's paywall revenue in 2013 was US$156 million, representing 22 percent of the FT Group's total sales of US$707 million. This demonstrates a clear increase in its paywall income as the paywall revenue in 2012 was estimated as 13 percent of the company's total revenue (Myllylahti, 2014). In 2013, digital subscriptions made almost two thirds of the *Financial Times'* total paying audience (Pearson, 2013).

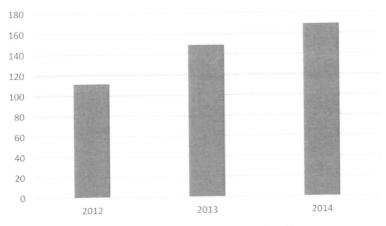

Figure 16.2 The NYT Company paywall revenue 2012–2014/US$ million.

Sources: The New York Times Annual Reports 2012–2014.

In 2014, Schibsted reported that its online newspapers in Norway and Sweden made 1,956 million Norwegian kronor in revenue compared to the company's total revenue of 14,975 million Norwegian kronor (Schibsted, 2014). Based on these figures, it can be estimated that the company's online newspapers contributed 13 percent toward its total earnings. However, the figures do not reveal anything about Schibsted's digital-only subscription revenue. If we calculate number of digital subscriptions and multiply them with the digital subscription package price, we can estimate that the paywall income of *Helsingin Sanomat* (Sanoma) is approximately 26 million euros, representing 1.4 percent of its total revenue; *Die Welt*'s (Axel Springer) 8.7 million euros, 0.2 percent of the company's total revenue; and *The Times & The Sunday Times* (News Corp) 29.8 million euros, representing 0.39 percent of News Corp's total revenue. A 2014 study estimated that in 2012 the digital subscription revenue of the two News Corp papers was 8.9 percent of the company's publishing revenue (Myllylahti, 2014). Substantial difference between these two estimates is most likely due to the changes in the News Corp organizational structure and revenue reporting. In 2013, News Corporation was split into two separate companies: News Corp and Twenty-First Century Fox Inc. News Corp's tabloid the *Sun* launched a paywall in 2013. In 2014, the paper had 225,000 digital subscribers. Based on the pricing of its most common digital package of 11 euros, its paywall income was approximately 29.95 million euros—as much as the combined revenue of *The Times* and *The Sunday Times*.

The National Business Review (in New Zealand) has argued that a paywall advances its advertising income, as the paper is able to "Deliver qualified audiences to advertisers," and therefore it can "Charge more for ads" (Keall, 2014). Also content sales manager Johanna Suhonen of *Kauppalehti* (the Finnish business daily) argues that paywall aids advertising as it can be modified according to advertiser's needs. "It is so easy to generate advertising revenue by loosening the paywall restrictions for content that is more in demand among advertisers" (Hantula, 2015). The *Financial Times* has also claimed to benefit from digital charges, as they have enabled collection of reader specific data, adding value for its advertisers (Bilton, 2014). However, some publishers have found that a paywall is ineffective in building audience and advertising income. In 2015, Canadian newspaper the *Toronto Star* abolished its paywall. The paper's chief operating officer Sandy Macleod stated that after a good start, its digital subscription growth came to a sudden halt: "Within about 90 days we seem to have plateaued—we spent about probably six months trying pretty aggressively trying to move the number and found that was expensive and a relatively high churn rate" (Christensen, 2015).

The digital advertising income of The New York Times Company has declined after its paywall implementation. The company's digital advertising income shrank 15.3 percent after charges were introduced for the digital content. In 2012, the company made US$215 million dollar revenue from digital advertising, but in 2014 it had fallen to US$182 million (The New York Times Company, 2014). Similarly, digital advertising income of Sanoma declined from EUR779.6 million in 2013 to EUR651 million in 2014, a decline of 16.4 percent (Sanoma, 2014). The way FT Group reports its income makes evaluating its digital advertising income difficult. What the company has stated is that its digital income as a whole is increasing, and its advertising income is shrinking compared to its subscription revenue. In 2010, the group's advertising income was 181 million British pounds, but in 2013 it was 166 million British pounds (Financial Times Group, 2013). However, it is not possible to tell how much of this advertising income comes from digital and print sources.

In contrast, Axel Springer has gained in advertising dollars, and its digital advertising revenue rose 10.8 percent after it launched paywall in Norway (Axel Springer, 2014). Fairfax also gained 5.6 percent in digital revenue after introducing digital charges for its general newspapers (Fairfax Media, 2014). It should be noted that these figures do not prove that paywalls advance digital advertising, neither have they proved that digital subscriptions hinder build up in advertising revenue. It is not possible to know how digital charges affect advertising without consulting news publishers. The advances in Axel Springer's and Fairfax's digital advertising income are more likely to do with diversification of their advertising portfolios. Schibsted, News Corp, Axel Springer, and Fairfax have all invested in online classified advertising and listing services, and this has most likely given a boost to their revenues. For example, in the first quarter of 2015, Schibsted increased its revenue from classified advertising by 13 percent from the same time in previous year (Schibsted, 2015).

Additional revenue, but newsrooms keep shrinking

The National Business Review states that a paywall aids journalism as it "Helps to fund professional newsroom" (Keall, 2014). The paper argues that it would not have been able to "replace every departing journalist on ad revenue alone" (Keall, 2014). However, it can be argued that in general income derived from paywalls would be only sufficient to fund substantially smaller newsrooms. To illustrate, in 2014, Fairfax's paywalls made AUD$24 million in revenue. In the same year, the company employed 7,043 people, and its staff costs were AUD$731 million (Fairfax Media, 2014). The company's staff-related expenses were over 30 times its paywall revenue. Looking at this from a different angle: in 2014, an average journalists' salary in Australia was AUD$48,313 per year. A very simplified calculation shows that the company would have been able to support 496 journalists with its paywall-only income (if assumed that all the workers were paid the average salary). Based on this scenario, Fairfax would need to cut 93 percent of its workforce if its operations were funded from digital subscriptions. In 2014, the *New York Times*' digital revenue was estimated at US$312 million. Bourgeault noted that this "Amount of revenue would only be able to support about 200 journalists, which is only about 20 percent of the current total" (Bourgeault, 2014).

What is clear is that paywalls provide additional revenue for newspaper publishers, although it is not substantial enough to sustain newsroom structures as print advertising and circulation incomes continue to shrink. To compensate for these declines, newspaper companies have continued redundancies: The New York Times Company, Fairfax Media, Sanoma, and Schibsted have all cut their workforces prior to and after paywalls were implemented. Cuts have also been felt in the FT Group: in 2013, 35 editorial posts were lost in the *Financial Times* newsroom after 'voluntary redundancies' (Turnvill, 2013).

Fairfax Media has shed 633 jobs since it introduced digital subscriptions, a reduction of 27 percent in its employee numbers. The company has cut editorial and photographic jobs in its Australian newsrooms. The number of the New York Times Group employees fell from 7,273 in 2011 to 3,529 in 2013, representing a 51 percent drop. In 2008, the *New York Times* cut 100 editorial jobs, in 2009 additional 100, and over 30 newsroom jobs were reduced in 2013. At the end of 2013, the newsroom had 1,330 workers. In 2014, more journalists were laid-off as the paper introduced a further 100 redundancies (Somaiya, 2014). Sanoma's workforce has shrank from 9,035 to 7,583 after it introduced digital subscriptions, a reduction of 16 percent in its employee number. These cuts have been felt in its newspapers and magazines, most notably in its masthead, *Helsingin Sanomat*'s, newsroom. The number of Schibsted's workforce has fallen 11.5 percent, from 7,800 to 6,900, and some of these cuts have been editorial jobs.

These layoffs are worrying as they impact on journalists' ability to do their jobs, as newsrooms are left with fewer journalists, who are required to produce content for print and online newspapers, shoot videos, take photos, moderate online comments, feed social media sites, and sub-edit their colleagues' stories. Nevertheless, some news publishers have argued that they have increased their newsroom spending as journalists need new skills. Fairfax Media, for example, has emphasized that it is 'upskilling' its journalists. The company's New Zealand executive editor Sinead Boucher commented in 2015 that "We're investing in our people and systems to reinvigorate our newsrooms" (Read, 2015). The company said that it was training its journalists with new skills as well as employing new teams to produce video, social media, and reader-generated content (Read, 2015).

Alternative, pay-per-article payment systems emerge

As discussed, paywalls have become a popular model for online news monetizing, and they generate additional revenue for newspapers. They do not work for all publishers, as seen in the cases of *The Dallas Morning News*, *The Toronto Star*, and *The San Francisco Chronicle*, which all have dropped their paywall, and they are exploring alternative funding models. New news payment systems are also emerging. Dutch company Blendle, for example, has developed a model that allows readers to pay-per-article. Both The New York Times Company and Axel Springer have invested in Blendle, which takes 30 percent of money the publishers earn via its pay system. Publishers set the cost for their articles, and prices vary from 10 to 30 cents for a newspaper articles to 20–79 cents for a magazine article. the *New York Times*, *The Wall Street Journal*, and the *Washington Post* are among the newspapers which have signed global licenses with Blendle. In April 2015, the Dutch company had over 250,000 users and stated that "We're proving that people do want to pay for great journalism" (Klöpping, 2015). Yet at the same time, the company noted that micropayments do not work for general news content, but they worked for analysis, opinion pieces, and long interviews. Alex Klöpping, co-founder of Blendle, observed that "We don't sell a lot of news in Blendle. People apparently don't want to spend money on something they can get everywhere for free now" (Klöpping, 2015).

Other companies have also developed new pay systems to aid publishers' content monetization. For example, a Finnish team, Prejkfast, has created a new standardized micropayment system for digital newspaper and magazine publishers. Also, Finnish companies Prime and Aatos have invented paywall systems, which offer either bundled content packages from international and domestic sources or personalized content packages from multiple magazines (Finland Ministry of Transport and Communication, 2015). Already in 2011, Slovakian Piano Media launched its national paywall system, which offers readers digital news content from multiple publishers with one single subscription. In 2014, the company was one of the leading providers for paywall solutions in the world after it acquired American digital media service company Press+.

It is hard to envision that per-pay-article systems would replace monthly subscriptions. The increases in digital subscriptions demonstrate that people are willing to subscribe to certain papers perhaps because of the brand loyalty or content provided. Some have doubted sustainability of micropayment systems. Filloux, for example, has pointed out that, in the case of the *New York Times*, revenue from Blendle would only provide the paper with a "Fraction of a percentage point to the $200 million a year cost of operating the Grey Lady's 1,300-staff newsroom" (Filloux, 2014). He argues that micropayments may damage news publishers' advertising revenue as pay-per-article systems do not provide similar in depth data about their readers as monthly subscription do. He draws parallels with the music industry, which started to lose income after people were able to buy individual songs (Filloux, 2014). Filloux makes a valid point by stating that "Paid-for music was not competing against free content in the way that today's paid content has to face a profusion of free editorial" (Filloux, 2014).

Conclusions and discussion

Analyzing news publishers' paywall revenue is an unnerving task: only two out of the seven news publishers analyzed here provided transparent information about their digital subscription and advertising revenue. What is clear is that paywall income is not substantial enough to support news publishers' current newsrooms structures. As demonstrated, newspaper publishers including The New York Times Company, FT Group (Pearson), Sanoma, Schibsted, and Fairfax Media have continued to lay-off their editorial workforce. It is safe to conclude that, if newspapers were funded by paywall revenue alone, they could only sustain substantially smaller newsrooms. In the case of Fairfax, for example, it would need to cut 93 percent of its newsroom if its operations could only depend on paywall income.

Some conclusions can be drawn based on the analysis here. The newspapers examined, regardless of their target audience and type of the newspaper, have gained in digital subscriptions since they were introduced. the *Financial Times* gained 359 percent increase in its digital subscriptions in 7 years, the *New York Times* 36 percent in 3 years, and *The Times & The Sunday Times* 53 percent (combined) in 4 years. Interestingly, British tabloid the *Sun* gained 92 percent in digital subscriptions in the first year of paywall, and by 2014 its subscriptions had overtaken combined subscriptions of the *Times & The Sunday Times*.

The data suggest that the *New York Times* and the *Financial Times* have gained substantially in paywall revenue. The findings propose that in 2014 the *New York Times* paywall contributed 10.6 percent toward the company's total revenue (7.2 percent in 2011); and the *Financial Times'* 22 percent toward FT Group's total income (13 percent in 2012). Interestingly, only 1 year after paywall implementation the *Sun* produced as much as revenue as *The Times* and the *Sunday Times* together.

The analysis does not support the view that paywalls automatically advance publishers' advertising revenue. It should be noted that the information in this regard was lacking. The digital advertising income of The New York Times Company and Sanoma declined since they started to charge for digital access, but it is not possible to know if this relates to their paywall. Most likely their advertising revenues were affected by general economic trends. Digital advertising income of Axel Springer and Fairfax Media increased after paywall launch, but these advances are most likely due to increases in their classified advertising and listing services. The statement made by the *Financial Times* proposes that as a paywall helps publishers to gather more specific data about their readers, these data are more valuable for advertisers, implying it can charge for its advertisements. Without relevant data and management consultation, it is impossible establish if this is the case.

Paywalls have also come down. As the *Toronto Star* demonstrates, it abolished charges for its digital content after subscriptions stalled, and as it readers turned to free, alternative news sources. Canada's largest daily newspaper noted that retaining its digital readers was challenging as it had "a relatively high churn rate" (Christensen, 2015). The 'paywall tide' may have already turned, as a 2015 INMA survey suggests. In 2013, 48 percent of media executives regarded paywall as "absolutely crucial development", whereas in 2015 only 27 percent said so (Lichterman, 2015).

Competition between free and paid media outlets is also increasing, so creating revenue from digital subscriptions may prove more challenging in the future. Australia offers an example: recently news outlets, such as the *Guardian*, the *Mail Online*, the *Huffington Post* and *BuzzFeed*, have entered the Australian media market by launching Australian sites offering specific local content. These outlets compete directly with News Corp's subscription-based mastheads *The Australian*, and Fairfax's *The Age* and *The Sydney Morning Herald*.

References

Axel Springer (2014) *Annual Report 2014*. Available from: https://www.axelspringer.de/en/publikationen/cw_publikation_en_22817860.html.

Berliner, M. (2015) "Top Ten Media Trends for the Decade Ahead: Exclusive Survey Findings." *The Guardian*, 30 March. Available from: http://www.theguardian.com/media-network/2015/mar/30/top-ten-media-trends-next-decade-video.

Bilton, R. (2014) "Inside the Financial Times' Digital Strategy." *Digiday*, 5 May. Available from: http://digiday.com/publishers/inside-financial-timess-digital-strategy/.

Bourgeault, G. (2014) "New York Times: Digital Subscription Growth Slowing, Business No Longer Sustainable As Is." *Seeking Alpha*, August 27. Available from: http://seekingalpha.com/article/2453475-new-york-times-digital-subscription-growth-slowing-business-no-longer-sustainable-as-is.

Bowen, G. (2009) "Document Analysis as a Qualitative Research Method." *Qualitative Research Journal* 9(2): 27–40.

Brandstetter, B. and Schmalhofer, J. (2014) "Paid Content: A Successful Revenue Model for Publishing Houses in Germany?" *Journalism Practice* 8(5): 499–507.

Chiou, L. and Tucker, C. (2013) "Paywalls and the Demand for News." *Information Economics and Policy* 25(21013): 61–69.

Christensen, N. (2015) "Toronto Star Scrapped Digital Paywall as It Was 'Expensive' and Had a 'High Churn' Rate." *Mumbrella*, 11 May. Available from: http://mumbrella.com.au/toronto-star-scrapped-digital-paywall-as-it-was-expensive-and-had-a-high-churn-rate-292661.

Chyi, H.I. (2005) "Willingness to Pay for Online News: An Empirical Study of the Viability of the Subscription Model." *Journal of Media Economics* 18(2): 131–142.

Chyi, I. (2012) "Paying for What? How Much? And Why (Not)? Predictors of Paying Intent for Multiplatform Newspapers." *International Journal on Media Management* 14(3): 227–250.

Costa, C. (2013) "A Business Model for Digital Journalism: How Newspapers Should Embrace Technology, Social and Value Added Services." [Report] *Columbia Journalism School*. Available from: http://www.inma.org/blogs/keynote/post.cfm/6-pillars-of-a-revenue-generating-business-model-for-digital-journalism.

Fairfax Media (2014) *Annual Report 2014*. Available from: http://www.fairfaxmedia.com.au/Investors/annual-reports.

Filloux, F. (2014) "The New York Times and Axel Springer are Wrong about Blendle." *Monday Note*, 2 November. Available from: http://www.mondaynote.com/2014/11/02/the-new-york-times-and-springer-are-wrong-about-blendle/.

Financial Times Group (2013) *Financial Times Group—2013 Results*. Available from: http://aboutus.ft.com/2014/02/28/67012/#ixzz3ZVCM1IAH.

Finland Ministry of Transport and Communication (2015) *Mediainnovaatiokilpailun finalistit valittu*. Available from: http://www.lvm.fi/uutinen/4433751/mediainnovaatiokilpailun-finalistit-valittu#.VPd7NRwiu0U.twitter.

Hantula, K. (2015) "Four + One Truths about Paywalls." *Living Information*, 27 February. Available from: http://livinginformation.fi/en/articles/four-plus-one-truths-about-paywalls.

INMA (2014) *Aftenposten Transforming Print into Digital Readers*. Available from: http://www.inma.org/modules/campaignArchive/index.cfm?action=detail&zyear=2014&id=2613863C-8875-4954-B01FF579891BFFB1.

Jackson, J. and Plunkett, J. (2015) "Financial Times to Change Way It Charges for Online Content." *The Guardian*, 27 February. Available from: http://www.theguardian.com/media/2015/feb/27/financial-times-to-change-way-it-charges-for-online-content.

Keall, C. (2014) "10 Reasons to Love Paywall." *NBR*, 9 September. Available from: http://www.nbr.co.nz/paywall.

Klöpping, A. (2015) "Blendle: A Radical Experiment with Micropayments in Journalism, 365 Days Later." *Blendle blog*, 28 April. Available from: https://medium.com/on-blendle/blendle-a-radical-experiment-with-micropayments-in-journalism-365-days-later-f3b799022edc.

Lichterman, J. (2015) *NiemanLab*. 18 May. Available from: http://www.niemanlab.org/2015/05/survey-news-orgs-are-prioritizing-mobile-development-and-placing-less-emphasis-on-paywalls/.

Marsh, P. (2014) "The State of the Paid Content: For Free, for Fee, or Somewhere in Between." *INMA blog*, 4 November. Available from: http://www.inma.org/blogs/ahead-of-the-curve/post.cfm/the-state-of-paid-content-for-free-for-a-fee-or-somewhere-in-between#ixzz3TISeuynX.

Myllylahti, M. (2014) "Newspaper Paywalls—Hype and the Reality. A Study of How Paid News Content Impacts on Media Corporation Revenues." *Digital Journalism* 2(2): 179–194.

News Corp (2015) "Fiscal 2015 Third Quarter Financial Highlights." [Investor Statement] Available from: http://newscorp.com/2015/05/05/news-corp-reports-third-quarter-results-for-fiscal-2015/.

Pearson (2013) *Annual Report.* Available from: https://www.pearson.com/ar2013.html.

Pickard, V. and Williams, T. (2013) "Salvation or Folly? The Promises and Perils of Digital Paywalls." *Digital Journalism* 2(2): 195–213.

PwC (2014) "Global Entertainment and Media Outlook 2014–2018." Available from: http://www.pwc.com/gx/en/global-entertainment-media-outlook/index.jhtml.

Read, E. (2015) "Fairfax Newsrooms to Take 'Digital-Centric' Approach." *Stuff*, 17 March. Available from: http://www.stuff.co.nz/business/industries/67428664/fairfax-newsrooms-to-take-digitalcentric-approach.

Sanoma (2014) *Financial Statements and Board of Director's Report 2014.* Available from: https://www.sanoma.com/sites/default/files/reports/sanoma_financial_statements_2014.pdf.

Schibsted (2014) *Annual Report 2014.* Available from: http://hugin.info/131/R/1911430/682298.pdf.

Schibsted (2015) "Interim Financial Statement Q1 2015." [Market Release] Available from: http://www.schibsted.com/en/ir/Regulatory--and-pressreleases/Regulatory-and-Press-Releases-Archive1/2015/Schibsted-ASA-SCH---Interim-Financial-Statement-Q1-2015/.

Sjøvaag, H. (2015) "Introducing the Paywall." *Journalism Practice* 10(3): 1–19.

Somaiya, R. (2014) "Layoffs Begin at the Times after Buyouts Come Up Short." *The New York Times*, 16 December. Available from: http://www.nytimes.com/2014/12/17/business/layoffs-new-york-times.html.

The New York Times Company (2014) *Annual Report 2014.* Available from: http://investors.nytco.com/files/doc_financials/annual/2014/2014-Annual-Report-%28FINAL%29.pdf.

Turnvill, W. (2013) "FT Avoids Compulsory Redundancies as 30 Journalists Leave." *Pressgazzette*, 19 April. Available from: http://www.pressgazette.co.uk/ft-avoids-compulsory-redundancies-30-journalists-leave.

17

COMPUTATIONAL JOURNALISM AND THE EMERGENCE OF NEWS PLATFORMS

Nicholas Diakopoulos

In June 2014, the Coral Project launched with a $3.9m grant from the Knight Foundation. An ambitious effort to reimagine and create an open-source community platform, the goal was to enable publishers both large and small to cultivate and tap into their online communities, to support and empower contributors, and to provide for a productive and civic space for readers. Some might find this a curious endeavor given that analogous community platform software like Disqus or Livefyre already exists and are sold by such vendors to meet market needs. But what is particularly interesting and perhaps even paradigm shifting about the Coral Project is that it represents a collaboration between the *New York Times*, the *Washington Post*, and Knight-Mozilla OpenNews. It is a platform tailor-made for news publishers and the types of community needs that emerge in that context, with their interests and values designed into the core.

This chapter examines this shift in how news organizations are increasingly designing and creating their own tools, products, and even entire platforms through the lens of computational journalism (CJ). Current industry darlings like Buzzfeed, Vox Media, and Quartz, as well as incumbents like the *New York Times* are now leveraging technology and computing to create platforms that produce a competitive advantage by enabling scale and reducing marginal costs in the gathering, production, and dissemination of their content. I will explore how CJ and thinking factors into this shift, expound on examples of platforms that are emerging in the industry, and discuss the implications of platforms for media competition, scale, and independence.

Computational journalism

In this section, I motivate the emergence of news platforms by looking at antecedent concepts in CJ.

Recently, I have begun defining CJ as "Finding and telling news stories, with, by, or about algorithms," in an attempt to broaden the scope of the term to encompass the idea that journalism ought also to orient towards investigating and reporting about computation (Diakopoulos, 2015). But perhaps the most core, distinctive aspect of CJ is its focus on tooling, on designing "practices or services built around computational tools in the service of journalistic ends"

(Coddington, 2015: 6). Similar framings of CJ as tool oriented derive from Cohen, Hamilton, and Turner (2011) and from my own early writing in conceiving of the field as the application of computing and computational thinking to enable journalistic tasks such as information gathering, organization and sensemaking, storytelling, and dissemination (Diakopoulos, 2010). CJ largely inherits this focus from one of its parent fields—computer science—whose culture underscores the importance of engineering and the production of novel and inventive computational artifacts. Anderson (2013) points out the early focus on digital tooling in CJ research and the concomitant loss of a broader sociological approach to the field.

But it is precisely this focus on computational tools that help to solve real journalistic tasks that make it so appealing to the profession and to industry. New ways of producing quality news at greater speed and at lower cost are some of the fundamental 'promises' of CJ as articulated by Flew *et al.* (2012). Yet the speed and cost savings do not always materialize. Karlsen and Stavelin (2014) studied CJ in Norwegian newsrooms and found that contrary to the notion that it would be time-saving, it was rather an activity that required a heavy time investment (and thus human resource costs). These two views are not irreconcilable however. Recouping a time investment into a CJ endeavor can be accomplished through a process of abstraction that results in reusable pieces or even a platform around the core idea.

A key concept here, also important to definitions of CJ, is *computational thinking*. Jeannette Wing, the progenitor of the idea (2006) defines it as "The thought processes involved in formulating problems and their solutions so that the solutions are represented in a form that can be effectively carried out by an information-processing agent" (Wing, 2010). Relevant components of computational thinking include *abstraction* such as decomposition of problems, modeling, aggregation, and parameterization, *modularization*, and *automation* via algorithms to enable *scale*. Moving away from individual stories via a process of abstraction, parameterization, and modularization is what makes CJ pay as an investment. Importantly, computational thinking is distinctly not about programming per se, though programming is often the operationalization of that thinking into code. Code then becomes reusable, and the marginal costs of producing similar but different content from the same code-base are minimal. Creating platforms out of reusable code is the key economic benefit to CJ in the long term.

In addition to a general tool-orientation and an inclination toward computational thinking, other cultural distinctions in CJ also factor in to the emergence of news platforms. Coddington (2015) clarified nuances relating to the definitions of Computer-Assisted Reporting (CAR), Data-Driven Journalism (DDJ), and CJ by delineating differences along dimensions including professional orientation, openness, epistemology, and vision of the public. He concluded that CAR reflects a basis in social science methods and a public affairs orientation, whereas DDJ is marked by a different attitude towards story and to the role of the public, and CJ is rooted in applications of automation to information. The cultural underpinnings of DDJ and CJ are marked by a positive orientation towards open-source programming that privileges the creation of productive artifacts over one-off stories (Lewis and Usher, 2013). And the epistemological differences between CAR and DDJ or CJ are further underscored by Parasie's (2015) analysis of journalistic revelations in an investigation by the Center for Investigative Reporting which illuminated the tensions between the hypothesis-driven practice of CAR and the open attitude towards making data accessible of DDJ. Here we see a cultural shift that creates new opportunities for *data platforms* and the idea of news apps that can act as data appliances rather than specific story devices. Aitamurto and Lewis (Aitamurto and Lewis, 2013) have explored this more specifically in terms of the role of open APIs (Application Programming Interfaces) in news organizations. Such APIs essentially serve as content platforms on top of which other applications, services, and R&D innovation can take place.

What are platforms?

The use of the term 'platform' is sometimes vague and equivocal depending on its context. What exactly is the difference between a 'product platform' and a 'technology platform,' a 'brand platform' and a 'customer platform'? Gillespie (2010) shrewdly points out that the agnosticism to end-use and the semantic adaptability of the word is what makes it such a powerful appeal for technology companies to simultaneously communicate to different legal, user, and commercial constituencies. The term 'platform' connotes that some activity will be facilitated and take place as a result. Despite the semantic flexibility of the term when used by businesses for various audiences, others have sought to pin the term down more precisely. Kristjansson, Jensen, and Hildre (2004) analyzed a range of definitions from the product development literature to derive that platforms are "a collection of core assets that are reused to achieve a competitive advantage." Cusumano (2010) later posited that platforms are "a foundation or base of common components around which a company might build a series of related products." Key to both of these definitions is the idea of *reuse* of components, which is precisely what is enabled by computational thinking concepts like abstraction, modularization, and parameterization. CJ is thus conceptually primed to create platforms and to contribute reusable core technology assets to news organizations looking for a competitive advantage.

Cusumano (2011) enumerates some of the dimensions along which platforms vary, including the degree of openness of the interfaces to the platform, the degree of modularity, and the ease with which other organizations can leverage features of the platform to innovate. Platforms can be considered either internal product platforms or external industry platforms (Cusumano, 2010). Internal product platforms are those reusable tools that enable an organization to work more efficiently in their production processes. For news organizations, this might include everything from publishing tools, to information gathering and management systems, to analytics dashboards. An example of an internal product platform would be a homegrown Content-Management System (CMS) that is reconfigurable to produce different branded content sites under the umbrella organization's banner (e.g. Vox Media, or Huffington Post). On the other hand, we have industry-wide platforms that enable third party external organizations to build on top of the platform and create new forms of value. The more complementors there are in the platform ecosystem, the greater the value of the platform. An example of an industry content platform would be the early days of Twitter, when their APIs provided ample data and access for a burgeoning 3rd party apps ecosystem. Open APIs and plugin architectures are typical methods for creating industry platforms.

A third type of platform that is perhaps peculiar to the media industry is what I would call a *content platform*. Although still used internally to an organization, unlike internal product platforms, content platforms are not about component reuse but rather about streamlining the production of content through modularization, standardization, and parameterization of content in various ways. While a story is a single unitary output (or perhaps a series of related outputs), a platform for stories systematizes things like format, structure, style, and interaction. In essence, flexibility is traded off for efficiency in producing sets of content that are structurally similar yet perceptually and semantically distinct. In this sense, the product here *is* the content, the output of the use of a tool by a knowledgeable operator rather than the tool itself. The distinction between a tool and a platform blur somewhat here, but if you subscribe to the idea that content is the product, then authoring tools can certainly be considered the platform for the creation of that content. Just like other platforms, content platforms can be operated internally to an organization or be built as industry platforms.

Platform developments

Let us examine several specific examples of various types of platforms that are currently emerging in journalism to address tasks as wide ranging as collecting, organizing and making sense of, presenting, and disseminating news information.

The CMS is perhaps the quintessential example of a content platform and is often the locus for struggle as newsrooms evolve into pure digital organizations (Rodgers, 2015). Vox Media often touts its CMS, dubbed 'Chorus,' as one of its key assets. As Trei Bundrett writes on the Vox Product blog, "Unlike many media companies that delegated the web publishing problem to the IT department, we built a platform from the ground up by iterating with bloggers who knew how to tell stories and build communities on the web." (Brundrett, 2014). The Chorus CMS is used to organize and systematize the content production process and is used as the backend not only for Vox.com but also for Vox Media's other outlets, including SB Nation, The Verge, and Polygon. The repurposability of the platform allows the organization to create different branded experiences rapidly for niche audiences. In a bid to generalize its use further, in addition to the internal use of the platform, Vox is also experimenting with making Chorus available to external actors—advertisers—interested in creating native advertising content (Barr, 2015). Other extensions to Chorus are designed to meet specific news publisher needs. For instance, the Syllabus platform was inspired by a lack of products in the marketplace that could effectively be used for live blogging of events with large traffic (Reeder, 2012).

In addition to its CMS, which are proprietary platforms, Vox Media has periodically made its content open source, including everything from choropleth mapping tools, to meme generating interfaces, and quiz generators (MacWilliam, 2015; Lai, 2014; Victor, 2014). Quartz launched an open-source tool for creating simple graphics called Chartbuilder (Yanofsky, 2013), which has been taken up by other outlets like NPR, the Wall Street Journal, and the New Yorker. the *New York Times* has its own chart creation platform that is used internally to the organization called Mr. Chartmaker (Aisch, 2015). Such content platforms are about efficiency in content production. They take easily articulable templates of content: the map, the chart, the image meme, the quiz, and factor out design commonalities so that the authoring process can be systematized and potentially even carried out by less tech-savvy journalists. Tricky decisions like how to make the output content amenable to mobile devices or social media are handled by designers and developers that think through the abstract problem, solve it once, and bake that solution into code. The efficiency boost increases the amount of content that can be produced, speeds-up such output in a deadline situation, and enables less digitally skilled content creators to be productive.

Another area where content platforms have grown substantially is in what is often termed 'robot' journalism—the use of automation in the production of written news content. Automated Insights is a company that has been successful in selling the use of their platform to news organizations like the Associated Press, which in 2015 is set to produce and publish 3,000 earnings report articles per quarter written automatically using structured financial data (Kotecki, 2015). At the *LA Times*, the Homicide report used algorithmic reporting tools to produce short posts for the homicide blog as early as 2010 (Young and Hermida, 2015). This code was drawn from an even earlier project called Mapping LA and has since also been repurposed to write tailored posts about earthquakes in California. Essentially, internal code has been generalized and used in various different editorial products and domains.

Journalistic sensemaking of data and documents is also benefiting from new platforms being built that systematize analytic processes. If the result of this standardization is more content creation, these systems can also be considered content platforms. An example of this is the Story Discovery Engine (Broussard, 2014, this volume) which is a reporting tool that generates data visualizations of education data in Philadelphia, PA, as a mechanism to tip investigative journalists to areas where there are juicy stories to be reported. While it is designed to solve a problem on a specific beat and in a specific locality, the underlying model and visualization could be applied to other beats or jurisdictions given the availability of appropriate data. As Broussard writes, "Any newsroom can take the software, analyze local data, and generate dozens of original investigative stories that matter to the newsroom's specific audience" (Broussard, 2014: 11). Another effort along these lines, but oriented towards large investigative document analyses is the Overview project (Brehmer *et al.* 2014). As a tool, Overview offers the ability to cluster documents and visualize those clusters. But as a platform, Overview allows for others to build their *own* visualizations that plug into the underlying document storage and analytics, thus providing for a lot more flexibility and adaptability to the needs of different kinds of investigations. Another example of a sensemaking platform is the DocumentCloud project, which serves as a repository for collecting and annotating documents. The documents become a substrate for investigative journalism work that can be built upon using the API.

News organizations are also building sensemaking tools to facilitate journalism that is less directly tied to content creation. The BBC has developed a platform called Datastringer that can be set up by ostensibly non-coding journalists to monitor a dynamic data set over time (e.g. campaign contributions, or crime statistics). Calculations can be configured on the monitored data set and triggers then send alert emails to journalists when interesting patterns are observed by the algorithms (Shearer, Simon, and Geiger, 2014). In data journalism, there is much interest in crowdsourcing as a technique to help journalists make sense of large amounts of documents or data (Appelgren and Nygren, 2014). Hive, a journalistic platform built by the *New York Times*, has been built to facilitate such crowdsourcing projects (Ellis, 2014). Both Datastringer and Hive are platforms insofar as they are both open-source projects and can be built upon by others, yet there is little evidence that anyone has done so. This raises an interesting challenge for platform creation by news organizations: it is not enough to simply make a project open source. These platforms need to be cultivated as such, with ongoing resources and community development to maintain interest and momentum.

How content is disseminated—that is, the ways in which content finds its audience—is another area of platform development. Social media networking platforms like Facebook and Twitter now drive substantial amounts of traffic to content of all sorts, including news content. As a result, news organizations are developing their own data-driven content optimization platforms that seek to enhance the reach of their content. For instance, Buzzfeed is developing a tool they call Pound (Nguyen, Kelleher, and Kelleher, 2015) which is helping them to study how their content diffuses across social networks. They want to use it to drive traffic as much as to study and understand the content they are creating so that they can iterate on and tailor their content to make it maximally appealing (and shareable) to their audiences. Velocity is another platform in this category produced by Mashable. It ingests large amounts of data about how content is spreading on social media and then attempts to predict when something is about to go viral. Recognizing the value of content virality prediction, the company began opening up the platform to advertising and marketing agencies in mid-2014 (Anon, 2014). So in one case, Pound, we see an internal platform, but in the other case, Velocity, we see the inklings of what might shift from its beginning as an internal platform to something that is generalizable and valuable in other content production contexts.

Discussion

In this chapter, I have suggested that certain conceptual antecedents in CJ are undergirding shifts in the news industry towards the development of platforms. While not a systematic sampling of platforms that have been created by news organization, the examples I describe above suggest that much of this development is squarely targeted at content. The business of media is media, whether produced by people or with new technologically enhanced tools. But we also see little development of true industry platforms that are used broadly across multiple organizations. While there are initial stirrings of platforms like Velocity being used (and sold) outside of their initial design context and there is the promise of the Coral Project which may eventually materialize, most news industry platforms are still only used internally. Because of a focus on content and content differentiation, platforms and tools that enable more efficient and scalable creation of content are a key competitive advantage when competing in the news industry. Take a tool like Mr. Chartmaker, which the *New York Times* uses as a content platform for quickly creating charts to use on The Upshot. If this was made open source or even if it was sold, it might erode the distinctiveness of the Times' chart content. Tools and platforms are thus mechanisms to enable product/content differentiation.

The news industry needs to develop better mechanisms and models to leverage the internal tools it is creating into broader externally oriented platforms that third parties will build on. I can think of at least three strategies they might pursue: community development, cross-industry non-content products, and cultural reorientation.

Firstly, to build but also to launch a successful platform involves cultivating communities around the open source tools and platforms that are proffered to the market. Without leadership and ongoing resources to tend to those projects, others may not sense that they are sustainable or worthwhile enough to also invest in. There ought to be a palpable feeling that a platform is stable and supported by the originating organization.

Secondly, the industry should more seriously consider how to take tools that it uses for content production internally and find other information and knowledge domains where such tools also have value (e.g. education, legal services, corporate communications). Companies like Automated Insights sell their automated writing software into the news industry. But a homegrown automated content production platform, benefitting from the knowledge and experiences of professional content creators, could just as well be developed internally to a news organization and sold into other markets like business analytics or government and sales reports. Robot journalism, including things like news bots that seek to disseminate information on social networks, is an area ripe for a content-focused industry to leverage deep knowledge of effective communication into more broadly applicable automation platforms.

A third strategy would involve more of a cultural shift and adoption of an alternative mindset, from the CMS mentality of "this is the platform that helps *us* publish" to the idea of "this is a platform that helps *you* publish." We see this cultural shift already emerging in DDJ and CJ projects that are more open to user contribution and see the role of the public in a different light. Facebook and Twitter can be seen essentially as CMS platforms that enable the public to publish everything from status updates to photos and videos. I opened this chapter by introducing the Coral project, which is taking an initial step in this direction, by rethinking how to help the 'audience' to publish their content in a way that integrates with publishers' sites. If news organizations can see themselves as facilitators for the publication of content by the broader public in a way that is still in line with professional quality expectations, they stand a chance of becoming, essentially, the *platform for democracy.*

The potential economic advantages and new revenue streams afforded by successful platforms would of course be helpful to news organizations' financial viability. But what is really at stake here is the capacity to create platforms that are deeply interwoven with journalistic values. The liminal press that has proliferated as a result of the popularity of news apps and recommendation systems is sometimes crafted in a vacuum without any explicit journalistic values or understanding of public or civic media (Ananny and Crawford, 2015). Philip Napoli points out that social media platforms like Twitter and Facebook do not come from institutional origins in which providing for the news and information needs of communities were foundational (2015).

Yet such platforms have become absolutely essential to the dissemination of content, accounting for substantial traffic flows to news sites. As a result, corporate editorial decisions, algorithmic or otherwise, dictate the legitimacy of speech, the application of selective censorship, and the relevance of copyright and fair use laws (Ball, 2014; Ragusea, 2015). Topics like medical marijuana (Flamm, 2015) or sex education (Madison, 2015) may trigger algorithmic censors that increase the friction in making such important issues more widely visible. Emily Bell has argued that such platforms have commercial interests that are in conflict with those of journalism and, as a result, news organizations ought to work towards creating its own platforms (Bell, 2015). Platforms are power, and the owner of the platform sets the ground rules for whatever the platform does, including not only dissemination but also collection, making sense of, and presenting content. If the goal is to maintain a media environment with public interest motives like transparency, diversity, and an approach to free speech that does not unduly privilege corporatism, then news organizations might be well served in the long run if they became more cognizant of their ability to embed their own organizational and institutional values into technological developments that become widely used platforms.

Further reading

David Weinberger's paper "The Rise, Fall, and Possible Rise of Open News Platforms" provides a closer look particularly at the role of APIs within news organizations and includes interviews with industry insiders at NPR, the *Guardian*, and the *New York Times*. Jonathan Stray has also written thoughtfully about the functions of journalism that are still waiting to be productized and platformatized in "Take two steps back from journalism: What are the editorial products we are not building?" Some of my own earlier writing also attempts to connect approaches to journalism with computational thinking and what that means for innovation in the Tow-Knight report *Cultivating the Landscape of Innovation in Computational Journalism* (Diakopoulos, 2012).

References

Aisch, G.s (2015) "Seven Features You'll Want in Your Next Charting Tool." Available from: http://vis4.net/blog/posts/seven-features-youll-wantin-your-next-charting-tool/ (accessed 16 May 2015).

Aitamurto, T. and Lewis, S.C. (2013) "Open Innovation in Digital Journalism: Examining the Impact of Open APIs at Four News Organizations." *New Media & Society* 15(2): 314–331.

Ananny, M. and Crawford, K. (2015) "A Liminal Press: Situating News App Designers within a Field of Networked News Production." *Digital Journalism* 3(2): 192–208.

Anderson, C.W. (2013) "Towards a Sociology of Computational and Algorithmic Journalism." *New Media & Society* 15(7): 1005–1021.

Anon. (2014) "Mashable Signs Partnership with Leading Media Agency MEC to License its Proprietary Velocity Technology." Available from: http://mecglobal.com/news/mashable-signs-partnership-with-leading-media-agency-mec-to-license-its-proprietary-velocity-technology (accessed 21 May 2015).

Appelgren, E. and Nygren, G. (2014) "Data Journalism in Sweden: Introducing New Methods and Genres of Journalism into 'Old' Organizations." *Digital Journalism* 2(3): 394–405.

Ball, J. (2014) "Twitter: From Free Speech Champion to Selective Censor?" *The Guardian*, 21 August. Available from: http://www.theguardian.com/technology/2014/aug/21/twitter-free-speech-champion-selective-censor (accessed 16 May 2015).

Barr, J. (2015) "Vox Media Begins to Monetize Its 'Magical' Content Platform." *Capital New York*, 30 April. Available from: http://www.capitalnewyork.com/article/media/2015/04/8567039/vox-media-begins-monetize-its-magical-content-platform (accessed 16 May 2015).

Bell, E. (2015) "Google and Facebook are Our Frenemy. Beware." *Columbia Journalism Review*. Available from: http://www.cjr.org/analysis/google_facebook_frenemy.php (accessed 16 May 2015).

Brehmer, M., Ingram, S., Stray, J. and Munzner, T. (2014) "Overview: The Design, Adoption, and Analysis of a Visual Document Mining Tool for Investigative Journalists." *IEEE Transactions on Visualization and Computer Graphics (TVCG)* 20(12): 2271–2280.

Broussard, M. (2014) "Artificial Intelligence for Investigative Reporting: Using an Expert System to Enhance Journalists' Ability to Discover Original Public Affairs Stories." *Digital Journalism* 3(6): 814–831.

Brundrett, T. (2014) "Editorially Joins Vox Media." *Vox Product*, 24 June. Available from: http://product.voxmedia.com/2014/6/24/5837406/editorially-joins-vox-media (accessed 16 May 2015).

Coddington, M. (2015) "Clarifying Journalism's Quantitative Turn: A Typology for Evaluating Data Journalism, Computational Journalism, and Computer-Assisted Reporting." *Digital Journalism* 3(3): 331–348.

Cohen, S., Hamilton, J.T. and Turner, F. (2011) "Computational Journalism." *Communications of the ACM (CACM)* 54(10): 68–71.

Cusumano, M.A. (2010) "Technology Strategy and Management: The Evolution of Platform Thinking." *Communications of the ACM (CACM)* 53(1): 32–34.

Cusumano, M.A. (2011) "Technology Strategy and Management: Platform Wars Come to Social Media." *Communications of the ACM (CACM)* 54(4): 31–33.

Diakopoulos, N. (2010) *A Functional Roadmap for Innovation in Computational Journalism*. Available from: http://www.nickdiakopoulos.com/wp-content/uploads/2007/05/CJ_Whitepaper_Diakopoulos.pdf (accessed 12 May 2015).

Diakopoulos, N. (2012) "Cultivating the Landscape of Innovation in Computational Journalism." *CUNY Tow-Knight Center for Computational Journalism*. Available from: http://cdn.journalism.cuny.edu/blogs.dir/418/files/2012/04/diakopoulos_whitepaper_systematicinnovation.pdf (accessed 12 May 2015).

Diakopoulos, N. (2015) "Algorithmic Accountability: Journalistic Investigation of Computational Power Structures." *Digital Journalism* 3(3): 398–415.

Ellis, J. (2014) "The New York Times R&D Lab Releases Hive, an Open-Source Crowdsourcing Tool." *NiemanLab*. Available from: http://www.niemanlab.org/2014/12/the-new-york-times-rd-lab-releases-hive-an-open-source-crowdsourcing-tool/ (accessed 12 May 2015).

Flamm, M. (2015) "Facebook Banned Us for Writing about Pot." *Crain's New York Business*. Available from: http://www.crainsnewyork.com/article/20150430/TECHNOLOGY/150429875/did-facebook-block-us-for-writing-about-pot (accessed 16 May 2015).

Flew, T., Spurgeon, C.L., Daniel, A. and Swift, A. (2012) "The Promise of Computational Journalism." *Journalism Practice* 6(2): 157–171.

Gillespie, T. (2010) "The Politics of 'Platforms.'" *New Media & Society* 12(3): 347–364.

Karlsen, J. and Stavelin, E. (2014) "Computational Journalism in Norwegian Newsrooms." *Journalism Practice* 8(1): 34–38.

Kotecki, J. (2015) "Automation Helps AP Publish 10 Times More Earnings Stories." *Automated Insights Blog*. Available from: http://blog.automatedinsights.com/post/109491692518/automation-helps-ap-publish-10-times-more-earnings.

Kristjansson, A.H., Jensen, T. and Hildre, H.P. (2004) "The Term Platform in the Context of a Product Developing Company." In *Proceedings of DESIGN 2004, the 8th International Design Conference*. Dubrovnik, Croatia, pp. 325–330.

Lai, K.R. (2014) *Quiz Quartet*. Available from: https://github.com/voxmedia/quiz-generator.

Lewis, S.C. and Usher, N. (2013) "Open Source and Journalism: Toward New Frameworks for Imagining News Innovation." *Media, Culture & Society* 35(5): 602–619.

MacWilliam, G. (2015) "Choropleth Maps Made Easy." *Vox Product*. Available from: http://product. voxmedia.com/2015/4/17/8444633/choropleth-maps-made-easy (accessed 16 May 2015).

Madison, A. (2015) "When Social-Media Companies Censor Sex Education." *The Atlantic*. Available from: http://www.theatlantic.com/health/archive/2015/03/when-social-media-censors-sex-education/ 385576/ (accessed 16 May 2015).

Napoli, P.M. (2015) "Social Media and the Public Interest: Governance of News Platforms in the Realm of Individual and Algorithmic Gatekeepers." *Telecommunications Policy* 39(9): 751–760.

Nguyen, D., Kelleher, A. and Kelleher, A. (2015) "Introducing Pound: Process for Optimizing and Understanding Network Diffusion." *BuzzFeed Tech Blog*. Available from: https://www.buzzfeed.com/ daozers/introducing-pound-process-for-optimizing-and-understanding-n?utm_term=.baMADdzjx#. ksrPOJ3dQ (accessed 16 May 2015).

Parasie, S. (2015) "Data-Driven Revelation? Epistemological Tensions in Investigative Journalism in the Age of 'Big Data.'" *Digital Journalism* 3(3): 364–380.

Ragusea, A. (2015) "Journalists Shouldn't Lose Their Rights in Their Move to Private Platforms." *NiemanLab*. Available from: http://www.niemanlab.org/2015/04/journalists-shouldnt-lose-their-rights-in-their-move-to-private-platforms/ (accessed 16 May 2015).

Reeder, C. (2012) "Introducing Syllabus, Vox Media's S3-Powered Liveblog Platform." *Vox Product*. Available from: http://product.voxmedia.com/2012/6/15/5426782/introducing-syllabus-vox-medias-s3-powered-liveblog-platform (accessed 16 May 2015).

Rodgers, S. (2015) "Foreign Objects? Web Content Management Systems, Journalistic Cultures and the Ontology of Software." *Journalism* 16(1): 10–26.

Shearer, M., Simon, B. and Geiger, C. (2014) "Datastringer: Easy Dataset Monitoring for Journalists." In *Proceedings Symposium on Computation + Journalism*. New York, NY, October 24–25, 2014.

Stray, J. (2015) "Take Two Steps Back from Journalism: What are the Editorial Products We're Not Building?" *NiemanLab*. Available from: http://www.niemanlab.org/2015/03/take-two-steps-back-from-journalism-what-are-the-editorial-products-were-not-building/.

Victor, Y. (2014) "Meme Generation Made Easy." *Vox Product*. Available from: http://product.voxmedia.com/2014/6/27/5849812/meme-generation-made-easy (accessed 16 May 2015).

Weinberger, D. (2015) "The Rise, Fall, and Possible Rise of Open News Platforms." *Shorenstein Center*. Available from: http://shorensteincenter.org/open-news-platforms-david-weinberger/.

Wing, J.M. (2006) "Computational Thinking." *Communications of the ACM (CACM)* 49(3): 33–35.

Wing, J.M. (2010) *"Computational Thinking: What and Why?"* Available from: https://www.cs.cmu.edu/~CompThink/papers/TheLinkWing.pdf.

Yanofsky, D. (2013) "Chartbuilder." *Github*. Available from: https://github.com/Quartz/Chartbuilder (accessed 21 May 2015).

Young, M.L. and Hermida, A. (2015) "From Mr. and Mrs. Outlier to Central Tendencies: Computational Journalism and Crime Reporting at the *Los Angeles Times*." *Digital Journalism* 3(3): 381–397.

18
CROWDSOURCING IN OPEN JOURNALISM
Benefits, challenges, and value creation

Tanja Aitamurto

This chapter explores the role of the crowd in journalism for sourcing information and resources. Through crowdsourcing, journalists can harness the crowd's knowledge for journalism. Crowdsourcing has been widely used as a mechanism for problem solving by companies, and professional journalists have more recently began to crowdsource knowledge for their stories.

Crowdsourcing channels information to journalists quickly and from a large number of people, thus contributing to the journalistic process in several ways. Crowdsourcing requires opening up the journalistic process, and thus, crowdsourcing becomes an open journalistic practice. Crowdsourcing enhances both knowledge search and discovery, strengthens reader-relationships, and provides journalists with a window to readers' world and tacit knowledge about their preferences (Aitamurto, 2013, 2015a).

Crowdfunding is a subtype of crowdsourcing, and it channels the crowd's resources to journalism as funding, with a growing number of stories financed this way. When used to fund journalism, the consequent journalism product becomes a more open product with journalism being a shared economic venture (Aitamurto, 2015b).

Crowdsourcing, however, brings also costs and complexities to the journalistic process. The method requires substantial human resources and also challenges traditional journalistic practices, norms, and ideals. The balance between the benefits and costs create the value of crowdsourcing in journalism. In this chapter, I introduce a framework for analyzing the value of crowdsourcing as an open journalistic practice. I first define crowdsourcing and its boundaries between other methods of large-scale online collaboration and participatory journalistic practices, going on to illustrate how crowdsourcing has been used in journalism, before presenting a framework for analyzing the value of crowdsourcing in journalism.

Crowdsourcing: definition and boundaries

Crowdsourcing is increasingly used in journalistic contexts (Aitamurto, 2015c). Crowdsourcing is an open call online for anybody to participate in a task (Afuah and Tucci, 2012; Brabham, 2008, 2013; Howe, 2008), developed and defined by the crowdsourcer, which in the case of journalism is often a journalist or a group of journalists. Crowdsourced eyewitness stories about corruption and election fraud are shared on platforms like Ushahidi (Meier, 2011), and organizations across the world have initiated crowdsourced fact checking, including *Full Fact* in the United Kingdom and *Chequeado* in Argentina. National and local governments have applied crowdsourcing to identify solutions to issues through policies and laws (Aitamurto and Landemore, 2013, 2015; Brabham, 2015). Emergency management organizations crowdsource information in crises such as earthquakes and hurricanes (Liu, 2010; Starbird, 2011), and companies like Eli Lilly and Procter & Gamble also use crowdsourcing to find solutions to their more difficult R&D problems.

Crowdsourcing can be either paid or voluntary. In paid crowdsourcing, members of the crowd are paid for accomplishing tasks typically on virtual labor markets like Amazon's *Mechanical Turk* or on *oDesk*. On these platforms, crowdsourcers post tasks and crowdworkers select which ones they want to accomplish. The compensation is typically very small—a couple of cents per task. Another type of paid crowdsourcing is innovation challenges where companies and organizations reward certain submissions. Organizations post these challenges to innovation intermediaries and solvers are asked to post solutions either in public or in private to the company. In voluntary crowdsourcing, tasks are completed without financial compensation. Crowdsourced journalism, as well as crisis mapping, crowdsourced policymaking, and crowdsourced science, is typically based on voluntary contributions. The crowd participates in voluntary crowdsourcing because of intrinsically driven motivations, such as a sense of civic duty to contribute, ideological reasoning, or the fun derived from the activity (Aitamurto, 2015c; Brabham, 2010, 2012; Lietsala and Joutsen, 2007; Nov, Arazy, and Anderson, 2011).

Crowdsourcing differs from other popular forms of online collaboration, such as commons-based peer production in several fundamental ways. Commons-based peer production is used in open source software production and in Wikipedia creation (Benkler, 2002) and differs from crowdsourcing in terms of the locus of power and the mode of participation. In crowdsourcing, power is always with the crowdsourcer. In crowdsourced journalism, the power lies within the journalist who decides when, where, and how crowdsourcing happens. The journalist also decides how the crowd's input is used. In contrast, for commons-based peer production, the locus of power is with the online participants, and they have more say over the production process than the crowd does in crowdsourcing. Contributors, such as Wikipedia editors or open source software producers, are often self-organized, and there is less of a hierarchy than in crowdsourcing. It is debatable, however, whether commons-based peer production can ever be fully free from managerial hierarchies. Wikipedia, for instance, while relying on volunteer editors in content production, has a managerial hierarchy in place. Wikipedia is also not a wholly independent endeavor absent any sustaining forces behind it; the encyclopedia is managed and sustained by the Wikimedia Foundation, which has its own managerial hierarchy in place.

The mode of participation in crowdsourcing also differs from commons-based peer production. In crowdsourcing, the crowd is not part of the actual making of the end result—the crowd contributes their knowledge, but it is the crowdsourcer who uses the crowd input to produce the end result. In crowdsourced journalism, the journalist treats crowd input as raw material and weaves it into the story in the ways that she or he thinks is appropriate, but—it is the journalist who writes the story. In commons-based peer production, in contrast, the participants are active in the production of the end product, as with a Wikipedia article or open source software. They collaborate almost in real time and follow as the end product comes to reality. If commons-based peer production was to be used in journalism, it would mean that the contributors would be collaboratively writing a story together using collaborative spaces, such as a Wiki, Google Docs, or Etherpad type of a platform.

Crowdsourcing as an open journalistic practice

When journalists use crowdsourcing in journalism, they open up the journalistic process to the public. Crowdsourcing, thus, can be considered an open journalistic practice (Aitamurto, 2015a). In open journalism, openness comes into play in several parts of the journalistic process. The process can be open to the public in the beginning, like in the previous examples, or it can also be open later in the process, when the journalist wants to source more information from the crowd. The journalist can also ask for ideas for interviewees, subjects of visualizations, and so on. However, in open journalism, the journalistic process is accessible to the public only in certain parts, and the process is never fully open.

When journalists use crowdsourcing, they publish a call online for the information they want from the crowd. One of the best-known examples of crowdsourcing in journalism happened in 2009, when the British newspaper the *Guardian* crowdsourced a part of the investigation of the British Members' of Parliament's expenses scandal. The crowd was asked to categorize digitized expense receipts and thousands of people participated in the process. Since then, crowdsourcing has been used in several high-profile cases across the world. In Sweden, *Svenska Dagbladet*, one of the leading daily newspapers, successfully crowdsourced mortgage interest rates for an investigation about mortgages in 2013. About 50,000 Swedes submitted their information on a crowdmap on the newspapers' website, and dozens of stories were written based on the crowdsourced data. In Finland, the leading daily newspaper, *Helsingin Sanomat*, crowdsourced an investigation of stock short-selling in 2012. The investigation resulted in a scoop about a questionable holding company's arrangement with a Finnish bank, leading to the firing of a bank executive (Aitamurto, 2015). The British Broadcasting Company (BBC) in the United Kingdom has crowdsourced information for real-time traffic updates and for tracking the consequences of the public budget cuts in cities. the *New York Times* in the United States successfully crowdsourced information for identifying people in images during the Boston bombings coverage in 2013. WNYC, a public radio station in New York, crowdsourced information for prediction about re-emergent of cicada swarms, by asking the crowd to use soil monitors to track the soil temperature in 2014. Participants submitted the temperature information, which was then displayed on a crowdmap online. Thus, it was possible to track the soil temperature in hundreds of locations simultaneously. Apart from these, largely visible crowdsourcing efforts, newspapers, magazines, and journalists also crowdsource information, such as pictures, about news events and story tips regularly on their websites. Journalists also ask for story ideas and tips through their social networks and beyond.

Crowdsourcing can also be used as a knowledge search method in participatory and citizen journalism. Readers participate in participatory journalism as commentators or content producers (Bruns, 2005; Domingo, 2011; Holmes and Nice, 2012). In citizen journalism, people who are not journalists by profession can create content that can be considered as journalism (Gillmor, 2004). This content can be published on independent blogs and citizen-run news sites or even in publications run by professional journalists. Participatory or citizen journalism, however, does not use crowdsourcing by default as a knowledge search method. Citizen journalism often resembles commons-based peer production more than crowdsourcing as there is not necessarily a crowdsourcer who controls the process. Furthermore, the locus of power in citizen journalism published on institutionally independent websites (not affiliated with professional news sites), is within the peer producers who are more equal than in crowdsourcing.

Crowdfunding in journalism: aggregated donor judgments

Crowdfunding is a subtype of crowdsourcing. In crowdfunding, the crowdsourced task is to gather money for a certain purpose, rather than information, and in crowdfunded journalism, the task is to gather funding for a story pitched by a journalist. Donors show their support for a journalistic story idea by donating money, and donors' judgments are aggregated and accumulated into funding. These aggregated judgments are one manifestation of collective intelligence in crowdfunded journalism (Aitamurto, 2011, 2015b). Collective intelligence refers to the distributed talent and knowledge of large crowds (Lévy, 1997; Landemore, 2013).

Crowdfunding in journalism is typically *ex ante* crowdfunding: The crowd is asked to contribute to the story before it is produced. A journalist organizes a campaign for crowdfunding a story and asks the crowd to donate money so that the journalist can accomplish the project. The campaigns are often run on dedicated crowdfunding platforms like Beacon, Kickstarter, and IndieGoGo. The funders often get rewards for their donation. The value of the rewards rises in tiers, and the more the funder gives, the more valuable the reward is. The rewards are typically related to the article, for example, a handwritten note from the journalist, a signed photograph, or a T-shirt. In *ex post facto* crowdfunding, the funds are raised for a completed product. *Ex post facto* crowdfunding is more of a digital tip jar (Kappel, 2008). Funds can be raised for a story that is available for free online anyway, for instance, by using digital tipjars like Kachingle or Flattr.

There are four types of crowdfunding in journalism: Fundraising for a single story, fundraising for continuous coverage or beat coverage, fundraising for a new platform or publication, and fundraising for a service that supports journalism.

When a journalist raises funds for a single story, she or he sets up a campaign online for crowdfunding. In this model, the journalist pitches a story online for potential funders. The pitching often happens on a specific platform like Kickstarter, Contributoria, or Beacon. (Aitamurto, 2015b). Raising funds for a single story used to be the most common form of crowdfunding, but fundraising for a continuous beat is becoming increasingly common. In this type of crowdfunding, a journalist funds a more continuous coverage by crowdfunding. This type of crowdfunding is thus both *ex ante* and *ex post facto* crowdfunding: The funds are raised both for future stories about the beat, but also based on already published work on the beat. On the crowdfunding site Beacon, journalists raise funding for continuous coverage of topics like environmental issues and mass incarceration. For instance, during the Ferguson unrest in Missouri in the United States in 2014, a journalist gathered funding on Beacon to travel to Ferguson and undertake reporting there. The fundraising was ongoing across several weeks of unrest, and she was able to cover the news event for the whole period, thanks to successful crowdfunding. Crowdfunding for a continuous beat recalls artistic patronage in that the journalists ask the crowd to support their work in a more long-lasting form than just one story at a time. In the traditional artistic patronage, typically a small number of supporters donate large sums. In crowdfunded patronage, the support comes from a large crowd in small amounts instead.

Benefits of crowdsourcing: knowledge discovery, peer learning, and deliberation

Through crowdsourcing, journalists have access to a larger number of people than ever before. The online crowd is a huge potential source pool for the journalist with the size of the participant crowd, in theory, being almost limitless. In practice, limited access to the internet, language, and skill barriers make the process accessible only to a certain number of people. It is also limited in terms of the number of people who have knowledge about the open journalistic process and can thus participate.

Using crowdsourcing, journalists can tap into the collective intelligence of the crowds and channel that to their articles. The larger the number of participants, the more likely the journalist is to find useful information. Crowdsourcing hence supports knowledge search in journalism. Empirical studies show that crowdsourcing in journalism can bring in relevant information that helps journalists to proceed with their investigations and that the crowd-sourced knowledge search can lead to a fast knowledge discovery and even to a discovery of knowledge that the journalist did not know to search for (Aitamurto, 2013, 2015a).

Journalists can enhance the knowledge search aspects in crowdsourced journalistic processes by using several methods, depending on the goals of their investigations. By answering the question or prompt, online participants contribute to journalistic investigations. For example, in the crowdsourced mortgage interest investigation in Sweden, the crowd was asked to share their home loan interest rate by filling out a simple Google form online. The rates would then appear on the newspapers' website as a large crowdmap. In another case, a science journalist in a science magazine in Finland crowdsourced an investigation of gender bias in math and science education. She developed provocative prompts about common beliefs regarding the different genders' ability to learn math and science. She then asked the crowd to react to those and share their experiences about math and science education. After analyzing the crowd's input, she asked experts' opinion about the common beliefs and then incorporated the crowd's and experts' contributions to her article.

Journalists can also publish documents related to the investigations online and ask the crowd to check those documents and then submit their observations to the journalist. For example, Svenska *Dagbladet*, one of the leading daily newspapers in Sweden, crowdsourced an investigation of development aid use in Swedish municipalities. As part of their investigations, journalists published online documents about development aid and asked the crowd to peruse those documents and report back to the journalist if anything interesting was found. Similarly in the investigation of stock short-selling, the leading daily newspaper in Finland, the *Helsingin Sanomat*, asked the crowd to check hundreds of stock trading reports that the newspaper had published online. In these cases, the crowd identified relevant issues in the documents, and by reporting those back to the journalist they enabled the journalist to proceed with their investigations (Aitamurto, 2015a).

Journalists can also apply co-creation, a type of crowdsourcing, in their open journalistic process. Co-creation is a more interactive method in which the crowd and the crowdsourcer work collaboratively to create content or solutions (Piller, Ihl, and Vossen, 2011). In co-creation, the crowd is invited to participate in several parts of the story process—in contrast to basic crowdsourcing where the crowd participates in only one part of the process, and participation is a one-time act. One example of this is the Finnish lifestyle magazine *Olivia*, which co-created several magazine issues with their readers. The crowd was asked to participate in several parts of the story process, starting from developing topics, choosing the topic, brainstorming sources, and shooting contexts (Aitamurto, 2013). Co-creation involves a lot of interaction between the participants and the journalists and strengthens the reader relationship with the publication and the journalists. The online participants feel a strong sense of belonging to the journalistic process and product, even prompting participants to subscribe to the magazine (Aitamurto, 2013).

Costs in crowdsourced journalism: interaction, verification, and aggregation

Crowdsourcing when used as an open journalistic practice is never free. The method comes with many costs. Most of the costs are incurred in the synthesis and aggregation part of crowdsourcing, as analyzing and synthesizing a large number of submissions requires a good deal of human resources, especially when the data are unstructured. Other aspects of a crowdsourced journalistic process are also demanding on human resources, along with technical costs incurred. In this section, I introduce a five-point framework outlining the benefits and costs in certain parts of a crowdsourced journalistic process. The framework is summarized in Table 18.1.

First, the better the crowdsourced process is prepared, the more likely it will succeed. However, preparing a crowdsourcing initiative requires resources. To mention just a few of the preparative tasks: there might be documents that need to be digitized for publishing; the crowdsourcing platform has to be set up, whether it is a specific platform or a website on the publications' website; and when preparing a crowdfunding process, the campaign and the rewards have to planned, the pitch videos need to be produced, and so on.

Second, the overall process requires attention. If the process is designed for interaction between journalists and participants, the journalists need to be present on the platform and interact with the participants. If there is horizontal transparency in the process, there needs to be either pre- or post-moderation on the platform for removing inappropriate input. The prompt for participation may require iteration based on early user feedback, or, if nobody participates or the participation is low, the prompt might need to be revised. Fast and smart iteration can save the whole process.

Third, the crowd's input needs to analyzed, evaluated, and filtered. This is typically the most laborious part in crowdsourcing. Journalists often crowdsource unstructured data—that

Table 18.1 Benefits and costs of crowdsourcing in journalism in several parts of a journalistic process

Process part	Description	Benefit	Cost
Preparation	Process planning, digitizing documents, and setting up the technology	The more and better designed probes, the more likely there will be useful crowd input	Human resource costs, technical cost
Interaction, moderation, and iteration	Interaction with online participants, moderating the comments, and iterating the prompt	Interaction leads to a stronger reader-relationship, deliberation, peer learning, and iteration to a better process	Human resource costs and technical costs
Analysis and evaluation	Analyzing the crowd input, evaluating what are useful and relevant data	Analysis and evaluation filters out useful information	Human resource costs and computational analysis
Verification	Verifying the accuracy of the crowd input	Cross-checking shows what is correct data	Human resource costs
Synthesis and aggregation	Synthesizing the crowd's input, channeling input to article	Synthesis brings out the diverse voices of the crowd shows diverse perspectives and contradicting facts	Human resource costs and technical costs

is, free-form online comments as responses to their questions. The data are qualitative, and the format and content varies, so the analysis is typically conducted so that the journalist peruses all of the comments. When the data are structured quantified data, they can be analyzed faster by automated computations. In the home loan interest investigation in Sweden, for example, the data were people's home loan interest rates, so they were all quantified. Thus, the journalists could analyze the data at the newsroom through simple and fast computations. Similarly, in crowdfunded journalism, the aggregation of the crowd's input—the donations—is easy, because it is all quantified contributions and they are all in the same format.

Fourth, the crowd's input needs to be verified before journalists can use the information in news articles. Journalists use traditional cross-checking procedures to verify the accuracy of the crowdsourced information: they call the sources, check the documents, and so on. For instance, in the crowdsourced stock short-selling case, the journalist checked the accuracy of the crowd's observations of the selling reports by investigating on his own the particular stock reports that the crowd highlighted. When the volume of crowd submissions is not too high, it is possible to undertake fact checking using traditional human resource-intensive journalistic practices. However, when the number of submissions is high, verification proves to be impossible—as with the home loan interest case where the journalists received 50,000 contributions. In this case, journalists first tried to verify the data by calling the participants, but after about 80 phone calls they had to give up. Nevertheless, they decided to use the data and were clear in the articles that the data were unverified, thus pushing the responsibility about accuracy onto the public. Consequently, journalists took the risk of compromising one of the core norms of journalism, that the reported facts are accurate. However, this has resulted to a new norm that blends responsibility between the crowd and the journalist (Aitamurto, 2015a). This also illustrates that the volume of participation in crowdsourced journalism can turn into a paradox: The more actively the crowd participates, the better, but the more difficult it makes the data verification.

Finally, the synthesis of the crowd's input is a very important part of the process. This is the point when the journalist decides what information to use and how to use it. For instance, in a story on gender bias in math and science education, the journalist categorized the crowd's input and mapped the controversies, attempting to create a balanced and accurate overview of the crowd's input to the article. Successful synthesis requires understanding that the crowd's input is rather like raw material for the story and cannot or should not be used 'as is' in the stories. When the volume of submissions is high and there are many controversies and broad diversity in the voices and opinions, it is challenging and time consuming to synthesize the input. Synthesis also requires understanding that crowdsourced input always comes from self-selected group of people, so there is a selection bias. This means that the crowd's input cannot be taken as the de facto public opinion about an issue, as it is not a random sample of the population.

The value of crowdsourced journalism: balance between benefits and costs

When used as an open journalistic practice, crowdsourcing generates undeniable benefits to professional journalism. It can accelerate knowledge gathering, widen the journalists' perspective, and create a stronger reader-relationship, as the examples presented in this chapter illustrate. The crowd also learns from each other, and that peer learning contributes to wider knowledge about the issue the journalist is investigating. Crowdsourcing thus has a potential to create value in several ways as an open journalistic practice.

However, crowdsourcing also comes with challenges. One of the main difficulties concerns the analysis and evaluation of the crowd's input and verifying accuracy. This is where traditional journalistic practices are in conflict with the nature of crowdsourcing. Crowdsourcing delivers information quickly from large crowds, yet the journalistic practices used to process and verify inputs can only approach small amounts of data at a time. Therefore, analysis, synthesis, and verification of crowdsourced input in open journalism often collide with traditional journalistic practices. They also collide with the ideals of journalism, which strive for verified information to ensure data accuracy.

The benefits of open journalism are partially compromised, then, by the costs of open practices. As shown in Table 18.1, planning, implementing, analyzing, verifying, and synthesizing the crowdsourced input require a considerable amount of human resources for post-processing of that input, especially when the amount of submissions is high.

New technologies have proved helpful in resolving the bottleneck of analysis and synthesis of the crowdsourced input. By training algorithms in machine learning and developing better Natural Language Processing technologies, some of these issues may be resolved, as the processing can be made more automatic. However, even those technologies do not resolve the challenges in data verification. Perhaps it is the case that to benefit from open journalistic practices like crowdsourcing certain norms and ideals of traditional journalism need to be left behind, to be replaced by new ideals, like that of blended responsibility in open journalism.

Further reading

This chapter has greatly benefited from *Crowdfunding the Future—Media Industries, Ethics, and Digital Society* (2015), edited by Lucy Bennett, Bertha Chin, and Bethan Jones. For those interested in collective intelligence, I recommend Hélène Landemore's *Democratic Reason: Politics, Collective Intelligence and the Rule of the Many* (2013) and Pierre Lévy's *Collective Intelligence: Mankind's Emerging World in Cyberspace* (1997).

References

Afuah, A.N. and Tucci, C.L. (2012) "Crowdsourcing as a Solution to Distant Search." *Academy of Management Review* 37(3): 355–375.

Aitamurto, T. (2011) "The Impact of Crowdfunding on Journalism." *Journalism Practice* 5(4): 429–445.

Aitamurto, T. (2013) "Balancing Between Open and Closed: Co-Creation in Magazine Journalism." *Digital Journalism* 1(2): 229–251.

Aitamurto, T. (2015a) "Crowdsourcing as a Knowledge Search Method in Digital Journalism: Ruptured Ideals and Blended Responsibility." *Digital Journalism* 4(2): 280–297. DOI: 10.1080/21670811.2015.1034807.

Aitamurto, T. (2015b) "The Role of Crowdfunding as a Business Model in Journalism: A Model of Value Creation." In Chin, B., Bennett, L. and Jones, B. (eds) *Crowdfunding the Future: Media Industries, Ethics and Digital Society*. New York, NY: Peter Lang, pp. 189–205.

Aitamurto, T. (2015c) "Motivation Factors in Crowdsourced Journalism: Social Impact, Social Change and Peer Learning." *International Journal of Communication* 9: 3523–3543.

Aitamurto, T. and Landemore, H. (2013) "Democratic Participation and Deliberation in Crowdsourced Legislative Processes: The Case of the Law on Off-Road Traffic in Finland." *The 6th Conference on Communities and Technologies (C&T)*. Workshop: Large-Scale Idea Management and Deliberation Systems.

Aitamurto, T. and Landemore, H. (2015) "Five Design Principles for Crowdsourced Policymaking: Assessing the Case of Crowdsourced Off-Road Traffic Law in Finland." *Journal of Social Media for Organizations* 2(1): 1–19.

Benkler, Y. (2002) "Coase's Penguin, or, Linux and the Nature of the Firm." *The Yale Law Journal* 112(3): 369–446.

Brabham, D.C. (2008) "Crowdsourcing as a Model for Problem Solving: An Introduction and Cases." *Convergence* 14(1): 75–90.

Brabham, D.C. (2010) "Moving the Crowd at Threadless." *Information, Communication & Society* 13(8): 1122–1145.

Brabham, D.C. (2012) "Motivations for Participation in a Crowdsourcing Application to Improve Public Engagement in Transit Planning." *Journal of Applied Communication Research* 40(3): 307–328.

Brabham, D.C. (2013) *Crowdsourcing* (The MIT Press Essential Knowledge Series). Cambridge, MA: Massachusetts Institute of Technology.

Brabham, D.C. (2015) *Crowdsourcing in the Public Sector*. Washington DC: Georgetown University Press.

Bruns, A. (2005) *Gatewatching: Collaborative Online News Production*. New York, NY: Peter Lang.

Domingo, D. (2011) "Managing Audience Participation: Practices, Workflows and Strategies." In Singer, J., Hermida, A., Domingo, D., Heinonen, A., Paulussen, S., Quandt, T., Reich, Z. and Vujnovic, M. (eds) *Participatory Journalism: Guarding Open Gates at Online Newspapers*. Oxford, UK: Wiley-Blackwell, pp. 76–95.

Gillmor, D. (2004) *We the Media: Grassroots Journalism by the People, for the People*. Sebastopol, CA: O'Reilly Media.

Holmes, T. and Nice, L. (2012) *Magazine Journalism*. London, UK: Sage.

Howe, J. (2008) *Crowdsourcing: Why the Power of the Crowd is Driving the Future of Business*. New York, NY: Crown Business.

Kappel, T. (2008) "Ex Ante Crowdfunding and the Recording Industry: A Model for the U.S.?" *Loyola of Los Angeles Entertainment Law Journal* 29: 375–385.

Landemore, H. (2013) *Democratic Reason: Politics, Collective Intelligence, and the Rule of the Many*. Princeton, NJ: Princeton University Press.

Landemore, H. (2015) "Inclusive Constitution-Making: The Icelandic Experiment." *Journal of Political Philosophy* 23(2): 166–191.

Lévy P. (1997) *Collective Intelligence: Mankind's Emerging World in Cyberspace*. Cambridge, MA: Perseus Books.

Lietsala, K. and Joutsen, A. (2007) "Hang-a-Rounds and True Believers: A Case Analysis of the Roles and Motivational Factors of the Star Wreck Fans." In Lugmayr, A., Lietsala, K. and Kallenbach, J. (eds) *MindTrek 2007 Conference Proceedings*. Tampere, Finland: Tampere University of Technology, pp. 25–30.

Liu, S.B. and Palen, L. (2010) "The New Cartographers: Crisis Map Mashups and the Emergence of Neogeographic Practice." *Cartography and Geographic Information Science* 37(1): 69–90.

Meier, P. (2011) "Do 'Liberation Technologies' Change the Balance of Power between Repressive States and Civil Society?" PhD thesis, Fletcher School of Law and Diplomacy, MA. Available from: http://irevolution.files.wordpress.com/2011/11/meier-dissertation-final.pdf.

Nov, O., Arazy, O. and Anderson, D. (2011) "Dusting for Science: Motivation and Participation of Digital Citizen Science Volunteers." In *iConference 2011*. Seattle, WA, 8 February, pp. 68–74.

Piller, F., Ihl, C. and Vossen, A. (2011) "A Typology of Customer Co-Creation in the Innovation Process." In Wittke, V. and Hanekop, H. (eds) *New Forms of Collaborative Production and Innovation on the Internet: Interdisciplinary Perspective*. Göttingen: Universitätsverlag Göttingen, pp. 9–29.

Starbird, K. (2011) "Digital Volunteerism During Disaster: Crowdsourcing Information Processing." In *Conference on Human Factors in Computing Systems*, May, pp. 7–12.

19

COMMUNITY AND HYPERLOCAL JOURNALISM

A 'sustainable' model?

Kristy Hess and Lisa Waller

In the journalistic 'field,' very local news is like a wild pasture—metaphorically speaking. It grows organically, but can be cultivated in certain conditions and harvested for profit. Its diversity and social importance make it a key part of the wider ecology of news (Phillips, 2015). However, across the globe, traditional media companies with interests in this patch are slashing and burning—cutting costs, centralizing production, or even closing down operations. Small start-up news providers are popping up like field mushrooms in their place, wherever conditions seem fertile. And there are also 'hyperlocal' and 'community' publications more interested in local news subsistence than in making money. This chapter outlines the broad set of economic approaches that have been applied to support community, hyperlocal, and local news and their benefits given the technical, industrial, and cultural changes taking place in the field. We argue the keys to a sustainable future are embracing their diversity and cultivating their 'niche': localness.

The discussion is organized into two overarching themes—business models and sustainability models. A business model puts the motivation for profit ahead of all else, while sustainability models seek to preserve and protect journalism for the benefit of society. The latter looks toward the social, cultural, and civic advantages of local news ahead of financial yield. This raises aspects of what we term 'centralization and dispersion,' 'news niches,' and traditional and experimental models to support local news. We conclude by offering a critical-cultural argument that niche knowledge and experience of what makes a place and the people within it 'tick' is required to build a news outlet's legitimacy as an authoritative public voice and to meet the very local audience's special informational needs in the digital age.

A diverse subfield

We begin by performing some definitional work to cut a swath through this scholarly terrain. News produced for and about the very local level is among the most diverse subfields of journalism—from who owns it and produces it—to the forms it takes, its distribution, and the economic models that sustain it. 'Community journalism' and 'hyperlocal journalism' are common terms in the international literature for the variety of news produced and circulated at the very local level. However, both have different meanings across time, place, and research traditions. For example, in the United States 'community journalism' used to be strictly defined as news produced by small, commercial hometown newspapers (Byerly, 1961; Lauterer, 2000). More recently, US scholars have theorized the community journalist as anyone who shares a strong 'connectedness' to his or her audience (Reader, 2011) or challenges mainstream journalism and media power (Howley, 2010). In contrast, Moore and Gillis (2005) contend that in sub-Saharan Africa, 'community journalism' is a process for increased citizen empowerment and social interaction to help transform lives and communities. In Europe and Britain, 'hyperlocal' is mostly used to describe wholly online startups, whereas some Australian scholars have conceptualized it more broadly to include very local news across a range of media platforms, including online, radio, and print (Ewart, 2014; Hess and Waller, 2015).

To add to this complexity, both 'community' and 'hyperlocal' are used in discussions of journalism carried out for large media conglomerates, as well as not-for-profit operations, and by both professional journalists and amateurs. The purpose here is not to wade into the complex and sometimes confusing definitional debates, or investigate the political, social, and cultural differences, or significance, associated with both terms (see Hatcher, 2011; Hess and Waller, 2014a on these important topics). This chapter focuses on news at a very local level, where ideas of 'community' can be particularly powerful, so 'community media' scholars and practitioners (especially advocacy, ethnic and alternative journalism) may find this overview on funding models helpful as well.

Business models

Any business model has the pursuit for profit as its *modus operandi*, or as Chesbrough and Rosenbloom (2002) argue, "the heuristic logic that connects technical potential with the realization of economic value" (as cited in Akinfemisoye and Deffor, 2014: 89). Some of the popular business models for journalism are advertising, the use of paywalls, and more recently the centralization and standardization of news. Despite intense competition and a rapid decline in print ad revenues (Mitchell, 2014), advertising remains the major source of income for small commercial news outlets that operate at the most local level (Abernathy, 2014). Lacy (2011) argues if a local news provider meets a community's demands for news, information, and connectedness, people who sell products and services to that community will advertise with them because they see value in being identified with that trusted and popular news platform (Lacy, 2011: 176). Balance sheets and business forecasts for news companies around the world offer a less optimistic outlook (Mitchell, 2014), and while traditional advertising from local print and television still accounts for more than half of the total revenue, print ad revenues are in rapid decline. In many small communities in the United States, classified advertising has fallen by as much as 80 percent since the year 2000 (Abernathy, 2014). As we will discuss shortly, in trying to remain profitable with advertising revenues continuing to nose dive, media companies may be adopting strategies that make it difficult to satisfy the demand for 'connectedness' that Lacy identifies—and we agree—is the key to the sustainability of news at the local level.

Charging audiences for news in a digital environment provides another important revenue stream, but presents a challenge given the amount of free content available online. Very local news media organizations have the financial advantage of occupying a niche market (discussed later in this chapter). However, they also face difficult choices on pricing and managing access to their content. One of the strategies trialed and implemented by local news outlets across the globe is the paywall. A paywall refers to any type of "digital mechanism that separates free content from paid content on a website" (Chiou and Tucker, 2013: 62; see Myllylahti, this volume). They can be content-based, frequency-based, micropayment, or app-based. Chiou and Tucker (2013) found that paywall sites experienced a sharp drop in visits after their introduction, especially among young people. They also raised concerns that local media has presumably fewer substitutes and paywalls might lead to less local news consumption overall (Chiou and Tucker, 2013). Myllylahti (2014) argues that online news paywalls create additional income for news companies, but at the current revenue levels they do not offer a viable business model in the short term.

Centralization

The process of centralization and standardization of news has been a popular business strategy in the digital age, especially among major media players with interests in local news. When the traditional business model based on advertising began to crumble, many media companies looked for ways to cut costs and preserve profits. This has led to the rise of centralized production nodes—where news is gathered from a local area and sent to a central location outside the geographic space to be edited, produced, and packaged for audiences. In the United Kingdom, Barnett (2009) contends that for local media outlets owned by large conglomerates, the process of centralization, standardization of editorial approaches, and homogeneity of output are part of the process of maximizing shareholder value. Sjøvaag (2014) outlines how Norwegian media company Schibsted imposed serious cost-cutting measures in 2012, including staff reductions, content syndication, and centralization of core services. Only the content and the mastheads differ. In Australia, Fairfax Media has standardized its online space, with almost all of its 200 or so regional newspapers' editions using the same template to upload news and information. It is worth noting that in the United States, Hood's (2014) content analysis in six local television markets found significant differences between locally produced and outsourced newscasts, from the location focus of stories to production attributes and deployment of reporting resources. Well over half the stories on local stations pertained to local news and events, which was more than 9 percent higher than on stations that delivered local news from remote locations.

The process of centralization and standardization does not fully describe the way local media production has been sliced and diced in attempts to sustain profits across digital and physical spaces. As we discuss elsewhere, local news outlets are not confined to geographic territory alone—they are situated in a 'geo-social' context (Hess, 2013; Hess and Waller, 2014a). This means they hold influential positions in certain social flows and movements and act as nodes to the wider global media network connected to news media conglomerates or dependent upon new media empires such as Facebook, Apple, and Google to reach audiences. The outsourcing of the creation, production, and distribution of local news is much more complex than centralizing labor costs alone. The digital world has led to the rise of what we conceptualize as the 'dispersion' of local news.

Centralization and dispersion: a survival strategy?

Dispersion is a term used in mathematics, sciences, physics, and biology. In its simplest form it means the process of distributing something over an area. In statistics it is synonymous with scatter or spread and contrasted with location or central tendency (Nist/Sematech, 2012). In biology, dispersal refers to the movement of individuals from their birth site to their breeding site, as well as the movement from one breeding site to another (Bonte *et al.*, 2012).

We use 'dispersion' as a concept for understanding the changing nature of local news production in a globalized world. Dispersion is largely a cost-cutting mechanism when local news is taken from its natural habitat (i.e. a geographic area) and drawn into global power structures in order for it to be produced and distributed across wide geographic and digital spaces.

When a company expands in size and scope, one might expect it to deflate or contract in tough times. However, in a globalized and digitized world, companies are able to disperse costs outside a physical location to save money, outsourcing to other corporate entities located beyond the geographic areas that news outlets serve. In the United Kingdom in 2012, regional publisher Johnston Press announced plans to outsource half its advertising creation work to India with the loss of dozens of local jobs (Lambourne, 2012). In Australia, editorial and production functions of a small daily newspaper, *The Bendigo Advertiser*, have been dispersed by its owner Fairfax, which has engaged in savage cost-cutting strategies across its local media network. The *Advertiser* has retained a handful of journalists to produce news and upload it into an online news template discussed in the previous section. When people want to read a story online, they often rely on the search engine Google to find the website or are required to download an app for their smart device. The newspaper is printed in another regional location, and when people want to place a death notice over the telephone, they are transferred to a call center in the Philippines. Barnett (2009) argues these strategies might seem a sensible short-term approach to business, but they can sacrifice journalism that is rooted in local communities. It is very difficult to quantify the financial return on good journalism, but very easy to quantify the outgoing cost of journalists' salaries and expenses (Barnett, 2009: 10).

The problems with centralizing and dispersing local news can be seen most clearly at the hyperlocal level. Major media players have endured a tumultuous experiment with this form of online news, and there appears to be little evidence of success with attempts to roll out hyperlocal sites nationally (Barnett and Townend, 2014). Farhi (2007) highlights the rapid rise and fall of a series of local news websites called Backfence in the United States; and perhaps the world's best known hyperlocal venture, Patch, has also endured a rocky road in this space with questions raised over the network's future (see also Barnett and Townend, 2014). In the words of one hyperlocal publisher: "you can't Amazon local news" (Rieder, 2013). Significantly, a UK study has found that the most successful hyperlocal ventures have been independent (Barnett and Townend, 2014), and later in this chapter, we will discuss the importance of niche business models to the future of very local news. The hyperlocal experiment tells us that attempting to stretch the production of local news across space and time might work on some levels, but stretch it too far and it can snap.

Sustainability models

'Sustainability' is understood as the ability of something to be used without being exhausted or destroyed; as in agriculture, to describe a method of harvesting or using a resource so that it is not depleted or permanently damaged (Mason, 2003). A sustainable model of very local news moves the emphasis from profit to preservation. Here the attention shifts from profits to issues of media plurality, preserving the civic, social, and cultural value that local news provides. In nations where the public interest role of journalism appears under threat due to the collapse of local commercial media, governments and philanthropic bodies have been urged to subsidize news at the very local level because of its importance to democracy and civic life. Greenslade and Barnett (2014) give the example of a newspaper in Maidenhead in the United Kingdom that transformed into a charitable trust to ensure its independence and foster community spirit. They argue that it will take a few more similar initiatives before any kind of precedent is established:

but it is just possible that [this] defining step might … presage a new wave of journalism enterprises which are just as independent, just as dedicated to serving the local community, and maybe just as long-lived.

(Greenslade and Barnett, 2014: 67)

The Knight Foundation embraces a "hospital model of journalism"—the idea that news can be created by a collective, leveraging emerging technologies, and channels like social media (Scutari, 2015). It has developed a local media initiative identifying promising new journalism outlets and provides them with the necessary funding to achieve long-term sustainability. The US$5 million initiative includes US$1 million in microgrants to support non-profit online news outlets and public media across the United States. In the United Kingdom, a report for the Media Trust (Fenton *et al.*, 2010) has called for the introduction of local news hubs, supported with funds from local authorities and foundations, which could bring together communities and professional journalists. The hubs would provide training, volunteer mentors, and technical support for communities to engage in identifying, investigating, and reporting local news. The Media Trust report suggests subsidies could come from local government advertising—guaranteeing that their information campaigns reach the target audience/s while supporting and nurturing local media. However, maintaining a business for private gain with public money raises some critical questions that go to the heart of democratic governance. For example, subsidies can be used to create and perpetuate the same actors in power and undermine democratic efficacy and perceptions of accountability (Zahariadis, 2013: 69).

Merging business and sustainability models: the people's journalism

The audience for news, once considered passive consumers, is now recognized for its capabilities of gathering news, editing, publishing, and for helping fund professionals' ability to practice quality journalism. We will examine some of these approaches to finance and sustain the circulation and production of very local news and information.

User-generated content, ranging from comments posted after stories to people contributing reports, photographs, and footage of local events—is a key dimension of this dynamic. Knight and Cook (2013) argue the closer a journalist is to their audience, the easier it is to link up and involve the community in finding and sharing stories, and user-generated content offers one potential resource or lifeline for local news outlets that have experienced a decline in revenue, according to Canter (2013). This means volunteers can take on mundane parts of a journalist's job that currently use precious human resources and instead bring new voices into journalists' work (Singer, 2010: 285). However, this model raises concerns when collaborative journalism is market-driven rather than civic-oriented and with audiences being exploited for free content, allowing news organizations to cut back on staff (see also Paulussen *et al.*, 2007; Ornebring, 2008, and Aitamurto, in this volume).

The role of user-generated content warrants specific attention in relation to hyperlocals, especially in discussions about who produces hyperlocal news (see, e.g., Glaser, 2010), with the literature identifying and distinguishing between citizen journalists (Schaffer, 2007), user-generated content (Paulussen and D'heer, 2013; van Kerkhoven and Bakker, 2014), and professional journalists (Williams *et al.*, 2014; Bunch, 2007).

Considering these factors, citizen goodwill and collaboration become increasingly valued in community and hyperlocal journalism, even if they are difficult to harness. Crowdsourcing describes grassroots or citizen-led initiatives—where individuals are encouraged to share information gathered for the purpose of producing rigorous, comprehensive pieces of reporting (see Aitamurto, this volume). This can also be a simple way of tracking down unusual sources a journalist may not know. While establishing a community of content creators is key to success, it can be challenging to build and maintain, according to Howe (2009).

Crowdfunding—an offshoot of crowdsourcing—targets the public for money through various platforms and funding avenues. In 2008, entrepreneur David Cohn founded Spot.us, a platform that facilitated crowdfunding, promotion, publishing, and dissemination of journalism by (often) independent community news outlets and independent or citizen journalists, with the support of a Knight News Challenge grant (Gahran, 2015). The site was put on hold in 2014 after being sold to American Public Media in 2011. The company argued that most projects tended to be funded by friends and family, as opposed to community members with an interest or need for certain information. It also said people gave once and never returned and concluded that there were few reasons, business-wise, for sustaining a crowdfunding platform (Gahran, 2015).

The marketplace of niche

The hyperlocal movement can be understood as a shift towards a "marketplace of niche" (Cook and Sirkkunen, 2013: 63). This perspective offers a key to sustainability in the digital age that works across the diversity of very local media outlets and the full spectrum of finance and funding models that underpin them. The literature on niche marketing and product differentiation provides a useful starting point. It emphasizes that mass production provides opportunities for niche marketing (Loureiro and Hine, 2001). In other words, the abundance of online international and national news creates a niche in the market for news for and about specific places and people. Dalgic (2013) provides a detailed account of niche marketing strategies. He calls for companies to be 'vocal locals' that differentiate their product based on local culture/lifestyle, products, and services and that establishing a strong local identity is paramount. Simon (1996 in Dalgic 2006) advises niche businesses to be 'ultra-specialists' and define their markets narrowly, cultivate strong interdependence between themselves and their consumers, and avoid outsourcing their core activities. Bijoor (2008) stresses a niche product is almost always a variation of what is not being covered adequately by the mainstream. To be seen as central to news and information in a given locale is powerful for any major news media 'brand,' but it requires investment, even if the returns are not grand scale. There is scope to 'centralize and disperse' some aspects of local news production in a digital age (such as printing and some sub-editing), but the focus must be on recognizing the importance of, and growing the dimensions of, news that make it niche. Bijoor (2008) says a niche strategy can fail due to lack of understanding of what a niche is, unaffordable pricing, defective product/market orientation, or failure to invest in developing the product and the people selling the niche products.

Local habitus and 'niche' forms of capital

Our previous research highlights that to be local is to have a grounded connection with, and understanding of, a physical place and its social and cultural dimensions that is practical and embodied (Hess and Waller, 2014b). Importantly, it involves an investment of time and requires a continual presence in that place. We extend on the scholarship of Pierre Bourdieu to suggest this may be understood as 'local habitus'—a powerful set of dispositions and practical logic developed within a place—that the small news outlet is inherently tied to. For example, reading a community newspaper or listening to local radio in a small town in the United States is part of many long-time residents' 'local habitus,' while a journalist who possesses it will likely have a significant advantage in their day-to-day newsgathering practice that manifests as a niche form of cultural capital because they know the people, the issues, the history, and the geography of that locale.

Production and consumption of very local news may be shifting, but it is not the first time the news industry and technology have changed. Bourdieu (1990) contends that habitus evolves over time as fields transform. Our point is that 'local habitus' is complex and needs to be nurtured by news organizations and journalists as part of the change. It means media companies with local ambitions need representatives on the ground, tapping into the institutions, organizations, social networks, events, and personalities that make up the diversity of local life. 'Mediated social capital' (Hess, 2015) is also important in examining future journalistic practices that can build reputation and ultimately the economics of local news outlets. This involves understanding the importance of using local knowledge to bring people together and utilizing these connections to advocate on behalf of audiences.

Digital transformation may mean that most local news will be accessed through smart device applications in the future. Given the enduring news value of 'proximity,' the news apps consumers choose to access may very well reflect their 'sense of place' and/or where they consider themselves 'a local.' 'Local habitus' is therefore important to production and consumption in the digital marketplace for very local news and needs to be considered in the social, cultural, economic, and political interests of society.

Conclusion

Despite talk of a business model crisis (see Franklin, 2014), leading media economist Robert Picard says the digital age is a time for optimism:

> What is clear is that news providers are becoming less dependent on any one form of funding than they have been for about 150 years. Multiple revenue streams from readers and advertisers, from events and e-commerce, from foundations and sponsors, and from related commercial services such as web hosting and advertising services are all contributing income. It is too early to assess fully the efficacy and sustainability of these sources, but they provide reason to believe that workable new business models are appearing in news provision.
>
> *(Picard, 2014: 507)*

Not every hyperlocal start-up or small 'community' newspaper with an online presence will be sustainable in the long term, nor will every business or sustainability model prove successful. However, the cultural significance of the most local forms of news combined with the diversity of platforms and business models available make very local journalism a vibrant sector. Furthermore, while there may be significant variations across the field, providers of very local news enjoy a common advantage in the world of digital journalism—a niche market for authentically local news that is important to audiences and not widely available. Understanding the importance of 'local habitus' and investing in forms of social capital to maintain advantage has been suggested as an important niche marketing strategy for very local news providers seeking to shore up or establish their presence. Ultimately, we argue that small media in its hyperlocal, local, and community forms is not built to make big profits. The research to date suggests that very local journalism should not be viewed as a news patch to be cultivated for mass production; it remains highly sensitive and responsive to the conditions in which it evolves.

Further reading

This chapter can be complemented by reading Penny Abernathy's *Saving Community Journalism: The Path to Profitability* (2014) and Bill Reader and John Hatcher's *Foundations of Community Journalism* (2011). Our research into the hyperlocal sector has also found Williams, Harte, and Turner's overview of hyperlocals in the United Kingdom "The value of UK hyperlocal community news" (2014) published in *Digital Journalism* to be especially helpful.

References

Abernathy, P. (2014) *Saving Community Journalism: The Path to Profitability*. North Carolina: University of North Carolina Press.

Akinfemisoye, M. and Deffor, S. (2014) "Funding Viable Business Models for Intermediate and Developing World Broadcast, Print and Online Newspaper Sectors." In Anderson, P., Williams, M. and Ogola, G. (eds) *The Future of Quality News Journalism: A Cross-Continental Analysis*. New York, NY: Routledge, pp. 88–100.

Barnett, S. (2009) *Journalism, Democracy and the Public Interest: Rethinking Media Pluralism for the Digital Age* (Working paper). Oxford, UK: Reuters Institute for the Study of Journalism.

Barnett, S. and Townend, J. (2014) "Plurality, Policy and the Local: Can Hyperlocals fill the Gap?" *Journalism Practice* 9(3): 332–349.

Bijoor, H. (2008) "They're on Their Own Trip." *Outlook Business*, 9 August, pp. 74–75.

Bonte, D., Van Dyck, H., Bullock, J.M., Coulon, A., Delgado, M., Gibbs, M., et al. (2012) "Costs of Dispersal." *Biological Reviews* 87(2): 290–312.

Bourdieu, P. (1990) *The Logic of Practice*. Cambridge, UK: Polity Press.

Bunch, W. (2007) "Forgetting Why Reporters Choose the Work They Do." *Nieman Reports* 61(4): 28–30.

Byerly, K.R. (1961) *Community Journalism*. Philadelphia, PA: Chilton.

Canter, L. (2013) "The Source, the Resource and the Collaborator: The Role of Citizen Journalism in Local UK Newspapers." *Journalism: Theory Practice Criticism* 14(8): 1091–1109.

Chesbrough, H. and Rosenbloom, R.S. (2002) "The Role of the Business Model in Capturing Value from Innovation: Evidence from Xerox Corporation's Technology Spin-off Companies." *Industrial and Corporate Change* 11(3): 529–555.

Chiou, L. and Tucker, C. (2013) "Paywalls and the Demand for News." *Information Economics and Policy* 25(2): 61–69.

Cook, C. and Sirkkunen, E. (2013) "What's in a Niche? Exploring the Business Models of Online Journalism." *Journal of Media Business Studies* 10(4): 63–82.

Dalgic, T. (2006) *Handbook of Niche Marketing: Principles and Practice*. New York, NY: The Haworth Reference Press.

Dalgic, T. (2013) *Customer-Oriented Marketing Strategy Theory and Practice*. New York, NY: Business Expert Press.

Ewart, J. (2014) "Local People, Local Places, Local Voices and Local Spaces: How Talkback Radio in Australia Provides Hyperlocal News Through Mini-Narrative Sharing." *Journalism* 15(6): 790–807.

Farhi, P. (2007) "Rolling the Dice." *American Journalism Review* 29(3): 40–43.

Fenton, N., Metykova, M., Schloseberg, J. and Freedman, D. (2010) *Meeting the Needs of Local Communities*. London, UK: Media Trust.

Franklin, B. (2014) "The Future of Journalism: In an Age of Digital Media and Economic Uncertainty." *Journalism Studies* 15(5): 481–499.

Gahran, A. (2015) "As Spot.us Ends, Insights on Community News Crowdfunding." *Knight Digital Media Center*. Available from: http://www.knightdigitalmediacenter.org/blogs/agahran/2015/02/spotus-ends-insights-community-news-crowdfunding.

Glaser, M. (2010) "Citizen Journalism: Widening World Views, Extending Democracy." In Allen, S. (ed.) *The Routledge Companion to News and Journalism*. London, UK: Routledge, pp. 267–277.

Greenslade, R. and Barnett, S. (2014) "Can Charity Save the Local Press?" *British Journalism Review* 25(1): 62–67.

Hatcher, J. (2011) "A View from the Outside: What Other Social Science Disciplines Can Teach Us about Community Journalism." In Reader, B. and Hatcher, J.A. (eds) *Foundations of Community Journalism*. Thousand Oaks, CA: Sage Publications, pp. 129–149.

Hess, K. (2013) "Breaking Boundaries: Recasting the Small Newspaper as Geo-Social News." *Digital Journalism* 1(1): 45–60.

Hess, K. (2015) "Making Connections: Mediated Social Capital and the Small-Town Press." *Journalism Studies* 16(4): 482–496.

Hess, K. and Waller, L. (2014a) "Geo-Social Journalism: Reorienting the Study of Small Commercial Newspapers in a Digital Environment." In Robinson, S. (ed.) *Community Journalism Midst Media Revolution*. London, UK: Routledge, pp. 14–30.

Hess, K. and Waller, L. (2014b) "River Flows and Profit Flows: The Powerful Logic Driving Local News." *Journalism Studies* 17(3): 263–276. DOI: 10.1080/1461670X.2014.981099.

Hess, K. and Waller, L. (2015) "Hip To Be Hyper: The Subculture of Excessively Local News." *Digital Journalism* 4(2): 193–210. DOI: 10.1080/21670811.2014.1002859.

Hood, L. (2014) "Remote Delivery of Local TV News: When Local May Be Hundreds of Miles Away." *Electronic News* 8(4): 290–305.

Howe, J. (2009) *Crowdsourcing: Why the Power of the Crowd is Driving the Future of Business*. New York, NY: Three Rivers Press.

Howley, K. (2010) *Understanding Community Media*. Thousand Oaks, CA: Sage.

Knight, M. and Cook, C. (2013) *Social Media for Journalists: Principles and Practice*. Thousand Oaks, CA: Sage.

Lacy, S. (2011) "The Economics of Community Newspapers." In Hatcher, J. and Reader, B. (eds) *Foundations of Community Journalism*. London, UK: Sage, pp. 174–177.

Lambourne, H. (2012) "Jobs Go as Publisher Outsources Ad Creations Teams to India." *Hold the Front Page*. Available from: http://www.holdthefrontpage.co.uk/2012/news/publisher-to-outsource-ad-creation-teams-to-india/.

Lauterer, J. (2000) *Community Journalism: The Personal Approach*. Ames, IA: Iowa State University Press.

Loureiro, M. and Hine, S. (2001) "Discerning Niche Markets: A Comparison of Consumer Willingness to Pay for a Local Organic and GMO-Free Product." *American Agricultural Economics Association, Meeting Proceedings*, pp. 1–24.

Mason, J. (2003) *Sustainable Agriculture*. Collingwood, Victoria: Landlinks Press.

Mitchell, A. (2014) "State of the News Media 2014." Available from: http://www.journalism.org/2014/03/26/state-of-the-news-media-2014-overview/.

Moore, C. and Gillis, T. (2005) "Transforming Communities: Community Journalism in Africa." *Transformations* 10. Available from: http://www.transformationsjournal.org/issues/10/article_06.shtml

Myllylahti, M. (2014) "Newspaper Paywalls: The Hype and the Reality." *Digital Journalism* 2(2): 179–194.

Nist.Sematech (2012) *Nist/Sematecg e-Handbook of Statistical Methods*. Available from: http://www.itl.nist.gov/div898/handbook/.

Ornebring, H. (2008) "The Consumer as Producer—Of What?" *Journalism Studies* 9(5): 771–785.

Paulussen, S. and D'heer, E. (2013) "Using Citizens for Community Journalism." *Journalism Practice* 7(5): 588–603.

Paulussen, S., Heinonen, A., Domingo, D. and Quant, T. (2007) "Doing It Together: Citizen Participation in the News Making Process." *Observatorio* 1(3): 1–24.

Phillips, A. (2015) *Journalism in Context: Practice and Theory for the Digital Age*. New York, NY: Routledge.

Picard, R. (2014) "Twilight or New Dawn of Journalism?" *Journalism Studies* 15(5): 500–510.

Reader, B. (2011) "Community Journalism: A Concept of Connectedness." In Reader, B. and Hatcher, J.A. (eds) *Foundations of Community Journalism*. Thousand Oaks, CA: Sage, pp. 3–19.

Rieder, R. (2013) "Small Independent Local News Makes Headlines." *USA Today*, 21 August. Available from: http://www.usatoday.com/story/money/columnist/rieder/2013/08/20/small-independent-hyperlocal-news-websites/2676515/.

Schaffer, J. (2007) "Citizen Media: Fad or the Future of News? The Rise and Prospects of Hyperlocal Journalism." Available from: http://www.j-lab.org/_uploads/downloads/citizen_media-1.pdf.

Scutari, M. (2015) "A Closer Look at the Knight Foundation's 'Venture Capital' Fund for Local News Outlets." *Inside Philanthropy*. Available from: http://www.insidephilanthropy.com/journalism/2015/1/8/a-closer-look-at-the-knight-foundations-venture-capital-fund.html.

Singer, J. (2010) "Journalism in the Network." In Allan, S. (ed.) *Routledge Companion to News and Journalism*. London, UK: Routledge, pp. 277–286.

Sjøvaag, H. (2014) "Homogenisation or Differentiation? The Effects of Consolidation in Regional Newspaper Market." *Journalism Studies* 15(5): 511–521.

van Kerkhoven, M. and Bakker, P. (2014) "The Hyperlocal in Practice." *Digital Journalism* 2(3): 296–309.

Williams, A., Harte, D. and Turner, J. (2014) "The Value of UK Hyperlocal Community News: Findings from a Content Analysis, an Online Survey and Interviews with Producers." *Digital Journalism* 3(5): 680–703. DOI: 10.1080/21670811.2014.965932.

Zahariadis, N. (2013) "Industrial Subsidies: Surveying Macroeconomic Policy Approaches." In Murschetz, P. (ed.) *State Aid for Newspapers: Theories, Cases, Actions*. London, UK: Springer, pp. 59–72.

PART IV

Digital journalism studies: Issues and debates

20

MOBILE NEWS

The future of digital journalism

Oscar Westlund

You wake up by the alarm bell in the morning. The very second you turn off the clock, which is incorporated into your smartphone, you are most likely faced with a high-resolution screen displaying a variety of application icons. While still lying in bed—and with a tap of your finger—you can use news applications or news sites to get informed and entertained. There is a wealth of opportunities; you can choose among news applications provided by both international and national news providers, originating from newspapers or broadcasters or from news startups and automatized news aggregators. Many also have the opportunity to access local news reporting through applications and sites customized for their mobile device. Moreover, you can—while still lying in bed—embark on a journey into specific domains of social media (such as Facebook, Twitter, or Instagram) to see the activities of your friends and broader networks and also access the news these people and institutions have shared directly or indirectly with you. As of 2016, you may also access instant news from specific news providers directly from Facebook (i.e. Instant articles). By the time you get out of bed, you are potentially already feeling like you are an informed citizen. Although many people still maintain their habit of digesting news during breakfast—by reading newspapers, listening to radio news, or watching television news—this chapter explores the mounting evidence that points to significant changes in news consumption through mobile technologies. This applies to the morning routines, but also to the multitude of interstices in everyday life.

Personal and portable mobile devices, including but not limited to smartphones, tablets, and smartwatches, offer records of network access, allowing these so-called miniaturized mobilities (Elliott and Urry, 2010) to facilitate communication as well as the accessing, sharing, and production of information literally around the clock and seemingly without any constraints in space (although limitations in the internet's infrastructure clearly pose an important constraint in some geographical locations). This means mobile devices—this chapter focuses specifically on the smartphone—can be used in the folds of everyday life for various communicative and informative purposes.

Mobile devices have reached a level of diffusion far beyond that of the internet (although the convergence between the two reduces this gap) and have even surpassed the diffusion of electricity (Westlund, 2013). As it has become increasingly typical for citizens around the globe to have a mobile device within arm's reach, many aspects of people's private and professional lives have changed in several and significant ways. Although not adopting a technological deterministic perspective, it is nonetheless necessary to account for these changes and the tremendous technological innovation that has taken place, enabling citizens and organizations alike to do many more things with their mobile devices. In developed countries, feature phones have become replaced by more and more advanced and smart mobile devices. These are equipped with hardware and software that make possible functionalities previously associated with the computer, but also make possible functionalities earlier only dreamed of, even going beyond one's imagination. Smartphones offer a touchscreen interface to a mobile ecosystem encompassing access to a wealth of (customized) applications and responsive sites. These are—from a technological perspective—somewhat difficult to distinguish from tablets, as well as the so-called phablets sized between the two; as functionalities becoming increasingly similar, the most salient difference between these is screen size.

Ultimately, why is it important to analyze and understand mobile news? The reasons are many, including the future sustainability of journalism from editorial, business and technological perspectives. From a democratic perspective, normative theories of journalism have institutionalized the idea that journalists produce and publish news that enables informed citizenry. Moreover, a large body of research into political communication has followed the same line of thought. Studies show that the routines or non-routines of news consumption in contemporary high-choice media environments are closely connected to individual factors such as political interest (Strömbäck, Djerf-Pierre, and Shehata, 2013). However, as a growing number of recent studies have shown, there is a growing shift towards accessing more and more news via mobile devices (see review in Westlund, 2015). Following this line, one important question is whether access to mobile news will prove to be a qualitative complement or replacement for other news media and news platforms. This naturally depends on how and to what extent citizens access the news with mobile devices, which in turn is influenced by the ways in which news publishers shape their mobile news services. To date, there is a small but growing number of studies exploring the diverse initiatives made by news publishers (Westlund, 2013).

This chapter departs from extant literature on the production and consumption of mobile news, synthesizing these alongside updates of recent publications and industry developments. The chapter focuses on mobile news use on increasingly versatile smartphones. It also includes feature phones and phablets, which similarly have their offshoots in telecommunications and the telephone, as they enable calls through telecommunication networks. The potential of other mobile devices—such as smartwatches, smart glasses, and networked chips implanted into the human body—is indeed poised to become significant. However, these technologies are in the relatively early stages of their development and will not be discussed at length in this chapter.

Mobile news: consumption

This section offers a brief review of extant literature and research on mobile news consumption. It illustrates how the always-on connection, extending beyond time and space, has made it easy to use mobile devices in the folds and interstices of everyday life for different purposes and functions throughout the day (Dimmick *et al.*, 2011; c.f. Kormelink and Meijer, 2014; van Damme *et al.*, 2015). Nevertheless, a decade ago, the accessing of news with mobile devices was largely met with skepticism, even among the young and tech savvy citizens (Westlund, 2007). Representative and cross-sectional annual survey data in the case of Sweden has evidenced that the uptake of mobile news among the public (16–85 years) was relatively slow from 2005 to 2008. While in 2009–2010 there was a significant increase, it was in 2011 that adoption increased tremendously. The pace continued in 2012, but thereafter the growth pace has slowed (Westlund, 2014).

As of today, several research projects and industry observations point to the exceptional growth in mobile news accessing and also its impact on other forms of news consumption. In January 2015, a majority of the 50 most-visited websites in the United States received more traffic from mobile devices than from desktops, although mobile news users spent less time per visit than desktop-based users (Olmstead and Shearer, 2015). A guest editorial for a special section titled "mobile news consumption in an age of mobile media" in *Mobile Media & Communication* reviewed the literature in this area, summarizing notes on five key articles on mobile news consumption (see review in Westlund, 2015). The review discussed findings from the limited yet growing number of studies, which in recent years have included numerous cross-sectional studies in China, Denmark, Japan, Sweden, the United Kingdom, the United States, and other countries (see Chan, 2015; Chyi and Chadha, 2012; Newman, 2012; Newman and Levy, 2013; Sasseen *et al.*, 2013; Schrøder, 2015; Westlund, 2008, 2010, 2014). Importantly, mobile news consumption has gained significance in both the developed and developing world and in democratic and non-democratic countries (Goggin and Hjorth, 2009) and is being accessed via social media with mobile devices (Crawford, 2010).

In that research review, and playing on alliteration, research is synthesized into mobile news consumption along four distinct themes: *patterns, people, place,* and *participation* Westlund (2015). Although these themes do not cover all research conducted on mobile news consumption, they do indeed appear to capture most. Extant research has, for the most part, focused on *patterns* and *people* and less so on *place* and *participation*. Research into *patterns* of mobile news consumption has traced changes over time and includes the array of aforementioned studies. This line of study has also investigated how patterns of mobile news consumption interrelate with other forms of news consumption, involving the study of displacing and/or complementary effects. Some studies have suggested that mobile news is complementary to legacy news media (Kitamura, 2013), whereas other studies have found that mobile news has led to both displacing and complementary effects, varying among distinct groups (Westlund and Färdigh, 2015). The question of complementarity extends beyond that of news, with some scholars evidencing the strong correlation between mobile news consumption and other tasks performed with mobile devices (Thorson *et al.*, 2015). Literature on the nexus of mobile news consumption and people has shown—similar to research on other forms of news consumption—a great degree of difference among groups of people, depending on factors such as age, sex, and educational level (see Fortunati, Deuze, and de Luca, 2014; Westlund and Färdigh, 2015; Westlund and Weibull, 2013; Wolf and Schnauber, 2014). Moreover, the significance of *place* has been documented in studies investigating when and where people use their mobile device for news consumption. Some studies have stressed that mobile devices are mainly used while outside the home, while on the go (Dimmick *et al.*, 2011), and/or at work (Taneja *et al.*, 2012). Other scholarly accounts have suggested these mobile devices are being used for mobile news literally everywhere, not least while people are at home (Schrøder, 2015; van Damme *et al.*, 2015). Collectively, the places where people access news with their mobile devices fluctuate with the rhythms of everyday life (Jansson and Lindell, 2014). There is less 'context stability' in comparison to other platforms and media used to access the news (Wolf and Schnauber, 2014). The fourth theme is *participation*, which encompasses two lines of scholarship. On the one end is 'produsage' (Bruns, 2012), which is a portmanteau of the words 'producer' and 'user.' This line of scholarship focuses on research into the presence or absence of citizen journalism and participatory journalism (see Lewis, 2012). It includes a significant number of studies focusing on how citizens use smartphones to record and make videos, as well as communicate through texting and social media; this often leads to interactions with news media during important events (Westlund, 2013). This line of research also includes a growing number of studies on social media–related news accessing with mobile devices (Mihailidis, 2014; Wei *et al.*, 2013). On the other end, research focuses on the intersection of political participation and mobile news consumption. This research encompasses studies on democracy, information access, and mobilization (Liu, 2013) in general, and how distinct individual characteristics (Campbell and Kwak, 2010, 2011) and mobile media uses of political news (Kwak *et al.*, 2011; Lee *et al.*, 2014) relate to political participation.

The bottom line is that mobile news has gained in significance over the past couple of years in a number of different ways. Reports and discussions from various actors in the news media industry suggest the uptake of mobile news continues to evolve at a rapid pace. From the perspective of informed citizens and democracy, it is relevant to ask whether mobile news consumption is a sufficient alternative to newspaper reading, watching television newscasts, etc. Mobile news consumption can take place in many different ways, varying in orientation, quality, length, intensity, and so forth. Ultimately, many issues require further scrutiny.

A meta-analysis of several research projects on media use focuses on how citizens create and articulate their experience with the news themselves. Out of these, Kormelink and Meijer (2014) identify 16 different kinds of activities with the news: reading, watching, viewing, listening, checking, snacking, monitoring, scanning, searching, clicking, linking, sharing, liking, recommending, commenting, and voting. Importantly, these activities are each associated with different kinds of senses, different kinds of media and platforms, and different kinds of cognitive focus. However, while there are several assessments for the importance of mobile news and the future of digital journalism—and its relative importance for the future of democracy—it remains important to investigate more closely how each of these 16 activities correspond to mobile news consumption.

Kormelink and Meijer (2014; see also Chapter 34, this volume) write that traditional forms of news use—reading and watching—are perceived to be active and attention-rich activities, whereas listening is considered a background activity. Viewing, however, is judged to be a more relaxed and laidback form of digesting videos or television. Checking the news is an activity of efficiency if something interesting and new has occurred, whereas snacking is marked by diversion and involves gaining a basic overview of what is happening. Scanning, on the other hand, takes place when people keep themselves updated concerning developments about a specific topic or domain, including interactions about this event. By comparison, monitoring means citizens survey their news landscape, ready to access and digest more news if necessary. The searching of news takes place when citizens seek answers to distinct questions. Clicking is the activity of clicking on news items or links to access more information, while sharing involves sharing through social media and clicking on 'like' (on sites such as Facebook). Recommending is clicking on a 'recommend' function, and linking is when one pastes the URL of a news article into a new context. Commenting involves posting online comments and voting refers to responding to a news poll (Kormelink and Meijer, 2014).

Ultimately, as some of the previously mentioned studies have shown, networked mobile devices have lowered the threshold for news consumption. Consequently, the uptake of mobile news has had a displacing effect on other news media. In the case of citizens replacing their habit of spending extensive time *reading* a printed newspaper with *checking*, *scanning* or *snacking* mobile news, the result may be that citizens are less informed. Similar effects may occur if citizens replace the active watching of television news with viewing occasional videos on their smartphones. These lines of development of mobile news consumption could potentially lead to citizens—who have access to news all the time—becoming paradoxically less informed. On the other hand, if citizens use mobile news in such ways while still maintaining their established habits of news consumption, the outcome could be positive. Similarly, it is also possible for citizens to develop habits of truly engaging with news through their mobile devices, both in terms of cognitive efforts through *reading* or *watching*, as well as active participation through social media (*liking, commenting, sharing, recommending, and voting*). Citizens today are offered great opportunities to individualize their news consumption to become actively informed citizens. However, these opportunities result in fragmentation and do not necessarily result in positive or negative outcomes.

The production and distribution of mobile news

Parallel to the growth of mobile news consumption, an increasing number of news publishers have incorporated and developed ways to produce and distribute mobile news. Studies from Brazil, Canada, Italy, and Spain (Palacios *et al.*, 2016) as well as Germany (Wolf and Hohlfeld, 2012), Spain (López, Westlund, and Silva, 2015), Sweden (Westlund, 2011, 2012), the United Kingdom (Nel and Westlund, 2012), and the United States (Sasseen, Olmstead, and Mitchell, 2013), all explore different efforts concerning mobile news publishing. These efforts have seemingly accelerated alongside legacy news media, especially newspapers, which are struggling with a decline in readership and worsening financial conditions.

Most of the research into the production and distribution of mobile news—until mid-2012—has shown how mobile news was approached on an organizational level, with news publishers engaging in both manual and automated forms of mobile news publishing. Some efforts have been marked as repurposing, whereas others signify attempts towards customization, all of which fit into the so-called *model of journalism*. News publishers have utilized editorial content management systems for their management of news content. They have been able to develop their approaches to how editorial content is published across various platforms and media. These include news sites for desktops, native applications, responsive sites, and push messaging services for mobile devices (SMS, MMS, RSS, etc.). Moreover, on the level of individual journalists, initiatives such as iReport by *CNN* or the MoJo Kit (a collaboration between Reuters and Nokia) started paving the way for so-called mobile journalists (MoJos) to gain significance in news reporting. To date, smartphones such as Apple's iPhone and the Samsung Galaxy S series enable journalists to communicate easily with their colleagues, sources, and audiences through voice, SMS, e-mail, and various social media. They can also use these mobile devices for journalistic practices such as live blogging as well as capturing, editing, and publishing videos and photos (Westlund, 2013).

As of 2016, it has become relatively commonplace for news publishers in the developed world to offer their digital news for citizens to access through mobile devices. Nevertheless, the ways in which they do so varies significantly. Publishers employ different approaches to customization and repurposing and involve both human-led approaches and technology-led approaches, utilizing algorithms and editorial content management systems with automation functionalities. Similarly, programmatic advertising is gaining significance as an effective and widespread approach for the trade of digital advertising. Nevertheless, advertising avoiders create increasingly potent threats, especially as ad-blocking features has become easily available with the latest Apple iOS software (iOS9).

Among the member organizations of global newspaper associations—most notably the World Association of Newspapers (WAN-IFRA) and the International News Media Association (INMA)—the past few years have been marked by discussions of 'mobile-first strategies' (see Seale, 2012). These have emerged out of a conviction that modern news publishers need to reconfigure their operations towards mobile news publishing (and mobile advertising). While mobile news for smartphones continues to evolve gradually, perhaps the most significant changes currently taking place involve news publishers exploring and experimenting with additional mobile devices. For instance, in May 2015, several European legacy news publishers gathered in Copenhagen to discuss possible ways to approach mobile news for Apple's iWatch. These also expand to new non-proprietary arenas, such as with Swedish tabloid *Expressen* publishing news for Snapchat and WhatsApp since the spring of 2015. Importantly, the use of Snapchat and WhatsApp is closely linked to mobile devices, similar to Twitter and Instagram. Reflective of these dynamics, during the spring of 2015 *Expressen* built a digital showroom where employees and visitors could explore and obtain first-hand experience with new digital and mobile technologies. They also installed 130 large LCD screens throughout their offices. Their rationale for doing this involved pushing their organizational culture towards digital and mobile technologies. Their main source of inspiration was a visit to the Facebook office in Ireland.

Concluding discussion

This chapter has discussed how various actors and news industries around the world have utilized mobile devices in the production and distribution of news: moving from pushing manually crafted news alerts by SMS or MMS towards the auto-direction of news content free of charge, for mobile news sites, thereafter exploring news publishing via applications or sites either tailored entirely for the mobile or developed with responsive Web design.

Turning to the more significant question of the future of digital journalism, this chapter will now explore how distinct social actors inside news organizations—journalists, technologists, and businesspeople—can collaboratively shape the future of mobile news (Westlund, 2011, 2012). These social actors develop and negotiate their developments of mobile news with each other and with other social actors beyond the organization. However, they also concern the affordances of technologies and in relation to different assemblages of audiences (Lewis and Westlund, 2015; Westlund and Lewis, 2014) and the multitude of different ways these potentially develop experiences with mobile news (Kormelink and Meijer, 2014).

In an article conceptualizing different agents' involvement in media innovations, the so-called 4A matrix was posited (Westlund and Lewis, 2014). It charts seven typologies for strategic directions in media innovation activities on the basis of plausible combinations of actors, actants, and audiences regarding who takes the lead. The seven distinct typologies are: (1) Actor-led; (2) Actant-led; (3) Audience-led; (4) Actor/actant-led; (5) Actor/audience-led; (6) Actant/Audience-led; and (7) The 3A approach. The 4A matrix thus presents seven approaches that news publishers can choose as they shape their approach to the production and distribution of mobile news, as well as the forms for news consumption. These agents all have their significance concerning opportunities such as the personalization of mobile news services, as well as locative news. Personalization grants more significance to technology (e.g. algorithms and editorial CMS) to deliver relevant news to audiences based on preferences and online behaviors. Personalization can still make use of news produced by journalists, but it results in a situation in which journalists lose some of their power and control over what news gets the most visibility.

The last few years have seen the rise of personalized news services for mobile devices, both by legacy news media and startups, and they include applications such as Flipboard and Omni. These applications deliver news on the basis of both preferences and behaviors, from a large pool of news publishers (i.e. shaping personal filter bubbles). Also Apple News, Google News, and Facebook Instant Articles are examples of significant initiatives. From the perspective of news publishers, these news aggregators can function as non-proprietary platforms through which news is spread more widely and generates traffic to their sites, similar to social media and search engines. The reason is that typically only headlines and ingresses are displayed in these personalized applications of aggregated news. From an audience perspective, these applications make it possible to check, snack, monitor, and scan. However, if audiences wish to receive more news stories, then they need to engage in clicking. This directs them to a proprietary news platform from which they can possibly gain more in-depth information through reading, watching, and listening.

It is also worth noting that with the launch of Facebook's 'instant articles,' a collaboration that started in May 2015 with a set of major news publishers, news is published immediately on Facebook. That is, no traffic is directed to the news publishers' proprietary news platforms. This is beneficial for audiences, who can access the entire story without clicking to go to the original source of journalism at the publishers' proprietary news platforms. User-friendliness also improves through shorter page loading times. In other words, different news publishers (including tax-funded British public service broadcaster BBC) produce news that is published directly on American-based Facebook, and thus they create traffic on which Facebook can capitalize.

Importantly, the news articles selected for what can be called 'instant social media publishing' have the possibility of becoming truly important for citizens evolving news diets. They may have a displacing effect on news accessed directly from publishers' proprietary platforms. Legacy news media have entered a mobile media era in which social media and other non-proprietary platforms are also thriving. This situation presents both opportunities and threats to their existence and the success with which they contribute to informed citizenry. The future shaping of news publishing needs to involve the expertise of journalists, businesspeople, and technologists—as well as audiences and technologies—in developing and reconfiguring the production and distribution of news for diverse proprietary media and platforms. Considering that automated and technology-led forms of news publishing are likely to grow in significance in the future (Westlund, 2013), there is a need for 'democratic news algorithms.' This term has been coined for this chapter and refers to algorithms balancing individual preferences and behaviors (i.e. what the people want) with editorial judgments (i.e. what people should have). The democratic news algorithms should be designed to facilitate informed citizens and to avoid people intentionally or unintentionally developing to narrow exposure to the wealth of news available (i.e. filter bubbles).

Ultimately, the current shift to mobile news poses a significant, unfortunately even insurmountable, challenge to news publishers: how to develop successful and sustainable revenue models. The personal and portable features of mobile devices—and the intensive and increasing uses of mobile media—open the gateway for massive revenue potential from advertising as well as different fee-based services. The relative increases in mobile revenues are obviously growing, although few news publishers to date have succeeded in generating significant revenues. One exception is the Scandinavian-based Schibsted Media Group, which has increased mobile revenues significantly in recent years (million SEK): 9 (2010), 25 (2011), 86 (2012), 234 (2013) and 308 (2014). Revenues from the leading tabloids in Sweden (*Aftonbladet*) and Norway (*VG*) constitute a major portion of these steep increases (Ljungqvist, 2015).

However, this window of opportunity is open to any stakeholder that can succeed in attracting the attention of the public. *Google* and *Facebook* have together seized the main slice of the mobile advertising pie and, importantly, the shift to mobile advertising will probably also result in displacing effects in the advertising expenditure for other platforms. The bottom line is that the turn to mobile media represents a window of opportunity of which news publishers can take advantage to forward their positions in the mediascape. However, it may also become their deathblow.

Further reading

For more in this area, Westlund's articles "Mobile news: A review and model of journalism in an age of mobile media" (2013) and "News Consumption in an Age of Mobile Media: Patterns, People, Place and Participation" (2015) offer rich overviews of mobile technologies and news media. Thorson *et al.*'s 2015 article "News use of mobile media: A contingency view" addresses mobile news consumption considering people's news habits. Finally, Wolf and Schnauber's "News consumption in the mobile era" (2014) looks at the ubiquity of news on mobile devices.

References

Bruns, A. (2012) "Reconciling Community and Commerce? Collaboration between Produsage Communities and Commercial Operators." *Information, Communication & Society* 15(6): 815–835.

Campbell, S.W. and Kwak, N. (2010) "Mobile Communication and Civic Life: Linking Patterns of Use to Civic and Political Engagements." *Journal of Communication* 60: 536–555.

Campbell, S.W. and Kwak, N. (2011) "Political Involvement in 'Mobilized' Society: The Interactive Relationships among Mobile Communication, Network Characteristics, and Political Participation." *Journal of Communication* 61: 1005–1024.

Chan, M. (2015) "Examining the Influences of News Use Patterns, Motivations, and Age Cohort on Mobile News Use: The Case of Hong Kong." *Mobile Media & Communication* 3(2): 179–195.

Chyi, H.I. and Chadha, M. (2012) "News on New Devices." *Journalism Practice* 6(4): 431–449.

Crawford, K. (2010) "News to Me: Twitter and the Personal Networking of News." In Meikle, G. and Redden, G. (eds) *News Online: Transformations and Continuities*. London, UK: Macmillan, pp. 115–131.

Dimmick, J., Feaster, J.C. and Hoplamazian, G.J. (2011) "News in the Interstices: The Niches of Mobile Media in Space and Time." *New Media and Society* 13(1): 23–39.

Elliott, A. and Urry, J. (2010) *Mobile Lives*. London, UK: Routledge.

Fortunati, L., Deuze, M. and de Luca, F. (2014) "The News about News: How Print, Online, Free, and Mobile Co-Construct New Audiences in Italy, France, Spain, the UK, and Germany." *Journal of Computer-Mediated Communication* 19(2): 121–140.

Goggin, G. and Hjorth, L. (2009) "The Question of Mobile Media." In Goggin, G. and Hjorth, L. (eds) *Mobile Technologies: From Telecommunications to Media*. New York, NY: Routledge, pp. 3–8.

Jansson, A. and Lindell, J. (2014) "News Media Consumption in the Transmedia Age." *Journalism Studies* 16(1): 79–96. DOI: 10.1080/1461670X.2014.890337.

Kitamura, S. (2013) "The Relationship between Use of the Internet and Traditional Information Sources: An Empirical Study in Japan." *SAGE Open*, April–June, pp. 1–9.

Kormelink, T.G. and Meijer, I.C. (2014) "Checking, Sharing, Clicking and Linking." *Digital Journalism* 3(5): 664–679. DOI: 10.1080/21670811.2014.937149.

Kwak, N., Campbell, S.W., Choi, J. and Bae, S.Y. (2011) "Mobile Communication and Public Affairs Engagement in Korea: An Examination of Non-Linear Relationships between Mobile Phone Use and Engagement Across Age Groups." *Asian Journal of Communication* 21(5): 485–503.

Lee, H., Kwak, N., Campbell, S.W. and Ling, R. (2014) "Mobile Communication and Political Participation in South Korea: Examining the Intersections between Informational and Relational Uses." *Computers in Human Behavior* 38: 38–52.

Lewis, S.C. (2012) "The Tension between Professional Control and Open Participation." *Information, Communication & Society* 15(6): 836–866.

Lewis, S.C. and Westlund, O. (2015) "Actors, Actants, Audiences, and Activities in Cross-Media News Work." *Digital Journalism* 3(1): 19–37.

Liu, J. (2013) "Mobile Communication, Popular Protests and Citizenship in China." *Modern Asian Studies* 47(3): 995–1018.

Ljungqvist, K. (2015) "Strategies for Transforming Legacy Media to Digital. Digital Disruption and the Media—What Does the Future Hold?" (Conference speech), Stockholm, Sweden.

López, X., Westlund O., and Silva, A. (2015) "La industria de medios impresos se sube al periodismo móvil." *Telos Journal* 100(1): 1–14.

Mihailidis, P. (2014) "A Tethered Generation: Exploring the Role of Mobile Phones in the Daily Life of Young People." *Mobile Media & Communication* 2(1): 58–72.

Nel, F. and Westlund, O. (2012) "The 4C's of Mobile News: Channels, Conversation, Content and Commerce." *Journalism Practice* 6(5): 744–753.

Newman, N. (2012) *Reuters Institute Digital News Report 2012*. Oxford: Reuters Institute for the Study of Journalism, University of Oxford.

Newman, N. and Levy, D. (2013) *Reuters Institute Digital News Report 2013—Tracking the Future of News*. Oxford: Reuters Institute for the Study of Journalism, University of Oxford.

Olmstead, K. and Shearer, E. (2015) *Digital News—Audience: Fact Sheet*. PEW, State of the News Media.

Palacios, M., da Silva, F.F., Barbosa, S. and da Cuncha, R. (2016) "Mobile Journalism and Innovation: A Study on Content Formats of Autochthonous News Apps for Tablets." In Aguado, J.M., Feijóo, C. and Martínez, I.J. (eds) *Emerging Perspectives on the Mobile Content Evolution*. Hershey, PA: IGI Global, pp. 239–262.

Sasseen, J., Olmstead, K. and Mitchell, A. (2013) *Digital: As Mobile Grows Rapidly, the Pressures on News Intensify*. Washington, DC: Pew Research Center's Project for Excellence in Journalism.

Schrøder, K. (2015) "News Media Old and New: Fluctuating Audiences, News Repertoires and Locations of Consumption." *Journalism Studies* 16(1): 60–78.

Seale, S. (2012) *Emerging Mobile Strategies for News Publishers*. International Newsmedia Marketing Association (INMA).

Strömbäck, J., Djerf-Pierre, M. and Shehata, A. (2013) "The Dynamics of Political Interest and News Media Consumption: A Longitudinal Perspective." *International Journal of Public Opinion Research* 25(4): 414–435.

Taneja, H., Webster, J.G., Malthouse, E.C. and Ksiazek, T.B. (2012) "Media Consumption Across Platforms: Identifying User-Defined Repertoires." *New Media and Society* 14: 951–968.

Thorson, T., Karaliova, T., Shoenberger, H., Kim, E. and Fidler, R. (2015) "News Use of Mobile Media: A Contingency View." *Mobile Media & Communication* 3(2): 160–178.

Van Damme, K., Courtois, C., Verbrugge, K. and de Marez, L. (2015) "What's APPening to News? A Mixed-Method Audience-Centered Study on Mobile News Consumption." *Mobile Media & Communication* 3(2): 196–213.

Wei, R., Lo, V., Xu, X., Chen, Y.K. and Zhang, G. (2013) "Predicting Mobile News Use among College Students: The Role of Press Freedom in Four Asian Cities." *New Media & Society* 16(4): 637–654.

Westlund, O. (2007) "The Adoption of Mobile Media by Young Adults in Sweden." In Goggin, G. and Hjorth, L. (eds) *Mobile Media*. University of Sydney, Australia: Watson Ferguson and Company, pp. 116–124.

Westlund, O. (2008) "From Mobile Phone to Mobile Device: News Consumption on the Go." *Canadian Journal of Communication* 33(3): 443–463.

Westlund, O. (2010) "New(s) Functions for the Mobile." *New Media & Society* 12(1): 91–108.

Westlund, O. (2011) *Cross-Media News Work: Sensemaking of the Mobile Media (R)evolution*. Gothenburg, JMG Book Series no.64, University of Gothenburg.

Westlund, O. (2012) "Producer-Centric vs. Participation-Centric: On the Shaping Mobile Media." *Northern Lights* 10(1): 107–112.

Westlund, O. (2013) "Mobile News: A Review and Model of Journalism in an Age of Mobile Media." *Digital Journalism* 1(1): 6–26.

Westlund, O. (2014) "Mognande Mobil Multimedia." ("Mobile media saturation"). In Oscarsson, H. and Bergström, A. (eds) *Mittfåra & Marginal (Middle Groove & Marginal)*. Gothenburg, The SOM Institute, University of Gothenburg.

Westlund, O. (2015) "News Consumption in an Age of Mobile Media: Patterns, People, Place and Participation." *Mobile Media & Communication* 3(2): 151–159.

Westlund, O. and Färdigh, M.A. (2015) "Accessing the News in an Age of Mobile Media." *Mobile Media & Communication* 3(1): 53–74.

Westlund, O. and Lewis, S.C. (2014) "Agents of Media Innovations: Actors, Actants, and Audiences." *The Journal of Media Innovations* 1(2): 10–35.

Westlund, O. and Weibull, L. (2013) "Generation, Life Course and News Media Use in Sweden 1986–2011." *Northern Lights* 11: 147–173.

Wolf, C. and Hohlfeld, R. (2012) "Revolution in Journalism? Mobile Devices as a New Means of Publishing." In Martin, C. and von Pape, T. (eds) *Images in Mobile Communication*. Germany: VS Verlag für Sozialwissenschaften.

Wolf, C. and Schnauber, A. (2014) "News Consumption in the Mobile Era." *Digital Journalism* 3(5): 759–776. DOI: 10.1080/21670811.2014.942497.

21

DIGITAL JOURNALISM AND TABLOID JOURNALISM

Marco T. Bastos

Tabloid media and the process of tabloidization are terms that refer to the deterioration of serious news gathering and reporting associated with the quality press that resulted from successive concessions to market liberalism and individualism (Franklin, 1997; Rowe, 2011: 452; Sparks and Tulloch, 2000). Early incursions into the tabloid genre date from the nineteenth century with experimental publications designed to appeal to popular taste, but it was only during the ensuing century that the term gained specific application to print media. The fast and large acceptance of the term was arguably driven by the multiple and reinforced expressions of disapproval from public intellectuals (Greenberg, 1996).

The terms broadsheet and tabloid stem from paper format, with the earlier being printed on A1 paper and the later in variations of the smaller A3 paper. The terms were subsequently adopted to refer to editorial decisions that define newspapers' journalism standards, setting quality press (broadsheets) apart from popular press (tabloids). By the early twentieth century, through a process of metonymic transfer, the term was extended to embrace commercial media in general, especially television, in a context of widespread concern about the power of the media and the quality of journalism. The tabloid press became increasingly specialized in the techniques of connecting reports on consumer products to economics and celebrity gossip to popular culture.

The differences between the two formats of journalism are considerable. Broadsheet papers rely on investigative approaches to news that emphasize in-depth coverage and a sober tone in articles and editorials, with smaller headlines, fewer pictures, and lengthier texts that are staples of the quality press (Preston, 2004). Tabloid content, on the other hand, tends to expose sexual misconduct and explore conservative and iconoclast topical interests, with strong commercial emphasis and populist vernacular. The type of writer and the editorial emphasis on the subject matter are also considerably different in tabloid media compared to broadsheet newspapers, with readers' voices being amplified in different ways by different types of newspaper. In terms of article composition, tabloid news articles are on average shorter and place more emphasis on headline and image space (Rowe, 2011).

Tabloid and broadsheets appeal to different audiences with limited overlap. The readership of British broadsheets reacts mostly to articles dedicated to "substantive issues rather than human interest or life style themes" (Richardson and Stanyer, 2011: 991), with commentaries concentrated on domestic politics and party policy and lifestyle issues such as sport, celebrity, and gardening receiving comparatively fewer comments. On the other hand, most comments made on British online tabloids are concentrated on religion, with the bulk of online posts focusing on lifestyle themes such as sport, celebrity, and gardening. Moreover, dialogue and debate among online readers of British newspapers are limited almost entirely to broadsheet discussion threads (31.3 percent of broadsheet comments, compared to 2.3 percent for tabloid newspapers), with the lion's share of this debate taking place on Guardian Online (Richardson and Stanyer, 2011).

While broadsheet newspapers emphasize hard news coverage, fact-checking, and research based on a timeline in which the story unfolds, tabloid newspapers present on average lesser detailed articles often directed by marketing departments and heavily influenced by demographic appeal and audience share. The readership of the tabloid press is on average younger and less educated (Andersen, 2003; Rowe, 2011). On the other hand, the detailed coverage of political issues offered by broadsheets appeals to a readership more interested in politics and more likely to be well informed. Consistent with these differences in business model and audience demographics, tabloids generally have a larger circulation compared to broadsheets (Murphy, 2003).

Print press and tabloid journalism

In the early twenty-first century, tabloid journalism boomed with various newspapers moving from broadsheets toward compact, visually appealing, and commuter-friendly editions that featured fewer stories with fewer words on each page and made space for the use of photography in storytelling. Hard news stories disappeared from the front page, which increasingly featured large photographs and headlines, with other editorial changes prompting an emphasis on more personalized news and a focus on themes such as education, the environment, health, and housing, along with an enhanced focus on readers' letters and readers' pages (Franklin, 2008).

During this period, the priorities of journalism have undergone considerable change: "entertainment has superseded the provision of information; human interest has supplanted the public interest; measured judgment has succumbed to sensationalism; the trivial has triumphed over the weighty; the intimate relationships of celebrities from soap operas, the world of sport or the royal family are judged to be more 'newsworthy' than the reporting of significant issues and events of international consequence. Traditional news values have been undermined by new values" (Franklin, 1997: 4). The spread of infotainment across news outlets and the increasing simplification and spectacularization of news, traditional characteristics of tabloid media, led scholars to diagnose a generalized tabloidization of contemporary newspapers (Rowe, 2011).

Cultural studies scholars have welcomed the cultural role of tabloids and the ensuing power struggle it reveals, as the binary classification of newspapers is both horizontal (broadsheet versus tabloid) and hierarchical (broadsheet over tabloid). Turner (1999) acknowledged that the tabloid press sacrifices information for entertainment, accuracy for sensation, and that it employs tactics of representation that exploit audiences, but he also argued that the discourse of tabloid media is important and ranges from the explicitly playful or self-conscious (e.g. staged family conflicts) to the self-important gravitas of an issue of public interest (e.g. a politician's sex life). The criticism of tabloidization, still according to Turner (1999), is grounded in a conventional and long-standing hostility to popular culture. Another critical take on tabloidization has made the point that "broadcasters have not been sufficiently remorseful to change their practices, nor apparently have audiences felt enough shame to avert their eyes or demand alternatives" (Langer, 1998: 4).

This scholarship argues that tabloid is not necessarily a negative term, but a desirable infiltration into the news media of the everyday concerns of non-elite readers, who are often alienated by the traditional, patriarchal guardians of the serious press interested in maintaining cultural hegemony (Rowe, 2011). This alternative take on tabloid media, one with its own theoretical foundations, has been systematically challenged by studies that measured the connection between levels of consumption of tabloid media and political engagement. Couldry, Livingstone, and Markham (2007: 182) investigated patterns of media consumption in Britain and found a relationship between voting likelihood and attachment to celebrity culture, but interest in celebrities was negatively correlated with level of political interest. In fact, the study reported a substantial disconnect between celebrity culture and public political engagement and confronted authors celebrating popular culture as a force for democratization while ignoring the fundamental divide in how audiences orient themselves in the world.

The differences between broadsheet and tabloid content are deeply intertwined with the physical transmission medium. Newspapers that transitioned to tabloid formats to meet the needs of an increasingly mobile readership commuting long distances within constrained areas of public transport also suffered substantial changes in content, deliberately or inadvertently. Different forms of journalism practices are enabled by different physical media, which in turn enforce specific cultural and professional practices that feedback into the content. Rowe (2011) noted that while broadsheet journalists devote considerable professional time to refining codes of ethics, in the tabloid world there is less emphasis placed on how the product is collected, how it is presented, and on what basis it is presented.

The immediate inference from the relationship between form and content is that the simple and ordinary change of a newspaper from broadsheet to tabloid format can enable new practices in the newsroom, with tabloids reportedly enforcing discipline, but placing less emphasis on developing the skills of its workforce and not being as committed to the principles of quality journalism. In short, there is a tangible effect on the news content resulting from the physical transmission medium used to convey the news. In tabloids, for instance, the turnover of journalists is reportedly higher than on a broadsheet (Rowe, 2011). As online news grows to become the major source of news in Western countries (Pew Research Center, 2012a, 2013b, 2014b), the practices and standards of journalism are likely to experience further upheaval.

Tabloid transition to digital media

The growing integration of print and online newsrooms has been accompanied by the proliferation of free titles, followed by the process of increasing tabloidization that advanced on the space of online and free daily papers, both of which place an emphasis on rapid turnover of content, digest-style short stories, blogs, entertainment gossip, and a heavy reliance on the visual (Allan, 2006). In fact, the dominance of celebrity and social news, and the growth of reality shows and other forms of popular culture-oriented news, contributed to the blurring of credibility boundaries that once set traditional outlets apart from digital media (Johnson and Kayer, 2004). Furthermore, the sharp decline of paid newspapers created the expectation that free dailies, mostly published in tabloid format, would fill the gap. However, the broadsheets' continued circulation decline was not followed by an increase of free daily newspapers, particularly in the United States and Europe (Benton, 2015), where free daily circulation went down 50 percent between 2007 and 2012 (Bakker, 2013).

Common to tabloid and social media audiences is the relative youth of their readerships (Andersen, 2003; Pew Research Center, 2013a), though tabloid readers are on average less educated (Andersen, 2003) compared to social media audiences, which are also more likely to be urban and politically engaged (Pew Research Center, 2012b). Twitter and Facebook are especially appealing to urban adults aged 18–29, particularly Twitter, which attracts urban dwellers more than both suburban and rural residents. Instagram has a special appeal to adults between the ages of 18 and 29, and Pinterest is particularly attractive to women, but also to white, young, well-educated, and wealthier people (Pew Research Center, 2013a). One potential similarity of social media and the tabloid press is the role of audience share and feedback to articles, which is often driven by the appeal of the headline rather than the content of the article (Roston, 2015).

The transition from the printed press to online news websites represented a qualitative leap that changed readership and reflected structural transformations associated with platform design, section assignment, and website layout. These technical modifications exert a major influence on reading habits and change the way news is consumed. The integration of social networking technologies to online newspapers further changes the reading experience not only because of new standards of graphic design, illustrations, typography, and positioning but also because of the technical possibilities granted to audiences that can access, share, and recommend the content to large communities of users.

In fact, the impact of social networking sites to the news industry is likely to be of greater importance than generally acknowledged at the time of this writing, with recent scholarship documenting the effects of social networking sites on broadsheet newspapers. Bastos (2014) reported that the audiences of social networking sites engaging with the *New York Times* and *Guardian* content tend to favor hard over soft news articles, but also opinion pieces, when compared to the news editors' choices. The disruptive influence of social networking sites to the news industry is consistent with the impressions of social media editors at the *New York Times*, who gained followers at very fast rates by providing wall-to-wall coverage of newsworthy events on Twitter. The newsroom believed that "investing effort in using social media platforms to share news had a measurable impact in growing the audience for a desk's journalism" (Roston, 2015).

Audience feedback loop

Innovation in the newsmaking process has cut across the broadsheet/tabloid spectrum. Dowling and Vogan (2014) examined new genres of news reporting on the *New York Times*, ESPN, and Sports Illustrated and detailed how each news outlet leveraged new opportunities in digital long-form storytelling (cf. Dowling and Vogan, this volume). These new forms broke significantly with journalism's past by resorting to visual attributes, multimedia features, and innovative layout that "function as opportunities for these prominent media organizations to build a branded sense of renown in an increasingly competitive market" (Dowling and Vogan, 2014: 10–11) and noted that these elaborately produced stories "encourage reader-driven circulation via social media, a process that expands the products' reach and allows consumers to cultivate their own identities by associating with such artifacts" (Dowling and Vogan, 2014: 11).

Although the differences between broadsheet and tabloid inherited from legacy media remain relatively stable in terms of content shared on Twitter (Bastos and Zago, 2013), social media platforms have introduced modalities of newsmaking that disrupt the broadsheet/tabloid spectrum and challenge the current classification scheme. This is likely a result of the audience component in the networked architecture of journalism that displays considerably erratic behavior compared to the traditional readership of newspapers. News readership on social networks expresses a preference for a subset of content and information that is at odds with the decisions of newspaper editors regarding which topic to emphasize (Bastos, 2014).

The disagreement between social media audiences and news editors stems mostly from items about arts, science, technology, and opinion pieces, which are on average more frequent on social networking sites than on newspapers. Social media users also rely on several different platforms to retrieve news, thus presenting another point of departure from the context of print media with a strong editorial identity. Social networks that are primarily a visual medium (i.e. Pinterest and YouTube) can specialize in providing visual and audio information in a similar fashion to broadcast television and radio. This specialization can result in greater fragmentation and boost new types of attention paid to content, further stratifying readership according to the news format and the interests of like-minded groups.

The potential fragmentation of audiences prescribed by social networking sites is another significant point of departure from the context of tabloid print press. This sits side by side with the balkanization of readership according to interests of like-minded groups and has sprung a renewed debate on potential political polarization, echo chamber behavior, and ideological homogeneity resulting from news consumption on social media (Barberá, 2014; Pew Research Center, 2014a). Scholarly debate rages over whether online social networks increase ideological segregation or exert the opposite effect by providing higher exposure to opposing perspectives. By any measure, the role of social media in the potential fragmentation of audiences remains an unresolved point of contention.

The debate is long-running and reflects the public fear of a news ecosystem tailored to individual's interests and tastes. It also reproduces the conflicting preferences of news readerships compared to news professionals. Jian and Usher (2014) examined patterns of funding preferences in a database of story projects crowdfunded through Spot.Us, a nonprofit news platform that funds ideas by micropayments, and found that "compared to reporters, consumers favor stories that provide them with practical guidance for daily living (e.g. public health or city infrastructure), as opposed to stories from which they gain a general awareness of the world" (Jian and Usher, 2014: 164–165). This is overall consistent with the hypothesis that if consumers are to play a bigger role in news production, lesser articles covering general public affairs would be expected.

The differences between what newspaper editors have deemed to be of public interest and what is of interest to users of social networking sites needs be considered within the wider debate on press and the public sphere and the validity of liberal journalism's claims to freedom and objectivity. As readership agency begins to deliver critical feedback to news items and interfere with the coverage of news outlets, newsrooms are forced to strike a balance between news that answers the wishes of their increasingly interactive and demanding readers and news that is of public interest—arguably the moral imperative of professional journalism (Jacquette, 2007: 214). This change in the balance of power introduced by social media is not restricted to quality press. In fact, the tabloid press is facing changes that are potentially even more disruptive.

Digital tabloid journalism

Picard (2014) provided an overview of the current changes in the news industry and argued that journalism is drifting away from a relatively closed system of news creation dominated by official sources and professional journalists. These changes impact on the business of newsmaking, as news providers become less dependent on any one form of funding than they have been in the last century, and impose considerable challenges to tabloid media. In this transitional period of journalism practices, the influence of commercial advertisers is likely to be severely reduced, and tabloid media, a segment of newsmaking whose form, range, and practices of news provision are often directed by marketing departments and focused on audience share, is expected to experience considerable changes in the business model.

Such changes have been observed across various national contexts. The fierce competition between tabloid media in Sweden has extended to clickbait viral news sites. *Expressen* competes with *Aftonbladet* as the two national evening tabloids in the country. While the digital editions of tabloids are not particularly different from their print editions, tabloid's parent companies have developed BuzzFeed-like copycats featuring parents' advice, content that speaks to personal experience, ranking of celebrity-related events, feel-good-human-interest pieces, curiosity gap headlines, and memes or videos trending across the web. The viral news website Omtalat is a spinoff of the tabloid *Expressen*, which has a print circulation of 193,100 and controls two of the most visited news sites in the country (expressen.se and expressen.tv), while the viral news website Lajkat is affiliated with Schibsted, *Aftonbladet*'s parent company. The two websites (Lajkat and Omtalat) represent a substantive change in the tabloid format by publishing compilations of highly clickable content that rarely offers any news value.

At the time of this writing, none of the top three headlines at Lajkat.se reported news events: (1) "28 persons who will have a worse Christmas than you" (*28 personer som har en sämre jul än du kommer ha*); (2) "11 Swedes who must practice their compliments" (*11 svenskar som måste öva på sina komplimanger*); and (3) "The reason it was much nicer to fly during the 70s" (*Anledningen till att det var betydligt skönare att flyga på 1970-talet*). NiemanLab emphasized that this change in the Swedish media landscape reflects a global trend in tabloid media that has witnessed an explosion of viral news sites like BuzzFeed, Upworthy, Viralnova, and Mashable devoted to aggregating highly clickable web content. As readers' habits change and advertising revenue continues to decline, media organizations are investing in viral sites as a potential source of revenue that can reverse the business downturn. In a country with a population of just 9.6 million like Sweden, viral news websites have amassed an average of 1 million unique mobile browsers each. Omtalat has expanded the business model to other countries and languages by launching similar viral news sites in German, Turkish, and Norwegian, while rival viral site Newsner has started an English language version of the site (Lichterman, 2014).

Conversely, viral news sites aim at a pulverized audience with varying media sophistication and often incompatible lifestyles and political orientation. This newly developed variant of digital tabloid media explores crowd mechanism and develops controversial stories by meticulously testing potential content on the website and upholding or removing material according to the number of clicks retrieved from early testers. As Upworthy races for the social media attention, the team breaks down the content into 'seeds' and 'nuggets'—content to feature on the site and a list of 25 potential headlines that are streamlined for 'click testing' (Rohani, 2014). The distribution and potential success of any viral news site depends directly on peer-to-peer engagement on social networking sites, which exhibit demographics considerably different from the traditional readership of newspapers, but perhaps more in line with the traditional readership of tabloids, which is younger and places less emphasis on experience (Andersen, 2003; Pew Research Center, 2013a).

A recent such example is BuzzFeed's story "What Colors Are This Dress?" (Holderness, 2015). At the time of this writing, the piece has amassed a total of 38 million page views by asking readers to identify the colors of a dress. Individual differences in how the brain processes light and visual information provided fertile ground for polarizing responses to the color of the dress. The post rapidly went viral and surpassed Tumblr's and BuzzFeed's previous records for traffic. Like a considerable portion of BuzzFeed's content, the photo was not produced by BuzzFeed itself; it was actually discovered on Tumblr and made its way to Buzzfeed via Twitter and later Facebook (Mahler, 2015). The social media conflagration provided such exposure that at its peak nearly 1 million users were simultaneously viewing Buzzfeed's post, and yet few readers arrived to the post via BuzzFeed's homepage. The story speaks to BuzzFeed maturation from clickbait to a social news company and sheds light on BuzzFeed strategy to incentivize content curation that is both user-generated and created by paid staff members.

It is unclear whether viral news websites like BuzzFeed and Upworthy represent niche audience behavior or reflect broader, systemic changes in tabloid media. Viral news sites feed from social network websites, primarily Facebook, but also Twitter and Reddit, in an attempt to ride the organic conversation in the social web. Social media editors perform reverse-gatekeeping by pushing stories that are gaining momentum across the highly interactive audiences of social networking sites. The reverse-gatekeeping function performed by news editors consists of filtering content based on the expectation that audience feedback loops will kick in and move the story forward. Social media cascades usually happen in the first minutes after the post is published (Dow, Adamic, and Friggeri, 2013), and accordingly the expertise of social media teams revolves around the artistry of guesswork on which stories will go viral. This represents a clear point of departure from print tabloids with their content carefully tailored to large segments of the population.

Conclusion

In this article, I reviewed the fundamental differences between broadsheets and tabloids in terms of form and content and explored the impact of the physical transmission medium used to convey the news to the deontology of journalism. I also detailed how readership varies across the two types of news outlets and described the ongoing disruption in the ecosystem of tabloid press caused by digital and social media; changes that stem from a changing landscape of media production, shifting audience demographics, as well as structural modifications in the business model and funding strategies.

I also reviewed recent scholarship that assessed the impact of social networking sites on the news industry, particularly broadsheet newspapers, but also news outlets with greater emphasis on soft news items. I explored the increasingly important role played by audience feedback and connected these developments to changes in tabloid media formats posited to take place in response to the disruption caused by social networking technologies. These structural changes can be summarized in two main rationales. Firstly, social media users rely on several different platforms to retrieve news, which presents a point of departure from the context of print media with a strong editorial identity. Secondly, and more importantly, the changing business of newsmaking has lessened the influence of commercial advertisers in ways that are particularly hurtful to the tabloid press and the business model directed by marketing departments and focused on audience share.

These changes have forced tabloids to move into viral news sites like BuzzFeed that publish compilations of highly clickable content rarely covering news events. Although viral news websites represent a niche audience behavior at odds with the readership and content of tabloid media, clickbait news sites can also represent a phenomenon of extreme tabloidization, with celebrity news as an endemic phenomenon that has found a place across the entire news business and beyond the niche market of tabloid media. Journalists currently working between the divides of broadsheet and tabloid, online and print, are familiarized with such challenges and have to employ strategies to navigate a precarious and embattled professional workforce.

It seems that for such workers, and particularly for those working at the crossroads between digital and tabloid journalism, the reality of digital journalism is not entirely clear, and the future is even less so.

Further reading

This chapter has benefitted from David Rowe's *Obituary for the Newspaper? Tracking the Tabloid*. The piece depicts the process of tabloidization in contemporary newspapers, while Robert G. Picard's *Twilight or New Dawn of Journalism* provides an overview of the current changes in the news industry and Marco Bastos' *Shares, Pins, and Tweets: News Readership from Daily Papers to Social Media* details what news editors emphasize compared to social media users. For an extended treatment of journalism and the entertainment industry, see Bob Franklin's *Newszak and News Media*.

References

Allan, S. (2006) "Online News: Journalism and the Internet." *Journalism and the Internet*. New York, NY: McGraw-Hill International.

Andersen, R. (2003) "Do Newspapers Enlighten Preferences? Personal Ideology, Party Choice and the Electoral Cycle: The United Kingdom, 1992–1997." *Canadian Journal of Political Science/Revue canadienne de science politique* 36(3): 601–619.

Bakker, P. (2013) "The Life Cycle of a Free Newspaper Business Model in Newspaper-Rich Markets." *Journalistica-Tidsskrift for forskning i journalistik* (1): 33–51.

Barberá, P. (2014) *How Social Media Reduces Mass Political Polarization*. Evidence from Germany, Spain, and the US.

Bastos, M.T. (2014) "Shares, Pins, and Tweets: News Readership from Daily Papers to Social Media." *Journalism Studies* 16(3): 305–325.

Bastos, M.T. and Zago, G. (2013) "Tweeting News Articles: Readership and News Sections in Europe and the Americas." *SAGE Open* 3(3).

Benton, J. (2015) "The Future Still Looks Pretty Grim for Free Print Daily Newspapers." *NiemanLab*, 20 January.

Couldry, N., Livingstone, S.M. and Markham, T. (2007) *Media Consumption and Public Engagement: Beyond the Presumption of Attention*. Basingstoke: Palgrave.

Dow, P.A., Adamic, L.A. and Friggeri, A. (2013) *The Anatomy of Large Facebook Cascades*. Translated by Boston: AAAI.

Dowling, D. and Vogan, T. (2014) "Can We 'Snowfall' This?" *Digital Journalism* 1–16.

Franklin, B. (1997) *Newszak and News Media*. London, UK: Arnold.

Franklin, B. (2008) "The Future of Newspapers." *Journalism Practice* 2(3): 306–317.

Greenberg, G. (1996) *Tabloid Journalism: An Annotated Bibliography of English-Language Sources*. Westport, CT: Greenwood Press.

Holderness, C. (2015) "What Colors Are This Dress?" *BuzzFeed*, 26 February.

Jacquette, D. (2007) *Journalist Ethics: Moral Responsibility in the Media*. Upper Saddle River, NJ: Pearson/Prentice Hall.

Jian, L. and Usher, N. (2014) "Crowd-Funded Journalism." *Journal of Computer-Mediated Communication* 19(2): 155–170.

Johnson, T.J. and Kayer, B.K. (2004) "Wag the Blog: How Reliance on Traditional Media and the Internet Influence Credibility Perceptions of Weblogs among Blog Users." *Journalism and Mass Communication Quarterly* 81(3): 622–642.

Langer, J. (1998) *Tabloid Television: Popular Journalism and the "Other News"*. London, UK: Routledge.

Lichterman, J. (2014) "In Sweden, Traditional Tabloid Rivals are Taking Their Battle to Viral Sites." *NiemanLab*, 1 December.

Mahler, J. (2015) "The White and Gold (No, Blue and Black!) Dress That Melted the Internet." *The New York Times*, 27 February.

Murphy, G.L. (2003) "The Downside of Categories." *Trends in Cognitive Sciences* 7(12): 513–514.

Pew Research Center (2012a) *Changing News Landscape, Even Television is Vulnerable: Trends in News Consumption: 1991–2012*, Washington, DC: Pew Internet & American Life Project.

Pew Research Center (2012b) *Social Media and Political Engagement*. Washington, DC: Pew Internet & American Life Project.

Pew Research Center (2013a) *The Demographics of Social Media Users, 2012*. Washington, DC: Pew Research Center's Internet & American Life Project.

Pew Research Center (2013b) *The Role of News on Facebook: Common yet Incidental*. Washington, DC: Pew Research Center's Internet & American Life Project & John S. and James L. Knight Foundation.

Pew Research Center (2014a) *Political Polarization & Media Habits*, Washington, DC: Pew Research Center's Internet & American Life Project.

Pew Research Center (2014b) *State of the News Media 2014: Overview*. Washington, DC: Pew Research Center's Internet & American Life Project.

Picard, R.G. (2014) "Twilight or New Dawn of Journalism?" *Journalism Studies* 15(5): 500–510.

Preston, P. (2004) "Tabloids: Only the Beginning." *British Journalism Review* 15(1): 50–55.

Richardson, J.E. and Stanyer, J. (2011) "Reader Opinion in the Digital Age: Tabloid and Broadsheet Newspaper Websites and the Exercise of Political Voice." *Journalism* 12(8): 983–1003.

Rohani, A. (2014) "Upworthy and the Race for Your Attention." *Urban Times*.

Roston, M. (2015) "Don't Try Too Hard to Please Twitter—and Other Lessons from *The New York Times*' Social Media Desk." *NiemanLab*, 22 January.

Rowe, D. (2011) "Obituary for the Newspaper? Tracking the Tabloid." *Journalism* 12(4): 449–466.

Sparks, C. and Tulloch, J. (2000) *Tabloid Tales: Global Debates Over Media Standards*. Lanham, MD: Rowman and Littlefield.

Turner, G. (1999) "Tabloidization, Journalism and the Possibility of Critique." *International Journal of Cultural Studies* 2(1): 59–76.

22

AUTOMATED JOURNALISM

A posthuman future for digital news?

Matt Carlson

Whether or not a human author wrote these words is not a question that most readers will consciously ask. Writing has been an unambiguously human activity, one whose durability has persisted through the transition from the intimacy of the written word to the mass reproducibility of print to the explosion of digital media. Even as human–computer interaction has become normalized in daily life (Reeves and Nass, 1996), the creative act of composition has appeared cordoned off as something innately human. The very root of 'author' in the Latin *auctor*—creator—and its connection to *auctoritas*—a kind of authority (Höpfl, 1999)—bind humanness to the written word. Yet such close ties can no longer be assumed. Advances in artificial intelligence and natural language generation have moved nonhuman writing from theory to practice, with journalism at the forefront of industries being affected. Already, human-authored news stories are being joined by a growing number of stories created entirely by computer programs. Just one company alone, Automated Insights, announced on its web site it has surpassed the milestone of a billion stories authored annually. While a billion seems incredible, the company's current software has the capacity to produce 2,000 unique stories every *second*—or 63 billion stories annually. These numbers point not only to the qualitative shift from human to computer but also to a quantitative transformation that is difficult to comprehend when we still think of human journalists laboring over their computer screens. Accepting that machines work faster than humans is deeply embedded in understandings of technological innovation and contemporary labor in industrial applications; now these forces are descending on creative practices as well.

The argument offered in this chapter is not that humans will be displaced from journalism. Instead, the posthuman future of journalism alluded to in the title suggests a hybrid state in which computer- and human-authored stories intermingle in ways yet to be developed. Making sense of this shift begins by placing the rise of computer-written news stories within the larger turn toward the integration of journalism with 'big data' (Lewis and Westlund, 2015; Lewis, this volume) and the use of algorithms (Anderson, 2013). Journalistic uses of algorithms and data have steadily advanced from data analysis and news selection practices to the birth of automated journalism: programs capable of converting data into publishable news stories without human intervention (Carlson, 2015). Purveyors of automated journalism promise to transform news production practices, but more centrally the growing feasibility of computer-written news alters how journalism production and reception are being imagined.

This chapter endeavors to get beyond the technological or logistical facets that drive the development and implementation of automated journalism to attend to the slew of onto-logical, epistemological, and normative dimensions accompanying this shift. The sections below contextualize the advent of automated journalism, review its existing research, and suggest three emerging tensions for journalism, expressed as the dichotomies of scarcity versus abundance, monovocality versus pluralized personalization, and information transfer versus cultural interpretation.

Background: algorithms in journalism

An initial caution is necessary in order to contextualize automated journalism. When we think of news production—digital or otherwise—human practices are usually privileged. Newsgathering involves layers of human-to-human interactions from internal newsroom dynamics of hierarchical decision-making to external engagement with eager spokespersons, reluctant sources, and garrulous audiences. Certainly, accomplishing news involves numerous interpersonal (e.g. telephones, email), recording (e.g. cameras, recorders), and production (e.g. presses, servers) technologies, which we commonly understand to be tools used to aid humans in the reporting and presentation of news. Often this perspective paints an overly simplified picture by positing a one-way agency: humans shape their tools, which then allow them to work effectively. On the surface, this may seem intuitive and adequate, but a more critical perspective arising from science and technology studies (STS) confounds this perspective by emphasizing how tools shape practices. For example, computers have long been integral to news work to the point of escaping notice. Yet their arrival into the newsroom occasioned a range of reactions that included fear of what computerization would mean for journalistic labor and how it would affect core news practices (Powers, 2012). Computers were not a neutral addition of merely superior typewriters but a deeper reconfiguration of what doing the news meant. They came to structure the newsroom in new ways, creating new possibilities, shaping expectations, and adding new constraints (see Rodgers, 2015, for the case of content management systems). As 'objects of journalism,' these technologies should be studied as more than tools (Anderson and De Maeyer, 2015). Journalism and technology are deeply intertwined so that extracting the human elements from newsgathering technologies occludes a fuller picture of how news gets made.

From this perspective wedding journalism and technology lays the groundwork for studying the growing application of advanced computing technologies to news. The shift toward what has been labeled 'computational journalism' (Coddington, 2015) further extends journalistic uses for what has been dubbed 'big data'—the ability of algorithms to sort through enormous data sets to identify meaningful patterns. Optimistically, big data present journalists with new opportunities for carrying out their mission of holding society's major institutions accountable, albeit with significant investment in resources and training (Flew *et al.*, 2012). A more mixed picture arises around the growing role of algorithms in news selection. In this capacity, algorithms have for many years been part of the digital news presentation. The popular Google News service, for example, eschews human editors in favor of algorithmically derived news presentation, including personalized news based on user preferences (Carlson, 2007). As more and more media selection is accomplished through algorithms, attention has turned to what may be called the politics of algorithms. One fear is that of 'filter bubbles' (Pariser, 2011) or the shift from human information intermediaries to responsive algorithms that select which news items each user sees based on past preferences. In making invisible decisions about content, these filters can reinforce existing interests and beliefs by feeding more of this content while omitting other news or viewpoints deemed to be a poor match. On an individual level, filter bubbles reduce exposure to a wider range of topics. From a social level, the fear is that such filters reduce the spread of news stories or topics of importance to a wide audience. For example, Tufekci (2014) worries important stories will go unnoticed, citing as an example the lack of attention on Facebook newsfeeds of a controversial police shooting of an unarmed black teenager by a white officer in Ferguson, Missouri, in 2014.

This line of inquiry into the journalism-algorithm nexus presents useful perspectives for thinking about automated journalism. For example, Gillespie (2014) concludes his excellent overview of the questions that need to be asked about algorithms with a particular call to ask "why algorithms are being looked to as a credible knowledge logic, how they fall apart and are repaired when they come in contact with the ebb and flow of public discourse, and where political assumptions might not only be etched into their design, but also constitutive of their widespread use and legitimacy" (191). That is, algorithms are not merely tools emerging as handmaidens to human agency but point to entrenched knowledge practices with untold social consequences. Diakopoulos (2015) has responded to these conditions with a call for 'algorithmic accountability reporting' to reveal the hidden workings of the algorithmic decision making affecting content choices made for us.

In sum, the growing role of algorithms in determining what news users see has been accompanied by critical questions about the individual and social impact of this technology. The growing critical body of work rejects assumptions of algorithmic objectivity to instead highlight the inbuilt biases of any content production or selection software. It also directs attention to societal questions regarding news exposure, particularly as access to a diversity of content has exploded in the digital media environment. Yet this research has carried within it the assumption that these seen or unseen stories were written by human journalists—an assumption that now needs to be tested.

Automated journalism

The very idea that an original news story can be written by a computer program raises questions about the viability of automated journalism. Understanding how a computer can author a passable story requires confronting the rapid growth of artificial intelligence and natural language generation processes. The software works by analyzing a data set and then crafting a story based on a library of story types and an appropriate lexicon for the topic. For example, financial reporting and sports summaries employ different narrative themes and particular vocabularies. However, the companies behind the automation software stress that no templates are used; the software crafts customized stories each time.

The market for automated journalism has been pioneered by two companies—Narrative Science and Automated Insights. What started as a project wedding computer science and journalism at Northwestern University morphed into the company Narrative Science and its proprietary software Quill, an "automated narrative generation platform" capable of converting an input of information into an output of a narrative "indistinguishable from a human-written one" (http://www.narrativescience.com/quill). Similarly, Automated Insights began as a means of narrativizing sports stories and eventually created its own software, Wordsmith, which it also touts for its human-like output: "Automated Insights' patented Wordsmith platform transforms Big Data into narrative reports by spotting patterns, correlations and key insights in the data and then describing them in plain English, just like a human would." These products are more than theoretical: the Associated Press uses Automated Insights to write short stories on quarterly earnings reports. The Big Ten Network uses Narrative Science to write sports reports and the Forbes web site uses it for financial reporting. Both companies are bullish on their futures and have attracted ample press attention for their technologies (Carlson, 2015).

Current research

Because automated journalism has only recently become a feasible tool for news organizations to produce news stories for their web sites, empirical research on the topic has been scant to date (certainly future studies will follow). Within the existing research, the focus has been on either the quality of the automated news texts or how their arrival affects production. With regard to the former, researchers have utilized experimental models to compare human and nonhuman writing. The results have shown the early success of the software, as experiments by both Clerwall (2014) and van der Kaa and Krahmer (2014) found that readers could not discern automated stories from human-written ones. These findings suggest the software's adeptness at mimicking the writing conventions of objective news stories. What this lack of distinction between human- and machine-authored stories entails poses a more ambiguous quandary. Instrumentally, these findings signal to news organizations the viability of the software as part of news production—and the software companies have been quick to tout their findings as a means of legitimating their products and, presumably, drumming up sales. Yet this indistinguishability also raises concerns among journalists.

The second area of research into automated journalism has looked into issues of production mainly through the analysis of discourse about the new practices. Van Dalen (2012) considers how the arrival of Automated Insights's service affected perceptions of journalistic labor and news quality and found significant apprehension. Similarly, Lemelshtrich Latar (2015) connects automated journalism to advancements in artificial intelligence to suggest human journalists will only be able to compete by adapting their own contributions in response to the strengths of automated stories. Anderson, Bell, and Shirky (2012) take a more optimistic view that automated news processes will free up journalists to work on other, more labor- or writing-intensive stories, yet still raise questions regarding the transparency of such processes for news consumers (27). In a broader study of journalistic uses of algorithms, Napoli (2014) employs institutional theory to develop a theoretical framework for the growth of automated news processes.

My own work (Carlson, 2015) goes beyond questions of labor to consider larger issues related to journalistic authority through the lens of a 'technological drama' (Pfaffenberger, 1992). The advent of automated journalism strikes at core issues regarding journalism as a form of cultural production. Long simmering debates over appropriate news forms and the achievability of objectivity gain new vitality in discussions of the merits and possibilities of computer-written news. The sections below pick up from these points to examine a set of emerging critical issues for digital journalism accompanying the rise of automated journalism.

Critical issues

The coexistence of human authors and their algorithmic counterparts raises a number of critical issues for how to think about the news landscape. It is not merely the replacement of one kind of labor for another, but the introduction of new technological affordances that simultaneously give rise to new practices *and* new ways to think about news. Automated journalism, while still in its nascent state, provides an array of possibilities previously unavailable when only humans wrote news stories. Interrogating these critical issues now, at the forefront of the technology, provides the building blocks for establishing a critique of these practices. They are an attempt to construct what we may call, to borrow from Diakopoulos (2015), 'automated journalism accountability.'

To begin this conversation at the early stage of the technology's development, a starting point is to question how the newfound possibilities of automated journalism necessitate a reassessment of basic assumptions undergirding journalism. By treating automated journalism as an idea to think about, scholars can pursue a conceptual framework for analyzing automated journalism. Before delving in, a quick word about the theoretical landmines accompanying assessments of technological impact is needed. While what follows concerns the affordances of automated journalism (as well as speculation based on these affordances), this appraisal should not be reduced to a technological deterministic reading—that is, the assumption that the artifact is the main driver of social effects. Instead of simple causality, a confluence of mutually determining economic, cultural, and technological forces converge to shape digital journalism. Understanding the technology is not enough to predict its uses. Yet it would also be incorrect to assume that journalism can somehow swallow large-scale automated news generation without somehow being altered. Sensitivity is needed to assess the development of the technology, its deployment by news organizations, reactions from news audiences, and its role within the larger news ecosystem. In this spirit, this chapter presents three dichotomies that contextualize the emerging and potential effects of automated newswriting on the practices and meanings of journalism as a form of cultural production.

Scarcity versus abundance: One of the more prominent discourses concerning the development of digital media focuses on the shift from a scarcity of media content associated with legacy print and broadcast media to the abundance of content associated with digital platforms. For example, the commercial logic of television has shifted from a limited number of programmers seeking the largest possible audience to a fragmented, niche-conscious strategy (Ellis, 2002). This strategy has been mirrored in advertising by a move toward niche markets (Turow, 2006). For journalism, where news is costly to produce, space is limited, and audiences have few choices, scarcity imbues the limited supply of news stories with importance (Schudson, 1995). This is the essence of gatekeeping (Shoemaker and Vos, 2009). A news article is not an isolated text, but a part of a larger news product in which the meaning of any one item is partly determined by its placement within the overall news product (Carlson, 2007). Stylistically, this pattern has continued with online news, as many digital news sites use layouts that signal the relative importance of any one item.

The shift from news scarcity to news abundance began with the digitization of legacy news on the production side and the limitless access to news sites on the audience side. Yet while online news signaled the erasure of geographical restrictions and barriers to entry, the reliance on humans to author stories and the difficult economic situation of digital news continued to limit abundance. In this light, perhaps the most noticeable advantage of automated journalism concerns the quantity of stories that can be produced. The shift to abundance echoes the strategies of long tail economics (Anderson, 2006). On the back end, the refinement of the technology coupled with the uptick in available data makes it economically and technologically feasible to produce large amounts of content with any story likely to draw only a small number of readers. On the front end, the ubiquity of search engines connects readers with stories that would not necessarily be prominently displayed on a web site. Plus, there is a juggernaut aspect with the so-called internet of things (Howard, 2015) promising to deliver more data that can then be narrativized into more stories. The outcome is a rapidly expanding universe of news stories.

In this scenario, automated journalism's ability to exponentially increase news content fundamentally alters the interpretive work of news selection. By dropping the cost of news production to near-zero (assuming freely available data) and eliminating content limits, it shifts the cultural meaning of any news item as being worthy of public attention to instead appeal to the particularized desires of atomized audience members. This shift raises questions about the power of journalists to dictate the news agenda (McCombs and Shaw, 1972), which, as seen above, has already been the subject of critique with algorithmic selection practices. An abundance of automated digital news stories further separates the news product from news selection practices. At the same time, this supply of stories gives audiences more selection; what may be useful information for a handful of people now becomes news. This is a fundamental shift, even if it does not necessarily mean that all news will be atomized in the digital news environment. Nonetheless, the pertinent question remains how to balance individual desires and interests with the need for a common pool of knowledge across society.

Monovocality versus pluralized personalization: The march of journalism from a more partisan and pluralized era to a professionalized press brought with it the rise of what Barnhurst and Nerone (2001) call monovocality—the assertion that well-trained journalists following set procedures can produce an accurate (as possible) account. In this view, the news organization speaks in a single voice to provide an authoritative account of an incident. Such claims to authority are built on the ideals of journalistic professionalism as a means of legitimation and quality assurance (Waisbord, 2013).

The ability of automated journalism to increase the quantity of news stories does not alter this dynamic on the surface. If anything, the attempt by automated news accounts to mimic conventional news stories as perfectly as possible underscores entrenched monovocal tendencies. As Gillespie (2014) notes, algorithms often connote objectivity (despite their embedded values). Yet the expansion of automated journalism includes more than just the horizontal expansion of the total amount of stories. Another potential development is the creation of multiple—even personalized—versions of any story to appeal to different audiences. Doing so would combine audience data with story data so that the software would decide what any individual or group of digital news audiences would want to read. This is an extension of the filter bubble scenario discussed above, albeit one proactively generated by news organizations themselves rather than the result of a search engine or newsfeed algorithm choosing particular stories.

The use of automated narrative systems to produce customized news raises fundamental questions about how journalism works. On the one hand, the personalization of news encourages greater connection between news producer and consumer. It alters the one-way mass communication model through the growth of a responsive system. Yet, from a society-level perspective, the personalization of news threatens to atomize news readership in ways that challenge the basic normative commitments that undergird journalism.

Information transfer versus cultural interpretation: The third dichotomy regarding how automated news writing affects understandings of journalism taps into a deeper ambiguity about what news stories do. The divide in question differentiates between, on one side, the literary and community-making aspects of news as a form of cultural production, and, on the other, news as a form of information transfer from journalist to reader. Certainly these are not mutually exclusive aspects, nor should this be asserted to be the case. Instead, the conceptual value of invoking these positions lies in ensuring a sensitivity to a basic sense of just what the news is. The notion of news-as-information connects to journalism's democratic normative ideals of providing citizens with vital updates necessary for self-governance (Kovach and Rosenstiel, 2001). This is a legitimating social role as much as a discursive strategy. Yet it also makes burdensome demands on journalists and the public (Schudson, 1998) and omits much of what constitutes news content (Dahlgren, 1992). The alternative view is commensurate with Carey's

(1992) ritual view of mass communication as providing social cohesion and shared identity. It also finds space for journalism as an aesthetic feat, whether as a literary form or in crafting appealing visual and audio packages. Regardless, quality journalism is positioned as the product of human creativity rather than the adherence to standardized newswriting conventions.

Automated journalism enters into this fray in its basic assumption that the narrativization of data provides a superior means of information transfer. Data sets and spreadsheets contain hidden patterns that can be brought to light through story forms. This is not an incorrect assumption, but it is predicated on the mimicking of existing news forms to convey knowledge. The creation of an automated story involves interpretation through the software's algorithm, and this interpretation is encased in an adherence to formal conventions. Yet competing views situate journalism as an interpretive form of cultural production that should seek to transcend such conventions. The implication for journalistic labor are clear: the growing role of automated journalism in producing conventional stories will likely push human journalists to differentiate themselves as creative beings. Doing so will lead to further engagement with the questions associated with what has been termed the dichotomy between information transfer and cultural interpretation. This is not merely an aesthetic debate, but, in a larger sense, an epistemological question concerning how best to construct an argument for journalistic authority.

Recommendations for future directions

Given advances in artificial intelligence and natural language processing, an emerging online economic model adhering to the logic of the long tail, the growing role of algorithms in structuring everyday knowledge, and the epistemic traditions of neutral newswriting, it is difficult to conceive of a future in which automated news writing is not part of journalism. The interconnectedness of these conditions makes predicting the pace and breadth of expansion difficult, but nonetheless more research will be needed to interrogate automated journalism. In particular, three perspectives are needed. First, research taking a political economy or media industries perspective ought to investigate how automated journalism adheres to the profit imperatives of the owners of news organizations, with an emphasis on how this affects labor. Journalistic labor in the digital age is already marked by precarity, and new questions will certainly arise with viable automation. Second, studies adopting a sociology of news approach can map the emerging field of practices within newsrooms. From the development of automation software to decisions regarding story and resource allocation, this approach will illuminate the implementation—and negotiation—of automated journalism. Third, studies of textual patterns and audience consumption practices promise to round out a research program on automated journalism. Issues of output are important, but so too is the more thorny question of audience reception. Also outside the newsroom, the data practices of news sources should be examined for how they tailor data for automated journalism.

Apart from the close look at how automated journalism is being institutionalized, the topic provides entrée into a broader examination of the interaction between journalism as a set of actors engaged in knowledge production and technology as a set of material objects with accompanying protocols (Gitelman, 2006). Rather than holding technology to be somehow ancillary to the work of creating news, recent research has sought to collapse this distinction. Much of this work turns to actor network theory to privilege the interaction of various human and nonhuman agents—or 'actants'—over preconceived boundaries (see Turner, 2005; Plesner, 2009). The study of news-authoring software has much to contribute to this ongoing conversation.

The blending of human and nonhuman journalists brings the conclusion of this chapter back to where it began. The 'posthuman' in the title is not so much the model of the cyborg, but of a shift away from human embodiment as an unspoken assumption of what constitutes a journalist. Posthumanism, in its cybernetic view, suggests that enhanced connections between humans and machines radically alter our perspective of subjectivity. As Katherine Hayles (1999) writes, "In the posthuman, there are no essential differences or absolute demarcations between bodily existence and computer simulation, cybernetic mechanism and biological organism, robot teleology and human goals" (3). This is a bold vision, frequently associated with the often-dystopian tropes of science fiction. But, pulled into journalism studies, this view helps us sort through an emerging—albeit slowly—hybridity between human and robot journalists. Indeed, the retronymic appending of 'human' before journalist both forestalls and codifies the blurring between human- and algorithm-authored news stories. In the end, the posthuman world of journalism involves ontological questions of the boundaries between human and automated actors as well as what it means for the news served up to us human audiences.

Further reading

For further reading in this area, C. W. Anderson's paper, "Towards a sociology of computational and algorithmic journalism" (2013) lays out a conceptual framework for thinking about journalism and technology. My own piece, "The robotic reporter: Automated journalism and the redefinition of labor, compositional forms, and journalistic authority" (2015) examines the tensions in the discourse around automated journalism. To look at how practitioners engage with automated journalism, the 2014 article "Enter the robot journalist: Users' perceptions of automated content" offers an exploration of journalists' anxieties toward automated journalism. From a more critical take, Tarleton Gillespie's chapter "The relevance of algorithms" (2014) provides an excellent overview of how to examine algorithms from a critical perspective.

References

Anderson, C. (2006) *The Long Tail*. New York, NY: Random House.

Anderson, C.W. (2013) "Towards a Sociology of Computational and Algorithmic Journalism." *New Media and Society* 15(7): 1005–1021.

Anderson, C.W., Bell, E. and Shirky, C. (2012) *Post-Industrial Journalism: Adapting to the Present*. New York, NY: Tow Center for Digital Journalism.

Anderson, C.W. and De Maeyer, J. (2015) "Introduction: Objects of Journalism and the News." *Journalism* 16(1): 3–9.

Barnhurst, K.G. and Nerone, J. (2001) *The Form of News*. New York, NY: Guilford Press.

Carey, J.W. (1992) *Communication as Culture*. New York, NY: Routledge.

Carlson, M. (2007) "Order versus Access: News Search Engines and the Challenge to Traditional Journalistic Roles." *Media, Culture and Society* 29(6): 1014–1030.

Carlson, M. (2015) "The Robotic Reporter: Automated Journalism and the Redefinition of Labor, Compositional Forms, and Journalistic Authority." *Digital Journalism* 3(3): 416–431.

Clerwall, C. (2014) "Enter the Robot Journalist: Users' Perceptions of Automated Content." *Journalism Practice* 8(5): 519–531.

Coddington, M. (2015) "Clarifying Journalism's Quantitative Turn: A Typology for Evaluating Data Journalism, Computational Journalism, and Computer-Assisted Reporting." *Digital Journalism* 3(3): 331–348.

Dahlgren, P. (1992) "Introduction." In Dahlgren, P. and Sparks, C. (eds) *Journalism and Popular Culture*. London, UK: Sage (pp. 1–23).

Diakopoulos, N. (2015) "Algorithmic Accountability: Journalistic Investigation of Computational Power Structures." *Digital Journalism* 3(3): 398–415.

Ellis, J. (2002) *Seeing Things*. London, UK: IB Tauris.

Flew, T., Spurgeon, C., Daniel, A. and Swift, A. (2012) "The Promise of Computational Journalism." *Journalism Practice* 6(2): 157–171.

Gillespie, T. (2014) "The Relevance of Algorithms." In Gillespie, T., Boczkowski, P. and Foot, K. (eds) *Media Technologies*. Cambridge, MA: MIT Press.

Gitelman, L. (2006) *Always Already New*. Cambridge, MA: MIT Press.

Hayles, N.K. (1999) *How We Became Posthuman*. Chicago, IL: University of Chicago Press.

Höpfl, H.M. (1999) "Power, Authority and Legitimacy." *Human Resource Development International* 2(3): 217–234.

Howard, P.N. (2015) *Pax Technica*. New Haven, CT: Yale University Press.

Kovach, B. and Rosenstiel, T. (2001) *The Elements of Journalism*. New York, NY: Three Rivers Press.

Latar, N.L. (2015) "The Robot Journalist in the Age of Social Physics: The End of Human Journalism?" In Einav, G. (ed.) *The New World of Transitioned Media*. Cham, Switzerland: Springer International Publishing.

Lewis, S.C. and Westlund, O. (2015) "Big Data and Journalism: Epistemology, Expertise, Economics, and Ethics." *Digital Journalism* 3(3): 447–466.

McCombs, M.E. and Shaw, D.L. (1972) "The Agenda-Setting Function of Mass Media." *Public Opinion Quarterly* 176–187.

Napoli, P.M. (2014) "Automated Media: An Institutional Theory Perspective on Algorithmic Media Production and Consumption." *Communication Theory* 24(3): 340–360. DOI: 10.1111/comt.12039.

Pariser, E. (2011) *The Filter Bubble*. New York, NY: Penguin.

Pfaffenberger, B. (1992) "Technological Dramas." *Science, Technology and Human Values* 17(3): 282–312.

Plesner, U. (2009) "An Actor-Network Perspective on Changing Work Practices: Communication Technologies as Actants in Newswork." *Journalism* 10(5): 604–626.

Powers, M. (2012) "'In Forms That are Familiar and Yet-To-Be Invented': American Journalism and the Discourse of Technologically Specific Work." *Journal of Communication Inquiry* 36(1): 24–43.

Reeves, B. and Nass, C. (1996) *The Media Equation*. Cambridge, UK: Cambridge University Press.

Rodgers, S. (2015) "Foreign Objects? Web Content Management Systems, Journalistic Cultures and the Ontology of Software." *Journalism* 16(1): 10–26.

Schudson, M. (1995) *The Power of News*. Cambridge, MA: Harvard University Press.

Schudson, M. (1998) *The Good Citizen*. New York, NY: Free Press.

Shoemaker, P.J. and Vos, T. (2009) *Gatekeeping Theory*. New York, NY: Routledge.

Tufekci, Z. (2014) "What Happens to #Ferguson Affects Ferguson: Net Neutrality, Algorithmic Filtering and Ferguson." *The Message*. Available from: https://medium.com/message/ferguson-is-also-a-net-neutrality-issue-6d2f3db51eb0.

Turner, F. (2005) "Actor-Networking the News." *Social Epistemology* 19(4): 321–324.

Turow, J. (2006) *Niche Envy*. Cambridge, MA: MIT Press.

Van Dalen, A. (2012) "The Algorithms Behind the Headlines: How Machine-Written News Redefines the Core Skills of Human Journalists." *Journalism Practice* 6(5–6): 648–658.

van der Kaa, H. and Krahmer, E. (2014) "Journalist versus News Consumer: The Perceived Credibility of Machine Written News." In *Proceedings of the Computation+Journalism Conference*, New York, NY.

Waisbord, S. (2013) *Reinventing Professionalism*. Cambridge, UK: Polity Press.

23

CITIZEN JOURNALISM

Connections, contradictions, and conflicts

Melissa Wall

From watchdogging public institutions to witnessing disasters, citizen journalism is so much a part of the discourse about news today that its existence has come to be taken for granted. It has been described as a vehicle for silenced voices to be heard, for political and social movements to cover neglected issues, and for independent witnesses to capture powerful images of sudden catastrophes or other dramatic events (Allan, 2009; Deuze, 2009; Robinson, 2009). Proclaimed a civic responsibility by some, it is said to be a tool to enable people to take part in democracy (Cottle, 2014). Yet its roles and meanings are not always viewed so enthusiastically by less sanguine observers who argue that citizen journalism facilitates corporate manipulation by media companies, propaganda by governments and information warfare by those involved in armed conflicts (Al-Ghazzi, 2014; Kovačič and Erjavec, 2008; Örnebring, 2013; Turner, 2010). What is clear is that citizen journalism has been assigned contradictory meanings by professional journalists, scholars, and corporate manipulators not to mention citizens themselves. What follows is a consideration of the conflicting points of view about what constitutes citizen journalism, its potential for good and for ill, along with proposals for future directions for research on this much-debated form of reporting.

Delineations: defining citizen journalism

Citizen journalism is often viewed as synonymous with other labels for new genres of journalism: participatory journalism, networked journalism, hyperlocal journalism, crowd-sourced journalism, user-generated content (UGC), etc. But these terms are not necessarily interchangeable; the names we use matter. For example, UGC is said to be professional news media's chosen appellation to neutralize the potential of citizen journalism to challenge its authority (Cottle, 2014). Meanwhile, using the word 'citizen' ties the practice to broader concepts such as democracy and civil society (Campbell, 2014). Nevertheless, citizen journalism remains one of the key designations for the genre of journalism being considered here.

Many scholars focus their definition on who produces citizen journalism, arguing that the non-professional status of its creators is what makes it citizen journalism. Thus, Örnebring simply defines citizen journalism as "news produced by amateurs" (2013: 36), and Berger similarly notes that citizen journalism is "done by persons whose status is not that of hired hands in a media enterprise, but who are outsiders" (2011: 710). Likewise, Robinson and

DeShano write that a citizen journalist is "any person who does not get paid by a mainstream news organization to report and write online as a part of a blog, website or forum imparting information about a geographic community" (2011: 965).

Others focus on what is produced, defining citizen journalism as the creation of original content such as a video or even simply posting a comment on a professionally written news story (Goode, 2009). Among the broader definitions, Friedland and Kim (2009: 297) write that citizen journalism is a "contribution to discussion in the public sphere, whether in the form of simple information, synthesis, reporting or opinion." Among the disagreements over what it is, academics from the Global South argue that the richer Northern countries have an ideological bias in how they define citizen journalism with some suggesting the term 'citizen' itself does not hold its meaning in different contexts (Rodriguez, 2014; Khiabany and Sreberny, 2009). Rodriguez (2014) argues that the citizen journalism practiced in the Global South requires training and skills and results in sustained attempts to create social or political change. Like other researchers, she believes the wealthy countries of the North have allowed corporate media to denude the term of its radical potential.

Citizen journalism genealogies

Citizen journalism has multiple possible originations, including attempts to tie it to the communications of American revolutionaries in their independence war against Britain (Bentley, 2013). Others suggest its predecessor is civic or public journalism, a US-based movement in the late twentieth century that sought to bring news audiences into the news process through focus groups, community meetings, and other programs directed by mainstream, corporate news outlets (Ryfe and Mensing, 2010). However, this movement was more about mainstream journalists collecting news differently and not about citizens independently creating news content. Just as importantly, it came into existence before most digital tools, particularly those involved in social networking, became accessible to ordinary people.

The DNA of today's citizen journalism can be traced through one or more of the following family trees:

- *The Activist.* Digital citizen journalism might be pegged to the creation of the Independent Media Center during the 1999 World Trade Organization protests in the United States (Anderson, 2013). Many of those citizen journalists were activists affiliated with social movement groups seeking to tell an alternative story about globalization by using software tools and platforms of their own making prior to the creation of today's social media mechanisms. A related activist origination story ties citizen journalism to the creation of OhMyNews in South Korea, which used the voices of thousands of ordinary citizens to report in ways that contributed to the installation of a new government (Nip, 2006). Both initiatives relied on local grassroots reporting to challenge the status quo. Today's heirs of the activist lineage include the Arab Spring and the Occupy movements, which used networked organizational forms to collectively produce their own reportage on protests concerning economic inequality and social justice issues (DeLuca and Lawson, 2014).

This category is particularly emphasized by researchers working from within the Global South who suggest that citizen journalism has a more sustained, intentional political mission than the single capture of an image (Berger, 2011; Rodriguez, 2014). Of course, this ideal form of ongoing reporting may be easier said than done. Bock's (2011) research examining citizen video content producers in the United States found that they often cannot produce high quality work due to a lack of time and money. She notes that, "without significant support and resources, it is difficult for the occasional, unpaid citizen journalist to consistently produce counter-narratives" (2011: 651).

- The *Independent*. We can just as easily find the foundation for the origins of digital citizen journalism in the rise of independent social media producers, particularly bloggers. In this scenario, a new type of reporting, which used the tools (e.g. Blogger, Typepad, etc.) of the newly ascendant new media companies practiced what the Knight Center calls citizen editing or what Bruns (2005) dubs 'gatewatching' (Informing Communities, 2009). Here, ordinary people curate and critique reporting done by others, especially mainstream news media, but also draw on disparate, sometimes unexpected sources of information to compile evidence of wrongdoing or to present an alternative view of an issue or event (Carpenter, 2010). In some cases, the independents also produce original coverage. The independents gained credibility and authority in part through interaction with their audiences and by exhibiting a personalized voice (Robinson, 2009; Wall, 2015). Individuals reporting with Twitter, Reddit, and other similar platforms are their heirs (Murthy, 2013).
- *The Witness*. Still others suggest that citizen journalism's beginnings can be seen in the sudden surges of content from crises such the 9/11 terrorist attacks in the United States or the 2004 Asian tsunami (cf. Allan, 2009, this volume). In these cases, individuals on the scenes of sudden, dramatic events record what they are experiencing, thus giving rise to a form of citizen journalism that is labeled 'witnessing' (Allan, 2013; Mortensen, 2011). Their output is temporary and unexpected, claiming attention in the first moments or hours of disruptions such as natural disasters or political upheavals. Usually, the witness produces fragments or snippets of accidental journalism as they capture moments from the "right place at the right time" (Rodriguez, 2014: 205). Some researchers see in these images openings for changing dominant narratives (Pantti, 2013). Others argue this form of citizen journalism has become prominent because it is so easily incorporated into mainstream news content, which can shape it to fit existing norms and values (Sjøvaag, 2011). Still other critics question whether witnessing counts as journalism, arguing that a journalistic act "stems from an individual consciousness of the rights and responsibilities of citizenship [...] one-off or even thrice-off volunteering of journalistic content" does not make the person producing it a citizen journalist (Berger, 2011: 5).

Relationships with mainstream news media: not too close

One of the key areas of contention concerning citizen journalism is its relationship with mainstream news media and the ways in which it may or may not be able to contribute to professional news. This relationship embodies a tension between professional control and the need to respond to the rise of citizen-produced content (Lewis, 2012). Mainstream journalists are repeatedly described as unable or unwilling to share their production processes with those outside the profession (Scott, Millard, and Leonard, 2014). For example, Örnebring (2013) argues that professional journalists are constantly engaged in boundary work to differentiate themselves from citizen journalists, as they highlight their expertise in news judgment and the exercise of practices such as objectivity, fairness, and ethics (see also Eldridge, this volume). They draw such boundaries in order to maintain their authority as the source of legitimate news (Carlson and Lewis, 2015).

But we live in an era of participatory cultures in which citizens are constantly producing their own media content, sometimes in the form of what might be considered news

(Holton, Coddington, and de Zúñiga, 2013). In response, news outlets ranging from iReport at CNN to YouReport at Lebanon's MTV to Canada's My News at CTV News have created separate and unequal spaces within their own news operations for citizens to upload their content (Domingo, 2011). Such sites often promise a chance to be part of the mainstream news product, but the opportunities are usually small. For example, a mere 8 percent of iReport content is actually vetted by CNN (Silverman, 2012). Corralled into its own space or what Jönsson and Örnebring (2011) call the 'UGC ghetto,' citizen content does not seem to be viewed as real news by professional journalists (135). Indeed, some research suggests that perhaps citizen journalism does not deserve a seat at the table, finding that news produced by citizens generally consists of entertainment and popular culture materials, which professional news operations deem irrelevant or even meaningless (Holt and Karlsson, 2014; Jönsson and Örnebring, 2011). However, D'heer and Paulussen's (2013) study of citizen journalism content within smaller professional news operations instead finds citizens effectively cover hyperlocal events, publicizing seemingly minor (but important to community members) news and offering positive stories about their communities. This suggests that the size and focus of the news outlet making use of citizen content may have an effect on how useful and relevant citizen content is to traditional outlets.

Even when citizen content is deemed newsworthy, some researchers argue that it is often controlled entirely by the professional news outlet to which it is submitted, and this entity decides how visible the item is, how to frame it, etc. Thus, gatekeeping remains the prerogative of the professionals, which leads to much citizen journalism content following the narrative logic of the mainstream news media (Ali and Fahmy, 2013; Semati and Brookey, 2014). In some cases, professional television news outlets use amateur content but do so in ways that diminish it, incorporating it into their broadcasts but not crediting or even acknowledging the presence of citizen-produced images. This leaves the audience unaware of the origins of the image or suggests that the creator of it does not matter (Pantti and Andén-Papadopoulos, 2011; Sjøvaag, 2011). In fact, Jönsson and Örnebring (2011) argue that citizen participation in mainstream news sites simply provides an "illusion of participation" (141). For many news outlets, allowing citizen participation is merely a branding exercise or the chance to use free labor (Kovačič and Erjavec, 2008; Kperogi, 2011; Usher, 2011).

Yet again, other researchers do not share this pessimistic view. Some scholars who have studied mainstream media usage of citizen content see the relationship as more fluid, albeit uneven and limited (Canter, 2013). This has particularly been evident in the use of live blogs by professional outlets that need rapid, constantly updating content. They also often need to turn to citizens for hard-to-get content (Thurman and Rodgers, 2014). The live blog use of citizen videos has even been called the production of the 'collaborative news clip,' suggesting a more horizontal relationship between professional and citizen journalists is evolving within certain digitally native forms (Wall and El Zahed, 2015: 164).

Dark sides of citizen journalism

Less research has focused on the more controversial, even dangerous, aspects of citizen journalism. Critics suggest some citizen journalism is a means to 'commercialize audience participation' (Kovačič and Erjavec, 2008: 884) and that it can pander to populist tastes and lower ethical standards, serving as an excuse for displaying what Mythen (2010: 53) says are "gratuitously . . . macabre images of human tragedies." This line of thought suggests that at best citizen journalism does not support positive expressions of citizenship and at worst it can be propaganda and even be part of information warfare (Al-Ghazzi, 2014; Mythen, 2010; Watson, 2012).

While much has been made of citizen witnessing, skeptics argue such acts may work as citizen surveillance and monitoring of other citizens, encouraging voyeurism and crass exploitation of other people's tragedies (Samuel, 2011; Trottier and Schneider, 2012). These skeptics warn that some citizen journalists are increasingly violating other citizens' privacy and even using the information they collect to harass or threaten others (Watson *et al.*, 2014). Indeed, Mano (2010) argues that citizen journalists' pursuit of what they perceive as justice can in some cases become a type high-tech 'necklacing', referring to a form of vigilantism practiced in South Africa during apartheid.

Examples include citizen journalists capturing images of fans rioting in Vancouver after the 2011 Stanley Cup hockey match and then posting these to Twitter to aid the police in identifying people to arrest, and a Denver student posting information to Reddit after a mass shooting in a movie theater in Colorado in a "new style of citizen journalism" that played a role in monitoring the events on the ground but that also appeared to be a form of 'citizen policing' (Warzel, 2014: 4). In another instance, citizen journalists using Reddit sought to uncover the criminals who bombed the Boston Marathon, appointing themselves to an informal team of armchair detectives that misidentified an innocent man as the culprit.

In other cases, citizen journalism has been identified as supporting hypernationalism, whipping up anger and even hatred of outsiders (Xin, 2010). Meanwhile, state and non-state actors may pose as citizen journalists or seek to manipulate real ones in order to further their own agendas. For example, the U.S. military has sought to both intimidate and influence independent citizen bloggers posting about conflicts the United States is involved in. In cases of terrorist attacks, citizen journalists can contribute to spreading terrorists' messages of fear, doing so in a personal, intimate format that may intensify the reception of the terrorists' aims (Watson, 2012). Watson (2012) further argues that martyrdom videos can be viewed as a form of citizen journalism reproduced by professional news media and spread virally by ordinary people through social networking sites. In Syria, critics warn that the Syrian government and extremist groups are using what passes for citizen journalism as weapons of war (Al-Ghazzi, 2014; Carter, Maher, and Neumann, 2014.)

Future research directions

As citizen journalism is constantly evolving, much remains to be studied and better understood. Below, I suggest some potentially fruitful lines of inquiry.

- *Citizen journalism and propaganda.* Research on citizen journalism tends toward positive examples. Its uses as propaganda, information warfare, etc. have been less studied. While perhaps harder to research and also not matching a normative belief that citizen journalism is a contributor to democracy, this dark side of citizen journalism needs to be further explored.
- *Citizen reporting and apps.* From the Guardian Witness app to Uganda's #NTVGO citizen journalism app, we know little about the practices that applications such as these are creating specifically for citizen journalists. Yes, new tools increasingly make creating high quality content easy to accomplish, but what about the seemingly invisible influences of app creators?
- *Place, space and citizen journalism.* Placing-making (the reimagining of the ways public space can be created) and citizen participation in these processes have been increasingly used in city planning and other urban projects. Such work could productively inform research on citizen journalism and the ways it may contribute to understanding how public spaces are

created, maintained, and assigned meaning. Often on the move and on location, citizen journalists may also create new spatial practices of information collection, opening up new lines of journalism research.

- *Social capital and citizen journalism.* Building on some of the assumptions that originated with civic journalism, more recent research has focused on how citizen journalism could "enhance social capital and citizenship" (Nah and Chung, 2012: 2). This area of inquiry could help assess the potential of citizen journalism as a means of connecting citizens to each other and to decision makers whom they could hold accountable.

- *Marginalized communities and citizen journalism.* Ethnic media have a long history of close journalist–citizen relationships and activism on behalf of communities. This would suggest that they might be at the forefront of incorporating citizen content, but is that actually the fact? We need more research on how citizen journalism is practiced in minority and marginalized communities, but also in what ways if any the arguments about the roles of citizen journalism put forth by researchers from the Global South intersect with minority media practices in the Global North.

- *Research with intention.* Finally, the dramatic changes facing journalism mean educators need to employ transformational or action research by having students initiate or participate in existing citizen journalism projects and then study the results. Some researchers have already found that students are more receptive to citizen journalism than older audience members, so they would appear to be an ideal group to experiment with (Netzley and Hemmer, 2012; Nah, Namkoong, Van Stee, and Record, 2014).

Conclusion

No one can be certain what the future of citizen journalism holds but some new patterns are already emerging. Mainstream news organizations' solicitations for citizen journalism may soon dissipate in their current forms, eventually eliminating the standing contribution pages (referred to as 'ghettos.') These are labor intensive and do not appear to produce enough 'quality' content to justify their continued existence. Indeed, the professional–citizen journalism relationship appears headed in a different direction. Professional journalists are now fully present on social networking sites such as Twitter and Facebook, where they can identify and seek relevant citizen content within those networks. Thus, citizen content will continue to be used by professionals but in ways that are less tied to the largest news organizations' own online sites and more connected to networking with ordinary people via social media sites. (However, smaller professional publications may well see boundaries falling between professionals and citizen contributors due to their closer relationship and lower expectations for complicated content.) Likewise, the rise of a new crop of citizen reporting apps may serve as channels for citizen content to create professional–social media hybrid spaces. This type of heightened visibility is important because citizen journalism is only truly called into being when it is public.

Another area of concern centers on privacy issues and citizen journalism. The surveillance work being undertaken by citizens of other citizens appears to be increasing. The rise in wearable technology, cheap drones, etc. may lead to loss of privacy and omniscient citizen-to-citizen scrutiny. Citizen vigilantes appear particularly potent when joined in loose teams and this could generate both new forms of investigative journalism (for example, citizen journalist Eliot Higgins who taught himself how to be an expert on weapons reporting) while also risking being incorporated into the security apparatus of states, the commercial manipulations of corporations or political projects of other unidentifiable actors.

Perhaps the best hope for citizen journalism to continue to develop as a force in its own right is through citizen-to-citizen collaborations with social movements and civil society organizations working for the public good. These may or may not have a relationship with mainstream news organizations. Indeed, the citizen media activists that researchers in the Global South have said all along are authentic citizen journalists seem well positioned to model this form for others.

In sum, we can continue to highlight the ideals of citizen journalism such as bringing a more diverse range of voices and independent participation to news collection. We can spread these ideals among student journalists and other citizens who wish to create community, build social capital, and/or enact social responsibility. Ultimately, however, we should be under no illusion that the future of citizen journalism is a clear route to democracy, pluralism, or even the truth.

Further reading

Allan and Thorsen's (2009) and Thorsen and Allan's (2014) *Citizen Journalism: Global Perspectives* Volumes 1 and 2, respectively, collect a comprehensive range of studies by leading researchers. Andén-Papadopoulos and Pantti's (2011) edited volume *Amateur Images and Global News* explores citizen content through a visual lens. Clemencia Rodriguez' (2011) exceptional fieldwork is the basis for *Citizens' Media against Armed Conflict: Disrupting Violence in Colombia*, an in-depth examination of citizen media in a violent environment.

References

Al-Ghazzi, O. (2014) "'Citizen Journalism' in the Syrian Uprising: Problematizing Western Narratives in a Local Context." *Communication Theory* 24(4): 435–454.

Ali, S.R. and Fahmy, S. (2013) "Gatekeeping and Citizen Journalism: The Use of Social Media During the Recent Uprisings in Iran, Egypt, and Libya." *Media, War & Conflict* 6(1): 55–69.

Allan, S. (2009) "Histories of Citizen Journalism." In Allan, S. and Thorsen, E. (eds) *Citizen Journalism: Global Perspectives, Vol. 1*. New York, NY: Peter Lang, pp. 17–31.

Allan, S. (2013) *Citizen Witnessing: Revisioning Journalism in Times of Crisis*. Malden, MA: Polity Press.

Allan, S. and Thorsen, E. (eds) (2009) *Citizen Journalism: Global Perspectives, Vol. 1*. New York, NY: Peter Lang.

Andén-Papadopoulos, K. and Pantti, M. (2011) *Amateur Images and Global News*. Chicago, IL: University of Chicago Press.

Anderson, C.W. (2013) *Rebuilding the News: Metropolitan Journalism in the Digital Age*. Philadelphia, PA: Temple University.

Bentley, C. (2013) "US Citizen Journalism and Alternative Online News Sites." In Anderson, P. J., Williams, M. and Ogola, G. (eds) *The Future of Quality Journalism: A Cross Continental Analysis*. New York, NY: Routledge, pp. 184–200.

Berger, G. (2011) "Empowering the Youth as Citizen Journalists: A South African Experience." *Journalism* 12(6): 708–726.

Bock, M.A. (2011) "Citizen Video Journalists and Authority in Narrative: Reviving the Role of the Witness." *Journalism* 13(5): 639–653.

Bruns, A. (2005) *Gatewatching: Collaborative Online News Production*. New York, NY: Peter Lang.

Campbell, V. (2014) "Theorizing Citizenship in Citizen Journalism." *Digital Journalism* 3(5): 704–719.

Canter, L. (2013) "The Source, the Resource and the Collaborator: The Role of Citizen Journalism in Local UK Newspapers." *Journalism* 14(8): 1091–1109.

Carlson, M. and Lewis, S.C. (eds) (2015) *Boundaries of Journalism: Professionalism, Practices and Participation*. New York, NY: Routledge.

Carpenter, S. (2010) "A Study of Content Diversity in Online Citizen Journalism and Online Newspaper Articles." *New Media & Society* 12(7): 1064–1084.

Carter, J.A., Maher, S. and Neumann, P.R. (2014) #*Greenbirds: Measuring Importance and Influence in Syrian Foreign Fighter Networks*. The International Centre for the Study of Radicalisation and Political Violence. London, UK: Kings College.

Cottle, S. (2014) "Series Editor's Preface." In Thorsen, E. and Allan, S. (eds) *Citizen Journalism: Global Perspectives, Vol. 2*. New York, NY: Peter Lang, pp. ix–xii.

DeLuca, K.M. and Lawson, S. (2014) "Occupy Wall Street and Social Media Sharing After the Wake of Institutional Journalism." In Thorsen, E. and Allan, S. (eds) *Citizen Journalism: Global Perspectives, Vol. 2*. New York, NY: Peter Lang, pp. 361–375.

Deuze, M. (2009) "The Future of Citizen Journalism." In Allan, S. and Thorsen, E. (eds) *Citizen Journalism: Global Perspectives*. New York, NY: Peter Lang, pp. 255–264.

D'heer, E. and Paulussen, S. (2013) "The Use of Citizen Journalism for Hyperlocal News Production." *Recherches en Communication* 39: 151–164. Available from: http://sites.uclouvain.be/rec/index.php/rec/issue/view/623.

Domingo, D. (2011) "Managing Audience Participation: Practices, Workflows, Strategies." In Singer, J.B., Domingo, D., Heinonen, A., Hermida, A., Paulussen, S., Quandt, T., et al. (eds) *Participatory Journalism: Guarding Open Gates at Online Newspapers*. Malden, MA: Wiley Blackwell, pp. 76–95.

Friedland, L. and Kim, N. (2009) "Citizen Journalism." In *Encyclopedia of Journalism*. Thousand Oaks, CA: Sage, pp. 297–302.

Goode, L. (2009) "Social News, Citizen Journalism and Democracy." *New Media & Society* 11(8): 1287–1305.

Holt, K. and Karlsson, M. (2014) "'Random Acts of Journalism?' How Citizen Journalists Tell the News in Sweden." *New Media & Society*. DOI: 10.1177/1461444814535189.

Holton, A.E., Coddington, M. and de Zúñiga, H.G. (2013) "Whose News? Whose Values? Citizen Journalism and Journalistic Values through the Lens of Content Creators and Consumers." *Journalism Practice* 7(6): 720–737.

Informing Communities (2009) "Informing Communities: Sustaining Democracy in the Digital Age." *Aspen Institute*. Available from: http://www.knightcomm.org/wpcontent/uploads/2010/02/Informing_Communities_Sustaining_Democracy_in_the_Digital_Age.pdf.

Jönsson, A.M. and Örnebring, H. (2011) "User-Generated Content and the News: Empowerment of Citizens or Interactive Illusion?" *Journalism Practice* 5(2): 127–144.

Khiabany, G. and Sreberny, A. (2009) "The Iranian Story: What Citizens? What Journalism?" In Allan, S. and Thorsen, E. (eds) *Citizen Journalism: Global Perspectives*. New York, NY: Peter Lang, pp. 121–132.

Kovačič, M.P. and Erjavec, E. (2008) "Mobi Journalism in Slovenia: Is This Really Citizen Journalism?" *Journalism Studies* 9(6): 874–890.

Kperogi, F.A. (2011) "Cooperation with the Corporation? CNN and the Hegemonic Cooptation of Citizen Journalism through iReport.com." *New Media & Society* 13(2): 314–329.

Lewis, S.C. (2012) "The Tension between Professional Control and Open Participation: Journalism and Its Boundaries." *Information, Communication & Society* 15(6): 836–866.

Mano, W. (2010) "Between Citizen and Vigilante Journalism: ZimDaily's Fair Deal Campaign and the Zimbabwe Crisis." *Communicare: Journal for Communication Sciences in Southern Africa* 29: 57–7.

Mortensen, M. (2011) "The Eyewitness in the Age of Digital Transformation." In Andén-Papadopoulos, K. and Pantti, M. (eds) *Amateur Images and Global News*. Chicago, IL: The University of Chicago Press, pp. 63–75.

Murthy, D. (2013) *Twitter: Social Communication in the Twitter Age*. Malden, MA: Polity Press.

Mythen, G. (2010) "Reframing Risk? Citizen Journalism and the Transformation of News." *Journal of Risk Research* 13(1): 45–58.

Nah, S. and Chung, D.S. (2012) "When Citizens Meet Both Professional and Citizen Journalists: Social Trust, Media Credibility, and Perceived Journalistic Roles among Online Community News Readers." *Journalism* 13(6): 714–730.

Nah, S., Namkoong, K., Van Stee, S.K. and Record, R.A. (2014) "Unveiling the Effects of Citizen Journalism Practice on College Students' Social Capital." *Journalism & Mass Communication Educator* 69(4): 366–385.

Netzley, S.B. and Hemmer, M. (2012) "Citizen Journalism Just as Credible as Stories by Pros, Students Say." *Newspaper Research Journal* 33(3): 49–61.

Nip, J.Y.M. (2006) "Exploring the Second Phase of Public Journalism." *Journalism Studies* 7(2): 212–236.

Örnebring, H. (2013) "Anything You Can Do, I Can Do Better? Professional Journalists on Citizen Journalism in Six European Countries." *International Communication Gazette* 75(1): 35–53.

Pantti, M. (2013) "Getting Closer? Encounters of the National Media with Global Images." *Journalism Studies* 14(2): 201–218.

Pantti, M. and Andén-Papadopoulos, K. (2011) "Transparency and Trustworthiness: Strategies for Incorporating Amateur Photography into News Discourse." In Andén-Papadopoulos, K. and Pantti, M. (eds) *Amateur Images and Global News*. Chicago, IL: The University of Chicago Press, pp. 97–112.

Robinson, S. (2009) "'If You Had Been With Us': Mainstream Press and Citizen Journalists Jockey for Authority Over the Collective Memory of Hurricane Katrina." *New Media & Society* 11(5): 795–814.

Robinson, S. and DeShano, C. (2011) "'Anyone Can Know': Citizen Journalism and the Interpretive Community of the Mainstream Press." *Journalism* 12(8): 963–982.

Rodriguez, C. (2011) *Citizens' Media against Armed Conflict: Disrupting Violence in Colombia*. Minneapolis, MN: University of Minnesota Press.

Rodriguez, C. (2014) "A Latin American Approach to Citizen Journalism." In Thorsen, E. and Allan, S. (eds) *Citizen Journalism: Global Perspectives, Vol. 2*. New York, NY: Peter Lang, pp.199–210.

Ryfe, D.M. and Mensing, D. (2010) "Citizen Journalism in a Historical Frame." In Rosenberry, J. and St. John, B. (eds) *Public Journalism 2.0: The Promise and Reality of a Citizen Engaged Press*. New York, NY: Routledge, pp. 32–44.

Samuel, A. (2011) "After a Loss in Vancouver, Troubling Signals of Citizen Surveillance." *Harvard Business Review*. Available from: https://hbr.org/2011/06/in-vancouver-troubling-signals/.

Scott, J., Millard, D. and Leonard, P. (2014) "Citizen Participation in News: An Analysis of the Landscape of Online Journalism." *Digital Journalism* 3(5): 737–758.

Semati, S. and Brookey, R. (2014) "Not For Neda: Digital Media, (Citizen) Journalism, and the Invention of a Postfeminist Martyr." *Communication, Culture & Critique* 7(2): 137–153.

Silverman, C. (2012) "How CNN Verifies Its Citizen Content." *Poynter Institute*. Available from: http://www.poynter.org/news/mediawire/160045/how-cnns-ireport-verifies-its-citizen-content/.

Sjøvaag, H. (2011) "Amateur Images and Journalistic Authority." In Andén-Papadopoulos, K. and Pantti, M. (eds) *Amateur Images and Global News*. Chicago, IL: University of Chicago Press, pp. 81–95.

Thorsen, E. and Allan, S. (eds) (2014) *Citizen Journalism: Global Perspectives, Vol. 2*. New York, NY: Peter Lang.

Thurman, N. and Rodgers, J. (2014) "Citizen Journalism in Real Time? Live Blogging and Crisis Events." In Thorsen, E. and Allan, S. (eds) *Citizen Journalism: Global Perspectives, Vol. 2*. New York, NY: Peter Lang, pp. 81–95.

Trottier, D. and Schneider, C. (2012) "The 2011 Vancouver Riot and the Role of Facebook in Crowd-Sourced Policing." *BC Studies: The British Columbian Quarterly* 175: 57–72.

Turner, G. (2010) *Ordinary People and the Media: The Demotic Turn*. Thousand Oaks, CA: Sage.

Usher, N. (2011) "Professional Journalist, Hands Off! Citizen Journalism as Civic Responsibility." In McChesney, R. and Pickard, V. (eds) *Will the Last Reporter Please Turn Out the Lights?* New York, NY: The Free Press, pp. 264–276.

Wall, M. (2015) "Citizen Journalism: A Retrospective on What We Know, an Agenda for What We Don't." *Digital Journalism* 3(6): 797–813.

Wall, M. and El Zahed, S. (2015) "Embedding Content from Syrian Citizen Journalists: The Rise of the Collaborative News Clip." *Journalism* 16(2): 163–180.

Warzel, C. (2014) "Behind the Alarming Rise of the Online Vigilante Detective." *Buzzfeed*. Available from: http://www.buzzfeed.com/charliewarzel/behind-the-alarming-rise-of-the-online-vigilante-detective#.qg2D4NvZZL.

Watson, H. (2012) "Dependent Citizen Journalism and the Publicity of Terror." *Terrorism and Political Violence* 24(3): 465–482.

Watson, H., Baruh, L., Finn, R.L. and Scifo, S. (2014) "Citizen (In) Security? Social Media, Citizen Journalism and Crisis Response." In Hiltz, S.R., Pfaff, M.S., Plotnick, L. and Shih, P.C. (eds) *Proceedings of the 11th International ISCRAM Conference*. University PA, May 2014. Available from: http://www.iscram.org/legacy/ISCRAM2014/ISCRAM2014_proceedings.pdf.

Xin, X. (2010) "The Impact of 'Citizen Journalism' on Chinese Media and Society." *Journalism Practice* 4(3): 333–344.

24

USER COMMENTS AND CIVILITY ON YOUTUBE

Thomas B. Ksiazek and Limor Peer

Digital journalism enables people to interact in new ways, creating a user experience that blends traditional forms of mass communication with interpersonal communication and user-generated content creation. These new modes of interactivity with online news come in two main forms—user-content and user-user (Ksiazek, Peer, and Lessard, 2014)—where individuals can either interact with the content (e.g. liking or ranking) or with other users (e.g. commenting, sharing, or recommending).

The interactive capabilities of online news are often celebrated for the potential to facilitate discussion and dialogue, where comment sections offer the possibility of a virtual public sphere (Papacharissi, 2002; Ruiz *et al.*, 2011; Singer, 2009). By enabling user comments, online journalism offers a forum for productive deliberation, meeting Dewey's call for a 'journalism of conversation' and capturing the essence of the recent 'public journalism' movement (Haas, 2007; Rosen, 2001). However, research on this topic often finds that these discussions do not embody rational and civil democratic dialogue, thus failing to meet the standards expected of a public sphere (Papacharissi, 2002; Ruiz *et al.*, 2011; Singer, 2009). A healthy, deliberative public sphere is not likely to be nurtured if users are not civil toward one another, and online commenting is the site of hostile and contentious discussions that are better characterized as vitriolic than argumentative.

This chapter addresses concerns about hostility in online discussions of the news. While hostility is assumed to be widespread in these virtual spaces, much of the evidence is anecdotal. Moreover, the conceptual understandings of hostility and its counterpart, civility, need better integration of normative and contextual definitions. We begin this chapter by reviewing the literature on civility and hostility in user comments and offering conceptual definitions. Next, we develop operational definitions through a process of triangulation. By integrating analytical precedents, established word dictionaries, and a qualitative contextual analysis, we develop measures of civility and hostility. Finally, we implement the civility index and hostility index to analyze user comments posted to YouTube news videos.

Civility and hostility in online discourse

The study of civility and hostility in democratic discourse dates back centuries (Herbst, 2010). While research on civility has largely focused on elite discourse (e.g. Presidential rhetoric), we address public discourse in the online space, meeting a growing call for research in this area (Herbst, 2010). What follows is an integration of conceptual work on civility and hostility in user comments posted in response to the news.

Civility

Much of the recent scholarly literature on civility is situated in relation to the public sphere and democratic dialogue, where researchers argue that civil discussion is needed for proper development and operation of a public sphere (e.g. Himelboim, 2011; Zhou, Chan, and Peng, 2008). Yet, coming to conceptual terms with civility has been less than productive, as some scholars define civility in broad, normative terms, while others treat it as a phenomenon that is socially constructed and contextually situated (Herbst, 2010).

Normative definitions situate civility in the context of generally held standards for civil discourse. Here, civility is typically identified by the avoidance of personal attacks and harsh language used against other users or the content being discussed (Zhou, Chan, and Peng, 2008). Much of what we see in normative definitions of civility seems to require users to engage in polite interaction. For instance, Ng and Detenber (2005: 8) equate civility with politeness and considered any "rude comments, name-calling, and personal attacks" to be examples of incivility. However, others disagree with this general approach, arguing that civility and politeness should not be seen as the same thing (Papacharissi, 2004; Reader, 2012; Schudson, 1997). Furthermore, these scholars suggest that being overly concerned with politeness can actually stifle healthy deliberation.

Still, some scholars argue that a normative understanding of civility is too simplistic and favor a more contextual approach, highlighting the unique, socially constructed nature of what civility means for a given discussion group. For instance, Papacharissi (2004) conceptualizes civility as behavior that is not offensive to the social group(s) in which the behavior exists. Similarly, Hurrell (2005) argues that civility is discursively constructed within each community and common notions of civility can privilege certain types of people depending on their class, race, or educational background.

From the nuanced and contextual definitions of civility to more normative definitions, we identify a common theme running through the literature on civility—civility is understood as the counterpart of hostility. Instead of offering a clear picture of what constitutes civility, many discuss civility in terms of what it is *not*—ad hominem attacks, name-calling, offensive language, profanity, obscenity, or stereotyping. While we agree that civility is an inherently contextual phenomenon, concerns in popular media about online commenting (Singal, 2012; Tate, 2012) show a societal belief that certain types of language—name-calling, racist remarks—do not contribute to quality discussion. Therefore, while acknowledging contextual differences, a broadly applicable conceptual definition of a civil comment is one that moves a discussion forward without name-calling, stereotyping, or being written solely to incite anger from another side of the argument. In other words, it is a comment absent of hostility.

Hostility

Conceptualizations of hostility appear under the guise of various terms—flaming, incivility, and impoliteness—with the latter two clearly suggesting hostility as the counterpart to civility. Much like the civility literature, the scholarship on hostility also wrestles with normative versus contextual definitions. Normative conceptualizations define hostility as comments that are profane, insulting, obscene, or otherwise offensive (Alonzo and Aiken, 2004;

Lee, 2005; Moor, Heuvelman, and Verleur, 2010). Alternatively, contextual understandings of hostility highlight the set of interactional norms for the group in which a message exists (Neurauter-Kessels, 2011; O'Sullivan and Flanagin, 2003). Once again, we see contrasting schools of thought: one focusing on broadly applicable, normative definitions; the other arguing that hostility is emergent and socially constructed in unique contexts.

Here, we offer conceptual definitions for hostility and civility that seek to integrate the often-varied perspectives on these phenomena. A hostile message is one that is intentionally designed to attack someone or something and, in doing so, incite anger or exasperation through the use of profanity, name calling, character assassination, and/or insulting or offensive language. In turn, civility is commonly understood as discourse that is absent of these qualities. A person can be argumentative and still be civil, and as long as an argument is made without insulting or offensive language, it maintains its civility, even if it might not be considered 'polite' or 'nice.' While these are broadly applicable normative conceptualizations, we also embrace the need for contextual understandings of these phenomena and discuss them in the next section.

Measures of civility and hostility

To measure civility and hostility in specific contexts, we have developed a civility index and a hostility index through a process of triangulation. First, we gathered normative operational definitions from the literature (e.g. Alonzo and Aiken, 2004; Herbst, 2010; Lee, 2005; Ng and Detenber, 2005; Turnage, 2007). Next, we drew from existing dictionaries in the widely used textual analysis program Linguistic Inquiry and Word Count, or LIWC (Pennebaker, Booth, and Francis, 2007a; Pennebaker *et al.*, 2007b). The custom civility dictionary combined LIWC's dictionaries of positive emotion, assent, and insight words. The custom hostility dictionary combined negative emotion, anger, and swear words. The selection of dictionaries was guided by the existing literature and normative definitions discussed above. For example, Herbst (2010) argues that emotion is central to the notion of civility. Finally, we conducted a qualitative contextual analysis of comments posted to YouTube news videos. This process involved reading through the comments posted to a random selection of videos, searching for indicators of civility and hostility that may be unique to YouTube news videos. Developing these measures through triangulation effectively integrates normative (existing operational definitions and word dictionaries) and contextual (inductive qualitative analysis) definitions. The final dictionaries include 619 civil words and 351 hostile words (see Ksiazek, Peer, and Zivic, 2014).

The custom dictionaries can be implemented in LIWC to create numerical indices of civility and hostility. We recommend computing proportional measures, where scores are calculated for a set of comments posted to a news story. By choosing the individual story as the unit of analysis, we can compare the indices across stories (or videos) and thus account for context to some degree (i.e. those who choose to comment on a story are assumed to share an interest in that story, and perhaps also share an understanding of the norms/conventions of that particular discussion community). When applied to YouTube news videos, the measures capture the number of civil or hostile words, respectively, as a proportion of total words in the comment thread for each video. For instance, if LIWC identifies 20 hostile words in a set of comments containing 200 words, then the hostility score is 0.1 (or 10 percent) for that video. These proportional measures control for the number of comments, and thus the number of words in those comment threads, so that a video with 30 comments can have the same hostility score as one with 3,000 comments.

LIWC's dictionaries are both valid and reliable. First, the total set of dictionaries contains an average of 86 percent of all words people use in speech and text, establishing external validity (Pennebaker *et al.*, 2007b: 10). Second, the dictionaries have good internal validity, as demonstrated by comparisons between dictionaries of word categories and judges' ratings of those same categories. Finally, the measures have acceptable reliability scores (see Pennebaker *et al.*, 2007b: 8–10 and Table 24.1).

User comments and civility on YouTube

To illustrate this approach, we offer a study of user comments posted to YouTube news videos (Ksiazek, Peer, and Zivic, 2014). The broad research questions focus on the general degree of hostility and civility in comments, the relationship between hostility/civility in comments and popularity and engagement with online news videos, and how content features and the origin of videos may explain the level of hostility/civility in online discussion.

The study draws on a sample of news videos from YouTube during a three-month period in 2008. We created a composite week by randomly selecting a Sunday, Monday, Tuesday, Wednesday, Thursday, Friday, and Saturday during the period of March–June 2008. The top 100 videos from YouTube's 'News' category, ranked by views, were selected for each of those seven days. A web crawler was developed to collect the videos, comments, and publicly available popularity and engagement metrics. After removing videos with zero comments, as well as those with all comments in a foreign language, the initial data set included 515 videos and 28,341 comments. A subsample of 163 videos was hand-coded for content features, such as content topic and objectivity, and the origin of the video (i.e. produced by a professional news organization or by amateurs).

In addition to the civility and hostility measures discussed above, popularity was measured using four indicators—number of views, number of times a video was marked as a favorite by a user, number of ratings a video received, and the average rating (on a scale of 1–5). The level of engagement, or interactivity, was measured in two different ways: user-content and user-user (Ksiazek, Peer, and Lessard, 2014). First, the number of comments posted to a video gives a general indicator of user engagement with the content. Second, the ratio of replies to total comments in a given comment thread indicates the degree of user-user interactivity. Similar to the civility and hostility indices, the use of a proportional measure here captures the degree of user-user interactivity, controlling for the raw number of comments in a particular thread.

The content features and source of the video were hand-coded by four journalism graduate students. The coders achieved an overall percent agreement score of 82 percent with a K_n score of 0.72 (Peer and Ksiazek, 2011). For content features, we focused on election videos (content topic) and measures of objectivity. First, we restricted the analysis of civility/hostility to only those videos identified as 'election videos,' part of a broader categorical variable capturing the content topic of each video. We measured bias vs. objectivity with three variables: fairness, sourcing, and agenda. Fairness indicates whether or not a video includes multiple sides of a story, where multiple sides signal objectivity. Sourcing refers to whether a video utilizes outside, or secondary, sources of information, where the use of sources indicates objectivity. The coders were also asked to ascertain whether a video was promoting an agenda, with the lack of an agenda indicating an objective video. Finally, to explore the origin of the videos, we identified videos as originating with a "TV news or other public affairs program" (Professional) and those identified as 'user-generated' content (Amateur).

We found that language in user comments on YouTube is generally more civil than hostile. On average, 6.31 percent of the words that appear in user comments are civil and 2.07 percent of words are hostile. Analysis of the subset of election videos exhibits a similar pattern with more civil than hostile language (6.33 percent and 2.15 percent, respectively). Further tests show a weak, but significant correlation between hostility and civility ($r = 0.103$, $p < 0.05$), hinting at the potential for both hostile and civil discourse to co-exist in comment threads. In fact, 76 percent of all videos have both civility and hostility scores above zero. Nevertheless, the degree of civil language clearly outweighs hostile, by a ratio of about three to one. It is likely that some of the disparity between civil and hostile language is explained by the greater number of words in the civility dictionary (619 words vs. 351 in the hostility dictionary). Still, that ratio (1.76) is less than the ratio of civil to hostile language in the comments (3.05), suggesting that civility outweighs hostility even if we control for the number of words in the dictionaries.

Moving beyond descriptive data, we tested whether the degree of hostility and civility in comments is related to common popularity and engagement metrics (Table 24.1). Hostility was positively related to all six popularity and engagement measures. In other words, the more popular and engaging a video, the more likely the comments and conversation will be hostile. Civility was positively related to the number of times a video was marked as a favorite and the number of ratings a video receives, but was not significantly associated with any other popularity or engagement metrics. So, even though we find that comments to videos exhibit more civil than hostile language overall, more popular and engaging videos are more likely to exhibit hostile discussion.

Finally, we explored differences in hostility and civility based on the content and origin of the video. In terms of sourcing practices, biased videos (i.e. those that do not use sources) exhibit greater hostility in comment threads (M = 2.50 percent, SD = 1.52), while objective videos (those that do use sources) have lower levels of hostility (M = 2.04 percent, SD = 1.88) ($t(136) = 2.330$, $p < 0.05$). However, for the remaining measures of bias vs. objectivity, there were no significant differences in hostility or civility scores. We also find that user-generated

Table 24.1 Pearson correlation matrix for hostility, civility, popularity, and engagement variables (n = 515 videos)

	Hostility	Civility	Number of comments	Ratio of replies	Number of views	Number of favorites	Number of ratings	Average rating
Hostility	–	0.103*	0.461***	0.337***	0.194***	0.248***	0.141**	0.348***
Civility		–	0.082	0.056	0.056	0.122**	0.191***	–0.010
Number of comments			–	0.453***	0.514**	0.588***	0.600***	0.282***
Ratio of replies				–	0.030	0.078	0.082	0.127**
Number of views					–	0.578***	0.568***	0.290***
Number of favorites						–	0.719**	0.043
Number of ratings							–	0.043
Average rating								–

*$p < 0.05$, **$p < 0.01$, ***$p < 0.001$.

Source: Ksiazek, Peer, and Zivic (2014).

videos exhibit more hostile discussion ($M = 2.84$ percent, $SD = 1.56$) than professionally produced news videos ($M = 2.06$ percent, $SD = 1.84$) ($t(122) = 2.784$, $p < 0.01$). Despite these significant differences in the degree of hostile discussion, the findings continue to suggest that regardless of content type (election vs. general news; biased vs. objective) or origin (professional vs. amateur), user comments exhibit more civil language than hostile. The ratio of mean scores was approximately the same in all cases, at about three to one, civil to hostile language.

Discussion

Despite widespread assumptions about the hostile nature of online discussions, our findings show that civility outweighs hostility in comments posted to news videos, including news videos about the 2008 U.S. Presidential election. At the same time, we find that civility and hostility do co-exist in comment threads. The results also show that including sources in news coverage is associated with lower levels of hostility in user discussions and that professionally produced news videos exhibit lower hostility scores than user-generated videos. Finally, news videos scoring highly on popularity and engagement metrics are positively related to hostility.

These findings offer good news and bad news for the field of journalism. It seems the use of professional standards in news production, including the use of sources in reporting, is associated with more civil discussion among users. This is desirable from an applied perspective, as users are more likely to have a positive experience with the news, and from a normative perspective, since high quality news and civil discussion are the backbone of healthy deliberation. However, despite relatively higher levels of civility overall, we find that more popular and more engaging news videos exhibit more hostile conversation. This is portentous, as these metrics indicate not only what is attractive for users, but also for producers of news content. As news organizations struggle to remain financially solvent in an increasingly competitive news environment, they seek exposure (i.e. popularity) and engagement, which translate into increased revenue through higher ad rates and greater likelihood of being able to charge users for access to their online content. If the goal is to maximize popular and engaging content, news organizations may unintentionally serve up forms of journalism that generate more hostile discourse, regardless of any desire to promote civil discussion. The findings of this study suggest that these types of stories may integrate more user-generated content and fewer sources, since these characteristics are associated with greater hostility. This would be consistent with previous research that finds biased news videos are more popular (Peer and Ksiazek, 2011), and user-generated content is more engaging (Ksiazek, Peer, and Lessard, 2014).

This presents a quandary for news organizations, highlighting the tension between profit-seeking and public service motives: while popularity and engagement are highly desirable from a business perspective, hostility in user comments can undermine the deliberative potential of virtual news discussions. Some argue that establishing a set of rules for discussion and argumentation can facilitate more civil interaction (Herbst, 2010). To mitigate the likelihood of hostile user interactions, news websites employ a variety of tactics to discourage hostility. In fact, many organizations have policies to discourage inter-user hostility among commenters (Gsell, 2009; Pérez-Peña, 2010). Most require user registration, either on-site or through third-party platforms (e.g. Facebook, Google, Yahoo, etc.). The self-policing logic assumes that the registration process creates awareness among users that their personal information is known, even if only to the news organization, and this may decrease the likelihood of posting obscene or profane comments. A similar logic applies to anonymity among commenters, where prohibiting anonymous user names should promote more civil discussion (Santana, 2014b).

Thomas B. Ksiazek and Limor Peer

This seems to be the rationale behind the recent decision by Huffington Post to restrict the use of anonymous user accounts (Soni, 2013). Many news websites also have 'netiquette' guidelines that explicitly discourage hostility. Other strategies include active moderation of comments (through automated screening algorithms or regular review by digital media personnel), reporting protocols for flagging hostile comments, reputation management systems where users are rewarded for their discussion contributions (through liking and other recommendation metrics translating into 'badges' and other ranking systems for commenters), and encouraging journalists to participate in user discussions. A recent study of commenting policies across 20 news websites found that user registration, moderation, and reputation management discourage hostility in user comments (Ksiazek, 2015). Some sites are even replacing traditional commenting platforms with third-party social media platforms, such as the integration of Facebook or Twitter feeds. Beyond the general engagement benefit, this also has the potential to discourage hostility by holding commenters accountable to their broader social networks.

Efforts to discourage hostility are part of the broader normative goal of promoting healthy online deliberation and enabling the possibility of a virtual public sphere for discussing the news. Yet, civil and hostile discourse can and does co-exist and may be beneficial. Schudson (1997) suggests that democratic dialogue might be limited if people are too worried about being civil, and conversation sometimes needs to be robust and impolite. Similarly, Papacharissi argued, "It is not civility that limits the democratic potential of conversation, but rather, a confusion of politeness with civility. It is adherence to etiquette that frequently restricts conversation, by making it reserved, tepid, less spontaneous" (2004: 260). In other words, robust discussions could include impolite behavior and still be considered civil. Herbst (2010) argues for a 'culture of argument,' where civility is preferred, but incivility can also be productive in certain cases. All of this suggests that there is a place for both civility and hostility in healthy deliberation.

Future research

There is growing interest in studying the ways that users interact with the news in the digital environment. The conceptual/operational synthesis and analysis presented here suggest a number of future research opportunities for understanding civility and hostility in user comments. In our study, the civility and hostility indices combined to account for less than 10 percent of all language in user comments, on average. A more comprehensive linguistic or conversational analysis could shed light on the remaining 90 percent of words that appear in user comments. Related, this chapter did not address more extreme versions of hostility (e.g. libel/defamation; explicit, targeted threats of physical violence toward a fellow commenter). Research should explore the existence of these forms of hostility and the possibility of legal regulation of virtual discussion spaces. While the automated content analysis of comments offers good validity and reliability, as well as an efficient way to code such a large corpus of comments, a hand-coded content analysis would offer further insight into context-specific conventions. Future research would also benefit from replication across individual news websites to see if these results hold beyond YouTube (e.g. Ksiazek, 2015; Santana, 2014a). Another productive line of inquiry would involve testing whether organizational strategies for discouraging hostility actually lead to lower levels of hostile language. This would require data collection across multiple sites with varying policies in order to test which of those predict more civil discussion (Ksiazek, 2015). Researchers could also explore how varied story topics, as well as storytelling format (e.g. degree of multimedia features), explain the civil/hostile nature of comments. Finally, research should aim to better understand user motivations for commenting

250

on the news, as well as journalists' perceptions of user comments, whether they are engaging with users in comment platforms, and whether that has an impact on their own work.

Conclusion

Nearly a century ago, Dewey argued for a 'journalism of conversation' in which the news should inspire and facilitate active democratic participation and dialogue among citizens. Journalism is now deep in the throes of a digital transition, and interactive technologies offer greater potential to encourage active, not passive, citizens. Crucial to these efforts is the capacity for news organizations to integrate users into the journalistic process. As users increasingly expect to have their voice heard, news organizations should seek to provide a civil platform for users to engage with the news. Journalists and their audiences would benefit from continued implementation of strategies to discourage hostility, while acknowledging that some degree of hostile interaction can have a place alongside civility in healthy deliberation.

Acknowledgments

We thank four coders—Josephine Lee, Jon Sonnheim, Jessica Bobula, and Daniel Ellman—for their careful work and dedication, Susan Anderson and Beth Bennett for their guidance and experience, and Mike Smith and the Media Management Center at Northwestern University for financial and logistic support.

Further reading

The original analysis of user comments and civility on YouTube is available in Ksiazek, Peer, and Zivic's *Discussing the news: Civility and hostility in user comments*, published in *Digital Journalism*. For a comprehensive treatment of civility and incivility, see Susan Herbst's *Rude democracy: Civility and incivility in American politics*. Zizi Papacharissi has written at length about online discussions as a virtual public sphere, and Arthur Santana has done extensive work on civility in user comments on news websites (see references below).

References

Alonzo, M. and Aiken, M. (2004) "Flaming in Electronic Communication." *Decision Support Systems* 36(3): 205–213.

Gsell, L. (2009) "Comments Anonymous: Newspaper Web sites Wrestle with Offensive Blog Comments." *American Journalism Review*, February/March. Available from: http://www.ajr.org/article_printable.asp?id=4681 (accessed 18 May 2015).

Haas, T. (2007) *The Pursuit of Public Journalism*. New York, NY: Routledge.

Herbst, S. (2010) *Rude Democracy: Civility and Incivility in American Politics*. Philadelphia, PA: Temple University Press.

Himelboim, I. (2011) "Civil Society and Online Political Discourse: The Network Structure of Unrestricted Discussion." *Communication Research* 38: 634–659.

Hurrell, A.C. (2005) "Civility in Online Discussion: The Case of Foreign Policy Dialogue." *Canadian Journal of Communication* 30(4): 633–648. Available from: http://www.cjc-online.ca/index.php/journal/article/view/1585 (accessed 18 May 2015).

Ksiazek, T.B. (2015) "Civil Interactivity: How News Organizations' Commenting Policies Explain Civility and Hostility in User Comments." *Journal of Broadcasting & Electronic Media* 59(4): 556–573.

Ksiazek, T.B., Peer, L. and Lessard, K. (2014) "User Engagement with Online News: Conceptualizing Interactivity and Exploring the Relationship between Online News Videos and User Comments." *New Media & Society* 18(3): 502–520.

Ksiazek, T.B., Peer, L. and Zivic, A. (2014) "Discussing the News: Civility and Hostility in User Comments." *Digital Journalism* 3(6): 850–870.

Lee, H. (2005) "Behavioral Strategies for Dealing with Flaming in an Online Forum." *The Sociological Quarterly* 46(2): 385–403.

Moor, P.J., Heuvelman, A. and Verleur, R. (2010) "Flaming on Youtube." *Computers in Human Behavior* 26(6): 1536–1546.

Neurauter-Kessels, M. (2011) "Im/polite Reader Responses on British Online News Sites." *Journal of Politeness Research* 7(2): 187–214.

Ng, E.W.J. and Detenber, B.H. (2005) "The Impact of Synchronicity and Civility in Online Political Discussions on Perceptions and Intentions to Participate." *Journal of Computer Mediated Communication* 10(3): 1–27.

O'Sullivan, P.B. and Flanagin, A.J. (2003) "Reconceptualizing 'Flaming' and Other Problematic Communication." *New Media and Society* 5(1): 69–94.

Papacharissi, Z. (2002) "The Virtual Sphere: The Internet as a Public Sphere." *New Media & Society* 4(1): 9–27.

Papacharissi, Z. (2004) "Democracy Online: Civility, Politeness, and the Democratic Potential of Online Political Discussion Groups." *New Media & Society* 6(2): 259–283.

Peer, L. and Ksiazek, T.B. (2011) "YouTube and the Challenge to Journalism: New Standards for News Videos Online." *Journalism Studies* 12(1): 45–63.

Pennebaker, J.W., Booth, R.J. and Francis, M.E. (2007a) *Linguistic Inquiry and Word Count (LIWC): LIWC2007*. LIWC, Inc. Available from: http://www.liwc.net (accessed 18 May 2015).

Pennebaker, J.W., Chung, C.K., Ireland, M., Gonzales, A. and Booth, R.J. (2007b) *The Development and Psychometric Properties of LIWC2007*. LIWC, Inc. Available from: http://www.liwc.net/LIWC2007LanguageManual.pdf (accessed 18 May 2015).

Pérez-Peña, R. (2010) "News Sites Rethink Anonymous Online Comments." *The New York Times*, 11 April. Available from: http://www.nytimes.com/2010/04/12/technology/12comments.html?_r=0 (accessed 18 May 2015).

Reader, B. (2012) "Free Press vs. Free Speech? The Rhetoric of 'Civility' in Regard to Anonymous Online Comments." *Journalism & Mass Communication Quarterly* 89(3): 495–513.

Rosen, J. (2001) *What are Journalists For?* New Haven, CT: Yale University Press.

Ruiz, C., Domingo, D., Micó, J.L., Díaz-Noci, J., Meso, K. and Masip, P. (2011) "Public Sphere 2.0? The Democratic Qualities of Citizen Debates in Online Newspapers." *The International Journal of Press/Politics* 16(4): 463–487.

Santana, A.D. (2014a) "Controlling the Conversation: The Availability of Commenting Forums in Online Newspapers." *Journalism Studies* 17(2): 141–158.

Santana, A.D. (2014b) "Virtuous or Vitriolic: The Effect of Anonymity on Civility in Online Newspaper Reader Comment Boards." *Journalism Practice* 8(1): 18–33.

Schudson, M. (1997) "Why Conversation is Not the Soul of Democracy?" *Critical Studies in Mass Communication* 14(4): 297–309.

Singal, J. (2012) "Most Comments are Horrible—Sites Look for Ways to Make them Better." *The Daily Beast*, 16 July. Available from: http://www.thedailybeast.com/articles/2012/07/16/most-comments-are-horrible-sites-look-for-ways-to-make-them-better.html (accessed 18 May 2015).

Singer, J.B. (2009) "Separate Spaces: Discourse about the 2007 Scottish Elections on a National Newspaper Web Site." *The International Journal of Press/Politics* 14(4): 477–496.

Soni, J. (2013) "The Reason HuffPost is Ending Anonymous Accounts." *Huffington Post*, 26 August. Available from: http://www.huffingtonpost.com/jimmy-soni/why-is-huffpost-ending-an_b_3817979.html (accessed 18 May 2015).

Tate, R. (2012) "Youtube is Developing a Secret Weapon against the Internet's Worst Commenters." *Wired*, 29 June. Available from: http://www.wired.com/2012/06/youtube-commenters/ (accessed 18 May 2015).

Turnage, A.K. (2007) "Email Flaming Behaviors and Organizational Conflict." *Journal of Computer-Mediated Communication* 13(1): 43–59.

Zhou, X., Chan, Y-Y. and Peng, Z-M. (2008) "Deliberativeness of Online Political Discussion." *Journalism Studies* 9(5): 759–770.

25

DIGITAL TRANSPARENCY AND ACCOUNTABILITY

Martin Eide

Tradition is not a safe haven in late modernity, in general and in the press in particular. There is a need for justification and updated legitimation of journalistic practice. In the age of digital journalism, accountability and transparency have been radicalized, and as journalism faces new challenges and undergoes severe reorientations, questions of accountability and transparency are essential.

The basic idea that journalism must hold those in power accountable has been well established, but it is similarly imperative that journalism itself is held accountable by an informed citizenry. The thriving industry of digital transparency and accountability instruments bear witness to how serious the situation appears for agents in the journalistic field.

Justification required

The idea of accounting for journalism is not new. The Hutchins Commission (Commission on Freedom of the Press), expressed the concept in 1947: "If the press is to be accountable—and it must be if it is to remain free—its members must discipline one another by the only means they have available, namely, public criticism" (in Bennett, 2014: 105). Thus, a central role was attributed to the audience from an early stage in modernity. In order to fulfill this role in a meaningful way, transparency and accountability instruments have been required. Media accountability systems and transparency efforts can be interpreted as a reorientation to account for an increasing need for the justification and legitimation of journalism. The online environment for journalism radicalizes this situation and provides new opportunities for accountability by including audience members in a public discourse on journalism.

Transparency is conceived as a device to stimulate debate and reflection, build credibility, and maintain journalism as a public good. Journalism's social contract is a productive resource in this regard. Transparency also has the potential to challenge another core value, that of journalistic independence. It has even been labeled the 'new objectivity.'

This chapter reflects upon the possibilities and limitations of diverse transparency and accountability instruments in digital journalism. It also asks whether there can be too much transparency and investigates what transparency can and cannot achieve in order to explore a tendency to regard transparency as a somewhat magical idea with a capacity to maintain democracy.

In dialogue with empirical studies and academic reflections of Media Accountability Instruments (MAIs) and Transparency Devices, this chapter discusses current challenges for digital journalism as a public good. A critical question here is *how* accountability ambitions are realized, and to what extent such arrangements tend to degenerate into self-glorification and strategic communication. The chapter provides a few relevant perspectives for an updated understanding of transparency and accountability in theory and practice. Since accountability and transparency are becoming central maintenance tools in modern journalism, they require a critical analysis.

Digital challenges

"If you wanted to sum up the past decade of the news ecosystem in a single phrase, it might be this," Anderson *et al.* (2012: 1) suggest:

> Everybody suddenly got a lot more freedom. The newsmakers, the advertisers, the startups, and especially, the people formerly known as the audience have all been given new freedom to communicate, narrowly and broadly, outside the old strictures of the broadcast and publishing models.

A connected citizen often provides the first drafts of breaking news and also challenges and supplement journalistic story telling in many ways. Simultaneously, there are things professional journalists do better. Among them, Anderson *et al.* list accountability: "If journalism has an impact and part of its role is to force accountability in other institutions, then it must be able to produce accountability of its own" (2012: 27).

The internet delivers new opportunities for many kinds of user involvement and citizen journalism. It challenges journalistic rules and conventions and offers new instances of transparency to the lay public. We are provided with a chance to see how the sausage is made! New opportunities emerge for media criticism and new accountability instruments might follow. It is, of course, an exaggeration, to say that the internet makes everyone an editor and a journalist. It might, however, be more correct to say that "The internet made anyone a potential ombudsman," as Philip Bennett maintains (2014: 106). Or, as Heikkilä observes, "Media Accountability goes online" (2012: 3).

This move has prompted former *Guardian* editor, Alan Rusbridger, to reflect on the relationship between authority and involvement. He finds the second challenging the first so effectively that this old version is being demolished—the old version of journalistic authority being "we know, you don't" (Lloyd, 2014: 88).

The need to be open and transparent is paramount in this situation. "Journalism on the internet thus has no choice but to become more self-consciously provisional than it was before: open not just to correction, but to endless development, revision, and reformulation," John Lloyd contends in a forceful argument in favor of transparency (2014: 89). He sees transparency as linked to the enabling features of the technology and to the bias towards radical openness. The idea of transparency must also be connected to media criticism and media governance (von Krogh, 2012).

In a digital era, transparency and accountability furthermore apply in relation to automated devices like algorithms. As Nicholas Diakopoulos (2013: 2) maintains, it is important to recognize that algorithms operate with biases like the rest of us, and they make mistakes like the rest of us. Algorithms encode power and should therefore be subjected to algorithmic accountability reporting. The ways algorithms prioritize, classify, associate, and filter need to be properly assessed, even though there are severe limitations to transparency (see also Lewis, this volume). Corporations and governments are unlikely to be transparent about their proprietary systems, but need to be constantly challenged (Diakopoulos, 2013: 12).

In journalism, the gospel of openness derives as much of its inspiration from the tabloid tradition as from the liberal newspaper tradition. The tabloid or popular journalism version of transparency "believes that the public has a right to know the private behaviour of the political class—and of those prominent in every sphere of public life" (Lloyd, 2014: 82; see also Bastos, this volume).

The audience also seems to have a legitimate interest and voice in discussions concerning journalism. The so-called participatory turn in journalism also takes the form of an increasing willingness and ability to participate in debates over journalism. Often accountability measures are seen as means to improve relations with the audience and to restore professional prestige. Accountability instruments, then, appear as a kind of restoration project and as a tool for audience loyalty.

Openness appears as a crucial part of journalism in the digital age. Teamwork with the audience, dialogue, and interactivity are becoming more and more central in current conceptions of journalism. Digital journalism thereby runs a risk of blurring old distinctions between professionals and amateurs. Established traditions and conventions are challenged.

It has been argued that journalism, in a time when "we're all journalists," should simply be regarded as an activity, rather as an institution (Gant, 2007). The present chapter, however, defends an institutional perspective and stresses the need to conceive of journalism as an institution with a history and a possible future. Accountability assumes an institutional perspective. As citizens we cannot hold any blogger accountable. We are, however, entitled to hold professional journalists to account.

Definitions and dimensions

Claude-Jean Bertrand defines *accountability* as "any non-state means of making media responsible towards the public" (Bertrand, 2000: 108). Furthermore, he makes a distinction between internal, external, and cooperative media accountability systems (Bertrand, 2003).

It is, furthermore, important to distinguish accountability from self-regulation. The latter has a narrower focus, while media accountability also includes activities from outside the profession, like media-criticism and media watchblogs (Fengler *et al.*, 2014: 21). McQuail (2003) and others distinguish between four accountability mechanisms: political, market, professional, and public accountability.

Media transparency requires that media organizations "make information about editorial processes, as well as the journalistic actors involved in the making of news, available to the public" (Fengler *et al.*, 2014: 21). Karlsson (2010: 537) identifies two main kinds of transparency: *a disclosure transparency* and *a participatory transparency*. The second version implies audience involvement, while the first represents an openness, which could also be implemented in legacy media.

Comprehensive research on journalistic accountability and transparency is conducted through the project *MediaAct* (Media Accountability and Transparency in Europe). This EU-funded project traces emerging practices and innovations within the field—mainly in Europe, but also beyond, including many Arab countries and the United States.

The ambition is to foster a general culture of accountability and transparency. This should be easier in a digital and online context since, "the interactive nature of online media [...] involve[s] the audience in [the] moral reasoning process already during the information processing and editing" (Fengler *et al.*, 2014: 4). MediaAct distinguishes between MAIs along two dimensions: (1) from journalism-internal to journalism-external and (2) from a low degree of institutionalization to a high degree of institutionalization. Press councils will then, typically, represent a highly institutionalized and journalism internal instrument. Citizen blogs will, typically, possess a low degree of institutionalization and be journalism-external (Fengler *et al.*, 2014: 5).

Heikkilä *et al.* (2010) work with three forms of transparency: actor transparency, production transparency, and responsiveness. Actor transparency has to do with the journalists and agents behind the news, including transparency of ownership and publishing codes. Production transparency refers to "practices where media organizations disclose information about their sources and professional decisions made in the process of news production" (Fengler *et al.*, 2014: 6), while responsiveness is when media organizations engage in dialogue with the audience about journalism practice.

The three categories of media transparency processes and instruments can be conceptualized along a chronological line:

- Before publication (*actor transparency*): Public information on media ownership. Public mission statements. Published codes of ethics. Profiles of journalists.
- During the process of publication (*process transparency*): Authorship/bylines. Precise links to sources. Newsrooms blogs. Collaborative story writing with citizens.
- After publication (*media responsiveness*): Correction buttons. Ombudsperson. Online comments. Social media use. (Fengler *et al.*, 2014, adapted from Heikkilä/Domingo, 2012: 43)

In an international study of news people in the digital age, Fengler *et al.* (2014) conclude that MAIs are crucial parts of journalism culture.

In tracing journalism cultures, they shed light on how media across Europe cope with self-regulation and offer an instructive exploration of what impact is ascribed to different MAIs. An overview of MAIs in the project countries precedes the journalist's survey and focuses on (i) press councils, (ii) media criticism in the mass media, (iii) ombudsmen, and (iv) media blogs. This overview motivates a typology with the studied countries allocated to five tentative categories reflecting varying degrees of media accountability. The first of these is the most advanced countries, with a distinct culture of media accountability (the United Kingdom, Finland, the Netherlands, Germany, and Switzerland). The second category designates the advanced countries (Austria, Estonia, and Spain), where the authors, for instance, find that media criticism in Estonia and Spain is still in short supply, and, consequently, this category displays less transparency than in the most advanced countries. The third category includes the less-advanced countries (France and Italy), and the fourth, the in-transition countries, includes Poland and Romania, where the concept of an independent press council has not yet gained ground. Countries without any formal media accountability institutions constitute the fifth category in the typology and in the present sample are represented by the two Arab states, Jordan and Tunisia.

New media accountability and transparency instruments online are another key topic for Fengler *et al.* internet technologies have increased people's readiness to call news media to account, and it has become much easier for media users to be actively involved in media monitoring and criticism. This leads Fengler *et al.* to the following questions: "Is the time ripe for a participatory approach to media accountability? Are journalists ready to give the public a significant role in holding the media to account?" And the answer is: "Not yet, according to our data" (2014: 269).

Journalists across the survey countries observe increasing audience criticism online, but they still do not take their publics as seriously as they should, Fengler *et al.* conclude:

> While journalists strongly favour transparency about media ownership and also support the idea of publishing a journalistic code of ethics online, they are much less enthusiastic about explaining everyday news decisions in a newsroom blog.
>
> *(2014: 269)*

Journalists are still reluctant to open up their toolboxes to the public. Yet, Fengler *et al.* (2014) argue that media accountability and transparency remain vital in theory and in practice. Accountability and transparency can be a competitive advantage for quality journalism in a context with many new voices online fighting for our attention.

Accountability and transparency can, of course, also be used for self-legitimation and self-glorification. Nevertheless, the following recommendations for media companies, formulated by the editors, remain valid (Fengler *et al.*, 2014: 270f): (1) be transparent about who you are and what you stand for; (2) be transparent about what you are doing; (3) communicate and collaborate with your audience; and (4) accountability increases brand loyalty and the commitment to quality journalism.

If accountability and transparency are not reduced to a matter of strategic action, these recommendations might be good advice.

Agency

An accountability instrument is a particular manifestation of human agency; it can be read as documentation of an interplay between action and structure. In formulating and sustaining an editorial account, the agents draw on particular material and symbolic rules and resources. These features can be conceptualized in line with theoretical reflections on "the puzzle of human agency" (Abrams, 1982: x). I have argued elsewhere that journalism studies have to take into account theories addressing the interplay between structure and action (Eide, 2014) or "the process of social structuring" (Abrams, 1982: x).

From Anthony Giddens' writings, we know that the intimate interdependency of structure and action means that structure cannot be understood as synonymous with constraint (system compulsion). Structure is both force and choice, both restriction and incitement, both constraining and enabling (see, e.g., Giddens, 1979, 1984). In Giddens' structuration theory, structure is conceived as *rules and resources*, recursively implicated in the reproduction of social systems. In general, there are two kinds of rules in Giddens' account: *normative elements* and *codes of signification*. Resources are also of two kinds: authoritative (or symbolic) resources and allocative (or material) resources. I find it promising that this conception of resources includes both symbolic and material features. In order to understand journalism and journalistic reorientations, we have to take into account the different versions of rules and resources. We will have to consider the impact of the changing political economy as well as changing professional values. We will also realize that some resources, like economic ones, might be constraining, while others, like professional values, might be enabling.

In a working paper entitled "Media Accountability Goes Online" (2012), Heikkilä *et al.* conclude a transnational study (of 13 countries) by suggesting that it all "boils down to the level of economic and technological development" (2012: 69). The material resources available when establishing practices for media accountability are decisive and vary from one country to another. Correspondingly, we could assume that the supply of symbolic resources can constrain or enable the development of accountability instruments.

The most important and enabling symbolic resources for Western journalism is, probably, the objectivity norm. These days, transparency seems to replace objectivity not only as a symbolic resource but also as a strategic resource. When the implementation of objective journalism has been labeled a 'strategic ritual' (Tuchman, 1972), we could easily use the same phrase in relation to transparency. Transparency is the new objectivity. Transparency is a strategic ritual.

It is in this vein that Michael Karlsson (2010) investigates exactly how the media in the United Kingdom, United States, and Sweden utilize 'rituals of transparency' or working notions of transparency. He finds that transparency has begun to affect online news but is far from a fully fledged transparency norm (2010: 536). The online news portrayal "falls short of fully committing to the openness that is at the heart of transparency" (2010: 542).

What transparency can and cannot do

The flourishing of "Media Accountability Systems" and the celebration of transparency have also led to critical scrutiny and questioning whether there is "such [a] thing as too much transparency and what the impact of transparency might be on journalists and journalistic institutions" (Allen, 2008: 323). An even more basic question is: "Why has transparency, at this point in time, become an issue in today's journalism?" (2008: 323). David S. Allen suggests that transparency, "rather than serving as a normative standard, has become an instrumental value enlisted to protect institutional legitimacy and stave off criticism" (2008: 324).

Other researchers also find it in a certain sense reassuring that attempts to establish practices to hold media accountable are most numerous in countries where lack of media legitimacy seems most articulate (Heikkilä *et al.*, 2012: 70). A mobilization of accountability instruments is then a productive way of addressing a critical situation.

The critical question to prevailing accountability systems will always be *how* proclaimed ambitions to strengthen journalistic quality and credibility are realized. Do such endeavors promote a genuine public discourse on journalistic standards, or will the arrangement inevitably degenerate into just another example of strategic communication? Is the main objective from the editorial side mostly a concern with self-promotion and marketing? To what extent do accountability systems include genuine cooperation with the audience? Do such projects have a role to play in efforts to combat decreasing levels of trust in journalism? (cf. Eide, 2014).

Relevant answers to such questions are already provided in research on accountability and transparency. For instance, Kalyani Chadha and Michael Koliska (2014) examine how journalists in six leading news outlets in the United States grapple with 'transparency' in their newsrooms. Echoing Karlsson (2010) and others (Arant and Anderson, 2001; Cassidy, 2006; Singer, 2005), Chadha and Koliska's data indicate that the news outlets engage in a limited and strategic form of transparency but do not offer substantial insights into the journalistic process (2014: 1).

Allowing audiences 'backstage' information appears to be strategy to combat rising public distrust in journalism. With Joshua Meyrowitz (1985), we can see how new digital technology intensifies the changed relations between the traditional backstage and front-stage. A new side- or middle-stage is established (between the front- and backstage), where carefully selected aspects of the journalistic production process are represented and disseminated.

Transparency devices of different kinds, consequently, can be seen as answers to these structural shifts or this change in the 'situational geography' of social life.

Transparency can, under such circumstances, adopt a ritualistic and strategic character, accompanied by certain problems. Transparency might be reduced to "a promotional brand identity thing," as one of Chadha and Koliska's informants phrased it (2014: 7). This study also reports that there is "a tendency to employ social media more as a promotional tool rather than as a mechanism for enhanced transparency regarding the news production process" (Chadha and Koliska, 2014: 10).

As participants in journalistic teamwork, audience members also become involved in the profiling and image building of the journalistic institution. As Erving Goffman points out in his analysis of teamwork performances, "those who participate in the activity that occurs in a social establishment become members of a team when they cooperate together to present their activity in a particular light" (Goffman, 1959: 106). Simultaneously, there is more to teamwork than the performative and dramaturgical aspects. And "the individual need not cease to devote some of his effort to non-dramaturgical concerns, that is, to the activity itself of which the performance offers an acceptable dramatization," Goffman continues. But for how long will audiences accept being involved in teamwork that is exploited for marketing?

When the position of the participating citizen is reduced to what Goffman labels 'purely ceremonial roles' or 'window dressing,' the motivation for participatory journalism will probably be eroded.

Traditionally, cooperation and teamwork have been concealed. When Goffman analyzed teamwork and the presentation of self in everyday life, secrecy was the norm. "We have seen, and will see further," Goffman wrote, "that if a performance is to be effective it will be likely that the extent and character of the cooperation that makes this possible will be concealed and kept secret" (1959: 108). To some extent this has also been the case when the media have cooperated with their audience. Nowadays, however, the importance of *displaying* teamwork and cooperation seems to be a dominant trend. Audience involvement is then first and foremost a marketing asset and a matter of 'impression management' by the media institution.

Against this backdrop, it is important to understand what transparency can and cannot achieve. Transparency does not come with a guarantee for success from the relevant institution's point of view. Transparency does not always succeed, David S. Allen reminds us that: "Providing more information does not always build more trust, but rather provides more reasons to challenge the authority of the journalistic text. Transparency can provide the raw material to undermine trust" (Allen, 2008: 326). Following Stephen J. A. Ward, transparency can be conceived as a master norm and as a public good. But, when it is 'out of place,' "overhyped and replaces important values—it distorts the ethics of democracy and media" (Ward, 2013; see also Ward, this volume). According to Ward, transparency is more than a buzzword. Too often, it is a magical idea—a norm with seemingly magical powers to restore democracy. It is a "'god' of institutional ethics."

The value of transparency should not be overrated. It should, rather, be placed in a realistic perspective, as in Ward's following alternative:

- The basis of journalism ethics is not transparency. It is responsible publication for democracy. The latter is neither identical with, nor reducible to, transparency.
- Transparency is not sufficient for good journalism practice.
- Often, good journalism practice is non-transparent, like other democratic practices.
- Transparency cannot replace basic ideas, such as editorial independence. (Ward, 2013)

Is transparency replacing independence? A most popular slogan in journalistic quarters has for long been that of 'independence.' Independence from political parties was the first matter of concern. Later on, independence from sources became a proclaimed professional ideal. A problem emerged when the proclaimed independence did not contribute to providing journalistic qualities, but was reduced to a superficial posture and a cult of independence (cf. Eide, 1998, 2007).

As mentioned above, journalists furthermore have to use non-transparent policies in their work. For instance, shield laws—laws against revealing sources—is a non-transparent legal mechanism. The use of anonymous sources is not transparency but can be of great importance in accountability processes For the journalist to hold those in power accountable, it can be necessary not to reveal the identity of the sources involved. Transparency can be counterproductive under such circumstances, since it:

> includes revealing the background information not only regarding a source, but also the background information concerning a journalist. Bias is inevitable. However, what is more important is that a journalist or an organization reveals the background that they bring to a story.
>
> *(Carpenter, 2010: 194)*

Rachel Smolkin (2006) poses a productive question: Is the transparency movement getting out of hand? "You can almost hear the hot air seeping from our bloated egos, replaced by grovelling apologies and overwrought explanations to our fleeing readers." Smolkin writes in her vivid report, which imagines these addresses reading: "Let me tell you why I ran that story, made that decision, chose that lead, buried that other story that you, our readers (and bloggers and ideologues and cranks), thought was more important" (2006). Smolkin, in her critical take, asks the limits of news organizations' openness. At the core of Smolkin's report, she asks whether transparency is "always better, or are there dangers lurking within an otherwise healthy movement?" This represents a sea change in news organizations' approaches to presenting news. "We used to think that there was virtue in not focusing on ourselves, in treating the gathering of the news like the manufacturing of any product," former Philadelphia Inquirer Executive Editor and ex-Poynter Institute President James M. Naughton said to Smolkin in her report (2006: n.p.).

However, media-saturated audiences these days probably do care how journalism is made. And journalism seems prepared to provide the goods—through real dialogue as well as strategic approaches to justify its professional endeavor. In fact, it is decisive to identify and locate tension between strategic action on the one side and communicative action on the other. A democratic culture seems to be a prerequisite for instruments of accountability and transparency. Or as Heikkilä *et al.* put it: "Despite their inter-connectedness, it is clear that democratization is more decisive than media accountability. The latter may not develop without the other" (Heikkilä *et al.*, 2012: 70).

Conclusion

More than ever before, journalism faces demands for justification. The participatory turn in the digital era presents new opportunities and challenges for journalism. A wide range of accountability and transparency devices are developed and tested; dialogical forms of journalism and accountability have emerged, and transparency has become a proclaimed ambition in many social arenas. To media versions of accountability instruments and transparency devices, we need to ask: Do these devices promote a genuine public discourse on journalistic standards? Or will the arrangement inevitably degenerate into just another example of strategic communication through self-promotion and marketing?

Empirical research and further theoretical conceptualization are required in order to answer questions like these. As demonstrated through a comprehensive project by Fengler *et al.*, journalistic cultures matter a great deal in this instance. Transparency can provide insights in enabling and constraining resources for journalism. This challenge should be relevant both for journalism scholars and journalists.

Further reading

In *An Arsenal for Democracy* (2003), the editor Claude-Jean Bertrand promotes the concept of Media Accountability Systems and offers a productive overview of different MAS, or M*A*S, as he preferred to write. Bertrand's seminal ambition is followed by more research-based contributions, among which Fengler *et al.*'s (2014) are among the more comprehensive. A more general reflection of recent trends within the area is found in Bowles *et al.*'s *Transparency in Politics and the Media. Accountability and Open Government* (2014). In his PhD dissertation, *Understanding Media Accountability* (2012), Torbjörn von Krogh gives a thoughtful analysis of post war Sweden's handling of the phenomenon and the contested concept of media accountability.

References

Abrams, P. (1982) *Historical Sociology*. Bath, UK: Pitman Press.

Allen, D. (2008) "The Trouble With Transparency: The Challenge of Doing Journalism Ethics in a Surveillance Society." *Journalism Studies* 9(3): 323–340.

Anderson, C.W., Bell, E. and Shirky, C. (2012) *Post-Industrial Journalism: Adapting to the Present*. New York, NY: Tow Center for Digital Journalism, Columbia Journalism School. Available from: http://towcenter.org/wp-content/uploads/2012/11/TOWCenter-Post_Industrial_Journalism.pdf.

Arant, D. and Anderson, J.Q. (2001) "Newspaper Online Editors Support Traditional Standards." *Newspaper Research Journal* 22(4): 57–69.

Bennett, P. (2014) "Truth Vigilantes: On Journalism and Transparency." In Bowles, N., Hamilton, J. and Levy, D.A.L. (eds) *Transparency in Politics and the Media: Accountability and Open Government*. Oxford, UK: Reuters Institute for the Study of Journalism, pp. 103–122.

Bertrand, C.-J. (2000) *Media Ethics & Accountability Systems*. New Brunswick, London: Transaction Publishers.

Bowles, N., Hamilton, J. and Levy, D.A.L. (eds) (2014) *Transparency in Politics and the Media. Accountability and Open Government*. Oxford: Reuters Institute for the Study of Journalism.

Carpenter, S. (2010) "A Study of Journalistic and Source Transparency in US Online Newspaper and Online Citizen Journalism Articles." In Tunney, S. and Monaghan, G. (eds) *Web Journalism: A New Form of Citizenship*. Eastbourne: Sussex Academic Press, pp. 191–207.

Cassidy, W. (2006) "Gatekeeping Similar for Online, Print Journalists." *Newspaper Research Journal* 27(2): 6–23.

Chadha, K. and Koliska, M. (2014) "Newsrooms and Transparency in the Digital Age." *Journalism Practice* 9(2): 215–229. DOI: 10.1080/17512786.2014.924737.

Diakopoulos, N. (2013) *Algoritmic Accountability Reporting: On the Investigation of Black Boxes*. New York, NY: Tow Center for Digital Journalism.

Eide, M. (1998) Det journalistiske mistaket [The Journalistic Fallacy]. In *Sociologisk Forskning* no. 3/98. Örebro: Humanistiska institutionen, Örebro universitet, pp. 123–142.

Eide, M. (2007) "Encircling the Power of Journalism." *Nordicom Information* 29(2): 21–29 and *Nordicom Review* 28(jubilee issue): 21–29.

Eide, M. (2014) "Accounting for Journalism." *Journalism Studies* 15(5): 679–688.

Fengler, S., Eberwein, T., Mazzoleni, G., Porlezza, C. and Russ-Mohl, S. (eds) (2014) *Journalists and Media Accountability: An International Study of News People in the Digital Age*. New York, NY: Peter Lang Publishing.

Gant, S. (2007) *We're All Journalists Now: The Transformation of the Press and Reshaping of the Law in the Internet Age*. New York, NY: Free Press.

Giddens, A. (1979) *Central Problems in Social Theory*. London, UK: MacMillan.

Giddens, A. (1984) *The Constitution of Society. Outline of the Theory of Structuration*. Cambridge, UK: Polity Press.

Goffman, E. (1959) *The Presentation of Self in Everyday Life*. London, UK: Penguin.

Heikkilä, H., Domingo, D., Pies, J., Glowacki, M., Kus, M. and Baisnée, O. (2010) "Media Accountability Goes Online: A Transnational Study on Emerging Practices and Innovations." In Heikkilä, H. and Domingo, D. (eds) *MediaAcT Working Paper Series on Media Accountability Practices on the Internet*. Finland: Journalism Research and Development Centre, University of Tampere.

Heikkilä, H., Domingo, D., Pies, J., Glowacki, M., Kus, M. and Baisnée, O. (2012) "Media Accountability Goes Online: A Transnational Study of Emerging Practices and Innovations." Working paper. Tampere: MediaAct.

Karlsson, M. (2010) "Rituals of Transparency: Evaluating Online News Outlets' Uses of Transparency Rituals in the United States, United Kingdom and Sweden." *Journalism Studies* 11(4): 535–545.

Lloyd, J. (2014) "Transparencies." In Bowles, N., Hamilton, J. and Levy, D.A.L. (eds) *Transparency in Politics and the Media: Accountability and Open Government*. Oxford, UK: Reuters Institute for the Study of Journalism, pp. 73–94.

McQuail, D. (2003) *Media Accountability and Freedom of Publication*. Oxford, UK: Oxford University Press.

Meyrowitz, J. (1985) *No Sense of Plaze: The Impact of Electronic Media on Social Behavior*. New York, NY: Oxford University Press.

Singer, J.B. (2005) "The Political J-blogger. 'Normalizing' a New Media form to Fit Old Norms and Practices." *Journalism* 6(2): 173–198.

Smolkin, R. (2006) "Is the Transparency Movement Getting Out of Hand?" *American Journalism Review (AJR)*, April/May. Available from: http://ajrarchive.org/Article.asp?id=4073.

Tuchman, G. (1972) Objectivity as Strategic Ritual: An Examination of Newsmen's Notion of Objectivity. *The American Journal of Sociology* 77(4): 660–679.

Von Krogh, T. (2012) *Understanding Media Accountability. Media Accountability in Relation to Media Criticism and Media Governance in Sweden 1940–2010*. Sundsvall: Mid Sweden University Doctoral Thesis.

Ward, S.J.A. (2013) "Why Hyping Transparency Distorts Journalism Ethics." http://pbs.org/mediashift/2013/11 (accessed 12 November 2014).

PART V

Developing digital journalism practice

26

DATA, ALGORITHMS, AND CODE

Implications for journalism practice in the digital age[1]

John V. Pavlik

Since the earliest days of news reporting, data have served a fundamental role in the content of what is reported. The first newspaper, Caesar's *Acta Diurna,* in 59 BC publicly reported on notices of legal proceedings, marriages, and births (Wikipedia, 2015). In America's colonial press, newspapers such as the Virginia Gazette as early as 1736 published official government notices among other content (Virginiaplaces, 2014). It is not surprising then that twenty-first century journalism should place increasing emphasis on data-driven reporting. Yet the approach is dramatically different than in the past. Data are now Big, often on the scale of many billions (see Lewis, this volume). Today, computer code in the form of sophisticated mathematical and statistical models interprets and analyzes the data reported in the news. Moreover, human reporters, editors, and writers increasingly play a secondary role in generating the stories and visualizations based on the code-driven analysis of Big Data. Since the advent of precision journalism in the late 1960s (Meyer, 1971), computers and data analysis have played an increasingly vital role in journalism as a means to provide context for mostly anecdotal, event-centered news.

This chapter examines how the rise of Big Data and algorithm-based computer code are transforming journalism in the twenty-first century.

A code movement

Coding has emerged as a fundamental skill for working in the digital age in almost any walk of modern life. *Wired* magazine reports, "The UK is the first G8 country to include computer science education in its national curriculum, and the move could serve as a test case for so many other nations across the globe" (Lapowski, 2014). School teachers across the United States are joining code.org and the codeacademy.com in large numbers, for instance, to learn to code and to develop a fundamental understanding of how to bring coding, or basic computer programming, into the K-12 curriculum (Code, 2014; CodeAcademy, 2014). In fact, using the free mobile app from the Code Academy, anyone can learn in about one hour the basics of coding, including HTML and creating a web site.

The code movement is also making dramatic inroads into contemporary journalism, an industry itself undergoing a broad sea-change across the United States and abroad. As computers, digitization, and data have become fundamental to nearly every aspect of daily life, journalists and journalistic institutions have begun to recognize the central role that programming, or code, in the form of computerized algorithms or digital instructions especially via data-driven mathematical models, will play in news reporting and storytelling. The urgency is particularly acute in the domain of what has come to be known as Big Data, or data sets that often measure in the billions or more bits of information, often culled not just from government or big business transactional records. The latter has been a mainstay of investigative journalism since at least the 1980s, although it was born in the 1960s. Big Data often emerges from the world of social media, where millions or even billions of citizens across a community, the nation, or the world post messages for public consumption, consideration, and commentary. Oftentimes, researchers and reporters alike view these Big Data as sources of stories, sources, and trends.

Data-driven journalism

A world-wide leader in the Big Data news reporting endeavor is the *Guardian*. The UK-based news organization was once known as an important newspaper in the United Kingdom. But with the advent of Big Data and online journalism, the *Guardian* has become a global force in news and beyond. The *Guardian* cut its Big Data teeth in 2011 by using algorithm-driven digital analysis of massive volumes of Twitter and other social media resources to break down patterns and developments in the Tottenham riots that year (*The Guardian*, 2011). The *Guardian* made international headlines in 2013 when its reporter Glenn Greenwald broke the story about the digital spy program known as PRISM operated covertly by the US National Security Agency (NSA), as revealed through data provided by former NSA consultant Edward Snowden (Greenwald, 2014).

A confluence of data and algorithms executed through computer code and global network connectivity presents transformative implications for journalism in the age of digital, online technology. To do their reporting, journalists have for the most part over the previous century and beyond relied on interviews, press conferences, and first-hand observations of news events, supplemented by information culled from documents and other records of governmental agencies, big business, and other institutions. The rise of the internet and especially the connecting of nearly everyone and everything to the internet has fundamentally begun to change the foundations of how journalists gather the news, not to mention how they tell stories and deliver them to the public. As the public has become highly engaged in the arena of social media, especially enabled by the overwhelming public adoption of mobile devices such as smartphones and tablets connected to the internet, journalists have been confronted by at least two new realities. One is the public is no longer characterized by passivity when it comes to the world of media, especially news. Instead, the public is often actively engaged in helping to break news and re-transmit or 're-tweet' it. So-called citizen journalists or reporters act as a fifth estate, complementary to the fourth estate of professional journalists. William Dutton of the Oxford internet Institute (2009) calls these individuals networked individuals and underscores their role in sometimes gathering news but typically lacking any professional training in journalism. Lay reporters use their nearly ubiquitous presence while equipped with smartphones or other devices featuring high-resolution cameras and microphones to capture photos and video of breaking news events. They use broadband network connections to share their photos and videos almost instantly, often geo-tagged to provide exact locational information as well as time and date stamps in a digital watermark.

Second is the recognition that reporters can glean stories, trends, and sources by observing patterns of human behavior online, especially in the quasi-public arena of social media such as Facebook, Twitter, YouTube, Instagram, Weibo (popular Chinese version of Facebook and Twitter; Weibo, 2014) and beyond in massive databases available in the twenty-first century. The tricky part is that the volumes of data are often so extreme and potentially fast changing that a human acting alone or even in a team of two or three (the previously standard *modus operandi* of journalism) cannot efficiently or practically in any sort of narrow time frame such as a reporter's deadline hope to distill the patterns in those billions of Big Data—unless they can create and use computer code that implements problem-solving algorithms to sort through them. The code often takes the form of if/then instructions where if a certain condition is met, then additional instructions tell the computer what to do next with the data, possibly counting or performing other mathematical calculations that reveal patterns in the data or outliers to overall patterns or trends. Algorithms are the instructions that carry out the intellectual tasks identified by the journalist or computer programmer to analyze the data, answer the question, or solve the reporting problem at hand. An algorithm itself does not necessarily need a computer to execute it, but given the massive volumes of data involved, only a computer can carry out the task, or algorithm, via computer code in a relatively short period (Wikipedia, 2014).

In the late 1960s and 1970s, the early version of such data-driven computer-assisted reporting was labeled 'precision journalism' (Meyer, 1971). One reason for this label was that in the past, journalistic methods although revealing, were often somewhat hit or miss, anecdotal and subject to the vagaries of current events. News often broke and moved from one topic to another without journalists often making connections to broader trends or placing news events into context, historical, sociological, economic, or otherwise. News reporting was not systematic or often precise. Data, which reporters would analyze in spreadsheets or with other statistical tools adapted from the social sciences, enabled journalists to place current developments into more context, helping provide more explanation and sensemaking to the news. A wide spectrum of news organizations around the world is recognizing the core role that algorithms and coding will play in the future of journalism. This sentiment is reflected in the agenda of the Global Editors Network (GEN) 2014 Summit held in Barcelona, Spain. A main session at the three-day event was titled, "Algorithm is the name of the Game" (GEN, 2014).

The rise of Big Data and the corresponding use of algorithms implemented through computer code to interpret those massive sets of numbers have begun to transform not just the occasional investigative report but journalism on a daily basis. A compelling example is *The Upshot*, a new data-driven news feature launched in early 2014 by the *New York Times* (*The Upshot*, 2014a). Employing a combination of Big Data analysis and traditional news reporting, *The Upshot* provides "news analysis, data visualizations, commentary and historical context from a staff led by David Leonhardt" on politics, policy, and daily life. Illustrative is a story *The Upshot* published on 21 May 2014. The report was titled "More Hispanics Declaring Themselves White" (*The Upshot*, 2014b). It was based on data presented by the Pew Research Center and collected by the US Census Bureau (Pew, 2014a). Some 168 million persons were included in the database. *The Upshot* report reflects the capacity to use data to identify precisely the trends and patterns not accessible when relying on anecdotal news reporting such as that provided through interviews with individuals such as eyewitnesses to a breaking news event. *The Upshot* (2014b) stated, "An estimated net 1.2 million Americans of the

35 million Americans identified in 2000 as of 'Hispanic, Latino or Spanish origin,' as the census form puts it, changed their race from 'some other race' to 'white' between the 2000 and 2010 censuses, according to research presented at an annual meeting of the Population Association of America and reported by Pew Research." The numbers reported and analyzed here are far beyond the ability of an individual to process. But via computer code, it is a relatively simple, efficient, and rapid task to sort through the millions of records and identify key shifts and trends in the population—and to do so reliably, accurately, or with precision.

The new data journalist

Fundamental to the news code as illustrated in this Big Data example is the new qualities or intellectual skill sets journalists must have to be effective in conducting data analysis. Not only must a journalist have a clear sense of news and news judgment about what is newsworthy. But she or he must also understand numbers, what makes them valid and reliable, how to find them, and perhaps most importantly, how to interpret them. This means reporters must have or be able to work with persons who can create code, or computer programs or instructions to process large data sets. In the case of David Leonhardt, the managing editor of *The Upshot*, this combination of strong editorial skills and excellent mathematical literacy is clear. Leonhardt has extensive experience in journalism at both the *New York Times* and the *Washington Post*. He previously served as *The Times*' Washington bureau chief and was an economics columnist. "He is the author of the e-book, 'Here's the Deal: How Washington Can Solve the Deficit and Spur Growth,' published by The Times and Byliner." He also knows about numbers, having studied applied mathematics at Yale (Leonhardt, 2015).

Further underscoring its commitment to data-driven journalism and the central role of coding to the news process, *The Times* also in 2014 hired as its Chief Data Scientist Columbia University engineering school faculty member Dr Chris Wiggins, associate professor of applied mathematics (Engineering.columbia.edu, 2014). Co-founder of hackNY, Wiggens says the following about his new post. "the *New York Times* is creating a machine learning group to help learn from data about the content it produces and the way readers consume and navigate that content." Adding, "As a highly trafficked site with a broad diversity of typical user patterns, the *New York Times* has a tremendous opportunity to listen to its readers at web scale."

Four consequences for journalism

As indicated in Table 26.1, the emergence of coding, data, and online connectivity brings at least four sets of implications for journalism. First, coding, Big Data, and global connectivity are fueling fundamental shifts in the methods of doing journalism and news production. News media are increasingly relying on the use of computer algorithms to help in the analysis of large data sets. These computer instructions or code help to sort data, find patterns, and identify outliers that may signal newsworthiness in the data. Widespread public use of social media, particularly via mobile media and increasingly wearable devices (see Westlund, this volume), is enabling journalistic access to massive data sets generated by public sources such as Twitter, Facebook, and YouTube. Digital enterprises such as Facebook, Twitter, and Google are using data-driven algorithms to deliver customized news to their users, as well. Facebook's news feed, for instance, provides a stream of updates, photos, videos, and stories to users all based on computer code that tries to predict the news each user wants to see or might enjoy (Somaiya, 2014). With 30 percent of US adults getting their news from Facebook, this is an important development (Pew, 2014b).

Table 26.1 Impact of data, algorithms, and code on journalism

Technology	Methods of production	Content and storytelling	Management, finance, and law	Who is a journalist?
Coding and Big Data	Algorithms to analyze large data sets	Data-driven visualizations, precision and quality, machine-written stories	Changing culture, complexity	Applied mathematicians, programmers
Connectivity	Social media, mobile media, wearable media	Interactivity with public, context	Public engagement, First Amendment and public	Citizen reporters

Second, these same forces are triggering a series of changes in the content and storytelling in journalism. Data-driven visualizations are increasingly common in all forms of journalism. In addition, algorithms are generating an increasing array of news stories, from sports to finance to science and crime. The *Los Angeles Times*, for instance, in early 2014 used the 'Quakebot' to capture in real-time a data feed from the US Geological Survey about a 4.2 magnitude earthquake in Southern California, write the story, alert a human editor to the breaking news, and send a story for publication on LATimes.com within moments of the earthquake event (Slate, 2014). In addition, the level of interaction with the public in the news is rising dramatically as reporters, editors, and members of the public participate together in social media networks revolving around news and issues of public importance. Perhaps most importantly, data-driven reporting and analysis is generating qualitatively different news reporting that places current developments and trends into broader context. In contrast to much traditional reporting that often emphasized the anecdotal, data-driven reporting enabled by code or algorithms is helping journalists identify trends, patterns, and broad developments, giving the much-needed context often missing in the past. In one case, Craig Silverman, a journalist and fellow at the Tow Center for Digital Journalism at Columbia University, has developed Emergent (2014), an algorithm-based tool that tracks the dissemination of rumors online. One rumor started on 25 September and shared by 10,951 persons as of 27 September 2014 is the claim that the family of a female United Arab Emirates (UAE) pilot bombing ISIS disowned her. Emergent fact-checking confirmed this rumor was false.

The *AP* is also making increasing use of computer code and algorithms to automatically report financial news stories, as reported in January 2015 (McFarland, 2015; see also Carlson, Lewis, this volume). Using automation, the *AP* has been able to increase its coverage of financial news stories based on corporate earnings reports from 300 stories in the final quarter of the year to more than 3,000, without hiring any new human staff. Code is used to cull through the reports and generate narratives summarizing the key elements of each report. The use of code has enabled a 10-fold increase in reporting efficiency.

Third, coding, data, and connectivity are all driving change in the newsroom itself, fostering organizational, managerial, and financial changes. Although not framed as a result of news code, the 2014 firing of *The Times* Executive Editor Jill Abramson may very well have been at least a partial by-product of the rise of a new digital culture in the newsroom. Early evidence suggests Abramson may not have embraced some of the cultural shifts in the networked, digital newsroom that places an increasing premium on data and the public. As noted in his blog column, *New Yorker* media critic Ken Auletta (2014) wrote of Abramson, "She was, and is, in other words, a complicated person, who might have been, arguably, better suited to the work of an investigative reporter than the leader of a big, fractious, evolving newsroom in the modern era."

Furthermore, the rise of social networking media as a nearly ubiquitous phenomenon in the United States and globally has fostered unparalleled levels of public engagement in public communication. Fully 20 percent (1.3 billion) of the Earth's human population uses Facebook monthly, and most of them use the social media's algorithm-driven news feed (Pew, 2014b). Yet, it is unclear the extent to which First Amendment protections of freedom of speech will extend to members of the public, even when acting as reporters. There is yet to be enacted in the United States a national shield law to protect reporters and even if one should pass into law, it may not protect the public (Society of Professional Journalists, 2014).

And this speaks directly to the fourth area of impact: who is doing journalism. The world of journalism in the analog age was one largely dominated by professionally employed journalists working for news organizations both large and small, sometimes for profit and other times operating exclusively in the public interest. The rise of coding, Big Data, and network connectivity has ushered in at least two new classes of journalists. One is the applied mathematician, the computer programmer, who may have little formal background or experience in professional journalism. She or he may have extensive experience as a news consumer and may care greatly about the role of journalism in public life. But her or his first area of expertise likely is in processing data, creating code to process data, and interpreting and analyzing data.

A second is the citizen journalist or reporter who is often equipped with an internet-connected device and able to shoot pictures or video of possible breaking news and share it via social networks or directly with news media. These citizen reporters act as a fifth estate or branch of government complementary to the fourth estate, or professional journalism, that has long acted as a check on the other three branches of US government, the executive, legislative, and judicial.

Notable here is the September, 2014 introduction of Apple's iPhone 6, the first in a new generation of smart phones that locks out the National Security Administration (NSA). The *New York Times* reports that the phone encrypts email, photos, and contacts using an algorithm unique to each user and to which Apple does not hold the key (Sanger and Chen, 2014). This closes the door to NSA surveillance, previously revealed by former NSA subcontractor Edward Snowden.

Concluding reflections: deciphering data, algorithms, and code

Coding, Big Data, and public connectivity via the internet represent a shift in the tectonic plates that undergird modern journalism. The confluence of these three developments is reshaping journalism on at least four levels across the world. These include (1) basic changes in the way journalists and journalism organizations do their work, their news reporting, (2) new forms of content and storytelling, especially data visualizations and context to once predominantly anecdotal storytelling, (3) structural changes in the news industry, culture, financing, and regulation, and (4) the essential notion of who is a journalist, with coders and machine writing entering the news mainstream alongside citizen journalists and reporters (see Carlson, this volume). Fundamentally, these forces are leading to a transformation in the quality of journalism in the online, digital age. Context is emerging as an increasingly common feature of news reporting at leading innovative media. Further research is needed to determine the extent to which these developments characterize news organizations more generally around the world.

Yet, the news code is far more than just a set of algorithms that process Big Data. The news code is also a reference to the 'genetic code' that constitutes the essence of journalism. In other words, the news code refers to the values (Fuller, 1996; Kovach and Rosenstiel, 2007) and principles, ethics, and practices that define journalism, how it is practiced and its role in society. This code is also evolving as changing technologies fundamentally lead to a reshaping of the financial, cultural, legal, and regulatory context for journalism. The once hallowed separation of the editorial and business sides of journalism is an increasingly blurred boundary in the age of code, Big Data, and network connectivity. As commercial and even non-profit news organizations grope for new funding models, the line between news and entertainment, objective reporting and opinion are growing less distinct. When newspapers, television, and radio stations held near monopoly control over local or regional news markets and advertisers had few options for reaching their potential consumers, highly profitable and well-funded news organizations could establish firm and clear rules regarding the definition of news, the ethics that guided reporting and the separation of the business side of the operation.

In an age where algorithms and social media increasingly rule e-commerce and global leviathans such as Google, Facebook, and Twitter command the lion's share of the digital marketing space, traditional news operations are forced to adapt and play by increasingly new rules and protocols to keep from hemorrhaging staff and content enterprises.

As the practices and techniques evolve, it is essential to maintain a vigorous commitment to the central role of journalism in democracy. The pressure to deliver the news quickly, cheaply, and efficiently must not lead to a sacrifice in the pursuit of truth, excellence, and independence. Fact-checking, a once critical process to ensure the accuracy of reporting, has often suffered in an era of cutbacks and staff reductions. It is vital to restore quality, rigorous fact-checking. This may mean invigorating the news gathering process with more crowdsourcing and other creative approaches to further engage the public and diversify sources of news.

Journalism, journalists, and the public urgently need leadership that can offer not only an innovative vision for a new data-driven paradigm of journalism but also one that can find a solid financial foundation and an ethical compass that will restore, even strengthen the public trust. Public trust is the cornerstone of an effective news media system. Without trust, without credibility, the public will turn even further away from professional news media. Gallup polling data show that public trust in the media is at a near all-time low, with just 44 percent of the American public saying they have a "great deal or fair amount of trust and confidence in the mass media" (2014). Bold leadership that establishes a model for vigorous journalism combining the best of traditional reporting and news values with new approaches based on data, algorithms, and public engagement can build a viable new news code for the twenty-first century.

Finally, we might also consider the news code in the spirit of *The Da Vinci Code*, a bestselling mystery novel by Dan Brown (2003) and later a blockbuster movie in which a secret code is thought to be embedded in the work of Leonardo da Vinci. In the context of the news code, one might consider the central notion that the greatest journalism reveals the secrets many of those in power seek to keep secret, not just because they could prove embarrassing but because they would reveal some substantial wrong-doing. Unraveling those secrets is the detective work of Pulitzer Prize winning journalists such as Carl Bernstein and Bob Woodward in their investigation of the 1972 Watergate break-in that lead to the resignation of US President Richard M. Nixon. In the digital age, journalists around the world should find creative ways to employ data, code, and critical, independent thinking to decipher the myriad stories and secrets hidden in the activities of often-global enterprises, governments and other institutions, and individuals whose power and secrecy often exceed and overwhelms freedom of speech and press while masking criminal activity and other abuses.

Further reading

Informing this chapter are several works, including Ken Auletta's *New Yorker* column "Why Jill Abramson Was Fired" (12 March 2015) and William H. Dutton's *The Fifth Estate Emerging through the Network of Networks* (2009). Providing professional perspective on the impact of algorithms in global journalism is Matt McFarland's the *Washington Post* article, "Associated Press looks to expand its automated stories program following successful launch" (29 January 2015). The Pew study, "How Social Media is Reshaping News," offers insight on the impact of social media networks on journalism (24 September 2014).

Note

1 An earlier version of this paper was presented at the fourth annual conference on cyber-journalism in Porto, Portugal, 4 December 2014.

References

Auletta, K. (2014) "Why Jill Abramsom was Fired." *The New Yorker*. May. Available from: http://www.newyorker.com/online/blogs/currency/2014/05/why-jill-abramson-was-fired-part-three.html (12 March 2015).

Brown, D. (2003) *The da Vinci Code*. New York, NY: Doubleday.

Code (2014) Available from: http://code.org/ (12 March 2015).

CodeAcademy (2014) Available from: http://codeacademy.com (12 March 2015).

Dutton, W.H. (2009) "The Fifth Estate Emerging through the Network of Networks." *Prometheus* 27: 1–15.

Emergent (2014) Available from: http://www.emergent.info/ (12 March 2015).

Engineering.columbia.edu (2014) "NY Times Taps Prof. Wiggins as Chief Data Scientist." Available from: http://engineering.columbia.edu/ny-times-taps-prof-wiggins-chief-data-scientist (21 May 2015).

Fuller, J. (1996) *News Values: Ideas for an Information Age*. Chicago, IL: University of Chicago Press.

Gallup (2014) Available from: http://www.gallup.com/poll/164459/trust-media-recovers-slightly-time-low.aspx (21 May 2015).

GEN (2014) *Algorithm the Name of the Game*. Barcelona, Spain: GEN Summit.

Greenwald, G. *The Guardian*. Available from: http://www.theguardian.com/commentisfree/series/glenn-greenwald-security-liberty+world/the-nsa-files (21 May 2015).

Kovach, B. and Rosenstiel, T. (2007) *The Elements of Journalism: What Newspeople Should Know and the Public Should Expect*. New York, NY: Three Rivers Press.

Lapowski, I. (2014) "The Startup That's Bringing Coding to the World's Classrooms." *Wired*, 22 May. Available from: http://www.wired.com/2014/05/codecademy/ (22 May 2015).

Leonhardt, D. Available from: http://topics.nytimes.com/top/reference/timestopics/people/l/david_leonhardt/index.html (12 March 2015).

McFarland, M. (2015) "Associated Press Looks to Expand Its Automated Stories Program Following Successful Launch." *The Washington Post*, 29 January. Available from: http://www.washingtonpost.com/blogs/innovations/wp/2015/01/29/associated-press-looks-to-expands-its-automated-stories-program-following-successful-launch/ (29 January 2015).

Meyer, P. (1971) *Precision Journalism: A Reporter's Guide to Social Science Methods*. Washington, DC: Rowman & Littlefield (4th edition 2002).

Pew. (2014a) "Millions of Americans Changed Their Racial or Ethnic Identity from One Census to the Next." Available from: http://www.pewresearch.org/fact-tank/2014/05/05/millions-of-americans-changed-their-racial-or-ethnic-identity-from-one-census-to-the-next/ (21 May 2015).

Pew. (2014b) "How Social Media is Reshaping News." Available from: http://www.pewresearch.org/fact-tank/2014/09/24/how-social-media-is-reshaping-news/ (12 March 2015).

Sanger, D.E. and Chen, B.X. (2014) "Signaling Post-Snowden Era, New iPhone Locks Out N.S.A." *The New York Times*, 28 September. Available from: http://www.nytimes.com/2014/09/27/technology/iphone-locks-out-the-nsa-signaling-a-post-snowden-era-.html?hpw&rref=technology&action=click&pgtype=Homepage&version=HpHedThumbWell&module=well-region&region=bottom-well&WT.nav=bottom-well (12 March 2015).

Slate. (2014) "Quakebot." *Slate*, 17 March. Available from: http://www.slate.com/blogs/future_tense/2014/03/17/quakebot_los_angeles_times_robot_journalist_writes_article_on_la_earthquake.html (21 May 2015).

Society of Professional Journalists (2014) "Raise the Shield!" Available from: http://www.spj.org/shieldlaw.asp (22 May 2015).

Somaiya, R. (2014) "How Facebook Is Changing the Way Its Users Consume Journalism." *The New York Times*, 26 October. Available from: http://www.nytimes.com/2014/10/27/business/media/how-facebook-is-changing-the-way-its-users-consume-journalism.html?ref=business (12 March 2015)

The Guardian (2011) "Tottenham in Flames as Riot Follows Protest." Available from: http://www.theguardian.com/uk/2011/aug/06/tottenham-riots-protesters-police (21 May 2015).

The Upshot (2014a) Available from: http://www.nytimes.com/upshot/ (21 May 2015).

The Upshot (2014b) "More Hispanics Declaring Themselves White." *The New York Times*. 21 May. Available from: http://www.nytimes.com/2014/05/22/upshot/more-hispanics-declaring-themselves-white.html (21 May 2015).

Virginiaplaces (2014) "Virginia Newspapers – Where Did They Start?" Available from: http://www.virginiaplaces.org/population/newspaper.html (14 March 2015).

Weibo (2014) Available from: http://www.weibo.com/signup/mobile.php?lang=en-us (12 March 2015).

Wikipedia (2014) *Algorithm*. Available from: http://en.wikipedia.org/wiki/Algorithm (12 May 2015).

Wikipedia (2015) *Acta Diurna*. Available from: http://en.wikipedia.org/wiki/Acta_Diurna (12 May 2015).

27

SELF-REFERENTIAL PRACTICES IN JOURNALISM

Metacoverage and metasourcing

Nete Nørgaard Kristensen and Mette Mortensen[1]

Self-referentiality has been described as a general feature of late modern society and culture due to the loss of 'grand narratives' (Nöth, 2007: 3). This tendency has also left its decisive mark on journalism. Stories-behind-the-stories and stories-about-the stories occupy still more space in the news media. In response to this development, a number of terms have emerged within journalism studies incorporating the prefix 'meta,' such as metacommunication, metacoverage, and metasources. 'Meta,' according to the Oxford Dictionary, is commonly used about work, which refers "to itself or to the conventions of its genre." Along these lines, meta-concepts are used in journalism studies to designate self-referential practices, which point to the text itself, its production, the field of journalism, or the larger communicative circuit: *Metacommunication* concerns the "news media's self-referential reflections on the nature of the interplay between political public relations and political journalism" during electoral campaigns (Esser, Reinemann, and Fan, 2001: 39). *Metacoverage* is used almost synonymously to refer to stories focusing on changing conditions for the production of news, but it is also applied to coverage of related areas such as war and conflict reporting (Esser, 2009; Mortensen, 2012, 2015), which is why this chapter favors the term metacoverage over metacommunication. *Metasourcing*, the latest scholarly term (Kristensen and Mortensen, 2013), refers to the still more frequent sourcing pattern in today's 'connective culture' (Dijck, 2013) that elite sources are brought in to explain and verify non-elite sources. A fourth term, *Metajournalism*, has been deployed to coin websites, on which users post and comment on news stories (Goode, 2009); however, this concept is not included in this chapter, which focuses on meta-dynamics in mainstream news media and professional journalism. Scholarly interest in conceptualizing the 'metas' of journalism gives a strong indication that these practices are becoming more widespread and visible in today's media landscape, even though only few comparative studies have provided quantitative data to support this assumption (e.g. Esser, 2009).

This chapter provides an overview and discussion of meta-practices within journalism. In particular, we pay attention to the concepts metasourcing and metasources. This priority is motivated by how these concepts are less developed than the related 'meta'-terms and add nuances to an issue of continuous importance and scrutiny in journalism studies, i.e., source relations and source criticism. Moreover, these concepts are of special relevance for understanding the professional practices of *digital* journalism. The chapter builds on existing research on self-referentiality emerging from the early 2000s. Even if meta-terms are now commonly accepted and deployed in journalism studies, important research has been conducted on journalistic self-referentiality with preference for a different terminology. For instance, Bishop (2001: 24) introduces 'ritual sacrifice' and 'synthetic self-policing' to designate the news media's self-critical practices in stories about their own performances, including citation of pundits or journalists as sources. Tumber and Palmer make a similar observation about the British news media's coverage of the invasion of Iraq in 2003: "journalists themselves constantly examined their own and other journalists' efforts, and commented on the communications strategies of other actors" (2004: 7).

The chapter unravels across four sections and begins by identifying the professionalization of communication and intensified source competition as a main driving forces behind the rise of meta-practices in journalism. In the second section, political reporting, conflict reporting, and media scandals are presented as three journalistic turfs, in which self-referentiality is particularly pronounced. The third section offers in-depth analysis of the concepts metasources and metasourcing, which may help fine-tune analyses of contemporary meta-practices and sourcing patterns in digital journalism. Finally, the chapter concludes with a discussion of metacoverage and metasourcing as examples of stronger and weaker forms of self-referentiality in journalism.

Professionalized communication and competing sources

The normative estimation of self-referentiality is far from settled in the scholarship in the field. On the one hand, meta-practices have been attributed democratic value for making the conditions for presenting news to the public more explicit and thus educating audiences to become critical of the bulletins presented to them and better equipped to navigate the stream of news (e.g. Kristensen and Ørsten, 2007). On the other hand, self-referentiality has been criticized for being a symptom of the self-absorption of journalism and the tendency to pay attention to form and process at the expense of substance and context (e.g. Bishop, 2001; Gitlin, 1991). This difference of opinions points to fundamental disagreement concerning whether meta-practices create transparency or opacity. Moreover, it accentuates how meta-practices both reflect on and contribute to the complexity and scale of the current news supply.

Research in the field has identified two main reasons for the rise in meta-practices, which both concern changes to the larger communicative environment of which journalism is a part. First of all, research into metacommunication and metacoverage has emphasized that the professionalization of political communication has spurred self-referentiality (e.g. D'Angelo and Esser, 2014; Esser and D'Angelo, 2003; Esser, Reinemann, and Fan, 2001; Esser and Spanier, 2005). Journalism, in response, conveys the new conditions for covering political actors, events, and issues, including the communicative strategies and performances of politicians and the role played by actors such as spin doctors, political pundits, commentators etc. (e.g. Bennett and Mannheim, 2001; Kristensen, 2006; Negrine and Lilleker, 2002). In particular, metacommunication and metacoverage pay attention to the interplay between media and political actors, which is often described in terms of a game or battle for power and control over the public image of politicians and political parties (e.g. Aalberg, Strömbäck, and de Vreese, 2011).

While the first driving force behind meta-practices stems from elite actors and their professionalized interaction with the news media, the second emerges primarily from non-elites and their use of digital media technologies, which has intensified competition among sources for media visibility and framing (e.g. Carlson and Franklin, 2011; Kristensen and

Mortensen, 2013; Mortensen, 2015; Phillips, 2010a). As increasingly important sources of information, the news media deploy content submitted by users or appropriated from social network sites. The material may also originate from elite actors who operate independently of, or in opposition to, their employing institution, such as whistleblowers leaking documents from political and military administrations (Mortensen, 2015). Even if these sources may help to uncover phenomena or perspectives otherwise unknown to the public, they often pose challenges to the news media on account of their subjective and/or decontextualized form rendering fact-checking difficult (see Eldridge, this volume). When deploying these sources, the news media often explicitly reflect on their value and validity as well as their defiance of source criticism, the backbone of professional journalism.

These two main tendencies giving rise to meta-practices sometimes meet. For instance, in the aftermath of terror attacks, civic unrest, and other major conflict events, the news media pay attention to crisis communication and other pieces of information conveyed by government, police, military, and other authorities, while also looking to social network sites for alternative sources such as eyewitness images and eyewitness accounts. In some cases, elites and non-elites present contradictory information, which in itself becomes a subject for professional journalism to (meta)cover by focusing on their own role in sorting out the various interests and interpretations. An example of this surfaced in the media coverage of the shooting of Neda Agha Soltan during the 2009 uprising in Iran. The international news media reflected on the communicative attempts by Iranian authorities to frame and control the media coverage by denying that events had played out as they were documented in video footage taken by bystanders, which was circulated intensely among opponents of the Iranian regime and in the international news media (Mortensen, 2011, 2015). This case exemplifies how conflicting narratives on the part of elites and non-elites leave the global media circuit entangled in inconsistent reports, which prompt professional journalism to resort to metacoverage and other meta-practices.

The driving forces behind self-referentiality in journalism—professionalized communication and intensified source competition—may both be explained in light of contemporary macro-structural processes of *mediatization*. Organizations, institutions, and individuals have incorporated media technologies, practices, and logics into their mode of operation (e.g. Hjarvard, 2013; Lundby, 2014). As a parallel development, the boundaries between media production and media consumption become still more blurred as users take an active part in communicating current media and news events. Mediatization has made the communicative environment more complex and contributed to an increasingly dense and diffused flow of information, as exemplified by professionalized media interactions and users contributing to the news, let alone the meta-texts and meta-performances stimulated by these two developments.

Self-referentiality in the coverage of politics, conflicts, and media scandals

Meta-practices are to be found across different journalistic domains in differing forms and to differing degrees. Research on this subject has focused mainly on political journalism and to a lesser extent conflict and war journalism, which are both highly marked by professionalized communication and the emergence of alternative sources of information. We would like to add media scandals as a third journalistic domain distinguished by meta-reflections.

As already mentioned, researchers have emphasized how political news, not least in connection with electoral campaigns, is greatly distinguished by metacoverage (D'Angelo and Esser, 2014; Esser and D'Angelo, 2003; Esser, Reinemann, and Fan, 2001). According to Esser, Reinemann, and Fan (2001), metacoverage of political campaigning does not merely constitute a particular reporting form and style but reflects a stage in the gradual development of the press from descriptive reporting around 1900; to coverage of campaigning strategies from the 1972 US election; to metacoverage emerging during the 1988 election. Metacoverage was in fact first coined by Todd Gitlin (1991: 122) in connection with the 1988 US election when he observed a "postmodern fascination with surfaces and the machinery that cranks them out." Even if the outline by Esser, Reinemann, and Fan (2001) of the evolution of stages is based on press coverage of US elections, it is transferable to other Western contexts despite differences in political systems and media systems (Plasser and Plasser, 2002). Similar patterns, albeit delayed in their emergence, characterize changes in media coverage of election campaigns in Europe: Weakening ties between political parties and the press, increasingly volatile voters, and the introduction of television during the second half of the twentieth century caused the news media to play an increasingly independent and intervening role as agenda setters and agenda stagers in election campaigns. For example, Zeh and Hopmann (2013) show an increase in personalization and 'horse race' reporting based on longitudinal studies of media coverage of elections in Denmark and Germany (1990–2010), and Kristensen (2006) analyzes the news media's intense preoccupation with spin, spin doctors, and the political game during the Danish election in 2005 as a response to the professionalization of political campaigning.

War and conflict reporting constitutes another journalistic arena marked by rising meta-practices (Esser, 2009; Kristensen and Ørsten, 2007; Kristensen and Mortensen, 2013; Mortensen, 2012, 2015). Similar to political journalism, this is linked to the professionalization of communication, but also to an increase in the number and types of sources available from conflicts which is a drastic change compared to the thorough communication control traditionally exercised during war and conflict. On the one hand, professionalized and strategic communication in the form of propaganda, information warfare, public diplomacy, etc., has played a crucial part in political and military strategies since World War I. The institutionalized news media provide a major platform for belligerent parties to disseminate information and sometimes disinformation on the causes, progress, and goals of a given conflict. In many instances, this instigates the dual strategy on the part of the news media of conveying the information pushed by diverse actors/institutions while at the same time engaging in critical meta-reflections on the interests vested in it. On the other hand, adding to the complexity of war and conflict reporting, much of the information made available in the digital era originates from participants in the conflict providing subjective, partial, or one-sided accounts, such as eyewitness images, leaked documents, blog posts, or content on social network sites. Thus, when referring to or including these types of source material, the news media often use the explanatory frameworks of metacoverage or, as we shall return to, metasourcing to emphasize that this is not necessarily a reliable source or simple, straightforward documentation.

Media scandals, or what Bucy, D'Angelo, and Bauer (2014) coin 'press crises,' represent a third domain stimulating meta-practices. They have in recent years shaken the global media system by revolving around the news media and their professional (mis)conduct. To mention but two recent and conspicuous examples: the *News of the World* phone hacking scandal which led to the arrest of several editorial staff members and to the closure of the tabloid in 2011, and the BBC-scandal of the long-term TV host Jimmy Savile who, after his death in 2011, was accused of the sexual abuse of numerous children. Media scandals of this caliber prompt public outrage, sometimes even official investigations, and they typically nurture debate and persistent criticism within the news media themselves about professionalism and responsibilities. In this context, metacoverage constitutes a strategic attempt to restore the authority and legitimacy of the news institution and of professional journalism among the public and legislators, that is, by engaging in public debates about measures to remedy the professional misconduct and avoid similar incidents in the future. Metacoverage on scandals may contribute to enhanced transparency, which scholars have pointed to as an essential part of 'the new ethics' of professional journalism in the digital age (e.g. Eldridge, 2014; Phillips, 2010b).

Why politics, conflicts, and media scandals are particularly prone to cause meta-practices may, to an extent, be explained by factors specific to the respective areas. However, we would also like to call attention to a few common denominators. Strong and divergent interests are vested in these areas, since they frequently evoke challenges or changes to the national or international distribution of power—that is, within the political system, the juridical system, or the media system. All three areas are frequent suppliers of major news events, which seem to increase the likelihood of self-referentiality. Moreover, the news media have traditionally played a great role within these areas and continue to do so, either on account of early and thorough processes of mediatization by instrumentalization of the media (politics and conflict) or on account of the news media themselves being the center of attention and primary actor (media scandals).

Metasourcing and metasources

While meta-practices have so far been presented and discussed in general terms, the remainder of this chapter is dedicated to defining and delineating the concepts metasources and metasourcing, which are newly introduced terms in the research on journalistic self-referentiality (Kristensen and Mortensen, 2013).

As a noun, the term metasources refers to actors, that is, elite sources commenting on and evaluating non-elite sources. For example, politicians, experts, or representatives of the institutionalized news media are included in the news coverage on topical events to explain or assess the information provided by citizens, eyewitnesses, or participants. Metasources assume this role due to their authority and power, without necessarily possessing exclusive first-hand knowledge on the specific case.

As a verb in present participle, the term metasourcing refers to actions, that is, journalistic practices of using elite sources on non-elite sources. Metasourcing represents an explicit form of source criticism by referring to professional journalists' routine of including (credible) news sources in their coverage to reflect on, validate, and grant legitimacy to information provided by other (less credible) sources.

A recent example of news coverage distinguished by metasourcing is the capture and killing of Libya's former dictator Muammar Gaddafi in 2011 (Kristensen and Mortensen, 2013, 2014). When the story broke, the institutionalized news media to a large extent based their coverage on accounts and visuals provided by eyewitnesses to/participants in the violent event. At the same time, the news media let this information be commented on, verified, or contradicted by metasources, primarily military and political elites such as political leaders, delegates from the Libyan NTC, and representatives from NATO, UN, and EU as well as news agencies and news media (Kristensen and Mortensen, 2013: 360). During the past five years, a large number of breaking news events have occurred linked to natural disasters or various forms of terror attacks. These major events were also characterized by alternative sources playing a crucial part in the mainstream news media's coverage, which included metasources in their struggle to verify and sort out the diverse accounts of unfolding events.

While metasourcing and metasources reflect the digital media landscape's information excess and wide range of new sources, they also reproduce professional rituals in news production instigated long before digitalization. On the one hand, these circumstances have challenged and renewed existing procedures for performing source criticism in professional journalism. On the other hand, professional journalists turn to traditional procedures and patterns to cope with the changed conditions. Credibility is namely (still) the most influential factor—deemed more important than availability and time—when journalists choose which sources to include in their reporting (Reich, 2011: 19).

Based on extensive interview data, Reich (2011) presents various strategies in journalists' use of sources to minimize errors. Among these are *typecasting*, that is, journalists' network of credible sources whom they regularly draw into their reporting; *practical skepticism*, when more sources are included to verify less credible sources; and *prominent presentation*, which refers to supposed credible sources taking up more space in the news coverage than those seen as less credible. These strategies reiterate the 'old' dynamics in journalists' sourcing patterns as articulated by, among others, Gans (1980), who suggests that the selection of sources is influenced by past suitability, productivity, reliability, trustworthiness, authoritativeness, and articulateness. Metasourcing is aligned with these traditional patterns for attributing credibility in so far as metasources typically represent authority by their connection to society's influential institutions (politics, industry, military, media, and expertise) and thus usually make part of journalists' conventional and existing networks. Metasources have adopted the logics of industrialized journalism, for example by being productive, reliable, and available for commentary and quotes. As already indicated, metasources often do not have first-hand access to information, but are nonetheless included in the news coverage because of their ability to bring expertise, credibility, and experience to the reporting. Likewise, representatives of institutionalized news media such as news agencies or journalists may be included as metasources, even though they are primarily recycling information and engaging in self-referential performances (Kristensen and Mortensen, 2013). In all, metasourcing maintains the authority of elite sources to sort out the different pieces of information at hand and contribute to constructing the dominant frames and narratives.

Metasources are included to comment on types of sources, which typically do *not* represent institutional authority, but reside outside the elite frameworks of the media, politics, academia, etc. This is in accordance with Furedi's (2013: 9) argument that authority is attributed to those who "are presumed to have power 'over the opinions of others,' they have power to 'inspire belief' and 'a title to be believed.'" These 'non-authorities' go by terms such as 'amateur,' 'citizen,' 'participant,' 'non-professional,' or 'non-elite' in different contexts. When available, visual or verbal eyewitness testimonies by citizens or participants often constitute the pivotal point of the initial phases of breaking news events. They are relevant as first-hand sources on account of their closeness to occurrences, but the information offered is also characterized by a high degree of uncertainty and limited opportunities for verification.

Even though the inclusion of new types of sources in the news media exemplifies the general tendency to question traditional authorities in society (e.g. Giddens, 1991), metasourcing preserves traditional power structures. As a journalistic routine, metasourcing also encapsulates competing hierarchies in digital journalism: While 'amateurs,' 'participants,' or 'citizens' take precedence due to their ability to bring authenticity, immediacy, and proximity to the story, 'professionals,' 'elites,' or 'authorities' are valued as sources-on-other sources due to their authority, legitimacy, and credibility. Finally, metasourcing also implies a reversal of these roles: Citizens have long been included in news reporting to exemplify, test, or challenge the narratives, decisions, and endeavors of elites. Today, these elites are included as metasources to test and validate perspectives provided by 'citizens.'

Metasourcing reflects the increasingly open display of editorial processes in journalism. During the age of mass media dominance, news content summarized the outcome of journalistic research and presented an edited version of reality based on authoritative sources. Metasourcing exemplifies how news audiences are confronted with various types of more or less credible information, presented by a variety of more or less credible sources. As a consequence, the audience takes part in the filtering process formerly performed exclusively by journalists, who turn from gatekeepers to gatewatchers, to use Bruns' phrase (2008). On the other hand, metasourcing may also be regarded as a way of guiding the audiences' filtering process. Metasourcing, from this perspective, reaffirms the role of professional journalists in a convergent media environment distinguished by dissolving boundaries between professionals and non-professionals: By including metasources, journalists demonstrate their exclusive access to authorities and, thus, emphasize that the institutionalized news media still represent an important arena for gaining or fighting for legitimacy (Hjarvard, 2013).

In sum, echoing the democratic arguments voiced in relation to meta-practices in general, metasourcing can be interpreted as a sign of enhanced attention to transparency in journalism. It can, however, also be interpreted as a sign that editorial processes have come under the pressure of immediacy to the extent that verification of information takes place live and front stage rather than behind the scenes, especially during breaking news events.

Conclusion

Three main terms have been used by media and journalism scholars about meta-practices: *metacommunication*, *metacoverage*, and *metasources*. In the shortest possible definition, the three concepts concern communication about communication, coverage about coverage, and sources about sources. Even though the three terms overlap by addressing different levels of self-referentiality, they also provide nuances to the study of the 'metas' of journalism. This not least applies to the distinction between metacoverage and metasourcing. Metacoverage represents a *stronger* form of self-referentiality compared to metasourcing. News stories characterized by metacoverage focus on the changing conditions for news production in light of professionalized communication acts and spin strategies performed by, for example, military and political elites. Metacoverage may be interpreted as a response by professional journalism to the changed communication culture in a mediatized society. Metasourcing constitutes a *weaker* form of self-referentiality compared to metacoverage by denoting the way in which authorities or elites, including the professional news media, are drawn on extensively to grant validity to other sources and bring legitimacy and credibility to the reporting. Thus, metasourcing coins an emerging, professional sourcing strategy and a new approach to the performance of source criticism in digital journalism characterized by competing types of elite/non-elite sources but also by the status quo. While new voices may have been given the opportunity to enter the news circuit with unfiltered accounts that challenge official narratives, metasourcing does not fundamentally change existing sourcing patterns or hierarchies.

Though different in 'meta'-strength or -explicitness, metacoverage and metasourcing may both bring opacity and transparency to news reporting by adding to the increasing complexity of contemporary information flows while at the same time striving to display the circumstances for the production of specific stories. These meta- or self-referential practices illustrate how the news institution and its professional performances are a focus of public attention and scrutiny in line with society's other institutions of power, but they also illustrate the news institution's professional strategies to manage this public attention.

Further reading

D'Angelo and Esser's 2014 article "Metacoverage and Mediatization in US Presidential Elections," in *Journalism Practice* 8(3): 295–310, offers a useful text connecting metacoverage to mediatization, while Esser, Reinemann, and Fan's well-known 2001 study "Spin Doctors in the United States, Great Britain, and Germany—Metacommunication about Media Manipulation," in the *Harvard International Journal of Press-Politics* 6(1): 16–45, represents a classic text on metacommunication, metacoverage, and professionalized political communication. Kristensen and Mortensen's 2013 article "Amateur Sources Breaking the News, Metasources Authorizing the News of Gaddafi's Death. New Patterns of Journalistic Information Gathering and Dissemination in the Digital Age," in *Digital Journalism* 1(3): 352–367, introduces the concepts of metasourcing and metasources. Finally Mortensen's recent book (2015) *Eyewitness Images. Digital Media, Participation, and Conflict*, New York: Routledge, offers discussions of metacoverage in digital journalism.

Note

1 This article is the product of close collaboration between the two authors, and we are equally responsible for the content. Our names are listed alphabetically.

References

Aalberg, T., Strömbäck, J. and de Vreese, C. (2011) "The Framing of Politics as Strategy and Game: A Review of Concepts, Operationalizations and Key Findings." *Journalism* 13(2): 162–178.

Bennett, W.L. and Mannheim, J.B. (2001) "The Big Spin: Strategic Communication and the Transformation of Pluralist Democracy." In Bennett, W.L. and Entman, R. (eds) *Mediated Politics: Communication in the Future of Democracy*. Cambridge, UK: Cambridge University Press.

Bishop, R. (2001) "News Media, Heal Thyselves: Sourcing Patterns in News Stories about News Media Performance." *Journal of Communication Inquiry* 25(1): 22–37.

Bruns, A. (2008) *Blogs, Wikipedia, Second Life, and Beyond: From Production to Produsage*. New York, NY: Peter Lang.

Bucy, E.P., D'Angelo, P. and Bauer, N.M. (2014) "Crisis, Credibility, and the Press: A Priming Model of News Evaluation." *International Journal of Press/Politics* 19(4): 453–475. DOI: 10.1177/1940161214541682.

Carlson, M. and Franklin, B. (2011) "Introduction." In Franklin, B. and Carlson, M. (eds) *Journalists, Sources and Credibility: New Pespectives*. New York, NY: Routledge, pp. 1–18.

D'Angelo, P. and Esser, F. (2014) "Metacoverage and Mediatization in US Presidential Elections." *Journalism Practice* 8(3): 295–310. DOI: 10.1080/17512786.2014.889446.

Dijck, J.V. (2013) *The Culture of Connectivity*. New York, NY: Oxford University Press.

Eldridge, S.A. II (2014) "Boundary Maintenance and Interloper Media Reaction." *Journalism Studies* 15(1): 1–16.

Esser, F. (2009) "Metacoverage of Mediated Wars." *American Behavioral Scientist* 52(5): 709–734.

Esser, F. and D'Angelo, P. (2003) "Framing the Press and the Publicity Process: A Content Analysis of Meta-Coverage in Campaign 2000 Network News." *American Behavioral Scientist* 46(5): 617–641.

Esser, F., Reinemann, C. and Fan, D. (2001) "Spin Doctors in the United States, Great Britain, and Germany—Metacommunication about Media Manipulation." *Harvard International Journal of Press-Politics* 6(1): 16–45.

Esser, F. and Spanier, B. (2005) "News Management as News: How Media Politics Leads to Metacoverage." *Journal of Political Marketing* 4(4): 27–59.

Furedi, F. (2013) *Authority: A Sociological History*. Cambridge, UK: Cambridge University Press.

Gans, H. (1980) *Deciding What's News*. New York, NY: Vintage Books.

Giddens, A. (1991) *Modernity and Self-Identity*. Stanford, CA: Stanford University Press.

Gitlin, T. (1991) "Bites and Blips: Chunk News, Savvy Talk and the Bifurcation of American Politics." In Dahlgren, P. and Sparks, C. (eds) *Communication and Citizenship: Journalism and the Public Sphere.* New York, NY: Routledge (pp. 119–136).

Goode, L. (2009) "Social News, Citizen Journalism and Democracy." *New Media & Society* 11(8): 1287–1305.

Hjarvard, S. (2013) *The Mediatization of Culture and Society.* New York, NY: Routledge.

Kristensen, N.N. (2006) "Spin in the Media—the Media in a (Self-)Spin?" *MedieKultur* 22(40): 54–63.

Kristensen, N.N. and Mortensen, M. (2014) "Non-professional Visuals Framing the News Coverage of the Death of Muammar Gaddafi." In Christensen, D.R. and Sandvik, K. (eds) *Mediating and Remediating Death.* Farnham, UK: Ashgate, pp. 133–153.

Kristensen, N.N. and Mortensen, M. (2013) "Amateur Sources Breaking the News, Metasources Authorizing the News of Gaddafi's Death. New Patterns of Journalistic Information Gathering and Dissemination in the Digital Age." *Digital Journalism* 1(3): 352–367.

Kristensen, N.N. and Ørsten, M. (2007) "The Danish Media at War: The Danish Media Coverage of the Invation of Iraq 2003." *Journalism* 8(3): 323–343.

Lundby, K. (ed.) (2014) *Mediatization of Communication.* Berlin, Germany: De Gruyter Mouton.

Mortensen, M. (2011) "When Citizen Photojournalism Sets the News Agenda: Neda Agha Soltan as a Web 2.0 Icon of Post-Election Unrest in Iran." *Global Media and Communication* 7(1): 4–16.

Mortensen, M. (2012) "Metacoverage Taking the Place of Coverage: WikiLeaks as a Source for the Production of News in the Digital Age." *Northern Lights: Yearbook of Film and Media Studies* 10: 91–106.

Mortensen, M. (2015) *Eyewitness Images: Digital Media, Participation, and Conflict.* New York, NY: Routledge.

Negrine, R. and Lilleker, D.G. (2002) "The Professionalization of Political Communication: Continuity and Change in Media Practices." *European Journal of Communication* 17(3): 305–323.

Nöth, W. (2007) "Self-Reference in the Media: The Semiotic Framework." In Nöth, W. and Bishara, N. (eds) *Self-Reference in the Media.* Hague, Netherlands: Holland Mouton de Gruyter, pp. 3–30.

Phillips, A. (2010a) "Old Sources: New Bottles." In Fenton, N. (ed.) *New Media, Old News: Journalism and Democracy in the Digital Age.* London, UK: Sage, pp. 87–101.

Phillips, A. (2010b) "Transparency and the New Ethics of Journalism." *Journalism Practice* 4(3): 373–382.

Plasser, F. and Plasser G. (2002) *Global Political Campaining.* London, UK: Praeger.

Reich, Z. (2011) "Credibility as a Journalistic Work Tool." In Franklin, B. and Carlson, M. (eds) *Journalists, Sources and Credibility: New Perspectives.* New York, NY: Routledge, pp. 19–36.

Tumber, H. and Palmer, J. (2004) *Media at War: The Iraq Crisis.* London, UK: Sage.

Zeh, R. and Hopmann, D.H. (2013) "Indicating Mediatization? Two Decades of Election Campaign Television Coverage." *European Journal of Communication* 28(3): 225–240.

28

LIVE BLOGS, SOURCES, AND OBJECTIVITY

The contradictions of real-time online reporting

Neil Thurman and Aljosha Karim Schapals

On any given day, online news sites around the world are using live news pages or 'live blogs' to give their readers almost minute-by-minute updates on stories. The format is especially conspicuous during major breaking news events but is also used to cover sports matches, ongoing news topics, and scheduled news events such as elections or the Oscars. Live blogs make generous use of links; they mix facts with interpretation; and they are often informal in tone, involving conversations between reporters and between reporters and their readers. The format is a crucible for many of the contemporary developments in digital journalism practice. Indeed a BBC World News journalist interviewed for this chapter says that live blogs have "transformed the way we think about news, our sourcing, and everything" (personal communication, 16 September 2014). Are such transformations to be welcomed, how widespread are they, and just how different are live blogs from the more traditional news formats both online and offline? These are some of the questions we hope to address in our contribution to this handbook.

Live blogs appear to be prevalent. Looking at the home page of one of the UK's most popular news websites, BBC News Online, on a typical day—15 May 2015—shows that two of the three most prominent stories were covered by live blogs: a report on negotiations between the UK Prime Minister and the Scottish First Minister (BBC, 2015a) and a story on British politician Chuka Umunna (BBC, 2015b). However, as a pioneer of live blogging, BBC News Online is perhaps untypical. To assess the importance of the format more broadly, we can look at data from the annual digital news survey conducted by the Reuters Institute for the Study of Journalism, which tracks the use of live blogs by regular online news consumers on four continents. Data from the 2015 survey show that, across 17 countries, an average of approximately 14 percent of respondents said they had used a live blog in the previous week. Comparing the nine countries that were polled in both 2014 and 2015 reveals that usage grew in more than three-quarters of those countries with an overall increase in use of 41 percent year-on-year (see Figure 28.1).

Such data appear to confirm the belief that, for a growing number of news consumers, there is an appetite for live news pages. There are a number of possible reasons why this demand exists and is growing: the availability of the format and of devices (such

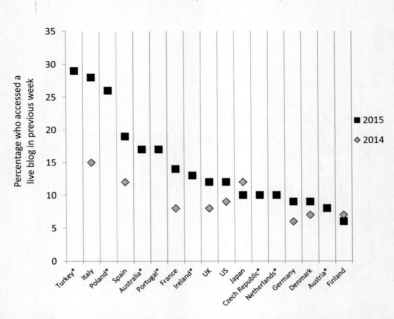

Figure 28.1 Popularity of live blogs with online news consumers in 17 countries, 2014–2015.

Source: Reuters Institute/YouGov.

Note: The survey was conducted using an online sample (2014, n = 17,822; 2015, n = 29,688) representative of the demographics in each country and excluding respondents who had not consumed news in the previous month (in most countries, this is negligible, but in the United States and United Kingdom it is between 5 and 7 percent).

*These eight countries were added to the survey in 2015.

as smartphones and computers at work) on which it can be viewed, a desire to be kept up-to-date with developments as they happen rather than simply receiving a summary in an evening broadcast bulletin or the next day's newspaper, and an appreciation of the format itself—its transparency, interactivity, and tone. While we do not present any new research on consumer perceptions of the format, we hope that this chapter will provide readers with a better understanding of the characteristics of live blogs and their production.

Historical perspectives

The lack of comprehensive historical archives of online news means that it is relatively difficult to trace the history of the format. Searching the Nexis online news database reveals no occurrences of the term 'live blog' until 2004, when the *St. Louis Post-Dispatch* alerted print readers to a live blog their reporter Gail Pennington would be writing during the last episode of the TV series *Friends* (*St. Louis Post-Dispatch*, 2004). In the same year, the *Ottawa Citizen* was promoting a live blog to be written by their National and World Editor, Peter Robb, from the *Canadian Antiques Roadshow* (*Ottawa Citizen*, 2004), and Washingtonpost. com linked out to a live blog (on an Alabama-based online news site), recommending it as a good way for their readers to follow Hurricane Ivan as it progressed through America's Southwest (Webb, 2004).

We do know, however, that the format was used even earlier, particularly to cover sports events. Thurman and Walters (2013: 99) mention an example from February 1999, which reported a Manchester United versus Arsenal soccer game. However, as in the United States and Canada, it seems that in the United Kingdom, it was not until the mid-2000s that the format started to be used more widely to cover breaking news and scheduled news events other than sports. Neil McIntosh, Guardian.com's former Head of Editorial Development, recalled that "the London bombings of 7 July 2005 was one of the first news stories [we] covered using the Live Blog format" (2013: 83).

Indeed the purely textual characteristics of live blogs find echoes as far back as 1923, when the *Manchester Guardian* published an 'Hour By Hour' story reporting the results of that year's general election. Although not containing hyperlinks—for obvious reasons—the story consisted of "chronological updates marked by timestamps" and had a "brisk, conversational, informal" tone similar to contemporary live blogs (Owen, 2012).

If we broaden the historical antecedents even further we can see the similarities between live blogging and live news broadcasting, not only in their shared concept of 'liveness'—with its "coincidence of three dimensions: spatial, temporal, and broadcast proximity" (Tereszkiewicz, 2014: 301)—but also in their shared tone, characterized, according to Tereszkiewicz, "by a loose frame and lack of fixed script [and an ...] interpersonal, multi-voiced character" (2014: 301). These shared characteristics are indicative of how live blogs are an archetypical example of media convergence. Powered by the fusion of video, telecoms, and computing, they are a place where textual forms and cultural practices are coming together in new ways.

Although he was writing before the emergence of live blogs, Roger Silverstone (1995: 11) worried about such textual convergence, which he called 'dangerous.' One of his concerns was that "fact and fantasy [would] lose their distinctiveness [... as] previously discrete categories of media content and function blend in an electronic hybridity" (2013: 11). Such concerns persist, including in the context of live blogs, and are discussed later in this chapter.

Definitions and characteristics

There is no universally agreed name for the phenomenon under discussion here. We, and some other authors (e.g. Sheller, 2015; Tereszkiewicz, 2014), use the term 'live blog,' echoing the usage found at news outlets including the *Wall Street Journal* (WSJ, 2011) and NBC (2011). However, other news organizations use different terminology. 'Live pages' is a popular designation at BBC News (Yolande Knell, personal communication, 29 September 2014) who also title their live blogs 'As It Happened' (BBC, 2013). Telegraph.co.uk (Hough, Chivers, and Bloxham, 2011) and Guardian.com also use the 'As It Happened' moniker (Clark *et al.*, 2014) or, sometimes, just 'Live' (Weaver *et al.*, 2015). ScribbleLive, one of the major suppliers of live blogging software, talk about 'real time publishing' (ScribbleLive, 2015a) and 'live content' (ScribbleLive, 2015b).

There is probably more consensus about the characteristics of the format. Thurman and Walters characterize live blogs as one of the "few web-native news artefacts" (2013: 87), in which "time-stamped content [on a specific topic] is progressively added for a finite period" (2013: 83). They go on to describe how live blogs include multimedia content and embedded material (e.g. tweets), how third-party content is usually clearly signposted (as are corrections), how the tone is informal and hyperlinks common, and how summary headlines are often used at the top of the story.

Anna Tereszkiewicz (2014) has built on Thurman and Walters' typology, producing what is, at the time of writing, probably the most complete attempt to define the format—based on an analysis of 56 live blogs published by two UK 'quality' news websites. Tereszkiewicz (2014: 302) says that live blogs typically have a macrostructure consisting of three main parts:

- "Introduction—general headline; background and context forming lead;
- Main body—episodes, up-dates on the event in question;
- Conclusion—summary of the report."

Like regular blogs, the episodic micro-reports are initially presented in reverse chronological order with "each block constituting an independent structure" which is "part of the larger whole" (2014: 302). The blocks vary widely in the content they contain. After text, Tereszkiewicz found that full size and thumbnail images were most prevalent, about 10 times more so than videos or audio clips (2014: 303).

Whereas Tereszkiewicz looked only at the internal characteristics of live blogs, we have compared the occurrence of multimedia elements across live blogs, traditional online news articles, *and* print articles. As Table 28.1 shows, live blogs—even with thumbnail images excluded—contain about 15 times more multimedia elements than print articles and nearly five and a half times more than traditional online articles. It should be noted, however, that live blogs are considerably—about 12 times—longer than the other article types, which means they have more space in which to accommodate non-textual elements. If we take

Table 28.1 Comparison (relative to articles' length and/or in absolute terms) of the number of external links and/or multimedia elements associated with quoted sources, number of quoted sources, and proportion of direct quotes appearing in the main body of live blogs, online articles, and print articles covering the Egyptian revolution in six* UK national news publishers, 25 January–11 February 2011

	Live blogs (n = 75)	Online news articles (n = 842)	Print articles (n = 148)
Average length (words)	7,241	593	618
Average number of external hyperlinks associated with quoted sources	22.39	0.456	n/a
Average length/average number of links	323	1,300	n/a
Average number of multimedia elements (photos, videos, and illustrations)	18.1	3.3	1.2
Average length/average number of multimedia elements	400	180	515
Average number of sources quoted	96	6.44	8.2
Average length/average number of sources quoted	75	92	75
Proportion of direct quotes (%)	68	57	54

Note: Thumbnail images were not counted in the analysis.

Daily Telegraph, Guardian, The Times, BBC News, Channel 4 News, and Reuters News.

these large variations in length into account, we see that live blogs have just 27 percent more multimedia elements per word than print articles and 55 percent *fewer* than traditional online articles.

Live blogs' divergence from traditional styles of news reporting may, then, be stronger in other ways, for example in their use of links. Tereszkiewicz (2014: 308) found an average of 20.6 links per live blog, comparable with Thurman and Walters' (2013: 91) equivalent figure of 16.25. By comparison the average number of links in traditional online articles has been in the low single figures (see, e.g., Stray, 2010). However, as we have already established, live blogs are more verbose than traditional online articles, providing more space for such links. So is their apparent tendency to link out more frequently simply a function of their length? Our research indicates not. The 75 live blogs we analyzed added external links to sources they quoted an average of 22 times per live blog. This compares with an average of just 0.46 links we found in 'traditional' online articles covering the same story. And even when the difference in word length is factored in, live blogs still linked out four times more frequently than traditional online articles (see Table 28.1).

In analyzing the sources of the quotations and the destinations of the links contained in live blogs, Tereszkiewicz's research (2014: 308) suggests that journalists and other media and news agencies are quoted most frequently, followed closely by governmental and political sources. According to Tereszkiewicz (2014: 308), live blogs' frequent quoting of other media sources "may be interpreted positively as a strategy aimed at providing readers with as complete a picture of an event as possible, together with various interpretations of the event." There are, however, other, less positive, explanations for such reliance on secondary sources, which include an increasing pressure to publish fast and frequently, and dwindling newsroom resources which keep journalists desk-bound and less able to cultivate specialist knowledge and independent sources.

Critical issues

The assessment of live blogs' potential to increase the quality, plurality, and transparency of news coverage is a key critical issue in any study of the format. Thurman and Newman (2014) found, in a survey of UK online news consumers, that those who agreed that live blogs were 'more balanced' outnumbered those who didn't by almost four to one. It has been suggested that this favorable reaction is, in part, due to live blogs' "provision of 'supporting evidence' and 'conflicting possibilities' from a relatively wide range of sources, and their transparent attribution practices" (Thurman and Walters, 2013: 98). There has, however, been no research that we are aware of that has tested this hypothesis by analyzing to what extent—if at all—live blogs actually quote original sources more frequently compared to other news formats.

A second critical issue relating to live blogs is the extent to which the material they publish has been verified. Angela Min-Chia Lee (2014: 47) has shown that US journalists believe speed-driven news formats like live blogs harm news credibility, as they demand journalists post "the newest information possible" even if that information has not been verified. Thurman and Walters (2013: 94) wrote about live blogs' "looser culture of corroboration" based on their interviews with live blogging journalists at Guardian.co.uk in 2011. There remains, however, very little work looking at live blogging journalists' working practices and the extent to which they are upholding established professional standards such as the UK Editors' Code of Practice which sets the 'benchmark' that members of the press shall not "publish inaccurate, misleading or distorted information, including pictures" (IPSO, n.d.). We present new research on this topic in the next section.

Current contributions and research

Our recent, and previously unpublished, interviews with journalists confirm Thurman and Walters' (2013: 94) assertion that live blogging has a relatively "loose culture of corroboration." A BBC World News journalist we interviewed told us that on live blogs there is 'less onus' to be 'close to 100 percent sure' about the accuracy of statements than there is on 'proper stories,' adding that it is more acceptable to use anonymous sources and to put out single, uncorroborated quotes. In the context of live blogging and using social media as a source, the two-source rule has become 'a bit more exploded,' they said (personal communication, 16 September 2014).

Yolande Knell, a BBC Middle East correspondent, also made the distinction between the demands of writing for definitive bulletins, like the BBC's 10 o'clock bulletin, and live tweeting or live blogging where—albeit with context—it is more acceptable to not be "fully accurate or give the full picture," because you are telling it as you see it at a particular moment, with the knowledge that the facts may not "stand the test of time" (personal communication, 29 September 2014). Laura Roberts, at the time a journalist with the *Daily Telegraph*, agreed that live blogs could carry unverified information as long as a caveat was given (personal communication, 2 October 2014).

We did, however, find evidence of discomfort with the developing culture around live blogging: "one tweet isn't a trusted news source," Krishnan Guru-Murthy of Channel 4 News told us, advocating that journalists should "always cross-reference with other sources" (personal communication, 21 September 2014). Indeed a BBC World News journalist thought that for live blogging journalists trying to reconcile the need for speed with the requirement to be accurate, the pendulum had started to swing back towards accuracy. Compared with "five years ago," they said, there is more acceptance that journalists can take an extra few minutes to "make sure this is factually right" (personal communication, 16 September 2014).

The pressure on journalists to report increasingly quickly was a major reason our interviewees gave for the looser culture of corroboration around live blogs. A BBC World News journalist (Ibid.) recalled rivalry with other news outlets—such as Sky News—about who could publish first, with 'competitions' sometimes decided by 'fractions of seconds.' Another reason was rolling news' incessant appetite for information. "You can't fill this hole on [live] news pages just through official sources, just through the old media—you have to look at social media," the journalist believed. Laura Roberts agreed, although she did not think the problem was unique to live blogs, drawing a parallel with 24-hour rolling TV news. "If you've got airtime to fill … you end up … elaborating on things that you shouldn't really be elaborating on … the focus on speed versus accuracy within journalism is a huge challenge," she said (personal communication, 2 October 2014).

The need to keep live blogs replete with regular updates is not only resulting, some evidence suggests, in a partial disintegration of previously established practices of verification but may also be increasing reliance on previously published media reports. Laura Roberts told us that when she was live blogging for Telegraph.co.uk she was using "Al Jazeera, Sky, and the BBC" as sources in order to be able to provide the live blog with what it needed as quickly as possible. In fact her impression was that live bloggers across a range of news providers were "looking at each other['s work]" for the same reasons (personal communication, 2 October 2014). Anne Alexander, an expert on the Middle East and occasional journalist for UK and Egyptian media, feels an important contributing factor is the "political economy of news production and the massive cull of journalistic jobs and the amount of work that journalists are expected to do without ever leaving the office, which tends to push towards using online sources." Part of the problem, she added, was that more generalists were covering international stories such as the Egyptian revolution. Generalists without "any specific connections with the country concerned are," she said, "probably more likely to fall back on mainstream sources" (personal communication, 16 September 2014).

This said, many of our interviewees still emphasized the value of 'being there.' Lindsey Hilsum, International Editor of the UK's Channel 4 News, recognizes the value of social media both in opening up "places that would otherwise be 100 percent dark" and in the provision of 'tip-offs' but maintains that she continues to do what she has always done: "Go somewhere. Talk to people. And watch. That is what journalism is" (personal communication, 15 September 2014). Krishnan Guru-Murthy (personal communication, 21 September 2014) agreed that the "best journalistic accounts are from the scene," as did *The Times*' Deputy Foreign Editor, Suzy Jagger, who worried about younger journalists thinking "Twitter is it … a replacement for actually going out and meeting people" (personal communication, 1 October 2014).

Such anecdotal evidence on the sourcing and reporting practices of live blogging journalists has not, to our knowledge, been triangulated qualitatively. We have attempted to do that and present some of the results here. Our method involved a content analysis of 75 live blogs, 842 online articles, and 148 print articles covering the Egyptian revolution of 2011 and published across six UK national news publishers. We found a total of 12,475 quotes that could be attributed to a source of some description. Given their length, it is no surprise that, on average, live blogs included 12 times more sourced quotes than print articles and 15 times more than traditional online news articles. However, when the differences between the average lengths of the formats are taken into account we observe that live blogs cited sources no more frequently than print articles (see Table 28.1). There were, however, differences in the proportion of direct quotes (as opposed to indirect quotes) between the three formats. Quotes in live blogs were 'direct' 68 percent of the time, compared with 57 percent for traditional online news articles and 54 percent for print articles (see Table 28.1).

Each source quoted in each article was assigned to one of 18 categories (e.g. 'Citizen,' 'NGO,' 'Foreign politician,' etc.) determined via a deductive explanatory approach. Because of the differences between both the number of articles we analyzed for each format and—as previously mentioned—the average length of each format, the results of this part of our content analysis are presented in a manner that allows for more direct comparison. Our method was as follows: separately for each format, we determined the frequency with which each source category was quoted and then divided that number by the average word count of each format.

The results reveal major differences between live blogs, online articles, and print articles, with journalists 'on the ground' and (foreign) media far more frequently found as sources in live blogs. Furthermore, live blogs—despite allowing the relatively easy integration of social media, such as tweets—actually quote citizen and activist sources less frequently (on a per word basis) than both traditional online articles and print articles (see Figure 28.2).

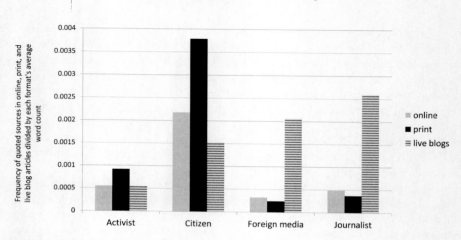

Figure 28.2 Frequency of quoted source divided by average word count in the main body of online, print, and live blog articles covering the Egyptian revolution in six UK national news publishers,* 25 January–11 February 2011 (n = 1,065).

Note: This graph shows results for four of the 18 source categories identified in the content analysis. The other sources were: Analyst/expert/academic, Anonymous source, Consultancy, Enterprise, EU official, Foreign government official, Lawyer, Leaked document, Military, National government official, National government opponent, National government supporter, Non-governmental organization, and State media organization.

*Daily Telegraph, Guardian, The Times, BBC News, Channel 4 News, and *Reuters News*.

Conclusion

The growing popularity of live blogs prompts questions about their appeal to digital news consumers as well as about how they are made and the extent to which they differ from established journalistic story formats. The new empirical data presented in this chapter—albeit in the particular context of a breaking international news story—suggest that live blogs differ materially not in their use of multimedia or even the frequency with which they quote sources but rather in their generous use of links and the first-hand nature of their reporting. Journalists 'on the ground' are their most common source. This may explain part of their attraction, because the links and first-handness give the format a transparency and directness that is likely to appeal to contemporary tastes. Furthermore, these qualities act as a counterbalance to live blogs' 'looser culture of corroboration' as described by Thurman and Walters (2013: 94) and further confirmed here.

Perhaps our most original contributions are on the extent to which live blogs rely on the media as a source and the relative absence in live blogs of first-hand, unofficial sources (such as citizens and activists). This is a reminder of how, as Pablo Boczkowski (2010) has so brilliantly identified, even in an age of information abundance the media tend towards imitation and mimicry to the disservice of plurality. It is also a reminder of how convergence is a 'contested and unpredictable' process (Jenkins, 2006). In the context of an exemplary example of media convergence—the live blog—we see only limited evidence that, as Jenkins and Deuze (2008: 6) and others hoped, there has been "a broadening of opportunities for individuals and grassroots communities to tell stories … to present arguments … to share information."

This analysis of a prevalent, influential, and increasingly popular news format has revealed some of what Murdock and Golding (2002: 111) call the "contradictions of communications convergence." Firstly, we see how, through real-time online reporting, journalism may be becoming more transparent yet also more speculative. Secondly, live news pages may be giving us a journalism that relies more on both journalists' first-hand accounts and on previously published media reports. We should, therefore, continue to monitor and analyze developments in journalism's forms and production and to debate how those developments are changing assessments and even definitions of media plurality and journalistic objectivity.

Further reading

There is no more comprehensive analysis of the structural conventions and discourse of live blogs than Anna Tereszkiewicz's "'I'm Not Sure What That Means Yet, But We'll Soon Find Out'—The Discourse of Newspaper Live Blogs" (2014). Angela Min-Chia Lee's PhD thesis, "How Fast Is Too Fast? Examining the Impact of Speed-Driven Journalism on News Production and Audience Reception" (2014), provided useful new context on the perceptual disconnect between what journalists and their readers think about speed-driven news practices, including live blogs. Finally, the key practical and ethical issues facing live blogging journalists are comprehensively covered in Neil Thurman's "Real-time Online Reporting: Best Practices for Live Blogging" (2014).

References

BBC (2013) "As It Happened: Algeria Hostage Crisis." *BBC News Online*, 19 January. Available from: http://www.bbc.co.uk/news/world-africa-21073655 (accessed 16 August 2015).

BBC (2015a) "Live Coverage: Cameron and Sturgeon Meeting." *BBC News Online*, 15 May. Available from: http://www.bbc.co.uk/news/live/uk-scotland-32747728 (accessed 15 May 2015).

BBC (2015b) "Live: Reaction as Umunna Withdraws Bid." *BBC News Online*, 15 May. Available from: http://www.bbc.co.uk/news/live/uk-politics-32726516 (accessed 15 May 2015).

Boczkowski, P.J. (2010) *News at Work: Imitation in an Age of Information Abundance*. Chicago, IL: University of Chicago Press.

Clark, S., Kingsland, J., Randerson, J. and Yuhas, A. (2014) "Rosetta Mission: Esa Weighs Options for Moving Philae Lander—As It Happened." *The Guardian*, 13 November. Available from: http://www.theguardian.com/science/across-the-universe/live/2014/nov/13/rosetta-mission-philae-lander-live-coverage-comet-esa (accessed 15 May 2015).

Hough, A., Chivers, T. and Bloxham, A. (2011) "Japan Earthquake and Tsunami: As It Happened March 11." *The Telegraph*, 11 March. Available from: http://www.telegraph.co.uk/news/world-news/asia/japan/8377742/Japanearthquake-and-tsunami-as-it-happened-March-11.html (accessed 16 August 2015).

Independent Press Standards Organisation (IPSO) (n.d.) *Editors' Code of Practice*. Available from: https://www.ipso.co.uk/IPSO/cop.html (accessed 15 May 2015).

Jenkins, H. (2006) *Convergence Culture*. New York, NY: New York University Press.

Jenkins, H. and Deuze, M. (2008) "Editorial: Convergence Culture." *Convergence: The International Journal of Research into New Media Technologies* 14(1): 5–12.

Lee, A.M. (2014) "How Fast Is Too Fast? Examining the Impact of Speed-Driven Journalism on News Production and Audience Reception." Texas ScholarWorks, PhD, University of Texas at Austin.

Murdock, G. and Golding, P. (2002) "Digital Possibilities, Market Realities: The Contradictions of Communications Convergence." *Socialist Register* 38: 111–29.

NBC (2011) "Live Blog: Huge Tsunami Hits Japan After 8.9 Quake." *World Blog, NBCnews*, 11 March. Available from: http://worldblog.nbcnews.com/_news/2011/03/11/6243734-live-blog-huge-tsunami-hits-japan-after-89-quake?lite (accessed 16 August 2015).

Ottawa Citizen (2004) "Peter and His Paddle." *News Section*, A2, 14 May. Available from: Nexis online database, 24 April 2015.

Owen, P. (2012) "When Was the First Live Blog? 1923, It Seems." *The Guardian*, 28 October. Available from: http://www.theguardian.com/media/shortcuts/2012/oct/28/when-first-live-blog-1923 (accessed 24 April 2015).

ScribbleLive (2015a) "Create and Publish Engaging Stories as they Unfold." *ScribbleLive*. Available from: http://www.scribblelive.com/book-demo-media/ (accessed 22 April 2015).

ScribbleLive (2015b) "ScribbleU." *ScribbleLive*. Available from: http://www.scribblelive.com/scribbleu/ (accessed 22 April 2015).

Sheller, M. (2015) "News Now: Interface, Ambience, Flow, and the Disruptive Spatio-Temporalities of Mobile News Media." *Journalism Studies* 16(1): 12–26.

Silverstone, R. (1995) "Convergence is a Dangerous Word." *Convergence: The International Journal of Research into New Media Technologies* 1(1): 11–13.

St. Louis Post-Dispatch (2004) "Online Today." *News Section*, A2, 6 May. Available from: Nexis online database (accessed 24 April 2015).

Stray, J. (2010) "Linking by the Numbers: How News Organizations are Using Links (Or Not)." *Nieman Lab*, 10 June. Available from: http://www.niemanlab.org/2010/06/linking-by-the-numbers-how-news-organizations-are-using-links-or-not (accessed 8 June 2015).

Tereszkiewicz, A. (2014) "'I'm Not Sure What that Means Yet, but We'll Soon Find Out' – The Discourse of Newspaper Live Blogs." *Studia Linguistica Universitatis Iagellonicae Cracoviensis* 131(3): 299–319.

Thurman, N. (2014) "Real-Time Online Reporting: Best Practices for Live Blogging." In Zion, L. and Craig, D.A. (eds) *Ethics for Digital Journalists: Emerging Best Practices*. New York, NY: Routledge, pp. 103–114.

Thurman, N. and Newman, N. (2014) "The Future of Breaking News Online? A Study of Live Blogs through Surveys of their Consumption, and of Readers' Attitudes and Participation." *Journalism Studies* 15(5): 655–667.

Thurman, N. and Walters, A. (2013) "Live Blogging – Digital Journalism's Pivotal Platform? A Case Study of the Production, Consumption, and Form of Live Blogs at Guardian.co.uk." *Digital Journalism* 1(1): 82–101.

Weaver, M., Gayle, D., Elgot, J. and Glenza, J. (2015) "Nepal Earthquake: US Helicopter Reported Missing as Dozens Reported Dead – Live." *The Guardian*, 12 May. Available from: http://www.the-guardian.com/world/live/2015/may/12/nepal-earthquake-74-tremor-hits-near-mount-everest-live-updates (accessed 15 May 2015).

Webb, C.L. (2004) "Digital Eye on Ivan." *The Washington Post*, 16 September. Available from: Nexis online database (accessed 24 April 2015).

WSJ (2011) "Live Blog: Japan Earthquake." *Japan Real Time*, 11 March. Available from: http://blogs.wsj.com/japanrealtime/2011/03/11/live-blog-japan-earthquake (accessed 16 August 2015).

29

FOLLOW THE CLICK?

Journalistic autonomy and web analytics

Edson C. Tandoc Jr.

This is the era of big data. Innovations in communication and information technology have allowed not just the collection but also the storage and analysis of big chunks of data recorded from almost our every move (Lewis and Westlund, 2014). Our purchase habits are recorded based on our credit card transactions. Our location points can be monitored courtesy of our smart phones. Our sentiments can be quantified via our social media posts. Important industry and policy decisions have been made by drawing on big data. Consequently, what is happening in the journalism industry is no exception.

Our news content preferences are recorded based on our clicks, thanks to web analytics. This explains why across many news sites, we see numerous articles about cats, dogs, and celebrity scandals. Through web analytics, journalists get a clear idea about which stories most audiences click on. Finding themselves having to compete with a multitude of alternative content online for our precious attention and for the online advertising dollars such attention can bring, news sites have to balance between giving what audiences want and what they need. This is why we get to read news about the violence in Syria along with Miley Cyrus' twerking (Tandoc, 2014a).

Of course, tracking audiences' news preferences is not new. Feedback from the audience traditionally came in the form of letters to the editor and phone calls to the newsroom (Gans, 1979; Schlesinger, 1978). Newspapers relied on circulation figures and broadcast stations turned to audience ratings (Beam, 1995; Gans, 1979). But while these forms of audience research provided some clues to audience preferences, they still left a good deal of room for editorial guesswork. Readership surveys relied on respondents' willingness and accuracy in reporting about their own media habits (Tewksbury, 2003) while television ratings took time to collect, analyze, and report (Gans, 1979). They also provided data based on a subset of the actual audience (Beam, 1995). Web analytics, by contrast, offers real-time and accurate collection and reporting of audience data—and journalists have taken notice.

What is web analytics?

The Digital Analytics Association (DAA, 2008) defines web analytics as "the measurement, collection, analysis and reporting of internet data for the purposes of understanding and optimizing web usage." The first commercial web analytics vendor was launched in 1994

(Chaffey and Patron, 2012). Since then, web analytics has become institutionalized, particularly for websites engaged in promotion and sales (Chaffey and Patron, 2012). Web analytics helps website owners to "learn more about how people use a site and why" (Miller, 2011). This is especially important for online businesses seeking to understand not only how many visitors come to their websites but also how they can convert these visits into purchases (Chaffey and Patron, 2012; Beri and Singh, 2013).

News organizations have similarly embraced web analytics. Surveys of journalists in the United States have shown that almost all newsrooms use one or more web analytics program (Lowrey and Woo, 2010; Jenner and Tandoc, 2013; Vu, 2013). An analysis of job ads published in 2010 also found that news organizations looked for web analytics experience from potential employees (Wenger and Owens, 2013). Many newsrooms use the free program Google Analytics while bigger newsrooms tend to use paid programs, such as Omniture, Chartbeat, and Visual Revenue for their web analytics (Yang, 2012). Such programs provide a wealth of information about what is happening in a website in real time. For example, analytics programs can report the actual number of unique and return visitors, which stories are getting the most number of clicks, how much time visitors are spending on the site and on each story, which other websites lead people to specific pages on the site, and which stories are being shared the most on social media, among other things (Napoli, 2011). These pieces of information are called *web metrics*, which refers to any quantitative measure of how internet users deal with content (Krall, 2009).

But what is the most important metric for news organizations? The use of web analytics is quite straightforward in online marketing, as conversion clearly refers to actual purchase, the most important metric for marketers (Beri and Singh, 2013). But conversion in the context of journalism is unclear. Indeed, the industry of web analytics has shifted its standard from hits, to page views, and to unique monthly visitors—each with inherent weaknesses in terms of accurately capturing what it is that journalists need and want to learn from web analytics (Krall, 2009). Hits measure the number of files loaded in a requested page. Since one web page can include a number of files (such as photos, texts, ads), hits tend to be inflated. Page views measure how many times a page is viewed, which means one user can also inflate the number of page views of a website if the user views multiple pages in one visit. Finally, unique monthly visitors refer to the number of individual visitors on the site. Many news organizations prioritize this metric. For example, a 2012 survey of news editors and managers in the United States ranked number of unique visitors as the most important metric (Jenner and Tandoc, 2013). Some newsrooms even make it an editorial goal to increase web traffic based on average number of unique monthly visitors (Tandoc, 2014a).

How do journalists use web analytics?

Web analytics influences numerous stages of the news construction process. While earlier research found that journalists initially used audience metrics to guide decisions on story placement (Anderson, 2011), recent studies found that data from web analytics are also being used to guide decisions in earlier stages of news construction, such as deciding which story topics to pursue and how to deploy newsroom resources (Tandoc, 2014a, 2014b; Vu, 2013). A few newsrooms have even started considering data from web analytics in evaluating the performance of their journalists, such as introducing a pay-per-click scheme (Fischer, 2014; Jenner and Tandoc, 2013).

In many newsrooms, only editors are given individual access to the web analytics program the company uses so they can view the results on their computers any time they want. Some

editors open the program at home, in the morning, after they wake up, to see what the numbers are even before reporting for work. In some newsrooms, a web analytics dashboard is usually projected on a main projector screen for everyone to see. Some newsrooms also send copies of weekly reports to their reporters, while a few others allow reporters full access to their analytics remotely and at any time.

Story placement and promotion

Online editors use web analytics to guide decisions about where to place particular stories on the homepage. Only a limited number of stories are placed on the homepage to make sure it remains uncluttered and readers can easily navigate the site. There is also a need to keep the website fresh by adding new stories and elements regularly. Readers are not expected to come back to the site if they will simply find the same stories on the homepage over and over again.

The homepage is often considered the prime space for a news site. It is where homepage editors exercise a lot of judgment in terms of story placement. This judgment is often based on audience metrics. Web analytics provides real-time information on the number of unique visitors on the site. When that number starts to dip, web editors see that as being the right time to update the homepage. Such updates involve moving around stories or adding new ones to replace others, or placing stories that are gaining a large number of clicks more prominently on the homepage. If a breaking story needs to be uploaded on the homepage, editors must decide which story must be taken out—a decision usually based on web analytics (Tandoc, 2014a).

However, for an increasing number of news outlets, the homepage is losing its relevance. Social media, particularly Facebook, account for an increasing number of referrals to news sites. Only a few online readers go directly to news sites. Instead, many readers are directed to these news sites through posts and links they come across on Facebook, Twitter, or other platforms. Thus, some news sites are shifting their focus from the homepage to promoting stories on social media. But such practice also requires editorial decision-making to determine which stories should be promoted on social media. Some editors turn to web analytics to guide these decisions—for example, some editors tend to promote stories that are already getting a lot of clicks, hoping that popular clickbait stories can bring more readers to their news sites (Tandoc, 2014a).

Story planning and selection

Budget meetings, in a newspaper context, refer to meetings at a specific time in the morning, usually before noon, when editors come together and decide what stories to pursue during the day. A similar meeting occurs for online newsrooms, but it tends to be more informal as online newsrooms do not operate on the same fixed deadlines as newspapers. But web analytics has also restructured budget meetings, even for newspapers with online outlets (Schlesinger and Doyle, 2015). Increasingly, budget meetings start with a brief discussion of the site's current analytics. Editors evaluate which stories are doing well, which stories are being shared, and what topics are trending on Twitter. Stories that are getting strong online traffic typically get updates and follow-ups. Topics that have done well in the past based on metrics are more likely to be assigned (Tandoc, 2014a). A survey of news editors in the United States found that 73 percent use web analytics "to decide if we will assign additional stories or coverage" (Jenner and Tandoc, 2013).

Web analytics also affects the selection of photos, videos, and graphics. A crime story that is not getting a lot of clicks might be updated with a photo, because stories that include photos tend to get more clicks. Photo galleries also tend to attract a lot of traffic and also help increase time spent on the site (Tandoc, 2014a).

Writing headlines

Google, the most popular search engine, has affected how online journalists write headlines (Dick, 2011). The competition for ranking high on a given search has redefined rules of headline writing. An online editor, for example, can see search engine rankings improve by adding the words 'video' and 'watch' to the headline for a story that includes a video component because readers searching Google for particular videos tend to use these words in their search. Web analytics have also influenced headline writing.

Take the analytics program Visual Revenue, which offers a headline-testing service. This is how it works: An online editor can write two headlines for the same story. Visual Revenue randomly exposes visitors to one of the two headlines. In a few minutes, Visual Revenue can provide a report about which headline got more clicks. The editor is then presented with a choice between the two headlines and often, editors follow the clicks: They go for the more popular headline (Tandoc, 2014a). Some editors also rewrite the headlines of stories that are not getting a lot of traffic. For example, some 38 percent of news editors who participated in a 2012 survey in the United States said they use web analytics to determine whether they would rewrite the headline of an underperforming story (Jenner and Tandoc, 2013). This orientation toward getting more traffic, coupled with the ability to monitor such traffic using web analytics, leads to clickbait headlines (Tandoc, 2014a).

Evaluating performance

The same 2012 survey found that 25 percent of news editors in the United States reported using web analytics to evaluate the performance of their employees. This might be in the form of setting goals for a particular newsroom unit, appraisals criteria for job promotion, and even strategies for pay schemes. For example, Gawker Media, an online media company with an extensive network of popular blogs, launched a program in 2014 where participants were paid $5 per 1,000 unique monthly visitors their contributions bring to the site (Fischer, 2014). The company's editorial director described this pay-per-click scheme as motivation for writers to come up with their 'best work' (Fischer, 2014). While this practice is not yet widespread, it highlights the fragile balancing act that journalists now find themselves having to perform: How should journalists balance the priority of getting more clicks with their social responsibility?

What factors affect how journalists use analytics?

Different news organizations use web analytics in different ways, but the main reasons for adopting analytics in the newsroom are clear. The first of these is the aggressive competition for audience attention that news outlets face. No longer do news organizations have to compete only among themselves, but now they also have to compete with a huge number of alternative information and entertainment sources online and offline. Second, the use of web analytics is a response to the changing nature of the "people formerly known as the audience" (Rosen, 2006). Now fragmented, with more control over their media use and with more choices for how they spend their time with the media (Napoli, 2011), audiences exert strong influences on the news construction process (Shoemaker and Reese, 2014). Knowing what audiences want then becomes more paramount for news organizations. This way, web analytics responds to, and further facilitates, the increasing influence of the audience on news construction.

In previous work, I argued that reliance on web analytics is largely motivated by a want to survive the bleak economic context that surrounds traditional news media (Tandoc, 2014a). Giving audiences what they want is seen as a way to survive, and this is made possible by measuring what audiences actually want in their media content through web analytics. Indeed, the higher the degree of economic uncertainty editors feel, the more they tend to monitor these audience metrics (Lowrey and Woo, 2010). Furthermore, editors who see the economic benefits of increased readership are also more willing to adjust editorial decisions based on web metrics (Vu, 2013). But not all news organizations are profit-oriented. For example, editors at the *Al Jazeera* newsroom often ignored audience metrics in their editorial decisions, even if they recognized web analytics as important (Usher, 2013). Funded by the Qatari government, *Al Jazeera* does not feel the same economic pressure to increase web traffic, which might explain how its editors use web analytics differently from profit-oriented news organizations (Usher, 2013).

What are the journalistic implications of web analytics?

News is an unusual product. It is often considered a 'public good' that exerts important intended and unintended individual and social consequences (Baker, 2002). But news consumption is not only about fulfilling needs for information and entertainment, the business of journalism also exerts macro-level effects, such as exposing corruption, focusing public attention on social problems, and amplifying risks. News organizations often serve two markets: audiences and advertisers (Baker, 2002). This aspect of news products makes it important to understand the larger implications of journalistic practices, such as the use of web analytics.

Supplying audiences with articles they want is not a novel practice. For example, sensationalism in news reporting is based on the belief that readers are drawn to emotional and scandalous stories. But prior to the widespread use of web analytics, journalists relied on their own editorial judgment and those of their superiors and peers to guess what actual audiences want (Gans, 1979). They received various forms of audience feedback in the past, but most journalists used to reject such feedback for various reasons. Some of them did not trust, and even disliked, decontextualized numbers from surveys and ratings (Beam, 1995; Schlesinger, 1978). Others had negative perceptions of their audiences, considering them as preoccupied with trivial and insignificant content (Atkin *et al.*, 1983). Finally, journalists also feared that incorporating the results of readership surveys in editorial decisions might compromise their valued editorial autonomy (Beam, 1995; Gans, 1979; Schlesinger, 1978).

But audience preference is now much harder to ignore, given the shaky economic context in which traditional news organizations find themselves and the omnipresence of audience feedback through new channels, such as web analytics. Journalists no longer have the option of ignoring the audience. But while increasing online traffic is good for business, we also have to consider how pursuing clicks affects the quality of the journalism we produce.

Faced with shrinking revenues that have triggered a spate of layoffs, many newsrooms are getting smaller and the journalists that remain find themselves having to juggle numerous tasks. They have to write, take photos, and capture videos. They have to edit and upload stories on their websites, compose tweets, and post stories on Facebook. Faced with these many tasks and a never-ending news cycle, online journalists rarely have the luxury of thoroughly reflecting on the editorial decisions they make (Tandoc, 2014a). For example, in one American newsroom I observed in May 2013, online editors were surprised one afternoon to suddenly realize they had uploaded three celebrity stories on their homepage: one about Beyonce, another about Amanda Bynes, and another about Justin Bieber. Focused on the numerous tasks they have to complete, journalists run the risk of missing the big picture. Indeed, a content analysis of news websites in the United States found that editorial judgment in terms of story placement tend to follow audiences' click patterns directly (Lee *et al.*, 2014).

News routines have long simplified the otherwise complicated processes of news construction (Tuchman, 1972, 1978). These can come through structural devices, such as the inverted pyramid format of news writing, which simplifies decision-making in ordering pieces of information that go into a story by requiring facts to be arranged in descending importance. Web analytics is also used to simplify editorial decision-making as it gets embedded in online news routines. An online editor trying to decide which story to either highlight or remove from the homepage can simply look at the constantly updated web analytics dashboard. The numbers offer immediate and easy recommendations—journalists can just follow the click. But understanding the impact of web analytics on journalism requires looking beyond the technology and focusing on how it is being used and for what purpose. It is therefore important to reflect constantly and discuss the theoretical and practical implications of the use of web analytics in journalism, as well as how we shall move forward from existing applications.

Theoretical implications

The complicated process of news construction operates under layers of influences that affect what gets published (Shoemaker and Reese, 2014). But in the context of online news, the news construction process no longer ends in publication. A published story has to be efficiently distributed on cyberspace or else other forms of content will overshadow it. Such distribution can come in the form of social media, although this process is outside any monopoly of journalistic control (Shoemaker and Reese, 2014). Web analytics influences what stories journalists promote on their social networks, and in turn journalists tend to share popular stories, or those that fit the mold of stories that tend to attract clicks (Tandoc, 2014a). But journalists can also choose to promote important stories, consistent with their normative roles and values.

Theorizing in news construction also used to prioritize the process of news selection, but gatekeeping now includes the process of *de-selection*. "De-selection refers to deciding which among articles that have made it through the gates will be taken out of the homepage to be replaced by a new story" (Tandoc, 2014a). This process tends to be heavily influenced by web analytics, and stories that do not perform well are usually replaced after a set period (Tandoc, 2014a). This also affects the range of topics and perspectives that reach public consciousness. Therefore, understanding and theorizing about journalism should focus equally on the process of distribution and de-selection. These processes, and not just news selection, have consequences in terms of what range of messages reaches, and ultimately affects, the public.

Practical implications

The use of web analytics should also be examined through the prism of journalistic roles and journalistic ethics. Web analytics allows journalists to know what audiences want, and while giving what audiences want is a way to attract traffic, it also treats audience choice as an end for an economic goal rather than as means to a journalistic mission (Tandoc and Thomas, 2014). Indeed: "Web analytics is a powerful tool, but how it is used is what determines the kind of power it can wield and to what end" (Tandoc and Thomas, 2014). Journalists must balance editorial autonomy and orientation to the audience, and these new tools and routines should not distract journalists from their journalistic roles.

Web analytics is not a bad tool. It helps journalists to be more aware and responsive to their audiences. However, the way journalists use this tool will determine how it will affect journalism. Indeed, there have been instances when editors used web analytics to support—rather than replace—their editorial judgment. For example, in one newsroom I observed, I came across an editor looking at the site's analytics. The editor noticed that the numbers for a particular story were not very good. The story was about a baby who was shot during a gang-related fight. For the editor, this story represented the social costs of seemingly uncontrolled gang-related violence in the community. Seeing that a story he thought was important was not getting clicks—information web analytics made available—he updated the story by adding a photo and by promoting the story on social media. Clicks then followed. This is an example of using a new tool to support normative beliefs about what journalism ought to be.

Moving forward

What should be at the heart of discussions on the use of web analytics in journalism is what journalists *should* measure. What should be journalism's most important metric? While the number of unique visitors has been the industry standard (Jenner and Tandoc, 2013), many argue that this metric is not useful. Hits, page views, and unique visits are all counted based on the cookies deposited in an online user's computer (Benkoil, 2010). But users can delete cookies before logging out and can be considered as new visitors when they visit the site again. They can also choose private browsing options available on some web browsers. Thus, news organizations and analytics companies are moving to a different metric: attention.

The online site Upworthy, known for its viral and inspirational posts, is advocating the measurement of 'attention minutes.' This metric "measures everything from video player signals about whether a video is currently playing to a user's mouse movements to which browser tab is currently open—all to determine whether the user is still engaged" (Upworthy, 2014). The content-hosting site Medium also measures 'total reading time' (Davies, 2013), saying: "We care less about clicks and more about actual reading. Time spent is a better reflection of this." (Sall, 2013). Web analytics company Chartbeat (2015) pushes for an 'attention web' metric, which is about optimizing measurements of 'audiences' true attention,' arguing that "online publishers know clicks don't always reflect content quality."

These updates and different approaches raise an important point: How can we best measure reader engagement? What does it mean for a reader to be engaged? So far, web analytics has been used in journalism mostly for business reasons. Monitoring the number of unique visitors is just a way of keeping an eye on the size of an audience, a size that can be sold to advertisers. But is this the only measure that matters in journalism? Or should we also ask how web analytics can measure—and ensure—journalistic quality? These questions are also about how we define these concepts. What do we mean by quality? Is getting a reader to click on another story a form of engagement? Or, in the end, is it just about what readers do with news content that matters?

Conclusion

Studies about journalists adopting new technologies have found that journalists tend to normalize them and try to fit new technologies into their existing journalistic norms and routines (Lasorsa *et al.*, 2011; Singer, 2005). But online news has also brought about new routines, including the process of story de-selection mentioned here (Tandoc, 2014a). Web analytics has modified traditional budget meetings, as newsrooms around the world have embraced web analytics. Therefore, we need to examine how web analytics affects how we do journalism and how it influences the kind of journalism we produce. It will be interesting and important to observe closely and examine how journalists continue to negotiate their way through economic, technological, cultural, and organizational transformations marking the journalistic field. In the process, we must also not lose sight of the social functions that have made journalism the important institution that it has become.

Further reading

This chapter is based on my research that started with my doctoral dissertation titled *Web analytics, social media, and the journalistic doxa: The impact of audience feedback on the evolving gatekeeping process* (2013) at the University of Missouri. The changes we see in journalism are largely triggered by how the audience is changing, and Philip Napoli's (2011) *Audience evolution: New technologies and the transformation of media audiences* provides a thorough discussion of the evolution of the audience. Other aspects of changes in the newsroom are also documented in a series of newsroom ethnographies and case studies compiled in the two volumes of *Making online news* (2008, 2011) edited by Chris Paterson and David Domingo.

References

Anderson, C.W. (2011) "Between Creative and Quantified Audiences: Web Metrics and Changing Patterns of Newswork in Local US Newsrooms." *Journalism* 12: 550–566.

Atkin, C.K., Burgoon, J.K. and Burgoon, M. (1983) "How Journalists Perceive the Reading Audience." *Newspaper Research Journal* 4: 51–63.

Baker, C.E. (2002) *Media, Markets, and Democracy*. New York, NY: Cambridge University Press.

Beam, R.A. (1995) "How Newspapers Use Readership Research." *Newspaper Research Journal* 16: 28–38.

Benkoil, D. (2010) "What Web Analytics Can—And Can't—Tell You about Your Site's Traffic and Audience." *Poynter.* Available from: http://www.poynter.org/how-tos/digital-strategies/e-media-tidbits/104772/what-web-analytics-can-and-cant-tell-you-about-your-sites-traffic-and-audience/ (accessed 10 October 2013).

Beri, B. and Singh, P. (2013) "Web Analytics: Increasing Website's Usability and Conversion Rate." *International Journal of Computer Applications* 72(6): 35–38.

Chaffey, D. and Patron, M. (2012) "From Web Analytics to Digital Marketing Optimization: Increasing the Commercial Value of Digital Analytics." *Journal of Direct, Data and Digital Marketing Practice* 14: 30–45.

Chartbeat. (2015) *What Is the Attention Web?* Available from: https://chartbeat.com/attention-web#. Vz6qFTV96Uk (accessed 12 May 2015).

DAA. (2008) *Web Analytics Definitions.* Available from: http://www.digitalanalyticsassociation.org/Files/PDF_standards/WebAnalyticsDefinitions.pdf (accessed 28 September 2013).

Davies, P. (2013) "Medium's Metric that Matters: Total Time Reading." *Data Lab.* Available from: https://medium.com/data-lab/mediums-metric-that-matters-total-time-reading-86c4970837d5 (accessed 21 November 2013).

Dick, M. (2011) "Search Engine Optimisation in UK News Production." *Journalism Practice* 5: 462–477.

Fischer, M.C. (2014) The Pay-Per-Visit Debate: Is Chasing Viral Traffic Hurting Journalism? *American Journalism Review.* Available from: http://ajr.org/2014/03/27/pay-per-visit-debate-chasing-viral-traffic-hurting-journalism/ (accessed 28 March 2014).

Gans, H. (1979) *Deciding What's News*. New York, NY: Pantheon Books.

Jenner, M. and Tandoc, E. (2013) "Newsrooms Using Web Metrics to Evaluate Staff, Guide Editorial Decisions." *Reynolds Journalism Institute.* Available from: http://www.rjionline.org/blog/newsrooms-using-web-metrics-evaluate-staff-guide-editorial-decisions (accessed 7 February 2014).

Krall, J. (2009) "Using Social Metrics to Evaluate the Impact of Online Healthcare Communications." *Journal of Communication in Healthcare* 2: 387–394.

Lasorsa, D.L., Lewis, S.C. and Holton, A.E. (2011) "Normalizing Twitter: Journalism Practice in an Emerging Communication Space." *Journalism Studies* 13: 19–36.

Lee, A.M., Lewis, S.C. and Powers, M. (2014) "Audience Clicks and News Placement: A Study of Time-Lagged Influence in Online Journalism." *Communication Research* 41: 505–530.

Lewis, S.C. and Westlund, O. (2014) "Big Data and Journalism: Epistemology, Expertise, Economics, and Ethics." *Digital Journalism* 3(3): 447–466.

Lowrey, W. and Woo, C.W. (2010) "The News Organization in Uncertain Times: Business or Institution?" *Journalism and Mass Communication Quarterly* 87: 41–61.

Miller, M. (2011) *The Ultimate Web Marketing Guide*. Indianapolis, IN: Pearson Education, Inc.

Napoli, P. (2011) *Audience Evolution: New Technologies and the Transformation of Media Audiences*. New York, NY: Columbia University Press.

Rosen, J. (2006) "The People Formerly Known as the Audience." *Huffington Post*, 25 May. Available from: http://www.huffingtonpost.com/entry/the-people-formerly-known_1_b_24113.html?section=india (Accessed 13 May 2013).

Sall, M. (2013) "The Optimal Post is 7 Minutes." *Data Lab*. Available from: https://medium.com/data-lab/the-optimal-post-is-7-minutes-74b9f41509b (accessed 2 December 2015).

Schlesinger, P. (1978) *Putting 'Reality' Together*. Beverly Hills, CA: Sage.

Schlesinger, P. and Doyle, G. (2015) "From Organizational Crisis to Multi-Platform Salvation? Creative Destruction and the Recomposition of News Media. *Journalism* 16: 305–323.

Shoemaker, P.J. and Reese, S.D. (2014) *Mediating the Message in the 21st Century: A Media Sociology Perspective*. New York, NY: Routledge.

Singer, J. (2005) "The Political J-Blogger." *Journalism* 6: 173–198.

Tandoc, E. (2014a) "Journalism is Twerking? How Web Analytics is Changing the Process of Gatekeeping." *New Media & Society* 16: 559–575.

Tandoc, E. (2014b) "Why Web Analytics Click: Factors Affecting the Ways Journalists Use Audience Metrics." *Journalism Studies* 16(6): 782–799.

Tandoc, E. and Thomas, R.J. (2014) "The Ethics of Web Analytics: Implications of Using Audience Metrics in News Construction." *Digital Journalism* 3: 243–258.

Tewksbury, D. (2003) "What Do Americans Really Want to Know? Tracking the Behavior of News Readers on the Internet." *Journal of Communication* 53: 694–710.

Tuchman, G. (1972) "Objectivity as Strategic Ritual: An Examination of Newsmen's Notions of Objectivity." *American Journal of Sociology* 77: 660–679.

Tuchman, G. (1978) *Making News: A Study in the Construction of Reality*. New York, NY: Free Press.

Upworthy. (2014) "The Code [Literally] to What Lies between the Click and the Share. Yours, for Free… Really." *Upworthy Insider*. Available from: http://blog.upworthy.com/post/89621755036/the-code-literally-to-what-lies-between-the (accessed 22 June 2015).

Usher, N. (2013) "Al Jazeera English Online: Understanding Web Metrics and News Production When a Quantified Audience is Not a Commodified Audience." *Digital Journalism* 1(2): 335–351.

Vu, H.T. (2013) "The Online Audience as Gatekeeper: The Influence of Reader Metrics on News Editorial Selection." *Journalism* 15(8): 1094–1110.

Wenger, D. and Owens, L.C. (2013) "An Examination of Job Skills Required by Top U.S. Broadcast News Companies and Potential Impact on Journalism Curricula." *Electronic News* 7: 22–35.

Yang, N. (2012) "How Web Analytics are Shaping Advertising Dollars and the Newsroom." *Editor & Publisher*. Available from: http://www.editorandpublisher.com/Features/Article/How-Web-Analytics-Are-Shaping-Advertising-Dollars-And-The-Newsroom (accessed 19 July 2013).

30

JOURNALISTS' USES OF HYPERTEXT

Juliette De Maeyer

In its celebratory 20-year anniversary issue, the magazine *Wired* proposed an inventory of all the keywords that mattered during the past two decades of the digital world. Somewhere between 'GIFs' and 'Jobs, Steve,' we find an entry for 'hypertext.' In it, writer Steven Johnson mulls over predictions about the "the transformative potential of journalism in a hypertext world" and how they proved to be wrong. Johnson points to a "strange mix of myopia and farsightedness that some of us experienced in the early 1990s" (2013: 92). Johnson includes himself in those who made predictions that hyperlinks "would allow us to jump suddenly to different textual locations—were about to become a central mode of communication. But many of us thought the primary impact of hypertext would be on storytelling" (2013). That optimism was pinned on an idea that "contributors would compose stories built out of small blocks of text—roughly the length of a blog post—that readers would navigate according to their own whims" (2013). This reimagined storytelling, predicted each reader's experience as differing from another's, and practices of reading being replaced by 'exploring.' As Johnson notes in his retelling: "That future never happened" (2013: 92).

This chapter addresses that potential future and how it never happened. It shows how digital journalism research first embraced the utopia of 'hyper-news' (Engebretsen, 1997), only to discover that news sites repeatedly failed to massively adopt hypertext. Instead of the deterministic view, which posits that a new technological feature necessarily needs it to be adopted, this chapter then shows how the story of hypertext in the news is one of normalization, where the many aspects of newsmaking may affect linking practices.

The (failed) adoption of hypertext by news websites

Research specifically devoted to digital journalism developed and gained momentum in the late 1990s and early 2000s. As hypertext was deemed as one of the fundamental assets of online journalism (Steensen, 2011), it figures quite prominently among the topics of interest. A first wave of research seemed primarily interested in gauging the success of technological innovation and the take-up of technological features. Many studies were concerned with the following question: Are news organization fully taking advantage of the possibilities of the web? Essentially descriptive, those studies often implicitly or explicitly posited that news production will naturally embrace the technological potential (interactive, multimedia, hypertextual) of the web (Boczkowski, 2002; Domingo, 2006; Mitchelstein and Boczkowski, 2009; Steensen and Ahva, 2015). They assumed that the seamless adoption of web-native tools and technologies represented the 'added value' of digital journalism and that innovation and progress would inevitably follow. That framing led first-wave studies about hypertext in the news to mostly adopt quantitative approaches, as they wanted to measure the extent to which news sites used new technological features. Scholars scrutinized the content of news websites and sought to assess if the 'features' of online journalism are actually used and, if so, to what extent (Quandt, 2008: 720).

Those analyses produced disappointing conclusions, by the standards of the utopian hopes that the digital brought to journalism. For instance, in their study entitled "Online newspapers: living up to the potential?," Tankard and Ban (1998) assessed the extent to which news sites use hypertext. Among the 196 news stories from the 135 US websites they analyzed, 94 percent contained no link at all. Online newspapers are "slow to start utilizing hypertext links and other web features," they concluded (Tankard and Ban, 1998: n.p.). Barnhurst (2001) found a similar, vast proportion (about three-quarter) of news stories contained no links at all in analysis of three US news sites. The absence of links is less striking in the 181 US television websites studied by Pitts in the early 2000s, but as more than half of the content examined contain no links at all, the verdict is similarly harsh: "Television stations are not using their web sites effectively to provide news information" (Pitts, 2003: 5). The same goes for studies that examine hypertext among other interactive features such as interactivity and the possibility to send e-mails to journalists, with scholars concluding that all those features are weakly represented in online news content (Kenney, Gorelik, and Mwangi, 2000). Furthermore, those grim findings are not reserved to the United States, with studies in Ireland (O'Sullivan, 2005) and in Belgium (Paulussen, 2004) showing similar trends.

A second wave of studies eventually acknowledged that hypertext had become a rather common feature of online news (Dimitrova and Neznanski, 2006; Quandt, 2008). However, the disappointing conclusion—that news sites do not live up to the potential—then slowly transformed as the content analyses proceeded not only to count the hyperlinks but also to take their destination into account. The distinction between *internal* and *external* links then becomes crucial, that is, the difference between links pointing to pages within the same websites (internal) and links pointing to other websites and resources (external). External links are, implicitly or explicitly, deemed more interesting, as they take part in the open, boundaryless myth of free-flowing information (Deuze, 2003: 212). Internal links, on the contrary, are often disregarded as crudely self-promotional. If internal links are abundantly present in news sites, external links are scarce (Dimitrova *et al.*, 2003; Engebretsen, 2006; Oblak, 2005; Quandt, 2008)—leading some to dub this trend the 'walled garden phenomenon' (Napoli, 2008) or 'gated cybercommunities' (Tremayne, 2005).

A slow take-up or a definitive failure?

The defeatist conclusions pile up: "Previous research studies and the professional literature have indicated that online newspapers have low levels of interactivity, and this study supports that finding" (Kenney, Gorelik, and Mwangi, 2000: n.p.), "online news media do not fully explore the potential of the internet yet" (Paulussen, 2004: n.p.), "[news] websites do not make use of the World Wide Web's potential for new types of writing, producing, linking and interacting" (Quandt, 2008: 735).

The premise that news sites will necessarily embrace technological progress in and of itself is proved wrong. But why is the use of hypertext by news organizations so deficient? Scholars propose several hypotheses. First, there is the 'shovelware' explanation, that was typical of late 1990s, early 2000s news production processes: news sites simply republish the articles that were created for other media, primarily for newspapers (Tankard and Ban, 1998) and those articles do not make use of hypertext.

Slowness to adapt to change and a cultural attachment to print is also highlighted as a possible cause of the scarcity of links (Dimitrova *et al.*, 2003), as well as overall constraints that weigh on news production processes, and especially immediacy, the pressure to produce a lot of content at high speed, and the lack of financial resources (Paulussen, 2004). As for the supremacy of internal links, it is explained by a will to tightly control the flow of readers. This control finds its source in the 'gatekeeping' role of news media (Dimitrova *et al.*, 2003; Tsui, 2008), as well as in the competitive economic context—news sites must keep readers within their own boundaries to accumulate page views, enhance their rankings in search engine results, and, more importantly, not send them to potential competitors (Himelboim, 2010: 384; Tsui, 2008: 82).

Some of those explanations indicate that the progress towards more hypertextual news is still plausible: it is only a matter of time and maturity. When news organizations stop relying on shovelware and when traditional mindsets have had the time to evolve, the rationale goes, news sites will finally live up to the potential of the web. This is a narrative of progress, of technological innovation necessarily being adopted, with challenging or difficult beginnings eventually deemed to make way for popularization. But as time goes by, the situation does not appear to improve.

Studies from the 2010s continue to produce the same finding: news sites link only occasionally, and they produce few external links (Barnhurst, 2012; Coddington, 2012; Paulussen and D'heer, 2013; Himelboim, 2010; Sjøvaag, Moe, and Stavelin, 2012). Even when the commercial pressure to keep readers within a site's own boundaries is less prominent, as it is the case with the public service broadcaster studied by Sjøvaag and her colleagues (2012), external links are used in a limited way.

If professional journalists repeatedly fail to incorporate (external) hyperlinks in their stories, alternative forms of news production—such a blogging or 'citizen journalism'—seem more incline to make use of hypertext features. For example, a study by Coddington (2012) compares the use of hyperlinks by six US news sites (the *New York Times*, the *Washington Post*, *The Wall Street Journal*, CNN, ABC News, and *TIME Magazine*) with that of blogs (whether independent blogs or blogs hosted by traditional media outlets). If the proportion of external links compared to internal links is, as usual, extremely feeble for the traditional news sites, that proportion grows for blogs hosted by traditional media, and it turns out that external links represent about 80 percent of all the links found on independent blogs (Coddington, 2012: 2014). Similar differences are found by D'heer and Paulussen (2013), who examined the content published on local news sites in Belgium that propose news stories produced by professional journalists alongside those written by 'citizens.' The former sweepingly contain internal links, whereas the latter are more balanced, with half of the news stories authored by citizens containing at least one external link.

The absence of standards in linking practices

So is that the story? Did news sites definitely fail to embrace hypertext? First, we should highlight that if some overall trends seem recurrent (the greater proportion of internal links over external links, for instance), there is no evidence of any standardization of linking practices. The aggregated results might seem to suggest that linking is perennially scarce, especially external linking, but notable exceptions always show up (De Maeyer, 2013). If we look beyond aggregated numbers, there are huge local differences from one news site to another. Not only does hypertext use vary across news sites in different national contexts (Quandt, 2008), but even when looking at only the online version of newspapers within a particular media market, the linking practices are far from homogeneous (De Maeyer, 2013; Karlsson, Clerwall, and Örnebring, 2015).

Research has tried to make sense of these differences by positing that linking practices may vary according to the targeted audience (local or national), the 'publishing tradition' ('quality' vs 'popular' media outlets), or the type of 'media channels,' that is, for news sites of traditional media, the fact that the parent company is primarily a newspaper or a television channel. Contrasts do appear, but they are minimal (Larsson, 2013), and they sometimes illustrate contradictory trends (Stroud, Scacco, and Curry, 2015). In other words, unsteady linking practices hardly make sense alongside traditional categories.

Longitudinal analyses also display the inconsistency of hypertext use. Some studies reveal a decrease in the proportion of external links over time (Tremayne, 2005) only to be contradicted by other studies that show only 'erratic' evolutions, with sharp peaks followed by decreases (Karlsson, Clerwall, and Örnebring, 2015). Inconsistency seem to rule, with some hypertext features that were present in the early 2000s disappearing in the middle of the decade, only to reappear in the 2010s (Barnhurst, 2002; Barnhurst, 2012). Consequently, it is difficult to talk about news linking practices in general, a unified and standardized phenomenon across news organizations and over time. So far, local differences and idiosyncratic linking practices seem to characterize the practice.

Multidimensional uses of hypertext

As the novelty of online news fades away, research on hypertext as a technological feature is less framed in terms of adoption, and more in terms of normalization (Coddington, 2014; Doudaki and Spyridou, 2015; Lasorsa, Lewis, and Holton, 2012; Vobič, 2014): after a brief period of hope that the internet and digital technologies were going to radically change existing practices, research started to question the radicalism of change and to show that "the internet became a new site for old activities" (Lasorsa, Lewis, and Holton, 2012: 21).

In this framework, scholarship attempts to make sense of hypertext quite differently to the studies mentioned above: the goal is not to measure the success of the adoption of a new technological feature but to understand how a technological feature may become incorporated in existing norms, reflect existing practices and potentially alter them. A new set of questions therefore emerges: how does hypertext take part in journalistic dynamics, such as the relation between journalists and their sources? How does the economy of newsmaking affect linking practices? Consequently, hyperlinks are not studied in and on themselves, as a feature that needs to be adopted, but as a trace of some other phenomena that may shape news production processes, a materialization of a relationship between a news organization and another entity (Anderson, 2013: 123). Those approaches do not assume more links are necessarily desirable, or even that there is necessarily one prescribed way of using hypertext. Instead, they take a step back and ask: if a hyperlink can be considered as "an inscribed acknowledgement of a networked relationship" (Ibid.), what kind of relationships do they reflect? Relying on diverse methods that range from newsroom ethnography to network analysis, they highlight a variety of factors that shape journalists' linking practices: sourcing routines, social and economic relations, and targeted and imagined audience.

Links show sources

A common perspective about the function of hyperlinks in journalism is that they closely reflect the sourcing practices of journalists. This parallel between links and sources embodies one of the greatest hopes associated with hypertext: by providing hyperlinks in their reports, journalists could directly connect readers to the sources, which would enhance the sense of facticity and credibility of news reports. The gain in credibility seems potentially huge, as illustrated by this quote by a *New York Times* columnist:

> [W]hy not give the reader, if he or she wants to, the opportunity to see the sources, or a source, when it's available? It helps bulletproof the column, because if they say 'He must be making that up,' they can look and see—here's the source, take a look and judge it for yourself …. If I'm citing a figure, at the most banal level, from the Labor Department or a poll or an economic report, [why not] link to the whole document it comes from?
>
> *(Delaney, 2008)*

The use of links to show sources is among the most important functions that journalists (De Maeyer and Holton, 2015) and journalism educators (De Maeyer, 2012) put forward when reflecting on the *raisons d'être* of hypertext in the news. But even if journalists claim to be open about how they use hypertext, the hyperlinks they actually produce show that they tend to rely on internal or well-established sources. In using links in that way, news producers reproduce existing routines in assessing the credibility and authority of sources.

Known characteristics of the relationship between journalists and sources then shine a light on linking practices. Sources that are traditionally dominant among the hierarchy of journalistic sources (such as official authorities, authoritative references) also permeate the linking practices of journalists. For instance, the linking practices of traditional news sites observed by Coddington "locates the nexus of online authority largely within the same institutions that constitute it offline" (Coddington, 2012: 2021).

If links closely correspond to sourcing practices, it might explain why significant differences were found between the linking practices of traditional journalists and those of alternative news producers such as bloggers or citizen journalists. The latter may be less prone to the long-established hierarchy of sources and hence may link more freely, to a wider variety of sources. Moreover, the sources that are traditionally at the core of journalistic reports, such as news wire copy, press releases, interviews, or field observation, may simply not be very 'linkable' (sometimes simply because they are not available online) (De Maeyer, 2012)—whereas citizen journalists and bloggers do not have access to these sources and therefore tend to rely on other sources, among which is the wide range of documents available online (Carpenter, 2008).

Existing routines that are valid for traditional media also affect how users perceive the credibility of news content: surveys show that 'traditional credibility factors' such as the assessed trustworthiness and expertise of a news outlet still matter the most in users' assessment of credibility, whereas technological features, such as the presence of hyperlinks, do not affect their judgment (Chung, Yoonjae, and Stefanone, 2012). Those findings present digital utopias in a sobering manner: even if there are great theoretical hopes that hypertext can enhance the credibility of news by showing the sources of a news report, both journalists and the audience seem to rely on traditional routines when assessing credibility—which means that so far, hypertext is not especially significant in the crafting and reception of credible news.

Links materialize social and economic relations

The fact that hypertext does not play as important a role as in fostering credibility as was initially anticipated does not mean, however, that it is of no use at all. Hyperlinks can have other functions, such as the materialization of social and economic relations.

The connections that are made with hyperlinks might reflect social relationships at an individual level. For instance, journalists or bloggers may create links that are friendly 'hat tips,' to convey a certain sense of comradeship with other writers (Coddington, 2012: 2016). Playful, Easter-egg type hyperlinks directed to knowing readers may also exist for the sheer enjoyment of both journalists and the audience (De Maeyer and Holton, 2015: 9). But in the context of news sites, the relations reflected by hyperlinks are also those of the organization, which operates in a commercial and competitive context. Strategic and economic interests are therefore also embedded in linking practices. Links on news websites sometimes closely mimic existing economic relations, notably when news sites tend to preferentially produce links that point to commercial partners or websites belonging to the same parent company (De Maeyer, 2013; Karlsson, Clerwall, and Örnebring, 2015; Ryfe *et al.*, 2012). In this regard, hypertext is seen as a direct gateway of traffic and page views, and therefore advertising revenue, that needs to be kept within a news organization's own borders (internal links) or only shared with allies and close partners (external links).

This economic reasoning, however, could equally plead for a more open hyperlinking strategy in the long term. Research has shown that when news organizations establish connections with other websites, and especially new entrants and potential competitors such as blogs, both the incoming hyperlinks they receive and their overall page views increase over time (Weber, 2012).

Links reflect representations of users

Another fundamental aspect of newsmaking manifested in journalists' uses of hypertext is how journalists imagine that users will appreciate and use hyperlinks. Theoretically, hypertext allows non-linear navigation and gives users the freedom to browse through informational content without following a predetermined path. As such, it may contribute to the positive perception of a news site by its users. Surveys show that the presence of hyperlinks is appreciated by news site users, even if that appreciation does not necessarily mean that readers actually use them (Larsson, 2011).

In contrast with that positive role, worries about the impact of hypertext on users also exist. On the one hand, non-linearity may have the potential to empower news readers by allowing them to customize what they read according to their informational needs. But on the other hand, it could also prove to be damaging to their reading experience by making news texts hard to read and affecting their overall comprehension (Doherty, 2014). Hypertext news will "demand more time and more attentive engagement on behalf of the user" (Engebretsen, 1997), which might be too much to ask, especially in a world of information overload. Even the sheer presence of a link in a text could have an undesirable cognitive load and distract users from their smooth reading experience (Carr, 2010).

Research on human–computer interactions has shown that readers confronted with non-linear hypertext indeed experiment a negative "lost in hyperspace phenomenon" (Theng and Thimbleby, 1998). However, these experiments mostly concern literary hypertexts, that is, pieces of fiction that display non-linear narratives and that are sometimes radically deconstructed—which does not correspond to most online news products, even those that contain hyperlinks. The actual impact of hypertext news on readers is an area that still need to be explored (Doherty, 2014).

In short, there are many uncertainties regarding how users receive, appreciate, and use hypertext. Those considerations therefore add up to the many factors that already shape how journalists use hypertext: depending on how they believe users will react, or even on the fact that they have formed an opinion about readers' use of hypertext at all, journalists and news organizations may show widely varying linking practices.

In a word, the factors that shape news production processes still matter when it comes to hypertext news. The variety of forces—economic and social relations, deeply entrenched sourcing practices, various ways of imagining the audience—may explain why hypertext use fluctuates so widely. Some challenges remain to be explored by digital journalism research. Notably, the extent to which hypertext impacts on users' reading experience still needs to be examined. Moreover, a holistic approach to the functions of hyperlinks, that would take into account the many factors shaping linking practices, could be further developed.

Hypertext remains a structuring element of digital journalism, a very simple and powerful feature of our digital world. Pieces of information are potentially more connected than ever, especially as the forms and channels of online news multiply. News apps, social media, and other forms of distributed content—all provide always-renewed opportunities of ubiquitously interconnecting bits and pieces, facts and data, articles and sources, and journalists and their audience.

Further reading

This chapter greatly benefitted from the essential work of Steensen (2011) and Domingo (2006) that provide a useful overview of digital journalism research. On the topic of hypertext and the news, Coddington (2012, 2014), Karlsson, Clerwall, and Örnebring (2015), Larsson (2013), and Vobič (2014) provide outstanding, empirical investigations in the everyday practices of journalists.

References

Anderson, C.W. (2013) *Rebuilding the News: Metropolitan Journalism in the Digital Age*. Philadelphia: Temple University Press.
Barnhurst, K. (2001) *The Form of News: A History*. New York, NY: Guilford Press.
Barnhurst, K. (2002) "News Geography & Monopoly: The Form of Reports on US Newspaper Internet Sites." *Journalism Studies* 3(4): 477–489.
Barnhurst, K. (2012) "The Form of Online News in the Mainstream U.S. Press 2001–2010." *Journalism Studies* 13(5): 791–800.
Boczkowski, P.J. (2002) "The Development and Use of Online Newspapers: What Research Tells Us and What We Might Want to Know." In Lievrouw, L. and Livingstone, S.M. (eds) *Handbook of New Media: Social Shaping and Consequences of ICTs*. Thousand Oaks, CA: Sage (pp. 270–286).
Carpenter, S. (2008) "Source Diversity in U.S. Online Citizen Journalism and Online Newspaper Articles." Paper presented at the International Symposium on Online Journalism, Austin, TX. Available from: https://online.journalism.utexas.edu/papers.php?year=2008.
Carr, N. (2010) *The Shallows: What the Internet Is Doing to Our Brains*. New York, NY: W.W. Norton.
Chung, C.J., Nam, Y. and Stefanone, M.A. (2012) "Exploring Online News Credibility: The Relative Influence of Traditional and Technological Factors." *Journal of Computer-Mediated Communication* 17(2): 171–186.
Coddington, M. (2012) "Building Frames Link by Link: The Linking Practices of Blogs and News Sites." *International Journal of Communication* 6: 2007–2026.
Coddington, M. (2014) "Normalizing the Hyperlink." *Digital Journalism* 2(2): 140–155.

Delaney, E.J. (2008) "Frank Rich: Why I Link." *Nieman Journalism Lab.* Available from: http://www.niemanlab.org/2008/12/frank-rich-why-i-link/.

De Maeyer, J. (2012) "The Journalistic Hyperlink." *Journalism Practice* 6(5–6): 692–701.

De Maeyer, J. (2013) "L'usage Journalistique Des Liens Hypertextes: Étude Des Représentations, Contenus et Pratiques À Partir Des Sites D'information de La Presse Belge Francophone." Available from: http://theses.ulb.ac.be/ETD-db/collection/available/ULBetd-06042013-151542/.

De Maeyer, J. and Holton, A.E. (2015) "Why Linking Matters: A Metajournalistic Discourse Analysis." *Journalism.* DOI: 10.1177/1464884915579330.

Deuze, M. (2003) "The Web and Its Journalisms: Considering the Consequences of Different Types of Newsmedia Online." *New Media Society* 5(2): 203–230.

Dimitrova, D.V., Connolly-Ahern, C., Williams, A.P., Kaid, L.L. and Reid, A. (2003) "Hyperlinking as Gatekeeping: Online Newspaper Coverage of the Execution of an American Terrorist." *Journalism Studies* 4(3): 401–414.

Dimitrova, D.V. and Neznanski, M. (2006) "Online Journalism and the War in Cyberspace: A Comparison Between U.S. and International Newspapers." *Journal of Computer-Mediated Communication* 12(1): 248–263.

Doherty, S. (2014) "Hypertext and Journalism." *Digital Journalism* 2(2): 124–139.

Domingo, D. (2006) *Inventing Online Journalism: Development of the Internet as a News Medium in Four Catalan Online Newsrooms.* Tarragona, Catalonia: Universita Rovira i Virgili. Available from: http://ddd.uab.cat/pub/tesis/2006/tdx-1219106-153347/dd1de1.pdf.

Doudaki, V. and Spyridou, L. (2015) "News Content Online: Patterns and Norms under Convergence Dynamics." *Journalism* 16(2): 257–277.

Engebretsen, M. (1997) "Hyper-News: Revolution or Contradiction?" In *Proceedings of the Eighth ACM Conference on Hypertext,* pp. 222–223. HYPERTEXT '97. New York, NY, USA: ACM.

Engebretsen, M. (2006) "Shallow and Static or Deep and Dynamic? Studying the State of Online Journalism in Scandinavia." *Nordicom Review* 27: 3–16.

Himelboim, I. (2010) "The International Network Structure of News Media: An Analysis of Hyperlinks Usage in News Web Sites." *Journal of Broadcasting & Electronic Media* 54(3): 373–390.

Johnson, S. (2013) "Hypertext." *Wired,* May.

Karlsson, M., Clerwall, C. and Örnebring, H. (2015) "Hyperlinking Practices in Swedish Online News 2007–2013: The Rise, Fall, and Stagnation of Hyperlinking as a Journalistic Tool." *Information, Communication & Society* 18(7): 847–863.

Kenney, K., Gorelik, A. and Mwangi, S. (2000) "Interactive Features of Online Newspapers." *First Monday* 5(1–3). DOI: 10.5210/fm.v5i1.720.

Larsson, A.O. (2011) "Interactive to Me—Interactive to You? A Study of Use and Appreciation of Interactivity on Swedish Newspaper Websites." *New Media & Society* 13(7): 1180–1197.

Larsson, A.O. (2013) "Staying In or Going Out?" *Journalism Practice* 7(6): 738–754.

Lasorsa, D.L., Lewis S.C. and Holton, A.E. (2012) "Normalizing Twitter." *Journalism Studies* 13(1): 19–36.

Mitchelstein, E. and Boczkowski, P.J. (2009) "Between Tradition and Change." *Journalism* 10(5): 562–586.

Napoli, P.N. (2008) "Hyperlinking and the Forces of 'Massification.'" In Turow, J. and Tsui, L. (eds) *The Hyperlinked Society.* Ann Arbor, MI: University of Michigan Press, pp. 56–69.

Oblak, T. (2005) "The Lack of Interactivity and Hypertextuality in Online Media." *Gazette* 67(1): 87–106.

O'Sullivan, J. (2005) "Delivering Ireland Journalism's Search for a Role Online." *Gazette* 67(1): 45–68.

Paulussen, S. (2004) "Online News Production in Flanders: How Flemish Online Journalists Perceive and Explore the Internet's Potential." *Journal of Computer-Mediated Communication* 9(4). DOI: 10.1111/j.1083-6101.2004.tb00300.x.

Paulussen, S. and D'heer, E. (2013) "Using Citizens for Community Journalism." *Journalism Practice* 7(5): 588–603.

Pitts, M.J. (2003) "Television Web Sites and Changes in the Nature of Storytelling." *SIMILE: Studies in Media & Information Literacy Education* 3(3): 1–8.

Quandt, T. (2008) "(No) News on the World Wide Web." *Journalism Studies* 9(5): 717–738.

Ryfe, D., Mensing, D., Ceker, H. and Gunes, M. (2012) "Popularity is Not the Same Thing as Influence: A Study of the Bay Area News System." Paper presented at the International Symposium on Online Journalism, Austin, TX. Available from: https://online.journalism.utexas.edu/2012/papers/Mensing.pdf.

Sjøvaag, H., Moe, H. and Stavelin, E. (2012) "Public Service News on the Web." *Journalism Studies* 13(1): 90–106.

Steensen, S. (2011) "Online Journalism and the Promises of New Technology." *Journalism Studies* 12(3): 311–327.

Steensen, S. and Ahva, L. (2015) "Theories of Journalism in a Digital Age." *Digital Journalism* 3(1): 1–18.

Stroud, N.J., Scacco, J.M. and Curry, A.L. (2015) "The Presence and Use of Interactive Features on News Websites." *Digital Journalism* 4(3): 339–358. DOI: 10.1080/21670811.2015.1042982.

Tankard, J.W. and Ban, H. (1998) "Online Newspapers: Living Up to the Potential?" Paper presented at the Annual Conference of the AEJMC, Baltimore, MD, August.

Theng, Y.L. and Thimbleby, H. (1998) "Addressing Design and Usability Issues in Hypertext and on the World Wide Web by Re-Examining the 'Lost in Hyperspace' Problem." *Journal of Universal Computer Science* 4(11): 839–855.

Tremayne, M. (2005) "News Websites as Gated Cybercommunities." *Convergence: The International Journal of Research into New Media Technologies* 11(3): 28–39.

Tsui, L. (2008) "The Hyperlink in Newspapers and Blogs." In Turow, J. and Tsui, L. (eds) *The Hyperlinked Society*. Ann Arbor, MI: University of Michigan Press, pp. 70–83.

Vobič, I. (2014) "Practice of Hypertext." *Journalism Practice* 8(4): 357–372.

Weber, M.S. (2012) "Newspapers and the Long-Term Implications of Hyperlinking." *Journal of Computer-Mediated Communication* 17(2): 187–201.

31

COMPUTER-MEDIATED CREATIVITY AND INVESTIGATIVE JOURNALISM

Meredith Broussard

In May 2015, journalist Maggie Lee posted the following to an email list of data journalists: "So, I'm a state gov't reporter learning CAR, hooray. Python and D3 and whatnot etc. But Lord, what should I make?" Lee's question, of what to write about, is a common one for digital journalists armed with tech skills but seeking an appropriate story on which to unleash them. Some journalists, asking themselves the same question, will undoubtedly answer, "I want to do an investigative story that uses government data to uncover potential fraud." Given the growing interest in computational analysis inside digital journalism and the resulting increase in questions such as Lee's, I offer a method for constructing a software system that will assist in developing a suite of story ideas on a single theme on a public affairs beat. The system, which I call a Story Discovery Engine, is a reporting tool. Like any specialized tool, its purpose is to help its user with a specific task, but it will also be useful for other as-yet-unimagined purposes. Creating a Story Discovery Engine and deploying it on a beat can help reporters to come up with a variety of story ideas based on data analysis.

In this chapter, I describe the Story Discovery Engine model for reporting. I explain what the Story Discovery Engine model is and offer an overview of the fields that the Story Discovery Engine draws on: artificial intelligence theory, cognition, and media management. I discuss how I developed a prototype for the system and deployed it for reporting, and what the impact was of that reporting. I conclude with suggestions for how the model might be usefully deployed in the future.

The Story Discovery Engine

The Story Discovery Engine is a model for a software system that accelerates the production of ideas and stories on a public affairs beat. It is intended as a tool to improve productivity in developing original investigative ideas and sources. The software model derives from a class of artificial intelligence programs called knowledge-based expert systems. Expert systems are designed to perform tasks at the level of a human expert. Benfer (1991) notes that expert systems typically incorporate artificial intelligence concepts, such as symbolic representation, inference, and heuristic search. Originally, the expert system was conceived as a black box that could deliver advice. It was imagined as a kind of doctor or other expert in a box. Some systems were developed for very specific, small-situation uses, as in web publishing (Lin, Hamalainen, and Whinston, 2002) or semiconductor factory monitoring (Fordyce *et al.*, 1989); efforts were also made to use expert systems in medicine (Buchanan and Shortliffe, 1984). These initiatives were largely abandoned over time, as machine experts proved far less effective than human experts. However, with new interest in artificial intelligence in recent years, expert systems have again emerged as an intriguing concept.

When most people think of artificial intelligence, they think of a fictional character: Commander Data from *Star Trek*, or Hal 5000 from *2001: A Space Odyssey*. It is important to remember that these characters are imaginary. There is no such thing as a sentient computer. In the realm of the real, we are constrained by the material realities of code, data, binary logic, and human beings.

A better way to think about artificial intelligence involves asking the question of how the computer can help reporters to come up with more ideas. Instead of thinking about a computer that can resemble or replace a human, think about ways that the computer can be inserted in the reporting process to make it easier for humans to do complex tasks.

The tool metaphor is helpful here. Imagine a carpenter who is building a house. When the carpenter has to drive a nail, he can use either a hammer or a nail gun fueled by an air compressor. Either way will work. However, the additional power that he gets from the compressor-fueled nail gun will allow him to build some things faster and more efficiently. The nail gun will likely spur him to build more complicated things because driving nails is so much easier with the additional power. He won't stop using the hammer and nail when appropriate—sometimes the simplest solution will be the most efficient solution. However, adding the nail gun to his arsenal of tools will help him to build a more elaborate, "innovative" house.

The nail gun is a specialized tool that does a single thing really well: it drives nails. The hypothetical carpenter can use it to create any number of houses, each of which could look very different. So it is with a Story Discovery Engine. It is a specialized reporting tool that does a single thing really well: it analyzes government data and presents scenarios. Reporters can use it to create any number of investigative stories, each of which will differ.

In the Story Discovery Engine model, the rules of the system are those articulated in law and public policy. The system executes the rules against the available data and creates visualizations representing each real-world site (such as a school) in a district, state, or country. The reporter looks at a scenario, identifies anomalies, and judges whether the anomaly is likely to represent a problem. Each potential problem is an opportunity for an investigative story.

Cognition

Developing an idea for an investigative story is a creative act. It is also a task of substantial cognitive complexity. A new idea, one that suggests change or difference, is harder to generate than an idea that comes out of an existing framework or knowledge base (Fischhoff and Kadvany, 2011; Slovic, 2000). Creativity is more difficult than most of us realize.

According to Boden (1994, 1998), creativity involves transforming a conceptual space. One type of creativity has to do with the storybook idea of a solitary genius engaging in contemplative activity. The other kind, less glamorous, is deliberative: a more practical sort of creativity on demand. Deliberative creativity is what reporters practice on deadline and in the newsroom. The demand of the job is that one must come up with new, story-worthy ideas every day or every few days or multiple times per day according to the news production cycle. An education reporter covers the education beat; this is thus the conceptual space in which they operate and in which they develop expertise.

Improved deliberative creativity will help a reporter create more ideas, which creates more sellable commodities for the media organization. So, as a reporter or editor, a useful system will allow the agent to come up with novel story ideas faster or more efficiently or just differently. This notion is related to what López-Ortega (2013) calls human in the loop creativity—it involves situating the computer and the human in a loop in order to facilitate the production of new ideas. The Story Discovery Engine diverges from Lopez-Ortega's system in its intent: unlike in Lopez-Ortega's model, the goal is not to get the computer to create original, creative ideas. Instead, the goal is to create a system to augment the human's capacity to engage in deliberate creativity in a specific conceptual space. This is computer-mediated communication in the sense that Chandler and Munday (2011) define, meaning that the user engages in a type of human–computer dialogue (as in the Turing test or the Eliza therapist simulator). Interacting with the Story Discovery Engine results in an idea for an original investigative story.

The rules embedded in the engine correspond to the rules articulated in laws and public policies. The system presents the reporter with a scenario, a data visualization showing how a single location in the system fares relative to the ideal. Ordinarily, only a subject matter expert would be able to render judgments about whether a scenario is reasonable or anomalous. The Story Discovery Engine makes some of these decisions for the reporter. The reporter is thus free to proceed to higher-level cognitive tasks such as coming up with a novel investigative story based on the scenario.

Media management and investigative reporting

Investigative reporting occupies a prominent place in news organizations' organizational hierarchies (Gans, 2004; Tuchman, 1978). I specifically refer here to investigative enterprise journalism produced over weeks or months that includes diverse sources (Hansen, 1991). Coming up with an original investigative idea is a creative act under Sternberg's (1999) definition of creativity as the production of work that is both novel (as in original) and appropriate (as in useful). Such ideas are also difficult—which explains why most investigative journalism results from tips by a whistleblower as opposed to a reporter's own initiative (Protess, 1991).

I specify investigative journalism, not routine journalism, because firms such as Automated Insights and Narrative Science have done fascinating work using artificial intelligence to generate routine news stories (see Carlson, this volume). The Associated Press uses Automated Insights technology to generate routine business and sports stories (Carlson, 2014). Both Automated Insights and Narrative Science currently rely on natural language generation (NLG), a different artificial intelligence concept, to create stories (Callaway and Lester, 2002; Fassler, 2012).

An NLG program will layer in some colloquialisms and a dash of the client's house writing style, and will concatenate these filler phrases along with new data. Concatenation, in the Boolean algebra that underscores most modern programming languages, means sticking things together. Usually two strings of text are concatenated. Concatenating A AND B results in the string AB. In ordinary arithmetic, 2 + 2 = 4. Concatenating 2 AND 2 results in 22.

Following is an example of the AP's October 2014 earnings report story for McCormick & Co, juxtaposed with the same story for a subsequent quarter. The similarity of the two stories suggests that the program concatenates raw financial data and stock phrases:

McCormick beats Street 3Q forecasts

McCormick tops 3Q earnings and revenue expectations

October 2, 2014 7:28 AM

SPARKS, Md. (AP)—McCormick & Co. (MKC) on Thursday reported profit of $122.9 million in its fiscal third quarter.

The Sparks, Maryland-based company said it had profit of 94 cents per share. Earnings, adjusted for non-recurring costs, came to 95 cents per share.

The results topped Wall Street expectations. The average estimate of analysts surveyed by Zacks Investment Research was for earnings of 81 cents per share.

The spices and seasonings company posted revenue of $1.04 billion in the period, which also topped Street forecasts. Analysts expected $1.03 billion, according to Zacks.

McCormick expects full-year earnings in the range of $3.30 to $3.37 per share.

McCormick shares have declined nearly 5 percent since the beginning of the year, while the Standard & Poor's 500 index has increased slightly more than 5 percent. The stock has increased 1 percent in the last 12 months.

This story was generated automatically by Automated Insights (http://automatedinsights.com/ap) using data from Zacks Investment Research. Full MKC report: http://www.zacks.com/ap/MKC

(AP/Automated Insights, 2014)

McCormick beats 4Q profit forecasts

McCormick tops 4Q net income expectations, misses revenue forecasts

January 28, 2015 6:49 AM

SPARKS, Md. (AP)—McCormick & Co. (MKC) on Wednesday reported fiscal fourth-quarter net income of $148 million.

On a per-share basis, the Sparks, Maryland-based company said it had profit of $1.14. Earnings, adjusted for non-recurring costs, were $1.16 per share.

The results topped Wall Street expectations. The average estimate of analysts surveyed by Zacks Investment Research was for earnings of $1.14 per share.

The spices and seasonings company posted revenue of $1.17 billion in the period, which fell short of Street forecasts. Analysts expected $1.2 billion, according to Zacks.

For the year, the company reported profit of $437.9 million or $3.34 per share. Revenue was reported as $4.24 billion.

McCormick expects full-year earnings in the range of $3.51 to $3.58 per share.

McCormick shares have decreased almost 2 percent since the beginning of the year, while the Standard & Poor's 500 index has decreased slightly more than 1 percent. The stock has increased 5.5 percent in the last 12 months.

This story was generated by Automated Insights (http://automatedinsights.com/ap) using data from Zacks Investment Research. Access a Zacks stock report on MKC at http://www.zacks.com/ap/MKC

(AP/Automated Insights, 2015)

Looking at the two stories next to each other, it is clear that the NLG program is running a very sophisticated version of filling in the blanks. The programmatic logic is simple. Human journalists write the skeleton of the story, and the program plugs in the new data each time earnings are released. The sentence container for the first paragraph is likely constructed and calculated as follows:

[Company name] [ticker symbol] on [day of the week on which earnings were released] reported [type of income] of [earnings amount]. (The [company city], [company state]-based company said it had profit of [per-share profit] per share.) OR (On a per-share basis, the [company city], [company state]-based company said it had profit of [per-share profit]) The results (IF [per-share profit]<[Zack's predicted per-share profit] THEN 'topped'; ELSE 'fell below') Wall Street expectations.

This is an extraordinarily useful program—few humans are interested in writing the same routine earnings report stories day in and day out. But the program is also extremely limited. Narrative Science CTO Kris Hammond explains:

> Though the platform can search for spikes and correlations—trends that might surprise clients in a 'Freakonomics' sense—it can only report on story possibilities that human programmers have trained it to 'see.' In looking at geological data, say, the software could potentially catch a surprising link between hydrofracking and increased earthquakes—but wouldn't, unless humans had asked for an assessment of this possibility.
>
> *(Fassler, 2012)*

Noting a surprising link or drawing a novel conclusion requires sentience, cognition, and theory of mind—none of which can be implemented computationally right now. A routine business story can be produced satisfactorily using concatenation, but it is hardly the kind of watchdog journalism that helps democracy thrive.

The difference between an original investigative story and a routine story has to do with ideas about the role of journalism in democracy. A free press functions to "help citizens gain the knowledge they need to self-govern and navigate their lives" (Kovach and Rosenstiel, 2014). Both routine and investigative stories inform, but the importance of each is different. Investigative stories shine light on potentially or actively harmful situations; routine stories are status updates. Synthesis, bringing together disparate ideas to form new knowledge, is what makes investigative journalism useful. Machines can concatenate, but they cannot synthesize.

Computational journalism offers abundant opportunities for innovative investigative reporting (Howard, 2014; McChesney, 2012; Meyer, 2002; Pavlik, 2013), especially when dealing with the large data sets commonly termed 'big data' (boyd and Crawford, 2012; Diakopoulos, 2014). As outlined by Hamilton and Turner (2009), computational journalism is a form of digital journalism practice in which practitioners use "the combination of algorithms, data, and knowledge from the social sciences to supplement the accountability function of journalism." Coddington (2014: 337) further differentiates between three computationally intensive strands of digital journalism practice that he calls computer-assisted reporting, data journalism, and computational journalism, writing:

> CAR is rooted in social science methods and the deliberate style and public-affairs orientation of investigative journalism, data journalism is characterized by

its participatory openness and cross-field hybridity, and computational journalism is focused on the application of the processes of abstraction and automation to information.

We can see computational journalism as a discipline at the intersection of computer science and journalism.

Computational systems that accelerate story idea production present a clear economic opportunity for newsrooms. Ideas are the commercial lifeblood of media organizations. Nylund (2013) writes: "Creativity lies at the heart of the media industry. Media firms are dependent on an ongoing supply of ideas that can be turned into saleable commodities. Therefore, creativity can be seen as one of the most important strategic issues in media management" (Küng, 2008: 144–145). A system that can help reporters generate more ideas is also a system that helps generate more 'saleable commodities' and thus has a direct impact on an organization's bottom line.

The prototype

As a proof of concept, I developed a prototype for a Story Discovery Engine and used it for reporting an investigative story series. Prototyping a computational system differs from traditional social science research methods, hewing closer to what might be called applied research in computational journalism. In computer science, developing a new software system *is* the experiment. I developed the system I describe above and deployed it in reporting on public education in Philadelphia. I also published the reporting tool online as open source software to increase transparency and to allow citizens to participate by developing their own stories out of the same tool.

Background

Philadelphia is the sixth largest city in the United States, and the School District of Philadelphia is the country's eighth largest school district. School funding issues are a major concern in Philadelphia and present a range of complicated, multifaceted issues. I focused one of these issues: textbooks. Specifically, I looked at whether a school had enough textbooks for all of its enrolled students.

In today's world, teachers use a combination of learning materials: books, workbooks, worksheets, manipulatives, online learning materials, and so on. However, the book remains the base unit of education. It is the minimum requirement for learning. It also serves as a canary in a coal mine: if there are not enough books in a school, there probably are not enough of any other resources, either (Broussard, 2014b). Well-organized, well-funded schools have enough books for their students and also have enough computers and additional learning materials. (Education Law Center of Pennsylvania, 2013; Finnigan *et al.*, 2009) Poorly funded or struggling schools can achieve sufficient outcomes with only books; schools and teachers were very effective operating this way for centuries. However, in America's struggling urban school districts like Philadelphia (and New York, Los Angeles, Chicago, and so on), if there are not enough books, there usually are not enough other resources either.

This last statement is an example of informal knowledge that would be possessed by an experienced education reporter. Formal knowledge refers to 'official' rules of a system, as in English language grammar; informal knowledge refers to domain expertise and rules of thumb

(Scribner and Cole, 1973). Reporters on a beat develop expertise in the subject, meaning that they possess a great deal of formal and informal knowledge. Novice reporters have not yet developed this expertise. To develop the Story Discovery Engine, I acquired formal and informal knowledge about the American public education system and embedded some of that knowledge into the system in the form of rules.

The rules-based system works beautifully as a model for identifying social inequality. Equality is a core principle in American government; equal access to education is guaranteed under law. Equality is also a calculable term. It is possible to compute whether students in American public schools have enough books and learning materials to achieve the educational goals outlined in law and policy.

This calculation is possible because of a massive standardization effort inside the American education system that has been gaining traction since the 1960s. Very briefly: The No Child Left Behind Act of 2001 mandated that states should develop a system of standardized testing in order to receive federal education funds. These tests were to be tied to state educational standards, outlining the content and educational goals that should be covered in each grade. Three companies now dominate the K-12 testing market: Pearson, Houghton Mifflin Harcourt, and CTB McGraw-Hill. These companies write the tests, grade the tests, and write the books that schools buy to prepare for the tests. The tests are written in such a way that it is difficult (if not impossible) to pass them unless a school has used the preparatory materials that correspond to the test. Houghton Mifflin Harcourt, according to its promotional materials, controls 42 percent of the educational publishing market. Its 2013 revenue was \$1.38 billion (Houghton Mifflin Harcourt, 2014).

The education system is designed to work in a particular way: the standards are supposed to inform the learning materials, and the tests are supposed to evaluate how well the students have absorbed the material. However, the way this works in practice is extremely haphazard (Steinberg and Quinn, 2013). While struggling schools themselves are often disorganized and the student population fluid, these problems are compounded by the fact that ill-funded school districts cannot afford to buy the test prep materials and, moreover, the standards change yearly, requiring ongoing investment in new materials (Broussard, 2014a). There is a huge gap between how the system is designed to work and how it actually works.

Informal knowledge of an investigative reporter suggests that each time there is a mismatch between *what should be* and *what is*, there is an opportunity for a story. This framework is formalized in the Story Discovery Engine. The rules of the system are articulated in law and policy: these comprise *what should be*. Data, primarily open data collected and provided by the school district, federal and state government, comprises *what is*. Holding up *what is* next to *what should be*, a reporter can perceive an anomaly. This anomaly should then be judged based on the reporter's formal and informal knowledge: is there an opportunity for a story? If so, what kind of story? This goes back to the idea of deliberative creativity. The system has revealed a potential story, but it remains up to the reporter to determine if the situation warrants further investigation. The lead that the system provides prompts the reporter to start imagining the shape of a potential story. Figure 31.1 is an illustration of the expert system with the reporter in the loop.

In the original paradigm, the user queries the expert system and receives 'expert advice' based on the rules encoded in the inference engine. Investigative journalism, as a profession that relies on creativity and craftsmanship, has too many rules to articulate reasonably. Instead, it is most efficient to rely on the substantial 'computing' power of the human brain—again, human-in-the-loop creativity.

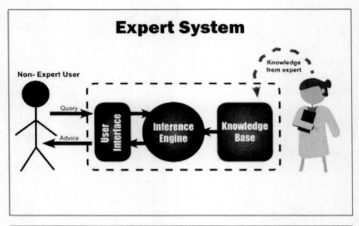

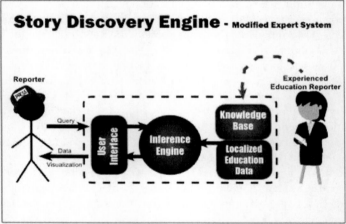

Figure 31.1 Expert system diagram.

The prototype tool I developed, which I call Stacked Up, is available online at stackedup. org. The program runs logical rules against 15 data sets comprising millions of pieces of data. A single reporter can generally analyze a single data set, and a team of data journalists can generally analyze two or three data sets together (Domingo, 2008; Parasie and Dagiral, 2012; Royal, 2010). Since I needed to pull together so many data sets in this case, it was necessary to build new software rather than using an off-the-shelf solution. Because large-scale data analysis is beyond the staffing capacity of most newsrooms (Fink and Anderson, 2014), I chose to make the Story Discovery Engine prototype available as open source software. Other reporters can use it to quickly run the same analysis in their states or districts and write multiple original investigative stories that matter to the newsroom's specific audience. Citizens can perform the same analysis as journalists, increasing transparency, and accountability.

Among the findings of the project were:

- Few schools had enough textbooks or learning materials to teach the students the material in the School District of Philadelphia's own educational guidelines.

- The School District of Philadelphia spent $111 million on textbooks between 2008 and 2013, yet was unable to locate or track most of these books.
- At least 10 schools appeared to have no books at all, according to the data in the textbook inventory system.
- Many schools were not using the textbook tracking system despite a District policy mandating its use.

These findings, once published, were shared widely on social media and received hundreds of comments. The findings also prompted a national conversation about books and tests, plus prompted changes in the School District of Philadelphia. Some of these changes included:

- At least two administrators involved in textbook tracking failures left the District.
- An internal investigation turned up additional corruption among book funds; this was eliminated and cost savings were achieved.
- When 24 Philadelphia schools were closed at the end of the 2013 school year, 4,000 students were reassigned to new schools. The District originally planned to send books from closing schools to the schools that were to receive the students; instead, they collected books from closing schools in a central location and attempted to reallocate them strategically.
- Administrators and principals audited schools to identify the curricula in use at each school.

This modest impact suggests that the model is effective and could be replicated in other US cities. Since many large US cities share the same urban problems and because government data are often collected in standardized formats, software solutions that work for one city can often be reused. In the future, the Story Discovery Engine model may be deployed in other public affairs realms such as transportation or campaign finance.

Further reading

A thorough explanation of expert systems may be found in R. A. Benfer's book *Expert Systems* (1991). Margaret Boden's book *Dimensions of Creativity* (1994) is an excellent resource for understanding creativity and its role in artificial intelligence. Nicholas Diakopoulos' work on algorithmic accountability, including a 2014 paper on the subject in the journal *Digital Journalism*, is useful for understanding the future of watchdog journalism in a data-driven culture.

References

AP/Automated Insights (2014) "McCormick Beats Street 3Q Forecasts." Available from: http://finance.yahoo.com/news/mccormick-beats-street-3q-forecasts-112854481.html (accessed 30 May 2015).
AP/Automated Insights (2015) "McCormick Beats 4Q Profit Forecasts." Available from: http://finance.yahoo.com/news/mccormick-beats-4q-profit-forecasts-114903717.html (accessed 30 May 2015).
Benfer, R.A. (1991) *Expert Systems*. Newbury Park, CA: Sage Publications. DOI: 10.4135/9781412984225.
Boden, M.A. (1994) *Dimensions of Creativity*. Cambridge, MA: MIT Press.
Boden, M.A. (1998) Creativity and Artificial Intelligence. *Artificial Intelligence* (103): 347–356.
boyd, danah and Crawford, K. (2012) "Critical Questions for Big Data: Provocations for a Cultural, Technological, and Scholarly Phenomenon." *Information, Communication & Society* 15(5): 662–679.
Broussard, M. (2014a) "Why Poor Schools Can't Win at Standardized Testing." *The Atlantic*. Available from: http://www.theatlantic.com/features/archive/2014/07/why-poor-schools-cant-win-at-standardized-testing/374287/.

Broussard, M. (2014b) "Artificial Intelligence for Investigative Reporting: Using an Expert System to Enhance Journalists' Ability to Discover Original Public Affairs Stories." *Digital Journalism* 3(6): 814–831.

Buchanan, B.G. and Shortliffe, E.H. (eds) (1984) *Rule-Based Expert Systems: The MYCIN Experiments of the Stanford Heuristic Programming Project*. Reading, MA: Addison-Wesley.

Callaway, C.B. and Lester, J.C. (2002) "Narrative Prose Generation." *Artificial Intelligence* 139(2): 213–252.

Carlson, M. (2014) "The Robotic Reporter: Automated Journalism and the Redefinition of Labor, Compositional Forms, and Journalistic Authority." *Digital Journalism* 3(3): 416–431.

Chandler, D. and Munday, R. (2011) *A Dictionary of Media and Communication*. Oxford, UK: Oxford University Press. Available from: http://www.oxfordreference.com/views/BOOK_SEARCH.html?book=t326 (accessed 26 May 2015).

Coddington, M. (2014) "Clarifying Journalism's Quantitative Turn: A Typology for Evaluating Data Journalism, Computational Journalism, and Computer-Assisted Reporting." *Digital Journalism* 3(3): 331–348.

Diakopoulos, N. (2014) "Algorithmic Accountability: Journalistic Investigation of Computational Power Structures." *Digital Journalism* 3(3): 398–415.

Domingo, D. (2008) "Interactivity in the Daily Routines of Online Newsrooms: Dealing with an Uncomfortable Myth." *Journal of Computer-Mediated Communication* 13(3): 680–704.

Education Law Center of Pennsylvania (2013) *Funding Public Schools in Pennsylvania: Law and Policy*. Available from: http://www.elc-pa.org/wp-content/uploads/2013/11/ELC_SchoolFunding_LawPolicy_11_6_13.pdf.

Fassler, J. (2012) "Can the Computers at Narrative Science Replace Paid Writers?" *The Atlantic*. Available from: http://www.theatlantic.com/entertainment/archive/2012/04/can-the-computers-at-narrative-science-replace-paid-writers/255631/ (accessed 26 May 2015).

Fink, K. and Anderson, C.W. (2014) "Data Journalism in the United States: Beyond the 'usual Suspects.'" *Journalism Studies* 16(4): 467–481.

Finnigan, K.S., Bitter, C. and O'Day, J. (2009) "Improving Low-Performing Schools through External Assistance: Lessons from Chicago and California." *education policy analysis archives* 17: 7.

Fischhoff, B. and Kadvany, J.D. (2011) *Risk: A Very Short Introduction*. Oxford, UK: Oxford University Press.

Fordyce, K., Norden, P. and Sullivan, G. (1989) "Artificial Intelligence and the Management Science Practitioner: One Definition of Knowledge-Based Expert Systems." *Interfaces* 19(5): 66–70.

Gans, H.J. (2004) *Deciding What's News: A Study of CBS Evening News, NBC Nightly News, Newsweek, and Time/Herbert J. Gans*. Evanston, IL: Northwestern University Press.

Hamilton, J.T. and Turner, F. (2009) *Accountability Through Algorithm: Developing the Field of Computational Journalism*. Center For Advanced Study in the Behavioral Sciences Summer Workshop: Stanford University. Available from: http://www.stanford.edu/~fturner/Hamilton%20Turner%20Acc%20by%20Alg%20Final.pdf (accessed 12 November 2013).

Hansen, K.A. (1991) "Source Diversity and Newspaper Enterprise Journalism." *Journalism & Mass Communication Quarterly* 68(3): 474–482.

Houghton Mifflin Harcourt (2014) *Houghton Mifflin Harcourt Media Kit*. Available from: http://www.hmhco.com/~/media/sites/home/media%20center/media-pdfs/hmh_media_kit_web-pdf_btn_hr.pdf?la=en (accessed 30 May 2015).

Howard, A.B. (2014) *The Art & Science of Data-Driven Journalism*. Tow Center for Digital Journalism: Columbia University. Available from: http://towcenter.org/wp-content/uploads/2014/05/Tow-Center-Data-Driven-Journalism.pdf

Kovach, B. and Rosenstiel, T. (2014) *The Elements of Journalism: What Newspeople Should Know and the Public Should Expect*. New York, NY: Three Rivers Press.

Küng, L. (2008) *Strategic Management in the Media: From Theory to Practice*. Thousand Oaks, CA: Sage.

Lin, Z., Hamalainen, M. and Whinston, A.B. (2002) "Knowledge-Based Approach for Automating Web Publishing from Databases." In Leondes, C.T. (ed.) *Expert Systems: The Technology of Knowledge Management and Decision Making for the 21st Century*. San Diego, CA: Academic Press, pp. 1155–1173.

López-Ortega, O. (2013) "Computer-Assisted Creativity: Emulation of Cognitive Processes on a Multi-Agent System." *Expert Systems with Applications* 40(9): 3459–3470.

McChesney, R.W. (2012) "Farewell to Journalism? Time for a Rethinking." *Journalism Practice* 6(5–6): 614–626.

Meyer, P. (2002) *Precision Journalism: A Reporter's Introduction to Social Science Methods.* Lanham, MD: Rowman & Littlefield Publishers.

Nylund, M. (2013) "Toward Creativity Management: Idea Generation and Newsroom Meetings." *International Journal on Media Management* 15(4): 197–210.

Parasie, S. and Dagiral, E. (2012) "Data-Driven Journalism and the Public Good: 'Computer-Assisted-Reporters' and 'Programmer-Journalists' in Chicago." *New Media & Society* 15(6): 853–871.

Pavlik, J.V. (2013) "Innovation and the Future of Journalism." *Digital Journalism* 1(2): 181–193.

Protess, D. (1991) *The Journalism of Outrage: Investigative Reporting and Agenda Building in America.* New York, NY: Guilford Press.

Royal, C. (2010) "The Journalist as Programmer: A Case Study of *The New York Times* Interactive News Technology Department." *International Symposium in Online Journalism.* Available from: https://online.journalism.utexas.edu/2010/papers/Royal10.pdf.

Scribner, S. and Cole, M. (1973) "Cognitive Consequences of Formal and Informal Education: New Accommodations Are Needed between School-Based Learning and Learning Experiences of Everyday Life." *Science* 182(4112): 553–559.

Slovic, P. (2000) *The Perception of Risk.* Sterling, VA: Earthscan Publications.

Steinberg, M.P. and Quinn, R. (2013) *Assessing Adequacy in Education Spending: A Summary of Key Findings from Pennsylvania and Philadelphia.* Available from: http://www.gse.upenn.edu/pdf/school_funding_summary_findings_steinberg_quinn.pdf.

Sternberg, R.J. (ed.) (1999) *Handbook of Creativity.* Cambridge, UK: Cambridge University Press.

Tuchman, G. (1978) *Making News: A Study in the Construction of Reality.* New York, NY: Free Press.

PART VI

Digital journalism and audiences

32

MAKING AUDIENCE ENGAGEMENT VISIBLE

Publics for journalism on social media platforms

Axel Bruns

Introduction: a second wave of citizen journalism?

The digitization of journalistic practice, which took off notably with the growing popularity of online media towards the end of the previous millennium, has brought about a number of profound changes for journalism, but arguably none is more significant than the transformation of the relationship between journalists and their audiences. Early in this process, the focus of scholars and practitioners alike turned to the rise of citizen journalism as an alternative form of collaborative news production. Popularized initially by *Indymedia* and similar online platforms and later by a myriad of news and commentary blogs engaging with the public debates of the day (Bruns, 2005), such citizen journalism activity was seen as a serious challenge to the authority of professional, industrial journalism which—depending on one's view—had to be combatted or embraced. Citizen journalists were demonized by some as 'upstarts' and 'armchair journalists' and embraced by others as valuable partners in the coverage and evaluation of news events—as Dan Gillmor famously put it, "my readers know more than I do" (2003: vi), especially on specialist topics beyond the general knowledge of the journalist.

But because the barriers to sustained, long-term participation in citizen journalism were almost as high as those to professional employment in the industry, citizen journalism in its conventional definition has remained a space populated by the usual suspects: "political junkies" (Coleman, 2003) who were already highly engaged in discussions about news and politics and simply shifted these debates to more visible online spaces. Some of them have managed to convert their amateur or semi-professional engagement into a more professional occupation over the past decade: such processes can be observed for practitioners from Matt Drudge to Arianna Huffington and from Guido Fawkes to Oh Yeon-ho. Far from a multitude of citizen journalists and news bloggers committing "random acts of journalism" (Lasica, 2003) as a continuous, distributed practice, citizen journalism itself has become increasingly professionalized, and a number of websites that started as citizen journalism sites must now be regarded simply as news organizations in their own right, even if they had a very different genesis and maintain journalistic practices and attitudes that diverge significantly from the leaders of the mainstream news industry.

But alongside these mainstream and alternative news outlets whose relationship mirrors the two-tier framework Herbert Gans sketched out as early as 1980, more recent developments have brought about a new wave of engagement with the news, which may be able to lay a more convincing claim to finally realizing the 'random acts of journalism' that Lasica envisaged (Bruns, 2016). This new wave is enabled largely by a further lowering of the barriers of entry to public discussion of the news, brought about by the widespread adoption of the current generation of mainstream social media platforms—such as Facebook and Twitter—for the public discussion of news and current affairs. For citizens to engage with the news—to share it with their social media friends and followers, to comment on and critique it, and even to add to it by contributing additional facts and interpretations and posting eyewitness accounts from the scene of news events—it is now no longer necessary to set up a content management system, create a blog site, or write lengthy commentary articles: all that is required is a Facebook or Twitter account that has an established 'personal public' (Schmidt, 2014) of friends and followers or can tap into the debate raging around a relevant topical hashtag.

The nature of such social media contributions to public debate is necessarily different from those made by the first wave of citizen journalists (and not just because of the specific techno-logical affordances and limitations of current social media spaces, such as Twitter's 140-character limit). Many in this second wave of contributors are truly committing *random* acts of journalism: 'drive-by' comments on news and politics that are interspersed with observations from their daily personal and political lives, comments on football scores, music and movies, and updates on other everyday activities. The role of Facebook and Twitter as general-purpose social networks—rather than providing spaces only for specific topics, themes, or groups of users—makes this unavoidable, and yet their fundamental character as algorithmically determined platforms (Gillespie, 2013) also always allows the automated or on-demand surfacing of specific discussion threads, themes, or communities from the billions of messages exchanged through these platforms every day.

This is what Hermida (2010, 2014) and Burns (2010) describe—for the case of Twitter—as the platforms' 'ambient news' function: much like ambient music in a physical environ-ment, ambient news discussion is always already happening in the background on such social media platforms, among self-selecting pockets of interested users or as part of overall, everyday activities—but when new stories break and major events unfold, this news discussion comes to the foreground and becomes considerably more visible (spawning topical Twitter hashtags or public Facebook pages set up to facilitate and contain it, for example). Such activities may be uncoordinated, decentralized, and in that sense truly random, but in this simply represent the predominant ways in which audiences have always engaged with the news, well before the advent of online and social media. As Habermas notes, "the public sphere is rooted in net-works for the wild flows of messages—news, reports, commentaries, talks, scenes and images" (2006: 415); social media merely make these 'wild flows' a great deal more visible by endow-ing them with digital, traceable, and quantifiable form. This chapter demonstrates how these processes may be investigated using advanced social media analytics research methods.

New opportunities for researching journalism audiences

These methods generate significant new opportunities for research that seeks to investigate how audiences use, engage with, and respond to news content. Advances in social media analytics over the past few years have enabled the unobtrusive study of patterns of public user activities at very large scale and in close to real time (as a prime example of developments in the wider field of 'big data' research, focusing here especially on 'big social data') and are making it possible to observe the dynamics of social media activities around given news stories or news outlets, for example. Some such research focuses especially on the participation of users in topical hashtags on Twitter that relate to specific world events, from the Arab Spring uprisings to political scandals (e.g. Bruns, Highfield, and Burgess, 2013; Maireder and Schlögl, 2014), but such approaches are generally able to capture only the tip of the iceberg of what is likely to be much more widespread engagement with these topics beyond the self-selecting group of hashtag participants (Burgess and Bruns, 2015); by contrast, more comprehensive (but also more complicated and resource-intensive) studies are able to generate a far more detailed picture of the full range of the 'wild flows of messages' that result from 'random acts of journalism' on social media (combining Habermas and Lasica).

This chapter draws on data from one such longitudinal study, the Australian Twitter News Index (ATNIX), as an illustrative case. Since mid-2012, ATNIX has captured all tweets that contain links to a list of (at the time of writing) 35 Australian news and commentary websites (independent of whether such links were shortened using services such as *t.co* or *bit.ly*). ATNIX covers virtually all Australian outlets of national or regional importance; however, it excludes recent overseas entries the *Guardian*, *Daily Mail*, and *Buzzfeed*. These outlets launched Australian versions in recent years, but continue to operate under their .com or .co.uk domains; it is therefore impossible to distinguish tweets that link to the Australian editions of these titles from those that link to the UK or international editions. Conversely, Australian-based commentary publication *The Conversation* continues to be tracked in ATNIX, but its recent expansion to the UK and US, and its shift from a.edu.au to a.com domain for all content, has meant that its numbers will now be inflated by tweets from overseas users that link to *Conversation* content. Studies similar to ATNIX are underway for Germany and the Nordic countries, and the same model could be applied to other national media markets as well.

Now capturing more than one million tweets each month, ATNIX still only constitutes a subset of the full range of audience engagement with the news on Twitter, of course: it will not capture tweets that mention newsworthy events but do not include a link to news articles covering them. What the dataset represents, then, is one specific form of news engagement: the sharing of articles deemed to be relevant or important with one's own network of Twitter followers, potentially also including some framing comments in the tweet (cf. Bruns, Highfield, and Harrington, 2013). Arguably such engagement constitutes a particularly important public function exercised by this second wave of citizen journalism: the evaluation, dissemination, and contextualization of mainstream news media content by everyday social media users who are thus acting as gatewatchers (Bruns, 2005, 2016; Bruns and Highfield, 2015).

The following discussion illustrates the uses of the ATNIX dataset—and, by extension, of similar empirical data that may be gathered from other social media platforms—in understanding the activities and dynamics of social media-based news audiences as they actively engage with and contribute to the news. It explores the temporal dynamics of news engagement over time, examines the specific social media footprints of different news organizations, and thus reveals social media audiences' overall role in disseminating, discussing, and evaluating the news. Finally, it also compares these patterns with other data about the general use of online news sources in Australia to highlight the similarities and differences between the active social media news audience and more general online news audiences.

The active social media news audience

Twitter-based engagement with Australian news and commentary sites has grown considerably over the timeframe covered by ATNIX. While 2012 and 2013 saw an average of some 675,000 tweets per month that shared links to the various sites, that number has grown consistently during the subsequent period to more than 1.5 million tweets identified in the most recent reporting period of March 2015. This increase is both an indicator of continuing growth in the user base for Twitter in Australia (with 2.8 million Australian Twitter accounts identified by September 2013, and an estimate of more than three million at the time of writing; cf. Bruns *et al.*, 2014), and of the increasing importance of Twitter in the national public debate. ATNIX data also show an increase from some 153,000 unique monthly users who shared news links during 2012 and 2013 to an average of 233,000 unique monthly users sharing the news since mid-2014 (but this number may be somewhat inflated by an increasing number of overseas users sharing *The Conversation* content, in particular).

Growth patterns for the various sites tracked by ATNIX are necessarily strongly divergent and reflect the relative success of different news organizations in a rapidly changing media environment in general and in the social media space in particular. Almost all Australian news sites now operate Twitter and Facebook presences as a matter of course and many of their journalistic and editorial staff have also developed a personal presence in social media environments. However, their success in doing so has been determined by a combination of factors including the traditional popularity and visibility of the parent imprint in the overall Australian news market; the overall thematic and ideological positioning of the news outlet, and its relevance to the demographics represented on Twitter; the impact of barriers to access and sharing, such as complete or partial paywalls; and the adequacy of the social media marketing strategies pursued by each outlet's institutional and staff social media accounts.

In particular, ATNIX data show a widening gap between joint market leaders *ABC News* (the major Australian public broadcaster) and *Sydney Morning Herald* (a leading quality newspaper) and the rest of the market. While monthly tweets for these leading sites have more than doubled from an average of 122,000 tweets per month during 2012 and 2013 to almost 270,000 tweets per month in the first quarter of 2015, results for other outlets have stagnated by comparison. Tweets linking to middle-of-the-road site *news.com.au*, for example, increased only by 29% between 2012/13 (67,000 per month) and Q1/2015 (87,000 per month)—given the growth in the number of Australian Twitter accounts over the same period this may even represent a loss of relative market share, in fact.

Such numbers document a substantial, and growing, engagement with the news via Twitter. Australian Twitter users actively seek out and share news information from a broad range of news and commentary sites, with specific relatively stable preferences for particular sites, and in doing so initiate and continue a lively, virtually permanent debate about news and current affairs ranging across all aspects of the news. This entirely user-driven process constitutes an example of Habermas's 'wild flows' of news, and substantially amplifies the visibility of the news reports and commentary articles published by these outlets: their sharing through the personal publics of each participating user enables them to reach an audience well beyond the readers who would visit these sites on a regular basis. Further, since we must assume that many users will share specific news items also because they believe them to be of particular interest to their imagined audiences of friends and followers, this on-sharing of news items constitutes a form of at least loosely targeted news dissemination and curation. Such social media analytics make visible, then, active audiencing practices which have long been recognized in the literature (e.g. Fiske, 1992) but have rarely been observed *in situ* in large-scale studies.

News outlets' social media footprints

Beyond tracking the overall sharing patterns to document the important role that social media now play in disseminating the news, thus augmenting the dissemination activities of the news outlets themselves, the approach outlined here also enables us to explore in more detail the specific audiences which exist around the various news organizations within the social media space. This approach addresses important questions relating to the relative fragmentation or interconnection of the Twittersphere and similar social networks: Are the sharers of links to specific news and commentary sites highly loyal and partisan towards those sites to the exclusion of all others, forming what some have described as 'filter bubbles' (Pariser, 2011), or is their news diet considerably more varied?

To address these questions, the following discussion examines ATNIX data for the first quarter of 2015 and focuses on the 10,000 Twitter accounts which are most actively sharing links to the sites of *ABC News*, the *Sydney Morning Herald*, *news.com.au*, the popular tabloid newspaper *Herald Sun*, and the conservative national quality newspaper *The Australian*. Collectively, the 10,000 most active *ABC News* users posted 605,988 tweets sharing links to that site; those linking to the *SMH* posted 583,838 tweets; those for *news.com.au* 184,021; those for *The Australian* 147,248; and those for the *Herald Sun* 124,025. These five groups of 10,000 users each are thus responsible for a substantial portion of all news links shared in the Australian Twittersphere; together, they posted 1,645,120 of the 2,295,238 tweets linking to these five sites during the first quarter of 2015.

Having identified these five groups, it is now possible to examine the extent of the overlap between them. This reveals a number of notable patterns. First, the cross-tabulation in Figure 32.1a indicates the overlap between these most active userbases for each publication. It shows, for example, that users sharing links to *ABC News* are most likely also to share links to quality newspaper sites *Sydney Morning Herald* and *The Australian* (more than 5,000 accounts belong to the userbase of top sharers for both ABC and SMH) and least likely to link to the tabloid *Herald Sun*; indeed, of all five sites examined here, prominent *ABC News* sharers are least likely to share *Herald Sun* links as well. Conversely, the most active *Herald Sun* sharers are most likely to also share the news articles published by *The Australian* and *news.com.au* (potentially as a result of cross-promotion across the News Corporation network to which all three sites belong). Most notably, however, *Herald Sun* sharers are the most likely of all five groups of users to limit their news diet to this one site only: more than 4,600 *Herald Sun* users—almost half of the 10,000 most active sharers considered here—did not also appear among the most active 10,000 users sharing links to one of the other sites. By contrast, those who shared links to *The Australian* or the *Sydney Morning Herald* were most likely also to frequently share links to one of the other sites; only just over 27% of SMH sharers chose to share links to that site alone.

Figure 32.1b converts these observations into a basic network graph indicating the interconnections between the five sites' userbases; it demonstrates the strong triangle of interrelationships between *ABC News*, the *Sydney Morning Herald*, and *The Australian* as well as the somewhat weaker connections within the NewsCorp stable between *news.com.au*, *The Australian*, and the *Herald Sun*, while pointing to the strong disconnects between the *Herald Sun* userbase and those of *ABC News* and the *Sydney Morning Herald*. Nodes in this network are sized by weighted degree, which affords *The Australian* particular prominence as it most uniformly shares its active users with the userbases of the other four sites examined here. This may boost the spread of its content beyond its comparatively limited market share as indicated by overall ATNIX metrics: while links to *The Australian*'s articles are not shared anywhere near as widely and frequently as those to *ABC News* or the *Sydney Morning Herald*, arguably they are shared by a more diverse range of users.

What emerges from this is that the processes of news engagement in the Australian Twittersphere are neither entirely random acts, where users tweet and retweet links to Australian news sites without considering the source of the information as they do so, nor

	SMH	news	HS	Aus	none
ABC	5,024	3,284	2,834	4,230	3,506
SMH		3,913	3,265	4,951	2,748
news			3,609	4,166	3,966
HS				3,734	4,681
Aus					2,932

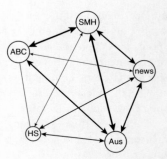

Figure 32.1 (a) Number of users shared between the userbases of the five sites, considering the top 10,000 most active Twitter users sharing links to each site in Q1/2015. Totals for each site are greater than 10,000 because double counts are possible. (b) Network graph of userbase overlaps between the 10,000 most active sharers of links to the five sites. Node size based on weighted degree; edge size based on weight of connection.

are they always predetermined by deep loyalties to specific news organizations over others. Instead, we may surmise that the specific preferences for some news outlets over others, and the divisions between the Twitter audiences of these outlets, and driven in part by broader habitual news repertoires well beyond online and social media themselves (habits which in turn may be related to factors such as thematic interest or socioeconomic status), and in part also by the network effects of social media-based news sharing itself (as widely shared news outlets are more likely to attract further sharers than more obscure sites). Further, the social media outreach activities of the news outlets and their staff, and internal cross-promotions between sites within the same media corporation, may also influence further user-driven sharing practices.

This points to the fact that the Australian Twittersphere is not strongly fragmented along political, socio-demographic, geographic, or other lines; there is no strong evidence of the formation of 'filter bubbles' (Pariser, 2011) or similar enclaves in the overall network which are hermetically sealed from the rest of the network and thus disconnected from information flows which may contradict their communities' commonly accepted beliefs and values. It is very much possible that the situation in other national Twitterspheres may differ considerably from this picture—and further research along the lines outlined here would be able to shed useful light on such questions. Australian news outlets clearly attract at least somewhat divergent audiences, but there appears to be enough overlap between these to avoid a fragmentation of the nationwide discourse into individual groupings, even on Twitter itself (and overlaps and interconnections in audiencing practices across other media forms should serve as further points of connection between these divergent audiences).

These distinctions between the different social media audiences for news outlets are also evident when the relative locations of the most active news sharers for each site are identified within the overall structure of the follower networks of the Australian Twittersphere. This builds on the comprehensive network map of the 140,000 most followed Australian Twitter accounts described in more detail in Bruns *et al.* (2014), which positions accounts relative to each other based on the structure of their follower relations; densely interconnected accounts will form close clusters, while loosely connected accounts will be placed at a greater distance from each other.

Identifying the locations of the most active 10,000 *ABC News* and *news.com.au* sharers on this map, it is immediately obvious that those accounts which share links to *ABC News* are more predominantly concentrated in a cluster of accounts related to Australian politics, while *news.com.au* sharers are less prominent in this politics cluster, somewhat more prominent in a cluster relating to various sports, and more generally dispersed throughout the map. This clearly points to the very different informational functions of these sites in the Australian public sphere in general, and in the Australian Twittersphere in particular—functions which can be explained fairly directly by their divergent editorial directions.

The fact that these news outlets cater to and seek to attract different audiences may not be particularly surprising. What is notable, however, is that the social media analytics approach outlined here is able to detect the effects of such editorial positioning on actual audience engagement; this represents a new metric—in addition to site visits, user registrations, and other data gathered by news organizations but rarely made publicly available in full—which can be used to assess the relative market positioning of individual sites. The use of such external data (generated by and available from the Application Programming Interfaces (APIs) of social media platforms such as Twitter) provides an important opportunity for researchers to generate solid independent data on the performance of news outlets at least among specific social media communities; further, if demographic information on such communities is available, more general societal news engagement patterns may also be able to be extrapolated.

Twitter news audiencing practices in context

One useful point of comparison in the Australian context is the data gathered by Experian Marketing Services, a company which captures anonymized information about the web searching and browsing activities of some 1.5 million Australian internet users. Its Experian Hitwise trends data, generated over the same timeframe as the ATNIX news sharing data and tracking the same set of news and commentary sites (with the addition of the *Guardian* and the *Daily Mail*), indicate that news *browsing* and news *sharing* practices in Australia differ considerably.

Figure 32.2 compares the number of tweets linking to the ATNIX sites, as determined by the ATNIX data themselves, with the number of total visits to the same sites, as identified by Experian Hitwise, for the first quarter of 2015. The comparison shows a number of very significant differences in the ranking of the sites, which can be explained in large part by the specific demographics of Twitter in Australia, where the platform's core userbase remains centered around comparatively affluent, well-educated, and urban users in the 25–55 age range, even though a considerable number of teenage users have joined the platform since 2012 (Bruns *et al.*, 2014; Sensis, 2014). Among the general population, middle-of-the-road news sites such as *news.com.au* and *ninemsn News*, UK tabloid spin-off *Daily Mail Australia*, and the site of quality newspaper *Sydney Morning Herald* are clearly leading the market—but the news that Twitter users choose to share with their followers is predominantly sourced from quality outlets *ABC News* and *Sydney Morning Herald*.

In addition to the demographic differences that are likely to be major drivers of these trends, other factors may also play an important role. It is probable, for example, that comparatively high-brow news content is shared disproportionately (and that less valued content is overlooked) if Twitter users are consciously taking into account the perceptions of their own imagined audiences as they make their sharing decisions: sharing news and commentary from quality publications could be seen as making the sharing users themselves appear more cultured and sophisticated, while sharing more low-brow content could have the opposite effect. (Such strategic decisions on how to position one's online persona are not limited to Twitter activities, of course.)

Website	Tweets
ABC News	847,517
Sydney Morning Herald	811,222
The Age	356,255
news.com.au	266,323
The Australian	202,326
The Conversation	186,418
Herald Sun	153,966
SBS World News	143,589
Daily Telegraph	133,319
Brisbane Times	124,741
Courier-Mail	87,698
Canberra Times	83,540
Yahoo!7 News	74,066
Australian Financial Review	66,344
Adelaide Now	39,666
Sky News	35,179
The West Australian	34,757
Crikey	33,971
Perth Now	32,967

Website	Total Visits
news.com.au	165,271,547
Sydney Morning Herald	114,343,374
Daily Mail	88,598,701
ninemsn News	75,772,762
The Age	73,188,461
ABC News	65,723,995
The Guardian	40,418,969
Herald Sun	38,987,455
Courier-Mail	36,795,376
Daily Telegraph	36,285,479
Perth Now	20,218,662
The Australian	18,532,520
Brisbane Times	16,718,828
Yahoo!7 News	10,868,806
Canberra Times	9,284,677
WA Today	8,533,372
Sky News	6,998,228
SBS World News	6,897,622
NT News	6,434,396

Figure 32.2   Tweets linking to the top 20 Australian news and commentary sites during Q1/2015 (left) and total visits to the top 20 Australian news and commentary sites during the same period (right; also contains data on the Australian editions of *Daily Mail* and *Guardian*, which cannot be tracked by ATNIX). Data on total visits courtesy of Experian Marketing Services Australia.

As a result, the ratios between visits and shares diverge widely across the different news outlets. Such ratios can be read in a number of ways, as it is difficult to ascribe a clear causal relationship between visits and shares: on the one hand, it may appear that a very substantial number of visits to a site such as *news.com.au* still results only in a comparatively low number of tweets sharing the content further; on the other hand, however, we might also say that a very high number of tweets linking to *ABC News* still appears to result in only a comparatively limited number of additional visits to the site. In the end, neither causal interpretation (visits result in shares; shares generate visits) is necessarily more likely than the other; what is most likely is simply that the ATNIX data on how news is being shared on Twitter represents a specific subset of audiencing practices that are very different from such practices as they unfold in other online spaces. (A brief glance at user practices on Facebook shows that the distribution of user activities across the various pages of Australian news outlets exhibits a different pattern yet again, for instance.) Any detailed investigation of causality would likely to have to trace user paths across specific websites and across the web as such.

Conclusion

What emerges from this brief study of the available data on news sharing in the Australian Twittersphere is a glimpse of the rich and diverse practices for news audiencing and engagement in social media. Such social media-based engagement necessarily constitutes only one component of a wider range of audience practices across multiple media forms, but—given the recognized amplifier effect of social media sharing and news curation—an increasingly important one. The analytics approach presented here can contribute significantly to our understanding of how audiences use the news, and of the effects that this may have on overall public debate and the democratic processes that depend on it; such analysis may then also come to affect the editorial and promotional strategies of news organizations themselves, for better or for worse. Already, some news outlets are actively exploring changes to their sites, content, or headlines that are designed to improve searchability and sharability, sometimes to the detriment of the journalistic quality of such content; the research methods outlined here are able to examine the impact of such changes on audience activities.

But beyond such more instrumental uses, the techniques outlined here also enable researchers to address some much more fundamental questions about what journalistic audiences do with the news. In a way that conventional methods are usually unable to do, these 'big data' analytics approaches are able to trace Habermas's 'wild flows of messages' well beyond their point of origin, and do so in ways that (unlike interviews, surveys, media diaries, or observational methods) are generally unobtrusive and do not disrupt or affect these flows themselves. They thus provide a useful counterpoint to the self-reporting of user activities which has been a common feature in many studies of audience attitudes and behaviors: they are able to test what news users tell us they do and fill in the gaps on what they fail to tell us. As a result of the combination of these diverse methods, a considerably more comprehensive picture of the processes by which publics for journalistic content form, act, and dissolve can be painted.

Further reading

Citizen journalism in its diversity of approaches, styles, and local adaptations is captured very successfully in the 2009 and 2014 volumes of *Citizen Journalism: Global Perspectives*, edited by Stuart Allan and Einar Thorsen. Further, Alfred Hermida's *Tell Everyone: Why We Share and Why It Matters* provides additional insights on the drivers of news sharing through social media. For more insights especially into the uses of Twitter and potential research approaches to this important platform, see *Twitter and Society*, edited by Katrin Weller *et al*.

Acknowledgment

This research was supported by the Australian Research Council through the Future Fellowship project "Understanding Intermedia Information Flows in the Australian Online Public Sphere."

References

Bruns, A. (2005) *Gatewatching: Collaborative Online News Production*. New York, NY: Peter Lang.

Bruns, A. (2016) "'Random Acts of Journalism' Redux: News and Social Media." In Jensen, J.L., Mortensen, M. and Ørmen, J. (eds) *News Across Media: The Production, Distribution and Consumption of News in a Cross-Media Perspective*. London, UK: Routledge (pp. 32–47).

Bruns, A. and T. Highfield. (2015) "From News Blogs to News on Twitter: Gatewatching and Collaborative News Curation." In Coleman, S. and Freelon, D. (eds) *Handbook of Digital Politics*. London, UK: Edward Elgar, pp. 325–339.

Bruns, A., Highfield, T. and Burgess, J. (2013) "The Arab Spring and Social Media Audiences: English and Arabic Twitter Users and Their Networks." *American Behavioral Scientist* 57(7): 871–898. DOI: 10.1177/0002764213479374.

Bruns, A., Highfield, T. and Harrington, S. (2013) "Sharing the News: Dissemination of Links to Australian News Sites on Twitter." In Gordon, J., Rowinski, P. and Stewart, G. (eds) *Br(e)aking the News: Journalism, Politics and New Media*. New York, NY: Peter Lang, pp. 181–210.

Bruns, A., Woodford, D., Sadkowsky, T. and Highfield, T. (2014) "Mapping a National Twittersphere: A 'Big Data' Analysis of Australian Twitter User Networks." Paper presented at the European Communication Conference (ECREA), Lisbon, 13 November.

Burgess, J. and Bruns, A. (2015) "Easy Data, Hard Data: The Politics and Pragmatics of Twitter Research after the Computational Turn." In Langlois, G., Redden, J. and Elmer, G. (eds) *Compromised Data: From Social Media to Big Data*. London, UK: Bloomsbury, pp. 68–88.

Burns, A. (2010) "Oblique Strategies for Ambient Journalism." *M/C Journal* 13(2). Available from: http://journal.media-culture.org.au/index.php/mcjournal/article/view/230 (accessed 18 April 2015).

Coleman, S. (2003) "A Tale of Two Houses: The House of Commons, the Big Brother House and the People at Home." *Parliamentary Affairs* 56(4): 733–758.

Fiske, J. (1992) "Audiencing: A Cultural Studies Approach to Watching Television." *Poetics* 21(4): 345–359.

Gans, H.J. (1980) *Deciding What's News: A Study of CBS Evening News, NBC Nightly News, Newsweek, and Time*. New York, NY: Vintage.

Gillespie, T. (2013) "The Relevance of Algorithms." In Gillespie, T., Boczkowski, P. and Foot, K. (eds) *Media Technologies*. Cambridge, MA: MIT Press, pp. 167–194.

Gillmor, D. (2003) "Foreword." In Bowman, S. and Willis, C. (eds) *We Media: How Audiences Are Shaping the Future of News and Information*. Reston, VA: The Media Center at the American Press Institute, p. vi. Available form: http://www.hypergene.net/wemedia/download/we_media.pdf (accessed 18 April 2015).

Habermas, J. (2006) "Political Communication in Media Society: Does Democracy Still Enjoy an Epistemic Dimension? The Impact of Normative Theory on Empirical Research." *Communication Theory* 16(4): 411–26.

Hermida, A. (2010) "From TV to Twitter: How Ambient News Became Ambient Journalism." *M/C Journal* 13(2). Available from: http://journal.media-culture.org.au/index.php/mcjournal/article/view/220 (accessed 18 April 2015).

Hermida, A. (2014) "Twitter as an Ambient News Network." In Weller, K., Bruns, A., Burgess, J., Puschmann, C. and Mahrt, M. (eds) *Twitter & Society*. New York, NY: Peter Lang, pp. 359–372.

Lasica, J.D. (2003) "Blogs and Journalism Need Each Other." *Nieman Reports* (Fall): 70–74. Available from: http://niemanreports.org/articles/blogs-and-journalism-need-each-other/ (accessed 18 March 2015).

Maireder, A. and Schlögl, S. (2014) "24 Hours of an #outcry: The Networked Publics of a Socio-Political Debate." *European Journal of Communication* 29(6): 687–702.

Pariser, E. (2011) *The Filter Bubble. What the Internet Is Hiding from You*. New York, NY: Viking.

Schmidt, J.-H. (2014) "Twitter and the Rise of Personal Publics." In Weller, K., Bruns, A., Burgess, J., Puschmann, C. and Mahrt, M. (eds) *Twitter & Society*. New York, NY: Peter Lang, pp. 3–14.

Sensis (2014) "Yellow™ Social Media Report: What Australian People and Business are Doing with Social Media." Available from: https://www.sensis.com.au/content/dam/sas/PDFdirectory/Yellow-Social-Media-Report-2014.pdf (accessed 18 April 2015).

33

CONSTRUCTING NEWS *WITH* AUDIENCES

A longitudinal study of CNN's integration of participatory journalism

You Li and Lea Hellmueller

Technology has not only changed how audiences consume information but it has also allowed them to construct information with journalists. The privilege of gathering and publishing news is no longer exclusively tied to the salaried work of professional journalism institutions (Deuze *et al.*, 2007; see Wall, this volume). While audiences welcome and celebrate the participatory culture, professional journalists maintain their gatekeeping role and normalize user-generated content mainly to fit existing editorial structures and procedures (Domingo *et al.*, 2008; Lewis *et al.*, 2010; Singer, 2005). Such participation in a restricted manner questions the extent to which the journalist–audience relationship has changed, and whether that relationship has been static or has evolved over time and across different editorial contexts.

This chapter presents a longitudinal study of CNN's iReport to examine the adoption of participatory journalism in mainstream media. It investigates in what context audience participation was encouraged and integrated into CNN, and how audience participation may shift the journalist–audience relationship over time. Pierre Bourdieu's field theory (1986), and in particular his concept of cultural capital, is applied to explain the institutionalizing process of participatory journalism in the case of CNN. The chapter departs from a dichotomous classification of journalism as either professional or nonprofessional, a major drawback seen in previous literature that misses the dynamic and hybrid character of a networked journalistic culture (Waisbord, 2013). This study is premised on the view that to understand how participatory culture becomes an integral addition to mainstream media like CNN, we should focus on the trajectory of integration over time.

CNN iReport presents an excellent landmark to document the progress of the professional-participatory relationship. Founded in 2006, CNN iReport has evolved from a stand-alone citizen journalism website into an integral part of the CNN brand that encourages audience around the world to contribute pictures and videos of breaking news. Our study analyzed news stories from CNN between 2006 and 2012 that relied partially or fully on iReports. The findings indicate that the integration of iReports in CNN news output conforms to journalists' gatekeeping function; audiences contributed post-hoc feedback and eyewitness accounts in most cases and occasionally acted as journalists' co-workers in covering foreign events. Audience materials were used as just another news source, routinized and institutionalized as organizational resources at a time when CNN was most vulnerable to economic challenges. While the newsroom was downsizing its editorial operations, iReport became the leading and sometimes only source of reporting extreme disasters in foreign lands. As participatory journalism compensated lost workforce or even substituted some newsroom positions in the aftermath of the recession (Ariens, 2011), it clearly shows that audience has now become part of that news-making process.

Participatory journalism

We conceptualize *participation* as a collaborative and collective action during which professional journalists work with audiences to create news (Singer *et al.*, 2011). Participation in that regard comes from both sides: audiences contribute their labor to the news-making process, while journalists share their organizational brand and resource. In this participatory culture, journalists are no longer confined to a physical space but rather build presence on whatever platforms popular with audience in order to remain as a relevant and authoritative news source (Robinson, 2011).

Despite their initial enthusiasm about the potential democratic opportunity provided by participatory journalism, researchers in recent years have found more disappointment with professional journalism's obduracy, economic motives to facilitate participatory journalism and audiences' passivity (Borger *et al.*, 2013). Mainstream media have been slow to adapt to the participatory culture, as they perceive user-generated content largely as a threat to editorial standards that would ultimately undermine journalistic norms and values (Harrison, 2010; Singer, 2010; Thurman, 2008). Though newspaper websites incorporated participatory features that invited audiences' commenting and blogging, they did not facilitate a meaningful and open participation and gradually discouraged audience involvement (Karlsson, 2011; Karlsson *et al.*, 2015). Newsrooms outsourced soft, good, and small local news to participatory journalists and preserved the hard and bad news as an exclusive territory to professional journalists (Karlsson, 2011; Paulussen and D'heer, 2013). Most journalists regard audience contributions, mostly in the forms of comments and experiences, as a source of news material to be processed the same way as traditional news sources (Wardle and Williams, 2010). Participation by and large is structured as a strategic experiment to solicit content subsidiaries for free and to generate traffic to websites (Borger *et al.*, 2013; Vujnovic *et al.*, 2010). A reciprocal relationship is expected and necessary to restore the relationship between news organizations and participatory audience in order to sustain many participatory journalistic projects (Borger *et al.*, 2014).

Journalists' attitude toward participatory journalism has shifted from suspicion to collaboration in recent years as citizens' reporting of emergencies and crises has become a complementary source to fill the vacuum of mainstream media coverage in resource-crunched newsrooms (Volkmer and Firdaus, 2013). BBC Persian and Arabic services relied heavily on protesters and amateur journalists to cover the 2009 Iran protests and the Arab uprising that followed when journalists' access on the ground was forbidden (Hänska-Ahy and Shapour, 2013). The *New York Times* has depended upon Syrian journalists' and non-journalist activists' insider knowledge to select and explain the events by incorporating their emotionally intensive video fragments in its blog 'the Lede,' which in a way allowed audience to co-frame the stories through a shared gatekeeping process (Wall and Zahed, 2014). In contrast to professional journalists' reporting, citizen journalists are more likely to report their own observations, personal experiences, and interview civilian sources rather than official sources of information (Bal and Baruh, 2015; Paulussen and D'heer, 2013). Participatory journalism has produced an alternative version of stories different from mainstream news (Bal and Baruh, 2015) and is welcomed by news consumers who regard it as giving ordinary people a chance to express themselves and covering important news that help them connect with other people (Holton *et al.*, 2013).

Through the lenses of Bourdieu's field theory (1986), the professional-participatory relationship can be understood as an ongoing struggle between agents occupying different positions within the journalistic field. Position is partially determined by the agent's pursuit of cultural capital that preserves one's identity and the extent of recognition in the journalistic field. To gain acceptance, new agents like participatory journalists need to acquire cultural capital in three interrelated forms: the embodied form, the objectified form, and the institutionalized form. The embodied form of cultural capital comprises "long-lasting dispositions of the mind and body" (Bourdieu, 1986: 249), such as education and practical experiences. The objectified form of cultural capital involves the transformation of the embodied state into a form that sets itself apart from its bearer and is hence visible to others—news output in general (Bourdieu, 1986). Finally, the institutionalized form of cultural capital neutralizes "some of the properties it derives from the fact that being embodied" (Bourdieu, 1986: 250). In its institutionalized form, cultural capital "confers on its holder a conventional, constant, legally guaranteed value with respect to culture" (Bourdieu, 1986: 250; see Table 33.1). It is cultural capital in its institutionalized form that defines a profession which, in the field of journalism, can refer to the fundamental norms and values widely shared and acknowledged by professional journalists which includes the principles of objectivity, newsworthiness, and verification.

In this chapter, we are mainly interested in how participatory journalists develop cultural capital in their collaboration with traditional journalists. Compared to established agents,

Table 33.1 Three forms of cultural capital adapted to the three stages of institutionalizing iReport.

	Embodied state	*Objectified state*	*Institutionalizing CNN iReport*
First stage: Definition	Incorporation	Properties defined by relationships with cultural capital in its embodied form	Audiences learn technical skills to produce visuals
Second stage: Investment	Time, personal cost	Transmissible in its materiality	CNN provides audiences with an access to a distribution channel that activates audiences' skills and knowledge of constructing news Audiences invest time and personal resource to transmit their skills in form of materiality to iReport
Third stage: Accumulation	Self-improvement	Presupposes economic capital Must have access to embodied cultural capital in person or by proxy	CNN reinforces and routinizes acceptable journalistic practices by training audiences in boot camps and by awarding best iReports

Source: Adapted from Bourdieu (1986).

new entrants to a field are more likely to introduce and create new forms of cultural capital because they are less familiar with the norms of the field (Kuhn, 1970). Consequently, to explain the extent to which participatory journalism has influenced the journalistic field, it is necessary to understand what form(s) of cultural capital participatory journalists have brought to the journalistic field and whether that capital differs from existing principles.

Method

A total of 3,589 newscast[1] transcripts and 2,750 online articles containing the keyword 'iReport' were archived by the database LexisNexis from August 2006 to September 2012. We selected the first 1,000 relevant articles ranked by LexisNexis's standard (i.e. the location, frequency and number of the search terms appear in the document). After deleting redundant messages and messages of promotional nature, we closely analyzed 316 broadcast transcripts and 353 online articles by tracking the story topic and story type associated with each use of iReport. The purpose was to contextualize and identify on what occasions CNN invited and integrated iReporters' participation. Two researchers coded 10 percent of the total sample to test for intercoder reliability. Using Cohen's *kappa* as a rather conservative measure, we reached almost perfect agreement for story topic (.90) and story type (.91). Moreover, iReporters' contribution to news production via composing stories was textually analyzed and weighed against the share of duties taken by professional journalists. Textual analysis pays attention to word choice, signs, voices, and related genre and context that give meanings to the language of users' discursive themes and strategies (Foss, 2004; Hall, 1980; McKee, 2003). By noting in what way CNN journalists refer to iReporters and their work, we intend to understand how, across the study period, iReporters' tasks and responsibilities became more similar to or differentiated from those of professional journalists.

Findings

We have written elsewhere that CNN assigned three primary positions to iReporters: commentators, eyewitnesses, and co-workers of professional journalists (Hellmueller and Li, 2014). However, not all positions arose around the same time or provided equal value to CNN. The following section will explain the three stages of institutionalizing participatory journalism.

The first stage (2006–2008): defining iReport as participatory journalism

Since the first day of operation, iReporters were motivated to become "reporter[s]" (CNN The Situation Room, 2006: August 1) and the "eyes and ears on the ground" for the network (CNN Live Today, 2006: August 2). Indeed, being an eyewitness to history was the first and most dominant position taken by iReporters who invested minimal professional or technological capital to cover breaking news of disasters and conflicts, including crisis in Middle East, tropical storms on the U.S. east coast, a snow storm in Buffalo, NY, wildfires in Florida and California, a bridge collapse in Minnesota, and many other stories. What CNN really wanted and considered valuable was audiences' proximity to news events that made their eyewitness accounts authentic, credible, and emotional. This kind of proximity not only allowed audiences to blend the roles of observer and participant but also to personalize the news. In that regard, eyewitness accounts function more like a news source in the traditional sense of illustrating or providing a perspective on a news event. Nevertheless, CNN often placed eyewitness accounts briefly in the later part of its programs, suggesting a marginal importance compared to traditional news sources. Moreover, CNN seldom included any iReporters' own narrative or interviews on the air to contextualize the incidents, even though the network staff often interviewed iReporters beforehand to collect background information.

A secondary position that emerged during this period was being a commentator who responded to CNN's solicitation of opinions and questions on political issues, including their voting experience, visions of the American dream, and thoughts about the presidential candidates. Audience members taking this position posted comment in text or video format on the website first, which were then screened and selected to air in the newscasts. CNN promoted this position around the 2006 mid-term election and then popularized it during the Democratic primary debate in 2007. The iReport in such cases offers an equivalent to more traditional avenues for engagement, such as an editor's mailbox or a discussion forum.

Overall, the integration of iReport in CNN mainstream news programs was still at a preliminary stage in these first two years. CNN set up a clear and intentional boundary between iReport and the rest of CNN programs in both organizational structure and editorial design. In 2007, CNN acquired the domain names iReport.com and i-Report.com to separate iReport from CNN.com (DN Journal, 2008: January 17). Moreover, the site used graphics and text to distinguish between the CNN brand and iReport content on the site. For instance, the CNN logo appeared nowhere in the iReport logo or in the site's tagline or page titles, but only in the lower right corner of pages and on content that was aired or posted on a CNN property (Hampel, 2008). CNN experimented with iReport as a strategic tool to engage audiences and crowdsource while keeping its traditional journalism practices remote and intact (see Aitamurto, this volume). Even when iReports were used in newscasts, their value to the whole program remained incremental if not marginal. The network had yet to fully embrace participatory culture.

The second stage (2008–2009): investing cultural capital in iReport

After two years of experimenting, the number of iReports included in both newscasts and online stories rose from a few hundred to more than a thousand per year, indicating a high investment of capital in the project by both CNN and its audiences. More collaboration took place at both organizational and editorial levels. In October 2009, iReport officially became part of CNN.com. CNN threw off the blue banner and separate URLs, indicating a formal recognition of iReport: "We did it because we know that together, CNN and iReport paint a more complete picture of the news" (CNN, 2009: October 30). The merging of iReport with CNN's main news website has shaped a model for "a news organization to report and tell the story of an event together with its audience" (King, 2011).

iReport added a considerable amount of user-generated content to CNN's editorial inventory. More than 800 transcripts were found mentioning 'iReport' in newscasts and online archives respectively in 2008, and more than 1,000 transcripts were found including 'iReport' for the two media platforms respectively in 2009.[2] For both platforms and in both years, being an eyewitness was a more prominent participatory position than being a commentator. The iReports about natural disasters were particularly popular with editors of the newscasts; nearly 40 percent of our sampled iReports aired in those two years featured coverage of weather or weather-related damages. Some prominent incidents included earthquakes in Sichuan, China (2008), Hurricane Dolly (2008), Hurricane Ike (2008), Hurricane Gustav (2008), wildfires in California (2009), and the protest in the Iranian presidential election (2009). The eyewitness accounts were no longer marginal to CNN reporting but becoming major and, on occasion, the only news source when CNN lacked access to the ground such as during the 2009 Iranian presidential election (CNN iReport, 2009: January 17). In contrast, website content trended toward entertainment and opinion. Political opinions often generated long threads of discussion, but very few of these would end up in newscasts unless an important political figure or issue was featured in the program. The topics that attracted high participation included the economic crisis, the Occupy Wall Street movement, the presidential election, gay marriage, health care reform, and the federal debt ceiling. Besides soliciting comments on political and business issues, CNN encouraged audiences to share personal stories on human interest topics. Those topics, such as the African Americans in America (2008), in memory of Michael Jackson (2009), Dr. Randy Pausch (2008), U.S. Senator Ted Kennedy (2008) and iReporters' Halloween photos (2009), added little news value, but engage audiences with diverse interests.

A third participatory position of being a co-worker of journalists emerged during this period when iReporters not only accessed and observed news events but also processed and interpreted information. The more journalistic capital an audience embodied, involving technical skill and professional knowledge, as well as the more objectified capital they produced—interview sources, edited stories and provision of context when interpreting the news—the more these audiences resembled professional journalists. One of the frequent contributors Desire Glover, described herself as a citizen journalist and a freelance illustrator (CNN Newsroom, 2009b: June 25). A super iReporter, Kyle Aevermann, was planning a career in journalism when asked what motivated him to submit an average of 10 stories per month: "This is what I want to do. I either want to be your co-anchor or your competition" (CNN Newsroom, 2009a: May 20).

Meanwhile, the unedited and unfiltered features of the iReport project had triggered a few controversial incidents where audiences posted marketing information or even untrue stories. Controversies like these damaged CNN's brand image and editorial integrity and questioned CNN's decision of not policing iReport or educating audiences on journalistic practices and ethics (Callan, 2008; Perez, 2008). To address these issues, CNN began to institutionalize iReport in the third stage by introducing a vetting system, a training boot camp, and a formal award system to regulate audience participation.

The third stage (2010–2012): accumulating institutional cultural capital

In the third stage, the number of iReports used in CNN declined to a third of its peak.[3] Within our sample, 97 stories were retrieved from newscast programs and 133 stories were found online. While the salience of integrating iReports on the web seemed to rise to and surpass its broadcast counterpart for the first time in years, the distribution of participants' positions in compiling various story topics were similar to that of previous years. CNN newscasts were more oriented toward integrating eyewitness accounts of disasters and accidents in breaking news coverage, whereas the website posted more audience comments on politics followed by features and human interest stories. CNN took advantage of iReporters' geographic proximity to news events and urged them to translate this capital into an immediate sharing of visuals and sound bites with CNN.com, which eventually contributed to CNN's story telling via broadcast. In this process, iReporters' eyewitness accounts (i.e. objectified cultural capital) helped to improve the organization's credibility (i.e. symbolic cultural capital) among audiences. In contrast, the website provided infinite space to host discussion about national politics and accumulated a large inventory of quotes to be cited in online articles. On both platforms, iReport did not bring a new form of objectified cultural capital but rather built upon CNN's existing practice and even filled the gap when the organization lacked resources to produce that form of objectified cultural capital.

The fact that CNN integrated fewer iReports in both newscasts and online articles may be due to several factors. For one, we speculate that CNN might become more selective and conservative about using user-generated content after seeing a series of unverified iReports misleading audiences and compromising the brand. In the third stage, CNN installed formal structures to regulate iReporters' journalistic practices. This is an important step toward transitioning iReporters from investing embodied cultural capital (i.e. journalistic skills and resources) to producing desirable objectified cultural capital (i.e. news stories, eyewitness accounts, and comments) that conforms to institutional norms and routines. The process started with CNN's launching of the iReport Awards in 2011 "to honor the best examples of participatory journalism" and to "showcase and recognize them for the impact they make on the news." (CNN, 2011: February 15). In addition, CNN educated iReporters on journalistic ethics and practices by training them in boot camps (Costello, 2011). iReporters who completed such training would have improved chances to work as journalists' co-workers in newscasts and even earn their individual bylines on CNN.com (CNN iReport, 2013: February 20). For example, when Charity Deane traveled to Uganda on a mission, she photographed her experiences and published them on CNN.com "after she participated in an iReport boot camp, an initiative aimed at improving iReporters' storytelling skills over a seven-week period" (CNN iReport, 2011: November 4). Meanwhile, the very act of standardizing user-generated content might discourage audiences from submitting content to CNN. After six years, the idea of participatory journalism was not as innovative or exciting to either journalists or audiences anymore. As more network competitors launched user-oriented programs, CNN iReport gradually became a regular audience engagement project with more online presence.

Conclusion

This study applied Bourdieu's concept of cultural capital to understand how participatory journalism became a part of the journalistic field through a case study of CNN's integration and institutionalization of iReport across six years. We found a broad variety of contributions from iReporters, ranging from eyewitnessing disasters to commenting on political and economic issues. Audiences' reporting and interpretation of news events would only become an exclusive source of news when CNN's journalists were absent. In other words, audience's proximity to and knowledge of those events, rather than their journalistic skills, contribute to the construction of news. Although CNN shared its platform and brand with participatory journalists and even championed them to become journalists' counterparts, CNN still weighed audiences' materials against professional principles and monopolized the editorial process of editing, interpreting, and analyzing hard news, i.e., the institutionalized form of cultural capital. As audiences learned more about 'defensive routines' (Shoemaker and Reese, 2014), such as verification and reporting, they gradually produced content that complies with professional norms. In essence, although audience's embodied capital may change with the use of different technological tools made possible by digitization, participatory journalism did not change the objectified cultural capital or challenge the institutionalized cultural capital of CNN, but rather helped to accumulate both forms of capital for CNN.

Our analysis also demonstrates that the integration of participatory culture is a long-term process. In our case, CNN intentionally separated iReport from its main operation at the outset and only established a standalone website for iReport a year later. CNN merged iReport with the main website in 2009, recognizing iReport as an integral corporate asset. Such collaboration, however, prompted criticism when unverified and unedited iReports caused damage to the editorial brand. Since then, CNN has installed more policing, training, and awarding systems to further regulate, educate, and reinforce standard journalistic practices. Now CNN only airs vetted iReports in its newscasts notwithstanding how urgent and newsworthy the piece may be (CNN iReport, 2014). As CNN journalists and producers became more articulate about the practice of CNN iReporters, the "new paradigm is moving past its infancy" (Elliot, 2008: 38). iReport has become a routine practice at CNN through which audiences can construct news most likely when they conform to the CNN principles.

Further reading

For more in this area, Singer *et al.*'s *Participatory Journalism: Guarding Open Gates at Online Newspapers* presents various challenges and issues facing most Western media in adopting user-generated content. Michael Borger, Anita Van Hoof, and Irene Costera Meijer's article *Constructing Participatory Journalism as a Scholarly Objects* summarizes the major themes and arguments of the scholarly research done between 1995 and 2011. Chris Peters and Marcel Broersma's (2013) *Rethinking Journalism: Trust and Participation in a Transformed News Landscape* highlights the vital functions of participatory journalism in regaining public trust and engagement while transforming the way public seek and receive news.

Notes

1 The newscast in the US broadcast system is equivalent to the news bulletin in the UK broadcast system.
2 803 broadcast transcripts and 863 online articles were archived in 2008; 1,134 news transcripts and 1,084 online articles were archived in 2009.
3 470 broadcast transcripts and 292 online articles were archived in 2010; 342 news transcripts and 234 online articles were found in 2011; and 370 news transcripts and 239 online articles were found from January to September 2012.

References

Ariens, C. (2011) "Dozens of Jobs Cut at CNN." *Mediabistro*, 11 November. Available from: http://www.mediabistro.com/tvnewser/dozens-of-jobs-cut-at-cnn-new-york-atlanta-washington-dc-miami-la-staffers-pink-slipped_b97876.

Bal, H.M. and Baruh, L. (2015) "Citizen Involvement in Emergency Reporting: A Study on Witnessing and Citizen Journalism." *Interactions: Studies in Communication & Culture* 6(2): 213–231.

Bourdieu, P. (1986) "The Forms of Capital." In Richardson, J.G. (eds) *Handbook of Theory and Research for the Sociology of Education*. New York, NY: Greenwood, pp. 241–258.

Borger, M., Hoof, A. and Meijer, I.C. (2013) "Construting Participatory Journalism as a Scholarly Object." *Digital Journalism* 1(1): 117–134.

Borger, M., Hoof, A. and Sanders, J. (2014) "Expecting Reciprocity: Torwards a Model of the Participants' Perspective on Participatory Journalism." *New Media & Society* 18(5): 708–725. DOI: 10.1177/1461444814545842.

Callan, J. (2008) "CNN's Citizen Journalism Goes 'Awry' with False Report on Jobs." *Bloomberg*, 4 October. Available from: http://www.bloomberg.com/apps/news?pid=newsarchive&sid=atekONWyM7As.

CNN (2009) *This Week in iReport: Welcome to the New CNN iReport*. Available from: http://www.cnn.com/2009/US/10/30/irpt.weekinireport/index.html

CNN (2011) *Press Release*. Available from: http://cnnpressroom.blogs.cnn.com/2011/02/15/cnn-launches-the-cnn-ireport-awards-2/

CNN iReport (2009) *Inaugural Segment for Don Lemon, CNN Newsroom.* Available from: http://ireport. cnn.com/docs/DOC-184216.

CNN iReport (2011) *iReporter Featured on New Photo Blog.* Available from: http://ireport.cnn.com/blogs/ ireport-blog/2011/11/04/ireporter-featured-on-new-photo-blog.

CNN iReport (2013) *How to Get a Byline on CNN.com.* Available from: http://ireport.cnn.com/blogs/ ireport-blog/2013/02/20/bylines-for-ireporters.

CNN iReport (2014) *From 'Vetted' to 'Verified'.* Available from: http://ireport.cnn.com/blogs/ireport-blog/2014/08/05/from-vetted-to-verified.

CNN Live Today (2006) *Transcript.* Available from: http://www.cnn.com/TRANSCRIPTS/0608/ 02/lt.02.html.

CNN Newsroom (2009a) *Transcript.* Available from: http://transcripts.cnn.com/TRANSCRIPTS/0905/ 20/cnr.03.html.

CNN Newsroom (2009b) *Transcript.* Available from: http://www.edition.cnn.com/TRANSCRIPTS/ 0906/25/cnr.07.html.

CNN the Situation Room (2006) *Transcript.* Available from: http://edition.cnn.com/TRANSCRIPTS/ 0608/01/sitroom.03.html.

Costello, C. (2011) "Welcome to CNN iReport Boot Camp." *CNN iReport,* 12 August. Available from: http://www.cnn.com/2011/IREPORT/08/05/boot.camp.irpt/.

Deuze, M., Bruns, A. and Neuberger, C. (2007) "Preparing for an Age of Participatory News." *Journalism Practice* 1(3): 322–338.

Domingo, D., Quandt, T., Heinonen, A., Paulussen, S., Singer, J.B. and Vujnovic, M. (2008) "Participatory Journalism Practices in the Media and Beyond." *Journalism Practice* 2(3): 326–342.

Elliot, D. (2008) "Essential Shared Values and 21st Century Journalism." In Wilkins, L. and Christians, C. (eds) *The Handbook of Mass Media Ethics.* Abingdon, UK: Routledge.

Foss, S.K. (2004) *Rhetorical Criticism: Exploration and Practice.* 3rd ed. Long Grove, IL: Waveland.

Hall, S. (1980) "Culture, Media, Language." In *Working Papers in Cultural Studies, 1972-79.* London, UK: Hutchinson.

Hampel, M. (2008) "iReport: Participatory Media Joins a Global Brand." *The Berkman Center for Internet & Society at Harvard University.* Available from: https://cyber.law.harvard.edu/sites/cyber.law. harvard.edu/files/iReport_MR.pdf.

Hänska-Ahy, M.T. and Shapour, R. (2013) "Who's Reporting the Protests?" *Journalism Studies* 14(1): 29–45.

Harrison, J. (2010) "User-Generated Content and Gatekeeping at the BBC Hub." *Journalism Studies* 11(2): 243–256.

Hellmueller, L. and Li, Y. (2014) "Contest Over Content: A Longitudinal Study of the CNN iReport Effect on the Journalistic Field." *Journalism Practice* 9(5): 617–633. DOI: 10.1080/17512786.2014.987553.

Holton, A.E., Coddington, M. and Gil de Zúñiga, H. (2013) "Whose News? Whose Values? Citizen Journalism and Journalistic Values through the Lens of Content Creators and Consumers." *Journalism Practice* 7(6): 720–737.

Jackson, R. (2008) "Daily Post." *DN Journal,* 17 January. Available from: http://www.dnjournal.com/ archive/lowdown/2008/dailyposts/01-17-08.htm.

Karlsson, M. (2011) "Flourishing but Restrained: The Evolution of Participatory Journalism in Swedish Online News, 2005–2009." *Journalism Practice* 5(1): 68–84.

Karlsson, M., Bergström, A., Clerwall, C. and Fast, K. (2015) "Participatory Journalism—The (R) evolution that Wasn't. Content and User Behavior in Sweden 2007–2013." *Journal of Computer-Mediated Communication* 20(3): 295–311.

King, L. (2011) "Five Years of iReport." *CNN iReport,* 2 August. Available from: http://www.cnn. com/2011/IREPORT/08/02/5years/.

Kuhn, T.S. (1970) *The Structure of Scientific Revolutions.* 2nd ed. Chicago, IL: University of Chicago Press.

Lewis, S.C., Kaufhold, K. and Lasorsa, D.L. (2010) "Thinking about Citizen Journalism." *Journalism Practice* 4(2): 163–179.

McKee, A. (2003) *Textual Analysis: A Beginner's Guide.* Thousand Oaks, CA: Sage.

Paulussen, S. and D'heer, E. (2013) "Using Citizens for Community Journalism." *Journalism Practice* 7(5): 588–603.

Perez, S. (2008) "Steve Jobs Had No Heart Attack... and Citizen Journalism Just Failed." *Readwrite,* 8 October. Available from: http://readwrite.com/2008/10/03/steve_jobs_had_no_heart_attack_ citizen_journalism_failed.

Robinson, S. (2011) "'Journalism as Process': The Organizational Implications of Participatory Online News." *Journalism & Communication Monographs* 13(3): 137–210.

Shoemaker, P.J. and Reese, S.D. (2014) *Mediating the Message in the 21st Century: A Media Sociology Perspective*. New York, NY: Routledge.

Singer, J.B. (2005) "The Political J-Blogger: 'Normalizing' a New Media Form to Fit Old Norms and Practices." *Journalism* 6(2): 173–198.

Singer, J.B. (2010) "Quality Control." *Journalism Practice* 4(2): 127–142.

Singer J.B., Domingo, D., Heinonen, A., Hermida, A., Paulussen, S., Quandt, T., et al. (2011) *Participatory Journalism: Guarding Open Gates at Online Newspapers*. Chichester, UK: Wiley-Blackwell.

Thurman, N.J. (2008) "Forums for Citizen Journalists? Adoption of User Generated Content Initiatives by Online News Media." *New Media & Society* 10(1): 139–157.

Volkmer, I. and Firdaus, A. (2013) "Between Networks and 'Hierarchies of Credibility': Navigating Journalistic Practice in a Sea of User-Generated Content." In Peters, C. and Broersma, M. (eds) *Rethinking Journalism: Trust and Participation in a Transformed News Landscape*. Abingdon, UK: Routledge, pp. 101–113.

Vujnovic, M., Singer, J.B., Paulussen, S., Heinonen, A., Reich, Z., Quandt, T., et al. (2010) "Exploring the Political-Economic Factors of Participatory Journalism." *Journalism Practice* 4(3): 285–296.

Waisbord, S. (2013) *Reinventing Professionalism: Journalism and News in Global Perspective*. Cambridge, UK: Polity Press.

Wall, M. and Zahed, S.E. (2014) "Embedding Content from Syrian Citizen Journalists: The Rise of the Collaborative News Clip." *Journalism* 16(2): 163–180. DOI: 10.1177/1464884914529213.

Wardle, C. and Williams, A. (2010) "Beyond User-Generated Content: A Production Study Examining the Ways in Which UGC is Used at the BBC." *Media, Culture & Society* 32(5): 781–799.

34

REVISITING THE AUDIENCE TURN IN JOURNALISM

How a user-based approach changes the meaning of clicks, transparency, and citizen participation

Irene Costera Meijer and Tim Groot Kormelink

Attention for audiences is growing. Yet, journalism too often runs on assumptions and gut feelings about what audiences want and how they consume news. While a decline in ratings and revenues and the introduction of new digital platforms has forced news organizations to become more considerate of their users, the habit of thinking for them rather than consulting the users themselves is still deeply ingrained. Journalism scholars are not much better, as Picone, Courtois, and Paulussen (2015) point out. The fact that even research dealing explicitly with digital audiences tends to rely on information provided by news professionals rather than audiences themselves (cf. Anderson, 2011b; MacGregor, 2007; Vu, 2014) is illustrative of the strength and persistence of the 'newsroom-centricity' of journalism studies (Wahl-Jorgensen, 2009). This pattern leads to biased results, as our user-centered studies show: news users' habits, demands, and experiences are often more layered, nuanced, and complex than news organizations can imagine. Drawing from these studies—conducted under the auspices of the first author—we will challenge three dominant assumptions about the impact of the digitization of journalism on its users. These assumptions illustrate how despite increasing attention for audiences, a genuine audience turn in journalism and journalism studies is needed to avoid systematic bias and to truly understand what journalism means from a user perspective.

The first assumption is that interest in news can be captured in clicking metrics; we present research results that illustrate what clicking and not clicking actually means for people and how clicks are a limited instrument for capturing users' interests. The second assumption is that users appreciate what the digitization of journalism can offer them: more transparency and insight into how news is constructed. We demonstrate that journalism scholars tend to overrate the value of transparency for audiences. The third assumption we will challenge is that citizen participation in professional journalism practices after initial enthusiasm is doomed to fail. We show that the limited success of participatory journalism is due to an underestimation of citizen journalists' capabilities and confusion of tongues between users and producers. Finally, we suggest that the systematic and automatic bias about news users is not only connected with the newsroom centricity of scholars, but may also be enhanced by single method research, often surveys or web metrics.

Assumption 1: Clicks are a reliable standard of users' interests

The recent availability of very large data sets ('Big Data') has enabled us to trace people's digital news practices. Tools like Google Analytics and Chartbeat let news organizations observe in real time how many users are clicking on their news items. News professionals are increasingly taking these clicks as a directive to their editorial choices and policies, including altering or removing poorly clicked headlines, keeping or placing heavily clicked stories prominently on the website, and expanding or following up popular stories (Anderson, 2011a; Boczkowski and Mitchelstein, 2013; Lee, Lewis, and Powers, 2012; Tandoc, 2014). Metrics are not only employed by commercial news media to generate more traffic; public news media use clicks as evidence of their public relevance (Karlsson and Clerwall, 2013), and journalists who do not have to deal with economic concerns still monitor metrics to see if their stories are doing well: "It's a gauge of my work. [...] If only five people are reading my stuff, I'm sad about it" (Usher, 2013). Throughout, web metrics are seen as reliable data to gauge user preferences: clicks as a measure of news interest. Because these metrics suggest that news readers are in essence primarily interested in so-called junk news (entertainment, sports, crime, etc.), becoming more responsive to news users' preferences is not without consequences. It might even endanger our democratic society, as argued by Boczkowski and Mitchelstein (2013) and Nieuwsmonitor (2013).

However, making use of news might not be equivalent to finding it important or even having an interest in it. And vice versa, nonuse may not mean people find it unimportant or do not have an interest in it, as we concluded in an earlier study (Costera Meijer, 2008). Still, measuring interest or value through usage frequency is a common research practice.

Rather than taking clicks at face value, in a recent study we not only employed the 'think-aloud-protocol' to follow people's digital news use closely and in real time but also used a sensory ethnographic approach in our interviews (N = 56) to investigate what clicking meant and when and why they clicked or did not click on news, resulting in a more complex story (Groot Kormelink and Costera Meijer, 2016). The results suggest that there is no one-to-one ratio between clicking behavior, demographic variables, and the level and type of interest in news. Illustrating that the reasons people have for clicking are much more diverse than the presence or absence of interest, we distinguished 30 distinct considerations, including *visual appeal*, *supersaturation*, and *informational completeness* (see Groot Kormelink and Costera Meijer, 2016, for full list).

Rather than their clicking patterns, people's browsing behavior (which cannot be automatically traced by web metrics) appears to be far more representative of their news interests. For instance, when browsing the *Al Jazeera* website, Jelena (age 26) shows a keen interest in the news, but this interest is not always captured in clicks:

> I just look what it says on the main page and those are usually things of which I'm already aware they're happening. [...] but then I just look at the headlines like uh, what has happened last night. [...] If I know a lot is happening, I'll check a couple of times per day to see if anything new has been added.

Jelena only needs to scan sentences and words to get the gist of what is going on, as she is already aware of the main developments behind the headlines. This browsing behavior updates her about important developments without involving any clicking. As a result, when looking purely at clicking patterns, one might erroneously conclude that Jelena has little interest in this news.

The participants were not inclined to click on informationally complete headlines that already told them all they wanted or needed to know about an event. Tessa (age 20) illustrates: "Very often you read the headline and then you already know, ok. [...] if you can kind of estimate what it says, [...] why would I read it?" This, however, as Jelena also illustrated, does not mean that the user does not pay attention to the headline itself. During the time of the interviews, the Syria conflict was featured heavily in the news. While many participants did not click on these news items, they did want to stay informed about the situation, gathering enough information from the headlines, and waiting to click until—from their perspective—something 'really new' happened.

Not accounting for browsing patterns without clicks, then, metrics tend to overrate the interest in headlines that invite users to click and underrate the significance of audiences' appreciation of headlines that simply inform. This leads to a no-win situation where journalists grudgingly give the audience more of the junk news they think it wants (Strömbäck, Karlsson, and Hopmann, 2012), whereas the users—while certainly also interested in clicking on funny or remarkable news—receive less of the important and recent news they expect professional journalists to present them with (Groot Kormelink and Costera Meijer, 2014). In addition, some of the reasons for (not) clicking we found suggest that on top of traditional journalistic values like relevance and topicality, users have additional criteria for what counts as 'valuable journalism' (Costera Meijer, 2013a; Costera Meijer and Groot Kormelink, 2015), including feeding their inquisitiveness by getting a different perspective on a well-known topic or finally understanding an issue by receiving the whole story rather than an isolated update. This mismatch between what journalists *think* they *know* the audience wants and what the audience *actually* wants, between perceived interest and actual interest, may lead to a downward spiral where, as O'Shea (2011) and Rosenstiel *et al.* (2007) suggest, journalism loses both quality and users.

Assumption 2: Transparency displaces 'objectivity' as primary standard for good journalism

Transparency is a new standard for journalism. The digitization of journalism and the dwindling trust in news media have "prompted calls for a normative shift from objectivity to transparency in journalism" (Karlsson, Clerwall, and Nord, 2014: 669). Most journalism scholars focus on what Karlsson (2010: 537) aptly named 'disclosure transparency,' which implies "that news producers can explain and be open about the way news is selected and produced." This kind of transparency has been ascribed the potential to (re-)establish the trust of the public and to enhance the credibility of journalism (Kovach and Rosenstiel, 2007; Hayes, Singer, and Geppos, 2007). When news organizations become more transparent about the newsmaking process, the character of news changes. From a finished product (published after it was found to be right and thus true) news becomes a continuous process of truth-seeking, enabling "the website audience to literally *see* in real time ... segments of the gathering and processing stages of news work" (Karlsson, 2011: 289). Research suggests that journalists themselves are hardly dying to let the audience see what is "hidden behind the curtain," but feel they have little choice due to decreasing audience trust and increasing competition (Chadha and Koliska, 2015: 225), as illustrated by a *Washington Post* editor:

> We are really aware that people have very high levels of suspicion about the media generally. Rightly or wrongly, the public does not trust us and so we have to make an effort to 'show' readers that we are professional in the way we do our job ... also there's definitely the aspect of competition.
>
> *(2015: 221)*

As Craft and Heim (2009: 226) rightly pointed out, this focus on credibility is a "focus on the needs of the news organization, not the readers or viewers." They suggested examining what methods of transparency work best for *them*. Following this suggestion, Doeve and Costera Meijer (2013) investigated two assumptions underlying most research: (1) transparency will enhance trust and credibility and (2) the user is interested in a look behind the scenes.

Contrary to scholarly and journalistic expectations, getting insight into the construction process of news was not appreciated by the majority of the respondents. In-depth user interviews (N = 19) (including cue card exercises to let participants rank transparency in relation to other news values like reliability and objectivity) suggest that both people's understanding as well as their appreciation of 'transparency' were limited. When the distribution of these findings was checked through a survey (N = 270), the majority of the participants preferred to experience news as a completed product, showing little interest in disclosure practices. These news users did not experience transparency as a positive value in its own right—like objectivity, for instance—and they preferred to hold on to the 'magic' quality of news. In line with the results of Van der Wurff and Schönbäch (2014: 128) who state that "[n]o more than 12 percent of the [Dutch] population would like to know how news items come about," "just getting the regular news" was more than enough for this majority. In fact, receiving updates all the time meant you could never be sure when the news you read represented the 'full story' and could therefore be trusted. As Stijn, a 25-year-old neuropsychology student, explained:

> When I read something, I often tend to believe it. And more so when it's in the paper than on the internet. I know that doesn't make sense [laughs], but that's just the way it feels. Because on the internet you can write something down so quickly, whrrrrr, enter [makes rapid typing movements on an imaginary keyboard], and there it is. ... They update the news *so* often. It's like: o, this is it. O, no, it isn't. We changed what we just said, again.
>
> *(Doeve and Costera Meijer, 2013: 5)*

Merely a small minority experienced disclosure transparency as increasing the reliability of news. These news users also loved being informed about the process of news production, preferably in real time, through hyperlinks, tweets from journalists, or alternative sources. What drove them to closely follow the news as process was the opportunity to learn something and to experience the news from the angle of the reporter, as if being a participant observer of journalism-in-action. This inclination resembles the 'body snatching' preference—experiencing the news through the 'body,' the perspective, of the protagonist of the news item—of news consumers (Costera Meijer, 2008).

If participants were able to experience news as permanent work in progress, which of course news is by its very nature, they welcomed strategies to enhance the transparency of its production process. If on the other hand participants demanded from news that it was a completed, finished (and thus 'true') product, they found it difficult to deal with disclosure transparency, because it emphasized the provisional, constructed, man-made nature of journalism. In the participants' experience, the digitization of journalism, including the increasing possibilities for the audience to question, contribute, and criticize its truth, challenges journalistic authority by the online exposition of the constructedness of news. Generally, participants did want to be sure news organizations were held accountable for any mistakes they might make, but apart from initiatives which would increase journalism's trustworthiness like actor and source transparency (Heise *et al.*, 2014), the vast majority had no desire to be confronted with disclosure transparency in their everyday news use (cf. Groenhart, 2012; van der Wurff and Schönbach, 2014).

Assumption 3: Citizens are unable to participate in professional journalism

As Borger *et al.* (2013b) point out, most academics initially agreed that digital technologies would enable and encourage audiences to participate in the making of news. However, as it turned out, one inhibitory factor is that the majority of journalists have a hard time incorporating participatory ideals and practices into their conventional journalistic values, roles, and routines (Borger *et al.*, 2013b; Deuze, Bruns, and Neuberger, 2007; Williams, Wardle, and Wahl-Jorgensen, 2011). Even frontrunners who pioneered user participation and who are therefore expected to be more open-minded than 'regular' editorial staff, reframed user participation—an active term which underscores users' agency—into a passive genre 'user generated content' (Borger *et al.*, 2013a; Costera Meijer, 2013a). This genre, as Hermida (2012: 313) concluded, is appreciated by professionals but only in exceptional circumstances like natural or man-made disasters. Ordinarily, as Heise *et al.* (2014: 422) suggest, journalists tend to assume that citizens are unable to participate in professional journalism, because they lack professional standards and routines like objectivity, and their motivations are "rather driven by affective and self-centered motivations (venting anger, self-display)." When we displace the focus in participatory journalism studies from the newsroom and the professionals involved to a citizen's point of view, a different picture surfaces.

Firstly, participation of citizens in professional journalism apparently works out when and if professionals and citizens have corresponding expectations of each other's roles and responsibilities. *Citizenside France* offers a good example (Nicey, 2013). This news photo agency pays amateurs for their original content, which is mediated, checked, and certified by professionals, who use classic gatekeeping procedures in addition to metadata, geolocation, and community management to transform "testimony into news information" (Nicey, 2013: 210).

When financial compensation is not available or sought after, Abma (2013), Costera Meijer *et al.* (2010), Costera Meijer (2013b), Heise *et al.* (2014), Fröhlich, Quiring, and Engesser (2012), and Borger *et al.* (2014) observed how citizens were willing to participate in professional journalism in return for learning the trade and improving one's job qualifications, a sizable audience, the expansion of one's network, recognition, or appreciation. When the news organization was unable or unwilling to provide such quid pro quo compensations, citizens would gradually lose interest.

Thirdly, it is not only journalists who accuse citizens of not being able to meet professional standards of factuality and objectivity. Allegations of routine subjectivity and self-centeredness also come from citizens. When interviewing citizen reporters participating in a hyperlocal project of a regional public broadcaster, they were critical about professional journalists who "only come if there are riots" (Costera Meijer, 2013c; Costera Meijer *et al.*, 2010). Citizen reporters accused their professional counterparts not only of a lack of facticity and objectivity, they also distanced themselves explicitly from the dominant conflict frame used by journalists to dramatize and spice up what happened in their neighborhood.

Paul:	Well, I think we are quite objective. In any case, more objective than the national journalists. (...)
Interviewer:	And why is that?
Paul:	Because we do not earn our bread with it.
Frank:	Right.
	(Everyone laughs)
Paul:	Because we don't necessarily have to get high ratings. We don't have to be liked.

These participatory journalists were proud that their amateur status gave them the freedom and independence to report about reality with an open mind instead of having to deliver news items within preconceived journalistic frames. Paradoxically, as we concluded, the success of this particular participatory journalism project depended on the regional broadcaster's willingness to grant them the freedom to produce their own weekly series and to provide technical support by professionals who understood the art of storytelling rather than newsmaking (Costera Meijer, 2013c; Costera Meijer *et al.*, 2010).

Yet, even in a situation where the professional news organization explicitly aims to integrate citizens' initiatives in its professional routines, citizen journalists will encounter numerous obstacles, as Abma (2013) found out through three case studies. Citizens have trouble getting heard by professionals when they do not conform to conventional roles as sources, tippers, PR, or activists. In one case, a citizen named Harry had made a video about an alderman's changing views about admitting new energy-generation windmills.[1] He had taken pains to shoot this video as if he were a journalist (and not an activist) and had followed journalistic procedures like hearing both sides and asking all the relevant questions. His story was, even in classical journalistic terms, an important one. Yet, weeks after he had e-mailed the video, he was still not contacted by the broadcaster. Abma (2013) retraced the entire process and asked an editor to explain what could have gone wrong. One explanation of why the message had remained unnoticed was that it was e-mailed to the broadcaster's general e-mail address; an address no one feels particularly responsible for. Second, even if the e-mail had been noticed, the regional newscaster might have had difficulties downloading it because it used a mail system that was not easily compatible with the file-sharing software "We-Transfer" Harry had used. A third and more viable explanation was that the message was not written in terms of a recognizable genre, for example, a press release, and on top of that contained as return address noreply@wetransfer.com. Although the message was accompanied by Harry's personal explanation and his mail address, both a press release format and a clear sender were indispensable to recognize valuable information. The editor explained: "If someone sends a press release about a big happening, I would have known what to do with it. In this case I had to find out for myself." This event illustrates how both the broadcaster and the citizen reporter need new conventions to recognize when and where citizens are acting as journalists and thus are stepping outside their accepted roles as source, tipper, PR, or activist. An expansion of journalistic discourse and citizens' and professionals' imagination of networked journalism is needed as a precondition for collaborating constructively in news making projects.

Conclusion

This chapter argued for a genuine audience turn in journalism studies by approaching web metrics, professional values, and user-generated content from the angle of audiences, users, and participants instead of journalism professionals as is customary. This approach enabled a debunking of three powerful assumptions about the meaning of clicks, transparency, and participatory journalism. First the newsroom centricity of journalism studies results in an incorrect assessment of audiences' news use practices. Journalists often assume that users' attention for news is reflected by their clicking patterns indicating a limited scope of news favorites: sports, crime, and celebrity news. We concluded, however, that browsing patterns (including checking, scanning, and snacking) provide more insight into what counts as useful or valuable journalism to its users. Ignoring browsing as yardstick for measuring users' concerns might lead to a downward spiral of both quality and use of journalism.

The second bias is the incorrect assessment of audiences' appreciation of particular news values. Contrary to newsroom expectations, disclosure transparency is not a convincing strategy to regain audiences' trust in news; only a small minority is able to enjoy its experience. The vast majority of the participants did not appreciate the uncertainty such openness results in and tended to trust news insofar as it reports rounded off events.

The third bias corresponds with an incorrect assessment of citizens' competences and willingness to participate in news production. From the participants' perspective, participatory journalism works if news organizations supply a free zone in which new gatekeeping procedures, new routines around networking and collaboration, and new forms of storytelling are developed to incorporate user-generated content into their professional news making procedures. In addition, a shared discourse is needed as a condition for collaborative journalism.

Finally, if we recognize that the digitization, the globalization, and the increasingly participatory character of journalism require us to listen more often and more carefully to audiences, users, and participants, we will need to radically alter our approach. A genuine audience turn in journalism studies may start from the principle of 'requisite variety,' or the need for tools and instruments "to be *at least as* complex, flexible, and multifaceted as the phenomena being studied" (Tracy, 2010: 841). Requisite variety may provide a better starting point for journalism research than the one-method approach (often surveys) that is habitually being used (cf. Costera Meijer, 2016). This is not only important from a scientific point of view but also because news media justify their policies and their financial and personal investments on the basis of these journalism studies.

Further reading

A prime example of a study that starts from a genuine audience perspective is *Media consumption and public engagement: Beyond the presumption of attention* (2007) by Nick Couldry, Sonia Livingstone, and Tim Markham. Kim Christian Schrøder's *News media old and new fluctuating audiences, news repertoires and locations of consumption* (2015) is also indispensable. Criteria and directives for good audience research are further discussed in *Practicing audience-centred journalism research* by Irene Costera Meijer (forthcoming). Pablo Boczkowski's and Eugenia Mitchelstein's *The news gap: When the information preferences of the media and the public diverge* (2013) provides further exploration of the differences in selection choices by news professionals and news users as measured through most clicked stories, whereas Tim Groot Kormelink's and Irene Costera Meijer's *What clicks actually mean: Exploring digital news users practices* (2016) provides a detailed account of clicking explored from a user perspective.

Note

1 An extensive version of this story can be read in Domingo, Masip, and Costera Meijer (2015).

References

Abma, C. (2013) "Tussen formeel en informeel: genetwerkte journalistiek met RTV N-H en lokale communities in Noord-Holland [Between Formal and Informal: Networked Journalism with RTV N-H and Local Communities in North-Holland]." Master thesis, Journalism Studies VU, Amsterdam.

Anderson, C.W. (2011a) "Between Creative and Quantified Audiences: Web Metrics and Changing Patterns of Newswork in Local US Newsrooms." *Journalism* 12(5): 550–566.

Anderson, C.W. (2011b) "Deliberative, Agonistic, and Algorithmic Audiences: Journalism's Vision of its Public in an Age of Audience Transparency." *International Journal of Communication* 5: 529–547.

Boczkowski, P.J. and Mitchelstein, E. (2013) *The News Gap: When the Information Preferences of the Media and the Public Diverge*. Cambridge, MA: MIT Press.

Borger, M., van Hoof, A., Costera Meijer, I. and Sanders, J. (2013a) "Constructing Participatory Journalism as a Scholarly Object: A Genealogical Analysis." *Digital Journalism* 1(1): 117–134.

Borger, M., van Hoof, A., Costera Meijer, I. and Sanders, J. (2013b) "It Really is a Craft': Repertoires in Frontrunners' Talk on Audience Participation." *Medijska istraživanja/Media Research* 19(2): 31–54.

Borger, M., van Hoof, A. and Sanders, J. (2016) "Expecting Reciprocity: Towards a Model of the Participants' Perspective on Participatory Journalism." *New Media & Society* 18(5): 708–725.

Chadha, K. and Koliska, M. (2015) "Newsrooms and Transparency in the Digital Age." *Journalism Practice* 9(2): 215–229.

Costera Meijer, I. (2008) "Checking, Snacking and Bodysnatching." In Lowe, G.F. and Bardoel, J. (eds) *From Public Service Broadcasting to Public Service Media RIPE@2007*. Gøteborg, Sweden: Nordicom, pp. 167–186.

Costera Meijer, I. (2013a) "Valuable Journalism: The Search for Quality from the Vantage Point of the User." *Journalism* 14(6): 754–770.

Costera Meijer, I. (2013b) "Beruchte buurten? Een journalistieke koorddans tussen kritiek en inspiratie in probleemwijken." In Tonkens, E. and de Wilde, M. (eds). *Als meedoen pijn doet. Affectief burgerschap in de wijk*. Amsterdam, Netherlands: Van Gennep, pp. 229–242.

Costera Meijer, I. (2013c) "When News Hurts: The Promise of Participatory Storytelling for Urban Problem Neighbourhoods." *Journalism Studies* 14(1): 13–28.

Costera Meijer, I. (2016) "Practicing Audience-Centred Journalism Research." In Witschge, T., Anderson, C.W., Domingo, D. and Hermida, A. (eds) *The SAGE Handbook of Digital Journalism*. London, UK: Sage, pp. 546–561.

Costera Meijer, I., Arendsen, J., van der Sluis, M. and Merks, M. (2010) *Een leesbare wijk. De impact van wijktelevisie*. Amsterdam, Netherlands: Lectoraat Media and Civil Society.

Costera Meijer, I. and Groot Kormelink, T. (2015) "Checking, Sharing, Clicking and Linking: Changing Patterns of News Use between 2004 and 2014." *Digital* Journalism 3(5): 664–679.

Craft, S. and Heim, K. (2009) "Transparency in Journalism: Meanings, Merits, and Risks." In Wilkins, L. and Christians, C.G. (eds) *The Handbook of Mass Media Ethics*. New York, NY: Routledge, pp. 217–228.

Deuze, M., Bruns, A. and Neuberger, C. (2007) "Preparing for an Age of Participatory News." *Journalism Practice* 1(3): 322–338.

Doeve, M. and Costera Meijer, I. (2013) "The Value of Transparency in Journalism for Audiences and (Public) Media Organizations." Paper presented at the conference Future of Journalism, Cardiff, 12–13 September.

Domingo, D., Masip, P. and Costera Meijer, I. (2015) "Tracing Digital News Networks: Towards an Integrated Framework of the Dynamics of News Production, Circulation and Use." *Digital Journalism* 3(1): 53–67.

Fröhlich, R., Quiring, O. and Engesser, S. (2012) "Between Idiosyncratic Self-Interests and Professional Standards: A Contribution to the Understanding of Participatory Journalism in Web 2.0. Results from an Online Survey in Germany." *Journalism: Theory, Practice, Criticism* 13(8): 1041–1063.

Groenhart, H. (2012) "Users' Perception of Media Accountability." *Central European Journal of Communication* 2: 190–203.

Groot Kormelink, T. and Costera Meijer, I. (2014) "Tailor-Made News: Meeting the Demands of News Users on Mobile and Social Media." *Journalism Studies* 15(5): 632–641.

Groot Kormelink, T. and Costera Meijer, I. (2016) "What Clicks Actually Mean: Exploring Digital News User Practices." Paper presented at ICA Conference 2016, Fukuoka, Japan, 9–13 June.

Hayes, A.S., Singer, J.B. and Ceppos, J. (2007) "Shifting Roles, Enduring Values: The Credible Journalist in a Digital Age." *Journal of Mass Media Ethics: Exploring Questions of Media Morality* 22(4): 262–279.

Heise, N., Loosen, W., Reimer, J. and Schmidt, J. (2014) "Including the Audience: Comparing the Attitudes and Expectations of Journalists and Users towards Participation in German TV News Journalism." *Journalism Studies* 15(4): 411–430.

Hermida, A. (2012) "Social Journalism: Exploring How Social Media is shaping Journalism." In Siapera, E. and Veglis, A. (eds) *The Handbook of Global Online Journalism*. Chichester, UK: Wiley, pp. 309–328.

Karlsson, M. (2010) "Rituals of Transparency: Evaluating Online News Outlets' Uses of Transparency Rituals in the United States, United Kingdom and Sweden." *Journalism Studies* 11(4): 535–545.

Karlsson, M. (2011) "The Immediacy of Online News, the Visibility of Journalistic Processes and a Restructuring of Journalistic Authority." *Journalism* 12(3): 279–295.

Karlsson, M. and Clerwall, C. (2013) "Negotiating Professional News Judgment and 'Clicks': Comparing Tabloid, Broadsheet and Public Service Traditions in Sweden." *Nordicom Review* 34(2): 65–76.

Karlsson, M., Clerwall, C. and Nord, L. (2014) "You ain't seen nothing yet." *Journalism Studies* 15(5): 668–678.

Kovach, B. and Rosenstiel, T. (2007) *The Elements of Journalism: What News People Should Know and the Public Should Expect*. New York, NY: Three Rivers Press.

Lee, A.M., Lewis, S.C. and Powers, M.J. (2014) "Audience Clicks and News Placement: A Study of Time-Lagged Influence in Online Journalism." *Communication Research* 41(1): 505–530.

MacGregor, P. (2007) "Tracking the Online Audience: Metric Data Start a Subtle Revolution." *Journalism Studies* 8(2): 280–298. DOI: 10.1080/14616700601148879.

Nicey, J. (2013) "Between Reactivity and Reactivation: User-Generated News, Photo Agencies, New Practices and Traditional Processes." In Storsul, T. and Krumsvik, A.H. (eds) *Media Innovations a Multidisciplinary Study of Change Gothenburg*. Gothenburg, Sweden: Nordicom/University of Gothenburg, pp. 207–218.

Nieuwsmonitor. (2013) "Seksmoord op horrorvakantie: De invloed van bezoekersgedrag op krantenwebsites op de nieuwsselectie van dagbladen en hun websites." *De Nederlandse Nieuwsmonitor*. Available from: http://www.nieuwsmonitor.net/d/244/Seksmoord_op_Horrorvakantie_pdf.

O'Shea, J. (2011) *The Deal from Hell: How Moguls and Wall Street Plundered Great American Newspapers*. New York, NY: Public Affairs.

Picone, I., Courtois, C. and Paulussen, S. (2015) "When News is Everywhere: Understanding Participation, Cross-Mediality and Mobility in Journalism from a Radical User Perspective." *Journalism Practice* 9(1): 35–49.

Rosenstiel, T., et al. (2007) *We Interrupt This Newscast: How to Improve Local News and Win Ratings, Too*. New York, NY: Cambridge University Press.

Strömbäck, J., Karlsson, M. and Hopmann, D.N. (2012) "Determinants of News Content." *Journalism Studies* 13(5–6): 718–728.

Tandoc Jr, E.C. (2014) "Journalism is Twerking? How Web Analytics is Changing the Process of Gatekeeping." *New Media and Society* 16(4): 559–575.

Tracy, S. (2010) "Qualitative Quality: Eight 'Big-Tent' Criteria for Excellent Qualitative Research." *Qualitative Inquiry* 16(10): 837–851.

Usher, N. (2013) "Understanding Web Metrics and News Production: When a Quantified Audience is not a Commodified Audience." *Digital Journalism* 1(3): 335–351.

van der Wurff, R. and Schönbach, K. (2014) "Audience Expectations of Media Accountability in the Netherlands." *Journalism Studies* 15(2): 121–137.

Vu, H.T. (2014) "The Online Audience as Gatekeeper: The Influence of Reader Metrics on News Editorial Selection." *Journalism* 15(8): 1094–1110.

Wahl-Jorgensen, K. (2009) "On the Newsroom-Centricity of Journalism Ethnography." In Bird, S.E. (ed.) *Journalism and Anthropology*. Bloomington, IN: Indiana University Press, pp. 21–35.

Williams, A., Wardle, C. and Wahl-Jorgensen, K. (2011) "'HAVE THEY GOT NEWS FOR US?' Audience Revolution or Business as Usual at the BBC?" *Journalism Practice* 5(1): 85–99.

35

BETWEEN PROXIMITY AND DISTANCE

Including the audience in journalism (research)

Wiebke Loosen and Jan-Hinrik Schmidt

Discussions about what journalism provides and what the audience selects have a long tradition in communications research and are also routinely a part of public debates on journalism's (in)ability to meet the demands and needs of its audience. Most would agree that journalism's purpose cannot be reduced to "giving the people what they want," while at the same time warning journalism not to ignore its audience's preferences. In essence, these debates are about the appropriate or functional degree of proximity and distance between journalism and its audience (Görke, 2014). But what does 'appropriate relation' mean, and who is going to decide on that and to what end? More generally, how do we define proximity and distance between journalism and audience, and how can we measure and assess it? And from a fundamentally theoretical perspective regarding journalism and the audience: What kind of relationship is it overall?

These questions are becoming even more pressing as media practices in the digital age blur the boundaries between news producers and consumers as well as between production and consumption (see Bruns, Costera Meijer and Groot Kormelink, this volume). In particular, the integration of social media into the media repertoires of individuals and media organizations urges us to rethink these categories, which are so fundamental, even constitutive, for journalism and audience research alike (see Hasebrink, this volume). Their fluidity and processuality have also been captured in hybrid terms: 'mass self-communication' (Castells, 2009: 58–70), 'produsage' (Bruns, 2008), 'personal media' (Lüders, 2008), or 'personal publics' (Schmidt, 2014), each of which offers new concepts that try to address the shifting relationship between professional journalism and active audiences and the 'de-boundarizing' of spheres that used to be regarded as separate (Loosen, 2015).

Given these developments, this chapter aims to provide an overview on current approaches to conceptualize and research the journalism/audience relationship. After a short glance at historical perspectives, we will address theoretical issues in more detail and discuss some ways the journalism/audience relationship has been conceptualized in empirical studies. The chapter concludes with reflections on the proximity and distance between journalism and audience and the role of journalism research in this respect.

Historical perspective

Paradoxically, the relation between journalism and its audience as a topic is both classical and emerging in journalism research. It is classical in the sense that the audience is (and has always been) constitutive for journalism and is therefore inherently interwoven in every conception or theory of journalism, its performance, and function for society. This is markedly visible in the case of journalism theories that are informed by social theories (Scholl, 2013; Löffelholz, 2008): Critical theories, for example, draw a picture of the audience as a mass that is both malleable and manipulated by media (industries). Cultural studies, on the other hand, ascribes the power over meaning and sensemaking to the user, who is subsequently making use of journalism and its products to their own end (Abercrombie and Longhurst, 1998).

At the same time, the journalism/audience relationship is an emerging topic as networked digital media have amplified the communicative forms which structure and reproduce it (Loosen and Schmidt, 2012). In other words: it makes a difference whether this relationship operates mainly under the conditions of mass media, or whether networked digital media provide additional and more varied channels of communication with different communicative modes. Print and broadcast media technologies have supported a 'communicative figuration' (Hepp and Hasebrink, 2014) that has been prominently described via theories of mass communication including 'gatekeeping' and the 'two-step-flow of communication' (McQuail, 2010). Within the mass media paradigm journalists act as 'senders' in the sense that they filter, aggregate and broadcast information for a dispersed and anonymous mass of people. Audience members act as 'receivers' of information who engage in interpersonal follow-up-communication on the news within smaller networks of families, friends, networks of shared interests, etc. These conversations, while important for the formation of opinion and social cohesion, do not gain the same visibility as journalistic content. Neither journalists nor most audience members take notice of them unless they are deliberately addressed in letters to the editors and subsequently chosen for publication, that is, for distribution to the mass audience, by journalists (da Silva 2012; Gans, 1977; Nielsen, 2010; Reader, 2015; Wahl-Jorgensen, 2007).

Digital media technologies, including social media as the most recent but surely not last wave of disruptive innovation, add new communicative options to this constellation. Now common on many news websites (Bachmann and Harlow, 2012; Netzer *et al.*, 2014; Jönsson and Örnebring, 2011), user comments supplement traditional reporting and make follow-up communication to news stories visible to journalists and other users alike. Readers or viewers might comment on the story by giving their own opinions, asking questions, calling the journalist's perspective into doubt or thanking them for their efforts, etc. (Witschge, 2011). Furthermore, they are not restricted to addressing journalists but can also engage in conversations with other audience members, eventually forming loose connections or even communities of people who gather regularly at a certain comment section to discuss the news (Mitchelstein, 2011).

Recent studies have investigated the changes and continuities in how journalists and audiences perceive, use, and manage user feedback via online comments (Boczkowski and Mitchelstein, 2011; McElroy, 2013; Nielsen, 2014; Springer *et al.*, 2015; Reich, 2011). User comments provide a 'meeting point' (Bergström and Wadbring, 2015: 140) for journalists and their audience with its own dynamics, emerging rules, and hierarchies (Rosenberry, 2011; Weber, 2013). They introduce an interface between the formerly separated modalities of interpersonal and mass communication, thus contributing to an overall paradigm shift from 'information supply and demand' to 'dialogue and participation' in public communications. And to manage these changes, journalistic organizations set up guidelines and create specific professional roles such as community managers or social media editors (Bakker, 2014). Thus, there is a considerable amount of empirical evidence that suggests a changing journalism/audience relationship. But how can we theorize these transformations of journalism and its audience?

Journalism and (its) audience: theorizing a complicated relationship

Journalism provides a service for which it needs an audience, not only in an economical sense. Information about and images of audiences 'help construct the news' (DeWerth-Pallmeyer, 1997: xi) and are 'flowing back' into the newsrooms (and more or less to individual journalists). So the relationship between journalism and audience is reflexive in a very practical sense: Journalism has to take information about its audience into account in order to produce news that has a chance to be noticed and will be consumed. But we need to take this reflexivity seriously in a theoretical sense as well. As Meusel (2014) argues, it falls short to understand the journalism/audience relationship just as an 'imaginary conversation' (Cooley, 1983) between (individual) journalists and their audiences. Instead she argues that a more appropriate conception can be achieved with reference to Max Weber's concept of a 'social relationship,' defined in "Basic Sociological Concepts" as

> behaviour of a plurality of actors insofar as, in its meaningful content, the action of each takes account of that of the others and is oriented in these terms […] Thus, as a defining criterion, it is essential that there should be at least a minimum of mutual orientation of the action of each to that of the others.
>
> *(Weber, 1978: 26/27)*

So the social relationship between journalism and audiences is based on a mutual orientation informed by reflexive and generalized expectations, that is, on what journalism should provide to its audience or on what the audience might expect from journalism (Borger *et al.*, 2014; Lewis *et al.*, 2014; Scholl, 2004). These generalized expectations can be addressed on a macro level by treating 'journalism' and 'audience' as social spheres which are interconnected to "a communicative unit called the public" (Görke and Scholl, 2006: 651). On the micro level, we might look at interdependencies between 'journalists' and 'audience members' (viewers, readers, listeners, users), conceiving them either in social roles which are constituted through a set of mutual expectations or focusing on individual actors who hold certain identifiable norms and beliefs. On all levels, though, reflexive generalized expectations should be treated as both a prerequisite to and a result of communication, that is, they are (re-)produced in mutual observation and interaction, and at the same time they frame these communicative processes.

So we can rephrase and specify the historical shift from mass media to digital networked media already mentioned in the previous section as a shift in the modes of mutual observation and interaction, which also affect the generalized expectations journalists and audiences have of each other. Under the conditions of mass media, journalism relied mainly on the observation modes of audience research and punctual feedback (e.g. via letters to the editor). Audience members, in turn, observed journalistic performance by selecting and consuming their products, with only little opportunity to engage in direct interaction and observe the 'other-audience.'

Online media have introduced new modes of observation to journalists, including monitoring and aggregating digital traces of audience members which reveal information about news preferences, appreciation, engagement, or recall (Anderson, 2011; Bermejo, 2009; Napoli, 2010). But they have also broadened the scope for audience members' observational practices towards journalism, as well as with respect to observing each other (Hautzer *et al.*, 2012; Schulz and Roessler, 2012; Wendelin, 2014). Online, media users can easily compare different takes on news events by checking different news outlets as well as by comparing perspectives shared via user comments, or they might gain insights into editorial decisions by following individual journalists on Twitter or reading editorial blogs offering a sense of transparency to the newsroom and its practices. Perhaps most important of all, digital media have introduced a conversational mode into the journalism–audience relationship by providing communication channels and spaces that afford direct interaction, whether dialogue- or conflict-oriented. Thus, with social media, journalism and audiences meet on 'uncommon ground.'

Based on these theoretical considerations, we can ask whether the shift in modes of mutual observation and communication lead to changing generalized expectations between journalism and audiences, or whether they are rather stable? Which values and norms do they include? Are these expectations, values, and norms congruent or is there a (growing) disparity between journalists and their audience?

Including the audience in journalism (studies): current contributions and research

Although the scholarly division between journalism studies and audience studies might suggest otherwise, journalism research is not restricted to journalists alone. Even if it usually treats 'the journalist' as the basic unit of empirical investigation, it contains many—more or less explicated—'traces of the audience.' This section will present a selection of research strategies used to investigate audiences from within the field of journalism studies.

The first strategy is to rely on concepts or research objects typical in journalism research, but also to probe them for *implicit information about the audience* they reveal, such as in research on journalistic role conceptions (Cassidy, 2005; Mellado, 2011; Mellado and van Dalen, 2013; van Dalen *et al.*, 2012; Weaver and Wilhoit, 1986). Even when not discussed explicitly, this research helps us understand whether journalists consider themselves as mainly independent from audience influence, as partners in a conversation with audiences, or as "stand[ing] up for the disadvantaged population" (Weischenberg *et al.*, 2012: 214).

A second strategy is to include instruments in the empirical design directed at extracting *explicit perspectives on the audience*. This refers to studies that include dimensions, categories, and/or constructs which relate directly to the audience, like asking journalists about their 'newsmen's fantasies' (Pool and Shulman, 1959) or 'image of the audience' (Weischenberg *et al.*, 2012: 215), on their perceived degree of the audience's influence on their work (Weischenberg *et al.*, 2012: 231), or on their general assessment of audience participation via social media (Robinson, 2010). A different approach, coming from the field of newsroom studies, is to observe daily work routines and focus on the instances when direct interaction with audience members takes place, for example, by reacting to readers' comments, monitoring Twitter, or answering phone calls from viewers (Domingo, 2011).

The third and final strategy is to *take both sides into account*. In a way, this is the most demanding strategy as it calls for the design of empirical instruments that address practices and expectations of journalists and audience members in a similar, comparable way. It can be realized with different methodological approaches, for example, different forms of qualitative or quantitative interviews, via content analysis or observation (see also

Loosen and Schmidt, 2016 on these three basic classes of scientific methods to access social reality). In addition, there are different possibilities available to relate findings for journalists and for audience members, for example, comparing them or developing a synthesis of the different partial aspects. Various studies have chosen this strategy, and they will be presented in more detail below.

An early example is a study by Martin, O'Keefe, and Nayman (1972) on the "opinion agreement and accuracy between editors and their readers." For a specific news event and a set of newspapers, they conducted interviews with editors and with readers, combining them with a content analysis of the news stories on the event. Thus, this approach departed from a simple 'supply/demand-gap' and worked with assumptions of the co-orientation model by McLeod and Chaffee (1972). What the authors found is that "editors perceive the views of their readers fairly closely, [...] [whereas] readers perceive newspapers as biased, and generally opposed to their views" (Martin *et al.*, 1972: 460); later on, such biased perceptions have been described by Vallone *et al.* (1985) as the 'hostile media phenomenon.'

Reader (2012) employs a different methodology to study online comments by comparing results from a textual analysis (with reference to Stuart Hall's Encoding/Decoding model) of six journalistic essays about anonymous online comments with 927 audience-member responses to these essays (that were partly quantitatively analyzed). The study concluded that "journalists and audiences have very different conceptualizations about 'civility' and the role of anonymity in civil discourse" (2012: 495): Whereas journalists seem to prefer quality over quantity, active commentators seem "willing to tolerate substandard writing and vitriol if it encourages broader public participation" (2012: 505).

A recent example investigating mutual co-orientation is the 'News Gap' study by Mitchelstein and Boczkowski (2013). They operationalized this news gap as the difference between the 'most newsworthy' and the 'most read'/'most emailed'/'most commented' stories on selected news sites. Instead of relying on self-reports gathered from interviewing journalists or users, they took data collected automatically and interpreted it as an outcome of aggregated selection decisions on the side of journalism and audiences. Similar approaches will probably become increasingly important, as journalists and journalism research increasingly deal with 'transparent audiences' that leave digital traces during their news practices (An *et al.*, 2013).

The most common approach to assess the journalism/audience relation in an integrated research design relies, however, on survey data. Tsfati, Meyers, and Peri (2006), for example, compared Israeli journalists' and the public's perceptions on "what constitutes good and bad journalism" (2006: 152) with the help of a "comparative survey strategy" (2006: 154): Using similarly worded questions and response options, they asked samples of both group questions on core journalistic goals, values, and practices as well as on a more general evaluation of the performance of Israeli media. Here one of the striking findings is that the public is slightly more positive in its general evaluation of Israeli media in comparison to journalists. One explanation given is that journalists are more familiar with the inner workings of the media and therefore may be more skeptical and critical (2006: 163). Furthermore, the authors highlight how perceptions of professional norms such as 'neutrality,' 'verifying facts,' and so on addressed in the survey most likely mean different things to journalists and audiences (2006: 168).

In a similar way, Bergström and Wadbring (2015) investigate the attitudes towards reader comments among the public and among journalists in Sweden. They conducted two surveys which included a set of statements (e.g. "Reader comments make news reporting more interesting") for assessment. Their findings show that journalists are less positive about reader comments and more critical of their quality than audience members (2015: 147). They found that a significant proportion of audience members (between 23 and 38 percent) stated 'no opinion' on certain items, indicating a noteworthy aspect of the journalism/audience relationship: Both methodologically and theoretically we have to account for the fact that not every audience member is knowledgeable, capable, or willing to express attitudes towards professional journalistic practices to the same degree.

In our own research on four news outlets in Germany, we encountered similar challenges. Based on a theoretical model of audience inclusion we set up a multi-method research design that aimed at the mutual co-orientation of practices and expectations (Loosen and Schmidt, 2012; Schmidt and Loosen, 2015). We operationalized constructs such as "journalistic self-image/external image" or "(assumed) motivations for audience participation" as parallel item sets which were included in standardized surveys among journalists and audience members. Among the latter, we found shares of "Don't know/no opinion" answers similar to Bergström and Wadbring (2015), pointing to the general methodological problem of comparing data from groups with different degrees of knowledge or interest in journalism as well as with different perspectives on journalism.

We were, however, able to assess the inclusion distance between journalists and their audiences by looking at the difference of the average scores for each item between both groups (see Heise *et al.*, 2014; Schmidt *et al.*, 2013 for detailed findings). Overall, we identified many areas of congruence between journalists' and users' expectations. However, disagreement (or, in theoretical terms, inclusion distance) was mostly found in two respects: Firstly, while journalists were more likely to assume ego-centered motivations for user participation such as 'blowing off steam' or 'self-expression and self-display,' they underestimated the degree to which audience members (stated that they) wanted to expand their own knowledge or aim to introduce topics that are important to them into public debate. Secondly, while journalists and audience members by and large agreed on the importance of traditional journalistic values of objective, fast, and reliable information on complex issues, they disagreed on the importance of new participatory practices for journalism. For example, in all cases journalists rejected notions such as "to provide opportunities for user-generated content to be published" or "to present own opinions on issues to the public" more strongly than audience members did.

Conclusion and outlook: between proximity and distance

Among the three strategies outlined above, there is no inherently 'better' perspective, because all help us to better understand the journalism/audience relationship—and all have their particular limitations. If we do, however, follow the theoretical consideration that this relationship consists of reflexive generalized expectations that frame actual practice (and are in turn reproduced by it), then we need to employ empirical designs and adequate theories that are able to assess and explain this social relationship. This is not only important in its own right but will also contribute to our understanding of the fundamental changes to the public sphere which networked digital media bring about.

Communicative options, opportunities for mutual observation, and channels for different modes of exchange have greatly increased in the past few years, but this development seems to be neither a linear nor a simultaneous process for all segments of journalism, for all journalists, or for all audience members. Instead, we witness that journalistic organizations as well as individual journalists differ in the enthusiasm or reluctance with which they embrace these developments, and in the resources they can employ to manage them.

We can also see a differentiation of audience segments in at least two respects: First, with respect to audience preferences and increasingly narrow interests which can be served better in the digital world; here, the highly personalized 'filter bubble' (Pariser, 2011) of algorithmically curated newsfeeds is regarded simultaneously as a promise and as a threat at the same time. Second, we see great differences with respect to the audience's interest in and capacity for participation: Not every user wants to have his or her say on current events, and not everyone is able to contribute to such debates, though for different, yet poorly understood reasons of (self-)exclusion. Some early evidence from our own research suggests that newsrooms do increasingly confront this differentiation when serving different communicative channels, that is, their print product reaches different audience segments than their online platform and their social media accounts do. Thus, it seems to be the case that journalists do not work with the operative fiction of 'a single audience,' but increasingly acknowledge that they serve 'multiple audiences' (Hasebrink, 2008, own translation) via different channels during their daily work routines.

Thus, we are led back to the fundamental questions posed in the introduction: Is there a 'right and functional relationship' between journalism and audience, and who is going to decide on what it should look like? If we accept the normative idea that journalism should represent principles such as diversity and controversy, then a more intensive contact between journalists and audience members does not necessarily result in 'better' journalism (Görke, 2014), especially if the opportunities for contact are skewed towards certain groups or interests. Journalists who only follow aggregated click data or who only follow the needs of those social groups that are articulating their demands and concerns online, might eventually neglect certain topics. But they could also reflect on the inherent bias built into these modes of observation and decide to report on events even though—or just because—they will not get many clicks, likes, and retweets.

So one major challenge for journalists is to reconcile the (assumed) demands of the dispersed and heterogeneous, yet often silent, mass media audience with the (verbalized) demands of the connected audiences they face in comment sections and social media. Journalism research which takes both sides into account can support journalism in this respect: Not because it will solve this challenge once and for all, but because it expands our knowledge of mutually oriented practices and expectations towards public communication—without being directly involved on either side. This way, journalism research can inform both sides about their values and expectations, helping journalists with their core task: To engage their audience with meaningful information about the world we share.

Further reading

For more on audiences, Nico Carpentier's (2011) chapter "New configuration of the audience? The challenge of user-generated content for audience theory and media participation" discusses the "core structural components of audience theory" such as active/passive and shows how they are challenged by participatory media practices. Seth Lewis' (2012) article "The tension between professional control and open participation: Journalism and its boundaries" explores the tension between professional control and open participation in the news process against the background of the sociology of professions. Our paper "(Re-)Discovering the audience: The relationship between journalism and audience in networked digital media" (2012) outlines key aspects of the sociological theory of inclusion and explicates them in a comprehensive heuristic model of audience inclusion in journalism.

References

Abercrombie, N. and Longhurst, B. (1998) *Audiences: A Sociological Theory of Performance and Imagination*. Thousand Oaks, CA: Sage.

An, J., Quercia, D., Cha, M., Gummadi, K. and Crowcroft, J. (2013) "Traditional Media Seen from Social Media." In *WebSci '13 Proceedings of the 5th Annual ACM Web Science Conference*, pp. 11–14. DOI: 10.1145/2464464.2464492.

Anderson, C.W. (2011) "Between Creative and Quantified Audiences: Web Metrics and Changing Patterns of Newswork in Local US Newsrooms." *Journalism* 12(5): 550–566.

Bachmann, I. and Harlow, S. (2012) "Opening the Gates." *Journalism Practice* 6(2): 217–232.

Bakker, P. (2014) "Mr. Gates Returns: Curation, Community Management and Other New Roles for Journalists." *Journalism Studies* 15(5): 596–606.

Bergström, A. and Wadbring, I. (2015) "Beneficial Yet Crappy: Journalists and Audiences on Obstacles and Opportunities in Reader Comments." *European Journal of Communication* 30(2): 137–151.

Bermejo, F. (2009) "Audience Manufacture in Historical Perspective: From Broadcasting to Google." *New Media and Society* 11(1–2): 133–154.

Boczkowski, P.J. and Mitchelstein, E. (2011) "How Users Take Advantage of Different Forms of Interactivity on Online News Sites: Clicking, E-mailing, and Commenting." In *Human Communication Research* 38(1): 1–22.

Borger, M., van Hoof, A. and Sanders, J. (2014) "Expecting Reciprocity: Towards a Model of the Participants' Perspective on Participatory Journalism." *New Media and Society* 18(5): 708–725.

Bruns, A. (2008) *Blogs, Wikipedia, Second Life, and Beyond. From Production to Produsage*. Oxford, UK: Peter Lang.

Carpentier, N. (2011) "New Configuration of the Audience? The Challenge of User-Generated Content for Audience Theory and Media Participation." In Nightingale, V. (ed.) *The Handbook of Media Audiences*. Oxford, UK: Wiley-Blackwell, pp. 190–212.

Cassidy, W.P. (2005) "Variations on a Theme: The Professional Role Conceptions of Print and Online Newspaper Journalists." *Journalism & Mass Communication Quarterly* 82(2): 264–280.

Castells, M. (2009) *Communication Power*. Oxford, UK: Oxford University Press.

Cooley, C.H. (1983) *Human Nature and the social order*. New Brunswick, London: Transaction Books.

da Silva, M.T. (2012) "Newsroom Practices and Letter-to-the-Editor. An Analysis of Selection Criteria." *Journalism Practice* 6(2): 250–263.

DeWerth-Pallmeyer, D. (1997) *The Audience in the News*. Mahwah, NJ: Lawrence Erlbaum.

Domingo, D. (2011) "Managing Audience Participation. Practices, Workflows and Strategies." In Singer, J.B., Hermida, A., Domingo, D., Heinonen, A., Paulussen, S., Quandt, T., et al. (eds) *Participatory Journalism: Guarding Open Gates at Online Newspapers*. Chichester, UK: Wiley-Blackwell, pp. 75–95.

Gans, H.J. (1977) "Audience Mail: Letters to an Anchorman." *Journal of Communication* 27(3): 86–91.

Görke, A. (2014) "Vom Hasen und vom Igel—oder warum der Journalismus sein Publikum stets erfolgreich und folgenreich verfehlen darf." In Loosen, W. and Dohle, M. (eds) *Journalismus und (sein) Publikum. Schnittstellen zwischen Journalismusforschung und Rezeptions- und Wirkungsforschung.* Wiesbaden, Germany: VS Verlag für Sozialwissenschaften, pp. 35–51.

Görke, A. and Scholl, A. (2006) "Niklas Luhmann's Theory of Social Systems and Journalism Research." *Journalism Studies* 7(4): 644–655.

Hasebrink, U. (2008) "Das multiple Publikum. Paradoxien im Verhältnis von Journalismus und Mediennutzung." In Pörksen, B., Loosen, W. and Scholl, A. (eds) *Paradoxien des Journalismus. Theorie—Empirie—Praxis. Festschrift für Siegfried Weischenberg*. Wiesbaden, Germany: VS Verlag für Sozialwissenschaften, pp. 512–530.

Hautzer, L., Lünich, M. and Rössler, P. (2012) *Social Navigation. Neue Orientierungsmuster bei der Mediennutzung im Internet*. Baden-Baden, Germany: Nomos.

Heise, N., Loosen, W., Reimer, J. and Schmidt, J.-H. (2014) "Including the Audience: Comparing the Attitudes and Expectations of Journalists and Users Towards Participation in German TV News Journalism." *Journalism Studies* 15(4): 411–430.

Hepp, A. and Hasebrink, U. (2014) "Human Interaction and Communicative Figurations: The Transformation of Mediatized Cultures and Societies." In Lundby, K. (ed.) *Mediatization of Communication*. New York, NY: de Gruyter, pp. 249–272.

Jönsson, A.M. and Örnebring, H. (2011) "User-Generated Content and the News. Empowerment of Citizens or Interactive Illusion." *Journalism Practice* 5(2): 127–144.

Lewis, S. (2012) "The Tension between Professional Control and Open Participation: Journalism and Its Boundaries." *Information, Communication & Society* 15(6): 836–866.

Lewis, S.C., Holton, A.E. and Coddington, M. (2014) "Reciprocal Journalism. A Concept of Mutual Exchange between Journalists and Audiences." *Journalism Practice* 8(2): 229–241.

Löffelholz, M. (2008) "Heterogeneous—Multidimensional—Competing: Theoretical Approaches to Journalism—An Overview." In Löffelholz, M. and Weaver, D.H. (eds) *Global Journalism Research: Theories, Methods, Findings, Future.* Malden, MA: Wiley-Blackwell, pp. 15–27.

Loosen, W. (2015) "The Notion of the 'Blurring Boundaries': Journalism as a (de-)Differentiated Phenomenon." *Digital Journalism* 3(1): 68–84.

Loosen, W. and Schmidt, J.-H. (2012) "(Re-)Discovering the Audience: The Relationship between Journalism and Audience in Networked Digital Media." *Information, Communication & Society* 15(6): 867–887.

Loosen, W. and Schmidt, J.-H. (2016) "Multi-Method Approaches in Journalism Research." In Witschge, T., Anderson, C.W., Domingo, D. and Hermida, A. (eds) *The Sage Handbook of Digital Journalism.* New York, NY: Sage, pp. 562–575.

Lüders, M. (2008) "Conceptualizing Personal Media." *New Media and Society* 10(5): 683–702.

Martin, R.K., O'Keefe, G.J. and Nayman, O.B. (1972) "Opinion Agreement and Accuracy between Editors and their Readers." *Journalism & Mass Communication Quarterly* 49(3): 460–468.

McElroy, K. (2013) "Where Old (Gatekeepers) Meets New (Media). Herding Reader Comments into Print." *Journalism Practice* 7(6): 755–771.

McLeod, J.M. and Chaffee, S.H. (1972) "The Construction of Social Reality." In Tedeschi, J.T. (ed.) *The Social Influence Process.* Chicago, IL: Aldine, pp. 50–99.

McQuail, D. (2010) *McQuail's Mass Communication Theory.* Los Angeles, CA: Sage.

Mellado, C. (2011) "Modeling Individual and Organizational Effects on Chilean Journalism: A Multilevel Analysis of Professional Role Conceptions." *Comunicación y Sociedad,* 24(2): 269–304.

Mellado, C. and van Dalen, A. (2013) "Between Rhetoric and Practice: Explaining the Gap between Role Conception and Performance in Journalism." *Journalism Studies* 15(6): 859–878.

Meusel, J. (2014) "Die Beziehung zwischen Journalisten und ihrem Publikum. Kritische Betrachtung und alternative theoretische Fundierung." In Loosen, W. and Dohle, M. (eds) *Journalismus und (sein) Publikum. Schnittstellen zwischen Journalismusforschung und Rezeptions- und Wirkungsforschung.* Wiesbaden, Germany: VS Verlag für Sozialwissenschaften, pp. 53–69.

Mitchelstein, E. (2011) "Catharsis and Community: Divergent Motivations for Audience Participation in Online Newspapers and Blogs." *International Journal of Communication* 5: 2014–2034.

Mitchelstein, E. and Boczkowski, P.J. (2013) *The News Gap: When the Information Preferences of the Media and the Public Diverge.* Cambridge, MA: MIT Press.

Napoli, P.M. (2010) *Audience Evolution: New Technologies and the Transformation of Media Audiences.* New York, NY: Columbia University Press.

Netzer, Y., Tenenboim-Weinblatt, K. and Shifman, L. (2014) "The Construction of Participation in News Websites: A Five-Dimensional Model." *Journalism Studies* 15(5): 619–631.

Nielsen, C.E. (2014) "Coproduction or Cohabitation: Are Anonymous Online Comments on Newspaper Websites Shaping News Content?" *New Media and Society* 16(3): 470–487.

Nielsen, R.K. (2010) "Participation through Letters to the Editor: Circulation, Considerations, and Genres in the Letters Institution." *Journalism* 11(1): 21–35.

Pariser, E. (2011) *The Filter Bubble: What the Internet is Hiding from You.* London, UK: Viking.

Pool, I.S. and Shulman, I. (1959) "Newsmen's Fantasies, Audiences and Newswriting." *Public Opinion Quarterly* 23(2): 145–158.

Reader, B. (2012) "Free Press vs. Free Speech? The Rhetoric of 'Civility' in Regard to Anonymous Online Comments." *Journalism & Mass Communication Quarterly* 89(30): 495–513.

Reader, B. (2015) *Audience Feedback in the News Media.* New York, NY: Routledge.

Reich, Z. (2011) "User Comments: The Transformation of Participatory Space." In Singer, J.B., Hermida, A., Domingo, D., Heinonen, A., Paulussen, S., Quandt, T., et al. (eds) *Participatory Journalism: Guarding Open Gates at Online Newspapers.* Chichester, UK: Wiley-Blackwell, pp. 96–117.

Robinson, S. (2010) "Traditionalists vs. Convergers. Textual Privilege, Boundary Work, and the Journalist-Audience Relationship in the Commenting Policies of Online News Sites." *Convergence: The International Journal of Research into New Media Technologies* 16(1): 125–143.

Rosenberry, J. (2011) "Users Support Online Anonymity Despite Increasing Negativity." *Newspaper Research Journal* 32(2): 6–19.

Schmidt, J.-H. (2014) "Twitter and the Rise of Personal Publics." In Weller, K., Bruns, A., Burgess, J., Mahrt, M. and Puschmann, C. (eds) *Twitter and Society*. New York, NY: Peter Lang, pp. 3–14.

Schmidt, J.-H. and Loosen, W. (2015) "Both Sides of the Story: Assessing Audience Participation in Journalism through the Concept of Inclusion Distance." *Digital Journalism* 3(2): 259–278.

Schmidt, J.-H., Loosen, W., Heise, N. and Reimer, J. (2013) "Journalism and Participatory Practices— Blurring or Reinforcement of Boundaries between Journalism and Audiences?" *Recherches en Communication* 39: 91–109.

Scholl, A. (2004) "Die Inklusion des Publikums. Theorien zur Analyse der Beziehungen von Journalismus und Publikum." In Löffelholz, M. (ed.) *Theorien des Journalismus. Ein diskursives Handbuch*. Wiesbaden, Germany: VS Verlag für Sozialwissenschaften, pp. 517–536.

Scholl, A. (2013) "Theorien des Journalismus im Vergleich." In Meier, K. and Neuberger, C. (eds) *Journalismusforschung: Stand und Perspektiven*. Baden-Baden, Germany: Nomos, pp. 167–194.

Springer, N., Engelmann, I. and Pfaffinger, C. (2015) "User Comments: Motives and Inhibitors to Write and Read." *Information, Communication & Society* 18(7): 798–815.

Schulz, A. and Roessler, P. (2012) "The Spiral of Silence and the Internet: Selection of Online Content and the Perception of the Public Opinion Climate in Computer-Mediated Communication Environments." *Public Opinion Research* 24(3): 346–367.

Tsfati, Y., Meyers, O. and Peri, Y. (2006) "What is Good Journalism? Comparing Israeli Public and Journalists' Perspectives." *Journalism* 7(2): 152–173.

Vallone, R.P., Ross, L. and Lepper, M. (1985) "The Hostile Media Phenomenon: Biased Perception and Perceptions of Media Bias in Coverage of the Beirut Massacre." *Journal of Personality and Social Psychology* 49(3): 577–585.

van Dalen, A., de Vreese, C.H. and Albæk, E. (2012) "Different Roles, Different Content? A Four-Country Comparison of the Role Conceptions and Reporting Style of Political Journalists." *Journalism* 13(7): 903–922.

Wahl-Jorgensen, K. (2007) *Journalists and the Public: Newsroom Culture, Letters to the Editor, and Democracy*. Cresskill, NJ: Hampton Press.

Weaver, D.H. and Wilhoit, G.C. (eds) (1986) *The American Journalist: A Portrait of U.S. News People and Their Work*. Bloomington, IN: Indiana University Press.

Weber, M. (1978) *Economy and Society: An Outline of Interpretive Sociology*. Los Angeles, CA: University of California Press.

Weber, P. (2013) "Discussions in the Comments Section: Factors Influencing Participation and Interactivity in Online Newspapers' Reader Comments." *New Media and Society* 16(6): 941–957.

Weischenberg, S., Malik, M. and Scholl, A. (2012) "Journalism in Germany in the 21st Century." In Weaver, D.H. and Willnat, L. (eds) *The Global Journalist in the 21st Century*. New York, NY: Routledge, pp. 205–219.

Wendelin, M. (2014): "Transparenz von Rezeptions- und Kommunikationsverhalten im Internet. Theoretische Überlegungen zur Veränderung der Öffentlichkeitsdynamiken zwischen Journalismus und Publikum." In Loosen, W. and Dohle, M. (eds) *Journalismus und (sein) Publikum*. Wiesbaden, Germany: VS Verlag für Sozialwissenschaften, pp.73–89.

Witschge, T. (2011) "From Confrontation to Understanding: In/Exclusion of Alternative Voices in Online Discussion." *Global Media Journal* 1(1): 2–22. Available from: http://www.db-thueringen.de/servlets/DerivateServlet/Derivate-22677/GMJ1_Witschge-final.pdf (accessed 10 April 2012).

36

AUDIENCES AND INFORMATION REPERTOIRES

Uwe Hasebrink

How do audiences make use of digital journalism in order to fulfill their information needs? In order to answer this question, this chapter provides a research overview along the following lines: Firstly, there is extensive empirical evidence with regard to the reach of particular forms of digital information services and to the technical platforms and devices that are used for accessing news. Secondly, due to technical convergence and cross-media strategies in the field of information services, research pays more and more attention to the interplay between different sources of information and how media users actually combine them within their everyday practices. Finally, based on a classification of information needs, the chapter discusses how people's information repertoires are changing.

The media-centered approach to audiences of digital journalism

Audiences have always been a highly risky and volatile component of media systems, whether in terms of their role as media consumers or in their role as citizens taking part in public affairs (Lunt and Livingstone, 2012; Hasebrink, 2011). The 'people out there' perform a wide range of highly individualistic practices of media use that are dependent on social context and situational conditions. Consequently, audiences are hard to control. In order to gain control media companies are—as Ien Ang expressed it as early as 1991—"desperately seeking the audience." This desperate search has led to a specific conceptualization of audiences that helped to construct them as countable and tradable commodities. In the second half of the twentieth century, a powerful research industry developed that focused on providing evidence on what people do with the media. The media industry has an existential interest in finding out how many people use their products; it is exactly this kind of audience data that media companies can sell to the advertising industry or to their shareholders. Beyond that these data have also gained importance as a feedback mechanism for improving journalistic strategies and as one indicator within the evaluation process of public service media.

The challenge for this kind of research is that media audiences cannot be regarded as a concrete and quantifiable group, in the way that is possible for the audience in a theater or cinema, for example. Instead, it is necessary to construct media audiences by certain operational definitions and methodological procedures. All over the world, the media and advertising industries have developed similar mechanisms to construct the 'audience' as the dominant model of research on exposure to media (Ang, 1991; McQuail, 1997; Webster and Phalen, 1997). The theoretical and empirical core of this model can be characterized along the following premises:

- Audience measurement focuses on *contacts* between users and specific media; thus the respective research is mainly based on behavioral measures as the frequency and duration of use.
- Audiences are described as *aggregate* behaviors for instance as the percentage of users that have been reached by a specific medium.
- Audiences refer to *single media*, so the respective research constructs television audiences or radio audiences or newspaper audiences or, with regard to digital journalism, audiences of particular online or mobile services.

This approach to audience research can be called media-centered, because its focus is on describing the audiences of particular media based on the size and the composition of the audiences they reach.

Recent findings on digital news use

With regard to digital journalism, there are plenty of studies from many countries providing evidence on the audiences for new digital services. At this point, we will mainly focus on one particular study that stands out because of its international and longitudinal scope, allowing for comparisons across countries and across time. The *Reuters Institute Digital News Survey* (Newman, Levy, and Nielsen, 2015) has been conducted annually since 2012. In the following section, we refer to the survey that was conducted by *YouGov* via online questionnaire at the end of January/February 2015. While data collection has been realized in many countries, the following findings refer to 12 that were included in the previous years and thus allow for comparisons across time: Australia, Brazil (only urban areas), Denmark, Finland, France, Germany, Ireland, Italy, Japan, Spain, United Kingdom, and the United States. Findings are based on people older than 17 years who use the internet. In 2015, this group represents on average about 85 to 90 percent of the population (highest: Denmark and Finland [97 percent], lowest: urban Brazil [54 percent] and Italy [59 percent]). Thus, the findings do not represent the total population, but those that have access to digital journalism and thus are particularly interesting for the overall topic of this volume. Among this group, only those who said they had used any news in the month prior to the interview were surveyed. On average the group of non-news users in this group makes up 5 percent of the original sample. Australia and Japan (6 percent) and France and UK (7 percent) were slightly higher; only the United States stands out with 11 percent saying they had not used any news in the last month—given the low threshold for news use (at least once in a month), this figure is interesting in itself and emphasizes that non-news use is an issue in today's societies (Trilling and Schönbach, 2013).

Table 36.1 provides an overview of the sources from which media users get their news. In 8 of the 12 countries involved online and mobile sources reach the highest figures, while TV news follows in second place. Exceptions are media users in Japan, the UK, France, and particularly Germany, where TV news (82 percent) still reaches substantially bigger audiences than online sources (60 percent). Figures for radio and printed newspapers reflect substantial differences between countries: For radio the range is between 50 percent in France, Germany, and Ireland and 17 percent in the United States; for printed newspapers, Finland, Spain,

Table 36.1 Sources of news by country

	AUS	BRA	DEN	ESP	FIN	FRA	GER	IRE	ITA	JP	UK	US
n	2042	2033	2019	2026	1509	1991	1969	1501	2006	2015	2149	2278
TV	72	81	75	82	75	80	82	75	78	73	75	64
Radio	41	39	50	40	45	28	50	50	23	17	37	26
Print	39	33	34	47	49	19	45	33	38	44	38	23
Online	85	91	85	86	90	71	60	85	81	70	73	74

Source: Reuters Institute Digital News Survey 2015 (Newman, Levy, and Nielsen, 2015: 51).

Q3. Which, if any, of the following have you used in the last week as a source of news? Please select all that apply. Base: Total sample in each country; in alphabetical order.

Germany, and Japan are highest (>40 percent) and France and the United States are lowest (<25 percent). These differences emphasize the need for news producers and suppliers to carefully reflect intercultural differences, and it is clear that the digital environment does not develop in a consistent and linear way (Hasebrink *et al.*, 2015).

Over the last few years, an obvious trend in news use has been the increase of the role of social media as sources of news (see Hermida, this volume) and smartphones as devices to access news (see Westlund, this volume). Table 36.2 mirrors the clear increase of social media use from 2014 to 2015 in almost all countries except Italy. In this respect, it is clear we are witnessing a rapid change in the digital media environment.

The same is true for the move towards smartphones as prominent devices for accessing online news. Table 36.3 shows how many users accessed digital news on a computer or laptop, on a smartphone, or on a tablet. While in 2015 the role of computers/laptops still topped other devices, smartphones have shown a very rapid diffusion in recent years. One important consequence for news providers is that the number of consumers using several digital devices has increased: In 2015, 45 percent of all respondents used more than two devices; in 2013, this figure was 33 percent (Newman, Levy, and Nielsen, 2015: 67). This presents a complication as users expect news to be delivered and optimized for different screens. In addition, there remain major groups who only receive their news on one particular device and therefore expect to receive the full range of information on that device.

Beyond the sources and devices used to access news, another relevant aspect of news-related practices is the way media users look for and access news. While for many years, it has been normal for users to turn directly to a trusted news brand—whether television, radio,

Table 36.2 Social media as source of news in 2014 and 2015

	BRA	AUS	ESP	IRE	ITA	DEN	FIN	US	UK	FRA	GER	JP
n	2033	2042	2026	1501	2006	2019	1509	2278	2149	1991	1969	2015
2014	50	n.d.	46	n.d.	48	35	36	30	23	19	23	16
2015	64	51	50	49	46	47	40	40	36	34	25	21

Source: Reuters Institute Digital News Survey 2014/2015 (Newman, Levy, and Nielsen, 2015: 52).

Q3. Which, if any, of the following have you used in the last week as a source of news? Please select all that apply. Base: Total sample in each country; ordered by social media percentage in 2015.

Table 36.3 Digital devices for accessing the news

	AUS	DEN	IRE	BRA	FIN	ESP	ITA	UK	US	FRA	GER	JP
n	2042	2019	1501	2033	1509	2026	2006	2149	2278	1991	1969	2015
Computer	67	67	74	71	75	66	65	59	64	58	57	78
Smartphone	59	57	52	50	50	48	44	42	41	37	34	33
Tablet	35	39	22	19	26	24	19	31	21	18	16	13

Source: Reuters Institute Digital News Survey 2015 (Newman, Levy, and Nielsen, 2015: 67).

Q8b. Which, if any, of the following devices have you used to access news in the last week? Please select all that apply. Base: Total sample in each country. Base: Total sample in each country; ordered by percentage of smartphone use.

newspaper, or online brand—there has been a differentiation in the ways leading to news as well. Search engines, direct email alerts or notifications via mobile apps, news aggregator sites or apps, and social media offer an increasing range of options to discover news. From the perspective of news producers and providers, this is obviously a highly relevant development as they need to redefine their branding and distribution strategies to ensure that they can be found by news-seekers. Table 36.4 shows how many news users access news by the different options. What is clear is the classic approach to news can no longer be regarded as dominant. The highest figures in this respect (>50 percent) are found for Denmark, Finland, and the UK, while in Japan, Italy, Germany, and France less than 30 percent of news users apply this strategy to access news. In 9 of the 12 countries accessing news through a search engine is the most popular approach to news, but there are intermediaries involved in the process of accessing news that also have a substantial reach and thus cause particular challenges for news brands in their efforts to be found and accessed.

Table 36.4 Starting points for news

	AUS	BRA	DEN	ESP	FIN	FRA	GER	IRE	ITA	JP	UK	US
n	2042	2033	2019	2026	1509	1991	1969	1501	2006	2015	2149	2278
Direct to news brand	33	46	54	36	63	27	26	44	20	15	52	36
Search	49	52	29	54	26	40	45	46	66	54	32	40
Social media	41	48	38	35	28	21	20	36	33	14	28	35
Email	20	23	24	14	9	21	15	9	17	15	10	25
Mobile alerts	9	11	9	8	7	14	9	9	7	7	10	13
Other news aggregator or App	8	17	9	11	12	6	5	7	6	27	4	5

Source: Reuters Institute Digital News Survey 2015 (Newman, Levy, and Nielsen, 2015: 75).

Q10. Thinking about how you got news online (via computer, mobile or any device) in the last week, which were the ways in which you came across news stories? Please select all that apply. Base: Total sample in each country; in alphabetical order.

A user-centered approach to audiences of digital journalism

The approach to audiences and their use of information media presented above is still limited in several respects. On the one hand, it does not consider the substantial interindividual differences of communications practices and it cannot help to understand the relationship between different media. Another large body of research on media use takes a user-centered perspective and examines why and how individuals or particular groups use particular media. This research is mostly rooted in approaches like uses and gratifications (Ruggiero, 2000) or selective exposure (Stroud, 2011). While this research is able to deal with interindividual differences and to provide fruitful insights into the motivation of media use and into the functions of these communicative practices for particular groups, it primarily focuses on single media types, such as television or newspapers or the internet, or on single genres, such as news or daily soaps, or of specific topics or products. In doing so, the entirety of different media that an individual uses and the interrelations among these different media are often ignored. However, we see a growing need for cross-media approaches in research on media use in order to meet the challenges of a changing media environment, including the increasing differentiation and convergence of media technologies, services and content, and the increasing importance of cross-media strategies for media industries.

In order to solve these conceptual problems, several researchers have emphasized the need for cross-media approaches to issues of media use (Bjur *et al.*, 2014; Schrøder, 2011). In the same line, we have proposed the concept of media repertoires (Hasebrink and Domeyer, 2012): The media repertoire of a person consists of the entirety of media he or she regularly uses. Media repertoires can be regarded as relatively stable cross-media patterns of media use. A repertoire-oriented approach to media use is characterized by the following principles:

- *User-centered perspective*: The concept of media repertoires moves the media user into the focus; rather than taking the media-centered perspective that asks which audiences a particular medium reaches, this concept emphasizes the question which media a particular person uses.
- *Entirety*: The repertoire-oriented approach stresses the need to consider the whole variety of media regularly assembled by a person; this helps to avoid misinterpretations resulting from approaches to single media.
- *Relationality*: Within a repertoire-oriented approach, the interrelations and specific functions of the components of a media repertoire are of particular interest since they represent the inner structure or coherence of a media repertoire; this reflects our basic assumption that the media repertoire of a user is not just the mere sum of different media he or she uses, but a meaningfully structured composition of media.

As seen above from the users' perspective, the digital media environment offers a wide range of information sources produced by different kinds of informants and distributed via different technical devices. The recent changes in the media environment have been analyzed as *convergence*, stressing the fact that the formerly clear boundaries between different kinds of technical services and information sources are increasingly blurred. As a consequence, information behavior can no longer be described as the reach a certain medium or service has, for example, a daily newspaper or television news. Instead any answer to questions of how people fulfill their information needs requires a more holistic view of information-oriented practices. The relevant question is: how do people combine the different options that are at their disposal and what does their personal *information repertoire* look like?

Table 36.5 Traditional users versus mainly digital users

	BRA	FIN	DEN	AUS	IRE	US	ESP	ITA	JP	UK	GER	FRAU
n	2033	1509	2019	2042	1501	2278	2026	2006	2015	2149	1969	1991
Mainly digital	54	51	46	44	43	41	40	39	36	35	26	25
Traditional	12	17	21	21	23	25	24	21	27	32	41	38

Source: Reuters Institute Digital News Survey 2015.

"Traditional users have been defined as those who consume more offline sources than online when we ask about specific newspaper, TV, radio, and online brands. (Q5a/b. Which, if any, of the following have you used to access news in the last week? Via TV, radio, or print/via online platforms?) Mainly Digital users are those who consume more online sources than offline. To pick up anomalies these segments were then further adjusted based on the number of digital devices used for news each week. Half & Half users who use more than two digital devices per week for news go into mainly digital segment and any traditionalists who use more than two devices for digital news go into the Half & Half category" (Newman, Levy, and Nielsen, 2015: 53). Base: Total sample in each country. Ordered by the percentage of *Mainly digital*.

To illustrate this conceptual framework using the Reuters Institute's Digital News Survey, a first step towards the concept of information repertoires is to segment the respondents into those who mainly focus on traditional sources (TV, radio, and print) and those who mainly use digital sources for news. This is based on the number of concrete (offline and online) media brands that have been used in the last week. Beyond these extreme repertoires, there is a third group of news users who turn to offline *and* online sources in a relatively balanced way. One might introduce a fourth segmentation by dividing the balanced group into those who generally use few news sources, neither online nor offline, and those who use many news sources, online and offline. Table 36.5 compares countries according to the relative size of these two unbalanced groups. Again the figures reflect substantial differences: France and Germany stand out as the only countries where the group of traditional users is bigger than the group of mainly digital users. Concerning the debates on the consequences of changing digital environments for the distribution and consumption of news, this small example shows that we should not focus on single indicators that suggest a linear shift from offline to online, which would ignore the multiple patterns of news use across sources, brands, and devices.

Towards a needs-based approach to the reconstruction of information repertoires

In order to reconstruct and understand people's information repertoires, it is helpful to combine two popular approaches to media and information use: information seeking on the one hand and uses and gratifications on the other.

According to research on *information seeking*, information needs emerge from people's insight that their current knowledge is insufficient for reaching a concrete objective. Therefore, they need particular information to fill this gap (see Bouwman and van de Wijngaert, 2002; Case, 2002). The intentional ambition to get missing information is conceptualized as information seeking. From this perspective, information needs can be classified against the concrete topics and knowledge domains they refer to. People have substantially different information needs, depending on their profession, their social contexts, and their individual characteristics, and these needs are strongly situation-bound: occurring in concrete situations.

In contrast, research within the uses and gratifications framework does not start from a concrete situation or a particular knowledge gap leading to information-seeking. Instead it starts from an observation that people use certain media and then ask for the needs, motives, and gratifications sought to explain why these media are used. In most cases, gratifications sought and obtained are not investigated via concrete episodes of use but rather to general patterns of media over longer periods of time—typical empirical indicators are estimations of the frequency or duration of use. From this perspective, a classification of information needs refers to general media functions. In order to operationalize information needs, many studies are using questions such as: "I use this medium in order to inform myself/to be able to take part in conversations/to get inspiration/to get some support in coping with everyday life" (see, e.g., Ridder and Engel, 2005: 426). However, the use of a concrete media service—for example, news—can fulfill a much wider range of functions beyond information. Contrary to information-seeking research, uses and gratifications research seeks to grasp the full range of functions.

Against the background of these two approaches, we can conceptually distinguish four levels of information needs. This classification might be illustrated by a pyramid (see Figure 36.1).

a) *Undirected information needs* represent people's wish to stay informed about any relevant public news agenda. The general need for information and surveillance as investigated by uses and gratifications research, referring to people's need to constantly monitor their environment in order to identify risks and opportunities for their coping with everyday life and to broader ambitions regarding the future. Those who miss certain opportunities or do not realize certain risks might encounter problems. This kind of information need does not lead to seeking particular information but to monitoring the environment for upcoming new issues that are relevant to the users. It can be regarded as an anthropological constant and to a lesser or greater degree it is shared by everybody. In order to fulfill this need

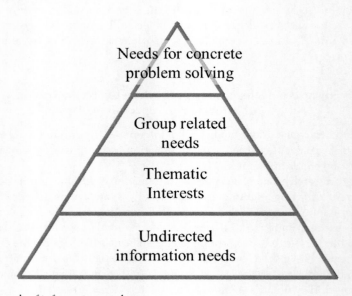

Figure 36.1 Levels of information needs.

in complex societies, the established instruments of public communication have been developed—in other words, this is what journalism is for.

b) *Thematic interests* make people look for certain information media dealing with their respective field of interest. These are active orientations towards certain topics and aspects of life. In this respect, people tend to specialize in order to acquire a certain expertise and to distinguish themselves from others. In this area, people differ dramatically and as a consequence, many different forms of targeted communication have been developed, e.g. special interest magazines and specialized channels, not to mention the many extremely specialized online services.

c) *Group-related needs* stress people's wish to have an idea of what their personal reference groups think about the world and about themselves. The exchange within these groups, including discussion about common interests and objectives leading to trust and feelings of belonging, is a core factor of community-building and thus an important prerequisite for the individual's identity and position in society. Before the digital age, this kind of information need was mainly fulfilled in personal networks, through face-to-face communication or personal forms of media-based communication, such as letters and phone. The new communication services offered by social media present a substantial increase in the opportunities for communications practices that serve group-related needs.

d) *Problem-oriented needs* refer to specific information that is needed in order to solve a particular problem. Thus, they match with the concept of information seeking identified above. These emerge from concrete challenges within concrete situations, which cannot be solved without particular information. These kinds of needs occur in everyone's everyday life, but the particular information needed is highly individualized and situationally bound. As a consequence, many forms of individualized services have been developed.

Assuming that all four information needs are relevant to a certain degree to all users, but that the importance of the four needs may differ for different users, this leads to different information repertoires. To illustrate the usefulness of this conceptual tool for analyzing ongoing changes in information-related practices, we can apply them to two questions concerning changing information audiences: How have audiences' information repertoires changed since the 1970s? How do information repertoires change as we grow older?

To explore changes to information repertoires since the 1970s, we have to consider the major societal and media-related changes. Assuming these changes lead to changes in the relative importance of the four information needs, we can illustrate the typical information repertoire in the 1970s by the relative importance of these information needs and assume that the basic level was by far the most important one. This phase was characterized by the dominant role of mass communication media provided by television, radio, and newspapers. Compared to this, the other three levels play minor roles. With regard to thematic interests, there was only a slight differentiation for magazines. Beyond small activist groups that developed their own alternative media, the existing media rarely fulfilled group-related needs. Opportunities for individualized services were rare; some special interest media offered a kind of counseling service for particular problems.

An important step in this development can be found in the period between the mid-1980s and mid-1990s, when many countries introduced commercial television and radio, which lead to a strong differentiation of broadcasting media among increasingly specific target groups. This process was mirrored by the launch of highly specialized magazines, leading to an increased prominence for thematic interests at the cost of mass media (as illustrated in the

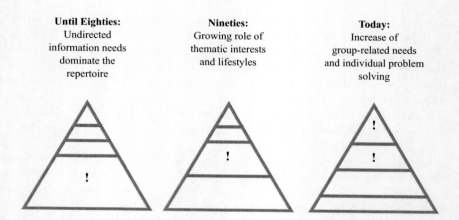

Until Eighties:
Undirected
information needs
dominate the
repertoire

Nineties:
Growing role of
thematic interests
and lifestyles

Today:
Increase of
group-related needs
and individual problem
solving

Figure 36.2 Changes of information repertoires related to major media developments.

middle pyramid in Figure 36.2). For group-related interests and individualized services, no major change occurred.

The last period from the mid-1990s is shaped by the diffusion of the internet and an increased digitization providing opportunities to substantially increase the relative role of these two levels of information needs in the audiences' media repertoires. Beyond trends in the media environment, this development was also fueled by basic societal changes, such as individualization. As a consequence, group-related and problem-related information needs have become stronger, while the role of thematic interest and undirected search lessened.

A second illustration of the usefulness of this analytical tool refers to the changes of information practices across the life course. Figure 36.3 shows typical information repertoires in three phases: adolescents, young adults, and mid-age adults. Within the process of socialization, people are confronted with particular developmental tasks (Havighurst, 1972) they have to cope with. These developmental tasks have specific implications for the four information needs. Key developmental tasks of adolescents include processes of developing one's identity and establishing their own relationships outside the family. Thus, group-related needs are the main driving force for their information repertoires as represented in the left triangle of Figure 36.3. Adolescents have a particular interest in finding out about being 'in' or 'out' and in monitoring the relationships within the peer group and their own position in it.

With the end of school and the entry into professional or academic qualification, new developmental tasks gain significance that stress the importance of identifying and developing particular interests and an idea of how to specialize. This developmental task goes along with specializing thematic interests. Group-related interests are still important, but they do not stand out among adolescents. Mid-age adults again are confronted with new developmental tasks. By then many have established a family and a professional career. In this phase, it can be assumed that undirected information needs will gain importance. The relatively stable position in different social contexts leads to decreased activity with regard to group-related needs and thematic interests. Instead they are confronted with increased expectations—in family, professional, and peer contexts—to be well informed on a broad range of issues and to be a well-integrated member of society. This requires an information repertoire that includes publicly relevant issues.

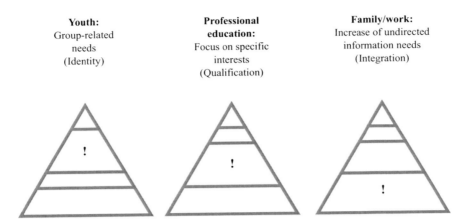

Youth:
Group-related
needs
(Identity)

**Professional
education:**
Focus on specific
interests
(Qualification)

Family/work:
Increase of undirected
information needs
(Integration)

Figure 36.3   Changes of information repertoires in the course of life.

This example of changing information repertoires in the life course demonstrates that the analytical distinction between four levels of information needs can help provide meaningful interpretations of empirical findings from audience research. While currently this conceptual model has not been tested empirically, the interpretations above can nevertheless contribute to explaining the complex and often contradictory evidence on information behaviors in the life course—such as why younger people do not use established journalism outlets very often. According to that interpretation, there are positive signals on the horizon that today's young people might turn to journalism when confronted with the developmental tasks of mid-age adults.

Conclusion

It is important to stress that the distinction between the four levels of information needs are analytical distinctions. The model is not for clearly attributing any concrete information behavior to exactly one of these levels, instead the objective is to provide a simple analytical tool that helps describe and understand transforming communication practices within the digital environment. As the current lines differentiating media services are increasingly blurring, the clear empirical distinctions between media services—addressing mass audiences following their undirected information needs, those that serve specialized interests, those that inform about news about the relevant reference groups, and those that help to solve particular problems—are increasingly complicated. Processes of convergence lead to all kinds of combinations of these services, and the increasing use of social media for news combines two levels of information needs—undirected search and group-related need. As journalists' work in the newsroom increasingly incorporates special services for particular interests, a lot of social media–related activities and sometimes also individualized services will come into focus. Therefore, it will be increasingly important to analyze how media users combine the different outlets and services that are at their disposal from a user-centered perspective.

Further reading

For more reading on putting patterns of media use into the broader context of public communication and participation, Nick Couldry, Sonia Livingstone, and Tim Markham's *Media*

Consumption and Public Engagement: Beyond the Presumption of Attention (2007) is useful. Meanwhile, Philip Napoli's book *Audience Evolution: New Technologies and the Transformation of Media Audiences* (2010) provides a broad overview and discussion of new technologies' consequences for audiences.

References

Ang, M.I. (1991) *Desperately Seeking the Audience*. London, UK: Routledge.

Bjur, J., Schrøder, K.C., Hasebrink, U., Courtois, C., Adoni, H. and Nossek, H. (2014) "Cross-Media Use: Unfolding Complexities in Contemporary Audiencehood." In Carpentier, N., Schrøder, K.C. and Hallett, L. (eds) *Audience Transformations: Shifting Audience Positions in Late Modernity*. New York, NY: Routledge, pp. 15–29.

Bouwman, H. and van de Wijngaert, L. (2002) "Content and Context: An Exploration of the Basic Characteristics of Information Needs." *New Media & Society* 4(3): 329–353.

Case, D.O. (2002) *Looking for Information: A Survey of Research on Information Seeking, Needs, and Behavior*. Amsterdam, Netherlands: Elsevier.

Couldry, N., Livingstone, S.M. and Markham, T. (2007) *Media Consumption and Public Engagement: Beyond the Presumption of Attention*. Houndmills, UK: Palgrave.

Hasebrink, U. (2011) "Giving the Audience a Voice: The Role of Research in Making Media Regulation More Responsive to the Needs of the Audience." *Journal of Information Policy* 1: 321–336.

Hasebrink, U. and Domeyer, H. (2012) "Media Repertoires as Patterns of Behaviour and as Meaningful Practices: A Multimethod Approach to Media Use in Converging Media Environments." *Participations* 9(2): 757–783.

Hasebrink, U., Jensen, K.B., van den Bulck, H., Hölig, S. and Maeseele, P. (2015) "Changing Patterns of Media Use Across Cultures: A Challenge for Longitudinal Research." *International Journal of Communication* 9: 435–457.

Havighurst, R.J. (1972) *Developmental Tasks and Education*. New York, NY: McKay.

Lunt, P. and Livingstone, S. (2012) *Media Regulation: Governance and the Interests of Citizens and Consumers*. London, UK: Sage.

McQuail, D. (1997) "Accountability of Media to Society: Principles and Means." *European Journal of Communication* 12: 511–529.

Napoli, P.M. (2010) *Audience Evolution: New Technologies and the Transformation of Media Audiences*. New York, NY: Columbia University Press.

Newman, N., Levy, D.A. and Nielsen, R.K. (2015) *Reuters Institute Digital News Report 2015: Tracking the Future of News*. Oxford, UK: Reuters Institute for the Study of Journalism.

Ridder, C.M. and Engel, B. (2005) "Massenkommunikation 2005: Images und Funktionen der Massenmedien im Vergleich. Ergebnisse der 9. Welle der ARD/ZDF-Langzeitstudie zur Mediennutzung und—bewertung." *Media Perspektiven* 9: 422–448.

Ruggiero, T.E. (2000) "Uses and Gratifications Theory in the 21st Century." *Mass Communication and Society* 3(1): 3–37.

Schrøder, K.C. (2011) "Audiences are Inherently Cross-Media: Audience Studies and the Cross-Media Challenge." *Communication Management Quarterly* 18: 5–27.

Stroud, N.J. (2011) *Niche News: The Politics of News Choice*. New York, NY: Oxford University Press.

Trilling, D. and Schönbach, K. (2013) "Skipping Current Affairs: The Non-Users of Online and Offline News." *European Journal of Communication* 28(1): 35–51.

Webster, J.G. and Phalen, P.F. (1997) *The Mass Audience: Rediscovering the Dominant Model*. Mahwah, NJ: Lawrence Erlbaum.

37

THE SPATIOTEMPORAL DYNAMICS OF DIGITAL NEWS AUDIENCES

Chris Peters

The changing patterns of news consumption in a digital era bring about new configurations between audiences, information, the devices upon which they consume it and the different (mobile) places and (shiftable) times when and where this is possible. Coupled with the rapid proliferation of news and informational sources arising alongside this—sometimes from the ashes of 'legacy' media, sometimes from Silicon Valley, occasionally via the goodwill of crowdsourced funding—trying to keep up with what 'news' and 'journalism' exactly 'is' in a digital era perplexes even the most avid and insightful observer. This is seemingly odd and somewhat paradoxical; as some commentators in recent years have wryly noted, journalism is like pornography or obscenity, 'we know it when we see it.' Yet while a good line, a reasonable question to ask ourselves is: do we? What we do seem to know fairly unequivocally is that much of the confusion and concern wrought by the changing media landscape is less about what journalism 'is' anymore but—quite crucially—what uses people still have for it, which functions are being created anew, and whether or not journalism 'as we knew it' will remain financially viable.

Journalism studies, and media and communication studies more broadly, have tried—and are still in the process of trying—to come to grips with these changing dynamics (e.g. Peters and Broersma, 2013; Zelizer, 2009). The contributions comprising this Companion trace such debates in the current age and try to look forward simultaneously. This particular chapter articulates a position that a constructive place to begin thinking through digital journalisms' possible futures and the impact of the shifts transforming the media landscape is, to start with, in Jay Rosen's (2006) phrase, "the people formerly known as the audience." Audiences matter if for no other reason than without them, the purpose of producing journalism in any era is somewhat meaningless, whether or not one is speaking economically, democratically, or socioculturally. So establishing what is happening in terms of audience or user dynamics should prove fairly central to digital journalism scholarship. Much of the academic focus over the past decade has attempted to do precisely this, considering the changing relationship between media producers and consumers, although typically focusing on what empowerment of the latter means for the former in terms of user-generated content and participation more broadly. However, there is a growing emphasis not just on the content people provide to news outlets but on the changing experiences of audiences in the contemporary digitalized age; an 'audience turn,' if you will, which posits the necessity of going beyond highly informative, but essentially descriptive, quantitative foci on changing patterns of use (e.g. Newman, Levy, and Nielsen, 2015) to consider novel meanings and experiences people associate with journalism (see Groot Kormelink and Costera Meijer, 2014; Heikkilä and Ahva, 2015).

Within this move toward the audience a crucial aspect, but one often overlooked, is the role space plays in the relation between journalism and audiences' experiences of consuming it (see Peters, 2015). This chapter highlights the need to address this absence by first focusing on interrelated changes in the media ecology necessary to grasp the newfound complexity of media consumption. Specifically, it outlines how audience engagement with news and different spatiotemporal configurations made possible by digital technology are trends that complement and reinforce one another in terms of changing the socially situated affordances of news use and the composition of our 'communication geography' (Adams and Jansson, 2012). Having sketched these contours, the chapter then highlights analytical challenges for understanding and conceptualizing the new interrelations between digital news content, production, and consumption, grounding this analysis with insights that emphasize the significance of spatiotemporal dynamics. The emphasis here is on the interrelations and mobilities of digital news audiences, based on a recognition of the productive impacts of media use while being careful to note the limitations of a paradigm shift that points solely to the possibilities generated by the ubiquitous presence of media in our everyday lives. The conclusion broadens this conversation to consider what this all means in terms of the societal role of journalism. Aspects of interaction and personalization beget by new media technologies certainly shape the possibilities, practices, and power audiences have to choose news wherever, whenever, and however they want. However, this simultaneously challenges the conventional routines and symbolic power of journalism as a place where, metaphorically, people can come together.

Changes in the digital media landscape

Expressed broadly, the places and spaces of news consumption matter, and matter significantly, for how people choose, interpret, and attend to the news. More specifically, we can say that changing spatiotemporal configurations of media use facilitated by technological developments tend to change how information are communicated and is oftentimes associated with significant sociocultural transformations (Meyrowitz, 1986). In this sense, the modification and emergence of different spaces of consumption, accompanying the rise of new media technologies, change what news 'is' (Peters, 2012). The slowly growing recognition of this in digital journalism studies touches upon the interrelation of audience engagement with media and our sense of place (see Banaji and Cammaerts, 2015; Dickens, Couldry, and Fotopoulou, 2015; Nyre, 2012; Picone, Courtois, and Paulussen, 2015; Schmitz Weiss, 2015). The manner in which both are transforming greatly impacts the media ecology in which news consumption occurs, as journalism transitions from its highly privileged institutional station to one that is increasingly situated—from the perspective of the audience—as merely one of many possible information providers designed to be informative, interactive, and civically and technologically engaging. Looking to the emerging practices of news audiences in this sense is instructive, because it encourages us to frame questions, "not to media considered as objects, texts, apparatuses of perception or production processes, but to what people are doing in relation to media in the contexts in which they act" (Couldry, 2012: 35). Conceptualizing such a media sociology means considering how audiences' old habits become 'de-ritualized' and re-evaluated in everyday life (Broersma and Peters, 2013). To do this robustly, attention to engagement and spatiotemporality is key.

Audience engagement (afforded by digital culture)

The story of journalism pre-digital technology was one where—pragmatically—interaction with the audience was fairly limited. While letters to the editor, call-ins to radio shows and the like existed, fundamentally news was primarily a one-way form of mass communication where "all the news that's fit to print" came down from media institutions on high. Classical notions about the different functions of the press in a democracy reflected such realities: news was an information source, a watchdog, a representative for the people, and so forth. Even though most accounts were quick to note that journalism should provide a 'public forum' to discuss issues—the classic idea of a public sphere, albeit interpreted in a variety of ways over the years—at best one could say that pre-digital journalism gave fodder for individuals to discuss issues of public concern among themselves; within the pages of the daily newspaper or on the nightly news, the space for members of the public to contribute meaningfully was in truth quite constrained. This, of course, is one of the great observations of the shift beget by web 2.0 technologies; by reducing the distance previously experienced between audiences and media institutions, this 'new wave' of journalism is said to promote interactivity by facilitating participation in the news.

This shift is certainly noteworthy for it potentially changes how audiences experience the news they encounter and how, conversely, encounters by audiences help to shape the news (Allan and Peters, 2015a). There has been a significant uptick in research in digital journalism studies which focuses on how journalism providers now marshal immediate, first-hand experience from, depending on analytic stress, amateurs, users, or citizens in different possible places. Similarly, the rise of manifest game-changing innovations, such as blogs, UGC hubs, crowdsourcing, Facebook, and Twitter, to name a few, have been studied, helping to broaden our understandings of how audiences—often in their role as citizens—increasingly find their way into news content (see Allan, 2013; Li and Hellmueller, this volume). These developments have prominent implications for journalism as a societal institution, recasting its boundaries (Carlson and Lewis, 2015), and potentially leading to a more collaborate ethos of connectivity in a digital era that, almost by necessity, is increasingly defined by and mandates co-operation between news organizations and audiences. "News organizations willing to recast journalism anew, namely by making the most of this potential to forge cooperative relationships between professionals and their citizen counterparts, will secure opportunities to rethink its forms, practices and epistemologies at a time of considerable scepticism about future prospects," remark Allan and Peters (2015b: 10). Such collaborative approaches demand not only innovation and creativity but also mutual respect and dialogue.

Understanding this fundamental shift in the relationship and power dynamics between news organizations and audiences is critical if we want to map the way digital audiences are changing their rituals and practices surrounding journalism. It is not enough to say what device a person chooses to get news or when they do it, the sociocultural functions served by consuming and potentially interacting with the news are dynamic, and what has transformed is indeed a greater possibility for locating ourselves within the story. In this regard, thinking spatiotemporally about audiences' uses of journalism has both literal and figurative associations—from the specific where and when of consumption, to the way we locate ourselves relationally against this information and, by association, within the wider world around us.

Spatiotemporal configurations (reconfigured by digital technology)

Bearing this in mind, when we speak of spatiotemporal configurations of news consumption we are not only speaking about the 'hard facts' of where, when, how often, and so forth, we are trying to plug into socially situated affordances from use. A basic insight of much spatial theory (see Lefebvre, 1991; Smith, 2008) is that trying to decouple the spatial—or perhaps more accurately, spatiotemporal—from the socio-political is erroneous, for space-time is simultaneously physical (locations and movement), conceptual (how we conceive of and 'map' it), and social (created and experienced by people). One brief example can highlight how these multifaceted and interrelated aspects are all necessary to appreciate the significance of media for communicative practices, including news consumption. The development of the smartphone and its associated apps, for instance, changes audiences' everyday patterns of news consumption and locations of news use (physical space), like checking news during the 'in between' periods of life such as waiting for public transit (Dimmick *et al.,* 2011). Such changes also prompt news organizations to rethink how they conceive of the audience (conceptual space); asking for crowdsourced, active contributions such as photos or videos as breaking news unfolds is now commonplace and relates to the ways audience engagement and news events themselves are conceived (Vis, 2013). And finally, the way people view socio-situational orientations of news consumption is impacted. Social media technologies such as the smartphone facilitate news streams, allowing people to infuse personal meaning into storytelling and, though its online and mobile capabilities, traverse public, private, and virtual spaces simultaneously (de Souza e Silva, 2006). In other words, smartphones allow novel experiential possibilities for news audiences, creating a liminal space that Papacharissi (2015: 36) terms electronic 'elsewheres,' which is to say geo-social, hybrid media environments that permit citizens to "access content in transition and find their own place in the story, alongside journalists, who already possess an institutionally assigned place in the story."

All these considerations come into play with the growing attention on locative media in journalism, a trend that highlights spatiotemporality as:

> a cardinal, orienting, and increasingly user-defined aspect of mobile news production and its consumption.[...] Locative technologies, such as geospatial positioning (GPS) data and geo-tagging, have been critical to the 'cartographic' turn in news, where events are mapped and user input invited to the construction of place through images or witness accounts. In turn audiences now expect to be able to search and aggregate news based on locational indicators and also to position themselves *vis-à-vis* events and places, via location annotated posts to social media.
>
> (Goggin, Martin, and Dwyer, 2015: 44)

Conceptually speaking, media consumption is thus both real and symbolic, shaping our spatiotemporal experiences of news in terms of positioning us simultaneously in relation to information as well as how we use it to engage, or disengage, with the world around us. And while the speed, scale, and complications of digital news reporting are complex and understandably invite suggestions that spatial aspects of (mobile, social, locational) news consumption matter more now than ever before, it is important to recall that such emerging configurations are not merely a property of the digital era. When thinking 'spatiotemporally' about news use, it is helpful to keep in mind that "the frameworks from within which we watch and listen, muse and remember, are defined in part by where we are in the world, and where we think we are, and sometimes too, of course, by where we might wish to be" (Silverstone, 1999: 86). Digital configurations of news use are different from what came before and worth specifying, but despite these shifting contours in the media environment, spatiotemporal configurations of consumption are in fact nothing new—they are merely more adaptable.

Analytical challenges for studying digital news audiences

It is not only within journalism studies that many are asking how transforming audience practices in the changing media and communication environment are correspondingly transforming societies (see COST, 2014). Concepts quickly (re)gaining currency within the broader field of media and communication research include mobility (e.g. Jones *et al.*, 2013), embodiment (e.g. Farman, 2013), and materiality (e.g. Packer and Wiley, 2013), representing attempts to come to grips with how people are using digital media, the societal significance of associated informational streams, and what meanings and experiences accompany contemporary media consumption. A consideration of spatiotemporally ties into all of these, demanding that analytic consideration be furnished on the pathways of information, and the different ways that audiences come to navigate within, challenge, and/or create such spaces simultaneously. In terms of journalism more specifically, a couple analytical prisms are worth considering in this regard, namely: the interrelations between people, places, and things, especially media devices and platforms; and mobilities, in the sense of how and where journalism fits with the flows of everyday life.

Interrelations (people, places, and things)

Many of the headlines that capture journalistic attention regarding the influence of new media devices on journalism tend to focus squarely on usage rates. X percent now use tablets, Y percent accessed a news story via Facebook last week, and Z percent paid for digital content. While intriguing, when viewed in isolation, such statistics on the use or preferences surrounding new media devices provide only a small glimpse of the overall picture. Rather than simply think about how people, news audiences in this case, use things—digital versus traditional media devices—conceptually there is a richer tapestry to be made from a relational view of media use that looks to interrelations within everyday life. As Pink and Leder Mackley (2013: 683) note of such a holistic perspective, conceptuality it makes sense to form research questions and design by considering three analytical prisms, "environment/place; movement/practice; [and] perception/sensory embodied experience." Related to recent 'turns' in contemporary social theory (i.e. spatial, mobility, sensorial, material), the point is that static theory which tries to compartmentalize uses of media to exclude these considerations will necessarily be somewhat impoverished. Of course, such in-depth analysis, typically afforded by ethnographic approaches, is time-consuming, costly, and intrusive, meaning that it suffers—in some eyes—from an inability to make claims on a grand scale. Even surveys, long derided for self-reporting biases and lack of depth but well received in policy circles, now face stiff competition in an age of 'big data' where 'hard evidence' from our digital footprint is but a click away and is said by some (e.g. Webster, 2014) to be the best foundation for robust knowledge of how people use the digital resources at their disposal. Nonetheless, it is worth embracing an 'ecological' perspective as a starting point despite these challenges and shortcomings, for if we want to address complex issues, or even know which questions to ask, we need to account for, among other considerations: the spatiotemporal contexts of consumption; engagement with the information itself ('decoding,' in Hall's [1980] classic sense); the emotional experience of involvement from engaging (Peters, 2011); and the feelings and preferences more broadly associated with media devices (Madianou and Miller, 2013). As Farman (2013: 17) notes:

> With mobile phones that connect to the internet or GPS receivers that are utilized for a wide array of purposes, locating one's self simultaneously in digital space and in material space has become an everyday action for many people. With this alteration of embodied space, the cultural objects we are producing and interacting with are also being transformed.

News is no exception. And while recognition of such impacts is essential, we must simultaneously be careful to note the limitations of a paradigm shift that points solely to the possibilities generated by the ubiquitous presence of media in our everyday lives. Many interrelations can be traced through digital approaches—for example, who uses an app, where, when, and potentially with whom—but considering how the consumption of news makes us orient toward different places, people, and issues, or conversely shy away, is a trickier business to capture with digital signals and storage alone. Similarly, speaking of the use of digital media artifacts to consume news (or any other form of media for that matter) as though they are neutral objects is also problematic. One should be wary of assuming mobile technologies or the spatial uses associated with them are sociologically neutral and it seems reasonable to assume that classic categories of analysis concerning social divisions and hierarchies—such as those associated with gender, class, ethnicity, sexuality, and so forth—bear upon not only how we understand the adaptation and material integration of technology to consume news but also, conversely, how the documenting capabilities of media themselves provide insight into the changing status of these categories themselves. To render problematic the uses of communication technology in everyday life demands multi-strand analyses, and thereby a renewed commitment to deploying creative methods to discern the interrelation between people, places, and things and their imbrication in a host of frequently ephemeral forms and practices.

Mobilities (movement and media)

Contemporary studies of media, including journalism, need to concern themselves with the 'emplaced' uses of media (Pink and Hjorth, 2012), in other words the way that media are both produced and consumed within the flow of everyday life, a life which is not static but one in which movement is key. Of course, movement is not unique to the digital era and historical precision demands that we recognize that the 'mobility' of computers and 4G telecommunications are not by themselves remarkable for journalism; newspapers, for instance, have also traditionally acted as a mobile interface that interacts both with the reader and with the surrounding social space in which it is consumed as have car radios. However, what is noteworthy about recent technological development is the way that they multiply and unshackle the places and times where people may choose to consume news, and the types of social interactions and functions this in turn makes possible. As Jansson and Lindell (2015: 8) note, the shift from a mass media environment to a more diversified, digital media ecology, "implies that virtual and corporeal mobilities are combined in increasingly diversified and open-ended ways as media users may access any virtual space (including 'news spaces') from any geographical location through their miniaturized transmedia technologies." The *sine qua non* of mobile technologies is this movement and reconfigured flows something which is not only confined to people of course but also to associated expectations and control over the speed, flow, and mobility of information in everyday life in general. In this respect, we should keep in mind that mobile media is only one aspect of a more broadly accelerated mobilization of life that encompasses goods, services, ideas, information, transport, travel, and communications (Elliott and Urry, 2010).

Considering current shifts in digital journalism through this analytic prism of mobility helps alert us to what has transformed, while still recognizing the fundamental fact that news consumption has always been a sociocultural (i.e. oriented to others), spatiotemporal (i.e. situated within everyday life), and material (i.e. requiring one's bodily presence and interface) practice. For instance, what is immediately apparent is how the rise of mobile technologies significantly impacts human interaction and communicative patterns. The rapid socialization of mobile phone usage, for instance, has altered a "bewildering and proliferating" array of cultural activities (Goggin, 2006: 2). Research illustrates how the introduction of the mobile phone transformed aspects of identity construction, community formation, and belonging as well as more quotidian aspects of life such as keeping in touch, working, parenting, flirting, bullying, and maintaining personal finance (see also Baym, 2010; Horst and Miller, 2006; Ling, 2004). A consideration of the influence of mobiles on journalism then benefits from looking holistically at news consumption within such a shifting informational ecology and asking what role 'news' (continues to) play in this equation. Schrøder's (2015) study about mobile news practices in Denmark, for instance, cautions that many other processes besides news consumption are equally if not more vital to how people traverse the terrain of everyday life. Digital cultures are interrelated, and in this respect it is difficult to quarantine attitudes people express towards journalism from other closely related considerations.

Keeping this caveat in mind, in a world where convenient, mobile updates are not just the norm but an expectation, how informational flows transect and shape the day has significant impact both on the expectations of journalism and its real-time integration by audiences. Moreover, these considerations dovetail. Sheller (2015: 20) has observed that what is telling about the data-sharing possibilities of contemporary digital technologies like smartphones is that they change the spatiotemporality of news events themselves; reporting becomes cotemporaneous and "may even precede the full unfolding of 'the news.'" This constantly updated flow of 'news now,' she argues, and mobile news practices such as agglomeration, curation, crowdsourcing, updating, tagging, and sharing go far beyond just remaking news. Such changes in how information circulates transform "the very ground beneath our feet: ambient flows of news re-situate how we understand where we are, who we are connected with, what our 'present' moment actually is. The now-ness of news, in other words, offers a new sense of the present" (Sheller, 2015). In this respect, as in other walks of life, new mobile ways of consuming news in 'always on,' itinerant societies correspond to shifts in the spatiotemporally situated and socially contextualized meanings individuals generate from such use as well as their assessment of the value of journalism as a cultural form.

Conclusion

Aspects of interaction and personalization beget by new media technologies certainly shape the possibilities and power audiences have to choose news wherever, whenever, and however they want. However, this simultaneously challenges the conventional routines and symbolic power of journalism as a place where, metaphorically, people can come together. Increasingly, the affordances of digital technology lead the creators of news content to valorize not only their informational aspects but also the benefits of consumption in terms of associated participatory possibilities. Such a shift is often seen as paradigmatic (see Livingstone, 2013), and media audiences in general are often now conceptualized in terms of being individual users who wish to have greater control over their media offerings. Social media, for instance, is premised on allowing users to orient to others and interact and share based on personal preferences. And yet if we apply the same logic to the production and consumption of news, there becomes a tipping point wherein individualistic rhetoric and empowerment becomes anathema to the idea of journalism's traditional collective, public ethos. While digital tools may promote connection in a very literal sense, when analyzing the current shifting dynamics of audiences it is crucial we do not forget the societally oriented discourses so ever-present during the previous era of mass media (see Peters and Witschge, 2015).

This is why spatiotemporal considerations of audiences are so important. News consumption, as is hopefully clear from above, is an associative practice whose importance derives from the connections it allows us to forge between places, people, and things. Such intersections are held together through cultural representations and flows of information as much as the technological networks which so often form the focal point of much contemporary scholarship. In other words, thinking through what makes news consumption meaningful demands relational thinking, and such thinking is—both literally and figuratively—spatiotemporal. The dynamics of how the everyday digital geographies of contemporary media, communication, and information flows intersect with the everywhere 'lived' geographies of individuals is a crucial consideration going forth if we want to grasp how current shifts impact audience perceptions of news, of storytelling, and of journalism. Increasingly, the idea of being able to communicate whenever, wherever, and while in motion is unremarkable, and the fact that one can combine and mix forms of auditory, oral, written, and visual communication while 'on the go' is expected. In such a seemingly 'fluid' mediascape, thinking 'spatiotemporally' helps us distinguish the unique from the routine, the extraordinary from the ordinary, the significant from the mundane, pointing to moments when metaphorically, we pause to think. This is imperative if we wish to capture the diverse meanings, connections, and experiences that audiences create out of the mediated content they consume, engage with, and augment. Day-by-day, month-by-month, year-by-year technology moves forward, and its development and integration, and the impact of this development and integration, means considering the fundamental shifts this imparts on how people conceive of informational integration within their everyday lives.

Further reading

Of the many helpful insights into spatial theory I have read, Henri Lefebvre's *The Production of Space* (1991) remains my go-to reference when pondering its significance. Consulting Phil Hubbard and Ron Kitchin's *Key Thinkers on Space and Place* (2011, although not cited in this chapter) is an effective introduction to other touchstones while Paul Adams and André Jansson (2012) successfully illustrate how this thinking can be applied to enrich studies of media and communication. Adriana de Souza e Silva's (2006) article on 'hybrid spaces' remains an inspiration in terms of the interrelation between urban, mobile, and online (social) spaces. Finally, the contributions comprising the special issue on "The Spaces and Places of News Audiences" (*Journalism Studies*, 2015) provide stimulating examples of how the related conceptual terrains of spatial and social theory, political communication and mobility research, and audience and journalism studies can inform each other to advantage.

References

Adams, P. and Jansson, A. (2012) "Communication Geography: A Bridge between Disciplines." *Communication Theory* 22(3): 299–318.

Allan, S. (2013) *Citizen Witnessing: Revisioning Journalism in Times of Crisis*. Cambridge, UK: Polity Press.

Allan, S. and Peters, C. (2015a) "The 'Public Eye' or 'Disaster Tourists': Investigating Public Perceptions of Citizen Smartphone Imagery." *Digital Journalism* 3(4): 477–494.

Allan, S. and Peters, C. (2015b) "Visual Truths of Citizen Reportage: Four Research Problematics." *Information, Communication & Society* 18(11): 1348–1361. DOI: 10.1080/1369118X.2015.1061576.

Banaji, S. and Cammaerts, B. (2015) "Citizens of Nowhere Land: Youth and News Consumption in Europe." *Journalism Studies* 16(1): 115–132.

Baym, N. (2010) *Personal Connections in the Digital Age*. Cambridge, UK: Polity Press.

Broermsa, M. and Peters, C. (2013). "Introduction. Rethinking Journalism: The structural transformation of a public good." In: C. Peters and M. Broersma (Eds.) *Rethinking Journalism*. Abingdon, UK: Routledge, 1–12

Carlson, M. and Lewis, S. (eds) (2015) *Boundaries of Journalism: Professionalism, Practices and Participation*. London, UK: Routledge.

COST Action, EU (2014) *Transforming Audiences, Transforming Societies*. Available from: http://www.cost-transforming-audiences.eu/.

Couldry, N. (2012) *Media, Society, World: Social Theory and Digital Media Practice*. Cambridge, UK: Polity Press.

De Souza e Silva, A. (2006) "From Cyber to Hybrid: Mobile Technologies as Interfaces of Hybrid Spaces." *Space and Culture* 9(3): 261–278.

Dickens, L., Couldry, N. and Fotopoulou, A. (2015) "News in the Community? Investigating Emerging Inter-Local Spaces of News Production/Consumption." *Journalism Studies* 16(1): 97–114.

Dimmick, J., Feaster, J. and Hoplamazian, G. (2011) "News in the Interstices: The Niches of Mobile Media in Space and Time." *New Media & Society* 13(1): 23–39.

Elliott, A. and Urry, J. (2010) *Mobile Lives*. Abingdon, UK: Routledge.

Farman, J. (2013) *Mobile Interface Theory: Embodied Space and Locative Media*. London, UK: Routledge.

Goggin, G. (2006) *Cell Phone Culture: Mobile Technology in Everyday Life*. Abingdon, UK: Routledge.

Goggin, G., Martin, F. and Dwyer, T. (2015) "Locative News: Mobile Media, Place Informatics, and Digital News." *Journalism Studies* 16(1): 41–59.

Groot Kormelink, T. and Costera Meijer, I. (2014) "Tailor-Made News: Meeting the Demands of News Users on Mobile and Social Media." *Journalism Studies* 15(5): 632–641.

Hall, S. (1980) "Encoding/Decoding." In Hall, S., Hobson, D., Lowe, A. and Willis, P. (eds) *Culture, Media, Language*. London, UK: Hutchinson, pp. 128–138.

Heikkilä, H. and Ahva, L. (2015) "The Relevance of Journalism: Studying News Audiences in a Digital Era." *Journalism Practice* 9(1): 50–64.

Horst, H. and Miller, D. (eds) (2006) *The Cell Phone: An Anthropology of Communication*. Oxford, UK: Berg.

Hubbard, P. and Kitchin, R. (eds) (2011) *Key Thinkers on Space and Place*. 2nd edn. London, UK: Sage.

Jansson, A. and Lindell, J. (2015) "News Media Consumption in the Transmedia Age: Amalgamations, Orientations and Geo-Social Structuration." *Journalism Studies* 16(1): 79–96.

Jones, S., Karnowski, V., Ling, R. and von Pape, T. (2013) "Welcome to Mobile Media & Communication." *Mobile Media & Communication* 1(1): 3–7.

Lefebvre, H. (1991) *The Production of Space*. Oxford, UK: Blackwell.

Ling, R. (2004) *The Mobile Connection: The Cell Phone's Impact on Society*. San Francisco, CA: Morgan Kaufmann.

Livingstone, S. (2013) "The Participation Paradigm in Audience Research." *The Communication Review* 16(1–2): 21–30.

Madianou, M. and Miller, D. (2013) "Polymedia: Towards a New Theory of Digital Media in Interpersonal Communication." *International Journal of Cultural Studies* 16(2): 169–187.

Meyrowitz, J. (1986) *No Sense of Place*. Oxford, UK: Oxford University Press.

Newman, N., Levy, D. and Kleis Nielsen, R. (2015) "Reuters Institute Digital News Report 2015." Available from: http://www.digitalnewsreport.org/.

Nyre, L., Bjørnestad, S., Tessem, B. and Vaage Øie, K. (2012) "Locative Journalism: Designing a Location-Dependent News Medium for Smartphones." *Convergence* 18(3): 297–314.

Packer, J. and Wiley, S. (2013) *Communication Matters: Materialist Approaches to Media, Mobility and Networks.* London, UK: Routledge.

Papacharissi, Z. (2015) "Toward New Journalism(s): Affective News, Hybridity, and Liminal Spaces." *Journalism Studies* 16(1): 27–40.

Peters, C. (2011) "Emotion Aside or Emotional Side? Crafting an 'Experience of Involvement' in the News." *Journalism* 12(3): 297–316.

Peters, C. (2012) "Journalism to Go: The Changing Spaces of News Consumption." *Journalism Studies* 13(5–6): 695–705.

Peters, C. (2015) "Introduction: The Places and Spaces of News Audiences." *Journalism Studies* 16(1): 1–11.

Peters, C. and Broersma, M. (eds) (2013) *Rethinking Journalism: Trust and Participation in a Transformed News Landscape.* London, UK: Routledge.

Peters, C. and Witschge, T. (2015) "From Grand Narratives of Democracy to Small Expectations of Participation: Audiences, Citizenship, and Interactive Tools in Digital Journalism." *Journalism Practice* 9(1): 19–34.

Picone, I., Courtois, C. and Paulussen, S. (2015) "When News is Everywhere: Understanding Participation, Cross-Mediality and Mobility in Journalism from a Radical User Perspective." *Journalism Practice* 9(1): 35–49.

Pink, S. and Hjorth, L. (2012) "Emplaced Cartographies: Reconceptualising Camera Phone Practices in an Age of Locative Media." *Media International Australia* 145: 145–155.

Pink, S. and Leder Mackley, K. (2013) "Saturated and Situated: Expanding the Meaning of Media in the Routines of Everyday Life." *Media, Culture & Society* 35(6): 677–691.

Rosen, J. (2006) "The People Formerly Known as the Audience." *PressThink.* Available from: http://archive.pressthink.org/2006/06/27/ppl_frmr.html.

Schmitz Weiss, A. (2015) "Place-Based Knowledge in the Twenty-First Century: The Creation of Spatial Journalism." *Digital Journalism* 3(1): 116–131.

Schrøder, K. (2015) "News Media Old and New: Fluctuating Audiences, News Repertoires and Locations of Consumption." *Journalism Studies* 16(1): 60–78.

Sheller, M. (2015) "News Now: Interface, Ambience, Flow, and the Disruptive Spatio-Temporalities of Mobile News Media." *Journalism Studies* 16(1): 12–26.

Silverstone, R. (1999) *Why Study the Media?* London, UK: Sage.

Smith, N. (2008) *Uneven Development: Nature, Capital, and the Production of Space.* Athens, GA: University of Georgia Press.

Vis, F. (2013) "Twitter as a Reporting Tool for Breaking News: Journalists Tweeting the 2011 UK Riots." *Digital Journalism* 1(1): 27–47.

Webster, F. (2014) *The Marketplace of Attention: How Audiences Take Shape in a Digital Age.* Cambridge, MA: MIT Press.

Zelizer, B. (2009) *The Changing Faces of Journalism: Tabloidization, Technology and Truthiness.* London, UK: Routledge.

PART VII

Digital journalism and social media

38

TRANSFORMATIONS OF
JOURNALISM CULTURE

Folker Hanusch

Journalism, particularly in the Western world, is currently undergoing a radical transformation in a variety of ways. News production in many societies has come under pressure reflecting cutbacks in editorial resources, increases in journalists' workloads as well as job losses, profit-making and advertising demands, the growing importance of audience measures, sensationalism, as well as shrinking editorial independence. Journalists increasingly face challenges posed by new media technologies, user-generated content, professionalized public relations, and other forces. All these developments, which have become apparent particularly over the past one to two decades, have led to the emergence of a 'crisis in journalism' frame (Franklin, 2012: 665). There is no doubt that the digital transformation of the creative industries has had fundamental implications for one of the key institutions of democratic societies, shaking up long-held beliefs about the nature of news and the professional practices of journalism (Zelizer, 2009).

As a result of these transformations, scholarship about journalism from across the globe has begun producing a considerable amount of evidence about the ways in which changes in new technologies are changing the industry. Yet, while there is a consensus that journalists' work is changing in quite fundamental ways, journalists and their practices themselves "have not often been the main objects of study" (Dickinson, Matthews, and Saltzis, 2013: 5). This is beginning to change, with an increasing number of studies focusing on journalists' experiences in the new environment, even though the focus has tended to be on the impact of technology on specific work practices, rather than broader understandings of journalism's changing role in society. In addition, for the most part, studies examining changes in journalism tend to focus on individual countries, most notably the United States, leading to a one-sided understanding through the relative lack of comparative evidence (Mitchelstein and Boczkowski, 2009: 577).

This chapter aims to provide an in-depth overview of how changes in news work are transforming journalism more broadly by focusing on their effect on journalism cultures. In doing so, it identifies three broader trends—cultural, economic, and technological changes—and argues that for a more comprehensive assessment of the transformation of journalism, scholars need to bear in mind all these aspects, rather than examining only one in isolation. Further, there is an urgent need for comparative studies of these transformations, both within and across nations or regions.

Journalism culture

Before exploring transformations in journalism culture, it is important to define what we mean by journalism culture, a term that is used often, though rarely well-defined. Despite a large variety of studies in this field emerging from around the world in recent times, a common conceptual approach to what the term journalism culture means had been missing from the analysis until relatively recently (Hanitzsch, 2007). One definition was provided by Dutch journalism scholar Mark Deuze (2005: 446), who saw journalism culture as a "shared occupational ideology among newsworkers." In a similar vein, German journalism scholar Thomas Hanitzsch proposed defining journalism culture as a "particular set of ideas and practices by which journalists legitimate their role in society and render their work meaningful" (Hanitzsch, 2007: 369). He focused on three essential constituents, which include journalism's functions in society (institutional roles), notions of reality and what constitutes evidence (epistemologies), as well as how journalists deal with ethical problems (ethical ideologies). Hanitzsch's framework has since been applied to a comparative study of journalists in 21 countries (Hanitzsch *et al.*, 2011), with Hanitzsch (2011) identifying four types of journalistic roles: journalists as populist disseminators, detached watchdogs, critical change agents, and opportunist facilitators. The importance of each of these roles differed quite widely between the different countries studied by Hanitzsch and his colleagues, showing the complexity of journalism's societal role across the globe. In the context of journalism's transformation in recent decades, it is interesting to note that rarely have studies examined the changes in the industry against the background of journalism culture in a comprehensive fashion, with most focusing on specific aspects of journalism culture.

A key focus in the scholarship on journalism in recent years has been the impact of digital technologies. Undoubtedly, the internet, Web 2.0, and social media have all presented enormous challenges to traditional journalistic authority and autonomy, blurring boundaries of media creation and media consumption in what some argue has become a 'convergence culture' (Jenkins, 2006). Yet, this focus has also come at the expense of other important changes at the broader societal level, which have been underexplored. This chapter argues that these changes are also important to explore if we want to arrive at a more comprehensive picture of how and why journalism culture is being transformed. The three key challenges include: social and cultural transformations, economic shifts, and technological developments.

Social and cultural transformations

Modernization processes around the globe have created a growing need for orientation in increasingly multi-optional societies. Three ongoing processes of social change—individualization, value change, and the mediatization of everyday life—can in this context be considered as having had an impact on journalism through an increased focus on lifestyle coverage and, more broadly, an increase in soft news (Hanusch and Hanitzsch, 2013). Individualization is considered to be removing individuals from historically prescribed social forms and commitments, leading to a loss of traditional security in relation to practical knowledge, faith and guiding norms, and new forms of social commitment (Beck, 1992: 128). As a result, audiences are confronted with increasing choices as regards their own identities, and they look—at least in part—to the media for guidance. Social value changes have seen a shift particularly in industrialized societies towards self-expression values, which go in line with increased freedom of choice, gender equality and personal autonomy, and a more general trend towards more flexibility in shaping one's lifestyle (Inglehart, 1997; Inglehart and Welzel, 2005).

Finally, media and media logic are increasingly important for social processes of any kind, a development typically called mediatization—"the process whereby society to an increasing degree is submitted to, or becomes dependent on, the media and their logic" (Hjarvard, 2008: 113). Expressed in a similar way, people do not live, any more, with the media—but increasingly in the media (Deuze, 2012).

While mediatization is now an established area of scholarship on the media, there still exists relatively little work in terms of how these larger social processes outlined here are impacting on journalistic culture. There is an increasing amount of scholarship on the rise of lifestyle and celebrity journalism, which is challenging traditional hard news reporting in new ways (see, e.g., Hanusch, 2013; Hanusch and Fürsich, 2014; Marshall, 2006; Turner, 2004). A further strand of research has focused on the reporting of political news through different formats, such as the rise of satirical news in many industrialized societies (Baym, 2005; Harrington, 2012), which can be seen as a response to the broader societal processes already outlined. While some criticize such types of journalism, others believe they can enhance journalism's contribution to the democratic process by popularizing knowledge (Hanusch, 2012; Hartley, 2000; McNair, 2009).

Arguably, the implications of modernization processes may be impacting on journalism culture in fundamental ways. Research on lifestyle journalism, in particular, has shown that journalism cultures may be shifting in their general orientation more towards a consumer orientation, where journalists give the public what they want to know, rather than necessarily what journalists think they should know (Hanusch and Hanitzsch, 2013). Yet, more research is necessary to better understand the impact of these societal trends on journalism culture.

Economic shifts

Among the key trends over the past few decades, we can observe immense economic implications for traditional journalism. Starr (2012: 236) points to recent data on revenues for newspapers, magazines, and other news media in the Western world, which typically show "a pattern of growth through the last three decades of the twentieth century, a peak around the year 2000, and then a decline in the past decade, accelerating in the last several years." Siles and Boczkowski (2012) note that generally a combination of interrelated economic factors is seen as responsible for the so-called crisis of newspapers and traditional business models. Scholars like Picard (2001) have argued that over time newspapers became too dependent on classified advertising. Starr (2012: 239) notes that US newspapers derived "80 percent of their revenue from advertising, and much of that advertising revenue has been irreversibly lost." Further, many news organizations began to focus more on their profit margins than on their news coverage (Downie and Kaiser, 2002), and generational changes have meant that newspaper circulation in the West has dropped steadily over the past decades, particularly in the United States (Starr, 2012). With the arrival of the internet, the former 'rivers of gold' of classified advertising moved online, leading to the establishment of 'pure-plays'—specialist websites dedicated to job searches, car sales, and real estate. Many established news media publishers missed these developments, leading to significant losses in their advertising revenues (Williams, 2013). The global financial crisis in 2008 made matters worse, massively affecting advertising revenues even further (Kaye and Quinn, 2010). One key problem is that advertising online generates far less revenue (Thurman and Myllylahti, 2009), and news organizations' attempts at introducing paywalls are not yet viable in the short term (Myllylahti, 2014, also this volume).

In a global context, it should be noted that most of the discussions on economic impacts and declines in newspaper circulation have focused on the Western world, most notably the United States, leading to "a curiously North American and Eurocentric view of the press" (Franklin, 2008: 631). Further, most studies were conducted from a single-country perspective, with very few comparative analyses of how news media may be experiencing crises differently in different national contexts. In their review of scholarship on the crisis in newspapers, Siles and Boczkowski (2012: 1387) note the lack of comparative studies and argue that possibly, "rather than a single, homogenous crisis affecting every national and regional setting in a uniform manner, countries might have experienced particular newspapers *crises*" (emphasis in original).

The economic shifts in news media have undoubted repercussions on journalism culture. Firstly, the economic downturn has led to enormous numbers of journalists losing their jobs in countries like Australia, Germany, the Netherlands, Norway, and the United States (O'Donnell, McKnight, and Este, 2012; Starr, 2012). Many scholars argue that this is affecting journalists' capacity to report the news, and, as a result, the overall quality of news. Surveys in Norway and Australia have noted that journalists find themselves increasingly overworked with fewer resources (Hanusch, 2015; Ottosen and Krumsvik, 2010).

Siles and Boczkowski (2012: 1380) note that it is generally agreed that "the crisis has had negative implications for democracy because it undermines the watchdog role traditionally played by the press and its significance as a vehicle for free speech." As the news media environment becomes increasingly commercialized with fewer players competing for reduced advertising share, some have identified a trend toward a more market-oriented approach in journalism and less political reporting in commercial news (Cohen, 2002; Franklin, 1997). In addition, Starr (2012) also argues that declines in circulation among US newspapers may also be leading to a more partisan journalism culture. By and large, however, analyses directly linking economic developments in news media to changes in journalism culture are still very rare.

Technological developments

The largest amount of attention in recent scholarship on journalism has been devoted to the impact of digital technologies on news work. Enabled by technologies, audiences are increasingly involved in influencing and creating news content and reshaping traditional definitions of journalism (Lewis, 2012). Despite the rapid pace of change, research into the challenges facing journalism was originally slow to emerge. Historically, studies of emerging technologies, such as the internet, Web 2.0, and social media, quickly focused on the pioneering work of participatory websites such as blogs or collaborative news sites (Bruns, 2005). Heralded as new opportunities for the reinvigoration of an idealized public sphere, these amateur sites received vastly more attention, while there was limited research on how mainstream journalism was changing with increased user involvement (Paulussen *et al.*, 2007). This situation has changed considerably, and there now exists a sizeable body of academic research into the way in which digital media are affecting journalism (for an overview, see Mitchelstein and Boczkowski, 2009).

Journalists, originally reluctant to embrace audience participation, appear to be slowly opening up to interaction (Anderson, 2011; Lasorsa, Lewis, and Holton, 2012), which appears to have some influence on news decisions, and digital technologies appear to be reshaping journalistic cultures more broadly. For example, studies of online journalists have shown that they may be less tied to the notion of objectivity than traditional journalists had been. Most recently, Agarwal and Barthel (2015: 381) interviewed 14 online journalists in the United States, who 'roundly rejected' the ideas of objectivity and neutrality, instead placing emphasis on the term 'fairness.' Journalists also developed new norms, emphasizing transparency, individualism, and risk taking. Thus, Agarwal and Barthel (2015: 387) argue that online journalists are "embracing a new set of norms while adapting and redefining traditional norms to their workplace routines and practices."

A key aspect in relation to digital technologies is the veritable explosion of social media over the past decade, fundamentally impacting established work practices. In particular, the impact of Twitter, and to a lesser extent Facebook, has been discussed in considerable depth in the recent literature. A key feature of these media has been the extent of interaction, participation, and connectivity they have offered, both for journalists in their work and for audiences in their ability to 'talk back' to journalists. Hermida (2012) notes that social media have been used by journalists and news organization in three key areas: (1) gathering news, such as for finding story ideas and sources; (2) reporting news, such as live coverage of events, either through original reporting or curating of other people's tweets; and (3) recommending news, such as the use of Twitter to extend an organization's reach. Canter (2014), in reviewing recent work on Twitter and journalism, notes that journalists use Twitter to test story ideas, follow sources for story leads, create informal, personal brands, enable greater transparency and accountability in their work, and as a research tool. Along with these various uses of Twitter, Hermida (2012) notes some key challenges, which include the difficulty of verifying news on Twitter, debates over objectivity in a medium that encourages personal expression, as well as how journalists manage their personal identity on social media.

Mostly, studies on the relationship between journalism and social media have focused on descriptive accounts of what journalists are actually doing on social media, with more explanatory accounts and investigations into how this may impact journalism only emerging recently. Yet, early evidence shows that social media in particular may be reshaping traditional journalistic cultures, particularly when it comes to the notion of objectivity, as well as journalism's market orientation.

Visibility on Twitter appears to a large degree reliant on individual personality, i.e. the way in which journalists successfully 'brand' their own presence through their activities on the social media platform (Bruns, 2012). Showing personality, of course, contravenes traditional notions of objectivity which stipulate that journalists refrain from offering their own opinions. As Canter (2014: 3) argues, Twitter practices "have seen journalists begin to cross the historic line between the professional and the personal, the objective and the subjective." Most scholarship finds that journalists in the main incorporate new technologies into traditional practices—thus 'normalizing' them (Singer, 2005; Lasorsa, Lewis, and Holton, 2012). Accordingly, Hermida (2012: 317) finds that "the research to date suggests that news organizations and journalists have yet to tap into the full potential of the 'social' aspect of social media technologies." Indeed, a study of Dutch newspapers' use of Facebook showed that "promotion and distribution of content seems more important than interaction and conversation" (Hille and Bakker, 2013).

Yet, some evidence is also emerging to suggest that frequent Twitter users are more likely to adapt. For example, Holton and Lewis' (2011: 1) study of the use of humor on Twitter shows that "journalists who become more accustomed to this social space are more apt to adopt its milieu of informality, conversation and humor." Similarly, Lasorsa, Lewis, and Holton's (2012) study of more than 22,000 journalist tweets showed while they normalized social media, they also more freely expressed opinions, provided accountability and transparency about their work practices, and shared user-generated content with followers. Hermida (2010; also this volume) has similarly noted that journalistic norms are bending as journalists adapt to social media and engage in practices such as live-tweeting. A study of Chinese journalists' use of Weibo—the Chinese equivalent of Twitter—showed that, while normalization patterns existed there as well, journalists active on Weibo also tended to be more politically involved, showed greater concern for social issues, and delivered unfiltered information. Thus, Weibo provided "journalists with the leeway to challenge traditional journalistic norms, and thus to conduct journalism in a non-traditional manner" (Fu and Lee, 2014: 17). Twitter may also be reformulating journalists' relationship with politicians. Broersma and Graham (2012) analyzed journalists' uses of Twitter in reporting, finding that tweets are becoming a regularly used source. This, they warned, could potentially lead to a higher power distance between journalists and politicians. With journalists increasingly only reporting journalists' statements rather than questioning them, it "might shift the power balance between journalists and politicians in benefit of the latter" (Broersma and Graham, 2012: 128), allowing a less mediated communication between politicians and the electorate.

At the same time, Hedman and Djerf-Pierre's (2013) survey of more than 1,400 Swedish journalists found little difference in journalists' professional ideals in relation to their social media use. While they found differences in attitudes to audience adaptation and branding, they found no significant differences with regard to traditional professional ideals such as objectivity, scrutiny, neutrality, and independence. This, they argue, "suggests that social media are indeed changing the journalistic profession in terms of how it relates to the audience/public, but not in terms of how it perceives its fundamental societal role as the fourth estate" (Hedman and Djerf-Pierre, 2013: 382).

Aside from social media, another area of technological change relates to the ability for news media to track audiences' uses of news in exceptional detail, potentially reshaping journalistic culture. Gone are the days when journalists—particularly at newspapers—had little feedback from audiences and news decisions were based solely on gut instinct. Today, comprehensive analytics (also called web metrics) software provides real-time feedback on online audiences' uses of news stories. Evidence shows that readership behavior may indeed be impacting on news decisions (Anderson, 2011; Lee *et al.*, 2012), a trend that can be seen as worrying if organizations simply chase clicks on their website and adopt a more populist, soft news style (Nguyen, 2013; Thurman and Myllylahti, 2009). Research on the impact of analytics is still in its early phase, however, and it remains to be seen to what extent such feedback may lead to more market-oriented journalism cultures or not.

Comparative studies are still rare when it comes to journalists and digital technologies and especially in relation to social media. The few that exist demonstrate the complexity of Twitter use, with Gulyás' (2013: 270) survey of Finnish, German, Swedish, and British journalists showing considerable variation in their patterns of use and opinions, leading her to argue that "journalists, similar to audiences, are increasingly fragmented and their professional practices are influence by a myriad of different variables." A further study found considerable differences in Twitter use among Dutch and British journalists (Broersma and Graham, 2012), again pointing to the need for more comparative studies to better understand the complexities of the relationship between journalists and social media.

Conclusion

This chapter has highlighted three key processes which are important to consider when examining changes in journalism culture: social and cultural transformations, economic shifts, and technological developments. While these three analytical categories were treated separately from one another in this overview, it is crucial to keep in mind that they are often interrelated. Economic shifts have been impacted to a considerable extent by technological developments, for example. Technological developments can also be seen to have generated some cultural shifts, such as the emergence of 'participatory' or 'digital' culture (Deuze, 2006; Jenkins, 2006), which is leading to an enduring tension between professional control and open participation (Lewis, 2012). Finally, social developments such as generational change are related to newspaper circulation declines, which in turn have economic consequences. These social developments are arguably enabled at the same time by technological developments as audiences increasingly get their news online.

This chapter has argued that these larger processes are in turn affecting journalists' work practices and role perceptions as encapsulated in the term journalism culture. While overall there is still very little research linking these developments explicitly to journalism culture as defined here, indications are that they may be leading to more market-oriented journalism, more involved, less objective, and less watchdog-oriented journalism. Clearly, however, future research needs to take account of these changes in comprehensive fashion, with an explicit link to an analytical conceptualization of journalism culture. This includes not only addressing the three developments outlined here simultaneously but also a comparative approach which takes account of differences across organizations as well as across media systems. The vast majority of studies on recent transformations in journalism have focused on the newspaper industry (Siles and Boczkowski, 2012), and even here different types of newspapers may be experiencing change in different ways. But there are also differences in relation to platform, such as television, radio, and print. Future studies could thus include analyses of journalism culture at broadsheet vs. tabloid newspapers, online-only vs. news organizations with an online and a traditional (e.g. newspaper, radio or TV) presence, and commercial vs. public service broadcasting media. Similarly, studies should take account of how these transformations play out in different media systems. Some research has been conducted in this regard, but this has mostly focused on different countries within one geographic region, rather than a more comprehensive approach taking account of media systems with very different contextual variables. There is an urgent need for more of such studies, which may broaden our understanding of how journalism culture is being transformed beyond the current US and Eurocentric view.

Further reading

This chapter's conceptualization of the term journalism culture is built around Thomas Hanitzsch's influential work outlined in "Deconstructing journalism culture: Towards a universal theory" (2007). Axel Bruns' (2005) *Gatewatching: Collaborative online news production* is an in-depth study of the early implications of technological change for news production, while, more recently, the ethnographic studies in C. W. Anderson's (2013) *Rebuilding the news: Metropolitan journalism in the digital age* and Nikki Usher's (2014) *Making news at the New York Times* have provided inside accounts of the impact of cultural, economic, and technological changes on journalism cultures. Seth Lewis' (2012) "The tension between professional control and open participation" gives a state-of-the art theoretical analysis of the impact of participation on journalism.

References

Agarwal, S.D. and Barthel, M.L. (2015) "The Friendly Barbarians: Professional Norms and Work Routines of Online Journalists in the United States." *Journalism* 16(3): 376–391.

Anderson, C.W. (2011) "Between Creative and Quantified Audiences: Web Metrics and Changing Patterns of Newswork in Local US Newsrooms." *Journalism* 12(5): 550–566.

Anderson, C.W. (2013) *Rebuilding the News: Metropolitan Journalism in the Digital Age.* Philadelphia, PA: Temple University Press.

Baym, G. (2005) "The Daily Show: Discursive Integration and the Reinvention of Political Journalism." *Political Communication* 22(3): 259–276.

Beck, U. (1992) *Risk Society: Towards a New Modernity*. London, UK: Sage.

Broersma, M. and Graham, T. (2012) "Social Media as Beat: Tweets as a News Source during the 2010 British and Dutch elections." *Journalism Practice* 6(3): 403–419.

Bruns, A. (2005) *Gatewatching: Collaborative Online News Production*. New York, NY: Peter Lang.

Bruns, A. (2012) "Journalists and Twitter: How Australian News Organisations Adapt to a New Medium." *Media International Australia* 144: 97–107.

Canter, L. (2014) "Personalised Tweeting: The Emerging Practices of Journalists on Twitter." *Digital Journalism* 3(6): 888–907. DOI: 10.1080/21670811.2014.973148.

Cohen, E.L. (2002) "Online Journalism as Market-Driven Journalism." *Journal of Broadcasting and Electronic Media* 46(4): 532–548.

Deuze, M. (2005) "What is Journalism? Professional Identity and Ideology of Journalists Reconsidered." *Journalism* 6(4): 442–464.

Deuze, M. (2006) "Participation, Remediation, Bricolage: Considering Principal Components of a Digital Culture." *The Information Society: An International Journal* 22(2): 63–75.

Deuze, M. (2012) *Media Life*. Cambridge, UK: Polity Press.

Dickinson, R., Matthews, J. and Saltzis, K. (2013) "Studying Journalists in Changing Times: Understanding News Work as Socially Situated Practice." *International Communication Gazette* 75(1): 3–18.

Downie, L. and Kaiser, R.G. (2002) *The News about the News: American Journalism in Peril*. New York, NY: A.A. Knopf.

Franklin, B. (1997) *Newszak and News Media*. London, UK: Arnold.

Franklin, B. (2008) "The Future of Newspapers." *Journalism Studies* 9(5): 630–641.

Franklin, B. (2012) "The Future of Journalism." *Journalism Studies* 13(5–6): 663–681.

Fu, J.S. and Lee, A.Y.L. (2014) "Chinese Journalists' Discursive Weibo Practices in an Extended Journalistic Sphere." *Journalism Studies* 17(1): 80–99. DOI: 10.1080/1461670X.2014.962927.

Gulyás, A. (2013) "The Influences of Professional Variables on Journalists' Uses and Views of Social Media: A Comparative Study of Finland, Germany, Sweden and the United Kingdom." *Digital Journalism* 1(2): 270–285.

Hanitzsch, T. (2007) "Deconstructing Journalism Culture: Towards a Universal Theory." *Communication Theory* 17(4): 367–385.

Hanitzsch, T. (2011) "Populist Disseminators, Detached Watchdogs, Critical Change Agents and Opportunist Facilitators: Professional Milieus, the Journalistic Field and Autonomy in 18 Countries." *International Communication Gazette* 73(6): 477–494.

Hanitzsch, T., Hanusch, F., Mellado, C., Anikina, M., Berganza, R., Cangoz, I., et al. (2011) "Mapping Journalism Cultures across Nations: A Comparative Study of 18 Countries." *Journalism Studies* 12(3): 273–293.

Hanusch, F. (ed.) (2013) *Lifestyle Journalism*. New York, NY: Routledge.

Hanusch, F. (2012) "Broadening the Focus: The Case for Lifestyle Journalism as a Field of Scholarly Inquiry." *Journalism Practice* 6(1): 2–11.

Hanusch, F. (2015) "Transformative Times: Australian Journalists' Perceptions of Changes in their Work." *Media International Australia* 155(1): 38–53.

Hanusch, F. and Fürsich, E. (eds) (2014) *Travel Journalism: Exploring Production, Impact and Culture*. Basingstoke, UK: Palgrave Macmillan.

Hanusch, F. and Hanitzsch, T. (2013) "Mediating Orientation and Self-Expression in the World of Consumption: Australian and German Lifestyle Journalists' Professional Views." *Media, Culture & Society* 35(8): 943–959.

Harrington, S. (2012) "The Uses of Satire: Unorthodox News, Cultural Chaos and the Interrogation of Power." *Journalism* 13(1): 38–52.

Hartley, J. (2000) "Communicative Democracy in a Redactional Society: The Future of Journalism Studies." *Journalism* 1(1): 39–48.

Hedman, U. and Djerf-Pierre, M. (2013) "The Social Journalist: Embracing the Social Media Life or Creating a New Digital Divide?" *Digital Journalism* 1(3): 368–385.

Hermida, A. (2010) "Twittering the News: The Emergence of Ambient Journalism." *Journalism Practice* 4(3): 297–308.

Hermida, A. (2012) "Social Journalism: Exploring How Social Media is Shaping Journalism." In Siapera, E. and Veglis, A. (eds) *The Handbook of Global Online Journalism*. Oxford, UK: Wiley-Blackwell, pp. 309–328.

Hille, S. and Bakker, P. (2013) "I Like News. Searching for the 'Holy Grail' of Social Media: The Use of Facebook by Dutch News Media and their Audiences." *European Journal of Communication* 28(6): 663–680.

Hjarvard, S. (2008) "The Mediatization of Society: A Theory of the Media as Agents of Social and Cultural Change." *Nordicom Review* 29(2): 105–134.

Holton, A.E. and Lewis, S.C. (2011) "Journalists, Social Media, and the Use of Humor on Twitter." *The Electronic Journal of Communication* 21(1–2). Available from: http://www.cios.org/EJCPUBLIC/021/1/021121.html

Inglehart, R. (1997) *Modernization and Postmodernization: Cultural, Economic and Political Change in 43 Societies*. Princeton, NJ: Princeton University Press.

Inglehart, R. and Welzel, C. (2005) *Modernization, Cultural Change and Democracy*. New York, NY: Cambridge University Press.

Jenkins, H. (2006) *Convergence Culture: Where Old and New Media Collide*. New York, NY: New York University Press.

Kaye, J. and Quinn, S. (2010) *Funding Journalism in the Digital Age: Business Models, Strategies, Issues and Trends*. New York, NY: Peter Lang.

Lasorsa, D.L., Lewis, S.C. and Holton, A.E. (2011) "Normalizing Twitter: Journalism Practice in an Emerging Communication Space." *Journalism Studies* 13(1): 19–36.

Lee, A., Lewis, S. and Powers, M. (2012) "Audience Clicks and News Placement: A Study of Time-Lagged Influence in Online Journalism." *Communication Research* 41(4): 505–530.

Lewis, S.C. (2012) "The Tension between Professional Control and Open Participation." *Information, Communication & Society* 15(6): 836–866.

Marshall, P.D. (ed.) (2006) *The Celebrity Culture Reader*. London, UK: Routledge.

McNair, B. (2009) "Journalism and Democracy." In Wahl-Jorgensen, K. and Hanitzsch, T. (eds) *The Handbook of Journalism Studies*. New York, NY: Routledge, pp. 237–249.

Mitchelstein, E. and Boczkowski, P.J. (2009) "Between Tradition and Change: A Review of Recent Research on Online News Production." *Journalism* 10(5): 562–586.

Myllylahti, M. (2014) "Newspaper Paywalls-the Hype and the Reality." *Digital Journalism* 2(2): 179–194.

Nguyen, A. (2013) "Online News Audiences: The Challenges of Web Metrics." In Fowler-Watt, K. and Allan, S. (eds) *Journalism: New Challenges*. Bournemouth, UK: Centre for Journalism and Communication Research, Bournemouth University, pp. 146–161.

O'Donnell, P., McKnight, D. and Este, J. (2012) *Journalism at the Speed of Bytes: Australian Newspapers in the 21st Century*. Sydney, Australia: Walkley Foundation.

Ottosen, R. and Krumsvik, A.H. (2010) "Digitization and Editorial Change in Online Media: Findings from a Norwegian Research Project." *Nordicom Information* 32(4): 17–26.

Paulussen, S., Heinonen, A., Domingo, D. and Quandt, T. (2007) "Doing It Together: Citizen Participation in the Professional News Making Process." *Observatorio* 3: 131–154.

Picard, R.G. (2001) "Effects of Recessions on Advertising Expenditures: An Exploratory Study of Economic Downturns in Nine Developed Nations." *Journal of Media Economics* 14(1): 1–14.

Siles, I. and Boczkowski, P.J. (2012) "Making Sense of the Newspaper Crisis: A Critical Assessment of Existing Research and an Agenda for Future Work." *New Media & Society* 14(8): 1375–1394.

Singer, J.B. (2005) "The Political J-Blogger: 'Normalizing' a New Media Form to Fit Old Norms and Practices." *Journalism* 6(2): 173–198.

Starr, P. (2012) "An Unexpected Crisis: The News Media in Postindustrial Democracies." *The International Journal of Press/Politics* 17(2): 234–242.

Thurman, N. and Myllylahti, M. (2009) "Taking the Paper Out of News: A Case Study of Taloussanomat, Europe's First Online-Only Newspaper." *Journalism Studies* 10(5): 691–708.

Turner, G. (2004) *Understanding Celebrity*. London, UK: Sage.

Usher, N. (2014) *Making News at The New York Times*. Ann Arbor, MI: University of Michigan Press.

Williams, P. (2013) *Killing Fairfax: Packer, Murdoch and the Ultimate Revenge*. Sydney, Australia: Harper Collins.

Zelizer, B. (ed.) (2009) *The Changing Faces of Journalism: Tabloidization, Technology and Truthiness*. New York, NY: Routledge.

39

SOCIAL MEDIA
AND JOURNALISM

Hybridity, convergence, changing relationship with the audience, and fragmentation

Ágnes Gulyás

Social media have been widely adopted by journalists and over a relatively short period of time. Industry research argues that social media have become part of the everyday toolkit of journalists (Cision, 2014) and most of the academic literature similarly suggests widespread adoption (Hermida, 2013). Indeed, this is occurring at such a rate that social media are seen as part of journalists' 'technological infrastructure' (Paulussen and Harder, 2014). Empirical data from research interviews further support the argument that social media have been firmly embedded in journalistic practices:

> "Social media have ... become far more prolific and more ingrained, ... where it was an added-on originally, a little something extra you used to do, now it's intrinsic to everyday life, it's completely woven into the newsroom." (Interviewee 3; see discussion of methods below)

Correspondingly, research on social media and journalism has received increased attention in academic literature. Studies so far have tended to focus on the effects of the tools and to what extent journalism produced with social media, or as some call it 'social journalism,' represents significant shifts in the profession. Characteristics of social media, especially their affordances for interactive dialogue, social interaction, and the creation and exchange of user-generated content, are cited as main factors in bringing about change. Social media do not merely represent a technological phenomenon but also a cultural one (Jenkins, 2006), where the "end-users feel enabled and encouraged to participate in the creation and circulation of media" (Lewis, 2012: 853). This also means that previous rationales for control over media production are challenged, as authority in the social media world is dispersed and shared. However, there is no agreement in this literature on the extent and nature of the shifts in journalism, partly because these are relatively new developments where long-term impacts are still unclear and partly because scholarship has tended to focus on dynamics of professional news practices (Hermida, 2013: 298).

This chapter explores the ways in which social media are adopted in journalistic practices, contributing to the debate about the extent and nature of the changes in the profession.

Rather than focusing on specific patterns of use or particular platforms, it seeks to explore social media adoption holistically, identifying four key features: hybridity, convergence, changing relationship with the audience, and fragmentation. The chapter provides analysis of each of these features and discusses their implications.

Methodological approach

A mixed methodological approach is applied to provide a theoretical contribution to the study area supported by empirical data. The four key features were identified partly from reviewing key literature and partly from the results of empirical studies about journalists' adoption of social media I have co-conducted during the past few years. One of these projects was a qualitative study involving interviews with 16 journalists between 2013 and 2014 exploring their views about social media and its impacts on their profession. The other projects were based on questionnaire surveys that were conducted across different countries between 2011 and 2014. Survey 1 (N = 1,560) included four countries, survey 2 (N = 2,822) eight countries, survey 3 (N = 2,301) was carried out in nine countries, and survey 4 (N = 1,716) in six countries. The six countries that were part of the final survey (Australia, Finland, Germany, Sweden, United Kingdom, and United States) were also part of at least three of the previous surveys. As some questions were repeated in the surveys, the data from the different years allow for comparative analysis. The findings from these surveys should be viewed as indicative, as samples were not representative, respondents were self-selected and recruited from CisionPoint Media Database, which contains contact details of majority of journalists in the studied countries.

Such a mixed methodological approach allows for observation and analysis of general trends, which are then supported by empirical findings. It also avoids some methodological challenges. One of these is that representative surveys including all types of journalists from all possible sectors have been notoriously difficult to achieve. Second, there is no agreed definition of social media in the literature, which makes measurement of its use problematic. Although scholars tend to agree about key characteristics of social media, notably interactivity and the enhanced role of the users, there are no clear boundaries between social media and other internet platforms. Additionally, as the social media sector is so diverse and quickly evolving, with new tools and providers constantly appearing, researching it remains complex and in flux. Third, there is also no agreement about what we mean by 'social media use' and how we measure that. Different academic and industry studies interpret the term differently according to their particularly agendas, some focusing on frequency of use, others on particular types of activities, yet others on engagement with specific platforms. Addressing these methodological issues is beyond the scope and focus of this chapter, but a key reason for taking a more holistic approach is to avoid some of these limitations.

Key features of social media adoption in journalistic practices

Hybridity

Hybridity has come to be commonly used to refer to processes and their outcomes of mixing and blending of hitherto distinctive elements. Chadwick (2011: 3) argues that the concept "highlights complexity, interdependence, and transition. Hybridity captures heterogeneity and things that are irreducible to simple, unified essences." Social media use by journalists, and the profession in the digital age in general, are often described in the literature in similar ways. For example, Vis (2013: 44) talks about the rise of new hybrid journalistic norms on Twitter as distinctive from traditional norms. Anderson (2013: 98) sees "institutional hybridity" and porousness of professional boundaries as key characteristics of contemporary journalism. Meanwhile Hermida (2013: 295) describes Twitter "as a networked communication space that results in a hybridity of old and new frames, values and approaches."

A number of researchers argue that social media and the internet, in general, have created conditions that led to the emergence of new hybrid forms of journalism where characteristics of traditional journalistic practices and cultures are in the process of being selectively recombined in new ways. The resulting new forms of journalism are genuinely novel, but they are also recognizable from their lineages. For example, Hermida (2010), analyzing Twitter in particular, identifies ambient journalism, which he defines as:

> an awareness system that offers diverse means to collect, communicate, share and display news and information, serving diverse purposes [....] The value does not lie in each individual fragment of news and information, but rather in the mental portrait created by a number of messages over a period of time.
>
> *(2010: 301)*

Assemblage journalism suggested by Anderson (2013: 172) is another example of a new form of journalism where work is becoming an "assemblage [...] a continuous process of networking the news" characterized by a process of hybridization of journalistic venues and practices as well as changes in understandings of the audience. For Rottwilm (2014: 4), a new significant form of journalism is entrepreneurial journalism, where journalists establish their own enterprises "to produce content, establishing their own distribution mechanisms through websites and blogs, and syndicating their content to other firms." Common to these assessments is the description of journalism in the digital age as more complex than previous forms, mixing hitherto distinctive platforms, processes, elements, and norms of the profession.

There are a number of indicators from the empirical studies discussed in this chapter that demonstrate that social media use by journalists is inherently diverse and hybrid. Although particular uses and platforms might be more significant than others, a key characteristic of social media adoption by journalists is that they use a variety of platforms for a diversity of purposes and professional tasks simultaneously, as the tools' affordances allow flexible use. As an example, Table 39.1 shows, on the basis of 2011–2013 survey data, that journalists use different types of social media tools and this diversity of use has increased over the studied

Table 39.1 Means for number of types of social media tools used by journalists in a typical week in the studied countries 2011–2013 (Min = 0, Max = 7)

	2013	2012	2011
United Kingdom	5.53	4.51	3.64
Australia	5.39	4.59	N/A
United States	5.31	5.05	N/A
Sweden	5.31	4.45	3.22
Finland	5.00	4.18	2.89
Germany	4.96	4.14	2.80

Note: The surveys asked respondents about their use of seven main types of social media: professional social networks (e.g. LinkedIn), blogs, social reader sites, social networking sites (e.g. Facebook), audio-visual sharing sites (e.g. YouTube), microblogs (e.g. Twitter), and content communities.

Table 39.2 Means for number of types of professional tasks social media is used for by journalists in a typical week in the studied countries 2011–2013 (Min = 0, Max = 5)

	2013	2012	2011
United Kingdom	3.72	3.67	3.50
Australia	3.70	3.54	N/A
Sweden	3.65	3.35	3.16
United States	3.45	3.68	N/A
Finland	3.10	3.03	2.77
Germany	2.62	3.16	2.98

Note: The surveys asked respondents about their social media use in relation to five main types of journalistic tasks: sourcing information, verifying information, publishing and promoting content, networking, and monitoring.

period. Similarly, when asked about purposes of social media use, respondents reported that they used the tools in their work for different professional tasks (Table 39.2).

Comparable findings were echoed in the qualitative study. In the interviews, journalists talked about how they used the tools variedly and for different reasons and how the tools offered new ways to carry out their work indicating hybrid nature of social media use.

> "It's a good newsgathering tool, a good promotion tool and a good way to talk to or reach our readers." (Interviewee 3)
>
> "I started using Twitter in order to tweet links to my articles as they were published ... That's just one of the ways in which I use Twitter, I use it generally to engage, and I also use it as a platform to network. ... My social media use actually depends on what I'm working on." (Interview 4)
>
> "Social media creates new ways to process information and gather information." (Interview 2)

Convergence

Convergence is seen as a key characteristic of digital transformation in the media and creative industries. In general, it refers to a process emerging from conditions created by digital technologies, including social media, where lines and boundaries that had existed before become blurred. However, definitions of convergence vary depending on particular focus and approach taken. Küng (2008) argues that there are three ways to understand convergence: network-focused definitions (convergence of delivery platforms), product- and service-focused definitions (convergence of devices), and sector-focused definitions (convergence of industries). Deuze (2010: 267), however, argues that convergence is not just a technological process but a cultural one too,

> blurring the lines between different channels, forms and formats, between different parts of the media enterprise, between the acts of production and consumption, between making media and using media, and between active or passive spectatorship of mediated culture.

Thus convergence affects the journalistic profession in a variety of ways. Nienstedt *et al.* (2013: 3) highlight that "not only does media convergence redefine the tasks of journalists and newsrooms, it also reshapes the business environments of media companies." Erdal (2011: 216), meanwhile, locates a key characteristic of changing professional practices in the increase of "cooperation and collaboration between formerly distinct media newsrooms."

The blurring of the lines between different media sectors is one of the convergence processes. Historic differences between media sectors are rooted in unique packaging and distribution of similarly obtained information (Reich, 2011). However, because of social media and other digital technologies packaging and distribution of news and information have become more similar. Although differences in journalistic practices between media sectors still remain (Gulyás, 2013; Reich, 2011), empirical findings indicate that, in terms of social media adoption, there are also significant similarities. As an example, Table 39.3 illustrates differences between media sectors from the 2013 UK survey data and shows that online journalists tend to use social media more and they tend to be more interactive. However, overall the figures reveal that social media adoption is prevalent across media sectors and respondents from different sectors were engaged in broadly similar activities with largely similar frequency patterns.

Empirical findings also reveal other convergence processes. A key theme that emerged from the interviews was that with social media adoption, the boundaries of journalists' work are blurring, as the distinctions between work and personal time as well as between professional and personal life are becoming obscured:

> "I am online 24/7, it's the first thing I do when I wake up and it's the last thing I do when I go to sleep." (Interview 7)
> "Sometimes I find myself actually working when I'm not supposed to be working; I think it's getting harder and harder to tell where the work starts and the spare time starts." (Interview 12)

A related dilemma was expressed in the interviews about the merging of personal and professional life on social media:

> "My personal activity interlinks with my professional life, so it's hard to tell where my personal life starts and where my professional life ends." (Interview 12)
> "They [the audience] know a lot more about me, thanks to my use of social media. They know my friends if they want to, they know how they look." (Interviewee 7)

Table 39.3 Percentage of respondents in the 2013 UK survey (N = 562) stating that they carry out following social media activities daily (% of respondent by media sector)

	Newspaper	Magazine	Broadcasting	Online
Post original comments on social networking or microblogging sites	61%	59%	54%	65%
Read postings of people they follow	64%	50%	51%	62%
Repost on microblogging site	44%	43%	43%	62%
Monitor discussions on social media about own content	44%	44%	43%	51%
Reply to comments received in relation to their work on social media sites	34%	30%	30%	42%
Use social media to make new contacts in their field of work	36%	24%	27%	31%
Publish a story based on information they found on social media	13%	11%	11%	12%

Convergence between the personal and the professional is a significant aspect of social media adoption and has meant a considerable shift from the institutional public face of journalists in the pre-digital era. By sharing fragments of their personal lives through social media, journalists appear more human (Lasorsa, Lewis, and Holton, 2012), which arguably can play a key role in how they interact with their audience.

Changing relationship with the audience

Interactivity is one of the key characteristics of social media widely seen to have transformed the relationship between journalists and their audience turning the traditionally one-way communication to two-way conversation. As social media changes the process of news diffusion and production (Quiring, 2013: 141), the boundaries between news producers and consumer are blurring, which is arguably another form of convergence. Paulussen and Harder (2014: 543) highlight that "in this open, interactive sphere, formerly distinct roles between sources, producers, and consumers of news and information are eroding, and the continuous streams of content can no longer be owned or controlled." For Hermida (2013: 306), the process means that the boundaries of journalism as a cultural field of production are questioned with "collaborative and collective newsgathering, production and management at play, facilitated by the sociotechnical dynamics of Twitter." On a similar line, Domingo (2008: 268) argues that the "increased transparency between readers and journalists may weaken the occupation's authority."

However, how and to what extent the relationship with the audience is changing varies according to journalists' backgrounds and attitudes. Empirical studies reveal a spectrum of interactivity between journalists and their audience on social media. However, "the extent to which this is happening is still largely dependent on individuals rather than being incorporated into organisational norms and routines" (Canter, 2013: 491), as "established news institutions have tended to rely on existing norms and practices as they have expanded into digital media" (Hermida, 2011: 30). Canter found that there was limited interaction with audiences on organizational social media accounts: "News organisations are largely sustaining a one-way communication model by creating automatic feeds or linkbots from their websites to social media platforms such as Facebook and Twitter and are rarely responding to readers" (Canter, 2013: 491).

Survey data used in this analysis also reveal differences in how the relationship with the audience is changing. Perceptions about the extent to which this relationship has changed varied greatly among respondents (Table 39.4) indicating diverse experiences, although most recognized at least some change. It is notable that these figures reveal significant differences between surveyed countries, suggesting that cultural factors are important in how relationship with the audience is developing.

Table 39.4 Perceptions about the extent to which social media changed journalists' relationship with their audience (% of respondents in surveyed countries, 2014)

	Australia	Finland	Germany	Sweden	UK	US
Not at all	8	8	19	12	7	5
To a small extent	15	18	20	12	11	14
To a moderate extent	18	34	24	23	20	21
To a large extent	28	28	30	41	38	32
Fundamentally	31	12	6	12	24	29

The relationship between journalists and their audience was also a key theme that emerged from the qualitative data, and the interviews revealed contrasting views. Some of the interviewees saw the changes as significant, resulting in a different type of relationship:

> "On social media ... you really do know your reader better even though it might be a smaller readership. But yeah you are way more engaged and they will tell you straight away if they hate something too." (Interviewee 4)
>
> "The readers ... are a lot more engaged and they are contributing, so they are more like a community, instead of what it was like ten years ago, sending a letter in and maybe getting a generic response, so you really do know your reader better." (Interviewee 3)
>
> "Now we talk to them much more on the same level, one to one, so there's a much closer relationship." (Interviewee 5)

But other interviewees expressed concerns. Some thought that journalists do not interact with audiences more and they have not found new audiences on social media. Other studies also found that the size of interacting and participating audiences has been limited (Canter, 2013).

> "It [social media] is changing the relationship ... but what concerns me is that the people that you hear from are the more motivated ones, that's always been an issue. ... You have a certain class of people ... of a certain mind set, they ... have a particular point of view about how journalism should be done, it's a classic case of you get a lot of feedback from those people." (Interviewee 2)

Another concern raised was that social media interactivity has a negative impact on other types of interaction with the audience, notably face-to-face contact is becoming less important.

> "I think that reporters can get into a habit of just talking to people on Twitter or on Facebook and they don't do quite as much getting out, face-to-face contact as they used to, so I think [the relationship] suffered in that way." (Interviewee 6)

Fragmentation

Fragmentation is another key feature of social media adoption by journalists, referring to a process of increased dispersion and differentiation of journalistic practices with multiple variables and factors. Rottwilm (2014: 20) argues that the root for the trend is that changes in the digital age promote "the rise of more flexible and often precarious forms of employment, a greater variety of organizations employing journalists, a greater degree of skills polarization and accompanying greater diversity in the risks and rewards for journalists." As these changes have led to "the convergence process, multi-skilling, the need to integrate digital network technologies, and a new producer-consumer relationship [...] the identity of journalism" has been diluted (Rottwilm, 2014: 20).

Empirical studies find that social media adoption is not homogenous but embedded in different ways in journalistic practices. Both Pole and Gulyás (2013), as well as Hedman and Djerf-Pierre (2013), find clusters of professionals in relation to social media adoption highlighting the differentiated ways the tools are used. Table 39.5 shows Pole and Gulyás' (2013) typology, grouping journalists into five categories by applying cluster analysis to the survey

Table 39.5 Five clusters of professional social media user types among journalists and their key characteristics (based on 2012 survey data, Pole and Gulyás, 2013)

Architects	Promoters	Hunters	Observers	Skeptics
They use social media the most and have highest self-rated knowledge about them. They have positive views about social media, which they use variedly and for diverse purposes. They are key content creators and often center of networks	They use social media a lot and have good self-rated knowledge about them. They have positive views about social media. They use a variety of social media forms, but prefer blogs, microblogs, and social networks. They use social media for different reasons, but publishing and promoting is a key function for them	They use social media regularly and have positive views about them, although they say they can carry out their work without them. Sourcing information and networking are the most important reasons why they use social media. They are keen users of social networks and microblogs but are not frequent content creators	They use social media at least weekly or more often. They tend to engage in more passive activities on social media, such as reading posts, and do not create content frequently. Their main reason for using social media for work is for sourcing information. Their views about social media are ambivalent	This group represents the least active users. They rarely, if ever, create content on social media and are poor networkers. Most of them use only one or two types of social media forms mainly for sourcing information or monitoring what is going on. They do not see social media necessary for their work

data. These five profile groups not only differ in terms of frequency of use but also regarding purposes and practices of use as well as attitudes to and views about social media.

Differentiated and dispersed social media use among journalists also emerged from the qualitative research. Interviewees were rarely discussing 'good' or 'common' practice on social media, the emphasis was more about the importance of finding their own voice and their own ways experimenting with the tools and self-teaching themselves.

> "It's sort of picking up and trying to see what works, testing out different kinds of tweets or Facebook messages and playing around with photos and going back and figuring out what works and what doesn't, I've never had any formal training." (Interviewee 8)

> "I know the [organisation] have organised social media training, which I actually haven't gone on. I don't see training anywhere near as useful as actually using it, I learn by using." (Interviewee 2)

Conclusion and implications

This chapter argues that hybridity, convergence, fragmentation, and the changing relationship with audiences are key features of social media adoption in journalistic practices. The analysis shows how social media use is inherently diverse and how it has contributed to an increasing complexity of journalists' work, where hitherto distinctive platforms, processes, elements, and norms are mixed and blended. Given the complexity, it is not surprising that views about the impacts of social media vary. Some see significant benefits:

"It's opening up my world of information and connections." (Interviewee 4)

"Overall I would say that journalists can react faster and they can be more relevant as social media makes that possible and they can get a wider audience for their stories." (Interviewee 8)

"All of it, newsgathering, picture gathering, audio, all of it has benefited from social media." (Interviewee 3)

On the other hand, social media have created additional pressures for journalists (Rottwilm, 2014) and are seen by some as jeopardizing traditional functions and values of the profession.

"It does increase the work load... reporters certainly now drive more words because there are more platforms to serve." (Interviewee 6)

"Very much in the last couple of years there was a lot of pressure on tweeting ... it's kind of working 24/7." (Interviewee 5)

"You can fall in to ... this analytics hole and ... spending too much on that side of it and then other projects don't get as much time." (Interviewee 8)

"A basic concern ... I would have with social media, is that it's very easy to be drawn into misinformation, for example on Twitter ... you can get something come up and it's tweeted by more than one source, and it's all very exciting and interesting and then it turns out to be a hoax, or a rumour, or ungrounded." (Interviewee 2)

Apart from the varied effects and different views about the impacts of the tools, another important implication of the ways in which social media have been adopted in journalistic practices is greater individualization in the profession. The analysis here illustrates that social media adoption is not homogenous, and the tools are appropriated into specific contexts of individual journalists utilizing social media affordances. As a result, there is a greater fragmentation of the profession along multiple lines and influenced by myriad of factors, including professional values, attitudes, industry background, and sociodemographic variables. Arguably, individualization is a structural characteristic of the profession in the digital age with complex and differentiated working practices.

Although there is a growing body of research on social media and journalism, it is still a relatively underdeveloped subject and further research is needed to fully understand the impacts of social media and the shifts in the profession. A particular limitation of social media research thus far has been a focus on specific platforms and on content (Zimmer and Proferes, 2014), and further research that investigates cross platform use and how the tools are embedded in practices would be especially beneficial. Additionally, social media research presents some challenging methodological questions, including: do we need new methods to study this area? Do we have appropriate tools to collect and analyze social media data? Do researchers have appropriate skills to research social media? Do we understand fully the ethical implications? Discussing and addressing these issues will help to develop the subject area.

Further reading

For more in this area, see my article "The influence of professional variables on journalists' uses and views of social media" (Gulyás, 2013) for an example of empirical research on the topic providing an international comparative analysis. Alfred Hermida's (2013) article '#Journalism' provides a very useful assessment of journalism research on Twitter, and Martin Löffelholz and David Weaver's collection *Global journalism research* (2008) offers a useful overview of theories and methods in journalism research for considering the changes of social media.

Acknowledgments

The author is grateful to Kristine Pole, Tammy Dempster, and Cision AB for their contribution to the empirical studies included in the analysis.

References

Anderson, C.W. (2013) *Rebuilding the News: Metropolitan Journalism in the Digital Age*. Philadelphia, PA: Temple University Press.

Canter, L. (2013) "The Interactive Spectrum: The Use of Social Media in UK Regional Newspapers." *Convergence: The International Journal of Research into New Media Technologies* 19(4): 472–495.

Chadwick, A. (2011) "The Hybrid Media System." Paper presented at the European Consortium for Political Research General Conference, Reykjavik, Iceland, 25 August.

Cision (2014) "Social Journalism-Studie 2013/2014 Internationaler Report." Available from: http://www.cision.com/de/wp-content/uploads/2014/04/SJS-13-14-Global-Report_deutsches-Deckblatt.pdf.

Deuze, M. (2010) "Journalism and Convergence Culture." In Allan, S. (ed.) *The Routledge Companion to News and Journalism*. London, UK: Routledge, pp. 267–276.

Domingo, D. (2008) "Interactivity in the Daily Routines of Online Newsrooms: Dealing with an Uncomfortable Myth." *Journal of Computer-Mediated Communication* 13(3): 680–704.

Erdal, I. (2011) "Coming to Terms with Convergence Journalism: Cross-Media as a Theoretical and Analytical Concept." *Convergence: The International Journal of Research into New Media Technologies* 17(2): 213–223.

Gulyás, Á. (2013) "The Influence of Professional Variables on Journalists' Uses and Views of Social Media." *Digital Journalism* 1(2): 270–285.

Hedman, U. and Djerf-Pierre, M. (2013) "The Social Journalist." *Digital Journalism* 1(3): 368–385.

Hermida, A. (2010) "Twittering the News: The Emergence of Ambient Journalism." *Journalism Practice* 4(3): 297–308.

Hermida, A. (2011) "Mechanisms of Participation: How Audience Options Shape the Conversation." In Singer, J., Hermida, A., Domingo, D., Heinonen, A., Paulussen, S., Quandt, T., Reich, Z. and Vujnovic, M. *Participatory Journalism: Guarding Open Gates at Online Newspapers*. Oxford, UK: Wiley-Blackwell, pp. 13–33.

Hermida, A. (2013) "#Journalism." *Digital Journalism* 1(3): 295–313.

Jenkins, H. (2006) *Convergence Culture: Where Old and New Media Collide*. New York, NY: New York University Press.

Küng, L. (2008) *Strategic Management in the Media*. London, UK: Sage.

Lasorsa, D., Lewis, S. and Holton, A. (2012) "Normalizing Twitter; Journalism Practice in an Emerging Communication Space." *Journalism Studies* 13(1): 19–36.

Lewis, S. (2012) "The Tension between Professional Control and Open Participation: Journalism and Its Boundaries." *Information, Communication & Society* 15(6): 836–866.

Löffelholz, M. and Weaver, D. (2008) *Global Journalism Research*. Oxford, UK: Wiley-Blackwell.

Nienstedt, H.-W., Russ-Mohl, S. and Wilczek, B. (eds) (2013) *Journalism and Media Convergence*. Berlin/Boston: Walter De Gruyter.

Paulussen, S. and Harder, R. (2014) "Social Media References in Newspapers." *Journalism Practice* 8(5): 542–551.

Pole, K. and Gulyás, Á. (2013) "An International Study of Social Media and Its Role within Journalism and the Journalists—PR Practitioner Relationship." Paper presented at the Academy of Marketing Annual Conference, 9–11 July, University of Glamorgan.

Quiring, O. (2013) "Journalists Must Rethink Their Roles." In Nienstedt, H.-W., Russ-Mohl, S. and Wilczek, B. (eds) *Journalism and Media Convergence*. Berlin/Boston: Walter De Gruyter, pp. 137–147.

Reich, Z. (2011) "Comparing Reporter Work Across Print, Radio, and Online." *Journalism & Mass Communication Quarterly* 88(2): 285–300.

Rottwilm, P. (2014) *The Future of Journalistic Work: Its Changing Nature and Implications*. Reuters Institute for the Study of Journalism report. Oxford, UK: University of Oxford.

Vis, F. (2013) "Twitter as a Reporting Tool for Breaking News." *Digital Journalism* 1(1): 27–47.

Zimmer, M. and Proferes, N. (2014) "A Topology of Twitter Research: Disciplines, Methods, and Ethics." *Aslib Journal of Information Management* 66(3): 250–261.

40

TWITTER, BREAKING THE NEWS, AND HYBRIDITY IN JOURNALISM

Alfred Hermida

Since its launch in March 2006, Twitter has become part of the media landscape, notably at times of breaking news events such as natural disasters, protests, or celebrity deaths. The social media technology has developed as a network for real-time news and information, impacting how news is reported, distributed, and consumed, such as during the 2008 Mumbai terror attacks, the 2009 Iranian election protests, and the 2011 Arab Spring and the 2011 London riots (Hermida, 2013; Knight, 2012; Newman, Dutton, and Blank, 2012).

Twitter has also become part of the journalist's arsenal, viewed as a valuable, if not vital, everyday tool due to its ease of use, immediacy, and reach. By 2015, 75 percent of UK journalists said they were using the service, with just under 54 percent stating that they could not do their job without social media (Cision, 2015). Twitter itself launched an official guide for newsrooms, followed by best practice guidelines for breaking news, live reporting, and engaging users.

For scholars, the use of Twitter by journalists in crisis reporting (Andén-Papadopoulos and Pantti, 2013), in covering street protests (Vis, 2013) and in reporting on political events (Chadwick, 2011) has developed apace. Much of the research into participatory technologies that enable publics to take on journalistic roles suggests that professional journalists apply established norms and practices (Singer et al., 2011), and emergent technologies such as Twitter tend to be normalized to fit within existing approaches (Lasorsa, Lewis, and Holton, 2012), highlighting the core tension between professional control and open participation (Lewis, 2012).

As a social media technology, Twitter is a networked, hybrid media space. It has become part of the fabric of everyday communication in areas as diverse as popular culture, sports, marketing, politics, activism, and crisis communication (see Weller et al., 2014). In this hybrid space, reports, commentary, and analysis from journalists jostle for attention with experiences, exclamations, and emotions of citizens. News, information, and comment circulate outside of the established order and hierarchy associated with traditional print or broadcast structures.

Services such as Twitter are open platforms that facilitate collaborative storytelling where users are fundamental in the production and dissemination of storytelling. The sociotechnical architecture of Twitter, combined with emerging social practices, have resulted in the collaborative co-creation of news through hybrid streams of information that blend fact, opinion, emotion, and experience, circulating outside of the structures of the news industry.

This chapter considers Twitter as a networked communication space that results in a mixture of old and new frames, values, and approaches, particularly at times of breaking news. It examines the dynamics of professional news practice on the social media platform and considers how far new, fluid forms of journalism are at play.

The affordances of Twitter

Of all the social media technologies, Twitter is most closely associated with news and journalism and not just due to its popularity among journalists. Users tend to view it as a source for news and are more likely to check Twitter for what's new, whereas audiences tend to stumble across news on Facebook (Newman, 2015). By April 2015, Twitter had 302 million monthly active users who post 500 million messages daily (Twitter, n.d.). Even though it started in San Francisco in 2006, the majority of users of its service are now outside the United States, accessing it primarily on mobile technologies.

Changes to Twitter since its launch in 2006 have sought to privilege informational messages designed for broader consumption, rather than more personal communication. As van Dijck notes, the "subtle but meaningful change in Twitter's interface indicates a strategy that emphasizes (global, public) news and information over (personal, private) conversation in restricted circles" (2012: 340–341). At the time of its launch in 2006, it prompted users with the question, "What are you doing?" This changed in 2009 to "What's happening?," signaling a shift towards a more news-focused medium. At the time, co-founder Biz Stone described the platform as a "discovery engine for finding out what is happening right now" (Stone, 2009).

By 2015, the company described its mission as "to give everyone the power to create and share ideas and information instantly, without barriers," (Twitter, n.d.). The architecture of Twitter also privileges event-based, event-driven social communication, much like the content that traditionally makes the news. The service is designed to encourage users to live in the present rather than the past, spurring instantaneity rather than reflection. This focus on the present is evident in how the company highlights popular issues through its 'Trends on Twitter' service. It identifies "topics that are immediately popular, rather than topics that have been popular for a while or on a daily basis" (Twitter, n.d.). The trends reflect the constantly updated public account of the experiences, interests, and opinions shared by the platform's users at a specific time.

For Bruns and Burgess (2012), Twitter is a leading example of a social media technology that brings together social networking, content production, and information sharing. The platform allows users to create their own "awareness system that offers diverse means to collect, communicate, share and display news and information, serving diverse purposes" (Hermida, 2010: 301). There is a persistent flow of information that is pervasive—a perpetual social awareness system that is always-on and moves from the background to the foreground as and when individuals on their own or collectively shift their attention. As Bruns and Burgess note, "when important news breaks and spreads across the Twittersphere, shifts in tone and topical focus of incoming tweets may cause that user to pay attention to the story" (2012: 2).

Twitter and journalism practice

A process of negotiation between the old and the new has marked the use of Twitter in journalism, the result of the affordances of new media technologies bumping up against established practices. Initial approaches sought to take advantage of the immediacy and reach of Twitter, with journalists using it to report the news, to distribute links to stories, to gather the news, and to find sources. It has become commonplace for reporters to share news snippets when covering political speeches, courtroom proceedings, conferences, or sports events (Hedman and Djerf-Pierre, 2013; Lasorsa *et al.*, 2012).

The 140-character limit of Twitter lends itself to sharing attention-grabbing headlines and links to longer stories, offering a promotional and branding tool for news organizations. At times, though, tweets have been little more than headlines designed as promotional messages to drive users to a website (Jeronimo and Duarte, 2010; Messner *et al.*, 2012). Individual journalists have also tended to share links that direct users to their own work or that of their news organization (Lasorsa *et al.*, 2012).

Twitter has proved to be a boon for journalists when it comes to newsgathering. They are able to monitor Twitter for eyewitness accounts, for tips including photos or videos of breaking news events, or tune into conversations on topical issues and find people to contact about a story. However, this does not necessarily lead to a greater diversity of voices in the media. Institutional Twitter accounts of elite sources tend to dominate journalistic practice (Bruno, 2011; Knight, 2012), and tweets from ordinary people are viewed as eyewitness material or a way of sampling the vox populi (Broersma and Graham, 2012; Knight, 2012). Engaging with readers is still far from the norm, even though most editors talk about the ability to interact with audiences on social media (Bullard, 2015), and using Twitter to ask for story ideas and information, find sources or involve the public in the co-creation of a story is a minority activity (Cozma and Chen, 2013; Noguera-Vivo, 2013).

Newsgathering and sourcing on Twitter, then, is pretty much journalism as usual. One notable exception to date has been NPR's Andy Carvin during the 2011 Arab Spring. He approached Twitter as his newsroom, rather than as a newswire, using the network to appeal for information, reach out to sources, and engage users in collaborative fact-checking (Hermida, Lewis, and Zamith, 2014). Since then, other journalists have expressed interest in adopting Carvin's sourcing methods. A recent study from South Korea found that more than half the journalists' tweets studied were interactions with other users (Lee, Kim, and Kim, 2015).

Twitter and journalism norms

The hybrid space of Twitter has strained the foundational norms of journalism, notably verification and objectivity. The real-time nature of Twitter has contributed to an acceleration of the news cycle, especially at times of breaking news when initial reports tend to come from people on the ground. Bruno argues that "even if the 1440-minute news-cycle facilitates the integration of citizen journalist contributions, it is also true that a similar acceleration is eroding the journalistic standards of the reliability and verification of the news" (2011: 66). (Verification being one of the key tenets of journalism as it validates a profession that claims an authority and jurisdiction over the news; Schudson and Anderson, 2009.)

The tension between being fast and being right is an age-old concern in journalism, but this has been brought to the fore by the volume and velocity of news flows on social media, above all on Twitter. News organizations and journalists have shared erroneous rumors, misidentified suspects, and declared politicians and celebrities dead on social media. As a result, verification is going through "processes of reinforcement, re-articulation and reinvention" (Hermida, 2015a: 41), with news organizations developing specific social media guidelines, investing in resources to check social media content, and making clear some material is labeled as unverified. There are indications that journalists are bending the rules in real-time reporting and willing to share some information before it is fully verified (Bruno, 2011; Newman, 2009). In such cases, journalistic authority relies less on steadfast verification and more on drawing from a wide range of sources, presenting supporting evidence, contradictory information, and attributing reports (Thurman and Walters, 2013).

Such an environment, where facts are fluid and journalists take a greater role in interpreting and contextualizing information, can also subvert notions of objectivity. While objectivity is a contested idea in journalism research, it remains central in U.S. journalism (Schudson and Anderson, 2008). Twitter, though, lends itself as a venue beyond the structures of a news organization's publication for journalists to blend professional and personal selves and show a human face to the audience (Ahmad, 2010). Research has highlighted that journalists mix in commentary, opinion, humor, and personal experiences on Twitter (Lasorsa *et al.*, 2012). As a consequence, "journalists are negotiating a space where the separation between the personal and private is fragile, and the hierarchical roles of reporter, editor and audience are blurred" (Hermida, 2013: 301).

Twitter beyond journalism

So far this chapter has considered the relationship between Twitter and journalism through the prism of the profession. Yet such social media platforms have developed as a hybrid space for the cultural production of journalism, with a broad range of actors involved in the filtering, framing, and interpretation of news. Papacharissi considers these as "complex and networked social awareness systems that evolve beyond traditional ecologies of journalism" (2015: 1).

A growing body of research points to how social media, and specifically Twitter, is reconfiguring news values, gatekeeping, and framing. As the lens through which journalists construct the news, news values are central to decisions about what events make the news and which do not (Galtung and Ruge, 1965). Much of what becomes big news on Twitter also reflects traditional news values of impact and tension, involving the unexpected and elite nations or people—the disappearance of Malaysia Airlines MH370 over the South China Sea in March 2014 or the re-election of Barack Obama in 2012 (Hermida, 2014).

The hybrid nature of the Twitter newsroom can impact how events become newsworthy. In their study of the Egyptian uprising of 2011, Papacharissi and de Fatima Oliveira (2012) argued that what made news on the platform was shaped by values of instantaneity, solidarity, and ambience. Events became news because details of what was happening were disseminated instantly, repeated, commented on, and filtered by the network, mixing lived experiences, opinions, and emotions. For Papacharissi, "news storytelling becomes increasingly dynamic and constantly evolving, driven by on-going conversations that turn events into evolving news stories" (2015: 31). She defines this process as affective news streams where the news is "collaboratively constructed out of subjective experience, opinion, and emotion, all sustained by and, in turn, sustaining ambient news environments" (2015: 34).

News, then, takes place outside the established logic of news institution and journalism practice. Instead, news morphs into fluid streams that blend fact, opinion, emotion, and experience, beyond journalistic practices, occurring in a networked communication space that results in a hybridity of old and new frames, values, and approaches (Chadwick, 2011; Hermida, 2013). Such affective news streams are at odds with established news values that define what tends to appear in the mainstream media.

Events and issues, from #Occupy to #Ferguson, gain prominence on social media due to the immediacy and intensity of tweets, where experience and emotion are just as important, if not more so, than facts and context. Viewed through a journalistic lens, such news streams are unreliable, unstable, and maybe even undesirable. But it highlights one of the challenges for journalists operating in a shared and hybrid media space. Time-honored norms and practices are ill suited to spaces where these norms and practices are redrawn and remediated.

Framing on Twitter

The networked newsroom of Twitter not only affects what becomes newsworthy. The collaborative co-construction of what makes the news also affects how events and issues are framed through a process of networked framing (Meraz and Papacharissi, 2013). Framing illustrates how different actors seek to influence how events are represented and interpreted. Media and societal elites tend to have disproportionate sway over media frames. But research into recent social movements such as the Arab Spring in the Middle East, #Occupy in the United States, and #IdleNoMore in Canada suggest that framing on Twitter is negotiated in a hybrid media space through interactions between journalists, activists, and citizens (Callison and Hermida, 2015; Meraz and Papacharissi, 2013; Papacharissi and Meraz, 2012).

Networked framing emerges through the sociotechnical practices of tweeting, retweeting, linking, and using hashtags on Twitter. As Papacharissi notes, "these spaces facilitate social conversations that produce user-generated arguments on what is news, or how a particular story might take the shape of news" (2014: 30). One example of how the volume of tweets can help to shape the media narrative came during the uprising in Egypt in 2011. At the time, bloggers, activists, and intellectuals tweeted in English in an attempt to get noticed in the West. During the key period between the first mass protest on January 25 and the fall of Hosni Mubarak on February 11, almost three-quarters of tweets from Egypt with #Jan25 or #Egypt hashtags were in English (Hermida, 2014). The tweets presented a seductive narrative for the West of a technologically savvy liberal youth brandishing camera phones and Facebook pages rising up against an unjust and corrupt regime. Western media reflected this aspiration in their coverage, providing far more space to pro-democracy voices than pro-government sources (AlMaskati, 2012). Egypt offers an example of hybridity in the framing of the news through complex interactions between a range of actors, with Twitter serving as one of the building blocks in the construction of meaning.

At other times, humor, sarcasm, and irony are employed to make sense of current events. In crisis situations, people circulate light-hearted jokes and mock the news as an emotional release and as a way of helping others cope in extreme situations (Sreenivasan, Lee, and Goh, 2011). At other times, snark becomes part of how an event is represented on Twitter, with contributions from journalists and the audience. The use of humor to reframe a news event bleeds into subsequent media coverage, such as in the case of tweets mocking teething troubles in the run-up to the Sochi Olympics or the 'binders of women' gaffe by Mitt Romney (Hermida, 2014). Such interactions between the media and the public are areas for further study.

The retweet mechanism provides a way for publics to add another layer of meaning to the news. Audiences routinely choose to select, comment on, and rebroadcast specific tweets, reframing or reinterpreting a message. In some cases, the volume of retweets can outweigh the number of original posts. In the aftermath of the loss of Malaysian Airlines flight MH370 in March 2014, 80 percent of the posts using the #MH370 hashtag were retweets by people fascinating by the disappearance of the Boeing 777. The retweet mechanism has been used to champion, contest, and condemn elite messages. During the Idle No More protests in Canada in December 2012 and January 2013, publics engaged through the #Idlenomore regularly retweeted stories from mainstream media, either to amplify stories that were broadly supportive of the Indigenous-led movement or to contest the media's narrative (Callison and Hermida, 2015).

The other sociotechnical affordance used as a framing device is the hashtag. The hashtag symbol, #, acts as a public marker to indicate a message is related to a specific topic, issue, or event. It also serves to make a tweet visible beyond a user's immediate network of followers as it becomes part of a broader stream of posts. Gruzd, Wellman, and Takhteyev (2011) suggest that hashtags enable publics to come together as information neighborhoods on Twitter. For example, hashtags were used in the United States to coalesce news and information from disparate protests across the United States by the Occupy movement such as #occupyBoston or #occupyoakland (Papacharissi and Meraz, 2012). The device is also used to connect events and causes with broader frames of reference. For example, Idle No More activists used hashtags such as #indigenous and #nokxl to link the protests to issues around the treatment of Indigenous peoples in Canada and the activism against the proposed Keystone XL pipeline (Hermida, 2015b).

The hashtag can also be appropriated to articulate a counter-narrative to mainstream media framing of a news event. In the aftermath of the Ferguson protests in the United States, people turned to Twitter to challenge media portrayals of Michael Brown, whose death at the hands of the police sparked the unrest. One of the hashtags, #HandsUpDontShoot, was used to highlight the way police tend to react to black youths as potential threats. Similarly, the hashtag #IfTheyGunnedMeDown was used to contest the images used by the mainstream media to represent black youths (Bonilla and Rosa, 2015). People shared images that juxtaposed respectable images with those that implied violence, such as a graduation photo next to one in a stereotypical thug pose. As Bonilla and Rosa explain, "social media participation becomes a key site from which to contest mainstream media silences and the long history of state-sanctioned violence against racialized populations" (2015: 12). In the context of contested events and issues, hashtags on Twitter can reveal user-led processes of networked framing.

Gatekeeping on Twitter

The persistent and pervasive stream of tweets could suggest that the role of gatekeeper is dead. However, the opposite is true. The sociotechnical affordances of Twitter, together with other social media platforms, mean that there are more gatekeepers than ever before as the core journalistic norm of gatekeeping is rearticulated (see Bro, this volume). Gatekeeping has been a central construct in journalism (Shoemaker and Vos, 2009; White, 1950). The journalist as gatekeeper decides not just what merits being defined as news, but also how it is evaluated and presented to the public. Networked gatekeeping, though, challenges the hierarchical construction of journalism and affects what stories are elevated through the individual actions of a crowd and the actors that rise to prominence.

The rise of social recommendation has impacted how people get the news and from whom. By 2015, Facebook, YouTube, and Twitter had emerged as significant platforms for news, with Twitter users in particular checking their feeds for the latest information (Newman, 2015). Editorially, the traditional gatekeeping function of the media has been weakened by the rise of social recommendation, introducing hybridity into gatekeeping. Singer *et al.* (2011: 821) suggest that "a person's social circle takes on the role of news editor, deciding whether a story, video or other piece of content is important, interesting or entertaining enough to recommend." Singer suggests that audiences have unprecedented power to act as secondary gatekeepers and "to make editorial judgments not only for themselves but also for others—and, importantly, to act on those judgments by serving as secondary distributors of the material they deem worthy" (2014: 66).

Research on the hyperlinks related to recent social movements illustrates how secondary gatekeeping shapes the circulation of the content on Twitter. An analysis of links shared on #Occupy tweets showed that only a third were to mainstream media (Bastedo, Chu, and Hilderman, 2012). The rest were to blogs, video-sharing sites, social media, and alternative news outlets. Comparable research by Callison and Hermida into the most circulated links on #Idlenomore indicated a similar breakdown; mainstream media accounted for a third of the links, while alternative media outlets accounted for another third (cited in Hermida 2015b). Activists used the retweet mechanism to share and contest media reports and commentaries critical of the movement were contested. But the shared links to mainstream media were to publications outside of Canada that shed a more positive light on the movement. As secondary gatekeepers, activists were reacting to the media in Canada, which at first ignored the Idle No More movement, before going on to largely criticize or dismiss it.

Networked gatekeeping also affects the range of sources that rise to prominence on the network due to the actions of a crowd. The retweet mechanism enables individuals to collectively assign authority to specific actors. For Meraz and Papacharissi, networked gatekeeping is a "process through which actors are crowdsourced to prominence through the use of conversational, social practices that symbiotically connect elite and crowd in the determination of information relevancy" (2013: 158). Studies into the dynamics of Twitter illustrate how an alternative set of actors can emerge compared to those cited in the media. Lotan *et al.* (2011: 1400) argue that "a particular kind of online press" emerged during the Egyptian uprising of 2011 as the mainstream media and actors outside of journalism co-created and curated news flows on Twitter. Callison and Hermida (2015) found that a diverse range of alternative and Indigenous voices were among the most influential on the #Idlenomore hashtag. The research points to how ad hoc publics can assign temporal and contextual authority to certain voices through the interactions and exchanges on Twitter.

Conclusion

Twitter has developed has a new space for storytelling with news as an essential part of the mix. It is not the only social media platform that plays host to public discourse, but it has become the one most closely associated with news and most used by people interested in the news—an always-on, event-driven ambient media space outside of the formal structures of journalism. Established media and professional journalists play a vital part in the circulation of information, views, and comment on Twitter. As established elites, they bring their institutional power to the network. But they operate in an open and horizontal space where ad hoc publics can influence how events and issues rise above the noise, how they are framed and interpreted, and who gets to speak about them.

Social media and Twitter specifically serve as a contested space where authority and power are continually being reinforced or undermined, questioned or endorsed. Through interactions on social media, journalists and publics collide, each bringing their own meaning of what is news from the perspective of their background and experience. Long-standing conventions of journalism—news values, gatekeeping, framing—are being reconfigured on the network.

Essentially, the networked architectures of news enable the emergence of collaborative forms of journalism emerge that at times break with existing notions of what is news. They may indeed break with what has traditionally being defined as journalism. Instead research points to the development of hybrid and innovative forms of news-gathering, production, dissemination, and consumption. The result may not be journalism as it has traditionally been known, but a range of nascent types of journalisms.

Further reading

The edited collection by Katrina Weller, Axel Bruns, Jean Burgess, Merja Mahrt, and Cornelius Puschmann, *Twitter and Society* (2014), offers an insightful overview of the emergence and impact of Twitter. For a broader take, Zizi Papacharissi examines the interplay between social media, activism, and politics in *Affective Publics: Sentiment, technology and politics* (2015), while Alfred Hermida offers a wide-ranging analysis of the contemporary culture of sharing in *Tell Everyone: Why We Share And Why It Matters* (2014). The annual *Reuters Institute Digital News Report* is unparalleled in offering valuable context about trends in digital news consumption across the world.

References

Ahmad A.N. (2010) "Is Twitter a Useful Tool for Journalists?" *Journal of Media Practice* 11(2): 145–155.
AlMaskati, N.A. (2012) "Newspaper Coverage of the 2011 Protests in Egypt." *International Communication Gazette* 74 (4): 342–366.
Andén-Papadopoulos, K. and Pantti, M. (2013) "Re-imagining Crisis Reporting: Professional Ideology of Journalists and Citizen Eyewitness Images." *Journalism* 14(7): 960–977.
Bastedo, H., Chu, W. and Hilderman, J. (2012) *Occupiers and Legislators: A Snapshot of Political Media Coverage*. Samara. Available from: http://www.samaracanada.com/docs/default-document-library/sam_occupiersandlegislators.pdf (accessed 15 May 2015).
Bonilla, Y. and Rosa, J. (2015) "#Ferguson: Digital Protest, Hashtag Ethnography, and the Racial Politics of Social Media in the United States." *American Ethnologist* 42(1): 4–17.
Broersma, M. and Graham, T. (2012) "Social Media as Beat." *Journalism Practice* 6(3): 403–419.
Bruno, N. (2011) *Tweet First, Verify Later: How Real-Time Information is Changing the Coverage of Worldwide Crisis Events*. Reuters Institute for the Study of Journalism. Available from: https://reutersinstitute.politics.ox.ac.uk/sites/default/files/Tweet%20first%20,%20verify%20later%20How%20real-time%20information%20is%20changing%20the%20coverage%20of%20worldwide%20crisis%20events.pdf (accessed 12 June 2011).
Bruns, A. and Burgess, J. (2012) "Researching News Discussion on Twitter." *Journalism Studies* 13 (5–6): 801–814.
Bullard, S.B. (2015) "Editors Use Social Media Mostly to Post Story Links." *Newspaper Research Journal*: 1–14. DOI: 10.1177/0739532915587288.
Callison, C. and Hermida, A. (2015) "Dissent and Resonance: #Idlenomore as an Emergent Middle Ground." *Canadian Journal of Communication* 40(4): 695–716.
Chadwick, A. (2011) "The Political Information Cycle in a Hybrid News System: The British Prime Minister and the 'Bullygate' Affair." *The International Journal of Press/Politics* 6(1): 3–29.
Cision (2015) *Social Journalism Study 2015*. Cision and Canterbury Christ Church University. Available from: http://cision-wp-files.s3.amazonaws.com/uk/wp-content/uploads/2015/02/Cision-Social-Journalism-Study-2015.pdf (accessed 3 June 2015).
Cozma, R. and Chen, K. (2013) "What's in a Tweet?" *Journalism Practice* 7(1): 33–46.
Galtung, J. and Ruge, M.H. (1965) "The Structure of Foreign News." *Journal of Peace Research* 2(1): 64–91.
Gruzd, A., Wellman, B. and Takhteyev, Y. (2011) "Imagining Twitter as an Imagined Community." *American Behavioral Scientist* 55(10): 1294–1318.
Hedman, U. and Djerf-Pierre, M. (2013) "The Social Journalist: Embracing the Social Media Life or Creating a New Digital Divide?" *Digital Journalism* 1(3): 368–385.
Hermida, A. (2010) "Twittering the News: The Emergence of Ambient Journalism." *Journalism Practice* 4(3): 297–308.

Hermida, A. (2013) "#Journalism: Reconfiguring Journalism Research about Twitter, One Tweet at a Time." *Digital Journalism* 1(3): 295–313.

Hermida, A. (2014) *Tell Everyone: Why We Share and Why It Matters*. Toronto, ON: DoubleDay Canada.

Hermida, A. (2015a) "Nothing But the Truth: Redrafting the Journalistic Boundary of Verification." In Carlson, M. and Lewis, S. (eds) *Boundaries of Journalism*. London, UK: Routledge, pp. 37–50.

Hermida, A. (2015b) "Networked Publics and the Remaking of the News." *GRCP International Workshop*. Available form: https://www.grcp.ulaval.ca/sites/grcp.ulaval.ca/files/ws_grcp_2015_-_hermida_a.pdf.

Hermida, A., Lewis, S.C. and Zamith, R. (2014) "Sourcing the Arab Spring: A Case Study of Andy Carvin's Sources on Twitter during the Tunisian and Egyptian Revolutions." *Journal of Computer-Mediated Communication* 19(3): 479–499.

Jerónimo, P. and Duarte, A. (2010) "Twitter e Jornalismo de Proximidade: Estudo de Rotinas de Produção nos Principais Titulos de Imprensa Regional em Portugal." *Prisma.com*, 12.

Knight, M. (2012) "Journalism as Usual: The Use of Social Media as a Newsgathering Tool in the Coverage of the Iranian Elections in 2009." *Journal of Media Practice* 12(1): 61–74.

Lasorsa, D.L., Lewis, S.C. and Holton, A.E. (2012) "Normalizing Twitter: Journalism Practice in an Emerging Communication Space." *Journalism Studies* 13(1): 19–36.

Lee, N.Y., Kim, Y. and Kim, J. (2015) "Tweeting Public Affairs or Personal Affairs? Journalists' Tweets, Interactivity, and Ideology." *Journalism*: 1–20. DOI: 10.1177/1464884915585954.

Lotan, G., Graeff, E., Ananny, M., Gaffney, D., Pearce, I. and boyd, d. (2011) "The Revolutions Were Tweeted: Information Flows during the 2011 Tunisian and Egyptian Revolutions." *International Journal of Communication* 5: 1375–1405.

Meraz, S. and Papacharissi, Z. (2013) "Networked Gatekeeping and Networked Framing on #Egypt." *International Journal of the Press and Politics* 18(2): 138–166.

Messner, M., Linke, M. and Esford, A. (2012) "Shoveling Tweets: An Analysis of the Microblogging Engagement of Traditional News Organizations." *#ISOJ: The Official Journal of the International Symposium on Online Journalism* 2(1): 74–87.

Newman, N. (2009) "The Rise of Social Media and Its Impact on Mainstream Journalism" (working paper). Reuters Institute for the Study of Journalism. Oxford University. Available from: https://reutersinstitute.politics.ox.ac.uk/sites/default/files/The%20rise%20of%20social%20media%20and%20its%20impact%20on%20mainstream%20journalism_0.pdf

Newman, N. (2015) "Executive Summary and Key Findings of the 2015 Report." Reuters Institute for the Study of Journalism. Available from: http://www.digitalnewsreport.org/survey/2015/executive-summary-and-key-findings-2015/ (accessed 18 June 2015).

Newman, N., Dutton, W.H. and Blank, G. (2012) "Social Media in the Changing Ecology of News: The Fourth and Fifth Estates in Britain." *International Journal of Internet Science* 7(1): 6–22.

Noguera-Vivo, J.M. (2013) "How Open are Journalists on Twitter? Trends Towards the End-User Journalism." *Communication & Society/Comunicacion y Sociedad* 26(1): 93–114.

Papacharissi, Z. (2015) "Toward New Journalism(s)." *Journalism Studies* 16(1): 27–40.

Papacharissi, Z. and de Fatima Oliveira, M. (2012) "Affective News and Networked Publics: The Rhythms of News Storytelling on# Egypt." *Journal of Communication* 62(2): 266–282.

Papacharissi, Z. and Meraz, S. (2012) "The Rhythms of Occupy: Broadcasting and Listening Practices on #ows." Paper presented at the annual convention of the Association of Internet Researchers 13, Salford, UK, 17–21 October.

Schudson, M. and Anderson, C.W. (2008) "Objectivity, Professionalism, and Truth-Seeking in Journalism." In Wahl-Jorgensen, K. and Hanitzsch, T. (eds) *The Handbook of Journalism Studies*. New York, NY: Routledge, pp. 88–101.

Schudson, M. and Anderson, C. (2009) "News Production and Organizations: Professionalism, Objectivity and Truth-Seeking." In Wahl-Jorgensen, K. and Hanitzch, T. (eds) *The Handbook of Journalism Studies*. New York, NY: Routledge, pp. 88–101.

Shoemaker, P.J. and Vos, T.P. (2009) *Gatekeeping Theory*. New York, NY: Routledge.

Singer, J. (2014) "User-Generated Visibility: Secondary Gatekeeping in a Shared Media Space." *New Media and Society* 16(1): 55–73.

Singer, J.B., Hermida, A., Domingo, D., Heinonen, A., Paulussen, S., Quandt, T., et al. (2011) *Participatory Journalism: Guarding Open Gates at Online Newspapers*. New York, NY: Wiley-Blackwell.

Sreenivasan, N.D., Lee, C.S. and Goh, D.H. (2011) "Tweet Me Home: Exploring Information Use on Twitter in Crisis Situations." In Ozok, A.A. and Zaphiris, P. (eds) *Online Communities and Social Computing*. Berlin, Germany: Springer-Verlag, pp. 120–129.

Stone, B. (2009) *Twitter Search for Everyone!* Available from: http://blog.twitter. com/2009/04/twitter-search-for-everyone.html (accessed 2 June 2015).

Thurman, N. and Walters, A. (2013) "Live Blogging: Digital Journalism's Pivotal Platform?" *Digital Journalism* 1(1): 82–101.

Twitter (n.d.) About. Available from: https://about.twitter.com/company.

van Dijck, J. (2012) "Tracing Twitter: The Rise of a Microblogging Platform." *International Journal of Media and Cultural Politics* 7(3): 333–348.

Vis, F. (2013) "Twitter as a Reporting Tool for Breaking News." *Digital Journalism* 1(1): 27–47.

Weller, K., Bruns, B., Burgess, J., Mahrt, M. and Puschmann, C. (2014) *Twitter and Society.* New York, NY: Peter Lang.

White, D.M. (1950) "The 'Gatekeeper': A Case Study in the Selection of News." *Journalism Quarterly* 27(3): 383–390.

41

JOURNALISTS' USES OF TWITTER

Ulrika Hedman and Monika Djerf-Pierre

Journalists' uses of Twitter have received considerable attention from scholars in recent years. There are good reasons for this surge in interest. Twitter is, possibly, the most important social medium for journalists. To have a Twitter account is virtually a professional obligation, journalism schools regard Twitter proficiency a 'must have' for aspiring journalists, and most news organizations have organizational accounts and also strongly encourage individual journalists to use Twitter for both personal and professional activities. The growing academic interest dovetails with the hype over social media in general, and Twitter in particular, in the news industry. The push and pull factors that attract journalists to Twitter derive from a range of personal, professional, and organizational motivations and requirements. In this chapter, we examine how much and why journalists use Twitter and how it influences their professional practices.

The J-tweeters: a generational gap

Despite the continuous production of metrics that can easily capture the totality of Twitter's networks and flows (Verweij, 2012), it is difficult to measure and assess Twitter activity among individual journalists. Most empirical studies of journalists' use of social media, such as Twitter, are either based on self-selected, non-representative large-N samples (e.g. Gulyás, 2013), or smaller, strategic samples (e.g. Artwick, 2013; Lasorsa, Lewis, and Holton, 2012). The former often suffer—besides the obvious lack of representativeness—from very low response rates; while the latter often target very active tweeters and are thus less suitable to assess the spread of Twitter among the wider group of journalist practitioners.

One of the few studies of journalists' use of Twitter that is based on a representative sample of journalists was conducted in Sweden (Hedman, 2015; Hedman and Djerf-Pierre, 2013). The study draws from a mail survey of a representative sample of Swedish journalists. The Swedish Journalist Survey (SJS) survey was conducted in collaboration between the Department of Journalism, Media and Communication at the University of Gothenburg and the Swedish Union of Journalists in the fall and winter of 2011 and 2012 and it targeted a sample of the members of the union. The representativeness of the survey derives from the very high degree of unionization among Swedish journalists. In 2011 the union had 17,500 members and the sample consisted of 2,500 individuals, selected through a random sample.

The net sample comprised of 2,362 journalists and 1,412 replied to the questionnaire, providing a net response rate of 60 percent. The group that responded to the survey was representative of the journalist population in terms of critical factors such as gender and workplace (see Hedman and Djerf-Pierre, 2013).

A key finding in this research is that most journalists are *not* active on Twitter (Hedman, 2015; Hedman and Djerf-Pierre, 2013), challenging the prevailing myth of the always-online, constantly chatting and tweeting journalist 2.0. This result is perhaps even more notable when we consider that the use of the internet and digital media in Sweden is among the highest in the world, and that Swedish media organizations have been keen to adopt digital and mobile technologies.

One study shows that the overall use of social media among Swedish journalists is indeed fairly high: 71 percent use social media privately or professionally on at least a daily basis and only 7 percent state that they never use social media (Table 41.1). Twitter use is considerably lower: only 22 percent use Twitter on a daily basis and 44 percent refrain from using Twitter—they do not tweet, nor follow the Twitter feeds of others; most journalists (74 percent) never send a tweet. These figures are from 2011 to 2012, but another study that also targets representative samples of journalists (Djerf-Pierre, Ghersetti, and Hedman, 2016), shows that the proportion that read tweets on a daily basis only increased slightly between 2012 and 2014, and the proportion of very active tweeters did not increase at all. Consequently, although Twitter is important to some journalists, most have not yet fully embraced the social media life on Twitter.

On the other hand, journalists are much more active on Twitter than the general population (Hedman and Djerf-Pierre, 2013; cf. Hindman, 2009). Large shares of those who are active Twitter users belong to the societal 'elite', that is, journalists, politicians, and celebrities (Farhi, 2009). The apparent elite character of this particular social network is certainly a key incentive for news organizations to encourage their journalists to be active on Twitter. With the help of Twitter, it is believed that journalists can quickly reach the 'right' people (Hedman, 2015). Other key incentives include Twitter's effectiveness in distribution of content, primarily via linking and retweeting (Messner, Linke, and Eford, 2012; Phillips, 2012), and its possibilities for interaction and dialog with audiences (Artwick, 2013; Hedman, 2016). For many journalists, organizational/managerial demands constitute an important push factor to use Twitter (cf. Revers, 2014).

Table 41.1 Journalists' use of Twitter and Facebook (2011/2012; percent)

	Write tweets	*Read tweets*	*Use Twitter (total)*	*Use social media**
Never	74	45	44	7
Monthly	8	17	17	7
Weekly	8	16	17	15
Daily	8	17	17	54
'24/7'	2	5	5	17
Sum	100	100	100	100
Responses (N)	1,412	1,412	1,412	1,412

The respondents were asked: "How often do you do the following in social media, for private and/or professional purposes?" The response alternatives were: 'Never,' 'Now and then each month' (Monthly), 'Now and then each week' (Weekly), 'Every day,' and 'All of the time' (24/7). *Includes reading or writing tweets, reading or writing blogs, or using other social networking sites (e.g. Facebook).

Table 41.2 Swedish journalists on Twitter: account information

Gender	*Women 48%* *Men 52%*
Number of followers	Range 0–81,000 Mean 1,714 Median 434
Number of followed	Range 0–45,000 Mean 631 Median 428
Number of updates (sent tweets)	Range 0–120,000 Mean 4,668 Median 1,488
Number of lists	Range 0–600 Mean 25 Median 10
States profession in bio (i.e. journalist, reporter, editor, etc.)	92%

The Twitter account information (N = 2,543) is collected from a sample of Swedish journalists on Twitter in May 2014.

An analysis of the available information from Swedish journalists' Twitter accounts (Table 41.2) shows a vast difference between high-end and low-end users, and further emphasizes the structural differences between groups of journalists. This analysis is based on a sample of 2,543 Swedish journalists on Twitter. There are obvious difficulties in drawing a randomized sample of journalists on Twitter, but a comparison with the SJS survey on key variables shows a high degree of representativeness of the Twitter sample (see Hedman, 2015). While 9 out of 10 journalists state their profession in their account presentations, some are just 'present' on Twitter and show no activity at all. At the same time, a relatively small group of journalists who are active 'all the time' represents a large proportion of all tweeting.

It is perhaps therefore unsurprising that journalists who are active users of other social media, such as Facebook, are also active on Twitter (Hedman and Djerf-Pierre, 2013). Equally predictable are the very large generational differences in social media use among journalists. This generational gap is even more pronounced when it comes to Twitter. The youngest journalists (≤29 years old) are by far the most active; 52 percent are active daily on Twitter (Table 41.3). The differences are even more pronounced among those who use Twitter 'all the time' (24/7): 16 percent of the youngest journalists use Twitter 24/7, compared to just 2 percent of the oldest age group of journalists. However, even among the youngest journalists in the study, one out of five never uses Twitter. In the oldest group of journalists (≥60 years old), 7 out of 10 avoid Twitter. There is clearly a wide generational gap in Twitter usage among journalists.

We also find other structural differences in journalists' Twitter activity that relate to their work tasks (web/online journalists are the most active and print journalists the least active) and workplace (journalists in tabloid and public service radio (SR) are most active and the local/regional press reporters least active). Swedish tabloids are at the forefront of the transition from print to online/mobile publishing; this is reflected in the journalists' relation to Twitter. At public SR, the persistent call from the management that all the company's journalists 'should be on Twitter' is indeed observed (Hedman, 2015).

Table 41.3 Generational gaps in journalists' use of Twitter (2011/2012; percent)

	Never	Occasionally	Daily	24/7	Sum	Responses (N)
≤29	19	39	26	16	100	136
30–39	28	38	27	7	100	363
40–49	41	38	17	4	100	329
50–59	57	30	12	1	100	336
≥60	69	24	5	2	100	245

The respondents were asked: "How often do you use Twitter, for private and/or professional purposes?" The response alternatives were: 'Never,' 'Now and then each month,' 'Now and then each week,' 'Every day,' and 'All of the time' (24/7).

Moreover, Twitter usage is primarily a metropolitan phenomenon, which further strengthens the argument that Twitter is indeed a key medium for the (national) political and cultural 'elite.' The level of Twitter activity is considerably higher among journalists working in the capital region of Stockholm. This argument is also substantiated by the differences in Twitter activity related to type of beat; the most active journalists on Twitter are those writing editorials, commentaries, and opinion pieces (Table 41.4), followed by those in entertainment and sports. The least likely tweeters work on the family pages and with feature material.

Interestingly, we find no gender gap with regard to Twitter use in the survey. However, in a content analysis of Swedish journalists' tweets, based on a representative sample of journalists, significant gender differences appear. While men seem to be more active in the sense that they send more tweets, female journalists are far more personal and private in their tweets,

Table 41.4 Journalists' use of Twitter in 2011 and 2012 related to beat (percent)

	Never	Occasionally	Daily	Sum	Responses (N)
Opinion/editorial	33	28	39	100	36
Entertainment	32	33	35	100	94
Sports	40	30	30	100	134
Politics	38	39	23	100	385
Business and finance	40	37	23	100	149
International	40	37	23	100	48
Culture	42	35	23	100	181
General assignment reporter	45	35	20	100	458
Crime	36	45	19	100	64
Science	42	40	18	100	40
Feature	55	29	16	100	179
Family	74	21	5	100	38

The respondents were asked: "How often do you use Twitter, for private and/or professional purposes?" The response alternatives were: 'Never,' 'Now and then each month,' 'Now and then each week,' 'Every day,' and 'All of the time' (24/7). The response alternatives 'Now and then each month' and 'Now and then each week' = Occasionally; 'Every day,' and 'All of the time' (24/7) = Daily.

Table 41.5 Gender gaps in how journalists tweet (2014; percent)

	Women	*Men*	*All*
Job talk, 'how news are made'	14	14	14
Talk about personal or private life	15	8	10
Picture or link to picture (i.e. Instagram)	7	7	7
Contains link(s)	19	23	21
Is a retweet	24	23	24
Contains mention(s)	61	67	65
Number of tweets (N)	559	939	1,500

The sample of tweets (N = 1,500) is collected from a representative sample of Swedish journalists in May 2014.

revealing more about their personal lives and everyday activities (Hedman, 2016; cf. Lasorsa, 2012; Russel *et al.*, 2015). While 15 percent of female journalists' tweets contain personal and/or private information, the same can be said of about only 8 percent of men's tweets (Table 41.5). There is also a significant difference in the share of tweets that contain a mention (@); men appear to be more engaged in dialog or (perhaps) 'name dropping.'

Why journalists use Twitter: researching, networking, and branding

To understand why journalists use Twitter, we need to identify its specific affordances. Twitter is indeed different from other social media; it shares networking features, but the communication pattern consists of a massive, continuous stream of updates where professional and private matters, serious debate and everyday chatting, self-promotion and crowd-sourcing are mixed (Bruns and Burgess, 2012). Twitter can thus be regarded as "both a social networking site and an ambient information stream" (Bruns and Burgess, 2012: 803); and it is the communication as a whole (i.e. the flow), not the individual tweets, that brings value to the users.

Hermida (2010a, 2010b) aptly describes how Twitter functions as an always-on asynchronous awareness system for both journalists and audiences. For journalists, the Twitter ambience is twofold: on one hand, many active Twitter users are journalists who are also active contributors to the stream of tweets; on the other hand, some journalists only follow the flow of tweets produced by others within their networks (Hedman and Djerf-Pierre, 2013).

The networking function is a key pull factor that draws journalists to Twitter (Artwick, 2013; Gulyás, 2013; Hedman, 2015; Hedman and Djerf-Pierre, 2013). Networking has always been considered an important professional asset for journalists. A well-maintained professional network can provide access to information and sources, invitations and career opportunities, and professional support (Brake, 2011; Deuze, 2007a; Örnebring, 2010; Tuchman, 1978). The expansion of social media makes networking skills even more important (van der Haak, Parks, and Castells, 2012: 2927).

The measurability of Twitter is also, possibly, a pull factor—at least for the very active users. Despite its amorphous appearance, Twitter activities are easier to measure than other social media actions (Verweij, 2012). Who is addressing, retweeting, following, and commenting on whom—all is made public. The very configuration of Twitter openly visualizes individual networks (Verweij, 2012), thus making the network a highly observable professional asset. This transparency, coupled with the ease of access to ostensibly hard metrics, endows prominent

Twitter statistics (i.e. many followers and retweets) with considerable status and prestige. In short, Twitter usage combines symbolic and material (practical usability) affordances.

The symbolic value of visibility on Twitter is also an asset when the network is used as a vehicle for personal branding (Marwick, 2011; Molyneux, 2014). Twitter allows individual journalists to display not only their professional performance, but also their networking competence and ability to build strong personal brands (Bruns, 2012; Hermida *et al.*, 2012). Personal branding on social media is indeed a recommended career strategy, especially for freelancers and aspiring young journalists (Chamberlain, 2011; Gynnild, 2005; Knight and Cook, 2013). Twitter is also important for the organizational branding of news organizations, in which the visibility of individual journalists in social media plays an important part (Ferguson and Greer, 2011; Greer and Ferguson, 2011).

Bearing in mind the social media hype that prods journalists to start a Twitter account, it comes as no surprise that the active j-tweeters are characterized by an overall positive attitude toward using social media as part of their work (Hedman, 2015). According to our research, Swedish journalists turn to social media (including Twitter) to follow ongoing discussions, find new ideas and angles for stories, spot trends, and for research, all of which can be categorized as traditional professional tasks. Even light and moderate users find Twitter useful for such purposes. Interestingly, the primary function of Twitter to date is to provide new means for doing traditional journalistic tasks: finding and researching stories (Hedman and Djerf-Pierre, 2013).

The heavy Twitter users, however, also use Twitter for tasks that to a lesser extent are part of the traditional repertoire of journalistic work. Using social media for the purpose of organizational branding, getting feedback from the audience, and distributing their own work/ stories or stories produced by others are additional areas where the active j-tweeters find social media useful but where light and moderate users do not see the benefit (Hedman, 2015). Our research indicates that, overall, it is the very active j-tweeters who take full advantage of and embrace all the new affordances that Twitter provides in terms of building networks, interacting with others, and seizing opportunities for personal branding.

Twitter use and professional norms

A key question for research on digital journalism is how social media in general might affect the profession of journalism. Many studies of Twitter and journalism have focused on social media's relation to professional practices and norms (e.g. Armstrong, 2010; Artwick, 2013; Bruns, 2012; Broersma and Graham, 2012; Chu, 2012; Cozma and Chen, 2012; Gulyás, 2013; Hermida, 2009, 2010b, 2012; Hedman and Djerf-Pierre, 2013; Knight and Cook, 2013; Lasorsa, 2012; Lasorsa, Lewis, and Holton, 2012; Lawrence *et al.*, 2013; Lowrey and Burleson Mackay, 2008; Noguera-Vivo, 2013; Parmelee, 2013; Phillips, 2012; Robinson, 2006; Singer, 2005). Hermida (2013: 306) recapitulates this research, concluding that there are "new paradigms of collaborative and collective newsgathering, production and management at play" as news organizations and journalists incorporate social media into their everyday routines and practices.

Several scholars, including Singer (2005) and Lasorsa, Lewis, and Holton (2012), argue that journalists 'normalize' social media to fit traditional professional practices and norms, while simultaneously adjusting some of those practices to fit the emerging 'new' media.

With regard to Twitter, we find that both heavy users and non-users of Twitter (and other social media) are indeed very similar with regard to their core professional ideals and norms

(Hedman, 2015; Hedman and Djerf-Pierre, 2013). The observable differences are not related to traditional professional ideals such as objectivity, scrutiny, neutrality, or independence. If social media are changing the journalistic profession, it is in terms of how journalism relates to the audience/public, and not how it recognizes its essential societal role as the fourth estate. Above all, active j-tweeters are more positive about interacting with audiences, but also more optimistic about increasing audience orientation overall.

The way that journalism relates to the audience/public is closely related to the idea of transparency. Transparency is often described as one of the most important ideals in journalism (cf. Chadha and Koliska, 2015). The argument is that social media like Twitter, with journalists tweeting about their jobs and family lives, 'foster trust relationships' (Feighery, 2011: 172; cf. Meier and Reimer, 2011; Phillips, 2010). Being on Twitter can be regarded as being transparent *per se*. In our studies, we find that Swedish journalists tweet about their jobs, how news is made, journalism, and so on (14 percent of all tweets), but also about their personal and private lives (10 percent) (Table 41.3). In being transparent, journalists explain the rationale behind the news and 'humanize' the reporter; thus not only building trust relationships, but also gaining accountability and credibility (Hedman, 2016; cf. Hayes, Singer, and Ceppos, 2007).

The other side of twitter: boundary-blurring and online threats

Despite the benefits of transparency, there are more troubling sides of the blurred lines between the private and the professional on Twitter. Journalists must find ways to cope with the liquid boundaries of work and off-work, work and play, professional and private, that Twitter epitomizes (Deuze, 2007b; Lasorsa, 2012; Williams, Wardle, and Wahl-Jorgensen, 2010).

Many journalists are critical of the increased focus on personal branding that derives from social media. Indeed, about one-third of the daily users of Twitter support the notion that "personal branding among journalists is incompatible with quality journalism" (Hedman, 2015; Hedman and Djerf-Pierre, 2013).

Not all journalists are keen to display their private lives online or be available to respond to public comments and criticisms at all times. Journalists who are heavy users of Twitter generally have a more positive attitude to interaction with audiences, and a more accepting view of the boundary-blurring of journalists' private and professional lives in social media (Hedman, 2015, 2016; Hedman and Djerf-Pierre, 2013). But both non-users and heavy users, to a large extent, say that the strong focus on audience dialog through social media may have the downside of increasing threats against journalists.

While personalization on Twitter contributes to an increasing—and perhaps even necessary—transparency, and builds connections with audiences, it also exposes individual journalists to public criticism and threats. Social media are indeed vehicles for verbal attacks, negative and abusive comments, and even overt threats directed at journalists. A study of how Swedish journalists experience threats and abusive comments in their work, conducted in 2013 and based on a representative sample of journalists (Löfgren-Nilsson and Örnebring, 2015), showed that hostile comments and threats are a fact of life for most journalists. Almost four out of five have received abusive comments, and one in three has received threats. Interestingly, however, all means of communication are used for dispensing hate and threats, not just social media. Most threats are received by email, but other prevalent channels are the article commentary sections, internet discussion forums, and social media (the study did not specify Twitter).

The professional divide: enthusiasts, pragmatics, and skeptics

In our research we identify three general stances regarding social media among journalists: the active enthusiasts, the pragmatic conformists, and the skeptical shunners (Hedman and Djerf-Pierre, 2013). These are clearly present in relation to Twitter users as well. The skeptical shunners are journalists who never use Twitter. This stance is quite common (about 45 percent of all journalists in our study), but most frequently found among older journalists working in the printed press (particularly the local press). Journalists in this group are generally skeptical of all of uses and impacts of social media.

The pragmatic conformists are journalists who regularly follow Twitter, but mostly use it for information collection and environmental scanning of what is going on online. They invest a certain amount of time in following the Twitter flow, but they seldom send a tweet themselves. Their attitudes toward social media are often marked by ambivalence. On one hand, they appreciate the new opportunities of using Twitter as a journalistic tool; on the other hand, they are less convinced of the virtues of audience adaptation and more ambivalent to personal branding and to the boundary blurring of the private and public in social media. This pragmatic stance is shared by about 50 percent of all journalists.

The enthusiastic activists are those who fully lead a life online, being connected and tweeting continuously. This approach is usually found among younger journalists, and among those working with digital and cross-media platforms, particularly in metropolitan areas. Their usage clearly goes beyond the information and environmental scanning functions, and they frequently use Twitter for networking, personal branding, and collaboration. The Twitter enthusiast group is still small (about 5 percent of all journalists in our study), but it is nevertheless a group that is quite distinctive in its overall positive attitude toward how social media influence the professional lives of journalists. They share most of the fundamental professional ideals of other journalists, but differ in their approach to audience interaction and personal branding.

Extant research clearly points to the wide reach of Twitter among journalists. At the same time, there are significant differences between social groups of journalists when it comes to Twitter use. These are mainly associated with age and type of work, but the division is also visible in other professional attitudes and practices: the level, range, and type of Twitter usage; attitudes toward social media in general; and attitudes toward audience interaction and branding specifically. In these respects, there is indeed a professional digital divide between 24/7 users and non-users of Twitter among journalists. The ongoing generational shift, with older print journalists leaving and younger multimedia journalists entering the newsrooms, will surely have wide implications for journalism as a profession.

Further reading

An article, '#Journalism,' by Hermida (2013) provides a comprehensive research overview of Twitter in journalism. The concept of 'normalizing,' how Twitter is normalized in journalism (and vice versa), is discussed in Lasorsa, Lewis, and Holton's article 'Normalizing Twitter' (2012). In 'Reporters on Twitter,' Artwick (2013) discusses a possible shift in journalism, from journalism as a product to journalism as a service. Barnard (2014) analyzes Twitter's impact on journalistic practices, norms, and values from a field theory point of view in the article 'Tweet or Be Sacked.'

References

Armstrong, C.L. and Gao, F. (2010) "Now Tweet This: How News Organizations Use Twitter." *Electronic News* 4(4): 218–235.

Artwick, C.G. (2013) "Reporters on Twitter." *Digital Journalism* 1(2): 212–228.

Barnard, S.R. (2014) "Tweet or Be Sacked: Twitter and the New Elements of Journalistic Practice." *Journalism*. DOI: 10.1177/1464884914553079.

Brake, L. (2011) "Time's Turbulence: Mapping Journalism Networks." *Victorian Periodicals Review* 44(2): 115–127.

Broersma, M. and Graham, T. (2012) "Social Media as Beat." *Journalism Practice* 6(3): 403–419.

Bruns, A. (2012) "Journalists and Twitter: How Australian News Organisations Adapt to a New Medium." *Media International Australia* 144: 97–107.

Bruns, A. and Burgess, J. (2012) "Researching News Discussion on Twitter." *Journalism Studies* 13(5–6): 801–814.

Chadha, K. and Koliska, M. (2015) "Newsrooms and Transparency in the Digital Age." *Journalism Practice* 9(2): 215–229.

Chamberlain, K. (2011) "Branded. How Do I Make My Reputation as Big as I Can? A Young Journalist Looks into the Wisdom of Branding." *Ryerson Review of Journalism*, March 10.

Chu, D. (2012) "Interpreting News Values in J-Blogs." *Journalism* 13(3): 371–387.

Cozma, R. and Chen, K-J. (2012) "What's in a Tweet?" *Journalism Practice* 7(1): 33–46.

Deuze, M. (2007a) *Media Work*. Cambridge, UK: Polity Press.

Deuze, M. (2007b) "Convergence Culture in the Creative Industries." *International Journal of Cultural Studies* 10(2): 243–263.

Djerf-Pierre, M., Ghersetti, M. and Hedman, U. (2016) "Appropriating Social Media: The Changing Uses of Social Media Among Journalists Across Time". *Digital Journalism*. DOI: 10.1080/21670811.2016.1152557.

Farhi, P. (2009) "The Twitter Explosion." *American Journalism Review* 31(3): 26–31.

Feighery, G. (2011) "Conversation and Credibility." *Journal of Mass Media Ethics* 26(2): 158–175.

Ferguson, D.A. and Greer, C.F. (2011) "Local Radio and Microblogging." *Journal of Radio & Audio Media* 18(1): 33–46.

Greer, C.F. and Ferguson, D.A. (2011) "Using Twitter for Promotion and Branding." *Journal of Broadcasting & Electronic Media* 55(2): 198–214.

Gulyás, Á. (2013) "The Influence of Professional Variables on Journalists' Uses and Views of Social Media." *Digital Journalism* 1(2): 270–285.

Gynnild, A. (2005) "Winner Takes It All: Freelance Journalism on the Global Communication Market." *Nordicom Review* 2005(1): 111–120.

Hayes, A.S., Singer, J.B. and Ceppos, J. (2007) "Shifting Roles, Enduring Values: The Credible Journalist in a Digital Age." *Journal of Mass Media Ethics* 22(4): 262–279.

Hedman, U. (2015) "J-tweeters." *Digital Journalism* 3(2): 297–297.

Hedman, U. (2016) "When Journalists Tweet: Disclosure, Participatory, and Personal Transparency." *Social Media + Society* 2(1): 1–13.

Hedman, U. and Djerf-Pierre, M. (2013) "The Social Journalist." *Digital Journalism* 1(3): 368–385.

Hermida, A. (2009) "The Blogging BBC." *Journalism Practice* 3(3): 268–284.

Hermida, A. (2010a) "From TV to Twitter." *Media/Culture Journal* 13(2): 1–6.

Hermida, A. (2010b) "Twittering the News." *Journalism Practice* 4(3): 297–308.

Hermida, A. (2012) "Tweets and Truth." *Journalism Practice* 6(5–6): 659–668.

Hermida, A. (2013) "#Journalism." *Digital Journalism* 1(3): 295–313.

Hermida, A., Fletcher, F., Korell, D. and Logan, D. (2012) "Share, Like, Recommend." *Journalism Studies* 13(5–6): 815–824.

Hindman, M.S. (2009) *The Myth of Digital Democracy*. Princeton, NJ: Princeton University Press.

Knight, M. and Cook, C. (2013) *Social Media for Journalists*. London, UK: Sage.

Lasorsa, D. (2012) "Transparency and Other Journalistic Norms on Twitter." *Journalism Studies* 13(3): 402–417.

Lasorsa, D., Lewis, S.C. and Holton, A.H. (2012) "Normalizing Twitter." *Journalism Studies* 13(1): 19–36.

Lawrence, R.G., Molyneux, L., Coddington, M. and Holton, A. (2013) "Tweeting Conventions." *Journalism Studies* 15(6): 789–806.

Lowrey, W. and Burleson Mackay, J. (2008) "Journalism and Blogging." *Journalism Practice* 2(1): 64–81.

Löfgren-Nilsson, M. and Örnebring, H. (2016) "Journalism Under Threat: Intimidation and Harassment of Swedish Journalists". *Journalism Practice*. DOI:10.1080/17512786.2016.1164614.

Marwick, A. (2011) *Status Update: Celebrity, Publicity and Self-branding in Web 2.0*. New York, NY: New York University.

Meier, K. and Reimer, J. (2011) "Transparenz im Journalismus" [Transparency in Journalism]. *Publizistik* 56(1): 133–155.

Messner, M., Linke, M. and Eford, A. (2012) "Shoveling Tweets." *ISOJ Journal* 2(1): 76–90.

Molyneux, L. (2014) "What Journalists Retweet: Opinion, Humor, and Brand Development on Twitter." *Journalism*. DOI: 10.1177/1464884914550135.

Noguera-Vivo, J.M. (2013) "How Open are Journalists on Twitter? Trends towards the End-user Journalism." *Communication & Society* 26(1): 93–114.

Örnebring, H. (2010) *The Skills of Journalism: Some Results from a Six-nation Comparative Project (Draft Only)*. Paper presented at 2010 IAMCR Conference, Braga, Portugal, 18–22 July.

Parmelee, J.H. (2013) "Political Journalists and Twitter: Influences on Norms and Practices." *Journal of Media Practice* 14(4): 291–305.

Phillips, A. (2010) "Transparency and the New Ethics of Journalism." *Journalism Practice* 4(3): 373–382.

Phillips, A. (2012) "Sociability, Speed and Quality in the Changing News Environment." *Journalism Practice* 6(5–6): 669–679.

Revers, M. (2014) "The Twitterization of News Making." *Journal of Communication* 64(5): 806–826.

Robinson, S. (2006) "The Mission of the J-Blog: Recapturing Journalistic Authority Online." *Journalism* 7(1): 65–83.

Russel, F.M., Hendricks, M.A., Choi, H. and Conner Stephens, E. (2015) "Who Sets the News Agenda on Twitter?" *Digital Journalism* 3(6): 925–943.

Singer, J.B. (2005) "The Political J-Blogger: 'Normalizing' a New Media Form to Fit Old Norms and Practices." *Journalism* 6(2): 173–198.

Tuchman, G. (1978) *Making News: A Study in the Construction of Reality*. New York, NY: Free Press.

van der Haak, B., Parks, M. and Castells, M. (2012) "The Future of Journalism: Networked Journalism." *International Journal of Communication* 6: 2923–2938.

Verweij, P. (2012) "Twitter Links between Politicians and Journalists." *Journalism Practice* 6(5–6): 680–691.

Williams, A., Wardle, C. and Wahl-Jorgensen, K. (2010) "Have They Got News for Us?" *Journalism Practice* 5(1): 85–99.

42

FACEBOOK AND NEWS JOURNALISM

Steve Paulussen, Raymond A. Harder, and Michiel Johnson

Let us start this chapter with two maybe obvious, but important notes of caution. First, focusing on the relationship between Facebook and journalism may lead to an overstatement of the direct, visible, and short-term impact of social media, but at the same time also to an understatement of the role of technology in reshaping journalism in the long term and in less tangible ways. There is indeed a risk of viewing technological changes in journalism through a myopic lens that clouds our vision on the (longer) historical and (broader) social and economic context in which both journalism and technology evolve (see also Paulussen, 2012). Therefore, understanding the relationship between social media and journalism requires an awareness of the past and ongoing changes in news production and consumption due to the commercialization and digitization of the media industry. More concretely, while current discussions about Facebook and the news media concentrate on trends and issues of distributed news publishing, personalized news streams, the changing journalist–audience relationship, and the 'datafication' of news consumption and delivery, it is good to be reminded that none of these trends or issues are completely 'new' in the literature on journalism (see, respectively, for example, Newhagen and Levy, 1998; Thurman, 2011; Hermida *et al.*, 2011; Anderson, 2011). To avoid technological determinism or myopia, it is thus important to recognize that, throughout the history of journalism, changes in news production and news usage have been entangled with and often amplified by technological innovations, but these changes were mostly incremental and never merely technologically driven (Conboy and Eldridge, 2014; Örnebring, 2010).

Second, when talking about Facebook—or any other social media—it is useful to differentiate between social media as (1) technological tools employed by users (including journalists and news organizations) to fulfill certain goals; (2) social platforms or spaces where 'networked publics' participate in processes of both public and private communication and information exchange; and (3) commercial organizations that make money from advertising and the commodification of user data. We elaborate on this in the next section, but here we want to emphasize that this distinction is relevant because the way we look at social media determines what we see and what might be overlooked. This, too, may seem an obvious point, yet much of the confusion, contradiction, and discussion in the literature on social media stems precisely from the fact that authors depart from different perspectives that highlight—and potentially overexpose—only a part of the whole story.

These two ideas will be borne in mind throughout this chapter. After a brief discussion of two major paradigms for understanding the relationship between social media and journalism, the chapter presents a review of the current literature on the role of Facebook—as a tool, as a social space, and as a company—in reshaping the processes of news selection, news presentation, and news distribution in the digital media ecology.

Two perspectives on Facebook and news journalism

It would, of course, be unwise to suggest that there are only two possible approaches to the study of new media and journalism (for other perspectives, see, e.g., Anderson, 2013). However, for the purpose of this chapter, we find it useful to make such a general distinction between what we regard as the two major and most fruitful theoretical approaches to the analysis of digital journalism: the first one is the social shaping of technology (SST) perspective and the other one is the perspective of critical political economy (CPE).

Facebook and journalism in the networked news ecology

SST is arguably the dominant paradigm in the current literature on digital journalism. From an SST perspective, the relationship between journalism and technology is understood in terms of 'mutual shaping': Instead of assuming a linear effect of technology on society, researchers in the SST tradition investigate the daily social and cultural practices that shape the uses of technology, and consequently the potentially new practices that emerge from these social interactions with technology (Lievrouw, 2006).

Applied to the study of social media and journalism, the SST perspective implies that social media cannot be considered merely as *enabling* technologies, but rather as platforms that also *shape*—and are, in turn, being reshaped by—the ways in which these new technologies are being used, resulting in new communication practices and patterns. In this regard, researchers tend to view social media platforms as 'networked public spheres,' which can be described as "spaces for audiences to share, discuss and contribute to the news" (Hermida *et al.*, 2012: 817; see also Hermida, this volume). The authors continue that the major implication of these networked public spheres for journalism lies in the assumption that it shifts the control over the flow and experience of news further away from the professional journalists towards the users, thus weakening the traditional editorial gatekeeping function of professional journalism. Even though many studies stress that the democratizing effects of the supposedly increased user control over the news process should not be exaggerated (Borger *et al.*, 2013), it is fair to say that legacy news media have become more aware of the active and participatory role that users can (and increasingly do) play in the creation as well as the curation of news (Singer *et al.*, 2011; Villi, 2012).

In a theoretically rich essay, Papacharissi (2015) suggests that social media influence not only the flow but also the form of news. To define the networked news ecology, she draws on Chadwick's concept of the 'hybrid media system' (2013); Hermida's view of social media as an 'ambient' news environment (2010); and Bruns' notion of 'produsage' (2008). She then goes on to argue that in the increasingly hybrid and ambient media ecosystem, 'producers' and 'users' of both old and new media engage in new processes of collaborative storytelling, which alter 'the shape news takes on.' News streams on social media, she argues, can be described as 'liminal' and 'affective'—that is, "driven by intensity and not factuality, instantaneity and not graduality" (Papacharissi, 2015: 35).

The political economy of Facebook and journalism

While conceptualizing the digital media environment as a networked public sphere is useful to grasp how social media is becoming an integral part of public communication, ultimately empowering users to influence the flow and even the form of news, several authors criticize this view for its failure to acknowledge how this new realm of communication is essentially being defined and confined by (neoliberal) market logic (Hardy, 2014; Poell and van Dijck, 2014). In this respect, it is relevant to complement the SST approach with the perspective of CPE (see Hardy, this volume). Simply put, media research in the CPE tradition focuses on "the influence of advertising and ownership on the content and role of the media" (Curran, 2014: x). As defined by Fenton (2007: 7):

> CPE is based upon a concern with the structural inequalities of production and the consequences for representation and access to consumption. By placing issues of economic distribution at its centre, it prioritizes the relationship between the economy and forms of democratic politics.

A thorough and comprehensive critical assessment of the political economy of social media is provided by Poell and van Dijck (2014) in which they vividly show why social media platforms, such as Facebook and Twitter, cannot be regarded as "*neutral* technologies that merely *enable* user activity," but rather as commercial services that "very much *shape* how users share information, curate news, and express their points of views" (Poell and van Dijck, 2014: 182). They give several examples of how social media platforms actively intervene in the production and dissemination of news. This happens directly through opaque algorithms that structure users' personal news feeds, but also indirectly, by advising and selling services to support news organizations to engage their audiences and boost traffic to their websites. News organizations increasingly use social media data and metrics to see what kind of content 'works best' on social media and to optimize the 'sociability' of their news stories (Phillips, 2012). As a consequence, news production and dissemination increasingly become subject to the 'algorithmic logic' of social media technologies rather than to the 'editorial logic' of professional news media (Gillespie, 2014). In this algorithmic logic, instead of being empowered, social media users are much rather "the products of algorithmic steering, pushed towards particular content and sold to advertisers" (Poell and van Dijck, 2014: 196).

It is important to note that the SST and CPE approaches in new media research complement, rather than oppose, each other. Indeed, both perspectives have in common a view that the digital media environment is being *shaped* by social and economic dynamics. Whereas the SST perspective emphasizes the social and cultural practices of users in this shaping process, CPE reminds us of the fact that agency is limited by the economic structures of the media industry. To investigate this tension between agency and structure in the networked news ecology, some authors propose and promote a holistic approach that regards social media platforms as a 'public sphere,' but also at the same time as a 'private' and 'corporate sphere' (van Dijck, 2012; see also Fenton, 2007).

Taking such a holistic approach, the remainder of this chapter will explore the influence of Facebook—and, more specifically, its cultural and commercial uses and articulations—on the processes of news selection, news presentation, and news distribution.

Facebook and news selection

Studies abound showing the rapid adoption of social media among journalists, so it is safe to say that the majority of today's news journalists use social networking sites, such as Facebook and Twitter, for professional purposes (Gulyás, 2013 and this volume; Hedman and Djerf-Pierre, 2013). Journalists' motivations for doing so vary, but a primary one is that it has become a tool for newsgathering. Still, the use of social media as a news source should not be exaggerated, as social media compete with a wide arsenal of information channels at a journalist's disposal (Raeymaeckers *et al.*, 2015). A study on social media citations in two Belgian newspapers found that they carry, on average, only one or two articles per day in which Facebook is referred to as a source (Paulussen and Harder, 2014). If newspaper journalists use social media as a source, they seem to do so to cite both unknown and well-known sources not available or easily accessible other than on social media, a finding in line with previous studies on the use of Twitter as a news source (e.g. Broersma and Graham, 2013).

As far as routine news coverage is concerned, Facebook appears to be, at first glance, not much more than just another easy-to-use tool for journalists to find stories that fill the news hole with limited resources and under increasing time pressures. However, the picture changes, to a certain extent, in the case of breaking news and media events. Although the majority of studies on the use of social media by journalists for breaking news coverage concentrate on Twitter (Hermida, 2013 and this volume), journalists also turn to Facebook when big news stories break. A study on the Arab Spring coverage in Belgian mainstream news media found that one out of ten news articles or TV items explicitly mentioned social media as a source, with Facebook as the most frequently cited social media site, followed by Twitter and YouTube (Van Leuven, Heinrich, and Deprez, 2015: 583). Another study on Belgian television coverage of the same event showed that in cases where social media were used as a news source, the content itself was not directly taken from the social media platforms but filtered by international news agencies and broadcast media from which the television stations derived most of their footage for their foreign news reporting. This finding led the authors to conclude that despite the increased visibility of social media in the news, conventional routines and standards of professional gatekeeping still seem to shape the use of social media in the news selection process (De Dobbelaer, Paulussen, and Maeseele, 2013).

Generally speaking, we can conclude from these studies that the impact of Facebook on journalists' news selection routines is still rather limited. However, what may be overlooked here, is that journalists use Facebook not only as a direct source for their news stories, but also as a tool for monitoring the 24/7 news stream. The results of a survey on social media use among Swedish journalists give support to Hermida's (2010) argument that social media function as an awareness system to journalists, who primarily use them for 'various forms of environmental scanning,' such as 'following ongoing discussions,' 'finding ideas,' and 'trend-spotting' (Hedman and Djerf-Pierre, 2013: 376). Later in their article, Hedman and Djerf-Pierre (2013: 377) ask whether it matters if journalists use social media or not: "More specifically, does social media usage impact upon and change professional identities and ideals?" While their answer is ambivalent and somewhat inconclusive, the question is pertinent and certainly requires further investigation.

Further research is indeed needed on how journalists' use of social media influences their perceptions of what—as well as who—counts as newsworthy. The topics that trigger journalists' attention on social media, for instance because they are 'trending' or going 'viral' in their social networks, may influence their news values (Tandoc, 2014, also this volume). Moreover, as argued by Hermida (2015: 1–2), certain actors on social media increasingly tend to be elevated by 'ad hoc publics' (rather than by professional gatekeepers) to the status of credible sources "on specific issues at specific times, within specific contexts or domains," thus potentially influencing the power play between journalists and their sources. The implications of this may not be directly visible in journalists' daily newsroom routines or in the sources they cite in their news stories, but it is likely that a closer examination of their news output may reveal traits of social media logic prevalent in their sourcing practices and their perceptions of newsworthiness (see also Bro and Wallberg, 2014).

Facebook and news presentation

Studies show that legacy news media tend to view Facebook as a platform to present and promote their content by engaging users in a process of 'audience distribution' (Hille and Bakker, 2013). According to Phillips (2012: 669), next to speed and quality, sociability has become a third pillar of 'good' online journalism: "It is no longer enough to be 'first with the news', nor is it sufficient to be comprehensive and trustworthy. It is now increasingly necessary to ensure that news is produced in a form that is capable of spreading virally." News organizations are increasingly using techniques of 'social media optimization' (SMO) to maximize the 'virality' of their news stories, even to a point where it threatens professional standards of accuracy (Riordan, 2014). It is worth noting in this respect that the term 'click bait' has entered the vocabulary of digital journalism. A Danish study shows that the increasing use of forward-references in online news headlines to generate curiosity and suspense can be seen as a form of 'tabloidization,' as journalists engage in it for commercial rather than editorial reasons, and therefore it "should not be ignored or considered collateral damage in the war for readers if considered ethically and not financially" (Blom and Hansen, 2015: 99).

Tandoc (2014) found that web analytics seem to give rise to a 'new' gatekeeping practice online, which he calls 'de-selection,' a process that takes place when online journalists decide, on the basis of audience metrics instead of relevance, to take stories out of the homepage of their website to replace them by a new story. This becomes even more problematic on social media platforms such as Facebook, where this process of de-selection is automated and directly based on opaque computer algorithms (Gillespie, 2014). Rather than considering such processes of de-selection and SMO as a mere reflection of news media's attempts to better serve the news interests and preferences of their users, some authors stress that these practices increase the commercial pressures on journalists, thus undermining their editorial independence and, eventually, the democratic role and responsibility of the press as a fourth estate (Poell and van Dijck, 2014).

It is indeed clear that, from a CPE point of view, the blurring 'news-business boundary' in journalism (Coddington, 2015), and more specifically the intensification of the commercial pressures on journalism due to social media, should not be considered as just a side effect of the increased user control over the news process. Journalism scholars raise concerns over the news media's tendency to confuse relevance with popularity when evaluating newsworthiness (Heinderyckx, 2015: 260). At the same time, several researchers stress that changes in people's news tastes and consumption behavior can and should not be ignored either. As users' news preferences and practices evolve, news media have to evolve as well if they want to retain their democratic role and create public value (Costera Meijer, 2013; Picone, Courtois, and Paulussen, 2015). Hence, it is again important to look at both sides of the coin: future research should, on the one hand, acknowledge the changing social and cultural practices in news usage due to social media and how they influence the shape of news in a networked news ecology (Papacharissi, 2015). On the other hand, research should be aware that these changes are manipulated by the commercial strategies of media organizations aimed at monetizing the likes, clicks, and shares of their users (Poell and van Dijck, 2014).

Facebook and news distribution

As we have tried to argue above, Facebook is more than just another newsgathering tool for journalists or an extra platform for news dissemination. Rather, the impact of Facebook lies in its potential to reshape the flow of news. The cultural and commercial interactions between social and legacy media, as well as between the 'producers/suppliers' and 'users/recipients' of news, are shifting the power relations in the news distribution process. According to Singer (2014: 55), users are becoming 'secondary gatekeepers' of the content published on news websites, as they increasingly become involved in the recommendation and "selective re-dissemination of that content." The result, she continues, is "a two-step gatekeeping process, in which initial editorial decisions to make an item part of the news product are followed by user decisions to upgrade or downgrade the visibility of that item for a secondary audience" (Singer, 2014: 55). This vision is in line with the often repeated notion that social media users would increasingly rely on their (opinion leading) 'friends' to tell them what news is worth paying attention to (Hermida *et al.*, 2012; Turcotte *et al.*, 2015), but it falls short of recognizing that news feeds on social networking sites are not 'edited' by other users, but, in fact, mediated by computational intervention (Gillespie, 2014). Since our knowledge of how social media technologies intervene in prioritizing certain content over other content is still limited, scholars and media critics urge Facebook to create more transparency about their algorithms and strategic decisions made to 'optimize' and channel the news streams on its platform (Napoli, 2015; Tufekci, 2014).

In sum, given the shifting power plays in the networked news ecology, the fundamental question arises regarding to what extent professional journalism will be capable of retaining its editorial independence and gatekeeping control over the *distribution* of news in times when (1) more and more users (though still a minority) are relying on social networking sites as their main gateway to find and access the news (Newman, Levy, and Nielsen, 2015; Nielsen and Schröder, 2014), and (2) social and legacy media organizations are increasingly implementing an algorithmic logic in the process of news dissemination, a logic that is entirely market-driven as it is based on traffic and user data and not concerned with the public interest (Napoli, 2015).

Conclusion

From a holistic point of view, combining insights from both SST and CPE approaches in digital journalism research, this chapter has discussed how Facebook is affecting journalism and the news in different ways. First, social networking sites, like Facebook and Twitter, seem to give journalists quick and easy access to a range of sources not readily and immediately available other than on social media. Particularly during breaking news events, but also during routine news coverage, journalists refer to Facebook as a source of information. Moreover, it can be assumed that 'networked publics,' through their social interactions on Facebook, can influence journalists' perceptions of who and what is deemed newsworthy. Secondly, Facebook seems to push news media organizations to replace their 'editorial logic' by an 'algorithmic logic' for the presentation of news to their publics. To stand out amidst the vast and constant stream of content on social media, news stories and headlines are presented in such a way as to increase their sociability and their virality—which leads to concerns about the intensification of the commercial pressures on journalism. Thirdly and finally, Facebook is increasingly capable to manipulate the dissemination of news on the social media platform and prioritize certain news stories over others, which further challenges professional journalists' editorial independence and gatekeeping control over the distribution of news.

Further reading

Zizi Papacharissi's (2015) essay "Toward New Journalism(s)," points out that the collaborative 'produsage' of news in the hybrid and ambient digital media ecology affects not only the flow but also the shape of news. Thomas Poell and José van Dijck (2014), in "Social Media and Journalistic Independence," provide a comprehensive critical analysis of how social media, such as Facebook and Twitter, further intensify commercial pressures on journalism. Finally, Jane Singer's article (2014), "User-Generated Visibility: Secondary Gatekeeping in a Shared Media Space," reflects on the distribution of news on social media, arguing that users have become 'secondary gatekeepers' of the editorial content published by professional media.

References

Anderson, C.W. (2011) "Between Creative and Quantified Audiences." *Journalism* 12(5): 550–566.

Anderson, C.W. (2013) "Towards a Sociology of Computational and Algorithmic Journalism." *New Media and Society* 15(7): 1005–1021.

Blom, P.N. and Hansen, K.R. (2015) "Click Bait: Forward-Reference as Lure in Online News Headlines." *Journal of Pragmatics* 76: 78–100.

Borger, M., van Hoof, A., Costera Meijer, I. and Sanders, J. (2013) "Constructing Participatory Journalism as a Scholarly Object." *Digital Journalism* 1(1): 117–134.

Bro, P. and Wallberg, F. (2014) "Digital Gatekeeping." *Digital Journalism* 2(3): 446–454.

Broersma, M. and Graham, T. (2013) "Twitter as a News Source." *Journalism Practice* 6(3): 403–419.

Bruns, A. (2008) *Blogs, Wikipedia, Second Life, and Beyond: From Production to Produsage*. New York, NY: Peter Lang.

Chadwick, A. (2013) *The Hybrid Media System*. New York, NY: Oxford University Press.

Coddington, M. (2015) "The Wall becomes a Curtain: Revisiting Journalism's News-Business Boundary." In Carlson, M. and Lewis, S.C. (eds) *Boundaries of Journalism*. Abingdon, UK: Routledge, pp. 67–82.

Conboy, M. and Eldridge, S. (2014) "Morbid Symptoms." *Journalism Studies* 15(5): 566–575.

Costera Meijer, I. (2013) "Valuable Journalism: A Search for Quality from the Vantage Point of the User." *Journalism* 14(6): 754–770.

Curran, J. (2014) "Foreword." In Hardy, J. (ed.) *Critical Political Economy of the Media*. Abingdon, UK: Routledge, pp. x–xx.

De Dobbelaer, R., Paulussen, S. and Maeseele, P. (2013) "Social Media and Old Routines." *Tijdschrift voor Communicatiewetenschap* 41(3): 265–279.

Fenton, N. (2007) "Bridging the Mythical Divide: Political Economy and Cultural Studies Approaches to the Analysis of the Media." In Devereux, E. (ed.) *Media Studies: Key Issues and Debates*. London, UK: Sage, pp. 7–31.

Gillespie, T. (2014) "The Relevance of Algorithms." In Gillespie, T., Boczkowski, P.J. and Foot, K.A. (eds) *Media Technologies*. Cambridge, MA: MIT Press, pp. 167–194.

Gulyás, Á. (2013) "The Influence of Professional Variables on Journalists' Uses and Views of Social Media." *Digital Journalism* 1(2): 270–285.

Hardy, J. (2014) *Critical Political Economy of the Media: An Introduction*. Abingdon, UK: Routledge.

Hedman, U. and Djerf-Pierre, M. (2013) "The Social Journalist." *Digital Journalism* 1(3): 368–385.

Heinderyckx, F. (2015) "Gatekeeping Theory Redux." In Vos, T.P. and Heinderyckx, F. (eds) *Gatekeeping in Transition*. Abingdon, UK: Routledge, pp. 253–267.

Hermida, A. (2010) "Twittering the News." *Journalism Practice* 4(3): 297–308.

Hermida, A. (2013) "#Journalism." *Digital Journalism* 1(3): 295–313.

Hermida, A. (2015) "Power Plays on Social Media." *Social Media + Society* 1(1). Available from: http://sms.sagepub.com/content/1/1/2056305115580340.

Hermida, A., Domingo, D., Heinonen, A., Paulussen, S., Quandt, T., Reich, Z., et al. (2011) "The Active Recipient: Participatory Journalism through the Lens of the Dewey-Lippmann Debate." *#ISOJ* 1(2): 129–152.

Hermida, A., Fletcher, F., Korell, D. and Logan, D. (2012) "Share, Like, Recommend." *Journalism Studies* 13(5): 815–824.

Hille, S. and Bakker, P. (2013) "I Like News: Searching for the 'Holy Grail' of Social Media: The Use of Facebook by Dutch News Media and their Audiences." *European Journal of Communication* 28(6): 663–680.

Lievrouw, L.A. (2006) "New Media Design and Development: Diffusion of Innovations vs Social Shaping of Technology." In Lievrouw, L.A. and Livingstone, S. (eds) *The Handbook of New Media*. London, UK: Sage, pp. 246–265.

Napoli, P.M. (2015) "Social Media and the Public Interest: Governance of News Platforms in the Realm of Individual and Algorithmic Gatekeepers." *Telecommunications Policy* 39(9): 751–760.

Newhagen, J.E. and Levy, M.R. (1998) "The Future of Journalism in a Distributed Communication Architecture." In Borden, D.L. and Harvey, K. (eds) *The Electronic Grapevine*. Mahwah, NJ: Lawrence Erlbaum, pp. 9–21.

Newman, N., Levy, D.A.L. and Nielsen, R.K. (2015) *Reuters Institute Digital News Report 2015*. Oxford, UK: Reuters Institute for the Study of Journalism. Available from: http://papers.ssrn.com/sol3/papers.cfm?abstract_id=2619576.

Nielsen, R.K. and Schröder, K.C. (2014) "The Relative Importance of Social Media for Accessing, Finding, and Engaging with News." *Digital Journalism* 2(4): 472–489.

Örnebring, H. (2010) "Technology and Journalism-as-Labour: Historical Perspectives." *Journalism* 11(1): 57–74.

Papacharissi, Z. (2015) "Toward New Journalism(s)." *Journalism Studies* 16(1): 27–40.

Paulussen, S. (2012) "Technology and the Transformation of News Work." In Siapera, E. and Veglis, A. (eds) *The Handbook of Global Online Journalism*. Malden, MA: Wiley-Blackwell, pp. 192–208.

Paulussen, S. and Harder, R.A. (2014) "Social Media References in Newspapers." *Journalism Practice* 8(5): 542–551.

Phillips, A. (2012) "Sociability, Speed and Quality in the Changing News Environment." *Journalism Practice* 6(5–6): 669–679.

Picone, I., Courtois, C. and Paulussen, S. (2015) "When News is Everywhere." *Journalism Practice* 9(1): 35–49.

Poell, T. and van Dijck, J. (2014) "Social Media and Journalistic Independence." In Bennett, J. and Strange, N. (eds) *Media Independence: Working with Freedom or Working for Free?* Abingdon, UK: Routledge, pp. 182–201.

Raeymaeckers, K., Deprez, A., De Vuyst, S. and De Dobbelaer, R. (2015) "The Journalist as a Jack of all Trades." In Vos, T.P. and Heinderyckx, F. (eds) *Gatekeeping in Transition*. Abingdon, UK: Routledge, pp. 104–119.

Riordan, K. (2014) *Accuracy, Independence, and Impartiality: How Legacy Media and Digital Natives Approach Standards in the Digital Age*. Oxford, UK: Reuters Institute for the Study of Journalism. Available from: http://reutersinstitute.politics.ox.ac.uk/publication/accuracy-independence-and-impartiality.

Singer, J.B. (2014) "User-Generated Visibility: Secondary Gatekeeping in a Shared Media Space." *New Media and Society* 16(1): 55–73.

Singer, J.B., Hermida, A., Domingo, D., Heinonen, A., Paulussen, S., Quandt, T., et al. (2011) *Participatory Journalism: Guarding Open Gates at Online Newspapers*. Malden, MA: Wiley-Blackwell.

Tandoc, E. (2014) "Journalism is Twerking? How Web Analytics is Changing the Process of Gatekeeping." *New Media and Society* 16(4): 559–575.

Thurman, N. (2011) "Making 'The Daily Me': Technology, Economics and Habit in the Mainstream Assimilation of Personalized News." *Journalism* 12(4): 395–415.

Tufekci, Z. (2014) "What Happens to #Ferguson Affects Ferguson: Net Neutrality, Algorithmic Filtering and Ferguson." *The Message*, 14 August. Available from: https://medium.com/message/ferguson-is-also-a-net-neutrality-issue-6d2f3db51eb0.

Turcotte, J., York, C., Irving, J., Scholl, R.M. and Pingree, R.J. (2015) "News Recommendations from Social Media Opinion Leaders: Effects on Media Trust and Information Seeking." *Journal of Computer-Mediated Communication* 20(5): 520–535.

van Dijck, J. (2012) "Facebook as a Tool for Producing Sociality and Connectivity." *Television and New Media* 13(2): 160–176.

Van Leuven, S., Heinrich, A. and Deprez, A. (2015) "Foreign Reporting and Sourcing Practices in the Network Sphere." *New Media and Society* 17(4): 573–591.

Villi, M. (2012) "Social Curation in Audience Communities: UDC (User-Distributed Content) in the Networked Media Ecosystem." *Participations* 9(2): 614–632.

43

THE SOLO VIDEOJOURNALIST AS SOCIAL STORYTELLER

Capturing subjectivity and realism with a digital toolkit and editorial vision

David Hedley

Since the birth of photojournalism in the battlefields of the Crimean Peninsula and during the American Civil War, two conditions have defined the news photographer's craft: how the technology of the day shapes the qualities of the images captured, and how society understands those images. For example, photographers in 1862, using bulky equipment and the cumbersome wet-plate imaging process, relied on exposure times ranging from a few seconds to 10 minutes as they documented the aftermath of the Antietam battle in northern Maryland (Harris, 2013). The emotionally charged still images from that period were a revelation to audiences, perceived as "truthful as the record of heaven" (2013: 87). Across the decades, technological disruption has been journalism's constant companion, affecting and shaping journalistic practice for photographers and writers alike (Meyer, 2009). This study focuses on solo videojournalism, the practice of a single journalist using role-blurring digital technologies to photograph, narrate, and edit a video production. The chapter asks: How does an award-winning solo videojournalist deploy mobile digital tools and his personal skills to shape a distinct story?

Arguably, photographers have experienced more disruption to their work than any other single professional group within the newsroom, as they adapt to emerging technology and communication networks. Today's photojournalists are more tethered to electronic equipment than their colleagues are as they handle most of the video shooting and editing, produce photo galleries and slideshows (Santana and Russial, 2013), and often write and narrate a script (Bock, 2008). Even as they negotiate the expanded identity thrust upon them, videojournalists work in a marketplace where their value as professional eyewitnesses on behalf of society is less central (Zelizer, 2007). The proliferation of smartphone cameras has the dual effect of democratizing as well as deprofessionalizing photojournalism (Santana and Russial, 2013). The "witness-bearing power of video" turns anyone who has access to a smartphone and a video-sharing site such as YouTube into a kind of journalist (Tripp, 2012: 11), although they may not share the professionals' values or intentions (Mäenpää, 2014). Peer and Ksiazek see how news videos uploaded to YouTube by non-professionals generate more page views when the productions depart from the content standards of quality journalism (2011, also Ksiazek and Peer, this volume). Nonetheless, in the face of so much change in working conditions and the marketplace, Santana and Russial's survey finds that many photographers regard the added responsibilities as offering new opportunities and greater job flexibility and satisfaction.

The concept of replacing a two- or three-person news crew with one highly skilled journalist to shoot news videos is not new. A variety of terms have arisen to describe the profession, based on personal preference, employer context, academic setting, and era: solo videojournalist (SoJo or SVJ), mobile journalist (MoJo), one-man band, backpack journalist, digital journalist, multimedia journalist, and platypus. I agree with Smith (2011: xii) that the designation 'solo videojournalist' most accurately describes what they do, while avoiding the gender difficulty of the popular 'one-man band' nickname. As the practice of solo videojournalism gains wider acceptance within mainstream news publishing on the Web, Rosenblum (2008), Penniman (2009), and Drew (2010) are among visionaries who believe digital technology creates an opportunity for reporters to produce breakthrough forms of videojournalism distinct from the anchor-centred conventions of broadcast television. This qualitative study considers the visual and social meaning of videojournalism through an analysis of one award-winning production, with the aim of learning whether this storytelling practice "creates its own forms of emphasis and registers of style," to use Cole's terms (2015: para. 8). The video *Being There for Betty*, shot by Dave Delozier of KUSA-TV in Denver, Colorado, for broadcast on television and publication on the Web, won an award of excellence from the National Press Photographers Association in 2010. The story, archived by the Poynter Institute for Media Studies on Vimeo at <http://vimeo.com/9867974>, describes the support offered by a war veteran bikers' group for a dying senior.

This study finds that Delozier calls upon the tools of video technology and his personal editorial vision in a 'social role' as a journalist (Costera Meijer, 2010: 328) as he reports about how the war veterans construct their social reality. The literature review briefly considers three topics related to the solo videojournalist mode of expression: how photojournalists' work as recorders of visual truth has been understood by culture and explored by scholars; how journalism negotiates the tension between notions of objectivity and more subjective emotional content; and recent research on how journalism contributes to the emotional sphere.

Method and framework

Two theoretical frameworks guide my analysis of both the content and the form of Delozier's exemplary video production. I apply social semiotics to examine the embedded social structure in the messages. Social semiotics is an understanding of semiotics constructed around the Piercean notion of signs as containing three elements: the sign, its object, and an interpretant (Jensen, 1991: 40). Social semiotics sheds light on how the images, language, gestures, and themes presented in the video function as 'semiotic resources' or as a communicative grammar to suggest audience meaning (van Leeuwen, 2005: 4). To examine the form of the story, or the shaping effect of the communicative environment, I turn to media theory, which holds that each medium dictates its own physical, psychological, social, and communicative possibilities. Theorists McLuhan (1964) and Meyrowitz (1985) show how the distinct characteristics of prevailing media at a given time in history affect users, individually and collectively, making emerging forms of news presentation on the Web a fertile area for study.

I regard Delozier's 2-minute video as a mobile 'multimodal communication' in which one multi-skilled person, operating in and across multiple semiotic modes, weaves together a boundary-crossing production for presentation on one interface (Kress and van Leeuwen,

2001: 20). I examine how the modes work individually and in concert to both articulate the content of the news story and structurally suggest audience meaning.

I conducted a semi-structured, taped interview with Delozier on February 7, 2012, to learn more about his research method and personal editorial vision.

During my analysis, I identified the emotions present across the 38 frames, according to Ekman and Friesen's guide to recognizing emotions from facial expressions (2003). I also noted a significant presence of social messages, suggesting the need for a more refined understanding of the embedding social structures. I coded each of the frames for *discourse*, *subjectivity*, and/ or *context*—three codes inspired by the three "basic constituents of the communication process" described by Jensen (1991: 18–20). *Discourse* refers to the use of everyday interaction, especially dialogue, to socially construct reality. *Subjectivity* refers to messages that infer social position, identity, or a perspective on the world. *Context* refers to messages that reflect the underlying, dominant structures or stories prevalent in a period of history.

The overarching framework of the study follows Rodriguez and Dimitrova's (2008) semiotic model, which operationalizes the three-term model of sign use within semiotics, but adds a fourth layer useful for this study: how editorial and stylistic conventions within journalism inform and shape the production. Applying this model, I develop a qualitative, structured, progressively sensitive semiotic analysis of how the solo video assigns meaning.

Photojournalism's contested role as visual interpreter

Photojournalists through history have sought an identity as trusted and authoritative visual interpreters of the world, anchored in realism but with an emphasis on the treatment or style (Aker, 2012). News photographers view objectivity as representing people and scenes in a transparent, natural manner immediately understood by the viewer (Schwartz, 1992). The truth claims of photojournalism were premised on the enlightenment view of vision's authoritative position in the structures of universal knowledge (Becker, 2007). Viewers were attracted to photojournalism in print and broadcast media by the assumptions of seeing-is-believing objectivity, artistry, experienced vision, and the practitioner's evident courage to get the shot (Newton, 2009). Yet, scholars also recognize the constructed, artistic nature of the image (Bock, 2009; Griffin, 2002; Sontag, 1973). The essayist Barthes draws a distinction between the 'mythical' status of the press photograph as a mechanical analogue of reality, and its 'coded' or symbolic meaning as a message that has been composed, selected, framed, processed, and displayed according to professional, aesthetic, and ideological norms (1977: 18–20). "Thanks to its code of connotation, the reading of the photograph is thus always historical; it depends on the readers 'knowledge' just as though it were a matter of real language," Barthes writes (1977: 28). Thus, the meaning of a news image in a given context relies on a shared understanding between the photographer and the viewer.

Early practitioners of solo videojournalism set out to capitalize on the expressive potential of the nimble new tool. Smith traces the origins of the solo videojournalism craft to the mid-1990s, when Rosenblum, a former CBS producer, launched a video newsmagazine network for combination reporter-photographers, advocating a more up-close and personal ethic in the development of stories (2011: 9–10). A few studies explore the forms and practices of videojournalism, revealing glimpses of a new craft establishing its boundaries. Following the introduction of videojournalism at three television newsrooms, news workers worry the demands of multiskilling may compromise journalistic rigour; they also see how the small video cameras facilitate more intimate, innovative storytelling (Wallace, 2009).

Solo videojournalists employed by television stations create narratives much like those produced by conventional two-person crews, whereas videojournalists at newspaper online sites invent a style closer to documentary filmmaking (Bock, 2009). The videojournalist's reliance on physical presence and social interaction leads to a shift of power into the hands of sources (Bock, 2011).

As an emerging field of practice, videojournalism presents a new venue for photographers to establish a distinctive voice as trusted interpreters. As they add their own social awareness to their storytelling toolkits, solo videojournalists find themselves balancing traditional notions of objectivity and transparency with shifting cultural understandings of what counts as truth.

Journalism's uneasy relationship with emotional content

Whether they work mainly with words, sound, or images, journalists must negotiate ideals of objectivity and style as they practice their profession. This review considers one thread within the larger scholarly discussion about objectivity: how journalists understand and manage more subjective types of content, such as emotional expression, everyday experience, social context, and the perspectives of ordinary citizens.

The objectivity ethic evolved as a constructed set of practices within the journalistic interpretive community in the United States in the early twentieth century, reflecting broader culture's high regard for science and non-partisanship (Schudson, 2001). The objectivity norm guides writers to report only the facts, set aside values, and adopt a cool rather than an emotional tone. Objectivity functions as a fact-centred workplace discipline and ideal but falls short in its ability to convey context and perspective (Hanson, 1997; Tuchman, 1972). Some writers in the 1960s turned to narrative realism as an alternative to the objective form, in an effort to "make the reader call forth his or her own experiences and emotions and apply them to the story at hand" (Hanson, 1997: 390).

On the front lines, reporters often feel conflicted as they negotiate emotional content, seeing it as 'fact and feeling' journalism (Kitch, 2009: 31) calculated to snag readers (Shapiro, 2006). A binary definition of news as either rational/serious or popular/light has shaped mainstream journalism practice for decades. 'Quality' journalism implies hard topics, a rational/critical approach, and an orientation toward the public sphere; 'popular' journalism is seen to emphasize everyday life and emotions over understanding (Pantti, 2010: 170). Yet, postmodern society is infatuated with emotion, passion, feeling, sentiment, and mood (Greco and Stenner, 2008). Recent scholarship makes the case that less traditional, more experiential forms of storytelling can contribute to greater societal understanding and a greater sense of involvement in the news.

Journalism's contribution to the emotional sphere

This literature review briefly considers how journalism is responding to the rise of the emotional public sphere, defined by Richards as "the nature and distribution of emotion in the mediatised public sphere" (2009: 59). While politicians and celebrities account for much of the content of the emotional sphere, journalists also make a major contribution through their own 'emotional labour,' or in how they process and present emotion (Richards and Rees, 2011: 853).

A handful of scholars explore the societal meaning of emotional content in journalism. Research finds that news coverage provides opportunities for ordinary people to express themselves politically and make claims for justice (Pantti and Wahl-Jorgensen, 2011); strengthens collective feeling and the ideal of working though emotion together (Pantti and Sumiala, 2009);

fulfils viewers' social expectations of community life (Costera Meijer, 2010); and reflects the role of the private sphere in an effective democracy (Costera Meijer, 2001). Other studies look at how subjective techniques in narrative influence the user experience. Pulitzer Prize-winning stories often engage readers by using narrative techniques such as anecdotal leads, personalized storytelling, and invocations of emotion, presented in a heavily policed manner acceptable to the journalistic establishment (Wahl-Jorgensen, 2013). Several American newsmagazines replicated the ritual stages of a funeral in their coverage during the month following the September 11 attacks (Kitch, 2003).

Researchers make the case that audiences not satisfied by traditional definitions of news can find meaning in respectful, subjective forms of journalistic discourse. Research taking place at the intersection of journalism and the emotional sphere equips writers and photographers with new strategies for connecting with readers.

Results

Level 1: Signs as denotative systems

Corresponding to Barthes' concept of a 'denoted' message (1977: 17), this level describes in basic terms the discrete visual elements appearing within the frame. Delozier relies on six modes for storytelling purposes: (1) moving visuals; (2) still photographs; (3) the subjects' words; (4) the journalist's narration; (5) ambient sounds; and (6) camera proximity. Delozier structures his video chronologically around the action of the funeral, using a sequential technique for heightened realism (Shook, Larson, and DeTarsio, 2009: 9). Delozier's sparse off-camera narrations provide 14 basic facts as well as bridges between scenes.

Level 2: Signs as stylistic semiotic systems

Rodriguez and Dimitrova define this level to delineate editorial and design conventions. Delozier recreates how viewers would experience the funeral if they were there. Delozier himself never appears on-camera; he becomes a 'fly on the wall' (Kobre, 2000: 47) who uses his camera unobtrusively to capture character, relationships, and atmosphere on film. Delozier says a key element in his reporting is establishing a relationship with the source, "so that they trust you enough to let you be there and capture the moments that really tell the story" (interview, February 7, 2012). Delozier employs another foundational news technique, the recording of natural sound, to add realism. Much of the 'persuasive' quality of documentaries stems from the sound track (Nichols, 2010: 26), while natural sounds remind viewers of their own life experiences (Shook, Larson, and DeTarsio, 2009). Delozier creates a more memorable story by emphasizing the emotional reactions of his subjects. By focusing on feelings, expressions, and gestures, the producer conveys the character's inner state, stirring in viewers a parallel emotional state (Nichols, 2010).

Level 3: Signs as symbolic systems

This level corresponds to Barthes' concept of a 'connoted' message (1977: 17), or how society thinks of an image. Images of American flags, guns, and military crests provide constant metaphorical reminders of the funeral as a social event with patriotic overtones. In this context, the photographer's use of the flag and other institutional emblems connotes the complex, deeply felt values about military service held by those who have served. In stark contrast to the institutional symbols, the emblems of biker culture express a layer of counter-cultural solidarity: leather jackets, baseball caps, bandanas, Harley-Davidson logos, and a skull-and-crossbones crest.

Delozier uses the playing of *Taps* as ambient sound in 15 frames. Music accompanying an event can function as religious ritual and means of social integration, powerfully symbolizing group structure and values (Danesi, 1999: 172).

The conversations depicted in the video offer a glimpse of the underlying attitudes, beliefs, and socially constructed reality of the war veterans. They convey attitudes on a wide range of topics as they reflect on Betty's life and death, such as: loyalty in friendship, characteristics of a fiercely independent personality, gender relations, reaching out to shut-ins, maintaining a sense of humour through adversity, carrying on despite poor weather, recognition of war veterans, the existence of an afterlife, fear of dying alone, and being there for someone who is dying. The emotions visible on the subjects' faces (Ekman and Friesen, 2003: 37, 50, 68, 103, 117) include: happiness, often conveyed in personal snapshots; sadness; disgust with the weather; surprise; and fear, while recalling Betty's fear of dying alone.

Level 4: Signs as ideological representations

Following from Barthes' 'third reading' (1997: 54), this level of analysis goes beyond the stylistic and symbolic features to identify the deeper attitudes of a nation, class, religious or philosophical persuasion, or period of history. Betty is portrayed as the unsung American war hero, an icon of individualism and patriotic service who is approaching anonymous death in a small-town nursing home. She is rescued from her worst fear by a group of individualistic, patriotic men and women who share her values and who reach out to protect her, extending the Soldier's Creed to "never leave a fallen comrade" (United States Army, 2011). The emotional eulogies focus on how the veterans came together like family in her time of need. When a biker says, "She's a veteran, and, uh, she deserves not to be alone or forgotten," he frames her identity as a soldier as her defining quality. The act of rescuing gives their lives meaning. In answering the call to serve, Betty's friends become quiet heroes themselves, perpetuating the values of social cohesion and loyalty shared by veterans.

Discussion: journalism in a social role

This analysis demonstrates how Delozier's production relies on the visual conventions of television broadcasting, documentary filmmaking, and photojournalism to tell the story of a war veteran's funeral. On technical grounds, I find the production cannot be considered groundbreaking in visual terms, compared to a story produced by a multi-person crew. However, the story is illustrative of three videojournalist craft values articulated by Smith as the 'Rosenblum Model': devote more time to a single story, develop a rapport between the videojournalist and subjects, and provide a detailed visual representation of the subjects' perspectives (2011: 9, 14, 27). Drawing on the same reporting techniques of narrative realism described by Wolfe (1973: 31–32), Delozier constructs the story scene by scene, uses extensive dialogue, tells the story through the eyes of the characters, and includes symbolic details. Delozier says operating as a solo videojournalist enhances his ability to capture what he refers to as 'storytelling' qualities:

> The fewer people that are around, the fewer distractions that are around, the easier it is for the story subject to just be themselves and let the moments happen, and not be distracted by a crew. That's not to say working as a two- or a three-person crew,

great stories can't happen. I just personally think it's easier whenever there are fewer distractions. If it's just me, just my camera, and I'm able to establish a relationship with them, it's pretty easy for those natural moments to happen.

(Interview, February 7, 2012)

By emphasizing relational perspectives in his reporting, and by focusing all of the digital tools at his disposal to achieve his editorial objective, Delozier extends his role as photographer into a social realm, beyond the more familiar position as a recorder of visual truth. For example, consider this comment by Henri Cartier-Bresson (in Kobre, 2000: 350): "To me, photography is the simultaneous recognition, in a fraction of a second, of the significance of an event as well as of a precise organization of forms which give that event its proper expression." In contrast, Delozier's production is more concerned with representations of extended moments, portraying what Meyrowitz describes as "that 'nebulous stuff' we learn about each other in acts of communication" (1985: 37). Delozier says he typically tries to orient his reports around social and emotional elements of the story:

To me it's far less important about the facts and figures of the story necessarily, as much just it is about peoples' feelings and their emotions and what's going on in their hearts and their heads. That story about Betty wasn't about where she served in World War Two, or what her role was in World War Two, or where she lived after World War Two. It was about why she lived and why the people who surrounded her cared about her.

(Interview, February 7, 2012)

What contribution does Delozier's story make to the emotional sphere? In Pantti and Wahl-Jorgensen's broad analysis, emotions are important to the constitution of citizenship and public life in three ways: (1) for the construction of collective identities and social bonds; (2) as motivators to political action; and (3) as a means of making political and moral judgments (2011: 105–106). I believe the Betty story falls into the first category. Delozier casts journalism in a 'social role,' to use Costera Meijer's term (2010: 328), exploring the perspectives and emotional values of war veterans through a portrayal of everyday social interactions, rather than through rational claims. The story fosters a sense of community among veterans while transforming the funeral from a private event to a public event. Ultimately, the account widens our imagination of citizenship as it depicts war veterans negotiating conflicts between individual and society.

Conclusion

At a time in journalism history when the ubiquitous smartphone camera and social media sharing networks have tended to dilute the value of professionally produced eyewitness news photos in the marketplace, productions such as Delozier's *Betty* illustrate how news photographers can leverage digital technology, expand their role, and reclaim a distinct professional identity. Delozier functions as a social as well as a visual interpreter, by capturing and portraying emotion, gestures, vocabulary, personal values, sound, posture, dress codes, pace of activity, and a sense of presence. Thus, the solo videojournalist creates what I describe as 'social moments' as he or she negotiates mobile digital technologies for a journalistic storytelling purpose.

In the final production, the subjects themselves are seen to construct their social reality, in their use of language, their personal and political values, and their social positions within the veteran community. The multimodal streams each affect the viewer's senses differently, conveying potential ways of knowing. In a Barthesian analysis, the production could be considered both constructed and as mechanical analogue; the story provides enough rich content for viewers to make up their own minds about its meaning. Such storytelling, according to research by Costera Meijer (2007), is especially meaningful to younger people, who find generic news unappealing, but who value the opportunity to live through an event, be part of the news, and feel associated emotions. The transparent, experiential qualities inherent in solo videojournalism productions of this caliber offer a promising means of connecting with postmodern audiences.

In his emphasis on realism, Delozier produces a story that ultimately reflects qualities described by Carey in his call for a more humble journalism modeled on conversation rather than on the metaphor of objectivity and science (1993: 20). The solo videojournalist harnesses his formidable skills as an observer of the human condition, and as an interpreter in multiple media modes; it then gets out of the way of a great story.

Further reading

For readers wishing to learn more about semiotics, I recommend Marcel Danesi's *The Quest for Meaning: A Guide to Semiotic Theory and Practice* (2007), published by Toronto Studies in Semiotics and Communications, Toronto. *Reading Television*, by John Fiske and John Hartley (London: Routledge, 2005), offers an authoritative deep-dive into the medium, its impact on culture (and vice-versa), and semiotics itself. *The Changing Faces of Journalism: Tabloidization, Technology and Truthiness* (London: Routledge), edited by Barbie Zelizer (2009), captures multiple academic perspectives on journalism's future and will introduce readers to many of the world's leading communication scholars and their fields of inquiry.

References

Aker, P. (2012) "Photography, Objectivity, and the Modern Newspaper." *Journalism Studies* 13(3): 325–329.

Barthes, R. (1977) *Image, Music, Text.* New York, NY: Hill and Wang.

Becker, K. (2007) *Visual Cultures of Journalism.* Paper presented at the International Communication Association Annual Convention, San Francisco, CA, 23 May.

Bock, M.A. (2008) "Together in the Scrum." *Visual Communication Quarterly* 15(3): 169–179.

Bock, M.A. (2009) *One-Man Band: The Process and Product of Videojournalism.* Unpublished PhD dissertation, Annenberg School for Communication, University of Pennsylvania.

Bock, M.A. (2011) "You Really, Truly, Have to 'Be There': Video Journalism as a Social and Material Construction." *Journalism & Mass Communication Quarterly* 88(4): 705–718.

Carey, J. (1993) "The Mass Media and Democracy: Between the Modern and the Postmodern." *Journal of International Affairs* 47(1): 1–21.

Cole, T. (2015) "A Visual Remix." *The New York Times Magazine*, 12 May. Available from: http://www.nytimes.com/2015/04/19/magazine/a-visual-remix.html

Costera Meijer, I. (2001) "The Public Quality of Popular Journalism: Developing a Normative Framework." *Journalism Studies* 2(2): 189–205.

Costera Meijer, I. (2007) "The Paradox of Popularity: How Young People Experience the News." *Journalism Studies* 8(1): 96–116.

Costera Meijer, I. (2010) "Democratizing Journalism? Realizing the Citizen's Agenda for Local News Media." *Journalism Studies* 11(3): 327–342.

Danesi, M. (1999) *Of Cigarettes, High Heels, and Other Interesting Things*. New York, NY: St. Martin's Press.

Drew, J. (2010) "See It Now!" *Columbia Journalism Review* 49(3): 38–43.

Ekman, P. and Friesen, W. (2003) *Unmasking the Face: A Guide to Recognizing Emotions from Facial Expressions*. Cambridge, MA: Malor Books.

Greco, M. and Stenner, P. (2008) *Emotions: A Social Science Reader*. London, UK: Routledge.

Griffin, M. (2002) "Sociocultural Perspectives on Visual Communication." *Journal of Visual Literacy* 22(1): 29–52.

Hanson, R.E. (1997) "Objectivity and Narrative in Contemporary Reporting: A Formal Analysis." *Symbolic Interaction* 20(4): 385–396.

Harris, J.M. (2013) "'Truthful as the Record of Heaven': The Battle of Antietam and the Birth of Photojournalism." *Southern Cultures* 19(3): 79–94.

Jensen, K.B. (1991) "Humanistic Scholarship as Qualitative Science: Contributions to Mass Communication Research." In Jensen, K.B. and Jankowski, N.W. (eds) *A Handbook of Qualitative Methodologies for Mass Communication Research*. London, UK: Routledge, pp. 17–42.

Kitch, C. (2003) "'Mourning in America': Ritual, Redemption, and Recovery in News Narrative after September 11." *Journalism Studies* 4(2): 213–224.

Kitch, C. (2009) "Tears and Trauma in the News." In Zelizer, B. (ed.) *The Changing Faces of Journalism: Tabloidization, Technology and Truthiness*. London, UK: Routledge, pp. 29–39.

Kobre, K. (2000) *Photojournalism: The Professionals' Approach*. 4th edn. Boston, MA: Focal Press.

Kress, G. and van Leeuwen, T. (2001) *Multimodal Discourse: The Modes and Media of Contemporary Communication*. London, UK: Hodder Arnold.

Mäenpää, J. (2014) "Rethinking Photojournalism: The Changing Work Practices and Professionalism of Photojournalists in the Digital Age." *Nordicom Review* 35(2): 91–104.

McLuhan, M. (1964) *Understanding Media: The Extensions of Man*. Cambridge, MA: MIT Press.

Meyer, P. (2009) "Journalism History is Merely a List of Surprises." *Quill* 97(2): 18–21.

Meyrowitz, J. (1985) *No Sense of Place: The Impact of Electronic Media on Social Behaviour*. Oxford, UK: Oxford University Press.

Newton, J.H. (2009) "Photojournalism: Do People Matter? Then Photojournalism Matters." *Journalism Practice* 3(2): 233–243.

Nichols, B. (2010) *Introduction to Documentary*. 2nd edn. Bloomington, IN: Indiana University Press.

Pantti, M. (2010) "The Value of Emotion: An Examination of Television Journalists' Notions on Emotionality." *European Journal of Communication* 25(2): 168–181.

Pantti, M. and Sumiala, J. (2009) "Till Death Do Us Join: Media, Mourning Rituals and the Sacred Centre of the Society." *Media, Culture & Society* 31(1): 119–135.

Pantti, M. and Wahl-Jorgensen, K. (2011) "'Not an Act of God': Anger and Citizenship in Press Coverage of British Man-Made Disasters." *Media, Culture & Society* 33(1): 105–122.

Peer, L. and Ksiazek, T. (2011) "YouTube and the Challenge to Journalism." *Journalism Studies* 12(1): 45–63.

Penniman, N. (2009) "Video News Reporting: New Lessons in New Media." *Nieman Reports* 63(1): 25–27.

Richards, B. (2009) "Explosive Humiliation and News Media." In Sclater, S.D., Jones, D., Price, H. and Yates, C. (eds) *Emotion: New Psychosocial Perspectives*. New York, NY: Palgrave Macmillan, pp. 59–79.

Richards, B. and Rees, G. (2011) "The Management of Emotion in British Journalism." *Media, Culture & Society* 33(6): 851–867.

Rodriguez, L. and Dimitrova, D. (2008) *The Levels of Visual Framing*. Paper presented at the International Communication Association Annual Conference, Montreal, May.

Rosenblum, M. (2008) "Video News: The Videojournalist Comes of Age." *Nieman Reports* (Winter): 75–77.

Santana, A. and Russial, J. (2013) "Photojournalists' Role Expands at Most Daily U.S. Newspapers." *Newspaper Research Journal* 34(1): 74–88.

Schudson, M. (2001) "The Objectivity Norm in American Journalism." *Journalism* 2(2): 149–170.

Schwartz, D. (1992) "To Tell the Truth: Codes of Objectivity in Photojournalism." *Communication* 13(2): 95–109.

Shapiro, S. (2006) "Return of the Sob Sisters." *American Journalism Review* 28(3): 50.

Shook, F., Larson, J. and DeTarsio, J. (2009) *Television Field Production and Reporting*. 5th edn. Boston, MA: Pearson Education.

Smith, S. (2011) *Going Solo: Doing Videojournalism in the 21st Century*. Columbia, MO: University of Missouri Press.

Sontag, S. (1973) *On Photography*. New York, NY: Picador.

Tripp, S. (2012) "From TVTV to YouTube: A Genealogy of Participatory Practices in Video." *Journal of Film and Video* 64(1): 5–16.

Tuchman, G. (1972) "Objectivity as Strategic Ritual: An Examination of Newsmen's Notions of Objectivity." *American Journal of Sociology* 77(4): 660–679.

United States Army (2011) "Soldier's Creed." Available from: http://www.army.mil/values/soldiers.html.

van Leeuwen, T. (2005) *Introducing Social Semiotics*. London, UK: Routledge.

Wahl-Jorgensen, K. (2013) "The Strategic Ritual of Emotionality: A Case Study of Pulitzer Prize-Winning Articles." *Journalism* 14(1): 129–145.

Wallace, S. (2009) "Watchdog or Witness? The Emerging Forms and Practices of Videojournalism." *Journalism* 10(5): 684–701.

Wolfe, T. (1973) "Seizing the Power." In Wolfe, T. and Johnson, E.W. (eds) *The New Journalism*. New York, NY: Harper and Row, pp. 23–36.

Zelizer, B. (2007) "On 'Having Been There': Eyewitnessing as a Journalistic Key Word." *Critical Studies in Media Communication* 24(5): 408–428.

Zelizer, B. (ed.) (2009) *The Changing Faces of Journalism: Tabloidization, Technology and Truthiness*. London: Routledge.

PART VIII

Digital journalism content

44

CONVERGED MEDIA CONTENT

Reshaping the 'legacy' of legacy media in the online scenario

Jose A. García-Avilés, Klaus Meier, and Andy Kaltenbrunner

Journalism is currently in a state of flux, as it is undergoing structural changes which are reshaping it as a practice, as a product, and as a profession (Spyridou *et al.*, 2013: 77). In the context of rapid transformation, legacy media have been credited with preservation of the ideals of journalism and its community-building purposes (Kelly, 2010). Accordingly, legacy media are said to preserve quality and professional standards, while their future is jeopardized both by a business and an identity crisis. Such an assessment, however, needs to also explain important variations in distinctive national settings and market sectors (Franklin, 2012). Besides, legacy and online media still share common ground in many aspects as they cover similar issues, use similar sources, and share common practices (Maier, 2010).

The convergence of legacy and online media: a challenging scenario

Online media, understood as 'post-industrial' journalism, pose a tremendous challenge to legacy media and its professionals (Anderson *et al.*, 2012). As the BBC's *Future of News Report* (2015) emphasizes, collaborative journalism is crucial for strengthening an outlet's relationship with its audience, as well as for pursuing a broader range of stories. Thus, legacy media implement strategies that respond to disruptive changes in the industry, as outlined in the *New York Times'* 'Innovation Report' (2014: 1), whose objective is to "to expand the reach and impact of our journalism at a time when technology, user behavior and our competitors are evolving more rapidly than ever."

The transformation of journalism has attracted research interest from different perspectives, including media management (Killebrew, 2005; Dal Zotto and van Kranenburg, 2008), interactive technologies (Gynnild, 2014), the shifting relationships with active audiences and social media users (Singer *et al.*, 2011), emerging business models (Carvajal *et al.*, 2012; Nee, 2013), and media innovation (Krumsvik and Storsul, 2013), to name just a few. The popularity of Web 2.0, both as a technological and a societal development (Jenkins, 2006), has opened up new ways of engagement, self-expression, and media consumption. It has also expanded what has been described as 'networked' journalism (Beckett and Mansell, 2008), 'participatory' journalism (Singer *et al.*, 2011), or 'convergent' journalism (Erdal, 2007).

Media convergence takes different dimensions that shape communication, including technological, professional, structural, and operational (Erdal, 2007). Technological convergence implies that digital devices equipped with displays—smartphones, tablets, watches, etc.—enable the sharing of any kind of content, with broad cultural and trans-media implications (Jenkins, 2006; see also Westlund, this volume). Professional convergence tends to focus on the changes in organization, professional practices, and content production in media houses. The process of digitization has obliged legacy media corporations to migrate from a production model that was constrained by the medium of reception to another model, which is relatively independent of this factor.

In a world of globalizing media markets, knowledge about convergence and news content production for several platforms can best be gained with an international perspective. Cases of media convergence occur with varying degrees of complexity, depending on the different cultures, companies, and countries that are involved (Kaltenbrunner and Meier, 2013). Newsrooms are undergoing a makeover process whose main catalysts are the complex changes taking place in the market, along with a shift towards the digital domain within media value creation chains.

The key consideration this chapter addresses is how legacy media have managed the transition into the digital world, reshaping the 'legacy' in the online scenario. Therefore, we are focusing on three crucial factors: (1) the basic preconditions for convergence and the pressure for legacy media enterprises to move into the digital world, (2) the description of different models and cases of newsroom convergence, and (3) innovation management and entrepreneurship.

In our research, we compare parameters and cases from different countries, mainly Austria, Germany, and Spain, but also from other countries, such as the United States and United Kingdom. The case study method offers a valid tool for analyzing a complex phenomenon in its own context. Case studies have frequently been used as a methodological tool to examine the implications of newsroom convergence (Erdal, 2011; García-Avilés, Kaltenbrunner, and Meier, 2014; García-Avilés *et al.*, 2009). To validate its conclusions, this type of qualitative method relies on sources such as direct observation, interviews, written records, and other documents.

Media landscapes as basic preconditions for convergence

Convergence development and the pressure for legacy media enterprises to move into the digital world are not only affected by the economic and strategic interests of publishers and broadcasters, but also by national parameters: general economic conditions and market situations for media enterprises, regulation or deregulation of communication legislation, and traditions and cultures of user behavior. We discuss these basic parameters as exemplified by three different media markets: Austria, Germany, and Spain.

The media in Austria: basic parameters

Austria was characterized as part of the Democratic Corporatist Model of journalistic cultures by Hallin and Mancini (2004). Some key features included a strong party press, press subsidies to support pluralism since the 1970s, and the prominence of the public broadcaster *ORF* in the audiovisual market. Yet, following reluctant changes in Austrian media politics (Kaltenbrunner, 2006) after the privatization of radio (1994) and television (2001), *ORF* is losing audience to the benefit of new national competitors and to the German commercial channels (e.g. *Sat1* and *RTL*).

High newspaper circulation (readership at levels above 70 percent of the population) places Austria in a top international position in terms of daily newspaper consumption (*Media-Analyse*, 2014). At the same time, only 15 newspapers remain in the market, which is a clear sign of national oligopolies and regional monopolies with ongoing concentration processes (Karmasin *et al.*, 2011: 22–35). The strongest groups of media owners, the German Funke-group (former WAZ group), Bertelsmann's Gruner+Jahr, the Austrian Raiffeisen Group, and the Dichand family (who control, along with other media operations, the largest national paper *Kronen Zeitung*) are interlinked in ownerships in multiple ways, cooperating in media production and distribution, and acting as partners in media printing (Steinmaurer, 2002). While over the last decades many newspapers have had to shut down, one success story of a printed medium was the foundation in 2004 of the free daily *heute*, which has become the most widely read tabloid in Austria's capital, Vienna. It too is owned by a foundation of members of the Dichand family, in partnership with a foundation strongly influenced and supported by the City of Vienna.

Advertising income in the Austrian newspaper market has been declining steadily, but at a lesser rate than in most European countries. The general forecast in the OECD's *The Evolution of News and the internet* in 2010 saw Austria in a more comfortable position than most other OECD countries with regard to the estimated decline of newspaper markets (OECD, 2010: 18). Losses in legacy media have largely been substituted by an increasing amount of public spending for campaigns run by ministries, publicly (co-)owned companies, and regional governments. While official Austrian press subsidies for newspapers have fallen to an all-time low of 8 million Euros per year, the advertisement expenses of federal and regional authorities, cities, and public bodies have exceeded 200 million Euros a year (*Medientransparenz Austria*, 2014). This has further condensed the *Beziehungsgeflecht* (Kaltenbrunner, 2006), that is, the interwoven web of relationships between politics and media in Austria.

The media in Germany: basic parameters

The German daily newspaper market is characterized by a large number of regional titles (336, with a total sold circulation of 12.6 million copies) and seven national papers (1.2 million), of which the vast majority is sold by subscription. Only eight daily newspapers are regularly sold at the newsstand (3.1 million) (BDZV, 2015; Meier, 2009). The ongoing decline in circulation (down 30 percent between 2000 and 2015) and advertising income (down 56 percent between 2000 and 2013) shows significant differences (Meier, 2015): while papers in economically strong regions record virtually no decline in circulation (e.g. *Donaukurier* from Ingolstadt had almost the same circulation in 2014 as in 2000), the regional papers in weak regions and some metropolises, as well as the tabloids, are losing circulation overall (e.g. *Bild* from 4.3 million in 2000 to 2.1 million in 2014). The main task of German newspaper publishers in the last two years has been erecting paywalls: At the end of 2014, more than 100 online editions of newspapers were using pay models (see Myllylahti, this volume). The most important forerunner was Axel Springer Verlag, Berlin, with paywalls for *bild.de* (2013) and *welt.de* (2012). In 2015, the internet reached 76 percent of the population (56 million online users) (www.agof.de); with about 50 percent of them using mobile devices for internet access (www.ard-zdf-onlinestudie.de).

The online advertising market is currently growing by about 7–15 percent per year, significantly slowing down from up to a 100 percent growth at the beginning of the millennium (www.zaw.de). The TV and radio sector is characterized by the dual system of two strong public broadcasting corporations (ARD and ZDF, with a market share of about 40 percent in TV and over 50 percent in radio) and a successful commercial broadcasting sector. ARD and ZDF suffer from government-mandated limits on online activities intended to prevent unfair competition between the online platforms of commercial media enterprises and stations funded by public license fees.

The media in Spain: basic parameters

The Spanish media are undergoing a severe crisis, following a decline in advertising revenue that accompanied the adaptation to the digital world and global recession. This has obliged them to rethink their future. Since 2008, print media have suffered a steady decline in circulation and advertising income. According to official figures, advertising spending in 2014 was divided between 41.7 percent in television, 21.1 percent online, 14.5 percent in print, and 9.3 percent in radio. A decline of almost 20 percent from 2008 to 2014 in print advertising income has shrunk the number of local editions of both pay and free newspapers and, similarly, reduced the number of copies distributed in the big cities.

Commercial broadcast media takeovers and mergers have reduced pluralism and increased market concentration, and only two large companies remain in the field: Mediaset and Atresmedia (Llorens, Luzón, and Grau, 2013). Online-only editions are proliferating in an unstable environment and lack clear business models. Since 2008, over 300 journalism startups have been launched (APM, 2015), staffed by a mix of veteran journalists laid off during the economic crisis and young journalists trying to gain a foothold in the industry. This reshuffling has added more uncertainty to an already precarious labor market: massive lay-offs were common in the media between 2008 and 2011, and have continued on a smaller scale since 2012 (APM, 2015).

Despite the growing popularity of social media, especially among young people, the majority of the viewing audience remains faithful to television as the main entertainment and news source, and the level of consumption has actually increased. At the same time, Spain has the second-highest mobile broadband and smart phone penetration levels in the EU after Italy: market research indicates that 81.7 percent of people access the internet from a smart phone (Fundación Telefónica, 2015: 34).

The most visited news media websites seem to replicate the market shares of publishers and broadcasters offline. They include the sports daily *Marca*; quality newspapers such as *El País*, *El Mundo*, and *ABC*; commercial networks Telecinco.es and Antena3.com, and public broadcaster Rtve.es. Legacy media outlets are the only ones still practicing investigative journalism, because of three key elements: budgets, staff and contacts. Many online-only news outlets concentrate not on producing original news, but rather on selecting and disseminating stories from the traditional media.

Newsroom convergence

Convergent newsrooms use the opportunities of digitization to conserve or even to increase their reach within a highly competitive audience market. Legacy media enterprises attempt to make up for the continuous losses in young patrons and to reach the stationary and mobile internet audiences, which hardly acknowledge conventional publications. Therefore, newsroom managers shift resources from legacy publications to digital publications; but the possibilities for newsroom convergence are multifaceted. In previous studies (García-Avilés, Kaltenbrunner, and Meier, 2014; García-Avilés *et al.*, 2009), we developed a matrix based on descriptors designed to measure the effectiveness of newsroom convergence: project focus, editorial management, journalists' practices, and work organization. Larrondo *et al.* (2014)

used this matrix to analyze the convergence processes of five European mid-sized public broadcasting corporations.

Each media house implements a different kind of convergence model. Thus, it is possible to distinguish models ranging from full integration to the coordination of isolated platforms, including different cross-media strategies (García-Avilés *et al.*, 2009). Large companies and public corporations have typically adopted a cross-media model, with distinct newsrooms for each media outlet and no contact between them. While in some cases newsroom redesign involves high technological standards and brings together journalists from all platforms into one common space, the editorial staff's approach towards convergence is often still reluctant and training programs in multiskilling have hardly been implemented.

In a comparative research project in several European media companies, we examined the implications of producing content for multiple platforms (García-Avilés, Kaltenbrunner, and Meier, 2014). News production for several platforms is rapidly changing the conditions of newsroom organization and journalists' practices. The shift towards the digital domain within the media value-creation chain engenders new debates on newsroom strategies. Early adopters of integration environments are remodeling their workflows, gearing them towards content and section logic, following the commandments of ultra-fast web dissemination. At the same time, high-quality formats are being developed, involving longer research, deeper content production, and more elaborate graphic processing. Media professionals are increasingly taking into account the redefinition of their job profiles and the consequences for their companies' business models, as well as the changing demands of their audiences.

Journalistic convergence, then, should not be regarded as just an 'effect' of corporate or technological trends (Fagerjord and Storsul, 2007). Technical innovation is usually based on professional and economic decisions, and journalists adapt new tools to their own expectations, skills, and routines. Therefore, journalistic convergence must be discussed not as a technology-driven process, but rather as a process that uses technological innovation to achieve specific goals in particular settings, and that is why each convergence project can reach a different outcome.

Newsroom convergence in Austria

Some Austrian media enterprises were early in embracing digital change. The daily *Der Standard* started its Web presence with *DerStandard.at* in 1994, the first online edition of a German language newspaper (García-Avilés *et al.*, 2009: 298–299). With its print and online operations, the *Vorarlberger Medienhaus* (today: *Russ Media*) was also very active in promoting a fast-growing regional internet service as early as the mid-1990s. The *Austria Presse Agentur* (APA), after developing many digital services for new customers, successfully moved its staff into a new multimedia newsroom in 2005 (Meier, 2007). The newly-founded newspaper *Österreich* and its digital outlet *oe24.at* started their newspaper, online and Web-TV editing activities in a large newsroom in 2006—but with clearly separated editorial staff and some cross-media cooperation (García-Avilés *et al.*, 2009).

Despite such pioneering endeavors, embracing the internet as a new channel for journalism newsroom convergence was not *the* media strategy a decade ago. It was only after 2010 that Austrian newspapers started discussing integration processes in state-of-the-art newsrooms. The small business daily *WirtschaftsBlatt* brought print and online news closer together on its news desks in 2012. *Der Standard* moved into new premises at the beginning of 2013. The original plan to keep online and print journalists separated was scrapped only a few weeks after migrating to the new newsroom, and editorial staff was fully amalgamated (García-Avilés, Kaltenbrunner, and Meier, 2014).

In a survey for the Austrian *Journalisten-Report IV* (Kaltenbrunner, Karmasin and Kraus, 2013), 85 percent of the 131 media managers interviewed considered the convergence of legacy and new digital channels very important for their companies' economic success. Additional media jumped on the bandwagon: *Tiroler Tageszeitung* moved into a newsroom in Innsbruck's city center and encouraged step-by-step, cross-media operations of its 100-journalist editorial staff. *Styria*, Austria's biggest publishing group by circulation, opened its new headquarters and newsroom in Graz in the spring of 2015. Its *Kleine Zeitung*, market leader in Styria and Carinthia, is set to continue as the profitable editorial flagship in a more integrated newsroom environment including Styria's radio and television operations, for "fast creative communication," its editor-in-chief explains (Styria, 2015).

The public broadcaster *ORF* announced plans to move hundreds of TV, radio, and online journalists into a new integrated newsroom, an annex of its current television center, by 2020. As with many broadcasters undergoing difficult integration processes in other countries, this announcement provoked discussions, hopes, and fears among the editorial staff of Austria' biggest media company (see *DerStandard.at*, 2015). After the decision of ORF's Stiftungsrat [steering committee] to finance said newsroom building, ORF CEO argues that the integration process is irreversible and he characterizes media convergence as 'today's most challenging scenario.'

This will be the case for all Austrian legacy media in the coming years, following a decade of rather slow digitization and very cautious access to integration processes, particularly when compared to the media industries of the Anglo-Saxon and Northern European countries.

Newsroom convergence in Germany

In Germany, legacy media enterprises hesitated to rush into the digital world. Among the publishers of daily newspapers, Axel Springer Verlag, Berlin, was one of the forerunners, integrating the editorial departments of several print and online publications as early as 2006 within the *Welt* Group (García-Avilés, Kaltenbrunner, and Meier, 2014: 576–577). True to the motto 'online first,' the online department uploads all articles onto the web as soon as they are completed—for free. Since 2012, the scope of news products has undergone significant diversification. 'Digital' has replaced 'online,' with an independent mobile browser range rounded off by various apps for smart phones and tablets. In December 2013, around 120 journalists moved into a large central newsroom geared to digital production. The motto 'online first' gave way to the 'digital to print' strategy: The journalists work for digital publishing first, and then produce daily papers out of what they had initially produced for digital channels. In newsroom staff meetings, 'issues' take center-stage—a shift from 'the printed page logic.' A change in the business model is at the root of this new approach: After the introduction of a 'metered paywall,' online publications pushed to reach quality standards high enough to loosen users' purse strings. In April 2015, CEO Mathias Döpfner said that *Die Welt* had reached 60,000 digital subscribers (W&V, 2015).

Whereas respected weekly publications like *Die Zeit* or *Der Spiegel* work with relatively distinct print and online editorial departments and free websites, the largest national quality daily *Süddeutsche Zeitung* followed the Springer strategy by introducing a paywall and a bundle of digital publications in 2015. At the same time, it launched an editorial cross-media strategy built around a central hub for print and online managing editors. The public broadcaster ARD—a consortium of nine autonomous (state-independent, but publicly funded) regional corporations—has taken several steps toward digital publications and cross-media integration of newsroom teams. The most transformative processes are occurring at the *Bayerischer*

Rundfunk, developing a topic-oriented newsroom structure instead of the old program logic (Spanner-Ulmer, 2014). New buildings featuring an integrated architecture for TV, radio, and digital platforms staffed by hundreds of journalists have been erected in Nuremberg and are planned for Munich.

Newsroom convergence in Spain: the case of El Mundo

El Mundo was launched in 1989 and is the flagship publication of Unidad Editorial, which is owned by the Italian group RCS Rizzoli. Its print edition reached a circulation of 134,000 in March 2015 (OJD's audit bureau); its web edition *Elmundo.es* is Spain's online market leader, with over 7.3 million unique users in January 2015, according to ComScore.

The integration process was initiated in *El Mundo's* newsroom in July 2007, when the print and online sections of Science, Communication, Infographics, and Sports were merged to produce content across media boundaries. Newspaper journalists showed initial reticence towards working for the web, due to the traditional importance given to the print edition. But this attitude changed as print journalists realized the importance of the website in reaching a broader audience, achieving more visibility, and receiving instant feedback.

El Mundo's newsroom integration blurred the lines between print and online operations, with newspaper journalists now expected to work on online projects. Multiskilled journalists gather information using multiple tools (such as audiovisual recording, photography, and database mining) and combine multiple-format elements into one story, or adapt the materials to the specific requirements of different outlets. Multiskilling may give reporters more control over the final products, but can, on the other hand, overload them with technical procedures. Editors say there is no difference any more between online and print journalists.

According to management, the integrated newsroom has not changed the principles of the editorial process drastically. Instead, integration has changed staffers' perception of the process: they are now thinking in terms of the content's suitability for a specific medium. All print and online sections are integrated, with information pooled in a central 'breaking news' desk to be rerouted to the various sections. Setting the news priorities at any given time, that same central hub issues all decisions on breaking news and the home page.

The differences between print journalists and their web counterparts in terms of their labor contracts have also disappeared: they all belong to the same company now and benefit from similar remuneration agreements. Print and online journalists have been grouped by area of specialization into so-called sections, such as health, education, politics or media, and technology, and can upload their articles autonomously, straight to the web. The picture desk is now fully integrated as a multimedia department made up of 30 professionals and photographers trained in video.

Innovation management and entrepreneurship

The success of newsroom innovation strategies depends on a variety of factors (see Meier, 2007). Case studies have shown that innovation in multiplatform newsrooms is linked to the roll-out of projects involving people and resources for the purposes of the production processes, and not the other way round (García-Avilés, 2012). The ability of newsroom leaders to innovate in cross-media management is just as important as innovation in products or services, as management has a direct bearing on journalistic standards and the quality of the news output. In media outlets that have implemented strategies to develop multiplatform products and improve content quality, innovation has required effective communication from management, as well as a general upgrade of production processes (Killebrew, 2005). A survey in Switzerland has explored that a multi-platform strategy is effective in overcoming procedural inertia and can contribute to maximize the innovative capacities of a news organization (Lischka, 2015).

A number of quality news organizations, such as the *New York Times* and the *Washington Post,* have created entrepreneurial units as in-house innovation labs in order to infuse new ideas, experimentation, and creativity across the newsroom. But as Boyles (2015) argues, there are several barriers toward their success, particularly the way media labs are insulated and isolated from the lifeblood of the broader news organization. To remove the tensions between the traditional and entrepreneurial news cultures, it is recommended to at least integrate employees from the traditional newsroom into the lab for a short rotation, to give reporters more time and freedom to experiment, and to pair entrepreneurial employees with news workers in teams, "forcing a linkage of skills" (Boyles, 2015: 13). Furthermore, a "capability to be innovative" is becoming more and more important in the education and training of journalists (Meier *et al.*, 2012: 313). Thus, labs at university journalism programs should connect the development of innovative products with innovation research which empirically evaluates journalists' output and work practices (Meier, 2014: 171–172).

At the same time, such investments into experiments in newsroom and cross-media laboratories are becoming increasingly difficult for legacy media, as Ken Doctor analyzes for Harvard's Nieman Lab, using business data from 10 of the largest US newspaper companies. The permanent loss of profits is "cutting into newspapers' chances at innovation" (Doctor, 2015).

The pace and scope of technological progress in the media industry urgently demands innovation and organizational change. But innovation must involve something more than the standard routines and practices of news production. As the need for newsroom coordination and integration grows, media professionals are learning to take into account its consequences for their economic survival and the redefinition of their jobs, as well as the changing demands of their audiences. Legacy media companies have no other choice than to transform themselves, to act strategically in order to improve their editorial processes and products, as well as their business models and organizational structures.

Further reading

This chapter has benefited from Andy Kaltenbrunner's and Klaus Meier's "Convergent Journalism—Newsrooms, Routines, Job Profiles and Training" (2013). In 2009, José A. García-Avilés *et al.* published a newsroom convergence matrix for analysis and comparison, which could be applied to legacy media. The models and matrix were confirmed later (García-Avilés, Kaltenbrunner, and Meier, 2014)—and enriched with new details and descriptors. Larrondo *et al.* (2014) used this matrix to analyze the convergence processes of public broadcasting corporations. Boyles' "The isolation of innovation" (2015) also throws light on intrapreneurship and implementing in-house innovation labs in order to infuse new ideas, experimentation, and creativity.

References

Anderson, C.W., Bell, E. and Shirky, C. (2012) *Post-industrial Journalism: Adapting to the Present: A Report.* New York, NY: Columbia Journalism School. Available from: http://towcenter.org/research/post-industrial-journalism/.

Asociación de la Prensa de Madrid (APM) (2015) *Informe Anual de la Profesión Periodística 2015.* Madrid, Spain: APM.

BBC (2015) *Future of News Report*. Available from: http://newsimg.bbc.co.uk/1/shared/bsp/hi/pdfs/28_01_15futureofnews.pdf.

BDZV (2015) *Die deutschen Zeitungen in Zahlen und Daten 2015*. Available from: http://www.bdzv.de/fileadmin/bdzv_hauptseite/aktuell/publikationen/2014/assets/Zahlen_Daten_2015.pdf.

Beckett, C. and Mansell, R. (2008) "Crossing Boundaries: New Media and Networked Journalism." *Communication, Culture and Critique* 1(1): 92–104.

Boyles, J.L. (2015) "The Isolation of Innovation: Restructuring the Digital Newsroom through Intrapreneurship." *Digital Journalism* 4(2): 229–246.

Carvajal, M., García-Avilés, J.A. and González, J.L. (2012) "Crowdfunding and Non-Profit Media: The Emergence of New Models for Public Interest Journalism." *Journalism Practice* 6(5–6): 638–647.

Dal Zotto, C. and van Kranenburg, H. (eds) (2008) *Management and Innovation in the Media Industry*. Cheltenham, UK: Edward Elgar.

DerStandard.at (2015) "ORF-Newsroom: Bornemann—Nicht in jede Geschichte hineinregieren." 19.3.2015. Available from: http://derstandard.at/2000013178316/Wrabetz-Newsroom-Pluralismus-schon-alleine-durch-Personenzahl.

Doctor, K. (2015) *Newsonomics: Razor-Thin Profits are Cutting into Newspapers' Chances at Innovation*. Available from: http://www.niemanlab.org/2015/05/newsonomics-razor-thin-profits-are-cutting-into-newspapers-chances-at-innovation/.

Erdal, I.J. (2007) "Researching Media Convergence and Crossmedia News Production. Mapping the Field." *Nordicom Review* 28(2): 51–16.

Erdal, I.J. (2011) "Coming to Terms with Convergence Journalism: Cross-Media as a Theoretical and Analytical Concept." *Convergence: The International Journal of Research into New Media Technologies* 17(2): 213–223.

Fagerjord, A. and Storsul, T. (2007) "Questioning Convergence." In Storsul, T. and Stuedahl, D. (eds) *Ambivalence Towards Convergence: Digitalization and Media Change*. Goteborg, Sweden: Nordicom, pp. 19–31.

Franklin, B. (2012) "The Future of Journalism: Developments and Debates." *Journalism Studies* 13(5–6): 663–681.

Fundación Telefónica (2015) *Informe de la Sociedad de la Información en España*. Available from: http://www.fundaciontelefonica.com/arte_cultura/publicaciones-listado/pagina-item-publicaciones/?itempubli=323.

García-Avilés, J.A. (2012) "Innovation Management in Crossmedia Production: Leading Change in the Newsroom." In Ibrus, I. and Scolari, C.A. (eds) *Crossmedia Innovations: Texts, Markets, Institutions*. Frankfurt, Germany: Peter Lang, pp. 259–276.

García-Avilés, J.A., Kaltenbrunner, A. and Meier, K. (2014) "Media Convergence Revisited: Lessons Learned on Newsroom Integration in Austria, Germany and Spain." *Journalism Practice* 8(5): 573–584.

García Avilés, J.A., Meier, K., Kaltenbrunner, A., Carvajal, M. and Kraus, D. (2009) "Newsroom Integration in Austria, Spain and Germany. Models of Media Convergence." *Journalism Practice* 3(3): 285–303.

Gynnild, A. (2014) "Journalism Innovation Leads to Innovation Journalism: The Impact of Computational Exploration on Changing Mindsets." *Journalism* 15(6): 713–730.

Hallin, D. and Mancini, P. (2004) *Comparing Media Systems: Three Models of Media and Politics*. Cambridge, UK: Cambridge University Press.

Jenkins, H. (2006) *Convergence Culture. Where Old and New Media Collide*. New York, NY: New York University Press.

Kaltenbrunner, A. (2006) "Medienpolitik." In Tálos, E. (ed.) *Schwarz-Blau. Eine Bilanz des Neu-Regierens*. Wien: Lit Verlag, pp. 117–136.

Kaltenbrunner, A. and Meier, K. (2013) "Convergent Journalism—Newsrooms, Routines, Job Profiles and Training." In Diehl, S. and Karmasin, M. (eds) *Media and Convergence Management*. Berlin: Springer, pp. 285–298.

Kaltenbrunner, A., Karmasin, M. and Kraus, D. (eds) (2013) *Der Journalisten-Report IV. Medienmanagement in Österreich*. Wien: Facultas.

Karmasin, M., Kraus, D., Kaltenbrunner, A. and Bichler, K. (2011) "Austria: A Border-Crosser." In Eberwein, T., Fengler, S., Lauk, E. and Leppik-Bork, T. (eds) *Mapping Media Accountability—in Europe and Beyond*. Köln: Herbert von Halem Verlag, pp. 22–35.

Kelly, J. (2010) "Parsing the Online Ecosystem: Journalism, Media, and the Blogosphere." In Einav. G. (ed.) *Transitioned Media*. New York, NY: Springer, pp. 93–108.

Killebrew, K.C. (2005) *Managing Media Convergence: Pathways to Journalistic Cooperation*. Ames, Iowa: Blackwell.

Krumsvik, A. and Storsul, T. (eds) (2013) *Media Innovations: A Multidisciplinary Study of Change*. Göteborg: Nordicom.

Larrondo, A., Domingo, D., Erdal, I.J., Masip, P. and Van den Bulck, H. (2014) "Opportunities and Limitations of Newsroom Convergence. A comparative study on European Public Service Broadcasting Organisations." *Journalism Studies* 17(4): 277–300. DOI: 10.1080/1461670X.2014.977611.

Lischka, J.A. (2015) "How Structural Multi-Platform Newsroom Features and Innovative Values Alter Journalistic Cross-Channel and Cross-Sectional Working Procedures." *Journal of Media Business Studies* 12: 7–28.

Llorens, C., Luzón, V. and Grau, H.P. (2013) "Mapping Digital Media and Journalism in Spain." *Anàlisi: Quaderns de comunicació i cultura* 49: 43–64.

Maier, S. (2010) "All the News Fit to Post? Comparing News Content on the Web to Newspapers, Television and Radio." *Journalism & Mass Communication Quarterly* 87(3–4): 548–562.

Media-Analyse (2014) MA 2014—*Tageszeitungen Total*. Available from: http://www.mediaanalyse.at/studienPublicPresseTageszeitungTotal.do?year=2014&title=Tageszeitungen&subtitle=Total.

Medientransparenz Austria (2014) *Eine Übersicht über steuerfinanzierte Medien-Kooperationen und – Förderungen*. Available from: http://www.medien-transparenz.at/#!/overview.

Meier, K. (2007) "Innovations in Central European Newsrooms: Overview and Case Study." *Journalism Practice* 1(1): 4–19.

Meier, K. (2009) "Germany: Newsroom Innovations and Newsroom Convergence." In Ruß-Mohl, St. and Fioretti, N. (eds) *Merging Media, Converging Newsrooms*. Bellinzona, Switzerland: Casagrande, pp. 37–49.

Meier, K. (2014) "Transfer empirischer Evidenz. Entwurf eines reformierten Leitbilds und Programms der Journalistik." *Publizistik* 59(2): 159–178.

Meier, K. (2015) *Zwischen Hofberichterstattung und kritischer Öffentlichkeit. Lokale Medienlandschaft und kommunale Demokratie im digitalen Zeitalter*. Düsseldorf: Heinrich Böll Stiftung. Available from: http://gutvertreten.boell.de/2015/02/28/klaus-meier-zwischen-hofberichterstattung-und-kritischer-offentlichkeit.

Meier, K., Giese, V. and Schweigmann, T. (2012) "Das, Kreuzen' der Medien: Das Konzept des crossmedialen Labors." In Dernbach, B. and Loosen, W. (eds) *Didaktik der Journalistik. Konzepte, Methoden und Beispiele aus der Journalistenausbildung*. Wiesbaden: Springer Fachmedien, pp. 311–322.

Nee, R.C. (2013) "Creative Destruction: An Exploratory Study of How Digitally Native News Nonprofits are Innovating Online Journalism Practices." *International Journal on Media Management* 15(1): 3–22.

The New York Times (2014) "The New York Times Innovation Report." Available from: http://visualdays.no/files/2014/05/224608514-The-Full-New-York-Times-Innovation-Report.pdf.

OECD (2010) *The Evolution of News and the Internet*. Available from: http://www.oecd.org/sti/ieconomy/45559596.pdf.

Singer, J.B., Hermida, A., Domingo, D., Heinonen, A., Quandt, T., Paulussen, S. et al. (2011) *Participatory Journalism: Guarding Open Gates at Online Newspapers*. Chichester, UK: Wiley-Blackwell.

Spanner-Ulmer, B. (2014) "Transformation und Management: Wie lässt sich ein etabliertes Medienunternehmen in die crossmediale Welt führen?" *Medienwirtschaft* 11(4): 45–46.

Spyridou, L.-P., Matsiola, M., Veglis, A., Kalliris, G. and Dimoulas, C. (2013) "Journalism in a State of Flux: Journalists as Agents of Technology Innovation and Emerging News Practices." *International Communication Gazette* 75(1): 76–98.

Steinmaurer, T. (2002) *Konzentriert und verflochten. Österreichs Mediensysteme im Überblick*. Innsbruck: Studien Verlag.

Styria (2015) *Die neuen DJs im Raumschiff Enterprise*. Available from: http://www.styria.com/-/im-focus-newsroom.

W&V (2015) "Döpfner: Paid Content Klappt Immer Besser." *w&v*, 16 April. Available from: http://www.wuv.de/medien/doepfner_paid_content_klappt_immer_besser.

45

NEWSPAPERS AND REPORTING

Keystones of the journalistic field

David Ryfe

Observers have noted for years that print reporters have had difficulty adapting to the digital world (e.g. Anderson *et al.*, 2014; Ryfe, 2012). The point remains valid. Take a moment to examine the website of any mainstream newspaper in the United States. For illustrative purposes, I have chosen sfgate.com—the website of the *San Francisco Chronicle*. It is May 5, 2015 at 6:00 a.m., Pacific Time. What do we find? We find a navigation strip at the top that replicates sections of the print product (e.g. news, sports, business, A&E, Food, Living, Travel, etc.). We find the page populated by conventional news stories. These stories are mostly about time-honored topics, like real estate development, an earthquake, a murder, a mayor's legislative proposal, a lawsuit filed by a local city. Public officials and experts serve as sources for these stories, as they have done for decades. And the stories are written mostly in conventional forms, like the 'who, what, when, where' lead: "In her first budget since being elected on the promise that she would strengthen public safety in Oakland," one such lead begins, "Mayor Libby Shaaf is pushing a plan to boost the city's police force..." What do we find, in other words? We find persistence, specifically, the persistence of 'reporting news,' by which I mean the set of practices associated with patrolling beats, interacting with officials and experts, applying standards of newsworthiness, and packaging information in story formulas to produce conventional news stories.

What does it mean that newspapers, and the reporters who work for them, have not adapted much of their work to the new environment they face? It does not mean that they remain passive. Newspapers and newspaper journalists *are* changing. Compared to a decade ago, their work is more collaborative and distributed. It is more data-driven and is faster-paced. It contains more interactive and multimedia elements. Even the job titles are different. I walked into a newspaper newsroom recently and was greeted by a 'community engagement manager' and a 'consumer experience coordinator.' More importantly, it does not mean that journalists alone are responsible for the persistence of longstanding practices and values. Of course, journalists embrace these practices and values, but so do actors outside of newsrooms—public officials and advertisers, managers of community news sites, and audiences. I have found that these individuals often have an investment in newspapers and reporting that nearly matches that of print journalists.

The reporting that takes place at newspapers, this is to say, is a *keystone* of the journalistic field. I borrow the term from Nielsen (2015), who shows, as others have done (e.g. Pew, 2015;

Waldman, 2011), that newspapers produce and circulate the vast majority of news in local communities, in his case a local Danish community. Just as an actual keystone locks the pieces of a crown in place, so reporting—and the newspapers where it is practiced—continues to lend a degree of coherence to the field of journalism. It is an activity that allows everything else, and everyone else, to find their place in the field. As such, it is as important to non-journalists in the field of journalism as it is to print reporters.

That, in any event, is the argument I pursue in this chapter. Drawing on my own research inside and outside of newsrooms, as well as the wider literature, I show that newspaper reporting remains a crucial set of practices and values within the field—for journalists and for others who now find themselves in the field's orbit. I end the chapter with an effort to explain why reporting continues to have traction in a fast-changing field. This explanation, I believe, lies in understanding how journalism works as a field of cultural production. I begin, however, with a brief discussion of changes that have taken place in newspaper journalism as it migrates to digital environments.

Changes in newspaper journalism

As much as any actor, newspapers have been forced to adapt to the turmoil that has enveloped the journalistic field. To my mind, five changes in particular stand out. These changes do not affect every kind of newspaper in every society; some describe regional newspapers better than small town papers. Some changes are taking place more quickly in some societies, like the United States, and less quickly in others, like Scandinavia. Still, together they represent five of the most pervasive trends in newspaper journalism in the transition to digital journalism.

First, and perhaps most obviously, *newspapers are smaller* than they once were, in some cases much smaller. In the United States, for instance, the regional daily newspaper still employs 60–70 percent of working journalists in any given region—but it is half the size it once was (e.g. Pew, 2015). Again, this is less true elsewhere (Krumsvik, 2012; Levy and Nielsen, 2010; Nossek *et al.*, 2015). Still, the general arc of the story throughout Western Europe is the same: circulation declines beget revenue slides that translate into a smaller number of working journalists.

Second, news production at newspapers is more *collaborative and distributed*. In the United States, it was once unthinkable for national dailies to cooperate with one another. Today, just as an illustration, the *Washington Post* partners with over 120 news organizations. The *New York Times* runs a similar program, as does *USA Today* (e.g. Doctor, 2014).

Third, news production is *more multi-media* and distributed across a *wider set of platforms*. Once, newspaper reporters attended events, interviewed sources, took notes, wrote news stories, and left it at that. Today, they carry backpacks filled with video recorders, microphones, and cameras. And they are required to distribute content across a wider variety of platforms, from Twitter to Instagram to Facebook.

With fewer reporters producing more and different kinds of content across a wider variety of platforms, a natural result follows: *news production speeds up*. This is a fourth change in contemporary newspaper journalism. Dean Starkman (2010: n.p.) famously calls this the 'hamster wheel' effect of digital journalism. "The Hamster Wheel," he writes, "isn't speed; it's motion for motion's sake [it] is volume without thought […]an inability to say no."

Finally, news production is *more data-driven* (e.g. Petre, 2015). The modern newspaper newsroom increasingly resembles the bridge of the Starship Enterprise. Desks often are arranged to face a front wall, on which monitors display a raft of constantly changing real-time statistics (bought through subscriptions to software like Google Analytics and ChartBeat). Editors have access to these data. Inevitably, it has begun to influence their decisions about which stories to cover, and how to cover those stories (e.g. Boczkowski and Mitchelstein, 2013).

These five changes mark the contemporary newspaper newsroom as different from the past, in some respects dramatically so.

The persistence of reporting

The changes I list above do not obscure the deep reservoir of stability that underlies newspaper journalism. That reservoir is filled with the practices and values of 'reporting.' By 'reporting' I mean the five elements of the modern news paradigm described by Høyer (2005): stories pegged to discrete events; values of newsworthiness (e.g. timeliness, immediacy, impact, proximity, relevance, and so on); the inverted pyramid style of writing; the interview; and objectivity. In the United States, it is often called 'shoe leather' reporting, which is the act of moving from source to source (whether people or documents) to collect the relevant facts of a news story. Typically, shoe leather reporting takes place on news beats, which are institutions (e.g. city hall) or subjects (e.g. health) a journalist covers on an ongoing basis. In the last few decades, even the modern news paradigm has morphed a bit. Newspaper stories are pegged somewhat less to events (e.g. Barnhurst and Mutz, 1997). Moreover, compared to the past, stories tend to be longer and more interpretive (e.g. Fink and Schudson, 2014). Still, Rosen (2015) is correct to observe that reporting remains the "one god an American journalist can officially pray to." Reporting, in other words, remains at the center of journalism, and specifically newspaper journalism.

Anderson's (2013: 159) study of the *Philadelphia News Inquirer*, and the online ecosystem of news that developed around it, illustrates the pull of reporting within journalism. After devoting chapters to documenting the 'vortex of events' swirling around the newspaper, Anderson (2013: 98) observes that reporting remains the 'jurisdictional core' of the profession: "The bulk of daily reporting" in this ecosystem, he writes, "continue[s] to be carried out by traditional newsroom professions [and] reporting [is] the most rhetorically valorized form of newswork inside Philadelphia newsrooms." The result, he concludes, is a degree of unexpected 'stasis' (2013: 159). "For all the fragmentation of journalism in Philadelphia," he writes, "a distinct center of gravity remains … that center was the *Inquirer*… [and that organization was] *concerned with reporting the news in a particularly traditionalist sense*" [italics in original] (2013: 161).

The broader literature bears out these ethnographic observations. Content analyses, for instance, consistently show that newspapers remain the most common source of news in most communities (e.g. Nielsen, 2015b; Pew, 2015). Reporting remains the common manner of producing this news. 'Online journalism,' Quandt (2008: 735) writes, "is basically good old news journalism." This is true across European and Anglo-American newspaper news sites. A 2008 study of European and American news sites conducted by Domingo and colleagues found a few that core news practices "remain largely unchanged" (2008: 339). More recent analyses of sources in online news arrive at much the same conclusion. Tiffen *et al*.'s (2014: 382) study of eleven countries ends with the thought that "political sources [still]…dominate in all countries." And Reich's (2015: 788) study of sources in Israeli online news indicates that officials remain core news sources while "ordinary citizens remain a minor news source."

Another literature on new technology use among journalists comes to similar findings. Many of these studies show reporters using new tools to pursue traditional reporting practices, or not using them at all. Consider, for instance, reporters' use of Twitter. Lawrence *et al*.'s (2014) study of reporters' use of Twitter during the 2012 presidential campaign finds that "reporters and commentators [rarely allowed] Twitter to disrupt traditional one-way gatekeeping flows." A study of German federal elections (Jungherr, 2014: 254) discovers much the same thing: "coverage of the leading candidates [...] on Twitter and traditional media followed largely similar dynamics..." Similarly, Moon and Hadley's (2014: 302) examination of how several American news organizations use Twitter to discover sources ends with this thought: "Journalists still throw their news nets to the same spots as they did in the pre-internet age."

Of course, as other chapters in this volume attest (see Starkey, among others), the literature is not unequivocal. Scholars detect many new practices and values in online news—even among newspaper journalists. Still, the extant literature strongly supports the general conclusion that reporting remains a pervasive practice as newspapers and other media move online.

This literature, however, tends to focus primarily on professional journalists. Perhaps this is natural, but it is no longer sufficient. One of the consequences of the great turmoil in journalism is that the field's boundaries have become more porous and permeable (see Eldridge, this volume). Journalists now find themselves working alongside many new news producers, only some of whom have experience, much less interest, in journalism. What do we find when we examine this broader community?

In answer to this question, let me present a small set of data on journalists working in two regional online news systems in the western part of the United States (Ryfe *et al.*, 2012; Ryfe, 2016). This investigation includes interviews with 34 individuals who operate news sites. A good number of these individuals are former journalists, but many have no background in the field. I have found that for these individuals, journalism, coded as reporting, exercises a strong gravitational pull.

This pull is different for people who are positioned differently in the field. Many of the former journalists with whom I have talked see reporting as an *opportunity*. After being laid off from a job at a startup technology company, for instance, one person recalled that she began looking around for opportunities. She soon realized that one existed right in her neighborhood: "I can provide something to the community" she said, "that [the small local newspaper] is not providing...and so I jumped on it." Others, who have a background in professional writing but not journalism, have no initial interest in reporting. Still, they found themselves pressured to do it anyway. For them, it is a *necessity*. One person with whom I talked wanted to write broadly about arts, culture, and community. "As soon as I jumped in," she told me, "it became very obvious that our readers wanted news. And so I had to adapt to our readers demands...and very rapidly I started veering toward harder core news like crime, and fires and you name it...I started functioning as a more traditional news site..." Other professional writers found themselves gravitating to journalism to enhance their *credibility* with sources or advertisers. "They didn't know who I was," one person says of people at the first city meeting she covered. "They were like, 'oh,' blank stare."

Over time, I have interviewed individuals who are farther and farther afield from traditional journalism. All along the way, the connection between journalism and reporting has remained. Some of these people run news sites for non-profit organizations or government agencies. Others are hobbyists, or news entrepreneurs. When I first approached these individuals, I sent an email that read in part: "I am conducting research on news sites of various kinds in the [San Francisco] Bay Area, and I would very much like to include your site in my study." Many of them responded in puzzlement. "Thanks for your interest in my website," a book editor turned blogger wrote back. "I just wanted to point out that my site [...] is a gardening blog. Although I do sometimes post links to news items [...] I don't really think of it as a news site." More tersely, the manager of a non-profit website wrote back: "We're not really a news site. Just a community organization." After some interaction, most admitted that their sites produce news. As one put it, "the content [on my site] is actual news in terms of new information you didn't know before and that may not have appeared anywhere else." However, all agreed that, in any event, they were not journalists.

What is the difference? What makes some kinds of news production journalism and other kinds not? As I orbited around this question with respondents, they turned to two kinds of distinctions. A first has to do with values: *journalists, my respondents wished to say, are detached from the issues they cover.* Why aren't you a journalist? I asked one interviewee. She responded that to her, journalists deliver "news objectively in a disinterested manner…" A second has to do with practice. *Journalists, they believed, report the news.* A respondent who manages a gardening blog told me that, in her mind, journalists produce 'time-linked' information. Early in her career as a blogger, she tried to cover daily news about her topic, but she "couldn't keep up with it." Journalists, she said, produce factual 'timely writing.' Another respondent echoed this theme. "Journalism is an occupation where you work under the supervision of an editor," he told me. While admitting that he "bring[s] information to a public" for the purpose of 'educat[ion],' this interviewee maintained that he did not 'cover current events' or work for a 'regularly published publication.' Still another said that his site was not a 'definitive news source.' Why? "If you can't have all the news and if you can't get to things quickly, it's very difficult to be a news site."

In sum, as I have talked with individuals positioned across the newly diversified field of journalism, it is clear that newspapers and reporting remain vital. But why?

Reporting and newspapers are keystones of the journalistic field

To understand newspaper reporting's continued relevance, it helps to place it within the broad context of the journalistic field. This is not the place to present a detailed description of institutional and field theories (but see Martin, 2003), or of how they have been applied to journalism (but see Benson and Neveu, 2005; Ryfe 2006; Ryfe and Blach-Ørsten, 2011). Instead, it is enough to draw on these resources to present a brief sketch of the field.

Much like a natural field (e.g. gravity or electromagnetism), a social field contains properties that lend it cohesion (e.g. Bourdieu, 1985). Within journalism, these properties are core practices and values of the kind listed by Høyer (2005) in his discussion of the 'news paradigm.' Like gravity in a gravitational field, these elements push and pull journalists toward one another. Due to this pushing and pulling, over time journalists come to look and act more like one another than like individuals in other occupational fields. In this way, the field of journalism gains a degree of cohesion and autonomy from other social fields. Historically, the field of journalism arose first in the early twentieth-century United States (e.g. Chalaby, 1996; Kaplan, 2002; McGerr, 1986; Schudson, 1998), and a bit later across Europe and other industrialized societies (Høyer and Pöttker, 2005; Wiener and Hampton, 2007).

For our purposes, two aspects of this history are important. First, journalism emerged amid a broader transformation of public life. Specifically, it inflated in the friction caused by a national industrial economy, an administrative state, and the growth of modern professions. All three of these forces were key to its emergence, but *it was the relation between them that was crucial* (see Figure 45.1). Much as a tent rises when its poles push and pull against one another, so journalism inflated in the pushing and pulling between the state, the market, and the profession. Journalism's distinctive properties (e.g. detachment, independence, facticity, and the inverted pyramid style of writing) are ways that journalists came to manage their complicated existence, pulled in the one direction by their sources (mostly public officials), in another by the imperatives of the market, and in still another by the demands of their own profession.

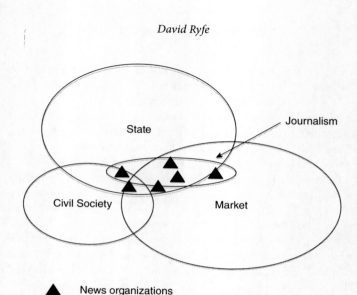

▲ News organizations

Figure 45.1   The journalistic field in the United States.

Second, *journalism emerged first and foremost within newspapers*, especially large urban newspapers. They are not the same thing—journalism and newspapers—but the culture of journalism grew up in and around the practices and processes developed in newspapers, and the field's core practices and values are entangled with this medium. This is easy to show. Think, for instance, of the notion, "journalists ought to get the facts right." This is a cardinal value of the field, one that is put into jeopardy daily by the permanency of print: a published error is visible and enduring evidence that a journalist has violated this rule. Because this is the case, newspapers have developed complex processes for ensuring the accuracy of their stories. In newspaper newsrooms, reporters are required to verify every significant fact in their stories, and once the stories leave reporters' hands they travel a circuitous route through a series of editors before they appear in the newspaper. At each step, editors check their accuracy. Print reporters see little distinction between these processes and the underlying value. To them, the processes merely make the value concrete.

When the internet arrived in the early 1990s, two things happened in the field of journalism at once. First, more people gained the ability to publish news. The sphere of public communication, in other words, enlarged. Second, the commercial underpinnings of modern journalism were severely damaged. Even today, there is no clear business model for digital news. Return to the tent metaphor I offered above. A tent inflates when its poles push and pull against one another. If one of the poles is taken way, the tent loses tension, and begins to sag. Essentially, this is what has happened to American journalism, and to a lesser extent journalism elsewhere. As the force of the market has weakened, there is less for the forces of the state and of the profession to push against. In the event, the field of journalism has lost integrity. Its boundaries have become more permeable, and there are fewer journalists available to patrol those boundaries.

The growth of published news coupled with the destabilization of journalism has had predictable consequences for newspapers. They now find themselves 'cheek to jowl' with more and different kinds of news publishers (e.g. Carlson and Lewis, 2015). Figure 45.2 presents a visual illustration of what has happened. New publishers have entered the journalistic field

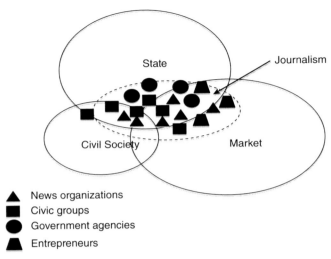

Figure 45.2   A more porous field of journalism.

from contiguous social fields, especially political (in the form of interest groups) and civil (in the form of non-profits) society and the market. This is most pronounced at the national level, but it is also true in regional and local markets. The new entrants are producing news in novel ways. They are adapting new technologies to news production and establishing new relationships with their audiences. Internally, the field has become less ordered. The occupational ladder (from small town weekly to city daily, from city daily to regional daily, and so on) has disintegrated and hierarchies within newsrooms have become destabilized. The result is a great deal more heterogeneity within the field, and permeability between it and contiguous social fields.

Within this more variegated field, reporting serves as a keystone. For current and former print journalists, it imbues their activities with *intention*. Geertz (1973: 90) makes the point that culture "establishes ... motivations in men by formulating conceptions of a general order of existence and clothing these conceptions with such an aura of factuality that the ... motivations seem uniquely realistic." In this context, a motivation is a "tendency ... to perform certain sorts of acts...in certain sorts of situations" (1973: 96). Geertz is saying that culture informs intention and produces passion. This is what I have witnessed with current and former print journalists. At a time when many journalistic verities have been challenged, reporting serves as a reminder of who they are, what they do, and why they do it.

Reporting also lends journalists *distinction*. In a more variegated field, more than ever it is incumbent upon journalists to distinguish their work. It is in this context that I interpret my respondent's suggestion that if I called her a blogger she would hit me. Bloggers express opinions; journalists, she wished to say, report the news. This was not only a matter of pride for her. It had tangible benefits. Sources were more likely to talk with her if they considered her a reporter, and advertisers were more likely to place ads on her site. Even as so much has changed within and around journalism, the act of reporting is still seen as more credible, and more valuable, than news produced in other ways.

For actors who are not journalists, reporting plays an *orienting* function. Again, so much in the field of journalism has been disrupted that it is difficult for actors to know who they are supposed to be and how they are supposed to relate to others. In this context, reporting is a set of practices that people recognize. It serves as a touchstone of sorts for them, helping them to orient themselves to the environment in which they find themselves. My respondents tell me that sources and advertisers, for instance, recognize reporting as journalism. When respondents do not approach such individuals as journalists, they do not know how to go on. That is, they do not know how to act and interact with a news producer who is not a journalist. In a different way, news producers who are not journalists often use reporting to establish who they are by making it clear who they are not. In this instance, they are NOT professional journalists who report the news (and, they seem to suggest, no one should expect them to be). In both instances, reporting helps non-journalists establish identity in relation to one another.

Perhaps reporting has always played this role; perhaps the uncertainties that afflict the field today have amplified it. It is difficult to say. What is certain, however, is this: even as newspapers lose economic value, they and the reporting that takes place in them retain great symbolic value. That is why they persist even as so much else within the journalistic field morphs around them.

Further reading

This chapter is built on the foundation of the 'golden age' ethnographies of news produced in the 1970s, foremost among them Gay Tuchman, *Making News: A Study in the Construction of Reality* (1978) and Herbert Gans' *Deciding What's News: A Study of CBS Evening News, NBC Nightly News, Newsweek, and Time* (1979). Timothy Cook's *Governing with the News: The News Media as a Political Institution* (1998) details the institutionalist perspective adopted in this chapter. Also see Rodney Benson, *Shaping Immigration News: A French-American Comparison* (2014), who offers a companion field theory perspective on the news. I have found Svennik Høyer and Horst Pöttker's *Diffusion of the News Paradigm, 1850-1900* (2005) central for understanding how modern news practices migrated through Europe. Among the spate of recent ethnographies of news production, see my *Can Journalism Survive? An Inside Look in American Newsrooms* (2012), C. W. Anderson's *Rebuilding the News: Metropolitan Journalism in the Digital Age* (2013), and Nikki Usher's *Making News at the New York Times* (2014).

References

Anderson, C.W. (2013) *Rebuilding the News: Metropolitan Journalism in the Digital Age.* Philadelphia, PA: Temple University Press.

Anderson, C.W., Bell, E. and Shirky, C. (2014) *Post-Industrial Journalism: Adapting to the Present.* New York, NY: The Tow Center for Digital Journalism.

Barnhurst, K. and Mutz, D. (1997) "American Journalism and the Decline of Event-Centered Reporting." *Journal of Communication* 47(4): 27–53.

Benson, R. (2014) *Shaping Immigration News: A French-American Comparison.* New York, NY: Cambridge University Press.

Benson, R. and Neveu, E. (eds) (2005) *Bourdieu and the Journalistic Field.* Cambridge, UK: Polity Press.

Boczkowski, P. and Mitchelstein, E. (2013) *The News Gap: When the Information Preferences of the Media and the Public Diverge.* Cambridge, MA: MIT Press.

Bourdieu, P. (1985) "The Genesis of Concepts of Habitus and of Field." *Sociocriticism* 2: 11–24.

Carlson, M. and Lewis, S. (eds) (2015) *The Boundaries of Journalism: Professionalism, Practices and Participation.* New York, NY: Routledge.

Chalaby, J. (1996) "Journalism as an Anglo-American Invention: A Comparison of the Development of French and Anglo-American Journalism, 1830s-1920s." *European Journal of Communication* 11(3): 303–326.

Cook, T. (1998) *Governing with the News: The News Media as a Political Institution*. Chicago, IL: University of Chicago Press.

Doctor, K. (2014) "The Newsonomics of the Washington Post and New York Times Network Wars." Available from: http://www.niemanlab.org/2014/09/the-newsonomics-of-the-washington-post-and-new-york-times-network-wars/ (accessed 27 May 2015).

Fink, K. and Schudson, M. (2014) "The Rise of Contextual Journalism, 1950s–2000s." *Journalism* 15(1): 3–20.

Geertz, C. (1973) *The Interpretation of Cultures: Selected Essays*. New York, NY: Basic Books.

Høyer, S. (2005) "The Anglo-American Background." In Høyer, S. and Pöttker, H. (eds) *Diffusion of the News Paradigm, 1850–1900*. Gothenborg: Nordicom, pp. 9–19.

Høyer, S. and Pöttker, H. (eds) (2005) *Diffusion of the News Paradigm, 1850–1900*. Gothenborg: Nordicom.

Jungherr, A. (2014) "The Logic of Political Coverage on Twitter: Temporal Dynamics and Content." *Journal of Communication* 64: 239–259.

Kaplan, R.L. (2002) *Politics and the American Press: The Rise of Objectivity, 1865–1920*. Cambridge, UK: Cambridge University Press.

Krumsvik, A.H. (2012) "Why Old Media Will Be Funding Journalism in the Future." *Journalism Studies* 13(5–6): 729–741.

Lawrence, R., Molyneux, L., Coddington, M. and Holton, A. (2014) "Tweeting Conventions." *Journalism Studies* 15(6): 789–806.

Levy, D. and Nielsen, R. (eds) (2010) *The Changing Business of Journalism and Its Implications for Democracy*. Oxford, UK: Reuters Institute for the Study of Journalism.

Martin, J.L. (2003) "What Is Field Theory?" *American Journal of Sociology* 109: 1–149.

McGerr, M.E. (1986) *The Decline of Popular Politics: The American North, 1865–1928*. New York, NY: Oxford University Press.

Moon, S.J. and Hadley, P. (2014) "Routinizing a New Technology in the Newsroom: Twitter as a News Source in Mainstream Media." *Journal of Broadcasting & Electronic Media* 58(2): 289–305.

Nielsen, R. (2015) "Local Newspapers as Keystone Media: The Increased Importance of Diminished Newspapers for Local Political Information Environments." In Nielsen, R. (ed.) *The Uncertain Future of Local Journalism: The Decline of Newspapers and the Rise of Digital Media*. Oxford, UK: Reuters Institute for the Study of Journalism, pp. 35–48.

Nossek, H., Adoni, H. and Nimrod, G. (2015) "Is Print Really Dying? The State of Print Media in Europe." *International Journal of Communication* 9: 365–385.

Petre, C. (2015) *The Traffic Factories: Metrics at Charbeat, Gawker Media, and The New York Times*. New York, NY: The Tow Center for Digital Journalism. Available from: http://towcenter.org/research/traffic-factories/ (accessed 27 May 2015).

Pew Research Center (2015) "The State of the Media 2015." Available from: http://www.journalism.org/2015/04/29/state-of-the-news-media-2015/ (accessed 27 May 2015).

Quandt, T. (2008) "(No) News on the World Wide Web? A Comparative Content Analysis of Online News in Europe and the United States." *Journalism Studies* 9: 717–738.

Reich, Z. (2015) "Why Citizens Still Rarely Serve as News Sources: Validating a Tripartite Model of Circumstantial, Logistical, and Evaluative Barriers." *International Journal of Communication* 9: 773–795.

Rosen, J. (2015) "Good Old Fashioned Shoe Leather Reporting." *Pressthink*. Available from: http://pressthink.org/2015/04/good-old-fashioned-shoe-leather-reporting/ (accessed 27 May 2015).

Ryfe, D. (2006) "Guest Editors Introduction: New Institutionalism and the News." *Political Communication* 23(2): 135–144.

Ryfe, D. (2012) *Can Journalism Survive? An Inside Look in American Newsrooms*. London, UK: Polity Press.

Ryfe, D. (2016) "Journalism in American Regional Online News Systems." In Alexander, J., Breese, E. and Luengo, M. (eds) *The Crisis of Journalism Reconsidered: From Technology to Culture*. Cambridge, UK: Cambridge University Press.

Ryfe, D. and Blach-Ørsten, M. (2011) "Introduction." *Journalism Studies* 12(1): 3–9.

Ryfe, D, Mensing, D., Cekker, M. and Gunes, M. (2012) "Popularity Is Not the Same Thing as Influence: A Study of the Bay Area News System." *International Society on Online Journalism* 2(2): 152–165.

Schudson, M. (1998) *The Good Citizen: A History of American Civic Life*. New York, NY: Martin Kessler Books.

Starkman, D. (2010) "The Hamster Wheel: Why Running as Fast as We Can Is Getting Us Nowhere." *Columbia Journalism Review*, October. Available from: http://www.cjr.org/cover_story/the_hamster_ wheel.php (accessed 27 May 2015).

Tiffen, R., Jones, P.K., Roe, D., Aalberg, T., Coen, S., Curran, J., et al. (2014) "Sources in the News." *Journalism Studies* 15(4): 374–391.

Usher, N. (2014) *Making News at The New York Times*. Ann Arbor, MI: University of Michigan Press.

Waldman, S. (2011) *The Information Needs of Communities: The Changing Media Landscape in a Broadband Age*. Washington, DC: Federal Communications Commission. Available from: http://www.fcc.gov/ infoneedsreport (accessed 27 May 2015).

Wiener, J.H. and Hampton, M. (2007) *Anglo-American Media Interactions, 1850–2000*. Basingstoke, UK: Palgrave Macmillan.

46

THE NEW KIDS ON THE BLOCK

The pictures, text, time-shifted audio, and podcasts of digital radio journalism online

Guy Starkey

Radio journalism has evolved dramatically since the mid-1990s, when computer technology began to invade its newsrooms and studios, and when the term mainly referred to the preparation and presentation of hourly news bulletins. At that time, in the United Kingdom some music-orientated commercial radio stations still broadcast daily or perhaps twice-daily longer-form news programs at lunchtime or early evening of up to 15 or perhaps 30 minutes, as did a number of BBC local radio stations. Today, a relatively small number of dedicated speech radio stations, albeit mainly in the public sector (such as the BBC's national network Radio 4), still produce longer news and current affairs programs, magazine programs with such themes as consumer affairs, women's issues and the arts, and even documentaries. Sport was, and still is, featured extensively on some stations, including live commentaries, sports news, and phone-ins, with one national commercial station, TalkSPORT, dedicated to it. But radio journalism has changed considerably since the 1990s, although within the context of continuity. The traditional broadcast genres are still the main products of radio journalism, even though the amount of relatively costly speech on music stations has been significantly eroded as less rigorous regulation of the commercial sector in the UK has made possible cost-cutting by the owners of whole groups of local and regional stations who are keen to maximize their profits (Starkey, 2015). The primary platform for the delivery of what is now termed radio 'content' is still the analog FM transmissions, which became the most popular way of receiving radio during the 1990s, and will remain so in almost every developed country in the world for at least several years (Berry, 2014: 3–15). There are, however, some new kids on the block—born out of radio journalism, raised on a steady diet of digitization and more than likely here to stay. Just as digital production practices involved in content research, in storing and communicating text, and in capturing and manipulating audio have replaced many traditional techniques of the former, exclusively analogue world of radio journalism, the development of what has become known as Web 2.0 as a platform for user-accessed and then user-generated content, and the birth of the podcast as a non-linear form of communicating content to listeners, have also revolutionized some aspects of distribution.

Tech talk and how radio journalism has not changed

Another term, 'technological determinism,' has often been used pejoratively in the associated fields of media, communication journalism studies, being commonly attributed to the economist and sociologist Thorstein Veblen (Riesman, 1953) but frequently criticized as over-simplistic for its contention that much dramatic change in society can be attributed solely to the intervention of new technologies. Other technological determinists have included the communications theorist Marshall McLuhan (2001: 334), with his categorization in the 1960s of 'hot' and 'cool' media and his prediction that the world would shrink in communication terms to the size of a 'global village,' in which media enable individuals to feel they are close neighbors to others many thousands of miles away. The critics of technological determinism make a good case against Veblen. It is reasonable, of course, to acknowledge that the societal role of journalism, and in particular *radio* journalism, is today largely unchanged since the 1990s and, indeed, its beginnings in the 1920s—despite the relatively recent development of digital audio recording and editing, the disappearance of magnetic tape, the emergence of the website, the proliferation of the podcast, the adoption by audiences of new, digital distribution platforms, and some erosion of the traditional linearity of radio. Radio journalism is still about relaying true narratives to specific target audiences who are unable to personally witness and comprehend significant events around the world (Starkey, 2007: 5–13), providing them with a range of information they might consider essential (such as which motorway traffic jams to avoid), and holding people in authority to account. Those are the purposes and objectives of all professional journalism, and they are unaffected in essence by the arrival of some new technologies, and with them some new techniques and the requirement for radio journalists to acquire some additional skills. Nonetheless, at a time of dramatic change inspired by rapid developments in the technologies of media production and distribution, it is difficult to deny the influence of technology on a wide range of current practices in radio journalism. It would be difficult to claim that some individuals subscribe to podcasts or visit radio station websites *despite*, rather than *as a consequence of* their invention, or that radio journalists continue to carry large, heavy analogue tape recorders to location interviews (they don't!) because they are resistant to the economies of size and time which digitization has brought to the tools of their trade. Similarly, while McLuhan's notion of the global village might once have been easier to refute, it is not so easy to do so now, with the ease of viewing distant strangers' amusing pets in their homes—*without* the intervention of any form of journalism. Lacking the filtering of what Galtung and Ruge (1965) and others call news values, this is a combination of exhibitionism and voyeurism that the development of social media has brought in its wake and which even McLuhan, if he were alive today, might regard with some disbelief. The world has changed, even since the 1990s, and this is particularly evident in the world of mediatized content distributed to sometimes large and often distant audiences. This chapter, though, is *not* written in the tradition of technological determinism. It does, however, attempt to rationalize some of the technological developments of the past 20 years in terms of their impact on the practice and consumption of radio journalism of several kinds.

First with the news—no, really: the greater immediacy of radio journalism

The introduction of digital production practices to the busy radio newsroom has considerably enhanced one of the key characteristics of radio journalism: its relative immediacy. That immediacy is relative to other 'traditional' or 'legacy' news media born in the analogue age of print and electronic communication. When it was first proposed in the 1920s that early BBC radio should carry news bulletins, the objections of the Newspaper Proprietors' Association to it doing so before 6 p.m. were well founded (Starkey and Crisell, 2009: 5–7). The newspaper owners quickly realized that this new electronic medium was unconstrained by the fixed print deadlines of the press or the cumbersome processing and distribution delays inherent in distributing cinema newsreels. A breakfast time news bulletin could have quickly rendered some stories in the morning newspapers redundant, because distribution by the new phenomenon of broadcasting was so much more immediate. From the receipt of information in the newsroom to its being broadcast in the next bulletin could take only a matter of minutes, once any appropriate checks on information coming from external sources had been made, and the most significant of breaking news did not even need to wait for the hourly bulletin once the newsflash became accepted practice, interrupting normal programming to 'flash' the top line of the story with the promise of more detail coming soon. So, the BBC's initial compliance with the demands of the newspaper industry to delay broadcasting any such news coverage until tea time, left the currency of the morning newspapers intact throughout the working day—and, crucially, the newsagents' opening hours—and this great potential of radio untapped. Like the cinema newsreel, television news was initially similarly encumbered by the need to chemically develop and then dry reels of film before it could be edited and subsequently shown, until the switch to electronic news gathering (ENG) in the 1970s introduced video recording tape to location shoots, with its obvious advantage of instant playback. Editing video tape, however, was almost as cumbersome as processing film, because it relied on real-time playback of the recordings to dub a finished version onto a second spool of tape. The magnetic audio tape used in radio journalism, which we have already noted as now having been eclipsed by digital recording techniques, had already brought greater speed to the broadcasting on radio of location reports, interview material, and other actuality. No real-time dubbing was needed, because the original recording could be cut, unwanted material edited out, and sections of the tape reassembled, even in a different order. With the development of digital audio recording media, though, the need to physically mark audio tape with a chinagraph pencil at each edit point and then to physically cut the tape with a razor blade and stick the two wanted sides of an edit together with a specialized form of adhesive tape—splicing tape—itself became redundant. Even though experienced radio journalists had learned to cut and splice tape with great speed and accuracy, the cut and paste operations that are now familiar to us all within word processing software, when applied to the various different audio editing software programs available since the early 2000s, such as Adobe Audition or Audacity, are considerably faster (Starkey, 2014: 22–4).

In what is sometimes called a digital revolution, then, what was once already a relatively immediate news medium, recently became much more immediate for a number of other reasons. Firstly, the digital recording equipment used for sound capture today often has editing capabilities built into it (Starkey, 2014: 6–11). An obvious example would be the iPad with its internal microphone and on-board audio editing software, and the ability to send audio straight back to the newsroom providing there is wifi or perhaps mobile phone network connectivity. Although many consider the audio quality from such an arrangement to be perfectly acceptable, other permutations of essentially the same hardware configuration include connecting a better-quality external microphone to the iPad, to a laptop, or to some other communication device with that almost instantaneous wireless connectivity, in order to achieve a recording of what in radio broadcasting we almost universally consider to be of broadcast quality. That is, a quality of sound that is not distorted or altered in any way from that which the ear of a near bystander would hear through the ears alone, as opposed to its being compromised, for example, by being heard by the listener via an ordinary telephone call to the newsroom. Alternatively, the microphone chosen for such a purpose might resemble a traditional handheld one, but with the recording technology built into the stem, as with the Flashmic, which provided a USB socket for downloading the audio files recorded. A further option is for one or two microphones to be built into a small hand-held recorder with button-operated editing functions and similar connectivity to other devices as the Flashmic, depending on the availability of equipment and the preference of the reporter. With two microphones come not only the reassurance of a contingency in case one of them should fail, but also the possibility of making a stereo recording with slightly differing left and right channels to give listeners listening in stereo a modest sense of spatial positioning along a left/right continuum that is still more familiar in music or radio drama broadcasts than in the output of radio journalism.

Secondly, because audio may be digitally compressed as .mp3 files, sending it back to the newsroom via wifi or the mobile network means reporting from on location no longer requires specialized equipment, the use of enhanced telephone lines (formerly referred to as 'music lines' to reflect the studio-quality sound they produced by being bundled expensively together by prior arrangement with the telephone company) nor indeed the cumbersome paraphernalia of television location reporting: the outside broadcast truck, the portable satellite dish, and the heavy-duty battery pack or petrol generator. In radio journalism sometimes a reporter will indeed use a mobile phone, and while this may not be ideal in terms of the audio quality, doing so may lend additional authenticity to the report, in that being phoned back to the studio might connote a sense of urgency, recency, or even conditions on location that are, for some reason, arduous and challenging to this kind of journalism. Seldom, though, is the phoned-in radio report as lacking in aesthetic quality as most television reports in which the contributor is seen via the video messaging service, Skype, which look grainier the greater the size of high-definition and soon ultra HD flat-screen televisions become.

In the radio newsroom, too, as well as on location, the traditional processes of newsgathering and bulletin editing have sped up with the adoption of digital technology. Data storage and retrieval provide greater ease of access on local hard drives or the internet to what would previously have consisted of newspaper cuttings in a filing cabinet (i.e. selected copy kept for easy future reference from past scripts or cut out of newspapers). So researching stories and their background, checking facts, and finding sources can be faster than ever before. Social networking provides a quick and relatively easy route to people and their pronouncements on line, but also to potential contributions from among listeners who just might provide useful leads, eyewitness comment, or even useable audio from videos they might have taken as a result of quick-witted serendipity, should rare happenstance position them at the scene of breaking news. Monitoring the output of rival news organizations is now much easier than recording their news bulletins off air or waiting for a teletext service such as the BBC's Ceefax to slowly scroll through pages of mostly unwanted information, because today they probably put their best content, including breaking news, online—while monitoring news media in other countries which are suddenly in the news through armed conflict, disasters, or other geopolitical developments is now easily achievable even for small regional or local newsrooms which would previously have found such access well beyond their reach in terms of logistics and budget. Some of the newsroom developments described above are, though, generic to all forms of professional journalism. More specific to radio journalism, getting studio-quality audio from reporters in remote contribution points around the editorial area, perhaps in a sports venue or a town hall, or from other contributors (such as businesses with in-house media facilities to enable them to provide expert opinion to enhance or at least manage their own public relations), is much easier using such digital solutions as the now already quite dated ISDN technology introduced in the 2000s.

Furthermore, digital technology brings considerable advantages for radio journalism in terms of the network supply-and-contribute model found in the UK and elsewhere. Typically, this is a central news service, probably located in the capital, feeding national and international news to satellite local and regional newsrooms which mix that content with their own regionally or locally originated copy and audio according to their own news values which might consider the potential loss of jobs at a local factory more important than a national story on power broking at Westminster. When a local newsroom has content of interest to others in the network or its proximity to a breaking story of national importance means it can cover it faster than a reporter from the center could make it down to what would inevitably be an unfamiliar patch, that local newsroom in turn has something to contribute back to the center. Not only is the written copy sent to these distant newsrooms easily editable on screen, with all the possibilities of electronic cutting and pasting that would have been too time consuming to achieve using the previous 'rip and read' technology of teleprinters chattering away on a desk as rolls of paper scrolled through them, but more modern software for bulletin compilation allows easy editing of accompanying audio cuts and almost instant reordering, updating, removal, and replacement of stories that are then instantly accessible in the news booth and even editable while the newsreader is live on air. The increases in immediacy here represent significant step changes to the agility of radio journalism in serving its audiences. Not surprisingly, though, there is at least one downside to going digital. The technology which enables such agility in the newsgathering and bulletin presentation processes described above has been seized upon by the management of different groups of local and regional radio stations in the UK and elsewhere to effectively take liberties with local news. Just as the network supply-and-contribute model rationalized from the outset the provision of international, national, and local or regional news to local or regional audiences, so significant relaxation of broadcasting regulation has allowed a new model to emerge, one which has been adopted enthusiastically in the UK by a number of radio groups. This has resulted in local newsrooms being closed down and their functions being carried out in regional news 'hubs' serving multiple local radio stations from outside their editorial areas. Depending on the commitment of the group to attempting to properly serve those editorial areas, there may or may not be reporters working the patch every day and sending reports to the hub.

Those new kids on the block: what else has going digital done for us?

In what ways, though, has radio journalism begun to change in terms of its *output*, as opposed to the developments in *process* we have already identified, which are largely hidden from its audiences? Most apparent is the way in which radio in all its genres has suddenly acquired pictures. These are not the imagined, all-in-the-mind pictures which result from a carefully constructed mixture of description, dialogue, ambient sound, and spot effects broadcast as an audio stream in the traditional manner of the medium often characterized as 'blind' and for which radio is, some say, rightly famed because the vitality and robustness of the mental image can be more powerful than anything on a printed page or a screen (Crisell, 2004a: 5–19). Such observations remain as undiminished today as those basic principles of journalism we identified earlier, because they relate to essential characteristics of a medium which is still listened to far more than it is looked at. This new manifestation, or bi-product, of radio journalism is the *given* image, more fixed in its meaning than the aural image conveyed by the radio broadcast because it is accessed with the eyes—that is, posted online by the radio journalist to accompany a report by way of illustration. This given image is as incontrovertible as any of those on the pages of a newspaper or a magazine, on a television or cinema screen, or on a website of whatever provenance. Which is to say, of course, that it is controvertible, but a lot less so than the image that exists only in someone's mind, and which may be quite different in the mind of every other listener to the same broadcast. The given image, by contrast, has an appearance which its audiences must share, even if the meanings they give to it will tend to differ from person to person. What, then, of these new radio images? Like the rest of the traditional media, most radio stations seek a web presence and aim to provide as compelling an experience for its visitors as possible, in order that visitors will share its content, thus publicizing its existence more widely in an asymmetrical act of reciprocity for whatever benefit they have derived from it, and then return at some future stage. For the radio station, just as for the television channel or the newspaper, the website is not an end in itself, but an accompaniment to the main manifestation of the brand designed to, on the one hand, promote that brand and on the other to bolster its share of media attention—that hard to define but nonetheless important measure of a media organization's success which, one way or another, plays some role in determining the finances at its disposal: in the case of the private, commercial sector through the advertising, sponsorship, and subscription income it attracts, and in that of the public sector, through the level of public subsidy or mandatory license fee income it is able to justify or subscription income it can earn. In the case of the United Kingdom, since the incorporation of the BBC under its first royal charter in 1927, the BBC has always been funded mainly through the license fee, and it is not surprising that as exploitation of the internet grew apace in the late 1990s and early 2000s the corporation diverted sufficient resources for bbc.co.uk to achieve a dominant position on the UK's online media landscape.

The still image, then, on the radio station website, accompanying a report either on the home page, a dedicated news page, or potentially any number of subsequent pages accessed via hyperlinks, is intended to supplement the radio journalism which lay behind the story as broadcast. This discussion does of course also relate in many ways to the audio clip, the video clip, or the discussion board which the journalist might attach to the story, and all of this supplementary material requires of the radio journalist a range of new skills in digital authorship that simply were not needed in the radio newsroom until a relatively short time ago. Performing those skills, even in relation to a selected minority of the stories the journalist is working on, takes up additional time that must now be integrated into the routines of an already busy workday, right from the initial origination of the story through to its posting online, probably via the putting to air of the arguably more important broadcast version. A reporter out on location who would previously have made sure to collect not only some essential facts and perhaps quotes in written form as well as the audio to use in a straightforward report or a more elaborate package or documentary, now has also to collect appropriate still images and perhaps video for the online iteration of the story. The audio posted online may be a fuller, longer version of an interview than there was time to include in a bulletin or as an item for a magazine program, so listeners can discover more by visiting the website if they so wish. Alternatively, it may be supplementary material in the true sense of the word, in that it is additional material that does not make it to the broadcast. This does raise the issue of whether the radio station perceives the radio broadcast or the website to be the primary concern, although in many cases it will still be the broadcast. There is an argument to be made in favor of each strategy: that the radio broadcast is the primary concern because it is more listened to than the website is visited, even though listeners must normally wait until the next bulletin to hear some new content, or that the website might develop a reputation for breaking news sooner than any other outlet, and thus it might drive new listeners to the radio station. In addition to the website, there are of course a number of different social media platforms with insatiable appetites for being fed with content that might similarly draw new listeners to the radio station, or, alternatively to engage the existing radio audience with a richer content experience, even drawing them into a dialogue with the station and with each other. This requires further content management, which can include moderation if the public can post content that risks inviting legal action or damaging the brand. There is now scope for some original research into the priorities of different radio stations (and in the case of longer-form radio journalism, individual production teams), and these are priorities which may of course change over time, but the books *Radio Content in the Digital Age* (Gazi, Starkey, and Jedrzejewski, 2011) and *Radio: The Resilient Medium* (Oliveira, Stachyra, and Starkey, 2014) present a number of case studies of how different stations deal with these new challenges.

A final new kid on the block is the podcast. After Richard Berry posed the question "Will the iPod kill the radio star?" in the journal *Convergence* in 2006 (143–162), it subsequently became one of the journal's most accessed articles, and central to his question was the then quite new phenomenon of the podcast. The new technology offering listeners the opportunity to escape the time-based linearity of radio and simply order regular downloads of something akin to a radio broadcast, but which is stored and played back on demand from an iPod, seemed then to be potentially damaging enough to one day cause the demise of the radio 'star.' With the audio available for playback at each listener's convenience, it was thought, what would be the need for live radio broadcasts that present speech only fleetingly and according to the producer's schedules and not the consumer's? Podcasting has indeed proven very popular, but not, alas, as popular as live radio. Because all forms of radio journalism—including the regular news bulletin—may justifiably be considered 'stars' of radio in their own ways, undoubtedly featuring among the many reasons why listeners tune in to radio stations, it should be a matter of some relief to us that they are not, now, deceased. Significantly, the news bulletin is a particularly time-sensitive example of journalistic radio content. It is often broadcast as part of a regular pattern of hourly or even half-hourly bulletins—in rare instances even more frequently than that—so the process of downloading it and timeshifting the act of listening to it later is rendered rather pointless because the information in it may well have been superseded even a short while after its creation. Like the website and the social media presence, where podcasting by professional radio producers has been particularly successful has been where it is offered as *additional* content intended to be complementary to the broadcast, in the manner of the very successful *Best of Chris Moyles* that strung together clips from the eponymous presenter's daily breakfast show on BBC Radio 1. Until the program's demise it was consistently one of the top podcasts downloaded in the UK. Some of the BBC's factual programming, such as the historical discussion program *In Our Time* (Radio 4), has also been repackaged as podcasts, but it does tend to be entertainment, rather than news, which most consistently receives this treatment. In this age of so-called citizen journalism, though (and this is where we finally add some quite literal, as opposed to metaphorical, new kids to the block), podcasting is perhaps more the preserve of the niche enthusiast, from the trainspotter to the electronic game player, than the professional radio journalist. Of the thousands of podcasts uploaded to online stores for subsequent download, perhaps upon payment of a modest fee, it is in this area of niche—to borrow a now near-redundant term from the early days of analogue cable television—*narrow* casting that podcasting mostly appears to thrive. That making and listening to audio-only content should find such enthusiastic audiences in a new, digital age, in which so many different media compete directly with radio journalism for attention, ought to be a cause for celebration, particularly as even amateur podcasting tends to mimic the stylistic and aesthetic conventions of the news bulletin, the radio interview, and the discussion program.

Conclusion

The profession of *radio* journalism is alive and well, despite the challenges of renewed competition for the attention of its audiences from new media and other reinvigorated traditional media. Radio journalists who practice it benefit from the considerable efficiencies gained from widespread adoption of digital technologies in the processes of originating and manipulating journalistic content, but face additional daily challenges from being required to originate and produce—and often moderate—complementary content for a number of different platforms. In the associated field of podcasting, traditional and digital practices of radio journalism, mainly serving niche audiences, are needed in work routines that have even been adopted by amateurs or self-styled citizen journalists. Despite the temptation to rationalize the relatively recent changes to radio journalism according to the paradigm known as technological determinism, the core principles and practices of radio journalism remain unchanged, if transformed in many ways to reflect the changed technological and even regulatory contexts in which they exist today.

Further reading

In addition to the works cited above, the study of radio journalism and the primary field within which it exists, radio, would benefit greatly from selected reading among the following books: Chignell's *Key Concepts in Radio Studies* (2009), Crisell's seminal work *Understanding Radio* (1994), and Wilby and Conroy's first edition of *The Radio Handbook* (1994). Various histories exist, from Asa Briggs' detailed chronicles of the history of the BBC from the birth of broadcasting—*The History of Broadcasting in the United Kingdom* (1961), to more concise versions by Crisell, *An Introductory History of British Broadcasting* (1997) and *Street A Concise History of British Radio* (2002). Crisell's edited volume *More than a Music Box* (2004b) examines the many manifestations of speech on radio, Mitchell's *Women and Radio* (2001) explores gender issues in radio, and the former radio journalist Tim Crook has also written authoritatively on radio journalism in *International Radio Journalism* (1997), as have Crisell and Starkey in their chapter "News on Local Radio" (2006).

References

Barnard, S. (2000) *Studying Radio*. London, UK: Arnold.
Baron, M. (1975) *Independent Radio*. Lavenham, UK: The Lavenham Press.
Berry, R. (2006) "Will the iPod Kill the Radio Star? Profiling Podcasting as Radio." *Convergence* 12(2): 143–162.
Berry, R. (2014) "The Future of Radio is the Internet, Not on the Internet." In Oliveira, M., Stachyra, G. and Starkey, G. (eds) *Radio: The Resilient Medium*. Sunderland: Centre for Research in Media and Cultural Studies, pp. 3–16.
Briggs, A. (1961) *The History of Broadcasting in the United Kingdom: Volume I—The Birth of Broadcasting*. Oxford, UK: Oxford University Press.
Chignell, H. (2009) *Key Concepts in Radio Studies*. London, UK: Sage.
Crisell, A. (1994) *Understanding Radio*. 2nd edn. London, UK: Routledge.
Crisell, A. (1997) *An Introductory History of British Broadcasting*. London, UK: Routledge.
Crisell, A. (2004a) "Look with Thine Ears: BBC Radio 4 and Its Significance in a Multi-Media Age." In Crisell, A. (ed.) *More than a Music Box: Radio Cultures and Communities in a Multi-Media World*. Oxford, UK: Berghahn.
Crisell, A. (ed.) (2004b) *More than a Music Box: Radio Cultures and Communities in a Multi-Media World*. Oxford, UK: Berghahn.
Crisell, A. and Starkey, G. (2006) "News on Local Radio." In Franklin, B. (ed.) *Local Journalism and Local Media: Making the Local News*. London, UK: Routledge.

Crook, T. (1997) *International Radio Journalism*. London, UK: Routledge.

Galtung, J. and Ruge, M. (1965) "The Structure of Foreign News: The Presentation of the Congo, Cuba and Cyprus Crises in Four Foreign Newspapers." *Journal of International Peace Research* 2(1): 64–91.

Gazi, A., Starkey, G. and Jedrzejewski, S. (eds). (2011) *Radio Content in the Digital Age*. Chicago, IL: University of Chicago Press.

Hendy, D. (2007) *Life on Air: A History of Radio Four*. Oxford, UK: Oxford University Press.

McLuhan, M. (2001) *Understanding Media: The Extensions of Man*. London, UK: Routledge. (First published 1964)

McWhinnie, D. (1959) *The Art of Radio*. London, UK: Faber & Faber.

Mitchell, C. (ed.). (2001) *Women and Radio*. London, UK: Routledge.

Oliveira, M., Stachyra, G. and Starkey, G. (2014) *Radio: The Resilient Medium*. Sunderland: Centre for Research in Media and Cultural Studies.

Riesman, D. (1953) *Thorstein Veblen: A Critical Interpretation*. New York, NY: Scribner.

Rudin, R. (2011) *Broadcasting in the 21st Century*. Basingstoke, UK: Palgrave Macmillan.

Shingler, M. and Wieringa, C. (1998) *On Air: Methods and Meanings of Radio*. London, UK: Hodder Arnold.

Starkey, G. (2007) *Balance and Bias in Journalism: Representation, Regulation and Democracy*. Basingstoke, UK: Palgrave Macmillan.

Starkey, G. (2014) *Radio in Context*. 2nd edn. Basingstoke, UK: Palgrave Macmillan.

Starkey, G. (2015) *Local Radio, Going Global*. 2nd edn. Basingstoke, UK: Palgrave Macmillan.

Starkey, G. and Crisell, A. (2009) *Radio Journalism*. London, UK: Sage.

Stoller, T. (2010) *Sounds of Your Life: A History of Independent Radio in the UK*. New Barnet, UK: John Libbey.

Street, S. (2002) *A Concise History of British Radio*. Tiverton, UK: Kelly Publications.

Wilby, P. and Conroy, M. (1994) *The Radio Handbook*. London, UK: Routledge.

47

LONGFORM NARRATIVE JOURNALISM

"Snow Fall" and beyond

David Dowling and Travis Vogan

Announcing that she was stepping aside as the *New York Times* editor-in-chief, in July 2013, Jill Abramson heralded her replacement, Sam Sifton, as the publication's new "Snowfaller-in-Chief." The designation carried the prestige of the December 2012 publication of John Branch's Pulitzer Prize-winning "Snow Fall: The Avalanche at Tunnel Creek," which recounts an avalanche that killed three skiers in the Cascade Mountains. It also pointed to what she viewed as Sifton's most vital role: to guide the newspaper toward the digital magazine market. Sifton's 'first assignment,' Abramson wrote, "is to create an immersive digital magazine experience, a lean back read that will include new multimedia narratives in the tradition of Snow Fall" (Pompeo, 2013). "Snow Fall's" profound success transformed the work's title into a verb used by editors who want to create similarly flashy and high-profile projects. When faced with a major story, editors reportedly began to ask their staff: "Can we 'Snow Fall' this?" (Abramson as quoted in NetNewsCheck, 2013).

Setting the stage for "Snow Fall's" publication and digital longform's consequent popularization was the 2010 introduction of the Apple iPad, a device promoted as "more intimate than a laptop, and more capable than a smartphone" (Jobs, 2010). The tablet market this precipitated, propelled a metamorphosis of electronic reading into an immersive experience that focuses rather than scatters attention, in contrast to Web discourse's stereotypical dissonance and ephemerality (Carr, 2011). Tablet-inspired stories form a 'cognitive container,' a reading environment featuring embedded multimedia elements that "maintains the feel of a container associated with print newspapers" as opposed to the distracting linked nature of the web (Dowling and Vogan, 2015: 2). "Snow Fall" showcased the tablet's storytelling potential and no doubt hastened the technology's popularization. From May 2010 to January 2014, tablet ownership among American adults skyrocketed from 3 to 42 percent (Rainie and Smith, 2014). In the heart of this period was "Snow Fall's" 2012 release, which was quickly followed by the production of more than two hundred digital longform pieces (Hiatt, 2014).

After the initial fervor surrounding "Snow Fall" cooled, Abramson claimed that the broader question preoccupying publications hungry for readers—particularly the relatively affluent demographic of tablet users—is not whether they can mimic the celebrated piece's format (Boynton, 2013: 130). Many have—inexpensively and effectively. Instead, the concern is how to move forward in the wake of such a work to capture the coveted tablet market, build the media outlet's brand, and compete for market share with other outlets that are also "Snow Falling" their most compelling stories.

"Snow Fall" emerged among the first wave of born-digital works of longform narrative journalism. Although it has attracted the most attention, the December 2012 piece actually followed the genre's first installations that year, ESPN.com's "The Long Strange Trip of Doc Ellis" in August and BuzzFeed's "Atari Teenage Riot: The Inside Story of Pong and the Video Game Industry's Big Bang" in November. "Snow Fall's" design, however, stood out among its generic bedfellows and went on to revolutionize digital storytelling through employing parallax scrolling and embedding multimedia add-ons. Parallax scrolling, or the 'curtain effect,' occurs when full-screen images—usually animated on video loops—yield to rising text, often automatically activating multimedia add-ons. This transition from visual to textual content draws the reader into an immersive interactive experience in an environment that contains cognitive attention through the feel of a closed application. Advertising, if included at all, is minimal and discretely positioned to avoid interrupting the narrative flow.

The *Times'* success in these areas inspired a wave of imitators the year following "Snow Fall," which included work from sites ranging from legacy print magazines like *Sports Illustrated* to newer digital outlets such as ESPN's boutique Grantland.com (Dowling and Vogan, 2015). Perhaps most notable was the *Guardian*'s 2013 piece, "NSA Files: Decoded," a work designed to match and even exceed "Snow Fall's" revolutionary achievement through combining its technological prowess with a focus on hard news.

This chapter details the cultural and industrial logic informing the recent upsurge of online longform journalism that surrounded "Snow Fall's" emergence and took inspiration from it. Paying particular attention to BuzzFeed's "Atari Teenage Riot" and the *Guardian*'s "NSA Files: Decoded," we contrast the institutional, journalistic, and commercial ends that informed BuzzFeed's and the *Guardian*'s respective entries into the digital longform market. We then consider how the "Snow Fall" template has migrated into the television industry through the award-winning "Blood and Water," a digital longform project designed to promote the cable TV channel Animal Planet's documentary program *Whale Wars*. All three cases aim to build brands for the media outlets that create them. This branding function bears significance for the rise of longform content in the digital journalism industry because it shows that snowfalling is not merely an aesthetic practice, but also a marketing strategy for a competitive online environment where dynamics like native advertising (content marketing) blur the line between advertising and editorial content. Digital longform's design and market strategy viewed in light of media's spreadability (Jenkins, Ford, and Green, 2013) in contemporary consumer culture has important implications for the genre's development away from traditional divisions, including those that separate editorial and advertising content.

Native advertising in narrative journalism

Digital longform represents the capacity for depth in an online environment otherwise seen as encouraging shallow journalistic content. But many have condemned 'longform' journalism as a fad that enables digital outlets to 'go long' rather than to produce work that demands or even deserves extended attention. The *New York Times'* Jonathan Mahler (2014) critiques a 'cult of longform' that compels publications to overlook the production of credible content in favor of capitalizing on the symbolic capital (Bourdieu, 1993) that the genre has recently acquired in the industry and in popular culture.

BuzzFeed, for instance, used the production of longform articles to signal its 2012 rebranding from an entertainment-driven news aggregator into a site that generates thoughtful, penetrating journalism (Selter, 2011). BuzzFeed frequently offsets the considerable cost of its longform works by integrating native advertising within them. Like product placement in film and television, native advertising blends editorial and advertising content (Dunn, 2005: 147). BuzzFeed's "Atari Teenage Riot" (not to be confused with the rock band), for instance, is ostensibly an in-depth digital feature story that reads in a single scroll of white text on a black background with humorous visuals of the gaming industry in 1970s culture, many on video loops. This history of Atari details the invention of Pong, the first coin-operated arcade video game. The article also promotes the mobile phone application Pongworld—a quirky update of Pong—within the space of the story. Pongworld struck a deal with Buzzfeed to commission the piece on Pong and the early history of video games, which unsurprisingly focuses on Pongworld producer Atari. This sponsored content is subtle and indeed intended to resemble editorial material. Near the end of this history of Atari's launch of Pong, "a game ubiquitous in culture high and low," what amounts to a convincing argument on behalf of the company's contribution to and significance in American culture sets up the product placement: "To celebrate the game's 40th anniversary, Atari has licensed a commemorative title, *Pongworld*," as promotional language announces "the game will be available in the app store—although playing it on your iPad or iPhone isn't the same as a hulking, whirring, arcade machine" (Stokel-Walker, 2012). In a nostalgic and humorously ironic tone matching that of the piece as a whole, the persuasive emphasis is on how the retro-game can be enjoyed on the latest digital mobile devices. Pongworld receives a full paragraph in the story with an animated visual graphic beside the text directing traffic to the application's website and demo video. Appearing soon after Atari launched its campaign for the product, BuzzFeed's feature was clearly designed to channel audiences toward the commercial posted on YouTube.

Unlike the overt attempts to attract reader attention with banners and popups, native advertising such as Atari's is etched into the story in a way that seems organic. This method does not attempt to divert reader attention, but capitalizes on its establishment within the narrative. To this end, time on site, rather than clicks, is what the new premium advertisers such as Atari now desire. Time spent on advertisements amounted to 57 percent of digital publishers' revenues followed by traffic at 33 percent, brand lift at 24 percent, comments at 19 percent, and cost per view or click at 10 percent (Kaye, 2013). Native advertising is thus most effective when embedded within immersive media products, especially in the metric of scroll depth, or, how far one scrolls down before clicking away (Kaye, 2013). The factor of length of engagement has become a goal of both news organizations and advertisers in their efforts to adapt to mobile device users' immersive habits. Time on page thus represents "a clear departure from the dominant business model in online journalism, which has been driven by advertising revenue based on page views" (Ray, 2013: 439). It is indeed difficult to be distracted by seemingly 'native' material within a product in which one is already immersed.

Traditional advertising's concern with page views only indicates how many people loaded the page, rather than how many read it and to what extent. Companies such as Chartbeat now cater directly to this new premium for engaged time by offering services that "highlight insights for editorial action" specifically to "convert first-time readers to lifetime loyalists" (2014). The goal is to foster not only exposure to the brand, but identification with and even affection for it. Banner ads and shorter native ads do not fare as well in this new commercial climate, as only half of readers personally identify with brands advertised in banner ads compared to 71 percent in native ads (IPG Lab, 2013).

After establishing itself as a major success in harnessing the first wave of the 'attention economy'—characterized by intense competition and demand for reader attention in a digital ecosystem where "there is seemingly no limit to the supply of free content"—BuzzFeed has now ventured into pieces with slower production schedules that make greater time demands on readers (Briggs, 2012: 153). Its repertoire of 'listicles' and video diversions now shares space with its expanding list of longform titles. BuzzFeed CEO Jonah Peretti has pursued long-form based on the assumption that "any smart brand would absolutely prefer a single native page view to a dozen banner ad impressions. The difference between the two isn't something marginal, on the order of 20 or 30 percent: it's *huge*" (as cited in Salmon, 2013).

Analytics reveal "readers were 25 percent more likely to look at a native ad than they were at a banner, and they looked at them 53 percent more frequently" (IPG Lab, 2013). The key feature that makes native advertising so conducive to longform is in its 'duration and story-telling arc' (Salmon, 2013). Indeed, digital longform's sponsored paragraphs, pullouts, and infographics function much in the same way product placement does in the film and television industries. These segments stand alone as individual promotions, as with "Atari Teenage Riot's" Pongworld advertisement, while simultaneously contributing to a larger piece. This, Salmon (2013) astutely points out, is precisely the function of traditional television advertising. Viewers consume a TV ad the same way they consume a TV show, "if you're not ignoring them, they command attention." Indeed, as high-end magazines shift to digital and enter the longform market they seek to carry over readers' tendency to "spend as much time with the ads—if not more—as with the edit" (Salmon, 2013). Analytics corroborate this claim by indicating that the average amount of time on editorial content exceeded that of native ads by only 20 percent (IPG Lab, 2013). Native ad quality can even exceed that of editorial content, as in the case of glossy fashion ads in magazines such as *Vogue* (Marris and Thornham, 1996: 480–488). Design strategies for digital longform stories likewise focus on creating an immersive environment without distracting advertising. Thus, as Salmon (2013) explains, an effective native advertisement "is something that readers read, interact with and even share—it fills up their attention space for a period of time, in a way that banner ads never do."

Though they do not contain native ads for other products, digital longform outputs such as "Snow Fall" and "NSA Files" function similarly to advertise the publications' brands. These branding practices suggest "it is an artificial distinction to keep editorial copy and advertising copy in the one magazine strictly apart in any analysis" (Huisman, 2005: 295). Indeed, when readers shared "Snow Fall" at record speed through social media—10,000 tweets, the most for a story not on the *New York Times*' main website—the *Times* profited handsomely from the publicity (Romenesko, 2012). The piece attracted half a million visits, half of which were "from new *Times* users … lured to our journalism by this feature," according to Abramson (as cited in Romenesko, 2012). The aim was to cultivate what Jenkins (2007) calls 'loyals,' emotionally dedicated consumers who spread and participate creatively with the brand according to the new industrial logic of the digital ecosystem (Jenkins, Ford, and Green, 2013).

Spreading the *Guardian*'s hard news brand

When the *Guardian* entered the digital longform market with "NSA Files," it did so in a way that would both provide an immersive reading experience like "Snow Fall" and display the publication's investigative capabilities. A contrast to "Snow Fall's" focus on sport and human interest, "NSA Files" sheds light on the United States government's questionable surveillance activities. The argument of the piece is that Edward Snowden was just one of many figures testifying to the activities of NSA. It thus opens a more comprehensive view of the files from which Snowden's story emerged. The story highlights how each use of social media and digital communication in online citizens' everyday lives discloses personal data to communications companies and governments alike. "NSA Files" reflects "Snow Fall's" efforts to mold the *New York Times'* brand. However, it does so by associating the *Guardian* with rigorous and politically resonant investigative reporting, particularly through its status as legacy media's main beneficiary of leaked government documents. The company has taken perhaps its most significant story of recent memory and showcased the tremendous archive of interview and documentary data it received from its former reporter, Glenn Greenwald, and other key players in the surveillance scandal. Thus the *Guardian* has designed "NSA Files" precisely as a tool to illuminate an important and complex story with real-world implications, and not simply as a means of visual pyrotechnics. Analytics indicated that "time on site has been fantastic" for the piece, according to *Guardian* interactive editor Gabriel Dance. "There are more than 23,000 visits that lasted over 30 minutes. That's more than 11,500 hours, or 479 days spent on the story. And that's just a slice of the users" (as cited in Titlow, 2013).

In its branded association with hard news, the *Guardian* has designed its marquee digital feature with an eye toward spreadability. Unlike "Snow Fall," "NSA Files" contains no internal advertising and is designed more aggressively than its predecessor to circulate through social media. Deep-linking social media icons are positioned next to every paragraph, graphic, and document for easy sharing of either the work as a whole or in segments. In "Snow Fall," social sharing options are only available at the top menu bar. "Snow Fall" thus circulated as a complete feature, unlike "NSA Files," which coursed through the internet both intact and in parts. "The deep linking was a huge asset" in "NSA Files," according to *Guardian* journalist and coder Feilding Cage, because it so effectively leveraged social media to politically engage readers (as cited in Titlow, 2013). This design acknowledges that "content is more likely to be shared" that is quotable, portable, "easily reusable in a variety of ways," and "relevant to multiple audiences" (Jenkins, Ford, and Green, 2013: 197–198). Thus, the *Guardian*'s strategy with "NSA Files" flies in the face of "traditional branding theory that has valued controlling meaning rather than inspiring circulation." Such circulation 'pluralize[s]' and 'multiplie[s] brands' because "each new viewer encounters the original content afresh and is reminded of the brand and its potential meanings" (Jenkins, Ford, and Green, 2013: 201–202).

Deep linking the story with social media enhances the *Guardian*'s reputation for empowering readers with leaked or previously classified data, reinforced in 2012 by its Cannes Lion Award winning promotional video "The Three Little Pigs." The commercial is a retelling of the children's fable in the context of open-source media. In it, citizen-driven exposure via social media of the pigs' insurance fraud led to the destruction of the house, triggering widespread blame and eventual global rebellion against the banks for placing them under such financial pressure in the first place. The allegorical narrative is a witty yet powerful articulation of the company's emphasis on open source citizen journalism and spreadable media as a form of digital activism. We find a similar motive in "NSA Files," especially in its discussion of how data reveals 'your digital trail' and its illustration of "what the revelations mean for you" in spreadable infographics indicating that a simple Google search reveals 'user name,' 'unique id,' and 'subscriptions' (Macaskill and Dance, 2013). While the *Times* reinvented the online news story as a space free of banner ads in "Snow Fall" to spur much of its success as a spreadable product, the *Guardian* set a new standard for digital longform with social media. In doing so, the *Guardian* radically socialized the otherwise typically solitary activity of extended deep reading. Further, the creator of every infographic and embedded element in "NSA Files" is named in the margins, an innovation in contrast to "Snow Fall's" more traditional single by-line of John Branch, who was uninvolved in "Snow Fall's" technological design and largely incapable of answering to reader feedback on the story's multimedia elements (Q&A, 2012). The *Guardian*'s decision to credit the many involved in the production of "NSA Files" gestures toward the project's unusual enormity and exceptional status among the publication's general flow of content. More importantly, it allows readers to commune with the designers and coders, and, in doing so, encourages more interaction with the piece through social media. The heavily connected environment both socializes the reading process and improves on highly publicized attempts by Amazon Kindle to bring a communal dimension to reading through its Popular Highlights feature, which displays how many readers mark specific passages as significant. This spreadability not only creates a shared experience, but also ensures the circulation of this brand that, in the *Guardian*'s case, is associated with hard news.

The televisual in digital longform

Many of the *Guardian*'s spreadable multimedia add-ons for "NSA Files" consist of video interviews. Digital longform borrows from both print feature writing and documentary film, just as television news has, according to Dunn (2005: 150), steadily become "more cinematic and less traditionally journalistic." "Snow Fall" and "NSA Files," for instance, employ televisual properties through film clips as well as moving illustrations and graphics on video loops that are automatically activated by scrolling. As the *New York Times* and the *Guardian* use televisual practices to build their celebrated works of digital longform, Animal Planet decided it might usefully promote itself and its documentary television program *Whale Wars* by "Snow Falling" it. *Whale Wars* follows the adventures of the Sea Shepherds—a renegade whale activist group led by Paul Watson—as it travels the globe to protect whales from harm. Animal Planet's digital longform piece on the show, "Blood and Water," situates the Sea Shepherds within a brief cultural history of whaling and activism against it. Indeed, *Whale Wars*' dramatic nautical themes, which often include the small Sea Shepherds crew taking on enormous whaling vessels, reflects "Snow Fall's" focus on outdoor adventure.

"Blood and Water's" design features background of spectacular ocean vistas against which parallax scrolling activates full-screen video. This has the effect of scrolling through two layers of photography, some still and some in motion, with the top layer in full vivid color and the background in muted hues. Audio comes on automatically as background music and airy oceanic tones with snatches of radio communication to enhance "Blood and Water's" cinematic effect. This also distinguishes it from "Snow Fall" and "NSA Files," neither of which employs a running soundtrack. Appropriately for a piece that grows out of TV, "Blood and Water's" written portion plays a supporting role to videos, maps, pullouts, and biographical profiles. The piece is organized chapter by chapter into a powerful assembly of data visualization in which documentary video functions as the main storytelling medium. Each video and graphic is carefully arranged to create a narrative that follows Watson's career and confrontations with would-be whale killers. While it outlines critiques against Watson's controversial tactics, it ultimately paints a sympathetic portrait of *Whale Wars*' protagonist and his devoted crew. Though informative and engaging, "Blood and Water" is, of course, ultimately an advertisement for *Whale Wars* and Animal Planet. The piece's only explicit mention of the show or channel appears following the conclusion, which includes *Whale Wars*' logo, a link to its webpage, and an image of a giant whale tail extending above the water as a menacing ship painted to look like a shark lurks menacingly nearby. Despite the piece's aggressive valorization of whale activism, it does not highlight the many other organizations dedicated to this cause, although their links are present on the site. Indeed, the audience of "Blood and Water" is not encouraged to politically engage their sympathy for the Sea Shepherds upon completion of the piece, but instead are urged to consume Animal Planet's TV product.

While its marketing for *Whale Wars* is subtle, "Blood and Water" employs the "Snow Fall" template to inflect the program with a literary quality seldom associated with television—a medium often derided as lowbrow. Situating *Whale Wars* and the Sea Shepherds within such a detailed history of whaling and the ethical debates surrounding it also works to distinguish the program from the less serious reality programs that surround it on Animal Planet, a collection that includes *Finding Bigfoot* and *Pit Bulls and Parolees*. It suggests that *Whale Wars* is more thoughtful—but no less engaging—than these brazenly outlandish reality programs. In doing so, it adds a degree of respectability to Animal Planet, which began in 1996 as a documentary-driven channel devoted to wildlife and nature programming. Low ratings, however, constrained the struggling channel to relaunch in 2008 with a focus on provocative reality programs. "The goal [of the re-launch]," claimed *Broadcasting & Cable*'s Anne Becker (2008), "is to move from being perceived by viewers as paternalistic, preachy, and observation-based to being seen as active, entertaining and edgy." While these shifts certainly helped Animal Planet to expand its audience, they did not enhance its respectability. Indeed, *Whale Wars* shares much of the sensationalism in which Animal Planet's other programs revel. The Sea Shepherds' missions are peppered with reality TV's common conventions, such as crewmembers' arguments and moments of comic relief. However, "Snow Falling" *Whale Wars* through "Blood and Water" exploits digital longform's cultural caché to mark the program as exceptional and to suggest Animal Planet can be both edgy and edifying.

Beyond simply promoting *Whale Wars* and Animal Planet, "Blood and Water's" front page illuminates digital longform's diverse uses across media. It features insignias representing two major awards the piece won in 2014: a Webby and an Addy. Webbys are awarded by the International Academy of Digital Arts and Sciences for general "Excellence on the Internet" and include both editorial and promotional works. Addys are given by the American Advertising Federation and, as the award's name implies, are limited to the advertisements. "Blood and Water's" dual recognition as an exceptional longform feature and an outstanding advertisement is a telling sign of the eroding wall between editorial content and advertising. It suggests digital longform can simultaneously serve both functions. Moreover, it indicates that a digital longform work's promotional status does not necessarily negate its value as editorial content. Pieces like "Blood and Water" and "Atari Teenage Riot" can, it seems, offer useful meditations on history and culture while promoting the organizations driving their creation.

But this perhaps should not be a surprise given the reliance of powerful media outlets like the *New York Times*, the *Guardian*, and BuzzFeed on digital longform projects to fashion their brands. These well-funded and immersive works are common in the promotional ends they serve. Moreover, they suggest that digital longform, and the "Snow Fall" template in particular, are as much promotional and branding strategies as they are aesthetic practices. The milestone achievement of "Snow Fall" has so profoundly influenced the evolution of digital journalism toward news branding that the BBC has recently attempted as well with its piece, "Future of the News," which ends with the chapter, "The Future of BBC News," to publicize the company (Harding, 2015). These developments all point toward the marketing and editorial convergence of digital longform toward brand promotion through spreadable multimedia products designed for the tablet. Sensational new designs continue to shape digital longform's latest narrative content, as the business of immersive media continues to boom.

Further reading

This chapter builds on research in David Dowling and Travis Vogan's (2015) "Can We 'Snowfall' This? Digital Longform and the Race for the Tablet Market" in *Digital Journalism*.

For more on the development of digital longform, especially in platforms such as *The Big Round Table* leveraging unconventional online business models, see Anna Hiatt and Michael Shapiro's (2015) *Tales from the Great Disruption: Insights and Lessons from Journalism's Technological Transformation*. An excellent study of the televisual and cinematic design of narrative online storytelling, particularly filmic transitions in the website medium, is Tuomo Hiippala's (2016) *The Structure of Multimodal Documents: An Empirical Approach*. See also Maria Lassila-Merisako's (2014) "Story First: Publishing Narrative Long-Form Journalism in Digital Environments" in the *Journal of Magazine and New Media Research*; Joe Pulizzi's (2012) "The Rise of Storytelling as the New Marketing" in *Publishing Research Quarterly*; and Vin Ray's (2013) "News Storytelling in a Digital Landscape" in the edited collection *Journalism: New Challenges*.

References

Becker, A. (2008) "Animal Planet Changes its Stripes." *Broadcasting & Cable*. 13 January. Available from: http://www.broadcastingcable.com/news/news-articles/animal-planet-changes-its-stripes/84207.

Bourdieu, P. (1993) *The Field of Cultural Production*. Trans. Randal Johnson. New York, NY: Columbia University Press.

Boynton, R. (2013) "Notes toward a Supreme Nonfiction: Teaching Literary Reportage in the Twenty-First Century." *Literary Journalism Studies* 5(2): 125–131.

Briggs, M. (2012) *Entrepreneurial Journalism: How to Build What's Next for News*. London, UK: Sage.

Carr, N. (2011) *The Shallows: What the Internet is Doing to Our Brains*. New York, NY: Norton.

Chartbeat (2014) "Understanding Engaged Time." *Chartbeat Publishing*. Available from: https://chartbeat.com/publishing/for-editorial/understanding-engaged-time#section-2.

Dowling, D. and Vogan, T. (2015) "Can We 'Snowfall' This? Digital Longform and the Race for the Tablet Market." *Digital Journalism* 3(2): 209–224.

Dunn, A. (2005) "Television News as Narrative." In Fulton, H. (ed.) *Narrative and Media*. Cambridge, UK: Cambridge University Press, pp. 140–152.

Harding, J. (2015) "Future of News." BBC, 28 January. Available from: http://www.bbc.co.uk/news/resources/idt-bbb9e158-4a1b-43c7-8b3b-9651938d4d6a.

Hiatt, A. (2014) "The Future of Digital Longform: All the Space in the World." *Tow Center for Digital Journalism*. Available from http://research.thebigroundtable.com.

Hiatt, A. and Shapiro, M. (2015) *Tales from the Great Disruption: Insights and Lessons from Journalism's Technological Transformation*. New York, NY: Big Roundtable Books.

Hiippala, T. (2016) *The Structure of Multimodal Documents: An Empirical Approach*. Abingdon, UK: Routledge.

Huisman, R. (2005) "Advertising Narratives." In Fulton, H. (ed.) *Narrative and Media*. Cambridge, UK: Cambridge University Press, pp. 285–299.

IPG Lab. (2013) "Exploring the Effectiveness of Native Ads." *IPG Media Lab*, 18 June. Available from: http://www.ipglab.com/2013/06/18/ipg-lab-sharethrough-exploring-the- effectiveness-of-native-ads/.

Jenkins, H. (2007) *Convergence Culture: Where Old and New Media Collide*. New York, NY: New York University Press.

Jenkins, H., Ford, S. and Green, J. (2013) *Spreadable Media: Creating Value and Meaning in a Networked Culture*. New York, NY: New York University Press.

Jobs, S. (2010) "Steve Jobs Announces iPad." *Apple World Wide Developers Conference*, 27 January. Available from: https://www.youtube.com/watch?v=_KN-5zmvjAo.

Kaye, K. (2013) "How Publishers are Measuring Native Ads Today." *Ad Age*, 25 July. Available from: http://adage.com/article/datadriven-marketing/study-publishers-measuring-native-ads-today/243287/.

Lassila-Merisako, M. (2014) "Story First: Publishing Narrative Long-Form Journalism in Digital Environments." *Journal of Magazine and New Media Research* 15(2): 1–15.

Macaskill, E. and Dance, G. (2013) "NSA Files: Decoded." the *Guardian*, 1 November. Available from: http://www.theguardian.com/world/interactive/2013/nov/01/snowden-nsa-files-surveillance-revelations-decoded#section/1.

Mahler, J. (2014) "When 'Long-Form' is Bad Form." *The New York Times*, 24 January. Available from: http://www.nytimes.com/2014/01/25/opinion/when-long-form-is-bad-form.html.

Marris, P. and Thornham, S. (ed.) (1996) *Media Studies: A Reader*. Edinburgh, UK: University of Edinburgh Press.

NetNewsCheck (2013) "Abramson Talks Snow Fall, NYT Digital." *NetNewsCheck*, 30 April. Available from: http://www.netnewscheck.com/article/25878/abramson-talks-snow-fall-nyt-digital.

The New York Times (2012) "Q. & A.: The Avalanche at Tunnel Creek." 21 December. Available from: http://www.nytimes.com/2012/12/22/sports/q-a-the-avalanche-at-tunnel-creek.html

Pompeo, J. (2013) "Jill Abramson Announces Big Leadership Changes at *The New York Times*." *Capital New York*, 12 July. Available from: https://www.youtube.com/watch?v=_KN- 5zmvjAo.

Pulizzi, J. (2012) "The Rise of Storytelling as the New Marketing." *Publishing Research Quarterly* 28(2): 116–123.

Rainie, L. and Smith, A. (2014) "Tablet and E-Readership Owner Update." *Pew Research Internet Project*, 18 January. Available from: http://www.pewinternet.org/2013/10/18/tablet-and-e-reader-ownership-update/.

Ray, V. (2013) "News Storytelling in a Digital Landscape." In Fowler-Watt, K. and Allen, S. (eds) *Journalism: New Challenges*. Bournemouth, UK: Bournemouth University Press, pp. 435–443.

Romenesko, J. (2012) "More than 3.5 Million Page Views for New York Times' 'Snow Fall' Feature." *Jimromenesko.com*, 27 December. Available from: http://jimromenesko.com/2012/12/27/morethan-3-5-million-page-views-for-nyts-snow fall/.

Salmon, F. (2013) "The Disruptive Potential of Native Advertising." *Reuters*, 9 April. Available from: http://blogs.reuters.com/felix-salmon/2013/04/09/the-disruptive-potential-of-native advertising/.

Selter, B. (2011) "BuzzFeed add Politico Writer." *The New York Times*, 12 December. Available from: http://mediadecoder.blogs.nytimes.com/2011/12/12/buzzfeed-adds-politico-writer/?_r=2.

Stokel-Walker, C. (2012) "Atari Teenage Riot: The Inside Story of Pong and the Video Game Indusry's Big Bang." *BuzzFeed*, 29 November. Available from: https://www.buzzfeed.com/chrisstokelwalker/atari-teenage-riot-the-inside-story-of-pong-and-t?utm_term=.ajl1PJ0Gg8#.xkd3opgOLk.

Titlow, J.P. (2013) "How Journalists at the Guardian Built that Epic NSA Story." *Fast Company & Inc.*, 18 November. Available from: http://www.fastcolabs.com/3021837/how-journalists-at-theguardian-built-that-epic-nsa-story.

48

PHOTOJOURNALISM AND CITIZEN WITNESSING

Stuart Allan

Taking a photograph or video clip with a camera-equipped cell or mobile telephone—more likely a smartphone these days—has become so normalized in everyday life in industrialized countries, it may be surprising to recall how disruptive the technology was perceived to be when it became available in the early years of this century. Viewed from the present vantage point, we may be forgiven a sense of nostalgia when reading how camera phones were celebrated by *Time* in 2003 as one of the 'coolest inventions' of the year (the magazine having awarded "Invention of the Year" to Apple's iTunes Music Store). "Take two popular gadgets," namely a cell or mobile telephone and a digital camera, it declared; "Merge them into a single point-and-click device. Then watch the world go nuts over it." *Time* writer Anita Hamilton proceeded to elaborate:

> Like the Internet before them, camera phones open up a new and surprisingly spontaneous way to communicate. Because they are inconspicuous—many look like regular cell phones—you can snap pictures as discreetly as any spy and, with the push of a few buttons, pop them into an e-mail or upload them to the Web in less than a minute. No wires or computer hookups necessary.
>
> (Hamilton, 2003)

While camera phones typically were being used to document ordinary events—"taking impromptu pictures of friends, family, babies and pets"—she also pointed out how several recent incidents had signaled their potential for more serious purposes. "In Italy, police nabbed two robbers after a shop owner snapped their pictures and e-mailed them to authorities. In Britain, what looked like a rape in progress at a pub was caught on a camera phone," she observed. "And in Osaka, Japan, police set up an e-mail address citizens can use to submit shots of suspicious activities." At the same time, however, a backlash of sorts seemed to be setting in, with fears mounting that camera phones would prove too intrusive where people's right to privacy was concerned. "But with an estimated 80 million camera phones sold this year—6 million in the US alone—the cat may already be out of the camera bag," Hamilton concluded. "Like it or not, these hot new gadgets are here to stay."

The implications these 'hot new gadgets' posed for professional photojournalism were not lost on media commentators either. "Amateur photogs part of breaking news; Media hunt pictures from witnesses on spot at right time" read one headline in Canada's *Globe & Mail* in April 2003. The newspaper's journalist, Sarah Lambert (2003), posed two key questions in response: "In this new digital world, how does this apparent deluge of images affect the news-gathering business? Will viewers and readers increasingly take the place of traditional reporters and photographers?" Over the years since, major news organizations have gradually—albeit in some cases reluctantly—reconciled themselves to the challenge of innovation through experimentation, and in so doing become increasingly open to pragmatic improvisation. Reportorial boundaries are being actively redrawn with the aim of securing new, creative ways to facilitate individuals' precipitous involvement—what I have described elsewhere as 'citizen witnessing' (Allan, 2013a)—in visual reportage. This chapter, in striving to contribute to current debates regarding the issues at stake for digital photojournalism, briefly traces the evolution of professional–citizen relationships negotiated through varied, uneven affordances and constraints associated with cameraphone technologies and their uses. We begin in the next section by identifying a 'Eureka!' moment in this history, one which—with the benefit of hindsight—set in motion repercussions of continuing significance today.

"Everyone is an embedded reporter"

In October 2000, *Wired* magazine's Bob Parks published a profile of the 'software maverick' Philippe Kahn and his plans for a niche company, LightSurf, and its 'ePhoto' process. Innovative projects were underway, Parks (2000) explained, including "a camera the size of a keychain charm that snaps onto a cell phone and transmits a photo over a cellular network directly to the Web." While other companies were pushing ahead with similar initiatives, their thinking was device centered—"a tiny camera piggybacking on a phone"—in contrast with LightSurf's end-to-end solution, which promised to instantly relay images across wireless networks where they would be filtered and stored in the billions. "To Kahn, nothing is outside the realm of imagination, because, in a world where anyone can instantly publish pictures on the Web, everyone becomes a photojournalist," Parks wrote. "And in Kahn's view, a camera could be our most powerful weapon."

Evidently this conception of "instant wireless digital photography" came to Kahn three years earlier in a hospital maternity center, where his wife, Sonia Lee, was in labor. "I'd gone to the Lamaze classes," he later recalled. "And the second time I said, 'Breathe!' Sonia said, 'Shut up!' So I said, 'OK, I'll sit at this desk and find something to do'." Left alone with his Toshiba laptop computer, Motorola Startac mobile phone, and Casio QV-10 digital camera, his mind turned to consider whether there might be a faster, easier way to share photographs. As his wife's labor continued over 18 hours, Kahn busied himself writing code and adjusting the hardware. "I had time to make a couple trips to RadioShack to get soldering wire," he added, otherwise "I just stayed in the room and made that thing work" (cited in Maney, 2007). It eventually did, in time for him to take a photograph of newborn daughter Sophie and wirelessly transmit it from the hospital room to distant family members, friends, and acquaintances around the world via a website. "The ah-ha moment was really the moment I realized that 2,000 people were going to get that very first picture," he remembered. "It's not like people hadn't put lenses in phones yet [by 11 June, 1997] but what I had done is basically built the Polaroid of the 21st century, the first camera, the first phone that can point, shoot and share instantly" (Kahn, 2012).

The anticipated implications for the fledgling device—"everyone becomes a photojournalist"—proved surprisingly close to the mark, with its capacity for documenting moments of personal significance to the user engendering intense interest.[1] When this

LightSurf 'picture messaging' service was launched in March 2003, Kahn realized citizen journalism was the first of several purposes for the real-time conveyance of digital photography attracting public attention (Kahn, 2007). Even before cameraphones became widely available, predictions that the proliferation of digital technologies in the hands of ordinary citizens signaled the imminent "death of professional photojournalism." Howard Rheingold in his 2002 book *Smart Mobs: The Next Social Revolution* described several experiments "on the fringes of mobile communications," such as the possibility of 'peer-to-peer journalism' emerging from the prospect of "phones that make it easy to send digital video directly to the Web" (2002: 165). He surmised the potential to transform the top-down dictates of the surveillance society and thereby the influence of the media monopolies. "Putting cameras and high-speed Net connections into telephones," he wrote, "moves blogging to the streets" (2002: 169).

By autumn 2003, camera phones were beginning to outsell digital cameras in Asia, Europe, and North America, despite the marked limitations of imagery with modest pixel resolution. In October, the *New York Times*' Amy Harmon (2003) reported on 'millions of surreptitious snapshots' being 'phoned into cyberspace,' the "product of cellphones with built-in cameras that are suddenly peeping out from every shirt pocket." Everyone's pocket was an overstatement, of course, but her point that 'an army of amateurs' wielding 'James Bond technology' was "quietly redrawing the boundaries of privacy in public spaces" underscored a major concern at the time. 'Phonecams' were being widely criticized for their possible misuse, particularly the danger of invading unsuspecting individuals' privacy in courtrooms, fitness centers and public swimming pools, or the risk of espionage in government or corporate workplaces (see also Johnstone, 2003; Kageyama, 2003). "The trend started innocuously a few years ago, when novelty cameras that plugged into mobile handsets were marketed to gadget-obsessed kids in Japan and Europe," XeniJardin (2003) observed in *Wired* magazine. "But in the past few months, a global phonecam revolution has begun to emerge." Jardin argued the growing ubiquity of the portable devices linked to the web represented a "cheap, fast strain of DIY publishing in which everyone is an embedded reporter." In rather colorful language, she envisioned 'mobile imaging hordes' able to 'colonize the globe,' capturing and sending news before 'conventional media' could react. "Minutes after a story breaks, television and Web sources will gather phonecam shots from the scene and disseminate them to viewers," she prophesized. "The world will be one big reality show."

These implications continue to play out today. Industry statistics indicated some 350 billion images were posted online in 2013, with major sites including Facebook (350 million), Instagram (55 million), and Flickr (3.5 million) leading the way.[2] By May 2015, Facebook reported that two billion photos were being shared daily on its services alone (Bandaru and Patiejunas, 2015). For photojournalism, the implications continue to reverberate as ordinary individuals document events unfolding before them, most being satisfied to receive due credit for their contribution to newsmaking by way of recompense (see Allan, 2013a, 2013b; Allan and Peters, 2015; Blaagaard, 2013; Mortensen, 2015; Ritchin, 2013; Solaroli, 2015). Growing numbers of so-called 'accidental photojournalists' provoke disquiet amongst wary professionals struggling to cope with uncertainty to protect their livelihoods (see also Allan, 2014; Becker, 2015; Brennen and Brennen, 2015; Caple, 2014; Mortensen, 2014; Yaschur, 2012).

'Citizen snappers'

"It's fair game—you can't stop people taking pictures with mobile phones," *Guardian* photographer David Levene has observed. So-called 'citizen snappers' may be lucky enough now and then, but "I just have to trust that my paper will show a certain amount of loyalty to me" (cited in Booth, 2011). Recent years have seen the active participation of amateur photographers in the news-gathering process correspond to the growing ubiquity of cheaper, easier to handle digital cameras. Where in the past it was typically the case that a photojournalist would be dispatched to the field following a tip called into the newsroom, now it is likely 'amateur snapshooters' or 'citizen shutterbugs' are making the most of opportunities when they are first on the scene.

The significance of bottom-up, inside-out contributions from increasingly image-savvy publics—in contrast with the top-down, outside-in imperatives of professional news reporting—was being regarded as indicative of a broader 'citizen journalism movement' (Schechter, 2005). The summer of 2005 year saw a crisis unfold that appeared to consolidate the role of mobile phones in citizen newsmaking, effectively dispensing with claims that it was a passing 'fad' or 'gimmick' for all but its fiercest critics. The immediate aftermath of the bombs that exploded in London on July 7, destroying three underground trains and a bus, leaving 56 people dead and over 700 injured, was precipitously recorded by citizens making use of digital technologies. In the face of official denials that anything was amiss, news organizations seized upon diverse forms of citizen witnessing to piece together the story. "What you're doing is gathering material you never could have possibly got unless your reporter happened by chance to be caught up in this," BBC News's Vicky Taylor maintained on the day (cited in Jesdanun, 2005). Mobile telephones captured the scene of fellow commuters trapped underground, with many of the resultant images resonating with what some aptly described as an eerie, even claustrophobic, quality. Video clips were judged to be all the more compelling because they were dim, grainy, and shaky, and because they were documenting an angle on an event as it was actually unfolding. Citizens were proffering a firsthand, personal vantage point. "The value of this is you'll know more about what's actually happening, why you should care, what it means," online editor Will Tacy said at the time. "You know about what's happening to individuals. That's always been the best of journalism" (cited in Matheson and Allan, 2009; Parry, 2005; Weiner, 2005). Remarking on this transition of news source to news gatherer, he added: "We aren't even close to where this is going to end up in inviting the public into our world."

In the days that followed, opinions of the changing dynamics between professional journalism and amateur, citizen-led alternatives were widespread. "With the camera phone and digital wizardry any idiot can snap a great news photo. Or can they?" photojournalist Nick Danziger (2005) asked in *The Times*. "Recording the extremes of human existence is not a job for amateurs," he argued. "All good reportage photographers go beyond being an eyewitness," Danziger insisted. "They establish evidence through a spirit of inquiry, compassion and communion." Elsewhere more accommodating views were rehearsed, some employing a discourse of partnership, albeit cautiously so. "We are in the earliest stages of a revolutionary relationship, and its current urgency is bound to be tempered by setbacks," said Emily Bell (2005), then of the *Guardian*. The rewards to be gained by "opening doors and distribution platforms to everybody" were substantial, she believed, but not without risk. "It might take only one faked film, one bogus report to weaken the bond of trust, and, conversely, one misedited report or misused image to make individuals wary once again of trusting their material to television or newspapers."

Inventing conventions

News organizations wasted little time fashioning strategies to verify the authenticity of this 'user-generated content,' even when this offered no absolute guarantees. Still, over a range of crisis events, assessments of how the news-gathering process was being effectively democ-ratized by 'digital snappers' tended to be upbeat. "Have Camera Phone? Yahoo and Reuters want you to work for their news service," announced a *New York Times* headline (Hansell, 2006). Commentators pointed to 'milestones' of how such imagery surpassed—or 'scooped'—alternatives offered by professional. Images shared from the French riots in the autumn of 2005, the Buncefield oil terminal explosions, and the execution of Saddam Hussein a year later. "It very much shows that citizen journalism's time is now," Feargall Kenny of Citizen Image said of a security guard's mobile footage of Hussein's execution, distributed anony-mously over the web, proffering chilling detail. "You're going to see this more and more, especially as the phones get better" (cited in Lang, 2007).

For those welcoming this "new army of citizen reporters," to use the *Independent*'s Guy Clapperton's (2006) phrase, a paradigm shift appeared to be underway. Traditional photo-reportage, with its adherence to common principles of dispassionate relay, seemed increasingly open to the charge of being formulaic in its appeal to the codified strictures of objectivity (Allan, 2006). Moreover, its polished aesthetic qualities risked being perceived as bland, even contrived, particularly amongst those disinclined to reaffirm official source-led news as rel-evant to their personal concerns or circumstances.

Citizen photojournalism, in marked contrast, inspired a celebratory language of revolution in the view of advocates. Journalism by the people for the people was heralded for its alter-native framings, values, and priorities; it was immediate, independent, and unapologetically subjective. "It's important to be open to receiving images from new, non-traditional sources" said Dave Boyle in 2007, photo editor at the *New York Post* (cited in *Business Wire*, 2007). Camera-equipped bystanders had long provided news organizations with this type of imagery (Abraham Zapruder's home-movie of the Kennedy assassination in 1963 or George Holliday's videotaping of the LAPD beating of Rodney King in 1991, being two of the more noteworthy historical precedents; see Allan, 2013a), simply not at this volume nor at such speed. "While this genre will never replace the award-winning photojournalism for which we're known, it's a highly complementary offering that enables us to meet the evolving imagery needs of a broad customer base," said Jonathan Klein of Getty Images (cited in *PR Newswire*, 2007).

Most agreed that citizen photojournalism was proving cheap and popular, and held con-siderable appeal for cash-strapped newsrooms. For critics, however, its dangers outweighed its merits. News organizations, they warned, were at serious risk of losing credibility in their rush to embrace seemingly newsworthy material they could not always independently verify. "Editorially they don't want it to happen but financially they want to let it happen because it increases page views," Marketwatch.com editor Bambi Francisco remarked in March 2007 (cited in Chapman, 2007). For Thomas Sutcliffe (2007), writing in the *Independent*, concerns revolve around the way such imagery "necessarily skews the definition of news towards the contingent and the unexpected." He added, "since photographs and footage of such catas-trophes are so compelling to most of us, the increased supply of them is likely to distort news bulletins and coverage towards the visually dramatic and away from the unphotogenic cogs and levers which actually move the world."

Still, even in a world where everyone is an 'incorrigible sensationalist'—to use Sutcliffe's phrase—for most news organizations facts, ethical codes, and audience trust remain para-mount. Debates over how best to be more accessible and interactive in rapidly converging digital environments recognized a hard truth, namely that citizens were intent on storming the ramparts of what was once considered the exclusive domain of the professional. Moreover, 'crowd-sourcing amateurs' were exhibiting a sharply competitive edge on online platforms such as Flickr, Citizen Image, Scoopt, and iStockPhoto.

Among wary professionals, there were pressing anxieties their livelihoods were at risk. "What if everybody in the world were my stringers?," Chris Ahearn, President of Reuters media group, asked in December 2006. One answer—photojournalism would cease to exist as a paid profession—was worrying, to say the least. Compounding matters for what might otherwise have been a welcome democratization of the medium was the apparent indifference to evaluative judgments of quality amongst audiences. "People don't say, 'I want to see user-generated content,'" Lloyd Braun of Yahoo News observed, they want to see interesting, preferably sensational imagery. "If that happens to be from a cellphone, they are happy with a cellphone. If it's from a professional photographer, they are happy for that, too" (cited in Hansell, 2006, Walker, 2006). 'Traditional' standards were shifting under this pressure, the implications coming to the fore in the autumn of 2008 when speculation grew that social networking would be the next challenge to photojournalism's news authority.

Digital witnesses

The precipitous rise of social networking cast these transitional features into ever-sharper relief. The imperative to be the first to bear witness, a defining lynchpin of professionalism, has been all but ceded to ordinary citizens engaged in 'accidental photojournalism' by simple virtue of being first on the scene, equipped with the means to circulate cameraphone reportage in real time. Often the immediacy of the raw, blurry imagery generated in these instances is prized for offering a compelling eyewitness perspective, in effect espousing a moral integrity engendered by its technical deficiencies.

Examples abound where news media commentary proclaimed startling incidents as pivotal moments in this emergent ecology. Citizen photo-reportage, shared via platforms such as Twitter, figured prominently in breaking news coverage of the Mumbai terror attacks in November 2008, particularly on 24-hour news networks (see Allan, 2013a; Bahador and Tng, 2010; Ibrahim, 2014). A dramatic image of a US Airways passenger jet following its emergency landing in the Hudson River in January 2009 was shot by Janis Krums—using his iPhone to upload it to TwitPic—onboard a diverted commuter ferryboat coming to its rescue. The image, showing passengers standing on one of the wings and on the inflatable chute, was shared with such intensity it caused the service to crash (see David, 2010; Hermida, 2010). TwitPic and related micro-blogging strategies proved similarly indispensable during the G20 summit in London 3 months later. Amongst the estimated 35,000 people demonstrating peacefully were a small number of protestors, some involved with anarchist groups intent on violent confrontations with the police. Citizen-shot still and video imagery recorded several clashes in shocking detail. One incident, in particular, ignited a major controversy—namely, the actions of a police officer knocking passer-by Ian Tomlinson to the ground. Tomlinson collapsed and died after being hit by a baton (see Greer and McLaughlin, 2011). The Metropolitan Police's initial denial that an officer had been involved was flatly contradicted by evidence in a video clip documenting the assault, handed over to the *Guardian* by an American visitor to the London and revealed six days later. For journalist Nik Gowing (2009), the citizen bystander who "happened to bear witness electronically" showed how non-professional 'information doers' were redefining the nature of power. "The new ubiquitous transparency they create," he contended, "sheds light where it is often assumed officially there will be darkness."

For understanding the reasons ordinary people find themselves compelled to engage in first-person reportage, these and related examples usefully raise further issues. To describe those involved as 'citizen photojournalists' may be advantageous at times, acknowledging that their actions are recognizable journalistic activity, but such a label brings with it certain heuristic difficulties too. More than a question of semantics, the person inclined to self-identify as someone engaging in a journalistic role—perhaps an independent blogger, photographer, or videographer—is likely to differentiate themselves from those who just happen to be nearby when a potentially newsworthy incident happens (see also Eldridge, this volume). Having the presence of mind to engage in citizen witnessing may well be a laudable achievement under trying constraints, but this represents a different level of engagement. "Let's face it, most of the people who capture this imagery have jobs to work, errands to run, houses to maintain and families to take care of," crowdsourcing analyst Eric Taubert (2012) has observed. "If asked, they don't consider themselves citizen journalists," he adds, although they will often welcome the opportunity to have their imagery shared with a wider audience. "Great content captured by smartphone-wielding citizens can die on the vine without ever being seen," unless it "finds its way into the hands of journalists who know how to wrap a story around it, fact-check it and place it into the distribution chain." In other words, unless the citizen in question is prepared to assume this responsibility for themselves—admittedly, an easier task to do via digital media—they will likely turn to a news organization to act on their behalf.

An emergent albeit uneven collaborative ethos between professional and citizen photojournalists was also apparent during the 'London Riots' of 2011. News coverage of a city 'under siege,' where certain neighborhoods were designated as 'battle zones' with protestors 'in control of the streets,' revolved around alarming imagery. Mindful of the need to blend into the crowds, photojournalists recognized their phone cameras helped considerably, but still raised suspicions. Photojournalist Fil Kaler left the protection of the police line in Brixton to enter a crowd outside an electronics store. "Once I got in, I knew it didn't feel safe to film," he stated; "I had my camera down by my side and took some shots on my phone and sent a few tweets and then out of nowhere I got punched in my face, my glasses were knocked off and my camera was nicked" (cited in L. O'Carroll, 2011). The *New York Times*' London reporter Ravi Somaiya said in an interview that the "rioters didn't like being photographed for obvious reasons, so I had to be subtle about the way I went about it." He added: "In those circumstances—where there were no police to be seen—it wouldn't be possible for [a television crew] to be protected. It was difficult enough for me to send Tweets and discreetly take photographs on my phone." In many ways, "it was a story made for Twitter" (cited in Kemp and Turner, 2011). Paul Lewis (2011) of the *Guardian* later described how his and film-maker colleague Mustafa Khalili's efforts to document "what felt like a country at war with itself" had been facilitated by social networking including Twitter. "It enabled us to deliver real-time reports from the scene, but more importantly enabled other users of Twitter to provide constant feedback and directions to trouble spots" (see also Lewis *et al.*, 2011).

In April 2013, ordinary citizens near the finishing line of the Boston Marathon suddenly found themselves bearing witness to the human devastation left in the wake of two bomb explosions. Many of their images represented personal, impromptu contributions to real-time reportage. In the eyes of some, however, the very legitimacy of citizen photo-reportage was morally problematic. "You're not a journalist just because you have your smartphone in your pocket and can take pictures of someone who has just had their leg blown off and their life shattered," read one Facebook comment that went 'viral' online (cited in Geleff, 2013). Further criticisms denounced the callousness of individuals taking images of victims instead of lending assistance or the irresistible prospect of media celebrity, while others expressed concerns that such depictions of carnage and panic were fulfilling the perpetrators' narcissistic desire for notoriety, or even inviting 'copy-cat' responses. Such graphic imagery was defended by others, counterpoising it against visually sanitized treatments proffered by corporate media. "Reporters have been normalizing the abnormal for so long that they've created well-worn catastrophe templates to convey their stories," Jack Shafer (2013) of Reuters argued. In contrast, these 'amateurs' offer 'unfiltered' news as a vivid alternative to the repetitive sameness of template-centered coverage (see also Allan, 2014; Meikle, 2014; Mortensen, 2015).

Conclusion

Disputes over what counts as photojournalism—and who qualifies to be a photojournalist—are hardly new, of course, but there is little doubt the types of crisis events highlighted above underscore the extent to which photo editors find themselves relying upon imagery shot by non-professionals. The very amateurness of citizen imagery tempers normalized conventions of journalistic authority, its up-close affirmation of presence, 'I am here' and this is 'what it means to be there,' intimately conveys a rawness of experience that can claim an emotional, often poignant purchase. News objectivity, it follows, is effectively shored up—that is to say, visually anchored—in normative terms to the extent emotional expression is contained within certain narrative conventions ritualized into consistency. As Wahl-Jorgensen (2013) has pointed out, this is a longstanding feature of tacit appeals to impartiality: "journalists rely on the outsourcing of emotional labor to non-journalists—the story protagonists and other sources, who are (a) authorized to express emotions in public, and (b) whose emotions journalists can authoritatively describe without implicating themselves" (2013: 2; see also Chouliaraki, 2014, this volume; Peters, 2011). Managing this proliferation of imagery thus invites fresh thinking about how to best perform a curatorial role, one consistent with professional standards and procedures while, at the same time, benefiting from the news value associated with the emotive, visceral immediacy of citizen witnessing.

Photo editors scrambling to figure out the guiding imperatives of this role are understandably wary of the reputational risk for their news organizations posed by decisions hurriedly made under seemingly incessant pressure to push ahead of the competition. Safely ensuring a professional's ostensibly credible image was trustworthy, its captioning accurate, or its placement properly contextualized demands close and methodical scrutiny, yet sifting through citizen imagery in search of deeper understanding has proven to be a curatorial challenge of an altogether different order. Meanwhile, the changing political economy of news organizations has engendered widespread cost-cutting, compelling time-pressed photo editors to prioritize certain types of visual story-telling consistent with managerial conceptions of efficiency (cf. Nilsson and Wadbring, 2015; Pantti and Sirén, 2015; Sasseen, 2012; Sheller, 2015; Solaroli, 2015). The ever-growing demand for visual representation—a "pix or it didn't happen" regimen—compels editors to refashion their commissioning practices, engaging with a diverse array of prospective sources with an eye to ad hoc communities of interest, if not impromptu coalition building. However, while few would dispute this rapid forging of points of connectivity between journalists and mobile-equipped citizens is increasingly important, not least where generating alternative types of photo-reportage is concerned, how best to enrich and deepen it over time is an open question. A first step in formulating strategic initiatives, as this chapter has argued, is to invite a rethinking of what it means to bear witness, and in so doing encourage photojournalism's civic responsibilities to be envisaged anew in a digital age.

Further reading

May I recommend two special issues of journals published in 2015—one in *Journalism Practice* (9:4), the other in *Digital Journalism* (3:4)—which explore the convergence of citizen journalism and photojournalism. Mortensen (2015) examines the use of eyewitness images in the reporting of conflict. Ritchin (2013) investigates "the complex new ecosystem of the image" in order to assess alternative forms of visual storytelling. Lastly, my *Citizen Witnessing* pursues several related issues in greater depth.

Notes

1 Press reports recurrently credited Kahn for being the first to demonstrate the potential of a cameraphone to relay digital photographs near-instantly. Kevin Kanellos (2007) of CNET News. com emphasized earlier developments, however, such as a digital camera with built-in transmission capabilities—at the rate of one frame every one to six minutes on the basis of picture quality—released by Olympus in 1994, called the Deltis VC-1100. "One could argue that the Deltis is really a camera that can connect to a cell phone, while Kahn made a camera phone," he noted. "Kahn, though, admits that he didn't come up with a unified piece of hardware that could be called a camera phone. Kyocera did that in 1999, followed by Sharp in 2000" (see also Flynn, 2001).
2 For these and related figures, see George (2014), who adds: "Every two minutes, we take as many photos as were taken in the whole of the 19th century" (2014: 30).

References

Allan, S. (2006) *Online News: Journalism and the Internet*. Maidenhead and New York: Open University Press.

Allan, S. (2013a) *Citizen Witnessing: Revisioning Journalism in Times of Crisis*. Cambridge, UK: Polity Press.

Allan, S. (2013b) "Blurring Boundaries: Professional and Citizen Photojournalism in a Digital Age." In Lister, M. (ed.) *The Photographic Image in Digital Culture*, 2nd edn. London and New York: Routledge, pp. 183–200.

Allan, S. (2014) "Witnessing in Crisis: Photo-Reportage of Terror Attacks in Boston and London." *Media, War & Conflict* 7(2): 131–151.

Allan, S. and Peters, C. (2015) "The 'Public Eye' or 'Disaster Tourists': Investigating Public Perceptions of Citizen Smartphone Imagery." *Digital Journalism* 3(4): 477–494.

Bahador, B. and Tng, S. (2010) "The Changing Role of the Citizen in Conflict Reporting." *Pacific Journalism Review* 16(2): 178–194.

Bandaru, K. and Patiejunas, K. (2015) "Under the Hood: Facebook's Cold Storage System." *Facebook.com*, 4 May. Available from: https://code.facebook.com/posts/1433093613662262/-under-the-hood-facebook-s-cold-storage-system-/.

Becker, K. (2015) "Gestures of Seeing: Amateur Photographers in the News." *Journalism* 16(4): 451–469.

Bell, E. (2005) "Media: Opinion." *The Guardian*, 11 July.

Blaagaard, B. (2013) "Post-Human Viewing: A Discussion of the Ethics of Mobile Phone Imagery." *Visual Communication* 13(3): 359–374.

Booth, H. (2011) "Citizen Snappers." *Design Week*, 3 February.

Brennen, B. and Brennen, J.S. (2005) "Taking Our Pictures: Citizen Photojournalism in Traditional US News Media." *Journalism Practice* 9(4): 520–535. DOI:10.1080/17512786.2015.1030138

Business Wire. (2007) "Citizen Image Turns Photo Sharing Social Networks Users into Global Corps of Photojournalists." *Business Wire*, 12 March.

Caple, H. (2014) "Anyone Can Take a Photo, but: Is there Space for the Professional Photographer in the Twenty-First Century Newsroom?" *Digital Journalism* 2(3): 355–365.

Chapman, G. (2007) "Internet Age Lets Anyone Play News Reporter." *Agence France Presse*, 28 March.

Chouliaraki, L. (2014) "'I have a Voice': The Cosmopolitan Ambivalence of Convergent Journalism." In Thorsen, E. and Allan, S. (eds) *Citizen Journalism: Global Perspectives*, Vol. 2. New York, NY: Peter Lang, pp. 51–66.

Clapperton, G. (2006) "Anytime, Any Place, Anywhere." *The Independent*, 16 January.

Danziger, N. (2005) "History in the Raw." *The Times*, 3 September.

David, G. (2010) "Camera Phone Images, Videos and Live Streaming: A Contemporary Visual Trend." *Visual Studies* 25(1): 89–98.

Flynn, L.J. (2001) "LightSurf Piggbacks a Tiny Camera on a Cell Phone." *The New York Times*, 9 July.

Geleff, A. (2013) "Citizen Journalism and Social Media in 2013: Is there a 'Too Much' or Is it just What We Need?" *ByteNow*, 17 April.

George, C. (2014) "The Digital Era." *Digital Camera* 155: 3–30.

Gowing, N. (2009) "Real-Time Media is Changing Our World." *The Guardian*, 11 May.

Greer, C. and McLaughlin, E. (2011) "'This is Not Justice': Ian Tomlinson, Institutional Failure and the Press Politics of Outrage." *British Journal of Criminology* 52(2): 274–293.

Hamilton, A. (2003) "Camera Phones." *Time*, 16 November.

Hansell, S. (2006) "Have Camera Phone? Yahoo and Reuters Want You to Work for Their News Service." *The New York Times*, 4 December.

Harmon, A. (2003) "Smile, You're on Candid Cellphone Camera." *The New York Times*, 12 October.

Hermida, A. (2010) "From TV to Twitter: How Ambient News Became Ambient Journalism." *M/C Journal* 13(2). Available from: http://journal.media-culture.org.au/index.php/mcjournal/article/viewArticle/220.

Ibrahim, Y. (2014) "Social Media and the Mumbai Terror Attack: The Coming of Age of Twitter." In Thorsen, E. and Allan, S. (eds) *Citizen Journalism: Global Perspectives*, Vol.2. New York, NY: Peter Lang, pp. 15–26.

Jardin, X. (2003) "Phonecam Nation." *Wired* 11(7), 1 July.

Jesdanun, A. (2005) "Proliferation of Digital Imaging Tech Broadens Newsgathering." *Associated Press*, 7 July.

Johnstone, L. (2003) "Hello Phone Cams, Goodbye Privacy." *CBSNews*, 2 December. Available from: http://www.cbsnews.com/news/hello-phone-cams-goodbye-privacy/.

Kageyama, Y. (2003) "Smile ... You're on a Candid Camera Phone: New Technology Breeding New Brands of Misbehaviourthroughout Asia." *Montreal Gazette*, 10 July.

Kahn, P. (2007) "Father of the Camera Phone." Transcript of Interview with B. Radke on Weekend America. *American Public Media*, 6 January.

Kahn, P. (2012) "Best Buy Super Bowl Advertisement Featuring Philippe Kahn." *NBC Network*, broadcast 5 February. Available from:http://www.youtube.com/watch?v=wMVuFybjkf0.

Kanellos, M. (2007) "Perspective: Who Invented the Camera Phone? It Depends." CNET, 3 April.

Kemp, S. and Turner, M. (2011) "London Riots: Journalists under Attack Share Stories from the Front Lines." *Hollywood Reporter*, 10 August.

Lambert, B. (2003) "Media Column." *Saint Paul Pioneer Press*, 5 February.

Lang, D. (2007) "Hussein Execution is Another Milestone for Cell Phone Cameras." *Photo District News*, 3 January.

Lewis, P., et al. (2011) "Reading the Riots: Investigating England's Summer of Disorder." London, UK: The LSE and The Guardian. Available from: http://eprints.lse.ac.uk/46297/1/Reading%20the%20riots%28published%29.pdf.

Maney, K. (2007) "Baby's Arrival Inspires Birth of Cellphone Camera—and Societal Evolution." *USA Today*, 23 January.

Matheson, D. and Allan, S. (2009) *Digital War Reporting*. Cambridge, UK: Polity Press.

Meikle, G. (2014) "Citizen Journalism, Sharing, and the Ethics of Visibility." InThorsen, E. and Allan, S. (eds)*Citizen Journalism: Global Perspectives*, Vol.2. New York, NY: Peter Lang, pp. 171–182.

Mortensen, M. (2015) *Journalism and Eyewitness Images*. London, UK: Routledge.

Mortensen, T.M. (2014) "Blurry and Centered or Clear and Balanced? Citizen Photojournalists and Professional Photojournalists'Understanding of Each Other's Visual Values." *Journalism Practice*8(6): 704–725.

Nilsson, M. and Wadbring, I. (2015) "Not Good Enough?: Amateur Images in the Regular News Flow of Print and Online Newspapers." *Journalism Practice* 9(4): 484–501. DOI:10.1080/17512786.2015.1030135

O'Carroll, L. (2011) "London Riots: Photographers Targeted by Looters." *Guardian Unlimited*, 9 August.

Pantti, M. and Sirén, S. (2015) "The Fragility of Photo-Truth: Verification of Amateur Images in Finnish Newsrooms." *Digital Journalism* 3(4): 495–512.

Parks, B. (2000) "The Big Picture." *Wired*, 8.10, October.

Parry, K. (2005) "When Citizens become the Journalists'." *Star Tribune*, 17 July.

Peters, C. (2011) "Emotion Aside or Emotional Side? Crafting an 'Experience of Involvement' in the News." *Journalism* 12(3): 297–316.

PR Newswire. (2007) "Getty Images Acquires Scoopt with Vision of Making Citizen Photojournalism more Accessible to the Mainstream Media." *PR Newswire*, 12 March.

Rheingold, H. (2002) *Smart Mobs: The Next Social Revolution*. New York, NY: Basic Books.

Ritchin, F. (2013) *Bending the Frame: Photojournalism, Documentary, and the Citizen*. New York, NY: Aperture.

Sasseen, J. (2012) "A Report to the Center for International Media Assistance."*The Video Revolution.* Washington, DC: Center for International Media Assistance.

Schechter, D. (2005) "Helicopter Journalism." *MediaChannel*, 5 January. Available from: http://www. asiamedia.ucla.edu/tsunami/1yearlater/article.asp?parentID=19220.

Shafer, J. (2013) "Terror and the Template of Disaster Journalism." *Reuters*, 15 April.

Sheller, M. (2015) "News Now: Interface, Ambience, Flow, and the Disruptive Spatio-Temporalities of Mobile News Media." *Journalism Studies* 16(1): 12–26.

Solaroli, M. (2015) "Toward a New Visual Culture of the News: Professional Photojournalism, Digital Post-Production, and the Symbolic Struggle for Distinction." *Digital Journalism* 3(4): 513–532.

Sutcliffe, T. (2007) "Ethics Aside, Citizen Reporters get Scoops." *The Independent*, 2 January.

Taubert, E. (2012) "So, You're Still Using the Phrase Citizen-Journalism." *DailyCrowdsource*, 14 May.

Wahl-Jorgensen, K. (2013) "The Strategic Ritual of Emotionality: A Case Study of Pulitzer Prize-winning Articles." *Journalism* 14(1): 129–145.

Walker, D. (2006) "Reuters and Yahoo Calling all Citizen Photojournalists."*Photo District News*, 4 December.

Weiner, E. (2005) "'Citizen Journalists' at the Point of Breaking News." *National Public Radio, Day to Day show*, broadcast 12 August.

Yaschur, C. (2012) "Shooting the Shooter: How Experience Level Affects Photojournalistic Coverage of a Breaking News Event." *Visual Communication Quarterly*19(3): 161–177.

49

DEVELOPMENTS IN INFOGRAPHICS

Murray Dick

Infographics are a constant presence in media today. They adorn the pages of national and regional newspapers around the world; they are popular across quality, mid-market, and tabloid formats, and they are routinely found in our television news. They are especially popular online, where freely available software makes it possible for anyone to create slick-looking charts. It has been suggested that news stories with infographics can generate up to 30 times more pageviews than stories without (So, 2012). The search term 'infographic' has been steadily rising in popularity since 2009, and is predicted to continue rising beyond 2015 (Google.co.uk, 2015).

How can we make sense then, of the rise of the infographic? Scholarship in the field of visual culture offers one possible explanation. Television, it is argued, is pervasive; we are constantly appraised by video surveillance, and our modern life, work, and leisure are mediated by visual media. Today, it is argued, our lives are best understood by means of this visual media, just as the nineteenth century is best understood by means of its newspapers and novels (Dikovitskaya in Heywood and Sandywell, 2012). After the 'visual turn' then, the significance of infographics in news and journalism acquires a new significance.

Elsewhere, other academic fields offer a research basis that may explain the increasing popularity of the form in news. Picture Superiority Effect, a theory derived from empirical studies in cognitive psychology, shows that concepts learned using pictures are recalled more easily and more frequently than their equivalent expressed in word form (Paivio and Kalman, 1973). Infographics offer news media a means of establishing a more lasting impact on their audiences than text alone.

Today's graphic design professionals are more confident, and more engaged in the making of our news than once they were in the news industry (Dick, 2014). Infographic design (where static) and development (where interactive) is the work of various specialisms, as reflected in the wide variety of job titles that now exist in the newsroom, including: interactive news developer, programmer/data specialist, software developer, data scientist, multimedia producer, and interactive producer (see McNair and Flew, this volume). The emergence of these new roles coincides with a working culture at leading media companies that actively privileges interactive (and hence visual data) journalism. In 2014, the *Guardian* merged its visual journalism, data journalism, and audience development teams, inspired by examples from native digital start-ups, in order to enhance its digital output (Reid, 2014). In the same year, the

BBC established its Visual Journalism Unit, a working structure that integrates designers and journalists across broadcast and online mediums (BBC, 2014).

A host of awards, including new categories within traditional journalism awards, now exist to recognize excellence in infographic design, including The Society of News Design Malofiej Awards (since 1993); The Online News Association Online Journalism Awards (since 2000); The Best of Digital Design, formerly known as the SND.ies (since 2002); and the Global Editor's Network Data Journalism Awards (since 2012). The range of participants and winners in some of these awards offers an insight into the rise of the form globally. In 2012 alone, work by 154 different media companies from 28 countries was submitted to the Malofiej awards (Malofiejgraphics, 2011). American and Spanish media tend to dominate this particular contest (and in particular the *New York Times*); nonetheless, there exists a spread of talent in the field that extends globally; the current year's awards saw gold medals for *South China Morning Post* (3) and the *Times of Oman* (2) (Malofiejgraphics, 2015).

For their advocates, the infographic (when designed responsibly and well) represents a highly functional means of communicating data efficiently to a wide audience (Cairo, 2012; Tufte, 1983; Tukey, 1990). However, when designed badly infographics can become a dangerously seductive means of propaganda (Dick, 2015). For some the use of graphs to prove a point in argument is considered a modern form of sophistry; a visual manifestation of lies, damned lies, and statistics; the big lie that belies big data:

Evan Davis: "Let me bring up a graph..."

Russell Brand: "I don't wanna look at a graph mate, I ain't got time for a bloody graph... this is the kind of stuff people like you use to confuse people like us."

(*BBC Newsnight*, 2014: 8:57–9:15)

How then can we reconcile the evident distrust this medium evokes in some, with the fact that it is today a highly specialized, professionalized, and firmly established manifestation of modern, networked news?

Infographics in Journalism Studies literature

Scholarship on infographics in the field of Journalism Studies falls broadly into three categories:

1 Studies of how users interact with infographics in news;
2 Content analyses of infographics in news;
3 Organizational studies concerned with the role of the visual journalist in the newsroom.

The first of these categories comprises research concerning the transgression of standards in newspaper infographics (Reavy, 2003); why audiences read particular infographics (Pasternack and Utt, 1990; Prabu, 1992); and the perceived dualism of visual attraction and understanding in audience engagement (Stone and Hall, 1997). The second of these categories comprises case studies and surveys concerned with the use of infographics in American (Smith and Hajash, 1988; Utt and Pasternack, 2000), United Arab Emirates (Bekhit, 2009), and Indian (Ghode, 2012) newspapers. The third category is largely the product of one scholar: Wilson Lowrey (1999; 2002; 2003). Situated within an organizational studies approach, Lowrey's research problematizes the creation of textual/visual journalism in the context of the conflicting norms held by competing professional subgroups in the newsroom.

Notable by its absence in this literature is a critical account of the problem of public trust in news infographics. Here I will explore this issue by setting out a series of competing (and at times overlapping) approaches to definitions, standards, and theorization in infographic design.

What is an infographic?

Infographics come in many forms; bar charts, pie charts, histograms, pictograms, statistical maps, process diagrams, experimental visualizations, or composites of any (or all) of the above, and more. So what, if anything, can we say collectively defines them?

The rudimentary (common-sense) definition of an infographic is formalistic; it is predicated on the compounding of the terms 'info' and 'graphic.' Alternatively, some definitions include an additional purposive dimension:

> Charts, graphs, maps, diagrams and tables whose primary function is to consolidate and display information graphically in an organized way so a viewer can readily retrieve the information and make specific and/or overall observations from it.
>
> *(Harris, 1999: 198)*

Today infographics are largely associated with mass media and with the notion of making concepts easily understandable (OED Online, 2006). In the practitioner literature, definitions tend to separate infographics according to those that serve decorative and informational ends (hence 'flavour' or 'fact or information') with the use of informational, or sign systems seen as the key distinction between 'illustrations' and 'graphics' (Evans and Taylor, 1997: 289). Moreover, some practitioners compound the term in order to draw out a more particular meaning; for example, Nigel Holmes prefers the term 'explanation graphics' (1984).

From definitions to standards

Some definitions of infographics are manifest in typological approaches to the form. A normative list of graphical forms (with accompanying standards of best practice) is presented in British Standard 7581 (1992). It comprises:

- Table
- Bar graph
- Line graph
- Area graph
- Pie graph
- Isotope graph
- Scatter graph
- Histogram
- Three-dimensional graph
- Superimposed graph
- Thematic map
- Illustrated graph
- Pictorial graph.

This approach may be considered the latest (or rather one of the latest) in a series of attempts to set out universal standards for the visual presentation of data.

The need for infographic standards first emerged during the second half of the nineteenth century, in the context of a perceived need to limit the 'babelisation' (Palsky, 1999) arising from inconsistencies in scientific practice across European borders. However, it would take until the second decade of the twentieth century before the first formal manifestation of rules around infographic design would emerge in the United States (Brinton, 1914; 1915). These early standards remain useful (and broadly relevant) today, but in some respects they are problematic. For example, The American Society of Mechanical Engineers' first principal of graphic presentation states that: "The general arrangement of a diagram should proceed from left to right." (Brinton, 1915: 791). But functionalist perceptual theories such as this, that take no cognizance of the contexts in which media are consumed, tend to ignore affective reasoning, and the cultural expectations different audiences hold (Brasseur, 2003: 18). This is problematic because experiments in cognitive psychology show that representations of temporal concepts are influenced by the directionality of written language (for example, where left-to-right is found to be dominant for speakers of English, and right-to-left is found to be dominant for speakers of Arabic) (Tversky, Kugelmass, and Winter, 1991). In short, far from being universal, this approach unduly privileges the Western mindset.

Elsewhere, in relation to time-series charts, Brinton's fourth principle states: "If the zero line of the vertical scale will not normally appear on the curve diagram, the zero line should be shown by the use of a horizontal break in the diagram" (Brinton, 1915: 792). But there is no allowance made here for those who would adhere to strict application of the rules, while misleading in other ways. For example, the use of a vertical line break across variables in time-series charts is a misleading method commonly found amongst early tabloid news infographics in the UK (Dick, 2015). This omission suggests a certain naivety; these early guidelines are directed merely at correcting (well-intended) misuse.

Standards in infographics: competing narratives

In the absence of internationally agreed standards today, best practice in infographic design is instead subject to a range of competing (and at times overlapping) approaches; and it is between and amongst these approaches that an informed understanding of infographics is best understood. Here I will set out four discourses that may be detected (to varying degrees) amongst the guides and text books that shape debate about infographics:

- Functionalist-idealist
- Pragmatist-realist
- Expressionist-aesthete
- Didactic-persuasive.

In doing so, I will outline how argumentation between these positions creates space for a deeper (and more nuanced) understanding of the value of infographics in our news; that goes some way to explaining the diverging views on the form that exist today.

Functionalist-idealist

The first of these discourses, the functionalist-idealist, is largely critical of newspaper infographics. It is most clearly articulated in the works of statisticians, mathematicians, and scientists, and in particular Edward Tufte (1983, 1997); though elements may also be found in the works of Willard Cope Brinton (1914, 1915, 1939), Darrell Huff (1954) and John Allen

Paulos (1996). For Tufte, graphics necessarily deal in complex, 'multivariate' (1983: 51) ideas (even if news does not), and they must explain clearly and efficiently: "telling the truth about the data" (1983: 51). The notion that designer and audience may not share a common and irreducible understanding of what 'the truth' means, is not countenanced here. This discourse is unapologetically positivist, Tufte states: "If the statistics are boring, then you've got the wrong numbers" (1983: 80). Yet some have long questioned the lack of evidence behind Tufte's claims and norms, and not least the suitability of his approach to infographics in news (Prabu, 1992).

In turn, Tufte expresses a low opinion of newspaper graphics: lies in these, he argues, are: "systematic and quite predictable, nearly always exaggerating the rate of recent change" (1983: 76). This criticism dovetails with some political economy critiques of news values more generally, and the undue emphasis placed on events and 'news hooks' in mainstream coverage (McChesney, 2000). In this reading, the rise of the infographic represents not so much an appeal to universalism per se, but rather a means of satisfying an international and rapacious audience of 'clicks' seeking out 'news you can use,' which in turn embodies the utilitarian short-sightedness of modern, globalized online news.

Tufte presents a (perhaps tongue in cheek?) method of verifying the 'truth' of infographics:

Lie factor = size of effect shown in graphic/size of effect in data (1983: 57)

It should be noted that Tufte's approach is not without its detractors from within the mathematical-statistical field. For example, it has been argued that Tukey's (1990) emphasis on the impact of graphical display poses a direct challenge to Tufte's Bauhausian minimalism (Wainer, 1990: 341). This graphical fidelity/graphical impact dichotomy represents a point of departure to the second discourse.

Pragmatist-realist

This discourse finds voice, by degrees, in the work and thoughts of infographics practitioners working in the news, including; Peter Sullivan (1987), Nigel Holmes (1984), Alberto Cairo (2012), and Dona Wong (2013). This approach involves conceiving of infographics as 'visual journalism,' and standards in this field are drawn both from traditional, liberal journalistic ethics and values, as well as the positivist canon that informs the first discourse.

For Sullivan, space is an invitation to experiment and move beyond statistical charts, into the realms of imaginative visual form (1987: 41). In turn, the availability of white space (in newspapers) he considered directly proportional to the potential for graphical story-telling. Sullivan was concerned with the audience that is, not the audience that ought to be (practitioners, after all, have a material interest in ensuring the audience understands their work). His designs at *The Sunday Times* speak to the shortcomings he perceived in the wider UK education system, in terms of instilling graphical literacy in the wider population.

In this view infographics are a tool or a technology (Cairo, 2012) rather than a communicative abstraction. This approach emerges from the contested professional and organizational values found in the newsroom (Lowrey, 1999). It accommodates practical realities; publication schedule, audience need, and constraints on materials and resources, as constraints upon infographic production. Best practice is constructed as part of an ongoing debate—something that requires constant vigilance. In 2011, international coverage of the 'raid' on Osama bin Laden's compound in Abbottabad, Pakistan, inspired so many wildly misleading infographics that practitioners sought to define the integrity of the medium publicly. In an open letter to Nieman Watchdog, Juan Antonio Giner and Alberto Cairo (supported by a number of other visual artists and experts) set out a six-point charter of ethical considerations graphic artists should aspire to, to obviate poor, misleading (even propagandistic) coverage in future (Niemanwatchdog, 2011).

Expressive-aesthetic

The third discourse, expressive-aesthetic, is informed by both post-modern thought and by fin de siècle aesthetic sensibilities, and may be detected in the graphical work (and thinking) of one of today's infographic 'superstars'—David McCandless. For McCandless, the potential in infographics is bound up in expressive experimentalism, with a premium on aesthetics, and an emphasis on the importance of play (Torran, 2015) and fun. McCandless' approach represents a challenge both to the positivism of the functionalist-idealist, and to the pragmatist-realist liberal ideal of journalism as fourth estate:

> I'm interested in how designed information can help us understand the world, cut through BS and reveal the hidden connections, patterns and stories underneath. Or, failing that, it can just look cool!
>
> (McCandless, 2009)

This approach foregrounds aesthetic impact at the expense of all other considerations. As such, it is subject to criticism within both the first and second discourses; prompting one media critic to question (rhetorically) whether it is "the illegitimate pop culture offspring of real analysis" (Maitlis, 2012: 1:53–1:57). Nonetheless, the pioneering aspects of this approach are popular amongst some in the media industry (Dick, 2014).

Didactic-persuasive

A fourth discourse in infographics, which may be called the didactic-persuasive approach, is given clearest expression in the work of logical positivist Otto Neurath and his artistic collaborators in 1930s Vienna. His pioneering ISOTYPE 'picture language' embodies a key organizing design principle in pictograms; namely that the repeated use of figure icons affords a means of achieving graphic fidelity better than resizing icons. This fourth discourse has long been criticized amongst statisticians as being unduly reductive, at the expense of full numerical accuracy (Burke, 2013: 197), and it is distinct from the others in so far as it conceives infographics as being ideologically purposive. ISOTYPE was intended to inform a socialist conception of adult education (Hartmann, 2006: 279), within the wider struggle for a fairer (socialist) society (Hartmann, 2006: 280). The idea of purposive infographics didn't necessarily begin with Neurath—some of the most celebrated infographic pioneers (including Florence Nightingale), it has been suggested, were more concerned with affecting persuasion in their intended audience, than with explaining reality 'objectively' (Small, 1998).

'Chartjunk': Good or bad?

Tufte coined the pejorative term 'chartjunk' to define (or rather to condemn) infographics incorporating, in his terms, a high 'lie factor':

Lurking behind chartjunk is contempt both for information and for the audience. Chartjunk promoters imagine that numbers and details are boring, dull and tedious, requiring ornament to enliven ... Credibility vanishes in a cloud of chartjunk; who would trust a chart that looks like a video game? ... Disrespect for the audience will leak through, damaging communication.

(Tufte, 1997: 34)

Recent empirical studies do not support this position. On the contrary, audiences often prefer (Inbar, Tractinsky, and Meyer, 2007), can better recall (Bateman *et al.*, 2010), and are in any case not necessarily hindered from interpreting (Blasio and Bisantz, 2002) data in 'chartjunk' form. Nevertheless, the concept of 'chartjunk' continues to shape debates around infographics. One of the most intractable of these debates, stretching back at least as far as Brinton (1914: 5), concerns the use of circles, circular data presentations, and proportional circle graphics (Christiansen, 2011). At the heart of this debate lies a tension in infographic design; the balance between maintaining the fundamental integrity, the accuracy of visual display, and the need to engage the viewer (or audience) in the data. At the BBC today, this tension is keenly felt, not least because the corporation has a stated duty (bound by Royal Charter) to appeal to all of the public, not just a select demographic. Internal research at the corporation has shown that a proportion of the public are entirely off-put by charts due to unhappy memories of studying mathematics at school, while on the other hand, circles are considered much more visually appealing (Dick, 2014). This debate in turn raises an interesting paradox with regard to high and low forms in journalism; complicating the perceived differences between populist (or tabloid) and quality coverage; between dumbed down content, and fourth-estate, public interest journalism.

The Guardian's Tax Gap interactive (2009), an interactive tool intended to help the audience obtain a comparative sense of the tax liabilities of FTSE 100 companies, embodies this paradox. Though purists may question the integrity (or rather, the lack of interpretive potential) in the use made of proportional circles in this interactive, it is clear that the mode of presentation lends itself well to engaging the public in the esoteric (perhaps even dull) process of comparing company financials. It may indeed be argued that the same information displayed in small multiples of bar graphs would not be nearly so engaging for a wide sweep of the reading public; thus limiting the story's full civic potential.

On the other hand, in terms of the more populist form of news infographics, the fun and (in some cases) frivolous stories found in online media brands like Ampp3d.com (started in December 2013) represent the latest (online) manifestation of tabloid 'explanatory' journalism, which found earlier expression in *Time* Magazine (during the 1990s), the *Daily Mirror's* Mirrorscope (of the late 1960s), the *Daily Express*' 'Expressographs' (from the 1950s onwards), and the Isotype-influenced 'Telefact' range of infographics published by Pictorial Statistics Inc in 1930s America.

But in one important sense this new manifestation of tabloid data journalism represents a departure from the past: here 'chartjunk' is notable by its absence. On the contrary, most infographics employed in this medium bear the mark of traditional, minimalist graphic displays (many are unadorned bar graphs and fever charts). In eschewing visual bells and whistles, the debate about what is 'tabloid' in this form of journalism, is not so much a matter of form as of content. Data journalists at quality newspapers and educators have criticized some of the tabloid data journalism emerging from media like Ampp3d.com (Ball, 2014) and FiveThirtyEight.com (Cairo, 2014); questioning the news values and journalistic integrity in the construction of these stories, but not necessarily the graphical formats used.

Today we see quality press employing what may be termed 'chartjunk' (or tabloid) characterizations in their use of infographics; whereas those tabloid sources online now tell sensational (occasionally erroneous, even misleading) news stories using sober, simple, standardized graphical configurations. Here 'chartjunk' has been interpolated into the ideal of classic liberal, fourth-estate journalism, while functionalist-idealist best practice has been interpolated into tabloid infographic news coverage.

Future directions

In 2010, the then President of The Society for News Design, Kris Viesselman, observed a recent shift away from narrative illustrated graphics, towards statistic-rich, data-driven visualizations (Datajournalism.stanford.edu, 2009: 4:42–4:54). This took place in the context of newly available data sources at the time; driven in the first instance by national governments (both data.gov and data.gov.uk were launched in 2009), allowing new opportunities for investigation and exploration to emerge. However, today it is argued that the general level of creativity in these large-scale data visualizations has slowed, due to the absorption of creative talent into the (conservative) organizational norms of industry (Wilson, 2015). Where does the truth lie here? And what types of news are most commonly expressed in infographic form? Are there any emerging trends, and if so what do they say about modern news? All of these issues merit further empirical research.

The integrity of (and audience engagement with) infographics in contemporary, networked media poses a serious civic challenge. In America, the Association of College and Research Libraries has argued that the visual nature of modern lived culture is "changing what it means to be literate in the 21st century" (Ala.org, 2011). As modern life is increasingly saturated with images, and infographics (both static and interactive), and as these images mediate our lived experience (and our democratic engagement), how can we be sure that the public has the critical faculties to interpret, critically appraise and make sense of it all? There is much demand for more empirical studies of audience engagement with news infographics. Moreover, a critical history of infographics, setting out the emergence of the form as a modern communicative medium would go some way towards informing scholarship (and policy) in this field.

Conclusion

Today infographics constitute a popular form in our news, and their purpose and function is subject to tensions between several competing discourses. One of the most intractable problems arises out of a conflict between a form of positivist puritanism that foregrounds and idealizes communicative fidelity, and a form of pragmatic populism that is concerned with balancing professional and organizational norms with the needs of the modern mass media audience. Though infographics may, at first glance, seem a relatively new (and understudied) field in wider journalism studies, it is nevertheless possible to discern traces of earlier themes and issues here, such as the tabloidization debate of the 1990s.

Further reading

This chapter builds upon three organizational studies of infographics production in the pre-converged newsroom, all by Wilson Lowrey: "Routine news: The power of the organization in visual journalism," published in *Visual Communication Quarterly* (1999); "Word People vs. Picture People: Normative Differences and Strategies for Control Over Work

Among Newsroom Subgroups," published in *Mass Communication and Society* (2002); and "Normative Conflict in the Newsroom: The Case of Digital Photo Manipulation," published in *Journal of Mass Media Ethics* (2003). More on best practice in the design of news infographics may be gleaned from Peter Sullivan's (1987) seminal *Newspaper Graphics*, and from Alberto Cairo's (2012) up-to-date, and theoretically engaged *The Functional Art*. More on the perceived shortcomings of newspaper infographics may be gleaned from John Allen Paulos's (1996) *A Mathematician Reads the Newspaper*; from Edward Tufte's (1983) *The Visual Display of Quantitative Information*; and from Darrell Huff's (1954) *How to Lie with Statistics*.

References

Ala.org (2011) "ACRL Visual Literacy Competency Standards for Higher Education." Available from: http://www.ala.org/acrl/standards/visualliteracy.

Ball, J. (2014) "Giving Up on Tabloid Data Journalism, or Giving up on Ampp3d." Available from: http://jbsidenotes.tumblr.com/post/100234161848/giving-up-on-tabloid-data-journalism-or-giving-up.

Bateman, S., Mandryk, R., Gutwin C., Genest, A., McDine, D. and Brooks, C. (2010) "Useful Junk? The Effects of Visual Embellishment on Comprehension and Memorability of Charts." *CHI 2010 Conference*, April 10–15, Atlanta, Georgia, USA.

BBC. (2014) "Visual Journalism Unit: Multiplatform Collaboration." *Academy*. Available from: http://www.bbc.co.uk/academy/journalism/article/art20140923115024680.

BBC Newsnight. (2014) "I Don't Trust Politicians & Corporations in this Country." Available from: https://www.youtube.com/watch?v=VqsFp0J22Hc

Bekhit, E. (2009) "Infographics in the United Arab Emirates Newspapers." *Journalism: Theory, Practice and Criticism* 10(4): 492–508.

Blasio, A. and Bisantz, A. (2002) "A Comparison of the Effects of Dataink Ratio on Performance with Dynamic Displays in a Monitoring Task." *Journal of Industrial Ergonomics* 30: 89–101.

Brasseur, L. (2003) *Visualizing Technical Information: A Cultural Critique*. Amityville, NY: Baywood.

Brinton, W. (1914) *Graphic Methods for Presenting Facts*. New York, NY: Engineering magazine company.

Brinton, W. (1915) "Joint Committee on Standards for Graphic Presentation Source." *Publications of the American Statistical Association* 14(112): 790–797.

Brinton, W. (1939) *Graphic Presentation*. New York, NY: Brinton Associates.

BSI (British Standards Institution). (1992) *British Standard 7581:1992 A Guide to the Presentation of Tables & Graphs*. London, UK: BSI.

Burke, C. (2013) "The atlas Gesellschaft und Wirtschaft (Society and the Economy), 1930." In Burke, C., Kindel, E. and Walker, S. (eds) *Isotype: Design and Contexts, 1925–1971*. London, UK: Hyphen, pp. 186–215.

Cairo, A. (2012) *The Functional Art: An Introduction to Information Graphics and Visualization*. New Riders.

Cairo, A. (2014) "Alberto Cairo: Data Journalism Needs to up its Own Standards." *Nieman Lab*. Available from: http://www.niemanlab.org/2014/07/alberto-cairo-data-journalism-needs-to-up-its-own-standards/.

Christiansen, J. (2011) "Infographics: The Great Circle Debate." *Scientific American*, 28 February. Available from: http://blogs.scientificamerican.com/observations/2011/03/28/infographics-the-great-circle-debate/.

Datajournalism.stanford.edu. (2009) "Journalism in the Age of Data: IV A New Era in Infographics." Available from: http://datajournalism.stanford.edu/.

Dick, M. (2014) "Interactive Infographics and News Values." *Digital Journalism* 2(4): 490–506.

Dick, M. (2015) "Just Fancy That: An Analysis of Infographic Propaganda in the *Daily Express*, 1956–1959." *Journalism Studies* 16(2): 1–23.

Dikovitskaya, M. (2012) "Major Theoretical Frameworks in Visual Culture." In Heywood, I. and Sandywell, B. (eds) *The Handbook of Visual Culture*. New York, NY: Berg.

Evans, H. and Taylor, E. (1997) *Pictures on a Page: Photo-Journalism, Graphics and Picture Editing*. London, UK: Pimlico.

Ghode, R. (2012) "Infographics in News Presentation: A Study of its Effective Use in Times of India and Indian Express the Two Leading Newspapers in India." *Journal of Business Management & Social Sciences Research* 1(1): 35–43.

Google. (2015) *Google Trends*. Available from: https://www.google.co.uk/trends/.

Guardian. (2009) "Tax Gap Interactive—Big Business: What they make, What they pay." Available from: http://www.theguardian.com/business/interactive/2009/feb/02/tax-database.

Harris, R. (1999) *Information Graphics: A Comprehensive Illustrated Reference*. New York, NY: Oxford University Press.

Hartmann, F. (2006) "After Neurath: The Quest for an Inclusive Form of the Icon." 31 October. Available from: http://www.medienphilosophie.net/texte/neurath.html.

Holmes, N. (1984) *Designer's Guide to Creating Charts and Diagrams*. New York, NY: Watson-Guptill Publications Inc.

Huff, D. (1954) *How to Lie with Statistics*. WW Norton & Company.

Inbar, O., Tractinsky, N. and Meyer, J. (2007) "Minimalism in Information Visualization: Attitudes towards Maximizing the Data-Ink Ratio." Proceedings of the 14th European Conference on Cognitive Ergonomics: Invent! Explore! ECCE, ACM Press, pp. 185–188.

Lowrey, W. (1999) "Routine News: The Power of the Organization in Visual Journalism." *Visual Communication Quarterly* 6(2): 10–15.

Lowrey, W. (2002) "Word People vs. Picture People: Normative Differences and Strategies for Control Over Work Among Newsroom Subgroups." *Mass Communication and Society* 5(4): 411–432.

Lowrey, W. (2003) "Normative Conflict in the Newsroom: The Case of Digital Photo Manipulation." *Journal of Mass Media Ethics* 18(2): 123–142.

Malofiejgraphics. (2011) "Awards—About—Malofiej Infographic World Summit Infographic Awards." Available from: http://www.malofiejgraphics.com/awards/.

Malofiejgraphics. (2015) "Times of Oman and The New York Times win Peter Sullivan Award / Best of Show in Print and Online Categories Respectively." Available from: http://www.malofiejgraphics.com/times-of-oman-and-the-new-york-times-win-peter-sullivan-award-best-of-show-in-print-and-online-categories-respectively/.

Maitlis, E. (2012) "Is Data Visualisation Just Style over Substance?" *BBC News*, 26 September. Available from: http://www.bbc.co.uk/news/technology-19731014.

McCandless, D. (2009) "Hello." *Information Is Beautiful*. Available from: http://www.informationisbeautiful.net/about/.

McChesney, R. (2000) *Rich Media Poor Democracy: Communications Politics in Dubious Times*. New York, NY: The New Press.

Niemanwatchdog. (2011) "Editors, Artists Chafe at the Errors and Hype in Bin Laden Death Story Graphics." Available from: http://www.niemanwatchdog.org/index.cfm?fuseaction=Showcase.view&showcaseid=152.

OED (Oxford English Dictionary). (2006) *OED Online*. Oxford: Oxford University Press. Available from: http://www.oed.com.

Paivio, A. and Kalman, C. (1973) "Picture Superiority in Free Recall: Imagery or Dual Coding?" *Cognitive Psychology* 5(2): 176–206.

Palsky, G. (1999) "The Debate on the Standardization of Statistical Maps and Diagrams (1857–1901): Elements for the History of Graphical Language." *Cybergeo: European Journal of Geography*. Available from: http://cybergeo.revues.org/148.

Pasternack, S. and Utt, S. (1990) "Reader Use and Understanding of Newspaper Infographics." *Newspaper Research Journal* 11(2): 28–41.

Paulos, J. (1996) *A Mathematician Reads the Newspaper*. New York, NY: Doubleday.

Prabu, D. (1992) "Accuracy of Visual Perception of Quantitative Graphics: An Exploratory Study." *Journalism Quarterly* 69(Summer): 273–292.

Reavy, M. (2003) "Rules and the Real World an Examination of Information Graphics in Time and Newsweek." *Visual Communication Quarterly* 10(4): 4–10.

Reid, A. (2014) "Guardian Forms New Editorial Teams to Enhance Digital Output." *Journalism.co.uk*, 10 October. Available from: https://www.journalism.co.uk/news/guardian-forms-new-editorial-teams-to-enhance-digital-output/s2/a562755/.

Small, H. (1998) "Florence Nightingale's Statistical Diagrams." Paper presented at Stats & Lamps Research Conference, organised by the Florence Nightingale Museum at St. Thomas' Hospital, 18 March.

Smith, E. and Hajash, D. (1988) "Informational Graphics in 30 Daily Newspapers." *Journalism & Mass Communication Quarterly* 65(3): 714–718.

So, A. (2012) "You Suck at Infographics." *Wired*, 23 July. Available from: http://www.wired.com/2012/07/you-suck-at-infographics/.

Stone, G. and Hall, P. (1997) "Do Newspapers Graphics have Two Dimensions?" *Visual Communication Quarterly* 4(4): 4–10.

Sullivan, P. (1987) *Newspaper Graphics*. Darmstadt, Germany: IFRA.

Torran, B. (2015) "Knowledge in Focus: A Q&A with David McCandless." *Statslife*, 12 January. Available from: http://www.statslife.org.uk/culture/1983-knowledge-in-focus-an-interview-with-david-mccandless.

Tufte, E. (1983) *The Visual Display of Quantitative Information*. Cheshire, CT: Graphics Press.

Tufte, E. (1997) *Visual Explanations: Images and Quantities, Evidence and Narrative*. Cheshire, CT: Graphics Press.

Tukey, J. (1990) "Data-Based Graphics: Visual Display in the Decades to Come." *Statistical Science* 5(3): 327–339.

Tversky, B., Kugelmass, S. and Winter, A. (1991) "Cross-Cultural and Developmental Trends in Graphic Productions." *Cognitive Psychology* 23(4): 515–557.

Utt, S. and Pasternak, S. (2000) "Update on Infographics to in American Newspapers." *Newspaper Research Journal* 21(2): 55–67.

Wainer, H. (1990) "Graphical Visions from William Playfair to John Tukey." *Statistical Science* 5(3): 340–346.

Wilson, M. (2015) "What Killed The Infographic?" *FastcoDesign*, 26 May. Available from: http://www.fastcodesign.com/3045291/what-killed-the-infographic.

Wong, D. (2013) *The Wall Street Journal Guide to Information Graphics: The Dos and Don'ts of Presenting Data, Facts, and Figures*. WW Norton & Company.

PART IX

Global digital journalism

50

SOCIAL MEDIA TRANSFORMING NEWS

Increasing public accountability in China—within limits

Joyce Y. M. Nip

On July 23, 2011, a message posted by a passenger four minutes after the crash of a high-speed train in Wenzhou, southeast China, on the Twitter-like platform Sina Weibo became the first of millions that were to follow about the crash, where 35 people died and 211 were injured. It also became an original source for news organizations. The government sacked three senior rail officials immediately and launched an investigation into the event, which has become cited as a watershed for the expression of public opinion using Weibo.

Nearly a year before, on September 16 2010, two sisters were intercepted by county officials of the Jiangxi province, southeast China, on their way to a news interview about the forced demolition of their home. They called the reporter for assistance when hiding in a public toilet, and the reporter then published a Weibo post seeking urgent help. Despite the desire for an exclusive story, he spread the word among other reporters of the happening to try to get help for the sisters. Reporters then interviewed the sisters via mobile phone, and the sisters broadcast their entrapment live on Weibo. Within an hour and a half, local officials suggested 'talking' to the sisters after reporters arrived at the scene. After a further half-hour, Sina Weibo had received clear instructions to delete the live broadcast messages. This turn of events resulting from the use of Weibo was described as the opening of a new page in citizen rights protection.

Events like these are examples of how Weibo has ushered in a new era of news production and dissemination in China with the use of the social media platform as both a medium for news but significantly as a source of news itself. With users of Weibo jumping from 13.8 percent of China's internet population to 48.7 percent from 2010 to 2011, users have broken news stories, opinion leaders have emerged, and critical voices, including citizen action, against unpopular projects and corrupt officials, have appeared. In some cases, this has resulted in projects being scrapped and officials being sacked. Alarmed by these developments, Chinese authorities have responded by cracking down on many of Weibo's more famous users, tightening control over how the platforms are used, and co-opting the space of Weibo for their own purposes. The adoption of Weibo peaked in June 2013 at 56.0 percent of internet users (44.1 percent of the Chinese population was online at that time), after which it declined (although remaining users seemed to have become more active) (Sina.com.cn, 2014) even as the adoption of the internet has continued to grow. In mid-2014, at least one major commercial player, Tencent, announced it would stop developing its Weibo service. By contrast, an alternative social media platform, Weixin, has grown exponentially.

While the democratizing role of social media has attracted a good deal of academic interest, this chapter looks specifically at that dynamic and the impact of Weibo on news in the context of China. The rise of Weibo over the past few years offers a concrete case for examining the possibilities as well as the limitations of the public role of social media in authoritarian China, where all forms of media are tightly controlled. This chapter draws on literature in Chinese and English and primary data from the author's own research. It offers a brief overview of the use of social media by news organizations and journalists and contextualizes their role in the system of media control in China (see Gulyás, and Djerf-Pierre and Hedman, this volume).

Weibo catches on

Weibo was first available commercially in China in 2006 but the services were closed by the Chinese authorities following the 2009 Ürümqi riots, when access to Facebook and Twitter was also blocked. Sina Weibo was launched in August 2009 as a free commercial service. Similar to Twitter, users could publish messages of up to 140 characters, but this renders a much richer message than 140 characters in English. Other features like 'long Weibo,' photo and video uploads (features that were later adopted by Twitter) further add to the communicative capacity of the platform. Users bring their offline social networks online as well as acquire new connections by 'following' and being 'followed' by other users. At the time of writing, the top user account on Sina Weibo, for a long time held by the out-spoken actress Yao Chen, had over 77 million followers. Building on its success as a privately owned and commercially run news portal, Sina repeated its strategy of enlisting celebrities to its Sina Weibo blogging service and managed to enroll 100 million registered users in its first 18 months. Since then, more than 100 other Weibo services have been offered by commercial and official media groups. By the end of 2010, there were more than 1.2 billion Weibo accounts in China (among a population of 1.3 billion), and Weibo had become the first choice of exposing information among Chinese internet users (People.com.cn, 2010). A survey in 2010 found that over 73 percent of Weibo users considered it an important supplier of news (Zhou, Liu, and Wang, 2011). Seventy-one percent of users said Weibo usage had increased their concern about politics (Wang, 2011).

Weibo as key public space in controlled mediascape

The public role of Weibo upsets the system of ideological formation, where the ruling Chinese Communist Party controls the production of news media content. Publications have to be licensed and newspapers at county level or above require an official agency as sponsor. Broadcasting is owned and run by various levels of government. Commercialization of the media that started in the 1990s only means that news media now serve two masters—the Communist Party and the audience. Within a newspaper group, the long-time 'mother' (Party) paper would focus on propagating the Party's messages and agenda, and the newer 'offspring' (commercial) papers would focus on winning the audience by social and even investigative news reports. Even commercial papers are not exempt from the task of official propaganda so some pages of a paper may be devoted to official announcements and campaign stories and other pages to non-official news (Lee, He, and Huang, 2006). Regional and local television stations are required to carry the 30-minute China Central Television evening news program every evening. The Communist Party controls the content of news through a multipronged mechanism that includes the appointment of editors, licensing of journalists, periodic political training of journalists, briefings, guidelines, and directives about news agenda and perspective, prepublication clearance of major stories, and reviews after publication.

Controls over the internet and Weibo

The internet has been publicly accessible in China since 1995. The internet infrastructure is officially owned and is subject to a multilayered system of technical blockage and filtering that came to be known as the Great Firewall. Institutional media, as well as Party and government agencies established their websites from the 1990s. Unofficial websites need registration and non-news sites are not allowed to publish news. Privately owned and commercially-run news portals, which were used mainly as sources of news until Weibo's popularity, are not permitted to conduct original news reporting but can aggregate news produced by traditional news organizations. Companies that provide internet services are held responsible for the content published on their interfaces so the regulation generates a mechanism of self-censorship.

From the end of 2011, regulations were passed in various cities to require Weibo users to register with their real names. In 2012, this became law and real-name registration was required of all internet users. In 2013, celebrities with huge followings on Weibo were targeted and a few were arrested to keep their Weibo use in line with the official ideology. Later that year, a judicial interpretation made people who publish slanderous comments online liable to defamation charges if their posts are read by 5,000 or more users or reposted 500 times or more. Party/government agencies were urged to increase interaction with the public, and as a result the number of Party/government accounts on Sina Weibo jumped by more than 200 percent from February 2011 to 2013 (Chinalabs.com and China Internet and Society Studies Centre, 2013). To reassert its dominance in public opinion, China Central Television (CCTV) started at least four new commentary segments in their news programs (Qian, 2012). Various levels of government also pay to have supportive posts published online. While the number of Weibo users has fallen, it remains the main platform on which Chinese citizens regularly publish public information, express their views, and share their sentiments on news issues. Writer Chen Shuqing contrasted Weibo to the recently popular Weixin, describing Weixin as like a private banquet, while Weibo acted like a public square (NTDTV, 2014).

Weibo usage for news

As of 2013, 'hot social events'—including natural disasters, public health, government corruption, and social security (as classified by the authors)—made up 21.9 percent of heavily reposted (more than 1,000 times) Weibo posts, just second to posts on 'leisure and mood' (42.6 percent) (Li *et al.*, 2015). At that time, 64.9 percent of users searched Weibo for news, and 59.2 percent searched for hot topics (Lei, 2011). Sina Weibo stands out from other service providers by attracting the urban elite and politically aware, with 80.3 percent of its users following news and hot social events on the platform (CNNIC, 2014).

The millions of news-savvy Weibo users have become a rich source of information for news organizations. Given the ineffectiveness of the government petition office and executive interference of courts, even in the pre-internet era Chinese citizens looked to the news media to redress their grievances. The investigative journalism programs of CCTV, for example, were known for drawing petitioners who tried to get their grievances reported. This occurred despite the party-state's control of media, as news organizations tried to appeal to their audiences and journalists struggled to tell the truth. With the rise of Weibo, journalists describe their Weibo accounts as 'online petition offices' (Bei, 2013). In 2010, 22 percent of the top 50 major social events originated on Weibo (People.com.cn, 2010).

Weibo transforms news process

While Weibo offers a novel platform for citizens to participate in news, news media and journalists use Weibo for their own purposes. By the end of 2013, Chinese newspapers, television stations, broadcast radio, and news agencies were running more than 37,000 organizational accounts on Sina and Tencent Weibo alone (People.com.cn, 2013). Weibo has also become the first space where news stories are being published ahead of news websites or portals, and ahead of the traditional media; sometimes as live broadcasting on Weibo. Weibo accounts are used to publicize stories and the organizations that provide them. Newspapers create new sections that source content from Weibo (Peng, 2011; Shen, 2011), and news magazines start new topics on Weibo to discuss with their followers and formulate stories. (Liao and Li, 2011). In 2010, more than 90 percent of reporters were using Weibo to help news-gathering and connect with their peers. More than 60 percent of reporters said they had completed enterprise stories with the help of tip-offs or interviews solicited on Weibo (PR Newswire, 2010). The changes in the process and organization of news production, and the news products themselves have been the main concern of Chinese-language studies about the impact of social media on journalism. Bei's (2013) report is one of the few in English that discusses these changes.

The Weibo platform has given journalists and news organizations a space that goes outside the logic of their usual operation. Individual journalists and the official Xinhua News Agency and CCTV have been found to publish content on their Weibo accounts that could not be published via their usual channels (Zhang, 2014; Zhang, Cai, and Zhang 2011). Journalists have also commented on news issues (Bei, 2013). However, this behavior is often considered deviant by the Party and has drawn penalties in some cases; as a result, many journalists have become more cautious of their use of Weibo (Bei, 2013).

Weibo vs. institutional news in agenda and frame setting

The effects of Weibo citizen content on news content in general have attracted little academic attention. Some studies have identified an agenda-setting effect for Weibo on institutional news (Tang and Sampson, 2012; Tong 2013). For example, Wu *et al.* (2013) found that Sina Weibo messages influenced the number of stories, type of content (information versus opinion), and topics covered by institutional media on the 2011 high-speed train crash. Beyond the first level of agenda setting, a comparison of the attributes of the train crash reportage in China's news and on Sina Weibo suggested that attribute agenda-setting power (McCombs, 2005) for Sina Weibo on institutional news was limited. In contrast, news media in Hong Kong and Macau—which enjoy press freedom under a different—'one country, two systems'—political system reported more of the attributes of the incident posted by Weibo users (Zhu, 2011). This suggests that a more nuanced understanding of the impact of Weibo citizen content on institutional news setting in China would need to take into account news control mechanisms. In other words, given the official requirement to downplay negativity, news organizations can only address audience interests and concerns within limits.

Depending on whether the news organization is oriented more to the Party or the audience, how they respond to Weibo citizen posts also differs. In reporting the 2011 train crash, a Party-oriented newspaper was found to have mainly sourced human stories and charity donations from Sina Weibo, whereas an outspoken audience-oriented paper sourced Weibo content that queried the government's actions and account of what really happened (Tong, 2013). In a second case in 2011 a two-year girl in Guangdong province was run over by two vehicles, with passers-by making no attempt to help, the perspectives presented in institutional media and on Weibo were opposed: Weibo messages mainly presented a negative image of the city involved, while the majority of institutional news reports presented a positive image (Xin and Lai, 2011).

It is important to note that the power of Weibo users can be easily over-estimated. Even in its early months, professional media had a significant presence on Weibo. Messages published by media organizations and journalists were the second most reposted (22.2 percent), just after individual personal home pages (32.9 percent) (Greer and Yan, 2012). Nip and Fu's (2016) more recent study conducted in early 2013 on a series of corruption exposés similarly found that news organizations and the Sina news headline aggregator were the most reposted Weibo accounts. Tong (2013) concluded in her study of newspaper and Weibo content about the train crash that Weibo's advantage was in releasing early information about the incident and facilitating citizens' efforts to hold the government accountable but newspapers maintained their authority in giving an interpretation of the incident.

User participation in news on earlier internet platforms

Weibo is the latest platform on which Chinese internet users have participated in the news process. The website was the earliest internet space used. Since the 1990s, activists have established "large numbers of websites containing news content and independent commentary." Examples are the June 4th Network (64tianwang.com), started in 1999, and the China Media Supervision Network, launched in 2003. Online magazines and online versions of independent magazines (such as *Minjian*) were also published (Wen, 2008–2009). Predictably, operators of these independent media have faced crackdowns from Chinese authorities. The founder of the June 4th Network, Huang Qi, for example, was arrested and jailed several times. Both the June 4th Network and the China Media Supervision Network were permanently closed; the former moved to a server overseas.

For most citizens who are not politically committed but might have something to say, online forums hosted on Bulletin Board Systems (BBSs) were the earliest space of their news participation. From 1995, when the Shuimu Tsinghua was started by Tsinghua University (open to non-members of the University), commercial and official forums including the very popular Tianya Forum and the Strong Nation Forum (hosted at *People's Daily Online*) began in 1998–2000, and blogs became popular in 2005 (Hu, 2010). The 2003 case of Sun Zhigang, a young graduate who migrated to the southern city of Guangzhou and who died while in custody for not carrying his residence permit, sparked an early storm of online protest. The outspoken *Southern Metropolis Daily* first reported the case, which was amplified on BBSs and citizen websites, eventually leading to the abolition of the government regulation that required migrants to always carry their residence permits. The building of a paraxylene chemical plant in Xiamen in 2007 offered an example of a journalist's blog providing alternative information and views, and mobilizing protest actions in collaboration with readers of his blog. On the anonymous online forums and video sharing sites, it was ordinary internet users who first published the report, photographs, and video of the 2008 Wenchuan earthquake.

By then, reporters were already sourcing ideas and contacts from blogs and online forums (Tang and Sampson, 2012). Some investigative reporters announced reporting projects on their personal blogs and online forums to invite user participation (Zhang, 2011). At the same time, traditional news media also influenced content on online spaces. From 1998 to 2010, traditional media were the source of information for 43 percent of the 210 issues that aroused heated public opinion online, with 34 percent from online spaces (forums at the top) (Zhong and Yu, 2011). However, while internet users were sourcing information from media coverage, this did not mean media were framing online talk. Perspectives on BBSs and media reports were more interactive (Zhou and Moy, 2007). Likewise, BBS forums and blogs sometimes sustained and other times acted against the agenda of traditional media (Tang and Sampson, 2012). In the last few years, as Weibo has grown in popularity, adoption of BBS among Chinese internet users decreased from 32.4 percent at the end of 2010 to 19.9 percent at the end of 2014.

Issues and discussion

At the end of 2014 the adoption rate of Weibo stood at 38.4 percent of Chinese Internet users (CNNIC, 2015). While the implications of the recent decline of Weibo's usage on journalism and the public at large have yet to be assessed, the developments relating to Weibo in the last few years in China have raised many important questions. A central question for English-language scholarship has been the implications of online technology for facilitating freedom and democracy. This is a contemporary version of the same concern about press freedom in the newspaper era. Scholars seem divided between the utopian perspective, arguing that civil society can use digital technology to achieve greater freedom, and the dystopian perspective, where rulers use the same technology to gain more control, while some consider these two dynamics as competing. The question can only be answered by examining uses of the specific technology in the particular cultural context—in the China case, taking into account the tension placed by both the Chinese Communist Party and the market on news organizations and the commercial Weibo service operators, mediated by the norms and practices of journalists. While Weibo has been able to play a role in news origination, the immediacy of citizen's postings is crucial for its popularity and, even at its height, institutional news media held an advantage in the interpretation of news events. Weibo's decline was widely interpreted to be the result of government action to rein it in, but some analysts have also suggested the novelty attraction of Weixin (Bei, 2013) and users have cited abundant advertising and marketing by faked accounts as other factors.

By merely offering a digital public space not previously available, the internet offers the opportunity of greater freedom of expression and communication to Chinese citizens. While the user registration requirement is often seen as inhibiting public expression, the trust associated with real identity also encourages public engagement and collective action, at least on mobile phones (Liu, 2014). The optional system of user verification on Weibo (which allows users to acquire a 'V' sign next to their displayed user name after their offline identity is verified by the service provider)—not related to the official user registration requirement—encourages the transfer of offline credibility to the online world. While this re-establishes the social hierarchy to online, it also allows journalists to emerge as opinion leaders on public issues. With news organizations and online news aggregators showing an ability to maintain their dominance as the most reposted accounts in public issues, and party and government accounts also active on Weibo, the extent to which the status quo of power has been upset needs further investigation.

News organizations source stories from Weibo and other social media platforms. They also seek input through interaction with Weibo users. This raises the question of whether this has resulted in news organizations reinforcing their power in public information or democratizing it, and consequently enabling greater freedom for public information or not. Weibo has offered new freedom to news organizations as well, which has led to incongruity between the identity of the Weibo account and that of the news organization. Questions about personnel and organizational control processes have also been raised. Bei (2013) identified a recent trend on Weibo for investigative journalists to become online social activists. Driven by a confluence of the traditional Confucian ideal of intellectuals and the Western liberal professional norm, while struggling against the controls of the party-state, Chinese journalists often support (rather than compete against) each other on the platform to report sensitive stories. The relationship between journalists and their news organizations as well as their public audience has changed with the rise of Weibo.

Tong (2013) asserts that Weibo has put traditional journalism on the defensive, as it forces the latter to safeguard its authority and legitimacy. Zhou (2013) agrees that the new media environment challenges some basic norms of journalistic professionalism and authority, but considers this greater transparency of journalism as an opportunity for the relationship between journalism and political control to be reconfigured by helping to construct the authority of journalism as a more independent profession.

The power of Weibo, of course, does not stand on its own. Messages are often cross-posted on various online forums and social networking sites. The degree of Weibo's interconnectivity with other social media platforms, however, is not fully known. What is known is that internet users in China are more social than in many other countries, due in part to the large number of users online at any one time. The dense social networks on Weibo—connecting family, friends, and strangers—makes it a unique, nationwide, and instantaneously interactive public space (though with much lower adoption in rural areas). However, news organizations also complain that they are getting the same news tips every other organization receives, leading to homogeneity of news coverage. The implication of this on the development of a Chinese public sphere also warrants study.

Speedy digital connections on Weibo work for dissemination, but they also work against interpretation or deliberation. The fact that nearly 80 percent of users access Weibo on mobile devices tends to encourage instantaneous rather than careful and deliberative responses. The technological characteristics of the platform and the mode of access fit well into the daily life of busy urban dwellers—most internet users in China are urban—who can afford little time for thinking about the news. This makes the formation of a 'public sphere' unlikely. Indeed, the author's own research about 21 corruption exposés on Sina Weibo found the communicative function of the majority of source posts was 'information provision' (81 percent), while that of the reposts was "disseminating/attending to the case" (56.3 percent). "Analysis/interpretation/opinion/judgment provision" was not found among the source posts and only among 16.5 percent of the reposts.

With the websites of Amnesty International and even the BBC blocked for Chinese internet users, and the most popular international social media platforms not accessible, some describe the Chinese internet as a giant intranet, filled with Chinese content produced by various levels of government and news organizations of every medium. A study on the democratic potential of online forums in the early years of the Chinese internet suggested that Chinese internet users were able to fly freely, but within a cage—where BBSs were merely virtual classrooms in which participants learned the meaning of democracy (Huang, 1999). Is Weibo an up-to-day version of this classroom? How has learning on earlier platforms of social media informed innovation this time around? Has the new technology provided conditions for users to step out of the classroom and make things real? Or has the government learned better and is able to confine the students to the classroom? What will new platforms of digital networked social media mean for the public dissemination of information and formation of opinion?

Further reading

Yuezhi Zhao's (2008) *Communication in China: Political economy, power and conflict* provides an excellent analysis and rich facts about China's media and culture sectors under the control of the party-state. Guobin Yang's (2009) *The power of the Internet in China: Citizen activism online* analyzes citizen contention from several perspectives. Jens Damm and Simona Thomas' (2006) *Chinese cyberspaces: Technological changes and political effects* provides a historical overview.

References

Bei, J. (2013) "How Chinese Journalists use Weibo Microblogging for Investigative Reporting." Reuters Institute for the study of Journalism. Available from: https://reutersinstitute.politics.ox.ac.uk/sites/default/files/How_Chinese_journalists_use_Weibo_microblogging_for_investigative_reportingpercent281percent29.pdf.

Chinalabs.com and China Internet and Society Studies Centre. (2013) *2012–2013 Weibo Development Research Report* [Chinese]. Available from: http://video.zj.com/cns/20122013weibo.pdf.

CNNIC. (2014) *2014 Research Report on User Behaviour of Chinese Social Applications.* Available from: http://www.cnnic.cn/hlwfzyj/hlwxzbg/201408/P020140822379356612744.pdf.

CNNIC. (2015) *35th Statistical Report on Internet Development in China* [Chinese]. Available from: http://www.cnnic.cn/hlwfzyj/hlwxzbg/201502/P020150203551802054676.pdf.

Damm, J. and Thomas, S. (eds). (2006) *Chinese Cyberspaces: Technological Changes and Political Effects.* London, UK: Routledge.

Greer, J.D. and Yan, Y. (2012) "Agenda-Setting and the Two-Step Flow of Communication on Microblogs: A Cross-Cultural Analysis of Opinion Leader Activities on U.S. Twitter and China's Sina Weibo." In Xue, L. (ed.) *The Illusions of Intercultural Communication in Global Media.* Wuhan, China: Wuhan University.

Hu, Y. (2010) "BBS Sites on China's Changing Web." 1 June. Available from: http://cmp.hku.hk/2010/06/01/6158/.

Huang, E. (1999) "Flying Freely but in the Cage: An Empirical Study of Using Internet for the Democratic Development in China." *Information Technology for Development* 8(3): 145–162.

Lee, C.C., He, Z. and Huang, Y. (2006) "'Chinese Party Publicity Inc.' Conglomerated: The Case of the Shenzhen Press Group." *Media Culture & Society* 28(4): 581–602.

Lei, B. (2011) "Study on the Issues and Strategies of Weibo Uses by Traditional Media" [Chinese]. *News World* 3: 76–77.

Li, Y., et al. (2015) "What are Chinese Talking about in Hot Weibos?" *Physica A: Statistical Mechanics and its Applications* 419: 546–557.

Liao, J. and Li, C. (2011) "Investigation into the Current Uses of Weibo by Traditonal Media" [Chinese]. *Editorial Friend* 5: 74–77.

Liu, J. (2014) "Communicating beyond Information? Mobile Phones and Mobilization to Offline Protests in China." *Television & New Media.* 20 August. DOI:10.1177/1527476414544972.

McCombs, M. (2005) "A Look at Agenda-Setting: Past, Present and Future." *Journalism Studies* 6(4): 543–557.

Nip, J.Y.M. and Fu, K.W. (2016) "Challenging Official Propaganda? Public Opinion Leaders on Sina Weibo." *The China Quarterly* 225: 122–144.

NTDTV. (2014, Feb 5) "Weibo Posts Drop by 70 percent: Will Weixin replace it?" [Chinese]. Available from: https://www.youtube.com/watch?v=vNzrOYyEkgI.

Peng, J. (2011) "Newspaper Weibo: Impact on the Production Mechanism of Newspaper Journalism and Competition" [Chinese]. *Xin Wen Jie* 4: 51–53.

People.com.cn. (2010) "2010 Weibo Annual Report Released: Weibo has become Internet Users' First Choice of Exposure" [Chinese]. 29 December. Available from: http://media.people.com.cn/GB/13605622.html.

People.com.cn. (2013) "2013 Media Weibo's New Force" [Chinese]. 13 December. Available from: http://media.people.com.cn/n/2013/1212/c14677-23816388.html.

PR Newswire. (2010) "Chinese Journalists Social Media Engagement Survey Report" [Chinese]. Available from: http://www.slideshare.net/strategythinker/china-journalist-socialmediaengagementsurveyreportprnewswire2010.

Qian, X. (2012) "Exploration and Analysis of the 'Weibotization' of News Commentary" [Chinese]. *Shanghai Journalism Review* 2: 71–74.

Shen, L. (2011) "The Weibo Road of Traditional Media: Empirical Analysis of the Weibo of Five Traditional Media" [Chinese]. *Xin Wen Jie* 4: 49–50, 53.

Sina.com.cn. (2014) "Sina Reports Third Quarter 2014 Financial Results." *Press Releases*, 13 November. Available from: http://corp.sina.com.cn/eng/news/2014-11-14/160.html.

Tang, L. and Sampson, H. (2012) "The Interaction between Mass Media and the Internet in Non-Democratic States: The Case of China." *Media, Culture & Society* 34(4): 457–471.

Tong, J. (2013) "Weibo Communication and the Epistemic Authority of Chinese Journalism: A Case Study of the 2011 Wenzhou High-Speed Train Incident" [Chinese]. *Communication & Society* 25: 73–101.

Wang, W. (2011) "Mainstream Ideology Needs to Act in Weibo Era" [Chinese]. *Red Flag Manuscript*. Available from: http://theory.people.com.cn/GB/16412773.html.

Wen, Y. (2008–2009) "China: Grass that Grows through the Cracks." Available from: http://www.scribd.com/doc/14626501/Mainland-China-English.

Wu, Y., Atkin, D., Lau, T.Y., Lin, C. and Mou, Y. (2013) "Agenda Setting and Micro-Blog Use: An Analysis of the Relationship between Sina Weibo and Newspaper Agendas in China." *The Journal of Social Media in Society* 2(2): 8–25.

Xin, W. and Lai, H. (2011) "Comparison and Contrast of the Agenda Setting of Traditional Media and Weibo: The Case of Hit-and-Run of Two-Year Old Xiao Yueyue in Foshan, Guangdong" [Chinese]. *Xin Wen Jie* 9: 27–30.

Zhang, H. (2014) "Could Weibo Save Decline" [Chinese]. *Tan Suo Jing Wei* 1: 61–65.

Zhang, X., Cai, M. and Zhang, J. (2011) "Examining the 5W Model: Convergence and Development of Traditional Media and Weibo" [Chinese]. *China Newspaper Industry* 9, 30–32.

Zhang, Z. (2011) "Revolution of News Production: From Organizational to Social—A Study on How Weibo has Impacted Investigative Journalism" [Chinese]. *Xin Wen Jie zhe*. Available from: http://xwjz.eastday.com/eastday/xwjz/node528384/node528385/u1a5749666.html.

Zhao, Y. (2008) *Communication in China: Political Economy, Power, and Conflict*. Maryland: Rowman & Littlefield Publishers.

Zhong, Y. and Yu, X. (2011) "Communication Characteristics of Significant Online Public Opinion Cases in China (1998–2010)." In Yin, Y., Wu, X. and Liu, R. (ed.) *Annual Report of Development on New Media in China 2011* [Chinese]. Beijing: Social Sciences Academic Press (China).

Zhou, B. (2013) "From Backstage to Frontstage: The Visualization of Journalism in the New Media Environment" [Chinese]. *Communication & Society* 25: 35–71.

Zhou, S., Liu, R. and Wang, W. (2011) "Reflection on Hot Phenomenon of Microblog in 2010" [Chinese]. In Yin, Y., Wu, X. and Liu, R. (eds) *Annual Report of Development on New Media in China 2011* [Chinese]. Beijing: Social Sciences Academic Press (China).

Zhou, Y. and Moy, P. (2007) "Parsing Framing Processes: The Interplay between Online Public Opinion and Media Coverage." *Journal of Communication* 57(1): 79–98.

Zhu, H. (2011) "Hold your Glass Tight! Advantages and Disadvantages of New and Old Media Revealed in the Reporting of the 7.23 High-Speed Train Incident" [Chinese]. *Observations from Internet* 6: 113–115.

51

SOCIAL MEDIA AND RADIO JOURNALISM IN SOUTH AFRICA

Tanja Bosch

Radio remains the most available, widespread, and affordable medium in Africa, compared to print and television channels. Circulation of mainstream broadsheets is on the decline internationally as well as in South Africa (Stassen, 2010), while radio listenership figures for mainstream and community radio stations are continually growing. Together with the growth of radio audiences, there is a concomitant growth in the number of internet users, and a corresponding shift in how radio stations have begun to extend their presence into the online realm, through websites and live streaming. In recent years, this has come through social networking sites, particularly Facebook and Twitter. Twitter especially supports multiple opportunities for participation, including creating, tagging, and sharing content, as well as reading, watching, and following hashtags (Gleason, 2013). The radio industry has found new ways to adapt to the changing needs of listeners and to address their new patterns of media consumption (Rosales, 2013).

When we examine the relationship between radio as 'traditional' or 'legacy media' and the internet and social media as 'new' media, we see how the 'new' media achieve cultural significance by refashioning the old media. This 'remediation' (Bolter and Grusin, 2001) allows radio broadcasters to draw on mutually constructive strategies of generating immediacy and making users hyperaware of the original medium of radio.

While there has been a significant growth of digital journalism in the form of online newspapers (Bosch, 2010), this chapter focuses only on commercial and public radio broadcasting and its engagement with social media. The online networking site Facebook and micro-blogging service Twitter are increasingly intersecting with mainstream news applications in South Africa. Social media have scooped traditional media in reporting breaking news, and mainstream reporters often use social networks to release news stories or to add detail outside of the usual news cycle. News production has become increasingly participatory, with producers and consumers using social media to produce, edit, and distribute news items. Similarly, the increased prevalence of the mobile phone has changed the practice of newsgathering in a number of ways. The most notable has been the rise of citizen journalism, and the spread of news not subject to gatekeeping or editorial processes. In Africa in particular, the penetration of mobile phones above fixed lines has reduced the digital divide, as more people also have access to online social networking sites via their phones.

Drawing on a qualitative approach, reflecting interviews with radio journalists together with a qualitative content analysis of tweets and Facebook posts from commercial talk and music radio stations, this chapter explores how radio journalists and listeners use social media (usually accessed via mobile phones). Moreover, this chapter considers whether stations organize less along the lines of identity politics and communal social relations and more on the basis of network sociality, whether digital technologies have impacted on the daily routines of radio journalists in South Africa, and how we can draw on theories of political listening (Bickford, 1996, 2011) to understand the listener engagements taking place in social media, perhaps as an extension of the public spheres created by radio stations.

Background: the internet and social media in South Africa

Internet penetration in Africa stands at 26.5 percent compared to the world average of 42.3 percent. In South Africa, internet penetration is at 51.3 percent (http://www.internetworldstats.com/stats1.htm). Country-specific data show that only 40.9 percent of South African households have internet access (http://mg.co.za/article/2014-06-24-a-tale-of-two-internet-connections), which means that many of those reflected in the former statistic are accessing the internet at work or in public spaces such as libraries. The issue of the digital divide is thus still very relevant in the South African context, where there is uneven access to broadband access. Moreover, the dominance of English on the internet means that many South Africans are excluded; among 11 official languages, English is not the most commonly spoken. High levels of poverty and inequality means that the majority of working class people probably do not have regular internet access. The growth of mobile telephony has been listed as one way to combat the digital divide in South Africa, and published internet statistics usually do not take the mobile internet into account. Donner and Gitau (2009) have shown how low-income mobile users frequently access the internet primarily on mobiles (versus desktop computers) and often see social media as low cost substitutes to other communication channels. They argue that in South Africa cost is a driver towards mobile internet usage as it is usually cheaper to access the internet using a mobile phone than to go to an internet cafe. In addition, the so-called pay-as-you-go system allows users to add airtime and data in small financial increments, together with the widespread possibility of purchasing smartphones on credit via clothing store accounts, for example.

Facebook is the most popular social networking site in South Africa with 11.8 million users and 8.8 million users accessing it on their mobile phones. Twitter is the third most popular social networking site in South Africa (after Facebook and YouTube) with 6.6 million users, though Twitter has more intensive engagement than Facebook (South African Social Media Landscape 2015, www.worldwideworx.com). While South African consumers also use other social networking sites such as Instagram, LinkedIn, and many others, Facebook and Twitter are the most prevalent, and the ones most used by media outlets, radio stations in particular. For this reason, the present study focuses only on these two sites. Audiences can now not only listen to their favorite radio stations using their mobile phones, if they stream live or if it is an online station, but they can also go online and 'follow' their radio stations and favorite presenters via Facebook and Twitter to get access to a host of contextual and follow-up information. While nearly all South African radio stations stream online, listening to these in real time requires a high-speed internet connection. Social networking sites thus become an easy way for radio stations to enhance their broadcast content and interact with audience members, particular as they already use these sites in large numbers. In some cases, these sites have been used to strengthen the relationship between listeners and radio stations (Taylor, 2010).

It should also be noted that while there is widespread prevalence of digital media, one should recognize the persistence of a digital divide—not only between South Africa and the global North but also within the global South itself. While South Africa is fairly well resourced by African standards, there are varying levels of internet access within the country. Much like radio set ownership and usage, smartphones and tablets with internet access are often shared within and between households, and thus choice of radio station and the choice to interact with these radio stations via social media can often be dependent upon availability. Much of the scholarship on radio and ICTs has focused on Western contexts, and as such the affordances of the new social media can be quite different. As Moyo (2012: 214) warns:

> the digital turn and the demotic turn on radio therefore must not be seen as synony-
> mous with the participatory turn, especially in African countries where the regulation
> of corporate power in mass media is weak and where multiple forms of the digital
> divide that impede on consistent and meaningful use of digital media still persist.

Background: radio in South Africa

The South African radio landscape is complex, with a range of public, commercial, and community radio stations offering audiences a wide range of listening choices. During the apartheid era, media were state-owned and controlled, but since 1994 with the liberaliza-tion of the airwaves, the range of options has widened. The state-owned radio broadcasting service was converted to a public service broadcaster (SABC) with an English service and an additional 11 stations broadcasting in local African languages. The PSB also operates a com-mercial arm with several commercial music radio stations. There are also independently owned and operated commercial music stations, and over 150 community radio stations owned and operated by community-based groups. Moreover, a number of online only radio stations exist and are thriving.

Traditional mass media, such as radio, are increasingly using the internet, through blogs, social media, and mobile phones to distribute their content and interact with the audience by combining vertical and horizontal communication methods. The majority of scholarship on new media technologies and the public sphere focuses on the political dimension of social media, but as Barton (2005) argues, social networking sites are not often used for political purposes. These sites are also used for exchanging mundane information and perspectives that sometimes influence public opinion. In this regard, we find the notion of 'cultural citizenship' (Urrichio, 2004) useful to problematize new participatory cultures in radio. Urrichio argues that the blurring of boundaries between production and consumption occasioned by online networks has implications for the practice of citizenship. New media technologies create not only dynamic online public spheres but also enable average citizens to participate in the appropriation, creation, transformation, and recirculation of media content (Urrichio, 2004).

Journalists' use of social media

Much of the research on Twitter and journalism has focused on the dynamics of professional news practices on the platform, with journalism considered as a cultural field of production (Hermida, 2013). When Twitter is used to spread and comment on the news, it results in a stream of information, opinions, and emotions related to current events, a phenomenon

Hermida (2010) refers to as 'ambient journalism'—a journalism derived from the absorption and negotiation of micro-content within complex media environments. Previous research has shown that most reporters engage in a 'journalism of service,' while also adhering to conventions of product and 'lecture by professional authorities.' Evidence for service includes live tweeting news events and re-tweeting citizen voices. 'Journalism as product' is supported by a significant number of reporters' links to their own newsroom content and by their heavy reliance on official sources, despite the networked audience afforded by Twitter. As studies in other countries show (e.g. Lasorsa, 2012), South African journalists freely express their opinions, and though this is a common micro-blogging practice it contests the normative journalistic mandate of objectivity. Similarly, radio journalists share user-generated content with their listeners and followers by re-tweeting posts by other users or sharing links to external websites.

In the present study, journalists interviewed described how they often take the lead from social media for story ideas, and although they are hesitant to acknowledge their use of social media as a news source, they admit to relying on it for story ideas. Their daily journalistic routine is also affected, as they turn more frequently to social media sources and contacts to source and supplement their research for existing stories. Most journalists were skeptical of the practice of quoting directly from social media sites, but indicated that they often turned to social networks to find out what was happening with respect to conflict events or to gauge citizen opinion on news events, which often shaped their reporting practices. They indicated that the volume of social media discussions, particularly on Twitter, was more likely to result in stories being followed up, showing its power as an agenda setting tool.

Besides sharing political opinions, radio journalists sometimes also write about their personal lives, giving listeners insights into their personalities beyond the normative 'objectivity' of their identities as journalists and creating an increased intimacy with their listeners. This was usually not a deliberate choice on their part, and they did not see this blurring of their roles as impacting on their credibility in any way. In most cases, journalists added a disclaimer that they were posting in their private capacities. However, their disclosures never extended to the political realm. While posts often pertained to aspects of their private lives, they never expressed political views openly on social media. Despite feeling free to share their opinions, journalists still felt bound by normative values of objectivity and impartiality, though their selection of mainstream news items to retweet or post, usually involved choosing a common frame which could ultimately shape public opinion. Posting private preferences about everyday topics, such as the weather, clothing, or restaurant choices, was also seen as closing the gap between journalist and audience, with the latter coming to know them much more intimately than usual.

Radio listeners and citizen journalism

Radio listeners often used their mobile phones to engage in citizen journalism, particularly now that social media affords the possibility for direct engagement with radio station staff. ICTs have expanded communicative radio spaces and transformed the nature of audience engagement (Chiumbu and Ligaga, 2013). Whereas in the past the mobile phone allowed listeners to participate by calling in to the station to interact with the host on air during phone-in programs, this new level of participation allows listeners to interact via stations' social media platforms.

The first level of engagement is through citizen journalism, referring to a wide range of practices in which citizens engage in journalistic practices which could include blogging, video and photo sharing, posting eyewitness commentary on current events, or a range of other practices in which they become content creators (Goode, 2009). This kind of user-generated content is frequently seen on the social media feeds of radio stations and often plays an agenda setting role. During citizen-driven conflicts such as the national service delivery protests, for example, or during periods of xenophobic violence, there were high levels of engagement on Facebook and Twitter. Radio stations would tweet their own news items, but when listeners posted or tweeted citizen commentary, they would also retweet these posts. The widespread nature of mobile technology and social media has thus allowed listeners to become active participants in creating radio content and to contribute to setting the news agendas. This happens in a number of ways. Listeners often use their mobile phones to record video footage of certain events considered newsworthy, then later post these videos on the Facebook site of a radio station to generate on-air discussion. This happens frequently on talk and music radio. Examples of this include mobile phone footage documenting incidences of police brutality and racist attacks by citizens on each other. The radio host would then engage in a conversation about these issues on the air, and direct listeners to the station's Facebook page to view with footage. "This so-called 'crowdsourcing' strategy provides a sense of ownership on the part of the audience and results in heightened engagement with the media" (Rosales, 2013: 253). As Good has argued, "Citizen journalism allows members of the public to engage in agenda-setting not merely by producing original content (though this is certainly a significant development) but also by rendering the agenda-setting processes of established professional media outlets radically provisional, malleable and susceptible to critical intervention" (2009: 7). Listeners call or SMS in to radio stations as they always have, but now it is increasingly common for not only their SMSes but also their social media posts to be read out on air as a routine part of programming.

Social media and radio

Audiences no longer need to interact directly with 'live' radio, but can also engage with broadcast content via social media after a show has been broadcast. On-air discussions often flow into social media discussions with a continuum between the two. Presenters refer to listener tweets on the air, listeners tweet directly to radio presenters or their callers, and the social media discussions that result show engagement and discussion between listeners, serving as an extension of the medium (and precisely because radio often does not allow enough space for such listener interaction).

However, the discussions that take place on social media are often highly emotive, and do not fall into the category of the normative notion of deliberation as "dispassionate, reflective exchange that obscures or undervalues the role of emotion in political interaction and the mix of motives with which citizens legitimately approach such interaction" (Bickford, 2011: 1025). Listeners often enter into heated exchanges with each other around various sociopolitical issues, ranging from race and gender to specific news-related issues such as the Oscar Pistorius trial or the "Rhodes Must Fall" campaign. They often accuse each other of falling short of reasoned debate and being overly emotional in their reactions to sensitive topics such as race. But as Bickford (2011: 1025) argues, contemporary theories of deliberation fail to take into account "the conflictual, impassioned and power-laden character of politics." Bickford instead argues for emotion and partisan thinking as morally appropriate elements of democratic communication. If we look at the political conversations which take place on Twitter particularly, as spin-offs of radio station broadcasts, we see the actualization of Bickford's arguments that, emotional talk is one of the central ways in which people negotiate and dispute meaning and value in political communication. It is a means of challenging and reinforcing power, and it can be used to expand or constrict relations between citizens, groups of citizens, and publics.

(2011: 1029)

What is occurring here is that when a topic is raised on the air, the conversation is continued on social media sites, but it takes a different form in that space, particularly as newcomers to the conversation may not have listened to the original broadcast. Social media conversations thus include listeners and non-listeners (or new listeners) in this process of remediation (Bolter and Grusin, 2001). The online conversations can often draw attention to a radio station, presenter of a particular program, but also result in greater intimacy between radio station, radio presenter, and listener—a kind of intimacy that is not afforded through the brief impersonal nature of call-ins.

Social media, radio, and publics

In general, radio stations draw groups of people together as a public by virtue of their listening choices. Bickford (1996) sees listening as a central activity of citizenship, and through both radio listening and listening to each other, audiences participate in the practice of citizenship. However, through further engagement on social media, the complexities of listening are heightened. Bickford asserts that it is precisely the presence of conflict and difference that makes communicative interaction necessary, and this often happens on social media, via radio stations. The 'publicness' of participation enacted via social media is thus turning "what was once an opaque audience into a transparent public" (Easton, 2005: 25). This visibility of the audience demands a reconfiguration of ideas of participation in radio listenership. Audiences can now produce, circulate, and share information in ways that allow them to form communities of 'strangerhoods' and open up dialogues within and beyond the radio station (Warner, 2002: 414). The social media engagement shows that listeners are beginning to organize less along the lines of identity politics and communal social relations and more on the basis of network sociality.

Social networking sites could thus be seen as the "latest generation of mediated publics" (boyd, 2007: 2) or as a networked public sphere. Peripheral involvement on social media has been likened to radio listening, a process that occurs in most online spaces. Crawford (2009) argues that posting, commenting, and direct interaction are not the only significant forms of participation and that lurkers or listening participants can feel a deep sense of connection in online spaces. The ongoing social media news feed, and listeners who simply scan through this feed, engage in a type of background listening, which results in ambient intimacy, similar to what happens when they listen to the radio. When listeners also engage with their favorite radio stations via social media (as well as listening on the airwaves), social media can become a natural extension of the listening experience. In some ways, it expands the listening experience, adding another dimension and making radio less of a flat, one-dimensional medium. Being able to instantly get responses on Twitter, or seeing photographs of in-studio activities on Facebook, rounds out the experience of only hearing a presenter's voice. Tacchi (1998) has previously argued that radio sound fills empty space and time with a routine that is familiar and thus unremarkable and naturalized. In this way, she argues that radio sound provides a texture in which everyday life can take place. In the same way, social media engagement by listeners and the constant interaction between them show that a kind of indifferent detachment and intimate comfort between citizens can co-exist, a kind of 'warm impersonality' that is central to the possibility of democratic politics in a diverse and unequal polity (Bickford, 2000).

While radio as a medium is immediate, intimate, and direct (Tacchi, 1998), so too is social media, and thus while radio is consumed or experienced as part of the material culture of the home or workplace, so too is social media consumption. While Tacchi (1998) argues that radio sound can reinforce sociality and a sense of social self, radio listeners' interactions with radio station staff and with each other can do the same. One might argue that different radio stations, with their different loyal audiences, create particular publics. But when these publics begin to engage within and between each other, this results in a new form of networked public.

The very form of radio requires the act of listening. Culturally and geographically diverse and disparate listeners listen privately but also together. While the academic focus on radio has often been on voice and the notion of citizens having voice to speak out on certain topics, media can also enable or constrain listening across multiculturalism and diversity (Dreher, 2009). When social media and radio intersect, it expands the possibilities for audiences to listen to each other. As Bickford (1996: 129) argues:

> A particular kind of listening can serve to break up linguistic conventions and create a public realm where a plurality of voices, faces, and languages can be heard and seen and spoken.

Social media spaces set up by radio stations serve as more than just additional arenas for individual stations or the expansion of specific stations' public spheres. When listeners across radio stations begin to interact with each other with the radio station as a kind of intermediary, it results in a kind of listening across difference. Social media expands the one-dimensional radio space into an even more interactive space in which those historically excluded from public communication can be listened to.

Conclusion

It is clear that radio convergence has reconfigured traditional radio to create new spaces that augment audience participation (Moyo, 2012). ICTs, and more importantly the social media platforms Facebook and Twitter, have become integral to South Africa's radio culture, as they provide valuable channels of communication and interaction between listeners and producers. These platforms transform listeners from being only audiences into becoming networked publics, formed around debates and discourses about current political and social issues, and result in a significant expansion of the discursive space (Chiumbu and Ligaga, 2013). This discursive social media space created as an extension of the radio station broadcasts also allows audiences the possibilities not only of having voice but also of listening—a key component of citizenship.

Further reading

This chapter has drawn on Tacchi's "Radio texture: between self and others" (1998) in Daniel Miller's *Material cultures: Why some things matter*, as a useful starting point for the nature of radio, in order to consider how it is changed by the introduction of social media. Moyo's (2012) article "The digital turn in radio: A critique of institutional and organizational modeling of new radio practices and cultures" provides a critical analysis of the use of the internet and mobile phone technologies in an African context. Similarly Rosales'

(2013) *Citizen participation and the uses of mobile technology in radio broadcasting* provides a good overview of the challenges of using social media and mobile technology in radio broadcasting.

References

Barton, M. (2005) "The Future of Rational-Critical Debate in Online Public Sphere." *Computers and Composition* 22(2): 177–190.

Bickford, S. (1996) *Listening, Conflict and Citizenship: The Dissonance of Democracy.* Ithaca, NY: Cornell University Press.

Bickford, S. (2011) "Emotional Talk and Political Judgement." *The Journal of Politics* 73(4): 1025–1037.

Bolter, R. and Grusin, D. (2001) *Remediation.* Cambridge, MA: MIT Press.

Bosch, T. (2010) "Digital Journalism and Online Public Spheres in South Africa." *Communicatio* 36(2): 265–275.

boyd, d. (2007) "Social Network Sites: Public, Private, or What?" *Knowledge Tree,* 13. Available from: http://www.danah.org/papers/KnowledgeTree.pdf

Chiumbu, S.H. and Ligaga, D. (2013) "Communities of Strangerhoods? Internet, Mobile Phones and the Changing Nature of Radio Cultures in South Africa." *Telematics and Informatics* 30(3): 242–251.

Crawford, K. (2009) "Following You: Disciplines of Listening in Social Media." *Continuum: Journal of Media & Cultural Studies* 23(4): 525–535.

Donner, J. and Gitau, S. (2009) "New Paths: Exploring Mobile-Centric Internet use in South Africa." In *International Communication Association Conference,* Chicago, IL, 20–21 May. Available from: http://citeseerx.ist.psu.edu/viewdoc/download?doi=10.1.1.147.9623&rep=rep1&type=pdf (accessed 1 June 2015).

Dreher, T. (2009) "Listening Across Difference: Media and Multiculturalism beyond the Politics of Voice." *Continuum: Journal of Media & Cultural Studies* 23(4): 445–458.

Easton, J. (2005) *High Interactivity Radio: Using the Internet to enhance Community among Radio Listeners.* Unpublished MA Thesis, Cambridge, MA: Massachusetts Institute of Technology.

Gleason, B. (2013) "#Occupy Wall Street: Exploring Informal Learning about a Social Movement on Twitter." *American Behavioral Scientist* 1–17.

Goode, L. (2009) "Social News, Citizen Journalism and Democracy." *New Media & Society* 11(8): 1–19.

Hermida, A. (2010) "Twittering the News: The Emergence of Ambient Journalism." *Journalism Practice* 4(3): 297–308.

Hermida, A. (2013) "#JOURNALISM: Reconfiguring Journalism Research about Twitter, One Tweet at a Time." *Digital Journalism* 1(3): 295–313.

Lasorsa, D., Lewis, S. and Holton, A. (2012) "Normalizing Twitter: Journalism Practice in an Emerging Communication Space." *Journalism Studies* 13(1): 19–36.

Moyo, L. (2012) "The Digital Turn in Radio: A Critique of Institutional and Organizational Modeling of New Radio Practices and Cultures." *Telematics and Informatics* 30: 214–222.

Rosales, R. (2013) "Citizen Participation and the Uses of Mobile Technology in Radio Broadcasting." *Telematics and Informatics* 30: 252–257.

Stassen, W. (2010) "Your News in 140 Characters: Exploring the Role of Social Media in Journalism." *Global Media Journal-African Edition* 4(1): 116–131.

Tacchi, J. (1998) "Radio Texture: Between Self and Others." In Miller, D. (ed.) *Material Cultures: Why Some Things Matter.* London, UK: University College London Press, pp. 25–45.

Tacchi, J. (2000) "The Need for Radio Theory in the Digital Age." *International Journal of Cultural Studies* 3(2): 289–298.

Taylor, T. (2010) "Radio the Way to go." Available from: http://www.marketingmix.co.za/pebble.asp?relid=11428 (accessed 20 January 2012).

Urrichio, W. (2004) "Cultural Citizenship in the Age of P2P Networks." In Bondebjerg, I. and Golding, P. (eds) *European Culture and the Media.* Bristol, UK: Intellect Books.

Warner, M. (2002) "Publics and Counter-Publics." *Quarterly Journal of Speech* 88(4): 413–425.

52

A CONUNDRUM OF CONTRAS

The 'Murdochization' of Indian journalism in a digital age

Prasun Sonwalkar

Journalism is one of the enduring legacies of British colonialism in India, along with cricket, the English language, railways and universities. The 'technology' of journalism, as it were, was first introduced in a vibrant local culture of oral-based social communication during the late eighteenth century with *Hicky's Bengal Gazette* in Calcutta. This early British link to Indian journalism remained influential, as the Indian press grew in size exponentially, through the long freedom struggle and after independence in 1947. The link also ensured that print journalism in India developed in a shorter period than any other former British colony. In terms of the ideas, ideology and idealism of journalism—if not content—the pathways of journalism in the two countries demonstrated many similarities, especially as reflected in India's English-language press. The good, the bad, and the ugly in the British press had their counterparts in India. Until the 1980s, trainee print journalists in India were told to emulate the standards of British journalism, with *The Times* and *The Sunday Times* under the editorship of Harold Evans held up as a reference point. But as *Times* saw seismic changes under its new owner, Rupert Murdoch, there were equally seismic changes in Indian journalism even though he did not have a presence in India at the time. Murdoch's market-oriented methods, introduced and tested in Australia, the United States, and Britain, were introduced by Indian newspaper owners from the late 1980s onwards, initially by *Times of India*, and quickly adopted by others.

This long British link, however, has faced challenges since the early 1990s as India liberalized its economy. The 'mediascape' that was until then dominated by print and state-owned radio and television, witnessed a proliferation of satellite television and was further complicated by the rapid spread of digital media since the 2000s. From citizens receiving news through a state-controlled radio and television and the long-established tradition of print journalism, the very nature of news underwent a major change, as American-style television news channels soon dominated the public sphere. India's first private television journalists—most of them moving from print (including this writer)—were trained by an American company, Frank N. Magid Associates, in 1994. Soon, sharp reductions in capital costs and entry barriers enabled the launch of several new channels, in various languages, so that by 2015, there were more than 400 news channels—all vying for a slice of a shrinking advertising pie. Newspapers that until then set the news agenda began to follow television's news leads and idioms.

By 2015, the size of India's news media infrastructure had become one of the largest in the world. India is the only country besides China where newspaper circulation continues to grow and thrive alongside television, radio, and new media. Besides more than 400 news channels in English, Hindi, and various languages, there were 99,660 registered publications, including 13,350 daily papers and 86,310 periodicals in 2014. The latest figures show that the number of internet users in India is fast approaching 300 million, which would overtake the United States and make it the second largest internet-enabled market after China. As a percentage of the population, internet penetration in India continues to be low, but is set to grow dramatically as millions of new users log in every month. Industry estimates project 640 million users by 2019, mostly driven by mobile internet usage. There has been similar growth in private FM radio stations across India, but regulation does not allow news on private radio. Television tops for advertising revenue, followed by print, but the fastest growth—44.5 percent—is in digital advertising (figures, projections from FICCI-KPMG, 2015). Besides the privately owned media infrastructure, the state owns and operates one of the largest television and radio networks, broadcasting across the subcontinent and beyond in various languages through Doordarshan (television) and All India Radio. Some key reasons for the continuing growth are enhanced literacy (from 12 percent in 1947 to over 74 percent in 2011), new technology, intense competition to capture new media markets, and a growing middle class with increasing purchasing power.

However, this 'good news' about growth in the media infrastructure is tempered by much 'bad news' about the quality of journalism; in other words, the quality of Indian journalism has been inversely proportionate to the growth of the news media infrastructure, as normative values are sacrificed at the altar of commerce and compromise. Growing corporatization has resulted in large industrial houses acquiring direct and/or indirect interest in media groups, both leveraging and feeding off each other to maximize profits. There are already allegations that crony capitalism is leading to 'crony journalism' (Jagannathan, 2012). Murdoch's methods may have assumed new and extreme forms in the Indian context, leading to widespread frustration and disappointment about the quality of journalism; journalists are among the fiercest critics of news output. Another key trend is political parties and individuals allied to political ideologies owning or controlling influential sections of the news media. Any attempt to restrict ownership and curb monopoly is strongly resisted in the name of freedom of the press. As T. N. Ninan, editorial director of *Business Standard*, a leading financial daily, put it: "We have never had such a vast audience or readership, but our credibility has never been so tested. We have never seen such a flowering of TV channels and such a spreading footprint for newspaper titles, but the market is more consolidated than ever around the top few players" (Ninan, 2011). Ninan went on to argue the impact of this change on India's public discourse was both fast moving and widespread, "The quality of what we offer to our public has never been better, but that same public can see that the ethical foundations of our actions have plumbed new depths" (2011).

As this chapter suggests, by 2015 a tipping point in financial and ethical corruption may have been reached, as journalism and journalists face a serious crisis of credibility, ridicule, and worse, with serious implications for the world's largest democracy of 1.3 billion facing serious challenges in poverty alleviation, education, health, and security. The situation is also reflected in popular culture; in Bollywood films such as *Rann* ('Battle', 2010) and thinly disguised novels such as 'Newsroom Live' (2012) by journalist Prabhat Shunglu. However, an encouraging aspect is the corrective role played by users of digital media to instantly point out errors of fact, bias, and perspective in mainstream journalism. By 2015, several news websites were providing an alternative to the dumbing down of news in the mainstream news media by focusing on a range of opinions, news, and features. Internet penetration is low but increasing and is creating new spaces for India's ancient tradition of argument and debate through, for example, citizen journalism, which has the potential to extend forms of 'recognition' to regions and minorities that are usually marginalized or ignored in mainstream news discourse (Sonwalkar, 2009). But the corrective role of news websites and their ability to provide a range of opinions remains limited due to issues of internet access and the wide reach of the traditional news media.

The next section discusses the idea of 'Murdochization' as a base to set out two major contemporary challenges: 'paid news' and the 'convergence' of interests of the ruling party and large dominant sections of news organizations after the 2014 general elections.

The idea of 'Murdochization'

Framed within the discourse of political economy, the commercialization of news (Picard, 2005; McManus, 2009) and journalism's central role in a democracy (McNair, 2000; Curran, 2005), 'Murdochization' is a useful term to unpack the role of corporate culture in journalism, where readers and viewers are treated as consumers instead of citizens. The term is based on the corporate culture devised by Murdoch to drive profits from his various titles in Australia, the United States, and the United Kingdom. It means privileging the 'marketing' or 'business' side of journalism over the 'editorial,' which takes the form of catering to the lowest common denominator, tabloidization, pricing wars, non-unionized workforce, journalists employed on short-term contracts, and censorship to suppress negative news about business partners or advertisers or political parties. Commentator Praful Bidwai (1996) in India and journalist-academic Granville Williams (1998) in Britain were among the first to use the term to describe the state of journalism in their countries.

As editor of *Free Press*, a publication of the Campaign for Press and Broadcasting Freedom, Williams wondered in an editorial in its March–April 1998 issue if there would soon be a new entry in the *Oxford Dictionary of New Words*: 'Murdochization (noun).' Stating that it was "an ugly sounding word to describe an ugly phenomenon," the editorial said the word emerged in the 1990s to describe the use and abuse of media power by Murdoch's News Corporation. 'Murdochization,' the editorial said, was coined following a number of high-profile cases which demonstrated the dangers of excessive media power in the hands of one person, which included predatory pricing to weaken other newspapers, preempting press freedom with commercial priorities, and strategic (and cynical) alignment with political parties to influence media policy. Williams described murdochization as "a process which impacted on the day to day lives of journalists so that the quality and range of journalism was diminished" (Williams, 1998).

In the Indian context, Bidwai wrote about 'Mudochization without Murdoch,' as his principles and methods were uncritically adopted by newspaper owners going back to the late 1980s, at a time when the media baron did not have a significant presence in India. He described 'Murdochization' as "the very destruction of the media as a responsible institution that disseminates information and promotes debate" (1996: 6). Bidwai sees this trend as 'total,' arguing it has removed the barrier between editorial and business functions: "The point is not so much that Murdoch is about to take over the bulk of the Indian media, but simply that Indian publishers are now doing roughly what he has already accomplished" (1996: 6). Bidwai notes how even at a time when Murdoch did not have a large foothold in the country, three of the largest newspaper companies had mimicked his corporate approach to newspaper ownership. "This silent 'Murdochization' has transformed notions of what is acceptable as news and the range of views that are permitted expression. Serious analytical writing is at a discount" (Bidwai, 1996: 7).

By the early 1990s, beginnings of a paradigm shift were evident within the *Times of India* (established 1838). The newspaper is owned by Bennett, Coleman & Co Ltd (BCCL), a company controlled by the Jain family. I have been witness to the changes in the newspaper, having worked on it as a senior sub-editor, chief sub-editor, and special correspondent from 1986 to 1994. The effect of several Murdoch-style marketing-oriented changes introduced by the company's vice-chairman Samir Jain has been so deep and far-reaching that Indian journalism is seen to divided into pre-Samir Jain and post-Samir Jain eras. Jain, who interned at the *New York Times* and the *Times*, London, before taking over, has been credited with single-handedly 'Americanizing' the *Times of India* and changing the face of Indian journalism. As Coleridge observed in his book on global newspaper barons, "Of all the newspaper owners in the world, I met no one so single-mindedly wedded to marketing as Samir Jain" (1993). Coinciding with the liberalization of the Indian economy in the early 1990s, he initiated and effected the shift from the "by-line to the bottom-line" (Sonwalkar, 2002), which soon burgeoned into widespread financial and ethical corruption at the institutional and individual levels.

Setting out his ethical compass in the early 1990s, Jain famously told top editors and journalists of the *Times of India* that news was no different from soap or any other commodity. He had little patience with the traditional wall between the editorial and marketing departments. As several editors and journalists resigned after their positions were downgraded and beats viewed as down-market abolished, Jain asked for 'light' editorial content. He set up trendy marketing departments and offered attractive packages to advertisers. The changes attracted much criticism, but as circulation, revenue and profits of the *Times of India* soared, others were quick to adopt similar practices and reap profits. Jain also replicated the kind of price wars unleashed by Murdoch in London. The *Times of India* soon faced accusations of ceasing to be a journal of record and distancing itself from journalism's normative functions in a democracy. The keyword in its newsroom was 'aspirational,' content was to be targeted at a young, urban readership, which meant ignoring events and issues that were considered 'down-market.'

The result was what India's vice-president Hamid Ansari termed 'sunshine journalism,' where "the role of the media as a defender and upholder of public interest is relegated to the background and its commercial persona takes over, replete with its allegiances to the market and the shareholders" (Ansari, 2011).

Shah (1997) detailed the shift towards marketing within the *Times of India* over the years, of how a former cigarette company executive was designated the managing editor; how, when the editor went on leave, his place was filled by an executive; and how, finally, the editor's post was scrapped altogether. Sainath, a senior journalist who worked on the *Times of India*, observed that the last decade of the twentieth century saw "the decline of the press as a public forum." He attributed this to a trend of corporate takeovers and concentration of ownership, with seven large companies controlling the majority of English language newspaper circulation.

Most other large Indian newspapers are eagerly following *The Times'* philosophy, inspired by the press baron Rupert Murdoch: a newspaper is a business like any other, not a public forum. Monopoly ownership has imposed a set of values entirely at odds with the traditional role of the Indian press.

(Sainath, 2001)

the *Times of India* group went on to introduce more marketing initiatives amidst continuing concerns over falling standards in journalism. In 2003, it set up Medianet, a company that offered space in the form of 'advertorials' in the *Times of India*'s supplements for a price. The supplements, sold and distributed with the main paper, are called 'Delhi Times,' 'Bombay Times,' or after the name of the city where the edition is published. Anyone desiring visual and/or textual coverage in the brightly produced supplements could do so for a fee. Again, the initiative attracted much criticism, but financially it was considered a success as would-be celebrities, individuals seeking to register on the party circuit, PR and 'brand' professionals, and others rushed to buy newspaper space. The 'advertorial' content is produced by staff reporters, and the masthead of supplements carry four words in tiny print: "Advertorial, entertainment promotional feature," which, critics say, need a magnifying glass to be seen. According to Santosh Desai, CEO of a brand consulting firm, "As far as advertising is concerned, it has always wanted to penetrate the sacred space of editorial, because that is where credibility lies. And now, here was editorial saying, penetrate me. So, of course advertising did just that, as PR" (Puri, 2012).

Another BCCL initiative was what is called 'private treaties' or 'brand capital,' under which a deal is offered to companies seeking to advertise in the *Times of India* group: BCCL accepts advertisements from companies in exchange for equity in them. One-third of the amount decided is accepted in cash and the rest in equity or real-estate ownership, constituting a delicate relationship between a leading player of the fourth estate and real estate. As a result, BCCL is now supposed to have a stake in more than 150 companies. Conflict of interest is obvious, with staff reporters unlikely to write against such companies. The initiative prompted renewed concern about journalism ethics, including from the regulator Securities and Exchange Board of India (SEBI), which wrote to the Press Council of India, "Private Treaties may lead to commercialisation of news reports since the same would be based on the subscription and advertising agreement entered into between the Media group and the company" (Sainath, 2010). Specified concerns of regulators included:

> Biased and imbalanced reporting [that] may lead to inaccurate perceptions of the companies which are the beneficiaries of such private treaties [which may; result in dilution of the independence of the press vis-a-vis the nature and content of the news/editorials in the media of companies promoting such agreements.
>
> *(2014)*

Undeterred by mounting criticism from journalists and others, Vineet Jain, younger brother of Samir Jain and the company's managing director, believes that "we are not in the newspaper business, we are in the advertising business[…] if ninety percent of your revenues come from advertising, you're in the advertising business" (Auletta, 2012). According to an analysis of BCCL's performance, it is not only one of the biggest media companies in India, but one of the most profitable companies of its kind anywhere in the world: "While its flexible ethical standards have attracted criticism, BCCL's aggressive marketing strategies and marketing clout have often been successful in stifling competition" (Guha Thakurta, 2012). The analysis quotes an interaction between Samir Jain and Inder Malhotra, who resigned as the resident editor of the New Delhi edition of the *Times of India* in 1986: "I told Samir that although he was fond of describing the newspaper as a product that was no different from a cake of soap, I had never seen a cake of soap that had to worry about its credibility and integrity. His reply to me was curt: 'Only profit matters, nothing else.'"

'Paid news' of India

As the practice of offering news space for money through Medianet became an established feature, it assumed larger and more ominous proportions by 2009, this time in the charged atmosphere of electoral politics. After elections in April–May of that year, it was revealed that large sums of money were paid by some candidates to media companies for favorable coverage or to ignore or publish negative content on rival candidates. The practice was termed 'paid news,' leading to another round of hand-wringing and concern about falling standards of journalism. A report by a sub-committee of the Press Council of India named newspapers and media companies, including the *Times of India* group and other prominent news organizations. According to the report titled "Paid News: How corruption in the Indian media undermines democracy," the deception or fraud takes place at three levels: First, the reader of the publication or the viewer of the television program is deceived into believing that what is essentially an advertisement is in fact, independently produced news content. Secondly, by not officially declaring the expenditure incurred on planting paid news items, the candidate standing for election violates the Conduct of Election Rules, 1961, which are meant to be enforced by the Election Commission of India under the Representation of the People Act, 1951. Finally, by not accounting for the money received from candidates, the concerned media company or its representatives are violating the provisions of the Companies Act, 1956 as well as the Income Tax Act, 1961, among other laws. The 71-page report described practice as clandestine and widespread malpractice:

> What is worse, these illegal operations have become "organized" and involve advertising agencies and public relations firms, besides journalists, managers and owners of media companies. Marketing executives use the services of journalists—willingly or otherwise—to gain access to political personalities.
>
> *(PCI, 2010: 5)*

The report is an important contribution to the ongoing debate about the quality of journalism, even if it did not lead to any action against the news organizations named. It cited several examples across the country and quoted several candidates describing their experience of 'paid news,' describing a practice where,

> So-called "rate cards" or "packages" are distributed that often include "rates" for publication of "news" items that not merely praise particular candidates but also criticize their political opponents. Candidates who do not go along with such "extortionist" practices on the part of media organizations are denied coverage.
>
> *(PCI, 2010: 5)*

The Election Commission issued new guidelines after the 2009 revelations and set up monitoring committees in constituencies for future elections. In 2011, for the first time, Umlesh Yadav, a legislator elected in the North Indian state of Uttar Pradesh, was disqualified by the commission for not disclosing expenditure to gain favorable media coverage. She was found guilty of exceeding the limit on election expenses. To prevent 'paid news' further impeding democratic processes, there are suggestions that election laws be amended to declare exchange of money for 'paid news' as a corrupt electoral practice, but as of late-2015 there was little legislative or executive movement on this issue. As Ram observed, 'paid news' was "every bit of a rogue practice as the UK's phone hacking affair was. [...] It also led to some critical debate on a wider phenomenon—paid news not as a rogue practice but as a deeper and industry-wide phenomenon that was not confined to election coverage" (2012).

'Paid news' is an extreme example of the philosophy behind 'Murdochization,' which had become so widespread that it lost the element of surprise by the 2014 general election. Parties, candidates, and news organizations devised ingenuous ways to avoid the commission's notice, while the 'paid news' route was also adopted by companies launching new products. As the vast news media infrastructure enlarged its reach across the vast country, 'paid news' became one of the key ways of influencing news media coverage.

2014 election: media—politics 'convergence'

After the general election in May, the commission reported nearly 700 cases of 'paid news.' The elections brought the Bharatiya Janata Party (BJP) and its allies to power in New Delhi, but attracted much criticism that it was fought largely on presidential lines, around the personality, promises, and record of Narendra Modi, who went on to become India's prime minister. American-style branding of candidates and parties was taken to new highs as BJP's multipronged campaign included the use of hologram technology provided by a British company that enabled Modi to appear and address large public meetings simultaneously across locations and cities. In the context of the now almost institutionalized corruption in the form of 'paid news,' Modi added to journalism's crisis of credibility by famously calling editors and journalists who were critical of him as 'news traders' during the election campaign (one of his ministers later added to the lexicon by calling journalists "presstitutes"). Editors and journalists critical of Modi and the BJP were denied access or came under much pressure from owners whose interests merged with Modi's.

The result was a dominating presence of Modi and BJP candidates in the pre-election news discourse, including in digital media. Large number of candidates, constituencies, parties, and issues were systematically marginalized in news discourse. One of the most digital media-savvy politicians, Modi's speeches were telecast live to millions as he promised "Achche din aney wale hai" (good days are coming) to an electorate seeking change after a decade of Congress-led government marked by a series of scams and perceptions of inertia. It was widely called "India's first social media election." Manoj Ladwa, who was the head of public relations of BJP's campaign, claimed after the party's landslide electoral victory: "We studied the Barack Obama and Tony Blair campaigns, but this was a (Narendra) Modi campaign and it will be seen as a benchmark in political communication on media courses" (Sonwalkar, 2014: 11).

The election and post-election periods saw ever closer concentration of media ownership in fewer hands. A large number of entities own media organizations, but a closer look reveals market domination by less than 100 groups that control what is heard, read, or watched at the national and state levels. The absence of cross-media ownership means that the main players dominate content across platforms, and most owners have traditionally held business interests outside the media. Reliance, an Indian conglomerate with interests in petrochemicals, energy, textiles, retail, and communications, bought over, or into, various news organizations, while other business and political interests took over or launched new news outlets. As the Modi government focused on its pro-business approach, there were renewed accusations of convergence of interests across business, politics, and the mainstream news media.

There is an unstated expectation that the news media should do nothing to affect the pro-business and pro-growth actions of the Modi government. According to A. Surya Prakash, a senior journalist appointed chairman of Prasar Bharati after the BJP came to power, there was now a "convergence between the State and the media." Prasar Bharati controls the state-owned networks of Doordarshan (television) and All India Radio. As Prakash put it, "the State, media and people are anxious about developmental programmes that were not implemented in the last 50 to 60 years. People are impatient and they want things to be done, and quickly too. The media, too, is of the same view" (quoted in: Rao Jr, 2014). He goes on to argue, "the private channels on their own are focusing on developmental agenda because they know that is what the people want" (ibid.).

The so-called 'convergence' under the Modi government conceals the expectation that the news media are called upon to act as cheerleaders of the state instead of holding it to account. Space for dissent is seen to have shrunk due to the wider 'convergence' of interests between business and the Modi government, while editors and journalists remain unsettled by tenuous employment terms and growing criticism and ridicule from the public. Unlike previous governments, the Modi government is perceived to be less tolerant of criticism, while holding tight control over information and access to journalists, reflecting another extreme aspect of the 'bottom-line' philosophy behind the idea of 'Murdochization.' It is in this context that the role of the growing number of news websites—such as thewire.in, thenewsminute.com, scroll.in, thequint.com, dailyo.in, and the media watch website, thehoot.org—assumes critical importance to provide correctives and alternative perspectives.

Conclusion

A conundrum of contra trends is evident as the last 25 years have witnessed a loosening of the old British link with Indian journalism and growing adoption of American-style formats, styles, and idioms. There has been a proliferation of what I call the 'hardware' of journalism (enabling factors such as technology, capital, rising literacy, access, and laws), which offers new opportunities for the 'software' of journalism—the quality of editorial content that empowers citizens, holds those in power to account, and strengthens democratic institutions—to flourish. But this 'software' faces serious challenges to use the 'hardware' of journalism to fulfill its social and normative functions in a democracy. Facing a serious crisis of credibility, the trajectory of Indian journalism over the last 25 years suggests that "more is not necessarily better," particularly in a country where there is much headroom for the traditional media to grow alongside the proliferating digital media. There is much potential for quality journalism through the internet, with examples of community journalism in villages and small towns in existence, but for the moment, the story of the quality of Indian journalism is similar to that of Indian democracy: imperfect, chaotic, diverse, compromised, noisy, corrupt, and in some aspects—as evident from much of the content of the news websites named above—magnificent.

Further reading

For research covering recent developments in Indian journalism, including digital media, see the special issue of *Journalism Studies* (Vol. 16, Issue 5; 2015). *The Indian Media Business* by Vanita Kohli-Khandekar, now in its third edition, provides a useful overview of the media infrastructure. Several key aspects of how the *Times of India* changed Indian journalism are covered in *The TOI Story* by Sangita P. Menon Malhan, while Nalini Rajan's *Practising Journalism* includes perceptive chapters by journalists and Indian academics on the values, constraints, and implications of Indian journalism.

References

Ansari, M.H. (2011) "Indian Media in a Challenging Environment". *The Hindu,* 16 July.

Auletta, K. (2012) "Citizens Jain: Why India's Newspaper Industry is Thriving". *The New Yorker,* 8 October.

Bidwai, P. (1996) "Whose Truth? Indian Media in the Global Village." *Humanscape,* 6–8 December.

Coleridge, N. (1993) *The Paper Tigers: The Latest, Greatest Newspaper Tycoons.* London, UK: Heinemann.

Curran, J. (2005) "Mediations of Democracy." In Curran, J. and Gurevitch, M. (eds) *Mass Media & Society,* 4th edn. London, UK: Arnold, pp. 122–149.

FICCI-KPMG. (2015) *#shootingforthestars: Indian Media and Entertainment Industry Report.* Mumbai: KPMG in Association with the Federation of Indian Chambers of Commerce and Industry.

Guha Thakurta, P. (2012) "The Times, the Jains and BCCL." *The Hoot* (Indian mediawatch website), 12 November.

Jagannathan, R. (2012) "Rise of Crony Journalism and Tainted Money in Media." *Firstpost,* 10 September. Available from: www.firstpost.com.

Kohli-Khandekar, V. (2010) "The Indian Media Business." New Delhi: Response.

McManus, J.H. (2009) "The Commercialization of News." In Wahl-Jorgensen, K. and Hanitzsch, T. (eds) *The Handbook of Journalism Studies.* London, UK: Routledge.McNair, B. (2000) "Journalism & Democracy: An Evaluation of the Political Public Sphere." London, UK: Routledge.

Menon Malhan, S.P. (2013) "The TOI Story: How a Newspaper Changes the Rules of the Game." New Delhi: HarperCollins.

Ninan, T.N. (2011) "Indian Media's Dickensian Age." *CASI Working Paper Series No. 11-03, Centre for the Advanced Study of India.* Philadelphia, PA: University of Pennsylvania.

PCI. (2010) "Paid News: How Corruption in the Indian Media Undermines Democracy." *Citizen's Issues.* New Delhi.

Picard, R.G. (2005) "Money, Media and the Public Interest." In Overhosler, G. and Hall Jamieson, K. (eds) *The Press.* New York, NY: Oxford University Press.

Puri, A. (2012) "Spotting the Astro Turf." *The Hoot* (Indian mediawatch website), 26 September.

Rajan, N. (2005) "Practising Journalism: Values, Constraints, Implications." New Delhi: Sage.

Ram, N. (2012) "Sharing the Best and the Worst: The Indian News Media in a Global Context." *James Cameron Memorial Lecture, 2012.* London, UK: City University.

Rao Jr, P.V. (2014) "There is Need for Public Broadcaster: A Surya Prakash." *DNA,* 20 November.

Sainath, P. (2001) "None So Blind as Those Who Will Not See." *UNESCO Courier,* 20 July.

Sainath, P. (2010) "Private Treaties Harm Fair, unbiased News: SEBI." *The Hindu,* 19 June.

Shah, A. (1997) *Hype, Hypocrisy and Television in Urban India.* New Delhi, India: Vikas.

Sonwalkar, P. (2002) "Murdochisation of the Indian Press: From Byline to Bottom Line." *Media, Culture & Society* 24(6): 821–834.

Sonwalkar, P. (2009) "Citizen Journalism in India: The Politics of Recognition." In Allan, S. and Thorsen, E. (eds) Citizen Journalism: Global Perspectives. New York, NY: Peter Lang, pp. 75–84.

Sonwalkar, P. (2014) "Narendra Modi's Victory Compared to '1979 Thatcher moment' in UK." *Hindustan Times,* 2 June.

Williams, G. (1998) "Editorial." *Free Press: Journal of the Campaign for Press and Broadcasting Freedom,* March–April.

53

DATA TRUMPS INTUITION EVERY TIME[1]

Computational journalism and the digital transformation of punditry

Brian McNair and Terry Flew

This essay explores the implications of digital transformation for the status and role of the journalistic expert, or 'pundit' (the term 'pundit' is rooted in the Sanskrit term meaning 'learned man, master, teacher or scholar'). The rise of data journalism, as exemplified by much discussed initiatives such as Nate Silver's 2012 US presidential election forecasts, has challenged the self-proclaimed status of mainstream political pundits as authoritative experts and exposed in rather stark manner the limits and flaws of journalistic commentary and prediction. At the same time, the rise of user-generated content in a variety of formats such as blogs and social media, globalized and accessed through digital channels, has produced a new 'online commentariat' of amateurs, semi-professionals, and activist-critics, often contesting the accuracy and relevance of professional journalists working on traditional platforms. This chapter explores the implications of those challenges for the concept of the journalist as privileged definer of meanings in a world of proliferating online sources of news and commentary. It will do this with particular reference to recent developments in Australian online journalism from both mainstream media and alternative sources.

The digitalization of journalism

In recent times journalism has been subject to far-reaching processes of digital transformation that have radically impacted on the production and consumption of the form. For example, the traditional roles and functions of journalism in the public sphere—in particular, for the purposes of this essay, those of the 'pundit,' or expert commentator (McNair, 2008)—are being challenged by a new type of digitally enabled producer, an 'online commentariat,' as the *Guardian* newspaper described them at an early stage of their evolution in 2005 (Burkeman, 2005).

Traditional political punditry associated with election forecasting has been a notable victim of this trend. In the run up to the 2012 US presidential election, the blogger and statistician Nate Silver emerged as a more accurate source of forecasts about the outcome than the established print and broadcast journalists of the mainstream media (Silver, 2011). Silver's statistics-based blog, *FiveThirtyEight*, launched in 2008 then taken up by other outlets before being licensed by the the *New York Times* in 2012, represents an example of what Coddington

(2015) has termed the 'quantitative turn' in journalism, variously referred to as *computational journalism*, *data journalism*, and *digital journalism*.[2] The critical response to Silver's work from some journalists in the United States and elsewhere illustrates many of the tensions around the growing role of big data in journalistic work, and the challenge computational journalism (CJ) poses to the knowledge status of punditry.

Historicizing data journalism

We should acknowledge at the outset that journalists have always used data of various kinds in their work. The nineteenth century publication of weather forecasts in newspapers, for example, was a form of 'data-based' journalism. Since the 1980s, digital tools for the acquisition, preparation, and presentation of journalism have been a familiar feature of newsrooms (Flew *et al.*, 2011). Scholarly articles about the implications of something called computer-assisted reporting (CAR) were being written in 1997, noting that CAR techniques had become "an essential element of every news organisation and reporter's toolkit" (Granato and Tapsall, 1997).

But the current ubiquity of terms such as *computational* and *data journalism* reflects the perception of a qualitative shift from an environment in which data gathering and management were essentially analogue processes of the type depicted in *All The President's Men* (Pakula, 1976) to the digitally enabled present. A key scene in Alan Pakula's iconic film shows Bob Woodward spending what we might assume to be days sifting through hard copy library borrowing records in search of information to advance his and Carl Bernstein's investigation of White House corruption. They worked slowly and methodically, sifting data by eye and hand, taking months if not years to complete their investigation. Computers existed in the 1970s, of course, but they were large and heavy, and thus of little practical value to a working journalist, as opposed to a NASA scientist.

Half a century after the Watergate scandal, 'Big Data' is everywhere, and as the UK *Telegraph*'s release of digitized British MPs expense claims showed in 2009, digitized data sets have emerged as a source of hugely important stories going to the heart of political, economic, and social systems. Nate Silver's statistical methods themselves became a major story in the 2012 US election, as noted. Earlier, the global profile of WikiLeaks, and its release of vast quantities of military, diplomatic, and corporate data—in the period before Julian Assange was driven to take refuge in the Ecuadorian embassy in London—exemplifies the transformation from an analogue environment in which data is regularly deployed to support a story to one in which, by virtue of both the unprecedented quantity and quality of the data involved, they routinely *become* or at least *trigger* the story (a story with, in the case of WikiLeaks, many and diffuse consequences in the real world to which the data refer). The WikiLeaks 'data dumps' were a running story from 2009 until 2011 and have generated highly newsworthy responses from governments, security agencies, and other authority figures in countries all over the world. In this case the unauthorized, digitally enabled release of data, and the risk they allegedly posed to national security in the countries affected, *was* the news, as much as the information they contained (see Thorsen, this volume).

In other cases, as the new newsroom category of 'programmer journalist' attests (Layser, 2016), journalists now routinely turn to publicly available data sets for leads on particular stories or for pointers to new stories. They 'mine' data for patterns and structures of significance, searching for newsworthy nuggets of information. Data sources themselves become the subject of news reporting, rather than serving the secondary function of validating particular journalistic or political claims.

At the same time as digital data have become more integral to the production of journalistic content, they have become more threatening to the traditional roles and functions of journalism in the public sphere. It has been widely noted that Julian Assange has broken more stories about US war fighting and diplomacy in recent times than the great majority of professional journalists, but his status as a journalist is contentious. Despite his claims to a new genre of factuality called 'scientific journalism' (Assange, 2010; Manne, 2011), many of his journalistic critics refuse to regard him as a journalist of any kind, as if anxious to demonstrate that the inadequacies of their own collective performance as watchdogs and scrutineers of the powerful (in reaction to the US invasion of Iraq, for example) have been exposed not by another journalist—which would be damaging to reputations and professional pride—but by a committed information activist working outside the ethical codes and practices of journalism as traditionally defined (see Eldridge, this volume). The legal theorist Yochai Benkler has identified WikiLeaks as an archetypal case of wider tensions between traditional mass media and what he terms the 'networked fourth estate,' and between the established practices of incumbent journalism and the emergent 'open source' approaches (Benkler, 2013). Edward Snowden's 2013 leaks of confidential data held by the US National Security Agency, channeled mainly through the medium of investigative reporter Glenn Greenwald in the *Guardian*, had a similarly critical response from many in the journalistic profession, who have labeled him as a 'spy' and a 'traitor' rather than, as Greenwald (2013) argued, a whistle-blower to be welcomed in the best traditions of the Fourth Estate.

Both Assange and Snowden were reliant upon professional journalists working for established titles to get their messages to a wider public. Assange worked with the *New York Times*, the *Guardian*, *Le Monde*, and *El País* in getting WikiLeaks' data out to the public, while Snowden worked with Glenn Greenwald and the *Guardian* and Barton Gellman and the *Washington Post*, then the *New York Times*. Nonetheless, their deployment of big data to set global news agendas has blurred the journalism/not-journalism boundary in ways which appear to threaten the professional identity of the established news-making class.

In the 2012, US presidential election, for example, the blogger and statistician Nate Silver's mathematically generated forecasts about the outcome turned out to be more accurate than most of the established pundits. Silver was not the only forecaster to get the outcome right, but the majority tended to overstate the likely performance of the Republican challenger Mitt Romney. More threatening to the mainstream commentariat than Silver's forecasting, however, were his methods in generating them. Using publicly available polling data and applying techniques for estimating probabilities that he had honed in US baseball analysis, Silver correctly forecast the outcomes of contests in all 50 states (plus the District of Columbia), and on the basis of those, that re-election for Obama was the most likely outcome.

Prior to the election, the majority of established political pundits of the US press and broadcast media simply refused to take Silver seriously as a peer and maintained that the election result was too close to call. As noted above, many overestimated the Republican contender's likely vote. After the results were in, and his success clear, there was a different kind of response, in which mainstream commentators sought to minimize the significance of Silver's work, characterizing it as a fluke, or as something other than expert journalism. As Ezra Klein (2012) put it in the *Washington Post*, such criticisms reflected the fact that "Silver's work poses a threat to more traditional—and, in particular, to more excitable—forms of political punditry and horse-race journalism."

The frequently defensive response to Silver's work by other pundits and journalists illustrates many of the tensions around the growing centrality of data-driven news in the public sphere and raises a key question for practitioners. The sense-making, analytical, interpretative functions of journalism have been fundamental to its role in democratic societies, where informed electorates and functioning civil societies are recognized to depend not just on the availability of true and accurate information, or reportage, but authoritative and credible interpretation of 'the facts' reported in news media. The performance of such sense-making practices has been historically linked to more or less subjective qualities of the journalist or pundit—such as 'insider status,' 'intuition,' and 'experience' (McNair, 2011). Does the rise of data-driven journalism mean that such skills are becoming redundant, or marginal, replaced by a facility with computational methods and data manipulation? What kinds of expertise can a journalist be said to provide in the digital era that is unique or distinctive, and is that expertise still required when the application of computer algorithms and statistical formulae can generate knowledge of a quality that is comparable to, or even superior to, that arising from more conventional journalistic techniques?

Philip Tetlock's (2005) study of 284 pundits' forecasts (journalists and others engaged in "commenting or offering advice on political or economic trends") found in a sample of 82,361 predictions made over a 20-year period that their rate of accuracy was less than would have been expected of random guess work. Long before the rise of computational journalism and big data, therefore, journalistic punditry was far from scientific, and frequently wrong, although its practitioners routinely asserted the superiority of their analyses and predictions, with public acceptance of such claims being the basis of their privileged place in the media ecology. The example of Silver in 2012, however, requires renewed consideration of the relationship between fact and knowledge in journalism and the implications of big data for socially useful knowledge production. It exposes in a particularly stark way the flaws and limitations of traditional punditry and the hubris of its practitioners: this was seen again in the 2015 UK general election, where virtually all forecasters got the result significantly wrong, overestimating the likely Labour vote and discounting the possibility of the Conservatives winning a majority of seats in their own right (Franks, 2015). It may also require a revised definition of journalism itself, fitter for purpose in a digitized media environment where large data sets are no longer only a support in the pursuit of journalistic truth, but central to it.

Data-driven journalism in Australia

Australia has one of the most concentrated commercial media sectors in the Western world (Papandrea and Tiffen, 2016), and its mainstream media outlets have not for the most part been particularly innovative. But applications of data-driven journalism, combined with the emergence of new entrants into the Australian news media industry, have generated new ways of telling stories and undertaking analysis of public affairs that make use of computational techniques.

A number of independent, online-only news and opinion sites have been developed in Australia since the mid-2000s, which have ranged across the political left (*New Matilda*) to the political right (*On Line Opinion*), have included niche sites targeted at women (*Mamamia*, *The Hoopla*) and business readership (*Business Spectator*), and also include the university-supported site *The Conversation*, which commenced in Australia in March 2011 and has expanded to the

United States and the United Kingdom. One of the more significant and long-lasting sites has been *Crikey*. First established in 2000, *Crikey* draws together commentary from its journalists in the areas of politics, business, media, and culture and combines this with an aggregated blog site, with topics ranging across urban planning (*The Urbanist*), airlines (*Plane Talking*) and health (*Croakey*). One well-established blog site has been *The Poll Bludger*, which was first established in 2004 and which applies the 'poll of polls' methodology used by Nate Silver to capture medium-term trends in the electoral prospects of Australia's political parties at both state and Federal levels.

The *Guardian Australia* was launched in May 2013 and has quickly established itself as a significant news site in Australia, ranking among the top 10 online news media sites by the end of 2014. In a manner similar to its UK parent site, it combines contributions by a number of established journalists with a 'Comment is Free' section that solicits wider public contributions, including those from a group of semi-regular contributors. It employs specialist data journalists, and its 'Data Blog' site has drawn upon publicly available data to develop interactive accounts of topics where there is wide public debate, including trends in the number of asylum seekers coming to Australia, public versus private schooling, severe weather events, the distribution of Australia's foreign aid budget, and political donations. It has also developed a feature that allows its readers to develop their own Federal Budget, using the Treasury's figures to make taxation and expenditure decisions that can balance the budget in different ways to those proposed by the current Liberal-National Party government.

Perhaps the most significant data-driven innovation in Australian journalism has been undertaken by the Australian Broadcasting Corporation (ABC), Australia's leading national public broadcaster, with its *Vote Compass* site. *Vote Compass* was originally developed by Canadian political scientists in 2011 for the Canadian Broadcasting Corporation (CBC) and allows its users to assess how their own views on a range of prominent policy issues align with the platforms of the major political parties contesting an election. It was refined by Australian political scientists and used in the 2013 Australian Federal election and is now used regularly by the ABC in both state and Federal elections. In the 2013 election, it garnered over 1.4 million responses or 10 percent of Australian registered voters, thereby generating an extraordinarily rich data set of voter views across a range of issues, which are then mapped at both an aggregate level and that of individual electorates.

From punditry to data?

The growing role of computational technologies and methods in the journalistic production process at all levels is accompanied by the emergence of forms of journalism founded less upon the cultivation of personal contacts, access to the views of elites and 'insiders,' and the expression of subjective opinion as to what things mean and more upon the apparently objective and factually grounded insights provided by the huge quantities of data now available to journalists and non-journalists alike. Computation is argued by many to enable more objective and accurate reportage and commentary of problematic reality, partly because it bypasses the news values and professional ideologies of journalists themselves. From this perspective, journalism is becoming a more scientific practice, with the truth claims of journalists increasingly backed up and verified by publicly available data.

In advocating computational journalism, Cohen, Hamilton, and Turner (2011) look forward to a renaissance of investigative work enabled by computer technologies and premised upon reader empowerment: "adaptation of algorithms and technology, rolled into free and open source tools, will level the playing field between powerful interests and the public by helping uncover leads and evidence that can trigger investigations by reporters" (Cohen, Hamilton, and Turner, 2011: 71). This would be a transition within journalism from analysis driven by punditry and insider sources to one driven by big data and the application of computational techniques or, as Mecklin (2009) puts it, "Deep Throat meets data mining."[3] Coddington (2015: 20) has observed that quantitatively oriented journalism has 'deep democratic roots,' being tied to "open government advocacy [...] and the public-service tradition of investigative journalism."

Beyond journalism, the rise of Big Data has been associated with what Chris Anderson, the former editor of *Wired*, termed 'the end of theory,' or the rise of a world where "massive amounts of data and applied mathematics replace [...] every theory of human behaviour, from linguistics to sociology" (Anderson, 2008). For Anderson, the exemplar of where data science replaces humanistic knowledge has been Google's intervention into the advertising market, which it "conquered ... with nothing more than applied mathematics. It didn't pretend to know anything about the culture and conventions of advertising—it just assumed that better data, with better analytical tools, would win the day."

The former News Corp Australia CEO, Kim Williams, argued at a public lecture after his resignation from the company in September 2013 that "data trumps punditry every time." In the contemporary newsroom, Williams argued, the solidity and ease of computerized access to data was making many of the more intuitive tasks of the journalist redundant. On the other hand, as boyd and Crawford (2012) remind us, the conclusions and inferences drawn from computerized data are not free of human intervention. Human subjects design the computer programs used to collect data and formulate the questions to be asked of it. Beyond the most basic 'facts,' such as air temperature or stock prices at a given moment in a day, the identification of 'truth' in data remains an essentially subjective, human process.[4]

It would be an error, therefore, to use the rise of computation and data in journalism to reinforce the long-standing binary opposition between fact and opinion, objectivity and subjectivity, and between data and its interpretation. boyd and Crawford note that "working with Big Data is still subjective, and what it quantifies does not necessarily have a closer claim on objective truth" (2012: 667). While noting how Big Data and computational techniques challenge the privileged truth claims of professional journalists, we should not fall into a neo-positivist trap of fetishizing data and their representation in journalism, seeing computational journalism as inherently more 'factual' and thus superior to other modes of storytelling and interpretation. It can be, and in many cases will be, but the complexities of interpretation and meaning will always remain a key element in the narrativization of problematic reality that we call news and journalism more broadly.

Conclusion

An important question raised by the rise of computational and data-driven journalism is whether we are seeing an end to that tradition of punditry based upon insider knowledge, experience and other subjective elements of a pundit's profile, and the rise of a 'scientific' journalism, which draws upon the computing and analytical powers of digital technology. A related question is whether this trend challenges the oft-criticized power of mainstream media with what Benkler (2013) terms the 'Networked Fourth Estate.'

We conclude by suggesting that this reading of the trends is an over-simplification. On the one hand, critical media studies has long questioned the supposed objectivity and superiority of liberal journalism. From the work of the Glasgow Media Group onwards, scholars have argued that journalistic discourse is deeply rooted in ideology and subjectivity, even as it is legitimized by claims to neutrality, impartiality, and objectivity. The rise of computational journalism has added another set of arguments to that general critique, as the value of 'insiderness' and other structural traits hitherto presumed to enable *primary definition*, or *dominant readings* of events, has been fundamentally challenged by the application of algorithms and formulae.

This does not negate the value of opinion journalism, however, nor the journalism of interpretation and analysis. Numbers are notoriously open to diverse readings of significance and easy to manipulate for political advantage, as any news bulletin or election campaign will show. There are many more opportunities for such manipulation, now that Big Data is ubiquitous and accessible to anyone with a point to make or public anxieties to stoke up. The current global debate on the causes and consequences of climate change is a good example of how routine the deployment of numbers in public debate now is and how difficult it can be to reach agreement on their meaning.

We can certainly argue, with heightened confidence, that journalists cannot presume to 'tell' us what things mean, or how they will turn out, in a definitive way, anymore than they were able to accurately predict the global credit crunch or the 2012 presidential election. But many of them have analytical-interpretative skills which are crucial to the public understanding of numbers and of the events, processes, and issues to which the data speak. Karppi and Crawford (2015) discuss the role of financial algorithms and automated reporting of price fluctuations in generating dangerously volatile stock markets and 'hack crashes.' With reference to a short-lived but precipitous fall in the Dow Jones Industrial Average in April 2013, these authors note the heightened risk of economic catastrophe associated with growing reliance on automated data journalism.

In this sense, computational journalism should not be viewed as the replacement of traditional commentary journalism by highly numerate geeks, but the augmentation of familiar journalistic skills with new ones based on the ability to acquire, process, and package digital data in the pursuit of reportage, analysis, interpretation, and commentary. We may hope that the increasing use of big data in journalism can improve the latter's quality as a diagnostic instrument, a predictive tool, and a democratic resource. We must not, however, replace the worship of journalistic expertise with an equally exaggerated fetishization of numbers as a 'magic' route toward the telling of journalistic truth. Data are part of the analytical apparatus of commentary and interpretative journalism, not their death knell.

Further reading

For more on computational journalism, Terry Flew, Christina Spurgeon, Anna Daniel, and Adam Swift's article "The Promise of Computational Journalism" in *Journalism Practice* reflects on the key challenges facing journalism which computational journalism addresses. Alternatively, Tero Karppi and Kate Crawford's explore in "Social Media, Financial Algorithms and the Hack Crash" the real-world implications of computational approaches to news sharing. For more discussion on punditry, Brian McNair's article "I, Columnist" establishes key discussions in journalism punditry and opinion writing.

Notes

1 From a public lecture delivered by former CEO of News Corporation in Australia, Kim Williams, delivered at Queensland University of Technology, Brisbane, Australia on October 2013. The authors would like to thank Andrew King for research assistance in the preparation of this essay.

2 These terms are used interchangeably in the literature, although they tend to place emphasis on different aspects of the journalistic production process. We do not have space here for a detailed discussion of the various terms but will tend to refer to *computational* journalism in this essay (CJ), by which we mean journalism that depends for its existence on the application of computer technology. CJ is not itself *computation*, but uses data that have been processed by computers, often visualized by computer-generated graphics, to tell its stories or to make computer-generated predictions and forecasts. Coddington (2015) provides a useful taxonomy of these terms.

3 'Deep Throat' refers here not to the 1970s porn film, but rather to the source from within the White House who gave the *Washington Post* journalists Bob Woodward and Carl Bernstein access to secret information about the Nixon administration, leading ultimately to Richard Nixon's resignation as US president.

4 Similar questions have arisen in debates surrounding the digital humanities. In her work on artificial intelligence and its implications for thinking about human creativity, Margaret Boden (2003) distinguished between 'transformational creativity,' which remains a uniquely human capacity, and 'combinational creativity,' or the capacity to combine or make associations between familiar ideas, which machines as well as people can undertake.

References

Anderson, C.W. (2008) "The End of Theory." *WIRED*, June. Available from: http://archive.wired.com/science/discoveries/magazine/16-07/pb_theory/.

Assange, J. (2010) "Don't Shoot the Messenger for Revealing Uncomfortable Truths." *The Australian*, 8 December, p. 14.

Benkler, Y. (2013) "WikiLeaks and the Networked Fourth Estate." In Brevini, B., Hintz, A. and McCurdy, P. (eds) *Beyond WikiLeaks: Implications for the Future of Communications, Journalism and Society*. Basingstoke, UK: Palgrave Macmillan, pp. 11–34.

Boden, M. (2003) *The Creative Mind: Myths and Mechnisms*. 2nd edn. London, UK: Routledge.

boyd, d. and Crawford, K. (2012) "Critical Questions for Big Data." *Information, Communication & Society* 15(5): 662–679.

Burkeman, O. (2005) "The New Commentariat." *The Guardian*, 17 November. Available from: http://www.theguardian.com/media/2005/nov/17/newmedia.politicsandthemedia.

Coddington, M. (2015) "Clarifying Journalism's Quantitative Turn." *Digital Journalism* 3(3): 331–348.

Cohen, S., Hamilton, J.T. and Turner, F. (2011) "Computational Journalism." *Communications of the ACM* 54(10): 66–71.

Flew, T., Spurgeon, C., Daniels, A. and Swift, A. (2011) "The Promise of Computational Journalism." *Journalism Practice* 6(2): 157–171.

Franks, S. (2015) "How Could the Polls Have Been So Wrong?" In Jackson, D. and Thorsen, E. (eds) *UK Election Analysis 2015: Media, Voters and the Campaign*. Bournemouth: Centre for the Study of Journalism, Culture and the Community, Bournemouth University, p. 28.

Granato, L. and Tapsall, S. (1997) "The CAR Curriculum will Influence the Practice of Journalism." *Australian Journalism Review* 19(2): 14–23.

Greenwald, G. (2013) "The Perfect Epitaph for Establishment Journalism." *The Guardian*, 14 October. Available from: http://www.theguardian.com/commentisfree/2013/oct/14/independent-epitaph-establishment-journalism.

Karppi, T. and Crawford, K. (2015) "Social Media, Financial Algorithms and the Hack Crash." *Theory, Culture & Society* 33(1): 73–92. DOI:10.1177/0263276415583139.

Klein, E. (2012) "The Nate Silver Backlash." *The Washington Post*, 30 October. Available from: http://www.washingtonpost.com/blogs/wonkblog/wp/2012/10/30/the-nate-silver-backlash/.

Layser, N. (2016) *Interactive Journalists: Hackers, Data and Code*. Urbana-Champaign, IL: University of Illinois Press.

Manne, R. (2011) "Juilian Assange the Sypherpubnk Revolutionary." *The Monthly*, March. Available from: https://www.themonthly.com.au/issue/2011/march/1324265093/robert-manne/cypherpunk-revolutionary.

McNair, B. (2008) "I, Columnist." In Franklin, B. (ed.) *Pulling Newspapers Apart: Analysing Print Journalism*. London, UK: Routledge, pp. 106–114.

McNair, B. (2011) *An Introduction to Political Communication*. London, UK: Routledge.

Mecklin, J. (2009) "Deep Throat Meets Data Mining." 20 December 2013, Available from: http://www. psmag.com/politics/deep-throat-meets-data-mining-4015/.

Papandrea, F. and Tiffen, R. (2016) "Australia." In Noam, E.I. (ed.) *Who Owns the World's Media? Media Concentration and Ownership around the World*. Oxford, UK: Oxford University Press (pp. 703–739).

Silver, N. (2011) *The Signal and the Noise: The Art and Science of Prediction*. New York, NY: Allen Lane.

Tetlock, P. (2005) *Expert Political Judgment*. New York, NY: Princeton University Press.

54

SOCIAL MEDIA USE, JOURNALISM, AND VIOLENCE IN THE NORTHERN MEXICO BORDER

Celeste González de Bustamante and Jeannine E. Relly

Mexico is ranked among the most dangerous countries in the world for journalists to work. Journalists in the northern border states, where drug trafficking and human smuggling are routine, often face perilous conditions when working in the field. This chapter is based on a study of social media use by journalists and bloggers reporting in the northern states and uses the conceptual framework of scale-shifting to analyze how journalists from both the United States and Mexico overcome information scarcity while also avoiding digital security risks in the northern Mexican states. The chapter describes how social media is utilized in an environment of heightened violence and indicates that numerous journalists from 18 cities often use social media to forge cross-border relationships with colleagues. The research in this chapter advances scale-shifting as a conceptual area by including transnational criminal organizations in the framework and investigates ways that journalists utilize or avoid social media in a landscape of propaganda and misinformation.

Why study social media among journalists in Mexico and Latin America?

In Mexico, almost half of the country's residents—49.2 percent of the country's 120 million inhabitants—now have access to the internet (Internet World Stats, 2014). With the digital divide among citizens narrowing, journalists have more opportunities to create news content online, enabling the country's residents to participate in the production of news through social media such as Facebook and Twitter. At the same time, citizens and journalists alike have had to endure ongoing violence in various regions of Mexico, including the northern part of the nation, and high levels of corruption and impunity (Committee to Protect Journalists, 2014). According to Freedom House, the country is considered 'not free,' and the organization rates freedom of expression online as considered 'partly free' (Freedom House, 2014). These realities create enormous challenges for journalists and those who rely on news and information online to make decisions. This chapter describes how some journalists from Mexico and the United States, covering northern Mexico use social media for their work. In northern Mexico, where bloggers and journalists continue to be threatened, social media present both opportunities and challenges.

Over the last decade and a half more than 100 journalists have been murdered in Mexico, while news media workers and citizens have increased their use of social media in an attempt to get their messages out and inform the public (Reporters Without Borders, 2013). Members of organized crime groups and corrupt government officials sometimes respond to what is published online through acts of violence and aggression. In 2014, a citizen-journalist was murdered in the state of Tamaulipas, Mexico in the US–Mexico border city of Reynosa, and the perpetrators of the crime are reported to have used the citizen's Twitter account to post images and messages about her death (Del Bosque, 2014). A few years prior to that incident, on September 24, 2011, the decapitated body of 39-year-old María Elizabeth Macías Castro was found in a public square, along with a computer keyboard and a note stating that she was killed because of information she posted in an online chat room (Greenslade, 2011; Centro de Periodismo y Ética Pública, 2011). Online media and social media sites such as Facebook and Twitter, enabled these local events to 'go viral' online and become global stories, resulting in a scale-shift in the pathways of information flows.

The concept of scale-shifting explores how, in some instances, the power of traditional media, such as newspapers, television and radio, and governmental agencies can be reduced, and how the digital landscape permits anyone with access to the internet to produce news content (Livingston and Asmolov, 2010). As Tarrow explains, one defining element of scale-shifting is collective action with "instances for cross-spatial collaboration" that include support of "spatial proximity, interpersonal networks, and institutional linkages within particular societies" (2005: 122), all potential characteristics of the US–Mexico border region.

In northern Mexico, where the majority of Mexican journalists were killed in the decade leading up to our 2011 study, journalists and bloggers scale-shifted traditional informational pathways in an environment of information scarcity and online security risks (Committee to Protect Journalists, 2010; Sierra, 2013). In a survey of 102 journalists in Mexico, including those who work in some of the violent states, most Mexican journalists assumed they were being watched by either members of organized crime groups or government officials and sometimes by both (Sierra, 2013).

Historically, politicians have used various news media to defame journalists, and online and social media have given them more tools to apply pressure to those they would like to silence (Sin Embargo, 2013). Undoubtedly, this situation can result in grave economic and social consequences for Mexican journalists, but it also presents additional challenges for some US journalists who rely solely on Twitter and other social media to cover northern Mexico (González de Bustamante and Relly, 2014).

Journalism, social media, and violence on the periphery

For several years, Mexico has ranked as one of the most dangerous places in the world for journalists (Committee to Protect Journalists, 2012a). Violence and aggression against journalists increased after President Felipe Calderón Hinojosa (2006–2012) launched a 'war' against organized crime groups, and his administration used the military to a greater extent than his predecessors to clamp down on drug cartels (Camp, 2010). During Calderón's presidency, 630 attacks were reported against the press, and from 2000 to July 2012, 82 journalists were killed and 16 others were 'disappeared' (Human Rights Watch, 2013: 1), with the majority of journalists murdered in northern Mexico between 2001 and 2011 (Committee to Protect Journalists, 2010). The term 'disappeared' refers to the intentionally violent act of disappearing a person, so that their whereabouts are unknown. The type of aggressions, specifically the phenomenon of members organized crime members directing and dictating media content, represented a new phase of violence against journalists and bloggers. (Antonio Mazzitelli, personal interview, November 20, 2013).

For some US-based journalists who cover Mexico, increased violence has posed new obstacles for attempting to obtain reliable information—they are directed to cover news across the border without going south of the border (Relly and González de Bustamante, 2014). As a result, some journalists have turned to Facebook and Twitter posts as a way to establish the veracity and accuracy of information. Furthermore, a lack of reporting regarding organized crime in legacy news media in Mexico (Arana and Guazo, 2011), alongside the limits on the mobility of reporters to cross into northern Mexico, has led to a increased chance of misinformation. In contrast, on-the-ground circumstances have generated opportunities for 'collective action' among journalists and citizens who use social media to gather and publish news and information.

Conducting research on social media in an environment of violence

Given the situation described, our study examines the uses of social media by US and Mexican journalists covering news in northern Mexico. We utilized the conceptual framework of scale-shifting (Livingston and Asmolov, 2010). The qualitative study is based on an analysis of 41 in-depth interviews gathered in autumn 2011 from journalists from 18 cities along the US–Mexico border. We focus on outlets from the western border cities and states of San Diego (California, USA) and Tijuana (Baja California Norte, Mexico) to the eastern Brownsville (Texas, USA) and Matamoros (Tamaulipas, Mexico; see Figure 54.1). The research questions include:

RQ1:   Given the online and physical security risks and the professional and geographic constraints for journalists covering northern Mexico, how are journalists on both sides of the border using social media to circumvent (scale-shift) and to overcome these constraints? And, as a subquestion, RQ1a: How is the use of social media by US and Mexican journalists covering northern Mexico distinct or similar?

RQ2:   In an atmosphere of heightened violence, to what extent have social media influenced cross-border relations and collective action among journalists?

Journalists we interviewed for this study work in television and radio, print publications, and online. The blogger is self-employed. Occupational titles of the study's participants are newspaper, online, television, and radio reporter; editor; anchor; and photojournalist. All participants in the study agreed that interviews could be audio recorded and were offered the option of anonymity for the study; every journalist opted for anonymity. Twenty-seven audio files were translated from Spanish to English and were transcribed, as were 15 English-language files. Below we present a condensed summary of our findings.

Findings related to social media use among journalists
covering northern Mexico

Both Mexican and US journalists agreed that the murders of bloggers in fall 2011 in Nuevo Laredo, Tamaulipas, had a noticeable effect on how they chose to either use, or in some cases, avoid using social media. Journalists from both sides of the border noted that they were very aware of the dangers of reporting in Mexico and in the period of our study, which included

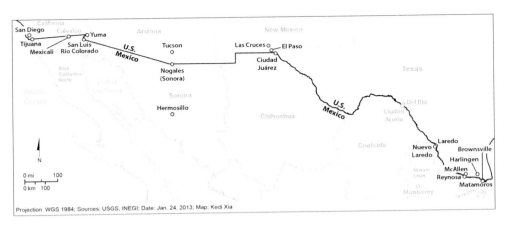

Figure 54.1 Map of US–Mexico border cities.

the months after the bridge hangings in Nuevo Laredo, journalists discussed particular caution with respect to social media use.

Given the online and physical security risks and the professional and geographic constraints for journalists covering northern Mexico and through analysis of our in-depth interviews, we found that in some cases, most notably in the area of the East Texas—Tamaulipas section of the border, heightened levels of violence are seriously affecting journalists' work and increasing their reliance on social media. For the purposes of our study, the East Texas–Tamaulipas section of the US–Mexico border begins in Laredo (Texas, USA)/Nuevo Laredo (Tamaulipas, Mexico), and ends at Brownsville (Texas, USA)/Matamoros (Tamaulipas, Mexico).

In response to the increased risks to safety that online media pose, journalists are developing innovative ways of utilizing social media. Some of these innovations suggest that journalists are circumventing (scale-shifting) various institutions, including government officials, *de facto* authorities such as criminal organizations, and at times their own news media organizations. Journalists on both sides of the border feel that they are at greater risk than they were prior to President Calderón's decision in late 2006 to send military troops to parts of the border in an attempt to cripple the criminal organizations (Camp, 2010). Our findings point to Mexican and US journalists making dramatic changes in practice, many of which include innovations that scale-shift and therefore bypass avenues of ongoing threat and constraint. Other key findings related to how social media have influenced cross-border journalists' relations with one another and collective action in this zone of conflict and violence.

Scale-shifting as an innovation in an environment of information scarcity

Mexican journalists. In general, Mexico-based journalists agreed that because of a decrease in news coverage on 'hot topics' such as organized crime in traditional media of newspapers and on television and radio, social media have become more important platforms in the way that journalists produce and find news. Social media use, including Twitter and Facebook, seemed more marked among reporters and photojournalists in Tamaulipas state. A Tamaulipas journalist said:

> Yes, they (social media) play a determining role. I think social networks right now have already taken work, I don't want to say it like that, but with their capacity to inform, they've already taken work from TV, from print media, and from radio … Here in Tamaulipas, you're not going to get anything from news organizations. Whatever you can find will be direct and personal information that's put up on social networks.

Despite continued heightened levels of violence in the state of Tamaulipas, combined with aggression and violence towards journalists and bloggers who use social media, reporters in this state said that they have frequently used Facebook and Twitter to inform the public. Given this environment, these journalists create innovative ways to use social media. When posting online, reporters have altered the manner in which they describe events and have changed the terminology that they use to explain violent acts or events. A Tamaulipas journalist gave an example of how journalists write about violent occurrences without divulging too much information: "You don't even say 'shooting' anymore. 'Blockade in this area.' Or 'this and this is blocked.' Not 'this neighborhood is in conflict,'—no, because people already know."

In an attempt to gather information when verifiable information is scarce, some journalists have gone so far as to create Facebook and Twitter accounts under false identities to use as reporting tools. On the other hand, there remain limitations to scale-shifting and social media use in the midst of a violent environment, as a Baja California Norte investigative reporter, who said he uses made-up accounts on social media, said he cancelled these accounts after he received threats.

Social media use can certainly put individual journalists at increased risk (Sierra, 2013). Keenly aware of these personal dangers, some journalists said they severely limit what they post on Facebook and Twitter, as one Sonoran radio reporter noted, "I'll upload 'such-and-such has just happened right now.' And that's it. I don't use it to debate or to talk badly about anyone or to say that this cartel does this and this cartel doesn't do this. I mean, I just share bits of news and that's it."

US journalists and the one blogger we interviewed acknowledged that even with the proliferation of social media, there was a scarcity of information in legacy media and a general lack of reliable information on social media sites. In cases when newspapers and television stations ignore news events, a blogger from the East Texas border noted that:

> People would pick up on that or people would just discuss what's going on … It (social media) has to be one of the most important outlets for us here, in hearing about those things, and the media has to pick up on those reports from Facebook or Twitter and things like that because sometimes government officials might not be all that forthcoming.

US reporters acknowledged that their Mexican colleagues were in a much more dangerous position for reporting, though some admitted fear or avoidance, at times, in crossing for work assignments in Mexico, and they sometimes curtailed activity there. Despite this acknowledgment, US reporters covering the northern border are taking precautions and developing their own innovative ways of using social media. As one Arizona reporter noted:

> I'm super, probably over-cautious on what I'm tweeting. […] I don't exactly want people to associate me with [mentions specific assignment] with my wife and son. I don't want to be a target.

As an added safety measure, some US journalists said they refrain from using social media while they are reporting south of the border and will use Facebook and Twitter only once they are back on US soil. One Texas-based reporter stated:

> I don't generally tweet when I am over there (in Mexico); I usually do it after I am back … I don't want to paint a target of where I'm at. I don't want to get kidnapped or assassinated or something.

For US-based journalists whose news organizations have prohibited them from crossing south into Mexico for reasons of liability and safety, social media have taken on increased importance because they are unable to witness or conduct interviews about events or activities as they occur in northern Mexico. This has exacerbated the problem of information scarcity in particular for some journalists based in the East Texas section of the border. As a result of information scarcity and continued responsibility of covering events in northern Mexico, these journalists also have developed innovations related to social media.

In response to geographical constraints, journalists said they use social media, including Twitter, YouTube, Facebook, and online chats, to get news tips, as a beginning, to get breaking news. One US-based journalist who covers the entire border stated: "You use it to figure out what might be happening and then you have to verify everything. Because we know also that criminal groups use it effectively as well to send misinformation."

US journalists who must rely on social media recognize their dependency on Facebook and Twitter presents some ethical concerns. For example, their reliance on social media made it extremely challenging for them to verify information. As one East Texas journalist stated:

> It's not the way I like to do journalism. And you can't do anything real extensive. You can't use any sound bites or anything, any interviews. It's basically, we're reading reports this is what we saw. This is what we heard…So, it's more you're doing play-by-play analysis. It's like you're at a football game and you're just doing it that way. To me it's not quality journalism. It's just a notch above hearsay and rumors.

Amid these challenges and concerns, some US journalists longed to be able to cross the border south to cover Mexico. One journalist from East Texas remarked, "We need to go back there."

Mexican and US journalists' relations and the potential for collective action

The use of social media has provided journalists with another way, and sometimes the only way, to develop or to continue cross-border relations. For example, journalists on both sides of the East Texas–Tamaulipas border said they share information via social media and texting. Journalists on both sides of the border consider these relations as an important part of the way they practice the profession. Communication between journalists that used to take place on the phone or in person now begins with social media. For example, a Brownsville journalist described how they keep abreast of events south of the border in Matamoros:

> We follow their tweets and once we see their tweets, then we'll try to contact them. We'll try to send an email or Tweet back to them. Sometimes they don't answer. So basically we take what they put on there at face value. Then the second tier of reporting is we call people that we know and we'll ask them what's going on and they look into it and call us back and say, "This is what we found."

An Arizona-based journalist said he follows certain Sonoran reporters on social media sites. Using Twitter, he noted that he follows one Mexican reporter's Tweets in particular:

> He's completely focused on getting out what happened. Like the other day they found this house with these sorts of torture instruments in Nogales Sonora, like a cattle prod and this stick with nails coming out of it and he was the one who tweeted about it. So yeah, I follow his Tweets really closely.

Mexico-based journalists seemed less dependent on social media to communicate with their counterparts north of the border. At the same time, communication and information via social media have proven to be vital for collaborations and support among those journalists based and living in Mexico's northern states. A Ciudad Juárez journalist commented that social media have helped strengthen solidarity among journalists:

> Social media help Mexican journalists keep in touch with journalists from other regions. For example, there have been people from Veracruz who don't know what to do. When they see the reality they're in, they call you and ask you, "What did you guys do? How could you go on doing your work?" People from Tamaulipas— fortunately right now social networks (laughter) have helped us be in touch with everyone right now. And the exchange is, "What do they do? What are they doing?" So we've understood that. The situation has united us, bit by bit. It's also made us wake up and say, "I'm also an affected citizen. I'm also that living victim of the violence, as a journalist."

In addition, reporters who are members of the journalism advocacy organization in Juárez known as *la Red de Periodistas de Juárez* (Juárez Journalist Network) have a Facebook site that the group utilizes to inform the public about aggressions and threats against journalists by government officials. According to founders of the Juárez group, members established the organization following the model of the national journalism advocacy group, *Periodistas de a Pié* (Journalists on Foot).

Discussion

Information scarcity, scale-shifting, and collective action

The 2011 study examined the ways in which journalists on both sides of the US–Mexico border were using social media in a region struggling with heightened levels of violence. The authors adapted the concept of scale-shifting with a broad interpretation of collective action to investigate both how journalists might circumvent institutions, through innovations in scale shifting, as well as to examine the ways in which social media influence cross-border relations among journalists.

Similar to Hänska-Ahy and Shapour (2013), we found that journalists have incorporated the use of social media into their daily news routines, yet these news routines regarding social media along the US–Mexico border were subject to change because of the volatility and fluidity of violence in the region. Further, our findings demonstrated that the salience of social media for newsgathering became more pronounced for US and Mexican journalists along the East Texas, USA–Tamaulipas, Mexico section of the border. This can be partly attributed to an increase in the overall level of violence in the state of Tamaulipas in 2011. The increased levels of violence along this part of the border, along with aggressions against journalists and bloggers, and a history of a less antagonistic press (Arana and Guazo, 2011) fostered a distinct environment for journalists reporting in the state of Tamaulipas.

We maintain that scale-shifting (Livingston and Asmolov, 2010) provides a useful framework for advancing understanding of how journalists and citizens, as a collective and in violent regions, can side step the state as well as members of organized crime through the use of Facebook, Twitter, and other social media venues. These findings suggest that journalists, even in some of the most dangerous regions of Mexico, have not been silenced.

Cross-border relations and collective action

The ways that social media influenced cross-border relations and the potential for collective action varied along the US–Mexico border. US journalists seemed more inclined to use social media to develop ties with their counterparts to the south. This was especially evident among East Texas journalists who were banned from crossing the border, but Arizona journalists also relied on Facebook and Twitter as a way to keep in contact with Mexican journalists. On the other hand, Mexico-based journalists seemed less dependent on social media to communicate with their counterparts north of the border. This is not surprising, given that Mexican journalists often are asked by their news organizations to cover events north of the border, and they can freely travel north in most cases, with presumably less risk.

With respect to using social media for collaboration and collective action, Mexican journalists appeared to use social media less for developing ties north of the border, and instead used Facebook to strengthen solidarity among their national counterparts in northern Mexico. The establishment of the organization *la Red de Periodistas de Juárez* (The Juarez Journalist Network) illustrates that these journalists are working together to advocate for increased press freedom.

Future directions

The implications of the findings of our study make apparent the presence of a negative side of networked society (Tarrow, 2005). Evidence of a cross-border networked society in the US–Mexico border region warrants further research, given that the US–Mexico border has long been a place of economic and cultural collaboration, and a local for personal interaction among transnational citizens, where family and business ties are abundant (González de Bustamante, 2013; Jones, 1992). In some cases, the ease with which US reporters crossed into Mexico diminished, presenting opportunities for 'virtual communities' to develop. However, the potential for cross-border interaction through social media was not uniform and, in some cases, opportunities for collective action seemed to decrease.

By employing a transnational approach to explore the connections between social media and journalism practice along the US–Mexico border, the research discussed in this chapter has set the groundwork for future projects regarding social media in the region. Nevertheless, a continued digital divide in Mexico causes the authors to remain circumspect regarding the significance and influence of social media in the region. Despite the inequities in media, and given current trends, more Mexicans will likely be relying on mobile telephones and the internet for communication. These on-the-ground circumstances provide clear justification for additional research about social media and journalism in zones of conflict.

Further reading

For more on social media in areas of conflict in other parts of the world, Berenger's edited collection (2013) *Social Media Go to War: Rage, Rebellion and Revolution in the Age of Twitter* offers a good compendium, while Waisbord's 2002 article "Antipress Violence and the Crisis of the State," discusses some of the factors that influence antipress violence in peripheral regions. Correa-Cabrera and Nava's chapter "Drug Wars, Social Networks and the Right to Information" (cited below) offers a thought provoking examination of citizen journalism in the region of northern Mexico, and Lasorsa, Lewis, and Holton's 2012 article 'Normalizing Twitter' (cited below) reflects on the way reporters use Twitter to follow news and news outlets. Finally, Manuel Castells' *The Rise of the Network Society* (2010, 2nd edn.), also cited below, offers key reflection and theorization on the development of the internet and the way networks form in society.

References

Arana, A. and Guazo, D. (2011) "Journalism Falls Victim to Mexico Narco Wars." México, DF: Fundación MEPI. Available from: http://www.fundacionmepi.org/index.php?option=com_content&view=article&id=755:mexicos-intensifying-drug-war-kills-journalism&catid=92:media-x-violence-&Itemid=344.

Berenger, R.D. (ed.) (2013) *Social Media Go to War: Rage, Rebellion and Revolution in the Age of Twitter*. Milwaukee, WI: Marquette Books.

Camp, R.A. (2010) "Armed Forces and Drugs: Public Perceptions and Institutional Challenges." In Olson, E.L., Selee, A. and Shirk, D.A. (eds) *Shared Responsibility: U.S.-Mexico Policy Options for Confronting Organized Crime*. Washington, DC: Mexico Institute, Woodrow Wilson International Center for Scholars and Trans-border Institute. Available from: http://www.wilsoncenter.org/publication/shared-responsibility.

Castells, M. (2010) *The Rise of the Network Society*. 2nd edn. Malden, MA: Blackwell Publishing.

Centro de Periodismo y Ética Pública. (2011) "Asesinan a María Elizabeth Macías, Periodista de Nuevo Laredo, Tamaulipas." Mexico City: Centro de Periodismo y Ética Pública. Available from: https://libexmexico.wordpress.com/2011/09/27/asesinan-a-maria-elizabeth-macias-periodista-de-nuevo-laredo-tamaulipas/.

Committee to Protect Journalists (2010) *Silence or Death: Crime, Violence and Corruption are Destroying the Country's Journalism*. New York, NY: Committee to Protect Journalists. Available from: http://www.cpj.org/reports/2010/09/silence-or-death-in-mexicos-press.php.

Committee to Protect Journalists. (2012a) *Anti-Press Crime Amendment Offers Hope for Mexican Press*. New York, NY: Committee to Protect Journalists. Available from: http://cpj.org/2012/06/anti-press-crime-amendment-offers-hope-for-mexican.php.

Committee to Protect Journalists. (2012b) *Getting Away with Murder: CPJ's 2012 Impunity Index*. New York, NY: Committee to Protect Journalists. Available from: http://www.cpj.org/reports/2012/04/impunity-index-2012.php.

Committee to Protect Journalists. (2014) *Getting Away with Murder: CPJ's 2014 Impunity Index*. New York, NY: Committee to Protect Journalists. Available from: http://www.cpj.org/reports/2012/04/impunity-index-2012.php.

Correa-Cabrera, G. and Nava, J. (2013) "Drug Wars, Social Networks and the Right to Information: The Rise of Informal Media as the Freedom of Press's Lifeline in Northern Mexico." In Payan, T., Staudt, K. and Kruszewski, Z.A. (eds) *A War that Can't Be Won: A Journey through the War on Drugs*. Tucson, AZ: University of Arizona Press (pp. 95–118).

Del Bosque, M. (2014) "Another Citizen-Journalist Silenced in Tamaulipas." *Texas Observer*, 17 October. Available from: http://www.texasobserver.org/reynosafollow-twitter-user-citizen-journalist-murdered/.

Freedom House (2014) *Freedom on the Net*. Washington, DC: Freedom House. Available from: https://freedomhouse.org/report/freedom-net/2014/mexico.

González de Bustamante, C. (2013) "Transnational Lives, Domestic Media: A History of Violence and Journalism along the U.S./Mexico Border." Paper presented at the American Historical Association Annual Meeting, New Orleans, LA, 5 January.

González de Bustamante, C. and Relly, J.E. (2014) "Journalism in Times of Violence: Social Media Use by U.S. and Mexican Journalists Working in Northern Mexico." *Digital Journalism* 2(4): 507–523.

Greenslade, R. (2011) "Mexican Journalist Decapitated." *The Guardian*, 29 September. Available from: http://www.guardian.co.uk/media/greenslade/2011/sep/29/journalist-safety-mexico?INTCMP=SRCH.

Hänska-Ahy, M.T. and Shapour, R. (2013) "Who's Reporting the Protests?" *Journalism Studies* 14(1): 29–45.

Human Rights Watch (2013) *World Report 2013: Mexico*. New York, NY: Human Rights Watch. Available from: http://www.hrw.org/world-report/2013/country-chapters/mexico?page=2.

Internet World Stats (2014) *Internet Users in the Americas*. Available from: http://www.internetworldstats.com/stats2.htm#americas.

Jones, R. (1992) "A Content Comparison of Daily Newspapers in the El Paso-Juarez Circulation Area." *Journal of Borderland Studies* 7(2): 93–100.

Lasorsa, D.L., Lewis, S.C. and Holton, A.E. (2012) "Normalizing Twitter." *Journalism Studies* 13(1): 19–36.

Livingston, S. and Asmolov, G. (2010) "Networks and the Future of Foreign Affairs Reporting." *Journalism Studies* 11(5): 745–760.

Mazzitelli, A. (2013) *Personal Interview*. Mexico City, 20 November.

Relly, J.E. and González de Bustamante, C. (2014) "Silencing Mexico: A Study of Influences on Journalists in the Northern States." *International Journal of Press/Politics* 19(1): 108–131.

Reporters Without Borders (2013) "A Journalist Forced to Flee: Another Murdered in Lawless Mexico." 4 July. Available from: http://en.rsf.org/mexico-a-journalist-forced-to-flee-04-07-2013,44894.html.

Sierra, J.L. (2013) *Digital and Mobile Security for Mexican Journalists and Bloggers*. New York, NY: Freedom House and International Center for Journalists. Available from: http://www.freedomhouse.org/report/special-reports/digital-and-mobile-security-mexican-journalists-and-bloggers.

Sin Embargo (2013) "El Pulso de San Luis Denuncia Campaña de Desprestigio en Redes Sociales, Operada Desde Oficinas de Gobierno del Estado." Mexico City: Sin Embargo, 19 February. Available from: http://www.sinembargo.mx/19-02-2013/533301.

Tarrow, S. (2005) *The New Transnational Activism*. Cambridge, NY: Cambridge University Press.

Waisbord, S. (2002) "Antipress Violence and the Crisis of the State." *International Journal of Press/Politics* 7(3): 90–109.

55

NEWSROOM CONVERGENCE

A comparative study of European public service broadcasting organizations in Scotland, Spain, Norway, and Flemish Belgium

Ainara Larrondo, Ivar John Erdal, Pere Masip, and Hilde Van den Bulck

Digitization has been one of the main energizing factors in innovation processes in mass media. At the present time, after more than two decades of the web's existence, this technological advance is significant, but only insofar as it is enabling different processes of change and improvement that affect the way news is conceived and journalism is practiced. These processes, directly linked to the phenomenon of 'media convergence' (see also García Avilés *et al.*, this volume), are of maximum importance today at the academic and professional level due to the opportunities and challenges they entail.

Among the multiple opportunities created by technological evolution, multiple media or multiplatform distribution—press and/or radio and/or television and online and/or mobile—has been emphasized until now because of its simplicity and validity in exploiting the competitive advantages of each medium. Content distribution across media has also been understood as a helpful strategy to make the most of the resources of the news organization, obtaining "a maximum value of outputs for given values of inputs" (Doyle, 2010: 40). In the current mass media context, this type of strategy necessarily promotes a growing interrelation or connection among different media divisions within the news organizations (print and/or broadcasting and online) (Deuze, 2004: 140).

This multimedia or cross-media approach implies greater coordination and synergistic cooperation among independent newsrooms and, as a result, among the journalists responsible for content on an everyday basis. This has been, in fact, one of the main impacts of technological convergence in news organizations to date. On the one hand, it obliges a confluence of different cultures and work rhythms; on the other, it increases the level of journalists' multiskilling, at both the technical level and the level of content, so that in some cases they are able to report across two or more media. These inner changes are usually accompanied by adaptations in the organizational structure of the newsroom. In some cases, these changes have resulted in the creation of single and integrated newsrooms that manage multiplatform production and distribution, which implies a different way of working, thinking of all the media in unison (Dailey, Demo, and Spillman, 2005; Silcock and Keith, 2006).

Analysis of these questions has made it possible to throw light on the changes that convergence is generating at the level of production routines and in the role of journalists

556

(Boczkowski and Ferris, 2005; Domingo *et al.*, 2007; Erdal, 2009; Killebrew, 2003, 2005; Klinenberg, 2005; Meier, 2007; Saltzis and Dickinson, 2008; Singer, 2004; Tameling and Broersma, 2013); so much so that 'newsroom integration' is today one of the main lines for approaching the phenomenon of convergence in the journalistic field.

Research circumscribed to this area of study describes different models of activity, which set out two basic scenarios: a scenario of an integrated type, which is normal in press companies; and another less advanced scenario of a 'cross-media' type, characteristic of broadcasting organizations, each with a different production system, newsroom organization, degree of journalists' multiskilling, and business strategy (García Avilés and Carvajal, 2008). While analyses of convergence processes in the press industry have predominated to date, in the specific case of broadcasting organizations we now have available an increasingly numerous *corpus*, which was initiated approximately 10 years ago, thanks to several pioneering studies (Cottle and Ashton, 1999; Duhe, Mortimer, and Chow, 2004; Dupagne and Garrison, 2006).

This body of research has also highlighted evidence on the impact of convergence in the newsrooms of public service broadcasters, equally affected by this change of scenario, symbolized by the transition from *broadcast* to *broadband*; a "Fourth Broadcasting Revolution" (Davies Report, 1999), leading Public Service Broadcasting (PSB) to achieve a new status as Public Service Media (PSM) (Ferrell and Bardoel, 2007).

On the basis of data from surveys and semi-structured interviews with managers, editorial heads, and journalists (Larrondo *et al.*, 2014), this chapter offers a basic, systemic, and professional view of current newsroom convergence processes in those mid-sized European public service broadcasting corporations that have initiated changes in this respect. Concretely, it considers representative cases of the three media models conceptualized by Hallin and Mancini (2004): the United Kingdom's BBC Scotland (Liberal Model), Spain's CCMA and EITB (Polarised Pluralist Model), and Norway's NRK and Flemish-Belgian VRT (Democratic Corporatist Model) (Table 55.1). These five public corporations have a strong position in their respective media landscapes and have shown a clear determination to adjust their news operations, carrying out projects for change that have impacted upon their newsrooms' established sociology. Table 55.2 summarizes the main steps given by these news organizations in their convergence processes, starting around 2006 and 2007 years.

Table 55.1 Analyzed cases

	Foundation	News outlets	Audience shares	Language
BBC Scotland	1923	TV: BBC One Scotland, BBC Two Scotland, BBC Alba Radio: BBC Radio Scotland Online: BBC.co.uk/ Scotland	BBC One Scotland: 21.2% BBC Scotland Radio: 20.4% Online: 11.02 m unique UK users (BBC Scotland Management Review, 2014)	English/ Gaelic
CCMA	1983	TV: TV3, 324 Radio: Catalunya Ràdio, Catalunya Informació Online: 324.cat	TV3: 13.5% Catalunya Ràdio: 25.5% Online: 1.2 m unique users (CCMA Annual Report, 2013)	Catalan

(Continued)

Table 55.1 (Continued)

	Foundation	News outlets	Audience shares	Language
EITB	1982	TV: ETB-1, ETB-2, ETB-3, ETB-4, ETB Basque Channel, ETBSat Radio: Euskadi Irratia, Radio Euskadi, Radio Vitoria, Gaztea y EiTB Musika Online: Eitb.eus	Overall TV: 13% Overall radio: 35% Online: 19 m unique users (EITB Annual Report, 2014)	Spanish/ Basque
VRT	1930 (radio) 1953 (TV)	TV: één, Canvas, Ketnet/ Op12 Radio: four general channels with news bulletin, one (Radio 1) with focus on news and information, digital Nieuws+ channel Online: Deredactie.be, Sporza.be, Cobra.be	TV: daily 2.1 m viewers for news and current affairs Radio: daily 2.9 m listeners for news and current affairs Online: 600.000 daily (VRT Annual Report, 2013)	Flemish
NRK	1933	TV: NRK1, NRK2, NRK3 Radio: P1, P2, P3, NRK Always News (+10 more special interest channels on DAB+) Online: NRK.no	87% of population uses one or more NRK's outputs on any given day (=4.5 m people) (NRK Annual Report, 2014)	Norwegian

Table 55.2 Major landmarks toward journalistic convergence

British Broadcasting Corporation Scotland (BBC Scotland)

2007
- Move to new headquarters: medium-specific desks together on one newsroom floor
- Introduction 'Digital Library' system (input–output accessible for everyone in newsroom; access to content editing software for all platforms)
- 'News organizer' harmonizes news flows between media
- In-house training for journalists and technicians
2009
- First multiplatform-purpose products
- Synergies with other broadcasting news organizations
2012–2016
- Constant revision of convergent operation and of organization's needs according to its public commitment ("Delivering Quality First for Scotland")

Corporació Catalana de Mitjans Audiovisuals (CCMA) (Catalan Broadcasting Corporation)

2007
- Five newsrooms: one for TV newscasts, one for radio newscasts, two for 24-hour news operations (TV and radio), and one for online
- News channel director: in charge of developing convergence project
- Revamped news portal

2008
– (Partial) sharing of internet and Radio newsroom. Online journalist at 3/24 TV newsroom and weekly TV planning meetings. Online journalist at radio daily news meetings
2010
– Sharing space of online newsroom and 24-hour TV newsroom, but separate television and internet teams
2011
– TV journalists trained to publish content on news website
– Managers renew aspiration of merging all media in single building, but project cut short due to budget cuts

---

Euskal Irrati Telebista (EITB) (Basque Public Radio and Television)

2007
– New headquarters: medium-specific desks (radio, television, and online) grouped on one newsroom floor
2008 and 2011
– Redesign of website and creation of a unique brand (*Eitb.com*) to improve on-demand service
2013
– Introduction 'Multimedia organizer' to harmonize workflows among media
2013–2016
– Convergence remains major objective

Norsk rikskringkasting (NRK) (Norwegian Public Broadcasting Corporation)

1997
– Establishment of NYDI, a separate division for news and regional services
2000
– Reorganization towards 'broadcaster model'/'the BBC model,' separating roles of broadcaster and program production
– Reorganization of medium-specific desks (radio, television, and online) on one newsroom floor
2013
– Introduction 'News Centre': central news desk as 'hub' of workflow of all newsroom desks (radio, TV, web, and mobile media)
– Web and mobile publishing platform (*NRK.no/nyheter*) tested as shared resource for fast publication

---

Vlaamse Radio-en Televisieomroeporganisatie (VRT) (Flemish Radio and Television Broadcasting Organization)

2007
– Moves from medium-specific (radio, TV, and online) newsrooms to one integrated newsroom (VRT News)
– Introduction *iNews*: newsroom digital platform for intake, editing and sharing of resources in radio, TV, and online media
– Management structured based on the news process (five chief editors)
2008
– Intermediary evaluation of convergence
2011
– Restructuring management to three chief editors according to medium

---

The chapter focuses on the positions adopted by management and newsroom staff facing questions like definitions of convergence, perceived benefits and risks, and general attitudes toward the phenomenon. These aspects would explain why certain convergent outcomes represent both an opportunity and a limitation, as it is, for example, the case of multiskilling, a key question in the current debate on journalistic convergence.

One medium different definitions

There does not exist a single and unanimous definition of convergence. Academic literature often offers systemic definitions of convergence, more complex and multidimensional than those coming from the professional world. Professional definitions are usually reductionist and limited to logistical aspects, mainly referring to the physical structure of newsrooms and to the production processes by which editorial teams are merged together (Erdal, 2007; Infotendencias Group, 2012).

That divergence in defining convergence is reproduced in the public broadcasters studied in this research. Top managers offer general definitions and consider convergence as a strategic objective. Thus, convergence acts as a key element of their discourse on modernity, quality, and improved service and is useful for promoting the identity and the brand of the news organization. In this sense, at BBC Scotland, for example, convergence is seen as a project of global change that affects all the physical spaces, the way of working, and also the relation with the public. In similar terms, expressed in the CCMA: "The driving force behind the project are adaptation to new media consumption habits, achieving a more efficient production by sharing information and resources, and by coordinating the distribution of content."

Beyond general discussion, top managers opt for a flexible conception of convergence, based on promoting greater cooperative work and connectivity among newsrooms and platforms. Although to lesser or greater extents all companies considered a reorganization of physical spaces, in no case is convergence understood as total integration of newsroom teams and content production processes. In BBC Scotland, VRT, NRK, and EITB newsrooms were moved to new headquarters where medium-specific desks (radio, television and online) are grouped together at the same newsroom floor. CCMA did not adopt a merging of the newsrooms, but planned specific practices in order to promote the collaboration among them, such as the exchange of content between media and the presence of journalists from one newsroom in the editorial meetings of the others.

Top managers from all the public corporations share a similar vision of journalistic practice in a convergent newsroom. The head of news project at BBC Scotland summarizes it in the adagio "together when possible, separate when necessary" and his counterpart at the CCMA states "reporter have to work once, but thinking on all the platforms." Also the VRT and EITB preferred safeguarding medium specificity to completing the cross-media integration.

Nevertheless, management's idea of convergence is contrasted with how reality is perceived on a daily basis; while for management convergence is understood to flow in a natural way once the journalists of radio, television, and online share a common newsroom physical space and common content sharing platforms, journalists see convergence as a somewhat more difficult process that requires effective coordination between media. As well as time, for journalists convergence involves creating a new journalistic culture based on the conjunction of already existing cultures, each with its own routines and self-perceptions. In this sense, many journalists understand convergence mainly as multiskilling. "We are not superman", argues a manager in the television newsroom at CCMA, highlighting the prevalence of convergence as multiskilling among many of the interviewees. Although this vision of convergence, shared to a greater or lesser degree by most of the news workers of the five newsrooms analyzed, convergence has been seen as being a moderate integration with limited multiskilling, where reporters worked predominantly for one medium.

The discourses adopted by news workers are the result of a limited or even nonexistent preparation via communication and in-house training. Likely, this has been one of the reasons of the prevalent journalists' reluctant reaction towards convergence-induced changes. It should also be noted that online journalists offer a slightly more positive appreciation of the convergence process; they relate it to innovation and to a major role of the website, as the hub of a new content distribution strategy aiming to join radio, television, and web-specific contents. Nowadays, the web platform is no longer marginalized, and television and radio cultures do not dominate newsroom organization and news practices with the same intensity as they once did.

In short, different interpretations of managers and workers for and against convergence processes are closely related to their individual or collective expectations of benefits or perceived risks. In this sense, convergence is seen as a strategy that advances insofar as certain achievements are reached and certain difficulties overcome.

Perceived benefits

While a number of generally held beliefs in the advantages of convergence can be identified, individuals' perceived benefits differ according to institution, their place in the hierarchy (management vs. newsroom workers), or where their organization was in the process of transition.

In general, there is a feeling that convergence allows for the introduction of new digital work facilities, in the case of EITB this is explicitly mentioned as modernization but in general believed to improve faster access to cross-media inputs and confluence in newsgathering. Together with closer physical proximity from the restructuration of the newsroom space (in most cases), this is believed to increase efficiency. Management generally underline this efficiency, noting convergence encourages faster and easier workflows and supports a more efficient operation and a better news service. Newsroom workers generally confirm the belief in increased efficiency but do not necessarily consider this a benefit. While management in several cases stress that improved efficiency allows for better quality in news, newsroom workers appear much more skeptical about this, although a few years into the transition VRT newsroom workers confirm that convergence had not led to more desk work as some had feared. Management in general was reluctant to discuss efficiency in relationship to cost reduction. Newsroom workers stressed the perceived link more explicitly and in a negative way, fearing layoffs.

The merging of newsrooms and physical proximity was believed in general to lead to being better informed about what colleagues of other media and programs are doing. It was hoped this would lessen competition and foster better understanding and mutual respect among newsroom workers. Indeed, prior to convergence, it was often felt that internet journalists were less respected (made most explicit in the BBC Scotland case), but in some cases (e.g. VRT) it appeared there were also prejudices between radio and television news workers. A few years into the transition, in several cases there was indeed a perception among managers and newsroom workers that communication and consultation had improved and that there was an increase in social contact between colleagues of diverse media and between people covering the same themes. The integration to some extent also resulted in more mutual respect for people working for other media. However, competition did not fully subside, as continued fights over scoops in the Flemish case illustrated.

In some cases, such as NRK and VRT, it was believed that convergence could lead to multiskilled reporters who could either be shuffled between media platforms (NRK) or could take care of the entire news production process. However, a few years into the transition, expectations in this regard were modified. Other benefits mentioned are the career opportunities such as the possibility to develop a different professional expertise (EITB), the opportunity to improve working conditions and salaries (CCMA), increased flexibility for managers in the daily planning of news production (NRK), and the opportunity to create a united news brand for the institution (EITB).

Perceived risks and disadvantages

It is possible to identify different beliefs about the disadvantages and risks related to convergence in broadcasting, and these also differ across institutions and different levels of the organization. The risks can roughly be put into two categories: professional risks and risks related to working conditions.

When it comes to working conditions, journalists worry about the increase of their workload from convergence, something they associate with factors such as cutting costs, reducing the number of working positions, the increased publishing pace of the web, multiskilling, and multitasking. Another risk journalists perceive is the possibility of job cuts, even where initial plans did not include layoffs. Journalists in all the organizations studied report a heavier workload as a result of convergence. The main reasons they give for this is an increase in the number of programs and platforms they are required to work for and the amount of time for cooperation. Relatedly, as integrated newsrooms are often noisy, a more chaotic work environment and leading to concentration problems were noted as risks (VRT). Journalists perceive convergence as something that demands both changes in familiar tasks and adoption of new tasks. Even if this poses an interesting challenge, at the same time it is a cause of concern and uncertainty (EITB, NRK), leading to uncertainty over the harmonization of technical and journalistic profiles. Thus, there is concern among professionals regarding difficulties in recycling skills required for using the new technical devices and applications.

In the professional risks category, one of the prominent disadvantages journalists perceived is the possibility for lower journalistic and technical quality. One of the culprits here is the increased speed of publication, which many journalists see as threatening professional standards of accuracy and objectivity, ranging from quality not increasing as a result of integration (VRT) to a perception of quality diminishing as a direct result of integration (NRK, EITB, CCMA, BBC Scotland). Related to quality, journalists also perceive a risk for increased uniformity across platforms, especially towards diminishing the uniqueness of each medium. In this study, the risks were identified as cooperation leading to journalists on different platforms imitating each other (VRT) to web journalists spending time repurposing television and radio content for online publication (NRK). This concern is voiced in all the organizations, even if cooperation and internal competition (so-called 'coopetition') coexisted in the newsrooms.

For broadcast journalists in particular, the weight of the web as a medium with greater projection is seen as a risk. In their opinion, the destabilization of traditional broadcast media influence could be one of the main threats involving convergence, even if for the management, the genuine convergent philosophy implies a balance in the weight and role that each medium and its workers play within the organization.

The majority of journalists thus perceive risks concerning the renovation of the traditional *modus operandi* that convergence entails, as they consider that effective convergence is not compatible with the current structure of the organization. The broadcasters in the study all have a relatively long history of strong radio and television cultures within the newsrooms. While not a convergence risk as such, the conflicts between different journalistic cultures get more prominent as a result of increased cooperation between previously separate media. However, this is a complex matter, and at the NRK, these 'cultural clashes' are not as prominent today as they were in 2006 (Erdal, 2009). To some degree, this is echoed at VRT, CCMA, and EITB, as more and more traditional broadcast journalists acknowledge the value of integration.

Attitudes toward change

Top managers we spoke with show a particularly enthusiastic attitude, advocating the intrinsic potential of digital facilities and the new organizational structures to promote effective multiplatform operations. They assume that having put significant effort into the preparation of the convergence process, changes in the day-to-day operations will fall to the mid-level managers and newsroom staff. However, when we spoke with journalists they are far less enthusiastic, a consequence of poor communication between top management down through to the newsroom. While this communication has increased in the last years, with change ongoing, as management admit, it has been necessary to diminish some resistance and even fears on job cuts.

Apart from more senior and experienced staff, who have shown more resistance to change, the majority of journalists have not openly resisted adapting to a new scenario, including greater multiskilling and collaboration with other journalists and teams. Web journalists are the most excited about management's support of the convergence, as it brings greater consideration of their extant multipurpose roles. In their opinion, a more convergent operation leads radio and television reporters to adopt a more active attitude towards web content.

Even so, newsroom workers remain more skeptical than management, particularly when it comes to reporting across the three media on a regular basis. Many still believe television, radio, and internet have very different rhythms, logistical needs, and narratives styles and that these need clear criteria to converge. In this respect, journalists feel very positive about the incorporation of a figure to orchestrate coordination and information flows among staff from the different media. They are constructive about erasing previous professional clashes, while recognizing the foundation of a new journalistic cross-media culture still needs time to establish itself, and it does not necessarily mean the extinction of radio, television, and online-only cultures. In fact, as managers and journalists recognize, modifying radio and television traditional self-perceptions is not an easy endeavor (see Figure 55.3).

Final remarks

This multiple comparative case study approach highlights the human and professional factors key to understanding the current challenges of *journalistic convergence* for public service broadcasters across Europe. Managers, editors, and reporters agree on defining this phenomenon as an opportunity to renovate content strategy and to produce better for less across all media. Nevertheless, their viewpoints differ on the requirements for accomplishing this synergy at the newsroom floor in an effective and consistent way.

While management tends to consider technological modernization and the physical proximity of formerly separate media newsrooms as a sufficient condition to promote interchange, editors and journalists recognize barriers that require time and further steps, without minimizing the efforts made to date by analyzed organizations. In fact, increasingly coordinated newsrooms should be considered a genuine achievement in all studied cases, regardless of the integration level attained at the newsroom. At the same time, professional differences remain a present challenge, to a greater or lesser degrees. These disparities affect the involvement

Table 55.3 Synopsis

	BBC-S	CCMA	EITB	NRK	VRT
Definition	Project of global change affecting physical spaces, ways of working and relationship with public	Common definition: collaboration, efficiency, mutual enhancement... But no consensus between journalists and managers and between different newsrooms' staff	Greater connection between platforms and newsroom teams	Moving towards shared workflow across media platforms	An integrated production project, aimed at "together when possible, separate when necessary"
Convergence-related general ideas	Change of mentality; reporting across media; multiskilling; improved service and quality	Multiskilling; internal communication	Confluence; modernity; strategy	Cooperative work and synergies	New journalistic culture
Perceived benefits	Proximity between radio, television, and online teams; restraining competition between media	Career opportunities; harmonization of working conditions and salaries	Confluence and coordination in newsgathering; faster and easier information flow between radio, TV, and online journalists	More efficient operation; less duplicities in content; cost reduction	Better news service
Perceived risks	Job cuts	Difficulties in recycling skills; loss of quality	Multiskilling	Uniformity; diminishing each medium's uniqueness	Workload increase
Management attitudes	Promoter	Confident	Enthusiastic	Promoter	Promoter
Journalists' attitudes	Skeptical and constructive	Skeptical and fearful	Uncertain and fearful	Constructive	Demanding

of the staff and their motivation to cooperate with others. The cases studied here suggest the need for management to continuously reinforce the convergent philosophy, for example, by strengthening at the newsroom the role of the web, since this is the medium with the greatest potential for mixing content in different media formats. This online platform plays a dual role; a medium in its own right and a supporting distribution channel for radio and television content. However, a higher awareness of these dynamics by those working within radio and television formats could help diminish long-standing medium-specific identities and hierarchies, as well as increasing broadcast journalists digital culture and consciousness towards the ground-breaking implications of the process of convergence.

This prospect on reinforcing the role of the web generates some worry, mainly among broadcast journalists who tend to relate convergence to a 'feared' multiskilling—particularly 'tri-media' reporting—with a higher workload and greater time pressures. As some of the cases explored here show, internal communication tends to be useful in lessening these fears and reporting across the three media remains quite an exceptional requirement, even when multiskilling and flexibility are considered to be determinant characteristics of journalists' new professional profile.

In short, this chapter reminds us that European public broadcasters are showing a proactive attitude towards convergence, as a way of redefining their position in a market of growing rivalry. That is why, even if current structures and practices are still inadequate to ensure genuine *newsroom convergence*, the reorganization efforts have proven highly meaningful. They illustrate how institutions, characterized by massive established structures, have the strength to introduce changes affecting the core of what they are (from PSB to PSM). Attention to these and other cases of PSB newsroom convergence can be instrumental in understanding how cross-media strategies continue to be negotiated on the newsroom floor, in a setting of renovated competences and concerns about quality of journalism.

Further reading

For a more in-depth analysis of these cases, please consult the authors' previous work in Larrondo *et al.* (2014) "Opportunities and limitations of newsroom convergence." This chapter has also benefitted from preceding conceptual discussions of Dailey, Demo, and Spillman (2005) on the models and implications of newsroom convergence, as well as from specific contributions on broadcasting companies, as Doyle's (2010) "From television to multiplatform." From a broader stance, G. Ferrell's and J. Bardoel's (2007) *From Public Service Broadcasting to Public Service Media* provides useful context for understanding how convergence and online media ongoing makeover are affecting PSB in a many-sided way.

Acknowledgments

The authors are grateful to the interviewed staff of the studied public broadcasting organizations for their time and commitment to sharing their insights and practices with us.

References

Boczkowski, P.J. sand Ferris, J.A. (2005) "Multiple Media, Convergent Processes, and Divergent Products: Organizational Innovation in Digital Media Production at a European Firm." *The Annals of the American Academy of Political and Social Science* 597(1): 32–47.

Cottle, S. and Ashton, M. (1999) "From BBC Newsroom to BBC Newscentre: On Changing Technology and Journalist Practices." *Convergence* 5(3): 22–43.

Dailey, L., Demo, L. and Spillman, M. (2005) "The Convergence Continuum: A Model for Studying Collaboration Between Media Newsrooms." *Atlantic Journal of Communication* 13(3): 150–168.

Davies, G. (1999) "The Future Funding of the BBC: Report of the Independent Review Panel." Available from: http://news.bbc.co.uk/hi/english/static/bbc_funding_review/reviewco.pdf.

Deuze, M. (2004) "What is Multimedia Journalism?" *Journalism Studies* 5(2): 139–152.

Domingo, D., Aguado, J.M., Cabrera, M.A., Edo, C., Masip, P., Meso, K., et al. (2007) "Four Dimensions of Journalistic Convergence: A Preliminary Approach to Current Media Trends at Spain." Paper presented at the "International Symposium of Online Journalism" (University of Austin). Available from: http://online.journalism.utexas.edu/2007/papers/Domingo.pdf.

Doyle, G. (2010) "From Television to Multi-Platform. Less from More or More for Less?" *Convergence* 16(4): 431–449.

Duhe, S., Mortimer, M. and Chow, S. (2004) "Convergence in TV Newsrooms: A Nationwide Look." *Convergence* 10(2): 81–89.

Dupagne, M. and Garrison, B. (2006) "The Meaning and Influence of Convergence: A Qualitative Case Study of Newsroom Work at the Tampa News Center." *Journalism Studies* 7: 237–255.

Erdal, I.J. (2007) "Researching Media Convergence and Crossmedia News Production. Mapping the Field." *Nordicom Review* 28(2): 51–16.

Erdal, I.J. (2008) "*Cross-Media News Journalism. Institutional, Professional and Textual Strategies and Practices in Multi-Platform News Production.*" PhD Dissertation, University of Oslo, Norway.

Erdal, I.J. (2009) "Cross-Media (Re) Production Cultures." *Convergence* 15(2): 215–231.

Ferrell, G. and Bardoel, J. (2007) *From Public Service Broadcasting to Public Service Media.* Göteborg: Nordicom.

García Avilés, J.A. and Carvajal, M. (2008) "Integrated and Cross-Media Newsroom Convergence." *Convergence* 14(2): 221–241.

Hallin, P. and Mancini, D.C. (2004) *Comparing Media Systems: The Three Models of Media and Politics.* Cambridge, UK: Cambridge University Press.

Infotendencias Group. (2012) "Media Convergence." In Siapera, E. and Veglis, A. (eds) *The Handbook of Global Online Journalism.* Oxford, UK: Willey & Sons, pp. 21–38.

Killebrew, K.C. (2003) "Culture, Creativity and Convergence: Managing Journalists in a Changing Information Workplace." *International Journal on Media Management* 5(1): 39–46.

Killebrew, K.C. (2005) *Managing Media Convergence: Pathways to Journalistic Cooperation.* Ames, IA: Blackwell.

Klinenberg, E. (2005) "Convergence: News Production in a Digital Age." *Annals of the American Academy of Political and Social Science* 597(1): 48–64.

Larrondo, A., Domingo, D., Erdal, I.J., Masip, P. and Van den Bulck, H. (2014) "Opportunities and Limitations of Newsroom Convergence: A Comparative Study on European Public Service Broadcasting Organizations." *Journalism Studies* 17(3): 1–24.

Meier, K. (2007) "Innovations in Central European Newsrooms: Overview and Case Study." *Journalism Practice* 1(1): 4–19.

Saltzis, K. and Dickinson, R. (2008) "Inside the Changing Newsroom: Journalists' Responses to Media Convergence." *Aslib Proceedings: New Information Perspectives* 60(3): 216–228.

Silcock, B.W. and Keith, S. (2006) "Translating the Tower of Babel? Issues of Definition, Language, and Culture in Converged Newsrooms." *Journalism Studies* 7(4): 610–627.

Singer, J.B. (2004) "Strange Bedfellows? The Diffusion of Convergence in Four News Organizations." *Journalism Studies* 5(1): 3–18.

Tameling, K. and Broersma, M. (2013) "De-Converging the Newsroom: Strategies for Newsroom Change and their Influence on Journalism Practice." *International Communication Gazette* 75(1): 19–34.

VRT (2013) *Jaarverslag 2013.* Brussels: VRT.

PART X

Future directions

56

WHISTLEBLOWING IN A DIGITAL AGE

Journalism after Manning and Snowden

Einar Thorsen

On 15 October 2015, *The Intercept* published a major national security leak dubbed The Drone Papers (The Intercept, 2015). While it only attracted moderate media attention, the leak highlighted how whistleblowing has been transformed in a digital age. First, The Drone Papers exposed the grim realities of modern warfare with remote-controlled assassinations conducted using Unmanned Aerial Vehicles (UAV), by detailing the secretive process by which people are selected for execution enabling a wider discussion about the Obama administration's use of state power. It also documented a heavy dependency on unreliable mobile phone 'signal intelligence' metadata to pinpoint 'targets' and a frightening scale of civilian casualties for every 'target' murdered.

Second, the leak confirmed that *The Intercept* had access to a senior source within the NSA besides Edward Snowden. To preserve the whistleblower's anonymity, he was simply referred to as 'the source.' Explaining his motivations, 'the source' argued that the public had a right to know the process by which the US government conducts assassinations on foreign soil. "This outrageous explosion of watchlisting—of monitoring people and racking and stacking them on lists, assigning them numbers, assigning them 'baseball cards,' assigning them death sentences without notice, on a worldwide battlefield—it was, from the very first instance, wrong" (cited in Scahill, *The Intercept*, 15 October 2015). Third, for such a major leak to be published by *The Intercept*, an online media initiative launched only in February 2014, was remarkable. Financed by eBay founder, Pierre Omidyar, as the first of his First Look Media ventures. The editors were equally avant-garde: lawyer and former *Guardian* journalist Glenn Greenwald, award-winning documentary maker Laura Poitras, and former *Democracy Now!* investigative journalist Jeremy Scahill. This was, in other words, a leak not just *in* the digital age, but *of* the digital age.

This chapter explores ways in which the relationship between whistleblowers, journalists, and political power has transformed over the past 5 years. Three core themes will be covered: a historical overview of the evolution of whistleblowing and associated legal frameworks; the disruptive scale of the leaks stemming from Chelsea Manning and Edward Snowden, and their motivations; the chapter examines tensions between protective and punitive frameworks used in different national contexts to define both whistleblowers and journalists who use leaked material as a source. I demonstrate how these frameworks are applied unevenly, in order to prevent challenges to established forms of political power. Finally, the chapter focuses on emerging communication security and source protection practices required to mitigate risks associated with whistleblowing in a digital age.

From informants to whistleblowers

The idea of citizens helping uncover fraudulent activity to aid prosecution has a longstanding history through so-called qui tam laws, which enable a private individual assisting in a prosecution to receive some, or all, of the penalty imposed. In England, the earliest example was the declaration of King Wihtred of Kent in 695 AD, who decreed that "If a freeman works during the forbidden time [...] the man who informs against him shall have half the fine" (Doyle, 2009: 2). This was followed by further provisions during King Edward II and Henry VIII's reigns, and qui tam laws had by fourteenth to sixteenth centuries become a common feature of the English legal framework—later to be superseded by the Common Informers Act 1951. Given the central premise of motivating informants financially, these laws sparked an unintended and unpopular movement of bounty hunters who were widely derided and castigated. In the United States, Congress passed the False Claims Act in 1863 (also referred to as the 'Lincoln Law') as a way of combating fraud and wartime contractor profiteering during the American Civil War (Johnson, 2003). Again this law relied on ordinary citizens to act as informants to expose wrongdoing, and sue companies making 'false claims' with the promise of a share in the money saved.

'Whistleblowing' emerged during the 1960s as a way of describing an act of 'ethical dissent,' which avoided the negative connotations associated with words such as *informant, snitch, traitor*, associated with the mafia and Communist informers of the time (Johnson, 2003). It was popularized by US civic rights activist Ralph Nader who included it in the title of the seminal book *Whistleblowing: The Report of the Conference on Professional Responsibility* (Nader, Petkas, and Blackwell, 1972). Nader and his colleagues described 25 different examples of whistleblowers, primarily concerned directly or indirectly with Government wrongdoing, and highlighted the great risk and personal cost to those who act on their conscience to blow the whistle. Crucially, the motivation of those highlighted was not financial—as with the bounty hunter informants—but arose from a sense of civic duty. Consequently, today the term whistleblowing is generally understood to mean the activity of calling attention to wrongdoing (Calland and Dehn, 2004: 2) through a distinct act of dissent (Elliston *et al.*, 1985) or ethical dissidence where "a member or former member of an organization goes outside the organization or outside normal organizational channels to reveal organizational wrongdoing, illegality, or actions that threaten the public" (Petersen and Farrell, 1986: 5). Typically whistleblowers are inside informants who want to expose 'actual nontrivial wrongdoing,' often in collaboration with journalists or media organizations (Johnson, 2003: 3–4).

Whistleblowing in the context of news reporting is not uncommon and is one of the few areas where an 'anonymous source' is considered acceptable in journalism practice (Duffy and Freeman, 2011). Anonymous sources are not always whistleblowers, and a culture of strategic leaking by government and corporate officials in both the United Kingdom and United States bears little resemblance to "the lone whistleblower doing what is right in a malevolent bureaucracy" (Duffy and Freeman, 2011: 302). Whistleblowing may therefore be classified as just one of several actions under the umbrella term of 'leak,' which emerged in the early twentieth century to describe "an inadvertent slip of information picked up by reporters" and today broadly means "an array of practices involving the accidental and strategic sharing of information, including whistle-blowing, settling grudges, culling favours, drawing attention to policy initiatives, signalling foreign governments, and releasing trial balloons so as to discern early public response" (Zelizer and Allan, 2010: 68). As a particular form of leaking, whistleblowing is a deliberate act driven by an idealistic motive—"a person uncovering a compelling injustice who needs protection from reprisal by powerful parties" (Duffy and Freeman, 2011: 310).

One of the most famous whistleblowers is Daniel Ellsberg, the former US military analyst who together with his friend Anthony Russo released the Pentagon Papers to the *New York Times* journalist Neil Sheehan in 1971. Ellsberg and Russo had slowly photocopied a 47-volume Department of Defense study—approximately 7,000 pages—revealing the true nature of US involvement in the Vietnam War. Charges were brought against Ellsberg and Russo under the Espionage Act of 1917, but the case was dismissed when during the Watergate scandal in 1972 clandestine operations by the Nixon administration were revealed. The *Washington Post*'s covert informant in Watergate, 'Deep Throat', was later revealed to be FBI deputy director, Mark Felt.

These are just two in a series of high-profile examples over the past 45 years of people with access to otherwise secret or classified information acting on their consciences to make that knowledge public. Other prominent whistleblowers who worked with journalists include: Peter Buxton, the US Public Health Service epidemiologist who collaborated with Associated Press reporter Jean Heller to expose the Tuskegee syphilis experiment in 1972; Mordechai Vanunu, the nuclear technician who leaked details of the Israeli nuclear program to the *Sunday Times* in 1985; Jeffrey Wigand, who worked with CBS's *60 Minutes* in 1996 to allege how the tobacco company Brown & Williamson manipulated nicotine content in cigarettes to addict smokers (see Brenner, 1996); David Shayler and Annie Machon who both resigned from MI5 and in 1997 worked with the *Mail on Sunday* to expose criminal activities within the UK secret intelligence services, including spying on Government ministers and an attempted assassination of Muammar Gaddafi in Libya (see Machon, 2005); David Kelley, the former UN weapons inspector who in 2003 leaked information to BBC journalist Andrew Gillingan detailing how the UK Government's dossier exaggerated claims about weapons of mass destruction in Iraq (see Barnett, 2005).

These are only some of the more prominent whistleblowers to emerge, and there is a plethora of individuals who have contributed to exposing wrongdoing—not least on a local or regional scale—that rarely attract the attention they deserve. I now turn to examine the massive scale of recent leaks and the whistleblowers behind them.

Digital leaking on a mass scale

Over the past 5 years, there have been dramatic shifts in forms and practices of whistleblowing, with digital information storage and complex networked communication flows playing an increasingly central role. Two whistleblowers have come to symbolize this new era of information leaking: Chelsea Manning and Edward Snowden. Both have attracted significant global attention for their roles in facilitating mass leaks of classified information that exposed excessive government surveillance, cover-ups, war crimes, and diplomatic secrecy.

Manning first established contact with WikiLeaks and Julian Assange in November 2009, whom she eventually supplied with a range of classified material acquired from her army base in Iraq. She had initially sought out the *Washington Post* with the information, but confessed at her tribunal that: "Although we spoke for about 5 minutes concerning the general nature of what I possessed, I do not believe she took me seriously" (see O'Brien, 2013). Manning also left a message on the *New York Times* news tips answer machine, without ever receiving a response so she decided to upload the material to WikiLeaks via the TOR anonymizer network instead. WikiLeaks published information from Manning independently, including the Collateral

Murder video, and developed partnerships with established news organizations for the sub-sequent cable leaks (initially the *Guardian*, the *New York Times*, and *Der Spiegel*). Manning would later describe the material in a confessional chat to Adrian Lamo (a grey-hat hacker and threat analyst who would, in turn, blow the whistle on Manning), as "almost criminal political backdealings [...] the non-PR-versions of world events and crises" (cited in Hansen, 2011).

The first published leak from Manning, was a US Embassy cable dubbed Reykjavik13 com-menting on Icelandic bank, IceSave, closely followed in March by the release of a 32-page Pentagon report written in 2008 about WikiLeaks, to "assesses the counterintelligence threat posed to the U.S. Army" (Horvath, 2008). In April 2010, WikiLeaks released the Collateral Murder video, which reveals a US helicopter indiscriminately killing civilians in a Baghdad street and the crew's cavalier banter about it (see Sreedharan, Thorsen, and Allan, 2012). The Collateral Murder publication propelled the organization into global limelight, but this was only the beginning.

Ellsberg's 7,000 pages in the Pentagon Papers seem modest compared to the massive vol-ume of information leaked by Manning (McCurdy, 2013: 129). The Pentagon Papers might have fitted in a 10Mb PDF file if they were leaked today (Ibid), while the Afghan War Diaries contained 91,000+ military communications in a 75.7 Mb file, the Iraq War Logs contained some 391,000+ military communications in a 354.18 Mb file, and finally the Cablegate leak contained 251,000+ diplomatic cables from 274 US embassies in a 1.61 Gb file (Sreedharan, Thorsen, and Allan, 2012). While both Ellsberg and Manning's leaks revealed hitherto unknown aspects of US government's involvement in contentious wars, the volume of infor-mation and methods used to extract that information from military organizations differed significantly. Ellsberg painstakingly photocopied page-by-page, whereas Manning simply extracted the information on a few rewritable CDs.

The full extent of Edward Snowden's NSA leak is not yet known, but it is estimated that he has turned over at least 58,000 documents—about 500 have been made public at the time of writing (the Snowden Archive keeps a record of releases at http://cjfe.org/snowden). He acquired the documents while working at the NSA on behalf of Booz Allen Hamilton, one of the largest US defense and intelligence contractors. This was a job he had taken after work-ing directly for the NSA, specifically so that he could access additional classified information. Snowden then worked with documentary film-maker, Laura Poitras, and *Guardian* journalists Glenn Greenwald and Ewen MacAskill. He also sent information to the *Washington Post*'s Barton Gellman.

At the center of Snowden's revelations was the coordinated global mass surveillance by the NSA, GCHQ and allied intelligence services (e.g. the Five Eyes Group that also included Australia, Canada, and New Zealand) indiscriminately targeting *all* citizens' communica-tions. The scale of NSA surveillance was actually hinted at by Manning in her exchange with Adrian Lamo a couple of years earlier although widely overlooked at the time: "I know that approximately 85-90% of global transmissions are sifted through by NSA ... but the vast majority is noise ... so its getting harder and harder for them to track anything down" (cited in Hansen, 2011). The first Snowden exposé was published in June 2013 by the *Guardian* and revealed the NSA had collected mobile phone records and metadata from more than 120 million Verizon subscribers. Following this came a string of secret programs, each detail-ing the pervasive data gathering techniques deployed by intelligence services—some of which went beyond metadata to include *content* of telephone calls, email messages, and other personal online activities.

The size of the Manning and Snowden leaks illustrate the unprecedented access afforded to individuals working with sensitive or classified information and has laid bare the excess and secrecy of military, diplomatic, and surveillance powers operations. Indeed, witnessing what Manning and Snowden perceived as excessive use of power and operational secrecy was central to their motivations for leaking. Manning described in her trial statement how she "read more of the diplomatic cables published on the Department of State Net Centric Diplomacy server" and then:

> With my insatiable curiosity and interest in geopolitics I became fascinated with them. I read not only the cables on Iraq, but also about countries and events I found interesting. [...] The more I read, the more I was fascinated by the way that we dealt with other nations and organizations. I also began to think that the documented backdoor deals and seemingly criminal activity didn't seem characteristic of the de facto leader of the free world.
>
> *(O'Brien, 2013)*

Snowden was similarly disillusioned by the pervasive operations of US government surveillance. "The government has granted itself power it is not entitled to," he argued in the interview that first disclosed his identity as the NSA whistleblower. "There is no public oversight," he bemoaned that: "The result is people like myself have the latitude to go further than they are allowed to" (cited in Roberts *et al.*, *The Guardian*, 10 June 2013). Leaking information about classified intelligence operations was a deliberate act for Snowden, driven by an idealistic cause of correcting a perceived injustice. "My sole motive is to inform the public as to that which is done in their name and that which is done against them," he concluded (2013).

Central to both revelations is a recurring concern that secrecy is in fact an operational mechanism designed to protect established forms of power (see Hintz *et al.*, this volume). Snowden poignantly proclaiming that: "If we can't understand the policies and the programs of our government, we cannot grant our consent" (Snowden's "Sam Adams Award" speech, 11 October 2013). This is similar to Assange's view of authoritarian power, which he argued in his early writings is maintained by "conspiratorial interactions among the political elite not merely for preferment or favor within the regime but as the primary planning methodology behind maintaining or strengthening authoritarian power" (Assange, 2006: 2). The logical antidote to which was a radical form of transparency, realized through WikiLeaks. This echoes Manuel Castell's assessment of power in contemporary society, contending, "if we do not know the forms of power in the network society, we cannot neutralize the unjust exercise of power" (Castells, 2009: 431; cf. Sreedharan, Thorsen, and Allan, 2012). In such an environment, competing assertions about what constitutes whistleblowing is a constant source of tension—especially where it undermines established forms of power, as the final section will explore.

Journalists, whistleblowing, and source protection

Several countries have legislation to protect whistleblowers from dismissal or lawsuits— typically imbued in statues covering labor standards, employment rights, trading regulations, or protection against discrimination. Such laws afford protection for employees or agency workers who speak out against: health and safety violations, environmental damage, criminal offences, or wrongdoing being covered up. However, there are a number of caveats that limit or blur the legal position of whistleblowers. According to the UK Government guidance for employees, for example, a worker will only be eligible for protection if:

- "they honestly think what they're reporting is true"
- "they think they're telling the right person"
- "they believe that their disclosure is in the public interest" (GOV.UK, 2014).

The UK Department for Business Innovation and Skills has published a "list of prescribed persons and bodies," ostensibly a series of watchdogs and regulators, to whom workers can turn if they wish to blow the whistle to someone other than their employer—none of those listed include news organizations or journalists. There are, however, various legal assurances in approximately 100 countries (Banisar, 2007) that allow journalists to protect their sources from identification. Thus, potentially affording an additional safeguard against persecution for any would be whistleblower. Journalists meanwhile gain access to privileged information and the opportunity for a scoop. They also shoulder the responsibility of conveying the significance of the leak to the public—making sense of often highly complex and codified material, and intricate value judgments about what constitutes 'in the public interest.'

Whistleblowers themselves have historically been cast in a positive light by news media and depictions in popular culture. That is, a person who discloses confidential information somewhat reluctantly, guided by the belief that public attention must be directed to perceived wrongdoing or injustice. This is the case in a range of fictional portrayals of whistleblowers as heroes and experts (Johnson, 2003: 4), and news media sometimes construct whistleblowers "as heroic, selfless individuals to establish the legitimacy of their claims of systemic wrongdoing in the public interest" (Wahl-Jorgensen and Hunt, 2012: 399). Systematic analysis of UK news coverage of whistleblowers from 1997 to 2009, however, reveals that they are "mostly covered in neutral or positive ways" (ibid). This was also the case in news frames used to refer to Manning, with the *Guardian*, the *New York Times*, and *Der Spiegel* all depicting her in neutral terms as a whistleblower—avoiding frequent use of both villain and hero angles (Thorsen, Sreedharan, and Allan, 2013). The coverage was at times sympathetic, however, especially when Manning was framed as a victim during the pre-trial solitary confinement. The *Guardian* reported Snowden in a similar way, explicitly labeling him a whistleblower or leaker and focusing on his act of disclosure (Di Salvo and Negro, 2015). The *New York Times*, however, emphasized Snowden's previous work with the NSA and only used the term 'whistleblower' *once* in their coverage (Ibid). Despite the global reach of the NSA/GCHQ revelations, news reporting appeared preoccupied with US legal and political debates. Salter argues the discursive framing in news reports of national security leaks such as those stemming from Manning and Snowden are ostensibly designed to reinforce rather than disrupt established forms of power. "When such threats to the state arise, discursive closure is almost total," he found. "The scandal must be reported because of its gravity but it is clear that its reporting takes the view of the state above all else" (Salter, 2015: 198).

Regardless of protective legislation, whistleblowers and journalists working with them are frequently persecuted and sanctioned. The status of the source as a whistleblower is contested, and the organizations they leaked information from call for punitive actions for breaking the law or failing to follow prescribed procedures. According to Martin, whistleblower legislation "serve primarily as a form of symbolic politics that gives only the illusion of protection," and laws are "flawed through exemptions and built-in weaknesses," to an extent that they are "creating an illusion that is dangerous for whistleblowers who put their trust in law rather than developing skills to achieve their goals more directly" (Martin, 2003: n.p.). Such threats are particularly pronounced when the wrongdoing involves government, military, diplomatic, or intelligence material. The Committee to Protect Journalists in a recent report illustrated how the persecution of journalists and whistleblowers had intensified during the Obama administration. The authors highlight "a disturbing distinction that the Obama administration has made repeatedly," about what constitutes acceptable parameters for whistleblowers:

> Exposing 'waste, fraud and abuse' is considered to be whistle-blowing. But exposing questionable government policies and actions, even if they could be illegal or unconstitutional, is often considered to be leaking that must be stopped and punished.
>
> *(Downie and Rafsky, 2013)*

Indeed several countries have specific laws that prohibit the dissemination of information classified as vital to protect national security interests, including: the US Espionage Act; the Security of Information Act in Canada; or different Official Secrets Acts in India, Malaysia, New Zealand, Ireland, and the United Kingdom. Here 'national security interests' appear to supersede those of 'public interest.' Subsequently, Manning, Snowden, and some journalists they worked with have been subject to ferociously hostile attacks—particularly by those whose interests are served by preserving the operational secrecy of state governance.

Then US Secretary of State, Hillary Clinton, maintained that Manning's leak "puts people's lives in danger, threatens our national security and undermines our efforts to work with other countries to solve shared problems" (cited in American Forces Press Service, 29 November 2010). Others wanted to "determine whether WikiLeaks could be designated a foreign terrorist organization" (Republican Peter King cited in CNET News, 28 November 2010) or claimed whoever "leaked that information is guilty of treason" and that "anything less than execution is too kind a penalty" (Republican Mike Huckabee cited in Politico, 30 November 2010). Snowden was subjected to similar attacks, with then-House Speaker John Boehner describing him as a 'traitor' and that "the disclosure of this information puts Americans at risk," concluding that "it's a giant violation of the law" (cited in ABC News, 11 June 2013). The Chairwoman of the Senate Intelligence Committee, Democrat Dianne Feinstein, was similarly blunt in her assessment of Snowden: "I don't look at this as being a whistleblower. I think it's an act of treason" (cited in Herb and Sink, *The Hill*, 10 June 2013). Former CIA Director James Woolsey claimed Snowden "should be prosecuted for treason," and "If convicted by a jury of his peers, he should be hanged by his neck until he is dead" (cited in Tomlinson, *Fox News*, 17 December 2013).

Of course the degrading and inhumane treatment of Manning in solitary confinement during her pre-trial detention in 2010–2011, Assange's drawn-out political asylum in the Ecuadorian Embassy in London since June 2012, and Snowden's exile in Russia since June 2013, demonstrate that these threats are far from empty rhetoric. Persecution extends to the journalists working with the whistleblowers. In July 2013, for example, *the Guardian* was forced by GCHQ to destroy computer equipment storing files provided to them by Snowden. Two months later David Miranda, partner of then *Guardian* journalist Glenn Greenwald, was detained under the UK Terrorism Act—this was subsequently deemed lawful by the high court, even though the judges acknowledged the detention had been "an indirect interference with press freedom" (cited in Travis *et al.*, *The Guardian*, 19 February 2014).

In response to these pressures, changes to how journalists communicate with their sources are precipitated both by the digital communication flows of the network society *and* the illusive nature of the various legal frameworks designed to protect them. Of course both Manning and Snowden were highly skilled computer operatives working within the intelligence environment and as such were well-versed in information and communication security. Manning saved confidential information to recordable CDs and later uploaded it to WikiLeaks via TOR.

She communicated with Assange using secure IRC and encrypted Jabber messaging services. Snowden, having saved classified documents to USB drives, initially failed to establish contact with Glenn Greenwald because he did not have the time to work out how to communicate via encrypted email. Snowden therefore decided to contact documentary maker Laura Poitras, who he knew used encryption, but did so via an intermediary Micah Lee to obtain her public encryption key. He used the now defunct secure email provider, Lavabit, encrypted his messages using GNU Privacy Guard (GPG) and Off-the-Record (OTR) and used the TOR network to communicate—asking Lee to provide Greenwald with a Tails installation on a USB stick (a specialized version of Linux aimed at preserving privacy and anonymity). While this might seem like an impenetrable list of acronyms, the central component to all of this is straightforward: encryption and diligent communication security practices to aid source protection (see Henrichsen, Betz, and Lisosky, 2015). Of course, despite their best efforts, there are examples where both Manning and Snowden lapsed in their attention to security and potentially compromised themselves or associates: "I was a bit nervous at the time, and my wife was very nervous," confessed Lee, "because the government does not look kindly on whistleblowers and the people who work with them" (Lee, *The Intercept*, 28 October 2014).

Conclusion

Digital communication technologies have precipitated a dramatic shift in both the mechanisms and potential potency of whistleblowing. "Never before have so many geeks and hackers wielded their keyboards for the sake of political expression, dissent, and direct action," according to Coleman (2014: 382). The physical act of whistleblowing has become easier, the volume of information that can be released to the public seems boundless, and delineation of who can be a whistleblower and publisher has become increasingly blurred. Forms of communication we now take for granted are also rapidly eroding boundaries between 'public' and 'private' in our everyday lived realities. This extends to normative assumptions about transparency, governance, and our right as citizens to know what is done in our name. Such ideals are rarely afforded when it comes to understanding operational mechanisms of elite power, and whistleblowers are an integral part of exposing abuse of power or even criminal wrongdoing.

In the concluding moments of Laura Poitras's documentary about Snowden, *Citizenfour*, Greenwald reveals to him that a second NSA whistleblower has come forward. It is unclear if this source is indeed the whistleblower behind the Drone Papers, mentioned at the outset of this chapter. However, the publication of these revelations signals the start of high-profile leaks in the post-Manning and Snowden landscape. Another source with privileged information sought out Greenwald and his team—and was able to do so using secure communication technology to reveal a heavy dependency on unreliable 'signal intelligence' metadata and a frightening scale of civilian casualties for every 'target' murdered. "There's countless instances where I've come across intelligence that was faulty," the whistleblower said (cited in Scahill, *The Intercept*, 15 October 2015).

It remains to be seen if the identity of the whistleblower behind the Drone Papers will become public, and the repercussions this might have on his personal safety, but the threat to whistleblowers remains acute, especially when it concerns a challenge to national security. Following coordinated attacks by gunmen killing 129 people in Paris on 13 November 2015, several people extraordinarily sought to attribute partial blame for the atrocity on Snowden. "To some people the whistleblower Edward Snowden is a hero; not to me," proclaimed UK Conservative politician and former London Mayor, Boris Johnson. "It is pretty clear that his bean-spilling has taught some of the nastiest people on the planet how to avoid being caught"

(Johnson, *The Telegraph*, 16 November 2015). While such claims are easily debunked (cf. Greenwald, 2015), they demonstrate the extreme lengths to which members of the political elite are willing to go to discredit whistleblowers. Further research is needed to analyze the complex relationship between journalists, whistleblowers, citizens, and the state. We need to understand not just the networked power relations but also how to enhance digital safety and surveillance circumvention practices for both journalists and their sources. These are challenges for journalists across the globe, regardless if they are working on national security stories or their local beat. Speaking after the publication of the Drone Papers, Daniel Ellsberg noted, "hundreds could and should have done" what he did, what Chelsea Manning did, what Edward Snowden did. "They did the right thing. The others were wrong to keep those secrets" (cited in McCarthy, *Guardian*, 16 October 2015).

Further reading

Roberta Ann Johnson's *Whistleblowing: When It Works, and Why* (2003) remains an excellent introduction to the historical context and mechanisms of whistleblowing. For me the voice of whistleblowers is also central to understanding their motivations and actions, and here I would recommend Annie Machon's *Spies, Lies and Whistleblowers: MI5, MI6 and the Shayler Affair* (2005), Chelsea Manning's military trial testimony or any of Edward Snowden's interviews. Gabriella Coleman's *Hacker, Hoaxer, Whistleblower, Spy: The Many Faces of Anonymous* (2014) offers a great insight into digital activism and the role of computer hackers in information leaking. Finally, in relation to source protection, David Banisar's *Silencing Sources: An International Survey of Protections and Threats to Journalists' Sources* (2007) provides a great critique of legal challenges, whereas UNESCO recently published *Building Digital Safety For Journalism: A Survey of Selected Issues* (2015) that also examines source protection in a digital environment.

References

Assange, J. (2006) "State and Terrorist Conspiracies." 10 November. Available from: http://iq.org/conspiracies.pdf.

Banisar, D. (2007) *Silencing Sources: An International Survey of Protections and Threats to Journalists' Sources*. London, UK: Privacy International.

Barnett, S. (2005) "Opportunity or Threat? The BBC, Investigative Journalism and the Hutton Report." In Allan, S. (ed.) *Journalism: Critical Issues*. Maidenhead: Open University Press, pp. 328–341.

Brenner, M. (1996) "The Man Who Knew Too Much." *Vanity Fair*. Available from: http://www.vanityfair.com/magazine/archive/1996/05/wigand199605.

Calland, R. and Dehn, G. (2004) "Introduction." In Calland, R. and Dehn, G. (eds) *Whistleblowing around the World: Law, Culture and Practice*. Cape Town: ODAC and PCAW, pp. 2–20.

Castells, M. (2009) *Communication Power*. Oxford, UK: Oxford University Press.

Coleman, G. (2014) *Hacker, Hoaxer, Whistleblower, Spy: The Many Faces of Anonymous*. Brooklyn, NY: Verso Books.

Di Salvo, P. and Negro, G. (2015) "Framing Edward Snowden: A Comparative Analysis of Four Newspapers in China, United Kingdom and United States." *Journalism* 1–18. DOI: 10.1177/1464884915595472.

Downie Jr., L. and Rafsky, S. (2013) *The Obama Administration and the Press: Leak Investigations and Surveillance in Post-9/11 America*. New York, NY: Committee to Protect Journalists. Available from: https://www.cpj.org/reports/2013/10/obama-and-the-press-us-leaks-surveillance-post-911.php.

Doyle, C. (2009) *Qui Tam: The False Claims Act and Related Federal Statutes*. CRS Report for Congress: Congressional Research Service, US.

Duffy, M.J. and Freeman, C.P. (2011) "Unnamed Sources: A Utilitarian Exploration of their Justification and Guidelines for Limited Use." *Journal of Mass Media Ethics* 26(4): 297–315.

Elliston, F.A., Keenan, J.P., Lockhart, P. and Van Schaick, J. (1985) *Whistleblowing Research: Methodological and Moral Issues*. New York, NY: Praeger.

GOV.UK. (2014) *Whistleblowing for Employees*. UK Government Guidance. Available from: https://www.gov.uk/whistleblowing/what-is-a-whistleblower (accessed 1 November 2014).

Greenwald, G. (2015) "Exploiting Emotions about Paris to Blame Snowden, Distract from Actual Culprits Who Empowered ISIS." *The Intercept*, 15 November. Available from: https://theintercept.com/2015/11/15/exploiting-emotions-about-paris-to-blame-snowden-distract-from-actual-culprits-who-empowered-isis/.

Hansen, E. (2011) "Manning-Lamo Chat Logs Revealed." *Wired*, 13 July. Available from: http://www.wired.com/2011/07/manning-lamo-logs/.

Henrichsen, J.R., Betz, M. and Lisosky, J.M. (2015) *Building Digital Safety For Journalism: A Survey of Selected Issues*. Paris, France: UNESCO.

Horvath, M.D. (2008) *Wikileaks.org—An Online Reference to Foreign Intelligence Services, Insurgents, or Terrorist Groups?*. Army Counterintelligence Center, 18 March 2008. Available from: http://www.wired.com/images_blogs/threatlevel/2010/03/wikithreat.pdf.

The Intercept. (2015) "The Drone Papers." Available from: https://theintercept.com/drone-papers.

Johnson, R.A. (2003) *Whistleblowing: When it Works, and Why*. Boulder, CO: Lynne Rienner Publishers.

Machon, A. (2005) *Spies, Lies and Whistleblowers: MI5, MI6 and the Shayler Affair*. Kibworth, UK: Book Guild Publishing Ltd.

Martin, B. (2003) *Illusions of Whistleblower Protection*. UTS Law Review, No 5, pp. 119–130. Available from: http://www.uow.edu.au/arts/sts/bmartin/pubs/03utslr.html.

McCurdy, P. (2013) "From the Pentagon Papers to Cablegate: How the Network Society has Changed Leaking." In Brevini, B., Hintz, A. and McCurdy, P. (eds) *Beyond WikiLeaks: Implications for the Future of Communications, Journalism and Society*. Basingstoke, UK: Palgrave Macmillan.

Nader, R., Petkas, P.J. and Blackwell, K. (eds) (1972) *Whistle Blowing: The Report of the Conference on Professional Responsibility*. New York, NY: Grossman.

O'Brien, A. (2013) "Transcript | US v Pfc. Manning, Pfc. Manning's Statement for the Providence Inquiry, 2/28/13." *Alexa O'Brien* [personal website], 28 February. Available from: http://alexaobrien.com/archives/985.

Petersen, J.C. and Farrell, D. (1986) *Whistleblowing: Ethical and Legal Issues in Expressing Dissent*. Dubuque, IA: Kendall/Hunt Publishing Co.

Salter, L. (2015) "Framing Glenn Greenwald: Hegemony and the NSA/GCHQ Surveillance Scandal in a News Interview." *International Journal of Media and Cultural Politics* 11(2): 183–201.

Sreedharan, C., Thorsen, E. and Allan, S. (2012) "WikiLeaks and the Changing Forms of Information Politics in the 'Network Society.'" In Downey, E. and Jones, M.A. (eds) *Public Service, and Web 2.0 Technologies: Future Trends in Social Media*. Hershey, PA: IGI Global, pp. 167–180.

Thorsen, E., Sreedharan, C. and Allan, S. (2013) "WikiLeaks and Whistle-Blowing: The Framing of Bradley Manning." In Brevini, B., Hintz, A. and McCurdy, P. (eds) *Beyond WikiLeaks: Implications for the Future of Communications, Journalism and Society*. Basingstoke: Palgrave Macmillan, pp. 101–122.

Wahl-Jorgensen, K. and Hunt, J. (2012) "Journalism, Accountability and the Possibilities for Structural Critique: A Case Study of Coverage of Whistleblowing." *Journalism* 13(4): 399–416.

Zelizer, B. and Allan, S. (2010) *Keywords in News and Journalism Studies*. Maidenhead and New York: Open University Press.

57

SURVEILLANCE IN A DIGITAL AGE

Arne Hintz, Lina Dencik, and Karin Wahl-Jorgensen

The 'Snowden Era' has placed surveillance at the centre of political and public debate. When former system administrator for the Central Intelligence Agency (CIA) and information analyst at the National Security Agency (NSA), Edward Snowden, started to expose secret surveillance programs by the NSA and the British Government Communications Headquarters (GCHQ) in 2013, he revealed the unprecedented extent to which our every move in online environments is tracked, monitored, analyzed, and stored. While 'offline' surveillance, for example through Close Circuit Television (CCTV) cameras, and targeted surveillance of specific social groups had already caused debate, the Snowden revelations raised the stakes significantly as they demonstrated how current bulk collection and analysis of data concern the entire public. While the leaks have focused on surveillance by state agencies, they have also highlighted extensive data gathering by social media platforms and other commercial entities. In the words of John Perry Barlow, co-founder of the Electronic Frontier Foundation (EFF), the extent to which data is now collected, stored, and analyzed amounts to "monitoring the communication of the human race" (Barlow, 2013).

Journalism has been closely connected to the revelations and, at the same time, heavily affected by surveillance. News organizations such as the *Guardian* and the *Washington Post* have been vital in exposing readers to the reality of mass surveillance by publishing many of Snowden's revelations. Traditional media organizations such as *Der Spiegel* as well as new online publications such as *The Intercept* have investigated the claims and implications of data collection and analysis. However, other newspapers and broadcasters have heavily criticized the publications, pointing to concerns for national security, and there has been no common approach in the media sector on how to deal with this 'story.' Further, journalists have been among the most vulnerable groups due to their need for confidential communication (for example, with sources). Omnipresent surveillance has led to risks of journalists self-censoring their work and avoiding controversial topics (PEN, 2013), which means that critical and investigative reporting is perceived to be under threat (Rusbridger, 2013).

This chapter discusses the contemporary reality of digital mass surveillance and its implications for journalism and the wider public. We begin by briefly outlining key theoretical concepts from the academic field of surveillance studies. Secondly, we provide an overview of the practices of state surveillance, as highlighted by the Snowden leaks, as well as commercial surveillance, for example the extensive data gathering by internet companies. Thirdly, the chapter explores media coverage and implications for journalists and press freedom, before addressing responses by the wider public.[1]

Surveillance society

Theoretical approaches to surveillance have been heavily influenced by classic concepts such as Bentham's panopticon (Bentham, 1791) and Deleuze's assemblage (Deleuze, 1995). The panopticon is an architectural structure that would enable constant and pervasive monitoring of people within a specific space, such as prisons, and it was conceptualized by Foucault (1975) as a symbol for contemporary methods of social control that incorporate self-discipline and self-control. While this approach places a strong emphasis on a hierarchical model of surveillance (and the interactions by those who are surveilled), work on surveillance through data flows and in networks has often drawn on the idea of 'assemblage' (Haggerty and Ericson, 2000). Rather than building on fixed physical enclosure, it emphasizes data traces and communicative interactions as components of a more open and participatory control society. Highlighting the pervasiveness of contemporary surveillance, Braman suggests the 'panspectron' as a concept to understand how information is gathered about everything, everyone, and all the time (Braman, 2006).

According to surveillance scholars, ubiquitous monitoring is forming a 'surveillance society' in which "all manner of everyday activities are recorded, checked, traced and monitored" (Lyon, 2007: 454). Surveillance societies may be marked by a combination of the top-down panopticon and the networked assemblage. An increasing amount of data is generated by the users of digital communication networks and their devices, processed by commercial intermediaries, and analyzed by both commercial actors and state agencies (Trottier, 2015). Interactions of 'veillance,' for example, relations of mutual watching and monitoring, take place in the context of traditional power relationships between the watcher and the watched, as the classic centers of power, particularly the state and major corporations, enjoy a higher level of control than citizens, users, and social/professional groups, such as journalists (Bakir, 2015).

However, the emergence of tools and practices such as camera-phones, social media, and citizen journalism have equipped those at the lower end of these power relations with opportunities to observe the watchers and engage in their own monitoring and data collection (see Allan, this volume). This bottom-up 'sous-veillance' (Mann, Nolan, and Wellman, 2003) may document malpractice and confront authorities, or it may just provide a more self-controlled perspective on one's own life and activities. Finally, 'counterveillance' describes measures to detect and block surveillance, including practices such as the use of cryptography in digital communication or direct action against surveillance cameras.

Surveillance in practice

The Snowden revelations have pointed to a core actor in surveillance relations—the state—and demonstrated the diverse practices of state surveillance in the digital age. State agencies harvest data from the internet's backbone cables and intercept communication that passes through key nodes and pipes, for example, between the United Kingdom and North America (through programs such as *Tempora* and *Upstream*). They collect data from the servers of large internet companies such as Google, Facebook, Apple, and Yahoo—sometimes with their consent, sometimes without (through programs such as *Prism*, *Muscular*, and *Squeaky Dolphin*)—and they collect millions of text messages and users' geolocations a day (through programs such as *Dishfire* and *Co-traveller*). Analytical tools such as *Xkeyscore* allow them to sift through these vast amounts of data, search for specific types of communication and online activity, and profile people and networks. Complementing the interception of data flows, other programs have been developed to break the encryption that protects our data exchanges with, for example, social media platforms and online banking, to weaken the security of software products and to hack into telecommunications services (Fidler, 2015; *The Guardian*, 2015).

While the Snowden leaks point to the state as the main perpetrator of mass surveillance, several of the revealed programs also demonstrate the central role of social media and internet companies. The 'big data' generated through social media platforms for commercial profit is at the heart of current surveillance trends (Lyon, 2014). Corporate services like Facebook and Google operate on the basis of a business model of collecting and analyzing user data. Detailed knowledge about user locations, activities, brand preferences, and political orientations, as well as those of their friends and networks, is the foundation of their market value, and so they are designed to maximize (corporate) surveillance (Trottier and Lyon, 2012). Users are tracked as they move across the web, required to identify themselves (e.g. through Facebook's 'real name' policy), and subjected to automatic facial recognition. While social media have been praised as 'liberation technology' (Diamond, 2010) and celebrated for their support for protesters during uprisings such as the Arab Spring, their provision of a public sphere of democratic communicative interactions only goes so far as it offers the company increased access to user data and improves insights into the preferences, networks, and activities of people. Users are primarily customers rather than citizens (Leistert and Rohde, 2011).

The 'data mine' (Andrejevic, 2012: 71) of social media and other commercial internet platforms has garnered significant interest from state agencies. Even before Snowden, Google specified in its Transparency Report some of the official ways in which state agencies use social media to collect information on citizens. In the United States alone, Google receives over one hundred government requests for the data of its users every day (Google Transparency Report, 2014). In authoritarian countries, social media-based surveillance has often targeted protesters and dissidents. In Iran, Tunisia, Syria, and elsewhere, authorities have used social media to identify and arrest opposition activists and to infect the computers of dissidents with spying software to capture, for example, webcam activity (Hofheinz, 2011; Villeneuve, 2012). Most of the software tools that are used for these forms of targeted intrusion, monitoring, and analysis of user data are developed by companies based in the Western world—North America and Europe—from where they provide sophisticated tools for surveillance and internet censorship to governments around the world (The Citizen Lab, 2013; Marquis-Boire et al., 2013).

Surveillance practices expand as the technology spreads and develops. As capabilities for data collection, tracking, and monitoring are moving from our laptops and mobile phones to household appliances, cars, and clothes, questions of privacy and data control are becoming ever more prevalent and informed public debate about these issues ever more important.

Journalism in the context of surveillance

Despite the profound nature of shifts in surveillance practices and their implications for individuals and organizations, the extent to which these vital debates have been reflected in media coverage is uneven. The initial coverage of the Snowden revelations directed public attention towards programs of mass surveillance and brought about policy intervention and activist mobilization based on the evidence in the leaks. As Wright and Kreissl (2013: 35) argued:

The media have played an enormous role in raising citizen awareness of the surveillance revelations and its consequences. The reportage has had a strong ripple effect throughout society as civil society activists have mobilised against dragnet surveillance and other public figures have lent their support for reining back the extent to which the NSA and others are able conduct their activities with little effective oversight and massive budgets.

Nonetheless, research on coverage of surveillance after Snowden demonstrates that even if the issue of mass surveillance came to the forefront in the immediate aftermath of the revelations, the mediated public debate on the issue has, in the longer run, rendered these concerns largely invisible. Our research project "Digital Citizenship and Surveillance Society"—which focused on moments of peak coverage in the UK national press after Snowden—examined five key events that took place in the broader context of the revelations and crystallized mediated debates over surveillance. These events included, aside from the initial Snowden revelations, the disclosure of GCHQ and NSA's spying on world leaders and embassies; the detention of Glenn Greenwald's partner, David Miranda at Heathrow Airport; the parliamentary report around Facebook's actions in the case of the murder of Fusilier Lee Rigby; and intelligence debates surrounding the Charlie Hebdo tragedy in France. Our research demonstrates that debates over surveillance are largely framed by elites, with politicians being by far the most frequently used sources (Wahl-Jorgensen and Bennett, forthcoming, 2017).

This, in itself, is not a surprising finding and consistent with long-standing research on journalistic sourcing patterns (e.g. Berkowitz, 2009). Nonetheless, there is a clear relationship between the elite framing of surveillance debates and voices and views heard in these debates. We examined the most frequent opinions in the case studies and found them to be supportive of mass surveillance efforts by corporate and state actors. Surveillance, in other words, was frequently framed as a valuable activity. By contrast, views that were more critical of mass surveillance and took into consideration the rights of citizens were much less prominent in the debate. This implies that debates over surveillance unfold within a larger—and long-established—ideological framework, one which positions national security and concerns over terrorism as a key regime of justification (Boltanski and Thevenot, 1999) for forms of action that might otherwise be deemed ethically problematic.

These findings resonate in the work of Mols (2015), who carried out a frame analysis of media coverage of the NSA revelations in Dutch newspapers. Her analysis showed that the most frequent way of framing surveillance is that the 'end justifies the means'—that surveillance is acceptable because it is in the public interest, in ensuring security and protecting against terrorism.

This pattern, however, may not hold true around the world. A cross-national comparative study of opinionated journalism about the NSA's surveillance (Kunelius *et al.*, 2015) highlighted that debates over surveillance are profoundly shaped by social and political contexts. For example, German coverage showed that the role of surveillance technologies in violating privacy and freedom was a central theme, even though the amount of coverage and its salience remained low throughout the period of study. By contrast, in the case of Chinese coverage, much of it focused on taking a critical view of the US reaction to the Snowden case, including the characterization of American politicians as 'big mouths' and 'dictators' (Kunelius *et al.*, 2015).

Overall, the small body of research carried out on media coverage of surveillance—most of it focused in the relatively brief period since the Snowden leaks—demonstrates that the mediated debates have largely failed to ignite a broader debate around the democratic consequences of mass surveillance. As Bauman and his colleagues concluded about the journalistic treatment of the drip-feed of leaks from Snowden's files, "However earnestly they tried, leaking Snowden's exposures caused slight, hardly felt tremors, where earthquakes were expected" (Bauman *et al.*, 2014).

Although the debates around the Snowden leaks and the emergence of the surveillance society may have attracted limited coverage in the media, the increasing ubiquity of surveillance practices nonetheless has significant implications for journalistic work. On the one hand, collaborations between news organizations and whistleblowers have opened up for a reshaping of journalism's role in society. As Chadwick and Collister (2014) wrote, the "leak's mediation reveals professional news organizations' evolving power in an increasingly congested, complex, and polycentric hybrid media system where the number of news actors has radically increased" (see also Brevini, Hintz, and McCurdy, 2013; Coddington, 2012). For Chadwick and Collister (2014), the *Guardian*'s handling of the leaks and the newspaper's uncovering of state surveillance practices enabled it to reconfigure and renew its power.

The leaks may have enhanced the profile of key media organizations involved in their mediation. On the other hand, their *content* also highlighted the ways in which surveillance of actors—including journalists—is prevalent and normalized. For journalists, this has meant that it is increasingly difficult to secure the confidentiality of conversations—whether online or face-to-face with sources. Some journalists—particularly those who have covered surveillance—are very aware of the implications of widespread surveillance for their own communications practices (see Thorsen, this volume). As James Ball, formerly special projects editor for the *Guardian* and WikiLeaks employee, put it, if you are a journalist "and do not know how to communicate securely, you are negligent" (Ball, 2015). Investigative journalists are increasingly aware of practices of surveillance, with around two thirds of US investigative journalists believing the government has collected information about their activities and nearly half changing the ways they store sensitive information, according to the Pew Center's report, *Investigative Journalists and Digital Security* (Holcomb *et al.*, 2015).

Ultimately, the emergence of a surveillance society raises larger questions around transparency, which has long been a cornerstone of journalistic ethics. As Allen (2008) has argued, a rhetoric of transparency has become central to journalistic accounts of ethics—often as a defensive move against attacks. This leaves journalists in a paradoxical bind: As they commit themselves to goals of transparency, they are simultaneously "subjected to forces of discipline and surveillance that might, in the end, run counter to the very goals that they seek" (Allen, 2008: 336).

Public debate and social implications

The limits and distortions of the media coverage of the Snowden leaks are reflected in the (lack of) public knowledge and debate about digital surveillance. Although demonstrations and protests erupted in various parts of the world (such as the protests organized under the banner "Stop Watching Us" in the United States, Germany, and France), in the United Kingdom, which had emerged from the Snowden leaks as a leading country in the adoption of surveillance technology, there was notably little public response. This may initially be surprising as the dominant position of the British public showed support for Snowden and a belief that he was right to leak the documents, according to early opinion polls.

However, the polls also show that despite widespread recognition of the value of leaking the documents, concerns have persisted regarding the potential dangers of reporting on issues of state security, fearing that this might 'help the terrorists' (Cable, 2015). Post-Snowden public debate has centered on a perceived necessary trade-off between privacy and security, with a prominent narrative stating that "if you have nothing to hide, you have nothing to fear." Despite an increase in concern regarding online privacy among the British public (60 percent of people surveyed in January 2014 felt more worried about their online privacy than they did a year earlier), a majority of the public also felt that the balance of powers of intelligence services with regards to surveillance is 'about right' (Cable, 2015).

The attitudes and opinions towards digital surveillance that have emerged through various surveys and opinion polls conducted since the Snowden leaks speak to a broader, historical shift in what Turow, McGuigan, and Maris (2015) have referred to as our social imaginary. Data mining has become naturalized as part of a ubiquitous and incomprehensible architecture of surveillance entrenched into our everyday lives. Importantly, this has emerged not on the basis of public consent but rather through public resignation. As Hoofnagle *et al.* (2010) have found based on research in the United States, most people would like to know more about, and have more control over, what happens to their data, but they lack access to this information and therefore feel disempowered. This sentiment echoes focus group research that we conducted in the United Kingdom regarding the Snowden leaks.[2] Focus groups with different demographic sections of British society (based on age, income, gender, and ethnic background) revealed that initial public knowledge regarding Edward Snowden and the substance of the Snowden leaks was very limited. However, when people were provided with a space to reflect on digital surveillance, including the extensive forms of state surveillance revealed by Snowden, significant concerns became apparent regarding the lack of transparency and the legal safeguards in place for how and for what purpose personal data is collected. Yet this does not necessarily translate into changing online behavior or actively resisting and challenging developments in surveillance, not least as the architectures of surveillance are not very visible and remain fairly abstract (Dencik and Cable, forthcoming, 2017). Instead, (mass) surveillance has become internalized as the way society is and must be organized in current times. This speaks to a state of what we have termed 'Surveillance Realism,' borrowing from Mark Fisher's (2009) notion of 'Capitalist Realism,' a state in which, despite recognizing and fearing the fallacies of the system, people have difficulties imagining society without ubiquitous surveillance (Dencik, 2015).

In many ways, the "nothing to hide, nothing to fear" mantra and the limited discussion on issues concerning civil rights and democratic implications of digital surveillance in the post-Snowden media and public debate are exemplary of Surveillance Realism and its implications can be wide-reaching. As the United Nations Special Rapporteur on Freedom of Expression and Opinion has repeatedly emphasized, pervasive monitoring of people's movements, actions, and communication undermines critical debate and dissident voices (UN General Assembly, 2013). Snowden himself has raised concern with a potential 'chilling-effect' in societies under mass surveillance, particularly in terms of our ability to express dissent and resist structures of power and domination. Recent research has highlighted the subtle ways in which this may play out, not just with regards to journalistic practice but also in terms of broader forms of self-censorship or fear of controversy and critique in wider society (Hampton *et al.*, 2014; PEN, 2013).

As part of our research we also conducted interviews with political activists in the United Kingdom from a range of civil society organizations and activist groups, including environmental activists, anti-war groups, labor unions, community organizations, and civil liberties groups. We found that a general awareness of surveillance may serve to limit the scope and range of dissenting voices and activities by keeping civil society organizations within a relatively compliant position in relation to the state. That is, the realities of mass surveillance can in some instances translate into hesitancy and forms of self-regulation regarding any discourse or activity that might be seen to move outside an accepted 'mainstream' and into areas potentially considered more 'radical' by the state (Dencik and Cable, forthcoming, 2017). In a climate where definitions of what constitutes 'radical' are vague at best and continuously shifting in line with geopolitical concerns and agendas of dominant institutions of power (Sedgwick, 2010), such implications of mass surveillance speak to a troubling situation for any notion of democracy.

Conclusion

Surveillance in its various forms has become one of the key characteristics of contemporary digital communication environments. It is intrinsically linked to questions of media, journalism, and democracy: Its invisible and often secret practice requires informed public debate about its roles and limits; confidential communication outside the watchful eye of authorities is essential for investigative journalism and thus for fulfilling journalism's role as a watchdog and fourth estate; and mass surveillance challenges free expression.

The mediated public debate on the issue has been inconsistent and has demonstrated significant differences among journalists and media organizations on how issues of public safety and civic rights should be reported. By and large, the coverage of the Snowden leaks, in particular, has lacked detailed discussions of the implications of surveillance for citizens and has been framed by (political) elites. Accordingly, public knowledge of the leaks and their contents has been limited. While significant concerns exist about surveillance, and particularly the lack of transparency of its use and of legal safeguards, a powerless 'surveillance realism' prevails.

Despite these sobering findings, increased awareness of both state-based and commercial surveillance has also led to some growth in counter-surveillance practices. The adoption of anonymization and encryption tools has increased, and journalists have had to familiarize themselves with new digital communication practices. The use of encryption has become more widely accepted in the 'Snowden Era' (Greenwald, 2014) and is complemented by campaigns for digital rights and policy change.

The debate on surveillance is closely connected to core questions concerning democracy. It is embedded in a controversial conversation about the nature of civil rights in the context of security; the role of security agencies and the need for public oversight; and the balance between human security (that includes the safety and privacy of individual communication), public safety, and state security. These issues require a robust public debate, and media are essential for enhancing our understanding and facilitating information and exchange.

Further reading

A key thinker in the emerging field of surveillance studies has been David Lyon whose classic work on both online and offline surveillance has recently been complemented with discussions of the Snowden revelations in the book "Surveillance After Snowden" (2015). Insights from a range of scholars are also included in a special issue of *Surveillance & Society* called "Surveillance and Security Intelligence after Snowden" (vol. 13, no. 2, 2015). Mark Andrejevic has complemented debates on state surveillance with insights on commercial surveillance and online exploitation of internet users (e.g. in the volume on *Internet and Surveillance* by Fuchs *et al.*, 2012). A detailed account of the Snowden story and revelations was provided by Greenwald (2014) in his book *Nowhere to Hide* as well as in the Oscar-winning documentary by Laura Poitras, *CitizenFour* (2014). As the Snowden leaks have continued to emerge, research projects, such as "Digital Citizenship and Surveillance Society" by the authors of this chapter, are analyzing reactions and implications and will lead to further publications.

Notes

1 This chapter is based on our ongoing academic work at the intersection of journalism and surveil-lance studies. In particular, it draws from findings of a research project that stretched from 2014 to 2016—"Digital Citizenship and Surveillance Society: State-Media-Citizen Relations after the Snowden Leaks."
2 As Haggerty and Gazso (2005) have argued, the limitations of opinion polls are that they often pro-duce results that do not capture the extent of contradictory and ambivalent views on complex issues such as surveillance and privacy and there is therefore a need to include more qualitative forms of research.

References

Allen, D.S. (2008) "The Trouble with Transparency: The Challenge of Doing Journalism Ethics in a Surveillance Society." *Journalism Studies* 9(3): 323–340.
Andrejevic, M. (2012) "Exploitation in the Data Mine." In Fuchs, C., Boersma, K., Albrechtslund, A. and Sandoval, M. (eds) *Internet and Surveillance: The Challenges of Web 2.0 and Social Media.* Abingdon, UK: Routledge, pp. 71–88.
Bakir, V. (2015) "Veillant Panoptic Assemblage: Mutual Watching and Resistance to Mass Surveillance After Snowden." *Media and Communication* 3(3): 12–25.
Ball, J. (2015) "State-Media-Citizen Relations in the Surveillance Society." In *Surveillance and Citizenship Conference*, 18–19 June. Cardiff, UK: Cardiff University.
Barlow, J.P. (2013) Interview by Sky News with John Perry Barlow and Julian Assange, 10 June 2013. Available from: https://www.youtube.com/watch?v=ZyGRh0T0Ej0.
Bauman, Z., Bigo, D., Esteves, P., Guild, E., Jabri, V., Lyon, D., et al. (2014) "After Snowden: Rethinking the Impact of Surveillance." *International Political Sociology* 8(2): 121–144.
Bentham, J. (1791) *Panopticon.* Dublin: T. Payne.
Berkowitz, D.A. (2009) "Reporters and their Sources." In Wahl-Jorgensen, K. and Hanitzsch, T. (eds) *The Handbook of Journalism Studies.* London and New York: Routledge, pp. 102–115.
Boltanski, L. and Thévenot, L. (1999) "The Sociology of Critical Capacity." *European Journal of Social Theory* 2(3): 359–377.
Braman, S. (2006) *Change of State: Information, Policy, and Power.* Cambridge, MA: MIT Press.
Brevini, B., Hintz, A. and McCurdy, P. (2013) *Beyond WikiLeaks: Implications for the Future of Communications, Journalism and Society.* Basingstoke, UK: Palgrave Macmillan.
Cable, J. (2015) "Working Paper: An Overview of Public Opinion Polls since the Edward Snowden Revelations in June 2013." Cardiff University, Cardiff. Available from: https://sites.cardiff.ac.uk/dcssproject/files/2015/08/UK-Public-Opinion-Review-180615.pdf.
Chadwick, A. and Collister, S. (2014) "Boundary-Drawing Power and the Renewal of Professional News Organizations: The Case of the Guardian and the Edward Snowden NSA Leak." *International Journal of Communication* 8: 2420–2441.
The Citizen Lab (2013) *Planet Blue Coat: Mapping Global Censorship and Surveillance Tools.* Available from: https://citizenlab.org/wp-content/uploads/2013/01/Planet-Blue-Coat.pdf.
Coddington, M. (2012) "Defending a Paradigm by Patrolling a Boundary: Two Global Newspapers' Approach to WikiLeaks." *Journalism and Mass Communication Quarterly* 89: 377–396.
Deleuze, G. (1995) *Negotiations.* New York, NY: Columbia University Press.
Dencik, L. (2015) "The Advent of Surveillance Realism." *JOMEC@Cardiff University*, 23 January. Available from: http://www.jomec.co.uk/blog/the-advent-of-surveillance-realism-2/.

Dencik, L. and Cable, J. (2017, forthcoming) "The Advent of Surveillance Realism: Public Opinion and Activist Responses to the Snowden Leaks." *International Journal of Communication*.

Diamond, L. (2010) "Liberation Technology." *Journal of Democracy* 21(3): 69–83.

Fidler, D.P. (ed.). (2015) *The Snowden Reader*. Bloomington, IN: Indiana University Press.

Fisher, M. (2009) *Capitalist Realism: Is There No Alternative?* Winchester, UK: Zero Books

Foucault, M. (1975) *Discipline and Punish: The Birth of the Prison*. New York, NY: Vintage Books.

Fuchs, C., Boersma, K., Albrechtslund, A. and Sandoval, M. (eds) (2012) *Internet and Surveillance: The Challenges of Web 2.0 and Social Media*. Abingdon, UK: Routledge.

Google (2014) *Transparency Report 2014*. Available from: http://www.google.co.uk/transparencyreport/.

Greenwald, G. (2014) *No Place to Hide: Edward Snowden, the NSA and the U.S. Surveillance State*. New York, NY: Metropolitan Books.

The Guardian (2015) "The NSA Files." Available from: http://www.theguardian.com/us-news/the-nsa-files.

Haggerty, K.D. and Ericson, R.V. (2000) "The Surveillant Assemblage." *British Journal of Sociology* 51(4): 605–622.

Haggerty, K.D. and Gazso, A. (2005) "The Public Politics of Opinion Research on Surveillance and Privacy." *Surveillance & Society* 3(2/3): 173–180.

Hampton, K.N., Rainie, L., Lu, W., Dwyer, M., Shin, I. and Purcell, K. (2014) "Social Media and the 'Spiral of Silence.'" Washington, DC: Pew Research Center. Available from: http://www.pewinternet.org/files/2014/08/PI_Social-networks-and-debate_082614.pdf.

Hofheinz, A. (2011) "Nextopia? Beyond Revolution 2.0." *International Journal of Communication* 5. Available from: http://ijoc.org/ojs/index.php/ijoc/article/view/1186.

Holcomb, J., Mitchell, A. and Purcell, K. (2015) "Investigative Journalists and Digital Security." Pew Research Center report. Available from: http://www.journalism.org/2015/02/05/investigative-journalists-and-digital-security/.

Hoofnagle, C.J., King, J., Li, S. and Turow, J. (2010) *How Different are Young Adults from Older Adults When it Comes to Information Privacy Attitudes and Policies?* SSRN. DOI: 10.2139/ssrn.1589864.

Kunelius, R., Russell, A., Eide, E., Mollen, A., Moller, J., Wang, H., et al. (2015) "The Prism of NSA: Security, Privacy and Journalism in the Global Debate on the Snowden Affair." Paper presented at the Surveillance and Citizenship Conference, Cardiff University, 18–19 June.

Leistert, O. and Rohle, T. (2011) "Identifizieren, Verbinden, Verkaufen. Einleitendes zur Maschine Facebook, ihren Konsequenzen und den Beiträgen in diesem Band." In Leistert, O. and Rohle, T. (eds) *Generation Facebook: Über das Leben im Social Net*. Bielefeld: Transcript, pp. 7–30.

Lyon, D. (2007) "Surveillance, Power, and Everyday Life." In Mansell, R., Anthi Avgerou, C., Quah, D. and Silverstone, R. (eds) *The Oxford Handbook of Information and Communication Technologies*. Oxford and New York: Oxford University Press, pp. 449–472.

Lyon, D. (2014) "Surveillance, Snowden, and Big Data: Capacities, Consequences, Critique." *Big Data & Society*, July–December, pp. 1–13.

Lyon, D. (2015) *Surveillance after Snowden*. Malden, MA: Polity Press.

Mann, S., Nolan, J. and Wellman, B. (2003) "Sousveillance: Inventing and Using Wearable Computing Devices for Data Collection in Surveillance Environments." *Surveillance & Society* 1(3): 331–355.

Marquis-Boire, M., Marczak, B., Guarnieri, C. and Scott-Railton, J. (2013) *For Their Eyes Only: The Commercialization of Digital Spying*. Toronto, ON: The Citizen Lab.

Mols, A. (2015) "Not Interesting Enough to Be Followed by the NSA: A Frame Analysis of the Dutch Public Debate about the NSA Revelations in 2013." Paper presented at the Surveillance and Citizenship Conference, Cardiff University, 18–19 June.

PEN (2013) *Chilling Effects: NSA Surveillance Drives U.S. Writers to Self-Censor*. New York, NY: PEN American Center. Available from: http://www.pen.org/sites/default/files/Chilling%20Effects_PEN%20American.pdf.

Rusbridger, A. (2013) "David Miranda, Schedule 7, and the Danger That All Reporters Now Face." *The Guardian*, 19 August. Available from: http://www.theguardian.com/commentisfree/2013/aug/19/david-miranda-schedule7-danger-reporters.

Sedgwick, M. (2010) "The Concept of Radicalisation as a Source of Confusion." *Terrorism and Political Violence* 22(4): 479–494.

Trottier, D. (2015) "Open Source Intelligence, Social Media and Law Enforcement: Visions, Constraints and Critiques." *European Journal of Cultural Studies* 18(4–5): 530–547.

Trottier, D. and Lyon, D. (2012) "Key Features of Social Media Surveillance." In Fuchs, C., Boersma, K., Albrechtslund, A. and Sandoval, M. (eds) *Internet and Surveillance: The Challenges of Web 2.0 and Social Media*. Abingdon, UK: Routledge, pp. 89–105.

Turow, J., McGuigan, L. and Maris, E.R. (2015) "Making Data Mining a Natural Part of Life: Physical Retailing, Customer Surveillance and the 21st Century Social Imaginary." *European Journal of Cultural Studies* 18(4–5): 464–478.

UN General Assembly. (2013) "Report of the Special Rapporteur on the Promotion and Protection of the Right to Freedom of Expression." *Frank La Rue*, 17 April. Available from: http://www.ohchr.org/Documents/HRBodies/HRCouncil/RegularSession/Session23/A.HRC.23.40_EN.pdf.

Villeneuve, N. (2012) "Fake Skype Encryption Software Cloaks DarkComet Trojan." *Trend Micro Malware Blog*, 20 April. Available from: http://blog.trendmicro.com/fake-skype-encryption-software-cloaks-darkcomet-trojan/.

Wahl-Jorgensen, K. and Bennett, L. (forthcoming, 2017) "The Normalization of Surveillance and the Invisibility of Digital Citizenship: Media Debates After the Snowden Revelations." *International Journal of Communication*.

Wright, D. and Kreissl, R. (2013) "European Responses to the Snowden Revelations: A Discussion Paper." *Increasing Resilience in Surveillance Societies Project*. Available from: http://irissproject.eu/.

EPILOGUE: DIGITAL JOURNALISM

A golden age, a data-driven dream, a paradise for readers—or the proletarianization of a profession?

Toby Miller

In 2013, the late David Carr, a breathtakingly immodest chief drug confessor and solipsist from the *New York Times* who also acted as its principal technology booster, wrote this advice to young *anglo-parlante* journalists:

> Right now, being a reporter is a golden age. There may be a lack of business models to back it up, but having AKTOCA—All Known Thought One Click Away—on my desktop, tablet or phone makes it an immensely deeper, richer exercise than it used to be.
>
> *(Carr, 2013)*

It would be hard to think of a better example of armchair cybertarianism than this. Thinking about life on the other side of news, Tom Englehardt, a well-meaning critic of US imperialism (http://www.tomdispatch.com/authors/tom/) says we are living in a golden age of journalism because of what he dubs 'the rise of the reader' (2014). Perhaps unwittingly drawing on a discourse from decades ago in the work of Roland Barthes (1967) and Umberto Eco (1984), Englehardt celebrates our times because they supposedly signal the birth of readers as curators, splicing together stories from news sources that fly at the speed of thought across the globe to flit across their screens. Of course, Barthes and Eco were writing about textual and social relations and their impact on technology. Englehardt is writing about technological relations and their impact on texts and societies.

In addition to this new era of readers' hegemony over digital journalism, there is great excitement over such new technologies as 'drone journalism' and 'immersive journalism' (http://www.dronejournalismlab.org/; Nuwer, 2015). More importantly, Carr, Englehardt, and their ilk also celebrate this as an age of big data, when truth comes bundled in numbers that desk-bound journalists turn into graphs, which are visual and hence superior to other forms of knowledge. This epilogue interrogates these grand claims, engaging along the way in a rather somber critique of technological determinism.

I have some fragrant memories of technology and journalism over the years. I think the genre of an epilogue permits sharing such things. In the early 1970s, the phone ringing in the middle of the night meant that a telegram operator was about to read out a message from *The Economist* to my father, commissioning a story; my mother would take it down in shorthand and awake the next day with no memory of what she had done. I would go with my father to the telegram office late the following night so he could hand over his copy. In the late 1970s, walking into the radio station where I worked to read the morning bulletin and finding the journalist asleep on the floor or absent (drunk, in both cases), I would look for last year's carbon copy from the same calendar day to read, on the ground that at least seasonal stories might be similar. In 1981, as I waited for my first book review to appear in a newspaper, I opened up each Saturday's copy excitedly for weeks until it did so. In the late 1980s and early 1990s, I had regular radio slots commenting on the popular, where I was introduced as 'our culture czar.' The ABC gave me a taxi voucher to come to the studio because they did not like the sound quality over landlines.

When I moved to New York in 1993, TV stations interviewed me in my apartment via groups that included journalists, sound recordists, cinematographers, and producers. A decade later, the group of experts had transmogrified into one allegedly multiply skilled person, who of course had to write copy as well as film and voice it, and do so across several platforms that repeated and reworked their copy. For my part, today I send columns instantaneously to editors from across the world—but am frequently unable to read what I have written for them because of the requirement to subscribe to the newspaper or magazine to do so.

Perhaps unsurprisingly given this personal history, I have strong and multiple feelings of *déjà-vu* as I trudge through the stupefying claims made for big data by journalists, academics, and corporate hucksters. First, I am transported to the 1970s and the touching credulity of cliometrics. At the time, we were assured that data would reform history and historiography, freeing writers and readers alike from inaccurate morganatic and social history alike (Woodman, 1972). Then I am suddenly thrown into the twenty-first century and evidence-based public policy (better known as policy-based evidence), which seeks to transform political science into the *ur-* discourse of statecraft, displacing an allegedly warlock world of extremism and populism (Marmot, 2004). Just when I think I am stably ensconced there, the catapult hurls me into the early 1990s. I emerge as a faithful, dutiful subscriber to *Wired* magazine in its heyday, signing up for a brave new world of liberty (so memorably skewered by Streeter, 2005).

By now, it is clear to me that the memories will just keep on coming each time 'big data' are invoked. I usually end up in the 1970s, because somewhere vaguely nearby to cliometrics lurked the real master discourse emerging at that time: a heady mixture of Cold War techno-futurism and neoclassical economics. This was that moment—its dread work stays with us still—that incarnated neoliberalism and technological determinism.

The ever-so-certain, entirely predictable academic and media discourse on big data in journalism duly performs various maneuvers: it lists websites that explain analytics; is careful to admire forebears who, you know, spoke to people in order to find stuff out and did quaint things like read documents; incarnates cybertarian ideology; does not value qualitative social science, such as ethnography; ignores political economy; is dedicated to essentialist views (there really *are* cohorts such as Generation X and they really *do* process, for example, pictures differently from their elders); pays little attention to scholarship on journalism or the media in general; finds journalistic norms, traditions, and innovations outside the Global North to be of passing or no interest; and leaves spectacularly unattended changes in the labor process due to pressures exacted not by technology but share market pressure and lizard-shoed financial advisors (Mair *et al.*, 2013). Sometimes it goes so far as to be thrilled that big data will entirely transform journalism and put it into popular hands (Baack, 2015). (I think that means a technological elite within unaccountable social movements.)

Many journalists are complicit with these occupational hazards. Everybody's banging on about it these days, from the *Guardian*'s Sustainable Business podcast (*Guardian*, 2015) to the *Financial Times* (Harford, 2014) to AT&T (Neff, 2014). True believers see the potential for adding value to research and investigative journalism as a saving grace of technological change for those with the right skills to participate, thereby offsetting the negative impacts of job losses (Mair *et al.*, 2013). These information society chorines, many of them journalists, rejoice that a full 90 percent of all currently existing data was created between 2012 and 2013 alone (Hsu, 2013; Ramanathan, 2013; SINTEF, 2013). So much for Austen, Foucault, and Confucius. *Le Monde* has declared this the moment "When Mathematicians Became Sexy"—surely the most bathetic Romance-language headline of 2013 (Durut, 2013).

There are even obedient Schumpeterian celebrants of this new era, which supposedly clears out decadent, incompetent media companies (Brock, 2013 is a stereotypical example); earnest seekers after new business models (Braiker, 2014); or coin-operated managers engorging themselves in capitalist self-congratulation (D'Vorkin, 2012).

Such true believers would do well to consider the work of Justin Lewis (see Lansdall-Welfare *et al.*, this volume), a noted figure in media studies who works with the fundamental understanding that the most quantoid of quantoids works with words, which have meaning at both denotative and connotative levels, and must translate them into numbers in order to do computation and then back into words in order to make a point. At the same time, the most qualtoid of qualtoids selects phenomena to discuss because they matter in some way—and numbers will always be part of what matters (Lewis, 1996, 2001, and 2008). I suspect the true believers in big data won't read Lewis, because their world is so tightly encased in certainty that being reduced to textuality might make it all end in tears.

But alongside the comforting certitude of diligent chorines, there is a dystopic side to contemporary journalism, where the digital is said to have diminished workers' and readers' attention spans alike, deprofessionalized reporters by proletarianizing and deskilling them, stimulated public relations, generated churnalism, and jeopardized on-the-spot reportage (Jackson and Moloney, 2015 and Macnamara, 2015 are sweetly ambivalent about this trend). Bob Franklin brilliantly summarizes these trends somewhat less contentiously than I could with this helpful list:

> the continuing innovations in communication technologies; the harshly competitive and fragmenting markets for audiences and advertising revenues; dramatic reductions in the entry costs of some online outlets for news; the collapse of the traditional business model to resource journalism; an expansive role for social media as sources and drivers of news; dynamic changes in government media policy; as well as shifting audience requirements for news, the ways in which it is presented and, given the expansive number of (increasingly mobile) devices on which it is received, even the places and spaces where news is produced and consumed.
>
> *(2012: 663)*

Let us revisit the alleged birth of the newly empowered reader, the master of screen wizardry. It is certainly true that audience subscriptions are now much more financially important than advertising for journalism:

> Global newspaper circulation revenues are higher than advertising revenues for the first time this century. Audiences have become publishers' biggest source of revenue. The industry generated an estimated US$179 billion in circulation and advertising

revenue in 2014—which makes it larger than the book publishing, music or film industries. Ninety-two billion dollars came from print and digital circulation, while $87 billion came from advertising.

(World Association of Newspapers and
News Publishers, 2015)

But the US newspaper industry, for example, is 60 percent of the size it was 20 years ago, and digital subscriptions are worth much less money to papers than print ones (Franklin, 2014: 470–471). Is this what the chorines want?

And what are readers gleaning, given their much-vaunted mixed-media, multi-platform style of sovereign consumption? The science available is largely educational, and it shows that cell phones have a negative impact on learning. For "low-achieving and at-risk students," banning their use is "equivalent to an additional hour a week in school, or to increasing the school year by five days" (Murphy and Beland, 2015). And college? Cornell's renowned "Laptop and the Lecture" study, published in 2003, showed that lecture attendees remembered lessons better if they did not use laptops during class. Lots of research in the decade since has confirmed the risks of technological multitasking with smartphones and the value of note taking with pen and paper rather than digitally—and not only for those doing so; others get distracted by people typing in ways they do not when surrounded by old-style note-taking (Hembrooke and Gay, 2003; Sana, Weston, and Cepeda, 2013). The research even shows, paradoxically, that people who engage heavily in media multitasking are worse than others when given multiple tasks to do. Sending texts and engaging with social media seriously diminish these capacities and learning in general (David *et al.*, 2015; Gingerich and Lineweaver, 2014; Lawson and Henderson, 2015; Ophir *et al.*, 2009).

Now let us look at what is happening in job terms. Everybody knows about disemployment and underemployment in the Global North's journalism. How did this come about? In part because the conglomerates that have come to own much of the *bourgeois* media do not see what they do as part of a public trust, as business conducted in the public interest. Rather, they view all their properties as designed for profit, with margins determined by stock markets. Given the decision made so early on to post news free on line, this has made for large-scale lay-offs and proletarianization. Again, technology has been to the fore in enabling these activities.

Consider Mindworks Global Media, a company outside New Delhi that provides US and European newspapers with Indian-based journalists and copyeditors who work long distance. There are 35–40 percent cost savings on employing local reporters (Lakshman, 2008; Tady, 2008; http://www.mindworksglobal.com/). Or perhaps your firm of choice is LocaLabs, formerly Journatic, which has used stringers from outside and inside the United States, paid at best US$10 an hour without healthcare coverage to write allegedly 'hyper-local' stories they took from internet sources and published under *noms de plume* (Tarkov, 2012; http://www.locallabs.com/).

Either way, we are seeing the New International Division of Cultural Labor, first discerned over 25 years ago, ineluctably making its way into journalism. Latin America may be a model for this—in Brazil, for example, public intellectuals routinely have to take more than one job, and journalists frequently moonlight as PR writers (Paiva, Guerra, and Custódio, 2015). But the digital world is seen as a force disrupting the *clientelismo* that has dogged much of the region, where interlocking directorates and oligarchical tendencies have seen Colombia, for example, normally run by politicians with significant media interests. The prospect of instant, unedited, on-line access as an alternative has excited many (Montaña, 2014).

This is not entirely to be lamented. First, it is high time that those in the Global South turned the tables by delivering stories to the Global North about the latter, after a century that was mostly the other way round. That reorientation also serves to destabilize the narrative of decline centered on Europe and white settler colonies, because it is truly a golden age of journalism in the Global South with the growth of literate middle classes (World Association of Newspapers and News Publishers, 2015).

Finally, let us examine the deprofessionalization that accompanies the rise of public relations and churnalism and the demise of participant observation and research. Journalism is a long way behind the times in terms of ethics to cover prevailing social relations of technology and work arrangements. A study of 99 codes around the world found that fewer than 10 percent had evolved to address such questions (Díaz-Campo and Segado-Boj, 2015).

I am left with a profound sense of ambivalence. The utopic and dystopic poles of debate about the future are compelling, depending on your orientation to romance versus critique, techno-futurism versus techno-skepticism, capital versus labor, and Global North versus Global South. These discomforting antinomies have many midpoints, of course. A blend of history as well as contemporaneity, political economy and ethnography as well as early adoption and multiskilling, will be our best guides in these uncertain times.

References

Baack, S. (2015) "Datafication and Empowerment: How the Open Data Movement Re-Articulates Notions of Democracy, Participation, and Journalism." *Big Data & Society*. DOI: 10.1177/2053951715594634.

Barthes, R. (1967) "The Death of the Author." *Aspen: The Magazine in a Box* 5+6. Available from: http://www.ubu.com/aspen/aspen5and6/index.html.

Braiker, B. (2014) "Inside the *Texas Tribune* Model of Sustainable Journalism." *Digiday*, 12 March. Available from: http://digiday.com/publishers/texas-tribune-publisher-tim-griggs/.

Brock, G. (2013) "Journalism is Going to Survive this Era of Creative Destruction." *New Statesman*, 27 September. Available from: http://www.newstatesman.com/business/2013/09/journalism-going-survive-era-creative-destruction.

Carr, D. (2013) "Reddit: IAmA Columnist and Reporter on Media and Culture for the *New York Times*." Available from: https://www.reddit.com/r/IAmA/comments/16k598/iama_columnist_and_reporter_on_media_and_culture.

David, P., Kim, J.-H., Brickman, J.S., Ran, W. and Curtis, C.M. (2015) "Mobile Phone Distraction While Studying." *New Media & Society* 17(10): 1661–1679.

Díaz-Campo, J. and Segado-Boj, F. (2015) "Journalism Ethics in a Digital Environment: How Journalistic Codes of Ethics Have Been Adapted to the Internet and ICTs in Countries Around the World." *Telematics and Informatics* 32(4): 735–744.

Durut, M. (2013) "Big Data: Quand le Mathématicien Devient Sexy." *Le Monde*, 20 May. Available from: http://archives.lesclesdedemain.lemonde.fr/organisations/big-data-quand-le-statisticien-devient-sexy_a-12-1769.html.

D'Vorkin, L. (2012) "Sustainable Journalism." *Forbes*, 2 May. Available from: http://www.forbes.com/forbes/2012/0521/brief-word-entrepreneur-digital-sustainable-journalism-lewis-dvorkin.html.

Eco, U. (1984) *The Role of the Reader: Explorations in the Semiotics of Texts*. Bloomington, IN: Indiana University Press.

Englehardt, T. (2014) "The Rise of the Reader." *TomDispatch*, 21 January. Available from: http://www.tomdispatch.com/blog/175796/tomgram%3A_engelhardt,_the_rise_of_the_reader/.

Franklin, B. (2012) "The Future of Journalism: Developments and Debates." *Journalism Studies* 13(5–6): 663–681.

Franklin, B. (2014) "The Future of Journalism." *Journalism Practice* 8(5): 469–487.

Gingerich, A.C. and Lineweaver, T.T. (2014) "OMG! Texting in Class = U Fail: (Empirical Evidence that Text Messaging During Class Disrupts Comprehension." *Teaching of Psychology* 41(1): 44–51.

The Guardian (2015) "Sustainable Business Podcast." Available from: http://www.theguardian.com/sustainable-business/big-data-sustainability-podcast.

Harford, T. (2014) "Big Data: Are We Making a Terrible Mistake?" *The Financial Times*, 28 March. Available from: http://www.ft.com/cms/s/2/21a6e7d8-b479-11e3-a09a-00144feabdc0.html#axzz2xXga2LUN.

Hembrooke, H. and Gay, G. (2003) "The Laptop and the Lecture: The Effects of Multitasking in Learning Environments." *Journal of Computing in Higher Education* 15(1): 46–64.

Hsu, J. (2013) "Big Business, Big Data, Big Sustainability." *Carbontrust.com*, 31 October. Available from: http://www.carbontrust.com/news/2013/10/big-business-big-data-big-sustainability.

Jackson, D. and Moloney, K. (2015) "Inside Churnalism." *Journalism Studies*. DOI: 10.1080/1461670X.2015.1017597.

Lakshman, N. (2008) "Copyediting? Ship the Work Out to India." *Business Week*, 8 July. Available from: http://www.bloomberg.com/news/articles/2008-07-08/copyediting-ship-the-work-out-to-indiabusinessweek-business-news-stock-market-and-financial-advice.

Lawson, D. and Henderson, B.B. (2015) "The Costs of Texting in the Classroom." *College Teaching* 63(3): 119–124.

Lewis, J. (1996) "What Counts in Cultural Studies." *Media, Culture & Society* 19(1): 83–98.

Lewis, J. (2001) *Constructing Public Opinion.* New York, NY: Columbia University Press.

Lewis, J. (2008) "Thinking by Numbers: Cultural Analysis and the Use of Data." In Bennett, T. and Frow, J. (eds) *The SAGE Handbook of Cultural Analysis.* Los Angeles, CA: Sage Publications, pp. 654–673.

Macnamara, J. (2015) "The Continuing Convergence of Journalism and PR: New Insights for Ethical Practice from a Three-Country Study of Senior Practitioners." *Journalism & Mass Communication Quarterly* 93(1): 118–141. DOI: 10.1177/1077699015605803.

Mair, J., Keeble, R.L., Bradshaw, P. and Beleaga, T. (2013) *Data Journalism: Mapping the Future.* Bury St Edmunds, UK: Abramis.

Marmot, M.G. (2004) "Evidence Based Policy or Policy Based Evidence?" *British Medical Journal* 328(7445): 906–907.

Montaña, S. (2014) "*Case 2*: Colombia—An Ethnographic Study of Digital Journalistic Practices." In Kalyango, Jr. Y. and Mould, D.H. (eds) *Global Journalism Practice and New Media Performance.* London, UK: Palgrave, pp. 146–160.

Murphy, R. and Beland, L.-P. (2015) "How Smart is it to Allow Students to Use Mobile Phones at School?" *The Conversation*, 12 May. Available from: https://theconversation.com/how-smart-is-it-to-allow-students-to-use-mobile-phones-at-school-40621.

Neff, J. (2014) "How Big Data Shapes AT&T's Advertising Creative." *AdAge*, 25 March. Available from: http://adage.com/article/cmo-strategy/t-big-data-shape-tv-creative/292313/.

Nuwer, R. (2015) "Journalism's New Reality." *Pacific Standard*, 18 November. Available from: http://www.psmag.com/nature-and-technology/journalisms-new-reality.

Ophir, E., Nass, C. and Wagner, A.D. (2009) "Cognitive Control in Media Multitaskers." *Proceedings of the National Academy of Sciences of the United States of America* 106(37): 15583–15587.

Paiva, R., Guerra, M. and Custódio, L. (2015) "Professional, Social and Regulatory Characteristics of Journalism in Online and Traditional Media in Brazil." *African Journalism Studies* 36(3): 8–32.

Ramanathan, V.M. (2013) "Global IT Spending Pegged at $3.7 Trillion: Gadget Spending Forecast at $1.1 Trillion in 2013." *International Business Times*, January 7. Available from: http://www.ibtimes.com/global-it-spending-pegged-37-trillion-gadget-spending-forecast-11-trillion-2013-996132.

Sana, F., Weston, T. and Cepeda, N. (2013) "Laptop Multitasking Hinders Classroom Learning for Both Users and Nearby Peers." *Computers & Education* 62(1): 24–31.

SINTEF (2013) "Big Data, for Better or Worse: 90% of World's Data Generated Over Last Two Years." *ScienceDaily*, 22 May. Available from: http://www.sciencedaily.com/releases/2013/05/130522085217.htm.

Streeter, T. (2005) "The Moment of *Wired.*" *Critical Inquiry* 31(4): 755–779.

Tady, M. (2008) "Outsourcing Journalism." *FAIR*, 1 November. Available from: http://fair.org/extra-online-articles/outsourcing-journalism/.

Tarkov, A. (2012) "Journatic Worker Takes 'This American Life' Inside Outsourced Journalism." *Poynter*, 30 June. Available from: http://www.poynter.org/news/mediawire/179555/journatic-staffer-takes-this-american-life-inside-outsourced-journalism/.

Woodman, H. (1972) "Economic History and Economic Theory: The New Economic History in America." *Journal of Interdisciplinary History* 3(2): 323–350.

World Association of Newspapers and News Publishers (2015) *World Press Trends Report 2015: The Definitive Guide to the Global Newspaper Industry, in Numbers, Trends and Changes.* Available from: http://www.wan-ifra.org/reports/2015/10/01/world-press-trends-report-2015.

INDEX